Collins
French
Dictionary

HarperCollins Publishers
Westerhill Road
Bishopbriggs
Glasgow
G64 2QT
Great Britain

This Edition 2008

© HarperCollins Publishers 2008

ISBN 978-0-00-782844-9

www.collinslanguage.com

A catalogue record for this book is
available from the British Library

Typeset by Thomas Callan

Printed and bound by
Clays Ltd, St Ives plc

This book is set in Collins Fedra, a
typeface specially created for Collins
dictionaries by Peter Bil'ak

Acknowledgements
We would like to thank those authors
and publishers who kindly gave
permission for copyright material to
be used in the Collins Word Web. We
would also like to thank Times
Newspapers Ltd for providing
valuable data.

PUBLISHING DIRECTOR
Catherine Love

CONTRIBUTORS
Maree Airlie
Jean-François Allain
Gaëlle Amiot-Cadey
Cécile Aubinière-Robb
Sabine Citron
Wendy Lee
Catherine Love
Rose Rociola

SERIES EDITOR
Rob Scriven

BASED ON THE COLLINS FRENCH GEM
Pierre-Henri Cousin
Renée Birks
Elizabeth Campbell
Hélène Lewis
Claude Nimmo
Philippe Patry
Lorna Knight

TABLE DES MATIÈRES   CONTENTS

William Collins' dream of knowledge for all began with the publication of his first book in 1819. A self-educated mill worker, he not only enriched millions of lives, but also founded a flourishing publishing house. Today, staying true to this spirit, Collins books are packed with inspiration, innovation, and practical expertise. They place you at the centre of a world of possibility and give you exactly what you need to explore it.

Language is the key to this exploration, and at the heart of Collins Dictionaries is language as it is really used. New words, phrases, and meanings spring up every day, and all of them are captured and analysed by the Collins Word Web. Constantly updated, and with over 2.5 billion entries, this living language resource is unique to our dictionaries.

Words are tools for life. And a Collins Dictionary makes them work for you.

Collins. Do more

INTRODUCTION

Nous sommes très heureux que vous ayez choisi ce dictionnaire et espérons que vous aimerez l'utiliser et que vous en tirerez profit au lycée, à la maison, en vacances ou au travail.

INTRODUCTION

We are delighted that you have decided to buy this dictionary and hope you will enjoy and benefit from using it at school, at home, on holiday or at work.

abréviation	*ab(b)r*	abbreviation
adjectif, locution adjectivale	*adj*	adjective, adjectival phrase
administration	*Admin*	administration
adverbe, locution adverbiale	*adv*	adverb, adverbial phrase
agriculture	*Agr*	agriculture
anatomie	*Anat*	anatomy
architecture	*Archit*	architecture
article défini	*art déf*	definite article
article indéfini	*art indéf*	indefinite article
automobile	*Aut(o)*	the motor car and motoring
aviation, voyages aériens	*Aviat*	flying, air travel
biologie	*Bio(l)*	biology
botanique	*Bot*	botany
anglais britannique	*BRIT*	British English
chimie	*Chem*	chemistry
commerce, finance, banque	*Comm*	commerce, finance, banking
informatique	*Comput*	computing
conjonction	*conj*	conjunction
construction	*Constr*	building
nom utilisé comme adjectif	*cpd*	compound element
cuisine	*Culin*	cookery
article défini	*def art*	definite article
déterminant: article; adjectif démonstratif ou indéfini *etc*	*dét*	determiner: article, demonstrative *etc*
économie	*Écon, Econ*	economics
électricité, électronique	*Élec, Elec*	electricity, electronics
en particulier	*esp*	especially
exclamation, interjection	*excl*	exclamation, interjection
féminin	*f*	feminine
langue familière (! emploi vulgaire)	*fam(!)*	colloquial usage (! particularly offensive)
emploi figuré	*fig*	figurative use
(verbe anglais) dont la particule est inséparable	*fus*	(phrasal verb) where the particle is inseparable
généralement	*gén, gen*	generally
géographie, géologie	*Géo, Geo*	geography, geology
géométrie	*Géom, Geom*	geometry
langue familière (! emploi vulgaire)	*inf(!)*	colloquial usage (! particularly offensive)
infinitif	*infin*	infinitive
informatique	*Inform*	computing
invariable	*inv*	invariable
irrégulier	*irreg*	irregular
domaine juridique	*Jur*	law

ABRÉVIATIONS

ABBREVIATIONS

grammaire, linguistique	*Ling*	grammar, linguistics
masculin	*m*	masculine
mathématiques, algèbre	*Math*	mathematics, calculus
médecine	*Méd, Med*	medical term, medicine
masculin ou féminin	*m/f*	masculine or feminine
domaine militaire, armée	*Mil*	military matters
musique	*Mus*	music
nom	*n*	noun
navigation, nautisme	*Navig, Naut*	sailing, navigation
nom ou adjectif numéral	*num*	numeral noun or adjective
	o.s.	oneself
péjoratif	*péj, pej*	derogatory, pejorative
photographie	*Phot(o)*	photography
physiologie	*Physiol*	physiology
pluriel	*pl*	plural
politique	*Pol*	politics
participe passé	*pp*	past participle
préposition	*prép, prep*	preposition
pronom	*pron*	pronoun
psychologie, psychiatrie	*Psych*	psychology, psychiatry
temps du passé	*pt*	past tense
quelque chose	*qch*	
quelqu'un	*qn*	
religion, domaine ecclésiastique	*Rel*	religion
	sb	somebody
enseignement, système scolaire et universitaire	*Scol*	schooling, schools and universities
singulier	*sg*	singular
	sth	something
subjonctif	*sub*	subjunctive
sujet (grammatical)	*su(bj)*	(grammatical) subject
superlatif	*superl*	superlative
techniques, technologie	*Tech*	technical term, technology
télécommunications	*Tél, Tel*	telecommunications
télévision	*TV*	television
typographie	*Typ(o)*	typography, printing
anglais des USA	*US*	American English
verbe (auxiliare)	*vb (aux)*	(auxiliary) verb
verbe intransitif	*vi*	intransitive verb
verbe transitif	*vt*	transitive verb
zoologie	*Zool*	zoology
marque déposée	®	registered trademark
indique une équivalence culturelle	≈	introduces a cultural equivalent

TRANCRIPTION PHONÉTIQUE

CONSONNES — CONSONANTS

NB. **p, b, t, d, k, g** sont suivis d'une aspiration en anglais.

NB. **p, b, t, d, k, g** are not aspirated in French.

Français	Symbole	English
poupée	p	puppy
bombe	b	baby
tente thermal	t	tent
dinde	d	daddy
coq qui képi	k	cork kiss chord
gage bague	g	gag guess
sale ce nation	s	so rice kiss
zéro rose	z	cousin buzz
tache chat	ʃ	sheep sugar
gilet juge	ʒ	pleasure beige
	tʃ	church
	dʒ	judge general
fer phare	f	farm raffle
verveine	v	very revel
	θ	thin maths
	ð	that other
lent salle	l	little ball
rare rentrer	ʀ	
	r	rat rare
maman femme	m	mummy comb
non bonne	n	no ran
agneau vigne	ɲ	
	ŋ	singing bank
	h	hat rehearse
yeux paille pied	j	yet
nouer oui	w	wall wail
huile lui	ɥ	
	x	loch

DIVERS — MISCELLANEOUS

pour l'anglais: le r final se prononce en liaison devant une voyelle	r	in English transcription: final r can be pronounced before a vowel
pour l'anglais: précède la syllabe accentuée	'	in French wordlist: no liaison before aspirate h

En règle générale, la prononciation est donnée entre crochets après chaque entrée. Toutefois, du côté anglais-français et dans le cas des expressions composées de deux ou plusieurs mots non réunis par un trait d'union et faisant l'objet d'une entrée séparée, la prononciation doit être cherchée sous chacun des mots constitutifs de l'expression en question.

PHONETIC TRANCRIPTION

VOYELLES

NB. La mise en équivalence de certains sons n'indique qu'une ressemblance approximative.

VOWELS

NB. The pairing of some vowel sounds only indicates approximate equivalence.

ici vie lyrique	i i:	heel bead
	ɪ	hit pity
jouer été	e	
lait jouet merci	ɛ	set tent
plat amour	a æ	bat apple
bas pâte	ɑ ɑ:	after car calm
	ʌ	fun cousin
le premier	ə	over above
beurre peur	œ	
peu deux	ø ə:	urgent fern work
or homme	ɔ	wash pot
mot eau gauche	o ɔ:	born cork
genou roue	u	full hook
	u:	boom shoe
rue urne	y	

DIPHTONGUES

DIPHTHONGS

ɪə	beer tier
ɛə	tear fair there
eɪ	date plaice day
aɪ	life buy cry
au	owl foul now
əu	low no
ɔɪ	boil boy oily
uə	poor tour

NASALES

NASAL VOWELS

matin plein	ɛ̃
brun	œ̃
sang an dans	ɑ̃
non pont	ɔ̃

In general, we give the pronunciation of each entry in square brackets after the word in question. However, on the English-French side, where the entry is composed of two or more unhyphenated words, each of which is given elsewhere in this dictionary, you will find the pronunciation of each word in its alphabetical position.

LES NOMBRES

NUMBERS

un (une)	1	one
deux	2	two
trois	3	three
quatre	4	four
cinq	5	five
six	6	six
sept	7	seven
huit	8	eight
neuf	9	nine
dix	10	ten
onze	11	eleven
douze	12	twelve
treize	13	thirteen
quatorze	14	fourteen
quinze	15	fifteen
seize	16	sixteen
dix-sept	17	seventeen
dix-huit	18	eighteen
dix-neuf	19	nineteen
vingt	20	twenty
vingt et un (une)	21	twenty-one
vingt-deux	22	twenty-two
trente	30	thirty
quarante	40	forty
cinquante	50	fifty
soixante	60	sixty
soixante-dix	70	seventy
soixante-et-onze	71	seventy-one
soixante-douze	72	seventy
quatre-vingts	80	eighty
quatre-vingt-un (-une)	81	eighty-one
quatre-vingt-dix	90	ninety
cent	100	a hundred, one hundred
cent un (une)	101	a hundred and one
deux cents	200	two hundred
deux cent un (une)	201	two hundred and one
quatre cents	400	four hundred
mille	1000	a thousand
cinq mille	5000	five thousand
un million	1000000	a million

LES NOMBRES

premier (première), 1er (1ère)
deuxième, 2e or 2ème
troisième, 3e or 3ème
quatrième, 4e or 4ème
cinquième, 5e or 5ème
sixième, 6e or 6ème
septième
huitième
neuvième
dixième
onzième
douzième
treizième
quartorzième
quinzième
seizième
dix-septième
dix-huitième
dix-neuvième
vingtième
vingt-et-unième
vingt-deuxième
trentième
centième
cent-unième
millième

NUMBERS

first, 1st
second, 2nd
third, 3rd
fourth, 4th
fifth, 5th
sixth, 6th
seventh
eighth
ninth
tenth
eleventh
twelfth
thirteenth
fourteenth
fifteenth
sixteenth
seventeenth
eighteenth
nineteenth
twentieth
twenty-first
twenty-second
thirtieth
hundredth
hundred-and-first
thousandth

LES FRACTIONS ETC

un demi
un tiers
un quart
un cinquième
zéro virgule cinq, 0,5
trois virgule quatre, 3,4
dix pour cent
cent pour cent

FRACTIONS ETC

a half
a third
a quarter
a fifth
(nought) point five, 0.5
three point four, 3.4
ten per cent
a hundred per cent

EXEMPLES

elle habite au septième (étage)
il habite au sept
au chapitre/à la page sept
il est arrivé (le) septième

EXAMPLES

she lives on the 7th floor
he lives at number 7
chapter/page 7
he came in 7th

L'HEURE

THE TIME

quelle heure est-il?

what time is it?

il est ...

it's ou *it is ...*

minuit	midnight, twelve p.m.
une heure (du matin)	one o'clock (in the morning), one (a.m.)
une heure cinq	five past one
une heure dix	ten past one
une heure et quart	a quarter past one, one fifteen
une heure vingt-cinq	twenty-five past one, one twenty-five
une heure et demie, une heure trente	half-past one, one thirty
deux heures moins vingt-cinq, une heure trente-cinq	twenty-five to two, one thirty-five
deux heures moins vingt, une heure quarante	twenty to two, one forty
deux heures moins le quart, une heure quarante-cinq	a quarter to two, one forty-five
deux heures moins dix, une heure cinquante	ten to two, one fifty
midi	twelve o'clock, midday, noon
deux heures (de l'après-midi), quatorze heures	two o'clock (in the afternoon), two (p.m.)
sept heures (du soir), dix-sept heures	seven o'clock (in the evening), seven (p.m.)

à quelle heure?

(at) what time?

à minuit	at midnight
à sept heures	at seven o'clock
dans vingt minutes	in twenty minutes
il y a un quart d'heure	fifteen minutes ago

a [a] *vb voir* **avoir**

MOT-CLÉ

à [a] (*à + le* = **au**, *à + les* = **aux**) *prép* **1** (*endroit, situation*) at, in; **être à Paris/au Portugal** to be in Paris/Portugal; **être à la maison/à l'école** to be at home/at school; **à la campagne** in the country; **c'est à 10 km/20 minutes (d'ici)** it's 10 km/20 minutes away

2 (*direction*) to; **aller à Paris/au Portugal** to go to Paris/Portugal; **aller à la maison/à l'école** to go home/to school; **à la campagne** to the country

3 (*temps*): **à 3 heures/minuit** at 3 o'clock/midnight; **au printemps/mois de juin** in the spring/the month of June; **à Noël/Pâques** at Christmas/Easter; **à demain/lundi!** see you tomorrow/on Monday!

4 (*attribution, appartenance*) to; **le livre est à Paul/à lui/à nous** this book is Paul's/his/ours; **un ami à moi** a friend of mine; **donner qch à qn** to give sth to sb

5 (*moyen*) with; **se chauffer au gaz** to have gas heating; **à bicyclette** on a *ou* by bicycle; **à pied** on foot; **à la main/machine** by hand/machine

6 (*provenance*) from; **boire à la bouteille** to drink from the bottle

7 (*caractérisation, manière*): **l'homme aux yeux bleus** the man with the blue eyes; **à leur grande surprise** much to their surprise; **à ce qu'il prétend** according to him, from what he says; **à la russe** the Russian way; **à nous deux nous n'avons pas su le faire** we couldn't do it, even between the two of us

8 (*but, destination*): **tasse à café** coffee cup; **maison à vendre** house for sale; **je n'ai rien à lire** I don't have anything to read; **à bien réfléchir ...** thinking about it ..., on reflection ...

9 (*rapport, évaluation, distribution*): **100 km/unités à l'heure** 100 km/units per *ou* an hour; **payé au mois/à l'heure** paid monthly/by the hour; **cinq à six** five to six; **ils sont arrivés à quatre** four of them arrived

abaisser [abese] *vt* to lower, bring down; (*manette*) to pull down; **s'~** *vi* to go down; (*fig*) to demean o.s.

abandon [abɑ̃dɔ̃] *nm* abandoning; giving up; withdrawal; **être à l'~** to be in a state of neglect; **laisser à l'~** to abandon

abandonner [abɑ̃dɔne] *vt* (*personne*) to abandon; (*projet, activité*) to abandon, give up; (*Sport*) to retire *ou* withdraw from; (*céder*) to surrender; **s'~ à** (*paresse, plaisirs*) to give o.s. up to

abat-jour [abaʒuR] *nm inv* lampshade

abats [aba] *nmpl* (*de bœuf, porc*) offal *sg*; (*de volaille*) giblets

abattement [abatmɑ̃] *nm*: **abattement fiscal** ≈ tax allowance

abattoir [abatwaR] *nm* slaughterhouse

abattre [abatR] *vt* (*arbre*) to cut down, fell; (*mur, maison*) to pull down; (*avion, personne*) to shoot down; (*animal*) to shoot, kill; (*fig*) to wear out, tire out; to demoralize; **s'~** *vi* to crash down; **ne pas se laisser ~** to keep one's spirits up, not to let things get one down; **s'~ sur** to beat down on; (*fig*) to rain down on; **~ du travail** *ou* **de la besogne** to get through a lot of work

abbaye [abei] *nf* abbey

abbé [abe] *nm* priest; (*d'une abbaye*) abbot

abcès [apsɛ] *nm* abscess

abdiquer [abdike] *vi* to abdicate

abdominaux [abdɔmino] *nmpl*: **faire des ~** to do sit-ups

abeille [abɛj] *nf* bee

aberrant, e [abeRɑ̃, ɑ̃t] *adj* absurd

aberration [abeRasjɔ̃] *nf* aberration

abîme [abim] *nm* abyss, gulf

abîmer [abime] *vt* to spoil, damage; **s'~** *vi* to get spoilt *ou* damaged

aboiement [abwamɑ̃] *nm* bark, barking

abolir [abɔliR] *vt* to abolish

abominable [abɔminabl] *adj* abominable

abondance [abɔ̃dɑ̃s] *nf* abundance

abondant, e [abɔ̃dɑ̃, ɑ̃t] *adj* plentiful, abundant, copious; **abonder** *vi* to abound, be plentiful; **abonder dans le sens de qn** to concur with sb

abonné, e [abɔne] *nm/f* subscriber; season ticket holder

abonnement [abɔnmɑ̃] *nm* subscription; (*transports, concerts*) season ticket

abonner [abɔne] *vt*: **s'~ à** to subscribe to, take out a subscription to

abord [abɔR] *nm*: **au premier ~** at first sight, initially; **abords** *nmpl* (*environs*) surroundings; **d'~** first

abordable [abɔRdabl] *adj* (*prix*) reasonable; (*personne*) approachable

aborder [abɔRde] *vi* to land ▷ *vt* (*sujet, difficulté*) to tackle; (*personne*) to approach; (*rivage etc*) to reach

aboutir [abutiR] *vi* (*négociations etc*) to succeed; **~ à** to end up at; **n'~ à rien** to come to nothing

aboyer [abwaje] *vi* to bark

abréger [abReʒe] *vt* to shorten

abreuver [abRœve]: **s'~** *vi* to drink; **abreuvoir** *nm* watering place

abréviation [abRevjasjɔ̃] *nf* abbreviation

abri [abRi] *nm* shelter; **être à l'~** to be under cover; **se mettre à l'~** to shelter; **à l'~ de** (*vent, soleil*) sheltered from; (*danger*) safe from

abricot [abRiko] *nm* apricot

abriter [abRite] *vt* to shelter; **s'~** *vt* to shelter, take cover

abrupt, e [abʀypt] adj sheer, steep; (ton) abrupt
abruti, e [abʀyti] adj stunned, dazed ▷ nm/f (fam) idiot,
moron; **~ de travail** overworked
absence [apsɑ̃s] nf absence; (Méd) blackout; **avoir des
~s** to have mental blanks
absent, e [apsɑ̃, ɑ̃t] adj absent ▷ nm/f absentee;
absenter: s'absenter vi to take time off work; (sortir)
to leave, go out
absolu, e [apsɔly] adj absolute; **absolument** adv
absolutely
absorbant, e [apsɔʀbɑ̃, ɑ̃t] adj absorbent
absorber [apsɔʀbe] vt to absorb; (gén Méd: manger,
boire) to take
abstenir [apstəniʀ] vb: **s'~ de qch/de faire** to refrain
from sth/from doing
abstrait, e [apstʀɛ, ɛt] adj abstract
absurde [apsyʀd] adj absurd
abus [aby] nm abuse; **~ de confiance** breach of trust; **il y
a de l'~!** (fam) that's a bit much!; **abuser** vi to go too far,
overstep the mark; **abuser de** (duper) to take advantage
of; **s'abuser** vi (se méprendre) to be mistaken; **abusif,
-ive** adj exorbitant; (punition) excessive
académie [akademi] nf academy; (Scol: circonscription)
≈ regional education authority
acajou [akaʒu] nm mahogany
acariâtre [akaʀjɑtʀ] adj cantankerous
accablant, e [akablɑ̃, ɑ̃t] adj (chaleur) oppressive;
(témoignage, preuve) overwhelming
accabler [akable] vt to overwhelm, overcome; **~ qn
d'injures** to heap ou shower abuse on sb; **~ qn de travail**
to overwork sb
accalmie [akalmi] nf lull
accaparer [akapaʀe] vt to monopolize; (suj: travail etc)
to take up (all) the time ou attention of
accéder [aksede]: **~ à** vt (lieu) to reach; (accorder: requête)
to grant, accede to
accélérateur [akseleʀatœʀ] nm accelerator
accélérer [akseleʀe] vt to speed up ▷ vi to accelerate
accent [aksɑ̃] nm accent; (Phonétique, fig) stress;
mettre l'~ sur (fig) to stress; **~ aigu/grave/circonflexe**
acute/grave/circumflex accent; **accentuer** vt (Ling) to
accent; (fig) to accentuate, emphasize; **s'accentuer** vi
to become more marked ou pronounced
acceptation [akseptasjɔ̃] nf acceptance
accepter [aksepte] vt to accept; **~ de faire** to agree to
do; **acceptez-vous les cartes de crédit?** do you take
credit cards?
accès [aksɛ] nm (à un lieu) access; (Méd: de toux) fit; (:
de fièvre) bout; **d'~ facile** easily accessible; **facile d'~**
easy to get to; **accès de colère** fit of anger; **accessible**
adj accessible; (livre, sujet): **accessible à qn** within the
reach of sb
accessoire [akseswaʀ] adj secondary; incidental ▷ nm
accessory; (Théâtre) prop
accident [aksidɑ̃] nm accident; **par ~** by chance; **j'ai
eu un ~** I've had an accident; **accident de la route** road
accident; **accidenté, e** adj damaged; injured; (relief,
terrain) uneven; hilly; **accidentel, le** adj accidental
acclamer [aklame] vt to cheer, acclaim
acclimater [aklimate]: **s'~** vi (personne) to adapt (o.s.)
accolade [akɔlad] nf (amicale) embrace; (signe) brace
accommoder [akɔmɔde] vt (Culin) to prepare; **s'~ de** vt
to put up with; (se contenter de) to make do with
accompagnateur, -trice [akɔ̃paɲatœʀ, tʀis] nm/f

(Mus) accompanist; (de voyage: guide) guide; (de voyage
organisé) courier
accompagner [akɔ̃paɲe] vt to accompany, be ou go ou
come with; (Mus) to accompany
accompli, e [akɔ̃pli] adj accomplished; voir aussi **fait**
accomplir [akɔ̃pliʀ] vt (tâche, projet) to carry out;
(souhait) to fulfil; **s'~** vi to be fulfilled
accord [akɔʀ] nm agreement; (entre des styles, tons etc)
harmony; (Mus) chord; **d'~!** OK!; **se mettre d'~** to come
to an agreement; **être d'~ (pour faire qch)** to agree
(to do sth)
accordéon [akɔʀdeɔ̃] nm (Mus) accordion
accorder [akɔʀde] vt (faveur, délai) to grant; (harmoniser)
to match; (Mus) to tune; (valeur, importance) attach
accoster [akɔste] vt (Navig) to draw alongside ▷ vi to
berth
accouchement [akuʃmɑ̃] nm delivery, (child)birth;
labour
accoucher [akuʃe] vi to give birth, have a baby; **~ d'un
garçon** to give birth to a boy
accouder [akude]: **s'~** vi: **s'~ à/contre/sur** to rest one's
elbows on/against/on; **accoudoir** nm armrest
accoupler [akuple] vt to couple; (pour la reproduction) to
mate; **s'~** vt to mate
accourir [akuʀiʀ] vi to rush ou run up
accoutumance [akutymɑ̃s] nf (gén) adaptation; (Méd)
addiction
accoutumé, e [akutyme] adj (habituel) customary,
usual
accoutumer [akutyme] vt: **s'~ à** to get accustomed
ou used to
accroc [akʀo] nm (déchirure) tear; (fig) hitch, snag
accrochage [akʀoʃaʒ] nm (Auto) collision; (dispute)
clash, brush
accrocher [akʀoʃe] vt (fig) to catch, attract; **s'~** (se
disputer) to have a clash ou brush; **~ qch à** (suspendre) to
hang sth (up) on; (attacher: remorque) to hitch sth (up) to;
~ qch (à) (déchirer) to catch sth (on); **il a accroché ma
voiture** he bumped into my car; **s'~ à** (rester pris à) to
catch on; (agripper, fig) to hang on ou cling to
accroissement [akʀwasmɑ̃] nm increase
accroître [akʀwatʀ]: **s'~** vi to increase
accroupir [akʀupiʀ]: **s'~** vi to squat, crouch (down)
accru, e [akʀy] pp de **accroître**
accueil [akœj] nm welcome; **comité d'~** reception
committee; **accueillir** vt to welcome; (aller chercher) to
meet, collect
accumuler [akymyle] vt to accumulate, amass; **s'~** vi
to accumulate; to pile up
accusation [akyzasjɔ̃] nf (gén) accusation; (Jur) charge;
(partie): **l'~** the prosecution
accusé, e [akyze] nm/f accused; defendant; **accusé de
réception** acknowledgement of receipt
accuser [akyze] vt to accuse; (fig) to emphasize, bring
out; to show; **~ qn de** to accuse sb of; (Jur) to charge sb
with; **~ réception de** to acknowledge receipt of
acéré, e [aseʀe] adj sharp
acharné, e [aʃaʀne] adj (efforts) relentless; (lutte,
adversaire) fierce, bitter
acharner [aʃaʀne] vb: **s'~ contre** to set o.s. against;
(suj: malchance) to dog; **s'~ à faire** to try doggedly to do;
(persister) to persist in doing; **s'~ sur qn** to hound sb
achat [aʃa] nm purchase; **faire des ~s** to do some
shopping; **faire l'~ de qch** to purchase sth

acheter [aʃ(ə)te] vt to buy, purchase; (soudoyer) to buy; **~ qch à** (marchand) to buy ou purchase sth from; (ami etc: offrir) to buy sth for; **où est-ce que je peux ~ des cartes postales?** where can I buy (some) postcards?; **acheteur, -euse** nm/f buyer; shopper; (Comm) buyer

achever [aʃ(ə)ve] vt to complete, finish; (blessé) to finish off; **s'~** vi to end

acide [asid] adj sour, sharp; (Chimie) acid(ic) ▷ nm (Chimie) acid; **acidulé, e** adj slightly acid; **bonbons acidulés** acid drops

acier [asje] nm steel; **aciérie** nf steelworks sg

acné [akne] nf acne

acompte [akɔ̃t] nm deposit

à-côté [akote] nm side-issue; (argent) extra

à-coup [aku] nm: **par ~s** by fits and starts

acoustique [akustik] nf (d'une salle) acoustics pl

acquéreur [akerœr] nm buyer, purchaser

acquérir [akerir] vt to acquire

acquis, e [aki, iz] pp de **acquérir** ▷ nm (accumulated) experience; **son aide nous est ~e** we can count on her help

acquitter [akite] vt (Jur) to acquit; (facture) to pay, settle; **s'~ de** vt (devoir) to discharge; (promesse) to fulfil

âcre [ɑkr] adj acrid, pungent

acrobate [akrɔbat] nm/f acrobat; **acrobatie** nf acrobatics sg

acte [akt] nm act, action; (Théâtre) act; **prendre ~ de** to note, take note of; **faire ~ de candidature** to apply; **faire ~ de présence** to put in an appearance; **acte de naissance** birth certificate

acteur [aktœr] nm actor

actif, -ive [aktif, iv] adj active ▷ nm (Comm) assets pl; (fig): **avoir à son ~** to have to one's credit; **population active** working population

action [aksjɔ̃] nf (gén) action; (Comm) share; **une bonne ~** a good deed; **actionnaire** nm/f shareholder; **actionner** vt (mécanisme) to activate; (machine) to operate

activer [aktive] vt to speed up; **s'~** vi to bustle about; to hurry up

activité [aktivite] nf activity; **en ~** (volcan) active; (fonctionnaire) in active life

actrice [aktris] nf actress

actualité [aktualite] nf (d'un problème) topicality; (événements): **l'~** current events; **actualités** nfpl (Cinéma, TV) the news; **l'~ topical**

actuel, le [aktyɛl] adj (présent) present; (d'actualité) topical; **à l'heure ~le** at the present time; **actuellement** adv at present, at the present time

acuponcture [akypɔ̃ktyr] nf acupuncture

adaptateur [adaptatœr] nm (Élec) adapter

adapter [adapte] vt to adapt; **s'~ (à)** (suj: personne) to adapt (to); **~ qch à** (approprier) to adapt sth to (fit); **~ qch sur/dans/à** (fixer) to fit sth on/into/to

addition [adisjɔ̃] nf addition; (au café) bill; **l'~, s'il vous plaît** could I have the bill, please?; **additionner** vt to add (up)

adepte [adɛpt] nm/f follower

adéquat, e [adekwa(t), at] adj appropriate, suitable

adhérent, e [aderɑ̃, ɑ̃t] nm/f member

adhérer [adere]: **~ à** vt (coller) to adhere ou stick to; (se rallier à) to join; **adhésif, -ive** adj adhesive, sticky; **ruban adhésif** sticky ou adhesive tape

adieu, x [adjø] excl goodbye ▷ nm farewell

adjectif [adʒɛktif] nm adjective

adjoint, e [adʒwɛ̃, wɛt] nm/f assistant; **adjoint au maire** deputy mayor; **directeur adjoint** assistant manager

admettre [admɛtr] vt (laisser entrer) to admit; (candidat: Scol) to pass; (tolérer) to allow, accept; (reconnaître) to admit, acknowledge

administrateur, -trice [administratœr, tris] nm/f (Comm) director; (Admin) administrator

administration [administrasjɔ̃] nf administration; **l'A~** ≈ the Civil Service

administrer [administre] vt (firme) to manage, run; (biens, remède, sacrement etc) to administer

admirable [admirabl] adj admirable, wonderful

admirateur, -trice [admiratœr, tris] nm/f admirer

admiration [admirasjɔ̃] nf admiration

admirer [admire] vt to admire

admis, e [admi, iz] pp de **admettre**

admissible [admisibl] adj (candidat) eligible; (comportement) admissible, acceptable

ADN sigle m (= acide désoxyribonucléique) DNA

adolescence [adɔlesɑ̃s] nf adolescence

adolescent, e [adɔlesɑ̃, ɑ̃t] nm/f adolescent, teenager

adopter [adɔpte] vt to adopt; **adoptif, -ive** adj (parents) adoptive; (fils, patrie) adopted

adorable [adɔrabl] adj delightful, adorable

adorer [adɔre] vt to adore; (Rel) to worship

adosser [adose] vt: **~ qch à ou contre** to stand sth against; **s'~ à/contre** to lean with one's back against

adoucir [adusir] vt (goût, température) to make milder; (avec du sucre) to sweeten; (peau, voix) to soften; (caractère) to mellow

adresse [adrɛs] nf (domicile) address; (dextérité) skill, dexterity; **~ électronique** email address

adresser [adrese] vt (lettre: expédier) to send; (: écrire l'adresse sur) to address; (injure, compliments) to address; **s'~ à** (parler à) to speak to, address; (s'informer auprès de) to go and see; (: bureau) to inquire at; (suj: livre, conseil) to be aimed at; **~ la parole à** to speak to, address

adroit, e [adrwa, wat] adj skilful, skilled

ADSL sigle m (= asymmetrical digital subscriber line) ADSL, broadband

adulte [adylt] nm/f adult, grown-up ▷ adj (chien, arbre) fully-grown, mature; (attitude) adult, grown-up

adverbe [advɛrb] nm adverb

adversaire [advɛrsɛr] nm/f (Sport, gén) opponent, adversary

aération [aerasjɔ̃] nf airing; (circulation de l'air) ventilation

aérer [aere] vt to air; (fig) to lighten

aérien, ne [aerjɛ̃, ɛn] adj (Aviat) air cpd, aerial; (câble, métro) overhead; (fig) light; **compagnie ~ne** airline

aéro... [aero] préfixe: **aérobic** nm aerobics sg; **aérogare** nf airport (buildings); (en ville) air terminal; **aéroglisseur** nm hovercraft; **aérophagie** nf (Méd) wind, aerophagia (Méd); **aéroport** nm airport; **aérosol** nm aerosol

affaiblir [afeblir]: **s'~** vi to weaken

affaire [afɛr] nf (problème, question) matter; (criminelle, judiciaire) case; (scandaleuse etc) affair; (entreprise) business; (marché, transaction) deal; business no pl; (occasion intéressante) bargain; **affaires** nfpl (intérêts publics et privés) affairs; (activité commerciale) business sg; (effets personnels) things, belongings; **ce sont mes ~s** (cela me concerne) that's my business; **occupe-toi de**

tes ~s! mind your own business!; **ça fera l'~** that will do (nicely); **se tirer d'~** to sort it out ou things out for o.s.; **avoir ~ à** (être en contact) to be dealing with; **les A~s étrangères** Foreign Affairs; **affairer: s'affairer** vi to busy o.s., bustle about

affamé, e [afame] adj starving

affecter [afɛkte] vt to affect; **~ qch à** to allocate ou allot sth to; **~ qn à** to appoint sb to; (diplomate) to post sb to

affectif, -ive [afɛktif, iv] adj emotional

affection [afɛksjɔ̃] nf affection; (mal) ailment; **affectionner** vt to be fond of; **affectueux, -euse** adj affectionate

affichage [afiʃaʒ] nm billposting; (électronique) display; **"~ interdit"** "stick no bills"; **affichage à cristaux liquides** liquid crystal display, LCD

affiche [afiʃ] nf poster; (officielle) notice; (Théâtre) bill; **être à l'~** to be on

afficher [afiʃe] vt (affiche) to put up; (réunion) to put up a notice about; (électroniquement) to display; (fig) to exhibit, display; **"défense d'~"** "no bill posters"; **s'~** vr (péj) to flaunt o.s.; (électroniquement) to be displayed

affilée [afile]: **d'~** adv at a stretch

affirmatif, -ive [afirmatif, iv] adj affirmative

affirmer [afirme] vt to assert

affligé, e [afliʒe] adj distressed, grieved; **~ de** (maladie, tare) afflicted with

affliger [afliʒe] vt (peiner) to distress, grieve

affluence [aflyɑ̃s] nf crowds pl; **heures d'~** rush hours; **jours d'~** busiest days

affluent [aflyɑ̃] nm tributary

affolement [afɔlmɑ̃] nm panic

affoler [afɔle] vt to throw into a panic; **s'~** vi to panic

affranchir [afrɑ̃ʃir] vt to put a stamp ou stamps on; (à la machine) to frank (BRIT), meter (US); (fig) to free, liberate; **affranchissement** nm postage

affreux, -euse [afrø, øz] adj dreadful, awful

affront [afrɔ̃] nm affront; **affrontement** nm clash, confrontation

affronter [afrɔ̃te] vt to confront, face

affût [afy] nm: **à l'~ (de)** (gibier) lying in wait (for); (fig) on the look-out (for)

Afghanistan [afganistɑ̃] nm: **l'~** Afghanistan

afin [afɛ̃]: **~ que** conj so that, in order that; **~ de faire** in order to do, so as to do

africain, e [afrikɛ̃, ɛn] adj African ⊳ nm/f: **A~, e** African

Afrique [afrik] nf: **l'~** Africa; **l'Afrique du Nord/Sud** North/South Africa

agacer [agase] vt to irritate

âge [aʒ] nm age; **quel ~ as-tu?** how old are you?; **prendre de l'~** to be getting on (in years); **le troisième ~** (période) retirement; (personnes âgées) senior citizens; **âgé, e** adj old, elderly; **âgé de 10 ans** 10 years old

agence [aʒɑ̃s] nf agency, office; (succursale) branch; **agence de voyages** travel agency; **agence immobilière** estate (BRIT) ou real estate (US) agent's (office)

agenda [aʒɛ̃da] nm diary; **~ électronique** PDA

agenouiller [aʒ(ə)nuje]: **s'~** vi to kneel (down)

agent, e [aʒɑ̃, ɑ̃t] nm/f (aussi: **~(e) de police**) policeman (policewoman); (Admin) official, officer; **agent immobilier** estate agent (BRIT), realtor (US)

agglomération [aglɔmerasjɔ̃] nf town; built-up area; **l'~ parisienne** the urban area of Paris

aggraver [agrave]: **s'~** vi to worsen

agile [aʒil] adj agile, nimble

agir [aʒir] vi to act; **il s'agit de** (ça traite de) it is about; (il est important de) it's a matter ou question of; **il s'agit de faire** we (ou you etc) must do; **de quoi s'agit-il?** what is it about?

agitation [aʒitasjɔ̃] nf (hustle and) bustle; (trouble) agitation, excitement; (politique) unrest, agitation

agité, e [aʒite] adj fidgety, restless; (troublé) agitated, perturbed; (mer) rough

agiter [aʒite] vt (bouteille, chiffon) to shake; (bras, mains) to wave; (préoccuper, exciter) to perturb

agneau, x [aɲo] nm lamb

agonie [agɔni] nf mortal agony, death pangs pl; (fig) death throes pl

agrafe [agraf] nf (de vêtement) hook, fastener; (de bureau) staple; **agrafer** vt to fasten; to staple; **agrafeuse** nf stapler

agrandir [agrɑ̃dir] vt to enlarge; **s'~** vi (ville, famille) to grow, expand; (trou, écart) to get bigger; **agrandissement** nm (Photo) enlargement

agréable [agreabl] adj pleasant, nice

agréé, e [agree] adj: **concessionnaire ~** registered dealer

agréer [agree] vt (requête) to accept; **~ à** to please, suit; **veuillez ~, Monsieur/Madame, mes salutations distinguées** (personne nommée) yours sincerely; (personne non nommée) yours faithfully

agrégation [agregasjɔ̃] nf highest teaching diploma in France; **agrégé, e** nm/f holder of the agrégation

agrément [agremɑ̃] nm (accord) consent, approval; (attraits) charm, attractiveness; (plaisir) pleasure

agresser [agrese] vt to attack; **agresseur** nm aggressor, attacker; (Pol, Mil) aggressor; **agressif, -ive** adj aggressive

agricole [agrikɔl] adj agricultural; **agriculteur** nm farmer; **agriculture** nf agriculture, farming

agripper [agripe] vt to grab, clutch; **s'~ à** to cling (on) to, clutch, grip

agro-alimentaire [agroalimɑ̃tɛr] nm farm-produce industry

agrumes [agrym] nmpl citrus fruit(s)

aguets [agɛ] nmpl: **être aux ~** to be on the lookout

ai [ɛ] vb voir **avoir**

aide [ɛd] nm/f assistant; carer ⊳ nf assistance, help; (secours financier) aid; **à l'~ de** (avec) with the help ou aid of; **appeler (qn) à l'~** to call for help (from sb); **à l'~!** help!; **aide judiciaire** legal aid; **aide ménagère** ≈ home help (BRIT) ou helper (US); **aide-mémoire** inv memoranda pages pl; (key facts) handbook; **aide-soignant, e** nm/f auxiliary nurse

aider [ede] vt to help; **~ à qch** to help (towards) sth; **~ qn à faire qch** to help sb to do sth; **pouvez-vous m'~?** can you help me?; **s'~ de** (se servir de) to use, make use of

aie [aj] excl ouch!

aie etc [ɛ] vb voir **avoir**

aigle [ɛgl] nm eagle

aigre [ɛgr] adj sour, sharp; (fig) sharp, cutting; **aigre-doux, -ce** adj (sauce) sweet and sour; **aigreur** nf sourness; sharpness; **aigreurs d'estomac** heartburn sg

aigu, ë [egy] adj (objet, douleur) sharp; (son, voix) high-pitched, shrill; (note) high(-pitched)

aiguille [eguij] nf needle; (de montre) hand; **aiguille à tricoter** knitting needle

aiguiser [egize] vt to sharpen; (fig) to stimulate; (: sens) to excite

ail [aj] *nm* garlic

aile [ɛl] *nf* wing; **aileron** *nm* (*de requin*) fin; **ailier** *nm* winger

aille *etc* [aj] *vb voir* **aller**

ailleurs [ajœʀ] *adv* elsewhere, somewhere else; **partout/nulle part ~** everywhere/nowhere else; **d'~** (*du reste*) moreover, besides; **par ~** (*d'autre part*) moreover, furthermore

aimable [ɛmabl] *adj* kind, nice

aimant [ɛmɑ̃] *nm* magnet

aimer [eme] *vt* to love; (*d'amitié, affection, par goût*) to like; (*souhait*): **j'aimerais ...** I would like ...; **j'aime faire du ski** I like skiing; **je t'aime** I love you; **bien ~ qn/qch** to like sb/sth; **j'aime mieux Paul (que Pierre)** I prefer Paul (to Pierre); **j'aimerais mieux faire** I'd much rather do

aine [ɛn] *nf* groin

aîné, e [ene] *adj* elder, older; (*le plus âgé*) eldest, oldest ▷ *nm/f* oldest child *ou* one, oldest boy *ou* son/girl *ou* daughter

ainsi [ɛ̃si] *adv* (*de cette façon*) like this, in this way, thus; (*ce faisant*) thus ▷ *conj* thus, so; **~ que** (*comme*) (just) as; (*et aussi*) as well as; **pour ~ dire** so to speak; **et ~ de suite** and so on

air [ɛʀ] *nm* air; (*mélodie*) tune; (*expression*) look, air; **prendre l'~** to get some (fresh) air; **avoir l'~** (*sembler*) to look, appear; **il a l'~ triste/malade** he looks sad/ill; **avoir l'~ de** to look like; **il a l'~ de dormir** he looks as if he's sleeping; **en l'~** (*promesses*) empty

airbag [ɛʀbag] *nm* airbag

aisance [ɛzɑ̃s] *nf* ease; (*richesse*) affluence

aise [ɛz] *nf* comfort; **être à l'~** *ou* **à son ~** to be comfortable; (*pas embarrassé*) to be at ease; (*financièrement*) to be comfortably off; **se mettre à l'~** to make o.s. comfortable; **être mal à l'~** to be uncomfortable; (*gêné*) to be ill at ease; **en faire à son ~** to do as one likes; **aisé, e** *adj* easy; (*assez riche*) well-to-do, well-off

aisselle [ɛsɛl] *nf* armpit

ait [ɛ] *vb voir* **avoir**

ajonc [aʒɔ̃] *nm* gorse *no pl*

ajourner [aʒuʀne] *vt* (*réunion*) to adjourn; (*décision*) to defer, postpone

ajouter [aʒute] *vt* to add

alarme [alaʀm] *nf* alarm; **donner l'~** to give *ou* raise the alarm; **alarmer** *vt* to alarm; **s'alarmer** *vi* to become alarmed

Albanie [albani] *nf:* **l'~** Albania

album [albɔm] *nm* album

alcool [alkɔl] *nm:* **l'~** alcohol; **un ~** a spirit, a brandy; **bière sans ~** non-alcoholic *ou* alcohol-free beer; **alcool à brûler** methylated spirits (*BRIT*), wood alcohol (*US*); **alcool à 90°** surgical spirit; **alcoolique** *adj, nm/f* alcoholic; **alcoolisé, e** *adj* alcoholic; **une boisson non alcoolisée** a soft drink; **alcoolisme** *nm* alcoholism; **alco(o)test®** *nm* Breathalyser®; (*test*) breath-test

aléatoire [aleatwaʀ] *adj* uncertain; (*Inform*) random

alentour [alɑ̃tuʀ] *adv* around, round about; **alentours** *nmpl* (*environs*) surroundings; **aux ~s de** in the vicinity *ou* neighbourhood of, round about; (*temps*) round about

alerte [alɛʀt] *adj* agile, nimble; brisk, lively ▷ *nf* alert; warning; **alerte à la bombe** bomb scare; **alerter** *vt* to alert

algèbre [alʒɛbʀ] *nf* algebra

Alger [alʒe] *n* Algiers

Algérie [alʒeʀi] *nf:* **l'~** Algeria; **algérien, ne** *adj* Algerian ▷ *nm/f:* **Algérien, ne** Algerian

algue [alg] *nf* (*gén*) seaweed *no pl*; (*Bot*) alga

alibi [alibi] *nm* alibi

aligner [aliɲe] *vt* to align, line up; (*idées, chiffres*) to string together; (*adapter*): **~ qch sur** to bring sth into alignment with; **s'~** (*soldats etc*) to line up; **s'~ sur** (*Pol*) to align o.s. on

aliment [alimɑ̃] *nm* food; **alimentation** *nf* (*commerce*) food trade; (*magasin*) grocery store; (*régime*) diet; (*en eau etc, de moteur*) supplying; (*Inform*) feed; **alimenter** *vt* to feed; (*Tech*): **alimenter (en)** to supply (with); to feed (with); (*fig*) to sustain, keep going

allaiter [alete] *vt* to (breast-)feed, nurse; (*suj: animal*) to suckle

allécher [aleʃe] *vt:* **~ qn** to make sb's mouth water; to tempt *ou* entice sb

allée [ale] *nf* (*de jardin*) path; (*en ville*) avenue, drive; **~s et venues** comings and goings

allégé, e [aleʒe] *adj* (*yaourt etc*) low-fat

alléger [aleʒe] *vt* (*voiture*) to make lighter; (*chargement*) to lighten; (*souffrance*) to alleviate, soothe

Allemagne [alman] *nf:* **l'~** Germany; **allemand, e** *adj* German ▷ *nm/f:* **Allemand, e** German ▷ *nm* (*Ling*) German

aller [ale] *nm* (*trajet*) outward journey; (*billet: aussi:* **~ simple**) single (*BRIT*) *ou* one-way (*US*) ticket; **~ (et) retour** return (ticket) (*BRIT*), round-trip ticket (*US*) ▷ *vi* (*gén*) to go; (*convenir*) to suit; (*suj: forme, pointure etc*) to fit; **~ (bien) avec** (*couleurs, style etc*) to go (well) with; **je vais y ~/me fâcher** I'm going to go/to get angry; **~ chercher qn** to go and get *ou* fetch (*BRIT*) sb; **~ voir** to go and see, go to see; **allez!** come on!; **allons!** come now!; **comment allez-vous?** how are you?; **comment ça va?** how are you?; (*affaires etc*) how are things?; **il va bien/mal** he's well/not well, he's fine/ill; **ça va bien/mal** (*affaires etc*) it's going well/not going well; **~ mieux** to be better; **s'en ~** (*partir*) to be off, go, leave; (*disparaître*) to go away

allergie [alɛʀʒi] *nf* allergy

allergique [alɛʀʒik] *adj:* **~ à** allergic to; **je suis ~ à la pénicilline** I'm allergic to penicillin

alliance [aljɑ̃s] *nf* (*Mil, Pol*) alliance; (*bague*) wedding ring

allier [alje] *vt* (*Pol, gén*) to ally; (*fig*) to combine; **s'~** to become allies; to combine

allô [alo] *excl* hullo, hallo

allocation [alɔkasjɔ̃] *nf* allowance; **allocation (de) chômage** unemployment benefit; **allocations familiales** = child benefit

allonger [alɔ̃ʒe] *vt* to lengthen, make longer; (*étendre: bras, jambe*) to stretch (out); **s'~** *vi* to get longer; (*se coucher*) to lie down, stretch out; **~ le pas** to hasten one's step(s)

allumage [alymaʒ] *nm* (*Auto*) ignition

allume-cigare [alymsigaʀ] *nm inv* cigar lighter

allumer [alyme] *vt* (*lampe, phare, radio*) to put *ou* switch on; (*pièce*) to put *ou* switch the light(s) on in; (*feu*) to light; **s'~** *vi* (*lumière, lampe*) to come *ou* go on; **je n'arrive pas à ~ le chauffage** I can't turn the heating on

allumette [alymɛt] *nf* match

allure [alyʀ] *nf* (*vitesse*) speed, pace; (*démarche*) walk; (*aspect, air*) look; **avoir de l'~** to have style; **à toute ~**

at top speed
allusion [a(l)lyzjɔ̃] *nf* allusion; (*sous-entendu*) hint; **faire ~ à** to allude *ou* refer to; to hint at

 MOT-CLÉ

alors [alɔʀ] *adv* **1** (*à ce moment-là*) then, at that time; **il habitait alors à Paris** he lived in Paris at that time
2 (*par conséquent*) then; **tu as fini? alors je m'en vais** have you finished? I'm going then; **et alors?** so what?
▷ *conj*: **alors que 1** (*au moment où*) when, as; **il est arrivé alors que je partais** he arrived as I was leaving
2 (*tandis que*) whereas, while; **alors que son frère travaillait dur, lui se reposait** while his brother was working hard, HE would rest
3 (*bien que*) even though; **il a été puni alors qu'il n'a rien fait** he was punished, even though he had done nothing

alourdir [aluʀdiʀ] *vt* to weigh down, make heavy
Alpes [alp] *nfpl*: **les ~** the Alps
alphabet [alfabɛ] *nm* alphabet; (*livre*) ABC (book)
alpinisme [alpinism] *nm* mountaineering, climbing
Alsace [alzas] *nf* Alsace; **alsacien, ne** *adj* Alsatian ▷ *nm/f*: **Alsacien, ne** Alsatian
altermondialisme [altɛʀmɔ̃djalism] *nm* anti-globalism; **altermondialiste** *adj, nm/f* anti-globalist
alternatif, -ive [altɛʀnatif, iv] *adj* alternating; **alternative** *nf* (*choix*) alternative; **alterner** *vi* to alternate
altitude [altityd] *nf* altitude, height
alto [alto] *nm* (*instrument*) viola
aluminium [alyminjɔm] *nm* aluminium (BRIT), aluminum (US)
amabilité [amabilite] *nf* kindness
amaigrissant, e [amegʀisɑ̃, ɑ̃t] *adj* (*régime*) slimming
amande [amɑ̃d] *nf* (*de l'amandier*) almond; **amandier** *nm* almond (tree)
amant [amɑ̃] *nm* lover
amas [amɑ] *nm* heap, pile; **amasser** *vt* to amass
amateur [amatœʀ] *nm* amateur; **en ~** (*péj*) amateurishly; **amateur de musique/sport** music/sport lover
ambassade [ɑ̃basad] *nf* embassy; **l'~ de France** the French Embassy; **ambassadeur, -drice** *nm/f* ambassador(-dress)
ambiance [ɑ̃bjɑ̃s] *nf* atmosphere; **il y a de l'~** there's a great atmosphere
ambigu, ë [ɑ̃bigy] *adj* ambiguous
ambitieux, -euse [ɑ̃bisjø, jøz] *adj* ambitious
ambition [ɑ̃bisjɔ̃] *nf* ambition
ambulance [ɑ̃bylɑ̃s] *nf* ambulance; **appelez une ~!** call an ambulance!; **ambulancier, -ière** *nm/f* ambulance man(-woman) (BRIT), paramedic (US)
âme [ɑm] *nf* soul; **âme sœur** kindred spirit
amélioration [ameljɔʀasjɔ̃] *nf* improvement
améliorer [ameljɔʀe] *vt* to improve; **s'~** *vi* to improve, get better
aménager [amenaʒe] *vt* (*agencer, transformer*) to fit out; to lay out; (*: quartier, territoire*) to develop; (*installer*) to fix up, put in; **ferme aménagée** converted farmhouse
amende [amɑ̃d] *nf* fine; **faire ~ honorable** to make amends
amener [am(ə)ne] *vt* to bring; (*causer*) to bring about;

s'~ *vi* to show up (*fam*), turn up; **~ qn à faire qch** to lead sb to do sth
amer, amère [amɛʀ] *adj* bitter
américain, e [ameʀikɛ̃, ɛn] *adj* American ▷ *nm/f*: **A~, e** American
Amérique [ameʀik] *nf*: **l'~** America; **Amérique centrale/latine** Central/Latin America; **l'Amérique du Nord/Sud** North/South America
amertume [amɛʀtym] *nf* bitterness
ameublement [amœbləmɑ̃] *nm* furnishing; (*meubles*) furniture
ami, e [ami] *nm/f* friend; (*amant/maîtresse*) boyfriend/girlfriend ▷ *adj*: **pays/groupe ~** friendly country/group; **petit ~/petite ~e** boyfriend/girlfriend
amiable [amjabl]: **à l'~** *adv* (*Jur*) out of court; (*gén*) amicably
amiante [amjɑ̃t] *nm* asbestos
amical, e, -aux [amikal, o] *adj* friendly; **amicalement** *adv* in a friendly way; (*dans une lettre*) (with) best wishes
amincir [amɛ̃siʀ] *vt*: **~ qn** to make sb thinner *ou* slimmer; (*suj: vêtement*) to make sb look slimmer
amincissant, e [amɛ̃sisɑ̃, ɑ̃t] *adj*: **régime ~** (slimming) diet; **crème ~e** slimming cream
amiral, -aux [amiʀal, o] *nm* admiral
amitié [amitje] *nf* friendship; **prendre en ~** to befriend; **faire** *ou* **présenter ses ~s à qn** to send sb one's best wishes; **"~s"** (*dans une lettre*) "(with) best wishes"
amonceler [amɔ̃s(ə)le] *vt* to pile *ou* heap up; **s'~** *vi* to pile *ou* heap up; (*fig*) to accumulate
amont [amɔ̃]: **en ~** *adv* upstream
amorce [amɔʀs] *nf* (*sur un hameçon*) bait; (*explosif*) cap; primer; priming; (*fig: début*) beginning(s), start
amortir [amɔʀtiʀ] *vt* (*atténuer: choc*) to absorb, cushion; (*bruit, douleur*) to deaden; (*Comm: dette*) to pay off; **~ un achat** to make a purchase pay for itself; **amortisseur** *nm* shock absorber
amour [amuʀ] *nm* love; **faire l'~** to make love; **amoureux, -euse** *adj* (*regard, tempérament*) amorous; (*vie, problèmes*) love *cpd*; (*personne*): **être amoureux (de qn)** to be in love (with sb); **tomber amoureux (de qn)** to fall in love (with sb) ▷ *nmpl* courting couple(s); **amour-propre** *nm* self-esteem, pride
ampère [ɑ̃pɛʀ] *nm* amp(ere)
amphithéâtre [ɑ̃fiteɑtʀ] *nm* amphitheatre; (*d'université*) lecture hall *ou* theatre
ample [ɑ̃pl] *adj* (*vêtement*) roomy, ample; (*gestes, mouvement*) broad; (*ressources*) ample; **amplement** *adv*: **c'est amplement suffisant** that's more than enough; **ampleur** *nf* (*de dégâts, problème*) extent
amplificateur [ɑ̃plifikatœʀ] *nm* amplifier
amplifier [ɑ̃plifje] *vt* (*fig*) to expand, increase
ampoule [ɑ̃pul] *nf* (*électrique*) bulb; (*de médicament*) phial; (*aux mains, pieds*) blister
amusant, e [amyzɑ̃, ɑ̃t] *adj* (*divertissant, spirituel*) entertaining, amusing; (*comique*) funny, amusing
amuse-gueule [amyzgœl] *nm inv* appetizer, snack
amusement [amyzmɑ̃] *nm* (*divertissement*) amusement; (*jeu etc*) pastime, diversion
amuser [amyze] *vt* (*divertir*) to entertain, amuse; (*égayer, faire rire*) to amuse; **s'~** *vi* (*jouer*) to play; (*se divertir*) to enjoy o.s., have fun; (*fig*) to mess around
amygdale [amidal] *nf* tonsil
an [ɑ̃] *nm* year; **avoir quinze ans** to be fifteen (years old); **le jour de l'an, le premier de l'an, le nouvel an** New

Year's Day

analphabète [analfabɛt] nm/f illiterate

analyse [analiz] nf analysis; (Méd) test; **analyser** vt to analyse; to test

ananas [anana(s)] nm pineapple

anatomie [anatɔmi] nf anatomy

ancêtre [ɑ̃sɛtʀ] nm/f ancestor

anchois [ɑ̃ʃwa] nm anchovy

ancien, ne [ɑ̃sjɛ̃, jɛn] adj old; (de jadis, de l'antiquité) ancient; (précédent, ex-) former, old; (par l'expérience) senior ▷ nm/f (dans une tribu) elder; **ancienneté** nf (Admin) (length of) service; (privilèges obtenus) seniority

ancre [ɑ̃kʀ] nf anchor; **jeter/lever l'~** to cast/weigh anchor; **ancrer** vt (Constr: câble etc) to anchor; (fig) to fix firmly

Andorre [ɑ̃dɔʀ] nf Andorra

andouille [ɑ̃duj] nf (Culin) sausage made of chitterlings; (fam) clot, nit

âne [an] nm donkey, ass; (péj) dunce

anéantir [aneɑ̃tiʀ] vt to annihilate, wipe out; (fig) to obliterate, destroy

anémie [anemi] nf anaemia; **anémique** adj anaemic

anesthésie [anɛstezi] nf anaesthesia; **faire une ~ locale/générale à qn** to give sb a local/general anaesthetic

ange [ɑ̃ʒ] nm angel; **être aux ~s** to be over the moon

angine [ɑ̃ʒin] nf throat infection; **angine de poitrine** angina

anglais, e [ɑ̃glɛ, ɛz] adj English ▷ nm/f: **A~, e** Englishman(-woman) ▷ nm (Ling) English; **les A~** the English; **filer à l'~e** to take French leave

angle [ɑ̃gl] nm angle; (coin) corner; **angle droit** right angle

Angleterre [ɑ̃glətɛʀ] nf: **l'~** England

anglo... [ɑ̃glɔ] préfixe Anglo-, anglo(-); **anglophone** adj English-speaking

angoisse [ɑ̃gwas] nf anguish, distress; **angoissé, e** adj (personne) distressed

anguille [ɑ̃gij] nf eel

animal, e, -aux [animal, o] adj, nm animal

animateur, -trice [animatœʀ, tʀis] nm/f (de télévision) host; (de groupe) leader, organizer

animation [animasjɔ̃] nf (voir animé) busyness; liveliness; (Cinéma: technique) animation

animé, e [anime] adj (lieu) busy, lively; (conversation, réunion) lively, animated

animer [anime] vt (ville, soirée) to liven up; (mener) to lead

anis [ani(s)] nm (Culin) aniseed; (Bot) anise

ankyloser [ɑ̃kiloze] **s'~** vi to get stiff

anneau, x [ano] nm (de rideau, bague) ring; (de chaîne) link

année [ane] nf year

annexe [anɛks] adj (problème) related; (document) appended; (salle) adjoining ▷ nf (bâtiment) annex(e); (jointe à une lettre) enclosure

anniversaire [anivɛʀsɛʀ] nm birthday; (d'un événement, bâtiment) anniversary

annonce [anɔ̃s] nf announcement; (signe, indice) sign; (aussi: **~ publicitaire**) advertisement; **les petites ~s** the classified advertisements, the small ads

annoncer [anɔ̃se] vt to announce; (être le signe de) to herald; **s'~ bien/difficile** to look promising/difficult

annuaire [anɥɛʀ] nm yearbook, annual; **annuaire**

téléphonique (telephone) directory, phone book

annuel, le [anɥɛl] adj annual, yearly

annulation [anylasjɔ̃] nf cancellation

annuler [anyle] vt (rendez-vous, voyage) to cancel, call off; (jugement) to quash (BRIT), repeal (US); (Math, Physique) to cancel out; **je voudrais ~ ma réservation** I'd like to cancel my reservation

anonymat [anɔnima] nm anonymity; **garder l'~** to remain anonymous

anonyme [anɔnim] adj anonymous; (fig) impersonal

anorak [anɔʀak] nm anorak

anorexie [anɔʀɛksi] nf anorexia

anormal, e, -aux [anɔʀmal, o] adj abnormal

ANPE sigle f (= Agence nationale pour l'emploi) national employment agency

antarctique [ɑ̃taʀktik] adj Antarctic ▷ nm: **l'A~** the Antarctic

antenne [ɑ̃tɛn] nf (de radio) aerial; (d'insecte) antenna, feeler; (poste avancé) outpost; (petite succursale) sub-branch; **passer à l'~** to go on the air; **antenne parabolique** satellite dish

antérieur, e [ɑ̃teʀjœʀ] adj (d'avant) previous, earlier; (de devant) front

anti... [ɑ̃ti] préfixe anti...; **antialcoolique** adj anti-alcohol; **antibiotique** nm antibiotic; **antibrouillard** adj: **phare antibrouillard** fog lamp (BRIT) ou light (US)

anticipation [ɑ̃tisipasjɔ̃] nf: **livre/film d'~** science fiction book/film

anticipé, e [ɑ̃tisipe] adj: **avec mes remerciements ~s** thanking you in advance ou anticipation

anticiper [ɑ̃tisipe] vt (événement, coup) to anticipate, foresee

anti...: **anticorps** nm antibody; **antidote** nm antidote; **antigel** nm antifreeze; **antihistaminique** nm antihistamine

antillais, e [ɑ̃tijɛ, ɛz] adj West Indian, Caribbean ▷ nm/ f: **A~, e** West Indian, Caribbean

Antilles [ɑ̃tij] nfpl: **les ~** the West Indies; **les Grandes/ Petites ~** the Greater/Lesser Antilles

antilope [ɑ̃tilɔp] nf antelope

anti...: **antimite(s)** adj, nm: **(produit) antimite(s)** mothproofer; moth repellent; **antimondialisation** nf anti-globalization; **antipathique** adj unpleasant, disagreeable; **antipelliculaire** adj anti-dandruff

antiquaire [ɑ̃tikɛʀ] nm/f antique dealer

antique [ɑ̃tik] adj antique; (très vieux) ancient, antiquated; **antiquité** nf (objet) antique; **l'Antiquité** Antiquity; **magasin d'antiquités** antique shop

anti...: **antirabique** adj rabies cpd; **antirouille** adj inv anti-rust cpd; **antisémite** adj anti-Semitic; **antiseptique** adj, nm antiseptic

antivirus [ɑ̃tiviʀys] nm (Inform) antivirus; **antivol** adj, nm: **(dispositif) antivol** anti-theft device

anxieux, -euse [ɑ̃ksjø, jøz] adj anxious, worried

AOC sigle f (= appellation d'origine contrôlée) label guaranteeing the quality of wine

août [u(t)] nm August

apaiser [apeze] vt (colère, douleur) to soothe; (personne) to calm (down), pacify; **s'~** vi (tempête, bruit) to die down, subside; (personne) to calm down

apercevoir [apɛʀsəvwaʀ] vt to see; **s'~ de** vt to notice; **s'~ que** to notice that

aperçu [apɛʀsy] nm (vue d'ensemble) general survey

apéritif [apeʀitif] nm (boisson) aperitif; (réunion)

drinks pl

à-peu-près [apøpʀɛ] (péj) nm inv vague approximation

apeuré, e [apœʀe] adj frightened, scared

aphte [aft] nm mouth ulcer

apitoyer [apitwaje] vt to move to pity; **s'~ (sur)** to feel pity (for)

aplatir [aplatiʀ] vt to flatten; **s'~** vi to become flatter; (écrasé) to be flattened

aplomb [aplɔ̃] nm (équilibre) balance, equilibrium; (fig) self-assurance; nerve; **d'~** steady

apostrophe [apɔstʀɔf] nf (signe) apostrophe

apparaître [apaʀɛtʀ] vi to appear

appareil [apaʀɛj] nm (outil, machine) piece of apparatus, device; (électrique, ménager) appliance; (avion) (aero)plane, aircraft inv; (téléphonique) phone; (dentier) brace (BRIT), braces (US); **"qui est à l'~?"** "who's speaking?"; **dans le plus simple ~** in one's birthday suit; **appareil(-photo)** camera; **appareiller** vi (Navig) to cast off, get under way ▷ vt (assortir) to match up

apparemment [apaʀamɑ̃] adv apparently

apparence [apaʀɑ̃s] nf appearance; **en ~** apparently

apparent, e [apaʀɑ̃, ɑ̃t] adj visible; (évident) obvious; (superficiel) apparent

apparenté, e [apaʀɑ̃te] adj: **~ à** related to; (fig) similar to

apparition [apaʀisjɔ̃] nf appearance; (surnaturelle) apparition

appartement [apaʀtəmɑ̃] nm flat (BRIT), apartment (US)

appartenir [apaʀtəniʀ]: **~ à** vt to belong to; **il lui appartient de** it is his duty to

apparu, e [apaʀy] pp de **apparaître**

appât [apa] nm (Pêche) bait; (fig) lure, bait

appel [apɛl] nm call; (nominal) roll call; (: Scol) register; (Mil: recrutement) call-up; **faire ~ à** (invoquer) to appeal to; (avoir recours à) to call on; (nécessiter) to call for, require; **faire** ou **interjeter ~** (Jur) to appeal; **faire l'~** to call the roll; (Scol) to call the register; **sans ~** (fig) final, irrevocable; **faire un ~ de phares** to flash one's headlights; **appel d'offres** (Comm) invitation to tender; **appel (téléphonique)** (tele)phone call

appelé [ap(ə)le] nm (Mil) conscript

appeler [ap(ə)le] vt to call; (faire venir: médecin etc) to call, send for; **s'~** vi: **elle s'appelle Gabrielle** her name is Gabrielle, she's called Gabrielle; **comment vous appelez-vous?** what's your name?; **comment ça s'appelle?** what is it called?; **être appelé à** (fig) to be destined to

appendicite [apɛ̃disit] nf appendicitis

appesantir [apəzɑ̃tiʀ]: **s'~** vi to grow heavier; **s'~ sur** (fig) to dwell on

appétissant, e [apetisɑ̃, ɑ̃t] adj appetizing, mouth-watering

appétit [apeti] nm appetite; **bon ~!** enjoy your meal!

applaudir [aplodiʀ] vt to applaud ▷ vi to applaud, clap; **applaudissements** nmpl applause sg, clapping sg

application [aplikasjɔ̃] nf application

appliquer [aplike] vt to apply; (loi) to enforce; **s'~** vi (élève etc) to apply o.s.; **s'~ à** to apply to

appoint [apwɛ̃] nm (extra) contribution ou help; **avoir/faire l'~** to have/give the right change ou money; **chauffage d'~** extra heating

apporter [apɔʀte] vt to bring

appréciable [apʀesjabl] adj appreciable

apprécier [apʀesje] vt to appreciate; (évaluer) to estimate, assess

appréhender [apʀeɑ̃de] vt (craindre) to dread; (arrêter) to apprehend

apprendre [apʀɑ̃dʀ] vt to learn; (événement, résultats) to learn of, hear of; **~ qch à qn** (informer) to tell sb (of) sth; (enseigner) to teach sb sth; **~ à faire qch** to learn to do sth; **~ à qn à faire qch** to teach sb to do sth; **apprenti, e** nm/f apprentice; **apprentissage** nm learning; (Comm, Scol: période) apprenticeship

apprêter [apʀete] vt: **s'~ à faire qch** to get ready to do sth

appris, e [apʀi, iz] pp de **apprendre**

apprivoiser [apʀivwaze] vt to tame

approbation [apʀɔbasjɔ̃] nf approval

approcher [apʀɔʃe] vi to approach, come near ▷ vt to approach; (rapprocher): **~ qch (de qch)** to bring ou put sth near (to sth); **s'~ de** to approach, go ou come near to; **~ de** (lieu, but) to draw near to; (quantité, moment) to approach

approfondir [apʀɔfɔ̃diʀ] vt to deepen; (question) to go further into

approprié, e [apʀɔpʀije] adj: **~ (à)** appropriate (to), suited to

approprier [apʀɔpʀije]: **s'~** vt to appropriate, take over; **s'~ en** to stock up with

approuver [apʀuve] vt to agree with; (trouver louable) to approve of

approvisionner [apʀɔvizjɔne] vt to supply; (compte bancaire) to pay funds into; **s'~ en** to stock up with

approximatif, -ive [apʀɔksimatif, iv] adj approximate, rough; (termes) vague

appt abr = **appartement**

appui [apɥi] nm support; **prendre ~ sur** to lean on; (objet) to rest on; **l'~ de la fenêtre** the windowsill, the window ledge

appuyer [apɥije] vt (poser): **~ qch sur/contre** to lean ou rest sth on/against; (soutenir: personne, demande) to support, back (up) ▷ vi: **~ sur** (bouton) to press, push; (mot, détail) to stress, emphasize; **~ sur le frein** to brake, to apply the brakes; **s'~ sur** to lean on; (fig: compter sur) to rely on

après [apʀɛ] prép after ▷ adv afterwards; **2 heures ~** 2 hours later; **~ qu'il est** ou **soit parti** after he left; **~ avoir fait** after having done; **d'~** (selon) according to; **~ coup** after the event, afterwards; **~ tout** (au fond) after all; **et (puis) ~?** so what?; **après-demain** adv the day after tomorrow; **après-midi** nm ou nf inv afternoon; **après-rasage** nm inv aftershave; **après-shampooing** nm inv conditioner; **après-ski** nm inv snow boot

après-soleil [apʀɛsɔlɛj] adj inv after-sun cpd ▷ nm after-sun cream ou lotion

apte [apt] adj capable; **~ à qch/faire qch** capable of sth/doing sth; **~ (au service)** (Mil) fit (for service)

aquarelle [akwaʀɛl] nf watercolour

aquarium [akwaʀjɔm] nm aquarium

arabe [aʀab] adj Arabic; (désert, cheval) Arabian; (nation, peuple) Arab ▷ nm/f: **A~** Arab ▷ nm (Ling) Arabic

Arabie [aʀabi] nf: **l'~ (Saoudite)** Saudi Arabia

arachide [aʀaʃid] nf (plante) groundnut (plant); (graine) peanut, groundnut

araignée [aʀɛɲe] nf spider

arbitraire [aʀbitʀɛʀ] adj arbitrary

arbitre [aʀbitʀ] nm (Sport) referee; (: Tennis, Cricket) umpire; (fig) arbiter, judge; (Jur) arbitrator; **arbitrer** vt to referee; to umpire; to arbitrate

arbre [aʀbʀ] nm tree; (Tech) shaft

arbuste [aʀbyst] nm small shrub

arc [aʀk] nm (arme) bow; (Géom) arc; (Archit) arch; **en ~ de cercle** semi-circular

arcade [aʀkad] nf arch(way); **arcades** nfpl (série) arcade sg, arches

arc-en-ciel [aʀkɑ̃sjɛl] nm rainbow

arche [aʀʃ] nf arch; **arche de Noé** Noah's Ark

archéologie [aʀkeɔlɔʒi] nf arch(a)eology; **archéologue** nm/f arch(a)eologist

archet [aʀʃɛ] nm bow

archipel [aʀʃipɛl] nm archipelago

architecte [aʀʃitɛkt] nm architect

architecture [aʀʃitɛktyʀ] nf architecture

archives [aʀʃiv] nfpl (collection) archives

arctique [aʀktik] adj Arctic ▷ nm: **l'A~** the Arctic

ardent, e [aʀdɑ̃, ɑ̃t] adj (soleil) blazing; (amour) ardent, passionate; (prière) fervent

ardoise [aʀdwaz] nf slate

ardu, e [aʀdy] adj (travail) arduous; (problème) difficult

arène [aʀɛn] nf arena; **arènes** nfpl (amphithéâtre) bull-ring sg

arête [aʀɛt] nf (de poisson) bone; (d'une montagne) ridge

argent [aʀʒɑ̃] nm (métal) silver; (monnaie) money; **argent de poche** pocket money; **argent liquide** ready money, (ready) cash; **argenterie** nf silverware

argentin, e [aʀʒɑ̃tɛ̃, in] adj Argentinian ▷ nm/f: **A~, e** Argentinian

Argentine [aʀʒɑ̃tin] nf: **l'~** Argentina

argentique [aʀʒɑ̃tik] adj (appareil-photo) film cpd

argile [aʀʒil] nf clay

argot [aʀgo] nm slang; **argotique** adj slang cpd; (très familier) slangy

argument [aʀgymɑ̃] nm argument

argumenter [aʀgymɑ̃te] vi to argue

aride [aʀid] adj arid

aristocratie [aʀistɔkʀasi] nf aristocracy; **aristocratique** adj aristocratic

arithmétique [aʀitmetik] adj arithmetic(al) ▷ nf arithmetic

arme [aʀm] nf weapon; **armes** nfpl (armement) weapons, arms; (blason) (coat of) arms; **~s de destruction massive** weapons of mass destruction; **arme à feu** firearm

armée [aʀme] nf army; **armée de l'air** Air Force; **armée de terre** Army

armer [aʀme] vt to arm; (arme à feu) to cock; (appareil-photo) to wind on; **~ qch de** to reinforce sth with; **s'~ de** to arm o.s. with

armistice [aʀmistis] nm armistice; **l'A~** ≈ Remembrance (BRIT) ou Veterans (US) Day

armoire [aʀmwaʀ] nf (tall) cupboard; (penderie) wardrobe (BRIT), closet (US)

armure [aʀmyʀ] nf armour no pl, suit of armour; **armurier** nm gunsmith

arnaque [aʀnak] nf (fam) swindling; **c'est de l'~** it's a rip-off; **arnaquer** (fam) vt to swindle

arobase [aʀɔbaz] nf (symbole) at symbol; **"paul ~ société point fr"** "paul at société dot fr"

aromates [aʀɔmat] nmpl seasoning sg, herbs (and spices)

aromathérapie [aʀɔmateʀapi] nf aromatherapy

aromatisé, e [aʀɔmatize] adj flavoured

arôme [aʀom] nm aroma

arracher [aʀaʃe] vt to pull out; (page etc) to tear off, tear out; (légumes, herbe) to pull up; (bras etc) to tear off; **s'~** (article recherché) to fight over; **~ qch à qn** to snatch sth from sb; (fig) to wring sth out of sb

arrangement [aʀɑ̃ʒmɑ̃] nm agreement, arrangement

arranger [aʀɑ̃ʒe] vt (gén) to arrange; (réparer) to fix, put right; (régler: différend) to settle, sort out; (convenir à) to suit, be convenient for; **cela m'arrange** that suits me (fine); **s'~** vi (se mettre d'accord) to come to an agreement; **je vais m'~** I'll manage; **ça va s'~** it'll sort itself out

arrestation [aʀɛstasjɔ̃] nf arrest

arrêt [aʀɛ] nm stopping; (de bus etc) stop; (Jur) judgment, decision; **à l'~** stationary; **tomber en ~ devant** to stop short in front of; **sans ~** (sans interruption) non-stop; (très fréquemment) continually; **arrêt de travail** stoppage (of work)

arrêter [aʀete] vt to stop; (chauffage etc) to turn off, switch off; (fixer: date etc) to appoint, decide on; (criminel, suspect) to arrest; **s'~** vi to stop; **~ de faire** to stop doing; **arrêtez-vous ici/au coin, s'il vous plaît** could you stop here/at the corner, please?

arrhes [aʀ] nfpl deposit sg

arrière [aʀjɛʀ] nm back; (Sport) fullback ▷ adj inv: **siège/roue ~** back ou rear seat/wheel; **à l'~** behind, at the back; **en ~** behind; (regarder) back, behind; (tomber, aller) backwards; **arrière-goût** nm aftertaste; **arrière-grand-mère** nf great-grandmother; **arrière-grand-père** nm great-grandfather; **arrière-pays** nm inv hinterland; **arrière-pensée** nf ulterior motive; mental reservation; **arrière-plan** nm background; **à l'arrière-plan** in the background; **arrière-saison** nf late autumn

arrimer [aʀime] vt to secure; (cargaison) to stow

arrivage [aʀivaʒ] nm consignment

arrivée [aʀive] nf arrival; (ligne d'arrivée) finish

arriver [aʀive] vi to arrive; (survenir) to happen, occur; **il arrive à Paris à 8h** he gets to ou arrives in Paris at 8; **à quelle heure arrive le train de Lyon?** what time does the train from Lyons get in?; **~ à** (atteindre) to reach; **~ à faire qch** to succeed in doing sth; **en ~ à** (finir par) to come to; **il arrive que** it happens that; **il lui arrive de faire** he sometimes does

arrobase [aʀɔbaz] nf (Inform) @, 'at' sign

arrogance [aʀɔgɑ̃s] nf arrogance

arrogant, e [aʀɔgɑ̃, ɑ̃t] adj arrogant

arrondissement [aʀɔ̃dismɑ̃] nm (Admin) ≈ district

arroser [aʀoze] vt to water; (victoire) to celebrate (over a drink); (Culin) to baste; **arrosoir** nm watering can

arsenal, -aux [aʀsənal, o] nm (Navig) naval dockyard; (Mil) arsenal; (fig) gear, paraphernalia

art [aʀ] nm art

artère [aʀtɛʀ] nf (Anat) artery; (rue) main road

arthrite [aʀtʀit] nf arthritis

artichaut [aʀtiʃo] nm artichoke

article [aʀtikl] nm article; (Comm) item, article; **à l'~ de la mort** at the point of death

articulation [aʀtikylasjɔ̃] nf articulation; (Anat) joint

articuler [aʀtikyle] vt to articulate

artificiel, le [aʀtifisjɛl] adj artificial

artisan [aʀtizɑ̃] nm artisan, (self-employed) craftsman; **artisanal, e, -aux** adj of ou made by craftsmen; (péj) cottage industry cpd; **de fabrication artisanale** home-made; **artisanat** nm arts and crafts pl

artiste [aʀtist] nm/f artist; (de variétés) entertainer; (musicien etc) performer; **artistique** adj artistic

as¹ [a] vb voiravoir

as² [as] nm ace

ascenseur [asɑ̃sœʀ] nm lift (BRIT), elevator (US)

ascension [asɑ̃sjɔ̃] nf ascent; (de montagne) climb; **l'A~** (Rel) the Ascension

asiatique [azjatik] adj Asiatic, Asian ▷ nm/f: **A~** Asian

Asie [azi] nf: **l'~** Asia

asile [azil] nm (refuge) refuge, sanctuary; (Pol): **droit d'~** (political) asylum

aspect [aspɛ] nm appearance, look; (fig) aspect, side; **à l'~ de** at the sight of

asperge [aspɛʀʒ] nf asparagus no pl

asperger [aspɛʀʒe] vt to spray, sprinkle

asphalte [asfalt] nm asphalt

asphyxier [asfiksje] vt to suffocate, asphyxiate; (fig) to stifle

aspirateur [aspiʀatœʀ] nm vacuum cleaner; **passer l'~** to vacuum

aspirer [aspiʀe] vt (air) to inhale; (liquide) to suck (up); (suj: appareil) to suck up; **~ à** to aspire to

aspirine [aspiʀin] nf aspirin

assagir [asaʒiʀ]: **s'~** vi to quieten down, settle down

assaisonnement [asɛzɔnmɑ̃] nm seasoning

assaisonner [asɛzɔne] vt to season

assassin [asasɛ̃] nm murderer; assassin; **assassiner** vt to murder; (esp Pol) to assassinate

assaut [aso] nm assault, attack; **prendre d'~** to storm, assault; **donner l'~ à** to attack

assécher [asefe] vt to drain

assemblage [asɑ̃blaʒ] nm (action) assembling; (de couleurs, choses) collection

assemblée [asɑ̃ble] nf (réunion) meeting; (assistance) gathering; (Pol) assembly; **l'A~ nationale** the National Assembly (the lower house of the French Parliament)

assembler [asɑ̃ble] vt (joindre, monter) to assemble, put together; (amasser) to gather (together), collect (together); **s'~** vi to gather

asseoir [aswaʀ] vt (malade, bébé) to sit up; (personne debout) to sit down; (autorité, réputation) to establish; **s'~** vi to sit (o.s.) down

assez [ase] adv (suffisamment) enough, sufficiently; (passablement) rather, quite, fairly; **~ de pain/livres** enough ou sufficient bread/books; **vous en avez ~?** have you got enough?; **j'en ai ~!** I've had enough!

assidu, e [asidy] adj (appliqué) assiduous, painstaking; (ponctuel) regular

assied etc [asje] vb voirasseoir

assiérai etc [asjeʀe] vb voirasseoir

assiette [asjɛt] nf plate; (contenu) plate(ful); **il n'est pas dans son ~** he's not feeling quite himself; **assiette à dessert** dessert plate; **assiette anglaise** assorted cold meats; **assiette creuse** (soup) dish, soup plate; **assiette plate** (dinner) plate

assimiler [asimile] vt to assimilate, absorb; (comparer): **~ qch/qn à** to liken ou compare sth/sb to; **s'~** vr (s'intégrer) to be assimilated, assimilate

assis, e [asi, iz] pp de asseoir ▷ adj sitting (down), seated

assistance [asistɑ̃s] nf (public) audience; (aide) assistance; **enfant de l'A~ publique** child in care

assistant, e [asistɑ̃, ɑ̃t] nm/f assistant; (d'université) probationary lecturer; **assistant(e) social(e)** social worker

assisté, e [asiste] adj (Auto) power assisted; **~ par ordinateur** computer-assisted; **direction ~e** power steering

assister [asiste] vt (aider) to assist; **~ à** (scène, événement) to witness; (conférence, séminaire) to attend, be at; (spectacle, match) to be at, see

association [asɔsjasjɔ̃] nf association

associé, e [asɔsje] nm/f associate; (Comm) partner

associer [asɔsje] vt to associate; **s'~** vi to join together; **s'~ à qn pour faire** to join (forces) with sb to do; **s'~ à** (couleurs, qualités) to be combined with; (opinions, joie de qn) to share in; **~ qn à** (profits) to give sb a share of; (affaire) to make sb a partner in; (joie, triomphe) to include sb in; **~ qch à** (allier à) to combine sth with

assoiffé, e [aswafe] adj thirsty

assommer [asɔme] vt (étourdir, abrutir) to knock out, stun

Assomption [asɔ̃psjɔ̃] nf: **l'~** the Assumption

assorti, e [asɔʀti] adj matched, matching; (varié) assorted; **~ à** matching; **assortiment** nm assortment, selection

assortir [asɔʀtiʀ] vt to match; **~ qch à** to match sth with; **~ qch de** to accompany sth with

assouplir [asupliʀ] vt to make supple; (fig) to relax; **assouplissant** nm (fabric) softener

assumer [asyme] vt (fonction, emploi) to assume, take on

assurance [asyʀɑ̃s] nf (certitude) assurance; (confiance en soi) (self-)confidence; (contrat) insurance (policy); (secteur commercial) insurance; **assurance au tiers** third-party insurance; **assurance maladie** health insurance; **assurance tous risques** (Auto) comprehensive insurance; **assurances sociales** ≈ National Insurance (BRIT), ≈ Social Security (US); **assurance-vie** nf life assurance ou insurance

assuré, e [asyʀe] adj (certain: réussite, échec) certain, sure; (air) assured; (pas) steady ▷ nm/f insured (person); **assurément** adv assuredly, most certainly

assurer [asyʀe] vt (Finance) to insure; (victoire etc) to ensure; (frontières, pouvoir) to make secure; (service) to provide, operate; **s'~ (contre)** (Comm) to insure o.s. (against); **s'~ de/que** (vérifier) to make sure of/that; **s'~ (de)** (aide de qn) to secure; **~ à qn que** to assure sb that; **~ qn de** to assure sb of

asthmatique [asmatik] adj, nm/f asthmatic

asthme [asm] nm asthma

asticot [astiko] nm maggot

astre [astʀ] nm star

astrologie [astʀɔlɔʒi] nf astrology

astronaute [astʀɔnot] nm/f astronaut

astronomie [astʀɔnɔmi] nf astronomy

astuce [astys] nf shrewdness, astuteness; (truc) trick, clever way; **astucieux, -euse** adj clever

atelier [atəlje] nm workshop; (de peintre) studio

athée [ate] adj atheistic ▷ nm/f atheist

Athènes [atɛn] n Athens

athlète [atlɛt] nm/f (Sport) athlete; **athlétisme** nm athletics sg

atlantique [atlɑ̃tik] adj Atlantic ▷ nm: **l'(océan) A~** the Atlantic (Ocean)

atlas [atlɑs] nm atlas

atmosphère [atmɔsfɛʀ] nf atmosphere

atome [atom] nm atom; **atomique** adj atomic, nuclear

atomiseur [atɔmizœʀ] nm atomizer

atout [atu] nm trump; (fig) asset

atroce [atʀɔs] adj atrocious

attachant, e [ataʃɑ̃, ɑ̃t] adj engaging, lovable, likeable

attache [ataʃ] nf clip, fastener; (fig) tie

attacher [ataʃe] vt to tie up; (étiquette) to attach, tie on; (ceinture) to fasten ▷ vi (poêle, riz) to stick; **s'~ à** (par affection) to become attached to; **~ qch à** to tie ou attach sth to

attaque [atak] nf attack; (cérébrale) stroke; (d'épilepsie) fit

attaquer [atake] vt to attack ▷ vi to attack; **s'~ à** vt (personne) to attack; (problème) to tackle; **~ qn en justice** to bring an action against sb, sue sb

attarder [ataʀde]: **s'~** vi to linger

atteindre [atɛ̃dʀ] vt to reach; (blesser) to hit; (émouvoir) to affect; **atteint, e** adj (Méd): **être atteint de** to be suffering from; **atteinte** nf: **hors d'atteinte** out of reach; **porter atteinte à** to strike a blow at

attendant [atɑ̃dɑ̃] adv: **en ~** meanwhile, in the meantime

attendre [atɑ̃dʀ] vt (gén) to wait for; (être destiné ou réservé à) to await, be in store for ▷ vi to wait; **s'~ à (ce que)** to expect (that); **attendez-moi, s'il vous plaît** wait for me, please; **~ un enfant** to be expecting a baby; **~ de faire/d'être** to wait until one does/is; **attendez qu'il vienne** wait until he comes; **~ qch de** to expect sth of

attendrir [atɑ̃dʀiʀ] vt to move (to pity); (viande) to tenderize

attendu, e [atɑ̃dy] adj (visiteur) expected; (événement) long-awaited; **~ que** considering that, since

attentat [atɑ̃ta] nm assassination attempt; **attentat à la pudeur** indecent assault no pl; **attentat suicide** suicide bombing

attente [atɑ̃t] nf wait; (espérance) expectation

attenter [atɑ̃te]: **~ à** vt (liberté) to violate; **~ à la vie de qn** to make an attempt on sb's life

attentif, -ive [atɑ̃tif, iv] adj (auditeur) attentive; (examen) careful; **~ à** careful to

attention [atɑ̃sjɔ̃] nf attention; (prévenance) attention, thoughtfulness no pl; **à l'~ de** for the attention of; **faire ~ (à)** to be careful (of); **faire ~ (à ce que)** to be ou make sure that; **~!** careful!, watch out!; **~ à la voiture!** watch out for that car!; **attentionné, e** adj thoughtful, considerate

atténuer [atenɥe] vt (douleur) to alleviate, ease; (couleurs) to soften; **s'~** vi to ease; (violence etc) to abate

atterrir [ateʀiʀ] vi to land; **atterrissage** nm landing

attestation [atɛstasjɔ̃] nf certificate

attirant, e [atiʀɑ̃, ɑ̃t] adj attractive, appealing

attirer [atiʀe] vt to attract; (appâter) to lure, entice; **~ qn dans un coin/vers soi** to draw sb into a corner/towards one; **l'attention de qn** to attract sb's attention; **~ l'attention de qn sur** to draw sb's attention to; **s'~ des ennuis** to bring trouble upon o.s., get into trouble

attitude [atityd] nf attitude; (position du corps) bearing

attraction [atʀaksjɔ̃] nf (gén) attraction; (de cabaret, cirque) number

attrait [atʀɛ] nm appeal, attraction

attraper [atʀape] vt (gén) to catch; (habitude, amende) to get, pick up; (fam: duper) to con; **se faire ~** (fam) to be told off

attrayant, e [atʀɛjɑ̃, ɑ̃t] adj attractive

attribuer [atʀibɥe] vt (prix) to award; (rôle, tâche) to allocate, assign; (imputer): **~ qch à** to attribute sth to; **s'~** vt (s'approprier) to claim for o.s.

attrister [atʀiste] vt to sadden

attroupement [atʀupmɑ̃] nm crowd

attrouper [atʀupe]: **s'~** vi to gather

au [o] prép +dét = **à +le**

aubaine [obɛn] nf godsend

aube [ob] nf dawn, daybreak; **à l'~** at dawn ou daybreak

aubépine [obepin] nf hawthorn

auberge [obɛʀʒ] nf inn; **auberge de jeunesse** youth hostel

aubergine [obɛʀʒin] nf aubergine

aucun, e [okœ̃, yn] dét no, tournure négative +any; (positif) any ▷ pron none, tournure négative +any; any(one); **sans ~ doute** without any doubt; **plus qu'~ autre** more than any other; **il le fera mieux qu'~ de nous** he'll do it better than any of us; **~ des deux** neither of the two; **~ d'entre eux** none of them

audace [odas] nf daring, boldness; (péj) audacity; **audacieux, -euse** adj daring, bold

au-delà [od(ə)la] adv beyond ▷ nm: **l'~** the hereafter; **~ de** beyond

au-dessous [odsu] adv underneath; below; **~ de** under(neath), below; (limite, somme etc) below, under; (dignité, condition) below

au-dessus [odsy] adv above; **~ de** above

au-devant [od(ə)vɑ̃]: **~ de** prép: **aller ~ de** (personne, danger) to go (out) and meet; (souhaits de qn) to anticipate

audience [odjɑ̃s] nf audience; (Jur: séance) hearing

audiovisuel, le [odjovizɥɛl] adj audiovisual

audition [odisjɔ̃] nf (ouïe, écoute) hearing; (Jur: de témoins) examination; (Mus, Théâtre: épreuve) audition

auditoire [oditwaʀ] nm audience

augmentation [ɔgmɑ̃tasjɔ̃] nf increase; **augmentation (de salaire)** rise (in salary) (BRIT), (pay) raise (US)

augmenter [ɔgmɑ̃te] vt (gén) to increase; (salaire, prix) to increase, raise, put up; (employé) to increase the salary of ▷ vi to increase

augure [ogyʀ] nm: **de bon/mauvais ~** of good/ill omen

aujourd'hui [oʒuʀdɥi] adv today

aumône [omon] nf inv alms sg; **aumônier** nm chaplain

auparavant [oparavɑ̃] adv before(hand)

auprès [opʀɛ]: **~ de** prép next to, close to; (recourir, s'adresser) to; (en comparaison de) compared with

auquel [okɛl] prép +pron = **à +lequel**

aurai etc [ɔʀe] vb voir **avoir**

aurons etc [ɔʀɔ̃] vb voir **avoir**

aurore [ɔʀɔʀ] nf dawn, daybreak

ausculter [ɔskylte] vt to sound (the chest of)

aussi [osi] adv (également) also, too; (de comparaison) as ▷ conj therefore, consequently; **~ fort que** as strong as; **moi ~** me too

aussitôt [osito] adv straight away, immediately; **~ que** as soon as

austère [ostɛʀ] adj austere

austral, e [ɔstʀal] adj southern

Australie [ɔstʀali] nf: **l'~** Australia; **australien, ne** adj Australian ▷ nm/f: **Australien, ne** Australian

autant [otɑ̃] adv (intensité) so much; **je ne savais pas que tu la détestais ~** I didn't know you hated her so much; (comparatif): **~ (que)** as much (as); (nombre) as many (as); **~ (de)** so much (ou many); as much (ou many); **~ partir** we (ou you etc) may as well leave; **~ dire que ...** one might as well say that ...; **pour ~** for all that; **d'~ plus/mieux (que)** all the more/the better (since)

autel [otɛl] nm altar

auteur [otœʀ] nm author

authentique [otɑ̃tik] adj authentic, genuine

auto [oto] nf car

auto...: **autobiographie** nf autobiography; **autobronzant** nm self-tanning cream (or lotion etc); **autobus** nm bus; **autocar** nm coach

autochtone [ɔtɔktɔn] nm/f native

auto...: **autocollant, e** adj self-adhesive; (enveloppe) self-seal ▷ nm sticker; **autocuiseur** nm pressure cooker; **autodéfense** nf self-defence; **autodidacte** nm/f self-taught person; **auto-école** nf driving school; **autographe** nm autograph

automate [ɔtɔmat] nm (machine) (automatic) machine

automatique [ɔtɔmatik] adj automatic ▷ nm: **l'~** direct dialling

automne [ɔtɔn] nm autumn (BRIT), fall (US)

automobile [ɔtɔmɔbil] adj motor cpd, car cpd ▷ nf (motor) car; **automobiliste** nm/f motorist

autonome [ɔtɔnɔm] adj autonomous; **autonomie** nf autonomy; (Pol) self-government, autonomy

autopsie [ɔtɔpsi] nf post-mortem (examination), autopsy

autoradio [otoʀadjo] nm car radio

autorisation [ɔtɔʀizasjɔ̃] nf permission, authorization; (papiers) permit

autorisé, e [ɔtɔʀize] adj (opinion, sources) authoritative

autoriser [ɔtɔʀize] vt to give permission for, authorize; (fig) to allow (of)

autoritaire [ɔtɔʀitɛʀ] adj authoritarian

autorité [ɔtɔʀite] nf authority; **faire ~** to be authoritative; **les ~s** the authorities

autoroute [otoʀut] nf motorway (BRIT), highway (US); **~ de l'information** (Inform) information superhighway

auto-stop [otostɔp] nm: **faire de l'~** to hitch-hike; **prendre qn en ~** to give sb a lift; **auto-stoppeur, -euse** nm/f hitch-hiker

autour [otuʀ] adv around; **~ de** around; **tout ~** all around

 MOT-CLÉ

autre [otʀ] adj **1** (différent) other, different; **je préférerais un autre verre** I'd prefer another ou a different glass **2** (supplémentaire) other; **je voudrais un autre verre d'eau** I'd like another glass of water

3: **autre chose** something else; **autre part** somewhere else; **d'autre part** on the other hand

▷ pron: **un autre** another (one); **nous/vous autres** us/you; **d'autres** others; **l'autre** the other (one); **les autres** the others; (autrui) others; **l'un et l'autre** both of them; **se détester l'un l'autre/les uns les autres** to hate each other ou one another; **d'une semaine à l'autre** from one week to the next; (incessamment) any week now; **entre autres** (personnes) among others; (choses) among other things

autrefois [otʀəfwa] adv in the past

autrement [otʀəmɑ̃] adv differently; (d'une manière différente) in another way; (sinon) otherwise; **~ dit** in

other words

Autriche [otʀiʃ] nf: **l'~** Austria; **autrichien, ne** adj Austrian ▷ nm/f: **Autrichien, ne** Austrian

autruche [otʀyʃ] nf ostrich

aux [o] prép +dét **= à +les**

auxiliaire [ɔksiljɛʀ] adj, nm/f auxiliary

auxquelles [okɛl] prép +pron **= à +lesquelles**

auxquels [okɛl] prép +pron **= à +lesquels**

avalanche [avalɑ̃ʃ] nf avalanche

avaler [avale] vt to swallow

avance [avɑ̃s] nf (de troupes etc) advance; progress; (d'argent) advance; (sur un concurrent) lead; **avances** nfpl (amoureuses) advances; **(être) en ~** (to be) early; (sur un programme) (to be) ahead of schedule; **à l'~, d'~** in advance

avancé, e [avɑ̃se] adj advanced; (travail) well on, well under way

avancement [avɑ̃smɑ̃] nm (professionnel) promotion

avancer [avɑ̃se] vi to move forward, advance; (projet, travail) to make progress; (montre, réveil) to be fast; to gain ▷ vt to move forward, advance; (argent) to advance; (montre, pendule) to put forward; **s'~** vi to move forward, advance; (fig) to commit o.s.

avant [avɑ̃] prép, adv before ▷ adj inv: **siège/roue ~** front seat/wheel ▷ nm (d'un véhicule, bâtiment) front; (Sport: joueur) forward; **~ qu'il (ne) parte** before he goes ou leaves; **~ de partir** before leaving; **~ tout** (surtout) above all; **à l'~** (dans un véhicule) in (the) front; **en ~** (se pencher, tomber) forward(s); **partir en ~** to go on ahead; **en ~ de** in front of

avantage [avɑ̃taʒ] nm advantage; **avantages sociaux** fringe benefits; **avantager** vt (favoriser) to favour; (embellir) to flatter; **avantageux, -euse** adj (prix) attractive

avant...: **avant-bras** nm inv forearm; **avant-coureur** adj inv: **signe avant-coureur** advance indication ou sign; **avant-dernier, -ière** adj, nm/f next to last, last but one; **avant-goût** nm foretaste; **avant-hier** adv the day before yesterday; **avant-première** nf (de film) preview; **avant-veille** nf: **l'avant-veille** two days before

avare [avaʀ] adj miserly, avaricious ▷ nm/f miser; **~ de** (compliments etc) sparing of

avec [avɛk] prép with; (à l'égard de) to(wards), with; **et ~ ça?** (dans magasin) anything else?

avenir [avniʀ] nm future; **à l'~** in future; **politicien/ métier d'~** politician/job with prospects ou a future

aventure [avɑ̃tyʀ] nf adventure; (amoureuse) affair; **aventureux, -euse** adj adventurous, venturesome; (projet) risky, chancy

avenue [avny] nf avenue

avérer [aveʀe]: **s'~** vb +attrib to prove (to be)

averse [avɛʀs] nf shower

averti, e [avɛʀti] adj (well-)informed

avertir [avɛʀtiʀ] vt: **~ qn (de qch/que)** to warn sb (of sth/that); (renseigner) to inform sb (of sth/that); **avertissement** nm warning; **avertisseur** nm horn, siren

aveu, x [avø] nm confession

aveugle [avœgl] adj blind ▷ nm/f blind man/woman

aviation [avjasjɔ̃] nf aviation; (sport) flying; (Mil) air force

avide [avid] adj eager; (péj) greedy, grasping

avion [avjɔ̃] nm (aero)plane (BRIT), (air)plane (US); **aller (quelque part) en ~** to go (somewhere) by plane, fly (somewhere); **par ~** by airmail; **avion à réaction** jet (plane)

aviron [aviʀɔ̃] nm oar; (sport): **l'~** rowing

avis [avi] nm opinion; (notification) notice; **à mon ~** in my opinion; **changer d'~** to change one's mind; **jusqu'à nouvel ~** until further notice

aviser [avize] vt (informer): **~ qn de/que** to advise ou inform sb of/that ▷ vi to think about things, assess the situation; **nous ~ons sur place** we'll work something out once we're there; **s'~ de qch/que** to become suddenly aware of sth/that; **s'~ de faire** to take it into one's head to do

avocat, e [avɔka, at] nm/f (Jur) barrister (BRIT), lawyer ▷ nm (Culin) avocado (pear); **~ de la défense** counsel for the defence; **avocat général** assistant public prosecutor

avoine [avwan] nf oats pl

⊙ MOT-CLÉ

avoir [avwaʀ] nm assets pl, resources pl; (Comm) credit ▷ vt **1** (posséder) to have; **elle a 2 enfants/une belle maison** she has (got) 2 children/a lovely house; **il a les yeux bleus** he has (got) blue eyes; **vous avez du sel?** do you have any salt?; **avoir du courage/de la patience** to be brave/patient

2 (âge, dimensions) to be; **il a 3 ans** he is 3 (years old); **le mur a 3 mètres de haut** the wall is 3 metres high; voir aussi **faim**; **peur** etc

3 (fam: duper) to do, have; **on vous a eu!** (dupé) you've been done ou had!; (fait une plaisanterie) we ou they had you there

4: **en avoir après** ou **contre qn** to have a grudge against sb; **en avoir assez** to be fed up; **j'en ai pour une demi-heure** it'll take me half an hour

5 (obtenir, attraper) to get; **j'ai réussi à avoir mon train** I managed to get ou catch my train; **j'ai réussi à avoir le renseignement qu'il me fallait** I managed to get (hold of) the information I needed

6 (éprouver): **avoir de la peine** to be ou feel sad

▷ vb aux **1** to have; **avoir mangé/dormi** to have eaten/slept

2 (avoir à +infinitif): **avoir à faire qch** to have to do sth; **vous n'avez qu'à lui demander** you only have to ask him

▷ vb impers **1**: **il y a** (+singulier) there is; (+pluriel) there are; **il y avait du café/des gâteaux** there was coffee/there were cakes; **qu'y-a-t-il?, qu'est-ce qu'il y a?** what's the matter?, what is it?; **il doit y avoir une explication** there must be an explanation; **il n'y a qu'à ...** we (ou you etc) will just have to ...; **il ne peut y en avoir qu'un** there can only be one

2 (temporel): **il y a 10 ans** 10 years ago; **il y a 10 ans/longtemps que je le sais** I've known it for 10 years/a long time; **il y a 10 ans qu'il est arrivé** it's 10 years since he arrived

avortement [avɔʀtəmɑ̃] nm abortion

avouer [avwe] vt (crime, défaut) to confess (to); **~ avoir fait/que** to confess ou admit to having done/that

avril [avʀil] nm April

axe [aks] nm axis; (de roue etc) axle; (fig) main line; **axe routier** main road, trunk road (BRIT), highway (US)

ayons etc [ɛjɔ̃] vb voir **avoir**

bâbord [babɔʀ] nm: **à ~** to port, on the port side

baby-foot [babifut] nm table football

bac [bak] abr m = **baccalauréat**; (récipient) tub

baccalauréat [bakalɔʀea] nm high school diploma

bâcler [bakle] vt to botch (up)

baffe [baf] (fam) nf slap, clout

bafouiller [bafuje] vi, vt to stammer

bagage [bagaʒ] nm piece of luggage; (connaissances) background, knowledge; **nos ~s ne sont pas arrivés** our luggage hasn't arrived; **bagage à main** piece of hand-luggage

bagarre [bagaʀ] nf fight, brawl; **bagarrer**: **se bagarrer** vi to have a fight ou scuffle, fight

bagnole [baɲɔl] (fam) nf car

bague [bag] nf ring; **bague de fiançailles** engagement ring

baguette [baget] nf stick; (cuisine chinoise) chopstick; (de chef d'orchestre) baton; (pain) stick of (French) bread; **baguette magique** magic wand

baie [bɛ] nf (Géo) bay; (fruit) berry; **baie (vitrée)** picture window

baignade [beɲad] nf bathing; **"~ interdite"** "no bathing"

baigner [beɲe] vt (bébé) to bath; **se ~** vi to have a swim, go swimming ou bathing; **baignoire** nf bath(tub)

bail [baj, bo] (pl baux) nm lease

bâiller [baje] vi to yawn; (être ouvert) to gape

bain [bɛ̃] nm bath; **prendre un ~** to have a bath; **se mettre dans le ~** (fig) to get into it ou things; **bain de bouche** mouthwash; **bain moussant** bubble bath; **bain de soleil: prendre un bain de soleil** to sunbathe; **bain-marie** nm: **faire chauffer au bain-marie** (boîte etc) to immerse in boiling water

baiser [beze] nm kiss ▷ vt (main, front) to kiss; (fam!) to screw (!)

baisse [bɛs] nf fall, drop; **être en ~** to be falling, be declining

baisser [bese] vt to lower; (radio, chauffage) to turn down ▷ vi to fall, drop, go down; (vue, santé) to fail, dwindle; **se ~** vi to bend down

bal [bal] *nm* dance; (*grande soirée*) ball; **bal costumé** fancy-dress ball

balade [balad] (*fam*) *nf* (*à pied*) walk, stroll; (*en voiture*) drive; **balader** (*fam*): **se balader** *vi* to go for a walk or stroll; to go for a drive; **baladeur** *nm* personal stereo, Walkman®

balai [balɛ] *nm* broom, brush

balance [balɑ̃s] *nf* scales *pl*; (*signe*): **la B~** Libra; **balance commerciale** balance of trade

balancer [balɑ̃se] *vt* to swing; (*fam: lancer*) to fling, chuck; (: *jeter*) to chuck out; **se ~** *vi* to swing, rock; **se ~ de** (*fam*) not to care about; **balançoire** *nf* swing; (*sur pivot*) seesaw

balayer [balɛje] *vt* (*feuilles etc*) to sweep up, brush up; (*pièce*) to sweep; (*objections*) to sweep aside; (*suj: radar*) to scan; **balayeur, -euse** *nm/f* roadsweeper

balbutier [balbysje] *vi, vt* to stammer

balcon [balkɔ̃] *nm* balcony; (*Théâtre*) dress circle; **avez-vous une chambre avec ~?** do you have a room with a balcony?

Bâle [bal] *n* Basle, Basel

Baléares [baleaR] *nfpl*: **les ~** the Balearic Islands, the Balearics

baleine [balɛn] *nf* whale

balise [baliz] *nf* (*Navig*) beacon; (*marker*) buoy; (*Aviat*) runway light, beacon; (*Auto, Ski*) sign, marker; **baliser** *vt* to mark out (with lights *etc*)

balle [bal] *nf* (*de fusil*) bullet; (*de sport*) ball; (*fam: franc*) franc

ballerine [bal(ə)Rin] *nf* (*danseuse*) ballet dancer; (*chaussure*) ballet shoe

ballet [balɛ] *nm* ballet

ballon [balɔ̃] *nm* (*de sport*) ball; (*jouet, Aviat*) balloon; **ballon de football** football

balnéaire [balneeR] *adj* seaside *cpd*; **station ~** seaside resort

balustrade [balystRad] *nf* railings *pl*, handrail

bambin [bɑ̃bɛ̃] *nm* little child

bambou [bɑ̃bu] *nm* bamboo

banal, e [banal] *adj* banal, commonplace; (*péj*) trite; **banalité** *nf* banality

banane [banan] *nf* banana; (*sac*) waist-bag, bum-bag

banc [bɑ̃] *nm* seat, bench; (*de poissons*) shoal; **banc d'essai** (*fig*) testing ground

bancaire [bɑ̃kɛR] *adj* banking; (*chèque, carte*) bank *cpd*

bancal, e [bɑ̃kal] *adj* wobbly

bandage [bɑ̃daʒ] *nm* bandage

bande [bɑ̃d] *nf* (*de tissu etc*) strip; (*Méd*) bandage; (*motif*) stripe; (*magnétique etc*) tape; (*groupe*) band; (: *péj*) bunch; **faire ~ à part** to keep to o.s.; **bande dessinée** comic strip; **bande sonore** sound track

bande-annonce [bɑ̃danɔ̃s] *nf* trailer

bandeau, x [bɑ̃do] *nm* headband; (*sur les yeux*) blindfold

bander [bɑ̃de] *vt* (*blessure*) to bandage; **~ les yeux à qn** to blindfold sb

bandit [bɑ̃di] *nm* bandit

bandoulière [bɑ̃duljɛR] *nf*: **en ~** (slung *ou* worn) across the shoulder

Bangladesh [bɑ̃gladɛʃ] *nm*: **le ~** Bangladesh

banlieue [bɑ̃ljə] *nf* suburbs *pl*; **lignes/quartiers de ~** suburban lines/areas; **trains de ~** commuter trains

bannir [baniR] *vt* to banish

banque [bɑ̃k] *nf* bank; (*activités*) banking; **banque de données** data bank

banquet [bɑ̃kɛ] *nm* dinner; (*d'apparat*) banquet

banquette [bɑ̃kɛt] *nf* seat

banquier [bɑ̃kje] *nm* banker

banquise [bɑ̃kiz] *nf* ice field

baptême [batɛm] *nm* christening; baptism; **baptême de l'air** first flight

baptiser [batize] *vt* to baptize, christen

bar [baR] *nm* bar

baraque [baRak] *nf* shed; (*fam*) house; (*dans une fête foraine*) stall, booth; **baraqué, e** (*fam*) *adj* well-built, hefty

barbare [baRbaR] *adj* barbaric

barbe [baRb] *nf* beard; **la ~!** (*fam*) damn it!; **quelle ~!** (*fam*) what a drag *ou* bore!; **à la ~ de qn** under sb's nose; **barbe à papa** candy-floss, cotton candy (*us*)

barbelé [baRbəle] *adj, nm*: **(fil de fer) ~** barbed wire *no pl*

barbiturique [baRbityRik] *nm* barbiturate

barbouiller [baRbuje] *vt* to daub; **avoir l'estomac barbouillé** to feel queasy

barbu, e [baRby] *adj* bearded

barder [baRde] (*fam*) *vi*: **ça va ~** sparks will fly, things are going to get hot

barème [baRɛm] *nm* (*Scol*) scale; (*table de référence*) table

baril [baRi(l)] *nm* barrel; (*poudre*) keg

bariolé, e [baRjɔle] *adj* gaudily-coloured

baromètre [baRɔmɛtR] *nm* barometer

baron, ne [baRɔ̃, ɔn] *nm/f* baron(ess)

baroque [baRɔk] *adj* (*Art*) baroque; (*fig*) weird

barque [baRk] *nf* small boat

barquette [baRkɛt] *nf* (*pour repas*) tray; (*pour fruits*) punnet

barrage [baRaʒ] *nm* dam; (*sur route*) roadblock, barricade

barre [baR] *nf* bar; (*Navig*) helm; (*écrite*) line, stroke

barreau, x [baRo] *nm* bar; (*Jur*): **le ~** the Bar

barrer [baRe] *vt* (*route etc*) to block; (*mot*) to cross out; (*chèque*) to cross; (*Navig*) to steer; **se ~** (*fam*) ▷ *vi* to clear off

barrette [baRɛt] *nf* (*pour cheveux*) (hair) slide (*BRIT*) *ou* clip (*us*)

barricader [baRikade]: **se ~** *vi* to barricade o.s.

barrière [baRjɛR] *nf* fence; (*obstacle*) barrier; (*porte*) gate

barrique [baRik] *nf* barrel, cask

bar-tabac [baRtaba] *nm* bar (which sells tobacco and stamps)

bas, basse [bɑ, bas] *adj* low ▷ *nm* bottom, lower part; (*vêtement*) stocking ▷ *adv* low; (*parler*) softly; **au ~ mot** at the lowest estimate; **de ~** down below; (*d'une liste, d'un mur etc*) at the bottom; (*dans une maison*) downstairs; **en ~ de** at the bottom of; **un enfant en ~ âge** a young child; **à ~ ...!** down with ...!

bas-côté [bakote] *nm* (*de route*) verge (*BRIT*), shoulder (*us*)

basculer [baskyle] *vi* to fall over, topple (over); (*benne*) to tip up ▷ *vt* (*contenu*) to tip out; (*benne*) to tip up

base [baz] *nf* base; (*Pol*) rank and file; (*fondement, principe*) basis; **de ~** basic; **à ~ de café** *etc* coffee *etc*-based; **base de données** database; **baser** *vt* to base; **se baser sur** *vt* (*preuves*) to base one's argument on

bas-fond [bafɔ̃] *nm* (*Navig*) shallow; **bas-fonds** *nmpl* (*fig*) dregs

basilic [bazilik] *nm* (*Culin*) basil

basket [baskɛt] *nm* trainer (*BRIT*), sneaker (*us*); (*aussi*: **~-ball**) basketball

basque [bask] *adj* Basque ▷ *nm/f*: **B~** Basque; **le Pays Basque** the Basque Country

basse [bas] *adj voir* **bas** ▷ *nf* (*Mus*) bass; **basse-cour** *nf* farmyard

bassin [basɛ̃] *nm* (*pièce d'eau*) pond, pool; (*de fontaine,: Géo*) basin; (*Anat*) pelvis; (*portuaire*) dock

bassine [basin] *nf* (*ustensile*) basin; (*contenu*) bowl(ful)

basson [basɔ̃] *nm* bassoon

bat [ba] *vb voir* **battre**

bataille [bataj] *nf* (*Mil*) battle; (*rixe*) fight; **elle avait les cheveux en ~** her hair was a mess

bateau, x [bato] *nm* boat, ship; **bateau-mouche** *nm* passenger pleasure boat (*on the Seine*)

bâti, e [bati] *adj*: **bien ~** well-built; **terrain ~** piece of land that has been built on

bâtiment [batimɑ̃] *nm* building; (*Navig*) ship, vessel; (*industrie*) building trade

bâtir [batiʀ] *vt* to build

bâtisse [batis] *nf* building

bâton [batɔ̃] *nm* stick; **parler à ~s rompus** to chat about this and that

bats [ba] *vb voir* **battre**

battement [batmɑ̃] *nm* (*de cœur*) beat; (*intervalle*) interval; **10 minutes de ~** 10 minutes to spare

batterie [batʀi] *nf* (*Mil, Élec*) battery; (*Mus*) drums *pl*, drum kit; **batterie de cuisine** pots and pans *pl*, kitchen utensils *pl*

batteur [batœʀ] *nm* (*Mus*) drummer; (*appareil*) whisk

battre [batʀ] *vt* to beat; (*blé*) to thresh; (*passer au peigne fin*) to scour; (*cartes*) to shuffle ▷ *vi* (*cœur*) to beat; (*volets etc*) to bang, rattle; **se ~** *vi* to fight; **~ la mesure** to beat time; **~ son plein** to be at its height, to be going full swing; **~ des mains** to clap one's hands

baume [bom] *nm* balm

bavard, e [bavaʀ, aʀd] *adj* (very) talkative; gossipy; **bavarder** *vi* to chatter; (*commérer*) to gossip; (*divulguer un secret*) to blab

baver [bave] *vi* to dribble; (*chien*) to slobber; **en ~** (*fam*) to have a hard time (of it)

bavoir [bavwaʀ] *nm* bib

bavure [bavyʀ] *nf* smudge; (*fig*) hitch; (*policière etc*) blunder

bazar [bazaʀ] *nm* general store; (*fam*) jumble; **bazarder** (*fam*) *vt* to chuck out

BCBG *sigle adj* (= *bon chic bon genre*) preppy, smart and trendy

BD *sigle f* = **bande dessinée**

bd *abr* = **boulevard**

béant, e [beɑ̃, ɑ̃t] *adj* gaping

beau, bel, belle [bo, bɛl] (*mpl* **~x**) *adj* beautiful, lovely; (*homme*) handsome; (*femme*) beautiful ▷ *adv*: **il fait ~** the weather's fine ▷ *nm*: **faire le ~** (*chien*) to sit up and beg; **un ~ jour** one (fine) day; **de plus belle** more than ever, even more; **on a ~ essayer** however hard we try; **bel et bien** well and truly; **le plus ~ c'est que ...** the best of it is that ...

beaucoup [boku] *adv* **1** a lot; **il boit beaucoup** he drinks a lot; **il ne boit pas beaucoup** he doesn't drink much *ou* a lot

2 (*suivi de plus, trop etc*) much, a lot; **il est beaucoup plus grand** he is much *ou* a lot taller; **c'est beaucoup plus cher** it's a lot *ou* much more expensive; **il a beaucoup plus de temps que moi** he has much *ou* a lot more time than me; **il y a beaucoup plus de touristes ici** there are a lot *ou* many more tourists here; **beaucoup trop vite** much too fast; **il fume beaucoup trop** he smokes far too much

3: **beaucoup de** (*nombre*) many, a lot of; (*quantité*) a lot of; **beaucoup d'étudiants/de touristes** a lot of *ou* many students/tourists; **beaucoup de courage** a lot of courage; **il n'a pas beaucoup d'argent** he hasn't got much *ou* a lot of money

4: **de beaucoup** by far

beau...: **beau-fils** *nm* son-in-law; (*remariage*) stepson; **beau-frère** *nm* brother-in-law; **beau-père** *nm* father-in-law; (*remariage*) stepfather

beauté [bote] *nf* beauty; **de toute ~** beautiful; **finir qch en ~** to complete sth brilliantly

beaux-arts [bozaʀ] *nmpl* fine arts

beaux-parents [boparɑ̃] *nmpl* wife's/husband's family, in-laws

bébé [bebe] *nm* baby

bec [bɛk] *nm* beak, bill; (*de théière*) spout; (*de casserole*) lip; (*fam*) mouth; **bec de gaz** (street) gaslamp

bêche [bɛʃ] *nf* spade; **bêcher** *vt* to dig

bedaine [bədɛn] *nf* paunch

bedonnant, e [bədɔnɑ̃, ɑ̃t] *adj* potbellied

bée [be] *adj*: **bouche ~** gaping

bégayer [begeje] *vi, vt* to stammer

beige [bɛʒ] *adj* beige

beignet [bɛɲɛ] *nm* fritter

bel [bɛl] *adj voir* **beau**

bêler [bele] *vi* to bleat

belette [bəlɛt] *nf* weasel

belge [bɛlʒ] *adj* Belgian ▷ *nm/f*: **B~** Belgian

Belgique [bɛlʒik] *nf*: **la ~** Belgium

bélier [belje] *nm* ram; (*signe*): **le B~** Aries

belle [bɛl] *adj voir* **beau** ▷ *nf* (*Sport*): **la ~** the decider; **belle-fille** *nf* daughter-in-law; (*remariage*) stepdaughter; **belle-mère** *nf* mother-in-law; (*remariage*) stepmother; **belle-sœur** *nf* sister-in-law

belvédère [belvedɛʀ] *nm* panoramic viewpoint (*or small building there*)

bémol [bemɔl] *nm* (*Mus*) flat

bénédiction [benediksjɔ̃] *nf* blessing

bénéfice [benefis] *nm* (*Comm*) profit; (*avantage*) benefit; **bénéficier: bénéficier de** *vt* to enjoy; (*situation*) to benefit by *ou* from; **bénéfique** *adj* beneficial

Benelux [benelyks] *nm*: **le ~** Benelux, the Benelux countries

bénévole [benevɔl] *adj* voluntary, unpaid

bénin, -igne [benɛ̃, iɲ] *adj* minor, mild; (*tumeur*) benign

bénir [beniʀ] *vt* to bless; **bénit, e** *adj* consecrated; **eau bénite** holy water

benne [bɛn] *nf* skip; (*de téléphérique*) (cable) car; **benne à ordures** (*amovible*) skip

béquille [bekij] *nf* crutch; (*de bicyclette*) stand

berceau, x [bɛʀso] *nm* cradle, crib

bercer [bɛʀse] *vt* to rock, cradle; (*suj: musique etc*) to lull; **~ qn de** (*promesses etc*) to delude sb with; **berceuse** *nf* lullaby

béret [beʀɛ] *nm* (*aussi*: **~ basque**) beret

berge [bɛʀʒ] *nf* bank

berger, -ère [bɛʀʒe, ɛʀ] nm/f shepherd(-ess); **berger allemand** alsatian (BRIT), German shepherd
Berlin [bɛʀlɛ̃] n Berlin
Bermudes [bɛʀmyd] nfpl: **les (îles) ~** Bermuda
Berne [bɛʀn(ə)] n Bern
berner [bɛʀne] vt to fool
besogne [bəzɔɲ] nf work no pl, job
besoin [bəzwɛ̃] nm need; **avoir ~ de qch/faire qch** to need sth/to do sth; **au ~** if need be; **le ~** (pauvreté) need, want; **être dans le ~** to be in need ou want; **faire ses ~s** to relieve o.s.
bestiole [bɛstjɔl] nf (tiny) creature
bétail [betaj] nm livestock, cattle pl
bête [bɛt] nf animal; (bestiole) insect, creature ▷ adj stupid, silly; **il cherche la petite ~** he's being pernickety ou over fussy; **bête noire** pet hate; **bête sauvage** wild beast ou animal
bêtise [betiz] nf stupidity; (action) stupid thing (to say ou do)
béton [betɔ̃] nm concrete; **(en) ~** (alibi, argument) cast iron; **béton armé** reinforced concrete
betterave [bɛtʀav] nf beetroot (BRIT), beet (US); **betterave sucrière** sugar beet
Beur [bœʀ] nm/f person of North African origin living in France
beurre [bœʀ] nm butter; **beurrer** vt to butter; **beurrier** nm butter dish
biais [bjɛ] nm (moyen) device, expedient; (aspect) angle; **en ~, de ~** (obliquement) at an angle; **par le ~ de** by means of
bibelot [biblo] nm trinket, curio
biberon [bibʀɔ̃] nm (feeding) bottle; **nourrir au ~** to bottle-feed
bible [bibl] nf bible
biblio... [bibli] préfixe: **bibliobus** nm mobile library van; **bibliothécaire** nm/f librarian; **bibliothèque** nf library; (meuble) bookcase
bic® [bik] nm Biro®
bicarbonate [bikaʀbɔnat] nm: **~ (de soude)** bicarbonate of soda
biceps [bisɛps] nm biceps
biche [biʃ] nf doe
bicolore [bikɔlɔʀ] adj two-coloured
bicoque [bikɔk] (péj) nf shack
bicyclette [bisiklɛt] nf bicycle
bidet [bidɛ] nm bidet
bidon [bidɔ̃] nm can ▷ adj inv (fam) phoney
bidonville [bidɔ̃vil] nm shanty town
bidule [bidyl] (fam) nm thingumajig

MOT-CLÉ

bien [bjɛ̃] nm **1** (avantage, profit): **faire du bien à qn** to do sb good; **dire du bien de** to speak well of; **c'est pour son bien** it's for his own good
2 (possession, patrimoine) possession, property; **son bien le plus précieux** his most treasured possession; **avoir du bien** to have property; **biens de consommation etc)** (consumer etc) goods
3 (moral): **le bien** good; **distinguer le bien du mal** to tell good from evil
▷ adv **1** (de façon satisfaisante) well; **elle travaille/mange bien** she works/eats well; **croyant bien faire, je/il ...** thinking I/he was doing the right thing, I/he ...;

tiens-toi bien! (assieds-toi correctement) sit up straight!; (debout) stand up straight!; (sois sage) behave yourself!; (prépare-toi) wait for it!; **c'est bien fait!** it serves him (ou her etc) right!
2 (valeur intensive) quite; **bien jeune** quite young; **bien assez** quite enough; **bien mieux** (very) much better; **j'espère bien y aller** I do hope to go; **je veux bien le faire** (concession) I'm quite willing to do it; **il faut bien le faire** it has to be done; **Paul est bien venu, n'est-ce pas?** Paul did come, didn't he?; **où peut-il bien être passé?** where can he have got to?
3 (beaucoup): **bien du temps/des gens** quite a time/a number of people
4 (au moins) at least; **cela fait bien deux ans que je ne l'ai pas vu** I haven't seen him for at least ou a good two years
▷ adj inv **1** (en bonne forme, à l'aise): **je me sens bien** I feel fine; **je ne me sens pas bien** I don't feel well; **on est bien dans ce fauteuil** this chair is very comfortable
2 (joli, beau) good-looking; **tu es bien dans cette robe** you look good in that dress
3 (satisfaisant) good; **elle est bien, cette maison/secrétaire** it's a good house/she's a good secretary; **c'est bien?** is that ou it O.K.?; **c'est très bien (comme ça)** it's fine (like that)
4 (moralement) right; (: personne) good, nice; (respectable) respectable; **ce n'est pas bien de ...** it's not right to ...; **elle est bien, cette femme** she's a nice woman, she's a good sort; **des gens bien** respectable people
5 (en bons termes): **être bien avec qn** to be on good terms with sb
▷ préfixe: **bien-aimé, e** adj, nm/f beloved; **bien-être** nm well-being; **bienfaisance** nf charity; **bienfait** nm act of generosity, benefaction; (de la science etc) benefit; **bienfaiteur, -trice** nm/f benefactor/benefactress; **bien-fondé** nm soundness; **bien que** conj (al)though; **bien sûr** adv certainly

bientôt [bjɛ̃to] adv soon; **à ~** see you soon
bienveillant, e [bjɛ̃vɛjɑ̃, ɑ̃t] adj kindly
bienvenu, e [bjɛ̃vny] adj welcome; **bienvenue** nf: **souhaiter la bienvenue à** to welcome; **bienvenue à** welcome to
bière [bjɛʀ] nf (boisson) beer; (cercueil) bier; **bière blonde** lager; **bière brune** brown ale (BRIT), dark beer (US); **bière (à la) pression** draught beer
bifteck [biftɛk] nm steak
bigorneau, x [bigɔʀno] nm winkle
bigoudi [bigudi] nm curler
bijou, x [biʒu] nm jewel; **bijouterie** nf jeweller's (shop); **bijoutier, -ière** nm/f jeweller
bikini [bikini] nm bikini
bilan [bilɑ̃] nm (fig) (net) outcome; (: de victimes) toll; (Comm) balance sheet(s); **un ~ de santé** a (medical) checkup; **faire le ~ de** to assess, review; **déposer son ~** to file a bankruptcy statement
bile [bil] nf bile; **se faire de la ~** (fam) to worry o.s. sick
bilieux, -euse [biljø, øz] adj bilious; (fig: colérique) testy
bilingue [bilɛ̃g] adj bilingual
billard [bijaʀ] nm (jeu) billiards sg; (table) billiard table
bille [bij] nf (gén) ball; (du jeu de billes) marble
billet [bijɛ] nm (aussi: **~ de banque**) (bank)note; (de

cinéma, de bus etc) ticket; *(courte lettre)* note; **billet électronique** e-ticket; **billetterie** nf ticket office; *(distributeur)* ticket machine; *(Banque)* cash dispenser

billion [biljɔ̃] nm billion (BRIT), trillion (US)

bimensuel, le [bimɑ̃sɥɛl] adj bimonthly

bio [bjo] adj inv organic

bio... [bjo] préfixe bio...; **biochimie** nf biochemistry; **biographie** nf biography; **biologie** nf biology; **biologique** adj biological; *(produits, aliments)* organic; **biométrie** nf biometrics; **biotechnologie** nf biotechnology; **bioterrorisme** nm bioterrorism

Birmanie [birmani] nf Burma

bis [bis] adv: **12 ~ 12a** ou A ▷ excl, nm encore

biscotte [biskɔt] nf toasted bread *(sold in packets)*

biscuit [biskɥi] nm biscuit (BRIT), cookie (US)

bise [biz] nf *(fam: baiser)* kiss; *(vent)* North wind; **grosses ~s (de)** *(sur lettre)* love and kisses (from)

bisexuel, le [bisɛksɥɛl] adj bisexual

bisou [bizu] *(fam)* nm kiss

bissextile [bisɛkstil] adj: **année ~** leap year

bistro(t) [bistro] nm bistro, café

bitume [bitym] nm asphalt

bizarre [bizar] adj strange, odd

blague [blag] nf *(propos)* joke; *(farce)* trick; **sans ~!** no kidding!; **blaguer** vi to joke

blaireau, x [blɛro] nm *(Zool)* badger; *(brosse)* shaving brush

blâme [blɑm] nm blame; *(sanction)* reprimand; **blâmer** vt to blame

blanc, blanche [blɑ̃, blɑ̃ʃ] adj white; *(non imprimé)* blank ▷ nm/f white, white man(-woman) ▷ nm *(couleur)* white; *(espace non écrit)* blank; *(aussi:* **~ d'œuf)** (egg-)white; *(aussi:* **~ de poulet)** breast, white meat; *(aussi:* **vin ~)** white wine; **~ cassé** off-white; **chèque en ~** blank cheque; **à ~** *(chauffer)* white-hot; *(tirer, charger)* with blanks; **blanche** nf *(Mus)* minim (BRIT), half-note (US); **blancheur** nf whiteness

blanchir [blɑ̃ʃir] vt *(gén)* to whiten; *(linge)* to launder; *(Culin)* to blanch; *(fig: disculper)* to clear ▷ vi *(cheveux)* to go white; **blanchisserie** nf laundry

blason [blazɔ̃] nm coat of arms

blasphème [blasfɛm] nm blasphemy

blazer [blazɛr] nm blazer

blé [ble] nm wheat; **blé noir** buckwheat

bled [blɛd] *(péj)* nm hole

blême [blɛm] adj pale

blessé, e [blese] adj injured ▷ nm/f injured person, casualty

blesser [blese] vt to injure; *(délibérément)* to wound; *(offenser)* to hurt; **se ~** to injure o.s.; **se ~ au pied** to injure one's foot; **blessure** nf *(accidentelle)* injury; *(intentionnelle)* wound

bleu, e [blø] adj blue; *(bifteck)* very rare ▷ nm *(couleur)* blue; *(contusion)* bruise; *(vêtement: aussi:* **~s)** overalls pl; *(fromage)* blue cheese; **bleu marine** navy blue; **bleuet** nm cornflower

bloc [blɔk] nm *(de pierre etc)* block; *(de papier à lettres)* pad; *(ensemble)* group, block; **serré à ~** tightened right down; **en ~** as a whole; **bloc opératoire** operating ou theatre block; **blocage** nm *(des prix)* freezing; *(Psych)* hang-up; **bloc-notes** nm note pad

blog, blogue [blɔg] nm blog; **bloguer** vi to blog

blond, e [blɔ̃, blɔ̃d] adj fair, blond; *(sable, blés)* golden

bloquer [blɔke] vt *(passage)* to block; *(pièce mobile)* to jam; *(crédits, compte)* to freeze

blottir [blɔtir]: **se ~** vi to huddle up

blouse [bluz] nf overall

blouson [bluzɔ̃] nm blouson jacket; **blouson noir** *(fig)* = rocker

bluff [blœf] nm bluff

bobine [bɔbin] nf reel; *(Élec)* coil

bobo [bɔbo] abr m/f = **bourgeois bohème**; *(fam)* boho

bocal, -aux [bɔkal, o] nm jar

bock [bɔk] nm glass of beer

bœuf [bœf] nm ox; *(Culin)* beef

bof [bɔf] *(fam)* excl don't care!; *(pas terrible)* nothing special

bohémien, ne [bɔemjɛ̃, -ɛn] nm/f gipsy

boire [bwar] vt to drink; *(s'imprégner de)* to soak up; **~ un coup** *(fam)* to have a drink

bois [bwa] nm wood; **de ~, en ~** wooden; **boisé, e** adj woody, wooded

boisson [bwasɔ̃] nf drink

boîte [bwat] nf box; *(fam: entreprise)* firm; **aliments en ~** canned ou tinned (BRIT) foods; **boîte à gants** glove compartment; **boîte à ordures** dustbin (BRIT), trashcan (US); **boîte aux lettres** letter box; **boîte d'allumettes** box of matches; *(vide)* matchbox; **boîte de conserves** can ou tin (BRIT) of food; **boîte (de nuit)** night club; **boîte de vitesses** gear box; **boîte postale** PO Box; **boîte vocale** *(Tél)* voice mail

boiter [bwate] vi to limp; *(fig: raisonnement)* to be shaky

boîtier [bwatje] nm case

boive etc [bwav] vb voir **boire**

bol [bɔl] nm bowl; **un ~ d'air** a breath of fresh air; **j'en ai ras le ~** *(fam)* I'm fed up with this; **avoir du ~** *(fam)* to be lucky

bombarder [bɔ̃barde] vt to bomb; **~ qn de** *(cailloux, lettres)* to bombard sb with

bombe [bɔ̃b] nf bomb; *(atomiseur)* (aerosol) spray

○ **MOT-CLÉ**

bon, bonne [bɔ̃, bɔn] adj 1 *(agréable, satisfaisant)* good; **un bon repas/restaurant** a good meal/restaurant; **être bon en maths** to be good at maths (BRIT) ou math (US)

2 *(charitable):* **être bon (envers)** to be good (to)

3 *(correct)* right; **le bon numéro/moment** the right number/moment

4 *(souhaits):* **bon anniversaire!** happy birthday!; **bon voyage!** have a good trip!; **bonne chance!** good luck!; **bonne année!** happy New Year!; **bonne nuit!** good night!

5 *(approprié, apte):* **bon à/pour** fit to/for; **à quoi bon?** what's the use?

6: **bon enfant** adj inv accommodating, easy-going; **bonne femme** *(péj)* woman; **de bonne heure** early; **bon marché** adj inv, adv cheap; **bon mot** witticism; **bon sens** common sense; **bon vivant** jovial chap; **bonnes œuvres** charitable works, charities

▷ nm 1 *(billet)* voucher; *(aussi:* **bon cadeau)** gift voucher; **bon d'essence** petrol coupon; **bon du Trésor** Treasury bond

2: **avoir du bon** to have its good points; **pour de bon** for good

▷ adv: **il fait bon** it's ou the weather is fine; **sentir bon** to

smell good; **tenir bon** to stand firm
▷ *excl* second! **ah bon?** really?; **bon, je reste** right then, I'll
stay; *voir aussi* **bonne**

bonbon [bɔ̃bɔ̃] *nm* (boiled) sweet
bond [bɔ̃] *nm* leap; **faire un ~** to leap in the air
bondé, e [bɔ̃de] *adj* packed (full)
bondir [bɔ̃diʀ] *vi* to leap
bonheur [bɔnœʀ] *nm* happiness; **porter ~ (à qn)** to
bring (sb) luck; **au petit ~** haphazardly; **par ~** fortunately
bonhomme [bɔnɔm] (*pl* **bonshommes**) *nm* fellow;
bonhomme de neige snowman
bonjour [bɔ̃ʒuʀ] *excl, nm* hello; (*selon l'heure*) good
morning/afternoon; **c'est simple comme ~!** it's easy
as pie!
bonne [bɔn] *adj voir* **bon** ▷ *nf* (*domestique*) maid
bonnet [bɔnɛ] *nm* hat; (*de soutien-gorge*) cup; **bonnet de
bain** bathing cap
bonsoir [bɔ̃swaʀ] *excl* good evening
bonté [bɔ̃te] *nf* kindness *no pl*
bonus [bɔnys] *nm* no-claims bonus; (*de DVD*) extras *pl*
bord [bɔʀ] *nm* (*de table, verre, falaise*) edge; (*de rivière, lac*)
bank; (*de route*) side; (*de* (**monter**) **à ~** (to go) on board; **jeter
par-dessus ~** to throw overboard; **le commandant
de/les hommes du ~** the ship's master/crew; **au ~ de
la mer** at the seaside; **au ~ de la route** at the roadside;
être au ~ des larmes to be on the verge of tears
bordeaux [bɔʀdo] *nm* Bordeaux (wine) ▷ *adj inv*
maroon
bordel [bɔʀdɛl] *nm* brothel; (*fam!*) bloody mess (!)
border [bɔʀde] *vt* (*être le long de*) to line; (*qn dans son lit*)
to tuck up; (*garnir*): **~ qch de** to edge sth with
bordure [bɔʀdyʀ] *nf* border; **en ~ de** on the edge of
borne [bɔʀn] *nf* boundary stone; (*aussi*: **~ kilométrique**)
kilometre-marker, ≈ milestone; **bornes** *nfpl* (*fig*) limits;
dépasser les ~s to go too far
borné, e [bɔʀne] *adj* (*personne*) narrow-minded
borner [bɔʀne] *vt*: **se ~ à faire** (*se contenter de*) to content
o.s. with doing; (*se limiter à*) to limit o.s. to doing
bosniaque [bɔsnjak] *adj* Bosnian ▷ *nm/f*: **B~** Bosnian
Bosnie-Herzégovine [bɔsniɛʀzegɔvin] *nf* Bosnia-
Herzegovina
bosquet [bɔskɛ] *nm* grove
bosse [bɔs] *nf* (*de terrain etc*) bump; (*enflure*) lump; (*du
bossu, du chameau*) hump; **avoir la ~ des maths** *etc* (*fam*)
to have a gift for maths *etc*; **il a roulé sa ~** (*fam*) he's
been around
bosser [bɔse] (*fam*) *vi* (*travailler*) to work; (*travailler dur*)
to slave (away)
bossu, e [bɔsy] *nm/f* hunchback
botanique [bɔtanik] *nf* botany ▷ *adj* botanic(al)
botte [bɔt] *nf* (*soulier*) (high) boot; (*gerbe*): **~ de paille**
bundle of straw; **botte de radis/d'asperges** bunch of
radishes/asparagus; **bottes de caoutchouc** wellington
boots
bottin [bɔtɛ̃] *nm* directory
bottine [bɔtin] *nf* ankle boot
bouc [buk] *nm* goat; (*barbe*) goatee; **bouc émissaire**
scapegoat
boucan [bukɑ̃] (*fam*) *nm* din, racket
bouche [buʃ] *nf* mouth; **faire du ~ à ~ à qn** to give sb
the kiss of life *ou* mouth-to-mouth resuscitation (BRIT);
rester ~ bée to stand open-mouthed; **bouche d'égout**
manhole; **bouche d'incendie** fire hydrant; **bouche de

métro métro entrance
bouché, e [buʃe] *adj* (*flacon etc*) stoppered; (*temps, ciel*)
overcast; (*péj fam: personne*) thick (*fam*); **c'est un secteur
~** there's no future in that area; **avoir le nez ~** to have a
blocked(-up) nose; **l'évier est ~** the sink's blocked
bouchée [buʃe] *nf* mouthful; **bouchées à la reine**
chicken vol-au-vents
boucher, -ère [buʃe, ɛʀ] *nm/f* butcher ▷ *vt* (*trou*) to fill up;
(*obstruer*) to block (up); **se ~** *vi* (*tuyau etc*) to block up, get
blocked up; **j'ai le nez bouché** my nose is blocked; **se ~
le nez** to hold one's nose; **boucherie** *nf* butcher's (shop);
(*fig*) slaughter
bouchon [buʃɔ̃] *nm* stopper; (*de tube*) top; (*en liège*) cork;
(*fig: embouteillage*) holdup; (*Pêche*) float
boucle [bukl] *nf* (*forme, figure*) loop; (*objet*) buckle;
boucle (de cheveux) curl; **boucle d'oreille** earring
bouclé, e [bukle] *adj* (*cheveux*) curly
boucler [bukle] *vt* (*fermer: ceinture etc*) to fasten;
(*terminer*) to finish off; (*fam: enfermer*) to shut away;
(*quartier*) to seal off ▷ *vi* to curl
bouder [bude] *vi* to sulk ▷ *vt* to stay away from
boudin [budɛ̃] *nm*: **~ (noir)** black pudding; **boudin
blanc** white pudding
boue [bu] *nf* mud
bouée [bwe] *nf* buoy; **bouée (de sauvetage)** lifebuoy
boueux, -euse [bwø, øz] *adj* muddy
bouffe [buf] (*fam*) *nf* grub (*fam*), food
bouffée [bufe] *nf* (*de cigarette*) puff; **une ~ d'air pur** a
breath of fresh air; **bouffée de chaleur** hot flush (BRIT)
ou flash (US)
bouffer [bufe] (*fam*) *vi* to eat
bouffi, e [bufi] *adj* swollen
bouger [buʒe] *vi* to move; (*dent etc*) to be loose; (*s'activer*)
to get moving ▷ *vt* to move; **les prix/les couleurs n'ont
pas bougé** prices/colours haven't changed
bougie [buʒi] *nf* candle; (*Auto*) spark(ing) plug
bouillabaisse [bujabɛs] *nf* type of fish soup
bouillant, e [bujɑ̃, ɑ̃t] *adj* (*qui bout*) boiling; (*très chaud*)
boiling (hot)
bouillie [buji] *nf* (*de bébé*) cereal; **en ~** (*fig*) crushed
bouillir [bujiʀ] *vi, vt* to boil; **~ d'impatience** to seethe
with impatience
bouilloire [bujwaʀ] *nf* kettle
bouillon [bujɔ̃] *nm* (*Culin*) stock *no pl*; **bouillonner** *vi* to
bubble; (*fig: idées*) to bubble up
bouillotte [bujɔt] *nf* hot-water bottle
boulanger, -ère [bulɑ̃ʒe, ɛʀ] *nm/f* baker; **boulangerie**
nf bakery
boule [bul] *nf* (*gén*) ball; (*de pétanque*) bowl; **boule de
neige** snowball
boulette [bulɛt] *nf* (*de viande*) meatball
boulevard [bulvaʀ] *nm* boulevard
bouleversement [bulvɛʀsəmɑ̃] *nm* upheaval
bouleverser [bulvɛʀse] *vt* (*émouvoir*) to overwhelm;
(*causer du chagrin*) to distress; (*pays, vie*) to disrupt;
(*papiers, objets*) to turn upside down
boulimie [bulimi] *nf* bulimia
boulimique [bulimik] *adj* bulimic
boulon [bulɔ̃] *nm* bolt
boulot, te [bulo, ɔt] *adj* plump, tubby ▷ *nm* (*fam:
travail*) work
boum [bum] *nm* bang ▷ *nf* (*fam*) party
bouquet [bukɛ] *nm* (*de fleurs*) bunch (of flowers),
bouquet; (*de persil etc*) bunch; **c'est le ~!** (*fam*) that takes

the biscuit!

bouquin [bukɛ̃] (fam) nm book; **bouquiner** (fam) vi to read

bourdon [burdɔ̃] nm bumblebee

bourg [bur] nm small market town

bourgeois, e [burʒwa, waz] (péj) adj ≈ (upper) middle class; **bourgeoisie** nf ≈ upper middle classes pl

bourgeon [burʒɔ̃] nm bud

Bourgogne [burgɔɲ] nf: **la ~** Burgundy ▷ nm: **bourgogne** burgundy (wine)

bourguignon, ne [burgiɲɔ̃, ɔn] adj of ou from Burgundy, Burgundian

bourrasque [burask] nf squall

bourratif, -ive [buratif, iv] (fam) adj filling, stodgy (pej)

bourré, e [bure] adj (fam: ivre) plastered, tanked up (BRIT); (rempli): **~ de** crammed full of

bourrer [bure] vt (pipe) to fill; (poêle) to pack; (valise) to cram (full)

bourru, e [bury] adj surly, gruff

bourse [burs] nf (subvention) grant; (porte-monnaie) purse; **la B~** the Stock Exchange

bous [bu] vb voir **bouillir**

bousculade [buskylad] nf (hâte) rush; (cohue) crush; **bousculer** (t heurter) to knock into; (fig) to push, rush

boussole [busɔl] nf compass

bout [bu] vb voir **bouillir** ▷ nm bit; (d'un bâton etc) tip; (d'une ficelle, table, rue, période) end; **au ~ de** at the end of, after; **pousser qn à ~** to push sb to the limit; **venir à ~ de** to manage to finish; **à ~ portant** (at) point-blank (range)

bouteille [butɛj] nf bottle; (de gaz butane) cylinder

boutique [butik] nf shop

bouton [butɔ̃] nm button; (sur la peau) spot; (Bot) bud; **boutonner** vt to button up; **boutonnière** nf buttonhole; **bouton-pression** nm press stud

bovin, e [bɔvɛ̃, in] adj bovine; **bovins** nmpl cattle pl

bowling [bulin] nm (tenpin) bowling; (salle) bowling alley

boxe [bɔks] nf boxing

BP abr = **boîte postale**

bracelet [braslɛ] nm bracelet

braconnier [brakɔnje] nm poacher

brader [brade] vt to sell off; **braderie** nf cut-price shop/stall

braguette [bragɛt] nf fly ou flies pl (BRIT), zipper (US)

braise [brɛz] nf embers pl

brancard [brɑ̃kar] nm (civière) stretcher; **brancardier** nm stretcher-bearer

branche [brɑ̃ʃ] nf branch

branché, e [brɑ̃ʃe] (fam) adj trendy

brancher [brɑ̃ʃe] vt to connect (up); (en mettant la prise) to plug in

brandir [brɑ̃dir] vt to brandish

braquer [brake] vi (Auto) to turn (the wheel) ▷ vt (revolver etc) to aim, point; **~ qch sur** to aim sth at, point sth at; (mettre en colère): **~ qn** to put sb's back up

bras [brɑ] nm arm; **~ dessus, ~ dessous** arm in arm; **se retrouver avec qch sur les ~** (fam) to be landed with sth; **bras droit** (fig) right hand man

brassard [brasar] nm armband

brasse [bras] nf (nage) breast-stroke; **brasse papillon** butterfly (stroke)

brassée [brase] nf armful

brasser [brase] vt to mix; **~ l'argent/les affaires** to

handle a lot of money/business

brasserie [brasri] nf (restaurant) café-restaurant; (usine) brewery

brave [brav] adj (courageux) brave; (bon, gentil) good, kind

braver [brave] vt to defy

bravo [bravo] excl bravo ▷ nm cheer

bravoure [bravur] nf bravery

break [brɛk] nm (Auto) estate car

brebis [brəbi] nf ewe; **brebis galeuse** black sheep

bredouiller [brəduje] vi, vt to mumble, stammer

bref, brève [brɛf, ɛv] adj short, brief ▷ adv in short; **d'un ton ~** sharply, curtly; **en ~** in short, in brief

Brésil [brezil] nm Brazil

Bretagne [brətaɲ] nf Brittany

bretelle [brətɛl] nf (de vêtement, de sac) strap; (d'autoroute) slip road (BRIT), entrance/exit ramp (US); **bretelles** nfpl (pour pantalon) braces (BRIT), suspenders (US)

breton, ne [brətɔ̃, ɔn] adj Breton ▷ nm/f: **B~, ne** Breton

brève [brɛv] adj voir **bref**

brevet [brəvɛ] nm diploma, certificate; **brevet des collèges** exam taken at the age of 15; **brevet (d'invention)** patent; **breveté, e** adj patented

bricolage [brikɔlaʒ] nm: **le ~** do-it-yourself

bricoler [brikɔle] vi (petits travaux) to do DIY jobs; (passe-temps) to potter about ▷ vt (réparer) to fix up; **bricoleur, -euse** nm/f handyman(-woman), DIY enthusiast

bridge [bridʒ] nm (Cartes) bridge

brièvement [brijɛvmɑ̃] adv briefly

brigade [brigad] nf (Police) squad; (Mil) brigade; **brigadier** nm sergeant

brillamment [brijamɑ̃] adv brilliantly

brillant, e [brijɑ̃, ɑ̃t] adj (remarquable) bright; (luisant) shiny, shining

briller [brije] vi to shine

brin [brɛ̃] nm (de laine, ficelle etc) strand; (fig): **un ~ de** a bit of

brindille [brɛ̃dij] nf twig

brioche [brijɔʃ] nf brioche (bun); (fam: ventre) paunch

brique [brik] nf brick; (de lait) carton

briquet [brikɛ] nm (cigarette) lighter

brise [briz] nf breeze

briser [brize] vt to break; **se ~** vi to break

britannique [britanik] adj British ▷ nm/f: **B~** British person, Briton; **les B~s** the British

brocante [brɔkɑ̃t] nf junk, second-hand goods pl; **brocanteur, -euse** nm/f junkshop owner; junk dealer

broche [brɔʃ] nf brooch; (Culin) spit; (Méd) pin; **à la ~** spit-roasted

broché, e [brɔʃe] adj (livre) paper-backed

brochet [brɔʃɛ] nm pike inv

brochette [brɔʃɛt] nf (ustensile) skewer; (plat) kebab

brochure [brɔʃyr] nf pamphlet, brochure, booklet

broder [brɔde] vt to embroider ▷ vi: **~ sur les faits ou une histoire)** to embroider the facts; **broderie** nf embroidery

bronches [brɔ̃ʃ] nfpl bronchial tubes; **bronchite** nf bronchitis

bronze [brɔ̃z] nm bronze

bronzer [brɔ̃ze] vi to get a tan; **se ~** to sunbathe

brosse [brɔs] nf brush; **coiffé en ~** with a crewcut; **brosse à cheveux** hairbrush; **brosse à dents** toothbrush; **brosse à habits** clothesbrush; **brosser** vt (nettoyer) to brush; (fig: tableau etc) to paint; **se brosser les dents** to brush one's teeth

brouette [bʀuɛt] nf wheelbarrow

brouillard [bʀujaʀ] nm fog

brouiller [bʀuje] vt (œufs, message) to scramble; (idées) to mix up; (rendre trouble) to cloud; (désunir: amis) to set at odds; **se ~** vi (vue) to cloud over; (gens): **se ~ (avec)** to fall out (with)

brouillon, ne [bʀujɔ̃, ɔn] adj (sans soin) untidy; (qui manque d'organisation) disorganized ▷ nm draft; **(papier)** ~ rough paper

broussailles [bʀusaj] nfpl undergrowth sg; **broussailleux, -euse** adj bushy

brousse [bʀus] nf: **la ~** the bush

brouter [bʀute] vi to graze

brugnon [bʀyɲɔ̃] nm (Bot) nectarine

bruiner [bʀuine] vb impers: **il bruine** it's drizzling, there's a drizzle

bruit [bʀui] nm: **un ~** a noise, a sound; (fig: rumeur) a rumour; **le ~** noise; **sans ~** without a sound, noiselessly; **bruit de fond** background noise

brûlant, e [bʀylã, ãt] adj burning; (liquide) boiling (hot)

brûlé, e [bʀyle] adj (fig: démasqué) blown ▷ nm: **odeur de ~** smell of burning

brûler [bʀyle] vt to burn; (suj: eau bouillante) to scald; (consommer: électricité, essence) to use; (feu rouge, signal) to go through ▷ vi to burn; (jeu): **tu brûles!** you're getting hot!; **se ~** to burn o.s.; (s'ébouillanter) to scald o.s.

brûlure [bʀylyʀ] nf (lésion) burn; **brûlures d'estomac** heartburn sg

brume [bʀym] nf mist

brun, e [bʀœ̃, bʀyn] adj (gén, bière) brown; (cheveux, tabac) dark; **elle est ~e** she's got dark hair

brunch [bʀœntʃ] nm brunch

brushing [bʀœʃiŋ] nm blow-dry

brusque [bʀysk] adj abrupt

brut, e [bʀyt] adj (minerai, soie) raw; (diamant) rough; (Comm) gross; **(pétrole)** ~ crude (oil)

brutal, e, -aux [bʀytal, o] adj brutal

Bruxelles [bʀysɛl] n Brussels

bruyamment [bʀuijamã] adv noisily

bruyant, e [bʀuijã, ãt] adj noisy

bruyère [bʀyjɛʀ] nf heather

BTS sigle m (= brevet de technicien supérieur) vocational training certificate taken at the end of a higher education course

bu, e [by] pp de **boire**

buccal, e, -aux [bykal, o] adj: **par voie ~e** orally

bûche [byʃ] nf log; **prendre une ~** (fig) to come a cropper; **bûche de Noël** Yule log

bûcher [byʃe] nm (funéraire) pyre; (supplice) stake ▷ vi (fam) to swot (BRIT), slave (away) ▷ vt (fam) to swot up (BRIT), slave away at

budget [bydʒɛ] nm budget

buée [bɥe] nf (sur une vitre) mist

buffet [byfɛ] nm (meuble) sideboard; (de réception) buffet; **buffet (de gare)** (station) buffet, snack bar

buis [bɥi] nm box tree; (bois) box(wood)

buisson [bɥisɔ̃] nm bush

bulbe [bylb] nm (Bot, Anat) bulb

Bulgarie [bylgaʀi] nf Bulgaria

bulle [byl] nf bubble

bulletin [byltɛ̃] nm (communiqué, journal) bulletin; (Scol) report; **bulletin d'informations** news bulletin; **bulletin**

(de vote) ballot paper; **bulletin météorologique** weather report

bureau, x [byʀo] nm (meuble) desk; (pièce, service) office; **bureau de change** (foreign) exchange office ou bureau; **bureau de poste** post office; **bureau de tabac** tobacconist's (shop); **bureaucratie** [byʀokʀasi] nf bureaucracy

bus¹ [by] vb voir **boire**

bus² [bys] nm bus; **à quelle heure part le ~?** what time does the bus leave?

buste [byst] nm (torse) chest; (seins) bust

but¹ [by] vb voir **boire**

but² [by(t)] nm (cible) target; (fig) goal, aim; (Football etc) goal; **de ~ en blanc** point-blank; **avoir pour ~ de faire** to aim to do; **dans le ~ de** with the intention of

butane [bytan] nm (camping) butane; (usage domestique) Calor gas®

butiner [bytine] vi (abeilles) to gather nectar

buvais etc [byvɛ] vb voir **boire**

buvard [byvaʀ] nm blotter

buvette [byvɛt] nf bar

C

c' [s] dét voir **ce**

ça [sa] pron (pour désigner) this; (: plus loin) that; (comme sujet indéfini) it; **ça m'étonne que ...** it surprises me that ...; **comment ça va?** how are you?; **ça va?** (d'accord?) O.K.?, all right?; **où ça?** where's that?; **pourquoi ça?** why's that?; **qui ça?** who's that?; **ça alors!** well really!; **ça fait 10 ans (que)** it's 10 years (since); **c'est ça** that's right; **ça y est** that's it

cabane [kaban] nf hut, cabin

cabaret [kabaʀɛ] nm night club

cabillaud [kabijo] nm cod inv

cabine [kabin] nf (de bateau) cabin; (de piscine etc)

cubicle; (de camion, train) cab; (d'avion) cockpit; **cabine d'essayage** fitting room; **cabine (téléphonique)** call ou (tele)phone box

cabinet [kabinɛ] nm (petite pièce) closet; (de médecin) surgery (BRIT), office (US); (de notaire etc) office; (: clientèle) practice; (POL) Cabinet; **cabinets** nmpl (w.-c.) toilet sg; **cabinet de toilette** toilet

câble [kɑbl] nm cable; **le ~** (TV) cable television, cablevision (US)

cacahuète [kakaɥɛt] nf peanut

cacao [kakao] nm cocoa

cache [kaʃ] nm mask, card (for masking)

cache-cache [kaʃkaʃ] nm: **jouer à ~** to play hide-and-seek

cachemire [kaʃmiʀ] nm cashmere

cacher [kaʃe] vt to hide, conceal; **se ~** vi (volontairement) to hide; (être caché) to be hidden ou concealed; **~ qch à qn** to hide ou conceal sth from sb

cachet [kaʃɛ] nm (comprimé) tablet; (de la poste) postmark; (rétribution) fee; (fig) style, character

cachette [kaʃɛt] nf hiding place; **en ~** on the sly, secretly

cactus [kaktys] nm cactus

cadavre [kadɑvʀ] nm corpse, (dead) body

caddie® [kadi] nm (supermarket) trolley (BRIT), (grocery) cart (US)

cadeau, x [kado] nm present, gift; **faire un ~ à qn** to give sb a present ou gift; **faire ~ de qch à qn** to make a present of sth to sb, give sb sth as a present

cadenas [kadnɑ] nm padlock

cadet, te [kadɛ, ɛt] adj younger; (le plus jeune) youngest ▷ nm/f youngest child ou one

cadran [kadʀɑ̃] nm dial; **cadran solaire** sundial

cadre [kadʀ] nm frame; (environnement) surroundings pl ▷ nm/f (ADMIN) managerial employee, executive; **dans le ~ de** (fig) within the framework ou context of

cafard [kafaʀ] nm cockroach; **avoir le ~** (fam) to be down in the dumps

café [kafe] nm coffee; (bistro) café ▷ adj inv coffee(-coloured); **café au lait** white coffee; **café noir** black coffee; **café tabac** tobacconist's ou newsagent's serving coffee and spirits; **cafetière** nf (pot) coffee-pot

cage [kaʒ] nf cage; **cage (d'escalier)** stairwell; **cage thoracique** rib cage

cageot [kaʒo] nm crate

cagoule [kagul] nf (passe-montagne) balaclava

cahier [kaje] nm notebook; **cahier de brouillon** jotter (BRIT), rough notebook; **cahier d'exercices** exercise book

caille [kaj] nf quail

caillou, x [kaju] nm (little) stone; **caillouteux, -euse** adj (route) stony

caire [kɛʀ] nm: **le ~** Cairo

caisse [kɛs] nf box; (tiroir où l'on met la recette) till; (où l'on paye) cash desk (BRIT), check-out; (de banque) cashier's desk; **caisse d'épargne** savings bank; **caisse de retraite** pension fund; **caisse enregistreuse** cash register; **caissier, -ière** nm/f cashier

cake [kɛk] nm fruit cake

calandre [kalɑ̃dʀ] nf radiator grill

calcaire [kalkɛʀ] nm limestone ▷ adj (eau) hard; (GÉO) limestone cpd

calcul [kalkyl] nm calculation; **le ~** (SCOL) arithmetic; **calcul (biliaire)** (gall)stone; **calculatrice** nf calculator; **calculer** vt to calculate, work out; **calculette** nf pocket

calculator

cale [kal] nf (de bateau) hold; (en bois) wedge

calé, e [kale] (fam) adj clever, bright

caleçon [kalsɔ̃] nm (d'homme) boxer shorts; (de femme) leggings

calendrier [kalɑ̃dʀije] nm calendar; (fig) timetable

calepin [kalpɛ̃] nm notebook

caler [kale] vt to wedge ▷ vi (moteur, véhicule) to stall

calibre [kalibʀ] nm calibre

câlin, e [kɑlɛ̃, in] adj cuddly, cuddlesome; (regard, voix) tender

calmant [kalmɑ̃] nm tranquillizer, sedative; (pour la douleur) painkiller

calme [kalm] adj calm, quiet ▷ nm calm(ness), quietness; **sans perdre son ~** without losing one's cool (inf) ou composure; **calmer** vt to calm (down); (douleur, inquiétude) to ease, soothe; **se calmer** vi to calm down

calorie [kalɔʀi] nf calorie

camarade [kamaʀad] nm/f friend, pal; (POL) comrade

Cambodge [kɑ̃bɔdʒ] nm: **le ~** Cambodia

cambriolage [kɑ̃bʀijɔlaʒ] nm burglary; **cambrioler** vt to burgle (BRIT), burglarize (US); **cambrioleur, -euse** nm/f burglar

camelote [kamlɔt] (fam) nf rubbish, trash, junk

caméra [kameʀa] nf (CINÉMA, TV) camera; (d'amateur) cine-camera

Cameroun [kamʀun] nm: **le ~** Cameroon

caméscope® [kameskɔp] nm camcorder®

camion [kamjɔ̃] nm lorry (BRIT), truck; **camion de dépannage** breakdown (BRIT) ou tow (US) truck; **camionnette** nf (small) van; **camionneur** nm (chauffeur) lorry (BRIT) ou truck driver; (entrepreneur) haulage contractor (BRIT), trucker (US)

camomille [kamɔmij] nf camomile; (boisson) camomile tea

camp [kɑ̃] nm camp; (fig) side

campagnard, e [kɑ̃paɲaʀ, aʀd] adj country cpd

campagne [kɑ̃paɲ] nf country, countryside; (MIL, POL, COMM) campaign; **à la ~** in the country

camper [kɑ̃pe] vi to camp ▷ vt to sketch; **se ~ devant** to plant o.s. in front of; **campeur, -euse** nm/f camper

camping [kɑ̃piŋ] nm camping; **faire du ~** to go camping; **(terrain de) camping** campsite, camping site; **camping-car** nm camper, motorhome (US); **camping-gaz®** nm inv camp(ing) stove

Canada [kanada] nm: **le ~** Canada; **canadien, ne** adj Canadian ▷ nm/f: **Canadien, ne** Canadian; **canadienne** nf (veste) fur-lined jacket

canal, -aux [kanal, o] nm canal; (naturel, TV) channel; **canalisation** nf (tuyau) pipe

canapé [kanape] nm settee, sofa

canard [kanaʀ] nm duck; (fam: journal) rag

cancer [kɑ̃sɛʀ] nm cancer; (signe): **le C~** Cancer

cancre [kɑ̃kʀ] nm dunce

candidat, e [kɑ̃dida, at] nm/f candidate; (à un poste) applicant, candidate; **candidature** nf (POL) candidature; (à poste) application; **poser sa candidature à un poste** to apply for a job

cane [kan] nf (female) duck

canette [kanɛt] nf (de bière) (flip-top) bottle

canevas [kanva] nm (COUTURE) canvas

caniche [kaniʃ] nm poodle

canicule [kanikyl] nf scorching heat

canif [kanif] nm penknife, pocket knife

canne [kan] nf (walking) stick; **canne à pêche** fishing rod; **canne à sucre** sugar cane

cannelle [kanɛl] nf cinnamon

canoë [kanɔe] nm canoe; (sport) canoeing; **canoë (kayak)** kayak

canot [kano] nm ding(h)y; **canot de sauvetage** lifeboat; **canot pneumatique** inflatable ding(h)y

cantatrice [kɑ̃tatʀis] nf (opera) singer

cantine [kɑ̃tin] nf canteen

canton [kɑ̃tɔ̃] nm district consisting of several communes; (en Suisse) canton

caoutchouc [kautʃu] nm rubber; **caoutchouc mousse** foam rubber

cap [kap] nm (Géo) cape; (promontoire) headland; (fig: tournant) watershed; (Navig): **changer de ~** to change course; **mettre le ~ sur** to head ou steer for

CAP sigle m (= Certificat d'aptitude professionnelle) vocational training certificate taken at secondary school

capable [kapabl] adj able, capable; **~ de qch/faire** capable of sth/doing

capacité [kapasite] nf (compétence) ability; (Jur, contenance) capacity

cape [kap] nf cape, cloak; **rire sous ~** to laugh up one's sleeve

CAPES [kapɛs] sigle m (= Certificat d'aptitude pédagogique à l'enseignement secondaire) teaching diploma

capitaine [kapitɛn] nm captain

capital, e, -aux [kapital, o] adj (œuvre) major; (question, rôle) fundamental ▷ nm (fig) stock; **d'une importance ~e** of capital importance; **capitaux** nmpl (fonds) capital sg; **capital (social)** authorized capital; **capitale** nf (ville) capital; (lettre) capital (letter); **capitalisme** nm capitalism; **capitaliste** adj, nm/f capitalist

caporal, -aux [kapɔʀal, o] nm lance corporal

capot [kapo] nm (Auto) bonnet (BRIT), hood (US)

câpre [kɑpʀ] nf caper

caprice [kapʀis] nm whim, caprice; **faire des ~s** to make a fuss; **capricieux, -euse** adj (fantasque) capricious, whimsical; (enfant) awkward

Capricorne [kapʀikɔʀn] nm: **le ~** Capricorn

capsule [kapsyl] nf (de bouteille) cap; (Bot etc, spatiale) capsule

capter [kapte] vt (ondes radio) to pick up; (fig) to win, capture

captivant, e [kaptivɑ̃, ɑ̃t] adj captivating

capturer [kaptyʀe] vt to capture

capuche [kapyʃ] nf hood

capuchon [kapyʃɔ̃] nm hood; (de stylo) cap, top

car [kaʀ] nm coach ▷ conj because, for

carabine [kaʀabin] nf rifle

caractère [kaʀaktɛʀ] nm (gén) character; **avoir bon/mauvais ~** to be good-/ill-natured; **en ~s gras** in bold type; **en petits ~s** in small print; **~s d'imprimerie** (block) capitals

caractériser [kaʀakteʀize] vt to be characteristic of; **se ~ par** to be characterized ou distinguished by

caractéristique [kaʀakteʀistik] adj, nf characteristic

carafe [kaʀaf] nf (pour eau, vin ordinaire) carafe

caraïbe [kaʀaib] adj Caribbean ▷ n: **les C~s** the Caribbean (Islands)

carambolage [kaʀɑ̃bɔlaʒ] nm multiple crash, pileup

caramel [kaʀamɛl] nm (bonbon) caramel, toffee; (substance) caramel

caravane [kaʀavan] nf caravan; **caravaning** nm caravanning

carbone [kaʀbɔn] nm carbon; (double) carbon (copy)

carbonique [kaʀbɔnik] adj: **gaz ~** carbon dioxide; **neige ~** dry ice

carbonisé, e [kaʀbɔnize] adj charred

carburant [kaʀbyʀɑ̃] nm (motor) fuel

carburateur [kaʀbyʀatœʀ] nm carburettor

cardiaque [kaʀdjak] adj cardiac, heart cpd ▷ nm/f heart patient; **être ~** to have heart trouble

cardigan [kaʀdigɑ̃] nm cardigan

cardiologue [kaʀdjɔlɔg] nm/f cardiologist, heart specialist

carême [kaʀɛm] nm: **le C~** Lent

carence [kaʀɑ̃s] nf (manque) deficiency

caresse [kaʀɛs] nf caress

caresser [kaʀese] vt to caress; (animal) to stroke

cargaison [kaʀgɛzɔ̃] nf cargo, freight

cargo [kaʀgo] nm cargo boat, freighter

caricature [kaʀikatyʀ] nf caricature

carie [kaʀi] nf: **la ~ (dentaire)** tooth decay; **une ~** a bad tooth

carnaval [kaʀnaval] nm carnival

carnet [kaʀnɛ] nm (calepin) notebook; (de tickets, timbres etc) book; **carnet de chèques** cheque book

carotte [kaʀɔt] nf carrot

carré, e [kaʀe] adj square; (fig: franc) straightforward ▷ nm (Math) square; **mètre/kilomètre ~** square metre/kilometre

carreau, x [kaʀo] nm (par terre) (floor) tile; (au mur) (wall) tile; (de fenêtre) (window) pane; (motif) check, square; (Cartes: couleur) diamonds pl; **tissu à ~x** checked fabric

carrefour [kaʀfuʀ] nm crossroads sg

carrelage [kaʀlaʒ] nm (sol) (tiled) floor

carrelet [kaʀlɛ] nm (poisson) plaice

carrément [kaʀemɑ̃] adv (franchement) straight out, bluntly; (sans hésiter) straight; (intensif) completely; **c'est ~ impossible** it's completely impossible

carrière [kaʀjɛʀ] nf (métier) career; (de roches) quarry; **militaire de ~** professional soldier

carrosserie [kaʀɔsʀi] nf body, coachwork no pl

carrure [kaʀyʀ] nf build; (fig) stature, calibre

cartable [kaʀtabl] nm satchel, (school)bag

carte [kaʀt] nf (de géographie) map; (marine, du ciel) chart (d'abonnement, à jouer) card; (au restaurant) menu; (aussi: **~ de visite**) (visiting) card; **pouvez-vous me l'indiquer sur la ~?** can you show me (it) on the map?; **à la ~** (au restaurant) à la carte; **est-ce qu'on peut voir la ~?** can we see the menu?; **donner ~ blanche à qn** to give sb a free rein; **carte bancaire** cash card; **Carte Bleue®** debit card; **carte à puce** smart card; **carte de crédit** credit card; **carte de fidélité** loyalty card; **carte d'identité** identity card; **carte de séjour** residence permit; **carte grise** (Auto) ≈ (car) registration book, logbook; **carte mémoire** (d'appareil-photo numérique) memory card; **carte postale** postcard; **carte routière** road map

carter [kaʀtɛʀ] nm sump

carton [kaʀtɔ̃] nm (matériau) cardboard; (boîte) (cardboard) box; **faire un ~** (fam) to score a hit; **carton (à dessin)** portfolio

cartouche [kaʀtuʃ] nf cartridge; (de cigarettes) carton

cas [kɑ] nm case; **ne faire aucun ~ de** to take no notice of; **en aucun ~** on no account; **au ~ où** in case; **en ~ de**

in case of, in the event of; **en ~ de besoin** if need be; **en tout ~** in any case, at any rate

cascade [kaskad] nf waterfall, cascade

case [kɑz] nf (hutte) hut; (compartiment) compartment; (sur un formulaire, de mots croisés etc) box

caser [kɑze] (fam) vt (placer) to put (away); (loger) to put up; **se ~** vi (se marier) to settle down; (trouver un emploi) to find a (steady) job

caserne [kazɛʀn] nf barracks pl

casier [kazje] nm (pour courrier) pigeonhole; (compartiment) compartment; (à clef) locker; **casier judiciaire** police record

casino [kazino] nm casino

casque [kask] nm helmet; (chez le coiffeur) (hair-)drier; (pour audition) (head-)phones pl, headset

casquette [kaskɛt] nf cap

casse...: **casse-croûte** nm inv snack; **casse-noix** nm inv nutcrackers pl; **casse-pieds** (fam) adj inv: **il est casse-pieds** he's a pain in the neck

casser [kɑse] vt to break; (Jur) to quash; **se ~** vi to break; **~ les pieds à qn** (fam: irriter) to get on sb's nerves; **se ~ la tête** (fam) to go to a lot of trouble

casserole [kasʀɔl] nf saucepan

casse-tête [kastɛt] nm inv (difficultés) headache (fig)

cassette [kasɛt] nf (bande magnétique) cassette; (coffret) casket

cassis [kasis] nm blackcurrant

cassoulet [kasulɛ] nm bean and sausage hot-pot

catalogue [katalɔg] nm catalogue

catalytique [katalitik] adj: **pot ~** catalytic convertor

catastrophe [katastʀɔf] nf catastrophe, disaster

catéchisme [kateʃism] nm catechism

catégorie [kategɔʀi] nf category; **catégorique** adj categorical

cathédrale [katedʀal] nf cathedral

catholique [katɔlik] adj, nm/f (Roman) Catholic; **pas très ~** a bit shady ou fishy

cauchemar [koʃmaʀ] nm nightmare

cause [koz] nf cause; (Jur) lawsuit, case; **à ~ de** because of, owing to; **pour ~ de** on account of; **(et) pour ~** and for (a very) good reason; **être en ~** (intérêts) to be at stake; **remettre en ~** to challenge; **causer** vt to cause ▷ vi to chat, talk

caution [kosjɔ̃] nf guarantee, security; (Jur) bail (bond); (fig) backing, support; **libéré sous ~** released on bail

cavalier, -ière [kavalje, jɛʀ] adj (désinvolte) offhand ▷ nm/f rider; (au bal) partner ▷ nm (Échecs) knight

cave [kav] nf cellar

CD sigle m (= compact disc) CD

CD-ROM [sederɔm] sigle m CD-ROM

○ **MOT-CLÉ**

ce, cette [sə, sɛt] (devant nm **cet** + voyelle ou h aspiré; pl **ces**) dét (proximité) this; these pl; (non-proximité) that; those pl; **cette maison(-ci/là)** this/that house; **cette nuit** (qui vient) tonight; (passée) last night
▷ pron 1: **c'est** it's ou it is; **c'est un peintre** he's ou he is a painter; **ce sont des peintres** they're ou they are painters; **c'est le facteur etc** (à la porte) it's the postman; **c'est toi qui lui a parlé** it was you who spoke to him; **qui est-ce?** who is it?; (en désignant) who is he/she?; **qu'est-ce?** what is it?

2: **ce qui, ce que**: **ce qui me plaît, c'est sa franchise**

what I like about him ou her is his ou her frankness; **il est bête, ce qui me chagrine** he's stupid, which saddens me; **tout ce qui bouge** everything ou that ou which moves; **tout ce que je sais** all I know; **ce dont j'ai parlé** what I talked about; **ce que c'est grand!** it's so big!; voir aussi **-ci**; **est-ce que**; **n'est-ce pas**; **c'est-à-dire**

ceci [səsi] pron this

céder [sede] vt (donner) to give up ▷ vi (chaise, barrage) to give way; (personne) to give in; **~ à** to yield to, give in to

CEDEX [sedɛks] sigle m (= courrier d'entreprise à distribution exceptionnelle) postal service for bulk users

cédille [sedij] nf cedilla

ceinture [sɛ̃tyʀ] nf belt; (taille) waist; **ceinture de sécurité** safety ou seat belt

cela [s(ə)la] pron that; (comme sujet indéfini) it; **~ m'étonne que ...** it surprises me that ...; **quand/où ~?** when/where (was that)?

célèbre [selɛbʀ] adj famous; **célébrer** vt to celebrate

céleri [sɛlʀi] nm: **~(-rave)** celeriac; **céleri en branche** celery

célibataire [selibatɛʀ] adj single, unmarried ▷ nm bachelor ▷ nf unmarried woman

celle, celles [sɛl] pron voir **celui**

cellule [selyl] nf (gén) cell; **~ souche** stem cell

cellulite [selylit] nf cellulite

○ **MOT-CLÉ**

celui, celle [səlɥi, sɛl] (mpl **ceux**, fpl **celles**) pron
1: **celui-ci/là, celle-ci/là** this one/that one; **ceux-ci, celles-ci** these (ones); **ceux-là, celles-là** those (ones)
2: **celui qui bouge** the one which ou that moves; (personne) the one who moves; **celui que je vois** the one (which ou that) I see; (personne) the one (whom) I see; **celui dont je parle** the one I'm talking about; **celui de mon frère** my brother's; **celui du salon/du dessous** the one in (ou from) the lounge/below
3 (valeur indéfinie): **celui qui veut** whoever wants

cendre [sɑ̃dʀ] nf ash; **cendres** nfpl (d'un défunt) ashes; **sous la ~** (Culin) in the embers; **cendrier** nm ashtray

censé, e [sɑ̃se] adj: **être ~ faire** to be supposed to do

censeur [sɑ̃sœʀ] nm (Scol) deputy-head (BRIT), vice-principal (US)

censure [sɑ̃syʀ] nf censorship; **censurer** vt (Cinéma, Presse) to censor; (Pol) to censure

cent [sɑ̃] num a hundred, one hundred ▷ nm (US, Canada etc) cent; (partie de l'euro) cent; **centaine** nf: **une centaine (de)** about a hundred, a hundred or so; **des centaines (de)** hundreds (of); **centenaire** adj hundred-year-old ▷ nm (anniversaire) centenary; (monnaie) cent; **centième** num hundredth; **centigrade** nm centigrade; **centilitre** nm centilitre; **centime** nm centime; **centime d'euro** euro cent; **centimètre** nm centimetre; (ruban) tape measure, measuring tape

central, e, -aux [sɑ̃tʀal, o] adj central ▷ nm: **~ (téléphonique)** (telephone) exchange; **centrale** nf power station; **centrale électrique/nucléaire** power/nuclear power station

centre [sɑ̃tʀ] nm centre; **centre commercial/sportif/culturel** shopping/sports/arts centre; **centre d'appels** call centre; **centre-ville** nm town centre, downtown (area) (US)

cèpe [sɛp] nm (edible) boletus
cependant [s(ə)pɑ̃dɑ̃] adv however
céramique [seramik] nf ceramics sg
cercle [sɛrkl] nm circle; **cercle vicieux** vicious circle
cercueil [sɛrkœj] nm coffin
céréale [sereal] nf cereal
cérémonie [seremɔni] nf ceremony; **sans ~** (inviter, manger) informally
cerf [sɛr] nm stag
cerf-volant [sɛrvɔlɑ̃] nm kite
cerise [s(ə)riz] nf cherry; **cerisier** nm cherry (tree)
cerner [sɛrne] vt (Mil etc) to surround; (fig: problème) to delimit, define
certain, e [sɛrtɛ̃, ɛn] adj certain ▷ dét certain; **d'un ~ âge** past one's prime, not so young; **un ~ temps** (quite) some time; **un ~ Georges** someone called Georges; **~s** pron some; **certainement** adv (probablement) most probably ou likely; (bien sûr) certainly, of course
certes [sɛrt] adv (sans doute) admittedly; (bien sûr) of course
certificat [sɛrtifika] nm certificate
certifier [sɛrtifje] vt: **~ qch à qn** to assure sb of sth; **copie certifiée conforme** certified copy of the original
certitude [sɛrtityd] nf certainty
cerveau, x [sɛrvo] nm brain
cervelas [sɛrvəla] nm saveloy
cervelle [sɛrvɛl] nf (Anat) brain; (Culin) brains
ces [se] dét voir **ce**
CES sigle m (= collège d'enseignement secondaire) ≈ (junior) secondary school (BRIT)
cesse [sɛs]: **sans ~** adv (tout le temps) continually, constantly; (sans interruption) continuously; **il n'a eu de ~ que** he did not rest until; **cesser** vt to stop ▷ vi to stop, cease; **cesser de faire** to stop doing; **cessez-le-feu** nm inv ceasefire
c'est-à-dire [sɛtadir] adv that is (to say)
cet, cette [sɛt] dét voir **ce**
ceux [sø] pron voir **celui**
chacun, e [ʃakœ̃, yn] pron each; (indéfini) everyone, everybody
chagrin [ʃagrɛ̃] nm grief, sorrow; **avoir du ~** to be grieved
chahut [ʃay] nm uproar; **chahuter** vt to rag, bait ▷ vi to make an uproar
chaîne [ʃɛn] nf chain; (Radio, TV: stations) channel; **travail à la ~** production line work; **réactions en ~** chain reaction sg; **chaîne de montagnes** mountain range; **chaîne (hi-fi)** hi-fi system
chair [ʃɛr] nf flesh; **avoir la ~ de poule** to have goosepimples ou gooseflesh; **bien en ~** plump, well-padded; **en ~ et en os** in the flesh; **~ à saucisse** sausage meat
chaise [ʃɛz] nf chair; **chaise longue** deckchair
châle [ʃɑl] nm shawl
chaleur [ʃalœr] nf heat; (fig: accueil) warmth; **chaleureux, -euse** adj warm
chamailler [ʃamaje]: **se ~** vi to squabble, bicker
chambre [ʃɑ̃br] nf bedroom; (Pol, Comm) chamber; **faire ~ à part** to sleep in separate rooms; **je voudrais une ~ pour deux personnes** I'd like a double room; **chambre à air** (de pneu) (inner) tube; **chambre à coucher** bedroom; **chambre à un lit/à deux lits** (à l'hôtel) single-/twin-bedded room; **chambre d'amis** spare ou guest room; **chambre d'hôte** ≈ bed and breakfast; **chambre meublée** bedsit(ter) (BRIT), furnished room; **chambre noire** (Photo) darkroom

chameau, x [ʃamo] nm camel
chamois [ʃamwa] nm chamois
champ [ʃɑ̃] nm field; **champ de bataille** battlefield; **champ de courses** racecourse
champagne [ʃɑ̃paɲ] nm champagne
champignon [ʃɑ̃piɲɔ̃] nm mushroom; (terme générique) fungus; **champignon de Paris** ou **de couche** button mushroom
champion, ne [ʃɑ̃pjɔ̃, jɔn] adj, nm/f champion; **championnat** nm championship
chance [ʃɑ̃s] nf: **la ~** luck; **chances** nfpl (probabilités) chances; **avoir de la ~** to be lucky; **il a des ~s de réussir** he's got a good chance of passing; **bonne ~!** good luck!
change [ʃɑ̃ʒ] nm (devises) exchange
changement [ʃɑ̃ʒmɑ̃] nm change; **changement de vitesses** gears pl
changer [ʃɑ̃ʒe] vt (modifier) to change, alter; (remplacer, Comm) to change ▷ vi to change, alter; **se ~** vi to change (o.s.); **~ de** (remplacer: adresse, nom, voiture etc) to change one's; (échanger: place, train etc) to change; **~ d'avis** to change one's mind; **~ de vitesse** to change gear; **il faut ~ à Lyon** you ou we etc have to change in Lyons; **où est-ce que je peux ~ de l'argent?** where can I change some money?
chanson [ʃɑ̃sɔ̃] nf song
chant [ʃɑ̃] nm song; (art vocal) singing; (d'église) hymn
chantage [ʃɑ̃taʒ] nm blackmail; **faire du ~** to use blackmail
chanter [ʃɑ̃te] vt, vi to sing; **si cela lui chante** (fam) if he feels like it; **chanteur, -euse** nm/f singer
chantier [ʃɑ̃tje] nm (building) site; (sur une route) roadworks pl; **mettre en ~** to put in hand; **chantier naval** shipyard
chantilly [ʃɑ̃tiji] nf voir **crème**
chantonner [ʃɑ̃tɔne] vi, vt to sing to oneself, hum
chapeau, x [ʃapo] nm hat; **~!** well done!
chapelle [ʃapɛl] nf chapel
chapitre [ʃapitr] nm chapter
chaque [ʃak] dét each, every; (indéfini) every
char [ʃar] nm (Mil): **~ (d'assaut)** tank; **~ à voile** sand yacht
charbon [ʃarbɔ̃] nm coal; **charbon de bois** charcoal
charcuterie [ʃarkytri] nf (magasin) pork butcher's shop and delicatessen; (produits) cooked meat products pl; **charcutier, -ière** nm/f pork butcher
chardon [ʃardɔ̃] nm thistle
charge [ʃarʒ] nf (fardeau) load, burden; (Élec, Mil, Jur) charge; (rôle, mission) responsibility; **charges** nfpl (du loyer) service charges; **à la ~ de** (dépendant de) dependent upon; (aux frais de) chargeable to; **prendre en ~** to take charge of; (suj: véhicule) to take on; (dépenses) to take care of; **charges sociales** social security contributions
chargement [ʃarʒəmɑ̃] nm (objets) load
charger [ʃarʒe] vt (voiture, fusil, caméra) to load; (batterie) to charge ▷ vi (Mil etc) to charge; **se ~ de** to see to, take care of
chariot [ʃarjo] nm trolley; (charrette) waggon
charité [ʃarite] nf charity; **faire la ~ à** to give (something) to
charmant, e [ʃarmɑ̃, ɑ̃t] adj charming
charme [ʃarm] nm charm; **charmer** vt to charm
charpente [ʃarpɑ̃t] nf frame(work); **charpentier** nm

carpenter

charrette [ʃaʀɛt] nf cart

charter [ʃaʀtɛʀ] nm (vol) charter flight

chasse [ʃas] nf hunting; (au fusil) shooting; (poursuite) chase; (aussi: **~ d'eau**) flush; **prendre en ~** to give chase to; (aussi) **tirer la ~ (d'eau)** to flush the toilet, pull the chain; **~ à courre** hunting; **chasse-neige** nm inv snowplough (BRIT), snowplow (US); **chasser** vt to hunt; (expulser) to chase away ou out, drive away ou out; **chasseur, -euse** nm/f hunter ▷ nm (avion) fighter

chat¹ [ʃa] nm cat

chat² [tʃat] nm (Internet) chat room

châtaigne [ʃatɛɲ] nf chestnut

châtain [ʃatɛ̃] adj inv (cheveux) chestnut (brown); (personne) chestnut-haired

château, x [ʃato] nm (forteresse) castle; (résidence royale) palace; (manoir) manor; **château d'eau** water tower; **château fort** stronghold, fortified castle

châtiment [ʃatimɑ̃] nm punishment

chaton [ʃatɔ̃] nm (Zool) kitten

chatouiller [ʃatuje] vt to tickle; **chatouilleux, -euse** adj ticklish

chatte [ʃat] nf (she-)cat

chatter [tʃate] vi (Internet) to chat

chaud, e [ʃo, ʃod] adj (gén) warm; (très chaud) hot; **il fait ~** it's warm; it's hot; **avoir ~** to be warm; to be hot; **ça me tient ~** it keeps me warm; **rester au ~** to stay in the warm

chaudière [ʃodjɛʀ] nf boiler

chauffage [ʃofaʒ] nm heating; **chauffage central** central heating

chauffe-eau [ʃofo] nm inv water-heater

chauffer [ʃofe] vt to heat ▷ vi to heat up, warm up; (trop chauffer: moteur) to overheat; **se ~** vi (au soleil) to warm o.s.

chauffeur [ʃofœʀ] nm driver; (privé) chauffeur

chaumière [ʃomjɛʀ] nf (thatched) cottage

chaussée [ʃose] nf road(way)

chausser [ʃose] vt (bottes, skis) to put on; (enfant) to put shoes on; **~ du 38/42** to take size 38/42

chaussette [ʃosɛt] nf sock

chausson [ʃosɔ̃] nm slipper; (de bébé) bootee; **chausson (aux pommes)** (apple) turnover

chaussure [ʃosyʀ] nf shoe; **chaussures basses** flat shoes; **chaussures montantes** ankle boots; **chaussures de ski** ski boots

chauve [ʃov] adj bald; **chauve-souris** nf bat

chauvin, e [ʃovɛ̃, in] adj chauvinistic

chaux [ʃo] nf lime; **blanchi à la ~** whitewashed

chef [ʃɛf] nm head, leader; (de cuisine) chef; **commandant en ~** commander-in-chief; **chef d'accusation** charge; **chef d'entreprise** company head; **chef d'État** head of state; **chef de famille** head of the family; **chef de file** (de parti etc) leader; **chef de gare** station master; **chef d'orchestre** conductor; **chef-d'œuvre** nm masterpiece; **chef-lieu** nm county town

chemin [ʃ(ə)mɛ̃] nm path; (itinéraire, direction, trajet) way; **en ~** on the way; **chemin de fer** railway (BRIT), railroad (US)

cheminée [ʃ(ə)mine] nf chimney; (à l'intérieur) chimney piece, fireplace; (de bateau) funnel

chemise [ʃ(ə)miz] nf shirt; (dossier) folder; **chemise de nuit** nightdress

chemisier [ʃ(ə)mizje] nm blouse

chêne [ʃɛn] nm oak (tree); (bois) oak

chenil [ʃ(ə)nil] nm kennels pl

chenille [ʃ(ə)nij] nf (Zool) caterpillar

chèque [ʃɛk] nm cheque (BRIT), check (US); **est-ce que je peux payer par ~?** can I pay by cheque?; **chèque sans provision** bad cheque; **chèque de voyage** traveller's cheque; **chéquier** [ʃekje] nm cheque book

cher, -ère [ʃɛʀ] adj (aimé) dear; (coûteux) expensive, dear ▷ adv: **ça coûte ~** it's expensive

chercher [ʃɛʀʃe] vt to look for; (gloire etc) to seek; **aller ~** to go for, go and fetch; **~ à faire** to try to do; **chercheur, -euse** nm/f researcher, research worker

chéri, e [ʃeʀi] adj beloved, dear; **(mon) ~** darling

cheval, -aux [ʃ(ə)val, o] nm horse; (Auto): **~ (vapeur)** horsepower no pl; **faire du ~** to ride; **à ~** on horseback; **à ~ sur** astride; (fig) overlapping; **cheval de course** racehorse

chevalier [ʃ(ə)valje] nm knight

chevalière [ʃ(ə)valjɛʀ] nf signet ring

chevaux [ʃəvo] nmpl de cheval

chevet [ʃ(ə)vɛ] nm: **au ~ de qn** at sb's bedside; **lampe de chevet** bedside lamp

cheveu, x [ʃ(ə)vø] nm hair; **cheveux** nmpl (chevelure) hair sg; **avoir les ~x courts** to have short hair

cheville [ʃ(ə)vij] nf (Anat) ankle; (de bois) peg; (pour une vis) plug

chèvre [ʃɛvʀ] nf (she-)goat

chèvrefeuille [ʃɛvʀəfœj] nm honeysuckle

chevreuil [ʃəvʀœj] nm roe deer inv; (Culin) venison

 MOT-CLÉ

chez [ʃe] prép **1** (à la demeure de) at; (: direction) to; **chez qn** at/to sb's house ou place; **je suis chez moi** I'm at home; **je rentre chez moi** I'm going home; **allons chez Nathalie** let's go to Nathalie's
2 (+profession) at; (: direction) to; **chez le boulanger/ dentiste** at ou to the baker's/dentist's
3 (dans le caractère, l'œuvre de) in; **chez ce poète** in this poet's work; **c'est ce que je préfère chez lui** that's what I like best about him

chic [ʃik] adj inv chic, smart; (fam: généreux) nice, decent ▷ nm stylishness; **~ (alors)!** (fam) great!; **avoir le ~ de** to have the knack of

chicorée [ʃikɔʀe] nf (café) chicory; (salade) endive

chien [ʃjɛ̃] nm dog; **chien d'aveugle** guide dog; **chien de garde** guard dog

chienne [ʃjɛn] nf dog, bitch

chiffon [ʃifɔ̃] nm (piece of) rag; **chiffonner** vt to crumple; (fam: tracasser) to concern

chiffre [ʃifʀ] nm (représentant un nombre) figure, numeral; (montant, total) total, sum; **en ~s ronds** in round figures; **chiffre d'affaires** turnover; **chiffrer** vt (dépense) to put a figure to, assess; (message) to (en)code, cipher; **se chiffrer à** to add up to, amount to

chignon [ʃiɲɔ̃] nm chignon, bun

Chili [ʃili] nm: **le ~** Chile; **chilien, ne** adj Chilean ▷ nm/f: **Chilien, ne** Chilean

chimie [ʃimi] nf chemistry; **chimiothérapie** [ʃimjɔteʀapi] nf chemotherapy; **chimique** adj chemical; **produits chimiques** chemicals

chimpanzé [ʃɛ̃pɑ̃ze] nm chimpanzee

Chine [ʃin] nf: **la ~** China; **chinois, e** adj Chinese ▷ nm/f:

Chinois, e Chinese ▷ *nm* (*Ling*) Chinese
chiot [ʃjo] *nm* pup(py)
chips [ʃips] *nfpl* crisps (BRIT), (potato) chips (US)
chirurgie [ʃiʀyʀʒi] *nf* surgery; **chirurgie esthétique** plastic surgery; **chirurgien, ne** *nm/f* surgeon
chlore [klɔʀ] *nm* chlorine
choc [ʃɔk] *nm* (*heurt*) impact, shock; (*collision*) crash; (*moral*) shock; (*affrontement*) clash
chocolat [ʃɔkɔla] *nm* chocolate; **chocolat au lait** milk chocolate
cœur [kœʀ] *nm* (*chorale*) choir; (*Opéra, Théâtre*) chorus; **en ~** in chorus
choisir [ʃwaziʀ] *vt* to choose, select
choix [ʃwa] *nm* choice, selection; **avoir le ~** to have the choice; **premier ~** (*Comm*) class one; **de ~** choice, selected; **au ~** as you wish
chômage [ʃomaʒ] *nm* unemployment; **mettre au ~** to make redundant, put out of work; **être au ~** to be unemployed *ou* out of work; **chômeur, -euse** *nm/f* unemployed person
choquer [ʃɔke] *vt* (*offenser*) to shock; (*deuil*) to shake
chorale [kɔʀal] *nf* choir
chose [ʃoz] *nf* thing; **c'est peu de ~** it's nothing (really)
chou, x [ʃu] *nm* cabbage; **mon petit ~** (my) sweetheart; **chou à la crème** choux bun; **chou de Bruxelles** Brussels sprout; **choucroute** *nf* sauerkraut
chouette [ʃwɛt] *nf* owl ▷ *adj* (*fam*) great, smashing
chou-fleur [ʃuflœʀ] *nm* cauliflower
chrétien, ne [kʀetjɛ̃, jɛn] *adj, nm/f* Christian
Christ [kʀist] *nm*: **le ~** Christ; **christianisme** *nm* Christianity
chronique [kʀɔnik] *adj* chronic ▷ *nf* (*de journal*) column, page; (*historique*) chronicle; (*Radio, TV*): **la ~ sportive** the sports review
chronologique [kʀɔnɔlɔʒik] *adj* chronological
chronomètre [kʀɔnɔmɛtʀ] *nm* stopwatch; **chronométrer** *vt* to time
chrysanthème [kʀizɑ̃tɛm] *nm* chrysanthemum
chuchotement [ʃyʃɔtmɑ̃] *nm* whisper
chuchoter [ʃyʃɔte] *vt, vi* to whisper
chut [ʃyt] *excl* sh!
chute [ʃyt] *nf* fall; (*déchet*) scrap; **faire une ~ (de 10 m)** to fall (10 m); **chute (d'eau)** waterfall; **chute libre** free fall; **chutes de pluie/neige** rainfall/snowfall
Chypre [ʃipʀ] *nm/f* Cyprus
-ci [si] *adv voir* **par** ▷ *dét*: **ce garçon~** this boy; **ces femmes~** these women
cible [sibl] *nf* target
ciboulette [sibulɛt] *nf* (small) chive
cicatrice [sikatʀis] *nf* scar; **cicatriser** *vt* to heal
ci-contre [sikɔ̃tʀ] *adv* opposite
ci-dessous [sidsu] *adv* below
ci-dessus [sidsy] *adv* above
cidre [sidʀ] *nm* cider
Cie *abr* (= *compagnie*) Co.
ciel [sjɛl] *nm* sky; (*Rel*) heaven
cieux [sjø] *nmpl de* **ciel**
cigale [sigal] *nf* cicada
cigare [sigaʀ] *nm* cigar
cigarette [sigaʀɛt] *nf* cigarette
ci-inclus, e [siɛ̃kly, yz] *adj, adv* enclosed
ci-joint, e [siʒwɛ̃, ɛ̃t] *adj, adv* enclosed
cil [sil] *nm* (eye)lash
cime [sim] *nf* top; (*montagne*) peak

ciment [simɑ̃] *nm* cement
cimetière [simtjɛʀ] *nm* cemetery; (*d'église*) churchyard
cinéaste [sineast] *nm/f* film-maker
cinéma [sinema] *nm* cinema
cinq [sɛ̃k] *num* five; **cinquantaine** *nf*: **une cinquantaine (de)** about fifty; **avoir la cinquantaine** (*âge*) to be around fifty; **cinquante** *num* fifty; **cinquantenaire** *adj, nm/f* fifty-year-old; **cinquième** *num* fifth ▷ *nf* (*Scol*) year 8 (BRIT), seventh grade (US)
cintre [sɛ̃tʀ] *nm* coat-hanger
cintré, e [sɛ̃tʀe] *adj* (*chemise*) fitted
cirage [siʀaʒ] *nm* (shoe) polish
circonflexe [siʀkɔ̃flɛks] *adj*: **accent ~** circumflex accent
circonstance [siʀkɔ̃stɑ̃s] *nf* circumstance; (*occasion*) occasion; **circonstances atténuantes** mitigating circumstances
circuit [siʀkɥi] *nm* (*Élec, Tech*) circuit; (*trajet*) tour, (round) trip
circulaire [siʀkylɛʀ] *adj, nf* circular
circulation [siʀkylasjɔ̃] *nf* circulation; (*Auto*): **la ~** (the) traffic
circuler [siʀkyle] *vi* (*sang, devises*) to circulate; (*véhicules*) to drive (along); (*passants*) to walk along; (*train, bus*) to run; **faire ~** (*nouvelle*) to spread (about), circulate; (*badauds*) to move on
cire [siʀ] *nf* wax; **ciré** *nm* oilskin; **cirer** *vt* to wax, polish
cirque [siʀk] *nm* circus; (*fig*) chaos, bedlam; **quel ~!** what a carry-on!
ciseau, x [sizo] *nm*: **~ (à bois)** chisel; **ciseaux** *nmpl* (*paire de ciseaux*) (pair of) scissors
citadin, e [sitadɛ̃, in] *nm/f* city dweller
citation [sitasjɔ̃] *nf* (*d'auteur*) quotation; (*Jur*) summons *sg*
cité [site] *nf* town; (*plus grande*) city; **cité universitaire** students' residences *pl*
citer [site] *vt* (*un auteur*) to quote (from); (*nommer*) to name; (*Jur*) to summon
citoyen, ne [sitwajɛ̃, jɛn] *nm/f* citizen
citron [sitʀɔ̃] *nm* lemon; **citron pressé** (fresh) lemon juice; **citron vert** lime; **citronnade** *nf* still lemonade
citrouille [sitʀuj] *nf* pumpkin
civet [sivɛ] *nm*: **~ de lapin** rabbit stew
civière [sivjɛʀ] *nf* stretcher
civil, e [sivil] *adj* (*mariage, poli*) civil; (*non militaire*) civilian; **en ~** in civilian clothes; **dans le ~** in civilian life
civilisation [sivilizasjɔ̃] *nf* civilization
clair, e [klɛʀ] *adj* light; (*pièce*) light, bright; (*eau, son, fig*) clear ▷ *adv*: **voir ~** to see clearly; **tirer qch au ~** to clear sth up, clarify sth; **mettre au ~** (*notes etc*) to tidy up ▷ *nm*: **~ de lune** moonlight; **clairement** *adv* clearly
clairière [klɛʀjɛʀ] *nf* clearing
clandestin, e [klɑ̃dɛstɛ̃, in] *adj* clandestine, secret; (*mouvement*) underground; (*travailleur, immigration*) illegal; **passager ~** stowaway
claque [klak] *nf* (*gifle*) slap; **claquer** *vi* (*porte*) to bang, slam; (*fam: mourir*) to snuff it ▷ *vt* (*porte*) to slam, bang; (*doigts*) to snap; (*fam: dépenser*) to blow; **il claquait des dents** his teeth were chattering; **être claqué** (*fam*) to be dead tired; **se claquer un muscle** to pull *ou* strain a muscle; **claquettes** *nfpl* tap-dancing *sg*; (*chaussures*) flip-flops
clarinette [klaʀinɛt] *nf* clarinet
classe [klas] *nf* class; (*Scol: local*) class(room); (: *leçon,*

élèves) class; **aller en ~** to go to school; **classement** *nm* (*rang*: *Scol*) place; (: *Sport*) placing; (*liste*: *Scol*) class list (in order of merit); (: *Sport*) placings *pl*

classer [klɑse] *vt* (*idées, livres*) to classify; (*papiers*) to file; (*candidat, concurrent*) to grade; (*Jur: affaire*) to close; **se ~ premier/dernier** to come first/last; (*Sport*) to finish first/last; **classeur** *nm* (*cahier*) file

classique [klasik] *adj* classical; (*sobre: coupe etc*) classic(al); (*habituel*) standard, classic

clavecin [klav(ə)sɛ̃] *nm* harpsichord

clavicule [klavikyl] *nf* collarbone

clavier [klavje] *nm* keyboard

clé [kle] *nf* key; (*Mus*) clef; (*de mécanicien*) spanner (BRIT), wrench (US); **prix ~s en main** (*d'une voiture*) on-the-road price; **clé de contact** ignition key; **clé USB** USB key

clef [kle] *nf* = **clé**

clergé [klɛʀʒe] *nm* clergy

cliché [kliʃe] *nm* (*fig*) cliché; (*négatif*) negative; (*photo*) print

client, e [klijɑ̃, klijɑ̃t] *nm/f* (*acheteur*) customer, client; (*d'hôtel*) guest, patron; (*du docteur*) patient; (*de l'avocat*) client; **clientèle** *nf* (*du magasin*) customers *pl*, clientèle; (*du docteur, de l'avocat*) practice

cligner [kliɲe] *vi*: **~ des yeux** to blink (one's eyes); **~ de l'œil** to wink; **clignotant** (*Auto*) indicator; **clignoter** *vi* (*étoiles etc*) to twinkle; (*lumière*) to flicker

climat [klima] *nm* climate

climatisation [klimatizasjɔ̃] *nf* air conditioning; **climatisé, e** *adj* air-conditioned

clin d'œil [klɛ̃dœj] *nm* wink; **en un clin d'œil** in a flash

clinique [klinik] *nf* private hospital

clip [klip] *nm* (*boucle d'oreille*) clip-on; (*vidéo*) **~** (pop) video

cliquer [klike] *vt* to click; **~ sur** to click on

clochard, e [kloʃaʀ, aʀd] *nm/f* tramp

cloche [klɔʃ] *nf* (*d'église*) bell; (*fam*) clot; **clocher** *nm* church tower; (*en pointe*) steeple ▷ *vi* to be ou go wrong; **de clocher** (*péj*) parochial

cloison [klwazɔ̃] *nf* partition (wall)

clonage [klonaʒ] *nm* cloning

cloner [klone] *vt* to clone

cloque [klɔk] *nf* blister

clore [klɔʀ] *vt* to close

clôture [klotyʀ] *nf* closure; (*barrière*) enclosure

clou [klu] *nm* nail; **clous** *nmpl* (*passage clouté*) pedestrian crossing; **pneus à ~s** studded tyres; **le ~ du spectacle** the highlight of the show; **clou de girofle** clove

clown [klun] *nm* clown

club [klœb] *nm* club

CNRS *sigle m* (= *Centre nationale de la recherche scientifique*) ≈ SERC (BRIT), ≈ NSF (US)

coaguler [kɔagyle] *vt, vi* (*aussi*: **se ~**: *sang*) to coagulate

cobaye [kɔbaj] *nm* guinea-pig

coca [kɔka] *nm* Coke®

cocaïne [kɔkain] *nf* cocaine

coccinelle [kɔksinɛl] *nf* ladybird (BRIT), ladybug (US)

cocher [kɔʃe] *vt* to tick off

cochon, ne [kɔʃɔ̃, ɔn] *nm* pig ▷ *adj* (*fam*) dirty, smutty; **cochon d'Inde** guinea pig; **cochonnerie** (*fam*) *nf* (*saleté*) filth; (*marchandise*) rubbish, trash

cocktail [kɔktɛl] *nm* cocktail; (*réception*) cocktail party

cocorico [kɔkɔriko] *excl, nm* cock-a-doodle-do

cocotte [kɔkɔt] *nf* (*en fonte*) casserole; **ma ~** (*fam*) sweetie (pie); **cocotte (minute)®** pressure cooker

code [kɔd] *nm* code ▷ *adj*: **phares ~s** dipped lights; **se mettre en ~(s)** to dip one's (head)lights; **code à barres** bar code; **code civil** Common Law; **code de la route** highway code; **code pénal** penal code; **code postal** (*numéro*) post (BRIT) ou zip (US) code

cœur [kœʀ] *nm* heart; (*Cartes: couleur*) hearts *pl*; (: *carte*) heart; **avoir bon ~** to be kind-hearted; **avoir mal au ~** to feel sick; **par ~** by heart; **de bon ~** willingly; **cela lui tient à ~** that's (very) close to his heart

coffre [kɔfʀ] *nm* (*meuble*) chest; (*d'auto*) boot (BRIT), trunk (US); **coffre-fort** *nm* safe; **coffret** *nm* casket

cognac [kɔɲak] *nm* brandy, cognac

cogner [kɔɲe] *vi* to knock; **se ~ contre** to knock ou bump into; **se ~ la tête** to bang one's head

cohérent, e [kɔeʀɑ̃, ɑ̃t] *adj* coherent, consistent

coiffé, e [kwafe] *adj*: **bien/mal ~** with tidy/untidy hair; **~ d'un chapeau** wearing a hat

coiffer [kwafe] *vt* (*fig: surmonter*) to cover, top; **se ~** *vi* to do one's hair; **~ qn** to do sb's hair; **coiffeur, -euse** *nm/f* hairdresser; **coiffeuse** *nf* (*table*) dressing table; **coiffure** *nf* (*cheveux*) hairstyle, hairdo; (*art*): **la coiffure** hairdressing

coin [kwɛ̃] *nm* corner; (*pour coincer*) wedge; **l'épicerie du ~** the local grocer; **dans le ~** (*aux alentours*) in the area, around about; (*habiter*) locally; **je ne suis pas du ~** I'm not from here; **au ~ du feu** by the fireside; **regard en ~** sideways glance

coincé, e [kwɛ̃se] *adj* stuck, jammed; (*fig: inhibé*) inhibited, hung up (*fam*)

coïncidence [kɔɛ̃sidɑ̃s] *nf* coincidence

coing [kwɛ̃] *nm* quince

col [kɔl] *nm* (*de chemise*) collar; (*encolure, cou*) neck; (*de montagne*) pass; **col de l'utérus** cervix; **col roulé** polo-neck

colère [kɔlɛʀ] *nf* anger; **une ~** a fit of anger; (**se mettre**) **en ~ (contre qn)** (to get) angry (with sb); **coléreux, -euse, colérique** *adj* quick-tempered, irascible

colin [kɔlɛ̃] *nm* hake

colique [kɔlik] *nf* diarrhoea

colis [kɔli] *nm* parcel

collaborer [kɔ(l)labɔʀe] *vi* to collaborate; **~ à** to collaborate on; (*revue*) to contribute to

collant, e [kɔlɑ̃, ɑ̃t] *adj* sticky; (*robe etc*) clinging, skintight; (*péj*) clinging ▷ *nm* (*bas*) tights *pl*; (*de danseur*) leotard

colle [kɔl] *nf* glue; (*à papiers peints*) (wallpaper) paste; (*fam: devinette*) teaser, riddle; (*Scol: fam*) detention

collecte [kɔlɛkt] *nf* collection; **collectif, -ive** *adj* collective; (*visite, billet*) group *cpd*

collection [kɔlɛksjɔ̃] *nf* collection; (*Édition*) series; **collectionner** *vt* to collect; **collectionneur, -euse** *nm/f* collector

collectivité [kɔlɛktivite] *nf* group; **collectivités locales** (*Admin*) local authorities

collège [kɔlɛʒ] *nm* (*école*) (secondary) school; (*assemblée*) body; **collégien** *nm* schoolboy

collègue [kɔ(l)lɛg] *nm/f* colleague

coller [kɔle] *vt* (*papier, timbre*) to stick (on); (*affiche*) to stick up; (*enveloppe*) to stick down; (*morceaux*) to stick ou glue together; (*Comput*) to paste; (*fam: mettre, fourrer*) to stick, shove; (*Scol: fam*) to keep in ▷ *vi* (*être collant*) to be sticky; (*adhérer*) to stick; **~ à** to stick to; **être collé à un examen** (*fam*) to fail an exam

collier [kɔlje] *nm* (*bijou*) necklace; (*de chien, Tech*) collar

colline [kɔlin] nf hill
collision [kɔlizjɔ̃] nf collision, crash; **entrer en ~ (avec)** to collide (with)
collyre [kɔliʀ] nm eye drops
colombe [kɔlɔ̃b] nf dove
Colombie [kɔlɔ̃bi] nf: **la ~** Colombia
colonie [kɔlɔni] nf colony; **colonie (de vacances)** holiday camp (for children)
colonne [kɔlɔn] nf column; **se mettre en ~ par deux** to get into twos; **colonne (vertébrale)** spine, spinal column
colorant [kɔlɔʀɑ̃] nm colouring
colorer [kɔlɔʀe] vt to colour
colorier [kɔlɔʀje] vt to colour(in)
coloris [kɔlɔʀi] nm colour, shade
colza [kɔlza] nm rape(seed)
coma [kɔma] nm coma; **être dans le ~** to be in a coma
combat [kɔ̃ba] nm fight, fighting no pl; **combat de boxe** boxing match; **combattant** nm: **ancien combattant** war veteran; **combattre** vt to fight; (épidémie, ignorance) to combat, fight against
combien [kɔ̃bjɛ̃] adv (quantité) how much; (nombre) how many; **~ de** (quantité) how much; (nombre) how many; **~ de temps** how long; **~ ça coûte/pèse?** how much does it cost/weigh?; **on est le ~ aujourd'hui?** (fam) what's the date today?
combinaison [kɔ̃binɛzɔ̃] nf combination; (astuce) scheme; (de femme) slip; (de plongée) wetsuit; (bleu de travail) boiler suit; (BRIT), coveralls pl (US)
combiné [kɔ̃bine] nm (aussi: **~ téléphonique**) receiver
comble [kɔ̃bl] adj (salle) packed (full) ▷ nm (du bonheur, plaisir) height; **combles** nmpl (Constr) attic sg, loft sg; **c'est le ~!** that beats everything!
combler [kɔ̃ble] vt (trou) to fill in; (besoin, lacune) to fill; (déficit) to make good; (satisfaire) to fulfil
comédie [kɔmedi] nf comedy; (fig) playacting no pl; **faire la ~** (fam) to make a fuss; **comédie musicale** musical; **comédien, ne** nm/f actor(-tress)
comestible [kɔmɛstibl] adj edible
comique [kɔmik] adj (drôle) comical; (Théâtre) comic ▷ nm (artiste) comic, comedian
commandant [kɔmɑ̃dɑ̃] nm (gén) commander, commandant; (Navig, Aviat) captain
commande [kɔmɑ̃d] nf (Comm) order; **commandes** nfpl (Aviat etc) controls; **sur ~** to order; **commander** vt (Comm) to order; (diriger, ordonner) to command; **commander à qn de faire** to command ou order sb to do; **je peux commander, s'il vous plaît?** can I order, please?

MOT-CLÉ

comme [kɔm] prép 1 (comparaison) like; **tout comme son père** just like his father; **fort comme un bœuf** as strong as an ox; **joli comme tout** ever so pretty
2 (manière) like; **faites-le comme ça** do it like this, do it this way; **comme ci, comme ça** so-so, middling; **comme il faut** (correctement) properly
3 (en tant que) as a; **donner comme prix** to give as a prize; **travailler comme secrétaire** to work as a secretary
▷ conj 1 (ainsi que) as; **elle écrit comme elle parle** she writes as she talks; **comme si** as if
2 (au moment où, alors que) as; **il est parti comme**

j'arrivais he left as I arrived
3 (parce que, puisque) as; **comme il était en retard, il ...** as he was late, he ...
▷ adv: **comme il est fort/c'est bon!** he's so strong/it's so good!

commencement [kɔmɑ̃smɑ̃] nm beginning, start
commencer [kɔmɑ̃se] vt, vi to begin, start; **~ à ou de faire** to begin ou start doing
comment [kɔmɑ̃] adv how; **~?** (que dites-vous) pardon?; **et ~!** and how!
commentaire [kɔmɑ̃tɛʀ] nm (remarque) comment, remark; (exposé) commentary
commerçant, e [kɔmɛʀsɑ̃, ɑ̃t] nm/f shopkeeper, trader
commerce [kɔmɛʀs] nm (activité) trade, commerce; (boutique) business; **~ électronique** e-commerce; **~ équitable** fair trade; **commercial, e, -aux** adj commercial, trading; (péj) commercial; **les commerciaux** the sales people; **commercialiser** vt to market
commissaire [kɔmisɛʀ] nm (de police) ≈ (police) superintendent; **commissaire aux comptes** (Admin) auditor; **commissariat** nm police station
commission [kɔmisjɔ̃] nf (comité, pourcentage) commission; (message) message; (course) errand; **commissions** nfpl (achats) shopping sg
commode [kɔmɔd] adj (pratique) convenient, handy; (facile) easy; (personne): **pas ~** awkward (to deal with) ▷ nf chest of drawers
commun, e [kɔmœ̃ yn] adj common; (pièce) communal, shared; (effort) joint; **ça sort du ~** it's out of the ordinary; **le ~ des mortels** the common run of people; **en ~ (faire)** jointly; **mettre en ~** to pool, share; **communs** nmpl (bâtiments) outbuildings; **d'un ~ accord** by mutual agreement
communauté [kɔmynote] nf community
commune [kɔmyn] nf (Admin) commune, ≈ district; (: urbaine) ≈ borough
communication [kɔmynikasjɔ̃] nf communication
communier [kɔmynje] vi (Rel) to receive communion
communion [kɔmynjɔ̃] nf communion
communiquer [kɔmynike] vt (nouvelle, dossier) to pass on, convey; (peur etc) to communicate ▷ vi to communicate; **se ~ à** (se propager) to spread to
communisme [kɔmynism] nm communism; **communiste** adj, nm/f communist
commutateur [kɔmytatœʀ] nm (Élec) (change-over) switch, commutator
compact, e [kɔ̃pakt] adj (dense) dense; (appareil) compact
compagne [kɔ̃paɲ] nf companion
compagnie [kɔ̃paɲi] nf (firme, Mil) company; **tenir ~ à qn** to keep sb company; **fausser ~ à qn** to give sb the slip, slip ou sneak away from sb; **compagnie aérienne** airline (company)
compagnon [kɔ̃paɲɔ̃] nm companion
comparable [kɔ̃paʀabl] adj: **~ (à)** comparable (to)
comparaison [kɔ̃paʀɛzɔ̃] nf comparison
comparer [kɔ̃paʀe] vt to compare; **~ qch/qn à ou et** (pour choisir) to compare sth/sb with ou and; (pour établir une similitude) to compare sth/sb to
compartiment [kɔ̃paʀtimɑ̃] nm compartment; **un ~ non-fumeurs** a non-smoking compartment (BRIT)

ou car (us)

compas [kɔ̃pa] *nm* (*Géom*) (pair of) compasses *pl*; (*Navig*) compass

compatible [kɔ̃patibl] *adj* compatible

compatriote [kɔ̃patrijɔt] *nm/f* compatriot

compensation [kɔ̃pɑ̃sasjɔ̃] *nf* compensation

compenser [kɔ̃pɑ̃se] *vt* to compensate for, make up for

compétence [kɔ̃petɑ̃s] *nf* competence

compétent, e [kɔ̃petɑ̃, ɑ̃t] *adj* (*apte*) competent, capable

compétition [kɔ̃petisjɔ̃] *nf* (*gén*) competition; (*Sport*: *épreuve*) event; **la ~ automobile** motor racing

complément [kɔ̃plemɑ̃] *nm* complement; (*reste*) remainder; **complément d'information** (*Admin*) supplementary *ou* further information; **complémentaire** *adj* complementary; (*additionnel*) supplementary

complet, -ète [kɔ̃plɛ, ɛt] *adj* complete; (*plein: hôtel etc*) full ▷ *nm* (*aussi*: **~-veston**) suit; **pain complet** wholemeal bread; **complètement** *adv* completely; **compléter** *vt* (*porter à la quantité voulue*) to complete; (*augmenter: connaissances, études*) to complement, supplement; (*: garde-robe*) to add to

complexe [kɔ̃plɛks] *adj, nm* complex; **complexe hospitalier/industriel** hospital/industrial complex; **complexé, e** *adj* mixed-up, hung-up

complication [kɔ̃plikasjɔ̃] *nf* complexity, intricacy; (*difficulté, ennui*) complication; **complications** *nfpl* (*Méd*) complications

complice [kɔ̃plis] *nm* accomplice

compliment [kɔ̃plimɑ̃] *nm* (*louange*) compliment; **compliments** *nmpl* (*félicitations*) congratulations

compliqué, e [kɔ̃plike] *adj* complicated, complex; (*personne*) complicated

comportement [kɔ̃pɔrtəmɑ̃] *nm* behaviour

comporter [kɔ̃pɔrte] *vt* (*consister en*) to consist of, comprise; (*inclure*) to have; **se ~** *vi* to behave

composer [kɔ̃poze] *vt* (*musique, texte*) to compose; (*mélange, équipe*) to make up; (*numéro*) to dial; (*constituer*) to make up, form ▷ *vi* (*transiger*) to come to terms; **se ~ de** to be composed of, be made up of; **compositeur, -trice** *nm/f* (*Mus*) composer; **composition** *nf* composition; (*Scol*) test

composter [kɔ̃poste] *vt* (*billet*) to punch

compote [kɔ̃pɔt] *nf* stewed fruit *no pl*; **compote de pommes** stewed apples

compréhensible [kɔ̃preɑ̃sibl] *adj* comprehensible; (*attitude*) understandable

compréhensif, -ive [kɔ̃preɑ̃sif, iv] *adj* understanding

comprendre [kɔ̃prɑ̃dr] *vt* to understand; (*se composer de*) to comprise, consist of

compresse [kɔ̃prɛs] *nf* compress

comprimé [kɔ̃prime] *nm* tablet

compris, e [kɔ̃pri, iz] *pp de* **comprendre** ▷ *adj* (*inclus*) included; **~ entre** (*situé*) contained between; **l'électricité ~e/non ~e, y/non ~ l'électricité** including/excluding electricity; **100 euros tout ~** 100 euros all inclusive *ou* all-in

comptabilité [kɔ̃tabilite] *nf* (*activité*) accounting, accountancy; (*comptes*) accounts *pl*, books *pl*; (*service*) accounts office

comptable [kɔ̃tabl] *nm/f* accountant

comptant [kɔ̃tɑ̃] *adv*: **payer ~** to pay cash; **acheter ~** to buy for cash

compte [kɔ̃t] *nm* count; (*total, montant*) count, (right) number; (*bancaire, facture*) account; **comptes** *nmpl* (*Finance*) accounts, books; (*fig*) explanation *sg*; **en fin de ~** all things considered; **s'en tirer à bon ~** to get off lightly; **pour le ~ de** on behalf of; **pour son propre ~** for one's own benefit; **régler un ~** (*s'acquitter de qch*) to settle an account; (*se venger*) to get one's own back; **rendre des ~s à qn** (*fig*) to be answerable to sb; **tenir ~ de** to take account of; **travailler à son ~** to work for oneself; **rendre ~ (à qn) de qch** to give (sb) an account of sth; *voir aussi* **rendre**; **compte à rebours** countdown; **compte courant** current account; **compte rendu** account, report; (*de film, livre*) review; **compte-gouttes** *nm inv* dropper

compter [kɔ̃te] *vt* to count; (*facturer*) to charge for; (*avoir à son actif, comporter*) to have; (*prévoir*) to allow, reckon; (*penser, espérer*): **~ réussir** to expect to succeed ▷ *vi* to count; (*être économe*) to economize; (*figurer*): **~ parmi** to be *ou* rank among; **~ sur** to count (up)on; **~ avec qch/qn** to reckon with *ou* take account of sth/sb; **sans ~ que** besides which

compteur [kɔ̃tœr] *nm* meter; **compteur de vitesse** speedometer

comptine [kɔ̃tin] *nf* nursery rhyme

comptoir [kɔ̃twar] *nm* (*de magasin*) counter; (*bar*) bar

con, ne [kɔ̃, kɔn] (*fam!*) *adj* damned *ou* bloody (BRIT) stupid (!)

concentrer [kɔ̃sɑ̃tre] *vt* to concentrate; **se ~** *vi* to concentrate

concerner [kɔ̃sɛrne] *vt* to concern; **en ce qui me concerne** as far as I am concerned

concert [kɔ̃sɛr] *nm* concert; **de ~** (*décider*) unanimously

concessionnaire [kɔ̃sesjɔnɛr] *nm/f* agent, dealer

concevoir [kɔ̃s(ə)vwar] *vt* (*idée, projet*) to conceive (of); (*comprendre*) to understand; (*enfant*) to conceive; **bien/mal conçu** well-/badly-designed

concierge [kɔ̃sjɛrʒ] *nm/f* caretaker

concis, e [kɔ̃si, iz] *adj* concise

conclure [kɔ̃klyr] *vt* to conclude; **conclusion** *nf* conclusion

conçois *etc* [kɔ̃swa] *vb voir* **concevoir**

concombre [kɔ̃kɔ̃br] *nm* cucumber

concours [kɔ̃kur] *nm* competition; (*Scol*) competitive examination; (*assistance*) aid, help; **concours de circonstances** combination of circumstances; **concours hippique** horse show

concret, -ète [kɔ̃krɛ, ɛt] *adj* concrete

conçu, e [kɔ̃sy] *pp de* **concevoir**

concubinage [kɔ̃kybinaʒ] *nm* (*Jur*) cohabitation

concurrence [kɔ̃kyrɑ̃s] *nf* competition; **faire ~ à** to be in competition with; **jusqu'à ~ de** up to

concurrent, e [kɔ̃kyrɑ̃, ɑ̃t] *nm/f* (*Sport, Écon etc*) competitor; (*Scol*) candidate

condamner [kɔ̃dane] *vt* (*blâmer*) to condemn; (*Jur*) to sentence; (*porte, ouverture*) to fill in, block up; **~ qn à 2 ans de prison** to sentence sb to 2 years' imprisonment

condensation [kɔ̃dɑ̃sasjɔ̃] *nf* condensation

condition [kɔ̃disjɔ̃] *nf* condition; **conditions** *nfpl* (*tarif, prix*) terms; (*circonstances*) conditions; **sans ~s** unconditionally; **à ~ de ou que** provided that; **conditionnel, le** *nm* conditional (tense)

conditionnement [kɔ̃disjɔnmɑ̃] *nm* (*emballage*) packaging

condoléances [kɔ̃dɔleɑ̃s] *nfpl* condolences

conducteur, -trice [kɔ̃dyktœʀ, tʀis] nm/f driver ▷ nm (Élec etc) conductor

conduire [kɔ̃dɥiʀ] vt to drive; (délégation, troupeau) to lead; **se ~** vi to behave; **~ à** to lead to; **~ qn quelque part** to take sb somewhere; to drive sb somewhere

conduite [kɔ̃dɥit] nf (comportement) behaviour; (d'eau, de gaz) pipe; **sous la ~ de** led by

confection [kɔ̃fɛksjɔ̃] nf (fabrication) making; (Couture): **la ~** the clothing industry

conférence [kɔ̃feʀɑ̃s] nf conference; (exposé) lecture; **conférence de presse** press conference

confesser [kɔ̃fese] vt to confess; **confession** nf confession; (culte: catholique etc) denomination

confetti [kɔ̃feti] nm confetti no pl

confiance [kɔ̃fjɑ̃s] nf (en l'honnêteté de qn) confidence, trust; (en la valeur de qch) faith; **avoir ~ en** to have confidence ou faith in, trust; **faire ~ à qn** to trust sb; **mettre qn en ~** to win sb's trust; **confiance en soi** self-confidence

confiant, e [kɔ̃fjɑ̃, jɑ̃t] adj confident; trusting

confidence [kɔ̃fidɑ̃s] nf confidence; **confidentiel, le** adj confidential

confier [kɔ̃fje] vt: **~ à qn** (objet, travail) to entrust to sb; (secret, pensée) to confide to sb; **se ~ à qn** to confide in sb

confirmation [kɔ̃fiʀmasjɔ̃] nf confirmation

confirmer [kɔ̃fiʀme] vt to confirm

confiserie [kɔ̃fizʀi] nf (magasin) confectioner's ou sweet shop; **confiseries** nfpl (bonbons) confectionery sg

confisquer [kɔ̃fiske] vt to confiscate

confit, e [kɔ̃fi, it] adj: **fruits ~s** crystallized fruits; **confit d'oie** nm conserve of goose

confiture [kɔ̃fityʀ] nf jam

conflit [kɔ̃fli] nm conflict

confondre [kɔ̃fɔ̃dʀ] vt (jumeaux, faits) to confuse, mix up; (témoin, menteur) to confound; **se ~** vi to merge; **se ~ en excuses** to apologize profusely

conforme [kɔ̃fɔʀm] adj: **~ à** (loi, règle) in accordance with; **conformément** adv: **conformément à** in accordance with; **conformer** vt: **se conformer à** to conform to

confort [kɔ̃fɔʀ] nm comfort; **tout ~** (Comm) with all modern conveniences; **confortable** adj comfortable

confronter [kɔ̃fʀɔ̃te] vt to confront

confus, e [kɔ̃fy, yz] adj (vague) confused; (embarrassé) embarrassed; **confusion** nf (voir confus) confusion; (voir confondre) confusion, mixing up

congé [kɔ̃ʒe] nm (vacances) holiday; **en ~** on holiday; **semaine/jour de ~** week/day off; **prendre ~ de qn** to take one's leave of sb; **donner son ~ à** to give in one's notice to; **congé de maladie** sick leave; **congé de maternité** maternity leave; **congés payés** paid holiday

congédier [kɔ̃ʒedje] vt to dismiss

congélateur [kɔ̃ʒelatœʀ] nm freezer

congeler [kɔ̃ʒ(ə)le] vt to freeze; **les produits congelés** frozen foods

congestion [kɔ̃ʒɛstjɔ̃] nf congestion

Congo [kɔ̃go] nm: **le ~** Congo, the Democratic Republic of the Congo

congrès [kɔ̃gʀɛ] nm congress

conifère [kɔnifɛʀ] nm conifer

conjoint, e [kɔ̃ʒwɛ̃, wɛ̃t] adj joint ▷ nm/f spouse

conjonctivite [kɔ̃ʒɔ̃ktivit] nf conjunctivitis

conjoncture [kɔ̃ʒɔ̃ktyʀ] nf circumstances pl; **la ~ actuelle** the present (economic) situation

conjugaison [kɔ̃ʒygɛzɔ̃] nf (Ling) conjugation

connaissance [kɔnɛsɑ̃s] nf (savoir) knowledge no pl; (personne connue) acquaintance; **être sans ~** to be unconscious; **perdre/reprendre ~** to lose/regain consciousness; **à ma/sa ~** to (the best of) my/his knowledge; **faire la ~ de qn** to meet sb

connaisseur, -euse [kɔnɛsœʀ, øz] nm/f connoisseur

connaître [kɔnɛtʀ] vt to know; (éprouver) to experience; (avoir: succès) to have, enjoy; **~ de nom/vue** to know by name/sight; **ils se sont connus à Genève** they (first) met in Geneva; **s'y ~ en qch** to know a lot about sth

connecter [kɔnɛkte] vt to connect; **se ~ à Internet** to log onto the Internet

connerie [kɔnʀi] (fam!) nf stupid thing (to do/say)

connexion [kɔnɛksjɔ̃] nf connection

connu, e [kɔny] adj (célèbre) well-known

conquérir [kɔ̃keʀiʀ] vt to conquer; **conquête** nf conquest

consacrer [kɔ̃sakʀe] vt (employer) to devote, dedicate; (Rel) to consecrate; **se ~ à qch** to dedicate ou devote o.s. to sth

conscience [kɔ̃sjɑ̃s] nf conscience; **avoir/prendre ~ de** to be/become aware of; **perdre ~** to lose consciousness; **avoir bonne/mauvaise ~** to have a clear/guilty conscience; **consciencieux, -euse** adj conscientious; **conscient, e** adj conscious

consécutif, -ive [kɔ̃sekytif, iv] adj consecutive; **~ à** following upon

conseil [kɔ̃sɛj] nm (avis) piece of advice; (assemblée) council; **des ~s** advice; **prendre ~ (auprès de qn)** to take advice (from sb); **conseil d'administration** board (of directors); **conseil des ministres** ≈ the Cabinet; **conseil municipal** town council

conseiller, -ère [kɔ̃seje, ɛʀ] nm/f adviser ▷ vt (personne) to advise; (méthode, action) to recommend, advise; **~ à qn de** to advise sb to; **pouvez-vous me ~ un bon restaurant?** can you suggest a good restaurant?

consentement [kɔ̃sɑ̃tmɑ̃] nm consent

consentir [kɔ̃sɑ̃tiʀ] vt to agree, consent

conséquence [kɔ̃sekɑ̃s] nf consequence; **en ~** (donc) consequently; (de façon appropriée) accordingly; **conséquent, e** adj logical, rational; (fam: important) substantial; **par conséquent** consequently

conservateur, -trice [kɔ̃sɛʀvatœʀ, tʀis] nm/f (Pol) conservative; (de musée) curator ▷ nm (pour aliments) preservative

conservatoire [kɔ̃sɛʀvatwaʀ] nm academy

conserve [kɔ̃sɛʀv] nf (gén pl) canned ou tinned food; **en ~** canned, tinned (BRIT)

conserver [kɔ̃sɛʀve] vt (faculté) to retain, keep; (amis, livres) to keep; (préserver, Culin) to preserve

considérable [kɔ̃sideʀabl] adj considerable, significant, extensive

considération [kɔ̃sideʀasjɔ̃] nf consideration; (estime) esteem

considérer [kɔ̃sideʀe] vt to consider; **~ qch comme** to regard sth as

consigne [kɔ̃siɲ] nf (de gare) left luggage (office) (BRIT), checkroom (US); (ordre, instruction) instructions pl; **consigne automatique** left-luggage locker

consister [kɔ̃siste] vi: **~ en/à faire** to consist of/in doing

consoler [kɔ̃sɔle] vt to console

consommateur, -trice [kɔ̃sɔmatœʀ, tʀis] nm/f

(*Écon*) consumer; (*dans un café*) customer

consommation [kɔ̃sɔmasjɔ̃] *nf* (*boisson*) drink; (*Écon*) consumption; **de ~** (*biens, sociétés*) consumer *cpd*

consommer [kɔ̃sɔme] *vt* (*suj: personne*) to eat *ou* drink, consume; (: *voiture, machine*) to use, consume; (*mariage*) to consummate ⊳ *vi* (*dans un café*) to (have a) drink

consonne [kɔ̃sɔn] *nf* consonant

constamment [kɔ̃stamɑ̃] *adv* constantly

constant, e [kɔ̃stɑ̃, ɑ̃t] *adj* constant; (*personne*) steadfast

constat [kɔ̃sta] *nm* (*de police, d'accident*) report; **~ (à l')amiable** jointly-agreed statement for insurance purposes; **~ d'échec** acknowledgement of failure

constatation [kɔ̃statasjɔ̃] *nf* (*observation*) (observed) fact, observation

constater [kɔ̃state] *vt* (*remarquer*) to note; (*Admin, Jur: attester*) to certify

consterner [kɔ̃stɛrne] *vt* to dismay

constipé, e [kɔ̃stipe] *adj* constipated

constitué, e [kɔ̃stitɥe] *adj:* **~ de** made up *ou* composed of

constituer [kɔ̃stitɥe] *vt* (*équipe*) to set up; (*dossier, collection*) to put together; (*suj: éléments: composer*) to make up, constitute; (*représenter, être*) to constitute; **se ~ prisonnier** to give o.s. up

constructeur, -trice [kɔ̃stryktœr, tris] *nm/f* manufacturer, builder

constructif, -ive [kɔ̃stryktif, iv] *adj* constructive

construction [kɔ̃stryksjɔ̃] *nf* construction, building

construire [kɔ̃strɥir] *vt* to build, construct

consul [kɔ̃syl] *nm* consul; **consulat** *nm* consulate

consultant [kɔ̃syltɑ̃] *adj, nm* consultant

consultation [kɔ̃syltasjɔ̃] *nf* consultation; **heures de ~** (*Méd*) surgery (BRIT) *ou* office (US) hours

consulter [kɔ̃sylte] *vt* to consult ⊳ *vi* (*médecin*) to hold surgery (BRIT), be in the office) (US)

contact [kɔ̃takt] *nm* contact; **au ~ de** (*air, peau*) on contact with; (*gens*) through contact with; **mettre/couper le ~** (*Auto*) to switch on/off the ignition; **entrer en** *ou* **prendre ~ avec** to get in touch *ou* contact with; **contacter** *vt* to contact, get in touch with

contagieux, -euse [kɔ̃taʒjø, jøz] *adj* infectious; (*par le contact*) contagious

contaminer [kɔ̃tamine] *vt* to contaminate

conte [kɔ̃t] *nm* tale; **conte de fées** fairy tale

contempler [kɔ̃tɑ̃ple] *vt* to contemplate, gaze at

contemporain, e [kɔ̃tɑ̃pɔrɛ̃, ɛn] *adj, nm/f* contemporary

contenir [kɔ̃t(ə)nir] *vt* to contain; (*avoir une capacité de*) to hold

content, e [kɔ̃tɑ̃, ɑ̃t] *adj* pleased, glad; **~ de** pleased with; **contenter** *vt* to satisfy, please; **se contenter de** to content o.s. with

contenu [kɔ̃t(ə)ny] *nm* (*d'un récipient*) contents *pl*; (*d'un texte*) content

conter [kɔ̃te] *vt* to recount, relate

conteste [kɔ̃tɛst]: **sans ~** *adv* unquestionably, indisputably; **contester** *vt* to question ⊳ *vi* (*Pol, gén*) rebel (against established authority)

contexte [kɔ̃tɛkst] *nm* context

continent [kɔ̃tinɑ̃] *nm* continent

continu, e [kɔ̃tiny] *adj* continuous; **faire la journée ~e** to work without taking a full lunch break; **(courant) continu** direct current, DC

continuel, le [kɔ̃tinɥɛl] *adj* (*qui se répète*) constant, continual; (*continu*) continuous

continuer [kɔ̃tinɥe] *vt* (*travail, voyage etc*) to continue (with), carry on (with), go on (with); (*prolonger: alignement, rue*) to continue ⊳ *vi* (*vie, bruit*) to continue, go on; **~ à** *ou* **de faire** to go on *ou* continue doing

contourner [kɔ̃turne] *vt* to go round; (*difficulté*) to get round

contraceptif, -ive [kɔ̃trasɛptif, iv] *adj, nm* contraceptive; **contraception** *nf* contraception

contracté, e [kɔ̃trakte] *adj* tense

contracter [kɔ̃trakte] *vt* (*muscle etc*) to tense, contract; (*maladie, dette*) to contract; (*assurance*) to take out; **se ~** *vi* (*muscles*) to contract

contractuel, le [kɔ̃traktɥɛl] *nm/f* (*agent*) traffic warden

contradiction [kɔ̃tradiksjɔ̃] *nf* contradiction; **contradictoire** *adj* contradictory, conflicting

contraignant, e [kɔ̃trɛɲɑ̃, ɑ̃t] *adj* restricting

contraindre [kɔ̃trɛ̃dr] *vt:* **~ qn à faire** to compel sb to do; **contrainte** *nf* constraint

contraire [kɔ̃trɛr] *adj, nm* opposite; **~ à** contrary to; **au ~** on the contrary

contrarier [kɔ̃trarje] *vt* (*personne: irriter*) to annoy; (*fig: projets*) to thwart, frustrate; **contrariété** *nf* annoyance

contraste [kɔ̃trast] *nm* contrast

contrat [kɔ̃tra] *nm* contract

contravention [kɔ̃travɑ̃sjɔ̃] *nf* parking ticket

contre [kɔ̃tr] *prép* against; (*en échange*) (in exchange) for; **par ~** on the other hand

contrebande [kɔ̃trəbɑ̃d] *nf* (*trafic*) contraband, smuggling; (*marchandise*) contraband, smuggled goods *pl*; **faire la ~ de** to smuggle

contrebas [kɔ̃trəba]: **en ~** *adv* (down) below

contrebasse [kɔ̃trəbas] *nf* (double) bass

contre...: **contrecoup** *nm* repercussions *pl*; **contredire** *vt* (*personne*) to contradict; (*faits*) to refute

contrefaçon [kɔ̃trəfasɔ̃] *nf* forgery

contre-...: **contre-indication** *nf* (*pl* **contre-indications**) *nf* (*Méd*) contra-indication; **"contre-indication en cas d'eczéma"** "should not be used by people with eczema"; **contre-indiqué, e** *adj* (*Méd*) contraindicated; (*déconseillé*) unadvisable, ill-advised

contremaître [kɔ̃trəmɛtr] *nm* foreman

contre-plaqué [kɔ̃trəplake] *nm* plywood

contresens [kɔ̃trəsɑ̃s] *nm* (*erreur*) misinterpretation; (*de traduction*) mistranslation; **à ~** the wrong way

contretemps [kɔ̃trətɑ̃] *nm* hitch; **à ~** (*fig*) at an inopportune moment

contribuer [kɔ̃tribɥe]: **~ à** *vt* to contribute towards; **contribution** *nf* contribution; **mettre à contribution** to call upon; **contributions directes/indirectes** direct/indirect taxation

contrôle [kɔ̃trol] *nm* checking *no pl*, check; (*des prix*) monitoring, control; (*test*) test, examination; **perdre le ~ de** (*véhicule*) to lose control of; **contrôle continu** (*Scol*) continuous assessment; **contrôle d'identité** identity check

contrôler [kɔ̃trole] *vt* (*vérifier*) to check; (*surveiller: opérations*) to supervise; (: *prix*) to monitor, control; (*maîtriser, Comm: firme*) to control; **contrôleur, -euse** *nm/f* (*de train*) (ticket) inspector; (*de bus*) (bus) conductor(-tress)

controversé, e [kɔ̃trɔvɛrse] *adj* (*personnage, question*) controversial

contusion [kɔ̃tyzjɔ̃] nf bruise, contusion

convaincre [kɔ̃vɛ̃kʀ] vt: ~ qn (de qch) to convince sb (of sth); ~ qn (de faire) to persuade sb (to do)

convalescence [kɔ̃valesɑ̃s] nf convalescence

convenable [kɔ̃vnabl] adj suitable; (assez bon, respectable) decent

convenir [kɔ̃vniʀ] vi to be suitable; ~ à to suit; ~ de (bien-fondé de qch) to admit (to), acknowledge; (date, somme etc) to agree upon; ~ que (admettre) to admit that; ~ de faire to agree to do

convention [kɔ̃vɑ̃sjɔ̃] nf convention; **conventions** nfpl (convenances) convention sg; **convention collective** (Écon) collective agreement; **conventionné, e** adj (Admin) applying charges laid down by the state

convenu, e [kɔ̃vny] pp de **convenir** ▷ adj agreed

conversation [kɔ̃vɛʀsasjɔ̃] nf conversation

convertir [kɔ̃vɛʀtiʀ] vt: ~ qn (à) to convert sb (to); se ~ (à) to be converted (to); ~ qch en to convert sth into

conviction [kɔ̃viksjɔ̃] nf conviction

convienne etc [kɔ̃vjɛn] vb voir **convenir**

convivial, e, -aux [kɔ̃vivjal, jo] adj (Inform) user-friendly

convocation [kɔ̃vɔkasjɔ̃] nf (document) notification to attend; (: Jur) summons sg

convoquer [kɔ̃vɔke] vt (assemblée) to convene; (subordonné) to summon; (candidat) to ask to attend

coopération [kɔɔpeʀasjɔ̃] nf co-operation; (Admin): **la C~** ≈ Voluntary Service Overseas (BRIT), ≈ Peace Corps (US)

coopérer [kɔɔpeʀe] vi: ~ (à) to co-operate (in)

coordonné, e [kɔɔʀdɔne] adj coordinated; **coordonnées** nfpl (adresse etc) address and telephone number

coordonner [kɔɔʀdɔne] vt to coordinate

copain [kɔpɛ̃] (fam) nm mate, pal; (petit ami) boyfriend

copie [kɔpi] nf copy; (Scol) script, paper; **copier** vt, vi to copy; **copier coller** (Comput) copy and paste; **copier sur** to copy from; **copieur** nm (photo)copier

copieux, -euse [kɔpjø, jøz] adj copious

copine [kɔpin] (fam) nf mate, pal; (petite amie) girlfriend

coq [kɔk] nm cock, rooster

coque [kɔk] nf (de noix, mollusque) shell; (de bateau) hull; **à la ~** (Culin) (soft-)boiled

coquelicot [kɔkliko] nm poppy

coqueluche [kɔklyʃ] nf whooping-cough

coquet, te [kɔkɛ, ɛt] adj appearance-conscious; (logement) smart, charming

coquetier [kɔk(ə)tje] nm egg-cup

coquillage [kɔkijaʒ] nm (mollusque) shellfish inv; (coquille) shell

coquille [kɔkij] nf shell; (Typo) misprint; **coquille St Jacques** scallop

coquin, e [kɔkɛ̃, in] adj mischievous, roguish; (polisson) naughty

cor [kɔʀ] nm (Mus) horn; (Méd): ~ (au pied) corn

corail, -aux [kɔʀaj, o] nm coral no pl

Coran [kɔʀɑ̃] nm: **le ~** the Koran

corbeau, x [kɔʀbo] nm crow

corbeille [kɔʀbɛj] nf basket; **corbeille à papier** waste paper basket ou bin

corde [kɔʀd] nf rope; (de violon, raquette) string; **usé jusqu'à la ~** threadbare; **corde à linge** washing ou clothes line; **corde à sauter** skipping rope; **cordes**

vocales vocal cords; **cordée** nf (d'alpinistes) rope, roped party

cordialement [kɔʀdjalmɑ̃] adv (formule épistolaire) (kind) regards

cordon [kɔʀdɔ̃] nm cord, string; **cordon de police** police cordon; **cordon ombilical** umbilical cord

cordonnerie [kɔʀdɔnʀi] nf shoe repairer's (shop); **cordonnier** nm shoe repairer

Corée [kɔʀe] nf: **la ~ du Sud/du Nord** South/North Korea

coriace [kɔʀjas] adj tough

corne [kɔʀn] nf horn; (de cerf) antler

cornée [kɔʀne] nf cornea

corneille [kɔʀnɛj] nf crow

cornemuse [kɔʀnəmyz] nf bagpipes pl

cornet [kɔʀnɛ] nm (paper) cone; (de glace) cornet, cone

corniche [kɔʀniʃ] nf (route) coast road

cornichon [kɔʀniʃɔ̃] nm gherkin

Cornouailles [kɔʀnwaj] nf Cornwall

corporel, le [kɔʀpɔʀel] adj bodily; (punition) corporal

corps [kɔʀ] nm body; **à ~ perdu** headlong; **prendre ~** to take shape; **corps électoral** the electorate; **corps enseignant** the teaching profession

correct, e [kɔʀɛkt] adj correct; (fam: acceptable: salaire, hôtel) reasonable, decent; **correcteur, -trice** nm/f (Scol) examiner; **correction** nf (voir corriger) correction; (voir correct) correctness; (coups) thrashing

correspondance [kɔʀɛspɔ̃dɑ̃s] nf correspondence; (de train, d'avion) connection; **cours par ~** correspondence course; **vente par ~** mail-order business

correspondant, e [kɔʀɛspɔ̃dɑ̃, ɑ̃t] nm/f correspondent; (Tél) person phoning (ou being phoned)

correspondre [kɔʀɛspɔ̃dʀ] vi to correspond, tally; ~ à to correspond to; ~ avec qn to correspond with sb

corrida [kɔʀida] nf bullfight

corridor [kɔʀidɔʀ] nm corridor

corrigé [kɔʀiʒe] nm (Scol: d'exercice) correct version

corriger [kɔʀiʒe] vt (devoir) to correct; (punir) to thrash; ~ qn de (défaut) to cure sb of

corrompre [kɔʀɔ̃pʀ] vt to corrupt; (acheter: témoin etc) to bribe

corruption [kɔʀypsjɔ̃] nf corruption; (de témoins) bribery

corse [kɔʀs] adj, nm/f Corsican ▷ nf: **la C~** Corsica

corsé, e [kɔʀse] adj (café) full-flavoured; (sauce) spicy; (problème) tough

cortège [kɔʀtɛʒ] nm procession

cortisone [kɔʀtizɔn] nf cortisone

corvée [kɔʀve] nf chore, drudgery no pl

cosmétique [kɔsmetik] nm beauty care product

cosmopolite [kɔsmɔpɔlit] adj cosmopolitan

costaud, e [kɔsto, od] (fam) adj strong, sturdy

costume [kɔstym] nm (d'homme) suit; (de théâtre) costume; **costumé, e** adj dressed up; **bal costumé** fancy dress ball

cote [kɔt] nf (en Bourse) quotation; **cote d'alerte** danger ou flood level; **cote de popularité** (popularity) rating

côte [kot] nf (rivage) coast(line); (pente) hill; (Anat) rib; (d'un tricot, tissu) rib, ribbing no pl; **~ à ~** side by side; **la Côte (d'Azur)** the (French) Riviera

côté [kote] nm (gén) side; (direction) way, direction; **de chaque ~ (de)** on each side (of); **de tous les ~s** from all directions; **de quel ~ est-il parti?** which way did he go?; **de ce/de l'autre ~** this/the other way; **du ~ de**

(provenance) from; (direction) towards; (proximité) near; **de ~** (regarder) sideways; **mettre qch de ~** to put sth aside; **mettre de l'argent de ~** to save some money; **à ~** (right) nearby; (voisins) next door; **à ~ de** beside, next to; (en comparaison) compared to; **être aux ~s de** to be by the side of

Côte d'Ivoire [kotdivwar] nf: **la Côte d'Ivoire** Côte d'Ivoire, the Ivory Coast

côtelette [kotlɛt] nf chop

côtier, -ière [kotje, jɛʀ] adj coastal

cotisation [kotizasjɔ̃] nf subscription, dues pl; (pour une pension) contributions pl

cotiser [kotize] vi: **~ (à)** to pay contributions (to); **se ~** vi to club together

coton [kotɔ̃] nm cotton; **coton hydrophile** cotton wool (BRIT), absorbent cotton (US); **Coton-tige®** nm cotton bud

cou [ku] nm neck

couchant [kuʃɑ̃] adj: **soleil ~** setting sun

couche [kuʃ] nf layer; (de peinture, vernis) coat; (de bébé) nappy (BRIT), diaper (US); **couches sociales** social levels ou strata

couché, e [kuʃe] adj lying down; (au lit) in bed

coucher [kuʃe] vt (personne) to put to bed; (: loger) to put up; (objet) to lay on its side ▷ vi to sleep; **~ avec qn** to sleep with sb; **se ~** vi (pour dormir) to go to bed; (pour se reposer) to lie down; (soleil) to set; **coucher de soleil** sunset

couchette [kuʃɛt] nf couchette; (pour voyageur, sur bateau) berth

coucou [kuku] nm cuckoo

coude [kud] nm (Anat) elbow; (de tuyau, de la route) bend; **~ à ~** shoulder to shoulder, side by side

coudre [kudʀ] vt (bouton) to sew on ▷ vi to sew

couette [kwɛt] nf duvet, quilt; **couettes** nfpl (cheveux) bunches

couffin [kufɛ̃] nm Moses basket

couler [kule] vi to flow, run; (fuir: stylo, récipient) to leak; (nez) to run; (sombrer: bateau) to sink ▷ vt (cloche, sculpture) to cast; (bateau) to sink; (faire échouer: personne) to bring down

couleur [kulœʀ] nf colour (BRIT), color (US); (Cartes) suit; **film/télévision en ~s** colo(u)r film/television; **de ~** (homme, femme: vieilli) colo(u)red

couleuvre [kulœvʀ] nf grass snake

coulisses [kulis] nfpl (Théâtre) wings; (fig): **dans les ~** behind the scenes

couloir [kulwaʀ] nm corridor, passage; (d'avion) aisle; (de bus) gangway; **~ aérien/de navigation** air/shipping lane

coup [ku] nm (heurt, choc) knock; (affectif) blow, shock; (agressif) blow; (avec arme à feu) shot; (de l'horloge) stroke; (tennis, golf) stroke; (boxe) blow; (fam: fois) time; **donner un ~ de balai** to give the floor a sweep; **boire un ~** (fam) to have a drink; **être dans le ~** (impliqué) to be in on it; (à la page) to be hip ou trendy; **du ~ ...** as a result; **d'un seul ~** (subitement) suddenly; (à la fois) at one go; **du premier ~** first time; **du même ~** at the same time; **à tous les ~s** (fam) every time; **tenir le ~** to hold out; **après ~** afterwards; **à ~ sûr** definitely, without fail; **~ sur ~** in quick succession; **sur le ~** outright; **sous le ~ de** (surprise etc) under the influence of; **coup de chance** stroke of luck; **coup de coude** nudge (with the elbow); **coup de couteau** stab (of a knife); **coup d'envoi** kick-off;

coup d'essai first attempt; **coup d'État** coup; **coup de feu** shot; **coup de filet** (Police) haul; **coup de foudre** (fig) love at first sight; **coup de frein** (sharp) braking no pl; **coup de grâce** coup de grâce, death blow; **coup de main: donner un coup de main à qn** to give sb a (helping) hand; **coup d'œil** glance; **coup de pied** kick; **coup de poing** punch; **coup de soleil** sunburn no pl; **coup de sonnette** ring of the bell; **coup de téléphone** phone call; **coup de tête** (fig) (sudden) impulse; **coup de théâtre** (fig) dramatic turn of events; **coup de tonnerre** clap of thunder; **coup de vent** gust of wind; **en coup de vent** (rapidement) in a tearing hurry; **coup franc** free kick

coupable [kupabl] adj guilty ▷ nm/f (gén) culprit; (Jur) guilty party

coupe [kup] nf (verre) goblet; (à fruits) dish; (Sport) cup; (de cheveux, de vêtement) cut; (graphique, plan) (cross) section

couper [kupe] vt to cut; (retrancher) to cut (out); (route, courant) to cut off; (appétit) to take away; (vin à table) to dilute ▷ vi to cut; (prendre un raccourci) to take a short-cut; **se ~** vi (se blesser) to cut o.s.; **~ la parole à qn** to cut sb short; **nous avons été coupés** we've been cut off

couple [kupl] nm couple

couplet [kuplɛ] nm verse

coupole [kupɔl] nf dome

coupon [kupɔ̃] nm (ticket) coupon; (reste de tissu) remnant

coupure [kupyʀ] nf cut; (billet de banque) note; (de journal) cutting; **coupure de courant** power cut

cour [kuʀ] nf (de ferme, jardin) (court)yard; (d'immeuble) back yard; (Jur, royale) court; **faire la ~ à qn** to court sb; **cour d'assises** court of assizes; **cour de récréation** playground

courage [kuʀaʒ] nm courage, bravery; **courageux, -euse** adj brave, courageous

couramment [kuʀamɑ̃] adv commonly; (parler) fluently

courant, e [kuʀɑ̃, ɑ̃t] adj (fréquent) common; (Comm, gén: normal) standard; (en cours) current ▷ nm current; (fig) movement; (: d'opinion) trend; **être au ~ (de)** (fait, nouvelle) to know (about); **mettre qn au ~ (de)** to tell sb (about); **se tenir au ~ (de)** (techniques etc) to keep o.s. up-to-date (on); **dans le ~ (de)** (pendant) in the course of; **le 10 ~** (Comm) the 10th inst.; **courant d'air** draught; **courant électrique** (electric) current, power

courbature [kuʀbatyʀ] nf ache

courbe [kuʀb] adj curved ▷ nf curve

coureur, -euse [kuʀœʀ, øz] nm/f (Sport) runner (ou driver); (péj) womanizer; manhunter

courge [kuʀʒ] nf (Culin) marrow; **courgette** nf courgette (BRIT), zucchini (US)

courir [kuʀiʀ] vi to run ▷ vt (Sport: épreuve) to compete in; (risque) to run; (danger) to face; **~ les magasins** to go round the shops; **le bruit court que** the rumour is going round that

couronne [kuʀɔn] nf crown; (de fleurs) wreath, circlet

courons etc [kuʀɔ̃] vb voir **courir**

courriel [kuʀjɛl] nm e-mail

courrier [kuʀje] nm mail, post; (lettres à écrire) letters pl; **est-ce que j'ai du ~?** are there any letters for me?; **courrier électronique** e-mail

courroie [kuʀwa] nf strap; (Tech) belt

courrons etc [kuʀɔ̃] vb voir **courir**

cours [kuʀ] nm (leçon) class; (: particulier) lesson; (série de leçons, cheminement) course; (écoulement) flow; (Comm: de devises) rate; (: de denrées) price; **donner libre ~ à** to give free expression to; **avoir ~** (Scol) to have a class ou lecture; **en ~** (année) current; (travaux) in progress; **en ~ de route** on the way; **au ~ de** in the course of, during; **le ~ de change** the exchange rate; **cours d'eau** waterway; **cours du soir** night school

course [kuʀs] nf running; (Sport: épreuve) race; (d'un taxi) journey, trip; (commission) errand; **courses** nfpl (achats) shopping sg; **faire des ~s** to do some shopping

court, e [kuʀ, kuʀt(ə)] adj short ▷ adv short ▷ nm: **~ (de tennis)** (tennis) court; **à ~ de** short of; **prendre qn de ~** to catch sb unawares; **court-circuit** nm short-circuit

courtoisie [kuʀtwazi] nf courtesy

couru, e [kuʀy] pp de **courir**

cousais etc [kuze] vb voir **coudre**

couscous [kuskus] nm couscous

cousin, e [kuzɛ̃, in] nm/f cousin

coussin [kusɛ̃] nm cushion

cousu, e [kuzy] pp de **coudre**

coût [ku] nm cost; **le ~ de la vie** the cost of living

couteau, x [kuto] nm knife

coûter [kute] vt, vi to cost; **combien ça coûte?** how much is it?, what does it cost?; **ça coûte trop cher** it's too expensive; **coûte que coûte** at all costs; **coûteux, -euse** adj costly, expensive

coutume [kutym] nf custom

couture [kutyʀ] nf sewing; (profession) dressmaking; (points) seam; **couturier** nm fashion designer; **couturière** nf dressmaker

couvent [kuvã] nm (de sœurs) convent; (de frères) monastery

couver [kuve] vt to hatch; (maladie) to be coming down with ▷ vi (feu) to smoulder; (révolte) to be brewing

couvercle [kuvɛʀkl] nm lid; (de bombe aérosol etc, qui se visse) cap, top

couvert, e [kuvɛʀ, ɛʀt] pp de **couvrir** ▷ adj (ciel) overcast ▷ nm place setting; (place à table) place; **couverts** nmpl (ustensiles) cutlery sg; **~ de** covered with ou in; **mettre le ~** to lay the table

couverture [kuvɛʀtyʀ] nf blanket; (de livre, assurance, fig) cover; (presse) coverage

couvre-lit [kuvʀəli] nm bedspread

couvrir [kuvʀiʀ] vt to cover; **se ~** vi (s'habiller) to cover up; (se coiffer) to put on one's hat; (ciel) to cloud over

cow-boy [kɔbɔj] nm cowboy

crabe [kʀab] nm crab

cracher [kʀaʃe] vi, vt to spit

crachin [kʀaʃɛ̃] nm drizzle

craie [kʀɛ] nf chalk

craindre [kʀɛ̃dʀ] vt to fear, be afraid of; (être sensible à: chaleur, froid) to be easily damaged by

crainte [kʀɛ̃t] nf fear; **de ~ de/que** for fear of/that; **craintif, -ive** adj timid

crampe [kʀãp] nf cramp; **j'ai une ~ à la jambe** I've got cramp in my leg

cramponner [kʀãpɔne] vb: **se ~ (à)** to hang ou cling on (to)

cran [kʀã] nm (entaille) notch; (de courroie) hole; (fam: courage) guts pl

crâne [kʀan] nm skull

crapaud [kʀapo] nm toad

craquement [kʀakmã] nm crack, snap; (du plancher) creak, creaking no pl

craquer [kʀake] vi (bois, plancher) to creak; (fil, branche) to snap; (couture) to come apart; (fig: accusé) to break down; (: fam) to crack up ▷ vt (allumette) to strike; **j'ai craqué** (fam) I couldn't resist it

crasse [kʀas] nf grime, filth; **crasseux, -euse** adj grimy, filthy

cravache [kʀavaʃ] nf (riding) crop

cravate [kʀavat] nf tie

crawl [kʀol] nm crawl; **dos ~é** backstroke

crayon [kʀɛjɔ̃] nm pencil; **crayon à bille** ball-point pen; **crayon de couleur** crayon, colouring pencil; **crayon-feutre** (pl **crayons-feutres**) nm felt(-tip) pen

création [kʀeasjɔ̃] nf creation

crèche [kʀɛʃ] nf (de Noël) crib; (garderie) crèche, day nursery

crédit [kʀedi] nm (gén) credit; **crédits** nmpl (fonds) funds; **payer/acheter à ~** to pay/buy on credit ou on easy terms; **faire ~ à qn** to give sb credit; **créditer** vt: **créditer un compte (de)** to credit an account (with)

créer [kʀee] vt to create

crémaillère [kʀemajɛʀ] nf: **pendre la ~** to have a house-warming party

crème [kʀɛm] nf cream; (entremets) cream dessert ▷ adj inv cream(-coloured); **un (café) ~** ≈ a white coffee; **crème anglaise** (egg) custard; **crème Chantilly** whipped cream; **crème à raser** shaving cream; **crème solaire** suntan lotion

créneau, x [kʀeno] nm (de fortification) crenel(le); (dans marché) gap, niche; (Auto): **faire un ~** to reverse into a parking space (between two cars alongside the kerb)

crêpe [kʀɛp] nf (galette) pancake ▷ nm (tissu) crêpe; **crêperie** nf pancake shop ou restaurant

crépuscule [kʀepyskyl] nm twilight, dusk

cresson [kʀesɔ̃] nm watercress

creuser [kʀøze] vt (trou, tunnel) to dig; (sol) to dig a hole in; (fig) to go (deeply) into; **ça creuse** that gives you a real appetite; **se ~ la cervelle** (fam) to rack one's brains

creux, -euse [kʀø, kʀøz] adj hollow ▷ nm hollow; **heures creuses** slack periods; (électricité, téléphone) off-peak periods; **avoir un ~** (fam) to be hungry

crevaison [kʀəvɛzɔ̃] nf puncture

crevé, e [kʀəve] (fam) adj (fatigué) shattered (BRIT), exhausted

crever [kʀəve] vt (ballon) to burst ▷ vi (pneu) to burst; (automobiliste) to have a puncture (BRIT) ou a flat (tire) (US); (fam) to die

crevette [kʀəvɛt] nf: **~ (rose)** prawn; **crevette grise** shrimp

cri [kʀi] nm cry, shout; (d'animal: spécifique) cry, call; **c'est le dernier ~** (fig) it's the latest fashion

criard, e [kʀijaʀ, kʀijaʀd] adj (couleur) garish, loud; (voix) yelling

cric [kʀik] nm (Auto) jack

crier [kʀije] vi (pour appeler) to shout, cry (out); (de douleur etc) to scream, yell ▷ vt (injure) to shout (out), yell (out)

crime [kʀim] nm crime; (meurtre) murder; **criminel, le** nm/f criminal; (assassin) murderer

crin [kʀɛ̃] nm (de cheval) hair no pl

crinière [kʀinjɛʀ] nf mane

crique [kʀik] nf creek, inlet

criquet [kʀike] nm grasshopper

crise [kʀiz] nf crisis; (Méd) attack; (d'épilepsie) fit; **piquer une ~ de nerfs** to go hysterical; **crise cardiaque** heart attack; **crise de foie: avoir une crise de foie** to have really bad indigestion

cristal, -aux [kʀistal, o] nm crystal

critère [kʀitɛʀ] nm criterion

critiquable [kʀitikabl] adj open to criticism

critique [kʀitik] adj critical ▷ nm/f (de théâtre, musique) critic ▷ nf criticism; (Théâtre etc: article) review

critiquer [kʀitike] vt (dénigrer) to criticize; (évaluer) to assess, examine (critically)

croate [kʀɔat] adj Croatian ▷ nm/f: **C~** Croat, Croatian

Croatie [kʀɔasi] nf: **la ~** Croatia

crochet [kʀɔʃɛ] nm hook; (détour) detour; (Tricot: aiguille) crochet hook; (: technique) crochet; **vivre aux ~s de qn** to live ou sponge off sb

crocodile [kʀɔkɔdil] nm crocodile

croire [kʀwaʀ] vt to believe; **se ~ fort** to think one is strong; **~ que** to believe ou think that; **~ à, ~ en** to believe in

croisade [kʀwazad] nf crusade

croisement [kʀwazmɑ̃] nm (carrefour) crossroads sg; (Bio) crossing; (: résultat) crossbreed

croiser [kʀwaze] vt (personne, voiture) to pass; (route) to cross, cut across; (Bio) to cross; **se ~** vi (personnes, véhicules) to pass each other; (routes, lettres) to cross; (regards) to meet; **~ les jambes/bras** to cross one's legs/fold one's arms

croisière [kʀwazjɛʀ] nf cruise

croissance [kʀwasɑ̃s] nf growth

croissant [kʀwasɑ̃] nm (à manger) croissant; (motif) crescent

croître [kʀwatʀ] vi to grow

croix [kʀwa] nf cross; **la Croix Rouge** the Red Cross

croque-monsieur [kʀɔkməsjø] nm inv toasted ham and cheese sandwich

croquer [kʀɔke] vt (manger) to crunch; (: fruit) to munch; (dessiner) to sketch; **chocolat à croquer** plain dessert chocolate

croquis [kʀɔki] nm sketch

crotte [kʀɔt] nf droppings pl; **crottin** nm dung, manure; (fromage) (small round) cheese (made of goat's milk)

croustillant, e [kʀustijɑ̃, ɑ̃t] adj crisp

croûte [kʀut] nf crust; (du fromage) rind; (Méd) scab; **en ~** (Culin) in pastry

croûton [kʀutɔ̃] nm (Culin) crouton; (bout du pain) crust, heel

croyant, e [kʀwajɑ̃, ɑ̃t] nm/f believer

CRS sigle fpl (= Compagnies républicaines de sécurité) state security police force ▷ sigle m member of the CRS

cru, e [kʀy] pp de **croire** ▷ adj (non cuit) raw; (lumière, couleur) harsh; (paroles) crude ▷ nm (vignoble) vineyard; (vin) wine; **un grand ~** a great vintage; **jambon ~** Parma ham

crû [kʀy] pp de **croître**

cruauté [kʀyote] nf cruelty

cruche [kʀyʃ] nf pitcher, jug

crucifix [kʀysifi] nm crucifix

crudités [kʀydite] nfpl (Culin) selection of raw vegetables

crue [kʀy] nf (inondation) flood

cruel, le [kʀyɛl] adj cruel

crus etc [kʀy] vb voir **croire**; **croître**

crûs etc [kʀy] vb voir **croître**

crustacés [kʀystase] nmpl shellfish

Cuba [kyba] nf Cuba; **cubain, e** adj Cuban ▷ nm/f:

Cubain, e Cuban

cube [kyb] nm cube; (jouet) brick; **mètre ~** cubic metre; **2 au ~** 2 cubed

cueillette [kœjɛt] nf picking; (quantité) crop, harvest

cueillir [kœjiʀ] vt (fruits, fleurs) to pick, gather; (fig) to catch

cuiller [kɥijɛʀ], **cuillère** [kɥijɛʀ] nf spoon; **cuiller à café** coffee spoon; (Culin) ≈ teaspoonful; **cuiller à soupe** soup-spoon; (Culin) ≈ tablespoonful; **cuillerée** nf spoonful

cuir [kɥiʀ] nm leather; **cuir chevelu** scalp

cuire [kɥiʀ] vt to cook; (au four) to bake ▷ vi to cook; **bien cuit** (viande) well done; **trop cuit** overdone

cuisine [kɥizin] nf (pièce) kitchen; (art culinaire) cookery, cooking; (nourriture) cooking, food; **faire la ~** to cook; **cuisiné, e** adj: **plat cuisiné** ready-made meal ou dish; **cuisiner** vt to cook; (fam) to grill ▷ vi to cook; **cuisinier, -ière** nm/f cook ▷ nf (poêle) cooker

cuisse [kɥis] nf thigh; (Culin) leg

cuisson [kɥisɔ̃] nf cooking

cuit, e [kɥi, kɥit] pp de **cuire**

cuivre [kɥivʀ] nm copper; **les cuivres** (Mus) the brass

cul [ky] (fam!) nm arse (!)

culminant, e [kylminɑ̃, ɑ̃t] adj: **point ~** highest point

culot [kylo] (fam) nm (effronterie) cheek

culotte [kylɔt] nf (de femme) knickers pl (BRIT), panties pl (US)

culte [kylt] nm (religion) religion; (hommage, vénération) worship; (protestant) service

cultivateur, -trice [kyltivatœʀ, tʀis] nm/f farmer

cultivé, e [kyltive] adj (personne) cultured, cultivated

cultiver [kyltive] vt to cultivate; (légumes) to grow, cultivate

culture [kyltyʀ] nf cultivation; (connaissances etc) culture; **les ~s intensives** intensive farming; **culture physique** physical training; **culturel, le** adj cultural

cumin [kymɛ̃] nm cumin

cure [kyʀ] nf (Méd) course of treatment; **cure d'amaigrissement** slimming (BRIT) ou weight-loss (US) course; **cure de repos** rest cure

curé [kyʀe] nm parish priest

cure-dent [kyʀdɑ̃] nm toothpick

curieux, -euse [kyʀjø, jøz] adj (indiscret) curious, inquisitive; (étrange) strange, curious ▷ nmpl (badauds) onlookers; **curiosité** nf curiosity; (site) unusual feature

curriculum vitae [kyʀikylɔmvite] nm inv curriculum vitae

cutané, e [kytane] adj skin

cuve [kyv] nf vat; (à mazout etc) tank

cuvée [kyve] nf vintage

cuvette [kyvɛt] nf (récipient) bowl, basin; (Géo) basin

CV sigle m (Auto) = **cheval vapeur**; (Comm) = **curriculum vitae**

cybercafé [sibɛʀkafe] nm Internet café

cyberespace [sibɛʀɛspas] nm cyberspace

cybernaute [sibɛʀnot] nm/f Internet user

cyclable [siklabl] adj: **piste ~** cycle track

cycle [sikl] nm cycle; **cyclisme** nm cycling; **cycliste** nm/f cyclist ▷ adj cycle cpd; **coureur cycliste** racing cyclist

cyclomoteur [siklomotœʀ] nm moped

cyclone [siklon] nm hurricane

cygne [siɲ] nm swan

cylindre [silɛ̃dʀ] nm cylinder; **cylindrée** nf (Auto) (cubic) capacity; **une (voiture de) grosse cylindrée** a big-engined car

cymbale [sɛ̃bal] nf cymbal
cynique [sinik] adj cynical
cystite [sistit] nf cystitis

d

d' [d] prép voir **de**
dactylo [daktilo] nf (aussi: **~graphe**) typist; (aussi: **~graphie**) typing
dada [dada] nm hobby-horse
daim [dɛ̃] nm (fallow) deer inv; (cuir suédé) suede
daltonien, ne [daltɔnjɛ̃, jɛn] adj colour-blind
dame [dam] nf lady; (Cartes, Échecs) queen; **dames** nfpl (jeu) draughts sg (BRIT), checkers sg (US)
Danemark [danmark] nm Denmark
danger [dɑ̃ʒe] nm danger; **être en ~** (personne) to be in danger; **mettre en ~** (personne) to put in danger; (projet, carrière) to jeopardize; **dangereux, -euse** adj dangerous
danois, e [danwa, waz] adj Danish ▷ nm/f: **D~, e** Dane ▷ nm (Ling) Danish

 MOT-CLÉ

dans [dɑ̃] prép 1 (position) in; (à l'intérieur de) inside; **c'est dans le tiroir/le salon** it's in the drawer/lounge; **dans la boîte** in ou inside the box; **je l'ai lu dans le journal** I read it in the newspaper; **marcher dans la ville** to walk about the town
2 (direction) into; **elle a couru dans le salon** she ran into the lounge; **monter dans une voiture/le bus** to get into a car/on to the bus
3 (provenance) out of, from; **je l'ai pris dans le tiroir/salon** I took it out of ou from the drawer/lounge; **boire dans un verre** to drink out of ou from a glass
4 (temps) in; **dans 2 mois** in 2 months, in 2 months' time

5 (approximation) about; **dans les 20 euros** about 20 euros

danse [dɑ̃s] nf: **la ~** dancing; **une ~** a dance; **la ~ classique** ballet; **danser** vi, vt to dance; **danseur, -euse** nm/f ballet dancer; (au bal etc) dancer; (: cavalier) partner
date [dat] nf date; **de longue ~** longstanding; **date de naissance** date of birth; **date limite** deadline; **dater** vt, vi to date; **dater de** to date from; **à dater de** (as) from
datte [dat] nf date
dauphin [dofɛ̃] nm (Zool) dolphin
davantage [davɑ̃taʒ] adv more; (plus longtemps) longer; **~ de** more

 MOT-CLÉ

de, d' [də] (de +le = **du**, de +les = **des**) prép 1 (appartenance) of; **le toit de la maison** the roof of the house; **la voiture d'Ann/de mes parents** Ann's/my parents' car
2 (provenance) from; **il vient de Londres** he comes from London; **elle est sortie du cinéma** she came out of the cinema
3 (caractérisation, mesure): **un mur de brique/bureau d'acajou** a brick wall/mahogany desk; **un billet de 50 euros** a 50 euro note; **une pièce de 2 m de large** ou **large de 2 m** a room 2m wide, a 2m-wide room; **un bébé de 10 mois** a 10-month-old baby; **12 mois de crédit/travail** 12 months' credit/work; **être payé 20 euros de l'heure** to be paid 20 euros an ou per hour; **augmenter de 10 euros** to increase by 10 euros; **de 14 à 18** from 14 to 18
4 (moyen) with; **je l'ai fait de mes propres mains** I did it with my own two hands
5 (cause): **mourir de faim** to die of hunger; **rouge de colère** red with fury
6 (devant infinitif) to; **il m'a dit de rester** he told me to stay
▷ dét 1 (phrases affirmatives) some (souvent omis); **du vin, de l'eau, des pommes** (some) wine, (some) water, (some) apples; **des enfants sont venus** some children came; **pendant des mois** for months
2 (phrases interrogatives et négatives) any; **a-t-il du vin?** has he got any wine? **il n'a pas de pommes/d'enfants** he hasn't (got) any apples/children, he has no apples/children

dé [de] nm (à jouer) die ou dice; (aussi: **dé à coudre**) thimble
déballer [debale] vt to unpack
débarcadère [debarkadɛr] nm wharf
débardeur [debardœr] nm (maillot) tank top
débarquer [debarke] vt to unload, land ▷ vi to disembark; (fig: fam) to turn up
débarras [debaʀa] nm (pièce) lumber room; (placard) junk cupboard; **bon ~!** good riddance!; **débarrasser** vt to clear; **se débarrasser de** vt to get rid of; **débarrasser qn de** (vêtements, paquets) to relieve sb of; **débarrasser (la table)** to clear the table
débat [deba] nm discussion, debate; **débattre** vt to discuss, debate; **se débattre** vi to struggle
débit [debi] nm (d'un liquide, fleuve) flow; (d'un magasin) turnover (of goods); (élocution) delivery; (bancaire) debit; **débit de boissons** drinking establishment; **débit de tabac** tobacconist's

déblayer [debleje] vt to clear

débloquer [debloke] vt (prix, crédits) to free

déboîter [debwate] vt (Auto) to pull out; **se ~ le genou** etc to dislocate one's knee etc

débordé, e [deborde] adj: **être ~ (de)** (travail, demandes) to be snowed under (with)

déborder [deborde] vi to overflow; (lait etc) to boil over; **~ (de) qch** (dépasser) to extend beyond sth; **~ de** (joie, zèle) to be brimming over with ou bursting with

débouché [debuʃe] nm (pour vendre) outlet; (perspective d'emploi) opening

déboucher [debuʃe] vt (évier, tuyau etc) to unblock; (bouteille) to uncork ▷ vi: **~ de** to emerge from; **~ sur** (études) to lead on to

debout [d(ə)bu] adv: **être ~** (personne) to be standing, stand; (: levé, éveillé) to be up; **se mettre ~** to stand up; **se tenir ~** to stand; **~!** stand up!; (du lit) get up!; **cette histoire ne tient pas ~** this story doesn't hold water

déboutonner [debutɔne] vt to undo, unbutton

débraillé, e [debraje] adj slovenly, untidy

débrancher [debrɑ̃ʃe] vt to disconnect; (appareil électrique) to unplug

débrayage [debrɛjaʒ] nm (Auto) clutch; **débrayer** vi (Auto) to declutch; (cesser le travail) to stop work

débris [debri] nmpl fragments; **des ~ de verre** bits of glass

débrouillard, e [debrujar, ard] (fam) adj smart, resourceful

débrouiller [debruje] vt to disentangle, untangle; **se ~** vi to manage; **débrouillez-vous** you'll have to sort things out yourself

début [deby] nm beginning, start; **débuts** nmpl (de carrière) début sg; **~ juin** in early June; **débutant, e** nm/f beginner, novice; **débuter** vi to begin, start; (faire ses débuts) to start out

décaféiné, e [dekafeine] adj decaffeinated

décalage [dekalaʒ] nm gap; **décalage horaire** time difference

décaler [dekale] vt to shift

décapotable [dekapɔtabl] adj convertible

décapsuleur [dekapsylœr] nm bottle-opener

décédé, e [desede] adj deceased

décéder [desede] vi to die

décembre [desɑ̃br] nm December

décennie [deseni] nf decade

décent, e [desɑ̃, ɑ̃t] adj decent

déception [desɛpsjɔ̃] nf disappointment

décès [desɛ] nm death

décevoir [des(ə)vwar] vt to disappoint

décharge [deʃarʒ] nf (dépôt d'ordures) rubbish tip ou dump; (électrique) electrical discharge; **décharger** vt (marchandise, véhicule) to unload; (tirer) to discharge; **décharger qn de** (responsabilité) to relieve sb of, release sb from

déchausser [deʃose] vt (skis) to take off; **se ~** vi to take off one's shoes; (dent) to come ou work loose

déchet [deʃɛ] nm (reste) scrap; **déchets** nmpl (ordures) refuse sg, rubbish sg; **~s nucléaires** nuclear waste

déchiffrer [deʃifre] vt to decipher

déchirant, e [deʃirɑ̃, ɑ̃t] adj heart-rending

déchirement [deʃirmɑ̃] nm (chagrin) wrench, heartbreak; (gén pl: conflit) rift, split

déchirer [deʃire] vt to tear; (en morceaux) to tear up; (arracher) to tear out; (fig: conflit) to tear (apart); **se ~** vi

to tear, rip; **se ~ un muscle** to tear a muscle

déchirure [deʃiryr] nf (accroc) tear, rip; **déchirure musculaire** torn muscle

décidé, e [deside] adj (personne, air) determined; **c'est ~** it's decided; **décidément** adv really

décider [deside] vt: **~ qch** to decide on sth; **~ de faire/que** to decide to do/that; **~ qn (à faire qch)** to persuade sb (to do sth); **se ~ (à faire)** to decide (to do), make up one's mind (to do); **se ~ pour** to decide on ou in favour of

décimal, e, -aux [desimal, o] adj decimal

décimètre [desimɛtr] nm decimetre

décisif, -ive [desizif, iv] adj decisive

décision [desizjɔ̃] nf decision

déclaration [deklarasjɔ̃] nf declaration; (discours: Pol etc) statement; **déclaration d'impôts** ou **de revenus** = tax return; **déclaration de vol: faire une déclaration de vol** to report a theft

déclarer [deklare] vt to declare; (décès, naissance) to register; **se ~** vi (feu) to break out

déclencher [deklɑ̃ʃe] vt (mécanisme etc) to release; (sonnerie) to set off; (attaque, grève) to launch; (provoquer) to trigger off; **se ~** vi (sonnerie) to go off

décliner [dekline] vi to decline ▷ vt (invitation) to decline; (nom, adresse) to state

décoiffer [dekwafe] vt: **~ qn** to mess up sb's hair; **je suis toute décoiffée** my hair is in a real mess

déçois etc [deswa] vb voir **décevoir**

décollage [dekɔlaʒ] nm (Aviat) takeoff

décoller [dekɔle] vt to unstick ▷ vi (avion) to take off; **se ~** vi to come unstuck

décolleté, e [dekɔlte] adj low-cut ▷ nm low neck(line); (plongeant) cleavage

décolorer [dekɔlɔre]: **se ~** vi to fade; **se faire ~ les cheveux** to have one's hair bleached

décommander [dekɔmɑ̃de] vt to cancel; **se ~** vi to cry off

déconcerter [dekɔ̃sɛrte] vt to disconcert, confound

décongeler [dekɔ̃ʒ(ə)le] vt to thaw

déconner [dekɔne] (fam) vi to talk rubbish

déconseiller [dekɔ̃seje] vt: **~ qch (à qn)** to advise (sb) against sth; **c'est déconseillé** it's not recommended

décontracté, e [dekɔ̃trakte] adj relaxed, laid-back (fam)

décontracter [dekɔ̃trakte]: **se ~** vi to relax

décor [dekɔr] nm décor; (paysage) scenery; **décorateur** nm (interior) decorator; **décoration** nf decoration; **décorer** vt to decorate

décortiquer [dekɔrtike] vt to shell; (fig: texte) to dissect

découdre [dekudr]: **se ~** vi to come unstitched

découper [dekupe] vt (papier, tissu etc) to cut up; (viande) to carve; (article) to cut out

décourager [dekuraʒe] vt to discourage; **se ~** vi to lose heart, become discouraged

décousu, e [dekuzy] adj unstitched; (fig) disjointed, disconnected

découvert, e [dekuvɛr, ɛrt] adj (tête) bare, uncovered; (lieu) open, exposed ▷ nm (bancaire) overdraft; **découverte** nf discovery; **faire la découverte de** to discover

découvrir [dekuvrir] vt to discover; (enlever ce qui couvre) to uncover; (dévoiler) to reveal; **se ~** vi (chapeau) to take off one's hat; (vêtement) to take something off; (ciel) to clear

décrire [dekʀiʀ] vt to describe
décrocher [dekʀɔʃe] vt (détacher) to take down; (téléphone) to take off the hook; (: pour répondre) to lift the receiver; (: fam: contrat etc) to get, land ▷ vi (fam: abandonner) to drop out; (: cesser d'écouter) to switch off
déçu, e [desy] pp de **décevoir**
dédaigner [dedɛɲe] vt to despise, scorn; (négliger) to disregard, spurn; **dédaigneux, -euse** adj scornful, disdainful; **dédain** nm scorn, disdain
dedans [dədɑ̃] adv inside; (pas en plein air) indoors, inside ▷ nm inside; **au ~** inside
dédicacer [dedikase] vt: **~ (à qn)** to sign (for sb), autograph (for sb)
dédier [dedje] vt: **~ à** to dedicate to
dédommagement [dedɔmaʒmɑ̃] nm compensation
dédommager [dedɔmaʒe] vt: **~ qn (de)** to compensate sb (for)
dédouaner [dedwane] vt to clear through customs
déduire [dedɥiʀ] vt: **~ qch (de)** (ôter) to deduct sth (from); (conclure) to deduce ou infer sth (from)
défaillance [defajɑ̃s] nf (syncope) (fatigue) (sudden) weakness no pl; (technique) fault, failure; **défaillance cardiaque** heart failure
défaire [defɛʀ] vt to undo; (installation) to take down, dismantle; **se ~** vi to come undone; **se ~ de** to get rid of
défait, e [defɛ, ɛt] adj (visage) haggard, ravaged; **défaite** nf defeat
défaut [defo] nm (moral) fault, failing, defect; (tissus) fault, flaw; (manque, carence): **~ de** shortage of; **prendre qn en ~** to catch sb out; **faire ~** (manquer) to be lacking; **à ~ de** for lack ou want of
défavorable [defavɔʀabl] adj unfavourable (BRIT), unfavorable (US)
défavoriser [defavɔʀize] vt to put at a disadvantage
défectueux, -euse [defɛktɥø, øz] adj faulty, defective
défendre [defɑ̃dʀ] vt to defend; (interdire) to forbid; **se ~** vi to defend o.s.; **~ à qn qch/de faire** to forbid sb sth/to do; **il se défend** (fam: se débrouille) he can hold his own; **se ~ de/contre** (se protéger) to protect o.s. from/against; **se ~ de** (se garder de) to refrain from
défense [defɑ̃s] nf defence; (d'éléphant etc) tusk; **ministre de la ~** Minister of Defence (BRIT), Defense Secretary (US); **"~ de fumer"** "no smoking"
défi [defi] nm challenge; **lancer un ~ à qn** to challenge sb; **sur un ton de ~** defiantly
déficit [defisit] nm (Comm) deficit
défier [defje] vt (provoquer) to challenge; (mort, autorité) to defy; **~ qn de faire qch** to challenge ou defy sb to do sth
défigurer [defigyʀe] vt to disfigure
défilé [defile] nm (Géo) (narrow) gorge ou pass; (soldats) parade; (manifestants) procession, march
défiler [defile] vi (troupes) to march past; (sportifs) to parade; (manifestants) to march; (visiteurs) to pour, stream; **faire ~ un document** (Comput) to scroll a document; **se ~** vi: **il s'est défilé** (fam) he wriggled out of it
définir [definiʀ] vt to define
définitif, -ive [definitif, iv] adj (final) final, definitive; (pour longtemps) permanent, definitive; (refus) definite; **définitive** nf: **en définitive** eventually; (somme toute) in fact; **définitivement** adv (partir, s'installer) for good
déformer [defɔʀme] vt to put out of shape; (pensée, fait) to distort; **se ~** vi to lose its shape

défouler [defule]: **se ~** vi to unwind, let off steam
défunt, e [defœ̃, œ̃t] adj (mort) late before n ▷ nm/f deceased
dégagé, e [degaʒe] adj (route, ciel) clear; **sur un ton ~** casually
dégager [degaʒe] vt (exhaler) to give off; (délivrer) to free, extricate; (désencombrer) to clear; (isoler: idée, aspect) to bring out; **~ qn de** (engagement, parole etc) to release ou free sb from; **se ~** vi (passage, ciel) to clear
dégâts [dega] nmpl damage sg; **faire des ~** to cause damage
dégel [deʒɛl] nm thaw; **dégeler** vt to thaw (out)
dégivrer [deʒivʀe] vt (frigo) to defrost; (vitres) to de-ice
dégonflé, e [degɔ̃fle] adj (pneu) flat
dégonfler [degɔ̃fle] vt (pneu, ballon) to let down, deflate; **se ~** vi (fam) to chicken out
dégouliner [deguline] vi to trickle, drip
dégourdi, e [deguʀdi] adj smart, resourceful
dégourdir [deguʀdiʀ] vt: **se ~ les jambes** to stretch one's legs (fig)
dégoût [degu] nm disgust, distaste; **dégoûtant, e** adj disgusting; **dégoûté, e** adj disgusted; **dégoûté de** sick of; **dégoûter** vt to disgust; **dégoûter qn de qch** to put sb off sth
dégrader [degʀade] vt (Mil: officier) to degrade; (abîmer) to damage, deface; **se ~** vi (relations, situation) to deteriorate
degré [dəgʀe] nm degree
dégressif, -ive [degʀesif, iv] adj on a decreasing scale
dégringoler [degʀɛ̃gɔle] vi to tumble (down)
déguisement [degizmɑ̃] nm (pour s'amuser) fancy dress
déguiser [degize]: **se ~ (en)** vi (se costumer) to dress up (as); (pour tromper) to disguise o.s. (as)
dégustation [degystasjɔ̃] nf (de fromages etc) sampling; **~ de vins** wine-tasting session
déguster [degyste] vt (vins) to taste; (fromages etc) to sample; (savourer) to enjoy, savour
dehors [dəɔʀ] adv outside; (en plein air) outdoors ▷ nm outside ▷ nmpl (apparences) appearances; **mettre ou jeter ~** (expulser) to throw out; **au ~** outside; **au ~ de** outside; **en ~ de** (hormis) apart from
déjà [deʒa] adv already; (auparavant) before, already
déjeuner [deʒœne] vi to (have) lunch; (le matin) to have breakfast ▷ nm lunch
delà [dəla] adv: **en ~ (de), au ~ (de)** beyond
délacer [delase] vt (chaussures) to undo
délai [delɛ] nm (attente) waiting period; (sursis) extension (of time); (temps accordé) time limit; **sans ~** without delay; **dans les ~s** within the time limit
délaisser [delese] vt to abandon, desert
délasser [delase]: **se ~** vt to relax; **se ~** vi to relax
délavé, e [delave] adj faded
délayer [deleje] vt (Culin) to mix (with water etc); (peinture) to thin down
delco(r) [dɛlko] nm (Auto) distributor
délégué, e [delege] nm/f representative
déléguer [delege] vt to delegate
délibéré, e [delibeʀe] adj (conscient) deliberate
délicat, e [delika, at] adj delicate; (plein de tact) tactful; (attention) thoughtful; **délicatement** adv delicately; (avec douceur) gently
délice [delis] nm delight
délicieux, -euse [delisjø, jøz] adj (au goût) delicious; (sensation) delightful

délimiter [delimite] vt (*terrain*) to delimit, demarcate

délinquant, e [delɛ̃kɑ̃, -ɑ̃t] adj, nm/f delinquent

délirer [delire] vi to be delirious; **tu délires!** (*fam*) you're crazy!

délit [deli] nm (criminal) offence

délivrer [delivre] vt (*prisonnier*) to (set) free, release; (*passeport*) to issue

deltaplane(r) [dɛltaplan] nm hang-glider

déluge [delyʒ] nm (*pluie*) downpour; (*biblique*) Flood

demain [d(ə)mɛ̃] adv tomorrow; **~ matin/soir** tomorrow morning/evening

demande [d(ə)mɑ̃d] nf (*requête*) request; (*revendication*) demand; (*d'emploi*) application; (*Écon*): **la ~** demand; **"~s d'emploi"** (*annonces*) "situations wanted"

demandé, e [d(ə)mɑ̃de] adj (*article etc*): **très ~** (very) much in demand

demander [d(ə)mɑ̃de] vt to ask for; (*chemin, heure etc*) to ask; (*nécessiter*) to require, demand; **~ qch à qn** to ask sb for sth; **~ un service à qn** to ask sb a favour; **~ à qn de faire qch** to ask sb to do sth; **je ne demande pas mieux que de ...** I'll be only too pleased to ...; **se ~ si/pourquoi** *etc* to wonder whether/why *etc*; **demandeur, -euse** nm/f: **demandeur d'emploi** job-seeker; **demandeur d'asile** asylum-seeker

démangeaison [demɑ̃ʒɛzɔ̃] nf itching; **avoir des ~s** to be itching

démanger [demɑ̃ʒe] vi to itch

démaquillant [demakijɑ̃] nm make-up remover

démaquiller [demakije] vt: **se ~** to remove one's make-up

démarche [demarʃ] nf (*allure*) gait, walk; (*intervention*) step; (*fig: intellectuelle*) thought processes pl; **faire les ~s nécessaires (pour obtenir qch)** to take the necessary steps (to obtain sth)

démarrage [demaraʒ] nm start

démarrer [demare] vi (*conducteur*) to start (up); (*véhicule*) to move off; (*travaux*) to get moving; **démarreur** nm (*Auto*) starter

démêlant [demelɑ̃] nm conditioner

démêler [demele] vt to untangle; **démêlés** nmpl problems

déménagement [demenaʒmɑ̃] nm move; **camion de déménagement** removal van

déménager [demenaʒe] vt (*meubles*) to (re)move ▷ vi to move (house); **déménageur** nm removal man

démerder [demɛrde] (*fam*): **se ~** vi to sort things out for o.s.

démettre [demɛtr] vt: **~ qn de** (*fonction, poste*) to dismiss sb from; **se ~ l'épaule** *etc* to dislocate one's shoulder *etc*

demeurer [d(ə)mœre] vi (*habiter*) to live; (*rester*) to remain

demi, e [dəmi] adj half ▷ nm (*bière*) ≈ half-pint (0,25 litres) ▷ préfixe: **~... half-, semi..., demi-; trois heures/bouteilles et ~es** three and a half hours/bottles, three hours/bottles and a half; **il est 2 heures et ~e/midi et ~** it's half past 2/half past 12; **à ~** half-; **à la ~e** (*heure*) on the half-hour; **demi-douzaine** nf half-dozen, half a dozen; **demi-finale** nf semifinal; **demi-frère** nm half-brother; **demi-heure** nf half an hour; **demi-journée** nf half-day, half a day; **demi-litre** nm half-litre, half a litre; **demi-livre** nf half-pound, half a pound; **demi-pension** nf (*à l'hôtel*) half-board; **demi-pensionnaire** nm/f: **être demi-pensionnaire** to take school lunches

démis, e [demi, iz] adj (*épaule etc*) dislocated

demi-sœur [dəmisœr] nf half-sister

démission [demisjɔ̃] nf resignation; **donner sa ~** to give *ou* hand in one's notice; **démissionner** vi to resign

demi-tarif [dəmitarif] nm half-price; **voyager à ~** to travel half-fare

demi-tour [dəmitur] nm about-turn; **faire ~** to turn (and go) back

démocratie [demɔkrasi] nf democracy; **démocratique** adj democratic

démodé, e [demɔde] adj old-fashioned

demoiselle [d(ə)mwazɛl] nf (*jeune fille*) young lady; (*célibataire*) single lady, maiden lady; **demoiselle d'honneur** bridesmaid

démolir [demɔlir] vt to demolish

démon [demɔ̃] nm (*enfant turbulent*) devil, demon; **le D~** the Devil

démonstration [demɔ̃strasjɔ̃] nf demonstration

démonter [demɔ̃te] vt (*machine etc*) to take down, dismantle; **se ~** (*meuble*) to be dismantled, be taken to pieces; (*personne*) to lose countenance

démontrer [demɔ̃tre] vt to demonstrate

démouler [demule] vt to turn out

démuni, e [demyni] adj (*sans argent*) impoverished; **~ de** without

dénicher [deniʃe] (*fam*) vt (*objet*) to unearth; (*restaurant etc*) to discover

dénier [denje] vt to deny

dénivellation [denivelasjɔ̃] nf (*pente*) slope

dénombrer [denɔ̃bre] vt to count

dénomination [denɔminasjɔ̃] nf designation, appellation

dénoncer [denɔ̃se] vt to denounce; **se ~** to give o.s. up, come forward

dénouement [denumɑ̃] nm outcome

dénouer [denwe] vt to unknot, undo

denrée [dɑ̃re] nf: **denrées alimentaires** foodstuffs

dense [dɑ̃s] adj dense; **densité** nf density

dent [dɑ̃] nf tooth; **dent de lait/de sagesse** milk/wisdom tooth; **dentaire** adj dental; **cabinet dentaire** dental surgery (BRIT), dentist's office (US)

dentelle [dɑ̃tɛl] nf lace no pl

dentier [dɑ̃tje] nm denture

dentifrice [dɑ̃tifris] nm toothpaste

dentiste [dɑ̃tist] nm/f dentist

dentition [dɑ̃tisjɔ̃] nf teeth

dénué, e [denɥe] adj: **~ de** devoid of

déodorant [deodɔrɑ̃] nm deodorant

déontologie [deɔ̃tɔlɔʒi] nf code of practice

dépannage [depanaʒ] nm: **service de ~** (*Auto*) breakdown service

dépanner [depane] vt (*voiture, télévision*) to fix, repair; (*fig*) to bail out, help out; **dépanneuse** nf breakdown lorry (BRIT), tow truck (US)

dépareillé, e [depareje] adj (*collection, service*) incomplete; (*objet*) odd

départ [depar] nm departure; (*Sport*) start; **au ~** at the start; **la veille de son ~** the day before he leaves/left

département [departəmɑ̃] nm department

dépassé, e [depase] adj superseded, outmoded; **il est complètement ~** he's completely out of his depth, he can't cope

dépasser [depase] vt (*véhicule, concurrent*) to overtake; (*endroit*) to pass, go past; (*somme, limite*) to exceed; (*fig*:

en beauté etc) to surpass, outshine ▷ *vi* (*jupon etc*) to show; **se ~** to excel o.s.

dépaysé, e [depeize] *adj* disoriented

dépaysement [depeizmɑ̃] *nm* (*changement*) change of scenery

dépêcher [depeʃe]: **se ~** *vi* to hurry

dépendance [depɑ̃dɑ̃s] *nf* dependence; (*bâtiment*) outbuilding

dépendre [depɑ̃dʀ]: **~ de** *vt* to depend on; (*financièrement etc*) to be dependent on; **ça dépend** it depends

dépens [depɑ̃] *nmpl*: **aux ~ de** at the expense of

dépense [depɑ̃s] *nf* spending *no pl*, expense, expenditure *no pl*; **dépenser** *vt* to spend; (*énergie*) to expend, use up; **se dépenser** *vi* to exert o.s.

dépeupler [depœple]: **se ~** *vi* to become depopulated

dépilatoire [depilatwaʀ] *adj*: **crème ~** hair-removing *ou* depilatory cream

dépister [depiste] *vt* to detect; (*voleur*) to track down

dépit [depi] *nm* vexation, frustration; **en ~ de** in spite of; **en ~ du bon sens** contrary to all good sense; **dépité, e** *adj* vexed, frustrated

déplacé, e [deplase] *adj* (*propos*) out of place, uncalled-for

déplacement [deplasmɑ̃] *nm* (*voyage*) trip, travelling *no pl*; **en ~** away

déplacer [deplase] *vt* (*table, voiture*) to move, shift; **se ~** *vi* to move; (*voyager*) to travel; **se ~ une vertèbre** to slip a disc

déplaire [deplɛʀ] *vt*: **ça me déplaît** I don't like this, I dislike this; **se ~** *vi* to be unhappy; **déplaisant, e** *adj* disagreeable

dépliant [deplijɑ̃] *nm* leaflet

déplier [deplije] *vt* to unfold

déposer [depoze] *vt* (*gén: mettre, poser*) to lay *ou* put down; (*à la banque, à la consigne*) to deposit; (*passager*) to drop (off), set down; (*roi*) to depose; (*plainte*) to lodge; (*marque*) to register; **se ~** *vi* to settle; **dépositaire** *nm/f* (*Comm*) agent; **déposition** *nf* statement

dépôt [depo] *nm* (*à la banque, sédiment*) deposit; (*entrepôt*) warehouse, store

dépourvu, e [depuʀvy] *adj*: **~ de** lacking in, without; **prendre qn au ~** to catch sb unprepared

dépression [depʀesjɔ̃] *nf* depression; **dépression (nerveuse)**, (nervous) breakdown

déprimant, e [depʀimɑ̃, ɑ̃t] *adj* depressing

déprimer [depʀime] *vi* to be/get depressed

MOT-CLÉ

depuis [dəpɥi] *prép* **1** (*point de départ dans le temps*) since; **il habite Paris depuis 1983/l'an dernier** he has been living in Paris since 1983/last year; **depuis quand?** since when?; **depuis quand le connaissez-vous?** how long have you known him?

2 (*temps écoulé*) for; **il habite Paris depuis 5 ans** he has been living in Paris for 5 years; **je le connais depuis 3 ans** I've known him for 3 years

3 (*lieu*): **il a plu depuis Metz** it's been raining since Metz; **elle a téléphoné depuis Valence** she rang from Valence

4 (*quantité, rang*) from; **depuis les plus petits jusqu'aux plus grands** from the youngest to the oldest

▷ *adv* (*temps*) since (then); **je ne lui ai pas parlé depuis** I haven't spoken to him since (then); **depuis que** *conj* (ever) since; **depuis qu'il m'a dit ça** (ever) since he said that to me

député, e [depyte] *nm/f* (*Pol*) ≈ Member of Parliament (*BRIT*), ≈ Member of Congress (*US*)

dérangement [deʀɑ̃ʒmɑ̃] *nm* (*gêne*) trouble; (*gastrique etc*) disorder; **en ~** (*téléphone, machine*) out of order

déranger [deʀɑ̃ʒe] *vt* (*personne*) to trouble, bother; (*projets*) to disrupt, upset; (*objets, vêtements*) to disarrange; **se ~** *vi*: **surtout ne vous dérangez pas pour moi** please don't put yourself out on my account; **est-ce que cela vous dérange si ...?** do you mind if ...?

déraper [deʀape] *vi* (*voiture*) to skid; (*personne, semelles*) to slip

dérégler [deʀegle] *vt* (*mécanisme*) to put out of order; (*estomac*) to upset

dérisoire [deʀizwaʀ] *adj* derisory

dérive [deʀiv] *nf*: **aller à la ~** (*Navig, fig*) to drift

dérivé, e [deʀive] *nm* (*Tech*) by-product

dermatologue [dɛʀmatɔlɔg] *nm/f* dermatologist

dernier, -ière [dɛʀnje, jɛʀ] *adj* last; (*le plus récent*) latest, last; **lundi/le mois ~** last Monday/month; **c'est le ~ cri** it's the very latest thing; **en ~** last; **ce ~** the latter; **dernièrement** *adv* recently

dérogation [deʀɔgasjɔ̃] *nf* (special) dispensation

dérouiller [deʀuje] *vt*: **se ~ les jambes** to stretch one's legs (*fig*)

déroulement [deʀulmɑ̃] *nm* (*d'une opération etc*) progress

dérouler [deʀule] *vt* (*ficelle*) to unwind; **se ~** *vi* (*avoir lieu*) to take place; (*se passer*) to go (off); **tout s'est déroulé comme prévu** everything went as planned

dérouter [deʀute] *vt* (*avion, train*) to reroute, divert; (*étonner*) to disconcert, throw (out)

derrière [dɛʀjɛʀ] *adv, prép* behind ▷ *nm* (*d'une maison*) back; (*postérieur*) behind, bottom; **les pattes de ~** the back *ou* hind legs; **par ~** from behind; (*fig*) behind one's back

des [de] *dét voir* **de** ▷ *prép +dét* = **de +les**

dès [de] *prép* from; **~ que** as soon as; **~ son retour** as soon as he was (*ou* is) back

désaccord [dezakɔʀ] *nm* disagreement

désagréable [dezagʀeabl] *adj* unpleasant

désagrément [dezagʀemɑ̃] *nm* annoyance, trouble *no pl*

désaltérer [dezalteʀe] *vt*: **se ~** to quench one's thirst

désapprobateur, -trice [dezapʀɔbatœʀ, tʀis] *adj* disapproving

désapprouver [dezapʀuve] *vt* to disapprove of

désarmant, e [dezaʀmɑ̃, ɑ̃t] *adj* disarming

désastre [dezastʀ] *nm* disaster; **désastreux, -euse** *adj* disastrous

désavantage [dezavɑ̃taʒ] *nm* disadvantage; **désavantager** *vt* to put at a disadvantage

descendre [desɑ̃dʀ] *vt* (*escalier, montagne*) to go (*ou* come) down; (*valise, paquet*) to take *ou* get down; (*étagère etc*) to lower; (*fam: abattre*) to shoot down ▷ *vi* to go (*ou* come) down; (*passager: s'arrêter*) to get out, alight; **~ à pied/en voiture** to walk/drive down; **~ de** (*famille*) to be descended from; **~ du train** to get out of *ou* get off the train; **~ de cheval** to dismount; **~ d'un arbre** to climb down from a tree; **~ à l'hôtel** to stay at a hotel

descente [desɑ̃t] nf descent, going down; (chemin) way down; (Ski) downhill (race); **au milieu de la ~** halfway down; **descente de lit** bedside rug; **descente (de police)** (police) raid

description [dɛskʀipsjɔ̃] nf description

déséquilibre [dezekilibʀ] nm (position): **en ~** unsteady; (fig: des forces, du budget) imbalance

désert, e [dezɛʀ, ɛʀt] adj deserted ▷ nm desert; **désertique** adj desert cpd

désespéré, e [dezɛspeʀe] adj desperate

désespérer [dezɛspeʀe] vi: **~ (de)** to despair (of); **désespoir** nm despair; **en désespoir de cause** in desperation

déshabiller [dezabije] vt to undress; **se ~** vi to undress (o.s.)

déshydraté, e [dezidʀate] adj dehydrated

désigner [dezipe] vt (montrer) to point out, indicate; (dénommer) to denote; (candidat etc) to name

désinfectant, e [dezɛ̃fɛktɑ̃, ɑ̃t] adj, nm disinfectant

désinfecter [dezɛ̃fɛkte] vt to disinfect

désintéressé, e [dezɛ̃teʀese] adj disinterested, unselfish

désintéresser [dezɛ̃teʀese] vt: **se ~ (de)** to lose · interest (in)

désintoxication [dezɛ̃tɔksikasjɔ̃] nf: **faire une cure de ~** to undergo treatment for alcoholism (ou drug addiction)

désinvolte [dezɛ̃vɔlt] adj casual, off-hand

désir [deziʀ] nm wish; (sensuel) desire; **désirer** vt to want, wish for; (sexuellement) to desire; **je désire ...** (formule de politesse) I would like ...

désister [deziste]: **se ~** vi to stand down, withdraw

désobéir [dezɔbeiʀ] vi: **~ (à qn/qch)** to disobey (sb/sth); **désobéissant, e** adj disobedient

désodorisant [dezɔdɔʀizɑ̃] nm air freshener, deodorizer

désolé, e [dezɔle] adj (paysage) desolate; **je suis ~** I'm sorry

désordonné, e [dezɔʀdɔne] adj untidy

désordre [dezɔʀdʀ] nm disorder(liness), untidiness; (anarchie) disorder; **en ~** in a mess, untidy

désormais [dezɔʀmɛ] adv from now on

desquelles [dekɛl] prép +pron = **de +lesquelles**

desquels [dekɛl] prép +pron = **de +lesquels**

dessécher [desefe]: **se ~** vi to dry out

desserrer [deseʀe] vt to loosen; (frein) to release

dessert [desɛʀ] nm dessert, pudding

desservir [desɛʀviʀ] vt (ville, quartier) to serve; (débarrasser): **~ (la table)** to clear the table

dessin [desɛ̃] nm (œuvre, art) drawing; (motif) pattern, design; **dessin animé** cartoon (film); **dessin humoristique** cartoon; **dessinateur, -trice** nm/f drawer; (de bandes dessinées) cartoonist; (industriel) draughtsman(-woman) (BRIT), draftsman(-woman) (US); **dessiner** vt to draw; (concevoir) to design; **se dessiner** vi (forme) to be outlined; (fig: solution) to emerge

dessous [d(ə)su] adv underneath, beneath ▷ nm underside ▷ nmpl (sous-vêtements) underwear sg; **en ~, par ~** underneath; **au-~ (de)** below; (peu digne de) beneath; **avoir le ~** to get the worst of it; **les voisins du ~** the downstairs neighbours; **dessous-de-plat** nm inv tablemat

dessus [d(ə)sy] adv on top; (collé, écrit) on it ▷ nm top;

en ~ above; **par ~** adv over it ▷ prép over; **au-~ (de)** above; **les voisins du ~** the upstairs neighbours; **avoir le ~** to get the upper hand; **sens ~ dessous** upside down; **dessus-de-lit** nm inv bedspread

destin [dɛstɛ̃] nm fate; (avenir) destiny

destinataire [dɛstinatɛʀ] nm/f (Postes) addressee; (d'un colis) consignee

destination [dɛstinasjɔ̃] nf (lieu) destination; (usage) purpose; **à ~ de** bound for, travelling to

destiner [dɛstine] vt: **~ qch à qn** (envisager de donner) to intend sb to have sth; (adresser) to intend sth for sb; **être destiné à** (usage) to be meant for; **se ~ à l'enseignement** to intend to become a teacher

détachant [detaʃɑ̃] nm stain remover

détacher [detaʃe] vt (enlever) to detach, remove; (délier) to untie; (Admin): **~ qn (auprès de ou à)** to post sb (to); **se ~** vi (se séparer) to come off; (: page) to come out; (se défaire) to come undone; **se ~ sur** to stand out against; **se ~ de** (se désintéresser) to grow away from

détail [detaj] nm detail; (Comm): **le ~** retail; **en ~** in detail; **au ~** (Comm) retail; **détaillant** nm retailer; **détaillé, e** adj (plan, explications) detailed; (facture) itemized; **détailler** vt (expliquer) to explain in detail

détecter [detɛkte] vt to detect

détective [detɛktiv] nm: **détective (privé)** private detective

déteindre [detɛ̃dʀ] vi (au lavage) to run, lose its colour; **~ sur** (vêtement) to run into; (fig) to rub off on

détendre [detɑ̃dʀ] vt (corps, esprit) to relax; **se ~** vi (ressort) to lose its tension; (personne) to relax

détenir [det(ə)niʀ] vt (record, pouvoir, secret) to hold; (prisonnier) to detain, hold

détente [detɑ̃t] nf relaxation

détention [detɑ̃sjɔ̃] nf (d'armes) possession; (captivité) detention; **détention préventive** custody

détenu, e [det(ə)ny] nm/f prisoner

détergent [detɛʀʒɑ̃] nm detergent

détériorer [deteʀjɔʀe] vt to damage; **se ~** vi to deteriorate

déterminé, e [detɛʀmine] adj (résolu) determined; (précis) specific, definite

déterminer [detɛʀmine] vt (fixer) to determine; **~ qn à faire qch** to decide sb to do sth; **se ~ à faire qch** to make up one's mind to do sth

détester [detɛste] vt to hate, detest

détour [detuʀ] nm detour; (tournant) bend, curve; **ça vaut le ~** it's worth the trip; **sans ~** (fig) plainly

détourné, e [detuʀne] adj (moyen) roundabout

détourner [detuʀne] vt to divert; (par la force) to hijack; (yeux, tête) to turn away; (de l'argent) to embezzle; **se ~** vi to turn away

détraquer [detʀake] vt to put out of order; (estomac) to upset; **se ~** vi (machine) to go wrong

détriment [detʀimɑ̃] nm: **au ~ de** to the detriment of

détroit [detʀwa] nm strait

détruire [detʀɥiʀ] vt to destroy

dette [dɛt] nf debt

DEUG sigle m (= diplôme d'études universitaires générales) diploma taken after 2 years at university

deuil [dœj] nm (perte) bereavement; (période) mourning; **être en deuil** to be in mourning

deux [dø] num two; **tous les ~** both; **ses ~ mains** both his hands, his two hands; **~ fois** twice; **deuxième** num second; **deuxièmement** adv secondly; **deux-pièces**

nm inv (tailleur) two-piece suit; *(de bain)* two-piece (swimsuit); *(appartement)* two-roomed flat (BRIT) ou apartment (US); **deux-points** *nm inv* colon *sg*; **deux-roues** *nm inv* two-wheeled vehicle

devais [dəvɛ] *vb voir* **devoir**

dévaluation [devalyasjɔ̃] *nf* devaluation

devancer [d(ə)vɑ̃se] *vt (coureur, rival)* to get ahead of; *(arriver)* to arrive before; *(prévenir: questions, désirs)* to anticipate

devant [d(ə)vɑ̃] *adv* in front; *(à distance: en avant)* ahead ▷ *prép* in front of; *(en avant)* ahead of; *(avec mouvement: passer)* past; *(en présence de)* before, in front of; *(étant donné)* in view of ▷ *nm* front; **prendre les ~s** to make the first move; **les pattes de ~** the forelegs, the forelegs; **par ~** *(boutonner)* at the front; *(entrer)* the front way; **aller au-~ de qn** to go out to meet sb; **aller au-~ de** *(désirs de qn)* to anticipate

devanture [d(ə)vɑ̃tyʀ] *nf (étalage)* display; *(vitrine)* (shop) window

développement [dev(ə)lɔpmɑ̃] *nm* development; **pays en voie de ~** developing countries

développer [dev(ə)lɔpe] *vt* to develop; **se ~** *vi* to develop

devenir [dəv(ə)niʀ] *vb +attrib* to become; **que sont-ils devenus?** what has become of them?

devez [dəve] *vb voir* **devoir**

déviation [devjasjɔ̃] *nf (Auto)* diversion (BRIT), detour (US)

devienne *etc* [dəvjɛn] *vb voir* **devenir**

deviner [d(ə)vine] *vt* to guess; *(apercevoir)* to distinguish; **devinette** *nf* riddle

devis [d(ə)vi] *nm* estimate, quotation

devise [dəviz] *nf (formule)* motto, watchword; **devises** *nfpl (argent)* currency *sg*

dévisser [devise] *vt* to unscrew, undo; **se ~** *vi* to come unscrewed

devoir [d(ə)vwaʀ] *nm* duty; *(Scol)* homework *no pl*; *(: en classe)* exercise ▷ *vt (argent, respect)*: **~ qch (à qn)** to owe (sb) sth; *(+infin: obligation)*: **il doit le faire** he has to do it, he must do it; *(: intention)*: **le nouveau centre commercial doit ouvrir en mai** the new shopping centre is due to open in May; *(: probabilité)*: **il doit être tard** it must be late; *(: fatalité)*: **cela devait arriver** it was bound to happen; **combien est-ce que je vous dois?** how much do I owe you?

dévorer [devɔʀe] *vt* to devour

dévoué, e [devwe] *adj* devoted

dévouer [devwe]: **se ~** *vi (se sacrifier)*: **se ~ (pour)** to sacrifice o.s. (for); *(se consacrer)*: **se ~ à** to devote ou dedicate o.s. to

devrai [dəvʀe] *vb voir* **devoir**

dézipper [dezipe] *vt* to unzip

diabète [djabɛt] *nm* diabetes *sg*; **diabétique** *nm/f* diabetic

diable [djabl] *nm* devil

diabolo [djabolo] *nm (boisson)* lemonade with fruit cordial

diagnostic [djagnɔstik] *nm* diagnosis *sg*; **diagnostiquer** *vt* to diagnose

diagonal, e, -aux [djagɔnal, o] *adj* diagonal; **diagonale** *nf* diagonal; **en diagonale** diagonally

diagramme [djagʀam] *nm* chart, graph

dialecte [djalɛkt] *nm* dialect

dialogue [djalɔg] *nm* dialogue

diamant [djamɑ̃] *nm* diamond

diamètre [djamɛtʀ] *nm* diameter

diapositive [djapozitiv] *nf* transparency, slide

diarrhée [djaʀe] *nf* diarrhoea

dictateur [diktatœʀ] *nm* dictator; **dictature** *nf* dictatorship

dictée [dikte] *nf* dictation

dicter [dikte] *vt* to dictate

dictionnaire [diksjɔnɛʀ] *nm* dictionary

dièse [djɛz] *nm* sharp

diesel [djezɛl] *nm* diesel ▷ *adj inv* diesel

diète [djɛt] *nf (jeûne)* starvation diet; *(régime)* diet; **diététique** *adj*: **magasin diététique** health food shop (BRIT) ou store (US)

dieu, x [djø] *nm* god; **D~** God; **mon D~!** good heavens!

différemment [difeʀamɑ̃] *adv* differently

différence [difeʀɑ̃s] *nf* difference; **à la ~ de** unlike; **différencier** *vt* to differentiate

différent, e [difeʀɑ̃, ɑ̃t] *adj (dissemblable)* different; **~ de** different from; *(divers)* different, various

différer [difeʀe] *vt* to postpone, put off ▷ *vi*: **~ (de)** to differ (from)

difficile [difisil] *adj* difficult; *(exigeant)* hard to please; **difficilement** *adv* with difficulty

difficulté [difikylte] *nf* difficulty; **en ~** *(bateau, alpiniste)* in difficulties

diffuser [difyze] *vt (chaleur)* to diffuse; *(émission, musique)* to broadcast; *(nouvelle)* to circulate; *(Comm)* to distribute

digérer [diʒeʀe] *vt* to digest; *(fam: accepter)* to stomach, put up with; **digestif** *nm* (after-dinner) liqueur; **digestion** *nf* digestion

digne [diɲ] *adj* dignified; **~ de** worthy of; **~ de foi** trustworthy; **dignité** *nf* dignity

digue [dig] *nf* dike, dyke

dilemme [dilɛm] *nm* dilemma

diligence [diliʒɑ̃s] *nf* stagecoach

diluer [dilɥe] *vt* to dilute

dimanche [dimɑ̃ʃ] *nm* Sunday

dimension [dimɑ̃sjɔ̃] *nf (grandeur)* size; *(dimensions)* dimensions

diminuer [diminɥe] *vt* to reduce, decrease; *(ardeur etc)* to lessen; *(dénigrer)* to belittle ▷ *vi* to decrease, diminish; **diminutif** *nm (surnom)* pet name

dinde [dɛ̃d] *nf* turkey

dindon [dɛ̃dɔ̃] *nm* turkey

dîner [dine] *nm* dinner ▷ *vi* to have dinner

dingue [dɛ̃g] *(fam) adj* crazy

dinosaure [dinozɔʀ] *nm* dinosaur

diplomate [diplɔmat] *adj* diplomatic ▷ *nm* diplomat; *(fig)* diplomatist; **diplomatie** *nf* diplomacy

diplôme [diplom] *nm* diploma; **avoir des ~s** to have qualifications; **diplômé, e** *adj* qualified

dire [diʀ] *nm*: **au ~ de** according to ▷ *vt* to say; *(secret, mensonge, heure)* to tell; **~ qch à qn** to tell sb sth; **~ à qn qu'il fasse** ou **de faire** to tell sb to do; **on dit que** they say that; **ceci** ou **cela dit** that being said; **si cela lui dit** *(plaire)* if he fancies it; **que dites-vous de** *(penser)* what do you think of; **on dirait que** it looks (ou sounds etc) as if; **dis/dites (donc)!** I say!; **se ~ (à soi-même)** to say to o.s.; **se ~ malade** *(se prétendre)* to claim one is ill; **ça ne se dit pas** *(impoli)* you shouldn't say that; *(pas en usage)* you don't say that

direct, e [diʀɛkt] *adj* direct ▷ *nm (TV)*: **en ~** live; **directement** *adv* directly

directeur, -trice [dirɛktœr, tris] nm/f (d'entreprise) director; (de service) manager(-eress); (d'école) head(teacher)(BRIT), principal (US)
direction [dirɛksjɔ̃] nf (sens) direction; (d'entreprise) management; (Auto) steering; **"toutes ~s"** "all routes"
dirent [dir] vb voir **dire**
dirigeant, e [diriʒɑ̃, ɑ̃t] adj (classe) ruling ▷ nm/f (d'un parti etc) leader
diriger [diriʒe] vt (entreprise) to manage, run; (véhicule) to steer; (orchestre) to conduct; (recherches, travaux) to supervise; **~ sur** (arme) to point ou level ou aim at; **~ son regard sur** to look in the direction of; **se ~** vi (s'orienter) to find one's way; **se ~ vers** ou **sur** to make ou head for
dis [di] vb voir **dire**
discerner [disɛrne] vt to discern, make out
discipline [disiplin] nf discipline; **discipliner** vt to discipline
discontinu, e [diskɔ̃tiny] adj intermittent
discontinuer [diskɔ̃tinɥe] vi: **sans ~** without stopping, without a break
discothèque [diskɔtek] nf (boîte de nuit) disco(thèque)
discours [diskur] nm speech
discret, -ète [diskrɛ, ɛt] adj discreet; (parfum, maquillage) unobtrusive; **discrétion** nf discretion; **à discrétion** as much as one wants
discrimination [diskriminasjɔ̃] nf discrimination; **sans ~** indiscriminately
discussion [diskysjɔ̃] nf discussion
discutable [diskytabl] adj debatable
discuter [diskyte] vt (débattre) to discuss; (contester) to question, dispute ▷ vi to talk; (protester) to argue; **~ de** to discuss
dise [diz] vb voir **dire**
disjoncteur [disʒɔ̃ktœr] nm (Élec) circuit breaker
disloquer [dislɔke]: **se ~** vi (parti, empire) to break up; (meuble) to come apart; (épaule) to be dislocated
disons [dizɔ̃] vb voir **dire**
disparaître [disparetr] vi to disappear; (se perdre: traditions etc) to die out; **faire ~** (tache) to remove; (douleur) to get rid of
disparition [disparisjɔ̃] nf disappearance; **espèce en voie de ~** endangered species
disparu, e [dispary] nm/f missing person ▷ adj: **être porté ~** to be reported missing
dispensaire [dispɑ̃ser] nm community clinic
dispenser [dispɑ̃se] vt: **~ qn de** to exempt sb from
disperser [dispɛrse] vt to scatter; **se ~** vi to break up
disponible [dispɔnibl(ə)] adj available
disposé, e [dispoze] adj: **bien/mal ~** (humeur) in a good/ bad mood; **~ à** (prêt à) willing ou prepared to
disposer [dispoze] vt to arrange ▷ vi: **vous pouvez ~** you may leave; **~ de** to have (at one's disposal); **se ~ à faire** to prepare to do, be about to do
dispositif [dispozitif] nm device; (fig) system, plan of action
disposition [dispozisjɔ̃] nf (arrangement) arrangement, layout; (humeur) mood; **prendre ses ~s** to make arrangements; **avoir des ~s pour la musique** etc to have a special aptitude for music etc; **à la ~ de qn** at sb's disposal; **je suis à votre ~** I am at your service
disproportionné, e [disprɔpɔrsjɔne] adj disproportionate, out of all proportion
dispute [dispyt] nf quarrel, argument; **disputer** vt (match) to play; (combat) to fight; **se disputer** vi to

quarrel
disqualifier [diskalifje] vt to disqualify
disque [disk] nm (Mus) record; (forme, pièce) disc; (Sport) discus; **disque compact** compact disc; **disque dur** hard disk; **disquette** nf floppy disk, diskette
dissertation [disɛrtasjɔ̃] nf (Scol) essay
dissimuler [disimyle] vt to conceal
dissipé, e [disipe] adj (élève) undisciplined, unruly
dissolvant [disɔlvɑ̃] nm nail polish remover
dissuader [disɥade] vt: **~ qn de faire** to dissuade sb from doing
distance [distɑ̃s] nf distance; (fig: écart) gap; **à ~** at ou from a distance; **distancer** vt to outdistance
distant, e [distɑ̃, ɑ̃t] adj (réservé) distant; **~ de** (lieu) far away from
distillerie [distilri] nf distillery
distinct, e [distɛ̃(kt), ɛ̃kt] adj distinct; **distinctement** adv distinctly, clearly; **distinctif, -ive** adj distinctive
distingué, e [distɛ̃ge] adj distinguished
distinguer [distɛ̃ge] vt to distinguish; **se ~ de** to be distinguished by
distraction [distraksjɔ̃] nf (inattention) absent-mindedness; (passe-temps) distraction, entertainment
distraire [distrer] vt (divertir) to entertain, divert; (déranger) to distract; **se ~** vi to amuse ou enjoy o.s.; **distrait, e** adj absent-minded
distrayant, e [distrɛjɑ̃, ɑ̃t] adj entertaining
distribuer [distribɥe] vt to distribute, hand out; (Cartes) to deal (out); (courrier) to deliver; **distributeur** nm (Comm) distributor; **distributeur (automatique)** (vending) machine; **distributeur de billets** (cash) dispenser
dit, e [di, dit] pp de **dire** ▷ adj (fixé): **le jour ~** the arranged day; (surnommé): **X, ~ Pierrot** X, known as Pierrot
dites [dit] vb voir **dire**
divan [divɑ̃] nm divan
divers, e [diver, ɛrs] adj (varié) diverse, varied; (différent) different, various; **~es personnes** various ou several people
diversité [diversite] nf (variété) diversity
divertir [divertir]: **se ~** vi to amuse ou enjoy o.s.; **divertissement** nm distraction, entertainment
diviser [divize] vt to divide; **division** nf division
divorce [divɔrs] nm divorce; **divorcé, e** nm/f divorcee; **divorcer** vi to get a divorce, get divorced; **divorcer de** ou **d'avec qn** to divorce sb
divulguer [divylge] vt to disclose
dix [dis] num ten; **dix-huit** num eighteen; **dix-huitième** num eighteenth; **dixième** num tenth; **dix-neuf** num nineteen; **dix-neuvième** num nineteenth; **dix-sept** num seventeen; **dix-septième** num seventeenth
dizaine [dizɛn] nf: **une ~ (de)** about ten, ten or so
do [do] nm (note) C; (en chantant la gamme) do(h)
docile [dɔsil] adj docile
dock [dɔk] nm dock; **docker** nm docker
docteur [dɔktœr] nm doctor; **doctorat** nm doctorate
doctrine [dɔktrin] nf doctrine
document [dɔkymɑ̃] nm document; **documentaire** adj, nm documentary; **documentation** nf documentation, literature; **documenter** vt: **se documenter (sur)** to gather information (on)
dodo [dodo] nm (langage enfantin): **aller faire ~** to go to beddy-byes

dogue [dɔg] nm mastiff

doigt [dwa] nm finger; **à deux ~s de** within an inch of; **un ~ de lait/whiskey** a drop of milk/whisky; **doigt de pied** toe

doit etc [dwa] vb voir **devoir**

dollar [dɔlaʀ] nm dollar

domaine [dɔmɛn] nm estate, property; (fig) domain, field

domestique [dɔmɛstik] adj domestic ▷ nm/f servant, domestic

domicile [dɔmisil] nm home, place of residence; **à ~** at home; **livrer à ~** to deliver; **domicilié, e** adj: **"domicilié à ..."** "address ..."

dominant, e [dɔminã, ãt] adj (opinion) predominant

dominer [dɔmine] vt to dominate; (sujet) to master; (surpasser) to outclass, surpass; (surplomber) to tower above, dominate ▷ vi to be in the dominant position; **se ~** vi to control o.s.

domino [dɔmino] nm domino; **dominos** nmpl (jeu) dominoes sg

dommage [dɔmaʒ] nm: **~s** (dégâts) damage no pl; **c'est ~!** what a shame!; **c'est ~ que** it's a shame ou pity that

dompter [dɔ̃(p)te] vt to tame; **dompteur, -euse** nm/f trainer

DOM-ROM [dɔmʀɔm] sigle m (= départements et régions d'outre-mer) French overseas departments and regions

don [dɔ̃] nm gift; (charité) donation; **avoir des ~s pour** to have a gift ou talent for; **elle a le ~ de m'énerver** she's got a knack of getting on my nerves

donc [dɔ̃k] conj therefore, so; (après une digression) so, then

donné, e [dɔne] adj (convenu: lieu, heure) given; (pas cher: fam): **c'est ~** it's a gift; **étant ~ que ...** given that ...; **données** nfpl data

donner [dɔne] vt to give; (vieux habits etc) to give away; (spectacle) to put on; **~ qch à qn** to give sb sth, give sth to sb; **~ sur** (suj: fenêtre, chambre) to look (out) onto; **ça donne soif/faim** it makes you (feel) thirsty/hungry; **se ~ à fond** to give one's all; **se ~ du mal** to take (great) trouble; **s'en ~ à cœur joie** (fam) to have a great time

○ **MOT-CLÉ**

dont [dɔ̃] pron relatif **1** (appartenance: objets) whose, of which; (appartenance: êtres animés) whose; **la maison dont le toit est rouge** the house the roof of which is red, the house whose roof is red; **l'homme dont je connais la sœur** the man whose sister I know

2 (parmi lequel(le)s): **2 livres, dont l'un est ...** 2 books, one of which is ...; **il y avait plusieurs personnes, dont Gabrielle** there were several people, among them Gabrielle; **10 blessés, dont 2 grièvement** 10 injured, 2 of them seriously

3 (complément d'adjectif, de verbe): **le fils dont il est si fier** the son he's so proud of; **le pays dont il est originaire** the country he's from; **la façon dont il l'a fait** the way he did it; **ce dont je parle** what I'm talking about

dopage [dɔpaʒ] nm (Sport) drug use; (de cheval) doping

doré, e [dɔʀe] adj golden; (avec dorure) gilt, gilded

dorénavant [dɔʀenavã] adv henceforth

dorer [dɔʀe] vt to gild; **(faire) ~** (Culin) to brown

dorloter [dɔʀlɔte] vt to pamper

dormir [dɔʀmiʀ] vi to sleep; (être endormi) to be asleep

dortoir [dɔʀtwaʀ] nm dormitory

dos [do] nm back; (de livre) spine; **"voir au ~"** "see over"; **de ~** from the back

dosage [dozaʒ] nm mixture

dose [doz] nf dose; **doser** vt to measure out; **il faut savoir doser ses efforts** you have to be able to pace yourself

dossier [dosje] nm (documents) file; (de chaise) back; (Presse) feature; (Comput) folder; **un ~ scolaire** a school report

douane [dwan] nf customs pl; **douanier, -ière** adj customs cpd ▷ nm customs officer

double [dubl] adj, adv double ▷ nm (2 fois plus): **le ~ (de)** twice as much (ou many) (as); (autre exemplaire) duplicate, copy; (sosie) double; (Tennis) doubles sg; **en ~ (exemplaire)** in duplicate; **faire ~ emploi** to be redundant; **double-cliquer** vi (Inform) to double-click

doubler [duble] vt (multiplier par 2) to double; (vêtement) to line; (dépasser) to overtake, pass; (film) to dub; (acteur) to stand in for ▷ vi to double

doublure [dublyʀ] nf lining; (Cinéma) stand-in

douce [dus] adj voir **doux**; **douceâtre** adj sickly sweet; **doucement** adv gently; (lentement) slowly; **douceur** nf softness; (de quelqu'un) gentleness; (de climat) mildness

douche [duʃ] nf shower; **prendre une ~** to have ou take a shower; **doucher: se doucher** vi to have ou take a shower

doué, e [dwe] adj gifted, talented; **être ~ pour** to have a gift for

douille [duj] nf (Élec) socket

douillet, te [duje, ɛt] adj cosy; (péj: à la douleur) soft

douleur [dulœʀ] nf pain; (chagrin) grief, distress; **douloureux, -euse** adj painful

doute [dut] nm doubt; **sans ~** no doubt; (probablement) probably; **sans aucun ~** without a doubt; **douter** vt to doubt; **douter de** (sincérité de qn) to have (one's) doubts about; (réussite) to be doubtful of; **douter que** to doubt if ou whether; **se douter de qch/que** to suspect sth/that; **je m'en doutais** I suspected as much; **douteux, -euse** adj (incertain) doubtful; (péj) dubious-looking

Douvres [duvʀ] n Dover

doux, douce [du, dus] adj soft; (sucré) sweet; (peu fort: moutarde, clément: climat) mild; (pas brusque) gentle

douzaine [duzɛn] nf (12) dozen; (environ 12): **une ~ (de)** a dozen or so

douze [duz] num twelve; **douzième** num twelfth

dragée [dʀaʒe] nf sugared almond

draguer [dʀage] vt (rivière) to dredge; (fam) to try to pick up

dramatique [dʀamatik] adj dramatic; (tragique) tragic ▷ nf (TV) (television) drama

drame [dʀam] nm drama

drap [dʀa] nm (de lit) sheet; (tissu) woollen fabric

drapeau, x [dʀapo] nm flag

drap-housse [dʀaus] nm fitted sheet

dresser [dʀese] vt (mettre vertical, monter) to put up, erect; (liste) to draw up; (animal) to train; **se ~** vi (obstacle) to stand; (personne) to draw o.s. up; **~ qn contre qn** to set sb against sb; **~ l'oreille** to prick up one's ears

drogue [dʀɔg] nf drug; **la ~** drugs pl; **drogué, e** nm/f drug addict; **droguer** vt (victime) to drug; **se droguer** vi (aux stupéfiants) to take drugs; (péj: de médicaments) to dose o.s. up; **droguerie** nf hardware shop; **droguiste**

e

nm keeper/owner of a hardware shop

droit, e [dʀwa, dʀwat] *adj* (*non courbe*) straight; (*vertical*) upright, straight; (*fig: loyal*) straight, straight(forward); (*opposé à gauche*) right, right-hand ▷ *adv* straight ▷ *nm* (*prérogative*) right; (*taxe*) duty, tax; (: *d'inscription*) fee; (*Jur*): **le ~** law; **avoir le ~ de** to be allowed to; **avoir ~ à** to be entitled to; **être dans son ~** to be within one's rights; **à ~e** on the right; (*direction*) (to the) right; **droits d'auteur** royalties; **droits d'inscription** enrolment fee; **droite** *nf* (*Pol*): **la droite** the right (wing); **droitier, -ière** *adj* right-handed

drôle [dʀol] *adj* funny; **une ~ d'idée** a funny idea

dromadaire [dʀomadɛʀ] *nm* dromedary

du [dy] *dét voir* **de** ▷ *prép* +*dét* = **de + le**

dû, due [dy] *vb voir* **devoir** ▷ *adj* (*somme*) owing, owed; (*causé par*): **dû à** due to ▷ *nm* due

dune [dyn] *nf* dune

duplex [dyplɛks] *nm* (*appartement*) split-level apartment, duplex

duquel [dykɛl] *prép* +*pron* = **de +lequel**

dur, e [dyʀ] *adj* (*pierre, siège, travail, problème*) hard; (*voix, climat*) harsh; (*sévère*) hard, harsh; (*cruel*) hard(-hearted); (*porte, col*) stiff; (*viande*) tough ▷ *adv* hard ▷ *nm* (*fam: meneur*) tough nut; **~ d'oreille** hard of hearing

durant [dyʀɑ̃] *prép* (*au cours de*) during; (*pendant*) for; **des mois ~** for months

durcir [dyʀsiʀ] *vt, vi* to harden; **se ~** *vi* to harden

durée [dyʀe] *nf* length; (*d'une pile etc*) life; **de courte ~** (*séjour*) short

durement [dyʀmɑ̃] *adv* harshly

durer [dyʀe] *vi* to last

dureté [dyʀte] *nf* hardness; harshness; stiffness; toughness

durit(r) [dyʀit] *nf* (*car radiator*) hose

duvet [dyvɛ] *nm* down; (*sac de couchage*) down-filled sleeping bag

DVD *sigle m* (= *digital versatile disc*) DVD

dynamique [dinamik] *adj* dynamic; **dynamisme** *nm* dynamism

dynamo [dinamo] *nf* dynamo

dyslexie [dislɛksi] *nf* dyslexia, word-blindness

eau, x [o] *nf* water; **eaux** *nfpl* (*Méd*) waters; **prendre l'~** to leak, let in water; **tomber à l'~** (*fig*) to fall through; **eau de Cologne** eau de Cologne; **eau courante** running water; **eau de javel** bleach; **eau de toilette** toilet water; **eau douce** fresh water; **eau gazeuse** sparkling (mineral) water; **eau minérale** mineral water; **eau plate** still water; **eau salée** salt water; **eau-de-vie** *nf* brandy

ébène [ebɛn] *nf* ebony; **ébéniste** *nm* cabinetmaker

éblouir [ebluiʀ] *vt* to dazzle

éboueur [ebwœʀ] *nm* dustman (BRIT), garbageman (US)

ébouillanter [ebujɑ̃te] *vt* to scald; (*Culin*) to blanch

éboulement [ebulmɑ̃] *nm* rock fall

ébranler [ebʀɑ̃le] *vt* to shake; (*affaiblir*) to weaken; **s'~** *vi* (*partir*) to move off

ébullition [ebylisjɔ̃] *nf* boiling point; **en ~** boiling

écaille [ekaj] *nf* (*de poisson*) scale; (*matière*) tortoiseshell; **écailler** *vt* (*poisson*) to scale; **s'écailler** *vi* to flake *ou* peel (off)

écart [ekaʀ] *nm* gap; **à l'~** out of the way; **à l'~ de** away from; **faire un ~** (*voiture*) to swerve

écarté, e [ekaʀte] *adj* (*lieu*) out-of-the-way, remote; (*ouvert*): **les jambes ~es** legs apart; **les bras ~s** arms outstretched

écarter [ekaʀte] *vt* (*séparer*) to move apart, separate; (*éloigner*) to push back, move away; (*ouvrir: bras, jambes*) to spread, open; (: *rideau*) to draw (back); (*éliminer: candidat, possibilité*) to dismiss; **s'~** *vi* to part; (*s'éloigner*) to move away; **s'~ de** to wander from

échafaudage [eʃafodaʒ] *nm* scaffolding

échalote [eʃalɔt] *nf* shallot

échange [eʃɑ̃ʒ] *nm* exchange; **en ~ de** in exchange *ou* return for; **échanger** *vt*: **échanger qch (contre)** to exchange sth (for)

échantillon [eʃɑ̃tijɔ̃] *nm* sample

échapper [eʃape]: **~ à** *vt* (*gardien*) to escape (from); (*punition, péril*) to escape; **s'~** *vi* to escape; **~ à qn** (*détail, sens*) to escape sb; (*objet qu'on tient*) to slip out of sb's hands; **laisser ~** (*cri etc*) to let out; **l'~ belle** to have a narrow escape

écharde [eʃaʀd] nf splinter (of wood)

écharpe [eʃaʀp] nf scarf; **avoir le bras en ~** to have one's arm in a sling

échauffer [eʃofe] vt (moteur) to overheat; **s'~** vi (Sport) to warm up; (dans la discussion) to become heated

échéance [eʃeɑ̃s] nf (d'un paiement: date) settlement date; (fig) deadline; **à brève ~** in the short term; **à longue ~** in the long run

échéant [eʃeɑ̃]: **le cas ~** adv if the case arises

échec [eʃɛk] nm failure; (Échecs): **~ et mat/au roi** checkmate/check; **échecs** nmpl (jeu) chess sg; **tenir en ~** to hold in check

échelle [eʃɛl] nf ladder; (fig, d'une carte) scale

échelon [eʃ(ə)lɔ̃] nm (d'échelle) rung; (Admin) grade; **échelonner** vt to space out

échiquier [eʃikje] nm chessboard

écho [eko] nm echo; **échographie** nf: **passer une échographie** to have a scan

échouer [eʃwe] vi to fail; **s'~** vi to run aground

éclabousser [eklabuse] vt to splash

éclair [eklɛʀ] nm (d'orage) flash of lightning, lightning no pl; (gâteau) éclair

éclairage [eklɛʀaʒ] nm lighting

éclaircie [eklɛʀsi] nf bright interval

éclaircir [eklɛʀsiʀ] vt to lighten; (fig: mystère) to clear up; (: point) to clarify; **s'~** vi (ciel) to clear; **s'~ la voix** to clear one's throat; **éclaircissement** nm (sur un point) clarification

éclairer [eklɛʀe] vt (lieu) to light (up); (personne: avec une lampe etc) to light the way for; (fig: problème) to throw light on ▷ vi: **~ mal/bien** to give a poor/good light; **s'~ à la bougie** to use candlelight

éclat [ekla] nm (de bombe, de verre) fragment; (du soleil, d'une couleur etc) brightness, brilliance; (d'une cérémonie) splendour; (scandale): **faire un ~** to cause a commotion; **éclats de voix** shouts; **éclat de rire** roar of laughter

éclatant, e [eklatɑ̃, ɑ̃t] adj brilliant

éclater [eklate] vi (pneu) to burst; (bombe) to explode; (guerre) to break out; (groupe, parti) to break up; **~ en sanglots/de rire** to burst out sobbing/laughing

écluse [eklyz] nf lock

écœurant, e [ekœʀɑ̃, ɑ̃t] adj (gâteau etc) sickly; (fig) sickening

écœurer [ekœʀe] vt: **~ qn** (nourriture) to make sb feel sick; (conduite, personne) to disgust sb

école [ekɔl] nf school; **aller à l'~** to go to school; **école maternelle** nursery school; **école primaire** primary (BRIT) ou grade (US) school; **école secondaire** secondary (BRIT) ou high (US) school; **écolier, -ière** nm/f schoolboy(-girl)

écologie [ekɔlɔʒi] nf ecology; **écologique** adj environment-friendly; **écologiste** nm/f ecologist

économe [ekɔnɔm] adj thrifty ▷ nm/f (de lycée etc) bursar (BRIT), treasurer (US)

économie [ekɔnɔmi] nf economy; (gain: d'argent, de temps etc) saving; (science) economics sg; **économies** nfpl (pécule) savings; **économique** adj (avantageux) economical; (Écon) economic; **économiser** vt, vi to save

écorce [ekɔʀs] nf bark; (de fruit) peel

écorcher [ekɔʀʃe] vt: **s'~ le genou/la main** to graze one's knee/one's hand; **écorchure** nf graze

écossais, e [ekɔsɛ, ɛz] adj Scottish ▷ nm/f: **É~, e** Scot

Écosse [ekɔs] nf: **l'~** Scotland

écouter [ekute] vt to listen to; **s'~** (malade) to be a bit of a hypochondriac; **si je m'écoutais** if I followed my instincts; **écouteur** nm (Tél) receiver; **écouteurs** nmpl (casque) headphones pl, headset

écran [ekʀɑ̃] nm screen; **petit ~** television; **~ total** sunblock

écrasant, e [ekʀazɑ̃, ɑ̃t] adj overwhelming

écraser [ekʀaze] vt to crush; (piéton) to run over; **s'~** vi to crash; **s'~ contre** to crash into

écrémé, e [ekʀeme] adj (lait) skimmed

écrevisse [ekʀəvis] nf crayfish inv

écrire [ekʀiʀ] vt to write; **s'~** to write to each other; **ça s'écrit comment?** how is it spelt?; **écrit** nm (examen) written paper; **par écrit** in writing

écriteau, x [ekʀito] nm notice, sign

écriture [ekʀityʀ] nf writing; **écritures** nfpl (Comm) accounts, books; **l'É~ (sainte), les É~s** the Scriptures

écrivain [ekʀivɛ̃] nm writer

écrou [ekʀu] nm nut

écrouler [ekʀule]: **s'~** vi to collapse

écru, e [ekʀy] adj (couleur) off-white, écru

écume [ekym] nf foam

écureuil [ekyʀœj] nm squirrel

écurie [ekyʀi] nf stable

eczéma [ɛgzema] nm eczema

EDF sigle f (= Électricité de France) national electricity company

Édimbourg [edɛ̃buʀ] n Edinburgh

éditer [edite] vt (publier) to publish; (annoter) to edit; **éditeur, -trice** nm/f publisher; **édition** nf edition; (industrie du livre) publishing

édredon [edʀədɔ̃] nm eiderdown

éducateur, -trice [edykatœʀ, tʀis] nm/f teacher; (en école spécialisée) instructor

éducatif, -ive [edykatif, iv] adj educational

éducation [edykasjɔ̃] nf education; (familiale) upbringing; (manières) (good) manners pl; **éducation physique** physical education

éduquer [edyke] vt to educate; (élever) to bring up

effacer [efase] vt to erase, rub out; **s'~** (inscription etc) to wear off; (pour laisser passer) to step aside

effarant, e [efaʀɑ̃, ɑ̃t] adj alarming

effectif, -ive [efɛktif, iv] adj real ▷ nm (Scol) (pupil) numbers pl; (entreprise) staff, workforce; **effectivement** adv (réellement) actually, really; (en effet) indeed

effectuer [efɛktɥe] vt (opération) to carry out; (trajet) to make

effervescent, e [efɛʀvesɑ̃, ɑ̃t] adj effervescent

effet [efɛ] nm effect; (impression) impression; **effets** nmpl (vêtements etc) things; **faire ~** (médicament) to take effect; **faire de l'~** (impressionner) to make an impression; **faire bon/mauvais ~ sur qn** to make a good/bad impression on sb; **en ~** indeed; **effet de serre** greenhouse effect

efficace [efikas] adj (personne) efficient; (action, médicament) effective; **efficacité** nf efficiency; effectiveness

effondrer [efɔ̃dʀe]: **s'~** vi to collapse

efforcer [efɔʀse]: **s'~ de** vi: **s'~ de faire** to try hard to do

effort [efɔʀ] nm effort

effrayant, e [efʀejɑ̃, ɑ̃t] adj frightening

effrayer [efʀeje] vt to frighten, scare; **s'~ (de)** to be frightened ou scared (by)

effréné, e [efʀene] adj wild

effronté, e [efʀɔ̃te] adj cheeky

effroyable [efʀwajabl] adj horrifying, appalling

égal, e, -aux [egal, o] adj equal; (constant: vitesse) steady ▷ nm/f equal; **être ~ à** (prix, nombre) to be equal to; **ça lui est ~** it's all the same to him, he doesn't mind; **sans ~** matchless, unequalled; **d'~ à ~** as equals; **également** adv equally; (aussi) too, as well; **égaler** vt to equal; **égaliser** vt (sol, salaires) to level (out); (chances) to equalize ▷ vi (Sport) to equalize; **égalité** nf equality; **être à égalité** to be level

égard [egar] nm: **~s** mpl consideration sg; **à cet ~** in this respect; **par ~ pour** out of consideration for; **à l'~ de** towards

égarer [egaʀe] vt to mislay; **s'~** vi to get lost, lose one's way; (objet) to go astray

églefin [egləfɛ̃] nm haddock

église [egliz] nf church; **aller à l'~** to go to church

égoïsme [egoism] nm selfishness; **égoïste** adj selfish

égout [egu] nm sewer

égoutter [egute] vt to drip; **s'~** vi to drip; **égouttoir** nm draining board; (mobile) draining rack

égratignure [egratiɲyʀ] nf scratch

Égypte [eʒipt] nf: **l'~** Egypt; **égyptien, ne** adj Egyptian ▷ nm/f: **Égyptien, ne** Egyptian

eh [e] excl hey!; **eh bien!** well!

élaborer [elabɔʀe] vt to elaborate; (projet, stratégie) to work out; (rapport) to draft

élan [elɑ̃] nm (Zool) elk, moose; (Sport) run up; (fig: de tendresse etc) surge; **prendre de l'~** to gather speed

élancer [elɑ̃se]: **s'~** vi to dash, hurl o.s.

élargir [elaʀʒiʀ] vt to widen; **s'~** vi to widen; (vêtement) to stretch

élastique [elastik] adj elastic ▷ nm (de bureau) rubber band; (pour la couture) elastic no pl

élection [elɛksjɔ̃] nf election

électricien, ne [elɛktʀisjɛ̃, jɛn] nm/f electrician

électricité [elɛktʀisite] nf electricity; **allumer/éteindre l'~** to put on/off the light

électrique [elɛktʀik] adj electric(al)

électrocuter [elɛktʀɔkyte] vt to electrocute

électroménager [elɛktʀomenaʒe] adj, nm: **appareils ~s, l'~** domestic (electrical) appliances

électronique [elɛktʀɔnik] adj electronic ▷ nf electronics sg

élégance [elegɑ̃s] nf elegance

élégant, e [elegɑ̃, ɑ̃t] adj elegant

élément [elemɑ̃] nm element; (pièce) component, part; **élémentaire** adj elementary

éléphant [elefɑ̃] nm elephant

élevage [el(ə)vaʒ] nm breeding; (de bovins) cattle rearing; **truite d'~** farmed trout

élevé, e [el(ə)ve] adj high; **bien/mal ~** well-/ill-mannered

élève [elɛv] nm/f pupil

élever [el(ə)ve] vt (enfant) to bring up, raise; (animaux) to breed; (hausser: taux, niveau) to raise; (édifier: monument) to put up, erect; **s'~** vi (avion) to go up; (niveau, température) to rise; **s'~ à** (suj: frais, dégâts) to amount to, add up to; **s'~ contre qch** to rise up against sth; **la voix** to raise one's voice; **éleveur, -euse** nm/f breeder

éliminatoire [eliminatwaʀ] nf (Sport) heat

éliminer [elimine] vt to eliminate

élire [eliʀ] vt to elect

elle [ɛl] pron (sujet) she; (: chose) it; (complément) her; it; **~s** (sujet) they; (complément) them; **~-même** herself; itself; **~s-mêmes** themselves; voir aussi **il**

éloigné, e [elwaɲe] adj distant, far-off; (parent) distant

éloigner [elwaɲe] vt (échéance) to put off, postpone; (soupçons, danger) to ward off; (objet): **~ qch (de)** to move ou take sth away (from); (personne): **~ qn (de)** to take sb away ou remove sb (from); **s'~ (de)** (personne) to go away (from); (véhicule) to move away (from); (affectivement) to grow away (from)

élu, e [ely] pp de **élire** ▷ nm/f (Pol) elected representative

Élysée [elize] nm: **(le palais de) l'~** the Élysée Palace (the French president's residence)

émail, -aux [emaj, o] nm enamel

e-mail [imɛl] nm e-mail; **envoyer qch par ~** to e-mail sth

émanciper [emɑ̃sipe]: **s'~** vi (fig) to become emancipated ou liberated

emballage [ɑ̃balaʒ] nm (papier) wrapping; (boîte) packaging

emballer [ɑ̃bale] vt to wrap (up); (dans un carton) to pack (up); (fig: fam) to thrill to bits; **s'~** vi (moteur) to race; (cheval) to bolt; (fig: personne) to get carried away

embarcadère [ɑ̃baʀkadɛʀ] nm wharf, pier

embarquement [ɑ̃baʀkəmɑ̃] nm (de passagers) boarding; (de marchandises) loading

embarquer [ɑ̃baʀke] vt (personne) to embark; (marchandise) to load; (fam) to cart off ▷ vi (passager) to board; **s'~** vi to board; **s'~ dans** (affaire, aventure) to embark upon

embarras [ɑ̃baʀa] nm (gêne) embarrassment; **mettre qn dans l'~** to put sb in an awkward position; **vous n'avez que l'~ du choix** the only problem is choosing

embarrassant, e [ɑ̃baʀasɑ̃, ɑ̃t] adj embarrassing

embarrasser [ɑ̃baʀase] vt (encombrer) to clutter (up); (gêner) to hinder, hamper; **~ qn** to put sb in an awkward position; **s'~ de** to burden o.s. with

embaucher [ɑ̃boʃe] vt to take on, hire

embêter [ɑ̃bete] vt to bother; **s'~** vi (s'ennuyer) to be bored

emblée [ɑ̃ble]: **d'~** adv straightaway

embouchure [ɑ̃buʃyʀ] nf (Géo) mouth

embourber [ɑ̃buʀbe]: **s'~** vi to get stuck in the mud

embouteillage [ɑ̃butɛjaʒ] nm traffic jam

embranchement [ɑ̃bʀɑ̃ʃmɑ̃] nm (routier) junction

embrasser [ɑ̃bʀase] vt to kiss; (sujet, période) to embrace, encompass

embrayage [ɑ̃bʀɛjaʒ] nm clutch

embrouiller [ɑ̃bʀuje] vt to muddle up; (fils) to tangle (up); **s'~** vi (personne) to get in a muddle

embruns [ɑ̃bʀœ̃] nmpl sea spray sg

embué, e [ɑ̃bɥe] adj misted up

émeraude [em(ə)ʀod] nf emerald

émerger [emɛʀʒe] vi to emerge; (faire saillie, aussi fig) to stand out

émeri [em(ə)ʀi] nm: **toile ou papier ~** emery paper

émerveiller [emɛʀveje] vt to fill with wonder; **s'~ de** to marvel at

émettre [emɛtʀ] vt (son, lumière) to give out, emit; (message etc: Radio) to transmit; (billet, timbre, emprunt) to issue; (hypothèse, avis) to voice, put forward ▷ vi to broadcast

émeus etc [emø] vb voir **émouvoir**

émeute [emøt] nf riot

émigrer [emigʀe] vi to emigrate

émincer [emɛ̃se] vt to cut into thin slices

émission [emisjɔ̃] nf (Radio, TV) programme, broadcast;

(d'un message) transmission; (de timbre) issue

emmêler [ãmele] vt to tangle (up); (fig) to muddle up; **s'~** vi to get in a tangle

emménager [ãmenaʒe] vi to move in; **~ dans** to move into

emmener [ãm(ə)ne] vt to take (with one); (comme otage, capture) to take away; **~ qn au cinéma** to take sb to the cinema

emmerder [ãmɛʀde] (fam!) vt to bug, bother; **s'~** vi to be bored stiff

émoticone [emotikon] nm smiley

émotif, -ive [emotif, iv] adj emotional

émotion [emosjɔ̃] nf emotion

émouvoir [emuvwaʀ] vt to move; **s'~** vi to be moved; (s'indigner) to be roused

empaqueter [ãpakte] vt to parcel up

emparer [ãpaʀe]: **s'~ de** vt (objet) to seize, grab; (comme otage, Mil) to seize; (suj: peur etc) to take hold of

empêchement [ãpɛʃmã] nm (unexpected) obstacle, hitch

empêcher [ãpeʃe] vt to prevent; **~ qn de faire** to prevent ou stop sb (from) doing; **il n'empêche que** nevertheless; **il n'a pas pu s'~ de rire** he couldn't help laughing

empereur [ãpʀœʀ] nm emperor

empiffrer [ãpifʀe]: **s'~** (fam) vi to stuff o.s.

empiler [ãpile] vt to pile (up)

empire [ãpiʀ] nm empire; (fig) influence

empirer [ãpiʀe] vi to worsen, deteriorate

emplacement [ãplasmã] nm site

emploi [ãplwa] nm (utilisation) use; (Comm, Écon) employment; (poste) job, situation; **mode d'~** directions for use; **emploi du temps** timetable, schedule

employé, e [ãplwaje] nm/f employee; **employé de bureau** office employee ou clerk

employer [ãplwaje] vt to use; (ouvrier, main-d'œuvre) to employ; **s'~ à faire** to apply ou devote o.s. to doing; **employeur, -euse** nm/f employer

empoigner [ãpwaɲe] vt to grab

empoisonner [ãpwazɔne] vt to poison; (empester: air, pièce) to stink out; (fam): **~ qn** to drive sb mad

emporter [ãpɔʀte] vt to take (with one); (en dérobant ou enlevant, emmener: blessés, voyageurs) to take away; (entraîner) to carry away; **s'~** vi (de colère) to lose one's temper; **l'~ (sur)** to get the upper hand (of); **plats à ~** take-away meals

empreinte [ãpʀɛ̃t] nf: **~ (de pas)** footprint; **empreintes (digitales)** fingerprints

empressé, e [ãpʀese] adj attentive

empresser [ãpʀese]: **s'~** vi: **s'~ auprès de qn** to surround sb with attentions; **s'~ de faire** (se hâter) to hasten to do

emprisonner [ãpʀizɔne] vt to imprison

emprunt [ãpʀœ̃] nm loan

emprunter [ãpʀœ̃te] vt to borrow; (itinéraire) to take, follow

ému, e [emy] pp de **émouvoir** ▷ adj (gratitude) touched; (compassion) moved

MOT-CLÉ

en [ã] prép 1 (endroit, pays) in; (direction) to; **habiter en France/ville** to live in France/town; **aller en France/ville** to go to France/town

2 (moment, temps) in; **en été/juin** in summer/June; **en 3**

jours in 3 days

3 (moyen) by; **en avion/taxi** by plane/taxi

4 (composition) made of; **c'est en verre** it's (made of) glass; **un collier en argent** a silver necklace

5 (description, état): **une femme (habillée) en rouge** a woman (dressed) in red; **peindre qch en rouge** to paint sth red; **en T/étoile** T/star-shaped; **en chemise/chaussettes** in one's shirt-sleeves/socks; **en soldat** as a soldier; **cassé en plusieurs morceaux** broken into several pieces; **en réparation** being repaired, under repair; **en vacances** on holiday; **en deuil** in mourning; **le même en plus grand** the same but ou only bigger

6 (avec gérondif) while, on, by; **en dormant** while sleeping, as one sleeps; **en sortant** on going out, as he etc went out; **sortir en courant** to run out

7 (comme) as; **je te parle en ami** I'm talking to you as a friend

▷ pron 1 (indéfini): **j'en ai/veux** I have/want some; **en as-tu?** have you got any?; **je n'en veux pas** I don't want any; **j'en ai 2** I've got 2; **combien y en a-t-il?** how many (of them) are there?; **j'en ai assez** I've got enough (of it ou them); (j'en ai marre) I've had enough

2 (provenance) from there; **j'en viens** I've come from there

3 (cause): **il en est malade/perd le sommeil** he is ill/can't sleep because of it

4 (complément de nom, d'adjectif, de verbe): **j'en connais les dangers** I know its ou the dangers; **j'en suis fier** I am proud of it ou him ou her ou them; **j'en ai besoin** I need it ou them

encadrer [ãkadʀe] vt (tableau, image) to frame; (fig: entourer) to surround; (personnel, soldats etc) to train

encaisser [ãkese] vt (chèque) to cash; (argent) to collect; (fam: coup, défaite) to take

en-cas [ãka] nm snack

enceinte [ãsɛ̃t] adj f: **~ (de 6 mois)** (6 months) pregnant ▷ nf (mur) wall; (espace) enclosure; **enceinte (acoustique)** (loud)speaker

encens [ãsã] nm incense

enchaîner [ãʃene] vt to chain up; (mouvements, séquences) to link (together) ▷ vi to carry on

enchanté, e [ãʃãte] adj (ravi) delighted; (magique) enchanted; **~ (de faire votre connaissance)** pleased to meet you

enchère [ãʃɛʀ] nf bid; **mettre/vendre aux ~s** to put up for (sale by)/sell by auction

enclencher [ãklãʃe] vt (mécanisme) to engage; **s'~** vi to engage

encombrant, e [ãkɔ̃bʀã, ãt] adj cumbersome, bulky

encombrement [ãkɔ̃bʀəmã] nm: **être pris dans un ~** to be stuck in a traffic jam

encombrer [ãkɔ̃bʀe] vt to clutter (up); (gêner) to hamper; **s'~ de** (bagages etc) to load ou burden o.s. with

MOT-CLÉ

encore [ãkɔʀ] adv 1 (continuation) still; **il y travaille encore** he's still working on it; **pas encore** not yet

2 (de nouveau) again; **j'irai encore demain** I'll go again tomorrow; **encore une fois** (once) again; **(et puis) quoi encore?** what next?

3 (en plus) more; **encore un peu de viande?** a little more meat?; **encore deux jours** two more days

4 (intensif) even, still; **encore plus fort/mieux** even louder/better, louder/better still

5 (restriction) even so then, only; **encore pourrais-je le faire si ...** even so, I might be able to do it if ...; **si encore** if only

encourager [ãkuRaʒe] vt to encourage; **~ qn à faire qch** to encourage sb to do sth

encourir [ãkuRiR] vt to incur

encre [ãkR] nf ink; **encre de Chine** Indian ink

encyclopédie [ãsiklɔpedi] nf encyclopaedia

endetter [ãdete]: **s'~** vi to get into debt

endive [ãdiv] nf chicory no pl

endormi, e [ãdɔRmi] adj asleep

endormir [ãdɔRmiR] vt to put to sleep; (suj: chaleur etc) to send to sleep; (Méd: dent, nerf) to anaesthetize; (fig: soupçons) to allay; **s'~** vi to fall asleep, go to sleep

endroit [ãdRwa] nm place; (opposé à l'envers) right side; **à l'~** (vêtement) the right way out; (objet posé) the right way round

endurance [ãdyRãs] nf endurance

endurant, e [ãdyRã, ãt] adj tough, hardy

endurcir [ãdyRsiR]: **s'~** vi (physiquement) to become tougher; (moralement) to become hardened

endurer [ãdyRe] vt to endure, bear

énergétique [enɛRʒetik] adj (aliment) energy-giving

énergie [enɛRʒi] nf (Physique) energy; (Tech) power; (morale) vigour, spirit; **énergique** adj energetic, vigorous; (mesures) drastic, stringent

énervant, e [enɛRvã, ãt] adj irritating, annoying

énerver [enɛRve] vt to irritate, annoy; **s'~** vi to get excited, get worked up

enfance [ãfãs] nf childhood

enfant [ãfã] nm/f child; **enfantin, e** adj (puéril) childlike; (langage, jeu etc) children's cpd

enfer [ãfɛR] nm hell

enfermer [ãfɛRme] vt to shut up; (à clef, interner) to lock up; **s'~** vi to shut o.s. away

enfiler [ãfile] vt (vêtement) to slip on, slip into; (perles) to string; (aiguille) to thread

enfin [ãfɛ̃] adv at last; (en énumérant) lastly; (toutefois) still; (pour conclure) in a word; (somme toute) after all

enflammer [ãflame]: **s'~** vi to catch fire; (Méd) to become inflamed

enflé, e [ãfle] adj swollen

enfler [ãfle] vi to swell (up)

enfoncer [ãfɔ̃se] vt (clou) to drive in; (faire pénétrer) **~ qch dans** to push (ou drive) sth into; (forcer: porte) to break open; **s'~** vi to sink; **s'~ dans** to sink into; (forêt, ville) to disappear into

enfouir [ãfwiR] vt (dans le sol) to bury; (dans un tiroir etc) to tuck away

enfuir [ãfɥiR]: **s'~** vi to run away ou off

engagement [ãgaʒmã] nm commitment; **sans ~** without obligation

engager [ãgaʒe] vt (embaucher) to take on; (: artiste) to engage; (commencer) to start; (lier) to bind, commit; (impliquer) to involve; (investir) to invest, lay out; (inciter) to urge; (introduire: clé) to insert; **s'~** vi (promettre) to commit o.s.; (Mil) to enlist; (débuter: conversation etc) to start (up); **s'~ à faire** to undertake to do; **s'~ dans** (rue, passage) to turn into; (fig: affaire, discussion) to enter into, embark on

engelures [ãʒlyR] nfpl chilblains

engin [ãʒɛ̃] nm machine; (outil) instrument; (Auto) vehicle; (Aviat) aircraft inv

engloutir [ãglutiR] vt to swallow up

engouement [ãgumã] nm (sudden) passion

engouffrer [ãgufRe] vt to swallow up, devour; **s'~ dans** to rush into

engourdir [ãguRdiR] vt to numb; (fig) to dull, blunt; **s'~** vi to go numb

engrais [ãgRe] nm manure; **engrais chimique** chemical fertilizer

engraisser [ãgRese] vt to fatten (up)

engrenage [ãgRanaʒ] nm gears pl, gearing; (fig) chain

engueuler [ãgœle] (fam) vt to bawl at

enhardir [ãaRdiR]: **s'~** vi to grow bolder

énigme [enigm] nf riddle

enivrer [ãnivRe] vt: **s'~** to get drunk

enjamber [ãʒãbe] vt to stride over

enjeu, x [ãʒø] nm stakes pl

enjoué, e [ãʒwe] adj playful

enlaidir [ãlediR] vt to make ugly ▷ vi to become ugly

enlèvement [ãlɛvmã] nm (rapt) abduction, kidnapping

enlever [ãl(ə)ve] vt (ôter: gén) to remove; (: vêtement, lunettes) to take off; (emporter: ordures etc) to take away; (kidnapper) to abduct, kidnap; (obtenir: prix, contrat) to win; (prendre): **~ qch à qn** to take sth (away) from sb

enliser [ãlize]: **s'~** vi to sink, get stuck

enneigé, e [ãneʒe] adj (route, maison) snowed-up; (paysage) snowy

ennemi, e [ɛnmi] adj hostile; (Mil) enemy cpd ▷ nm/f enemy

ennui [ãnɥi] nm (lassitude) boredom; (difficulté) trouble no pl; **avoir des ~s** to have problems; **ennuyer** vt to bother; (lasser) to bore; **s'ennuyer** vi to be bored; **si cela ne vous ennuie pas** if it's no trouble (to you); **ennuyeux, -euse** adj boring, tedious; (embêtant) annoying

énorme [enɔRm] adj enormous, huge; **énormément** adv enormously; **énormément de neige/gens** an enormous amount of snow/number of people

enquête [ãket] nf (de journaliste, de police) investigation; (judiciaire, administrative) inquiry; (sondage d'opinion) survey; **enquêter (sur)** vi to investigate

enragé, e [ãRaʒe] adj (Méd) rabid, with rabies; (fig) fanatical

enrageant, e [ãRaʒã, ãt] adj infuriating

enrager [ãRaʒe] vi to be in a rage

enregistrement [ãR(ə)ʒistRəmã] nm recording; **enregistrement des bagages** baggage check-in

enregistrer [ãR(ə)ʒistRe] vt (Mus etc) to record; (fig: mémoriser) to make a mental note of; (bagages: à l'aéroport) to check in

enrhumer [ãRyme] vt: **s'~, être enrhumé** to catch a cold

enrichir [ãRiʃiR] vt to make rich(er); (fig) to enrich; **s'~** vi to get rich(er)

enrouer [ãRwe]: **s'~** vi to go hoarse

enrouler [ãRule] vt (fil, corde) to wind (up); **s'~ (autour de qch)** to wind (around sth)

enseignant, e [ãsɛɲã, ãt] nm/f teacher

enseignement [ãsɛɲ(ə)mã] nm teaching; (Admin) education

enseigner [ãsɛɲe] vt, vi to teach; **~ qch à qn** to teach sb sth

ensemble [ãsãbl] adv together ▷ nm (groupement) set;

(*vêtements*) outfit; (*totalité*) **l'~ du/de la** the whole *ou* entire; (*unité, harmonie*) unity; **impression/idée d'~** overall *ou* general impression/idea; **dans l'~** (*en gros*) on the whole

ensoleillé [ɑ̃sɔleje] *adj* sunny

ensuite [ɑ̃sɥit] *adv* then, next; (*plus tard*) afterwards, later

entamer [ɑ̃tame] *vt* (*pain, bouteille*) to start; (*hostilités, pourparlers*) to open

entasser [ɑ̃tase] *vt* (*empiler*) to pile up, heap up; **s'~** *vi* (*s'amonceler*) to pile up; **s'~ dans** (*personnes*) to cram into

entendre [ɑ̃tɑ̃dʀ] *vt* to hear; (*comprendre*) to understand; (*vouloir dire*) to mean; **s'~** *vi* (*sympathiser*) to get on; (*se mettre d'accord*) to agree; **j'ai entendu dire que** I've heard (it said) that; **~ parler de** to hear of

entendu, e [ɑ̃tɑ̃dy] *adj* (*réglé*) agreed; (*au courant: air*) knowing; **(c'est)** ~ all right, agreed; **bien** ~ of course

entente [ɑ̃tɑ̃t] *nf* understanding; (*accord, traité*) agreement; **à double ~** (*sens*) with a double meaning

enterrement [ɑ̃tɛʀmɑ̃] *nm* (*cérémonie*) funeral, burial

enterrer [ɑ̃teʀe] *vt* to bury

entêtant, e [ɑ̃tɛtɑ̃, ɑ̃t] *adj* heady

en-tête [ɑ̃tɛt] *nm* heading; **papier à ~** headed notepaper

entêté, e [ɑ̃tete] *adj* stubborn

entêter [ɑ̃tete]: **s'~ vi (~ à faire)** to persist (in doing)

enthousiasme [ɑ̃tuzjasm] *nm* enthusiasm; **enthousiasmer** *vt* to fill with enthusiasm; **s'enthousiasmer (pour qch)** to get enthusiastic (about sth); **enthousiaste** *adj* enthusiastic

entier, ère [ɑ̃tje, jɛʀ] *adj* whole; (*total: satisfaction etc*) complete; (*fig: caractère*) unbending ▷ *nm* (*Math*) whole; **en ~** totally; **lait ~** full-cream milk; **entièrement** *adv* entirely, wholly

entonnoir [ɑ̃tɔnwaʀ] *nm* funnel

entorse [ɑ̃tɔʀs] *nf* (*Méd*) sprain; (*fig*): **~ au règlement** infringement of the rule

entourage [ɑ̃tuʀaʒ] *nm* circle; (*famille*) circle of family/friends; (*ce qui enclôt*) surround

entourer [ɑ̃tuʀe] *vt* to surround; (*apporter son soutien à*) to rally round; **~ de** to surround with; **s'~ de** to surround o.s. with

entracte [ɑ̃tʀakt] *nm* interval

entraide [ɑ̃tʀɛd] *nf* mutual aid

entrain [ɑ̃tʀɛ̃] *nm* spirit; **avec/sans ~** spiritedly/half-heartedly

entraînement [ɑ̃tʀɛnmɑ̃] *nm* training

entraîner [ɑ̃tʀene] *vt* (*charrier*) to carry *ou* drag along; (*Tech*) to drive; (*emmener: personne*) to take (off); (*influencer*) to lead; (*Sport*) to train; (*impliquer*) to entail; **s'~** *vi* (*Sport*) to train; **s'~ à qch/à faire** to train o.s. for sth/to do; **~ qn à faire** (*inciter*) to lead sb to do; **entraîneur, -euse** *nm/f* (*Sport*) coach, trainer ▷ *nm* (*Hippisme*) trainer

entre [ɑ̃tʀ] *prép* between; (*parmi*) among(st); **l'un d'~ eux/nous** one of them/us; **ils se battent ~ eux** they are fighting among(st) themselves; **~ autres (choses)** among other things; **entrecôte** *nf* entrecôte *ou* rib steak

entrée [ɑ̃tʀe] *nf* entrance; (*accès: au cinéma etc*) admission; (*billet*) (admission) ticket; (*Culin*) first course

entre...: **entrefilet** *nm* paragraph (*short article*); **entremets** *nm* (cream) dessert

entrepôt [ɑ̃tʀəpo] *nm* warehouse

entreprendre [ɑ̃tʀəpʀɑ̃dʀ] *vt* (*se lancer dans*) to undertake; (*commencer*) to begin *ou* start (upon)

entrepreneur, -euse [ɑ̃tʀəpʀənœʀ, øz] *nm/f*: **entrepreneur (en bâtiment)** (building) contractor

entreprise [ɑ̃tʀəpʀiz] *nf* (*société*) firm, concern; (*action*) undertaking, venture

entrer [ɑ̃tʀe] *vi* to go (*ou* come) in, enter ▷ *vt* (*Inform*) to enter, input; **(faire) ~ qch dans** to get sth into; **~ dans** (*gén*) to enter; (*pièce*) to go (*ou* come) into, enter; (*club*) to join; (*heurter*) to run into; **~ à l'hôpital** to go into hospital; **faire ~** (*visiteur*) to show in

entre-temps [ɑ̃tʀətɑ̃] *adv* meanwhile

entretenir [ɑ̃tʀət(ə)niʀ] *vt* to maintain; (*famille, maîtresse*) to support, keep; **~ qn (de)** to speak to sb (about)

entretien [ɑ̃tʀətjɛ̃] *nm* maintenance; (*discussion*) discussion, talk; (*pour un emploi*) interview

entrevoir [ɑ̃tʀəvwaʀ] *vt* (*à peine*) to make out; (*brièvement*) to catch a glimpse of

entrevue [ɑ̃tʀəvy] *nf* (*audience*) interview

entrouvert, e [ɑ̃tʀuvɛʀ, ɛʀt] *adj* half-open

énumérer [enymeʀe] *vt* to list

envahir [ɑ̃vaiʀ] *vt* to invade; (*suj: inquiétude, peur*) to come over; **envahissant, e** (*péj*) *adj* (*personne*) intrusive

enveloppe [ɑ̃v(ə)lɔp] *nf* (*de lettre*) envelope; (*crédits*) budget; **envelopper** *vt* to wrap; (*fig*) to envelop, shroud

enverrai *etc* [ɑ̃veʀe] *vb voir* **envoyer**

envers [ɑ̃vɛʀ] *prép* towards, to ▷ *nm* other side; (*d'une étoffe*) wrong side; **à l'~** (*verticalement*) upside down; (*pull*) back to front; (*chaussettes*) inside out

envie [ɑ̃vi] *nf* (*sentiment*) envy; (*souhait*) desire, wish; **avoir ~ de (faire)** to feel like (doing); (*plus fort*) to want (to do); **avoir ~ que** to wish that; **cette glace me fait ~** I fancy some of that ice cream; **envier** *vt* to envy; **envieux, -euse** *adj* envious

environ [ɑ̃viʀɔ̃] *adv*: **~ 3 h/2 km** (around) about 3 o'clock/2 km; *voir aussi* **environs**

environnant, e [ɑ̃viʀɔnɑ̃, ɑ̃t] *adj* surrounding

environnement [ɑ̃viʀɔnmɑ̃] *nm* environment

environs [ɑ̃viʀɔ̃] *nmpl* surroundings; **aux ~ de** (round) about

envisager [ɑ̃vizaʒe] *vt* to contemplate, envisage; **~ de faire** to consider doing

envoler [ɑ̃vɔle]: **s'~** *vi* (*oiseau*) to fly away *ou* off; (*avion*) to take off; (*papier, feuille*) to blow away; (*fig*) to vanish (into thin air)

envoyé, e [ɑ̃vwaje] *nm/f* (*Pol*) envoy; (*Presse*) correspondent; **envoyé spécial** special correspondent

envoyer [ɑ̃vwaje] *vt* to send; (*lancer*) to hurl, throw; **~ chercher** to send for; **~ promener qn** (*fam*) to send sb packing

épagneul, e [epaɲœl] *nm/f* spaniel

épais, se [epɛ, ɛs] *adj* thick; **épaisseur** *nf* thickness

épanouir [epanwiʀ]: **s'~** *vi* (*fleur*) to bloom, open out; (*visage*) to light up; (*personne*) to blossom

épargne [epaʀɲ] *nf* saving

épargner [epaʀɲe] *vt* to save; (*ne pas tuer ou endommager*) to spare ▷ *vi* to save; **~ qch à qn** to spare sb sth

éparpiller [epaʀpije] *vt* to scatter; **s'~** *vi* (*fig*) to dissipate one's efforts

épatant, e [epatɑ̃, ɑ̃t] (*fam*) *adj* super

épater [epate] (*fam*) *vt* (*étonner*) to amaze; (*impressionner*) to impress

épaule [epol] nf shoulder

épave [epav] nf wreck

épée [epe] nf sword

épeler [ep(ə)le] vt to spell

éperon [eprɔ̃] nm spur

épervier [epεrvje] nm sparrowhawk

épi [epi] nm (de blé, d'orge) ear; (de maïs) cob

épice [epis] nf spice

épicé, e [epise] adj spicy

épicer [epise] vt to spice

épicerie [episri] nf grocer's shop; (denrées) groceries pl; **épicerie fine** delicatessen; **épicier, -ière** nm/f grocer

épidémie [epidemi] nf epidemic

épiderme [epidεrm] nm skin

épier [epje] vt to spy on, watch closely

épilepsie [epilεpsi] nf epilepsy

épiler [epile] vt (jambes) to remove the hair from; (sourcils) to pluck

épinards [epinar] nmpl spinach sg

épine [epin] nf thorn, prickle; (d'oursin etc) spine

épingle [epɛ̃gl] nf pin; **épingle de nourrice** ou **de sûreté** safety pin

épisode [epizɔd] nm episode; **film/roman à ~s** serial; **épisodique** adj occasional

épluche-légumes [eplyʃlegym] nm inv (potato) peeler

éplucher [eplyʃe] vt (fruit, légumes) to peel; (fig) to go over with a fine-tooth comb; **épluchures** nfpl peelings

éponge [epɔ̃ʒ] nf sponge; **éponger** vt (liquide) to mop up; (surface) to sponge; (fig: déficit) to soak up

époque [epɔk] nf (de l'histoire) age, era; (de l'année, la vie) time; **d'~** (meuble) period cpd

épouse [epuz] nf wife; **épouser** vt to marry

épousseter [epuste] vt to dust

épouvantable [epuvãtabl] adj appalling, dreadful

épouvantail [epuvãtaj] nm scarecrow

épouvante [epuvãt] nf terror; **film d'~** horror film; **épouvanter** vt to terrify

époux [epu] nm husband ▷ nmpl (married) couple

épreuve [eprœv] nf (d'examen) test; (malheur, difficulté) trial, ordeal; (Photo) print; (Typo) proof; (Sport) event; **à toute ~** unfailing; **mettre à l'~** to put to the test

éprouver [epruve] vt (tester) to test; (marquer, faire souffrir) to afflict, distress; (ressentir) to experience

épuisé, e [epɥize] adj exhausted; (livre) out of print; **épuisement** nm exhaustion

épuiser [epɥize] vt (fatiguer) to exhaust, wear ou tire out; (stock, sujet) to exhaust; **s'~** vi to wear ou tire o.s. out, exhaust o.s.

épuisette [epɥizεt] nf shrimping net

équateur [ekwatœr] nm equator; **(la république de) l'É~** Ecuador

équation [ekwasjɔ̃] nf equation

équerre [ekεr] nf (à dessin) (set) square

équilibre [ekilibr] nm balance; **garder/perdre l'~** to keep/lose one's balance; **être en ~** to be balanced; **équilibré, e** adj well-balanced; **équilibrer** vt to balance

équipage [ekipaʒ] nm crew

équipe [ekip] nf team; **travailler en ~** to work as a team

équipé, e [ekipe] adj: **bien/mal ~** well-/poorly-equipped

équipement [ekipmã] nm equipment

équiper [ekipe] vt to equip; **~ qn/qch de** to equip sb/sth with

équipier, -ière [ekipje, jεr] nm/f team member

équitation [ekitasjɔ̃] nf (horse-)riding; **faire de l'~** to go riding

équivalent, e [ekivalã, ãt] adj, nm equivalent

équivaloir [ekivalwar]: **~ à** vt to be equivalent to

érable [erabl] nm maple

érafler [erafle] vt to scratch; **éraflure** nf scratch

ère [εr] nf era; **en l'an 1050 de notre ~** in the year 1050 A.D.

érection [erεksjɔ̃] nf erection

éroder [erɔde] vt to erode

érotique [erɔtik] adj erotic

errer [ere] vi to wander

erreur [erœr] nf mistake, error; **faire ~** to be mistaken; **par ~** by mistake

éruption [erypsjɔ̃] nf eruption; (Méd) rash

es [ε] vb voir **être**

ès [εs] prép: **licencié ès lettres/sciences** ≈ Bachelor of Arts/Science

ESB sigle f (= encéphalopathie spongiforme bovine) BSE

escabeau, x [εskabo] nm (tabouret) stool; (échelle) stepladder

escalade [εskalad] nf climbing no pl; (Pol etc) escalation; **escalader** vt to climb

escale [εskal] nf (Navig: durée) call; (endroit) port of call; (Aviat) stop(over); **faire ~ à** (Navig) to put in at; (Aviat) to stop over at; **vol sans ~** nonstop flight

escalier [εskalje] nm stairs pl; **dans l'~** ou **les ~s** on the stairs; **escalier mécanique** ou **roulant** escalator

escapade [εskapad] nf: **faire une ~** to go on a jaunt; (s'enfuir) to run away ou off

escargot [εskargo] nm snail

escarpé, e [εskarpe] adj steep

esclavage [εsklavaʒ] nm slavery

esclave [εsklav] nm/f slave

escompte [εskɔ̃t] nm discount

escrime [εskrim] nf fencing

escroc [εskro] nm swindler, conman; **escroquer** vt: **escroquer qch (à qn)** to swindle sth (out of sb); **escroquerie** nf swindle

espace [εspas] nm space; **espacer** vt to space out; **s'espacer** vi (visites etc) to become less frequent

espadon [εspadɔ̃] nm swordfish nm

espadrille [εspadrij] nf rope-soled sandal

Espagne [εspaɲ] nf: **l'~** Spain; **espagnol, e** adj Spanish ▷ nm/f: **Espagnol, e** Spaniard ▷ nm (Ling) Spanish

espèce [εspεs] nf (Bio, Bot, Zool) species inv; (gén: sorte) sort, kind, type; (péj): **~ de maladroit/de brute!** you clumsy oaf/you brute!; **espèces** nfpl (Comm) cash sg; **payer en ~** to pay (in) cash

espérance [εsperãs] nf hope; **espérance de vie** life expectancy

espérer [εspere] vt to hope for; **j'espère (bien)** I hope so; **~ que/faire** to hope that/to do

espiègle [εspjεgl] adj mischievous

espion, ne [εspjɔ̃, jɔn] nm/f spy; **espionnage** nm espionage, spying; **espionner** vt to spy (up)on

espoir [εspwar] nm hope; **dans l'~ de/que** in the hope of/that; **reprendre ~** not to lose hope

esprit [εspri] nm (intellect) mind; (humour) wit; (mentalité, d'une loi etc, fantôme etc) spirit; **faire de l'~** to try to be witty; **reprendre ses ~s** to come to; **perdre l'~** to lose one's mind

esquimau, de, -x [εskimo, od] adj Eskimo ▷ nm/f: **E~, de** Eskimo ▷ nm: **E~®** ice lolly (BRIT), popsicle (US)

essai [esɛ] *nm* (*tentative*) attempt, try; (*de produit*) testing; (*Rugby*) try; (*Littérature*) essay; **à l'~** on a trial basis; **mettre à l'~** to put to the test

essaim [esɛ̃] *nm* swarm

essayer [eseje] *vt* to try; (*vêtement, chaussures*) to try (on); (*méthode, voiture*) to try (out) ▷ *vi* to try; **~ de faire** to try *ou* attempt to do

essence [esɑ̃s] *nf* (*de voiture*) petrol (BRIT), gas(oline) (US); (*extrait de plante*) essence; (*espèce: d'arbre*) species *inv*

essentiel, le [esɑ̃sjɛl] *adj* essential; **c'est l'~** (*ce qui importe*) that's the main thing; **l'~ de** the main part of

essieu, x [esjø] *nm* axle

essor [esɔʀ] *nm* (*de l'économie etc*) rapid expansion

essorer [esɔʀe] *vt* (*en tordant*) to wring (out); (*par la force centrifuge*) to spin-dry; **essoreuse** *nf* spin-dryer

essouffler [esufle]: **s'~** *vi* to get out of breath

essuie-glace [esɥiglas] *nm inv* windscreen (BRIT) windshield (US) wiper

essuyer [esɥije] *vt* to wipe; (*fig: échec*) to suffer; **s'~** *vi* (*après le bain*) to dry o.s.; **~ la vaisselle** to dry up

est¹ [ɛ] *vb voir* **être**

est² [ɛst] *nm* east ▷ *adj inv* east; (*région*) east(ern); **à l'~** in the east; (*direction*) to the east, east(wards); **à l'~ de** (to the) east of

est-ce que [ɛskə] *adv*: **~ c'est cher/c'était bon?** is it expensive/was it good?; **quand est-ce qu'il part?** when does he leave?, when is he leaving?; *voir aussi* **que**

esthéticienne [ɛstetisjɛn] *nf* beautician

esthétique [ɛstetik] *adj* attractive

estimation [ɛstimasjɔ̃] *nf* valuation; (*chiffre*) estimate

estime [ɛstim] *nf* esteem, regard; **estimer** *vt* (*respecter*) to esteem; (*expertiser: bijou etc*) to value; (*évaluer: coût etc*) to assess, estimate; (*penser*): **estimer que/être** to consider that/o.s. to be

estival, e, -aux [ɛstival, o] *adj* summer *cpd*

estivant, e [ɛstivɑ̃, ɑ̃t] *nm/f* (summer) holiday-maker

estomac [ɛstɔma] *nm* stomach

estragon [ɛstʀagɔ̃] *nm* tarragon

estuaire [ɛstɥɛʀ] *nm* estuary

et [e] *conj* and; **et lui?** what about him?; **et alors!** so what!

étable [etabl] *nf* cowshed

établi [etabli] *nm* (work)bench

établir [etabliʀ] *vt* (*papiers d'identité, facture*) to make out; (*liste, programme*) to draw up; (*entreprise*) to set up; (*réputation, usage, fait, culpabilité*) to establish; **s'~** *vi* to be established; **s'~ (à son compte)** to set up in business; **s'~ à/près de** to settle in/near

établissement [etablismɑ̃] *nm* (*entreprise, institution*) establishment; **établissement scolaire** school, educational establishment

étage [etaʒ] *nm* (*d'immeuble*) storey, floor; **à l'~** upstairs; **au 2ème ~** on the 2nd (BRIT) *ou* 3rd (US) floor; **c'est à quel ~?** what floor is it on?

étagère [etaʒɛʀ] *nf* (*rayon*) shelf; (*meuble*) shelves *pl*

étai [etɛ] *nm* stay, prop

étain [etɛ̃] *nm* pewter *no pl*

étais *etc* [etɛ] *vb voir* **être**

étaler [etale] *vt* (*carte, nappe*) to spread (out); (*peinture*) to spread; (*échelonner: paiements, vacances*) to spread, stagger; (*marchandises*) to display; (*connaissances*) to parade; **s'~** *vi* (*liquide*) to spread out; (*fam*) to fall flat on one's face; **s'~ sur** (*suj: paiements etc*) to be spread out over

étalon [etalɔ̃] *nm* (*cheval*) stallion

étanche [etɑ̃ʃ] *adj* (*récipient*) watertight; (*montre, vêtement*) waterproof

étang [etɑ̃] *nm* pond

étant [etɑ̃] *vb voir* **être; donné**

étape [etap] *nf* stage; (*lieu d'arrivée*) stopping place; (*: Cyclisme*) staging point

état [eta] *nm* (*Pol, condition*) state; **en mauvais ~** in poor condition; **en ~ (de marche)** in (working) order; **remettre en ~** to repair; **hors d'~** out of order; **être en ~/hors d'~ de faire** to be in a/in no fit state to do; **être dans tous ses ~s** to be in a state; **faire ~ de** (*alléguer*) to put forward; **l'É~** the State; **état civil** civil status; **état des lieux** inventory of fixtures; **États-Unis** *nmpl*: **les États-Unis** the United States

etc. [ɛtseteʀa] *adv* etc

et c(a)etera [ɛtseteʀa] *adv* et cetera, and so on

été [ete] *pp de* **être** ▷ *nm* summer

éteindre [etɛ̃dʀ] *vt* (*lampe, lumière, radio*) to turn *ou* switch off; (*cigarette, feu*) to put out, extinguish; **s'~** *vi* (*feu, lumière*) to go out; (*mourir*) to pass away; **éteint, e** *adj* (*fig*) lacklustre, dull; (*volcan*) extinct

étendre [etɑ̃dʀ] *vt* (*pâte, liquide*) to spread; (*carte etc*) to spread out; (*linge*) to hang up; (*bras, jambes*) to stretch out; (*fig: agrandir*) to extend; **s'~** *vi* (*augmenter, se propager*) to spread; (*terrain, forêt etc*) to stretch; (*s'allonger*) to stretch out; (*se coucher*) to lie down; (*fig: expliquer*) to elaborate

étendu, e [etɑ̃dy] *adj* extensive

éternel, le [etɛʀnɛl] *adj* eternal

éternité [etɛʀnite] *nf* eternity; **ça a duré une ~** it lasted for ages

éternuement [etɛʀnymɑ̃] *nm* sneeze

éternuer [etɛʀnɥe] *vi* to sneeze

êtes [ɛt(z)] *vb voir* **être**

Éthiopie [etjɔpi] *nf*: **l'~** Ethiopia

étiez [etje] *vb voir* **être**

étinceler [etɛ̃s(ə)le] *vi* to sparkle

étincelle [etɛ̃sɛl] *nf* spark

étiquette [etikɛt] *nf* label; (*protocole*): **l'~** etiquette

étirer [etiʀe]: **s'~** *vi* (*personne*) to stretch; (*convoi, route*): **s'~ sur** to stretch out over

étoile [etwal] *nf* star; **à la belle ~** in the open; **étoile de mer** starfish; **étoile filante** shooting star; **étoilé, e** *adj* starry

étonnant, e [etɔnɑ̃, ɑ̃t] *adj* amazing

étonnement [etɔnmɑ̃] *nm* surprise, amazement

étonner [etɔne] *vt* to surprise, amaze; **s'~ que/de** to be amazed that/at; **cela m'~ait (que)** (*j'en doute*) I'd be very surprised (if)

étouffer [etufe] *vt* to suffocate; (*bruit*) to muffle; (*scandale*) to hush up ▷ *vi* to suffocate; **s'~** *vi* (*en mangeant etc*) to choke; **on étouffe** it's stifling

étourderie [eturdəri] *nf* (*caractère*) absent-mindedness *no pl*; (*faute*) thoughtless blunder

étourdi, e [eturdi] *adj* (*distrait*) scatterbrained, heedless

étourdir [eturdiʀ] *vt* (*assommer*) to stun, daze; (*griser*) to make dizzy *ou* giddy; **étourdissement** *nm* dizzy spell

étrange [etʀɑ̃ʒ] *adj* strange

étranger, -ère [etʀɑ̃ʒe, ɛʀ] *adj* foreign; (*pas de la famille, non familier*) strange ▷ *nm/f* foreigner; stranger ▷ *nm*: **à l'~** abroad

étrangler [etʁɑ̃gle] vt to strangle; **s'~** vi (en mangeant etc) to choke

O MOT-CLÉ

être [ɛtʁ] nm being; **être humain** human being
▷ vb +attrib **1** (état, description) to be; **il est instituteur** he is ou he's a teacher; **vous êtes grand/intelligent/fatigué** you are ou you're tall/clever/tired
2 (+à: appartenir) to be; **le livre est à Paul** the book is Paul's ou belongs to Paul; **c'est à moi/eux** it is ou it's mine/theirs
3 (+de: provenance): **il est de Paris** he's from Paris; (: appartenance): **il est des nôtres** he is one of us
4 (date): **nous sommes le 10 janvier** it's the 10th of January (today)
▷ vi to be; **je ne serai pas ici demain** I won't be here tomorrow
▷ vb aux **1** to have; to be; **être arrivé/allé** to have arrived/gone; **il est parti** he has left, he has gone
2 (forme passive) to be; **être fait par** to be made by; **il a été promu** he has been promoted
3 (+à: obligation): **c'est à réparer** it needs repairing; **c'est à essayer** it should be tried; **il est à espérer que ...** it is ou it's to be hoped that ...
▷ vb impers **1**: **il est** +adjectif it is +adjective; **il est impossible de le faire** it's impossible to do it
2 (heure, date): **il est 10 heures** it is ou it's 10 o'clock
3 (emphatique): **c'est moi** it's me; **c'est à lui de le faire** it's up to him to do it

étrennes [etʁɛn] nfpl Christmas box sg

étrier [etʁije] nm stirrup

étroit, e [etʁwa, wat] adj narrow; (vêtement) tight; (fig: liens, collaboration) close; **à l'~** cramped; **~ d'esprit** narrow-minded

étude [etyd] nf studying; (ouvrage, rapport) study; (Scol: salle de travail) study room; **études** nfpl (Scol) studies; **être à l'~** (projet etc) to be under consideration; **faire des ~s (de droit/médecine)** to study (law/medicine)

étudiant, e [etydjɑ̃, jɑ̃t] nm/f student

étudier [etydje] vt, vi to study

étui [etɥi] nm case

eu, eue [y] pp de **avoir**

euh [ø] excl er

euro [øʁo] nm euro

Europe [øʁɔp] nf: **l'~** Europe; **européen, ne** adj European ▷ nm/f: **Européen, ne** European

eus etc [y] vb voir **avoir**

eux [ø] pron (sujet) they; (objet) them

évacuer [evakɥe] vt to evacuate

évader [evade]: **s'~** vi to escape

évaluer [evalɥe] vt (expertiser) to appraise, evaluate; (juger approximativement) to estimate

évangile [evɑ̃ʒil] nm gospel; **É~** Gospel

évanouir [evanwiʁ]: **s'~** vi to faint; (disparaître) to vanish, disappear; **évanouissement** nm (syncope) fainting fit

évaporer [evapɔʁe]: **s'~** vi to evaporate

évasion [evazjɔ̃] nf escape

éveillé, e [eveje] adj awake; (vif) alert, sharp; **éveiller** vt to (a)waken; (soupçons etc) to arouse; **s'éveiller** vi to (a)waken; (fig) to be aroused

événement [evɛnmɑ̃] nm event

éventail [evɑ̃taj] nm fan; (choix) range

éventualité [evɑ̃tɥalite] nf eventuality; possibility; **dans l'~ de** in the event of

éventuel, le [evɑ̃tɥɛl] adj possible

éventuellement [evɑ̃tɥɛlmɑ̃] adv possibly

évêque [evɛk] nm bishop

évidemment [evidamɑ̃] adv (bien sûr) of course; (certainement) obviously

évidence [evidɑ̃s] nf obviousness; (fait) obvious fact; **de toute ~** quite obviously ou evidently; **être en ~** to be clearly visible; **mettre en ~** (fait) to highlight; **évident, e** adj obvious, evident; **ce n'est pas évident!** (fam) it's not that easy!

évier [evje] nm (kitchen) sink

éviter [evite] vt to avoid; **~ de faire** to avoid doing; **~ qch à qn** to spare sb sth

évoluer [evɔlɥe] vi (enfant, maladie) to develop; (situation, moralement) to develop, evolve; (aller et venir) to move about; **évolution** nf development, evolution

évoquer [evɔke] vt to call to mind, evoke; (mentionner) to mention

ex- [ɛks] préfixe ex-; **son ~mari** her ex-husband; **son ~femme** his ex-wife

exact, e [ɛgza(kt), ɛgzakt] adj exact; (correct) correct; (ponctuel) punctual; **l'heure ~e** the right ou exact time; **exactement** adv exactly

ex aequo [ɛgzeko] adj equally placed; **arriver ~** to finish neck and neck

exagéré, e [ɛgzaʒeʁe] adj (prix etc) excessive

exagérer [ɛgzaʒeʁe] vt to exaggerate ▷ vi to exaggerate; (abuser) to go too far

examen [ɛgzamɛ̃] nm examination; (Scol) exam, examination; **à l'~** under consideration; **examen médical** (medical) examination; (analyse) test

examinateur, -trice [ɛgzaminatœʁ, tʁis] nm/f examiner

examiner [ɛgzamine] vt to examine

exaspérant, e [ɛgzaspeʁɑ̃, ɑ̃t] adj exasperating

exaspérer [ɛgzaspeʁe] vt to exasperate

exaucer [ɛgzose] vt (vœu) to grant

excéder [ɛksede] vt (dépasser) to exceed; (agacer) to exasperate

excellent, e [ɛksɛlɑ̃, ɑ̃t] adj excellent

excentrique [ɛksɑ̃tʁik] adj eccentric

excepté, e [ɛksɛpte] adj, prép: **les élèves ~s, ~ les élèves** except for the pupils

exception [ɛksɛpsjɔ̃] nf exception; **à l'~ de** except for, with the exception of; **d'~** (mesure, loi) special, exceptional; **exceptionnel, le** adj exceptional; **exceptionnellement** adv exceptionally

excès [ɛksɛ] nm surplus ▷ nmpl excesses; **faire des ~** to overindulge; **excès de vitesse** speeding no pl; **excessif, -ive** adj excessive

excitant, e [ɛksitɑ̃, ɑ̃t] adj exciting ▷ nm stimulant; **excitation** nf (état) excitement

exciter [ɛksite] vt to excite; (suj: café etc) to stimulate; **s'~** vi to get excited

exclamer [ɛksklame]: **s'~** vi to exclaim

exclure [ɛksklyʁ] vt (faire sortir) to expel; (ne pas compter) to exclude, leave out; (rendre impossible) to exclude, rule out; **il est exclu que** it's out of the question that ...; **il n'est pas exclu que ...** it's not impossible that ...; **exclusif, -ive** adj exclusive; **exclusion** nf exclusion; **à l'exclusion de** with the exclusion ou exception of;

exclusivité nf (Comm) exclusive rights pl; **film passant en exclusivité à** film showing only at

excursion [ɛkskyRsjɔ̃] nf (en autocar) excursion, trip; (à pied) walk, hike

excuse [ɛkskyz] nf excuse; **excuses** nfpl (regret) apology sg, apologies; **excuser** vt to excuse; **s'excuser (de)** to apologize (for); **excusez-moi** I'm sorry; (pour attirer l'attention) excuse me

exécuter [ɛgzekyte] vt (tuer) to execute; (tâche etc) to execute, carry out; (Mus: jouer) to perform, execute; **s'~** vi to comply

exemplaire [ɛgzɑ̃plɛR] nm copy

exemple [ɛgzɑ̃pl] nm example; **par ~** for instance, for example; **donner l'~** to set an example

exercer [ɛgzɛRse] vt (pratiquer) to exercise, practise; (influence, contrôle) to exert; (former) to exercise, train; **s'~** vi (sportif, musicien) to practise

exercice [ɛgzɛRsis] nm exercise

exhiber [ɛgzibe] vt (montrer: papiers, certificat) to present, produce; (péj) to display, flaunt; **s'~** vi to parade; (suj: exhibitionniste) to expose o.s; **exhibitionniste** nm/f flasher

exigeant, e [ɛgziʒɑ̃, ɑ̃t] adj demanding; (péj) hard to please

exiger [ɛgziʒe] vt to demand, require

exil [ɛgzil] nm exile; **exiler** vt to exile; **s'exiler** vi to go into exile

existence [ɛgzistɑ̃s] nf existence

exister [ɛgziste] vi to exist; **il existe un/des** there is a/are (some)

exorbitant, e [ɛgzɔRbitɑ̃, ɑ̃t] adj exorbitant

exotique [ɛgzɔtik] adj exotic; **yaourt aux fruits ~s** tropical fruit yoghurt

expédier [ɛkspedje] vt (lettre, paquet) to send; (troupes) to dispatch; (fam: travail etc) to dispose of, dispatch; **expéditeur, -trice** nm/f sender; **expédition** nf sending; (scientifique, sportive, Mil) expedition

expérience [ɛksperjɑ̃s] nf (de la vie) experience; (scientifique) experiment

expérimenté, e [ɛksperimɑ̃te] adj experienced

expérimenter [ɛksperimɑ̃te] vt to test out, experiment with

expert, e [ɛkspɛR, ɛRt] adj, nm expert; **~ en objets d'art** art appraiser; **expert-comptable** nm ≈ chartered accountant (BRIT), ≈ certified public accountant (US)

expirer [ɛkspiRe] vi (prendre fin, mourir) to expire; (respirer) to breathe out

explication [ɛksplikasjɔ̃] nf explanation; (discussion) discussion; (dispute) argument

explicite [ɛksplisit] adj explicit

expliquer [ɛksplike] vt to explain; **s'~** to explain (o.s.); **s'~ avec qn** (discuter) to explain o.s. to sb; **son erreur s'explique** one can understand his mistake

exploit [ɛksplwa] nm exploit, feat; **exploitant, e** nm/f: **exploitant (agricole)** farmer; **exploitation** nf exploitation; (d'une entreprise) running; **exploitation agricole** farming concern; **exploiter** vt (personne, don) to exploit; (entreprise, ferme) to run, operate; (mine) to exploit, work

explorer [ɛksplɔRe] vt to explore

exploser [ɛksploze] vi to explode, blow up; (engin explosif) to go off; (personne: de colère) to flare up; **explosif, -ive** adj, nm explosive; **explosion** nf explosion; (de joie, colère) outburst

exportateur, -trice [ɛkspɔRtatœR, tRis] adj export cpd, exporting ▷ nm exporter

exportation [ɛkspɔRtasjɔ̃] nf (action) exportation; (produit) export

exporter [ɛkspɔRte] vt to export

exposant [ɛkspozɑ̃] nm exhibitor

exposé, e [ɛkspoze] nm talk ▷ adj: **~ au sud** facing south

exposer [ɛkspoze] vt (marchandise) to display; (peinture) to exhibit, show; (parler de) to explain, set out; (mettre en danger, orienter, Photo) to expose; **s'~ à** (soleil, danger) to expose o.s. to; **exposition** nf (manifestation) exhibition; (Photo) exposure

exprès¹ [ɛkspRɛ] adv (délibérément) on purpose; (spécialement) specially; **faire ~ de faire qch** to do sth on purpose

exprès², -esse [ɛkspRɛs] adj inv (lettre, colis) express

express [ɛkspRɛs] adj, nm: **(café) ~** espresso (coffee); **(train) ~** fast train

expressif, -ive [ɛkspRɛsif, iv] adj expressive

expression [ɛkspRɛsjɔ̃] nf expression

exprimer [ɛkspRime] vt (sentiment, idée) to express; (jus, liquide) to press out; **s'~** vi (personne) to express o.s.

expulser [ɛkspylse] vt to expel; (locataire) to evict; (Sport) to send off

exquis, e [ɛkski, iz] adj exquisite

extasier [ɛkstazje]: **s'~ sur** vt to go into raptures over

exténuer [ɛkstenɥe] vt to exhaust

extérieur, e [ɛksteRjœR] adj (porte, mur etc) outer, outside; (au dehors: escalier, w.-c.) outside; (commerce) foreign; (influences) external; (apparent: calme, gaieté etc) surface cpd ▷ nm (d'une maison, d'un récipient etc) outside, exterior; (apparence) exterior; **à l'~** outside; (à l'étranger) abroad

externat [ɛkstɛRna] nm day school

externe [ɛkstɛRn] adj external, outer ▷ nm/f (Méd) non-resident medical student (BRIT), extern (US); (Scol) day pupil

extincteur [ɛkstɛ̃ktœR] nm (fire) extinguisher

extinction [ɛkstɛ̃ksjɔ̃] nf: **extinction de voix** loss of voice

extra [ɛkstRa] adj inv first-rate; (fam) fantastic ▷ nm inv extra help

extraire [ɛkstRɛR] vt to extract; **~ qch de** to extract sth from; **extrait** nm extract; **extrait de naissance** birth certificate

extraordinaire [ɛkstRaɔRdinɛR] adj extraordinary; (Pol: mesures etc) special

extravagant, e [ɛkstRavagɑ̃, ɑ̃t] adj extravagant

extraverti, e [ɛkstRavɛRti] adj extrovert

extrême [ɛkstRɛm] adj, nm extreme; **d'un ~ à l'autre** from one extreme to another; **extrêmement** adv extremely; **Extrême-Orient** nm Far East

extrémité [ɛkstRemite] nf end; (situation) straits pl, plight; (geste désespéré) extreme action; **extrémités** nfpl (pieds et mains) extremities

exubérant, e [ɛgzybeRɑ̃, ɑ̃t] adj exuberant

f

F _abr_ = **franc**; (_appartement_): **un F2/F3** a one-/two-bedroom flat (_BRIT_) _ou_ apartment (_US_)

fa [fɑ] _nm inv_ (_Mus_) F; (_en chantant la gamme_) fa

fabricant, e [fabʀikɑ̃, ɑ̃t] _nm/f_ manufacturer

fabrication [fabʀikasjɔ̃] _nf_ manufacture

fabrique [fabʀik] _nf_ factory; **fabriquer** _vt_ to make; (_industriellement_) to manufacture; (_fig_): **qu'est-ce qu'il fabrique?** (_fam_) what is he doing?

fac [fak] (_fam_) _abr f_ (_Scol_) = **faculté**

façade [fasad] _nf_ front, façade

face [fas] _nf_ face; (_fig: aspect_) side ▷ _adj_: **le côté ~** heads; **en ~ de** opposite; (_fig_) in front of; **de ~** (_voir_) face on; **~** facing; (_fig_) faced with, in the face of; **faire ~ à** to face; **~ à ~** _adv_ facing each other ▷ _nm inv_ encounter

fâché, e [fɑʃe] (_fam_) _adj_ angry; (_désolé_) sorry

fâcher [fɑʃe] _vt_ to anger; **se ~ (contre qn)** _vi_ to get angry (with sb); **se ~ avec** (_se brouiller_) to fall out with

facile [fasil] _adj_ easy; (_caractère_) easy-going; **facilement** _adv_ easily; **facilité** _nf_ easiness; (_disposition, don_) aptitude; **facilités** (_possibilités_) facilities; (_Comm_) terms; **faciliter** _vt_ to make easier

façon [fasɔ̃] _nf_ (_manière_) way; (_d'une robe etc_) making-up, cut; **façons** _nfpl_ (_péj_) fuss _sg_; **de ~ à/à ce que** so as to/that; **de toute ~** anyway, in any case; **sans ~** (_accepter_) without fuss; **non merci, sans ~** no thanks, honestly

facteur, -trice [faktœʀ] _nm/f_ postman(-woman) (_BRIT_), mailman(-woman) (_US_) ▷ _nm_ (_Math, fig: élément_) factor

facture [faktyʀ] _nf_ (_à payer: gén_) bill; (_Comm_) invoice

facultatif, -ive [fakyltatif, iv] _adj_ optional

faculté [fakylte] _nf_ (_intellectuelle, d'université_) faculty; (_pouvoir, possibilité_) power

fade [fad] _adj_ insipid

faible [fɛbl] _adj_ weak; (_voix, lumière, vent_) faint; (_rendement, revenu_) low ▷ _nm_ (_pour quelqu'un_) weakness, soft spot; **faiblesse** _nf_ weakness; **faiblir** _vi_ to weaken; (_lumière_) to dim; (_vent_) to drop

faïence [fajɑ̃s] _nf_ earthenware _no pl_

faillir [fajiʀ] _vi_: **j'ai failli tomber** I almost _ou_ very nearly fell

faillite [fajit] _nf_ bankruptcy; **faire ~** to go bankrupt

faim [fɛ̃] _nf_ hunger; **avoir ~** to be hungry; **rester sur sa ~** (_aussi fig_) to be left wanting more

fainéant, e [fɛneɑ̃, ɑ̃t] _nm/f_ idler, loafer

⭕ **MOT-CLÉ**

faire [fɛʀ] _vt_ **1** (_fabriquer, être l'auteur de_) to make; **faire du vin/une offre/un film** to make wine/an offer/a film; **faire du bruit** to make a noise

2 (_effectuer: travail, opération_) to do; **que faites-vous?** (_quel métier etc_) what do you do?; (_quelle activité: au moment de la question_) what are you doing?; **faire la lessive** to do the washing

3 (_études_) to do; (_sport, musique_) to play; **faire du droit/du français** to do law/French; **faire du rugby/piano** to play rugby/the piano

4 (_simuler_): **faire le malade/l'innocent** to act the invalid/the innocent

5 (_transformer, avoir un effet sur_): **faire de qn un frustré/avocat** to make sb frustrated/a lawyer; **ça ne me fait rien** (_m'est égal_) I don't care ou mind; (_me laisse froid_) it has no effect on me; **ça ne fait rien** it doesn't matter; **faire que** (_impliquer_) to mean that

6 (_calculs, prix, mesures_): **2 et 2 font 4** 2 and 2 are ou make 4; **ça fait 10 m/15 euros** it's 10 m/15 euros; **je vous le fais 10 euros** I'll let you have it for 10 euros; **je fais du 40** I take a size 40

7 (_distance_): **faire du 50 (à l'heure)** to do 50 (km an hour); **nous avons fait 1000 km en 2 jours** we did ou covered 1000 km in 2 days; **faire l'Europe** to tour ou do Europe; **faire les magasins** to go shopping

8: **qu'a-t-il fait de sa valise?** what has he done with his case?

9: **ne faire que**: **il ne fait que critiquer** (_sans cesse_) all he (ever) does is criticize; (_seulement_) he's only criticizing

10 (_dire_) to say; **"vraiment?" fit-il** "really?" he said

11 (_maladie_) to have; **faire du diabète** to have diabetes _sg_

▷ _vi_ **1** (_agir, s'y prendre_) to act, do; **il faut faire vite** we (ou you etc) must act quickly; **comment a-t-il fait pour?** how did he manage to?; **faites comme chez vous** make yourself at home

2 (_paraître_) to look; **faire vieux/démodé** to look old/old-fashioned; **ça fait bien** it looks good

▷ _vb substitut_ to do; **ne le casse pas comme je l'ai fait** don't break it as I did; **je peux le voir? - faites!** can I see it? - please do!

▷ _vb impers_ **1**: **il fait beau** _etc_ the weather's fine _etc_; _voir aussi_ **jour**; **froid** _etc_

2 (_temps écoulé, durée_): **ça fait 2 ans qu'il est parti** it's 2 years since he left; **ça fait 2 ans qu'il y est** he's been there for 2 years

▷ _vb semi-aux_ **1**: **faire** (+_infinitif: action directe_) to make; **faire tomber/bouger qch** to make sth fall/move; **faire démarrer un moteur/chauffer de l'eau** to start up an engine/heat some water; **cela fait dormir** it makes you sleep; **faire travailler les enfants** to make the children work ou get the children to work; **il m'a fait traverser la rue** he helped me to cross the street

2 (_indirectement, par un intermédiaire_): **faire réparer qch** to get ou have sth repaired; **faire punir les enfants** to have the children punished

se faire _vi_ **1** (_être convenable_): **cela se fait beaucoup/ne se fait pas** it's done a lot/not done

2: **se faire** +*nom ou pron*: **se faire une jupe** to make o.s. a skirt; **se faire des amis** to make friends; **se faire du souci** to worry; **il ne s'en fait pas** he doesn't worry
3: **se faire** +*adj* (*devenir*): **se faire vieux** to be getting old; **se faire beau** to do o.s. up
4: **se faire à** (*s'habituer*) to get used to; **je n'arrive pas à me faire à la nourriture/au climat** I can't get used to the food/climate
5: **se faire** +*infinitif*: **se faire examiner la vue/opérer** to have one's eyes tested/have an operation; **se faire couper les cheveux** to get one's hair cut; **il va se faire tuer/punir** he's going to get himself killed/get punished; **il s'est fait aider** he got somebody to help him; **il s'est fait aider par Simon** he got Simon to help him; **se faire faire un vêtement** to get a garment made for o.s.
6 (*impersonnel*): **comment se fait-il/faisait-il que?** how is it/was it that?

faire-part [fɛʀpaʀ] *nm inv* announcement (*of birth, marriage etc*)
faisan, e [fəzɑ̃, an] *nm/f* pheasant
faisons [fəzɔ̃] *vb voir* **faire**
fait, e [fɛ, fɛt] *adj* (*mûr: fromage, melon*) ripe ▷ *nm* (*événement*) event, occurrence; (*réalité, donnée*) fact; **être au ~ (de)** to be informed (of); **au ~** (*à propos*) by the way; **en venir au ~** to get to the point; **du ~ de ceci/qu'il a menti** because of *ou* on account of this/his having lied; **de ce ~** for this reason; **en ~** in fact; **prendre qn sur le ~** to catch sb in the act; **c'est bien ~ pour lui** (*ou eux etc*) it serves him (*ou them etc*) right; **fait divers** news item
faites [fɛt] *vb voir* **faire**
falaise [falɛz] *nf* cliff
falloir [falwaʀ] *vb impers*: **il faut qu'il parte/a fallu qu'il parte** (*obligation*) he has to *ou* must leave/had to leave; **il a fallu le faire** it had to be done; **il faudrait qu'elle rentre** she should come *ou* go back, she ought to come *ou* go back; **il faut faire attention** you have to be careful; **il me faudrait 100 euros** I would need 100 euros; **il vous faut tourner à gauche après l'église** you have to turn left past the church; **nous avons ce qu'il (nous) faut** we have what we need; **il ne fallait pas** you shouldn't have (done); **comme il faut** (*personne*) proper; (*agir*) properly; **s'en ~**: **il s'en faut de 100 euros/5 minutes** we/they *etc* were 100 euros short/5 minutes late (*ou* early); **il s'en faut de beaucoup qu'il soit** he is far from being; **il s'en est fallu de peu que cela n'arrive** it very nearly happened
famé, e [fame] *adj*: **mal ~** disreputable, of ill repute
fameux, -euse [famø, øz] *adj* (*illustre*) famous; (*bon: repas, plat etc*) first-rate, first-class; (*valeur intensive*) real, downright
familial, e, -aux [familjal, jo] *adj* family *cpd*
familiarité [familjaʀite] *nf* familiarity
familier, -ère [familje, jɛʀ] *adj* (*connu*) familiar; (*atmosphère*) informal, friendly; (*Ling*) informal, colloquial ▷ *nm* regular (visitor)
famille [famij] *nf* family; **il a de la ~ à Paris** he has relatives in Paris
famine [famin] *nf* famine
fanatique [fanatik] *adj* fanatical ▷ *nm/f* fanatic
faner [fane] *se* **~** *vi* to fade
fanfare [fɑ̃faʀ] *nf* (*orchestre*) brass band; (*musique*) fanfare

fantaisie [fɑ̃tezi] *nf* (*spontanéité*) fancy, imagination; (*caprice*) whim ▷ *adj*: **bijou ~** costume jewellery
fantasme [fɑ̃tasm] *nm* fantasy
fantastique [fɑ̃tastik] *adj* fantastic
fantôme [fɑ̃tom] *nm* ghost, phantom
faon [fɑ̃] *nm* fawn
FAQ *sigle f* (= **foire aux questions**) FAQ
farce [faʀs] *nf* (*viande*) stuffing; (*blague*) (practical) joke; (*Théâtre*) farce; **farcir** *vt* (*viande*) to stuff
farder [faʀde] *se* **~** *vi* to make (o.s.) up
farine [faʀin] *nf* flour
farouche [faʀuʃ] *adj* (*timide*) shy, timid
fart [faʀt] *nm* (ski) wax
fascination [fasinasjɔ̃] *nf* fascination
fasciner [fasine] *vt* to fascinate
fascisme [faʃism] *nm* fascism
fasse *etc* [fas] *vb voir* **faire**
fastidieux, -euse [fastidjø, jøz] *adj* tedious, tiresome
fatal, e [fatal] *adj* fatal; (*inévitable*) inevitable; **fatalité** *nf* (*destin*) fate; (*coïncidence*) fateful coincidence
fatidique [fatidik] *adj* fateful
fatigant, e [fatigɑ̃, ɑ̃t] *adj* tiring; (*agaçant*) tiresome
fatigue [fatig] *nf* tiredness, fatigue; **fatigué, e** *adj* tired; **fatiguer** *vt* to tire, make tired; (*fig: agacer*) to annoy ▷ *vi* (*moteur*) to labour, strain; **se fatiguer** to get tired
fauché, e [foʃe] (*fam*) *adj* broke
faucher [foʃe] *vt* (*herbe*) to cut; (*champs, blés*) to reap; (*fig: véhicule*) to mow down; (*fam: voler*) to pinch
faucon [fokɔ̃] *nm* falcon, hawk
faudra [fodʀa] *vb voir* **falloir**
faufiler [fofile] *se* **~** *vi*: **se ~ dans** to edge one's way into; **se ~ parmi/entre** to thread one's way among/between
faune [fon] *nf* (*Zool*) wildlife, fauna
fausse [fos] *adj voir* **faux**; **faussement** *adv* (*accuser*) wrongly, wrongfully; (*croire*) falsely
fausser [fose] *vt* (*objet*) to bend, buckle; (*fig*) to distort; **~ compagnie à qn** to give sb the slip
faut [fo] *vb voir* **falloir**
faute [fot] *nf* (*erreur*) mistake, error; (*mauvaise action*) misdemeanour; (*Football etc*) offence; (*Tennis*) fault; **c'est de sa/ma ~** it's his *ou* her/my fault; **être en ~** to be in the wrong; **~ de** (*temps, argent*) for *ou* through lack of; **sans ~** without fail; **faute de frappe** typing error; **faute professionnelle** professional misconduct *no pl*
fauteuil [fotœj] *nm* armchair; (*au théâtre*) seat; **fauteuil roulant** wheelchair
fautif, -ive [fotif, iv] *adj* (*responsable*) at fault, in the wrong; (*incorrect*) incorrect, inaccurate; **il se sentait ~** he felt guilty
fauve [fov] *nm* wildcat ▷ *adj* (*couleur*) fawn
faux¹ [fo] *nf* scythe
faux², fausse [fo, fos] *adj* (*inexact*) wrong; (*voix*) out of tune; (*billet*) fake, forged; (*sournois, postiche*) false ▷ *adv* (*Mus*) out of tune ▷ *nm* (*copie*) fake, forgery; **faire ~ bond à qn** to let sb down; **faire un ~ pas** to trip; (*fig*) to make a faux pas; **fausse alerte** false alarm; **fausse couche** miscarriage; **faux frais** *nmpl* extras, incidental expenses; **faux mouvement** awkward movement; **fausse note** wrong note; **faux témoignage** (*délit*) perjury; **faux-filet** *nm* sirloin
faveur [favœʀ] *nf* favour; **traitement de ~** preferential treatment; **en ~ de** in favour of
favorable [favɔʀabl] *adj* favourable
favori, te [favɔʀi, it] *adj, nm/f* favourite

favoriser [favɔʀize] vt to favour

fax [faks] nm fax

fécond, e [fekɔ̃, ɔ̃d] adj fertile; **féconder** vt to fertilize

féculent [fekylɑ̃] nm starchy food

fédéral, e, -aux [federal, o] adj federal

fée [fe] nf fairy

feignant, e [fɛɲɑ̃, ɑ̃t] nm/f = **fainéant, e**

feindre [fɛ̃dʀ] vt to feign; **~ de faire** to pretend to do

fêler [fele] vt to crack; **se ~** to crack

félicitations [felisitasjɔ̃] nfpl congratulations

féliciter [felisite] vt: **~ qn (de)** to congratulate sb (on)

félin [felɛ̃, in] nm (big) cat

femelle [fəmɛl] adj, nf female

féminin, e [feminɛ̃, in] adj feminine; (sexe) female; (équipe, vêtements etc) women's ▷ nm (Ling) feminine; **féministe** adj feminist

femme [fam] nf woman; (épouse) wife; **femme au foyer** housewife; **femme de chambre** chambermaid; **femme de ménage** cleaning lady

fémur [femyʀ] nm femur, thighbone

fendre [fɑ̃dʀ] vt (couper en deux) to split; (fissurer) to crack; (traverser: foule, air) to cleave through; **se ~** vi to crack

fenêtre [f(ə)nɛtʀ] nf window

fenouil [fənuj] nm fennel

fente [fɑ̃t] nf (fissure) crack; (de boîte à lettres etc) slit

fer [fɛʀ] nm iron; **fer à cheval** horseshoe; **fer à friser** curling tongs pl; **fer (à repasser)** iron; **fer forgé** wrought iron

ferai etc [fəʀe] vb voir **faire**

fer-blanc [fɛʀblɑ̃] nm tin(plate)

férié, e [feʀje] adj: **jour ~** public holiday

ferions etc [fəʀjɔ̃] vb voir **faire**

ferme [fɛʀm] adj firm ▷ adv (travailler etc) hard ▷ nf (exploitation) farm; (maison) farmhouse

fermé, e [fɛʀme] adj closed, shut; (gaz, eau etc) off; (fig: milieu) exclusive

fermenter [fɛʀmɑ̃te] vi to ferment

fermer [fɛʀme] vt to close, shut; (cesser l'exploitation de) to close down, shut down; (eau, électricité, robinet) to turn off; (aéroport, route) to close ▷ vi to close, shut; (magasin: définitivement) to close down, shut down; **~ à clef** to lock; **se ~** vi to close, shut

fermeté [fɛʀməte] nf firmness

fermeture [fɛʀmətyʀ] nf closing; (dispositif) catch; **heures de ~** closing times; **fermeture éclair®** ou **à glissière** zip (fastener) (BRIT), zipper (US)

fermier [fɛʀmje] nm farmer

féroce [feʀɔs] adj ferocious, fierce

ferons [fəʀɔ̃] vb voir **faire**

ferrer [feʀe] vt (cheval) to shoe

ferroviaire [feʀɔvjɛʀ] adj rail(way) cpd (BRIT), rail(road) cpd (US)

ferry(-boat) [fɛʀe(-bot)] nm ferry

fertile [fɛʀtil] adj fertile; **~ en incidents** eventful, packed with incidents

fervent, e [fɛʀvɑ̃, ɑ̃t] adj fervent

fesse [fɛs] nf buttock; **fessée** nf spanking

festin [fɛstɛ̃] nm feast

festival [fɛstival] nm festival

festivités [fɛstivite] nfpl festivities

fêtard, e [fɛtaʀ, aʀd] (fam) nm/f high liver, merry-maker

fête [fɛt] nf (religieuse) feast; (publique) holiday; (réception) party; (kermesse) fête, fair; (du nom) feast day, name day;

faire la ~ to live it up; **faire ~ à qn** to give sb a warm welcome; **les ~s (de fin d'année)** the festive season; **la salle des ~s** the village hall; **la ~ des Mères/Pères** Mother's/Father's Day; **fête foraine** (fun) fair; **fêter** vt to celebrate; (personne) to have a celebration for

feu, x [fø] nm (gén) fire; (signal lumineux) light; (de cuisinière) ring; **feux** nmpl (Auto) (traffic) lights; **au ~!** (incendie) fire!; **à ~ doux/vif** over a slow/brisk heat; **à petit ~** (Culin) over a gentle heat; (fig) slowly; **faire ~** to fire; **ne pas faire long ~** not to last long; **prendre ~** to catch fire; **mettre le ~ à** to set fire to; **faire du ~** to make a fire; **avez-vous du ~?** (pour cigarette) have you (got) a light?; **feu arrière** rear light; **feu d'artifice** (spectacle) fireworks pl; **feu de joie** bonfire; **feu orange/rouge/vert** amber (BRIT) ou yellow (US)/red/green light; **feux de brouillard** fog lights ou lamps; **feux de croisement** dipped (BRIT) ou dimmed (US) headlights; **feux de position** sidelights; **feux de route** headlights

feuillage [fœjaʒ] nm foliage, leaves pl

feuille [fœj] nf (d'arbre) leaf; (de papier) sheet; **feuille de calcul** spreadsheet; **feuille d'impôts** tax form; **feuille de maladie** medical expenses claim form; **feuille de paie** pay slip

feuillet [fœjɛ] nm leaf

feuilleté, e [fœjte] adj: **pâte ~** flaky pastry

feuilleter [fœjte] vt (livre) to leaf through

feuilleton [fœjtɔ̃] nm serial

feutre [føtʀ] nm felt; (chapeau) felt hat; (aussi: **stylo-~**) felt-tip pen; **feutré, e** adj (atmosphère) muffled

fève [fɛv] nf broad bean

février [fevʀije] nm February

fiable [fjabl] adj reliable

fiançailles [fjɑ̃saj] nfpl engagement sg

fiancé, e [fjɑ̃se] nm/f fiancé(e) ▷ adj: **être ~ (à)** to be engaged (to)

fiancer [fjɑ̃se]: **se ~ (avec)** vi to become engaged (to)

fibre [fibʀ] nf fibre; **fibre de verre** fibreglass, glass fibre

ficeler [fis(ə)le] vt to tie up

ficelle [fisɛl] nf string no pl; (morceau) piece ou length of string

fiche [fiʃ] nf (pour fichier) (index) card; (formulaire) form; (Élec) plug; **fiche de paye** pay slip

ficher [fiʃe] vt (dans un fichier) to file; (Police) to put on file; (fam: faire) to do; (: donner) to give; (: mettre) to stick ou shove; **fiche-(moi) le camp!** (fam) clear off!; **fiche-moi la paix!** (fam) leave me alone!; **se ~ de** (fam: rire de) to make fun of; (être indifférent à) not to care about

fichier [fiʃje] nm file; **~ joint** (Comput) attachment

fichu, e [fiʃy] pp de **ficher** (fam) ▷ adj (fam: fini, inutilisable) bust, done for; (: intensif) wretched, darned ▷ nm (foulard) (head)scarf; **mal ~** (fam) feeling lousy

fictif, -ive [fiktif, iv] adj fictitious

fiction [fiksjɔ̃] nf fiction; (fait imaginé) invention

fidèle [fidɛl] adj faithful ▷ nm/f (Rel): **les ~s** (à l'église) the congregation sg; **fidélité** nf (d'un conjoint) fidelity, faithfulness; (d'un ami, client) loyalty

fier¹ [fje]: **se ~ à** vt to trust

fier², fière [fjɛʀ] adj proud; **~ de** proud of; **fierté** nf pride

fièvre [fjɛvʀ] nf fever; **avoir de la ~/39 de ~** to have a high temperature/a temperature of 39°C; **fiévreux, -euse** adj feverish

figer [fiʒe]: **se ~** vi (huile) to congeal; (personne) to freeze

fignoler [fiɲɔle] (fam) vt to polish up

figue [fig] nf fig; **figuier** nm fig tree

figurant, e [figyʀɑ̃, ɑ̃t] nm/f (Théâtre) walk-on; (Cinéma) extra

figure [figyʀ] nf (visage) face; (forme, personnage) figure; (illustration) picture, diagram

figuré, e [figyʀe] adj (sens) figurative

figurer [figyʀe] vi to appear ▷ vt to represent; **se ~ que** to imagine that

fil [fil] nm (brin, fig: d'une histoire) thread; (électrique) wire; (d'un couteau) edge; **au ~ des années** with the passing of the years; **au ~ de l'eau** with the stream ou current; **coup de ~** (fam) phone call; **donner/recevoir un coup de ~** to make/get ou receive a phone call; **fil de fer** wire; **fil de fer barbelé** barbed wire

file [fil] nf line; (Auto) lane; **en ~ indienne** in single file; **à la ~** (d'affilée) in succession; **file (d'attente)** queue (BRIT), line (US)

filer [file] vt (tissu, toile) to spin; (prendre en filature) to shadow, tail; (fam: donner) **~ qch à qn** to slip sb sth ▷ vi (bas) to run; (aller vite) to fly past; (fam: partir) to make ou be off; **~ doux** to toe the line

filet [file] nm net; (Culin) fillet; (d'eau, de sang) trickle; **filet (à provisions)** string bag

filiale [filjal] nf (Comm) subsidiary

filière [filjɛʀ] nf (carrière) path; **suivre la ~** (dans sa carrière) to work one's way up (through the hierarchy)

fille [fij] nf girl; (opposé à fils) daughter; **vieille ~** old maid; **fillette** nf (little) girl

filleul, e [fijœl] nm/f godchild, godson/daughter

film [film] nm (pour photo) (roll of) film; (œuvre) film, picture, movie

fils [fis] nm son; **fils à papa** daddy's boy

filtre [filtʀ] nm filter; **filtrer** vt to filter; (fig: candidats, visiteurs) to screen

fin¹ [fɛ̃] nf end; **fins** nfpl (but) ends; **prendre ~** to come to an end; **mettre ~ à** to put an end to; **à la ~** in the end, eventually; **en ~ de compte** in the end; **sans ~** endless; **~ juin** at the end of June; **fin prêt** quite ready

fin², e [fɛ̃, fin] adj (papier, couche, fil) thin; (cheveux, visage) fine; (taille) neat, slim; (esprit, remarque) subtle ▷ adv (couper) finely; **fines herbes** mixed herbs; **avoir la vue/ l'ouïe fine** to have keen eyesight/hearing; **repas/vin fin** gourmet meal/fine wine

final, e [final, o] adj final ▷ nm (Mus) finale; **finale** nf final; **quarts de finale** quarter finals; **finalement** adv finally, in the end; (après tout) after all

finance [finɑ̃s]: **finances** nfpl (situation) finances; (activités) finance sg; **moyennant ~** for a fee; **financer** vt to finance; **financier, -ière** adj financial

finesse [finɛs] nf thinness; (raffinement) fineness; (subtilité) subtlety

fini, e [fini] adj finished; (Math) finite ▷ nm (d'un objet manufacturé) finish

finir [finiʀ] vt to finish ▷ vi to finish, end; **~ par faire** to end up ou finish up doing; **~ de faire** to finish doing; (cesser) to stop doing; **il finit par m'agacer** he's beginning to get on my nerves; **en ~ avec** to be ou have done with; **il va mal ~** he will come to a bad end

finition [finisjɔ̃] nf (résultat) finish

finlandais, e [fɛ̃lɑ̃dɛ, ɛz] adj Finnish ▷ nm/f: **F~, e** Finn

Finlande [fɛ̃lɑ̃d] nf: **la ~** Finland

finnois, e [finwa, waz] adj Finnish ▷ nm (Ling) Finnish

fioul [fjul] nm fuel oil

firme [fiʀm] nf firm

fis [fi] vb voir **faire**

fisc [fisk] nm tax authorities pl; **fiscal, e, -aux** adj tax cpd, fiscal; **fiscalité** nf tax system

fissure [fisyʀ] nf crack; **fissurer** vt to crack; **se fissurer** vi to crack

fit [fi] vb voir **faire**

fixation [fiksasjɔ̃] nf (attache) fastening; (Psych) fixation

fixe [fiks] adj fixed; (emploi) steady, regular ▷ nm (salaire) basic salary; (téléphone) landline; **à heure ~** at a set time; **menu à prix ~** set menu

fixé, e [fikse] adj: **être ~ (sur)** (savoir à quoi s'en tenir) to have made up one's mind (about)

fixer [fikse] vt (attacher): **~ qch (à/sur)** to fix ou fasten sth (to/onto); (déterminer) to fix, set; (regarder) to stare at; **se ~** vi (s'établir) to settle down; **se ~ sur** (suj: attention) to focus on

flacon [flakɔ̃] nm bottle

flageolet [flaʒɔlɛ] nm (Culin) dwarf kidney bean

flagrant, e [flagʀɑ̃, ɑ̃t] adj flagrant, blatant; **en ~ délit** in the act

flair [flɛʀ] nm sense of smell; (fig) intuition; **flairer** vt (humer) to sniff (at); (détecter) to scent

flamand, e [flamɑ̃, ɑ̃d] adj Flemish ▷ nm (Ling) Flemish ▷ nm/f: **F~, e** Fleming

flamant [flamɑ̃] nm flamingo

flambant, e [flɑ̃bɑ̃, ɑ̃t] adv: **~ neuf** brand new

flambé, e [flɑ̃be] adj (Culin) flambé

flambée [flɑ̃be] nf blaze; (fig: des prix) explosion

flamber [flɑ̃be] vi to blaze (up)

flamboyer [flɑ̃bwaje] vi to blaze (up)

flamme [flam] nf flame; (fig) fire, fervour; **en ~s** on fire, ablaze

flan [flɑ̃] nm (Culin) custard tart ou pie

flanc [flɑ̃] nm side; (Mil) flank

flancher [flɑ̃ʃe] (fam) vi to fail, pack up

flanelle [flanɛl] nf flannel

flâner [flane] vi to stroll

flanquer [flɑ̃ke] vt to flank; (fam: mettre) to chuck, shove; (: jeter): **~ par terre/à la porte** to fling to the ground/chuck out

flaque [flak] nf (d'eau) puddle; (d'huile, de sang etc) pool

flash [flaʃ] (pl **~es**) nm (Photo) flash; **flash d'information** newsflash

flatter [flate] vt to flatter; **se ~ de qch** to pride o.s. on sth; **flatteur, -euse** adj flattering

flèche [flɛʃ] nf arrow; (de clocher) spire; **monter en ~** (fig) to soar, rocket; **partir en ~** to be off like a shot; **fléchette** nf dart

fléchir [fleʃiʀ]: **se ~** vi to wither

fleur [flœʀ] nf flower; (d'un arbre) blossom; **en ~** (arbre) in blossom; **à ~s** flowery

fleuri, e [flœʀi] adj (jardin) in flower ou bloom; (tissu, papier) flowery

fleurir [flœʀiʀ] vi (rose) to flower; (arbre) to blossom; (fig) to flourish ▷ vt (tombe) to put flowers on; (chambre) to decorate with flowers

fleuriste [flœʀist] nm/f florist

fleuve [flœv] nm river

flexible [flɛksibl] adj flexible

flic [flik] (fam: péj) nm cop

flipper [flipœʀ] nm pinball (machine)

flirter [flœʀte] vi to flirt

flocon [flɔkɔ̃] nm flake

flore [flɔʀ] nf flora

florissant, e [flɔʀisɑ̃, ɑ̃t] adj (économie) flourishing

flot [flo] nm flood, stream; **flots** nmpl (de la mer) waves; **être à ~** (Navig) to be afloat; **entrer à ~s** to stream ou pour in

flottant, e [flɔtɑ̃, ɑ̃t] adj (vêtement) loose

flotte [flɔt] nf (Navig) fleet; (fam: eau) water; (: pluie) rain

flotter [flɔte] vi to float; (nuage, odeur) to drift; (drapeau) to fly; (vêtements) to hang loose; (fam: pleuvoir) to rain; **faire ~** to float; **flotteur** nm float

flou, e [flu] adj fuzzy, blurred; (fig) woolly, vague

fluide [fluid] adj fluid; (circulation etc) flowing freely ▷ nm fluid

fluor [flyɔʀ] nm: **dentifrice au ~** fluoride toothpaste

fluorescent, e [flyɔʀesɑ̃, ɑ̃t] adj fluorescent

flûte [flyt] nf flute; (verre) flute (glass); (pain) (thin) French stick; **~!** I drat it! **flûte traversière/à bec** flute/recorder

flux [fly] nm incoming tide; (écoulement) flow; **le ~ et le reflux** the ebb and flow

foc [fɔk] nm jib

foi [fwa] nf faith; **digne de ~** reliable; **être de bonne/ mauvaise ~** to be sincere/insincere; **ma ~ ...** well ...

foie [fwa] nm liver; **crise de ~** stomach upset

foin [fwɛ̃] nm hay; **faire du ~** (fig: fam) to kick up a row

foire [fwaʀ] nf fair; (fête foraine) (fun) fair; **faire la ~** (fig: fam) to whoop it up; **~ aux questions** (Internet) FAQs; **foire (exposition)** trade fair

fois [fwa] nf time; **une/deux ~** once/twice; **2 ~ 2** 2 times 2; **une ~** (passé) once; (futur) sometime; **une ~ pour toutes** once and for all; **une ~ que** once; **des ~** (parfois) sometimes; **à la ~** (ensemble) at once

fol [fɔl] adj voir **fou**

folie [fɔli] nf (d'une décision, d'un acte) madness, folly; (état) madness, insanity; **la ~ des grandeurs** delusions of grandeur; **faire des ~s** (en dépenses) to be extravagant

folklorique [fɔlklɔʀik] adj folk cpd; (fam) weird

folle [fɔl] adj, nf voir **fou**; **follement** adv (très) madly, wildly

foncé, e [fɔ̃se] adj dark

foncer [fɔ̃se] vi to go darker; (fam: aller vite) to tear ou belt along; **~ sur** to charge at

fonction [fɔ̃ksjɔ̃] nf function; (emploi, poste) post, position; **fonctions** nfpl (professionnelles) duties; **voiture de ~** company car; **en ~ de** (par rapport à) according to; **faire ~ de** to serve as; **la ~ publique** the state ou civil service; **fonctionnaire** nm/f state employee, local authority employee; (dans l'administration) ≈ civil servant; **fonctionner** vi to work, function

fond [fɔ̃] nm (d'un récipient, trou) bottom; (d'une salle, scène) back; (d'un tableau, décor) background; (opposé à la forme) content; (Sport): **le ~** long distance (running); **au ~ de** at the bottom of; at the back of; **à ~** (connaître, soutenir) thoroughly; (appuyer, visser) right down ou home; **à ~ (de train)** (fam) full tilt; **dans le ~, au ~** (en somme) basically, really; **de ~ en comble** from top to bottom; **fond de teint** foundation (cream); voir aussi **fonds**

fondamental, e, -aux [fɔ̃damɑ̃tal, o] adj fundamental

fondant, e [fɔ̃dɑ̃, ɑ̃t] adj (neige) melting; (poire) that melts in the mouth

fondation [fɔ̃dasjɔ̃] nf founding; (établissement) foundation; **fondations** nfpl (d'une maison) foundations

fondé, e [fɔ̃de] adj (accusation etc) well-founded; **être à ~**

to have grounds for ou good reason to

fondement [fɔ̃dmɑ̃] nm: **sans ~** (rumeur etc) groundless, unfounded

fonder [fɔ̃de] vt to found; (fig) to base; **se ~ sur** (suj: personne) to base o.s. on

fonderie [fɔ̃dʀi] nf smelting works sg

fondre [fɔ̃dʀ] vt (aussi: **faire ~**) to melt; (dans l'eau) to dissolve; (fig: mélanger) to merge, blend ▷ vi (à la chaleur) to melt; (dans l'eau) to dissolve; (fig) to melt away; (se précipiter): **~ sur** to swoop down on; **~ en larmes** to burst into tears

fonds [fɔ̃] nm (Comm): **~ (de commerce)** business ▷ nmpl (argent) funds

fondu, e [fɔ̃dy] adj (beurre, neige) melted; (métal) molten; **fondue** nf (Culin) fondue

font [fɔ̃] vb voir **faire**

fontaine [fɔ̃tɛn] nf fountain; (source) spring

fonte [fɔ̃t] nf melting; (métal) cast iron; **la ~ des neiges** the (spring) thaw

foot [fut] (fam) nm football

football [futbol] nm football, soccer; **footballeur** nm footballer

footing [futiŋ] nm jogging; **faire du ~** to go jogging

forain, e [fɔʀɛ̃, ɛn] adj fairground cpd ▷ nm (marchand) stallholder; (acteur) fairground entertainer

forçat [fɔʀsa] nm convict

force [fɔʀs] nf strength; (Physique, Mécanique) force; **forces** nfpl (physiques) strength sg; (Mil) forces; **à ~ d'insister** by dint of insisting; as he (ou elle ou l etc) kept on insisting; **de ~** forcibly, by force; **dans la ~ de l'âge** in the prime of life; **les forces de l'ordre** the police no pl

forcé, e [fɔʀse] adj forced; **c'est ~** (fam) it's inevitable; **forcément** adv inevitably; **pas forcément** not necessarily

forcer [fɔʀse] vt to force; (voix) to strain ▷ vi (Sport) to overtax o.s.; **~ la dose** (fam) to overdo it; **se ~ (à faire)** to force o.s. (to do)

forestier, -ère [fɔʀestje, jɛʀ] adj forest cpd

forêt [fɔʀɛ] nf forest

forfait [fɔʀfɛ] nm (Comm) all-in deal ou price; **déclarer ~** to withdraw; **forfaitaire** adj inclusive

forge [fɔʀʒ] nf forge, smithy; **forgeron** nm (black)smith

formaliser [fɔʀmalize]: **se ~** vi: **se ~ (de)** to take offence (at)

formalité [fɔʀmalite] nf formality; **simple ~** mere formality

format [fɔʀma] nm size; **formater** vt (disque) to format

formation [fɔʀmasjɔ̃] nf (développement) forming; (apprentissage) training; **formation permanente** ou **continue** continuing education

forme [fɔʀm] nf (gén) form; (d'un objet) shape, form; **formes** nfpl (bonnes manières) proprieties; (d'une femme) figure sg; **en ~ de poire** pear-shaped, in the shape of a pear; **être en ~** (Sport etc) to be on form; **en bonne et due ~** in due form

formel, le [fɔʀmɛl] adj (catégorique) definite, positive; **formellement** adv (absolument) positively; **formellement interdit** strictly forbidden

former [fɔʀme] vt to form; (éduquer) to train; **se ~** vi to form

formidable [fɔʀmidabl] adj tremendous

formulaire [fɔʀmylɛʀ] nm form

formule [fɔʀmyl] nf (gén) formula; (expression) phrase; **formule de politesse** polite phrase; (en fin de lettre) letter ending

fort, e [fɔʀ, fɔʀt] adj strong; (intensité, rendement) high, great; (corpulent) stout; (dur) good, able ▷ adv (serrer, frapper) hard; (parler) loud(ly); (beaucoup) greatly, very much; (très) very ▷ nm (édifice) fort; (point fort) strong point, forte; **forte tête** rebel; **forteresse** nf stronghold

fortifiant [fɔʀtifjɑ̃] nm tonic

fortune [fɔʀtyn] nf fortune; **faire ~** to make one's fortune; **de ~** makeshift; **fortuné, e** adj wealthy

forum [fɔʀɔm] nm forum; **~ de discussion** (Internet) message board

fosse [fos] nf (grand trou) pit; (tombe) grave

fossé [fose] nm ditch; (fig) gulf, gap

fossette [fosɛt] nf dimple

fossile [fosil] nm fossil

fou (fol), folle [fu, fɔl] adj mad; (déréglé etc) wild, erratic; (fam: extrême, très grand) terrific, tremendous ▷ nm/f madman(-woman) ▷ nm (de roi) jester; **être fou de** to be mad ou crazy about; **avoir le fou rire** to have the giggles

foudre [fudʀ] nf: **la ~** lightning

foudroyant, e [fudʀwajɑ̃, ɑ̃t] adj (progrès) lightning cpd; (succès) stunning; (maladie, poison) violent

fouet [fwɛ] nm whip; (Culin) whisk; **de plein ~** (se heurter) head on; **fouetter** vt to whip; (crème) to whisk

fougère [fuʒɛʀ] nf fern

fougue [fug] nf ardour, spirit; **fougueux, -euse** adj fiery

fouille [fuj] nf search; **fouilles** nfpl (archéologiques) excavations; **fouiller** vt to search; (creuser) to dig ▷ vi to rummage; **fouillis** nm jumble, muddle

foulard [fulaʀ] nm scarf

foule [ful] nf crowd; **la ~** crowds pl; **une ~ de** masses of

foulée [fule] nf stride

fouler [fule] vt to press; (sol) to tread upon; **se ~ la cheville** to sprain one's ankle; **ne pas se ~** not to overexert o.s.; **il ne se foule pas** he doesn't put himself out; **foulure** nf sprain

four [fuʀ] nm oven; (de potier) kiln; (Théâtre: échec) flop

fourche [fuʀʃ] nf pitchfork

fourchette [fuʀʃɛt] nf fork; (Statistique) bracket, margin

fourgon [fuʀgɔ̃] nm van; (Rail) wag(g)on; **fourgonnette** nf (small) van

fourmi [fuʀmi] nf ant; **avoir des ~s dans les jambes/ mains** to have pins and needles in one's legs/hands; **fourmilière** nf ant-hill; **fourmiller** vi to swarm

fourneau, x [fuʀno] nm stove

fourni, e [fuʀni] adj (barbe, cheveux) thick; (magasin): **bien ~ (en)** well stocked (with)

fournir [fuʀniʀ] vt to supply; (preuve, exemple) to provide; (effort) to put in; **~ qch à qn** to supply sth to sb, supply ou provide sb with sth; **fournisseur, -euse** nm/f supplier; **fournisseur d'accès à Internet** (Internet) service provider, ISP; **fourniture** nf supply(ing); **fournitures scolaires** school stationery

fourrage [fuʀaʒ] nm fodder

fourré, e [fuʀe] adj (bonbon etc) filled; (manteau etc) fur-lined ▷ nm thicket

fourrer [fuʀe] (fam) vt to stick, shove; **se ~ dans/sous** to get into/under

fourrière [fuʀjɛʀ] nf pound

fourrure [fuʀyʀ] nf fur; (sur l'animal) coat

foutre [futʀ] (fam!) vt = **ficher; foutu, e** (fam!) adj = **fichu, e**

foyer [fwaje] nm (maison) home; (famille) family; (de cheminée) hearth; (de jeunes etc) (social) club; (résidence) hostel; (salon) foyer; **lunettes à double ~** bi-focals

fracassant, e [fʀakasɑ̃, ɑ̃t] adj (succès) thundering

fraction [fʀaksjɔ̃] nf fraction

fracture [fʀaktyʀ] nf fracture; **fracture du crâne** fractured skull; **fracturer** vt (coffre, serrure) to break open; (os, membre) to fracture; **se fracturer le crâne** to fracture one's skull

fragile [fʀaʒil] adj fragile, delicate; (fig) frail; **fragilité** nf fragility

fragment [fʀagmɑ̃] nm (d'un objet) fragment, piece

fraîche [fʀɛʃ] adj voir **frais; fraîcheur** nf coolness; (d'un aliment) freshness; **fraîchir** vi to get cooler; (vent) to freshen

frais, fraîche [fʀɛ, fʀɛʃ] adj fresh; (froid) cool ▷ adv (récemment) newly, fresh(ly) ▷ nm: **mettre au ~** to put in a cool place ▷ nmpl (gén) expenses; (Comm) costs; **il fait ~** it's cool; **servir ~** serve chilled; **prendre le ~** to take a breath of cool air; **faire des ~** to go to a lot of expense; **frais de scolarité** school fees (BRIT), tuition (US); **frais généraux** overheads

fraise [fʀɛz] nf strawberry; **fraise des bois** wild strawberry

framboise [fʀɑ̃bwaz] nf raspberry

franc, franche [fʀɑ̃, fʀɑ̃ʃ] adj (personne) frank, straightforward; (visage) open; (net: refus) clear; (: coupure) clean; (intensif) downright ▷ nm franc

français, e [fʀɑ̃sɛ, ɛz] adj French ▷ nm/f: **F~, e** Frenchman(-woman) ▷ nm (Ling) French

France [fʀɑ̃s] nf: **la ~** France; **~ 2, ~ 3** public-sector television channels

franche [fʀɑ̃ʃ] adj voir **franc; franchement** adv frankly; (nettement) definitely; (tout à fait: mauvais etc) downright

franchir [fʀɑ̃ʃiʀ] vt (obstacle) to clear, get over; (seuil, ligne, rivière) to cross; (distance) to cover

franchise [fʀɑ̃ʃiz] nf frankness; (douanière) exemption; (Assurances) excess

franc-maçon [fʀɑ̃masɔ̃] nm freemason

franco [fʀɑ̃ko] adv (Comm): **~ (de port)** postage paid

francophone [fʀɑ̃kɔfɔn] adj French-speaking

franc-parler [fʀɑ̃paʀle] nm inv outspokenness; **avoir son ~** to speak one's mind

frange [fʀɑ̃ʒ] nf fringe

frangipane [fʀɑ̃ʒipan] nf almond paste

frappant, e [fʀapɑ̃, ɑ̃t] adj striking

frappé, e [fʀape] adj iced

frapper [fʀape] vt to hit, strike; (étonner) to strike; **~ dans ses mains** to clap one's hands; **frappé de stupeur** dumbfounded

fraternel, le [fʀatɛʀnɛl] adj brotherly, fraternal; **fraternité** nf brotherhood

fraude [fʀod] nf fraud; (Scol) cheating; **passer qch en ~** to smuggle sth in (ou out); **fraude fiscale** tax evasion

frayeur [fʀɛjœʀ] nf fright

fredonner [fʀədɔne] vt to hum

freezer [fʀizœʀ] nm freezing compartment

frein [fʀɛ̃] nm brake; **mettre un ~ à** (fig) to curb, check; **frein à main** handbrake; **freiner** vi to brake ▷ vt (progrès etc) to check

frêle [fʀɛl] adj frail, fragile

frelon [fʀəlɔ̃] nm hornet

frémir [fʀemiʀ] vi (de peur, d'horreur) to shudder; (de colère) to shake; (feuillage) to quiver

frêne [fʀɛn] nm ash

fréquemment [fʀekamã] adv frequently

fréquent, e [fʀekã, ãt] adj frequent

fréquentation [fʀekãtasjõ] nf frequenting; **fréquentations** nfpl (relations) company sg; **avoir de mauvaises ~s** to be in with the wrong crowd, keep bad company

fréquenté, e [fʀekãte] adj: **très ~** (very) busy; **mal ~** patronized by disreputable elements

fréquenter [fʀekãte] vt (lieu) to frequent; (personne) to see; **se ~** to see each other

frère [fʀɛʀ] nm brother

fresque [fʀɛsk] nf (Art) fresco

fret [fʀɛ(t)] nm freight

friand, e [fʀijã, fʀijãd] adj: **~ de** very fond of ▷ nm: **~ au fromage** cheese puff

friandise [fʀijãdiz] nf sweet

fric [fʀik] (fam) nm cash, bread

friche [fʀiʃ]: **en ~** adj, adv (lying) fallow

friction [fʀiksjõ] nf (massage) rub, rub-down; (Tech, fig) friction

frigidaire® [fʀiʒidɛʀ] nm refrigerator

frigo [fʀigo] (fam) nm fridge

frigorifique [fʀigɔʀifik] adj refrigerating

frileux, -euse [fʀilø, øz] adj sensitive to (the) cold

frimer [fʀime] (fam) vi to show off

fringale [fʀɛ̃gal] (fam) nf: **avoir la ~** to be ravenous

fringues [fʀɛ̃g] (fam) nfpl clothes

fripé, e [fʀipe] adj crumpled

frire [fʀiʀ] vt, vi: **faire ~** to fry

frisé, e [fʀize] adj (cheveux) curly; (personne) curly-haired

frisson [fʀisõ] nm (de froid) shiver; (de peur) shudder; **frissonner** vi (de fièvre, froid) to shiver; (d'horreur) to shudder

frit, e [fʀi, fʀit] pp de **frire**; **frite** nf: **(pommes) frites** chips (BRIT), French fries; **friteuse** nf chip pan; **friteuse électrique** deep fat fryer; **friture** nf (huile) (deep) fat; (plat) **friture (de poissons)** fried fish

froid, e [fʀwa, fʀwad] adj, nm cold; **il fait ~** it's cold; **avoir/prendre ~** to be/catch cold; **être en ~ avec** to be on bad terms with; **froidement** adv (accueillir) coldly; (décider) coolly

froisser [fʀwase] vt to crumple (up), crease; (fig) to hurt, offend; **se ~** vi to crumple, crease; (personne) to take offence; **se ~ un muscle** to strain a muscle

frôler [fʀole] vt to brush against; (suj: projectile) to skim past; (fig) to come very close to

fromage [fʀomaʒ] nm cheese; **fromage blanc** soft white cheese

froment [fʀomã] nm wheat

froncer [fʀõse] vt to gather; **~ les sourcils** to frown

front [fʀõ] nm forehead, brow; (Mil) front; **de ~** (se heurter) head-on; (rouler) together (i.e. 2 or 3 abreast); (simultanément) at once; **faire ~ à** to face up to

frontalier, -ère [fʀõtalje, jɛʀ] adj border cpd, frontier cpd; **(travailleurs) ~s** people who commute across the border

frontière [fʀõtjɛʀ] nf frontier, border

frotter [fʀote] vi to rub, scrape ▷ vt to rub; (pommes de terre, plancher) to scrub; **~ une allumette** to strike a match

fruit [fʀɥi] nm fruit gen no pl; **fruits de mer** seafood(s); **fruits secs** dried fruit sg; **fruité, e** adj fruity; **fruitier, -ère** adj: **arbre fruitier** fruit tree

frustrer [fʀystʀe] vt to frustrate

fuel(-oil) [fjul(ɔjl)] nm fuel oil; (domestique) heating oil

fugace [fygas] adj fleeting

fugitif, -ive [fyʒitif, iv] adj (fugace) fleeting ▷ nm/f fugitive

fugue [fyg] nf: **faire une ~** to run away, abscond

fuir [fɥiʀ] vt to flee from; (éviter) to shun ▷ vi to run away; (gaz, robinet) to leak

fuite [fɥit] nf flight; (écoulement, divulgation) leak; **être en ~** to be on the run; **mettre en ~** to put to flight

fulgurant, e [fylgyʀã, ãt] adj lightning cpd, dazzling

fumé, e [fyme] adj (Culin) smoked; (verre) tinted; **fumée** nf smoke

fumer [fyme] vi to smoke; (soupe) to steam ▷ vt to smoke

fûmes [fym] vb voir **être**

fumeur, -euse [fymœʀ, øz] nm/f smoker

fumier [fymje] nm manure

funérailles [fyneʀaj] nfpl funeral sg

fur [fyʀ]: **au ~ et à mesure** adv as one goes along; **au ~ et à mesure que** as

furet [fyʀɛ] nm ferret

fureter [fyʀ(ə)te] (péj) vi to nose about

fureur [fyʀœʀ] nf fury; **être en ~** to be infuriated; **faire ~** to be all the rage

furie [fyʀi] nf fury; (femme) shrew, vixen; **en ~** (mer) raging; **furieux, -euse** adj furious

furoncle [fyʀõkl] nm boil

furtif, -ive [fyʀtif, iv] adj furtive

fus [fy] vb voir **être**

fusain [fyzɛ̃] nm (Art) charcoal

fuseau, x [fyzo] nm (pour filer) spindle; (pantalon) (ski) pants; **fuseau horaire** time zone

fusée [fyze] nf rocket

fusible [fyzibl] nm (Élec: fil) fuse wire; (: fiche) fuse

fusil [fyzi] nm (de guerre, à canon rayé) rifle, gun; (de chasse, à canon lisse) shotgun, gun; **fusillade** nf gunfire no pl, shooting no pl; **fusiller** vt to shoot; **fusiller qn du regard** to look daggers at sb

fusionner [fyzjone] vi to merge

fût [fy] vb voir **être** ▷ nm (tonneau) barrel, cask

futé, e [fyte] adj crafty; **Bison ~®** TV and radio traffic monitoring service

futile [fytil] adj futile; frivolous

futur, e [fytyʀ] adj, nm future

fuyard, e [fɥijaʀ, aʀd] nm/f runaway

Gabon [gabɔ̃] *nm*: **le ~** Gabon

gâcher [gaʃe] *vt* (*gâter*) to spoil; (*gaspiller*) to waste; **gâchis** *nm* waste *no pl*

gaffe [gaf] *nf* blunder; **faire ~** (*fam*) to be careful

gage [gaʒ] *nm* (*dans un jeu*) forfeit; (*fig: de fidélité, d'amour*) token; **gages** *nmpl* (*salaire*) wages; **mettre en ~** to pawn

gagnant, e [gaɲɑ̃, ɑ̃t] *adj*: **billet/numéro ~** winning ticket/number ▷ *nm/f* winner

gagne-pain [gaɲpɛ̃] *nm inv* job

gagner [gaɲe] *vt* to win; (*somme d'argent, revenu*) to earn; (*aller vers, atteindre*) to reach; (*envahir: sommeil, peur*) to overcome; (: *mal*) to spread to ▷ *vi* to win; (*fig*) to gain; **~ du temps/de la place** to gain time/save space; **~ sa vie** to earn one's living

gai, e [ge] *adj* cheerful; (*un peu ivre*) merry; **gaiement** *adv* cheerfully; **gaieté** *nf* cheerfulness; **de gaieté de cœur** with a light heart

gain [gɛ̃] *nm* (*revenu*) earnings *pl*; (*bénéfice: gén pl*) profits *pl*

gala [gala] *nm* official reception; **de ~** (*soirée etc*) gala

galant, e [galɑ̃, ɑ̃t] *adj* (*courtois*) courteous, gentlemanly; (*entreprenant*) flirtatious, gallant; (*scène, rendez-vous*) romantic

galerie [galʀi] *nf* gallery; (*Théâtre*) circle; (*de voiture*) roof rack; (*fig: spectateurs*) audience; **galerie de peinture** (*private*) art gallery; **galerie marchande** shopping arcade

galet [galɛ] *nm* pebble

galette [galɛt] *nf* flat cake; **galette des Rois** *cake eaten on Twelfth Night*

galipette [galipɛt] *nf* somersault

Galles [gal] *nfpl*: **le pays de ~** Wales; **gallois, e** *adj* Welsh ▷ *nm*: **Gallois, e** Welshman(-woman) ▷ *nm* (*Ling*) Welsh

galon [galɔ̃] *nm* (*Mil*) stripe; (*décoratif*) piece of braid

galop [galo] *nm* gallop; **galoper** *vi* to gallop

gambader [gɑ̃bade] *vi* (*animal, enfant*) to leap about

gamin, e [gamɛ̃, in] *nm/f* kid ▷ *adj* childish

gamme [gam] *nf* (*Mus*) scale; (*fig*) range

gang [gɑ̃g] *nm* (*de criminels*) gang

gant [gɑ̃] *nm* glove; **gant de toilette** face flannel (BRIT), face cloth

garage [gaʀaʒ] *nm* garage; **garagiste** *nm/f* garage owner; (*employé*) garage mechanic

garantie [gaʀɑ̃ti] *nf* guarantee; **(bon de) ~** guarantee *ou* warranty slip

garantir [gaʀɑ̃tiʀ] *vt* to guarantee; **~ à qn que** to assure sb that

garçon [gaʀsɔ̃] *nm* boy; (*célibataire*): **vieux ~** bachelor; **garçon (de café)** (*serveur*) waiter; **garçon de courses** messenger

garde [gaʀd(ə)] *nm* (*de prisonnier*) guard; (*de domaine etc*) warden; (*soldat, sentinelle*) guardsman ▷ *nf* (*soldats*) guard; **de ~** on duty; **monter la ~** to stand guard; **mettre en ~** to warn; **prendre ~ (à)** to be careful (of); **garde champêtre** *nm* rural policeman; **garde du corps** *nm* bodyguard; **garde à vue** *nf* (*Jur*) ≈ police custody; **garde-boue** *nm inv* mudguard; **garde-chasse** *nm* gamekeeper

garder [gaʀde] *vt* (*conserver*) to keep; (*surveiller: enfants*) to look after; (: *immeuble, lieu, prisonnier*) to guard; **se ~** *vi* (*aliment: se conserver*) to keep; **se ~ de faire** to be careful not to do; **~ le lit/la chambre** to stay in bed/indoors; **pêche/chasse gardée** private fishing/hunting (ground)

garderie [gaʀdəʀi] *nf* day nursery, crèche

garde-robe [gaʀdəʀɔb] *nf* wardrobe

gardien, ne [gaʀdjɛ̃, jɛn] *nm/f* (*garde*) guard; (*de prison*) warder; (*de domaine, réserve*) warden; (*de musée etc*) attendant; (*de phare, cimetière*) keeper; (*d'immeuble*) caretaker; (*fig*) guardian; **gardien de but** goalkeeper; **gardien de la paix** policeman; **gardien de nuit** night watchman

gare¹ [gaʀ] *nf* station; **gare routière** bus station

gare² [gaʀ] *excl*: **~ à ...!** mind ...!; **~ à toi!** watch out!

garer [gaʀe] *vt* to park; **se ~** *vi* to park

garni, e [gaʀni] *adj* (*plat*) served with vegetables (*and chips or rice etc*)

garniture [gaʀnityʀ] *nf* (*Culin*) vegetables *pl*; **garniture de frein** brake lining

gars [ga] (*fam*) *nm* guy

Gascogne [gaskɔɲ] *nf* Gascony; **le golfe de ~** the Bay of Biscay

gas-oil [gazɔjl] *nm* diesel (oil)

gaspiller [gaspije] *vt* to waste

gastronome [gastʀɔnɔm] *nm/f* gourmet; **gastronomique** *adj* gastronomic

gâteau, x [gɑto] *nm* cake; **gâteau sec** biscuit

gâter [gɑte] *vt* to spoil; **se ~** *vi* (*dent, fruit*) to go bad; (*temps, situation*) to change for the worse

gâteux, -euse [gɑtø, øz] *adj* senile

gauche [goʃ] *adj* left, left-hand; (*maladroit*) awkward, clumsy ▷ *nf* (*Pol*) left (wing); **le bras ~** the left arm; **le côté ~** the left-hand side; **à ~** on the left; (*direction*) (to the) left; **gaucher, -ère** *adj* left-handed; **gauchiste** *nm/f* leftist

gaufre [gofʀ] *nf* waffle

gaufrette [gofʀɛt] *nf* wafer

gaulois, e [golwa, waz] *adj* Gallic ▷ *nm/f*: **G~, e** Gaul

gaz [gaz] *nm inv* gas; **ça sent le ~** I can smell gas, there's a smell of gas

gaze [gaz] *nf* gauze

gazette [gazɛt] *nf* news sheet

gazeux, -euse [gazø, øz] *adj* (*boisson*) fizzy; (*eau*) sparkling

gazoduc [gazodyk] nm gas pipeline

gazon [gazɔ̃] nm (herbe) grass; (pelouse) lawn

geai [ʒɛ] nm jay

géant, e [ʒeɑ̃, ɑ̃t] adj gigantic; (Comm) giant-size ▷ nm/f giant

geindre [ʒɛ̃dʀ] vi to groan, moan

gel [ʒɛl] nm frost

gélatine [ʒelatin] nf gelatine

gelée [ʒ(ə)le] nf jelly; (gel) frost

geler [ʒ(ə)le] vt, vi to freeze; **il gèle** it's freezing

gélule [ʒelyl] nf (Méd) capsule

Gémeaux [ʒemo] nmpl: **les ~** Gemini

gémir [ʒemiʀ] vi to groan, moan

gênant, e [ʒenɑ̃, ɑ̃t] adj (irritant) annoying; (embarrassant) embarrassing

gencive [ʒɑ̃siv] nf gum

gendarme [ʒɑ̃daʀm] nm gendarme; **gendarmerie** nf military police force in countryside and small towns; their police station or barracks

gendre [ʒɑ̃dʀ] nm son-in-law

gêné, e [ʒene] adj embarrassed

gêner [ʒene] vt (incommoder) to bother; (encombrer) to be in the way; (embarrasser): **~ qn** to make sb feel ill-at-ease; **se ~** to put o.s. out; **ne vous gênez pas!** don't mind me!

général, e, -aux [ʒeneʀal, o] adj, nm general; **en ~** usually, in general; **généralement** adv generally; **généraliser** vt, vi to generalize; **se généraliser** vi to become widespread; **généraliste** nm/f general practitioner, G.P.

génération [ʒeneʀasjɔ̃] nf generation

généreux, -euse [ʒeneʀø, øz] adj generous

générique [ʒeneʀik] nm (Cinéma) credits pl

générosité [ʒeneʀozite] nf generosity

genêt [ʒ(ə)nɛ] nm broom no pl (shrub)

génétique [ʒenetik] adj genetic

Genève [ʒ(ə)nɛv] n Geneva

génial, e, -aux [ʒenjal, jo] adj of genius; (fam: formidable) fantastic, brilliant

génie [ʒeni] nm genius; (Mil): **le ~** the Engineers pl; **génie civil** civil engineering

genièvre [ʒənjɛvʀ] nm juniper

génisse [ʒenis] nf heifer

génital, e, -aux [ʒenital, o] adj genital; **les parties ~es** the genitals

génoise [ʒenwaz] nf sponge cake

genou, x [ʒ(ə)nu] nm knee; **à ~x** on one's knees; **se mettre à ~x** to kneel down

genre [ʒɑ̃ʀ] nm kind, type, sort; (Ling) gender; **avoir bon ~** to look a nice sort; **avoir mauvais ~** to be coarse-looking; **ce n'est pas son ~** it's not like him

gens [ʒɑ̃] nmpl (f in some phrases) people pl

gentil, le [ʒɑ̃ti, ij] adj kind; (enfant: sage) good; (endroit etc) nice; **gentillesse** nf kindness; **gentiment** adv kindly

géographie [ʒeɔgʀafi] nf geography

géologie [ʒeɔlɔʒi] nf geology

géomètre [ʒeɔmɛtʀ] nm/f (arpenteur) (land) surveyor

géométrie [ʒeɔmetʀi] nf geometry; **géométrique** adj geometric

géranium [ʒeʀanjɔm] nm geranium

gérant, e [ʒeʀɑ̃, ɑ̃t] nm/f manager(-eress); **gérant d'immeuble** (managing) agent

gerbe [ʒɛʀb] nf (de fleurs) spray; (de blé) sheaf

gercé, e [ʒeʀse] adj chapped

gerçure [ʒeʀsyʀ] nf crack

gérer [ʒeʀe] vt to manage

germain, e [ʒeʀmɛ̃, ɛn] adj: **cousin ~** first cousin

germe [ʒeʀm] nm germ; **germer** vi to sprout; (semence) to germinate

geste [ʒɛst] nm gesture

gestion [ʒɛstjɔ̃] nf management

Ghana [gana] nm: **le ~** Ghana

gibier [ʒibje] nm (animaux) game

gicler [ʒikle] vi to spurt, squirt

gifle [ʒifl] nf slap (in the face); **gifler** vt to slap (in the face)

gigantesque [ʒigɑ̃tɛsk] adj gigantic

gigot [ʒigo] nm leg (of mutton ou lamb)

gigoter [ʒigɔte] vi to wriggle (about)

gilet [ʒile] nm waistcoat; (pull) cardigan; **gilet de sauvetage** life jacket

gin [dʒin] nm gin; **~-tonic** gin and tonic

gingembre [ʒɛ̃ʒɑ̃bʀ] nm ginger

girafe [ʒiʀaf] nf giraffe

giratoire [ʒiʀatwaʀ] adj: **sens ~** roundabout

girofle [ʒiʀɔfl] nf: **clou de ~** clove

girouette [ʒiʀwɛt] nf weather vane ou cock

gitan, e [ʒitɑ̃, an] nm/f gipsy

gîte [ʒit] nm (maison) home; (abri) shelter; **gîte (rural)** (country) holiday cottage (BRIT), gîte (self-catering accommodation in the country)

givre [ʒivʀ] nm (hoar) frost; **givré, e** adj covered in frost; (fam: fou) nuts; **orange givrée** orange sorbet (served in peel)

glace [glas] nf ice; (crème glacée) ice cream; (miroir) mirror; (de voiture) window

glacé, e [glase] adj (mains, vent, pluie) freezing; (lac) frozen; (boisson) iced

glacer [glase] vt to freeze; (gâteau) to ice; (fig): **~ qn** (intimider) to chill sb; (paralyser) to make sb's blood run cold

glacial, e [glasjal, jo] adj icy

glacier [glasje] nm (Géo) glacier; (marchand) ice-cream maker

glacière [glasjɛʀ] nf icebox

glaçon [glasɔ̃] nm icicle; (pour boisson) ice cube

glaïeul [glajœl] nm gladiolus

glaise [glɛz] nf clay

gland [glɑ̃] nm acorn; (décoration) tassel

glande [glɑ̃d] nf gland

glissade [glisad] nf (par jeu) slide; (chute) slip; **faire des ~s sur la glace** to slide on the ice

glissant, e [glisɑ̃, ɑ̃t] adj slippery

glissement [glismɑ̃] nm: **glissement de terrain** landslide

glisser [glise] vi (avancer) to glide ou slide along; (coulisser, tomber) to slide; (déraper) to slip; (être glissant) to be slippery ▷ vt to slip; **se ~ dans/entre** to slip into/between

global, e, -aux [glɔbal, o] adj overall

globe [glɔb] nm globe

globule [glɔbyl] nm (du sang): **~ blanc/rouge** white/red corpuscle

gloire [glwaʀ] nf glory

glousser [gluse] vi to cluck; (rire) to chuckle

glouton, ne [glutɔ̃, ɔn] adj gluttonous

gluant, e [glyɑ̃, ɑ̃t] adj sticky, gummy

glucose [glykoz] nm glucose

glycine [glisin] *nf* wisteria
GO *sigle* (= *grandes ondes*) LW
goal [gol] *nm* goalkeeper
gobelet [gɔblɛ] *nm* (*en étain, verre, argent*) tumbler; (*d'enfant, de pique-nique*) beaker; (*à dés*) cup
goéland [gɔelɑ̃] *nm* (sea)gull
goélette [gɔelɛt] *nf* schooner
goinfre [gwɛ̃fʀ] *nm* glutton
golf [gɔlf] *nm* golf; (*terrain*) golf course; **golf miniature** crazy (BRIT) *ou* miniature golf
golfe [gɔlf] *nm* gulf; (*petit*) bay
gomme [gɔm] *nf* (*à effacer*) rubber (BRIT), eraser; **gommer** *vt* to rub out (BRIT), erase
gonflé, e [gɔ̃fle] *adj* swollen; **il est ~** (*fam: courageux*) he's got some nerve; (*impertinent*) he's got a nerve
gonfler [gɔ̃fle] *vt* (*pneu, ballon: en soufflant*) to blow up; (: *avec une pompe*) to pump up; (*nombre, importance*) to inflate ▷ *vi* to swell (up); (*Culin: pâte*) to rise
gonzesse [gɔ̃zɛs] (*fam*) *nf* chick, bird (BRIT)
gorge [gɔʀʒ] *nf* (*Anat*) throat; (*vallée*) gorge; **gorgée** *nf* (*petite*) sip; (*grande*) gulp
gorille [gɔʀij] *nm* gorilla; (*fam*) bodyguard
gosse [gɔs] (*fam*) *nm/f* kid
goudron [gudʀɔ̃] *nm* tar; **goudronner** *vt* to tar(mac) (BRIT), asphalt (US)
gouffre [gufʀ] *nm* abyss, gulf
goulot [gulo] *nm* neck; **boire au ~** to drink from the bottle
goulu, e [guly] *adj* greedy
gourde [guʀd] *nf* (*récipient*) flask; (*fam*) (clumsy) clot *ou* oaf ▷ *adj* oafish
gourdin [guʀdɛ̃] *nm* club, bludgeon
gourmand, e [guʀmɑ̃, ɑ̃d] *adj* greedy; **gourmandise** *nf* greed; (*bonbon*) sweet
gousse [gus] *nf*: **gousse d'ail** clove of garlic
goût [gu] *nm* taste; **avoir bon ~** to taste good; **de bon ~** tasteful; **de mauvais ~** tasteless; **prendre ~ à** to develop a taste *ou* a liking for
goûter [gute] *vt* (*essayer*) to taste; (*apprécier*) to enjoy ▷ *vi* to have (afternoon) tea ▷ *nm* (afternoon) tea; **je peux ~?** can I have a taste?
goutte [gut] *nf* drop; (*Méd*) gout; (*alcool*) brandy; **tomber ~ à ~** to drip; **une ~ de whisky** a drop of whisky; **goutte-à-goutte** *nm* (*Méd*) drip
gouttière [gutjɛʀ] *nf* gutter
gouvernail [guvɛʀnaj] *nm* rudder; (*barre*) helm, tiller
gouvernement [guvɛʀnəmɑ̃] *nm* government
gouverner [guvɛʀne] *vt* to govern
grâce [gʀɑs] *nf* (*charme, Rel*) grace; (*faveur, Jur*) pardon; **faire ~ à qn de qch** to spare sb sth; **demander ~** to beg for mercy; **~ à** thanks to; **gracieux, -euse** *adj* graceful
grade [gʀad] *nm* rank; **monter en ~** to be promoted
gradin [gʀadɛ̃] *nm* tier; step; **gradins** *nmpl* (*de stade*) terracing *sg*
gradué, e [gʀadɥe] *adj*: **verre ~** measuring jug
graduel, le [gʀadɥɛl] *adj* gradual
graduer [gʀadɥe] *vt* (*effort etc*) to increase gradually; (*règle, verre*) to graduate
graffiti [gʀafiti] *nmpl* graffiti
grain [gʀɛ̃] *nm* (*gén*) grain; (*Navig*) squall; **grain de beauté** beauty spot; **grain de café** coffee bean; **grain de poivre** peppercorn
graine [gʀɛn] *nf* seed

graissage [gʀɛsaʒ] *nm* lubrication, greasing
graisse [gʀɛs] *nf* fat; (*lubrifiant*) grease; **graisser** *vt* to lubricate, grease; (*tacher*) to make greasy; **graisseux, -euse** *adj* greasy
grammaire [gʀa(m)mɛʀ] *nf* grammar
gramme [gʀam] *nm* gramme
grand, e [gʀɑ̃, gʀɑ̃d] *adj* (*haut*) tall; (*gros, vaste, large*) big, large; (*long*) long; (*plus âgé*) big; (*adulte*) grown-up; (*important, brillant*) great ▷ *adv*: **~ ouvert** wide open; **au ~ air** in the open (air); **les grands blessés** the severely injured; **grand ensemble** housing scheme; **grand magasin** department store; **grande personne** grown-up; **grande surface** hypermarket; **grandes écoles** prestigious schools at university level; **grandes lignes** (*Rail*) main lines; **grandes vacances** summer holidays (BRIT) *ou* vacation (US); **grand-chose** *nm/f inv*: **pas grand-chose** not much; **Grande-Bretagne** *nf* (Great) Britain; **grandeur** *nf* (*dimension*) size; **grandeur nature** life-size; **grandiose** *adj* imposing; **grandir** *vi* to grow ▷ *vt*: **grandir qn** (*suj: vêtement, chaussure*) to make sb look taller; **grand-mère** *nf* grandmother; **grand-peine**: **à grand-peine** *adv* with difficulty; **grand-père** *nm* grandfather; **grands-parents** *nmpl* grandparents
grange [gʀɑ̃ʒ] *nf* barn
granit [gʀanit] *nm* granite
graphique [gʀafik] *adj* graphic ▷ *nm* graph
grappe [gʀap] *nf* cluster; **grappe de raisin** bunch of grapes
gras, se [gʀɑ, gʀɑs] *adj* (*viande, soupe*) fatty; (*personne*) fat; (*surface, main*) greasy; (*plaisanterie*) coarse; (*Typo*) bold ▷ *nm* (*Culin*) fat; **faire la ~se matinée** to have a lie-in (BRIT), sleep late (US); **grassement** *adv*: **grassement payé** handsomely paid
gratifiant, e [gʀatifjɑ̃, jɑ̃t] *adj* gratifying, rewarding
gratin [gʀatɛ̃] *nm* (*plat*) cheese-topped dish; (*croûte*) cheese topping; (*fam: élite*) upper crust; **gratiné, e** *adj* (*Culin*) au gratin
gratis [gʀatis] *adv* free
gratitude [gʀatityd] *nf* gratitude
gratte-ciel [gʀatsjɛl] *nm inv* skyscraper
gratter [gʀate] *vt* (*avec un outil*) to scrape; (*enlever: avec un outil*) to scrape off; (: *avec un ongle*) to scratch; (*enlever avec un ongle*) to scratch off ▷ *vi* (*irriter*) to be scratchy; (*démanger*) to itch; **se ~** to scratch (o.s.)
gratuit, e [gʀatɥi, ɥit] *adj* (*entrée, billet*) free; (*fig*) gratuitous
grave [gʀav] *adj* (*maladie, accident*) serious, bad; (*sujet, problème*) serious, grave; (*air*) grave, solemn; (*voix, son*) deep, low-pitched; **gravement** *adv* seriously; (*parler, regarder*) gravely
graver [gʀave] *vt* (*plaque, nom*) to engrave; (*CD, DVD*) to burn
graveur [gʀavœʀ] *nm* engraver; **graveur de CD/DVD** CD/DVD writer
gravier [gʀavje] *nm* gravel *no pl*; **gravillons** *nmpl* loose chippings *ou* gravel *sg*
gravir [gʀaviʀ] *vt* to climb (up)
gravité [gʀavite] *nf* (*de maladie, d'accident*) seriousness; (*de sujet, problème*) gravity
graviter [gʀavite] *vi* to revolve
gravure [gʀavyʀ] *nf* engraving; (*reproduction*) print
gré [gʀe] *nm*: **à son ~** to one's liking; **de bon ~** willingly; **contre le ~ de qn** against sb's will; **de son (plein) ~** of one's own free will; **bon ~ mal ~** like it or not; **de ~ ou de**

force whether one likes it or not; **savoir ~ à qn de qch** to be grateful to sb for sth

grec, grecque [gʀɛk] adj Greek; (classique: vase etc) Grecian ▷ nm/f: **G~, Grecque** Greek ▷ nm (Ling) Greek

Grèce [gʀɛs] nf: **la ~** Greece

greffe [gʀɛf] nf (Bot, Méd: de tissu) graft; (Méd: d'organe) transplant; **greffer** vt (Bot, Méd: tissu) to graft; (Méd: organe) to transplant

grêle [gʀɛl] adj (very) thin ▷ nf hail; **grêler** vb impers: **il grêle** it's hailing; **grêlon** nm hailstone

grelot [gʀǝlo] nm little bell

grelotter [gʀǝlɔte] vi to shiver

grenade [gʀǝnad] nf (explosive) grenade; (Bot) pomegranate; **grenadine** nf grenadine

grenier [gʀǝnje] nm attic; (de ferme) loft

grenouille [gʀǝnuj] nf frog

grès [gʀɛ] nm sandstone; (poterie) stoneware

grève [gʀɛv] nf (d'ouvriers) strike; (plage) shore; **se mettre en/faire ~** to go on/be on strike; **grève de la faim** hunger strike; **grève sauvage** wildcat strike

gréviste [gʀevist] nm/f striker

grièvement [gʀijɛvmɑ̃] adv seriously

griffe [gʀif] nf claw; (de couturier) label; **griffer** vt to scratch

grignoter [gʀiɲɔte] vt (personne) to nibble at; (souris) to gnaw at ▷ vi to nibble

gril [gʀil] nm steak ou grill pan; **faire cuire au ~** to grill; **grillade** nf (viande etc) grill

grillage [gʀijaʒ] nm (treillis) wire netting; (clôture) wire fencing

grille [gʀij] nf (clôture) wire fence; (portail) (metal) gate; (d'égout) (metal) grate; (fig) grid

grille-pain [gʀijpɛ̃] nm inv toaster

griller [gʀije] vt (pain) to toast; (viande) to grill; (fig: ampoule etc) to blow; **faire ~** to toast; (châtaignes) to roast; **~ un feu rouge** to jump the lights

grillon [gʀijɔ̃] nm cricket

grimace [gʀimas] nf grimace; (pour faire rire): **faire des ~s** to pull ou make faces

grimper [gʀɛ̃pe] vi, vt to climb

grincer [gʀɛ̃se] vi (objet métallique) to grate; (plancher, porte) to creak; **~ des dents** to grind one's teeth

grincheux, -euse [gʀɛ̃ʃø, øz] adj grumpy

grippe [gʀip] nf flu, influenza; **grippe aviaire** bird flu; **grippé, e** adj: **être grippé** to have flu

gris, e [gʀi, gʀiz] adj grey; (ivre) tipsy

grisaille [gʀizaj] nf greyness, dullness

griser [gʀize] vt to intoxicate

grive [gʀiv] nf thrush

Groenland [gʀɔenlɑ̃d] nm Greenland

grogner [gʀɔɲe] vi to growl; (fig) to grumble; **grognon, ne** adj grumpy

grommeler [gʀɔm(ǝ)le] vi to mutter to o.s.

gronder [gʀɔ̃de] vi to rumble; (fig: révolte) to be brewing ▷ vt to scold; **se faire ~** to get a telling-off

gros, se [gʀo, gʀos] adj big, large; (obèse) fat; (travaux, dégâts) extensive; (épais) thick; (rhume, averse) heavy ▷ adv: **risquer/gagner ~** to risk/win a lot ▷ nm/f fat man/woman ▷ nm (Comm): **le ~** the wholesale business; **le ~ de** the bulk of; **prix de gros/gros** at; **par ~ temps/grosse mer** in rough weather/heavy seas; **en ~** roughly; (Comm) wholesale; **gros lot** jackpot; **gros mot** swearword; **gros plan** (Photo) close-up; **gros sel** cooking salt; **gros titre** headline; **grosse caisse** big

drum

groseille [gʀozɛj] nf: **~ (rouge/blanche)** red/white currant; **groseille à maquereau** gooseberry

grosse [gʀos] adj voir **gros**; **grossesse** nf pregnancy; **grosseur** nf size; (tumeur) lump

grossier, -ière [gʀosje, jɛʀ] adj coarse; (insolent) rude; (dessin) rough; (travail) roughly done; (imitation, instrument) crude; (évident: erreur) gross; **grossièrement** adv (sommairement) roughly; (vulgairement) coarsely; **grossièreté** nf rudeness; (mot): **dire des grossièretés** to use coarse language

grossir [gʀosiʀ] vi (personne) to put on weight ▷ vt (exagérer) to exaggerate; (au microscope) to magnify; (suj: vêtement): **~ qn** to make sb look fatter

grossiste [gʀosist] nm/f wholesaler

grotesque [gʀɔtɛsk] adj (extravagant) grotesque; (ridicule) ludicrous

grotte [gʀɔt] nf cave

groupe [gʀup] nm group; **groupe de parole** support group; **groupe sanguin** blood group; **groupe scolaire** school complex; **grouper** vt to group; **se grouper** vi to gather

grue [gʀy] nf crane

GSM [ʒeesɛm] nm, adj GSM

guenon [gǝnɔ̃] nf female monkey

guépard [gepaʀ] nm cheetah

guêpe [gɛp] nf wasp

guère [gɛʀ] adv (avec adjectif, adverbe): **ne ... ~** hardly; (avec verbe: pas beaucoup): **ne ... ~** tournure négative +much; (pas souvent) hardly ever; (pas longtemps) tournure négative +(very) long; **il n'y a ~ que/de** there's hardly anybody (ou anything) but/hardly any; **ce n'est ~ difficile** it's hardly difficult; **nous n'avons ~ de temps** we have hardly any time

guérilla [geʀija] nf guerrilla warfare

guérillero [geʀijeʀo] nm guerrilla

guérir [geʀiʀ] vt (personne, maladie) to cure; (membre, plaie) to heal ▷ vi (malade, maladie) to be cured; (blessure) to heal; **guérison** nf (de maladie) curing; (de membre, plaie) healing; (de malade) recovery; **guérisseur, -euse** nm/f healer

guerre [gɛʀ] nf war; **en ~** at war; **faire la ~ à** to wage war against; **guerre civile/mondiale** civil/world war; **guerrier, -ière** adj warlike ▷ nm/f warrior

guet [gɛ] nm: **faire le ~** to be on the watch ou look-out; **guet-apens** [gɛtapɑ̃] nm ambush; **guetter** vt (épier) to watch (intently); (attendre) to watch (out) for; (hostilement) to be lying in wait for

gueule [gœl] nf (d'animal) mouth; (fam: figure) face; (: bouche) mouth; **ta ~!** (fam) shut up!; **avoir la ~ de bois** (fam) to have a hangover, be hung over; **gueuler** (fam) vi to bawl

gui [gi] nm mistletoe

guichet [giʃɛ] nm (de bureau, banque) counter; **les ~s** (à la gare, au théâtre) the ticket office sg

guide [gid] nm (personne) guide; (livre) guide (book) ▷ nf (éclaireuse) girl guide; **guider** vt to guide

guidon [gidɔ̃] nm handlebars pl

guignol [giɲɔl] nm ≈ Punch and Judy show; (fig) clown

guillemets [gijmɛ] nmpl: **entre ~** in inverted commas

guindé, e [gɛ̃de] adj (personne, air) stiff, starchy; (style) stilted

Guinée [gine] nf Guinea

guirlande [giʀlɑ̃d] nf (fleurs) garland; **guirlande de**

Noël tinsel garland
guise [giz] *nf*: **à votre ~** as you wish *ou* please; **en ~ de** by way of
guitare [gitar] *nf* guitar
Guyane [gчijan] *nf*: **la ~ (française)** French Guiana
gym [ʒim] *nf* (*exercices*) gym; **gymnase** *nm* gym(nasium); **gymnaste** *nm/f* gymnast; **gymnastique** *nf* gymnastics *sg*; (*au réveil etc*) keep-fit exercises *pl*
gynécologie [ʒinekɔlɔʒi] *nf* gynaecology; **gynécologique** *adj* gynaecological; **gynécologue** *nm/f* gynaecologist

habile [abil] *adj* skilful; (*malin*) clever; **habileté** [abilte] *nf* skill, skilfulness; cleverness
habillé, e [abije] *adj* dressed; (*chic*) dressy
habiller [abije] *vt* to dress; (*fournir en vêtements*) to clothe; (*couvrir*) to cover; **s'~** *vi* to dress (o.s.); (*se déguiser, mettre des vêtements chic*) to dress up
habit [abi] *nm* outfit; **habits** *nmpl* (*vêtements*) clothes; **habit (de soirée)** evening dress; (*pour homme*) tails *pl*
habitant, e [abitã, ãt] *nm/f* inhabitant; (*d'une maison*) occupant; **loger chez l'~** to stay with the locals
habitation [abitasjɔ̃] *nf* house; **habitations à loyer modéré** (block of) council flats
habiter [abite] *vt* to live in ▷ *vi*: **~ à/dans** to live in; **où habitez-vous?** where do you live?
habitude [abityd] *nf* habit; **avoir l'~ de qch** to be used to sth; **avoir l'~ de faire** to be in the habit of doing; (*expérience*) to be used to doing; **d'~** usually; **comme d'~** as usual
habitué, e [abitчe] *nm/f* (*de maison*) regular visitor; (*de café*) regular (customer)
habituel, le [abitчɛl] *adj* usual
habituer [abitчe] *vt*: **~ qn à** to get sb used to; **s'~ à** to

get used to
'hache [ʼaʃ] *nf* axe
'hacher [ʼaʃe] *vt* (*viande*) to mince; (*persil*) to chop; **'hachis** *nm* mince *no pl*; **hachis Parmentier** ≈ shepherd's pie
'haie [ʼɛ] *nf* hedge; (*Sport*) hurdle
'haillons [ʼajɔ̃] *nmpl* rags
'haine [ʼɛn] *nf* hatred
'haïr [ʼair] *vt* to detest, hate
'hâlé, e [ʼɑle] *adj* (sun)tanned, sunburnt
haleine [alɛn] *nf* breath; **hors d'~** out of breath; **tenir en ~** (*attention*) to hold spellbound; (*incertitude*) to keep in suspense; **de longue ~** long-term
'haleter [ʼalte] *vt* to pant
'hall [ʼol] *nm* hall
'halle [ʼal] *nf* (covered) market; **halles** *nfpl* (*d'une grande ville*) central food market *sg*
hallucination [alysinasjɔ̃] *nf* hallucination
'halte [ʼalt] *nf* stop, break; (*endroit*) stopping place ▷ *excl* stop!; **faire halte** to stop
haltère [altɛr] *nm* dumbbell, barbell; **haltères** *nmpl*: **(poids et) ~s** (*activité*) weightlifting *sg*; **haltérophilie** *nf* weightlifting
'hamac [ʼamak] *nm* hammock
'hameau, x [ʼamo] *nm* hamlet
hameçon [amsɔ̃] *nm* (fish) hook
'hanche [ʼɑ̃ʃ] *nf* hip
'handball [ʼɑ̃dbal] *nm* handball
'handicapé, e [ʼɑ̃dikape] *adj* disabled, handicapped ▷ *nm/f* handicapped person; **handicapé mental/physique** mentally/physically handicapped person; **'handicapé moteur** person with a movement disorder
'hangar [ʼɑ̃gar] *nm* shed; (*Aviat*) hangar
'hanneton [ʼantɔ̃] *nm* cockchafer
'hanter [ʼɑ̃te] *vt* to haunt
'hantise [ʼɑ̃tiz] *nf* obsessive fear
'harceler [ʼarsəle] *vt* to harass; **harceler qn de questions** to plague sb with questions
'hardi, e [ʼardi] *adj* bold, daring
'hareng [ʼarɑ̃] *nm* herring; **hareng saur** kipper, smoked herring
'hargne [ʼarɲ] *nf* aggressiveness; **'hargneux, -euse** *adj* aggressive
'haricot [ʼariko] *nm* bean; **'haricot blanc** haricot bean; **'haricot vert** green bean; **'haricot rouge** kidney bean
harmonica [armɔnika] *nm* mouth organ
harmonie [armɔni] *nf* harmony; **harmonieux, -euse** *adj* harmonious; (*couleurs, couple*) well-matched
'harpe [ʼarp] *nf* harp
'hasard [ʼazar] *nm*: **le hasard** chance, fate; **un hasard** a coincidence; **au hasard** (*aller*) aimlessly; (*choisir*) at random; **par hasard** by chance; **à tout hasard** (*en cas de besoin*) just in case; (*en espérant trouver ce qu'on cherche*) on the off chance (BRIT)
'hâte [ʼɑt] *nf* haste; **à la hâte** hurriedly, hastily; **en hâte** posthaste, with all possible speed; **avoir hâte de** to be eager *ou* anxious to; **'hâter** *vt* to hasten; **se hâter** *vi* to hurry; **'hâtif, -ive** *adj* (*travail*) hurried; (*décision, jugement*) hasty
'hausse [ʼos] *nf* rise, increase; **être en hausse** to be going up; **'hausser** *vt* to raise; **hausser les épaules** to shrug (one's shoulders)
'haut, e [ʼo, ʼot] *adj* high; (*grand*) tall ▷ *adv* high ▷ *nm* top (part); **de 3 m de haut** 3 m high, 3 m in height; **des**

hauts et des bas ups and downs; **en haut lieu** in high places; **à haute voix, (tout) haut** aloud, out loud; **du haut de** from the top of; **de haut en bas** from top to bottom; **plus haut** higher up, further up; (*dans un texte*) above; (*parler*) louder; **en haut** (*être/aller*) at/to the top; (*dans une maison*) upstairs; **en haut de** at the top of; **'haut débit** broadband

'hautain, e [ˈotɛ̃, ɛn] *adj* haughty

'hautbois [ˈobwa] *nm* oboe

'hauteur [ˈotœʀ] *nf* height; **à la hauteur de** (*accident*) near; (*fig: tâche, situation*) equal to; **à la hauteur** (*fig*) up to it

'haut-parleur [ˈopaʀlœʀ] *nm* (loud)speaker

Hawaï [awai] *n*: **les îles ~** Hawaii

'Haye [ˈɛ] *n*: **la Haye** the Hague

hebdomadaire [ɛbdɔmadɛʀ] *adj, nm* weekly

hébergement [ebɛʀʒəmɑ̃] *nm* accommodation

héberger [ebɛʀʒe] *vt* (*touristes*) to accommodate, lodge; (*amis*) to put up; (*réfugiés*) to take in

hébergeur [ebɛʀʒœʀ] *nm* (*Internet*) host

hébreu, x [ebʀø] *adj m, nm* Hebrew

Hébrides [ebʀid] *nf*: **les ~** the Hebrides

hectare [ɛktaʀ] *nm* hectare

'hein [ˈɛ̃] *excl* eh?

'hélas [ˈelas] *excl* alas! ▷ *adv* unfortunately

'héler [ˈele] *vt* to hail

hélice [elis] *nf* propeller

hélicoptère [elikɔptɛʀ] *nm* helicopter

helvétique [ɛlvetik] *adj* Swiss

hématome [ematɔm] *nm* nasty bruise

hémisphère [emisfɛʀ] *nm*: **l'~ nord/sud** the northern/ southern hemisphere

hémorragie [emɔʀaʒi] *nf* bleeding *no pl*, haemorrhage

hémorroïdes [emɔʀɔid] *nfpl* piles, haemorrhoids

'hennir [ˈeniʀ] *vi* to neigh, whinny

hépatite [epatit] *nf* hepatitis

herbe [ɛʀb] *nf* grass; (*Culin, Méd*) herb; **~s de Provence** mixed herbs; **en ~** unripe; (*fig*) budding; **herbicide** *nm* weed-killer; **herboriste** *nm/f* herbalist

héréditaire [eʀeditɛʀ] *adj* hereditary

'hérisson [ˈeʀisɔ̃] *nm* hedgehog

héritage [eʀitaʒ] *nm* inheritance; (*coutumes, système*) heritage, legacy

hériter [eʀite] *vi*: **~ de qch (de qn)** to inherit sth (from sb); **héritier, -ière** *nm/f* heir(-ess)

hermétique [ɛʀmetik] *adj* airtight; watertight; (*fig: obscur*) abstruse; (: *impénétrable*) impenetrable

hermine [ɛʀmin] *nf* ermine

hernie [ˈɛʀni] *nf* hernia

héroïne [eʀɔin] *nf* heroine; (*drogue*) heroin

héroïque [eʀɔik] *adj* heroic

'héron [ˈeʀɔ̃] *nm* heron

'héros [ˈeʀo] *nm* hero

hésitant, e [ezitɑ̃, ɑ̃t] *adj* hesitant

hésitation [ezitasjɔ̃] *nf* hesitation

hésiter [ezite] *vi*: **~ (à faire)** to hesitate (to do)

hétérosexuel, le [eteʀɔsɛkɥɛl] *adj* heterosexual

'hêtre [ˈɛtʀ] *nm* beech

heure [œʀ] *nf* hour; (*Scol*) period; (*moment*) time; **c'est l'~** it's time; **quelle ~ est-il?** what time is it?; **2 ~s** (*du matin*) 2 o'clock (in the morning); **être à l'~** to be on time; (*montre*) to be right; **mettre à l'~** to set right; **à une ~ avancée (de la nuit)** at a late hour (of the night); **de bonne ~** early; **à toute ~** at any time; **24 ~s sur 24** round the clock, 24 hours a day; **à l'~ qu'il est** at this time (of day); by now; **sur l'~** at once; **à quelle ~ ouvre le musée/magasin?** what time does the museum/shop open?; **heures de bureau** office hours; **heure de pointe** rush hour; (*téléphone*) peak period; **heures supplémentaires** overtime *sg*

heureusement [œʀøzmɑ̃] *adv* (*par bonheur*) fortunately, luckily

heureux, -euse [œʀø, øz] *adj* happy; (*chanceux*) lucky, fortunate

'heurt [ˈœʀ] *nm* (*choc*) collision; (*conflit*) clash

'heurter [ˈœʀte] *vt* (*mur*) to strike, hit; (*personne*) to collide with

hexagone [ɛgzagɔn] *nm* hexagon; **l'H~** (*la France*) France (*because of its shape*)

hiberner [ibɛʀne] *vi* to hibernate

'hibou, x [ˈibu] *nm* owl

'hideux, -euse [ˈidø, øz] *adj* hideous

hier [jɛʀ] *adv* yesterday; **~ matin/midi** yesterday morning/lunchtime; **~ soir** last night, yesterday evening; **toute la journée d'~** all day yesterday; **toute la matinée d'~** all yesterday morning

'hiérarchie [ˈjeʀaʀʃi] *nf* hierarchy

hindou, e [ɛ̃du] *adj* Hindu ▷ *nm/f*: **H~, e** Hindu

hippique [ipik] *adj* equestrian, horse *cpd*; **un club ~** a riding centre; **un concours ~** a horse show; **hippisme** *nm* (horse)riding

hippodrome [ipodʀom] *nm* racecourse

hippopotame [ipɔpɔtam] *nm* hippopotamus

hirondelle [iʀɔ̃dɛl] *nf* swallow

'hisser [ˈise] *vt* to hoist, haul up

histoire [istwaʀ] *nf* (*science, événements*) history; (*anecdote, récit, mensonge*) story; (*affaire*) business *no pl*; **histoires** *nfpl* (*chichis*) fuss *no pl*; (*ennuis*) trouble *sg*; **historique** *adj* historical; (*important*) historic ▷ *nm*: **faire l'historique de** to give the background to

'hit-parade [ˈitpaʀad] *nm*: **le hit-parade** the charts

hiver [ivɛʀ] *nm* winter; **hivernal, e, -aux** *adj* winter *cpd*; (*glacial*) wintry; **hiverner** *vi* to winter

HLM *nm ou f* (= *habitation à loyer modéré*) council flat; **des ~** council housing

'hobby [ˈɔbi] *nm* hobby

'hocher [ˈɔʃe] *vt*: **hocher la tête** to nod; (*signe négatif ou dubitatif*) to shake one's head

'hockey [ˈɔkɛ] *nm*: **hockey (sur glace/gazon)** (ice/ field) hockey

'hold-up [ˈɔldœp] *nm inv* hold-up

'hollandais, e [ˈɔlɑ̃dɛ, ɛz] *adj* Dutch ▷ *nm* (*Ling*) Dutch ▷ *nm/f*: **Hollandais, e** Dutchman(-woman)

'Hollande [ˈɔlɑ̃d] *nf*: **la Hollande** Holland

'homard [ˈɔmaʀ] *nm* lobster

homéopathique [ɔmeɔpatik] *adj* homoeopathic

homicide [ɔmisid] *nm* murder; **homicide involontaire** manslaughter

hommage [ɔmaʒ] *nm* tribute; **rendre ~ à** to pay tribute to

homme [ɔm] *nm* man; **homme d'affaires** businessman; **homme d'État** statesman; **homme de main** hired man; **homme de paille** stooge; **l'homme de la rue** the man on the street

homo...: **homogène** *adj* homogeneous; **homologue** *nm/f* counterpart; **homologué, e** *adj* (*Sport*) ratified; (*tarif*) authorized; **homonyme** *nm* (*Ling*) homonym; (*d'une personne*) namesake; **homosexuel, le** *adj* homosexual

'Hong Kong ['ɔ̃gkɔ̃g] n Hong Kong

'Hongrie ['ɔ̃gri] nf: **la Hongrie** Hungary; **'hongrois, e** adj Hungarian ▷ nm/f: **Hongrois, e** Hungarian ▷ nm (Ling) Hungarian

honnête [ɔnɛt] adj (intègre) honest; (juste, satisfaisant) fair; **honnêtement** adv honestly; **honnêteté** nf honesty

honneur [ɔnœʀ] nm honour; (mérite) credit; **en l'~ de** in honour of; (événement) on the occasion of; **faire ~ à** (engagements) to honour; (famille) to be a credit to; (fig: repas etc) to do justice to

honorable [ɔnɔʀabl] adj worthy, honourable; (suffisant) decent

honoraire [ɔnɔʀɛʀ] adj honorary; **professeur ~** professor emeritus; **honoraires** nmpl fees

honorer [ɔnɔʀe] vt to honour; (estimer) to hold in high regard; (faire honneur à) to do credit to

'honte ['ɔ̃t] nf shame; **avoir honte de** to be ashamed of; **faire honte à qn** to make sb (feel) ashamed; **'honteux, -euse** adj ashamed; (conduite, acte) shameful, disgraceful

hôpital, -aux [ɔpital, o] nm hospital; **où est l'~ le plus proche?** where is the nearest hospital?

'hoquet ['ɔkɛ] nm: **avoir le hoquet** to have (the) hiccoughs

horaire [ɔʀɛʀ] adj hourly ▷ nm timetable, schedule; **horaires** nmpl (d'employé) hours; **horaire souple** flexitime

horizon [ɔʀizɔ̃] nm horizon

horizontal, e, -aux [ɔʀizɔ̃tal, o] adj horizontal

horloge [ɔʀlɔʒ] nf clock; **l'~ parlante** the speaking clock; **horloger, -ère** nm/f watchmaker; clockmaker

'hormis ['ɔʀmi] prép save

horoscope [`skɔp] nm horoscope

horreur [ɔʀœʀ] nf horror; **quelle ~!** how awful!; **avoir ~ de** to loathe ou detest; **horrible** adj horrible; **horrifier** vt to horrify

'hors ['ɔʀ] prép: **hors de** out of; **hors pair** outstanding; **hors de propos** inopportune; **être hors de soi** to be beside o.s.; **'hors d'usage** out of service; **'hors-bord** nm inv speedboat (with outboard motor); **'hors-d'œuvre** nm inv hors d'œuvre; **'hors-la-loi** nm inv outlaw; **'hors-service** adj inv out of order; **'hors-taxe** adj (boutique, articles) duty-free

hortensia [ɔʀtɑ̃sja] nm hydrangea

hospice [ɔspis] nm (de vieillards) home

hospitalier, -ière [ɔspitalje, jɛʀ] adj (accueillant) hospitable; (Méd: service, centre) hospital cpd

hospitaliser [ɔspitalize] vt to take/send to hospital, hospitalize

hospitalité [ɔspitalite] nf hospitality

hostie [ɔsti] nf host (Rel)

hostile [ɔstil] adj hostile; **hostilité** nf hostility

hôte [ot] nm (maître de maison) host; (invité) guest

hôtel [otɛl] nm hotel; **aller à l'~** to stay in a hotel; **hôtel de ville** town hall; **hôtel (particulier)** (private) mansion; **hôtellerie** nf hotel business

hôtesse [otɛs] nf hostess; **hôtesse (de l'air)** stewardess, air hostess (BRIT)

'houblon ['ublɔ̃] nm (Bot) hop; (pour la bière) hops pl

'houille ['uj] nf coal; **'houille blanche** hydroelectric power

'houle ['ul] nf swell; **'houleux, -euse** adj stormy

'hourra ['uʀa] excl hurrah!

'housse ['us] nf cover

'houx ['u] nm holly

'hublot ['yblo] nm porthole

'huche ['yʃ] nf: **huche à pain** bread bin

'huer ['ɥe] vt to boo

huile [ɥil] nf oil

huissier [ɥisje] nm usher; (Jur) ≈ bailiff

'huit ['ɥi(t)] num eight; **samedi en huit** a week on Saturday; **dans huit jours** in a week; **'huitaine** nf: **une huitaine (de jours)** a week or so; **'huitième** num eighth

huître [ɥitʀ] nf oyster

humain, e [ymɛ̃, ɛn] adj human; (compatissant) humane ▷ nm human (being); **humanitaire** adj humanitarian; **humanité** nf humanity

humble [œ̃bl] adj humble

'humer ['yme] vt (plat) to smell; (parfum) to inhale

humeur [ymœʀ] nf mood; **de bonne/mauvaise ~** in a good/bad mood

humide [ymid] adj damp; (main, yeux) moist; (climat, chaleur) humid; (saison, route) wet

humilier [ymilje] vt to humiliate

humilité [ymilite] nf humility, humbleness

humoristique [ymɔʀistik] adj humorous

humour [ymuʀ] nm humour; **avoir de l'~** to have a sense of humour; **humour noir** black humour

'huppé, e ['ype] (fam) adj posh

'hurlement ['yʀləmɑ̃] nm howling no pl, howl, yelling no pl, yell

'hurler ['yʀle] vi to howl, yell

'hutte ['yt] nf hut

hydratant, e [idʀatɑ̃, ɑ̃t] adj (crème) moisturizing

hydraulique [idʀolik] adj hydraulic

hydravion [idʀavjɔ̃] nm seaplane

hydrogène [idʀɔʒɛn] nm hydrogen

hydroglisseur [idʀɔglisœʀ] nm hydroplane

hyène [jɛn] nf hyena

hygiène [iʒjɛn] nf hygiene

hygiénique [iʒenik] adj hygienic

hymne [imn] nm hymn

hyperlien [ipɛʀljɛ̃] nm hyperlink

hypermarché [ipɛʀmaʀʃe] nm hypermarket

hypermétrope [ipɛʀmetʀɔp] adj long-sighted

hypertension [ipɛʀtɑ̃sjɔ̃] nf high blood pressure

hypnose [ipnoz] nf hypnosis; **hypnotiser** vt to hypnotize

hypocrisie [ipɔkʀizi] nf hypocrisy; **hypocrite** adj hypocritical

hypothèque [ipɔtɛk] nf mortgage

hypothèse [ipɔtɛz] nf hypothesis

hystérique [isteʀik] adj hysterical

iceberg [ajsbɛʀɡ] nm iceberg

ici [isi] adv here; **jusqu'~** as far as this; (temps) so far; **d'~ demain** by tomorrow; **d'~ là** by then, in the meantime; **d'~ peu** before long

icône [ikon] nf icon

idéal, e, -aux [ideal, o] adj ideal ▷ nm ideal; **idéaliste** adj idealistic ▷ nm/f idealist

idée [ide] nf idea; **avoir dans l'~ que** to have an idea that; **se faire des ~s** to imagine things, get ideas into one's head; **avoir des ~s noires** to have black ou dark thoughts; **idées reçues** received wisdom sg

identifier [idãtifje] vt to identify; **s'~** vi: **s'~ avec** ou **à qn/qch** (héros etc) to identify with sb/sth

identique [idãtik] adj: **~ (à)** identical (to)

identité [idãtite] nf identity

idiot, e [idjo, idjɔt] adj idiotic ▷ nm/f idiot

idole [idɔl] nf idol

if [if] nm yew

ignoble [iɲɔbl] adj vile

ignorant, e [iɲɔʀã, ãt] adj ignorant; **~ de** ignorant of, not aware of

ignorer [iɲɔʀe] vt not to know; (personne) to ignore

il [il] pron he; (animal, chose, en tournure impersonnelle) it; **il fait froid** it's cold; **Pierre est-il arrivé?** has Pierre arrived?; **il a gagné** he won; voir **avoir**

île [il] nf island; **l'île Maurice** Mauritius; **les îles anglo-normandes** the Channel Islands; **les îles britanniques** the British Isles

illégal, e, -aux [i(l)legal, o] adj illegal

illimité, e [i(l)limite] adj unlimited

illisible [i(l)lizibl] adj illegible; (roman) unreadable

illogique [i(l)lɔʒik] adj illogical

illuminer [i(l)lymine] vt to light up; (monument, rue: pour une fête) to illuminate; (: au moyen de projecteurs) to floodlight

illusion [i(l)lyzjɔ̃] nf illusion; **se faire des ~s** to delude o.s.; **faire ~** to delude ou fool people

illustration [i(l)lystʀasjɔ̃] nf illustration

illustré, e [i(l)lystʀe] adj illustrated ▷ nm comic

illustrer [i(l)lystʀe] vt to illustrate; **s'~** to become

famous, win fame

ils [il] pron they

image [imaʒ] nf (gén) picture; (métaphore) image; **image de marque** brand image; (fig) public image; **imagé, e** adj (texte) full of imagery; (langage) colourful

imaginaire [imaʒinɛʀ] adj imaginary

imagination [imaʒinasjɔ̃] nf imagination; **avoir de l'~** to be imaginative

imaginer [imaʒine] vt to imagine; (inventer: expédient) to devise, think up; **s'~** vi (se figurer: scène etc) to imagine, picture; **s'~ que** to imagine that

imbécile [ɛ̃besil] adj idiotic ▷ nm/f idiot

imbu, e [ɛ̃by] adj: **~ de** full of

imitateur, -trice [imitatœʀ, tʀis] nm/f (gén) imitator; (Music-Hall) impersonator

imitation [imitasjɔ̃] nf imitation; (de personnalité) impersonation

imiter [imite] vt to imitate; (contrefaire) to forge; (ressembler à) to look like

immangeable [ɛ̃mãʒabl] adj inedible

immatriculation [imatʀikylasjɔ̃] nf registration

immatriculer [imatʀikyle] vt to register; **faire/se faire ~** to register

immédiat, e [imedja, jat] adj immediate ▷ nm: **dans l'~** for the time being; **immédiatement** adv immediately

immense [i(m)mãs] adj immense

immerger [imɛʀʒe] vt to immerse, submerge

immeuble [imœbl] nm building; (à usage d'habitation) block of flats

immigration [imigʀasjɔ̃] nf immigration

immigré, e [imigʀe] nm/f immigrant

imminent, e [iminã, ãt] adj imminent

immobile [i(m)mɔbil] adj still, motionless

immobilier, -ière [imɔbilje, jɛʀ] adj property cpd ▷ nm: **l'~** the property business

immobiliser [imɔbilize] vt (gén) to immobilize; (circulation, véhicule, affaires) to bring to a standstill; **s'~** (personne) to stand still; (machine, véhicule) to come to a halt

immoral, e, -aux [i(m)mɔʀal, o] adj immoral

immortel, le [imɔʀtɛl] adj immortal

immunisé, e [im(m)ynize] adj: **~ contre** immune to

immunité [imynite] nf immunity

impact [ɛ̃pakt] nm impact

impair, e [ɛ̃pɛʀ] adj odd ▷ nm faux pas, blunder

impardonnable [ɛ̃paʀdɔnabl] adj unpardonable, unforgiving

imparfait, e [ɛ̃paʀfɛ, ɛt] adj imperfect

impartial, e, -aux [ɛ̃paʀsjal, jo] adj impartial, unbiased

impasse [ɛ̃pas] nf dead end, cul-de-sac; (fig) deadlock

impassible [ɛ̃pasibl] adj impassive

impatience [ɛ̃pasjãs] nf impatience

impatient, e [ɛ̃pasjã, jãt] adj impatient; **impatienter: s'impatienter** vi to get impatient

impeccable [ɛ̃pekabl] adj (parfait) perfect; (propre) impeccable; (fam) smashing

impensable [ɛ̃pãsabl] adj (événement hypothétique) unthinkable; (événement qui a eu lieu) unbelievable

impératif, -ive [ɛ̃peʀatif, iv] adj imperative ▷ nm (Ling) imperative; **impératifs** nmpl (exigences: d'une fonction, d'une charge) requirements; (: de la mode) demands

impératrice [ɛ̃peratris] nf empress
imperceptible [ɛ̃persɛptibl] adj imperceptible
impérial, e, -aux [ɛ̃perjal, jo] adj imperial
impérieux, -euse [ɛ̃perjø, jøz] adj (caractère, ton) imperious; (obligation, besoin) pressing, urgent
impérissable [ɛ̃perisabl] adj undying
imperméable [ɛ̃permeabl] adj waterproof; (fig): ~ à impervious to ▷ nm raincoat
impertinent, e [ɛ̃pertinɑ̃, ɑ̃t] adj impertinent
impitoyable [ɛ̃pitwajabl] adj pitiless, merciless
implanter [ɛ̃plɑ̃te]: s'~ vi to be set up
impliquer [ɛ̃plike] vt to imply; ~ qn (dans) to implicate sb (in)
impoli, e [ɛ̃pɔli] adj impolite, rude
impopulaire [ɛ̃pɔpylɛr] adj unpopular
importance [ɛ̃pɔrtɑ̃s] nf importance; (de somme) size; (de retard, dégâts) extent; **sans ~** unimportant
important, e [ɛ̃pɔrtɑ̃, ɑ̃t] adj important; (en quantité: somme, retard) considerable, sizeable; (: dégâts) extensive; (péj: airs, ton) self-important ▷ nm: **l'~** the important thing
importateur, -trice [ɛ̃pɔrtatœr, tris] nm/f importer
importation [ɛ̃pɔrtasjɔ̃] nf importation; (produit) import
importer [ɛ̃pɔrte] vt (Comm) to import; (maladies, plantes) to introduce ▷ vi (être important) to matter; **il importe qu'il fasse** it is important that he should do; **peu m'importe** (je n'ai pas de préférence) I don't mind; (je m'en moque) I don't care; **peu importe (que)** it doesn't matter (if); voir aussi **n'importe**
importun, e [ɛ̃pɔrtœ̃ yn] adj irksome, importunate; (arrivée, visite) inopportune, ill-timed ▷ nm intruder; **importuner** vt to bother
imposant, e [ɛ̃pozɑ̃, ɑ̃t] adj imposing
imposer [ɛ̃poze] vt (taxer) to tax; s'~ (être nécessaire) to be imperative; ~ **qch à qn** to impose sth on sb; **en ~ à** to impress; s'~ **comme** to emerge as; s'~ **par** to win recognition through
impossible [ɛ̃pɔsibl] adj impossible; **il m'est ~ de le faire** it is impossible for me to do it, I can't possibly do it; **faire l'~** to do one's utmost
imposteur [ɛ̃pɔstœr] nm impostor
impôt [ɛ̃po] nm tax; **impôt foncier** land tax; **impôt sur le chiffre d'affaires** corporation (BRIT) ou corporate (US) tax; **impôt sur le revenu** income tax; **impôts locaux** rates, local taxes (US), ≈ council tax (BRIT)
impotent, e [ɛ̃pɔtɑ̃, ɑ̃t] adj disabled
impraticable [ɛ̃pratikabl] adj (projet) impracticable, unworkable; (piste) impassable
imprécis, e [ɛ̃presi, iz] adj imprecise
imprégner [ɛ̃preɲe] vt (tissu) to impregnate; (lieu, air) to fill; s'~ **de** (fig) to absorb
imprenable [ɛ̃prənabl] adj (forteresse) impregnable; **vue ~** unimpeded outlook
impression [ɛ̃presjɔ̃] nf impression; (d'un ouvrage, tissu) printing; **faire bonne/mauvaise ~** to make a good/bad impression; **impressionnant, e** adj (imposant) impressive; (bouleversant) upsetting; **impressionner** vt (frapper) to impress; (bouleverser) to upset
imprévisible [ɛ̃previzibl] adj unforeseeable
imprévu, e [ɛ̃prevy] adj unforeseen, unexpected ▷ nm (incident) unexpected incident; **des vacances pleines d'~** holidays full of surprises; **en cas d'~** if anything unexpected happens; **sauf ~** unless anything

unexpected crops up
imprimante [ɛ̃primɑ̃t] nf printer; **imprimante (à) laser** laser printer
imprimé [ɛ̃prime] nm (formulaire) printed form; (Postes) printed matter no pl; (tissu) printed fabric; ~ **à fleur** floral print
imprimer [ɛ̃prime] vt to print; (publier) to publish; **imprimerie** nf printing; (établissement) printing works sg; **imprimeur** nm printer
impropre [ɛ̃prɔpr] adj inappropriate; ~ **à** unfit for
improviser [ɛ̃prɔvize] vt, vi to improvise
improviste [ɛ̃prɔvist]: **à l'~** adv unexpectedly, without warning
imprudence [ɛ̃prydɑ̃s] nf (d'une personne, d'une action) carelessness no pl; (d'une remarque) imprudence no pl; **commettre une ~** to do something foolish
imprudent, e [ɛ̃prydɑ̃, ɑ̃t] adj (conducteur, geste, action) careless; (remarque) unwise, imprudent; (projet) foolhardy
impuissant, e [ɛ̃pɥisɑ̃, ɑ̃t] adj helpless; (sans effet) ineffectual; (sexuellement) impotent
impulsif, -ive [ɛ̃pylsif, iv] adj impulsive
impulsion [ɛ̃pylsjɔ̃] nf (Élec, instinct) impulse; (élan, influence) impetus
inabordable [inabɔrdabl] adj (cher) prohibitive
inacceptable [inaksɛptabl] adj unacceptable
inaccessible [inaksesibl] adj inaccessible; ~ **à** impervious to
inachevé, e [inaʃ(ə)ve] adj unfinished
inactif, -ive [inaktif, iv] adj inactive; (remède) ineffective; (Bourse: marché) slack
inadapté, e [inadapte] adj (gén): ~ **à** not adapted to, unsuited to; (Psych) maladjusted
inadéquat, e [inadekwa(t), kwat] adj inadequate
inadmissible [inadmisibl] adj inadmissible
inadvertance [inadvɛrtɑ̃s]: **par ~** adv inadvertently
inanimé, e [inanime] adj (matière) inanimate; (évanoui) unconscious; (sans vie) lifeless
inanition [inanisjɔ̃] nf: **tomber d'~** to faint with hunger (and exhaustion)
inaperçu, e [inapɛrsy] adj: **passer ~** to go unnoticed
inapte [inapt] adj: ~ **à** incapable of; (Mil) unfit for
inattendu, e [inatɑ̃dy] adj unexpected
inattentif, -ive [inatɑ̃tif, iv] adj inattentive; ~ **à** (dangers, détails) heedless of; **inattention** nf lack of attention; **une faute** ou **une erreur d'inattention** a careless mistake
inaugurer [inogyre] vt (monument) to unveil; (exposition, usine) to open; (fig) to inaugurate
inavouable [inavwabl] adj shameful; (bénéfices) undisclosable
incalculable [ɛ̃kalkylabl] adj incalculable
incapable [ɛ̃kapabl] adj incapable; ~ **de faire** incapable of doing; (empêché) unable to do
incapacité [ɛ̃kapasite] nf (incompétence) incapability; (impossibilité) incapacity; **dans l'~ de faire** unable to do
incarcérer [ɛ̃karsere] vt to incarcerate, imprison
incassable [ɛ̃kasabl] adj unbreakable
incendie [ɛ̃sɑ̃di] nm fire; **incendie criminel** arson no pl; **incendie de forêt** forest fire; **incendier** vt (mettre le feu à) to set fire to, set alight; (brûler complètement) to burn down
incertain, e [ɛ̃sɛrtɛ̃, ɛn] adj uncertain; (temps) unsettled; (imprécis: contours) indistinct, blurred;

incertitude nf uncertainty

incessamment [ɛ̃sesamã] adv very shortly

incident [ɛ̃sidã] nm incident; **incident de parcours** minor hitch ou setback; **incident technique** technical difficulties pl

incinérer [ɛ̃sineʀe] vt (ordures) to incinerate; (mort) to cremate

incisive [ɛ̃siziv] nf incisor

inciter [ɛ̃site] vt: **~ qn à (faire) qch** to encourage sb to do sth; (à la révolte etc) to incite sb to do sth

incivilité [ɛ̃sivilite] nf (grossièreté) incivility; **incivilités** nfpl antisocial behaviour sg

inclinable [ɛ̃klinabl] adj: **siège à dossier ~** reclining seat

inclination [ɛ̃klinasjɔ̃] nf (penchant) inclination

incliner [ɛ̃kline] vt (pencher) to tilt ▷ vi: **~ à qch/à faire** to incline towards sth/doing; **s'~** vr (se pencher) to bow; **s'~ devant** (qch) to pay one's respects

inclure [ɛ̃klyʀ] vt to include; (joindre à un envoi) to enclose

inclus, e [ɛ̃kly, -yz] pp de **inclure** ▷ adj included; (joint à un envoi) enclosed ▷ adv: **est-ce que le service est ~?** is service included?; **jusqu'au 10 mars ~** until 10th March inclusive

incognito [ɛ̃kɔɲito] adv incognito ▷ nm: **garder l'~** to remain incognito

incohérent, e [ɛ̃kɔeʀɑ̃, ɑ̃t] adj (comportement) inconsistent; (geste, langage, texte) incoherent

incollable [ɛ̃kɔlabl] adj (riz) non-stick; **il est ~** (fam) he's got all the answers

incolore [ɛ̃kɔlɔʀ] adj colourless

incommoder [ɛ̃kɔmɔde] vt (chaleur, odeur): **~ qn** to bother sb

incomparable [ɛ̃kɔ̃paʀabl] adj incomparable

incompatible [ɛ̃kɔ̃patibl] adj incompatible

incompétent, e [ɛ̃kɔ̃petã, ɑ̃t] adj incompetent

incomplet, -ète [ɛ̃kɔ̃plε, εt] adj incomplete

incompréhensible [ɛ̃kɔ̃pʀeɑ̃sibl] adj incomprehensible

incompris, e [ɛ̃kɔ̃pʀi, iz] adj misunderstood

inconcevable [ɛ̃kɔ̃s(ə)vabl] adj inconceivable

inconfortable [ɛ̃kɔ̃fɔʀtabl(ə)] adj uncomfortable

incongru, e [ɛ̃kɔ̃gʀy] adj unseemly

inconnu, e [ɛ̃kɔny] adj unknown ▷ nm/f stranger ▷ nm: **l'~** the unknown; **inconnue** nf unknown factor

inconsciemment [ɛ̃kɔ̃sjamã] adv unconsciously

inconscient, e [ɛ̃kɔ̃sjɑ̃, jɑ̃t] adj unconscious; (irréfléchi) thoughtless, reckless; (sentiment) subconscious ▷ nm (Psych): **l'~** the unconscious; **~ de** unaware of

inconsidéré, e [ɛ̃kɔ̃sideʀe] adj ill-considered

inconsistant, e [ɛ̃kɔ̃sistɑ̃, ɑ̃t] adj (fig) flimsy, weak

inconsolable [ɛ̃kɔ̃sɔlabl] adj inconsolable

incontestable [ɛ̃kɔ̃tεstabl] adj indisputable

incontinent, e [ɛ̃kɔ̃tinã, ɑ̃t] adj incontinent

incontournable [ɛ̃kɔ̃tuʀnabl] adj unavoidable

incontrôlable [ɛ̃kɔ̃tʀolabl] adj unverifiable; (irrépressible) uncontrollable

inconvénient [ɛ̃kɔ̃venjã] nm disadvantage, drawback; **si vous n'y voyez pas d'~** if you have no objections

incorporer [ɛ̃kɔʀpɔʀe] vt: **~ (à)** to mix in (with); **~ (dans)** (paragraphe etc) to incorporate (in); (Mil: appeler) to recruit (into); **il a très bien su s'~ à notre groupe** he was very easily incorporated into our group

incorrect, e [ɛ̃kɔʀεkt] adj (impropre, inconvenant)

improper; (défectueux) faulty; (inexact) incorrect; (impoli) impolite; (déloyal) underhand

incorrigible [ɛ̃kɔʀiʒibl] adj incorrigible

incrédule [ɛ̃kʀedyl] adj incredulous; (Rel) unbelieving

incroyable [ɛ̃kʀwajabl] adj incredible

incruster [ɛ̃kʀyste] vt (Art) to inlay; **s'~** vi (invité) to take root

inculpé, e [ɛ̃kylpe] nm/f accused

inculper [ɛ̃kylpe] vt: **~ (de)** to charge (with)

inculquer [ɛ̃kylke] vt: **~ qch à** to inculcate sth in ou instil sth into

Inde [ɛ̃d] nf: **l'~** India

indécent, e [ɛ̃desɑ̃, ɑ̃t] adj indecent

indécis, e [ɛ̃desi, iz] adj (par nature) indecisive; (temporairement) undecided

indéfendable [ɛ̃defɑ̃dabl] adj indefensible

indéfini, e [ɛ̃defini] adj (imprécis, incertain) undefined; (illimité, Ling) indefinite; **indéfiniment** adv indefinitely; **indéfinissable** adj indefinable

indélébile [ɛ̃delebil] adj indelible

indélicat, e [ɛ̃delika, at] adj tactless

indemne [ɛ̃dɛmn] adj unharmed; **indemniser** vt: **indemniser qn (de)** to compensate sb (for)

indemnité [ɛ̃dɛmnite] nf (dédommagement) compensation no pl; (allocation) allowance; **indemnité de licenciement** redundancy payment

indépendamment [ɛ̃depɑ̃damã] adv independently; **~ de** (abstraction faite de) irrespective of; (en plus de) over and above

indépendance [ɛ̃depɑ̃dɑ̃s] nf independence

indépendant, e [ɛ̃depɑ̃dɑ̃, ɑ̃t] adj independent; **~ de** independent of; **travailleur ~** self-employed worker

indescriptible [ɛ̃deskʀiptibl] adj indescribable

indésirable [ɛ̃dezirabl] adj undesirable

indestructible [ɛ̃dεstʀyktibl] adj indestructible

indéterminé, e [ɛ̃detεʀmine] adj (date, cause, nature) unspecified; (forme, longueur, quantité) indeterminate

index [ɛ̃dεks] nm (doigt) index finger; (d'un livre etc) index; **mettre à l'~** to blacklist

indicateur [ɛ̃dikatœʀ] nm (Police) informer; (Tech) gauge, indicator ▷ adj: **panneau ~** signpost; **indicateur des chemins de fer** railway timetable; **indicateur de rues** street directory

indicatif, -ive [ɛ̃dikatif, iv] adj: **à titre ~** for (your) information ▷ nm (Ling) indicative; (Radio) theme ou signature tune; (Tél) dialling code (BRIT), area code (US); **quel est l'~ de ...** what's the code for ...?

indication [ɛ̃dikasjɔ̃] nf indication; (renseignement) information no pl; **indications** nfpl (directives) instructions

indice [ɛ̃dis] nm (marque, signe) indication, sign; (Police: lors d'une enquête) clue; (Jur: présomption) piece of evidence; (Science, Écon, Tech) index; **~ de protection** (sun protection) factor

indicible [ɛ̃disibl] adj inexpressible

indien, ne [ɛ̃djɛ̃, jεn] adj Indian ▷ nm/f: **I~, ne** Indian

indifféremment [ɛ̃difeʀamã] adv (sans distinction) equally (well)

indifférence [ɛ̃difeʀɑ̃s] nf indifference

indifférent, e [ɛ̃difeʀɑ̃, ɑ̃t] adj (peu intéressé) indifferent; **ça m'est ~** it doesn't matter to me; **elle m'est ~e** I am indifferent to her

indigène [ɛ̃diʒεn] adj native, indigenous; (des gens du pays) local ▷ nm/f native

indigeste [ɛ̃diʒɛst] adj indigestible

indigestion [ɛ̃diʒɛstjɔ̃] nf indigestion no pl; **avoir une ~** to have indigestion

indigne [ɛ̃diɲ] adj unworthy

indigner [ɛ̃diɲe] vt: **s'~ de qch** to get annoyed about sth; **s'~ contre qn** to get annoyed with sb

indiqué, e [ɛ̃dike] adj (date, lieu) agreed; (traitement) appropriate; (conseillé) advisable

indiquer [ɛ̃dike] vt (suj: pendule, aiguille) to show; (: étiquette, panneau) to show, indicate; (renseigner sur) to point out, tell; (déterminer: date, lieu) to give, state; (signaler, dénoter) to indicate, point to; **~ qch/qn à qn** (montrer du doigt) to point sth/sb out to sb; (faire connaître: médecin, restaurant) to tell sb of sth/sb; **pourriez-vous m'~ les toilettes/l'heure?** could you direct me to the toilets/tell me the time?

indiscipliné, e [ɛ̃disipline] adj undisciplined

indiscret, -ète [ɛ̃diskʀɛ, ɛt] adj indiscreet

indiscutable [ɛ̃diskytabl] adj indisputable

indispensable [ɛ̃dispɑ̃sabl] adj indispensable, essential

indisposé, e [ɛ̃dispoze] adj indisposed

indistinct, e [ɛ̃distɛ̃(kt), ɛ̃kt] adj indistinct; **indistinctement** adv (voir, prononcer) indistinctly; (sans distinction) indiscriminately

individu [ɛ̃dividy] nm individual; **individuel, le** adj (gén) individual; (responsabilité, propriété, liberté) personal; **chambre individuelle** single room; **maison individuelle** detached house

indolore [ɛ̃dɔlɔʀ] adj painless

Indonésie [ɛ̃dɔnezi] nf Indonesia

indu, e [ɛ̃dy] adj: **à une heure ~e** at some ungodly hour

indulgent, e [ɛ̃dylʒɑ̃, ɑ̃t] adj (parent, regard) indulgent; (juge, examinateur) lenient

industrialisé, e [ɛ̃dystʀijalize] adj industrialized

industrie [ɛ̃dystʀi] nf industry; **industriel, le** adj industrial ▷ nm industrialist

inébranlable [inebʀɑ̃labl] adj (masse, colonne) solid; (personne, certitude, foi) unshakeable

inédit, e [inedi, it] adj (correspondance, livre) hitherto unpublished; (spectacle, moyen) novel, original; (film) unreleased

inefficace [inefikas] adj (remède, moyen) ineffective; (machine, employé) inefficient

inégal, e, -aux [inegal, o] adj unequal; (irrégulier) uneven; **inégalable** adj matchless; **inégalé, e** adj (record) unequalled; (beauté) unrivalled; **inégalité** nf inequality

inépuisable [inepɥizabl] adj inexhaustible

inerte [inɛʀt] adj (immobile) lifeless; (sans réaction) passive

inespéré, e [inɛspeʀe] adj unexpected, unhoped-for

inestimable [inɛstimabl] adj priceless; (fig: bienfait) invaluable

inévitable [inevitabl] adj unavoidable; (fatal, habituel) inevitable

inexact, e [inɛgza(kt), akt] adj inaccurate

inexcusable [inɛkskyzabl] adj unforgivable

inexplicable [inɛksplikabl] adj inexplicable

in extremis [inɛkstʀemis] adv at the last minute ▷ adj last-minute

infaillible [ɛ̃fajibl] adj infallible

infarctus [ɛ̃faʀktys] nm: **~ (du myocarde)** coronary (thrombosis)

infatigable [ɛ̃fatigabl] adj tireless

infect, e [ɛ̃fɛkt] adj revolting; (personne) obnoxious; (temps) foul

infecter [ɛ̃fɛkte] vt (atmosphère, eau) to contaminate; (Méd) to infect; **s'~** to become infected ou septic; **infection** nf infection; (puanteur) stench

inférieur, e [ɛ̃feʀjœʀ] adj lower; (en qualité, intelligence) inferior; **~ à** (somme, quantité) less ou smaller than; (moins bon que) inferior to

infernal, e, -aux [ɛ̃fɛʀnal, o] adj (insupportable: chaleur, rythme) infernal; (: enfant) horrid; (satanique, effrayant) diabolical

infidèle [ɛ̃fidɛl] adj unfaithful

infiltrer [ɛ̃filtʀe] vr: **s'~ dans** to get into; (liquide) to seep through; (fig: groupe, ennemi) to infiltrate

infime [ɛ̃fim] adj minute, tiny

infini, e [ɛ̃fini] adj infinite ▷ nm infinity; **à l'~** endlessly; **infiniment** adv infinitely; **infinité** nf: **une infinité de** an infinite number of

infinitif [ɛ̃finitif] nm infinitive

infirme [ɛ̃fiʀm] adj disabled ▷ nm/f disabled person

infirmerie [ɛ̃fiʀməʀi] nf medical room

infirmier, -ière [ɛ̃fiʀmje] nm/f nurse; **infirmière chef** sister

infirmité [ɛ̃fiʀmite] nf disability

inflammable [ɛ̃flamabl] adj (in)flammable

inflation [ɛ̃flasjɔ̃] nf inflation

influençable [ɛ̃flyɑ̃sabl] adj easily influenced

influence [ɛ̃flyɑ̃s] nf influence; **influencer** vt to influence; **influent, e** adj influential

informaticien, ne [ɛ̃fɔʀmatisjɛ̃, jɛn] nm/f computer scientist

information [ɛ̃fɔʀmasjɔ̃] nf (renseignement) piece of information; (Presse, TV: nouvelle) item of news; (diffusion de renseignements, Inform) information; (Jur) inquiry, investigation; **informations** nfpl (TV) news sg

informatique [ɛ̃fɔʀmatik] nf (technique) data processing; (science) computer science ▷ adj computer cpd; **informatiser** vt to computerize

informer [ɛ̃fɔʀme] vt: **~ qn (de)** to inform sb (of); **s'~** vr: **s'~ (de/si)** to inquire ou find out (about/whether); **s'~ sur** to inform o.s. about

infos [ɛ̃fo] nfpl: **les ~** the news sg

infraction [ɛ̃fʀaksjɔ̃] nf offence; **~ à** violation ou breach of; **être en ~** to be in breach of the law

infranchissable [ɛ̃fʀɑ̃ʃisabl] adj impassable; (fig) insuperable

infrarouge [ɛ̃fʀaʀuʒ] adj infrared

infrastructure [ɛ̃fʀastʀyktyʀ] nf (Aviat, Mil) ground installations pl; (Écon: touristique etc) infrastructure

infuser [ɛ̃fyze] vt, vi (thé) to brew; (tisane) to infuse; **infusion** nf (tisane) herb tea

ingénier [ɛ̃ʒenje] s'~ vi: **s'~ à faire** to strive to do

ingénierie [ɛ̃ʒeniʀi] nf engineering

ingénieur [ɛ̃ʒenjœʀ] nm engineer; **ingénieur du son** sound engineer

ingénieux, -euse [ɛ̃ʒenjø, jøz] adj ingenious, clever

ingrat, e [ɛ̃gʀa, at] adj (personne) ungrateful; (travail, sujet) thankless; (visage) unprepossessing

ingrédient [ɛ̃gʀedjɑ̃] nm ingredient

inhabité, e [inabite] adj uninhabited

inhabituel, le [inabitɥɛl] adj unusual

inhibition [inibisjɔ̃] nf inhibition

inhumain, e [inymɛ̃, ɛn] adj inhuman

inimaginable [inimaʒinabl] *adj* unimaginable

ininterrompu, e [inɛ̃tɛʀɔ̃py] *adj* (*file, série*) unbroken; (*flot, vacarme*) uninterrupted, non-stop; (*effort*) unremitting, continuous; (*suite, ligne*) unbroken

initial, e, -aux [inisjal, jo] *adj* initial; **initiales** *nfpl* (*d'un nom, sigle etc*) initials

initiation [inisjasjɔ̃] *nf*: **à** introduction to

initiative [inisjativ] *nf* initiative

initier [inisje] *vt*: **qn à** to initiate sb into; (*faire découvrir: art, jeu*) to introduce sb to

injecter [ɛ̃ʒɛkte] *vt* to inject; **injection** *nf* injection; **à injection** (*Auto*) fuel injection *cpd*

injure [ɛ̃ʒyʀ] *nf* insult, abuse *no pl*; **injurier** *vt* to insult, abuse; **injurieux, -euse** *adj* abusive, insulting

injuste [ɛ̃ʒyst] *adj* unjust, unfair; **injustice** *nf* injustice

inlassable [ɛ̃lasabl] *adj* tireless

inné, e [i(n)ne] *adj* innate, inborn

innocent, e [inɔsɑ̃, ɑ̃t] *adj* innocent; **innocenter** *vt* to clear, prove innocent

innombrable [i(n)nɔ̃bʀabl] *adj* innumerable

innover [inɔve] *vi* to break new ground

inoccupé, e [inɔkype] *adj* unoccupied

inodore [inɔdɔʀ] *adj* (*gaz*) odourless; (*fleur*) scentless

inoffensif, -ive [inɔfɑ̃sif, iv] *adj* harmless, innocuous

inondation [inɔ̃dasjɔ̃] *nf* flood

inonder [inɔ̃de] *vt* to flood; **de** to flood with

inopportun, e [inɔpɔʀtœ̃ yn] *adj* ill-timed, untimely

inoubliable [inublijabl] *adj* unforgettable

inouï, e [inwi] *adj* unheard-of, extraordinary

inox [inɔks] *nm* stainless steel

inquiet, -ète [ɛ̃kjɛ, ɛkjɛt] *adj* anxious; **inquiétant, e** *adj* worrying, disturbing; **inquiéter** *vt* to worry; **s'inquiéter** to worry; **s'inquiéter de** to worry about; (*s'enquérir de*) to inquire about; **inquiétude** *nf* anxiety

insaisissable [ɛ̃sezisabl] *adj* (*fugitif, ennemi*) elusive; (*différence, nuance*) imperceptible

insalubre [ɛ̃salybʀ] *adj* insalubrious

insatisfait, e [ɛ̃satisfɛ, ɛt] *adj* (*non comblé*) unsatisfied; (*mécontent*) dissatisfied

inscription [ɛ̃skʀipsjɔ̃] *nf* inscription; (*immatriculation*) enrolment

inscrire [ɛ̃skʀiʀ] *vt* (*marquer: sur son calepin etc*) to note ou write down; (*: sur un mur, une affiche etc*) to write; (*: dans la pierre, le métal*) to inscribe; (*mettre: sur une liste, un budget etc*) to put down; **s' (à)** (*club, parti*) to join; (*université*) to register ou enrol (at); (*examen, concours*) to register (for); **qn à** (*club, parti*) to enrol sb at

insecte [ɛ̃sɛkt] *nm* insect; **insecticide** *nm* insecticide

insensé, e [ɛ̃sɑ̃se] *adj* mad

insensible [ɛ̃sɑ̃sibl] *adj* (*nerf, membre*) numb; (*dur, indifférent*) insensitive

inséparable [ɛ̃separabl] *adj* inseparable ▷ *nm*: **s** (*oiseaux*) lovebirds

insigne [ɛ̃siɲ] *nm* (*d'un parti, club*) badge; (*d'une fonction*) insignia ▷ *adj* distinguished

insignifiant, e [ɛ̃siɲifjɑ̃, jɑ̃t] *adj* insignificant; trivial

insinuer [ɛ̃sinɥe] *vt* to insinuate; **s' dans** (*fig*) to worm one's way into

insipide [ɛ̃sipid] *adj* insipid

insister [ɛ̃siste] *vi* to insist; (*continuer à sonner*) to keep on trying; **sur** (*détail, sujet*) to lay stress on

insolation [ɛ̃sɔlasjɔ̃] *nf* (*Méd*) sunstroke *no pl*

insolent, e [ɛ̃sɔlɑ̃, ɑ̃t] *adj* insolent

insolite [ɛ̃sɔlit] *adj* strange, unusual

insomnie [ɛ̃sɔmni] *nf* insomnia *no pl*; **avoir des s** to sleep badly, not be able to sleep

insouciant, e [ɛ̃susjɑ̃, jɑ̃t] *adj* carefree; **du danger** heedless of danger

insoupçonnable [ɛ̃supsɔnabl] *adj* unsuspected; (*personne*) above suspicion

insoupçonné, e [ɛ̃supsɔne] *adj* unsuspected

insoutenable [ɛ̃sut(ə)nabl] *adj* (*argument*) untenable; (*chaleur*) unbearable

inspecter [ɛ̃spɛkte] *vt* to inspect; **inspecteur, -trice** *nm/f* inspector; **inspecteur d'Académie** (regional) director of education; **inspecteur des finances** ≈ tax inspector (BRIT), ≈ Internal Revenue Service agent (US); **inspecteur (de police)** (police) inspector; **inspection** *nf* inspection

inspirer [ɛ̃spiʀe] *vt* (*gén*) to inspire ▷ *vi* (*aspirer*) to breathe in; **s' vr**: **s' de** to be inspired by

instable [ɛ̃stabl] *adj* unstable; (*meuble, équilibre*) unsteady; (*temps*) unsettled

installation [ɛ̃stalasjɔ̃] *nf* (*mise en place*) installation; **installations** *nfpl* (*de sport, dans un camping*) facilities; **l'installation électrique** wiring

installer [ɛ̃stale] *vt* (*loger, placer*) to put; (*meuble, gaz, électricité*) to put in; (*rideau, étagère, tente*) to put up; (*appartement*) to fit out; **s'** (*s'établir: artisan, dentiste etc*) to set o.s. up; (*se loger*) to settle; (*emménager*) to settle in; (*sur un siège, à un emplacement*) to settle (down); (*fig: maladie, grève*) to take a firm hold

instance [ɛ̃stɑ̃s] *nf* (*Admin: autorité*) authority; **affaire en** matter pending; **être en de divorce** to be awaiting a divorce

instant [ɛ̃stɑ̃] *nm* moment, instant; **dans un** in a moment; **à l'** this instant; **je l'ai vu à l'** I've just this minute seen him, I saw him a moment ago; **pour l'** for the moment, for the time being

instantané, e [ɛ̃stɑ̃tane] *adj* (*lait, café*) instant; (*explosion, mort*) instantaneous ▷ *nm* snapshot

instar [ɛ̃staʀ]: **à l' de** *prép* following the example of, like

instaurer [ɛ̃stɔʀe] *vt* to institute; (*couvre-feu*) to impose; **s' vr** (*paix*) to be established; (*doute*) to set in

instinct [ɛ̃stɛ̃] *nm* instinct; **instinctivement** *adv* instinctively

instituer [ɛ̃stitɥe] *vt* to establish

institut [ɛ̃stity] *nm* institute; **institut de beauté** beauty salon; **Institut universitaire de technologie** ≈ polytechnic

instituteur, -trice [ɛ̃stitytœʀ, tʀis] *nm/f* (primary school) teacher

institution [ɛ̃stitysjɔ̃] *nf* institution; (*collège*) private school; **institutions** *nfpl* (*structures politiques et sociales*) institutions

instructif, -ive [ɛ̃stʀyktif, iv] *adj* instructive

instruction [ɛ̃stʀyksjɔ̃] *nf* (*enseignement, savoir*) education; (*Jur*) (preliminary) investigation and hearing; **instructions** *nfpl* (*ordres, mode d'emploi*) instructions; **instruction civique** civics *sg*

instruire [ɛ̃stʀɥiʀ] *vt* (*élèves*) to teach; (*recrues*) to train; (*Jur: affaire*) to conduct the investigation for; **s' to educate o.s.; **instruit, e** *adj* educated

instrument [ɛ̃stʀymɑ̃] *nm* instrument; **instrument à cordes/à vent** stringed/wind instrument; **instrument de mesure** measuring instrument; **instrument de musique** musical instrument; **instrument de travail**

(working) tool

insu [ɛsy] nm: **à l'~ de qn** without sb knowing (it)

insuffisant, e [ɛsyfizɑ̃, ɑ̃t] adj (en quantité) insufficient; (en qualité) inadequate; (sur une copie) poor

insulaire [ɛsylɛʀ] adj island cpd; (attitude) insular

insuline [ɛsylin] nf insulin

insulte [ɛsylt] nf insult; **insulter** vt to insult

insupportable [ɛsypɔʀtabl] adj unbearable

insurmontable [ɛsyʀmɔ̃tabl] adj (difficulté) insuperable; (aversion) unconquerable

intact, e [ɛ̃takt] adj intact

intarissable [ɛ̃taʀisabl] adj inexhaustible

intégral, e, -aux [ɛ̃tegʀal, o] adj complete; **texte ~** unabridged version; **bronzage ~** all-over suntan; **intégralement** adv in full; **intégralité** nf whole; **dans son intégralité** in full; **intégrant, e** adj: **faire partie intégrante de** to be an integral part of

intègre [ɛ̃tɛgʀ] adj upright

intégrer [ɛ̃tegʀe] **s'~** vr: **s'~ à** ou **dans qch** to become integrated into sth; **bien s'~** to fit in

intégrisme [ɛ̃tegʀism] nm fundamentalism

intellectuel, le [ɛ̃telɛktɥɛl] adj intellectual ▷ nm/f intellectual; (péj) highbrow

intelligence [ɛ̃teliʒɑ̃s] nf intelligence; (compréhension): **l'~ de** the understanding of; (complicité): **regard d'~** glance of complicity; (accord): **vivre en bonne ~ avec qn** to be on good terms with sb

intelligent, e [ɛ̃teliʒɑ̃, ɑ̃t] adj intelligent

intelligible [ɛ̃teliʒibl] adj intelligible

intempéries [ɛ̃tɑ̃peʀi] nfpl bad weather sg

intenable [ɛ̃t(ə)nabl] adj (chaleur) unbearable

intendant, e [ɛ̃tɑ̃dɑ̃] nm/f (Mil) quartermaster; (Scol) bursar

intense [ɛ̃tɑ̃s] adj intense; **intensif, -ive** adj intensive; **un cours intensif** a crash course

intenter [ɛ̃tɑ̃te] vt: **~ un procès contre** ou **à** to start proceedings against

intention [ɛ̃tɑ̃sjɔ̃] nf intention; (Jur) intent; **avoir l'~ de faire** to intend to do; **à l'~ de** (renseignement) for the benefit of; (film, ouvrage) aimed at; **à cette ~** with this aim in view; **intentionné, e** adj: **bien intentionné** well-meaning ou -intentioned; **mal intentionné** ill-intentioned

interactif, -ive [ɛ̃teʀaktif, iv] adj (Comput) interactive

intercepter [ɛ̃teʀsɛpte] vt to intercept; (lumière, chaleur) to cut off

interchangeable [ɛ̃teʀʃɑ̃ʒabl] adj interchangeable

interdiction [ɛ̃teʀdiksjɔ̃] nf ban; **interdiction de fumer** no smoking

interdire [ɛ̃teʀdiʀ] vt to forbid; (Admin) to ban, prohibit; (: journal, livre) to ban; **~ qch à qn** to forbid sb to do; (suj: empêchement) to prevent sb from doing

interdit, e [ɛ̃teʀdi, it] pp de **interdire** ▷ adj (stupéfait) taken aback; **film ~ aux moins de 18/12 ans** ≈ 18-/12A-rated film; **"stationnement ~"** "no parking"

intéressant, e [ɛ̃teʀesɑ̃, ɑ̃t] adj interesting; (avantageux) attractive

intéressé, e [ɛ̃teʀese] adj (parties) involved, concerned; (amitié, motifs) self-interested

intéresser [ɛ̃teʀese] vt (captiver) to interest; (toucher) to be of interest to; (Admin: concerner) to affect, concern; **s'~** vr: **s'~ à** to be interested in

intérêt [ɛ̃teʀe] nm interest; (égoïsme) self-interest; **tu as ~ à accepter** it's in your interest to accept; **tu as ~ à te**

dépêcher you'd better hurry

intérieur, e [ɛ̃teʀjœʀ] adj (mur, escalier, poche) inside; (commerce, politique) domestic; (cour, calme, vie) inner; (navigation) inland ▷ nm: **l'~** (d'une maison, d'un récipient etc) the inside; (d'un pays, aussi: décor, mobilier) the interior; **à l'~ (de)** inside; **ministère de l'l~e** ≈ Home Office (BRIT), ≈ Department of the Interior (US); **intérieurement** adv inwardly

intérim [ɛ̃teʀim] nm interim period; **faire de l'~** to temp; **assurer l'~ (de)** to deputize (for); **par ~** interim

intérimaire [ɛ̃teʀimɛʀ] adj (directeur, ministre) acting; (secrétaire, personnel) temporary ▷ nm/f (secrétaire) temporary secretary, temp (BRIT)

interlocuteur, -trice [ɛ̃teʀlɔkytœʀ, tʀis] nm/f speaker; **son ~** the person he was speaking to

intermédiaire [ɛ̃teʀmedjɛʀ] adj intermediate; (solution) temporary ▷ nm/f intermediary; (Comm) middleman; **sans ~** directly; **par l'~ de** through

interminable [ɛ̃teʀminabl] adj endless

intermittence [ɛ̃teʀmitɑ̃s] nf: **par ~** sporadically, intermittently

internat [ɛ̃teʀna] nm boarding school

international, e, -aux [ɛ̃teʀnasjɔnal, o] adj, nm/f international

internaute [ɛ̃teʀnot] nm/f Internet user

interne [ɛ̃teʀn] adj internal ▷ nm/f (Scol) boarder; (Méd) houseman

Internet [ɛ̃teʀnɛt] nm: **l'~** the Internet

interpeller [ɛ̃teʀpəle] vt (appeler) to call out to; (apostropher) to shout at; (Police, Pol) to question; (concerner) to concern

interphone [ɛ̃teʀfɔn] nm intercom; (d'immeuble) entry phone

interposer [ɛ̃teʀpoze] vt: **s'~** to intervene; **par personnes interposées** through a third party

interprète [ɛ̃teʀpʀɛt] nm/f interpreter; (porte-parole) spokesperson; **pourriez-vous nous servir d' ~?** could you act as our interpreter?

interpréter [ɛ̃teʀpʀete] vt to interpret; (jouer) to play; (chanter) to sing

interrogatif, -ive [ɛ̃teʀɔgatif, iv] adj (Ling) interrogative

interrogation [ɛ̃teʀɔgasjɔ̃] nf question; (action) questioning; **~ écrite/orale** (Scol) written/oral test

interrogatoire [ɛ̃teʀɔgatwaʀ] nm (Police) questioning no pl; (Jur, aussi fig) cross-examination

interroger [ɛ̃teʀɔʒe] vt to question; (Inform) to consult; (Scol) to test

interrompre [ɛ̃teʀɔ̃pʀ] vt (gén) to interrupt; (négociations) to break off; (match) to stop; **s'~** to break off; **interrupteur** nm switch; **interruption** nf interruption; (pause) break; **sans interruption** without stopping; **interruption (volontaire) de grossesse** termination (of pregnancy)

intersection [ɛ̃teʀsɛksjɔ̃] nf intersection

intervalle [ɛ̃teʀval] nm (espace) space; (de temps) interval; **dans l'~** in the meantime; **à deux jours d'~** two days apart

intervenir [ɛ̃teʀvəniʀ] vi (gén) to intervene; **~ auprès de qn** to intervene with sb; **intervention** nf intervention; (discours) speech; **intervention chirurgicale** (Méd) (surgical) operation

interview [ɛ̃teʀvju] nf interview

intestin [ɛ̃tɛstɛ̃] nm intestine

intime [ɛ̃tim] adj intimate; (vie) private; (conviction) inmost; (dîner, cérémonie) quiet ▷ nm/f close friend; **un journal ~** a diary

intimider [ɛ̃timide] vt to intimidate

intimité [ɛ̃timite] nf: **dans l'~** in private; (sans formalités) with only a few friends, quietly

intolérable [ɛ̃tɔlerabl] adj intolerable

intox [ɛ̃tɔks] (fam) nf brainwashing

intoxication [ɛ̃tɔksikasjɔ̃] nf: **intoxication alimentaire** food poisoning

intoxiquer [ɛ̃tɔksike] vt to poison; (fig) to brainwash

intraitable [ɛ̃tretabl] adj inflexible, uncompromising

intransigeant, e [ɛ̃trɑ̃ziʒɑ̃, ɑ̃t] adj intransigent

intrépide [ɛ̃trepid] adj dauntless

intrigue [ɛ̃trig] nf (scénario) plot; **intriguer** vt to puzzle, intrigue

introduction [ɛ̃trɔdyksjɔ̃] nf introduction

introduire [ɛ̃trɔdɥir] vt to introduce; (visiteur) to show in; (aiguille, clef): **~ qch dans** to insert ou introduce sth into; **s'~** vr (techniques, usages) to be introduced; **s'~ (dans)** to get in(to); (dans un groupe) to get o.s. accepted (into)

introuvable [ɛ̃truvabl] adj which cannot be found; (Comm) unobtainable

intrus, e [ɛ̃try, yz] nm/f intruder

intuition [ɛ̃tɥisjɔ̃] nf intuition

inusable [inyzabl] adj hard-wearing

inutile [inytil] adj useless; (superflu) unnecessary; **inutilement** adv unnecessarily; **inutilisable** adj unusable

invalide [ɛ̃valid] adj disabled ▷ nm: **~ de guerre** disabled ex-serviceman

invariable [ɛ̃varjabl] adj invariable

invasion [ɛ̃vazjɔ̃] nf invasion

inventaire [ɛ̃vɑ̃ter] nm inventory; (Comm: liste) stocklist; (: opération) stocktaking no pl

inventer [ɛ̃vɑ̃te] vt to invent; (subterfuge) to devise, invent; (histoire, excuse) to make up, invent; **inventeur** nm inventor; **inventif, -ive** adj inventive; **invention** nf invention

inverse [ɛ̃vers] adj opposite ▷ nm: **l'~** the opposite; **dans l'ordre ~** in the reverse order; **en sens ~** in (ou from) the opposite direction; **dans le sens ~ des aiguilles d'une montre** anticlockwise; **tu t'es trompé, c'est l'~** you've got it wrong, it's the other way round; **inversement** adv conversely; **inverser** vt to invert, reverse; (Élec) to reverse

investir [ɛ̃vestir] vt to invest; **~ qn de** (d'une fonction, d'un pouvoir) to vest ou invest sb with; **s'~** vr: **s'~ dans** (Psych) to put a lot into; **investissement** nm investment

invisible [ɛ̃vizibl] adj invisible

invitation [ɛ̃vitasjɔ̃] nf invitation

invité, e [ɛ̃vite] nm/f guest

inviter [ɛ̃vite] vt to invite; **~ qn à faire qch** to invite sb to do sth

invivable [ɛ̃vivabl] adj unbearable

involontaire [ɛ̃vɔlɔ̃ter] adj (mouvement) involuntary; (insulte) unintentional; (complice) unwitting

invoquer [ɛ̃vɔke] vt (Dieu, muse) to call upon, invoke; (prétexte) to put forward (as an excuse); (loi, texte) to refer to

invraisemblable [ɛ̃vresɑ̃blabl] adj (fait, nouvelle) unlikely, improbable; (insolence, habit) incredible

iode [jɔd] nm iodine

irai etc [ire] vb voir **aller**

Irak [irak] nm Iraq; **irakien, ne** adj Iraqi ▷ nm/f: **Irakien, ne** Iraqi

Iran [irɑ̃] nm Iran; **iranien, ne** adj Iranian ▷ nm/f: **Iranien, ne** Iranian

irions etc [irjɔ̃] vb voir **aller**

iris [iris] nm iris

irlandais, e [irlɑ̃dɛ, ɛz] adj Irish ▷ nm/f: **I~, e** Irishman(-woman)

Irlande [irlɑ̃d] nf Ireland; **la République d'~** the Irish Republic; **la mer d'~** the Irish Sea; **Irlande du Nord** Northern Ireland

ironie [irɔni] nf irony; **ironique** adj ironical; **ironiser** vi to be ironical

irons etc [irɔ̃] vb voir **aller**

irradier [iradje] vt to irradiate

irraisonné, e [irezɔne] adj irrational

irrationnel, le [irasjɔnel] adj irrational

irréalisable [irealizabl] adj unrealizable; (projet) impracticable

irrécupérable [irekyperabl] adj beyond repair; (personne) beyond redemption

irréel, le [ireel] adj unreal

irréfléchi, e [irefleʃi] adj thoughtless

irrégularité [iregylarite] nf irregularity; (de travail, d'effort, de qualité) unevenness no pl

irrégulier, -ière [iregylje, jer] adj irregular; (travail, effort, qualité) uneven; (élève, athlète) erratic

irrémédiable [iremedjabl] adj irreparable

irremplaçable [irɑ̃plasabl] adj irreplaceable

irréparable [ireparabl] adj (objet) beyond repair; (dommage etc) irreparable

irréprochable [ireprɔʃabl] adj irreproachable, beyond reproach; (tenue) impeccable

irrésistible [irezistibl] adj irresistible; (besoin, désir, preuve, logique) compelling; (amusant) hilarious

irrésolu, e [irezɔly] adj (personne) irresolute; (problème) unresolved

irrespectueux, -euse [irespektɥø, øz] adj disrespectful

irresponsable [irespɔ̃sabl] adj irresponsible

irriguer [irige] vt to irrigate

irritable [iritabl] adj irritable

irriter [irite] vt to irritate

irruption [irypsjɔ̃] nf: **faire ~ (chez qn)** to burst in (on sb)

Islam [islam] nm: **l'~** Islam; **islamique** adj Islamic; **islamophobie** nf Islamophobia

Islande [islɑ̃d] nf Iceland

isolant, e [izɔlɑ̃, ɑ̃t] adj insulating; (insonorisant) soundproofing

isolation [izɔlasjɔ̃] nf insulation; **~ acoustique** soundproofing

isolé, e [izɔle] adj isolated; (contre le froid) insulated

isoler [izɔle] vt to isolate; (prisonnier) to put in solitary confinement; (ville) to cut off, isolate; (contre le froid) to insulate; **s'~** vi to isolate o.s.

Israël [israel] nm Israel; **israélien, ne** adj Israeli ▷ nm/f: **Israélien, ne** Israeli; **israélite** adj Jewish ▷ nm/f: **Israélite** Jew (Jewess)

issu, e [isy] adj: **~ de** (né de) descended from; (résultant de) stemming from; **issue** nf (ouverture, sortie) exit; (solution) way out, solution; (dénouement) outcome; **à l'issue de** at the conclusion ou close of; **voie sans issue** dead end;

issue de secours emergency exit
Italie [itali] *nf* Italy; **italien, ne** *adj* Italian ⊳ *nm/f*: **Italien, ne** Italian ⊳ *nm* (*Ling*) Italian
italique [italik] *adj*: **en ~** in italics
itinéraire [itinerɛʀ] *nm* itinerary, route; **itinéraire bis** alternative route
IUT *sigle m* = **Institut universitaire de technologie**
IVG *sigle f* (= interruption volontaire de grossesse) abortion
ivoire [ivwaʀ] *nm* ivory
ivre [ivʀ] *adj* drunk; **~ de** (colère, bonheur) wild with; **ivrogne** *nm/f* drunkard

◆

j

j' [ʒ] *pron voir* **je**
jacinthe [ʒasɛ̃t] *nf* hyacinth
jadis [ʒadis] *adv* long ago
jaillir [ʒajiʀ] *vi* (liquide) to spurt out; (cris, réponses) to burst forth
jais [ʒɛ] *nm* jet; **(d'un noir) de ~** jet-black
jalousie [ʒaluzi] *nf* jealousy; (store) slatted blind
jaloux, -ouse [ʒalu, uz] *adj* jealous; **être ~ de** to be jealous of
jamaïquain, e [ʒamaikɛ̃, -ɛn] *adj* Jamaican ⊳ *nm/f*: **J~, e** Jamaican
Jamaïque [ʒamaik] *nf*: **la ~** Jamaica
jamais [ʒamɛ] *adv* never; (sans négation) ever; **ne ... ~** never; **je ne suis ~ allé en Espagne** I've never been to Spain; **si ~ vous passez dans la région, venez nous voir** if you happen to be/if you're ever in this area, come and see us; **à ~** for ever
jambe [ʒɑ̃b] *nf* leg
jambon [ʒɑ̃bɔ̃] *nm* ham
jante [ʒɑ̃t] *nf* (wheel) rim
janvier [ʒɑ̃vje] *nm* January
Japon [ʒapɔ̃] *nm* Japan; **japonais, e** *adj* Japanese ⊳ *nm/f*:

Japonais, e Japanese ⊳ *nm* (Ling) Japanese
jardin [ʒaʀdɛ̃] *nm* garden; **jardin d'enfants** nursery school; **jardinage** *nm* gardening; **jardiner** *vi* to do some gardening; **jardinier, -ière** *nm/f* gardener; **jardinière** *nf* planter; (de fenêtre) window box; **jardinière de légumes** (Culin) mixed vegetables
jargon [ʒaʀgɔ̃] *nm* (baragouin) gibberish; (langue professionnelle) jargon
jarret [ʒaʀɛ] *nm* back of knee; (Culin) knuckle, shin
jauge [ʒoʒ] *nf* (instrument) gauge; **jauge (de niveau) d'huile** (Auto) dipstick
jaune [ʒon] *adj, nm* yellow ⊳ *adv* (fam): **rire ~** to laugh on the other side of one's face; **jaune d'œuf** (egg) yolk; **jaunir** *vi, vt* to turn yellow; **jaunisse** *nf* jaundice
Javel [ʒavɛl] *nf voir* **eau**
javelot [ʒavlo] *nm* javelin
je, j' [ʒə] *pron* I
jean [dʒin] *nm* jeans pl
Jésus-Christ [ʒezykʀi(st)] *n* Jesus Christ; **600 avant/après ~ ou J.-C.** 600 B.C./A.D.
jet [ʒɛ] *nm* (lancer: action) throwing no pl; (: résultat) throw; (jaillissement: d'eaux) jet; (: de sang) spurt; **jet d'eau** spray
jetable [ʒ(ə)tabl] *adj* disposable
jetée [ʒ(ə)te] *nf* jetty; (grande) pier
jeter [ʒ(ə)te] *vt* (gén) to throw; (se défaire de) to throw away ou out; **~ qch à qn** to throw sth to sb; (de façon agressive) to throw sth at sb; **~ un coup d'œil (à)** to take a look (at); **~ un sort à qn** to cast a spell on sb; **se ~ sur qn** to rush at sb; **se ~ dans** (suj: fleuve) to flow into
jeton [ʒ(ə)tɔ̃] *nm* (au jeu) counter
jette *etc* [ʒɛt] *vb voir* **jeter**
jeu, x [ʒø] *nm* (divertissement, Tech: d'une pièce) play; (Tennis: partie, Football etc: façon de jouer) game; (Théâtre etc) acting; (série d'objets, jouet) set; (Cartes) hand; (au casino): **le ~** gambling; **remettre en ~** (Football) to throw in; **être en ~** (fig) to be at stake; **entrer/mettre en ~** (fig) to come/bring into play; **jeu de cartes** pack of cards; **jeu d'échecs** chess set; **jeu de hasard** game of chance; **jeu de mots** pun; **jeu de société** board game; **jeu télévisé** television quiz; **jeu vidéo** video game
jeudi [ʒødi] *nm* Thursday
jeun [ʒœ̃]: **à ~** *adv* on an empty stomach; **être à ~** to have eaten nothing; **rester à ~** not to eat anything
jeune [ʒœn] *adj* young; **jeunes** *nmpl*: **les ~s** young people; **jeune fille** girl; **jeune homme** young man; **jeunes gens** young people
jeûne [ʒøn] *nm* fast
jeunesse [ʒœnɛs] *nf* youth; (aspect) youthfulness
joaillier, -ière [ʒɔaje, -jɛʀ] *nm/f* jeweller
jogging [dʒɔgiŋ] *nm* jogging; (survêtement) tracksuit; **faire du ~** to go jogging
joie [ʒwa] *nf* joy
joindre [ʒwɛ̃dʀ] *vt* to join; (à une lettre): **~ qch à** to enclose sth with; (contacter) to contact, get in touch with; **se ~ à qn** to join sb; **se ~ à qch** to join in sth
joint, e [ʒwɛ̃, ɛ̃t] *adj*: **pièce ~e** (de lettre) enclosure; (de mail) attachment ⊳ *nm* joint; (ligne) join; **joint de culasse** cylinder head gasket
joli, e [ʒɔli] *adj* pretty, attractive; **une ~e somme/situation** a tidy sum/a nice little job; **c'est du ~!** (ironique) that's very nice!; **c'est bien ~, mais ...** that's all very well but ...
jonc [ʒɔ̃] *nm* (bul) rush

jonction [ʒɔ̃ksjɔ̃] nf junction
jongleur, -euse [ʒɔ̃glœʀ, øz] nm/f juggler
jonquille [ʒɔ̃kij] nf daffodil
Jordanie [ʒɔʀdani] nf: **la ~** Jordan
joue [ʒu] nf cheek
jouer [ʒwe] vt to play; (somme d'argent, réputation) to stake, wager; (simuler: sentiment) to affect, feign ▷ vi to play; (Théâtre, Cinéma) to act; (au casino) to gamble; (bois, porte: se voiler) to warp; (clef, pièce: avoir du jeu) to be loose; **~ sur** (miser) to gamble on; **~ de** (Mus) to play; **~ à** (jeu, sport, roulette) to play; **~ un tour à qn** to play a trick on sb; **~ serré** to play a close game; **~ la comédie** to put on an act; **à toi/nous de ~** it's your/our go ou turn; **bien joué!** well done!; **on joue Hamlet au théâtre X** Hamlet is on at the X theatre
jouet [ʒwe] nm toy; **être le ~ de** (illusion etc) to be the victim of
joueur, -euse [ʒwœʀ, øz] nm/f player; **être beau/mauvais ~** to be a good/bad loser
jouir [ʒwiʀ] vi (sexe: fam) to come ▷ vt: **~ de** to enjoy
jour [ʒuʀ] nm day; (opposé à la nuit) day, daytime; (clarté) daylight; (fig: aspect) light; (ouverture) gap; **de ~** (crème, service) day cpd; **travailler de ~** to work during the day; **voyager de ~** to travel by day; **au ~ le ~** from day to day; **de nos ~** these days; **du ~ au lendemain** overnight; **il fait ~** it's daylight; **au grand ~** (fig) in the open; **mettre au ~** to disclose; **mettre à ~** to update; **donner le ~ à** to give birth to; **voir le ~** to be born; **le J** J D-day; **jour férié** public holiday; **jour ouvrable** working day
journal, -aux [ʒuʀnal, o] nm (news)paper; (spécialisé) journal; (intime) diary; **journal de bord** log; **journal parlé/télévisé** radio/television news sg
journalier, -ière [ʒuʀnalje, jɛʀ] adj daily; (banal) everyday
journalisme [ʒuʀnalism] nm journalism; **journaliste** nm/f journalist
journée [ʒuʀne] nf day; **faire la ~ continue** to work over lunch
joyau, x [ʒwajo] nm gem, jewel
joyeux, -euse [ʒwajø, øz] adj joyful, merry; **~ Noël!** merry Christmas!; **~ anniversaire!** happy birthday!
jubiler [ʒybile] vi to be jubilant, exult
judas [ʒyda] nm (trou) spy-hole
judiciaire [ʒydisjɛʀ] adj judicial
judicieux, -euse [ʒydisjø, øz] adj judicious
judo [ʒydo] nm judo
juge [ʒyʒ] nm judge; **juge d'instruction** examining (BRIT) ou committing (US) magistrate; **juge de paix** justice of the peace
jugé [ʒyʒe] nm: **au ~** adv by guesswork
jugement [ʒyʒmɑ̃] nm judgment; (Jur: au pénal) sentence; (: au civil) decision
juger [ʒyʒe] vt to judge; (estimer) to consider; **~ qn/qch satisfaisant** to consider sb/sth (to be) satisfactory; **~ bon de faire** to see fit to do
juif, -ive [ʒɥif, ʒɥiv] adj Jewish ▷ nm/f: **J~, ive** Jew (Jewess)
juillet [ʒɥije] nm July
juin [ʒɥɛ̃] nm June
jumeau, -elle, x [ʒymo, ɛl] adj, nm/f twin
jumeler [ʒym(ə)le] vt to twin
jumelle [ʒymɛl] adj, nf voir **jumeau**; **jumelles** nfpl (appareil) binoculars
jument [ʒymɑ̃] nf mare

jungle nf jungle
jupe [ʒyp] nf skirt
jupon [ʒypɔ̃] nm waist slip
juré, e [ʒyʀe] nm/f juror ▷ adj: **ennemi ~** sworn enemy
jurer [ʒyʀe] vt (obéissance etc) to swear, vow ▷ vi (dire des jurons) to swear, curse; (dissoner): **~ (avec)** to clash (with); **~ de faire/que** to swear to do/that; **~ de qch** (s'en porter garant) to swear to sth
juridique [ʒyʀidik] adj legal
juron [ʒyʀɔ̃] nm curse, swearword
jury [ʒyʀi] nm jury; (Art, Sport) panel of judges; (Scol) board of examiners
jus [ʒy] nm juice; (de viande) gravy, (meat) juice; **jus de fruit** fruit juice
jusque: **jusqu'à** prép (endroit) as far as, (up) to; (moment) until, till; (limite) up to; **~ sur/dans** up to; (y compris) even on/in; **jusqu'à ce que** until; **jusqu'à présent** ou **maintenant** so far; **jusqu'où?** how far?
justaucorps [ʒystokɔʀ] nm leotard
juste [ʒyst] adj (équitable) just, fair; (légitime) just; (exact) right; (pertinent) apt; (étroit) tight; (insuffisant) on the short side ▷ adv rightly, correctly; (chanter) in tune; (exactement, seulement) just; **~ assez/au-dessus** just enough/above; **au ~** exactly; **le ~ milieu** the happy medium; **c'était ~** it was a close thing; **pouvoir tout ~ faire** to be only just able to do; **justement** adv justly; (précisément) just, precisely; **justesse** nf (précision) accuracy; (d'une remarque) aptness; (d'une opinion) soundness; **de justesse** only just
justice [ʒystis] nf (équité) fairness, justice; (Admin) justice; **rendre ~ à qn** to do sb justice
justificatif, -ive [ʒystifikatif, iv] adj (document) supporting; **pièce justificative** written proof
justifier [ʒystifje] vt to justify; **~ de** to prove
juteux, -euse [ʒytø, øz] adj juicy
juvénile [ʒyvenil] adj youthful

K l

K [ka] nm (Inform) K
kaki [kaki] adj inv khaki
kangourou [kɑ̃guʀu] nm kangaroo
karaté [kaʀate] nm karate
kascher [kaʃɛʀ] adj kosher
kayak [kajak] nm canoe, kayak; **faire du ~** to go canoeing
képi [kepi] nm kepi
kermesse [kɛʀmɛs] nf fair; (fête de charité) bazaar, (charity) fête
kidnapper [kidnape] vt to kidnap
kilo [kilo] nm = **kilogramme**
kilo...: **kilogramme** nm kilogramme; **kilométrage** nm number of kilometres travelled, ≈ mileage; **kilomètre** nm kilometre; **kilométrique** adj (distance) in kilometres
kinésithérapeute [kineziteʀapøt] nm/f physiotherapist
kiosque [kjɔsk] nm kiosk, stall
kir [kiʀ] nm kir (white wine with blackcurrant liqueur)
kit [kit] nm kit; **~ piéton** ou **mains libres** hands-free kit; **en ~** in kit form
kiwi [kiwi] nm kiwi
klaxon [klaksɔn] nm horn; **klaxonner** vi, vt to hoot (BRIT), honk (US)
km abr = **kilomètre**
km/h abr (= kilomètres/heure) ≈ mph
K.-O. (fam) adj inv shattered, knackered
Kosovo [kɔsɔvo] nm Kosovo
Koweït, Kuweit [kɔwɛt] nm: **le ~** Kuwait
k-way® [kawe] nm (lightweight nylon) cagoule
kyste [kist] nm cyst

l' [l] art déf voir **le**
la [la] art déf voir **le** ▷ nm (Mus) A; (en chantant la gamme) la
là [la] adv there; (ici) here; (dans le temps) then; **elle n'est pas là** she isn't here; **c'est là que** this is where; **là où** where; **de là** (fig) hence; **par là** (fig) by that; voir aussi **-ci; ce; celui; là-bas** adv there
laboratoire [labɔʀatwaʀ] nm laboratory; **laboratoire de langues** language laboratory
laborieux, -euse [labɔʀjø, jøz] adj (tâche) laborious
labourer vt to plough
labyrinthe [labiʀɛ̃t] nm labyrinth, maze
lac [lak] nm lake
lacet [lasɛ] nm (de chaussure) lace, (de route) sharp bend; (piège) snare
lâche [lɑʃ] adj (poltron) cowardly; (desserré) loose, slack ▷ nm/f coward
lâcher [lɑʃe] vt to let go of; (ce qui tombe, abandonner) to drop; (oiseau, animal: libérer) to release, set free; (fig: mot, remarque) to let slip, come out with ▷ vi (freins) to fail; **~ les amarres** (Navig) to cast off (the moorings); **~ prise** to let go
lacrymogène [lakʀimɔʒɛn] adj: **gaz ~** teargas
lacune [lakyn] nf gap
là-dedans [ladədɑ̃] adv inside (there), in it; (fig) in that
là-dessous [ladsu] adv underneath, under there; (fig) behind that
là-dessus [ladsy] adv on there; (fig: sur ces mots) at that point; (: à ce sujet) about that
lagune [lagyn] nf lagoon
là-haut [lao] adv up there
laid, e [lɛ, lɛd] adj ugly; **laideur** nf ugliness no pl
lainage [lɛnaʒ] nm (vêtement) woollen garment; (étoffe) woollen material
laine [lɛn] nf wool
laïque [laik] adj lay, civil; (Scol) state cpd ▷ nm/f layman(-woman)
laisse [lɛs] nf (de chien) lead, leash; **tenir en ~** to keep on a lead ou leash
laisser [lese] vt to leave ▷ vb aux: **~ qn faire** to let sb do; **se ~ aller** to let o.s. go; **laisse-toi faire** let me (ou him

etc) do it; **laisser-aller** *nm* carelessness, slovenliness; **laissez-passer** *nm inv* pass

lait [lɛ] *nm* milk; **frère/sœur de ~** foster brother/sister; **lait concentré/condensé** condensed/evaporated milk; **lait écrémé/entier** skimmed/full-cream (BRIT) *ou* whole milk; **laitage** *nm* dairy product; **laiterie** *nf* dairy; **laitier, -ière** *adj* dairy *cpd* ▷ *nm/f* milkman (dairywoman)

laiton [lɛtɔ̃] *nm* brass

laitue [lety] *nf* lettuce

lambeau, x [lɑ̃bo] *nm* scrap; **en ~x** in tatters, tattered

lame [lam] *nf* blade; (*vague*) wave; (*lamelle*) strip; **lame de fond** ground swell *no pl*; **lame de rasoir** razor blade; **lamelle** *nf* thin strip *ou* blade

lamentable [lamɑ̃tabl] *adj* appalling

lamenter [lamɑ̃te] *vb*: **se ~ (sur)** to moan (over)

lampadaire [lɑ̃padɛʀ] *nm* (*de salon*) standard lamp; (*dans la rue*) street lamp

lampe [lɑ̃p] *nf* lamp; (*Tech*) valve; **lampe à bronzer** sun lamp; **lampe à pétrole** oil lamp; **lampe de poche** torch (BRIT), flashlight (US); **lampe halogène** halogen lamp

lance [lɑ̃s] *nf* spear; **lance d'incendie** fire hose

lancée [lɑ̃se] *nf*: **être/continuer sur sa ~** to be under way/keep going

lancement [lɑ̃smɑ̃] *nm* launching

lance-pierres [lɑ̃spjɛʀ] *nm inv* catapult

lancer [lɑ̃se] *nm* (*Sport*) throwing *no pl*, throw ▷ *vt* to throw; (*émettre, projeter*) to throw out, send out; (*produit, fusée, bateau, artiste*) to launch; (*injure*) to hurl, fling; **se ~** *vi* (*prendre de l'élan*) to build up speed; (*se précipiter*): **se ~ sur** *ou* **contre** to rush at; **se ~ dans** (*discussion*) to launch into; (*aventure*) to embark on; **~ qch à qn** to throw sth to sb; (*de façon agressive*) to throw sth at sb; **~ un cri** *ou* **un appel** to shout *ou* call out; **lancer du poids** putting the shot

landau [lɑ̃do] *nm* pram (BRIT), baby carriage (US)

lande [lɑ̃d] *nf* moor

langage [lɑ̃gaʒ] *nm* language

langouste [lɑ̃gust] *nf* crayfish *inv*; **langoustine** *nf* Dublin Bay prawn

langue [lɑ̃g] *nf* (*Anat, Culin*) tongue; (*Ling*) language; **tirer la ~ (à)** to stick one's tongue out (at); **de ~ française** French-speaking; **quelles ~s parlez-vous?** what languages do you speak?; **langue maternelle** native language, mother tongue; **langues vivantes** modern languages

langueur [lɑ̃gœʀ] *nf* languidness

languir [lɑ̃giʀ] *vi* to languish; (*conversation*) to flag; **faire ~ qn** to keep sb waiting

lanière [lanjɛʀ] *nf* (*de fouet*) lash; (*de sac, bretelle*) strap

lanterne [lɑ̃tɛʀn] *nf* (*portable*) lantern; (*électrique*) light, lamp; (*de voiture*) (side)light

laper [lape] *vt* to lap up

lapidaire [lapidɛʀ] *adj* (*fig*) terse

lapin [lapɛ̃] *nm* rabbit; (*peau*) rabbitskin; (*fourrure*) cony; **poser un ~ à qn** (*fam*) to stand sb up

Laponie [laponi] *nf* Lapland

laps [laps] *nm*: **~ de temps** space of time, time *no pl*

laque [lak] *nf* (*vernis*) lacquer; (*pour cheveux*) hair spray

laquelle [lakɛl] *pron voir* **lequel**

larcin [laʀsɛ̃] *nm* theft

lard [laʀ] *nm* (*bacon*) (streaky) bacon; (*graisse*) fat

lardon [laʀdɔ̃] *nm*: **~s** chopped bacon

large [laʀʒ] *adj* wide, broad; (*fig*) generous ▷ *adv*:

calculer/voir ~ to allow extra/think big ▷ *nm* (*largeur*): **5 m de ~** 5 m wide *ou* in width; (*mer*): **le ~** the open sea; **au ~ de** off; **large d'esprit** broad-minded; **largement** *adv* widely; (*de loin*) greatly; (*au moins*) easily; (*généreusement*) generously; **c'est largement suffisant** that's ample; **largesse** *nf* generosity; **largesses** *nfpl* (*dons*) liberalities; **largeur** *nf* (*qu'on mesure*) width; (*impression visuelle*) wideness, width; (*d'esprit*) broadness

larguer [laʀge] *vt* to drop; **~ les amarres** to cast off (the moorings)

larme [laʀm] *nf* tear; (*fam: goutte*) drop; **en ~s** in tears; **larmoyer** *vi* (*yeux*) to water; (*se plaindre*) to whimper

larvé, e [laʀve] *adj* (*fig*) latent

laryngite [laʀɛ̃ʒit] *nf* laryngitis

las, lasse [lɑ, lɑs] *adj* weary

laser [lazɛʀ] *nm*: **(rayon) ~** laser (beam); **chaîne** *ou* **platine ~** laser disc (player); **disque ~** laser disc

lasse [lɑs] *adj voir* **las**

lasser [lɑse] *vt* to weary, tire; **se ~ de** *vt* to grow weary *ou* tired of

latéral, e, -aux [lateʀal, o] *adj* side *cpd*, lateral

latin, e [latɛ̃, in] *adj* Latin ▷ *nm/f*: **L~, e** Latin ▷ *nm* (*Ling*) Latin

latitude [latityd] *nf* latitude

lauréat, e [loʀea, at] *nm/f* winner

laurier [loʀje] *nm* (*Bot*) laurel; **feuille de ~** (*Culin*) bay leaf

lavable [lavabl] *adj* washable

lavabo [lavabo] *nm* washbasin; **lavabos** *nmpl* (*toilettes*) toilet *sg*

lavage [lavaʒ] *nm* washing *no pl*, wash; **lavage de cerveau** brainwashing *no pl*

lavande [lavɑ̃d] *nf* lavender

lave [lav] *nf* lava *no pl*

lave-linge [lavlɛ̃ʒ] *nm inv* washing machine

laver [lave] *vt* to wash; (*tache*) to wash off; **se ~** *vi* to have a wash, wash; **se ~ les mains/dents** to wash one's hands/clean one's teeth; **~ la vaisselle/le linge** to wash the dishes/clothes; **~ qn de** (*accusation*) to clear sb of; **laverie** *nf*: **laverie (automatique)** launderette; **lavette** *nf* dish cloth; (*fam*) drip; **laveur, -euse** *nm/f* cleaner; **lave-vaisselle** *nm inv* dishwasher; **lavoir** *nm* wash house; (*évier*) sink

laxatif, -ive [laksatif, iv] *adj, nm* laxative

layette [lɛjɛt] *nf* baby clothes

O   MOT-CLÉ

le [lə], **la, l'** (*pl* **les**) *art déf* **1** the; **le livre/la pomme/ l'arbre** the book/the apple/the tree; **les étudiants** the students

2 (*noms abstraits*): **le courage/l'amour/la jeunesse** courage/love/youth

3 (*indiquant la possession*): **se casser la jambe** *etc* to break one's leg *etc*; **levez la main** put your hand up; **avoir les yeux gris/le nez rouge** to have grey eyes/a red nose

4 (*temps*): **le matin/soir** in the morning/evening; **mornings/evenings**; **le jeudi** *etc* (*d'habitude*) on Thursdays *etc*; (*ce jeudi-là etc*) on (the) Thursday

5 (*distribution, évaluation*), a, an: **10 euros le mètre/kilo** 10 euros a *ou* per metre/kilo; **le tiers/quart de** a third/quarter of

▷ *pron* **1** (*personne: mâle*) him; (*: femelle*) her; (*: pluriel*) them; **je le/la/les vois** I can see him/her/them

2 (animal, chose: singulier) it; (: pluriel) them; **je le** (ou **la**) **vois** I can see it; **je les vois** I can see them

3 (remplaçant une phrase): **je ne le savais pas** I didn't know (about it); **il était riche et ne l'est plus** he was once rich but no longer is

lécher [leʃe] vt to lick; (laper: lait, eau) to lick ou lap up; **se ~ les doigts/lèvres** to lick one's fingers/lips; **lèche-vitrines** nm: **faire du lèche-vitrines** to go window-shopping

leçon [l(ə)sɔ̃] nf lesson; **faire la ~ à** (fig) to give a lecture to; **leçons de conduite** driving lessons; **leçons particulières** private lessons ou tuition sg (BRIT)

lecteur, -trice [lɛktœr, tris] nm/f reader; (d'université) foreign language assistant ▷ nm (Tech): **~ de cassettes/CD/DVD** cassette/CD/DVD player; **lecteur de disquette(s)** disk drive; **lecteur MP3** MP3 player

lecture [lɛktyr] nf reading

ledit [lədi], **ladite** (mpl **lesdits**, fpl **lesdites**) dét the aforesaid

légal, e, -aux [legal, o] adj legal; **légaliser** vt to legalize; **légalité** nf law

légendaire [leʒɑ̃dɛr] adj legendary

légende [leʒɑ̃d] nf (mythe) legend; (de carte, plan) key; (de dessin) caption

léger, -ère [leʒe, ɛr] adj light; (bruit, retard) slight; (personne: superficiel) thoughtless; (: volage) free and easy; **à la légère** (parler, agir) rashly, thoughtlessly; **légèrement** adv (s'habiller, bouger) lightly; (un peu) slightly; **manger légèrement** to eat a light meal; **légèreté** nf lightness; (d'une remarque) flippancy

législatif, -ive [leʒislatif, iv] adj legislative; **législatives** nfpl general election sg

légitime [leʒitim] adj (Jur) lawful, legitimate; (fig) rightful, legitimate; **en état de ~ défense** in self-defence

legs [lɛg] nm legacy

léguer [lege] vt: **~ qch à qn** (Jur) to bequeath sth to sb

légume [legym] nm vegetable; **légumes secs** pulses; **légumes verts** green vegetables, greens

lendemain [lɑ̃dmɛ̃] nm: **le ~** the next ou following day; **le ~ matin/soir** the next ou following morning/evening; **le ~ de** the day after

lent, e [lɑ̃, lɑ̃t] adj slow; **lentement** adv slowly; **lenteur** nf slowness no pl

lentille [lɑ̃tij] nf (Optique) lens sg; (Culin) lentil; **lentilles de contact** contact lenses

léopard [leɔpar] nm leopard

lèpre [lɛpr] nf leprosy

lequel, laquelle [ləkɛl, lakɛl] (mpl **lesquels**, fpl **lesquelles**) (à + lequel = **auquel**, de + lequel = **duquel** etc) pron **1** (interrogatif) which, which one; **lequel des deux?** which one?

2 (relatif: personne: sujet) who; (: objet, après préposition) whom; (: chose) which

▷ adj: **auquel cas** in which case

les [le] dét voir **le**

lesbienne [lɛsbjɛn] nf lesbian

léser [leze] vt to wrong

lésiner [lezine] vi: **ne pas ~ sur les moyens** (pour mariage etc) to push the boat out

lésion [lezjɔ̃] nf lesion, damage no pl

lessive [lesiv] nf (poudre) washing powder; (linge) washing no pl, wash; **lessiver** vt to wash; (fam: fatiguer) to tire out, exhaust

lest [lɛst] nm ballast

leste [lɛst] adj sprightly, nimble

lettre [lɛtr] nf letter; **lettres** nfpl (littérature) literature sg; (Scol) arts (subjects); **à la ~** literally; **en toutes ~s** in full; **lettre piégée** letter bomb

leucémie [løsemi] nf leukaemia

leur [lœr] adj possessif their; **leur maison** their house; **leurs amis** their friends

▷ pron **1** (objet indirect) (to) them; **je leur ai dit la vérité** I told them the truth; **je le leur ai donné** I gave it to them, I gave it them

2 (possessif): **le(la) leur, les leurs** theirs

levain [ləvɛ̃] nm leaven

levé, e [ləve] adj: **être ~** to be up; **levée** nf (Postes) collection

lever [l(ə)ve] vt (vitre, bras etc) to raise; (soulever de terre, supprimer: interdiction, siège) to lift; (impôts, armée) to levy ▷ vi to rise ▷ nm: **au ~** on getting up; **se ~** vi to get up; (soleil) to rise; (jour) to break; (brouillard) to lift; **ça va se ~** (temps) it's going to clear up; **lever de soleil** sunrise; **lever du jour** daybreak

levier [ləvje] nm lever

lèvre [lɛvr] nf lip

lévrier [levrije] nm greyhound

levure [l(ə)vyr] nf yeast; **levure chimique** baking powder

lexique [lɛksik] nm vocabulary; (glossaire) lexicon

lézard [lezar] nm lizard

lézarde [lezard] nf crack

liaison [ljɛzɔ̃] nf (rapport) connection; (transport) link; (amoureuse) affair; (Phonétique) liaison; **entrer/être en ~ avec** to get/be in contact with

liane [ljan] nf creeper

liasse [ljas] nf wad, bundle

Liban [libɑ̃] nm: **le ~** (the) Lebanon

libeller [libele] vt (chèque, mandat): **~ (au nom de)** to make out (to); (lettre) to word

libellule [libelyl] nf dragonfly

libéral, e, -aux [liberal, o] adj, nm/f liberal; **profession ~e** (liberal) profession

libérer [libere] vt (délivrer) to free, liberate; (relâcher: prisonnier) to discharge, release; (: d'inhibitions) to liberate; (gaz) to release; **se ~** vi (de rendez-vous) to get out of previous engagements

liberté [liberte] nf freedom; (loisir) free time; **libertés** nfpl (privautés) liberties; **mettre/être en ~** to set/be free; **en ~ provisoire/surveillée/conditionnelle** on bail/probation/parole

libraire [librɛr] nm/f bookseller

librairie [libreri] nf bookshop

libre [libr] adj free; (route, voie) clear; (place, salle) free; (ligne) not engaged; (Scol) non-state; **~ de qch/de faire** free from sth/to do; **la place est ~?** is this seat free?; **libre arbitre** free will; **libre-échange** nm free trade; **libre-service** nm self-service store

Libye [libi] nf: **la ~** Libya

licence [lisɑ̃s] nf (permis) permit; (diplôme) degree; (liberté) liberty; **licencié, e, licencié, e** nm/f (Scol): **licencié ès lettres/en droit** ≈ Bachelor of Arts/Law

licenciement [lisɑ̃simɑ̃] nm redundancy ≈

licencier [lisɑ̃sje] vt (débaucher) to make redundant, lay off; (renvoyer) to dismiss

licite [lisit] adj lawful

lie [li] nf dregs pl, sediment

lié, e [lje] adj: **très ~ avec** very friendly with ou close to

Liechtenstein [liʃtɛnʃtain] nm: **le ~** Liechtenstein

liège [ljɛʒ] nm cork

lien [ljɛ̃] nm (corde, fig: affectif) bond; (rapport) link, connection; **lien de parenté** family tie; **lien hypertexte** hyperlink

lier [lje] vt (attacher) to tie up; (joindre) to link up; (fig: unir, engager) to bind; **~ conversation (avec)** to strike up a conversation (with); **~ connaissance avec** to get to know

lierre [ljɛʀ] nm ivy

lieu, x [ljø] nm place; **lieux** nmpl (locaux) premises; (endroit: d'un accident etc) scene sg; **en ~ sûr** in a safe place; **en premier ~** in the first place; **en dernier ~** lastly; **avoir ~** to take place; **tenir ~ de** to serve as; **donner ~ à** to give rise to; **au ~ de** instead of; **arriver/être sur les ~x** to arrive at/be on the scene; **lieu commun** cliché; **lieu-dit** (pl **lieux-dits**) nm locality

lieutenant [ljøt(ə)nɑ̃] nm lieutenant

lièvre [ljɛvʀ] nm hare

ligament [ligamɑ̃] nm ligament

ligne [liɲ] nf (gén) line; (Transports: liaison) service; (: trajet) route; (silhouette) figure; **garder la ~** to keep one's figure; **entrer en ~ de compte** to come into it; **en ~** (Inform) online; **~ fixe** (Tél) land line (phone)

lignée [liɲe] nf line, lineage

ligoter [ligɔte] vt to tie up

ligue [lig] nf league

lilas [lila] nm lilac

limace [limas] nf slug

limande [limɑ̃d] nf dab

lime [lim] nf file; **lime à ongles** nail file; **limer** vt to file

limitation [limitasjɔ̃] nf: **limitation de vitesse** speed limit

limite [limit] nf (de terrain) boundary; (partie ou point extrême) limit; **à la ~ (au pire)** if the worst comes (ou came) to the worst; **vitesse/charge ~** maximum speed/load; **cas ~** borderline case; **date ~** deadline; **date ~ de vente/consommation** sell-by/best-before date; **limiter** vt (restreindre) to limit, restrict; (délimiter) to border; **limitrophe** adj border cpd

limoger [limɔʒe] vt to dismiss

limon [limɔ̃] nm silt

limonade [limɔnad] nf lemonade

lin [lɛ̃] nm (tissu) linen

linceul [lɛ̃sœl] nm shroud

linge [lɛ̃ʒ] nm (serviettes etc) linen; (lessive) washing; (aussi: **~ de corps**) underwear; **lingerie** nf lingerie, underwear

lingot [lɛ̃go] nm ingot

linguistique [lɛ̃gɥistik] adj linguistic ▷ nf linguistics sg

lion, ne [ljɔ̃, ljɔn] nm/f lion (lioness); (signe): **le L~** Leo; **lionceau, x** nm lion cub

liqueur [likœʀ] nf liqueur

liquidation [likidasjɔ̃] nf (vente) sale

liquide [likid] adj liquid ▷ nm liquid; (Comm): **en ~** in ready money ou cash; **je n'ai pas de ~** I haven't got any cash; **liquider** vt to liquidate; (Comm: articles) to clear, sell off

lire [liʀ] nf (monnaie) lira ▷ vt, vi to read

lis [lis] nm = **lys**

Lisbonne [lizbɔn] n Lisbon

lisible [lizibl] adj legible

lisière [lizjɛʀ] nf (de forêt) edge

lisons [lizɔ̃] vb voir **lire**

lisse [lis] adj smooth

liste [list] nf list; **faire la ~ de** to list; **liste de mariage** wedding (present) list; **liste électorale** electoral roll; **listing** nm (Inform) printout

lit [li] nm bed; **petit ~, ~ à une place** single bed; **grand ~, ~ à deux places** double bed; **faire son ~** to make one's bed; **aller/se mettre au ~** to go to/get into bed; **lit de camp** camp bed; **lit d'enfant** cot (BRIT), crib (US)

literie [litʀi] nf bedding, bedclothes pl

litige [litiʒ] nm dispute

litre [litʀ] nm litre

littéraire [liteʀɛʀ] adj literary ▷ nm/f arts student; **elle est très ~** she's very literary

littéral, e, -aux [liteʀal, o] adj literal

littérature [liteʀatyʀ] nf literature

littoral, -aux [litɔʀal, o] nm coast

livide [livid] adj livid, pallid

livraison [livʀɛzɔ̃] nf delivery

livre [livʀ] nm book ▷ nf (monnaie) pound; (poids) half a kilo, ≈ pound; **livre de poche** paperback

livré, e [livʀe] adj: **~ à soi-même** left to o.s. ou one's own devices

livrer [livʀe] vt (Comm) to deliver; (otage, coupable) to hand over; (secret, information) to give away; **se ~ à** (se confier) to confide in; (se rendre, s'abandonner) to give o.s. up to; (faire: pratiques, actes) to indulge in; (enquête) to carry out

livret [livʀɛ] nm booklet; (d'opéra) libretto; **livret de caisse d'épargne** (savings) bank-book; **livret de famille** (official) family record book; **livret scolaire** (school) report book

livreur, -euse [livʀœʀ, øz] nm/f delivery boy ou man/girl ou woman

local, e, -aux [lɔkal] adj local ▷ nm (salle) premises pl; voir aussi **locaux**; **localité** nf locality

locataire [lɔkatɛʀ] nm/f tenant; (de chambre) lodger

location [lɔkasjɔ̃] nf (par le locataire, le loueur) renting; (par le propriétaire) renting out, letting; (Théâtre) booking office; **"~ de voitures"** "car rental"; **habiter en ~** to live in rented accommodation; **prendre une ~ (pour les vacances)** to rent a house etc (for the holidays)

locomotive [lɔkɔmɔtiv] nf locomotive, engine

locution [lɔkysjɔ̃] nf phrase

loge [lɔʒ] nf (Théâtre: d'artiste) dressing room; (: de spectateurs) box; (de concierge, franc-maçon) lodge

logement [lɔʒmɑ̃] nm accommodation no pl (BRIT), accommodations pl (US); (appartement) flat (BRIT), apartment (US); (Pol, Admin): **le ~** housing no pl

loger [lɔʒe] vt to accommodate ▷ vi to live; **être logé, nourri** to have board and lodging; **se ~: trouver à se ~** to find somewhere to live; **se ~ dans** (suj: balle, flèche) to lodge itself in; **logeur, -euse** nm/f landlord(-lady)

logiciel [lɔʒisjɛl] nm software

logique [lɔʒik] adj logical ▷ nf logic

logo [logo] nm logo

loi [lwa] nf: **faire la ~** to lay down the law

loin [lwɛ̃] adv far; (dans le temps: futur) a long way off; (: passé) a long time ago; **plus ~** further; **~ de** far from; **c'est ~ d'ici?** is it far from here?; **au ~** far off; **de ~** from a distance; (fig: de beaucoup) by far

lointain, e [lwɛ̃tɛ̃, ɛn] adj faraway, distant; (dans le futur, passé) distant; (cause, parent) remote, distant ▷ nm: **dans le ~** in the distance

loir [lwar] nm dormouse

Loire [lwar] nf: **la ~** the (River) Loire

loisir [lwazir] nm: **heures de ~** spare time; **loisirs** nmpl (temps libre) leisure sg; (activités) leisure activities; **avoir le ~ de faire** to have the time ou opportunity to do; **à ~** at leisure

londonien, ne [lɔ̃dɔnjɛ̃, jɛn] adj London cpd, of London ▷ nm/f: **L~, ne** Londoner

Londres [lɔ̃dr] n London

long, longue [lɔ̃, lɔ̃g] adj long ▷ adv: **en savoir ~** to know a great deal ▷ nm: **de 3 m de ~** 3 m long, 3 m in length; **ne pas faire ~ feu** not to last long; **(tout) le ~ de** (all) along; **tout au ~ de** (année, vie) throughout; **de ~ en large** (marcher) to and fro, up and down; voir aussi **longue**

longer [lɔ̃ʒe] vt to go (ou walk ou drive) along(side); (suj: mur, route) to border

longiligne [lɔ̃ʒiliɲ] adj long-limbed

longitude [lɔ̃ʒityd] nf longitude

longtemps [lɔ̃tɑ̃] adv (for) a long time, (for) long; **avant ~** before long; **pour ou pendant ~** for a long time; **mettre ~ à faire** to take a long time to do; **il en a pour ~?** will he be long?

longue [lɔ̃g] adj voir **long** ▷ nf: **à la ~** in the end; **longuement** adv (longtemps) for a long time; (en détail) at length

longueur [lɔ̃gœr] nf length; **longueurs** nfpl (fig: d'un film etc) tedious parts; **en ~** lengthwise; **tirer en ~** to drag on; **à ~ de journée** all day long

loquet [lɔkɛ] nm latch

lorgner [lɔrɲe] vt to eye; (fig) to have one's eye on

lors [lɔr]: **~ de** prép at the time of; during

lorsque [lɔrsk] conj when, as

losange [lɔzɑ̃ʒ] nm diamond

lot [lo] nm (part) share; (de loterie) prize; (fig: destin) fate, lot; (Comm, Inform) batch; **le gros ~** the jackpot

loterie [lɔtri] nf lottery

lotion [losjɔ̃] nf lotion; **lotion après rasage** aftershave (lotion)

lotissement [lɔtismɑ̃] nm housing development; (parcelle) plot, lot

loto [lɔto] nm lotto

lotte [lɔt] nf monkfish

louanges [lwɑ̃ʒ] nfpl praise sg

loubard [lubar] (fam) nm lout

louche [luʃ] adj shady, fishy, dubious ▷ nf ladle; **loucher** vi to squint

louer [lwe] vt (maison: suj: propriétaire) to let, rent (out); (: locataire) to rent; (voiture etc: entreprise) to hire out (BRIT), rent (out); (: locataire) to hire, rent; (réserver) to book; (faire l'éloge de) to praise; **"à ~"** "to let" (BRIT), "for rent" (US); **je voudrais ~ une voiture** I'd like to hire (BRIT) ou rent (US) a car

loup [lu] nm wolf; **jeune ~** young go-getter

loupe [lup] nf magnifying glass; **à la ~** in minute detail

louper [lupe] (fam) vt (manquer) to miss; (examen) to flunk

lourd, e [lur, lurd] adj, adv heavy; **c'est trop ~** it's too heavy; **~ de** (conséquences, menaces) charged with; **il fait ~** the weather is close, it's sultry; **lourdaud, e** (péj) adj clumsy; **lourdement** adv heavily

loutre [lutr] nf otter

louveteau, x [luv(ə)to] nm wolf-cub; (scout) cub (scout)

louvoyer [luvwaje] vi (fig) to hedge, evade the issue

loyal, e, -aux [lwajal, o] adj (fidèle) loyal, faithful; (fair-play) fair; **loyauté** nf loyalty, faithfulness; fairness

loyer [lwaje] nm rent

lu, e [ly] pp de **lire**

lubie [lybi] nf whim, craze

lubrifiant [lybrifjɑ̃] nm lubricant

lubrifier [lybrifje] vt to lubricate

lubrique [lybrik] adj lecherous

lucarne [lykarn] nf skylight

lucide [lysid] adj lucid; (accidenté) conscious

lucratif, -ive [lykratif, iv] adj lucrative, profitable; **à but non ~** non profit-making

lueur [lɥœr] nf (pâle) (faint) light; (chatoyante) glimmer no pl; (fig) glimmer; gleam

luge [lyʒ] nf sledge (BRIT), sled (US)

lugubre [lygybr] adj gloomy, dismal

○ **MOT-CLÉ**

lui [lɥi] pron **1** (objet indirect: mâle) (to) him; (: femelle) (to) her; (: chose, animal) (to) it; **je lui ai parlé** I have spoken to him (ou to her); **il lui a offert un cadeau** he gave him (ou her) a present

2 (après préposition, comparatif: personne) him; (: chose, animal) it; **elle est contente de lui** she is pleased with him; **je la connais mieux que lui** I know her better than he does; I know her better than him; **ce livre est à lui** this book is his, this is his book; **c'est à lui de jouer** it's his turn ou go

3 (sujet, forme emphatique) he; **lui, il est à Paris** HE is in Paris; **c'est lui qui l'a fait** HE did it

4 (objet, forme emphatique) him; **c'est lui que j'attends** I'm waiting for HIM

5: **lui-même** himself; itself

luire [lɥir] vi to shine; (en rougeoyant) to glow

lumière [lymjɛr] nf light; **mettre en ~** (fig) to highlight; **lumière du jour** daylight

luminaire [lyminɛr] nm lamp, light

lumineux, -euse [lyminø, øz] adj luminous; (éclairé) illuminated; (ciel, couleur) bright; (rayon) of light, light cpd; (fig: regard) radiant

lunatique [lynatik] adj whimsical, temperamental

lundi [lœ̃di] nm Monday; **on est ~** it's Monday; **le(s) ~(s)** on Mondays; **"à ~"** "see you on Monday"; **lundi de Pâques** Easter Monday

lune [lyn] nf moon; **lune de miel** honeymoon

lunette [lynɛt] nf: **~s** nfpl glasses, spectacles; (protectrices) goggles; **lunette arrière** (Auto) rear window; **lunettes de soleil** sunglasses; **lunettes noires** dark glasses

lustre [lystr] nm (de plafond) chandelier; (fig: éclat) lustre; **lustrer** vt to shine

luth [lyt] nm lute

lutin [lytɛ̃] nm imp, goblin

lutte [lyt] nf (conflit) struggle; (sport) wrestling; **lutter** vi to fight, struggle

luxe [lyks] nm luxury; **de ~** luxury cpd

Luxembourg [lyksɑ̃buʀ] nm: **le ~** Luxembourg

luxer [lykse] vt: **se ~ l'épaule** to dislocate one's shoulder

luxueux, -euse [lyksɥø, øz] adj luxurious

lycée [lise] nm ≈ secondary school; **lycéen, ne** nm/f secondary school pupil

Lyon [ljɔ̃] n Lyons

lyophilisé, e [ljofilize] adj (café) freeze-dried

lyrique [liʀik] adj lyrical; (Opéra) lyric; **artiste ~** opera singer

lys [lis] nm lily

M abr = **Monsieur**

m' [m] pron voir **me**

ma [ma] adj voir **mon**

macaron [makaʀɔ̃] nm (gâteau) macaroon; (insigne) (round) badge

macaronis [makaʀoni] nmpl macaroni sg; **~ au fromage** ou **en gratin** macaroni cheese (BRIT), macaroni and cheese (US)

macédoine [masedwan] nf: **~ de fruits** fruit salad; **~ de légumes** mixed vegetables; **la M~** Macedonia

macérer [maseʀe] vi, vt to macerate; (dans du vinaigre) to pickle

mâcher [maʃe] vt to chew; **ne pas ~ ses mots** not to mince one's words

machin [maʃɛ̃] (fam) nm thing(umajig); (personne): **M~(e)** nm(f) what's-his-(ou her)-name

machinal, e, -aux [maʃinal, o] adj mechanical, automatic

machination [maʃinasjɔ̃] nf frame-up

machine [maʃin] nf machine; (locomotive) engine; **machine à laver/coudre** washing/sewing machine; **machine à sous** fruit machine

mâchoire [maʃwaʀ] nf jaw

mâchonner [maʃone] vt to chew (at)

maçon [masɔ̃] nm builder; (poseur de briques) bricklayer; **maçonnerie** nf (murs) brickwork; (pierres) masonry, stonework

Madagascar [madagaskaʀ] nf Madagascar

Madame [madam] (pl **Mesdames**) nf: **~ Dupont** Mrs Dupont; **occupez-vous de ~/Monsieur/ Mademoiselle** please serve this lady/gentleman/ (young) lady; **bonjour ~/Monsieur/Mademoiselle** good morning; (ton déférent) good morning Madam/Sir/ Madam; (le nom est connu) good morning Mrs/Mr/Miss X; **~/Monsieur/Mademoiselle!** (pour appeler) Madam/ Sir/Miss!; **~/Monsieur/Mademoiselle** (sur lettre) Dear Madam/Sir/Madam; **chère ~/cher Monsieur/chère Mademoiselle** Dear Mrs/Mr/Miss X; **Mesdames** Ladies; **mesdames, mesdemoiselles, messieurs** ladies and gentlemen

madeleine [madlɛn] nf madeleine, small sponge cake

Mademoiselle [madmwazɛl] (pl **Mesdemoiselles**) nf Miss; voir aussi **Madame**

madère [madɛʀ] nm Madeira (wine)

Madrid [madʀid] n Madrid

magasin [magazɛ̃] nm (boutique) shop; (entrepôt) warehouse; **en ~** (Comm) in stock

magazine [magazin] nm magazine

Maghreb [magʀɛb] nm: **le ~** North Africa; **maghrébin, e** adj North African ▷ nm/f: **Maghrébin, e** North African

magicien, ne [maʒisjɛ̃, jɛn] nm/f magician

magie [maʒi] nf magic; **magique** adj magic; (enchanteur) magical

magistral, e, -aux [maʒistʀal, o] adj (œuvre, adresse) masterly; (ton) authoritative; **cours ~** lecture

magistrat [maʒistʀa] nm magistrate

magnétique [maɲetik] adj magnetic

magnétophone [maɲetofɔn] nm tape recorder; **magnétophone à cassettes** cassette recorder

magnétoscope [maɲetɔskɔp] nm video-tape recorder

magnifique [maɲifik] adj magnificent

magret [magʀɛ] nm: **~ de canard** duck steaklet

mai [mɛ] nm May

maigre [mɛgʀ] adj (very) thin, skinny; (viande) lean; (fromage) low-fat; (végétation) thin, sparse; (fig) poor, meagre, skimpy; **jours ~s** days of abstinence, fish days; **maigreur** nf thinness; **maigrir** vi to get thinner, lose weight; **maigrir de 2 kilos** to lose 2 kilos

mail [mɛl] nm e-mail

maille [maj] nf stitch; **maille à l'endroit/l'envers** plain/purl stitch

maillet [majɛ] nm mallet

maillon [majɔ̃] nm link

maillot [majo] nm (aussi: **~ de corps**) vest; (de sportif) jersey; **maillot de bain** swimming ou bathing (BRIT) costume, swimsuit; (d'homme) **maigrir** (swimming ou bathing (BRIT)) trunks pl

main [mɛ̃] nf hand; **à la ~** (tenir, avoir) in one's hand; (faire, tricoter etc) by hand; **se donner la ~** to hold hands; **donner** ou **tendre la ~ à qn** to hold out one's hand to sb; **se serrer la ~** to shake hands; **serrer la ~ à qn** to shake hands with sb; **sous la ~** to ou at hand; **haut les ~s!** hands up!; **attaque à ~ armée** armed attack;

à remettre en ~s propres to be delivered personally; **mettre la dernière ~ à** to put the finishing touches to; **se faire/perdre la ~** to get one's hand in/lose one's touch; **avoir qch bien en ~** to have (got) the hang of sth; **main-d'œuvre** nf manpower, labour; **mainmise** nf (fig): **mainmise sur** complete hold on; **mains libres** adj inv (téléphone, kit) hands-free

maint, e [mɛ̃, mɛ̃t] adj many a; **~s** many; **à ~es reprises** time and (time) again

maintenant [mɛ̃t(ə)nɑ̃] adv now; (actuellement) nowadays

maintenir [mɛ̃t(ə)niʀ] vt (retenir, soutenir) to support; (contenir: foule etc) to hold back; (conserver, affirmer) to maintain; **se ~** vi (prix) to keep steady; (amélioration) to persist

maintien [mɛ̃tjɛ̃] nm (sauvegarde) maintenance; (attitude) bearing

maire [mɛʀ] nm mayor; **mairie** nf (bâtiment) town hall; (administration) town council

mais [mɛ] conj but; **~ non!** of course not!; **~ enfin** but after all; (indignation) look here!

maïs [mais] nm maize (BRIT), corn (US)

maison [mɛzɔ̃] nf house; (chez-soi) home; (Comm) firm ▷ adj inv (Culin) home-made; (fig) in-house, own; **à la ~** at home; (direction) home; **maison de repos** convalescent home; **maison de retraite** old people's home; **maison close** ou **de passe** brothel; **maison de santé** mental home; **maison des jeunes** ≈ youth club; **maison mère** parent company

maître, -esse [mɛtʀ, mɛtʀɛs] nm/f master (mistress); (Scol) teacher, schoolmaster(-mistress) ▷ nm (peintre etc) master; (titre): **M~** Maître, term of address gen for a barrister ▷ adj (principal, essentiel) main; **être ~ de** (soi, situation) to be in control of; **une ~sse femme** a managing woman; **maître chanteur** blackmailer; **maître d'école** schoolmaster; **maître d'hôtel** (domestique) butler; (d'hôtel) head waiter; **maître nageur** lifeguard; **maîtresse** nf (amante) mistress; **maîtresse (d'école)** teacher, (school)mistress; **maîtresse de maison** hostess; (ménagère) housewife

maîtrise [mɛtʀiz] nf (aussi: **~ de soi**) self-control, self-possession; (habileté) skill, mastery; (suprématie) mastery, command; (diplôme) ≈ master's degree; **maîtriser** vt (cheval, incendie) to (bring under) control; (sujet) to master; (émotion) to control, master; **se maîtriser** to control o.s.

majestueux, -euse [maʒɛstɥø, øz] adj majestic

majeur, e [maʒœʀ] adj (important) major; (Jur) of age ▷ nm (doigt) middle finger; **en ~e partie** for the most part; **la ~e partie de** most of

majorer [maʒɔʀe] vt to increase

majoritaire [maʒɔʀitɛʀ] adj majority cpd

majorité [maʒɔʀite] nf (gén) majority; (parti) party in power; **en ~** mainly; **avoir la ~** to have the majority

majuscule [maʒyskyl] adj, nf: (lettre) **~** capital (letter)

mal [mal, mo] (pl **maux**) nm (opposé au bien) evil; (tort, dommage) harm; (douleur physique) pain, ache; (maladie) illness, sickness no pl ▷ adv badly ▷ adj bad, wrong; **être ~ à l'aise** to be uncomfortable; **être ~ avec qn** to be on bad terms with sb; **il a ~ compris** he misunderstood; **se sentir** ou **se trouver ~** to feel ill ou unwell; **dire/penser du ~ de** to speak/think ill of; **ne voir aucun ~ à** to see no harm in, see nothing wrong in; **faire ~ à qn** to hurt sb; **se faire ~** to hurt o.s.; **avoir du ~ à faire qch** to have

trouble doing sth; **se donner du ~ pour faire qch** to go to a lot of trouble to do sth; **ça fait ~** it hurts; **j'ai ~ au dos** my back hurts; **avoir ~ à la tête/à la gorge/aux dents** to have a headache/a sore throat/toothache; **avoir le ~ du pays** to be homesick; voir aussi **cœur**; **maux** nmpl; **mal de mer** seasickness; **mal en point** in a bad state

malade [malad] adj ill, sick; (poitrine, jambe) bad; (plante) diseased ▷ nm/f invalid, sick person; (à l'hôpital etc) patient; **tomber ~** to fall ill; **être ~ du cœur** to have heart trouble ou a bad heart; **malade mental** mentally ill person; **maladie** nf (spécifique) disease, illness; (mauvaise santé) illness, sickness; **maladif, -ive** adj sickly; (curiosité, besoin) pathological

maladresse [maladʀɛs] nf clumsiness no pl; (gaffe) blunder

maladroit, e [maladʀwa, wat] adj clumsy

malaise [malɛz] nm (Méd) feeling of faintness; (fig) uneasiness, malaise; **avoir un ~** to feel faint

Malaisie [malɛzi] nf: **la ~** Malaysia

malaria [malaʀja] nf malaria

malaxer [malakse] vt (pétrir) to knead; (mélanger) to mix

malbouffe [malbuf] (fam) nf: **la ~** junk food

malchance [malʃɑ̃s] nf misfortune, ill luck no pl; **par ~** unfortunately; **malchanceux, -euse** adj unlucky

mâle [mal] adj (aussi Élec, Tech) male; (viril: voix, traits) manly ▷ nm male

malédiction [malediksjɔ̃] nf curse

mal...: **malentendant, e** nm/f: **les malentendants** the hard of hearing; **malentendu** nm misunderstanding; **il y a eu un malentendu** there's been a misunderstanding; **malfaçon** nf fault; **malfaisant, e** adj evil, harmful; **malfaiteur** nm lawbreaker, criminal; (voleur) burglar, thief; **malfamé, e** adj disreputable

malgache [malgaʃ] adj Madagascan, Malagasy ▷ nm/f: **M~** Madagascan, Malagasy ▷ nm (Ling) Malagasy

malgré [malgʀe] prép in spite of, despite; **~ tout** all the same

malheur [malœʀ] nm (situation) adversity, misfortune; (événement) misfortune; (: très grave) disaster, tragedy; **faire un ~** to be a smash hit; **malheureusement** adv unfortunately; **malheureux, -euse** adj (triste) unhappy, miserable; (infortuné, regrettable) unfortunate; (malchanceux) unlucky; (insignifiant) wretched ▷ nm/f poor soul

malhonnête [malɔnɛt] adj dishonest; **malhonnêteté** nf dishonesty

malice [malis] nf mischievousness; (méchanceté): **par ~** out of malice ou spite; **sans ~** guileless; **malicieux, -euse** adj mischievous

malin, -igne [malɛ̃, malin] adj (futé: f gén: aussi: **maline**) smart, shrewd; (Méd) malignant

malingre [malɛ̃gʀ] adj puny

malle [mal] nf trunk; **mallette** nf (small) suitcase; (porte-documents) attaché case

malmener [malməne] vt to manhandle; (fig) to give a rough handling to

malodorant, e [malɔdɔʀɑ̃, ɑ̃t] adj foul- ou ill-smelling

malpoli, e [malpoli] adj impolite

malsain, e [malsɛ̃, ɛn] adj unhealthy

malt [malt] nm malt

Malte [malt] nf Malta

maltraiter [maltʀete] vt to manhandle, ill-treat

malveillance [malvejɑ̃s] nf (animosité) ill will; (intention *de nuire)* malevolence

malversation [malvɛʀsasjɔ̃] *nf* embezzlement

maman [mamɑ̃] *nf* mum(my), mother

mamelle [mamɛl] *nf* teat

mamelon [mam(ə)lɔ̃] *nm (Anat)* nipple

mamie [mami] *(fam) nf* granny

mammifère [mamifɛʀ] *nm* mammal

mammouth [mamut] *nm* mammoth

manche [mɑ̃ʃ] *nf (de vêtement)* sleeve; *(d'un jeu, tournoi)* round; *(Géo):* **la M~** the Channel ▷ *nm (d'outil, casserole)* handle; *(de pelle, pioche etc)* shaft; **à ~s courtes/longues** short-/long-sleeved; **manche à balai** broomstick; *(Inform, Aviat)* joystick *m inv*

manchette [mɑ̃ʃɛt] *nf (de chemise)* cuff; *(coup)* forearm blow; *(titre)* headline

manchot [mɑ̃ʃo] *nm* one-armed man; armless man; *(Zool)* penguin

mandarine [mɑ̃daʀin] *nf* mandarin (orange), tangerine

mandat [mɑ̃da] *nm (postal)* postal *ou* money order; *(d'un député etc)* mandate; *(procuration)* power of attorney, proxy; *(Police)* warrant; **mandat d'arrêt** warrant for arrest; **mandat de perquisition** search warrant; **mandataire** *nm/f (représentant)* representative; *(Jur)* proxy

manège [manɛʒ] *nm* riding school; *(à la foire)* roundabout, merry-go-round; *(fig)* game, ploy

manette [manɛt] *nf* lever, tap; **manette de jeu** joystick

mangeable [mɑ̃ʒabl] *adj* edible, eatable

mangeoire [mɑ̃ʒwaʀ] *nf* trough, manger

manger [mɑ̃ʒe] *vt* to eat; *(ronger: suj: rouille etc)* to eat into *ou* away ▷ *vi* to eat; **donner à ~ à** *(enfant)* to feed; **est-ce qu'on peut ~ quelque chose?** can we have something to eat?

mangue [mɑ̃g] *nf* mango

maniable [manjabl] *adj (outil)* handy; *(voiture, voilier)* easy to handle

maniaque [manjak] *adj* finicky, fussy ▷ *nm/f (méticuleux)* fusspot; *(fou)* maniac

manie [mani] *nf (tic)* odd habit; *(obsession)* mania; **avoir la ~ de** to be obsessive about

manier [manje] *vt* to handle

manière [manjɛʀ] *nf (façon)* way, manner; **manières** *nfpl (attitude)* manners; *(chichis)* fuss *sg*; **de ~ à** so as to; **de cette ~** in this way *ou* manner; **d'une certaine ~** in a way; **de toute ~** in any case; **d'une ~ générale** generally speaking, as a general rule

maniéré, e [manjeʀe] *adj* affected

manifestant, e [manifɛstɑ̃, ɑ̃t] *nm/f* demonstrator

manifestation [manifɛstasjɔ̃] *nf (de joie, mécontentement)* expression, demonstration; *(symptôme)* outward sign; *(culturelle etc)* event; *(Pol)* demonstration

manifeste [manifɛst] *adj* obvious, evident ▷ *nm* manifesto; **manifester** *vt (volonté, intentions)* to show, indicate; *(joie, peur)* to express, show ▷ *vi* to demonstrate; **se manifester** *vi (émotion)* to show *ou* express itself; *(difficultés)* to arise; *(symptômes)* to appear

manigancer [manigɑ̃se] *vt* to plot

manipulation [manipylasjɔ̃] *nf* handling; *(Pol, génétique)* manipulation

manipuler [manipyle] *vt* to handle; *(fig)* to manipulate

manivelle [manivɛl] *nf* crank

mannequin [manke͂] *nm (Couture)* dummy; *(Mode)* model

manœuvre [manœvʀ] *nf (gén)* manoeuvre *(BRIT)*, maneuver *(US)* ▷ *nm* labourer; **manœuvrer** *vt* to manoeuvre *(BRIT)*, maneuver *(US)*; *(levier, machine)* to operate ▷ *vi* to manoeuvre

manoir [manwaʀ] *nm* manor *ou* country house

manque [mɑ̃k] *nm (insuffisance):* **~ de** lack of; *(vide)* emptiness, gap; *(Méd)* withdrawal; **être en état de ~** to suffer withdrawal symptoms

manqué, e [mɑ̃ke] *adj* failed; **garçon ~** tomboy

manquer [mɑ̃ke] *vi (faire défaut)* to be lacking; *(être absent)* to be missing; *(échouer)* to fail ▷ *vt* to miss ▷ *vb impers:* **il (nous) manque encore 10 euros** we are still 10 euros short; **il manque des pages (au livre)** there are some pages missing (from the book); **il/cela me manque** I miss him/this; **~ à** *(règles etc)* to be in breach of, fail to observe; **~ de** to lack; **je ne ~ai pas de le lui dire** I'll be sure to tell him; **il a manqué (de) se tuer** he very nearly got killed

mansarde [mɑ̃saʀd] *nf* attic; **mansardé, e** *adj:* **chambre mansardée** attic room

manteau, x [mɑ̃to] *nm* coat

manucure [manykyʀ] *nf* manicurist

manuel, le [manɥɛl] *adj* manual ▷ *nm (ouvrage)* manual, handbook

manufacture [manyfaktyʀ] *nf* factory; **manufacturé, e** *adj* manufactured

manuscrit, e [manyskʀi, it] *adj* handwritten ▷ *nm* manuscript

manutention [manytɑ̃sjɔ̃] *nf (Comm)* handling

mappemonde [mapmɔ̃d] *nf (plane)* map of the world; *(sphère)* globe

maquereau, x [makʀo] *nm (Zool)* mackerel *inv*; *(fam)* pimp

maquette [makɛt] *nf (à échelle réduite)* (scale) model; *(d'une page illustrée)* paste-up

maquillage [makijaʒ] *nm* making up; *(crème etc)* make-up

maquiller [makije] *vt (personne, visage)* to make up; *(truquer: passeport, statistique)* to fake; *(: voiture volée)* to do over *(respray etc)*; **se ~** *vi* to make up (one's face)

maquis [maki] *nm (Géo)* scrub; *(Mil)* maquis, underground fighting *no pl*

maraîcher, -ère [maʀeʃe, ɛʀ] *adj:* **cultures maraîchères** market gardening *sg* ▷ *nm/f* market gardener

marais [maʀɛ] *nm* marsh, swamp

marasme [maʀasm] *nm* stagnation, slump

marathon [maʀatɔ̃] *nm* marathon

marbre [maʀbʀ] *nm* marble

marc [maʀ] *nm (de raisin, pommes)* marc

marchand, e [maʀʃɑ̃, ɑ̃d] *nm/f* shopkeeper, tradesman(-woman); *(au marché)* stallholder; *(de vins, charbon)* merchant ▷ *adj:* **prix/valeur ~(e)** market price/value; **marchand de fruits** fruiterer *(BRIT)*; fruit seller *(US)*; **marchand de journaux** newsagent; **marchand de légumes** greengrocer *(BRIT)*, produce dealer *(US)*; **marchand de poissons** fishmonger *(BRIT)*, fish seller *(US)*; **marchander** *vi* to bargain, haggle; **marchandise** *nf* goods *pl*, merchandise *no pl*

marche [maʀʃ] *nf (d'escalier)* step; *(activité)* walking; *(promenade, trajet, allure)* walk; *(démarche)* walk, gait; *(Mil etc, Mus)* march; *(fonctionnement)* running; *(des événements)* course; **dans le sens de la ~** *(Rail)* facing the engine; **en ~** *(monter etc)* while the vehicle is moving *ou* in motion; **mettre en ~** to start; **se mettre en ~** (*personne*) to get moving; (*machine*) to start; **être en état de ~** to be in working order; **marche à suivre** (correct) procedure; **marche arrière** reverse (gear); **faire marche arrière** to reverse; (*fig*) to backtrack, back-pedal

marché [maʀʃe] *nm* market; (*transaction*) bargain, deal; **faire du ~ noir** to buy and sell on the black market; **marché aux puces** flea market

marcher [maʀʃe] *vi* to walk; (*Mil*) to march; (*aller: voiture, train, affaires*) to go; (*prospérer*) to go well; (*fonctionner*) to work, run; (*fam: consentir*) to go along, agree; (: *croire naïvement*) to be taken in; **faire ~ qn** (*taquiner*) to pull sb's leg; (*tromper*) to lead sb up the garden path; **comment est-ce que ça marche?** how does this work?; **marcheur, -euse** *nm/f* walker

mardi [maʀdi] *nm* Tuesday; **Mardi gras** Shrove Tuesday

mare [maʀ] *nf* pond; (*flaque*) pool

marécage [maʀekaʒ] *nm* marsh, swamp; **marécageux, -euse** *adj* marshy

maréchal, -aux [maʀeʃal, o] *nm* marshal

marée [maʀe] *nf* tide; (*poissons*) fresh (sea) fish; **marée haute/basse** high/low tide; **marée noire** oil slick

marelle [maʀɛl] *nf:* **(jouer à) la ~** (to play) hopscotch

margarine [maʀgaʀin] *nf* margarine

marge [maʀʒ] *nf* margin; **en ~ de** (*fig*) on the fringe of; **marge bénéficiaire** profit margin

marginal, e, -aux [maʀʒinal, o] *nm/f* (*original*) eccentric; (*déshérité*) dropout

marguerite [maʀgəʀit] *nf* marguerite, (oxeye) daisy; (*d'imprimante*) daisy-wheel

mari [maʀi] *nm* husband

mariage [maʀjaʒ] *nm* marriage; (*noce*) wedding; **mariage civil/religieux** registry office (*BRIT*) *ou* civil wedding/church wedding

marié, e [maʀje] *adj* married ▷ *nm* (bride)groom; **les ~s** the bride and groom; **les (jeunes) ~s** the newly-weds

marier [maʀje] *vt* to marry; (*fig*) to blend; **se ~ (avec)** to marry, get married (to)

marin, e [maʀɛ̃, in] *adj* sea *cpd*, marine ▷ *nm* sailor

marine [maʀin] *adj voir* **marin** ▷ *adj inv* navy (blue) ▷ *nm* (*Mil*) marine ▷ *nf* navy; **marine marchande** merchant navy

mariner [maʀine] *vt:* **faire ~** to marinade

marionnette [maʀjɔnɛt] *nf* puppet

maritalement [maʀitalmɑ̃] *adv:* **vivre ~** to live as husband and wife

maritime [maʀitim] *adj* sea *cpd*, maritime

mark [maʀk] *nm* mark

marmelade [maʀməlad] *nf* stewed fruit, compote; **marmelade d'oranges** marmalade

marmite [maʀmit] *nf* (cooking-)pot

marmonner [maʀmɔne] *vt, vi* to mumble, mutter

marmotter [maʀmɔte] *vt* to mumble

Maroc [maʀɔk] *nm:* **le ~** Morocco; **marocain, e** [maʀɔkɛ̃, ɛn] *adj* Moroccan ▷ *nm/f:* **Marocain, e** Moroccan

maroquinerie [maʀɔkinʀi] *nf* (*articles*) fine leather goods *pl*; (*boutique*) shop selling fine leather goods

marquant, e [maʀkɑ̃, ɑ̃t] *adj* outstanding

marque [maʀk] *nf* mark; (*Comm: de nourriture*) brand; (: *de voiture, produits manufacturés*) make; (*de disques*) label; **de ~** (*produits*) high-class; (*visiteur etc*) distinguished, well-known; **une grande ~ de vin** a well-known brand of wine; **marque de fabrique** trademark; **marque déposée** registered trademark

marquer [maʀke] *vt* to mark; (*inscrire*) to write down; (*bétail*) to brand; (*Sport: but etc*) to score; (: *joueur*) to mark; (*accentuer: taille etc*) to emphasize; (*manifester: refus, intérêt*) to show ▷ *vi* (*événement*) to stand out, be outstanding; (*Sport*) to score; **~ les points** to keep the score

marqueterie [maʀkɛtʀi] *nf* inlaid work, marquetry

marquis [maʀki] *nm* marquis, marquess

marraine [maʀɛn] *nf* godmother

marrant, e [maʀɑ̃, ɑ̃t] (*fam*) *adj* funny

marre [maʀ] (*fam*) *adv:* **en avoir ~ de** to be fed up with

marrer [maʀe]: **se ~** (*fam*) *vi* to have a (good) laugh

marron [maʀɔ̃] *nm* (*fruit*) chestnut ▷ *adj inv* brown; **marrons glacés** candied chestnuts; **marronnier** *nm* chestnut (tree)

mars [maʀs] *nm* March

Marseille [maʀsɛj] *n* Marseilles

marteau, x [maʀto] *nm* hammer; **être ~** (*fam*) to be nuts; **marteau-piqueur** *nm* pneumatic drill

marteler [maʀtəle] *vt* to hammer

martien, ne [maʀsjɛ̃, jɛn] *adj* Martian, of *ou* from Mars

martyr, e [maʀtiʀ] *nm/f* martyr ▷ *adj:* **enfants ~s** battered children; **martyre** *nm* martyrdom; (*fig: sens affaibli*) agony, torture; **martyriser** *vt* (*Rel*) to martyr; (*fig*) to bully; (*enfant*) to batter, beat

marxiste [maʀksist] *adj, nm/f* Marxist

mascara [maskaʀa] *nm* mascara

masculin, e [maskylɛ̃, in] *adj* masculine; (*sexe, population*) male; (*équipe, vêtements*) men's; (*viril*) manly ▷ *nm* masculine

masochiste [mazɔʃist] *adj* masochistic

masque [mask] *nm* mask; **masque de beauté** face pack *ou* mask; **masque de plongée** diving mask; **masquer** *vt* (*cacher: paysage, porte*) to hide, conceal; (*dissimuler: vérité, projet*) to mask, obscure

massacre [masakʀ] *nm* massacre, slaughter; **massacrer** *vt* to massacre, slaughter; (*fam: texte etc*) to murder

massage [masaʒ] *nm* massage

masse [mas] *nf* mass; (*Élec*) earth; (*maillet*) sledgehammer; (*péj*): **la ~** the masses *pl*; **une ~ de** (*fam*) masses *ou* loads of; **en ~** *adv* (*acheter*) in bulk; (*en foule*) en masse ▷ *adj* (*exécutions, production*) mass *cpd*

masser [mase] *vt* (*assembler: gens*) to gather; (*pétrir*) to massage; **se ~** *vi* (*foule*) to gather; **masseur, -euse** *nm/f* masseur(-euse)

massif, -ive [masif, iv] *adj* (*porte*) solid, massive; (*visage*) heavy, large; (*bois, or*) solid; (*dose*) massive; (*déportations etc*) mass *cpd* ▷ *nm* (*montagneux*) massif; (*de fleurs*) clump, bank; **le M~ Central** the Massif Central

massue [masy] *nf* club, bludgeon

mastic [mastik] *nm* (*pour vitres*) putty; (*pour fentes*) filler

mastiquer [mastike] *vt* (*aliment*) to chew, masticate

mat, e [mat] *adj* (*couleur, métal*) mat(t); (*bruit, son*) dull ▷ *adj inv* (*Échecs*): **être ~** to be checkmate

mât [mɑ] *nm* (*Navig*) mast; (*poteau*) pole, post

match [matʃ] *nm* match; **faire ~ nul** to draw; **match aller** first leg; **match retour** second leg, return match

matelas [mat(ə)la] *nm* mattress; **matelas pneumatique** air bed *ou* mattress

matelot [mat(ə)lo] *nm* sailor, seaman

mater [mate] *vt* (*personne*) to bring to heel, subdue; (*révolte*) to put down

matérialiser [materjalize]: **se ~** vi to materialize
matérialiste [materjalist] adj materialistic
matériau [materjo] nm material; **matériaux** nmpl
material(s)
matériel, le [materjɛl] adj material ▷ nm equipment
no pl; (de camping etc) gear no pl; (Inform) hardware
maternel, le [matɛrnɛl] adj (amour, geste) motherly,
maternal; (grand-père, oncle) maternal; **maternelle** nf
(aussi: **école maternelle**) (state) nursery school
maternité [maternite] nf (établissement) maternity
hospital; (état de mère) motherhood, maternity;
(grossesse) pregnancy; **congé de ~** maternity leave
mathématique [matematik] adj mathematical;
mathématiques nfpl (science) mathematics sg
maths [mat] (fam) nfpl maths
matière [matjɛr] nf matter; (Comm, Tech) material,
matter no pl; (fig: d'un livre etc) subject matter, material;
(Scol) subject; **en ~ de** as regards; **matières grasses** fat
content sg; **matières premières** raw materials
Matignon [matiɲɔ̃] nm: **(l'hôtel) ~** the French Prime
Minister's residence
matin [matɛ̃] nm, adv morning; **le ~** (pendant le
matin) in the morning; **demain/hier/dimanche ~**
tomorrow/yesterday/Sunday morning; **tous les ~s**
every morning; **une heure du ~** one o'clock in the
morning; **du ~ au soir** from morning till night; **de bon
ou grand ~** early in the morning; **matinal, e, -aux**
adj (toilette, gymnastique) morning cpd; **être matinal**
(personne) to be up early; to be an early riser; **matinée**
nf morning; (spectacle) matinée
matou [matu] nm tom(cat)
matraque [matrak] nf (de policier) truncheon (BRIT),
billy (US)
matricule [matrikyl] nm (Mil) regimental number;
(Admin) reference number
matrimonial, e, -aux [matrimɔnjal, jo] adj marital,
marriage cpd
maudit, e [modi, -it] (fam) adj (satané) blasted,
confounded
maugréer [mogree] vi to grumble
maussade [mosad] adj sullen; (temps) gloomy
mauvais, e [mɔvɛ, ɛz] adj bad; (faux): **le ~ numéro/
moment** the wrong number/moment; (méchant,
malveillant) malicious, spiteful ▷ adv: **il fait ~** the
weather is bad; **sentir ~** to have a nasty smell, smell
nasty; **la mer est ~e** the sea is rough; **mauvais joueur**
bad loser; **mauvaise herbe** weed; **mauvaise langue**
gossip, scandalmonger (BRIT); **mauvaise plaisanterie**
nasty trick
mauve [mov] adj mauve
maux [mo] nmpl de **mal**
maximum [maksimɔm] adj, nm maximum; **au ~** (le plus
possible) as much as one can; (tout au plus) at the (very)
most ou maximum; **faire le ~** to do one's level best
mayonnaise [majɔnɛz] nf mayonnaise
mazout [mazut] nm (fuel) oil
me, m' [m(ə)] pron (direct: téléphoner, attendre etc) me;
(indirect: parler, donner etc) (to) me; (réfléchi) myself
mec [mɛk] (fam) nm bloke, guy
mécanicien, ne [mekanisjɛ̃, jɛn] nm/f mechanic;
(Rail) (train ou engine) driver; **pouvez-vous nous
envoyer un ~?** can you send a mechanic?
mécanique [mekanik] adj mechanical ▷ nf (science)
mechanics sg; (mécanisme) mechanism; **ennui ~** engine

trouble no pl
mécanisme [mekanism] nm mechanism
méchamment [meʃamɑ̃] adv nastily, maliciously,
spitefully
méchanceté [meʃɑ̃ste] nf nastiness, maliciousness;
dire des ~s à qn to say spiteful things to sb
méchant, e [meʃɑ̃, ɑ̃t] adj nasty, malicious, spiteful;
(enfant: pas sage) naughty; (animal) vicious
mèche [mɛʃ] nf (de cheveux) lock; (de lampe, bougie)
wick; (d'un explosif) fuse; **se faire faire des ~s** to have
highlights put in one's hair; **de ~ avec** in league with
méchoui [meʃwi] nm barbecue of a whole roast sheep
méconnaissable [mekɔnɛsabl] adj unrecognizable
méconnaître [mekɔnɛtr] vt (ignorer) to be unaware of;
(mésestimer) to misjudge
mécontent, e [mekɔ̃tɑ̃, ɑ̃t] adj: **~ (de)** discontented
ou dissatisfied ou displeased (with); (contrarié) annoyed
(at); **mécontentement** nm dissatisfaction, discontent,
displeasure; (irritation) annoyance
Mecque [mɛk] nf: **la ~** Mecca
médaille [medaj] nf medal
médaillon [medajɔ̃] nm (bijou) locket
médecin [med(ə)sɛ̃] nm doctor
médecine [med(ə)sin] nf medicine
média [medja] nmpl: **les ~** the media; **médiatique** adj
media cpd
médical, e, -aux [medikal, o] adj medical; **passer une
visite ~e** to have a medical
médicament [medikamɑ̃] nm medicine, drug
médiéval, e, -aux [medjeval, o] adj medieval
médiocre [medjɔkr] adj mediocre, poor
méditer [medite] vi to meditate
Méditerranée [mediterane] nf: **la (mer) ~** the
Mediterranean (Sea); **méditerranéen, ne** adj
Mediterranean ▷ nm/f: **Méditerranéen, ne** native ou
inhabitant of a Mediterranean country
méduse [medyz] nf jellyfish
méfait [mefɛ] nm (faute) misdemeanour, wrongdoing;
méfaits nmpl (ravages) ravages, damage sg
méfiance [mefjɑ̃s] nf mistrust, distrust
méfiant, e [mefjɑ̃, jɑ̃t] adj mistrustful, distrustful
méfier [mefje]: **se ~** vi to be wary; to be careful; **se ~
de** to mistrust, distrust, be wary of
mégaoctet [megaɔktɛ] nm megabyte
mégarde [megard] nf: **par ~** (accidentellement)
accidentally; (par erreur) by mistake
mégère [meʒɛr] nf shrew
mégot [mego] (fam) nm cigarette end
meilleur, e [mɛjœr] adj, adv better ▷ nm: **le ~** the best;
le ~ des deux the better of the two; **il fait ~ qu'hier**
it's better weather than yesterday; **meilleur marché**
(inv) cheaper
mél [mɛl] nm e-mail
mélancolie [melɑ̃kɔli] nf melancholy, gloom;
mélancolique adj melancholic, melancholy
mélange [melɑ̃ʒ] nm mixture; **mélanger** vt to mix;
(vins, couleurs) to blend; (mettre en désordre) to mix up,
muddle (up)
mêlée [mele] nf mêlée, scramble; (Rugby) scrum(mage)
mêler [mele] vt (unir) to mix; (embrouiller) to muddle
(up), mix up; **se ~** to mix, mingle; **se ~ à** (personne: se
joindre) to join; (: s'associer à) to mix with; **se ~ de** (suj:
personne) to meddle with, interfere in; **mêle-toi de
ce qui te regarde** ou **de tes affaires!** mind your own

business!

mélodie [melɔdi] *nf* melody; **mélodieux, -euse** *adj* melodious

melon [m(ə)lɔ̃] *nm* (Bot) (honeydew) melon; (aussi: **chapeau ~**) bowler (hat)

membre [mãbr] *nm* (Anat) limb; (personne, pays, élément) member ▷ *adj* member cpd

mémé [meme] (fam) *nf* granny

MOT-CLÉ

même [mɛm] *adj* **1** (avant le nom) same; **en même temps** at the same time; **ils ont les mêmes goûts** they have the same ou similar tastes

2 (après le nom: renforcement): **il est la loyauté même** he is loyalty itself; **ce sont ses paroles mêmes** they are his very words

▷ *pron*: **le(la) même** the same one

▷ *adv* **1** (renforcement): **il n'a même pas pleuré** he didn't even cry; **même lui l'a dit** even HE said it; **ici même** at this very place; **même si** even if

2: **à même**: **à même la bouteille** straight from the bottle; **à même la peau** next to the skin; **être à même de faire** to be in a position to do, be able to do

3: **de même**: **faire de même** to do likewise; **lui de même** so does (ou did ou is) he; **de même que** just as; **il en va de même pour** the same goes for

mémoire [memwar] *nf* memory ▷ *nm* (Scol) dissertation, paper; **mémoires** *nmpl* (souvenirs) memoirs; **à la ~ de** to the ou in memory of; **de ~** from memory; **mémoire morte** read-only memory, ROM; **mémoire vive** random access memory, RAM

mémorable [memɔrabl] *adj* memorable, unforgettable

menace [mənas] *nf* threat; **menacer** *vt* to threaten

ménage [menaʒ] *nm* (travail) housework; (couple) (married) couple; (famille, Admin) household; **faire le ~** to do the housework; **ménagement** *nm* care and attention; **ménager, -ère** *adj* household cpd, domestic ▷ *vt* (traiter: personne) to handle with tact; (utiliser) to use sparingly; (prendre soin de) to take (great) care of, look after; (organiser) to arrange; **ménagère** *nf* housewife

mendiant, e [mãdjã, jãt] *nm/f* beggar

mendier [mãdje] *vi* to beg ▷ *vt* to beg (for)

mener [m(ə)ne] *vt* to lead; (enquête) to conduct; (affaires) to manage ▷ *vi*: **~ à/dans** (emmener) to take to/into; **~ qch à bien** to see sth through (to a successful conclusion), complete sth successfully

meneur, -euse [mənœr, øz] *nm/f* leader; (péj) agitator

méningite [menẽʒit] *nf* meningitis no pl

ménopause [menopoz] *nf* menopause

menottes [mənɔt] *nfpl* handcuffs

mensonge [mãsõʒ] *nm* lie; (action) lying no pl; **mensonger, -ère** *adj* false

mensualité [mãsɥalite] *nf* (traite) monthly payment

mensuel, le [mãsɥɛl] *adj* monthly

mensurations [mãsyrasjõ] *nfpl* measurements

mental, e, -aux [mãtal, o] *adj* mental; **mentalité** *nf* mentality

menteur, -euse [mãtœr, øz] *nm/f* liar

menthe [mãt] *nf* mint

mention [mãsjõ] *nf* (annotation) note, comment; (Scol) grade; **~ bien** ≈ grade B, ≈ good pass; (Université) ≈ upper

2nd class pass (BRIT), ≈ pass with (high) honors (US); (Admin): **"rayer les ~s inutiles"** "delete as appropriate"; **mentionner** *vt* to mention

mentir [mãtir] *vi* to lie

menton [mãtõ] *nm* chin

menu, e [məny] *adj* (personne) slim, slight; (frais, difficulté) minor ▷ *adv* (couper, hacher) very fine ▷ *nm* menu; **~ touristique/gastronomique** economy/gourmet's menu

menuiserie [mənɥizri] *nf* (métier) joinery, carpentry; (passe-temps) woodwork; **menuisier** *nm* joiner, carpenter

méprendre [meprãdr]: **se ~** *vi*: **se ~ sur** to be mistaken (about)

mépris [mepri] *nm* (dédain) contempt, scorn; **au ~ de** regardless of, in defiance of; **méprisable** *adj* contemptible, despicable; **méprisant, e** *adj* scornful; **méprise** *nf* mistake, error; **mépriser** *vt* to scorn, despise; (gloire, danger) to scorn, spurn

mer [mɛr] *nf* sea; (marée) tide; **en ~** at sea; **en haute** ou **pleine ~** off shore, on the open sea; **la ~ du Nord/Rouge/Noire/Morte** the North/Red/Black/Dead Sea

mercenaire [mɛrsənɛr] *nm* mercenary, hired soldier

mercerie [mɛrsəri] *nf* (boutique) haberdasher's shop (BRIT), notions store (US)

merci [mɛrsi] *excl* thank you ▷ *nf*: **à la ~ de qn/qch** at sb's mercy/the mercy of sth; **~ beaucoup** thank you very much; **~ de** thank you for; **sans ~** merciless(ly)

mercredi [mɛrkrədi] *nm* Wednesday; **~ des Cendres** Ash Wednesday; voir aussi **lundi**

mercure [mɛrkyr] *nm* mercury

merde [mɛrd] (fam!) *nf* shit (!) ▷ *excl* (bloody) hell (!)

mère [mɛr] *nf* mother; **mère célibataire** single parent, unmarried mother; **mère de famille** housewife, mother

merguez [mɛrgɛz] *nf* merguez sausage (type of spicy sausage from N Africa)

méridional, e, -aux [meridjɔnal, o] *adj* southern ▷ *nm/f* Southerner

meringue [mərɛ̃g] *nf* meringue

mérite [merit] *nm* merit; **avoir du ~ (à faire qch)** to deserve credit (for doing sth); **mériter** *vt* to deserve

merle [mɛrl] *nm* blackbird

merveille [mɛrvɛj] *nf* marvel, wonder; **faire ~** to work wonders; **à ~** perfectly, wonderfully; **merveilleux, -euse** *adj* marvellous, wonderful

mes [me] *adj* voir **mon**

mésange [mezãʒ] *nf* tit (mouse)

mésaventure [mezavãtyr] *nf* misadventure, misfortune

Mesdames [medam] *nfpl* de **Madame**

Mesdemoiselles [medmwazɛl] *nfpl* de **Mademoiselle**

mesquin, e [mɛskɛ̃, in] *adj* mean, petty; **mesquinerie** *nf* meanness; (procédé) mean trick

message [mesaʒ] *nm* message; **est-ce que je peux laisser un ~?** can I leave a message?; **~ SMS** text message; **messager, -ère** *nm/f* messenger; **messagerie** *nf* (Internet): **messagerie électronique** e-mail; **messagerie vocale** (service) voice mail; **messagerie instantanée** instant messenger

messe [mɛs] *nf* mass; **aller à la ~** to go to mass

Messieurs [mesjø] *nmpl* de **Monsieur**

mesure [m(ə)zyr] *nf* (évaluation, dimension) measurement; (récipient) measure; (Mus: cadence) time, tempo; (: *division*) bar; (*retenue*) moderation; (*disposition*) measure, step; **sur ~** (*costume*) made-to-measure; **dans la ~ où** insofar as, inasmuch as; **à ~ que** as; **être en ~ de** to be in a position to; **dans une certaine ~** to a certain extent

mesurer [məzyʀe] vt to measure; (*juger*) to weigh up, assess; (*modérer: ses paroles etc*) to moderate

métal, -aux [metal, o] nm metal; **métallique** adj metallic

météo [meteo] nf (*bulletin*) weather report

météorologie [meteˈlɔʒi] nf meteorology

méthode [metɔd] nf method; (*livre, ouvrage*) manual, tutor

méticuleux, -euse [metikylø, øz] adj meticulous

métier [metje] nm (*profession: gén*) job; (: *manuel*) trade; (*artisanal*) craft; (*technique, expérience*) (acquired) skill ou technique; (*aussi*: **à tisser**) (weaving) loom

métis, se [metis] adj, nm/f half-caste, half-breed

métrage [metʀaʒ] nm: **long/moyen/court ~** full-length/medium-length/short film

mètre [mɛtʀ] nm metre; (*règle*) (metre) rule; (*ruban*) tape measure; **métrique** adj metric

métro [metʀo] nm underground (BRIT), subway

métropole [metʀɔpɔl] nf (*capitale*) metropolis; (*pays*) home country

mets [mɛ] nm dish

metteur [metœʀ] nm: **~ en scène** (*Théâtre*) producer; (*Cinéma*) director

MOT-CLÉ

mettre [mɛtʀ] vt **1** (*placer*) to put; **mettre en bouteille/en sac** to bottle/put in bags ou sacks

2 (*vêtements: revêtir*) to put on; (: *porter*) to wear; **mets ton gilet** put your cardigan on; **je ne mets plus mon manteau** I no longer wear my coat

3 (*faire fonctionner: chauffage, électricité*) to put on; (: *réveil, minuteur*) to set; (*installer: gaz, eau*) to put in, lay on; **mettre en marche** to start up

4 (*consacrer*): **mettre du temps à faire qch** to take time to do sth ou over sth

5 (*noter, écrire*) to say, put (down); **qu'est-ce qu'il a mis sur la carte?** what did he say ou write on the card?; **mettez au pluriel ...** put ... into the plural

6 (*supposer*): **mettons que ...** let's suppose ou say that ...

7: **y mettre du sien** to pull one's weight

se mettre vi **1** (*se placer*): **vous pouvez vous mettre là** you can sit (ou stand) there; **où ça se met?** where does it go?; **se mettre au lit** to get into bed; **se mettre au piano** to sit down at the piano; **se mettre de l'encre sur les doigts** to get ink on one's fingers

2 (*s'habiller*): **se mettre en maillot de bain** to get into ou put on a swimsuit; **n'avoir rien à se mettre** to have nothing to wear

3: **se mettre à** to begin, start; **se mettre à faire** to begin ou start doing ou to do; **se mettre au piano** to start learning the piano; **se mettre au régime** to go on a diet; **se mettre au travail/à l'étude** to get down to work/one's studies

meuble [mœbl] nm piece of furniture; **des ~s** furniture; **meublé** nm furnished flatlet (BRIT) ou room; **meubler** vt to furnish

meuf [mœf] nf (*fam*) woman

meugler [møgle] vi to low, moo

meule [møl] nf (*de foin, blé*) stack; (*de fromage*) round; (*à broyer*) millstone

meunier [mønje] nm miller

meurs etc [mœʀ] vb voir **mourir**

meurtre [mœʀtʀ] nm murder; **meurtrier, -ière** adj (*arme etc*) deadly; (*fureur, instincts*) murderous ▷ nm/f murderer(-eress)

meurtrir [mœʀtʀiʀ] vt to bruise; (*fig*) to wound

meus etc [mœ] vb voir **mouvoir**

meute [møt] nf pack

mexicain, e [mɛksikɛ̃, ɛn] adj Mexican ▷ nm/f: **M~, e** Mexican

Mexico [mɛksiko] n Mexico City

Mexique [mɛksik] nm: **le ~** Mexico

mi [mi] nm (*Mus*) E; (*en chantant la gamme*) mi ▷ préfixe: **mi...** half(-); mid-; **à la mi-janvier** in mid-January; **à mi-jambes/corps** (up ou down) to the knees/waist; **à mi-hauteur** halfway up

miauler [mjole] vi to mew

miche [miʃ] nf round ou cob loaf

mi-chemin [miʃmɛ̃]: **à ~** adv halfway, midway

mi-clos, e [miklo, kloz] adj half-closed

micro [mikʀo] nm mike, microphone; (*Inform*) micro

microbe [mikʀɔb] nm germ, microbe

micro...: **micro-onde** nf: **four à micro-ondes** microwave oven; **micro-ordinateur** nm microcomputer; **microscope** nm microscope; **microscopique** adj microscopic

midi [midi] nm midday, noon; (*moment du déjeuner*) lunchtime; (*sud*) south; **à ~** at 12 (o'clock) ou midday ou noon; **le M~** the South (of France), the Midi

mie [mi] nf crumb (of the loaf)

miel [mjɛl] nm honey; **mielleux, -euse** adj (*personne*) unctuous, syrupy

mien, ne [mjɛ̃, mjɛn] pron: **le(la) ~(ne), les ~(ne)s** mine; **les ~s** my family

miette [mjɛt] nf (*de pain, gâteau*) crumb; (*fig: de la conversation etc*) scrap; **en ~s** in pieces ou bits

MOT-CLÉ

mieux [mjø] adv **1** (*d'une meilleure façon*): **mieux (que)** better (than); **elle travaille/mange mieux** she works/eats better; **aimer mieux** to prefer; **elle va mieux** she is better; **de mieux en mieux** better and better

2 (*de la meilleure façon*) best; **ce que je connais le mieux** what I know best; **les livres les mieux faits** the best-made books

▷ adj **1** (*plus à l'aise, en meilleure forme*) better; **se sentir mieux** to feel better

2 (*plus satisfaisant*) better; **c'est mieux ainsi** it's better like this; **c'est le mieux des deux** it's the better of the two; **le(la) mieux, les mieux** the best; **demandez-lui, c'est le mieux** ask him, it's the best thing

3 (*plus joli*) better-looking; **il est mieux que son frère** (*plus beau*) he's better-looking than his brother; (*plus gentil*) he's nicer than his brother; **il est mieux sans moustache** he looks better without a moustache

4: **au mieux** at best; **au mieux avec** on the best of terms with; **pour le mieux** for the best

▷ nm **1** (progrès) improvement
2: de mon/ton **mieux** as best I/you can (ou could);
faire de son mieux to do one's best

mignon, ne [miɲɔ̃, ɔn] adj sweet, cute
migraine [migʀɛn] nf headache; (Méd) migraine
mijoter [miʒɔte] vt to simmer; (préparer avec soin) to
cook lovingly; (fam: tramer) to plot, cook up ▷ vi to
simmer
milieu, x [miljø] nm (centre) middle; (Bio, Géo)
environment; (entourage social) milieu; (provenance)
background; (pègre): **le ~** the underworld; **au ~ de** in the
middle of; **au beau** ou **en plein ~ (de)** right in the middle
(of); **un juste ~** a happy medium
militaire [militɛʀ] adj military, army cpd ▷ nm
serviceman
militant, e [militɑ̃, ɑ̃t] adj, nm/f militant
militer [milite] vi to be a militant
mille [mil] num a ou one thousand ▷ nm (mesure): **~
(marin)** nautical mile; **mettre dans le ~** (fig) to be
bang on target; **millefeuille** nm cream ou vanilla slice;
millénaire nm millennium ▷ adj thousand-year-old;
(fig) ancient; **mille-pattes** nm inv centipede
millet [mijɛ] nm millet
milliard [miljaʀ] nm milliard, thousand million (BRIT),
billion (US); **milliardaire** nm/f multimillionaire (BRIT),
billionaire (US)
millier [milje] nm thousand; **un ~ (de)** a thousand or
so, about a thousand; **par ~s** in (their) thousands, by
the thousand
milligramme [miligʀam] nm milligramme
millimètre [milimɛtʀ] nm millimetre
million [miljɔ̃] nm million; **deux ~s de** two million;
millionnaire nm/f millionaire
mime [mim] nm/f (acteur) mime(r) ▷ nm (art) mime,
miming; **mimer** vt to mime; (singer) to mimic, take off
minable [minabl] adj (décrépit) shabby(-looking);
(médiocre) pathetic
mince [mɛ̃s] adj thin; (personne, taille) slim, slender;
(fig: profit, connaissances) slight, small, weak ▷ excl:
~ alors! drat it!, darn it! (US); **minceur** nf thinness;
(d'une personne) slimness, slenderness; **mincir** vi to get
slimmer
mine [min] nf (physionomie) expression, look; (allure)
exterior, appearance; (de crayon) lead; (gisement, explosif,
fig: source) mine; **avoir bonne ~** (personne) to look
well; (ironique) to look an utter idiot; **avoir mauvaise
~** to look unwell ou poorly; **faire ~ de faire** to make a
pretence of doing; **~ de rien** although you wouldn't
think so
miner [mine] vt (saper) to undermine, erode; (Mil) to
mine
minerai [minʀɛ] nm ore
minéral, e, -aux [mineral, o] adj, nm mineral
minéralogique [mineralɔʒik] adj: **plaque ~** number
(BRIT) ou license (US) plate; **numéro ~** registration (BRIT)
ou license (US) number
minet, te [minɛ, ɛt] nm/f (chat) pussy-cat; (péj) young
trendy
mineur, e [minœʀ] adj minor ▷ nm/f (Jur) minor,
person under age ▷ nm (travailleur) miner
miniature [minjatyʀ] adj, nf miniature
minibus [minibys] nm minibus
minier, -ière [minje, jɛʀ] adj mining

mini-jupe [miniʒyp] nf mini-skirt
minime [minim] adj minor, minimal
minimessage [minimesaʒ] nm text message
minimiser [minimize] vt to minimize; (fig) to play
down
minimum [minimɔm] adj, nm minimum; **au ~** (au
moins) at the very least
ministère [ministɛʀ] nm (aussi Rel) ministry; (cabinet)
government
ministre [ministʀ] nm (aussi Rel) minister; **ministre
d'État** senior minister ou secretary
Minitel® [minitɛl] nm videotext terminal and service
minoritaire [minɔʀitɛʀ] adj minority
minorité [minɔʀite] nf minority; **être en ~** to be in the
ou a minority
minuit [minɥi] nm midnight
minuscule [minyskyl] adj minute, tiny ▷ nf: **(lettre)
~** small letter
minute [minyt] nf minute; **à la ~** (just) this instant;
(faire) there and then; **minuter** vt to time; **minuterie**
nf time switch
minutieux, -euse [minysjø, jøz] adj (personne)
meticulous; (travail) minutely detailed
mirabelle [miʀabɛl] nf (cherry) plum
miracle [miʀakl] nm miracle
mirage [miʀaʒ] nm mirage
mire [miʀ] nf: **point de ~** (fig) focal point
miroir [miʀwaʀ] nm mirror
miroiter [miʀwate] vi to sparkle, shimmer; **faire ~ qch
à qn** to paint sth in glowing colours for sb, dangle sth in
front of sb's eyes
mis, e [mi, miz] pp de **mettre** ▷ adj: **bien ~** well-dressed
mise [miz] nf (argent: au jeu) stake; (tenue) clothing,
attire; **être de ~** to be acceptable ou in season; **mise à
jour** updating; **mise au point** (fig) clarification; **mise de
fonds** capital outlay; **mise en plis** set; **mise en scène**
production
miser [mize] vt (enjeu) to stake, bet; **~ sur** (cheval,
numéro) to bet on; (fig) to bank ou count on
misérable [mizeʀabl] adj (lamentable, malheureux)
pitiful, wretched; (pauvre) poverty-stricken; (insignifiant,
mesquin) miserable ▷ nm/f wretch
misère [mizɛʀ] nf (extreme) poverty, destitution;
misères nfpl (malheurs) woes, miseries; (ennuis) little
troubles; **salaire de ~** starvation wage
missile [misil] nm missile
mission [misjɔ̃] nf mission; **partir en ~** (Admin, Pol) to
go on an assignment; **missionnaire** nm/f missionary
mité, e [mite] adj moth-eaten
mi-temps [mitɑ̃] nf inv (Sport: période) half; (: pause)
half-time; **à ~** part-time
miteux, -euse [mitø, øz] adj (lieu) seedy
mitigé, e [mitiʒe] adj: **sentiments ~s** mixed feelings
mitoyen, ne [mitwajɛ̃, jɛn] adj (mur) common, party
cpd; **maisons ~nes** semi-detached houses; (plus de deux)
terraced (BRIT) ou row (US) houses
mitrailler [mitʀaje] vt to machine-gun; (fig) to pelt,
bombard; (: photographier) to take shot after shot of;
mitraillette nf submachine gun; **mitrailleuse** nf
machine gun
mi-voix [mivwa]: **à ~** adv in a low ou hushed voice
mixage [miksaʒ] nm (Cinéma) (sound) mixing
mixer [miksœʀ] nm (food) mixer
mixte [mikst] adj (gén) mixed; (Scol) mixed,

coeducational; **cuisinière ~** combined gas and electric cooker (BRIT) ou stove (US)

mixture [mikstyʀ] nf mixture; (fig) concoction

Mlle (pl **~s**) abr = **Mademoiselle**

MM abr = **Messieurs**

Mme (pl **~s**) abr = **Madame**

mobile [mɔbil] adj mobile; (pièce de machine) moving ▷ nm (motif) motive; (œuvre d'art) mobile; **(téléphone) ~** nm (phone)

mobilier, -ière [mɔbilje, jɛʀ] nm furniture

mobiliser [mɔbilize] vt to mobilize

mocassin [mɔkasɛ̃] nm moccasin

moche [mɔʃ] (fam) adj (laid) ugly; (mauvais) rotten

modalité [mɔdalite] nf form, mode

mode [mɔd] nf fashion ▷ nm (manière) form, mode; (Ling) mood; (Mus, Inform) mode; **à la ~** fashionable, in fashion; **mode d'emploi** directions pl (for use); **mode de paiement** method of payment; **mode de vie** lifestyle

modèle [mɔdɛl] adj, nm model; (qui pose: de peintre) sitter; **modèle déposé** registered design; **modèle réduit** small-scale model; **modeler** vt to model

modem [mɔdɛm] nm modem

modéré, e [mɔdeʀe] adj, nm/f moderate

modérer [mɔdeʀe] vt to moderate; **se ~** vi to restrain o.s.

moderne [mɔdɛʀn] adj modern ▷ nm (style) modern style; (meubles) modern furniture; **moderniser** vt to modernize

modeste [mɔdɛst] adj modest; **modestie** nf modesty

modifier [mɔdifje] vt to modify, alter; **se ~** vi to alter

modique [mɔdik] adj modest

module [mɔdyl] nm module

moelle [mwal] nf marrow

moelleux, -euse [mwalø, øz] adj soft; (gâteau) light and moist

mœurs [mœʀ] nfpl (conduite) morals; (manières) manners; (pratiques sociales, mode de vie) habits

moi [mwa] pron me; (emphatique): **~, je ...** for my part, I ..., I myself ...; **c'est ~ qui l'ai fait** I did it, it was me who did it; **apporte-le-~** bring it to me; **à ~** mine; (dans un jeu) my turn; **moi-même** pron myself; (emphatique) I myself

moindre [mwɛ̃dʀ] adj lesser; lower; **le(la) ~, les ~s** the least, the slightest; **merci - c'est la ~ des choses!** thank you - it's a pleasure!

moine [mwan] nm monk, friar

moineau, x [mwano] nm sparrow

⭕ **MOT-CLÉ**

moins [mwɛ̃] adv **1** (comparatif): **moins (que)** less (than); **moins grand que** less tall than, not as tall as; **il a 3 ans de moins que moi** he's 3 years younger than me; **moins je travaille, mieux je me porte** the less I work, the better I feel

2 (superlatif): **le moins** (the) least; **c'est ce que j'aime le moins** it's what I like (the) least; **le(la) moins doué(e)** the least gifted; **au moins, du moins** at least; **pour le moins** at the very least

3: **moins de** (quantité) less (than); (nombre) fewer (than); **moins de sable/d'eau** less sand/water; **moins de livres/gens** fewer books/people; **moins de 2 ans** less than 2 years; **moins de midi** not yet midday

4: **de moins, en moins: 100 euros/3 jours de moins** 100 euros/3 days less; **3 livres en moins** 3 books fewer;

3 books too few; de l'argent en moins less money; **le soleil en moins** but for the sun, minus the sun; **de moins en moins** less and less

5: **à moins de, à moins que** unless; **à moins de faire** unless we do (ou he does etc); **à moins que tu ne fasses** unless you do; **à moins d'un accident** barring any accident

▷ prép: **4 moins 2** 4 minus 2; **il est moins 5** it's 5 to; **il fait moins 5** it's 5 (degrees) below (freezing), it's minus 5

mois [mwa] nm month

moisi [mwazi] nm mould, mildew; **odeur de ~** musty smell; **moisir** vi to go mouldy; **moisissure** nf mould no pl

moisson [mwasɔ̃] nf harvest; **moissonner** vt to harvest, reap; **moissonneuse** nf (machine) harvester

moite [mwat] adj sweaty, sticky

moitié [mwatje] nf half; **la ~** half; **la ~ de** half (of); **la ~ du temps** half the time; **à la ~ de** halfway through; **à ~** (avant le verbe) half; (avant l'adjectif) half-; **~ prix** (at) half-price

molaire [mɔlɛʀ] nf molar

molester [mɔlɛste] vt to manhandle, maul (about)

molle [mɔl] adj voir **mou**; **mollement** adv (péj: travailler) sluggishly; (protester) feebly

mollet [mɔlɛ] nm calf ▷ adj m: **œuf ~** soft-boiled egg

molletonné, e [mɔltɔne] adj fleece-lined

mollir [mɔliʀ] vi (fléchir) to relent; (substance) to go soft

mollusque [mɔlysk] nm mollusc

môme [mom] (fam) nm/f (enfant) brat

moment [mɔmɑ̃] nm moment; **ce n'est pas le ~** this is not the (right) time; **au même ~** at the same time; (instant) at the same moment; **pour un bon ~** for a good while; **pour le ~** for the moment, for the time being; **au ~ de** at the time of; **au ~ où** just as; **à tout ~** (peut arriver etc) at any time ou moment; (constamment) constantly, continually; **en ce ~** at the moment; at present; **sur le ~** at the time; **par ~s** now and then, at times; **d'un ~ à l'autre** any time (now); **du ~ où ou que** seeing that, since; **momentané, e** adj temporary, momentary; **momentanément** adv (court instant) for a short while

momie [mɔmi] nf mummy

mon, ma [mɔ̃, ma] (pl **mes**) adj my

Monaco [mɔnako] nm Monaco

monarchie [mɔnaʀʃi] nf monarchy

monastère [mɔnastɛʀ] nm monastery

mondain, e [mɔdɛ̃, ɛn] adj (vie) society cpd

monde [mɔd] nm world; (haute société): **le ~** (high) society; **il y a du ~** (beaucoup de gens) there are a lot of people; (quelques personnes) there are some people; **beaucoup/peu de ~** many/few people; **mettre au ~** to bring into the world; **pas le moins du ~** not in the least; **mondial, e, -aux** adj (population) world cpd; (influence) world-wide; **mondialement** adv throughout the world; **mondialisation** nf globalization

monégasque [mɔnegask] adj Monegasque, of ou from Monaco ▷ nm/f: **M~** Monegasque, person from ou inhabitant of Monaco

monétaire [mɔnetɛʀ] adj monetary

moniteur, -trice [mɔnitœʀ, tʀis] nm/f (Sport) instructor(-tress); (de colonie de vacances) supervisor ▷ nm (écran) monitor

monnaie [mɔnɛ] nf (Écon, gén: moyen d'échange) currency; (petites pièces): **avoir de la ~** to have (some) change; **une pièce de ~** coin; **faire de la ~** to get (some) change; **avoir/faire la ~ de 20 euros** to have change of/get change for 20 euros; **rendre à qn la ~ (sur 20 euros)** to give sb the change (out of ou from 20 euros); **gardez la ~** keep the change; **désolé, je n'ai pas de ~** sorry, I don't have any change; **avez-vous de la ~?** do you have any change?

monologue [mɔnɔlɔɡ] nm monologue, soliloquy; **monologuer** vi to soliloquize

monopole [mɔnɔpɔl] nm monopoly

monotone [mɔnɔtɔn] adj monotonous

Monsieur [məsjø] (pl **Messieurs**) titre Mr ▷ nm (homme quelconque): **un/le monsieur** a/the gentleman; **~, ...** (en tête de lettre) Dear Sir, ...; voir aussi **Madame**

monstre [mɔstʀ] nm monster ▷ adj (fam: colossal): **un travail ~** a fantastic amount of work; **monstrueux, -euse** adj monstrous

mont [mɔ̃] nm: **par ~s et par vaux** up hill and down dale; **le Mont Blanc** Mont Blanc

montage [mɔ̃taʒ] nm (assemblage: d'appareil) assembly; (Photo) photomontage; (Cinéma) editing

montagnard, e [mɔ̃taɲaʀ, aʀd] adj mountain cpd ▷ nm/f mountain-dweller

montagne [mɔ̃taɲ] nf (cime) mountain; (région): **la ~** the mountains pl; **montagnes russes** big dipper sg, switchback sg; **montagneux, -euse** adj mountainous; (basse montagne) hilly

montant, e [mɔ̃tɑ̃, ɑ̃t] adj rising; **pull à col ~** high-necked jumper ▷ nm (somme, total) (sum) total, (total) amount; (de fenêtre) upright; (de lit) post

monte-charge [mɔ̃tʃaʀʒ] nm inv goods lift, hoist

montée [mɔ̃te] nf (des prix, hostilités) rise; (escalade) climb; (côte) hill; **au milieu de la ~** halfway up

monter [mɔ̃te] vt (escalier, côte) to go up (ou come) up; (valise, paquet) to take (ou bring) up; (étagère) to raise; (tente, échafaudage) to put up; (machine) to assemble; (Cinéma) to edit; (Théâtre) to put on, stage; (société etc) to set up ▷ vi to go (ou come) up; (prix, niveau, température) to go up, rise; (passager) to get on; **~ à cheval** (faire du cheval) to ride (a horse); **~ sur** to climb up onto; **~ sur ou à un arbre/une échelle** to climb (up) a tree/ladder; **se ~ à** (frais etc) to add up to

montgolfière [mɔ̃ɡɔlfjɛʀ] nf hot-air balloon

montre [mɔ̃tʀ] nf watch; **contre la ~** (Sport) against the clock

Montréal [mɔ̃real] n Montreal

montrer [mɔ̃tre] vt to show; **~ qch à qn** to show sb sth; **pouvez-vous me ~ où c'est?** can you show me where it is?

monture [mɔ̃tyʀ] nf (cheval) mount; (de lunettes) frame; (d'une bague) setting

monument [mɔnymɑ̃] nm monument; **monument aux morts** war memorial

moquer [mɔke]: **se ~ de** vt to make fun of, laugh at; (fam: se désintéresser de) not to care about; (tromper): **se ~ de qn** to take sb for a ride

moquette [mɔkɛt] nf fitted carpet

moqueur, -euse [mɔkœʀ, øz] adj mocking

moral, e, -aux [mɔʀal, o] adj moral ▷ nm morale; **avoir le ~** (fam) to be in good spirits; **avoir le ~ à zéro** (fam) to be really down; **morale** nf (mœurs) morals pl; (valeurs) moral standards pl, morality; (d'une fable etc) moral; **faire la morale à** to lecture, preach at; **moralité** nf morality; (de fable) moral

morceau, x [mɔʀso] nm piece, bit; (d'une œuvre) passage, extract; (Mus) piece; (Culin: de viande) cut; (de sucre) lump; **mettre en ~x** to pull to pieces ou bits; **manger un ~** to have a bite (to eat)

morceler [mɔʀsəle] vt to break up, divide up

mordant, e [mɔʀdɑ̃, ɑ̃t] adj (ton, remarque) scathing, cutting; (ironie, froid) biting ▷ nm (style) bite, punch

mordiller [mɔʀdije] vt to nibble at, chew at

mordre [mɔʀdʀ] vt to bite ▷ vi (poisson) to bite; **~ sur** (fig) to go over into, overlap into; **~ à l'hameçon** to bite, rise to the bait

mordu, e [mɔʀdy] (fam) nm/f enthusiast; **un ~ de jazz** a jazz fanatic

morfondre [mɔʀfɔ̃dʀ]: **se ~** vi to mope

morgue [mɔʀɡ] nf (arrogance) haughtiness; (lieu: de la police) morgue; (: à l'hôpital) mortuary

morne [mɔʀn] adj dismal, dreary

morose [mɔʀoz] adj sullen, morose

mors [mɔʀ] nm bit

morse [mɔʀs] nm (Zool) walrus; (Tél) Morse (code)

morsure [mɔʀsyʀ] nf bite

mort[1] [mɔʀ] nf death

mort[2], e [mɔʀ, mɔʀt] pp de **mourir** ▷ adj dead ▷ nm/f (défunt) dead man ou woman; (victime): **il y a eu plusieurs ~s** several people were killed, there were several killed; **~ de peur/fatigue** frightened to death/dead tired

mortalité [mɔʀtalite] nf mortality, death rate

mortel, le [mɔʀtɛl] adj (poison etc) deadly, lethal; (accident, blessure) fatal; (silence, ennemi) deadly; (péché) mortal; (fam: ennuyeux) deadly boring

mort-né, e [mɔʀne] adj (enfant) stillborn

mortuaire [mɔʀtɥɛʀ] adj: **avis ~** death announcement

morue [mɔʀy] nf (Zool) cod inv

mosaïque [mɔzaik] nf mosaic

Moscou [mɔsku] n Moscow

mosquée [mɔske] nf mosque

mot [mo] nm word; (message) line, note; **~ à ~** word for word; **mot de passe** password; **mots croisés** crossword (puzzle) sg

motard [mɔtaʀ] nm biker; (policier) motorcycle cop

motel [mɔtɛl] nm motel

moteur, -trice [mɔtœʀ, tʀis] adj (Anat, Physiol) motor; (Tech) driving; (Auto): **à 4 roues motrices** 4-wheel drive ▷ nm engine, motor; **à ~** power-driven, motor cpd; **moteur de recherche** search engine

motif [mɔtif] nm (cause) motive; (décoratif) design, pattern, motif; **sans ~** groundless

motivation [mɔtivasjɔ̃] nf motivation

motiver [mɔtive] vt to motivate; (justifier) to justify, account for

moto [mɔto] nf (motor)bike; **motocycliste** nm/f motorcyclist

motorisé, e [mɔtɔʀize] adj (personne) having transport ou a car

motrice [mɔtʀis] adj voir **moteur**

motte [mɔt] nf: **~ de terre** lump of earth, clod (of earth); **motte de beurre** lump of butter

mou (mol), molle [mu, mɔl] adj soft; (personne) lethargic; (protestations) weak ▷ nm: **avoir du mou** to be slack

mouche [muʃ] nf fly

moucher [muʃe]: **se ~** vi to blow one's nose

moucheron [muʃʀɔ̃] nm midge

mouchoir [muʃwaʀ] nm handkerchief, hanky; **mouchoir en papier** tissue, paper hanky

moudre [mudʀ] vt to grind

moue [mu] nf pout; **faire la ~** to pout; (fig) to pull a face

mouette [mwɛt] nf (sea)gull

moufle [mufl] nf (gant) mitt(en)

mouillé, e [muje] adj wet

mouiller [muje] vt (humecter) to wet, moisten; (tremper): **~ qn/qch** to make sb/sth wet ▷ vi (Navig) to lie ou be at anchor; **se ~** to get wet; (fam: prendre des risques) to commit o.s.

moulant, e [mulã, ãt] adj figure-hugging

moule [mul] nf mussel ▷ nm (Culin) mould; **moule à gâteaux** nm cake tin (BRIT) ou pan (US)

mouler [mule] vt (suj: vêtement) to hug, fit closely round

moulin [mulɛ̃] nm mill; **moulin à café** coffee mill; **moulin à eau** watermill; **moulin à légumes** (vegetable) shredder; **moulin à paroles** (fig) chatterbox; **moulin à poivre** pepper mill; **moulin à vent** windmill

moulinet [mulinɛ] nm (de canne à pêche) reel; (mouvement): **faire des ~s avec qch** to whirl sth around

moulinette® [mulinɛt] nf (vegetable) shredder

moulu, e [muly] pp de **moudre**

mourant, e [muʀã, ãt] adj dying

mourir [muʀiʀ] vi to die; (civilisation) to die out; **~ de froid/faim** to die of exposure/hunger; **~ de faim/d'ennui** (fig) to be starving/be bored to death; **~ d'envie de faire** to be dying to do

mousse [mus] nf (Bot) moss; (de savon) lather; (écume: sur eau, bière) froth, foam; (Culin) mousse ▷ nm (Navig) ship's boy; **mousse à raser** shaving foam

mousseline [muslin] nf muslin; **pommes ~** mashed potatoes

mousser [muse] vi (bière, détergent) to foam; (savon) to lather; **mousseux, -euse** adj frothy ▷ nm: **(vin) mousseux** sparkling wine

mousson [musɔ̃] nf monsoon

moustache [mustaʃ] nf moustache; **moustaches** nfpl (du chat) whiskers pl; **moustachu, e** adj with a moustache

moustiquaire [mustikɛʀ] nf mosquito net

moustique [mustik] nm mosquito

moutarde [mutaʀd] nf mustard

mouton [mutɔ̃] nm sheep inv; (peau) sheepskin; (Culin) mutton

mouvement [muvmã] nm movement; (fig: impulsion) gesture; **avoir un bon ~** to make a nice gesture; **en ~** in motion, on the move; **mouvementé, e** adj (vie, poursuite) eventful; (réunion) turbulent

mouvoir [muvwaʀ] **se ~** vi to move

moyen, ne [mwajɛ̃, jɛn] adj average; (tailles, prix) medium; (de grandeur moyenne) medium-sized ▷ nm (façon) means sg, way; **moyens** nmpl (capacités) means; **très ~** (résultats) pretty poor; **je n'en ai pas les ~s** I can't afford it; **au ~ de** by means of; **par tous les ~s** by every possible means, every possible way; **par ses propres ~s** all by oneself; **moyen âge** Middle Ages pl; **moyen de transport** means of transport

moyennant [mwajɛnã] prép (somme) for; (service, conditions) in return for; (travail, effort) with

moyenne [mwajɛn] nf average; (Math) mean; (Scol) pass mark; **en ~** on (an) average; **moyenne d'âge** average age

Moyen-Orient [mwajɛnɔʀjã] nm: **le ~** the Middle East

moyeu, x [mwajø] nm hub

MST sigle f (= maladie sexuellement transmissible) STD

mû, mue [my] pp de **mouvoir**

muer [mɥe] vi (oiseau, mammifère) to moult; (serpent) to slough; (jeune garçon): **il mue** his voice is breaking

muet, te [mɥɛ, mɥɛt] adj dumb; (fig): **~ d'admiration** etc speechless with admiration etc; (Cinéma) silent ▷ nm/f mute

mufle [myfl] nm muzzle; (fam: goujat) boor

mugir [myʒiʀ] vi (taureau) to bellow; (vache) to low; (fig) to howl

muguet [mygɛ] nm lily of the valley

mule [myl] nf (Zool) (she-)mule

mulet [mylɛ] nm (Zool) (he-)mule

multinationale [myltinasjɔnal] nf multinational

multiple [myltipl] adj multiple, numerous; (varié) many, manifold; **multiplication** nf multiplication; **multiplier** vt to multiply; **se multiplier** vi to multiply

municipal, e, -aux [mynisipal, o] adj (élections, stade) municipal; (conseil) town cpd; **piscine/bibliothèque ~e** public swimming pool/library; **municipalité** nf (ville) municipality; (conseil) town council

munir [myniʀ] vt: **~ qch de** to equip sth with; **se ~ de** to arm o.s. with

munitions [mynisjɔ̃] nfpl ammunition sg

mur [myʀ] nm wall; **mur du son** sound barrier

mûr, e [myʀ] adj ripe; (personne) mature

muraille [myʀaj] nf (high) wall

mural, e, -aux [myʀal, o] adj wall cpd; (art) mural

mûre [myʀ] nf blackberry

muret [myʀɛ] nm low wall

mûrir [myʀiʀ] vi (fruit, blé) to ripen; (abcès) to come to a head; (fig: idée, personne) to mature ▷ vt (projet) to nurture; (personne) to (make) mature

murmure [myʀmyʀ] nm murmur; **murmurer** vi to murmur

muscade [myskad] nf (aussi: **noix (de) ~**) nutmeg

muscat [myska] nm (raisins) muscat grape; (vin) muscatel (wine)

muscle [myskl] nm muscle; **musclé, e** adj muscular; (fig) strong-arm

museau, x [myzo] nm muzzle; (Culin) brawn

musée [myze] nm museum; (de peinture) art gallery

museler [myz(ə)le] vt to muzzle; **muselière** nf muzzle

musette [myzɛt] nf (sac) lunchbag

musical, e, -aux [myzikal, o] adj musical

music-hall [myzikɔl] nm (salle) variety theatre; (genre) variety

musicien, ne [myzisjɛ̃, jɛn] adj musical ▷ nm/f musician

musique [myzik] nf music

musulman, e [myzylmã, an] adj, nm/f Moslem, Muslim

mutation [mytasjɔ̃] nf (Admin) transfer

muter [myte] vt to transfer, move

mutilé, e [mytile] nm/f disabled person (through loss of limbs)

mutiler [mytile] vt to mutilate, maim

mutin, e [mytɛ̃, in] adj (air, ton) mischievous, impish ▷ nm/f (Mil, Navig) mutineer; **mutinerie** nf mutiny

mutisme [mytism] nm silence

mutuel, le [mytɥɛl] adj mutual; **mutuelle** nf voluntary insurance premiums for back-up health cover

myope [mjɔp] adj short-sighted

myosotis [mjɔzɔtis] nm forget-me-not
myrtille [miʀtij] nf bilberry
mystère [mistɛʀ] nm mystery; **mystérieux, -euse** adj mysterious
mystifier [mistifje] vt to fool
mythe [mit] nm myth
mythologie [mitɔlɔʒi] nf mythology

n

n' [n] adv voir **ne**
nacre [nakʀ] nf mother of pearl
nage [naʒ] nf swimming; (manière) style of swimming, stroke; **traverser/s'éloigner à la ~** to swim across/away; **en ~** bathed in sweat; **nageoire** nf fin; **nager** vi to swim; **nageur, -euse** nm/f swimmer
naïf, -ive [naif, naiv] adj naïve
nain, e [nɛ̃, nɛn] nm/f dwarf
naissance [nesɑ̃s] nf birth; **donner ~ à** to give birth to; (fig) to give rise to; **lieu de ~** place of birth
naître [nɛtʀ] vi to be born; (fig): **~ de** to arise from, be born out of; **il est né en 1960** he was born in 1960; **faire ~** (fig) to give rise to, arouse
naïveté [naivte] nf naïvety
nana [nana] (fam) nf (fille) chick, bird (BRIT)
nappe [nap] nf tablecloth; (de pétrole, gaz) layer; **napperon** nm table-mat
naquit etc [naki] vb voir **naître**
narguer [naʀge] vt to taunt
narine [naʀin] nf nostril
natal, e [natal] adj native; **natalité** nf birth rate
natation [natasjɔ̃] nf swimming
natif, -ive [natif, iv] adj native
nation [nasjɔ̃] nf nation; **national, e, -aux** adj national; **nationale** nf: **(route) nationale** ≈ A road (BRIT), ≈ state highway (US); **nationaliser** vt to nationalize;

nationalisme nm nationalism; **nationalité** nf nationality
natte [nat] nf (cheveux) plait; (tapis) mat
naturaliser [natyʀalize] vt to naturalize
nature [natyʀ] nf nature ▷ adj, adv (Culin) plain, without seasoning or sweetening; (café, thé) black, without sugar; (yaourt) natural; **payer en ~** to pay in kind; **nature morte** still life; **naturel, le** adj (gén, aussi enfant) natural ▷ nm (absence d'affectation) naturalness; (caractère) disposition, nature; **naturellement** adv naturally; (bien sûr) of course
naufrage [nofʀaʒ] nm (ship)wreck; **faire ~** to be shipwrecked
nausée [noze] nf nausea; **avoir la ~** to feel sick
nautique [notik] adj nautical, water cpd; **sports ~s** water sports
naval, e [naval] adj naval; (industrie) shipbuilding
navet [navɛ] nm turnip; (péj: film) rubbishy film
navette [navɛt] nf shuttle; **faire la ~ (entre)** to go to and fro ou shuttle (between)
navigateur [navigatœʀ] nm (Navig) seafarer; (Inform) browser
navigation [navigasjɔ̃] nf navigation, sailing
naviguer [navige] vi to navigate, sail; **~ sur Internet** to browse the Internet
navire [naviʀ] nm ship
navrer [navʀe] vt to upset, distress; **je suis navré** I'm so sorry
ne, n' [n(ə)] adv voir **pas**; **plus**; **jamais** etc; (sans valeur négative: non traduit): **c'est plus loin que je ne le croyais** it's further than I thought
né, e [ne] pp (voir naître): **né en 1960** born in 1960; **née Scott** née Scott
néanmoins [neɑ̃mwɛ̃] adv nevertheless
néant [neɑ̃] nm nothingness; **réduire à ~** to bring to nought; (espoir) to dash
nécessaire [neseseʀ] adj necessary ▷ nm necessary; (sac) kit; **je vais faire le ~** I'll see to it; **nécessaire de couture** sewing kit; **nécessaire de toilette** toilet bag; **nécessité** nf necessity; **nécessiter** vt to require
nectar [nɛktaʀ] nm nectar
néerlandais, e [neɛʀlɑ̃dɛ, ɛz] adj Dutch
nef [nɛf] nf (d'église) nave
néfaste [nefast] adj (nuisible) harmful; (funeste) ill-fated
négatif, -ive [negatif, iv] adj negative ▷ nm (Photo) negative
négligé, e [negliʒe] adj (en désordre) slovenly ▷ nm (tenue) negligee
négligeable [negliʒabl] adj negligible
négligent, e [negliʒɑ̃, ɑ̃t] adj careless, negligent
négliger [negliʒe] vt (tenue) to be careless about; (avis, précautions) to disregard; (épouse, jardin) to neglect; **~ de faire** to fail to do, not bother to do
négociant, e [negosjɑ̃, jɑ̃t] nm/f merchant
négociation [negosjasjɔ̃] nf negotiation
négocier [negosje] vi, vt to negotiate
nègre [nɛgʀ] nm (péj) (écrivain) ghost (writer)
neige [nɛʒ] nf snow; **neiger** vi to snow
nénuphar [nenyfaʀ] nm water-lily
néon [neɔ̃] nm neon
néo-zélandais, e [neozelɑ̃dɛ, ɛz] adj New Zealand cpd ▷ nm/f: **Néo-Zélandais, e** New Zealander
Népal [nepal] nm: **le ~** Nepal
nerf [nɛʀ] nm nerve; **être sur les ~s** to be all keyed up;

nerveux, -euse adj nervous; (irritable) touchy, nervy; (voiture) nippy, responsive; **nervosité** nf excitability, tenseness; (irritabilité passagère) irritability, nerviness

n'est-ce pas? [nɛspa] adv isn't it?, won't you? etc, selon le verbe qui précède

Net [nɛt] nm (Internet): **le ~** the Net

net, nette [nɛt] adj (sans équivoque, distinct) clear; (évident: amélioration, différence) marked, distinct; (propre) neat, clean; (Comm: prix, salaire) net ▷ adv (refuser) flatly ▷ nm: **mettre au ~** to copy out; **s'arrêter ~** to stop dead; **nettement** adv clearly, distinctly; (incontestablement) decidedly; **netteté** nf clearness

nettoyage [netwajaʒ] nm cleaning; **nettoyage à sec** dry cleaning

nettoyer [netwaje] vt to clean

neuf¹ [nœf] num nine

neuf², neuve [nœf, nœv] adj new; **remettre à ~** to do up (as good as new); (refaire) quoi de **~?** what's new?

neutre [nøtr] adj neutral; (Ling) neuter

neuve [nœv] adj voir **neuf²**

neuvième [nœvjɛm] num ninth

neveu, X [n(ə)vø] nm nephew

New York [njujɔrk] n New York

nez [ne] nm nose; **~ à ~ avec** face to face with; **avoir du ~** to have flair

ni [ni] conj: **ni ... ni** neither ... nor; **je n'aime ni les lentilles ni les épinards** I like neither lentils nor spinach; **il n'a dit ni oui ni non** he didn't say either yes or no; **elles ne sont venues ni l'une ni l'autre** neither of them came; **il n'a rien vu ni entendu** he didn't see or hear anything

niche [niʃ] nf (du chien) kennel; (de mur) recess, niche; **nicher** vi to nest

nid [ni] nm nest; **nid de poule** pothole

nièce [njɛs] nf niece

nier [nje] vt to deny

Nil [nil] nm: **le ~** the Nile

n'importe [nɛ̃pɔrt] adv: **n'importe qui/quoi/où** anybody/anything/anywhere; **n'importe quand** any time; **n'importe quel/quelle** any; **n'importe lequel/laquelle** any (one); **n'importe comment** (sans soin) carelessly

niveau, X [nivo] nm level; (des élèves, études) standard; **niveau de vie** standard of living

niveler [niv(ə)le] vt to level

noble [nɔbl] adj noble; **noblesse** nf nobility; (d'une action etc) nobleness

noce [nɔs] nf wedding; (gens) wedding party (ou guests pl); **faire la ~ (~** (fam) to go on a binge; **noces d'argent/ d'or/de diamant** silver/golden/diamond wedding (anniversary)

nocif, -ive [nɔsif, iv] adj harmful

nocturne [nɔktyrn] adj nocturnal ▷ nf late-night opening

Noël [nɔɛl] nm Christmas

nœud [nø] nm knot; (ruban) bow; **nœud papillon** bow tie

noir, e [nwar] adj black; (obscur, sombre) dark ▷ nm/f black man/woman ▷ nm: **dans le ~** in the dark; **travail au ~** moonlighting; **travailler au ~** to work on the side; **noircir** vt, vi to blacken; **noire** nf (Mus) crotchet (BRIT), quarter note (US)

noisette [nwazɛt] nf hazelnut

noix [nwa] nf walnut; (Culin): **une ~ de beurre** a knob

of butter; **à la ~** (fam) worthless; **noix de cajou** cashew nut; **noix de coco** coconut; **noix muscade** nutmeg

nom [nɔ̃] nm name; (Ling) noun; **nom de famille** surname; **nom de jeune fille** maiden name

nomade [nɔmad] nm/f nomad

nombre [nɔ̃br] nm number; **venir en ~** to come in large numbers; **depuis ~ d'années** for many years; **au ~ de mes amis** among my friends; **nombreux, -euse** adj many, numerous; (avec sens sg: foule etc) large; **peu nombreux** few; **de nombreux cas** many cases

nombril [nɔ̃bri(l)] nm navel

nommer [nɔme] vt to name; (élire) to appoint, nominate; **se ~; il se nomme Pascal** his name's Pascal, he's called Pascal

non [nɔ̃] adv (réponse) no; (avec loin, sans, seulement) not; **~ (pas) que** not that; **moi ~ plus** neither do I, I don't either; **c'est bon ~?** (exprimant le doute) it's good, isn't it?; **je pense que ~** I don't think so

non alcoolisé, e [nɔ̃alkɔlize] adj non alcoholic

nonchalant, e [nɔ̃ʃalɑ̃, ɑ̃t] adj nonchalant

non-fumeur, -euse [nɔ̃fymœr, øz] nm/f non-smoker

non-sens [nɔ̃sɑ̃s] nm absurdity

nord [nɔr] nm North ▷ adj northern; north; **au ~** (situation) in the north; (direction) to the north; **au ~ de** (to the) north of; **nord-africain, e** adj North-African ▷ nm/f: **Nord-Africain, e** North African; **nord-est** nm North-East; **nord-ouest** nm North-West

normal, e, -aux [nɔrmal, o] adj normal; **c'est tout à fait ~** it's perfectly natural; **vous trouvez ça ~?** does it seem right to you?; **normale** nf: **la normale** the norm, the average; **normalement** adv (en général) normally

normand, e [nɔrmɑ̃, ɑ̃d] adj of Normandy ▷ nm/f: **N~, e** (de Normandie) Norman

Normandie [nɔrmɑ̃di] nf Normandy

norme [nɔrm] nf norm; (Tech) standard

Norvège [nɔrvɛʒ] nf Norway; **norvégien, ne** adj Norwegian ▷ nm/f: **Norvégien, ne** Norwegian ▷ nm (Ling) Norwegian

nos [no] adj voir **notre**

nostalgie [nɔstalʒi] nf nostalgia; **nostalgique** adj nostalgic

notable [nɔtabl] adj (fait) notable, noteworthy; (marqué) noticeable, marked ▷ nm prominent citizen

notaire [nɔtɛr] nm solicitor

notamment [nɔtamɑ̃] adv in particular, among others

note [nɔt] nf (écrite, Mus) note; (Scol) mark (BRIT), grade; (facture) bill; **note de service** memorandum

noter [nɔte] vt (écrire) to write down; (remarquer) to note, notice; (devoir) to mark, grade

notice [nɔtis] nf summary, short article; (brochure) leaflet, instruction book

notifier [nɔtifje] vt: **~ qch à qn** to notify sb of sth, notify sth to sb

notion [nɔsjɔ̃] nf notion, idea

notoire [nɔtwar] adj widely known; (en mal) notorious

notre [nɔtr] (pl **nos**) adj our

nôtre [nɔtr] pron: **le ~, la ~, les ~s** ours ▷ adj ours; **les ~s** ours; (alliés etc) our own people; **soyez des ~s** join us

nouer [nwe] vt to tie, knot; (fig: alliance etc) to strike up

noueux, -euse [nwø, øz] adj gnarled

nourrice [nuris] nf (gardienne) child-minder

nourrir [nurir] vt to feed; (fig: espoir) to harbour, nurse; **nourrissant, e** adj nourishing, nutritious; **nourrisson** nm (unweaned) infant; **nourriture** nf food

nous [nu] *pron (sujet)* we; *(objet)* us; **nous-mêmes** *pron* ourselves

nouveau (nouvel), -elle, x [nuvo, nuvɛl] *adj* new ▷ *nm*: **y a-t-il du nouveau?** is there anything new on this? ▷ *nm/f* new pupil *(ou* employee); **de nouveau, à nouveau** again; **nouveau venu, nouvelle venue** newcomer; **nouveaux mariés** newly-weds; **nouveau-né, e** *nm/f* newborn baby; **nouveauté** *nf* novelty; *(objet)* new thing *ou* article

nouvel [nuvɛl] *adj voir* **nouveau**; **Nouvel An** New Year

nouvelle [nuvɛl] *adj voir* **nouveau** ▷ *nf (piece of)* news *sg*; *(Littérature)* short story; **les ~s** *(Presse, TV)* the news; **je suis sans ~s de lui** I haven't heard from him; **Nouvelle-Calédonie** *nf* New Caledonia; **Nouvelle-Zélande** *nf* New Zealand

novembre [nɔvɑ̃bʀ] *nm* November

noyade [nwajad] *nf* drowning *no pl*

noyau, x [nwajo] *nm (de fruit)* stone; *(Bio, Physique)* nucleus; *(fig: centre)* core

noyer [nwaje] *nm* walnut (tree); *(bois)* walnut ▷ *vt* to drown; *(moteur)* to flood; **se ~** *vi* to be drowned, drown; *(suicide)* to drown o.s.

nu, e [ny] *adj* naked, bare; *(membres)* naked, bare; *(pieds, mains, chambre, fil électrique)* bare ▷ *nm (Art)* nude; **tout nu** stark naked; **se mettre nu** to strip

nuage [nɥaʒ] *nm* cloud; **nuageux, -euse** *adj* cloudy

nuance [nɥɑ̃s] *nf (de couleur, sens)* shade; **il y a une ~ (entre)** there's a slight difference (between); **nuancer** *vt (opinion)* to bring some reservations *ou* qualifications to

nucléaire [nykleɛʀ] *adj* nuclear ▷ *nm*: **le ~** nuclear energy

nudiste [nydist] *nm/f* nudist

nuée [nɥe] *nf*: **une ~ de** a cloud *ou* host *ou* swarm of

nuire [nɥiʀ] *vi* to be harmful; **~ à** to harm, do damage to; **nuisible** *adj* harmful; **animal nuisible** pest

nuit [nɥi] *nf* night; **il fait ~** it's dark; **cette ~ (hier)** last night; *(aujourd'hui)* tonight; **de ~ (vol, service)** night *cpd*; **nuit blanche** sleepless night

nul, nulle [nyl] *adj (aucun)* no; *(minime)* nil, non-existent; *(non valable)* null; *(péj)*: **être ~ (en)** to be useless *ou* hopeless (at) ▷ *pron* none, no one; **match ou résultat ~** draw; **~le part** nowhere; **nullement** *adv* by no means

numérique [nymeʀik] *adj* numerical; *(affichage, son, télévision)* digital

numéro [nymeʀo] *nm* number; *(spectacle)* act, turn; *(Presse)* issue, number; **numéro de téléphone** (tele)phone number; **numéro vert** ≈ freefone® number *(BRIT)*, ≈ toll-free number *(US)*; **numéroter** *vt* to number

nuque [nyk] *nf* nape of the neck

nu-tête [nytɛt] *adj inv, adv* bareheaded

nutritif, -ive [nytʀitif, iv] *adj (besoins, valeur)* nutritional; *(nourrissant)* nutritious

nylon [nilɔ̃] *nm* nylon

oasis [ɔazis] *nf* oasis

obéir [ɔbeiʀ] *vi* to obey; **~ à** to obey; **obéissance** *nf* obedience; **obéissant, e** *adj* obedient

obèse [ɔbɛz] *adj* obese; **obésité** *nf* obesity

objecter [ɔbʒɛkte] *vt*: **~ que** to object that; **objecteur** *nm*: **objecteur de conscience** conscientious objector

objectif, -ive [ɔbʒɛktif, iv] *adj* objective ▷ *nm* objective; *(Photo)* lens *sg*, objective

objection [ɔbʒɛksjɔ̃] *nf* objection

objectivité [ɔbʒɛktivite] *nf* objectivity

objet [ɔbʒɛ] *nm* object; *(d'une discussion, recherche)* subject; **être ou faire l'~ de** *(discussion)* to be the subject of; *(soins)* to be given *ou* shown; **sans ~** purposeless; *(craintes)* groundless; **(bureau des) ~s trouvés** lost property *sg (BRIT)*, lost-and-found *sg (US)*; **objet d'art** objet d'art; **objets de valeur** valuables; **objets personnels** personal items

obligation [ɔbligasjɔ̃] *nf* obligation; *(Comm)* bond, debenture; **obligatoire** *adj* compulsory, obligatory; **obligatoirement** *adv* necessarily; *(fam: sans aucun doute)* inevitably

obliger [ɔbliʒe] *vt (contraindre)*: **~ qn à faire** to force *ou* oblige sb to do; **je suis bien obligé (de le faire)** I have to (do it)

oblique [ɔblik] *adj* oblique; **en ~** diagonally

oblitérer [ɔbliteʀe] *vt (timbre-poste)* to cancel

obnubiler [ɔbnybile] *vt* to obsess

obscène [ɔpsɛn] *adj* obscene

obscur, e [ɔpskyʀ] *adj* dark; *(méconnu)* obscure; **obscurcir** *vt* to darken; *(fig)* to obscure; **s'obscurcir** *vi* to grow dark; **obscurité** *nf* darkness; **dans l'obscurité** in the dark, in darkness

obsédé, e [ɔpsede] *nm/f*: **un ~ de jazz** a jazz fanatic; **obsédé sexuel** sex maniac

obséder [ɔpsede] *vt* to obsess, haunt

obsèques [ɔpsɛk] *nfpl* funeral *sg*

observateur, -trice [ɔpsɛʀvatœʀ, tʀis] *adj* observant, perceptive ▷ *nm/f* observer

observation [ɔpsɛʀvasjɔ̃] *nf* observation; *(d'un règlement etc)* observance; *(reproche)* reproof; **être en ~**

(*Méd*) to be under observation
observatoire [ɔpsɛʀvatwaʀ] *nm* observatory
observer [ɔpsɛʀve] *vt* (*regarder*) to observe, watch; (*scientifiquement; aussi règlement etc*) to observe; (*surveiller*) to watch; (*remarquer*) to observe, notice; **faire ~ qch à qn** (*dire*) to point out sth to sb
obsession [ɔpsesjɔ̃] *nf* obsession
obstacle [ɔpstakl] *nm* obstacle, (*Équitation*) jump, hurdle; **faire ~ à** (*projet*) to hinder, put obstacles in the path of
obstiné, e [ɔpstine] *adj* obstinate
obstiner [ɔpstine]: **s'~** *vi* to insist, dig one's heels in; **s'~ à faire** to persist (obstinately) in doing
obstruer [ɔpstʀye] *vt* to block, obstruct
obtenir [ɔptəniʀ] *vt* to obtain, get; (*résultat*) to achieve, obtain; **~ de pouvoir faire** to obtain permission to do
obturateur [ɔptyʀatœʀ] *nm* (*Photo*) shutter
obus [ɔby] *nm* shell
occasion [ɔkazjɔ̃] *nf* (*aubaine, possibilité*) opportunity; (*circonstance*) occasion; (*Comm: article non neuf*) secondhand buy; (: *acquisition avantageuse*) bargain; **à plusieurs ~s** on several occasions; **à l'~** sometimes, on occasions; **d'~** secondhand; **occasionnel, le** *adj* (*non régulier*) occasional
occasionner [ɔkazjɔne] *vt* to cause
occident [ɔksidɑ̃] *nm*: **l'O~** the West; **occidental, e, -aux** *adj* western; (*Pol*) Western ▷ *nm/f* Westerner
occupation [ɔkypasjɔ̃] *nf* occupation
occupé, e [ɔkype] *adj* (*personne*) busy; (*place, sièges*) taken; (*toilettes*) engaged; (*Mil, Pol*) occupied; **la ligne est ~e** the line's engaged (*BRIT*) *ou* busy (*US*)
occuper [ɔkype] *vt* to occupy; (*poste*) to hold; **s'~ de** (*être responsable de*) to be in charge of; (*se charger de: affaire*) to take charge of, deal with; (: *clients etc*) to attend to; **s'~ (à qch)** to occupy o.s. *ou* keep o.s. busy (with sth)
occurrence [ɔkyʀɑ̃s] *nf*: **en l'~** in this case
océan [ɔseɑ̃] *nm* ocean
octet [ɔktɛ] *nm* byte
octobre [ɔktɔbʀ] *nm* October
oculiste [ɔkylist] *nm/f* eye specialist
odeur [ɔdœʀ] *nf* smell
odieux, -euse [ɔdjø, jøz] *adj* hateful
odorant, e [ɔdɔʀɑ̃, ɑ̃t] *adj* sweet-smelling, fragrant
odorat [ɔdɔʀa] *nm* (sense of) smell
œil [œj] (*pl* **yeux**) *nm* eye; **avoir un ~ au beurre noir** *ou* **poché** to have a black eye; **à l'~** (*fam*) for free; **à l'~ nu** with the naked eye; **ouvrir l'~** (*fig*) to keep one's eyes open *ou* an eye out; **fermer les yeux (sur)** (*fig*) to turn a blind eye (to); **les yeux fermés** (*aussi fig*) with one's eyes shut
œillères [œjɛʀ] *nfpl* blinkers (*BRIT*), blinders (*US*)
œillet [œjɛ] *nm* (*Bot*) carnation
œuf [œf, *pl* ø] *nm* egg; **œuf à la coque** boiled egg; **œuf au plat** fried egg; **œuf dur** hard-boiled egg; **œuf de Pâques** Easter egg; **œufs brouillés** scrambled eggs
œuvre [œvʀ] *nf* (*tâche*) task, undertaking; (*livre, tableau etc*) work; (*ensemble de la production artistique*) works *pl* ▷ *nm* (*Constr*): **le gros ~** the shell; **mettre en ~** (*moyens*) to make use of; **œuvre de bienfaisance** charity; **œuvre d'art** work of art
offense [ɔfɑ̃s] *nf* insult; **offenser** *vt* to offend, hurt; **s'offenser de qch** to take offence (*BRIT*) *ou* offense (*US*) at sth
offert, e [ɔfɛʀ, ɛʀt] *pp de* **offrir**

office [ɔfis] *nm* (*agence*) bureau, agency; (*Rel*) service ▷ *nm ou nf* (*pièce*) pantry; **faire ~ de** to act as; **d'~** automatically; **office du tourisme** tourist bureau
officiel, le [ɔfisjɛl] *adj, nm/f* official
officier [ɔfisje] *nm* officer
officieux, -euse [ɔfisjø, jøz] *adj* unofficial
offrande [ɔfʀɑ̃d] *nf* offering
offre [ɔfʀ] *nf* offer; (*aux enchères*) bid; (*Admin: soumission*) tender; (*Écon*): **l'~ et la demande** supply and demand; **"~s d'emploi"** "situations vacant"; **offre d'emploi** job advertised; **offre publique d'achat** takeover bid
offrir [ɔfʀiʀ] *vt*: **~ (à qn)** to offer (to sb); (*faire cadeau de*) to give (to sb); **s'~** *vt* (*vacances, voiture*) to treat o.s. to; **~ (à qn) de faire qch** to offer to do sth (for sb); **~ à boire à qn** (*chez soi*) to offer sb a drink; **je vous offre un verre** I'll buy you a drink
OGM *sigle m* (= *organisme génétiquement modifié*) GMO
oie [wa] *nf* (*Zool*) goose
oignon [ɔɲɔ̃] *nm* onion; (*de tulipe etc*) bulb
oiseau, x [wazo] *nm* bird; **oiseau de proie** bird of prey
oisif, -ive [wazif, iv] *adj* idle
oléoduc [ɔleɔdyk] *nm* (oil) pipeline
olive [ɔliv] *nf* (*Bot*) olive; **olivier** *nm* olive (tree)
OLP *sigle f* (= *Organisation de libération de la Palestine*) PLO
olympique [ɔlɛ̃pik] *adj* Olympic
ombragé, e [ɔ̃bʀaʒe] *adj* shaded, shady
ombre [ɔ̃bʀ] *nf* (*espace non ensoleillé*) shade; (*ombre portée, tache*) shadow; **à l'~** in the shade; **dans l'~** (*fig*) in the dark; **ombre à paupières** eyeshadow
omelette [ɔmlɛt] *nf* omelette; **omelette norvégienne** baked Alaska
omettre [ɔmɛtʀ] *vt* to omit, leave out
omoplate [ɔmɔplat] *nf* shoulder blade

⬤ **MOT-CLÉ**

on [ɔ̃] *pron* **1** (*indéterminé*) you, one; **on peut le faire ainsi** you *ou* one can do it like this, it can be done like this
2 (*quelqu'un*): **on les a attaqués** they were attacked; **on vous demande au téléphone** there's a phone call for you, you're wanted on the phone
3 (*nous*) we; **on va y aller demain** we're going tomorrow
4 (*les gens*) they; **autrefois, on croyait ...** they used to believe ...
5: **on ne peut plus** *adv*: **on ne peut plus stupide** as stupid as can be

oncle [ɔ̃kl] *nm* uncle
onctueux, -euse [ɔ̃ktɥø, øz] *adj* creamy, smooth
onde [ɔ̃d] *nf* wave; **~s courtes/moyennes** short/medium wave *sg*; **grandes ~s** long wave *sg*
ondée [ɔ̃de] *nf* shower
on-dit [ɔ̃di] *nm inv* rumour
onduler [ɔ̃dyle] *vi* to undulate; (*cheveux*) to wave
onéreux, -euse [ɔneʀø, øz] *adj* costly
ongle [ɔ̃gl] *nm* nail
ont [ɔ̃] *vb voir* **avoir**
ONU *sigle f* (= *Organisation des Nations Unies*) UN
onze [ɔ̃z] *num* eleven; **onzième** *num* eleventh
OPA *sigle f* = **offre publique d'achat**
opaque [ɔpak] *adj* opaque
opéra [ɔpeʀa] *nm* opera; (*édifice*) opera house
opérateur, -trice [ɔpeʀatœʀ, tʀis] *nm/f* operator;

opérateur (de prise de vues) cameraman
opération [ɔperasjɔ̃] nf operation; (Comm) dealing
opératoire [ɔperatwaʀ] adj (choc etc) post-operative
opérer [ɔpeʀe] vt (personne) to operate on; (faire, exécuter) to carry out, make ▷ vi (remède: faire effet) to act, work; (Méd) to operate; **s'~** vi (avoir lieu) to occur, take place; **se faire ~** to have an operation
opérette [ɔpeʀet] nf operetta, light opera
opinion [ɔpinjɔ̃] nf opinion; **l'opinion (publique)** public opinion
opportun, e [ɔpɔʀtœ̃ yn] adj timely, opportune; **opportuniste** nm/f opportunist
opposant, e [ɔpozɑ̃, ɑ̃t] nm/f opponent
opposé, e [ɔpoze] adj (direction) opposite; (faction) opposing; (opinions, intérêts) conflicting; (contre): **~ à** opposed to, against ▷ nm: **l'~** the other ou opposite side (ou direction); (contraire) the opposite; **à l'~** (fig) on the other hand; **à l'~ de** (fig) contrary to, unlike
opposer [ɔpoze] vt (personnes, équipes) to oppose; (couleurs) to contrast; **s'~** vi (équipes) to confront each other; (opinions) to conflict; (couleurs, styles) to contrast; **s'~ à** (interdire) to oppose; **~ qch à** (comme obstacle, défense) to set sth against; (comme objection) to put sth forward against
opposition [ɔpozisjɔ̃] nf opposition; **par ~ à** as opposed to; **entrer en ~ avec** to come into conflict with; **faire ~ à un chèque** to stop a cheque
oppressant, e [ɔpʀesɑ̃, ɑ̃t] adj oppressive
oppresser [ɔpʀese] vt to oppress; **oppression** nf oppression
opprimer [ɔpʀime] vt to oppress
opter [ɔpte] vi: **~ pour** to opt for
opticien, ne [ɔptisjɛ̃, jɛn] nm/f optician
optimisme [ɔptimism] nm optimism; **optimiste** nm/f optimist ▷ adj optimistic
option [ɔpsjɔ̃] nf option; **matière à ~** (Scol) optional subject
optique [ɔptik] adj (nerf) optic; (verres) optical ▷ nf (fig: manière de voir) perspective
or [ɔʀ] nm gold ▷ conj now, but; **en or** (objet) gold cpd; **une affaire en or** a real bargain; **il croyait gagner or il a perdu** he was sure he would win and yet he lost
orage [ɔʀaʒ] nm (thunder)storm; **orageux, -euse** adj stormy
oral, e, -aux [ɔʀal, o] adj, nm oral; **par voie ~e** (Méd) orally
orange [ɔʀɑ̃ʒ] nf orange ▷ adj inv orange; **orangé, e** adj orangey, orange-coloured; **orangeade** nf orangeade; **oranger** nm orange tree
orateur [ɔʀatœʀ] nm speaker
orbite [ɔʀbit] nf (Anat) (eye-)socket; (Physique) orbit
Orcades [ɔʀkad] nfpl: **les ~** the Orkneys, the Orkney Islands
orchestre [ɔʀkestʀ] nm orchestra; (de jazz) band; (places) stalls pl (BRIT), orchestra (US)
orchidée [ɔʀkide] nf orchid
ordinaire [ɔʀdineʀ] adj ordinary; (qualité) standard; (péj: commun) common ▷ nm ordinary; (menus) everyday fare ▷ nf (essence) ≈ two-star (petrol) (BRIT), ≈ regular gas (US); **d'~** usually, normally; **comme à l'~** as usual
ordinateur [ɔʀdinatœʀ] nm computer; **ordinateur individuel** ou **personnel** personal computer; **ordinateur portable** laptop (computer)
ordonnance [ɔʀdɔnɑ̃s] nf (Méd) prescription; (Mil)

orderly, batman (BRIT); **pouvez-vous me faire une ~?** can you write me a prescription?
ordonné, e [ɔʀdɔne] adj tidy, orderly
ordonner [ɔʀdɔne] vt (agencer) to organize, arrange; (donner un ordre): **~ à qn de faire** to order sb to do; (Rel) to ordain; (Méd) to prescribe
ordre [ɔʀdʀ] nm order; (propreté et soin) orderliness, tidiness; (nature): **d'~ pratique** of a practical nature; **ordres** nmpl (Rel) holy orders; **mettre en ~** to tidy (up), put in order; **par ~ alphabétique/d'importance** in alphabetical order/in order of importance; **à l'~ de qn** payable to sb; **être aux ~s de qn/sous les ~s de qn** to be at sb's disposal/under sb's command; **jusqu'à nouvel ~** until further notice; **de premier ~** first-rate; **ordre du jour** (d'une réunion) agenda; **à l'ordre du jour** (fig) topical; **ordre publique** law and order
ordure [ɔʀdyʀ] nf filth no pl; **ordures** nfpl (balayures, déchets) rubbish sg, refuse sg; **ordures ménagères** household refuse
oreille [ɔʀej] nf ear; **avoir de l'~** to have a good ear (for music)
oreiller [ɔʀeje] nm pillow
oreillons [ɔʀejɔ̃] nmpl mumps sg
ores [ɔʀ]: **d'~ et déjà** already
orfèvrerie [ɔʀfevʀəʀi] nf goldsmith's (ou silversmith's) trade; (ouvrage) gold (ou silver) plate
organe [ɔʀgan] nm organ; (porte-parole) representative, mouthpiece
organigramme [ɔʀganigʀam] nm (tableau hiérarchique) organization chart; (schéma) flow chart
organique [ɔʀganik] adj organic
organisateur, -trice [ɔʀganizatœʀ, tʀis] nm/f organizer
organisation [ɔʀganizasjɔ̃] nf organization; **Organisation des Nations Unies** United Nations (Organization)
organiser [ɔʀganize] vt to organize; (mettre sur pied: service etc) to set up; **s'~** to get organized
organisme [ɔʀganism] nm (Bio) organism; (corps, Admin) body
organiste [ɔʀganist] nm/f organist
orgasme [ɔʀgasm] nm orgasm, climax
orge [ɔʀʒ] nf barley
orgue [ɔʀg] nm organ
orgueil [ɔʀgœj] nm pride; **orgueilleux, -euse** adj proud
oriental, e, -aux [ɔʀjɑ̃tal, -o] adj (langue, produit) oriental; (frontière) eastern
orientation [ɔʀjɑ̃tasjɔ̃] nf (de recherches) orientation; (d'une maison etc) aspect; (d'un journal) leanings pl; **avoir le sens de l'~** to have a (good) sense of direction; **orientation professionnelle** careers advisory service
orienté, e [ɔʀjɑ̃te] adj (fig: article, journal) slanted; **bien/mal ~** (appartement) well/badly positioned; **~ au sud** facing south, with a southern aspect
orienter [ɔʀjɑ̃te] vt (tourner: antenne) to direct, turn; (personne, recherches) to direct; (fig: élève) to orientate; **s'~** (se repérer) to find one's bearings; **s'~ vers** (fig) to turn towards
origan [ɔʀigɑ̃] nm oregano
originaire [ɔʀiʒineʀ] adj: **être ~ de** to be a native of
original, e, -aux [ɔʀiʒinal, o] adj original; (bizarre) eccentric ▷ nm/f eccentric ▷ nm (document etc, Art) original
origine [ɔʀiʒin] nf origin; **origines** nfpl (d'une personne)

origins; **d'~** (*pays*) of origin; **d'~ suédoise** of Swedish origin; (*pneus etc*) original; **à l'~** originally; **originel, le** *adj* original

orme [ɔʀm] *nm* elm

ornement [ɔʀnəmɑ̃] *nm* ornament

orner [ɔʀne] *vt* to decorate, adorn

ornière [ɔʀnjɛʀ] *nf* rut

orphelin, e [ɔʀfəlɛ̃, in] *adj* orphan(ed) ▷ *nm/f* orphan; **orphelin de mère/de père** motherless/fatherless; **orphelinat** *nm* orphanage

orteil [ɔʀtɛj] *nm* toe; **gros ~** big toe

orthographe [ɔʀtɔgʀaf] *nf* spelling

ortie [ɔʀti] *nf* (stinging) nettle

os [ɔs] *nm* bone; **os à moelle** marrowbone

osciller [ɔsile] *vi* (*au vent etc*) to rock; (*fig*): **~ entre** to waver *ou* fluctuate between

osé, e [oze] *adj* daring, bold

oseille [ozɛj] *nf* sorrel

oser [oze] *vi, vt* to dare; **~ faire** to dare (to) do

osier [ozje] *nm* willow; **d'~, en ~** wicker(work)

osseux, -euse [ɔsø, øz] *adj* bony; (*tissu, maladie, greffe*) bone *cpd*

otage [ɔtaʒ] *nm* hostage; **prendre qn comme ~** to take sb hostage

OTAN *sigle f* (= *Organisation du traité de l'Atlantique Nord*) NATO

otarie [ɔtaʀi] *nf* sea-lion

ôter [ote] *vt* to remove; (*soustraire*) to take away; **~ qch à qn** to take sth (away) from sb; **~ qch de** to remove sth from

otite [ɔtit] *nf* ear infection

ou [u] *conj* or; **ou ... ou** either ... or; **ou bien** or (else)

MOT-CLÉ

où [u] *pron relatif* **1** (*position, situation*) where, that (*souvent omis*); **la chambre où il était** the room (that) he was in, the room where he was; **la ville où je l'ai rencontré** the town where I met him; **la pièce d'où il est sorti** the room he came out of; **le village d'où je viens** the village I come from; **les villes par où il est passé** the towns he went through

2 (*temps, état*) that (*souvent omis*); **le jour où il est parti** the day (that) he left; **au prix où c'est** at the price it is ▷ *adv* **1** (*interrogation*) where; **où est-il/va-t-il?** where is he/is he going?; **par où?** which way?; **d'où vient que ...?** how come ...?

2 (*position*) where; **je sais où il est** I know where he is; **où que l'on aille** wherever you go

ouate [wat] *nf* cotton wool (*BRIT*), cotton (*US*)

oubli [ubli] *nm* (*acte*): **l'~ de** forgetting; (*trou de mémoire*) lapse of memory; (*négligence*) omission, oversight; **tomber dans l'~** to sink into oblivion

oublier [ublije] *vt* to forget; (*laisser quelque part: chapeau etc*) to leave behind; (*ne pas voir: erreurs etc*) to miss; **j'ai oublié ma clé/mon passeport** I've forgotten my key/passport

ouest [wɛst] *nm* west ▷ *adj inv* west; (*région*) western; **à l'~** in the west; (*direction*) (to the) west, westwards; **à l'~ de** (to the) west of

ouf [uf] *excl* phew!

oui [ˈwi] *adv* yes

ouï-dire [ˈwidiʀ]: **par ~** *adv* by hearsay

ouïe [wi] *nf* hearing; **ouïes** *nfpl* (*de poisson*) gills

ouragan [uʀagɑ̃] *nm* hurricane

ourlet [uʀlɛ] *nm* hem

ours [uʀs] *nm* bear; **ours blanc/brun** polar/brown bear; **ours (en peluche)** teddy (bear)

oursin [uʀsɛ̃] *nm* sea urchin

ourson [uʀsɔ̃] *nm* (bear-)cub

ouste [ust] *excl* hop it!

outil [uti] *nm* tool; **outiller** *vt* to equip

outrage [utʀaʒ] *nm* insult; **outrage à la pudeur** indecent conduct *no pl*

outrance [utʀɑ̃s]: **à ~** *adv* excessively, to excess

outre [utʀ] *prép* besides ▷ *adv*: **passer ~ à** to disregard, take no notice of; **en ~** besides, moreover; **~ mesure** to excess; (*manger, boire*) immoderately; **outre-Atlantique** *adv* across the Atlantic; **outre-mer** *adv* overseas

ouvert, e [uvɛʀ, ɛʀt] *pp de* **ouvrir** ▷ *adj* open; (*robinet, gaz etc*) on; **ouvertement** *adv* openly; **ouverture** *nf* opening; (*Mus*) overture; **heures d'ouverture** (*Comm*) opening hours; **ouverture d'esprit** open-mindedness

ouvrable [uvʀabl] *adj*: **jour ~** working day, weekday

ouvrage [uvʀaʒ] *nm* (*tâche, de tricot etc*) work *no pl*; (*texte, livre*) work

ouvre-boîte(s) [uvʀəbwat] *nm inv* tin (*BRIT*) *ou* can opener

ouvre-bouteille(s) [uvʀəbutɛj] *nm inv* bottle-opener

ouvreuse [uvʀøz] *nf* usherette

ouvrier, -ière [uvʀije, ijɛʀ] *nm/f* worker ▷ *adj* working-class; (*conflit*) industrial; (*mouvement*) labour *cpd*; **classe ouvrière** working class

ouvrir [uvʀiʀ] *vt* (*gén*) to open; (*brèche, passage, Méd: abcès*) to open up; (*commencer l'exploitation de, créer*) to open (up); (*eau, électricité, chauffage, robinet*) to turn on ▷ *vi* to open; to open up; **s'~** *vi* to open; **s'~ à qn** to open one's heart to sb; **est-ce ouvert au public?** is it open to the public?; **quand est-ce que le musée est ouvert?** when is the museum open?; **à quelle heure ouvrez-vous?** what time do you open?; **~ l'appétit à qn** to whet sb's appetite

ovaire [ɔvɛʀ] *nm* ovary

ovale [ɔval] *adj* oval

OVNI [ɔvni] *sigle m* (= *objet volant non identifié*) UFO

oxyder [ɔkside]: **s'~** *vi* to become oxidized

oxygène [ɔksiʒɛn] *nm* oxygen

oxygéné, e [ɔksiʒene] *adj*: **eau ~e** hydrogen peroxide

ozone [ozon] *nf* ozone; **la couche d'~** the ozone layer

p

pacifique [pasifik] *adj* peaceful ▷ *nm*: **le P~, l'océan P~** the Pacific (Ocean)

pack [pak] *nm* pack

pacotille [pakɔtij] *nf* cheap junk

PACS *sigle m* (= *pacte civil de solidarité*) contract of civil partnership; **pacser: se pacser** *vi* to sign a contract of civil partnership

pacte [pakt] *nm* pact, treaty

pagaille [pagaj] *nf* mess, shambles *sg*

page [paʒ] *nf* page ▷ *nm* page (boy); **à la ~** (*fig*) up-to-date; **page d'accueil** (*Inform*) home page; **page Web** (*Inform*) web page

paiement [pemɑ̃] *nm* payment

païen, ne [pajɛ̃, pajɛn] *adj, nm/f* pagan, heathen

paillasson [pajasɔ̃] *nm* doormat

paille [paj] *nf* straw

pain [pɛ̃] *nm* (*substance*) bread; (*unité*) loaf (of bread); (*morceau*): **~ de savon** *etc* bar of soap *etc*; **pain au chocolat** chocolate-filled pastry; **pain aux raisins** currant bun; **pain bis/complet** brown/wholemeal (*BRIT*) *ou* wholewheat (*US*) bread; **pain d'épice** ≈ gingerbread; **pain de mie** sandwich loaf; **pain grillé** toast

pair, e [pɛʀ] *adj* (*nombre*) even ▷ *nm* peer; **aller de ~** to go hand in hand *ou* together; **jeune fille au ~** au pair; **paire** *nf* pair

paisible [pezibl] *adj* peaceful, quiet

paix [pɛ] *nf* peace; **faire/avoir la ~** to make/have peace; **fiche-lui la ~!** (*fam*) leave him alone!

Pakistan [pakistɑ̃] *nm*: **le ~** Pakistan

palais [palɛ] *nm* palace; (*Anat*) palate

pâle [pɑl] *adj* pale; **bleu ~** pale blue

Palestine [palɛstin] *nf*: **la ~** Palestine

palette [palɛt] *nf* (*de peintre*) palette; (*produits*) range

pâleur [palœʀ] *nf* paleness

palier [palje] *nm* (*d'escalier*) landing; (*fig*) level, plateau; **par ~s** in stages

pâlir [paliʀ] *vi* to turn *ou* go pale; (*couleur*) to fade

pallier [palje] *vt* to offset, make up for

palme [palm] *nf* (*de plongeur*) flipper; **palmé, e** *adj* (*pattes*) webbed

palmier [palmje] *nm* palm tree; (*gâteau*) heart-shaped biscuit made of flaky pastry

pâlot, te [palo, ɔt] *adj* pale, peaky

palourde [paluʀd] *nf* clam

palper [palpe] *vt* to feel, finger

palpitant, e [palpitɑ̃, ɑ̃t] *adj* thrilling

palpiter [palpite] *vi* (*cœur, pouls*) to beat; (: *plus fort*) to pound, throb

paludisme [palydism] *nm* malaria

pamphlet [pɑ̃flɛ] *nm* lampoon, satirical tract

pamplemousse [pɑ̃pləmus] *nm* grapefruit

pan [pɑ̃] *nm* section, piece ▷ *excl* bang!

panache [panaʃ] *nm* plume; (*fig*) spirit, panache

panaché, e [panaʃe] *adj*: **glace ~e** mixed-flavour ice cream ▷ *nm* (*bière*) shandy

pancarte [pɑ̃kaʀt] *nf* sign, notice

pancréas [pɑ̃kreas] *nm* pancreas

pané, e [pane] *adj* fried in breadcrumbs

panier [panje] *nm* basket; **mettre au ~** to chuck away; **panier à provisions** shopping basket; **panier-repas** *nm* packed lunch

panique [panik] *nf, adj* panic; **paniquer** *vi* to panic

panne [pan] *nf* breakdown; **être/tomber en ~** to have broken down/break down; **être en ~ d'essence** *ou* **sèche** to have run out of petrol (*BRIT*) *ou* gas (*US*); **ma voiture est en ~** my car has broken down; **panne d'électricité** *ou* **de courant** power cut *ou* failure

panneau, x [pano] *nm* (*écriteau*) sign, notice; **panneau d'affichage** notice board; **panneau de signalisation** roadsign; **panneau indicateur** signpost

panoplie [panɔpli] *nf* (*jouet*) outfit; (*fig*) array

panorama [panɔrama] *nm* panorama

panse [pɑ̃s] *nf* paunch

pansement [pɑ̃smɑ̃] *nm* dressing, bandage; **pansement adhésif** sticking plaster

pantacourt [pɑ̃takuʀ] *nm* three-quarter length trousers *pl*

pantalon [pɑ̃talɔ̃] *nm* trousers *pl*, pair of trousers; **pantalon de ski** ski pants *pl*

panthère [pɑ̃tɛʀ] *nf* panther

pantin [pɑ̃tɛ̃] *nm* puppet

pantoufle [pɑ̃tufl] *nf* slipper

paon [pɑ̃] *nm* peacock

papa [papa] *nm* dad(dy)

pape [pap] *nm* pope

paperasse [papʀas] (*péj*) *nf* bumf *no pl*, papers *pl*; **paperasserie** (*péj*) *nf* paperwork *no pl*; (*tracasserie*) red tape *no pl*

papeterie [papetʀi] *nf* (*magasin*) stationer's (shop)

papi [papi] *nm* (*fam*) granddad

papier [papje] *nm* paper; (*article*) article; **papiers** *nmpl* (*aussi*) **~s d'identité**) (identity) papers; **papier à lettres** writing paper, notepaper; **papier (d')aluminium** aluminium (*BRIT*) *ou* aluminum (*US*) foil, tinfoil; **papier calque** tracing paper; **papier de verre** sandpaper; **papier hygiénique** *ou* **(de) toilette** toilet paper; **papier journal** newspaper; **papier peint** wallpaper

papillon [papijɔ̃] *nm* butterfly; (*fam: contravention*) (parking) ticket; **papillon de nuit** moth

papillote [papijɔt] *nf*: **en ~** cooked in tinfoil

papoter [papɔte] *vi* to chatter

paquebot [pak(ə)bo] *nm* liner

pâquerette [pakʀɛt] *nf* daisy

Pâques [pɑk] nm, nfpl Easter
paquet [pakɛ] nm packet; (colis) parcel; (fig: tas): ~
de pile ou heap of; **un ~ de cigarettes, s'il vous plaît**
a packet of cigarettes, please; **paquet-cadeau** nm:
**pouvez-vous me faire un paquet-cadeau, s'il vous
plaît?** can you gift-wrap it for me, please?
par [paR] prép by; **finir** etc **~ to** end etc with; **~ amour**
out of love; **passer ~ Lyon/la côte** to go via ou through
Lyons/along the coast; **~ la fenêtre** (jeter, regarder) out of
the window; **3 ~ jour/personne** 3 a ou per day/person; **~
2** in twos; **~ ici** this way; (dans le coin) round here; **~-ci,
~-là** here and there; **~ temps de pluie** in wet weather
parabolique [paRabɔlik] adj: **antenne ~** parabolic ou
dish aerial
parachute [paRaʃyt] nm parachute; **parachutiste**
nm/f parachutist; (Mil) paratrooper
parade [paRad] nf (spectacle, défilé) parade; (Escrime,
Boxe) parry
paradis [paRadi] nm heaven, paradise
paradoxe [paRadɔks] nm paradox
paraffine [paRafin] nf paraffin
parages [paRaʒ] nmpl: **dans les ~ (de)** in the area ou
vicinity (of)
paragraphe [paRagRaf] nm paragraph
paraître [paRɛtR] vb +attrib to seem, look, appear ▷ vi
to appear; (être visible) to show; (Presse, Édition) to be
published, come out, appear ▷ vb impers: **il paraît que** it
seems ou appears that, they say that
parallèle [paRalɛl] adj parallel; (non officiel) unofficial
▷ nm (comparaison): **faire un ~ entre** to draw a parallel
between ~ ▷ nf parallel (line)
paralyser [paRalize] vt to paralyse
paramédical, e, -aux [paRamedikal, o] adj:
personnel ~ paramedics pl, paramedical workers pl
paraphrase [paRafRaz] nf paraphrase
parapluie [paRaplɥi] nm umbrella
parasite [paRazit] nm parasite; **parasites** nmpl (Tél)
interference sg
parasol [paRasɔl] nm parasol, sunshade
paratonnerre [paRatɔnɛR] nm lightning conductor
parc [paRk] nm (public) park, gardens pl; (de château etc)
grounds pl; (d'enfant) playpen; **parc à thème** theme
park; **parc d'attractions** amusement park; **parc de
stationnement** car park
parcelle [paRsɛl] nf fragment, scrap; (de terrain) plot,
parcel
parce que [paRsk(ə)] conj because
parchemin [paRʃəmɛ̃] nm parchment
parc(o)mètre [paRkmɛtR] nm parking meter
parcourir [paRkuRiR] vt (trajet, distance) to cover;
(article, livre) to skim ou glance through; (lieu) to go all
over, travel up and down; (suj: frisson) to run through
parcours [paRkuR] nm (trajet) journey; (itinéraire) route
par-dessous [paRd(ə)su] prép, adv under(neath)
pardessus [paRdəsy] nm overcoat
par-dessus [paRd(ə)sy] prép over (the top of) ▷ adv
over (the top); **~ le marché** on top of all this; **~ tout**
above all; **en avoir ~ la tête** to have had enough
par-devant [paRd(ə)vɑ̃] adv (passer) round the front
pardon [paRdɔ̃] nm forgiveness no pl ▷ excl sorry!;
(pour interpeller etc) excuse me!; **demander ~ à qn (de)**
to apologize to sb (for); **je vous demande ~** I'm sorry;
(pour interpeller) excuse me; **pardonner** vt to forgive;
pardonner qch à qn to forgive sb for sth

pare...: pare-brise nm inv windscreen (BRIT),
windshield (US); **pare-chocs** nm inv bumper; **pare-feu** nm inv (de
foyer) fireguard; (Inform) firewall
pareil, le [paRɛj] adj (identique) the same, alike;
(similaire) similar; (tel): **un courage/livre ~** such
courage/a book, courage/a book like this; **faire ~** to do the same (thing); **~ à** the same
as; (similaire) similar to; **sans ~** unparalleled, unequalled
parent, e [paRɑ̃, ɑ̃t] nm/f: **un(e) ~(e)** a relative ou
relation; **parents** nmpl (père et mère) parents; **parenté** nf
(lien) relationship
parenthèse [paRɑ̃tɛz] nf (ponctuation) bracket,
parenthesis; (digression) parenthesis, digression; **entre
~s** in brackets; (fig) incidentally
paresse [paRɛs] nf laziness; **paresseux, -euse** adj lazy
parfait, e [paRfɛ, ɛt] adj perfect ▷ nm (Ling) perfect
(tense); **parfaitement** adv perfectly ▷ excl (most)
certainly
parfois [paRfwa] adv sometimes
parfum [paRfœ̃] nm (produit) perfume, scent; (odeur:
de fleur) scent, fragrance; (goût) flavour; **quels ~s
avez-vous?** what flavours do you have?; **parfumé, e**
adj (fleur, fruit) fragrant; (femme) perfumed; **parfumé au
café** coffee-flavoured; **parfumer** vt (suj: odeur, bouquet)
to perfume; (crème, gâteau) to flavour; **parfumerie** nf
(produits) perfumes pl; (boutique) perfume shop
pari [paRi] nm bet; **parier** vt to bet
Paris [paRi] n Paris; **parisien, ne** adj Parisian; (Géo,
Admin) Paris cpd ▷ nm/f: **Parisien, ne** Parisian
parité [paRite] nf (Pol): **~ hommes-femmes** balanced
representation of women and men
parjure [paRʒyR] nm perjury
parking [paRkiŋ] nm (lieu) car park
parlant, e [paRlɑ̃, ɑ̃t] adj (regard) eloquent; (Cinéma)
talking
parlement [paRləmɑ̃] nm parliament; **parlementaire**
adj parliamentary ▷ nm/f member of parliament
parler [paRle] vi to speak, talk; (avouer) to talk; **~ (à qn)
de** to talk ou speak (to sb) about; **~ le/en français** to
speak French/in French; **~ affaires** to talk business;
sans ~ de (fig) not to mention, to say nothing of; **tu
parles!** (fam: bien sûr) you bet!; **parlez-vous français?**
do you speak French?; **je ne parle pas anglais** I don't
speak English; **est-ce que je peux ~ à ...?** can I speak
to ...?
parloir [paRlwaR] nm (de prison, d'hôpital) visiting room
parmi [paRmi] prép among(st)
paroi [paRwa] nf wall; (cloison) partition
paroisse [paRwas] nf parish
parole [paRɔl] nf (faculté): **la ~** speech; (mot, promesse)
word; **paroles** nfpl (Mus) words, lyrics; **tenir ~** to keep
one's word; **prendre la ~** to speak; **demander la ~** to
ask for permission to speak; **je te crois sur ~** I'll take
your word for it
parquet [paRkɛ] nm (parquet) floor; (Jur): **le ~** the Public
Prosecutor's department
parrain [paRɛ̃] nm godfather; **parrainer** vt (suj:
entreprise) to sponsor
pars [paR] vb voir **partir**
parsemer [paRsəme] vt (suj: feuilles, papiers) to be
scattered over; **~ qch de** to scatter sth with
part [paR] nf (qui revient à qn) share; (fraction, partie) part;
à ~ adv (séparément) separately; (de côté) aside ▷ prép
apart from, except for; **prendre ~ à** (débat etc) to take

part in; (*soucis, douleur de qn*) to share in; **faire ~ de qch à qn** to announce sth to sb, inform sb of sth; **pour ma ~** as for me, as far as I'm concerned; **à ~ entière** full; **de ~ la de** (*au nom de*) on behalf of; (*donné par*) from; **de toute(s) ~(s)** from all sides ou quarters; **de ~ et d'autre** on both sides, on either side; **d'une ~ ... d'autre ~** on the one hand ... on the other hand; **d'autre ~** (*de plus*) moreover; **faire la ~ des choses** to make allowances

partage [paʀtaʒ] *nm* (*fractionnement*) dividing up; (*répartition*) sharing (out) *no pl*, share-out

partager [paʀtaʒe] *vt* to share; (*distribuer, répartir*) to share (out); (*morceler, diviser*) to divide (up); **se ~** *vt* (*héritage etc*) to share between themselves (ou ourselves)

partenaire [paʀtənɛʀ] *nm/f* partner

parterre [paʀtɛʀ] *nm* (*de fleurs*) (flower) bed; (*Théâtre*) stalls *pl*

parti [paʀti] *nm* (*Pol*) party; (*décision*) course of action; (*personne à marier*) match; **tirer ~ de** to take advantage of, turn to good account; **prendre ~ (pour/contre)** to take sides ou a stand (for/against); **parti pris** bias

partial, e, -aux [paʀsjal, jo] *adj* biased, partial

participant, e [paʀtisipɑ̃, ɑ̃t] *nm/f* participant; (*à un concours*) entrant

participation [paʀtisipasjɔ̃] *nf* participation; (*financière*) contribution

participer [paʀtisipe]: **~ à** *vt* (*course, réunion*) to take part in; (*frais etc*) to contribute to; (*chagrin, succès de qn*) to share (in)

particularité [paʀtikylaʀite] *nf* (distinctive) characteristic

particulier, -ière [paʀtikylje, jɛʀ] *adj* (*spécifique*) particular; (*spécial*) special, particular; (*personnel, privé*) private; (*étrange*) peculiar, odd ▷ *nm* (*individu: Admin*) private individual; **~ à** peculiar to; **en ~** (*surtout*) in particular, particularly; (*en privé*) in private; **particulièrement** *adv* particularly

partie [paʀti] *nf* (*gén*) part; (*Jur etc: protagonistes*) party; (*de cartes, tennis etc*) game; **une ~ de pêche** a fishing party ou trip; **en ~** partly, in part; **faire ~ de** (*suj: chose*) to be part of; **prendre qn à ~** to take sb to task; **en grande ~** largely, in the main; **partie civile** (*Jur*) party claiming damages in a criminal case

partiel, le [paʀsjɛl] *adj* partial ▷ *nm* (*Scol*) class exam

partir [paʀtiʀ] *vi* (*gén*) to go; (*quitter*) to go, leave; (*tache*) to go, come out; **~ de** (*lieu: quitter*) to leave; (: *commencer à*) to start from; **~ pour/à** (*lieu, pays etc*) to leave for/go off to; **à ~ de** from; **le train/le bus part à quelle heure?** what time does the train/bus leave?

partisan, e [paʀtizɑ̃, an] *nm/f* partisan ▷ *adj*: **être ~ de qch/de faire** to be in favour of sth/doing

partition [paʀtisjɔ̃] *nf* (*Mus*) score

partout [paʀtu] *adv* everywhere; **~ où il allait** everywhere ou wherever he went

paru [paʀy] *pp* de **paraître**

parution [paʀysjɔ̃] *nf* publication

parvenir [paʀvəniʀ]: **~ à** *vt* (*atteindre*) to reach; (*réussir*): **~ à faire** to manage to do, succeed in doing; **faire ~ qch à qn** to have sth sent to sb

pas¹ [pɑ] *nm* (*enjambée, Danse*) step; (*allure, mesure*) pace; (*bruit*) (foot)step; (*trace*) footprint; **~ à ~** step by step; **au ~** at walking pace; **marcher à grands ~** to stride along; **à ~ de loup** stealthily; **faire les cent ~** to pace up and down; **faire le premier ~** to make the first move; **sur le**

~ de la porte on the doorstep

MOT-CLÉ

pas² [pɑ] *adv* **1** (*en corrélation avec ne, non etc*) not; **il ne pleure pas** (*habituellement*) he does not ou doesn't cry; (*maintenant*) he's not ou isn't crying; **il n'a pas pleuré/ne pleurera pas** he did not ou didn't/will not ou won't cry; **ils n'ont pas de voiture/d'enfants** they don't have ou haven't got a car/any children; **il m'a dit de ne pas le faire** he told me not to do it; **non pas que ...** not that ...
2 (*employé sans ne etc*): **pas moi** not me, I don't (ou can't etc); **elle travaille, (mais) lui pas** ou **pas lui** she works but he doesn't ou does not; **une pomme pas mûre** an unripe apple; **pas du tout** not at all; **pas de sucre, merci** no sugar, thanks; **ceci est à vous ou pas?** is this yours or not?, is this yours or isn't it?
3: **pas mal** (*joli: personne, maison*) not bad; **pas mal fait** not badly done ou made; **comment ça va? — pas mal** how are things? — not bad; **pas mal de** quite a lot of

passage [pɑsaʒ] *nm* (*fait de passer*) voir **passer**; (*lieu, prix de la traversée, extrait*) passage; (*chemin*) way; **de ~** (*touristes*) passing through; **passage à niveau** level crossing; **passage clouté** pedestrian crossing; **passage interdit** no entry; **passage souterrain** subway (BRIT), underpass

passager, -ère [pɑsaʒe, ɛʀ] *adj* passing ▷ *nm/f* passenger

passant, e [pɑsɑ̃, ɑ̃t] *adj* (*rue, endroit*) busy ▷ *nm/f* passer-by; **en ~** in passing

passe [pɑs] *nf* (*Sport, Navig*) pass; **être en ~ de faire** to be on the way to doing; **être dans une mauvaise ~** to be going through a rough patch

passé, e [pɑse] *adj* (*révolu*) past; (*dernier: semaine etc*) last; (*couleur*) faded ▷ *prép* after ▷ *nm* past; (*Ling*) past (tense); **~ de mode** out of fashion; **passé composé** perfect (tense); **passé simple** past historic (tense)

passe-partout [pɑspaʀtu] *nm inv* master ou skeleton key ▷ *adj inv* all-purpose

passeport [pɑspɔʀ] *nm* passport

passer [pɑse] *vi* (*aller*) to go; (*voiture, piétons: défiler*) to pass (by), go by; (*facteur, laitier etc*) to come, call; (*pour rendre visite*) to call ou drop in; (*film, émission*) to be on; (*temps, jours*) to pass, go by; (*couleur*) to fade; (*mode*) to die out; (*douleur*) to pass, go away; (*Scol*): **~ dans la classe supérieure** to go up to the next class ▷ *vt* (*frontière, rivière etc*) to cross; (*douane*) to go through; (*examen*) to sit, take; (*visite médicale etc*) to have; (*journée, temps*) to spend; (*enfiler: vêtement*) to slip on; (*film, pièce*) to show, put on; (*disque*) to play, put on; (*commande*) to place; (*marché, accord*) to agree on; **se ~** *vi* (*avoir lieu: scène, action*) to take place; (*se dérouler: entretien etc*) to go; (*s'écouler: semaine etc*) to pass, go by; (*arriver*): **que s'est-il passé?** what happened?; **~ qch à qn** (*sel etc*) to pass sth to sb; (*prêter*) to lend sb sth; (*lettre, message*) to pass sth on to sb; (*tolérer*) to let sb get away with sth; **~ par** to go through; **~ avant qch/qn** (*fig*) to come before sth/sb; **~ un coup de fil à qn** (*fam*) to give sb a ring; **laisser ~** (*air, lumière, personne*) to let through; (*occasion*) to let slip, miss; (*erreur*) to overlook; **~ à la radio/télévision** to be on the radio/on television; **~ à table** to sit down to eat; **~ au salon** to go into the sitting-room; **~ son tour** to miss one's turn; **~ la seconde** (*Auto*) to change into second; **~ le balai/l'aspirateur** to sweep up/hoover; **je vous passe M. Dupont** (je vous mets en communication avec lui) I'm putting you through to Mr Dupont; (je lui passe l'appareil) here is Mr Dupont, I'll hand you over to Mr Dupont; **se ~ de** to go ou do without

passerelle [pasʀɛl] nf footbridge; (de navire, avion) gangway

passe-temps [pastɑ̃] nm inv pastime

passif, -ive [pasif, iv] adj, nm passive

passion [pasjɔ̃] nf passion; **passionnant, e** adj fascinating; **passionné, e** adj (personne) passionate; (récit) impassioned; **être passionné de** to have a passion for; **passionner** vt (personne) to fascinate, grip

passoire [paswaʀ] nf sieve; (à légumes) colander; (à thé) strainer

pastèque [pastɛk] nf watermelon

pasteur [pastœʀ] nm (protestant) minister, pastor

pastille [pastij] nf (à sucer) lozenge, pastille

patate [patat] nf (fam: pomme de terre) spud; **patate douce** sweet potato

patauger [patoʒe] vi to splash about

pâte [pat] nf (à tarte) pastry; (à pain) dough; (à frire) batter; **pâtes** nfpl (macaroni etc) pasta sg; **pâte à modeler** modelling clay, Plasticine® (BRIT); **pâte brisée** shortcrust pastry; **pâte d'amandes** almond paste, marzipan; **pâte de fruits** crystallized fruit no pl; **pâte feuilletée** puff ou flaky pastry

pâté [pate] nm (charcuterie) pâté; (tache) ink blot; **pâté de maisons** block (of houses); **pâté (de sable)** sandpie; **pâté en croûte** ≈ pork pie

pâtée [pate] nf mash, feed

patente [patɑ̃t] nf (Comm) trading licence

paternel, le [patɛʀnɛl] adj (amour, soins) fatherly; (ligne, autorité) paternal

pâteux, -euse [patø, øz] adj pasty; (langue) coated

pathétique [patetik] adj moving

patience [pasjɑ̃s] nf patience

patient, e [pasjɑ̃, jɑ̃t] adj, nm/f patient; **patienter** vi to wait

patin [patɛ̃] nm skate; (sport) skating; **patins (à glace)** (ice) skates; **patins à roulettes** roller skates

patinage [patinaʒ] nm skating

patiner [patine] vi to skate; (roue, voiture) to spin; **se ~ vi** (meuble, cuir) to acquire a sheen; **patineur, -euse** nm/f skater; **patinoire** nf skating rink, (ice) rink

pâtir [patiʀ]: **~ de** vt to suffer because of

pâtisserie [patisʀi] nf (boutique) cake shop; (gâteau) cake, pastry; (à la maison) pastry- ou cake-making, baking; **pâtissier, -ière** nf pastrycook

patois [patwa] nm dialect, patois

patrie [patʀi] nf homeland

patrimoine [patʀimwan] nm (culture) heritage

patriotique [patʀijɔtik] adj patriotic

patron, ne [patʀɔ̃, ɔn] nm/f boss; (Rel) patron saint ▷ nm (Couture) pattern; **patronat** nm employers pl; **patronner** vt to sponsor, support

patrouille [patʀuj] nf patrol

patte [pat] nf (jambe) leg; (pied: de chien, chat) paw; (: d'oiseau) foot

pâturage [patyʀaʒ] nm pasture

paume [pom] nf palm

paumé, e [pome] (fam) nm/f drop-out

paupière [popjɛʀ] nf eyelid

pause [poz] nf (arrêt) break; (en parlant, Mus) pause

pauvre [povʀ] adj poor; **les pauvres** nmpl the poor; **pauvreté** nf (état) poverty

pavé, e [pave] adj (cour) paved; (chaussée) cobbled ▷ nm (bloc) paving stone; cobblestone

pavillon [pavijɔ̃] nm (de banlieue) small (detached) house; pavilion; (drapeau) flag

payant, e [pejɑ̃, ɑ̃t] adj (spectateurs etc) paying; (fig: entreprise) profitable; (effort) which pays off; **c'est ~** you have to pay, there is a charge

paye [pɛj] nf pay, wages pl

payer [peje] vt (créancier, employé, loyer) to pay; (achat, réparations, fig: faute) to pay for ▷ vi to pay; (métier) to be well-paid; (tactique etc) to pay off; **il me l'a fait ~ 10 euros** he charged me 10 euros for it; **~ qch à qn** to buy sth for sb, buy sb sth; **~ la tête de qn** (fam) to take the mickey out of sb; **est-ce que je peux ~ par carte de crédit?** can I pay by credit card?

pays [pei] nm country; (région) region; **du ~** local

paysage [peizaʒ] nm landscape

paysan, ne [peizɑ̃, an] nm/f farmer; (péj) peasant ▷ adj (agricole) farming; (rural) country

Pays-Bas [peiba] nmpl: **les ~** the Netherlands

PC nm (Inform) PC

PDA sigle m (= personal digital assistant) PDA

PDG sigle m = **président directeur général**

péage [peaʒ] nm toll; (endroit) tollgate

peau, x [po] nf skin; (cuir) fine leather gloves; **être bien/mal dans sa ~** to be quite at ease/ill-at-ease; **peau de chamois** (chiffon) chamois leather, shammy

pêche [pɛʃ] nf (fruit) peach; (sport, activité) fishing; (poissons pêchés) catch; **pêche à la ligne** (en rivière) angling

péché [peʃe] nm sin

pécher [peʃe] vi (Rel) to sin

pêcher [peʃe] nm peach tree ▷ vi to go fishing ▷ vt (attraper) to catch; (être pêcheur de) to fish for

pécheur, -eresse [peʃœʀ, peʃʀɛs] nm/f sinner

pêcheur [peʃœʀ] nm fisherman; (à la ligne) angler

pédagogie [pedagoʒi] nf educational methods pl, pedagogy; **pédagogique** adj educational

pédale [pedal] nf pedal

pédalo [pedalo] nm pedal-boat

pédant, e [pedɑ̃, ɑ̃t] (péj) adj pedantic

pédestre [pedɛstʀ] adj: **randonnée ~** ramble; **sentier ~** pedestrian footpath

pédiatre [pedjatʀ] nm/f paediatrician, child specialist

pédicure [pedikyʀ] nm/f chiropodist

pègre [pɛgʀ] nf underworld

peigne [pɛɲ] nm comb; **peigner** vt to comb (the hair of); **se peigner** vi to comb one's hair; **peignoir** nm dressing gown; **peignoir de bain** bathrobe

peindre [pɛ̃dʀ] vt to paint; (fig) to portray, depict

peine [pɛn] nf (affliction) sorrow, sadness no pl; (mal, effort) trouble no pl, effort; (difficulté) difficulty; (Jur) sentence; **avoir de la ~** to be sad; **faire de la ~ à qn** to distress ou upset sb; **prendre la ~ de faire** to go to the trouble of doing; **se donner de la ~** to make an effort; **ce n'est pas la ~ de faire** there's no point in doing, it's not worth doing; **à ~** scarcely, barely; **à ~ ... que** hardly ... than, no sooner ... than; **peine capitale** capital punishment; **peine de mort** death sentence ou penalty; **peiner** vi (personne) to work hard; (moteur, voiture) to labour ▷ vt to grieve, sadden

peintre [pɛ̃tʀ] nm painter; **peintre en bâtiment**

painter (and decorator)

peinture [pɛ̃tyʀ] nf painting; (matière) paint; (surfaces peintes: aussi: **~s**) paintwork; "**~ fraîche**" "wet paint"

péjoratif, -ive [peʒɔʀatif, iv] adj pejorative, derogatory

Pékin [pekɛ̃] n Beijing

pêle-mêle [pɛlmɛl] adv higgledy-piggledy

peler [pəle] vt, vi to peel

pèlerin [pɛlʀɛ̃] nm pilgrim

pèlerinage [pɛlʀinaʒ] nm pilgrimage

pelle [pɛl] nf shovel; (d'enfant, de terrassier) spade

pellicule [pelikyl] nf film; **pellicules** nfpl (Méd) dandruff sg; **je voudrais une ~ de 36 poses** I'd like a 36-exposure film

pelote [p(ə)lɔt] nf (de fil, laine) ball; **pelote basque** pelota

peloton [p(ə)lɔtɔ̃] nm group, squad; (Cyclisme) pack

pelotonner [p(ə)lɔtɔne]: **se ~** vi to curl (o.s.) up

pelouse [p(ə)luz] nf lawn

peluche [p(ə)lyʃ] nf: (animal en) **~** fluffy animal, soft toy; **chien/lapin en ~** fluffy dog/rabbit

pelure [p(ə)lyʀ] nf peeling, peel no pl

pénal, e, -aux [penal, o] adj penal; **pénalité** nf penalty

penchant [pɑ̃ʃɑ̃] nm (tendance) tendency, propensity; (faible) liking, fondness

pencher [pɑ̃ʃe] vi to tilt, lean over ▷ vt to tilt; **se ~** vi to lean over; (se baisser) to bend down; **se ~ sur** (fig: problème) to look into; **~ pour** to be inclined to favour

pendant [pɑ̃dɑ̃] prép (au cours de) during; (indique la durée) for; **~ que** while

pendentif [pɑ̃dɑ̃tif] nm pendant

penderie [pɑ̃dʀi] nf wardrobe

pendre [pɑ̃dʀ] vt, vi to hang; **se ~** (se suicider) to hang o.s.; **~ qch à** (mur) to hang sth (up) on; (plafond) to hang sth (up) from

pendule [pɑ̃dyl] nf clock ▷ nm pendulum

pénétrer [penetʀe] vi, vt to penetrate; **~ dans** to enter

pénible [penibl] adj (travail) hard; (sujet) painful; (personne) tiresome; **péniblement** adv with difficulty

péniche [peniʃ] nf barge

pénicilline [penisilin] nf penicillin

péninsule [penɛ̃syl] nf peninsula

pénis [penis] nm penis

pénitence [penitɑ̃s] nf (peine) penance; (repentir) penitence; **pénitencier** nm penitentiary

pénombre [penɔ̃bʀ] nf (faible clarté) half-light; (obscurité) darkness

pensée [pɑ̃se] nf thought; (démarche, doctrine) thinking no pl; (fleur) pansy; **en ~** in one's mind

penser [pɑ̃se] vi, vt to think; **~ à** (ami, vacances) to think of ou about; (réfléchir à: problème, offre) to think about ou over; (prévoir) to think of; **faire ~ à** to remind one of; **~ faire qch** to be thinking of doing sth, intend to do sth; **pensif, -ive** adj pensive, thoughtful

pension [pɑ̃sjɔ̃] nf (allocation) pension; (prix du logement) board and lodgings, bed and board; (école) boarding school; **pension alimentaire** (de divorcée) maintenance allowance, alimony; **pension complète** full board; **pension de famille** boarding house, guesthouse; **pensionnaire** nm/f (Scol) boarder; **pensionnat** nm boarding school

pente [pɑ̃t] nf slope; **en ~** sloping

Pentecôte [pɑ̃tkot] nf: **la ~** Whitsun (BRIT), Pentecost

pénurie [penyʀi] nf shortage

pépé [pepe] (fam) nm grandad

pépin [pepɛ̃] nm (Bot: graine) pip; (ennui) snag, hitch

pépinière [pepinjɛʀ] nf nursery

perçant, e [pɛʀsɑ̃, ɑ̃t] adj (cri) piercing, shrill; (regard) piercing

percepteur, -trice [pɛʀsɛptœʀ, tʀis] nm/f tax collector

perception [pɛʀsɛpsjɔ̃] nf perception; (bureau) tax office

percer [pɛʀse] vt to pierce; (ouverture etc) to make; (mystère, énigme) to penetrate ▷ vi to break through; **perceuse** nf drill

percevoir [pɛʀsəvwaʀ] vt (distinguer) to perceive, detect; (taxe, impôt) to collect; (revenu, indemnité) to receive

perche [pɛʀʃ] nf (bâton) pole

percher [pɛʀʃe] vt, vi to perch; **se ~** vi to perch; **perchoir** nm perch

perçois etc [pɛʀswa] vb voir **percevoir**

perçu, e [pɛʀsy] pp de **percevoir**

percussion [pɛʀkysjɔ̃] nf percussion

percuter [pɛʀkyte] vt to strike; (suj: véhicule) to crash into

perdant, e [pɛʀdɑ̃, ɑ̃t] nm/f loser

perdre [pɛʀdʀ] vt to lose; (gaspiller: temps, argent) to waste; (personne: moralement etc) to ruin ▷ vi to lose; (sur une vente etc) to lose out; **se ~** vi (s'égarer) to get lost, lose one's way; (denrées) to go to waste; **j'ai perdu mon portefeuille/passeport** I've lost my wallet/passport; **je me suis perdu** I'm lost; (et je ne le suis plus) I got lost

perdrix [pɛʀdʀi] nf partridge

perdu, e [pɛʀdy] pp de **perdre** ▷ adj (isolé) out-of-the-way; (Comm: emballage) non-returnable; (malade): **il est ~** there's no hope left for him; **à vos moments ~s** in your spare time

père [pɛʀ] nm father; **père de famille** father; **le père Noël** Father Christmas

perfection [pɛʀfɛksjɔ̃] nf perfection; **à la ~** to perfection; **perfectionné, e** adj sophisticated; **perfectionner** vt to improve, perfect; **se perfectionner en anglais** to improve one's English

perforer [pɛʀfɔʀe] vt (poinçonner) to punch

performant, e [pɛʀfɔʀmɑ̃, ɑ̃t] adj: **très ~** high-performance cpd

perfusion [pɛʀfyzjɔ̃] nf: **faire une ~ à qn** to put sb on a drip

péril [peʀil] nm peril

périmé, e [peʀime] adj (Admin) out-of-date, expired

périmètre [peʀimɛtʀ] nm perimeter

période [peʀjɔd] nf period; **périodique** adj periodic ▷ nm periodical; **garniture** ou **serviette périodique** sanitary towel (BRIT) ou napkin (US)

périphérique [peʀifeʀik] adj (quartiers) outlying ▷ nm (Auto): **boulevard ~** ring road (BRIT), beltway (US)

périr [peʀiʀ] vi to die, perish

périssable [peʀisabl] adj perishable

perle [pɛʀl] nf pearl; (de plastique, métal, sueur) bead

permanence [pɛʀmanɑ̃s] nf permanence; (local) (duty) office; **assurer une ~** (service public, bureaux) to operate ou maintain a basic service; **être de ~** to be on call ou duty; **en ~** continuously

permanent, e [pɛʀmanɑ̃, ɑ̃t] adj permanent; (spectacle) continuous; **permanente** nf perm

perméable [pɛʀmeabl] *adj* (*terrain*) permeable; **~ à** (*fig*) receptive *ou* open to

permettre [pɛʀmɛtʀ] *vt* to allow, permit; **~ à qn de faire/qch** to allow sb to do/sth; **se ~ de faire** to take the liberty of doing

permis [pɛʀmi] *nm* permit, licence; **permis de conduire** driving licence (BRIT), driver's license (US); **permis de construire** planning permission (BRIT), building permit (US); **permis de séjour** residence permit; **permis de travail** work permit

permission [pɛʀmisjɔ̃] *nf* permission; (*Mil*) leave; **avoir la ~ de faire** to have permission to do; **en ~** on leave

Pérou [peʀu] *nm* Peru

perpétuel, le [pɛʀpetɥɛl] *adj* perpetual; **perpétuité** *nf*: **à perpétuité** for life; **être condamné à perpétuité** to receive a life sentence

perplexe [pɛʀplɛks] *adj* perplexed, puzzled

perquisitionner [pɛʀkizisjɔne] *vi* to carry out a search

perron [peʀɔ̃] *nm* steps *pl* (*leading to entrance*)

perroquet [peʀɔkɛ] *nm* parrot

perruche [peʀyʃ] *nf* budgerigar (BRIT), budgie (BRIT), parakeet (US)

perruque [peʀyk] *nf* wig

persécuter [pɛʀsekyte] *vt* to persecute

persévérer [pɛʀsevere] *vi* to persevere

persil [pɛʀsi] *nm* parsley

Persique [pɛʀsik] *adj*: **le golfe ~** the (Persian) Gulf

persistant, e [pɛʀsistɑ̃, ɑ̃t] *adj* persistent

persister [pɛʀsiste] *vi* to persist; **~ à faire qch** to persist in doing sth

personnage [pɛʀsɔnaʒ] *nm* (*individu*) character, individual; (*célébrité*) important person; (*de roman, film*) character; (*Peinture*) figure

personnalité [pɛʀsɔnalite] *nf* personality; (*personnage*) prominent figure

personne [pɛʀsɔn] *nf* person ▷ *pron* nobody, no one; (*avec négation en anglais*) anybody, anyone; **personne âgée** elderly person; **personnel, le** *adj* personal; (*égoïste*) selfish ▷ *nm* staff, personnel; **personnellement** *adv* personally

perspective [pɛʀspɛktiv] *nf* (*Art*) perspective; (*vue*) view; (*point de vue*) viewpoint, angle; (*chose envisagée*) prospect; **en ~** in prospect

perspicace [pɛʀspikas] *adj* clear-sighted, gifted with (*ou* showing) insight; **perspicacité** *nf* clear-sightedness

persuader [pɛʀsɥade] *vt*: **~ qn (de faire)** to persuade sb (to do); **persuasif, -ive** *adj* persuasive

perte [pɛʀt] *nf* loss; (*de temps*) waste; (*fig: morale*) ruin; **à ~ de vue** as far as the eye can (*ou* could) see; **pertes blanches** (vaginal) discharge *sg*

pertinent, e [pɛʀtinɑ̃, ɑ̃t] *adj* apt, relevant

perturbation [pɛʀtyʀbasjɔ̃] *nf*: **perturbation (atmosphérique)** atmospheric disturbance

perturber [pɛʀtyʀbe] *vt* to disrupt; (*Psych*) to perturb, disturb

pervers, e [pɛʀvɛʀ, ɛʀs] *adj* perverted

pervertir [pɛʀvɛʀtiʀ] *vt* to pervert

pesant, e [pəzɑ̃, ɑ̃t] *adj* heavy; (*fig: présence*) burdensome

pèse-personne [pɛzpɛʀsɔn] *nm* (bathroom) scales *pl*

peser [pəze] *vt* to weigh ▷ *vi* to weigh; (*fig: avoir de l'importance*) to carry weight; **~ lourd** to be heavy

pessimiste [pesimist] *adj* pessimistic ▷ *nm/f* pessimist

peste [pɛst] *nf* plague

pétale [petal] *nm* petal

pétanque [petɑ̃k] *nf* type of bowls

pétard [petaʀ] *nm* banger (BRIT), firecracker

péter [pete] *vi* (*fam: casser*) to bust; (*fam!*) to fart (*!*)

pétillant, e [petijɑ̃, ɑ̃t] *adj* (*eau etc*) sparkling

pétiller [petije] *vi* (*feu*) to crackle; (*champagne*) to bubble; (*yeux*) to sparkle

petit, e [p(ə)ti, it] *adj* small; (*avec nuance affective*) little; (*voyage*) short, little; (*bruit etc*) faint, slight ▷ *nm/f* (*petit enfant*) little boy/girl, child; **petits** *nmpl* (*d'un animal*) young *no pl*; **faire des ~s** to have kittens (*ou* puppies *etc*); **la classe des ~s** the infant class; **les tout~s** the little ones, the tiny tots (*fam*); **~ à ~** bit by bit, gradually; **petit(e) ami(e)** boyfriend/girlfriend; **petit déjeuner** breakfast; **le petit déjeuner est à quelle heure?** what time is breakfast?; **petit four** petit four; **petit pain** (bread) roll; **les petites annonces** the small ads; **petits pois** (garden) peas; **petite-fille** *nf* granddaughter; **petit-fils** *nm* grandson

pétition [petisjɔ̃] *nf* petition

petits-enfants [pətizɑ̃fɑ̃] *nmpl* grandchildren

pétrin [petʀɛ̃] *nm* (*fig*): **dans le ~** (*fam*) in a jam *ou* fix

pétrir [petʀiʀ] *vt* to knead

pétrole [petʀɔl] *nm* oil; (*pour lampe, réchaud etc*) paraffin (oil); **pétrolier, -ière** *nm* oil tanker

 MOT-CLÉ

peu [pø] *adv* **1** (*modifiant verbe, adjectif, adverbe*): **il boit peu** he doesn't drink (very) much; **il est peu bavard** he's not very talkative; **peu avant/après** shortly before/afterwards

2 (*modifiant nom*): **peu de: peu de gens/d'arbres** few *ou* not (very) many people/trees; **il a peu d'espoir** he hasn't (got) much hope, he has little hope; **pour peu de temps** for (only) a short while

3: **peu à peu** little by little; **à peu près** just about, more or less; **à peu près 10 kg/10 euros** approximately 10 kg/10 euros

▷ *nm* **1**: **le peu de gens qui** the few people who; **le peu de sable qui** what little sand, the little sand which

2: **un peu** a little; **un petit peu** a little bit; **un peu d'espoir** a little hope; **elle est un peu bavarde** she's quite *ou* rather talkative; **un peu plus de** slightly more than; **un peu moins de** slightly less than; (*avec pluriel*) slightly fewer than

▷ *pron*: **peu le savent** few know (it); **de peu** (only) just

peuple [pœpl] *nm* people; **peupler** *vt* (*pays, région*) to populate; (*étang*) to stock; (*suj: hommes, poissons*) to inhabit

peuplier [pøplije] *nm* poplar (tree)

peur [pœʀ] *nf* fear; **avoir ~ (de/de faire/que)** to be frightened *ou* afraid (of/of doing/that); **faire ~ à** to frighten; **de ~ de/que** for fear of/that; **peureux, -euse** *adj* fearful, timorous

peut [pø] *vb voir* **pouvoir**

peut-être [pøtɛtʀ] *adv* perhaps, maybe; **~ que** perhaps, maybe; **~ bien qu'il fera/est** he may well do/be

phare [faʀ] *nm* (*en mer*) lighthouse; (*de véhicule*) headlight

pharmacie [faʀmasi] *nf* (*magasin*) chemist's (BRIT), pharmacy; (*de salle de bain*) medicine cabinet; **pharmacien, ne** *nm/f* pharmacist, chemist (BRIT)

phénomène [fenɔmɛn] nm phenomenon
philosophe [filɔzɔf] nm/f philosopher ▷ adj philosophical
philosophie [filɔzɔfi] nf philosophy
phobie [fɔbi] nf phobia
phoque [fɔk] nm seal
phosphorescent, e [fɔsfɔresɑ̃, ɑ̃t] adj luminous
photo [foto] nf photo(graph); **prendre en ~** to take a photo of; **pourriez-vous nous prendre en ~, s'il vous plaît?** would you take a picture of us, please?; **faire de la ~** to take photos; **photo d'identité** passport photograph; **photocopie** nf photocopy; **photocopier** vt to photocopy; **photocopieuse** nf photocopier; **photographe** nm/f photographer; **photographie** nf (technique) photography; (cliché) photograph; **photographier** vt to photograph
phrase [fʀaz] nf sentence
physicien, ne [fizisjɛ̃, jɛn] nm/f physicist
physique [fizik] adj physical ▷ nm physique ▷ nf physics sg; **au ~** physically; **physiquement** adv physically
pianiste [pjanist] nm/f pianist
piano [pjano] nm piano; **pianoter** vi to tinkle away (at the piano)
pic [pik] nm (instrument) pick(axe); (montagne) peak; (Zool) woodpecker; **à ~** vertically; (fig: tomber, arriver) just at the right time
pichet [piʃɛ] nm jug
picorer [pikɔʀe] vt to peck
pie [pi] nf magpie
pièce [pjɛs] nf (d'un logement) room; (Théâtre) play; (de machine) part; (de monnaie) coin; (document) document; (fragment, de collection) piece; **dix euros ~** ten euros each; **vendre à la ~** to sell separately; **travailler à la ~** to do piecework; **un maillot une ~** a one-piece swimsuit; **un deux-~s cuisine** a two-room(ed) flat (BRIT) ou apartment (US) with kitchen; **pièce à conviction** exhibit; **pièce d'eau** ornamental lake ou pond; **pièce de rechange** spare (part); **pièce d'identité: avez-vous une pièce d'identité?** have you got any (means of) identification?; **pièce jointe** (Comput) attachment; **pièce montée** tiered cake; **pièces détachées** spares, (spare) parts; **pièces justificatives** supporting documents
pied [pje] nm foot; (de table) leg; (de lampe) base; **~s nus** ou **nus-~s** barefoot; **à ~** on foot; **au ~ de la lettre** literally; **avoir ~** to be able to touch the bottom, not to be out of one's depth; **avoir le ~ marin** to be a good sailor; **sur ~** (debout, rétabli) up and about; **mettre sur ~** (entreprise) to set up; **c'est le ~** (fam) it's brilliant; **mettre les ~s dans le plat** (fam) to put one's foot in it; **il se débrouille comme un ~** (fam) he's completely useless; **pied-noir** nm Algerian-born Frenchman
piège [pjɛʒ] nm trap; **prendre au ~** to trap; **piéger** vt (avec une bombe) to booby-trap; **lettre/voiture piégée** letter-/car-bomb
piercing [pjɛʀsiŋ] nm body piercing
pierre [pjɛʀ] nf stone; **pierre tombale** tombstone; **pierreries** nfpl gems, precious stones
piétiner [pjetine] vi (trépigner) to stamp (one's feet); (fig) to be at a standstill ▷ vt to trample on
piéton, ne [pjetɔ̃, ɔn] nm/f pedestrian; **piétonnier, -ière** adj: **rue** ou **zone piétonnière** pedestrian precinct
pieu, x [pjø] nm post; (pointu) stake

pieuvre [pjœvʀ] nf octopus
pieux, -euse [pjø, pjøz] adj pious
pigeon [piʒɔ̃] nm pigeon
piger [piʒe] (fam) vi, vt to understand
pigiste [piʒist] nm/f freelance(r)
pignon [piɲɔ̃] nm (de mur) gable
pile [pil] nf (tas) pile; (Élec) battery ▷ adv (fam: s'arrêter etc) dead; **à deux heures ~** at two on the dot; **jouer à ~ ou face** to toss up (for it); **~ ou face?** heads or tails?
piler [pile] vt to crush, pound
pilier [pilje] nm pillar
piller [pije] vt to pillage, plunder, loot
pilote [pilɔt] nm pilot; (de voiture) driver ▷ adj pilot cpd: **pilote de course** racing driver; **pilote de ligne** airline pilot; **piloter** vt (avion) to pilot, fly; (voiture) to drive
pilule [pilyl] nf pill; **prendre la ~** to be on the pill
piment [pimɑ̃] nm (aussi: **~ rouge**) chilli; (fig) spice, piquancy; **~ doux** pepper, capsicum; **pimenté, e** adj (plat) hot, spicy
pin [pɛ̃] nm pine
pinard [pinaʀ] (fam) nm (cheap) wine, plonk (BRIT)
pince [pɛ̃s] nf (outil) pliers pl; (de homard, crabe) pincer, claw; (Couture: pli) dart; **pince à épiler** tweezers pl; **pince à linge** clothes peg (BRIT) ou pin (US)
pincé, e [pɛ̃se] adj (air) stiff
pinceau, x [pɛ̃so] nm (paint)brush
pincer [pɛ̃se] vt to pinch; (fam) to nab
pinède [pined] nf pinewood, pine forest
pingouin [pɛ̃gwɛ̃] nm penguin
ping-pong® [piŋpɔ̃g] nm table tennis
pinson [pɛ̃sɔ̃] nm chaffinch
pintade [pɛ̃tad] nf guinea-fowl
pion [pjɔ̃] nm (Échecs) pawn; (Dames) piece; (Scol) supervisor
pionnier [pjɔnje] nm pioneer
pipe [pip] nf pipe; **fumer la ~** to smoke a pipe
piquant, e [pikɑ̃, ɑ̃t] adj (barbe, rosier etc) prickly; (saveur, sauce) hot, pungent; (détail) titillating; (froid) biting ▷ nm (épine) thorn, prickle; (fig) spiciness, spice
pique [pik] nf pike; (fig) cutting remark ▷ nm (Cartes) spades pl
pique-nique [piknik] nm picnic; **pique-niquer** vi to have a picnic
piquer [pike] vt (suj: guêpe, fumée, orties) to sting; (: moustique) to bite; (: barbe) to prick; (: froid) to bite; (Méd) to give a jab to; (: chien, chat) to put to sleep; (intérêt) to arouse; (fam: voler) to pinch ▷ vi (avion) to go into a dive
piquet [pikɛ] nm (pieu) post, stake; (de tente) peg
piqûre [pikyʀ] nf (d'épingle) prick; (d'ortie) sting; (de moustique) bite; (Méd) injection, shot (US); **faire une ~ à qn** to give sb an injection
pirate [piʀat] nm, adj pirate; **pirate de l'air** hijacker
pire [piʀ] adj worse; (superlatif): **le(la) ~ ...** the worst ... ▷ nm: **le ~ (de)** the worst (of); **au ~** at (the very) worst
pis [pi] nm (de vache) udder ▷ adj, adv worse; **de mal en ~** from bad to worse
piscine [pisin] nf (swimming) pool; **piscine couverte** indoor (swimming) pool
pissenlit [pisɑ̃li] nm dandelion
pistache [pistaʃ] nf pistachio (nut)
piste [pist] nf (d'un animal, sentier) track, trail; (indice) lead; (de stade) track; (de cirque) ring; (de danse) floor; (de patinage) rink; (de ski) run; (Aviat) runway; **piste cyclable** cycle track

pistolet [pistɔlɛ] nm (arme) pistol, gun; (à peinture) spray gun; **pistolet-mitrailleur** nm submachine gun

piston [pistɔ̃] nm (Tech) piston; **avoir du ~** (fam) to have friends in the right places; **pistonner** vt (candidat) to pull strings for

piteux, -euse [pitø, øz] adj pitiful, sorry (avant le nom); **en ~ état** in a sorry state

pitié [pitje] nf pity; **il me fait ~** I feel sorry for him; **avoir ~ de** (compassion) to pity, feel sorry for; (merci) to have pity ou mercy on

pitoyable [pitwajabl] adj pitiful

pittoresque [pitɔRɛsk] adj picturesque

PJ sigle f (= police judiciaire) ≈ CID (BRIT), ≈ FBI (US)

placard [plakaR] nm (armoire) cupboard; (affiche) poster, notice

place [plas] nf (emplacement, classement) place; (de ville, village) square; (espace libre) room, space; (de parking) space; (siège: de train, cinéma, voiture) seat; (emploi) job; **en ~** (mettre) in its place; **sur ~** on the spot; **faire ~ à** to give way to; **ça prend de la ~** it takes up a lot of room ou space; **à la ~ de** in place of, instead of; **à votre ~ ...** if I were you ...; **je voudrais réserver deux ~s** I'd like to book two seats; **la ~ est prise?** is this seat taken?; **se mettre à la ~ de qn** to put o.s. in sb's place ou in sb's shoes

placé, e [plase] adj: **haut ~** (fig) high-ranking; **être bien/mal ~** (spectateur) to have a good/a poor seat; (concurrent) to be in a good/bad position; **il est bien ~ pour le savoir** he is in a position to know

placement [plasmɑ̃] nm (Finance) investment; **agence ou bureau de ~** employment agency

placer [plase] vt to place; (convive, spectateur) to seat; (argent) to place, invest; **se ~ au premier rang** to go and stand (ou sit) in the first row

plafond [plafɔ̃] nm ceiling

plage [plaʒ] nf beach; **plage arrière** (Auto) parcel ou back shelf

plaider [plede] vi (avocat) to plead ▷ vt to plead; **~ pour** (fig) to speak for; **plaidoyer** nm (Jur) speech for the defence; (fig) plea

plaie [plɛ] nf wound

plaignant, e [plɛɲɑ̃, ɑ̃t] nm/f plaintiff

plaindre [plɛ̃dR] vt to pity, feel sorry for; **se ~** vi (gémir) to moan; (protester): **se ~ (à qn) (de)** to complain (to sb) (about); (souffrir): **se ~ de** to complain of

plaine [plɛn] nf plain

plain-pied [plɛ̃pje] adv: **de ~ (avec)** on the same level (as)

plainte [plɛ̃t] nf (gémissement) moan, groan; (doléance) complaint; **porter ~** to lodge a complaint

plaire [plɛR] vi to be a success, be successful; **ça plaît beaucoup aux jeunes** it's very popular with young people; **~ à: cela me plaît** I like it; **se ~ quelque part** to like being somewhere ou like it somewhere; **s'il vous plaît** please

plaisance [plɛzɑ̃s] nf (aussi: **navigation de ~**) (pleasure) sailing, yachting

plaisant, e [plɛzɑ̃, ɑ̃t] adj pleasant; (histoire, anecdote) amusing

plaisanter [plɛzɑ̃te] vi to joke; **plaisanterie** nf joke

plaisir [plɛziR] nm pleasure; **faire ~ à qn** (délibérément) to be nice to sb, please sb; **ça me fait ~** I like (doing) it; **j'espère que ça te fera ~** I hope you'll like it; **pour le ~** for pleasure

plaît [plɛ] vb voir **plaire**

plan, e [plɑ̃, an] adj flat ▷ nm plan; (fig) level, plane; (Cinéma) shot; **au premier/second ~** in the foreground/ middle distance; **à l'arrière ~** in the background; **plan d'eau** lake

planche [plɑ̃ʃ] nf (pièce de bois) plank, (wooden) board; (illustration) plate; **planche à repasser** ironing board; **planche (à roulettes)** skateboard; **planche (à voile)** (sport) windsurfing

plancher [plɑ̃ʃe] nm floor; floorboards pl ▷ vi (fam) to work hard

planer [plane] vi to glide; (fam: rêveur) to have one's head in the clouds; **~ sur** (fig: danger) to hang over

planète [planɛt] nf planet

planeur [planœR] nm glider

planifier [planifje] vt to plan

planning [planiŋ] nm programme, schedule; **planning familial** family planning

plant [plɑ̃] nm seedling, young plant

plante [plɑ̃t] nf plant; **la plante du pied** the sole (of the foot); **plante verte ou d'appartement** house plant

planter [plɑ̃te] vt (plante) to plant; (enfoncer) to hammer ou drive in; (tente) to put up, pitch; (fam: personne) to dump; **se ~** (fam: se tromper) to get it wrong

plaque [plak] nf plate; (de verglas, d'eczéma) patch; (avec inscription) plaque; **plaque chauffante** hotplate; **plaque de chocolat** bar of chocolate; **plaque tournante** (fig) centre

plaqué, e [plake] adj: **~ or/argent** gold-/silver-plated

plaquer [plake] vt (Rugby) to bring down; (fam: laisser tomber) to drop

plaquette [plakɛt] nf (de chocolat) bar; (beurre) pack(et); **plaquette de frein** brake pad

plastique [plastik] adj, nm plastic; **plastiquer** vt to blow up (with a plastic bomb)

plat, e [pla, -at] adj flat; (cheveux) straight; (style) flat, dull ▷ nm (récipient, Culin) dish; (d'un repas) course; **à ~ ventre** face down; **à ~** (pneu, batterie) flat; (fam: personne) dead beat; **plat cuisiné** pre-cooked meal; **plat de résistance** main course; **plat du jour** dish of the day

platane [platan] nm plane tree

plateau, x [plato] nm (support) tray; (Géo) plateau; (Cinéma) set; **plateau à fromages** cheese board

plate-bande [platbɑ̃d] nf flower bed

plate-forme [platfɔRm] nf platform; **plate-forme de forage/pétrolière** drilling/oil rig

platine [platin] nm platinum ▷ nf (d'un tourne-disque) turntable; **platine laser** compact disc ou CD player

plâtre [plɑtR] nm (matériau) plaster; (statue) plaster statue; (Méd) (plaster) cast; **avoir un bras dans le ~** to have an arm in plaster

plein, e [plɛ̃, plɛn] adj full ▷ nm: **faire le ~ (d'essence)** to fill up (with petrol); **à ~es mains** (ramasser) in handfuls; **à ~ temps** full-time; **en ~ air** in the open air; **en ~ soleil** in direct sunlight; **en ~e nuit/rue** in the middle of the night/street; **en ~ jour** in broad daylight; **le ~, s'il vous plaît** fill it up, please

pleurer [plœRe] vi to cry; (yeux) to water ▷ vt to mourn (for); **~ sur** to lament (over), to bemoan

pleurnicher [plœRniʃe] vi to snivel, whine

pleurs [plœR] nmpl: **en ~** in tears

pleut [plø] vb voir **pleuvoir**

pleuvoir [pløvwaR] vb impers to rain ▷ vi (coups) to rain down; (critiques, invitations) to shower down; **il pleut**

it's raining; **il pleut des cordes** it's pouring (down), it's raining cats and dogs

pli [pli] nm fold; (de jupe) pleat; (de pantalon) crease

pliant, e [plijā, plijāt] adj folding

plier [plije] vt to fold; (pour ranger) to fold up; (genou, bras) to bend ▷ vi to bend; (fig) to yield; **se ~ à** to submit to

plisser [plise] vt (jupe) to put pleats in; (yeux) to screw up; (front) to crease

plomb [plɔ̃] nm (métal) lead; (d'une cartouche) (lead) shot; (Pêche) sinker; (Élec) fuse; **sans ~** (essence etc) unleaded

plomberie [plɔ̃bʀi] nf plumbing

plombier [plɔ̃bje] nm plumber

plonge [plɔ̃ʒ] nf washing-up

plongeant, e [plɔ̃ʒã, ãt] adj (vue) from above; (décolleté) plunging

plongée [plɔ̃ʒe] nf (Sport) diving no pl; (sans scaphandre) skin diving; **~ sous-marine** diving

plongeoir [plɔ̃ʒwaʀ] nm diving board

plongeon [plɔ̃ʒɔ̃] nm dive

plonger [plɔ̃ʒe] vi to dive ▷ vt: **~ qch dans** to plunge sth into; **se ~ dans** (études, lecture) to bury ou immerse o.s. in; **plongeur** nm diver

plu [ply] pp de **plaire**; de **pleuvoir**

pluie [plɥi] nf rain

plume [plym] nf feather; (pour écrire) (pen) nib; (fig) pen

plupart [plypaʀ]: **la ~** pron the majority, most (of them); **la ~ des** most, the majority of; **la ~ du temps/d'entre nous** most of the time/of us; **pour la ~** for the most part, mostly

pluriel [plyʀjɛl] nm plural

plus¹ [ply] vb voir **plaire**

○ MOT-CLÉ

plus² [ply] adv 1 (forme négative): **ne ... plus** no more, no longer; **je n'ai plus d'argent** I've got no more money ou no money left; **il ne travaille plus** he's no longer working, he doesn't work any more

2 [ply, plyz + voyelle] (comparatif) more, ...+er; (superlatif): **le plus** the most, the ...+est; **plus grand/intelligent (que)** bigger/more intelligent (than); **le plus grand/intelligent** the biggest/most intelligent; **tout au plus** at the very most

3 [plys, plyz + voyelle] (davantage) more; **il travaille plus (que)** he works more (than); **plus il travaille, plus il est heureux** the more he works, the happier he is; **plus de 10 personnes/3 heures** more than ou over 10 people/3 hours; **3 heures de plus que** 3 hours more than; **de plus** what's more, moreover; **il a 3 ans de plus que moi** he's 3 years older than me; **3 kilos en plus** 3 kilos more; **en plus de** in addition to; **de plus en plus** more and more; **plus ou moins** more or less; **ni plus ni moins** no more, no less

▷ prép [plys]: **4 plus 2** 4 plus 2

plusieurs [plyzjœʀ] dét, pron several; **ils sont ~** there are several of them

plus-value [plyvaly] nf (bénéfice) surplus

plutôt [plyto] adv rather; **je préfère ~ celui-ci** I'd rather have this one; **~ que (de) faire** rather than ou instead of doing

pluvieux, -euse [plyvjø, jøz] adj rainy, wet

PME sigle f (= petite(s) et moyenne(s) entreprise(s)) small business(es)

PMU sigle m (= Pari mutuel urbain) system of betting on horses; (café) betting agency

PNB sigle m (= produit national brut) GNP

pneu [pnø] nm tyre (BRIT), tire (US); **j'ai un ~ crevé** I've got a flat tyre

pneumonie [pnømɔni] nf pneumonia

poche [pɔʃ] nf pocket; (sous les yeux) bag, pouch; **argent de ~** pocket money

pochette [pɔʃɛt] nf (d'aiguilles etc) case; (mouchoir) breast pocket handkerchief; (sac à main) clutch bag; **pochette de disque** record sleeve

poêle [pwal] nm stove ▷ nf: **~ (à frire)** frying pan

poème [pɔɛm] nm poem

poésie [pɔezi] nf (poème) poem; (art): **la ~** poetry

poète [pɔɛt] nm poet

poids [pwa] nm weight; (Sport) shot; **vendre au ~** to sell by weight; **perdre/prendre du ~** to lose/put on weight; **poids lourd** (camion) lorry (BRIT), truck (US)

poignant, e [pwaɲã, ãt] adj poignant

poignard [pwaɲaʀ] nm dagger; **poignarder** vt to stab, knife

poigne [pwaɲ] nf grip; **avoir de la ~** (fig) to rule with a firm hand

poignée [pwaɲe] nf (de sel etc, fig) handful; (de couvercle, porte) handle; **poignée de main** handshake

poignet [pwaɲɛ] nm (Anat) wrist; (de chemise) cuff

poil [pwal] nm (Anat) hair; (de pinceau, brosse) bristle; (de tapis) strand; (pelage) coat; (fam) starkers; **au ~** (fam) hunky-dory; **poilu, e** adj hairy

poinçonner [pwɛ̃sɔne] vt (bijou) to hallmark; (billet) to punch

poing [pwɛ̃] nm fist; **coup de ~** punch

point [pwɛ̃] nm point; (endroit) spot; (marque, signe) dot; (: de ponctuation) full stop, period (US); (Couture, Tricot) stitch ▷ adv = **pas²**; **faire le ~** (fig) to take stock (of the situation); **sur le ~ de faire** (just) about to do; **à tel ~ que** so much so that; **mettre au ~** (procédé) to develop; (affaire) to settle; **à ~** (Culin: viande) medium; **à ~ (nommé)** just at the right time; **deux ~s** colon; **point de côté** stitch (pain); **point d'exclamation/d'interrogation** exclamation/question mark; **point de repère** landmark; (dans le temps) point of reference; **point de vente** retail outlet; **point de vue** viewpoint; (fig: opinion) point of view; **point faible** weak spot; **point final** full stop, period (US); **point mort: au point mort** (Auto) in neutral; **points de suspension** suspension points

pointe [pwɛ̃t] nf point; (clou) tack; (fig): **une ~ de** a hint of; **être à la ~ de** (fig) to be in the forefront of; **sur la ~ des pieds** on tiptoe; **en ~** pointed, tapered; **de ~** (technique etc) leading; **heures de ~** peak hours

pointer [pwɛ̃te] vt (diriger: canon, doigt): **~ sur qch** to point at sth ▷ vi (employé) to clock in

pointillé [pwɛ̃tije] nm (trait) dotted line

pointilleux, -euse [pwɛ̃tijø, øz] adj particular, pernickety

pointu, e [pwɛ̃ty] adj pointed; (voix) shrill; (analyse) precise

pointure [pwɛ̃tyʀ] nf size

point-virgule [pwɛ̃viʀgyl] nm semi-colon

poire [pwaʀ] nf pear; (fam: péj) mug

poireau, X [pwaʀo] nm leek

poirier [pwaʀje] nm pear tree

pois [pwa] nm (Bot) pea; (sur une étoffe) dot, spot; **~**

chiche chickpea; **à ~** (*cravate etc*) spotted, polka-dot *cpd*
poison [pwazɔ̃] *nm* poison
poisseux, -euse [pwasø, øz] *adj* sticky
poisson [pwasɔ̃] *nm* fish *gén inv*; (*Astrol*): **P~s** Pisces;
~ d'avril April fool; (*blague*) April Fool's Day trick;
poisson rouge goldfish; **poissonnerie** *nf* fish-shop;
poissonnier, -ière *nm/f* fishmonger (BRIT), fish
merchant (US)
poitrine [pwatrin] *nf* chest; (*seins*) bust, bosom; (*Culin*)
breast
poivre [pwavR] *nm* pepper
poivron [pwavRɔ̃] *nm* pepper, capsicum
polaire [poleR] *adj* polar
pôle [pol] *nm* (*Géo*, *Élec*) pole; **le ~ Nord/Sud** the
North/South Pole
poli, e [poli] *adj* polite; (*lisse*) smooth
police [polis] *nf* police; **police judiciaire** ≈ Criminal
Investigation Department (BRIT), ≈ Federal Bureau of
Investigation (US); **police secours** ≈ emergency services
pl (BRIT), ≈ paramedics *pl* (US); **policier, -ière** *adj* police
cpd ▷ *nm* policeman; (*aussi*: **roman policier**) detective
novel
polir [poliR] *vt* to polish
politesse [polites] *nf* politeness
politicien, ne [politisjɛ̃, jɛn] (*péj*) *nm/f* politician
politique [politik] *adj* political ▷ *nf* politics *sg*; (*mesures,
méthode*) policies *pl*
politiquement [politikmɑ̃] *adv* politically; **~ correct**
politically correct
pollen [polɛn] *nm* pollen
polluant, e [pɔlyɑ̃, ɑ̃t] *adj* polluting ▷ *nm* (*produit*): **~**
pollutant; **non ~** non-polluting
polluer [pɔlɥe] *vt* to pollute; **pollution** *nf* pollution
polo [polo] *nm* (*chemise*) polo shirt
Pologne [pɔlɔɲ] *nf*: **la ~** Poland; **polonais, e** *adj* Polish
▷ *nm/f*: **Polonais, e** Pole ▷ *nm* (Ling) Polish
poltron, ne [pɔltRɔ̃, ɔn] *adj* cowardly
polycopier [pɔlikɔpje] *vt* to duplicate
Polynésie [pɔlinezi] *nf*: **la ~** Polynesia; **la ~ française**
French Polynesia
polyvalent, e [pɔlivalɑ̃, ɑ̃t] *adj* (*rôle*) varied; (*salle*)
multi-purpose
pommade [pɔmad] *nf* ointment, cream
pomme [pɔm] *nf* apple; **tomber dans les ~s** (*fam*) to
pass out; **pomme d'Adam** Adam's apple; **pomme de
pin** pine ou fir cone; **pomme de terre** potato
pommette [pɔmɛt] *nf* cheekbone
pommier [pɔmje] *nm* apple tree
pompe [pɔ̃p] *nf* pump; (*faste*) pomp (and ceremony);
pompe (à essence) petrol pump; **pompes funèbres**
funeral parlour *sg*, undertaker's *sg*; **pomper** *vt* to pump;
(*aspirer*) to pump up; (*absorber*) to soak up
pompeux, -euse [pɔ̃pø, øz] *adj* pompous
pompier [pɔ̃pje] *nm* fireman
pompiste [pɔ̃pist] *nm/f* petrol (BRIT) ou gas (US) pump
attendant
poncer [pɔ̃se] *vt* to sand (down)
ponctuation [pɔ̃ktɥasjɔ̃] *nf* punctuation
ponctuel, le [pɔ̃ktɥɛl] *adj* punctual
pondéré, e [pɔ̃deRe] *adj* level-headed, composed
pondre [pɔ̃dR] *vt* to lay
poney [pɔnɛ] *nm* pony
pont [pɔ̃] *nm* bridge; (*Navig*) deck; **faire le ~** to take the
extra day off; **pont suspendu** suspension bridge; **pont-**

levis *nm* drawbridge
pop [pɔp] *adj inv* pop
populaire [pɔpylɛR] *adj* popular; (*manifestation*)
mass *cpd*; (*milieux, quartier*) working-class; (*expression*)
vernacular
popularité [pɔpylaRite] *nf* popularity
population [pɔpylasjɔ̃] *nf* population
populeux, -euse [pɔpylø, øz] *adj* densely populated
porc [pɔR] *nm* pig; (*Culin*) pork
porcelaine [pɔRsəlɛn] *nf* porcelain, china; piece of
china(ware)
porc-épic [pɔRkepik] *nm* porcupine
porche [pɔRʃ] *nm* porch
porcherie [pɔRʃəRi] *nf* pigsty
pore [pɔR] *nm* pore
porno [pɔRno] *adj* porno ▷ *nm* porn
port [pɔR] *nm* harbour, port; (*ville*) port; (*de l'uniforme etc*)
wearing; (*pour lettre*) postage; (*pour colis, aussi*: *posture*)
carriage; **port d'arme** (*Jur*) carrying of a firearm; **port
payé** postage paid
portable [pɔRtabl] *adj* (*portatif*) portable; (*téléphone*)
mobile ▷ *nm* (*Comput*) laptop (computer); (*téléphone*)
mobile (phone)
portail [pɔRtaj] *nm* gate
portant, e [pɔRtɑ̃, ɑ̃t] *adj*: **bien/mal ~** in good/poor
health
portatif, -ive [pɔRtatif, iv] *adj* portable
porte [pɔRt] *nf* door; (*de ville, jardin*) gate; **mettre à la
~** to throw out; **porte-avions** *nm inv* aircraft carrier;
porte-bagages *nm inv* luggage rack; **porte-bonheur**
nm inv lucky charm; **porte-clefs** *nm inv* key ring; **porte-
documents** *nm inv* attaché ou document case
porté, e [pɔRte] *adj*: **être ~ à faire** to be inclined to
do; **être ~ sur qch** to be keen on sth; **portée** *nf* (*d'une
arme*) range; (*fig*: *effet*) impact, import; (: *capacité*) scope,
capability; (*de chatte etc*) litter; (*Mus*) stave, staff; **à/hors
de portée (de)** within/out of reach (of); **à portée de
(la) main** within (arm's) reach; **à la portée de qn** (*fig*) at
sb's level, within sb's capabilities
porte...: **portefeuille** *nm* wallet; **portemanteau, x** *nm*
(*cintre*) coat hanger; (*au mur*) coat rack; **porte-monnaie**
nm inv purse; **porte-parole** *nm inv* spokesman
porter [pɔRte] *vt* to carry; (*sur soi*: *vêtement, barbe, bague*)
to wear; (*fig*: *responsabilité etc*) to bear, carry; (*inscription,
nom, fruits*) to bear; (*coup*) to deal; (*attention*) to turn;
(*apporter*): **~ qch à qn** to take sth to sb ▷ *vi* (*voix*) to carry;
(*coup, argument*) to hit home; **se ~** *vi* (*se sentir*): **se ~ bien/
mal** to be well/unwell; **~ sur** (*recherches*) to be concerned
with; **se faire ~ malade** to report sick
porteur, -euse [pɔRtœR, øz] *nm/f* (*de bagages*) porter;
(*de chèque*) bearer
porte-voix [pɔRtəvwa] *nm inv* megaphone
portier [pɔRtje] *nm* doorman
portière [pɔRtjɛR] *nf* door
portion [pɔRsjɔ̃] *nf* (*part*) portion, share; (*partie*)
portion, section
porto [pɔRto] *nm* port (wine)
portrait [pɔRtRɛ] *nm* (*peinture*) portrait; (*photo*)
photograph; **portrait-robot** *nm* Identikit® ou photo-
fit® picture
portuaire [pɔRtɥɛR] *adj* port *cpd*, harbour *cpd*
portugais, e [pɔRtyɡɛ, ɛz] *adj* Portuguese ▷ *nm/f*: **P~, e**
Portuguese ▷ *nm* (Ling) Portuguese
Portugal [pɔRtyɡal] *nm*: **le ~** Portugal

pose [poz] *nf (de moquette)* laying; *(attitude, d'un modèle)* pose; *(Photo)* exposure

posé, e [poze] *adj* serious

poser [poze] *vt* to put; *(installer: moquette, carrelage)* to lay; *(rideaux, papier peint)* to hang; *(question)* to ask; *(principe, conditions)* to lay ou set down; *(formuler: problème)* to formulate ▷ *vi (modèle)* to pose; **se ~** *vi (oiseau, avion)* to land; *(question)* to arise; **~ qch (sur)** *(déposer)* to put sth down (on); **~ qch sur/quelque part** *(placer)* to put sth on/somewhere; **~ sa candidature à un poste** to apply for a post

positif, -ive [pozitif, iv] *adj* positive

position [pozisjɔ̃] *nf* position; **prendre ~** *(fig)* to take a stand

posologie [pozɔlɔʒi] *nf* dosage

posséder [posede] *vt* to own, possess; *(qualité, talent)* to have, possess; *(sexuellement)* to possess; **possession** *nf* ownership *no pl*, possession; **prendre possession de qch** to take possession of sth

possibilité [posibilite] *nf* possibility; **possibilités** *nfpl (potentiel)* potential *sg*

possible [posibl] *adj* possible; *(projet, entreprise)* feasible ▷ *nm*: **faire son ~** to do all one can, do one's utmost; **le plus/moins de livres ~** as many/few books as possible; **le plus vite ~** as quickly as possible; **aussitôt/dès que ~** as soon as possible

postal, e, -aux [postal, o] *adj* postal

poste¹ [post] *nf (service)* post, postal service; *(administration, bureau)* post office; **mettre à la ~** to post; **poste restante** poste restante (BRIT), general delivery (US)

poste² [post] *nm (fonction, Mil)* post; *(Tél)* extension; *(de radio etc)* set; **poste de police** police station; **poste de secours** first-aid post; **poste d'essence** filling station; **poste d'incendie** fire point; **poste de pilotage** cockpit, flight deck

poster [poste] *vt* to post; **où est-ce que je peux ~ ces cartes postales?** where can I post these cards?

postérieur, e [posterjœr] *adj (date)* later; *(partie)* back ▷ *nm (fam)* behind

postuler [postyle] *vi*: **~ à ou pour un emploi** to apply for a job

pot [po] *nm (en verre)* jar; *(en terre)* pot; *(en plastique, carton)* carton; *(en métal)* tin; *(fam: chance)* luck; **avoir du ~** *(fam)* to be lucky; **boire ou prendre un ~** *(fam)* to have a drink; **petit ~ (pour bébé)** (jar of) baby food; **~ catalytique** catalytic converter; **pot d'échappement** exhaust pipe

potable [potabl] *adj*: **eau (non) ~** (non-)drinking water

potage [potaʒ] *nm* soup; **potager, -ère** *adj*: **(jardin) potager** kitchen ou vegetable garden

pot-au-feu [potofø] *nm inv (beef) stew

pot-de-vin [podvɛ̃] *nm* bribe

pote [pot] *(fam)* nm pal

poteau, x [poto] *nm* post; **poteau indicateur** signpost

potelé, e [pot(ə)le] *adj* plump, chubby

potentiel, le [potɑ̃sjɛl] *adj, nm* potential

poterie [potri] *nf* pottery; *(objet)* piece of pottery

potier, -ière [potje, jɛr] *nm/f* potter

potiron [potirɔ̃] *nm* pumpkin

pou, x [pu] *nm* louse

poubelle [pubɛl] *nf* (dust)bin

pouce [pus] *nm* thumb

poudre [pudr] *nf* powder; *(fard)* (face) powder; *(explosif)* gunpowder; **en ~: café en ~** instant coffee; **lait en ~** dried ou powdered milk; **poudreuse** *nf* powder snow; **poudrier** *nm* (powder) compact

pouffer [pufe] *vi*: **~ (de rire)** to burst out laughing

poulailler [pulaje] *nm* henhouse

poulain [pulɛ̃] *nm* foal; *(fig)* protégé

poule [pul] *nf* hen; *(Culin)* (boiling) fowl; **poule mouillée** coward

poulet [pulɛ] *nm* chicken; *(fam)* cop

poulie [puli] *nf* pulley

pouls [pu] *nm* pulse; **prendre le ~ de qn** to feel sb's pulse

poumon [pumɔ̃] *nm* lung

poupée [pupe] *nf* doll

pour [pur] *prép* for ▷ *nm*: **le ~ et le contre** the pros and cons; **~ faire** (so as) to do, in order to do; **~ avoir fait** for having done; **~ que** so that, in order that; **fermé ~ (cause de) travaux** closed for refurbishment ou alterations; **c'est ~ ça que ...** that's why ...; **~ quoi faire?** what for?; **~ 20 euros d'essence** 20 euros' worth of petrol; **~ cent** per cent; **~ ce qui est de** as for

pourboire [purbwar] *nm* tip; **combien de ~ est-ce qu'il faut laisser?** how much should I tip?

pourcentage [pursɑ̃taʒ] *nm* percentage

pourchasser [purʃase] *vt* to pursue

pourparlers [purparle] *nmpl* talks, negotiations

pourpre [purpr] *adj* crimson

pourquoi [purkwa] *adv, conj* why ▷ *nm inv*: **le ~ (de)** the reason (for)

pourrai *etc* [pure] *vb voir* **pouvoir**

pourri, e [puri] *adj* rotten

pourrir [purir] *vi* to rot; *(fruit)* to go rotten ou bad ▷ *vt* to rot; *(fig)* to spoil thoroughly; **pourriture** *nf* rot

poursuite [pursɥit] *nf* pursuit, chase; **poursuites** *nfpl (Jur)* legal proceedings

poursuivre [pursɥivr] *vt* to pursue, chase (after); *(obséder)* to haunt; *(Jur)* to bring proceedings against, prosecute; *(: au civil)* to sue; *(but)* to strive towards; *(continuer: études etc)* to carry on with, continue; **se ~** to go on, continue

pourtant [purtɑ̃] *adv* yet; **c'est ~ facile** (and) yet it's easy

pourtour [purtur] *nm* perimeter

pourvoir [purvwar] *vt*: **~ qch/qn de** to equip sth/sb with ▷ *vi*: **~ à** to provide for; **pourvu, e** *adj*: **pourvu de** equipped with; **pourvu que** *(si)* provided that, so long as; *(espérons que)* let's hope (that)

pousse [pus] *nf* growth; *(bourgeon)* shoot

poussée [puse] *nf* thrust; *(d'acné)* eruption; *(fig: prix)* upsurge

pousser [puse] *vt* to push; *(émettre: cri, soupir)* to give; *(stimuler: élève)* to urge on; *(poursuivre: études, discussion)* to carry on (further) ▷ *vi* to push; *(croître)* to grow; **se ~** *vi* to move over; **~ qn à** *(inciter)* to urge ou press sb to; *(acculer)* to drive sb to; **faire ~** *(plante)* to grow

poussette [pusɛt] *nf* push chair (BRIT), stroller (US)

poussière [pusjɛr] *nf* dust; **poussiéreux, -euse** *adj* dusty

poussin [pusɛ̃] *nm* chick

poutre [putr] *nf* beam

MOT-CLÉ

pouvoir [puvwar] *nm* power; *(Pol: dirigeants)*: **le pouvoir** those in power; **les pouvoirs publics** the authorities; **pouvoir d'achat** purchasing power

▷ vb semi-aux **1** (être en état de) can, be able to; **je ne peux pas le réparer** I can't ou I am not able to repair it; **déçu de ne pas pouvoir le faire** disappointed not to be able to do it

2 (avoir la permission) can, may, be allowed to; **vous pouvez aller au cinéma** you can ou may go to the pictures

3 (probabilité, hypothèse) may, might, could; **il a pu avoir un accident** he may ou might ou could have had an accident; **il aurait pu le dire!** he might ou could have said (so)!

▷ vb impers may, might, could; **il peut arriver que** it may ou might ou could happen that; **il pourrait pleuvoir** it might rain

▷ vt can, be able to; **j'ai fait tout ce que j'ai pu** I did all I could; **je n'en peux plus** (épuisé) I'm exhausted; (à bout) I can't take any more

▷ vi: **se pouvoir: il se peut que** it may ou might be that; **cela se pourrait** that's quite possible

prairie [pʀeʀi] nf meadow
praline [pʀalin] nf sugared almond
praticable [pʀatikabl] adj passable, practicable
pratiquant, e [pʀatikã, ãt] nm/f (regular) churchgoer
pratique [pʀatik] nf practice ▷ adj practical;
  pratiquement adv (pour ainsi dire) practically, virtually;
  pratiquer vt to practise; (l'équitation, la pêche) to go in
  for; (le golf, football) to play; (intervention, opération) to
  carry out
pré [pʀe] nm meadow
préalable [pʀealabl] adj preliminary; **au ~** beforehand
préambule [pʀeãbyl] nm preamble; (fig) prelude; **sans
  ~** straight away
préau [pʀeo] nm (Scol) covered playground
préavis [pʀeavi] nm notice
précaution [pʀekosjɔ̃] nf precaution; **avec ~**
  cautiously; **par ~** as a precaution
précédemment [pʀesedamã] adv before, previously
précédent, e [pʀesedã, ãt] adj previous ▷ nm
  precedent; **sans ~** unprecedented; **le jour ~** the day
  before, the previous day
précéder [pʀesede] vt to precede
prêcher [pʀeʃe] vt to preach
précieux, -euse [pʀesjø, jøz] adj precious; (aide,
  conseil) invaluable
précipice [pʀesipis] nm drop, chasm
précipitamment [pʀesipitamã] adv hurriedly, hastily
précipitation [pʀesipitasjɔ̃] nf (hâte) haste
précipité, e [pʀesipite] adj hurried, hasty
précipiter [pʀesipite] vt (hâter: départ) to hasten; (faire
  tomber): **~ qn/qch du haut de** to throw ou hurl sb/sth
  off ou from; **se ~** vi to speed up; **se ~ sur/vers** to rush
  at/towards
précis, e [pʀesi, iz] adj precise; (mesures) accurate,
  precise; **à 4 heures ~es** at 4 o'clock sharp; **précisément**
  adv precisely; **préciser** vt (expliquer) to be more specific
  about, clarify; (spécifier) to state, specify; **se préciser**
  vi to become clear(er); **précision** nf precision; (détail)
  point ou detail; **demander des précisions** to ask for
  further explanation
précoce [pʀekɔs] adj early; (enfant) precocious
préconçu, e [pʀekɔ̃sy] adj preconceived
préconiser [pʀekɔnize] vt to advocate
prédécesseur [pʀedesesœʀ] nm predecessor

prédilection [pʀedileksjɔ̃] nf: **avoir une ~ pour** to be
  partial to
prédire [pʀediʀ] vt to predict
prédominer [pʀedɔmine] vi to predominate
préface [pʀefas] nf preface
préfecture [pʀefɛktyʀ] nf prefecture; **préfecture de
  police** police headquarters pl
préférable [pʀefeʀabl] adj preferable
préféré, e [pʀefeʀe] adj, nm/f favourite
préférence [pʀefeʀãs] nf preference; **de ~** preferably
préférer [pʀefeʀe] vt: **~ qn/qch (à)** to prefer sb/sth
  (to), like sb/sth better (than); **~ faire** to prefer to do; **je
  préférerais du thé** I would rather have tea, I'd prefer tea
préfet [pʀefɛ] nm prefect
préhistorique [pʀeistɔʀik] adj prehistoric
préjudice [pʀeʒydis] nm (matériel) loss; (moral) harm
  no pl; **porter ~ à** to harm, be detrimental to; **au ~ de** at
  the expense of
préjugé [pʀeʒyʒe] nm prejudice; **avoir un ~ contre** to
  be prejudiced ou biased against
prélasser [pʀelase]: **se ~** vi to lounge
prélèvement [pʀelɛvmã] nm (montant) deduction;
  faire un ~ de sang to take a blood sample
prélever [pʀel(ə)ve] vt (échantillon) to take; **~ (sur)**
  (montant) to deduct (from); (argent: sur son compte) to
  withdraw (from)
prématuré, e [pʀematyʀe] adj premature ▷ nm
  premature baby
premier, -ière [pʀəmje, jɛʀ] adj first; (rang) front; (fig:
  objectif) basic; **le ~ venu** the first person to come along;
  de ~ ordre first-rate; **Premier ministre** Prime Minister;
  première nf (Scol) year 12 (BRIT), eleventh grade (US);
  (Aviat, Rail etc) first class; **premièrement** adv firstly
prémonition [pʀemɔnisjɔ̃] nf premonition
prenant, e [pʀənã, ãt] adj absorbing, engrossing
prénatal, e [pʀenatal] adj (Méd) antenatal
prendre [pʀãdʀ] vt to take; (repas) to have; (se procurer)
  to get; (malfaiteur, poisson) to catch; (passager) to pick up;
  (personnel) to take on; (traiter: personne) to handle; (voix,
  ton) to put on; (ôter): **~ qch à** to take sth from; (coincer):
  se ~ les doigts dans to get one's fingers caught in ▷ vi
  (liquide, ciment) to set; (greffe, vaccin) to take; (feu: foyer)
  to go; (se diriger): **~ à gauche** to turn (to the) left; **~
  froid** to catch cold; **se ~ pour** to think one is; **s'en ~ à**
  to attack; **se ~ d'amitié pour** to befriend; **s'y ~** (procéder)
  to set about it
preneur [pʀənœʀ] nm: **être/trouver ~** to be willing to
  buy/find a buyer
prénom [pʀenɔ̃] nm first ou Christian name
préoccupation [pʀeɔkypasjɔ̃] nf (souci) concern; (idée
  fixe) preoccupation
préoccuper [pʀeɔkype] vt (inquiéter) to worry;
  (absorber) to preoccupy; **se ~ de** to be concerned with
préparatifs [pʀepaʀatif] nmpl preparations
préparation [pʀepaʀasjɔ̃] nf preparation
préparer [pʀepaʀe] vt to prepare; (café, thé) to make;
  (examen) to prepare for; (voyage, entreprise) to plan; **se ~** vi
  (orage, tragédie) to brew, be in the air; **~ qch à qn** (surprise
  etc) to have sth in store for sb; **se ~ (à qch/faire)** to
  prepare (o.s.) ou get ready (for sth/to do)
prépondérant, e [pʀepɔ̃deʀã, ãt] adj major,
  dominating
préposé, e [pʀepoze] nm/f employee; (facteur) postman
préposition [pʀepozisjɔ̃] nf preposition

près [pʀɛ] adv near, close; **~ de** near (to), close to; (environ) nearly, almost; **de ~** closely; **à 5 kg ~** to within about 5 kg; **il n'est pas à 10 minutes ~** he can spare 10 minutes; **est-ce qu'il y a une banque ~ d'ici?** is there a bank nearby?

présage [pʀezaʒ] nm omen

presbyte [pʀɛsbit] adj long-sighted

presbytère [pʀɛsbitɛʀ] nm presbytery

prescription [pʀɛskʀipsjɔ̃] nf prescription

prescrire [pʀɛskʀiʀ] vt to prescribe

présence [pʀezɑ̃s] nf presence; (au bureau, à l'école) attendance

présent, e [pʀezɑ̃, ɑ̃t] adj, nm present; **à ~ (que)** now (that)

présentation [pʀezɑ̃tasjɔ̃] nf presentation; (de nouveau venu) introduction; (allure) appearance; **faire les ~s** to do the introductions

présenter [pʀezɑ̃te] vt to present; (excuses, condoléances) to offer; (invité, conférencier): **~ qn (à)** to introduce sb (to) ▷ vi: **~ bien** to have a pleasing appearance; **se ~** vi (occasion) to arise; **se ~ à** (examen) to sit; (élection) to stand at, run for; **je vous présente Nadine** this is Nadine, could I introduce you to Nadine?

préservatif [pʀezɛʀvatif] nm condom, sheath

préserver [pʀezɛʀve] vt: **~ de** (protéger) to protect from

président [pʀezidɑ̃] nm (Pol) president; (d'une assemblée, Comm) chairman; **président directeur général** chairman and managing director; **présidentielles** nfpl presidential elections

présider [pʀezide] vt to preside over; (dîner) to be the guest of honour at

presque [pʀɛsk] adv almost, nearly; **~ personne** hardly anyone; **~ rien** hardly anything; **~ pas** hardly (at all); **~ pas (de)** hardly any

presqu'île [pʀɛskil] nf peninsula

pressant, e [pʀesɑ̃, ɑ̃t] adj urgent

presse [pʀɛs] nf press; (affluence): **heures de ~** busy times

pressé, e [pʀese] adj in a hurry; (travail) urgent; **orange ~e** freshly-squeezed orange juice

pressentiment [pʀesɑ̃timɑ̃] nm foreboding, premonition

pressentir [pʀesɑ̃tiʀ] vt to sense

presse-papiers [pʀɛspapje] nm inv paperweight

presser [pʀese] vt (fruit, éponge) to squeeze; (bouton) to press; (allure) to speed up; (inciter): **~ qn de faire** to urge ou press sb to do ▷ vi to be urgent; **se ~** vi (se hâter) to hurry (up); **se ~ contre qn** to squeeze up against sb; **le temps presse** there's not much time; **rien ne presse** there's no hurry

pressing [pʀesiŋ] nm (magasin) dry-cleaner's

pression [pʀesjɔ̃] nf pressure; (bouton) press stud; (fam: bière) draught beer; **faire ~ sur** to put pressure on; **sous ~** pressurized, under pressure; (fig) under pressure; **pression artérielle** blood pressure

prestataire [pʀɛstatɛʀ] nm/f supplier

prestation [pʀɛstasjɔ̃] nf (allocation) benefit; (d'une entreprise) service provided; (d'un artiste) performance

prestidigitateur, -trice [pʀɛstidiʒitatœʀ, tʀis] nm/f conjurer

prestige [pʀɛstiʒ] nm prestige; **prestigieux, -euse** adj prestigious

présumer [pʀezyme] vt: **~ que** to presume ou assume that

prêt, e [pʀɛ, pʀɛt] adj ready ▷ nm (somme) loan; **quand est-ce que mes photos seront ~es?** when will my photos be ready?; **prêt-à-porter** nm ready-to-wear ou off-the-peg (BRIT) clothes pl

prétendre [pʀetɑ̃dʀ] vt (affirmer): **~ que** to claim that; (avoir l'intention de): **~ faire qch** to mean ou intend to do sth; **prétendu, e** adj (supposé) so-called

prétentieux, -euse [pʀetɑ̃sjø, jøz] adj pretentious

prétention [pʀetɑ̃sjɔ̃] nf claim; (vanité) pretentiousness

prêter [pʀete] vt (livres, argent): **~ qch (à)** to lend sth (to); (supposer): **~ à qn** (caractère, propos) to attribute to sb; **pouvez-vous me ~ de l'argent?** can you lend me some money?

prétexte [pʀetɛkst] nm pretext, excuse; **sous aucun ~** on no account; **prétexter** vt to give as a pretext ou an excuse

prêtre [pʀɛtʀ] nm priest

preuve [pʀœv] nf proof, evidence no pl; **faire ~ de** to show; **faire ses ~s** to prove o.s. (ou itself)

prévaloir [pʀevalwaʀ] vi to prevail

prévenant, e [pʀev(ə)nɑ̃, ɑ̃t] adj thoughtful, kind

prévenir [pʀev(ə)niʀ] vt (éviter: catastrophe etc) to avoid, prevent; (anticiper: désirs, besoins) to anticipate; **~ qn (de)** (avertir) to warn sb (about); (informer) to tell ou inform sb (about)

préventif, -ive [pʀevɑ̃tif, iv] adj preventive

prévention [pʀevɑ̃sjɔ̃] nf prevention; **prévention routière** road safety

prévenu, e [pʀev(ə)ny] nm/f (Jur) defendant, accused

prévision [pʀevizjɔ̃] nf: **~s** predictions; (Écon) forecast sg; **en ~ de** in anticipation of; **prévisions météorologiques** weather forecast sg

prévoir [pʀevwaʀ] vt (anticiper) to foresee; (s'attendre à) to expect, reckon on; (organiser: voyage etc) to plan; (envisager) to allow; **comme prévu** as planned; **prévoyant, e** adj gifted with (ou showing) foresight; **prévu, e** pp de **prévoir**

prier [pʀije] vi to pray ▷ vt (Dieu) to pray to; (implorer) to beg; (demander): **~ qn de faire** to ask sb to do; **se faire ~** to need coaxing ou persuading; **je vous en prie** (allez-y) please do; (de rien) don't mention it; **prière** nf prayer; **"prière de ..."** "please ..."

primaire [pʀimɛʀ] adj primary ▷ nm (Scol) primary education

prime [pʀim] nf (bonus) bonus; (subvention) premium; (Comm: cadeau) free gift; (Assurances, Bourse) premium ▷ adj: **de ~ abord** at first glance; **primer** vt (récompenser) to award a prize to ▷ vi to dominate; to be most important

primevère [pʀimvɛʀ] nf primrose

primitif, -ive [pʀimitif, iv] adj primitive; (originel) original

prince [pʀɛ̃s] nm prince; **princesse** nf princess

principal, e, -aux [pʀɛ̃sipal, o] adj principal, main ▷ nm (Scol) principal, head(master); (essentiel) main thing

principe [pʀɛ̃sip] nm principle; **par ~** on principle; **en ~** (habituellement) as a rule; (théoriquement) in principle

printemps [pʀɛ̃tɑ̃] nm spring

priorité [pʀijɔʀite] nf priority; (Auto) right of way; **priorité à droite** right of way to vehicles coming from the right

pris, e [pʀi, pʀiz] pp de **prendre** ▷ adj (place) taken; (mains) full; (personne) busy; **avoir le nez/la gorge ~(e)** to have a stuffy nose/a hoarse throat; **être de**

panique to be panic-stricken

prise [priz] nf (d'une ville) capture; (Pêche, Chasse) catch; (point d'appui ou pour empoigner) hold; (Élec: fiche) plug; (: femelle) socket; **être aux ~s avec** to be grappling with; **prise de courant** power point; **prise de sang** blood test; **prise multiple** adaptor

priser [prize] vt (estimer) to prize, value

prison [prizɔ̃] nf prison; **aller/être en ~** to go to/be in prison ou jail; **prisonnier, -ière** nm/f prisoner ▷ adj captive

privé, e [prive] adj private; (en punition): **tu es ~ de télé!** no TV for you! ▷ nm (Comm) private sector; **en ~** in private

priver [prive] vt: **~ qn de** to deprive sb of; **se ~ de** to go ou do without

privilège [privilɛʒ] nm privilege

prix [pri] nm price; (récompense, Scol) prize; **hors de ~** exorbitantly priced; **à aucun ~** not at any price; **à tout ~** at all costs

probable [prɔbabl] adj likely, probable; **probablement** adv probably

problème [prɔblɛm] nm problem

procédé [prɔsede] nm (méthode) process; (comportement) behaviour no pl

procéder [prɔsede] vi (agir) to proceed; (moralement) to behave; **~ à** to carry out

procès [prɔsɛ] nm trial; (poursuites) proceedings pl; **être en ~ avec** to be involved in a lawsuit with

processus [prɔsesys] nm process

procès-verbal, -aux [prɔsɛverbal, o] nm (de réunion) minutes pl; (contravention): **P.-V.** parking ticket

prochain, e [prɔʃɛ̃, ɛn] adj next; (proche: départ, arrivée) impending ▷ nm fellow man; **la ~e fois/semaine ~e** next time/week; **prochainement** adv soon, shortly

proche [prɔʃ] adj nearby; (dans le temps) imminent; (parent, ami) close; **proches** nmpl (parents) close relatives; **être ~ (de)** to be near, be close (to)

proclamer [prɔklame] vt to proclaim

procuration [prɔkyrasjɔ̃] nf proxy

procurer [prɔkyre] vt: **~ qch à qn** (fournir) to obtain sth for sb; (causer: plaisir etc) to bring sb sth; **se ~** vt to get; **procureur** nm public prosecutor

prodige [prɔdiʒ] nm marvel, wonder; (personne) prodigy; **prodiguer** vt (soins, attentions): **prodiguer qch à qn** to give sb sth

producteur, -trice [prɔdyktœr, tris] nm/f producer

productif, -ive [prɔdyktif, iv] adj productive

production [prɔdyksjɔ̃] nf production; (rendement) output

productivité [prɔdyktivite] nf productivity

produire [prɔdɥir] vt to produce; **se ~** vi (événement) to happen, occur; (acteur) to perform, appear

produit [prɔdɥi] nm product; **produit chimique** chemical; **produits agricoles** farm produce sg; **produits de beauté** beauty products, cosmetics; **produits d'entretien** cleaning products

prof [prɔf] (fam) nm teacher

proférer [prɔfere] vt to utter

professeur, e [prɔfesœr] nm/f teacher; (de faculté) (university) lecturer; (: titulaire d'une chaire) professor

profession [prɔfesjɔ̃] nf occupation; **~ libérale** (liberal) profession; **sans ~** unemployed; **professionnel, le** adj, nm/f professional

profil [prɔfil] nm profile; **de ~** in profile

profit [prɔfi] nm (avantage) benefit, advantage; (Comm, Finance) profit; **au ~ de** in aid of; **tirer ~ de** to profit from; **profitable** adj (utile) beneficial; (lucratif) profitable; **profiter** vi: **profiter de** (situation, occasion) to take advantage of; (vacances, jeunesse etc) to make the most of

profond, e [prɔfɔ̃, ɔ̃d] adj deep; (sentiment, intérêt) profound; **profondément** adv deeply; **il dort profondément** he is sound asleep; **profondeur** nf depth; **l'eau à quelle profondeur?** how deep is the water?

programme [prɔgram] nm programme; (Scol) syllabus, curriculum; (Inform) program; **programmer** vt (émission) to schedule; (Inform) to program; **programmeur, -euse** nm/f programmer

progrès [prɔgrɛ] nm progress no pl; **faire des ~** to make progress; **progresser** vi to progress; **progressif, -ive** adj progressive

proie [prwa] nf prey no pl

projecteur [prɔʒɛktœr] nm (pour film) projector; (de théâtre, cirque) spotlight

projectile [prɔʒɛktil] nm missile

projection [prɔʒɛksjɔ̃] nf projection; (séance) showing

projet [prɔʒɛ] nm plan; (ébauche) draft; **projet de loi** bill; **projeter** vt (envisager) to plan; (film, photos) to project; (ombre, lueur) to throw, cast; (jeter) to throw up (ou off ou out)

prolétaire [prɔletɛr] adj, nmf proletarian

prolongement [prɔlɔ̃ʒmɑ̃] nm extension; **dans le ~ de** running on from

prolonger [prɔlɔ̃ʒe] vt (débat, séjour) to prolong; (délai, billet, rue) to extend; **se ~** vi to go on

promenade [prɔm(ə)nad] nf walk (ou drive ou ride); **faire une ~** to go for a walk; **une ~ en voiture/à vélo** a drive/(bicycle) ride

promener [prɔm(ə)ne] vt (chien) to take out for a walk; (doigts, regard): **~ qch sur** to run sth over; **se ~** vi to go for (ou be out for) a walk

promesse [prɔmɛs] nf promise

promettre [prɔmɛtr] vt to promise ▷ vi to be ou look promising; **~ à qn de faire** to promise sb that one will do

promiscuité [prɔmiskɥite] nf (chambre) lack of privacy

promontoire [prɔmɔ̃twar] nm headland

promoteur, -trice [prɔmɔtœr, tris] nm/f: **promoteur (immobilier)** property developer (BRIT), real estate promoter (US)

promotion [prɔmosjɔ̃] nf promotion; **en ~** on special offer

promouvoir [prɔmuvwar] vt to promote

prompt, e [prɔ̃(pt), prɔ̃(p)t] adj swift, rapid

prôner [prone] vt (préconiser) to advocate

pronom [prɔnɔ̃] nm pronoun

prononcer [prɔnɔ̃se] vt to pronounce; (dire) to utter; (discours) to deliver; **se ~** vi to be pronounced; **comment est-ce que ça se prononce?** how do you pronounce ou say it?; **se ~ (sur)** (se décider) to reach a decision (on ou about), give a verdict (on); **prononciation** nf pronunciation

pronostic [prɔnɔstik] nm (Méd) prognosis; (fig: aussi: **~s**) forecast

propagande [prɔpagɑ̃d] nf propaganda

propager [prɔpaʒe] vt to spread; **se ~** vi to spread

prophète [prɔfɛt] nm prophet

prophétie [prɔfesi] nf prophecy

propice [prɔpis] adj favourable

proportion [prɔpɔrsjɔ̃] nf proportion; **toute(s) ~(s)**

gardée(s) making due allowance(s)
propos [prɔpo] nm (intention) intention, aim; (sujet): **à quel ~?** what about? ▷ nmpl (paroles) talk no pl, remarks; **à - de** about, regarding; **à tout ~** for the slightest thing ou reason; **à -** by the way; (opportunément) at the right moment
proposer [prɔpoze] vt to propose; **~ qch (à qn)** (suggérer) to suggest sth (to sb), propose sth (to sb); (offrir) to offer (sb) sth; **se ~ (pour faire)** to offer one's services (to do); **proposition** nf (suggestion) proposal, suggestion; (Ling) clause
propre [prɔpr] adj clean; (net) neat, tidy; (possessif) own; (sens) literal; (particulier): **~ à** peculiar to; (approprié): **~ à** suitable for ▷ nm: **recopier au ~** to make a fair copy of; **proprement** adv (avec propreté) cleanly; **le village proprement dit** the village itself; **à proprement parler** strictly speaking; **propreté** nf cleanliness
propriétaire [prɔprijetɛr] nm/f owner; (pour le locataire) landlord(-lady)
propriété [prɔprijete] nf property; (droit) ownership
propulser [prɔpylse] vt to propel
prose [proz] nf (style) prose
prospecter [prɔspɛkte] vt to prospect; (Comm) to canvass
prospectus [prɔspɛktys] nm leaflet
prospère [prɔspɛr] adj prosperous; **prospérer** vi to prosper
prosterner [prɔstɛrne]: **se ~** vi to bow low, prostrate o.s.
prostituée [prɔstitɥe] nf prostitute
prostitution [prɔstitysjɔ̃] nf prostitution
protecteur, -trice [prɔtɛktœr, tris] adj protective; (air, ton: péj) patronizing ▷ nm/f protector
protection [prɔtɛksjɔ̃] nf protection; (d'un personnage influent: aide) patronage
protéger [prɔteʒe] vt to protect; **se ~ de/contre** to protect o.s. from
protège-slip [prɔtɛʒslip] nm panty liner
protéine [prɔtein] nf protein
protestant, e [prɔtɛstɑ̃, ɑ̃t] adj, nm/f Protestant
protestation [prɔtɛstasjɔ̃] nf (plainte) protest
protester [prɔtɛste] vi: **~ (contre)** to protest (against ou about); **~ de** (son innocence) to protest
prothèse [prɔtɛz] nf: **prothèse dentaire** denture
protocole [prɔtɔkɔl] nm (fig) etiquette
proue [pru] nf bow(s pl), prow
prouesse [prues] nf feat
prouver [pruve] vt to prove
provenance [prɔv(ə)nɑ̃s] nf origin; **avion en ~ de** plane (arriving) from
provenir [prɔv(ə)nir]: **~ de** vt to come from
proverbe [prɔvɛrb] nm proverb
province [prɔvɛ̃s] nf province
proviseur [prɔvizœr] nm ≈ head(teacher) (BRIT), ≈ principal (US)
provision [prɔvizjɔ̃] nf (réserve) stock, supply; **provisions** nfpl (vivres) provisions, food no pl
provisoire [prɔvizwar] adj temporary; **provisoirement** adv temporarily
provocant, e [prɔvɔkɑ̃, ɑ̃t] adj provocative;
provoquer [prɔvɔke] vt (défier) to provoke; (causer) to cause, bring about; (inciter): **~ qn à** to incite sb to
proxénète [prɔksenɛt] nm procurer
proximité [prɔksimite] nf nearness, closeness; (dans le

temps) imminence, closeness; **à ~** near ou close by; **à ~ de** near (to), close to
prudemment [prydamɑ̃] adv carefully; wisely, sensibly
prudence [prydɑ̃s] nf carefulness; **avec ~** carefully; **par ~** as a precaution
prudent, e [prydɑ̃, ɑ̃t] adj (pas téméraire) careful; (: en général) safety-conscious; (sage, conseillé) wise, sensible; **c'est plus ~** it's wiser
prune [pryn] nf plum
pruneau, x [pryno] nm prune
prunier [prynje] nm plum tree
PS sigle m = **parti socialiste**
pseudonyme [psødɔnim] nm (gén) fictitious name; (d'écrivain) pseudonym, pen name
psychanalyse [psikanaliz] nf psychoanalysis
psychiatre [psikjatr] nm/f psychiatrist; **psychiatrique** adj psychiatric
psychique [psiʃik] adj psychological
psychologie [psikɔlɔʒi] nf psychology; **psychologique** adj psychological; **psychologue** nm/f psychologist
pu [py] pp de **pouvoir**
puanteur [pɥɑ̃tœr] nf stink, stench
pub [pyb] nf (fam: annonce) ad, advert; (pratique) advertising
public, -ique [pyblik] adj public; (école, instruction) state cpd ▷ nm public; (assistance) audience; **en ~** in public
publicitaire [pyblisitɛr] adj advertising cpd; (film) publicity cpd
publicité [pyblisite] nf (méthode, profession) advertising; (annonce) advertisement; (révélations) publicity
publier [pyblije] vt to publish
publipostage [pyblipostaʒ] nm mailing m
publique [pyblik] adj voir **public**
puce [pys] nf flea; (Inform) chip; **carte à ~** smart card; **(marché aux) ~s** flea market sg
pudeur [pydœr] nf modesty; **pudique** adj (chaste) modest; (discret) discreet
puer [pɥe] (péj) vi to stink
puéricultrice [pɥerikyltris] nf p(a)ediatric nurse
puéril, e [pɥeril] adj childish
puis [pɥi] vb voir **pouvoir** ▷ adv then
puiser [pɥize] vt: **~ (dans)** to draw (from)
puisque [pɥisk] conj since
puissance [pɥisɑ̃s] nf power; **en ~** adj potential
puissant, e [pɥisɑ̃, ɑ̃t] adj powerful
puits [pɥi] nm well
pull(-over) [pyl(ɔvɛr)] nm sweater
pulluler [pylyle] vi to swarm
pulpe [pylp] nf pulp
pulvériser [pylverize] vt to pulverize; (liquide) to spray
punaise [pynɛz] nf (Zool) bug; (clou) drawing pin (BRIT), thumbtack (US)
punch [pɔ̃ʃ] nm (boisson) punch
punir [pynir] vt to punish; **punition** nf punishment
pupille [pypij] nf (Anat) pupil ▷ nm/f (enfant) ward
pupitre [pypitr] nm (Scol) desk
pur, e [pyr] adj pure; (vin) undiluted; (whisky) neat; **en ~e perte** to no avail; **c'est de la folie ~e** it's sheer madness
purée [pyre] nf: **~ (de pommes de terre)** mashed potatoes pl; **purée de marrons** chestnut purée
purement [pyrmɑ̃] adv purely
purgatoire [pyrgatwar] nm purgatory

purger [pyrʒe] vt (Méd, Pol) to purge; (Jur: peine) to serve
pur-sang [pyrsɑ̃] nm inv thoroughbred
pus [py] nm pus
putain [pytɛ̃] (fam!) nf whore (!)
puzzle [pœzl] nm jigsaw (puzzle)
P.-V. [peve] sigle m = **procès-verbal**
pyjama [piʒama] nm pyjamas pl (BRIT), pajamas pl (US)
pyramide [piramid] nf pyramid
Pyrénées [pirene] nfpl: **les ~** the Pyrenees

QI sigle m (= quotient intellectuel) IQ
quadragénaire [k(w)adraʒener] nm/f man/woman in his/her forties
quadruple [k(w)adrypl] nm: **le ~ de** four times as much as
quai [ke] nm (de port) quay; (de gare) platform; **être à ~** (navire) to be alongside; **de quel ~ part le train pour Paris?** which platform does the Paris train go from?
qualification [kalifikasjɔ̃] nf (aptitude) qualification
qualifier [kalifje] vt to qualify; **se ~** vi to qualify; **~ qch/qn de** to describe sth/sb as
qualité [kalite] nf quality
quand [kɑ̃] conj, adv when; **~ je serai riche** when I'm rich; **~ même** all the same; **~ même, il exagère!** really, he overdoes it!; **~ bien même** even though
quant [kɑ̃]: **~ à** prép (pour ce qui est de) as for, as to; (au sujet de) regarding
quantité [kɑ̃tite] nf quantity, amount; (grand nombre): **une ou des ~(s) de** a great deal of
quarantaine [karɑ̃ten] nf (Méd) quarantine; **avoir la ~** (âge) to be around forty; **une ~ (de)** forty or so, about forty

quarante [karɑ̃t] num forty
quart [kar] nm (fraction) quarter; (surveillance) watch; **un ~ de vin** a quarter litre of wine; **le ~ de** a quarter of; **quart d'heure** quarter of an hour; **quarts de finale** quarter finals
quartier [kartje] nm (de ville) district, area; (de bœuf) quarter; (de fruit) piece; **cinéma de ~** local cinema; **avoir ~ libre** (fig) to be free; **quartier général** headquarters pl
quartz [kwarts] nm quartz
quasi [kazi] adv almost, nearly; **quasiment** adv almost, nearly; **quasiment jamais** hardly ever
quatorze [katɔrz] num fourteen
quatorzième [katɔrzjɛm] num fourteenth
quatre [katr] num four; **à ~ pattes** on all fours; **se mettre en ~ pour qn** to go out of one's way for sb; **~ à ~** (monter, descendre) four at a time; **quatre-vingt-dix** num ninety; **quatre-vingts** num eighty; **quatrième** num fourth ▷ nf (Scol) year 9 (BRIT), eighth grade (US)
quatuor [kwatɥɔr] nm quartet(te)

O MOT-CLÉ

que [kə] conj **1** (introduisant complétive) that; **il sait que tu es là** he knows (that) you're here; **je veux que tu acceptes** I want you to accept; **il a dit que oui** he said he would (ou it was etc)
2 (reprise d'autres conjonctions): **quand il rentrera et qu'il aura mangé** when he gets back and (when) he has eaten; **si vous y allez et que vous ...** if you go there and if you ...
3 (en tête de phrase: hypothèse, souhait etc): **qu'il le veuille ou non** whether he likes it or not; **qu'il fasse ce qu'il voudra!** let him do as he pleases!
4 (après comparatif) than, as; voir aussi **plus**; **aussi**; **autant** etc
5 (seulement): **ne ... que** only; **il ne boit que de l'eau** he only drinks water
6 (temps): **il y a 4 ans qu'il est parti** it is 4 years since he left, he left 4 years ago
▷ adv (exclamation): **qu'il ou qu'est-ce qu'il est bête/ court vite!** he's so silly!/he runs so fast!; **que de livres!** what a lot of books!
▷ pron **1** (relatif: personne) whom; (: chose) that, which; **l'homme que je vois** the man (whom) I see; **le livre que tu vois** the book (that ou which) you see; **un jour que j'étais ...** a day when I was ...
2 (interrogatif) what; **que fais-tu?, qu'est-ce que tu fais?** what are you doing?; **qu'est-ce que c'est?** what is it?, what's that?; **que faire?** what can one do?

Québec [kebɛk] n: **le ~** Quebec; **québécois, e** adj Quebec ▷ nm/f: **Québécois, e** Quebecker ▷ nm (Ling) Quebec French

O MOT-CLÉ

quel, quelle [kɛl] adj **1** (interrogatif: personne) who; (: chose) what; **quel est cet homme?** who is this man?; **quel est ce livre?** what is this book?; **quel livre/ homme?** what book/man?; (parmi un certain choix) which book/man?; **quels acteurs préférez-vous?** which actors do you prefer?; **dans quels pays êtes-vous allé?** which ou what countries did you go to?

2 (exclamatif): **quelle surprise!** what a surprise!
3: **quel que soit le coupable** whoever is guilty; **quel que soit votre avis** whatever your opinion

quelconque [kɛlkɔ̃k] adj (indéfini): **un ami/prétexte ~** some friend/pretext or other; (médiocre: repas) indifferent, poor; (laid: personne) plain-looking

O **MOT-CLÉ**

quelque [kɛlk] adj **1** (au singulier) some; (au pluriel) a few, some; (tournure interrogative) any; **quelque espoir** some hope; **il a quelques amis** he has a few ou some friends; **a-t-il quelques amis?** does he have any friends?; **les quelques livres qui** the few books which; **20 kg et quelque(s)** a bit over 20 kg
2: **quelque ... que**: **quelque livre qu'il choisisse** whatever (ou whichever) book he chooses
3: **quelque chose** something; (tournure interrogative) anything; **quelque chose d'autre** something else; anything else; **quelque part** somewhere; anywhere; **en quelque sorte** as it were
▷ adv **1** (environ): **quelque 100 mètres** some 100 metres
2: **quelque peu** rather, somewhat

quelquefois [kɛlkəfwa] adv sometimes
quelques-uns, -unes [kɛlkəzœ̃, yn] pron a few, some
quelqu'un [kɛlkœ̃] pron someone, somebody; (+tournure interrogative) anyone, anybody; **quelqu'un d'autre** someone ou somebody else; (+ tournure interrogative) anybody else
qu'en dira-t-on [kɑ̃diRatɔ̃] nm inv: **le qu'en dira-t-on** gossip, what people say
querelle [kəRɛl] nf quarrel; **quereller: se quereller** vi to quarrel
qu'est-ce que [kɛskə] vb + conj voir **que**
qu'est-ce qui [kɛski] vb + conj voir **qui**
question [kɛstjɔ̃] nf question; (fig) matter, issue; **il a été ~ de** we (ou they) spoke about; **de quoi est-il ~?** what is it about?; **il n'en est pas ~** there's no question of it; **en ~** question; **hors de ~** out of the question; **remettre en ~** to question; **questionnaire** nm questionnaire; **questionner** vt to question
quête [kɛt] nf collection; (recherche) quest, search; **faire la ~** (à l'église) to take the collection; (artiste) to pass the hat round
quetsche [kwɛtʃ] nf kind of dark-red plum
queue [kø] nf tail; (fig: du classement) bottom; (: de poêle) handle; (: de fruit, feuille) stalk; (: de train, colonne, file) rear; **faire la ~** to queue (up) (BRIT), line up (US); **queue de cheval** ponytail; **queue de poisson** (Auto): **faire une queue de poisson à qn** to cut in front of sb

O **MOT-CLÉ**

qui [ki] pron **1** (interrogatif: personne) who; (: chose): **qu'est-ce qui est sur la table?** what is on the table?; **qui est-ce qui?** who?; **qui est-ce que?** who?; **à qui est ce sac?** whose bag is this?; **à qui parlais-tu?** who were you talking to?, to whom were you talking?; **chez qui allez-vous?** whose house are you going to?
2 (relatif: personne) who; (+prép) whom; **l'ami de qui je vous ai parlé** the friend I told you about; **la dame chez qui je suis allé** the lady whose house I went to
3 (sans antécédent): **amenez qui vous voulez** bring who you like; **qui que ce soit** whoever it may be

quiconque [kikɔ̃k] pron (celui qui) whoever, anyone who; (n'importe qui) anyone, anybody
quille [kij] nf: **(jeu de) ~s** skittles sg (BRIT), bowling (US)
quincaillerie [kɛ̃kajRi] nf (ustensiles) hardware; (magasin) hardware shop
quinquagénaire [kɛ̃kazenɛR] nm/f man/woman in his/her fifties
quinquennat [kɛ̃kena] nm five year term of office (of French President)
quinte [kɛ̃t] nf: **~ (de toux)** coughing fit
quintuple [kɛ̃typl] nm: **le ~ de** five times as much as
quinzaine [kɛ̃zɛn] nf: **une ~ (de)** about fifteen, fifteen or so; **une ~ (de jours)** a fortnight (BRIT), two weeks
quinze [kɛ̃z] num fifteen; **dans ~ jours** in a fortnight('s time), in two weeks(' time)
quinzième [kɛ̃zjɛm] num fifteenth
quiproquo [kipRɔko] nm misunderstanding
quittance [kitɑ̃s] nf (reçu) receipt
quitte [kit] adj: **être ~ envers qn** to be no longer in sb's debt; (fig) to be quits with sb; **~ à faire** even if it means doing
quitter [kite] vt to leave; (vêtement) to take off; **se ~** vi (couples, interlocuteurs) to part; **ne quittez pas** (au téléphone) hold the line
qui-vive [kiviv] nm: **être sur le ~** to be on the alert

O **MOT-CLÉ**

quoi [kwa] pron interrog **1** what; **quoi de neuf?** what's new?; **quoi?** (qu'est-ce que tu dis?) what?
2 (avec prép): **à quoi tu penses?** what are you thinking about?; **de quoi parlez-vous?** what are you talking about?; **à quoi bon?** what's the use?
▷ pron rel: **as-tu de quoi écrire?** do you have anything to write with?; **il n'y a pas de quoi** (please) don't mention it; **il n'y a pas de quoi rire** there's nothing to laugh about
▷ pron (locutions): **quoi qu'il arrive** whatever happens; **quoi qu'il en soit** be that as it may; **quoi que ce soit** anything at all
▷ excl what!

quoique [kwak] conj (al)though
quotidien, ne [kɔtidjɛ̃, jɛn] adj daily; (banal) everyday
▷ nm (journal) daily (paper); **quotidiennement** adv dail

r

r. abr = **route; rue**

rab [Rab] (fam) nm (nourriture) extra; **est-ce qu'il y a du ~?** are there any seconds?

rabâcher [Rabaʃe] vt to keep on repeating

rabais [Rabɛ] nm reduction, discount; **rabaisser** vt (déprécier) to belittle; (rabattre: prix) to reduce

Rabat [Raba(t)] n Rabat

rabattre [RabatR] vt (couvercle, siège) to pull down; (déduire) to reduce; **se ~** vi (se refermer: couvercle) to fall shut; (véhicule, coureur) to cut in; **se ~ sur** to fall back on

rabbin [Rabɛ̃] nm rabbi

rabougri, e [RabugRi] adj stunted

raccommoder [Rakɔmɔde] vt to mend, repair

raccompagner [Rakɔ̃paɲe] vt to take ou see back

raccord [RakɔR] nm link; (retouche) touch up; **raccorder** vt to join (up), link up; (suj: pont etc) to connect, link

raccourci [Rakursi] nm short cut

raccourcir [RakursiR] vt to shorten ▷ vi (jours) to grow shorter, draw in

raccrocher [RakRɔʃe] vt (tableau) to hang back up; (récepteur) to put down ▷ vi (Tél) to hang up, ring off

race [Ras] nf race; (d'animaux, fig) breed; **de ~** purebred, pedigree

rachat [Raʃa] nm buying; (du même objet) buying back

racheter [Raʃ(ə)te] vt (article perdu) to buy another; (après avoir vendu) to buy back; (d'occasion) to buy; (Comm: part, firme) to buy up; (davantage): **~ du lait/3 œufs** to buy more milk/another 3 eggs ou 3 more eggs; **se ~** vi (fig) to make amends

racial, e, -aux [Rasjal, jo] adj racial

racine [Rasin] nf root; **racine carrée/cubique** square/cube root

racisme [Rasism] nm racism

raciste [Rasist] adj, nm/f racist

racket [Raket] nm racketeering no pl

raclée [Rakle] (fam) nf hiding, thrashing

racler [Rakle] vt (surface) to scrape; **se ~ la gorge** to clear one's throat

racontars [Rakɔ̃taR] nmpl story, lie

raconter [Rakɔ̃te] vt: **~ (à qn)** (décrire) to relate (to sb),

tell (sb) about; (dire de mauvaise foi) to tell (sb); **~ une histoire** to tell a story

radar [RadaR] nm radar

rade [Rad] nf (natural) harbour; **rester en ~** (fig) to be left stranded

radeau, x [Rado] nm raft

radiateur [RadjatœR] nm radiator, heater; (Auto) radiator; **radiateur électrique** electric heater ou fire

radiation [Radjasjɔ̃] nf (Physique) radiation

radical, e, -aux [Radikal, o] adj radical

radieux, -euse [Radjø, jøz] adj radiant

radin, e [Radɛ̃, in] (fam) adj stingy

radio [Radjo] nf radio; (Méd) X-ray ▷ nm radio operator; **à la ~** on the radio; **radioactif, -ive** adj radioactive; **radiocassette** nf cassette radio, radio cassette player; **radiographie** nf radiography; (photo) X-ray photograph; **radiophonique** adj radio cpd; **radio-réveil** (pl **radios-réveils**) nm radio alarm clock

radis [Radi] nm radish

radoter [Radɔte] vi to ramble on

radoucir [RadusiR]: **se ~** vi (temps) to become milder; (se calmer) to calm down

rafale [Rafal] nf (vent) gust of wind); (tir) burst of gunfire

raffermir [RafɛRmiR] vt to firm up

raffiner [Rafine] vt to refine; **raffinerie** nf refinery

raffoler [Rafɔle]: **~ de** vt to be very keen on

rafle [Rafl] nf (de police) raid; **rafler** (fam) vt to swipe, nick

rafraîchir [RafReʃiR] vt (atmosphère, température) to cool (down); (aussi: **mettre à ~**) to chill; (fig: rénover) to brighten up; **se ~** vi (temps) to grow cooler; (en se lavant) to freshen up; (en buvant) to refresh o.s.; **rafraîchissant, e** adj refreshing; **rafraîchissement** nm (boisson) cool drink; **rafraîchissements** nmpl (boissons, fruits etc) refreshments

rage [Raʒ] nf (Méd): **la ~** rabies; (fureur) rage, fury; **faire ~** to rage; **rage de dents** (raging) toothache

ragot [Rago] (fam) nm malicious gossip no pl

ragoût [Ragu] nm stew

raide [Rɛd] adj stiff; (câble) taut, tight; (escarpé) steep; (droit: cheveux) straight; (fam: sans argent) flat broke; (osé) daring, bold ▷ adv (en pente) steeply; **~ mort** stone dead; **raideur** nf (rigidité) stiffness; **avec raideur** (répondre) stiffly, abruptly; **raidir** vt (muscles) to stiffen; **se raidir** vi (tissu) to stiffen; (personne) to tense up; (: se préparer moralement) to brace o.s.; (fig: to harden°

raie [Rɛ] nf (Zool) skate, ray; (rayure) stripe; (des cheveux) parting

raifort [RɛfɔR] nm horseradish

rail [Raj] nm rail; (chemins de fer) railways pl; **par ~** by rail

railler [Raje] vt to scoff at, jeer at

rainure [RɛnyR] nf groove

raisin [Rɛzɛ̃] nm (aussi: **~s**) grapes pl; **raisins secs** raisins

raison [Rɛzɔ̃] nf reason; **avoir ~** to be right; **donner ~ à qn** to agree with sb; (événement) to prove sb right; **perdre la ~** to become insane; **se faire une ~** to learn to live with it; **~ de plus** all the more reason; **à plus forte ~** all the more so; **en ~ de** because of; **à ~ de** at the rate of; **sans ~** for no reason; **raison sociale** corporate name; **raisonnable** adj reasonable, sensible

raisonnement [Rɛzɔnmã] nm (façon de réfléchir) reasoning; (argumentation) argument

raisonner [Rɛzɔne] vi (penser) to reason; (argumenter, discuter) to argue ▷ vt (personne) to reason with

rajeunir [ʀaʒœniʀ] vt (suj: coiffure, robe): **~ qn** to make sb look younger; (fig: personnel) to inject new blood into ▷ vi to become (ou look) younger

rajouter [ʀaʒute] vt to add

rajuster [ʀaʒyste] vt (vêtement) to straighten, tidy; (salaires) to adjust

ralenti [ʀalɑ̃ti] nm: **au ~** (fig) at a slower pace; **tourner au ~** (Auto) to tick over, idle

ralentir [ʀalɑ̃tiʀ] vt to slow down

râler [ʀale] vi to groan; (fam) to grouse, moan (and groan)

rallier [ʀalje] vt (rejoindre) to rejoin; (gagner à sa cause) to win over

rallonge [ʀalɔ̃ʒ] nf (de table) (extra) leaf

rallonger [ʀalɔ̃ʒe] vt to lengthen

rallye [ʀali] nm rally, (Pol) march

ramassage [ʀamasaʒ] nm: **ramassage scolaire** school bus service

ramasser [ʀamase] vt (objet tombé ou par terre, fam) to pick up; (recueillir: copies, ordures) to collect; (récolter) to gather; **ramassis** (péj) nm (de voyous) bunch; (d'objets) jumble

rambarde [ʀɑ̃baʀd] nf guardrail

rame [ʀam] nf (aviron) oar; (de métro) train; (de papier) ream

rameau, x [ʀamo] nm (small) branch; **les Rameaux** (Rel) Palm Sunday sg

ramener [ʀam(ə)ne] vt to bring back; (reconduire) to take back; **~ qch à** (réduire à) to reduce sth to

ramer [ʀame] vi to row

ramollir [ʀamɔliʀ] vt to soften; **se ~** vi to go soft

rampe [ʀɑ̃p] nf (d'escalier) banister(s pl); (dans un garage) ramp; (Théâtre): **la ~** the footlights pl; **rampe de lancement** launching pad

ramper [ʀɑ̃pe] vi to crawl

rancard [ʀɑ̃kaʀ] (fam) nm (rendez-vous) date

rancart [ʀɑ̃kaʀ] nm: **mettre au ~** (fam) to scrap

rance [ʀɑ̃s] adj rancid

rancœur [ʀɑ̃kœʀ] nf rancour

rançon [ʀɑ̃sɔ̃] nf ransom

rancune [ʀɑ̃kyn] nf grudge, rancour; **garder ~ à qn (de qch)** to bear sb a grudge (for sth); **sans ~!** no hard feelings!; **rancunier, -ière** adj vindictive, spiteful

randonnée [ʀɑ̃dɔne] nf (pédestre) walk, ramble; (: en montagne) hike, hiking no pl; **la ~** (activité) hiking, walking; **une ~ à cheval** a pony trek

rang [ʀɑ̃] nm (rangée) row; (grade, classement) rank; **rangs** nmpl (Mil) ranks; **se mettre en ~s** to get into ou form rows; **au premier ~** in the first row; (fig) ranking first

rangé, e [ʀɑ̃ʒe] adj (vie) well-ordered; (personne) steady

rangée [ʀɑ̃ʒe] nf row

ranger [ʀɑ̃ʒe] vt (mettre de l'ordre dans) to tidy up; (classer, grouper) to order, arrange; (mettre à sa place) to put away; (fig: classer): **~ qn/qch parmi** to rank sb/sth among; **se ~** vi (véhicule, conducteur) to pull over ou in; (piéton) to step aside; (s'assagir) to settle down; **se ~ à** (avis) to come round to

ranimer [ʀanime] vt (personne) to bring round; (douleur, souvenir) to revive; (feu) to rekindle

rapace [ʀapas] nm bird of prey

râpe [ʀɑp] nf (Culin) grater; **râper** vt (Culin) to grate

rapide [ʀapid] adj fast; (prompt: coup d'œil, mouvement) quick ▷ nm express (train); (de cours d'eau) rapid; **rapidement** adv fast; quickly

rapiécer [ʀapjese] vt to patch

rappel [ʀapɛl] nm (Théâtre) curtain call; (Méd: vaccination) booster; (deuxième avis) reminder; **rappeler** vt to call back; (ambassadeur, Mil) to recall; (faire se souvenir): **rappeler qch à qn** to remind sb of sth; **se rappeler** vt (se souvenir de) to remember, recall; **pouvez-vous rappeler plus tard?** can you call back later?

rapport [ʀapɔʀ] nm (lien, analogie) connection; (compte rendu) report; (profit) yield, return; **rapports** nmpl (entre personnes, pays) relations; **avoir ~ à** to have something to do with; **être/se mettre en ~ avec qn** to be/get in touch with sb; **par ~ à** in relation to; **rapports (sexuels)** (sexual) intercourse sg; **rapport qualité-prix** value (for money)

rapporter [ʀapɔʀte] vt (rendre, ramener) to bring back; (bénéfice) to yield, bring in; (mentionner, répéter) to report ▷ vi (investissement) to give a good return ou yield; (activité) to be very profitable; **se ~ à** to relate to

rapprochement [ʀapʀɔʃmɑ̃] nm (de nations) reconciliation; (rapport) parallel

rapprocher [ʀapʀɔʃe] vt (deux objets) to bring closer together; (fig: ennemis, partis etc) to bring together; (comparer) to establish a parallel between; (chaise d'une table): **~ qch (de)** to bring sth closer (to); **se ~** vi to draw closer ou nearer; **se ~ de** to come closer to; (présenter analogie avec) to be close to

raquette [ʀakɛt] nf (de tennis) racket; (de ping-pong) bat

rare [ʀɑʀ] adj rare; **se faire ~** to become scarce; **rarement** adv rarely, seldom

ras, e [ʀɑ, ʀɑz] adj (poil, herbe) short; (tête) close-cropped ▷ adv short; **en ~e campagne** in open country; **à ~ bords** to the brim; **en avoir ~ le bol** (fam) to be fed up

raser [ʀɑze] vt (barbe, cheveux) to shave off; (menton, personne) to shave; (fam: ennuyer) to bore; (démolir) to raz (to the ground); (frôler) to graze, skim; **se ~** vi to shave; (fam) to be bored (to tears); **rasoir** nm razor

rassasier [ʀasazje] vt: **être rassasié** to have eaten one's fill

rassemblement [ʀasɑ̃bləmɑ̃] nm (groupe) gathering; (Pol) union

rassembler [ʀasɑ̃ble] vt (réunir) to assemble, gather; (documents, notes) to gather together, collect; **se ~** vi to gather

rassurer [ʀasyʀe] vt to reassure; **se ~** vi to reassure o.s **rassure-toi** don't worry

rat [ʀa] nm rat

rate [ʀat] nf spleen

raté, e [ʀate] adj (tentative) unsuccessful, failed ▷ nm/f (fam: personne) failure

râteau, x [ʀɑto] nm rake

rater [ʀate] vi (affaire, projet etc) to go wrong, fail ▷ vt (fam: cible, train, occasion) to miss; (plat) to spoil; (fam: examen) to fail; **nous avons raté notre train** we missed our train

ration [ʀasjɔ̃] nf ration

RATP sigle f (= Régie autonome des transports parisiens) Paris transport authority

rattacher [ʀataʃe] vt (animal, cheveux) to tie up again; (fig: relier): **~ qch à** to link sth with

rattraper [ʀatʀape] vt (fugitif) to recapture; (empêcher de tomber) to catch (hold of); (atteindre, rejoindre) to catch up with; (réparer: erreur) to make up for; **se ~** vi to make up for it; **se ~ (à)** (se raccrocher) to stop o.s. falling (by catching hold of)

rature [ʀatyʀ] nf deletion, erasure
rauque [ʀok] adj (voix) hoarse
ravages [ʀavaʒ] nmpl: **faire des ~** to wreak havoc
ravi, e [ʀavi] adj: **être ~ de/que** to be delighted with/that
ravin [ʀavɛ̃] nm gully, ravine
ravir [ʀaviʀ] vt (enchanter) to delight; **à ~** adv beautifully
raviser [ʀavize]: **se ~** vi to change one's mind
ravissant, e [ʀavisɑ̃, ɑ̃t] adj delightful
ravisseur, -euse [ʀavisœʀ, øz] nm/f abductor, kidnapper
ravitailler [ʀavitaje] vt (en vivres, munitions) to provide with fresh supplies; (avion) to refuel; **se ~ (en)** to get fresh supplies (of)
raviver [ʀavive] vt (feu, douleur) to revive; (couleurs) to brighten up
rayé, e [ʀeje] adj (à rayures) striped
rayer [ʀeje] vt (érafler) to scratch; (barrer) to cross out; (d'une liste) to cross off
rayon [ʀejɔ̃] nm (de soleil etc) ray; (Géom) radius; (de roue) spoke; (étagère) shelf; (de grand magasin) department; **dans un ~ de** within a radius of; **rayon de soleil** sunbeam; **rayons X** X-rays
rayonnement [ʀejɔnmɑ̃] nm (fig: d'une culture) influence
rayonner [ʀejɔne] vi (fig) to shine forth; (personne: de joie, de beauté) to be radiant; (touriste) to go touring (from one base)
rayure [ʀejyʀ] nf (motif) stripe; (éraflure) scratch; **à ~s** striped
raz-de-marée [ʀadmaʀe] nm inv tidal wave
ré [ʀe] nm (Mus) D; (en chantant la gamme) re
réaction [ʀeaksjɔ̃] nf reaction
réadapter [ʀeadapte]: **se ~ (à)** vi to readjust (to)
réagir [ʀeaʒiʀ] vi to react
réalisateur, -trice [ʀealizatœʀ, tʀis] nm/f (TV, Cinéma) director
réalisation [ʀealizasjɔ̃] nf realization; (cinéma) production; **en cours de ~** under way
réaliser [ʀealize] vt (projet, opération) to carry out, realize; (rêve, souhait) to realize, fulfil; (exploit) to achieve; (film) to produce; (se rendre compte de) to realize; **se ~** vi to be realized
réaliste [ʀealist] adj realistic
réalité [ʀealite] nf reality; **en ~** in (actual) fact; **dans la ~** in reality
réanimation [ʀeanimasjɔ̃] nf resuscitation; **service de ~** intensive care unit
rébarbatif, -ive [ʀebaʀbatif, iv] adj forbidding
rebattu, e [ʀ(ə)baty] adj hackneyed
rebelle [ʀəbɛl] nm/f rebel ▷ adj (troupes) rebel; (enfant) rebellious; (mèche etc) unruly
rebeller [ʀ(ə)bele]: **se ~** vi to rebel
rebondir [ʀ(ə)bɔ̃diʀ] vi (ballon: au sol) to bounce; (: contre un mur) to rebound; (fig) to get moving again
rebord [ʀ(ə)bɔʀ] nm edge; **le ~ de la fenêtre** the windowsill
rebours [ʀ(ə)buʀ]: **à ~** adv the wrong way
rebrousser [ʀ(ə)bʀuse] vt: **~ chemin** to turn back
rebuter [ʀəbyte] vt to put off
récalcitrant, e [ʀekalsitʀɑ̃, ɑ̃t] adj refractory
récapituler [ʀekapityle] vt to recapitulate, sum up
receler [ʀ(ə)səle] vt (produit d'un vol) to receive; (fig) to conceal; **receleur, -euse** nm/f receiver

récemment [ʀesamɑ̃] adv recently
recensement [ʀ(ə)sɑ̃smɑ̃] nm (population) census
recenser [ʀ(ə)sɑ̃se] vt (population) to take a census of; (inventorier) to list
récent, e [ʀesɑ̃, ɑ̃t] adj recent
récépissé [ʀesepise] nm receipt
récepteur [ʀeseptœʀ] nm receiver
réception [ʀesɛpsjɔ̃] nf receiving no pl; (accueil) reception, welcome; (bureau) reception desk; (réunion mondaine) reception, party; **réceptionniste** nm/f receptionist
recette [ʀ(ə)sɛt] nf recipe; (Comm) takings pl; **recettes** nfpl (Comm: rentrées) receipts; **faire ~** (spectacle, exposition) to be a winner
recevoir [ʀ(ə)səvwaʀ] vt to receive; (client, patient) to see; **être reçu** (à un examen) to pass
rechange [ʀ(ə)ʃɑ̃ʒ]: **de ~** adj (pièces, roue) spare; (fig: solution) alternative; **des vêtements de ~** a change of clothes
recharge [ʀ(ə)ʃaʀʒ] nf refill; **rechargeable** adj (stylo etc) refillable; **recharger** vt (stylo) to refill; (batterie) to recharge
réchaud [ʀeʃo] nm (portable) stove
réchauffer [ʀeʃofe] vt (plat) to reheat; (mains, personne) to warm; **se ~** vi (température) to get warmer; (personne) to warm o.s. (up)
rêche [ʀɛʃ] adj rough
recherche [ʀ(ə)ʃɛʀʃ] nf (action) search; (raffinement) studied elegance; (scientifique etc): **la ~** research; **recherches** nfpl (de la police) investigations; (scientifiques) research sg; **la ~ de** the search for; **être à la ~ de qch** to be looking for sth
recherché, e [ʀ(ə)ʃɛʀʃe] adj (rare, demandé) much sought-after; (raffiné: style) mannered; (: tenue) elegant
rechercher [ʀ(ə)ʃɛʀʃe] vt (objet égaré, personne) to look for; (causes, nouveau procédé) to try to find; (bonheur, compliments) to seek
rechute [ʀ(ə)ʃyt] nf (Méd) relapse
récidiver [ʀesidive] vi to commit a subsequent offence; (fig) to do it again
récif [ʀesif] nm reef
récipient [ʀesipjɑ̃] nm container
réciproque [ʀesipʀɔk] adj reciprocal
récit [ʀesi] nm story; **récital** nm recital; **réciter** vt to recite
réclamation [ʀeklamasjɔ̃] nf complaint; **(service des) ~s** complaints department
réclame [ʀeklam] nf ad, advert(isement); **en ~** on special offer; **réclamer** vt to ask for; (revendiquer) to claim, demand ▷ vi to complain
réclusion [ʀeklyzjɔ̃] nf imprisonment
recoin [ʀəkwɛ̃] nm nook, corner
reçois etc [ʀəswa] vb voir **recevoir**
récolte [ʀekɔlt] nf harvesting, gathering; (produits) harvest, crop; **récolter** vt to harvest, gather (in); (fig) to collect
recommandé [ʀ(ə)kɔmɑ̃de] nm (Postes): **en ~** by registered mail
recommander [ʀ(ə)kɔmɑ̃de] vt to recommend; (Postes) to register
recommencer [ʀ(ə)kɔmɑ̃se] vt (reprendre: lutte, séance) to resume, start again; (refaire: travail, explications) to start afresh, start (over) again ▷ vi to start again; (récidiver) to do it again

récompense [Rekɔ̃pɑ̃s] nf reward; (prix) award; **récompenser** vt: **récompenser qn (de** ou **pour)** to reward sb (for)

réconcilier [Rekɔ̃silje] vt to reconcile; **se ~ (avec)** to make up (with)

reconduire [R(ə)kɔ̃dɥiR] vt (raccompagner) to take ou see back; (renouveler) to renew

réconfort [Rekɔ̃fɔR] nm comfort; **réconforter** vt (consoler) to comfort

reconnaissance [R(ə)kɔnɛsɑ̃s] nf (gratitude) gratitude, gratefulness; (action de reconnaître) recognition; (Mil) reconnaissance, recce; **reconnaissant, e** adj grateful; **je vous serais reconnaissant de bien vouloir ...** I would be most grateful if you would (kindly) ...

reconnaître [R(ə)kɔnɛtR] vt to recognize; (Mil: lieu) to reconnoitre; (Jur: enfant, torts) to acknowledge; **~ que** to admit ou acknowledge that; **~ qn/qch à** (l'identifier grâce à) to recognize sb/sth by; **reconnu, e** adj (indiscuté, connu) recognized

reconstituer [R(ə)kɔ̃stitɥe] vt (événement, accident) to reconstruct; (fresque, vase brisé) to piece together, reconstitute

reconstruire [R(ə)kɔ̃stRɥiR] vt to rebuild

reconvertir [R(ə)kɔ̃vɛRtiR]: **se ~ dans** vr (un métier, une branche) to go into

record [R(ə)kɔR] nm, adj record

recoupement [R(ə)kupmɑ̃] nm: **par ~** by cross-checking

recouper [R(ə)kupe]: **se ~** vi (témoignages) to tie ou match up

recourber [R(ə)kuRbe]: **se ~** vi to curve (up), bend (up)

recourir [R(ə)kuRiR]: **~ à** vt (ami, agence) to turn ou appeal to; (force, ruse, emprunt) to resort to

recours [R(ə)kuR] nm: **avoir ~ à = recourir à**; **en dernier ~** as a last resort

recouvrer [R(ə)kuvRe] vt (vue, santé etc) to recover, regain

recouvrir [R(ə)kuvRiR] vt (couvrir à nouveau) to re-cover; (couvrir entièrement, aussi fig) to cover

récréation [RekReasjɔ̃] nf (Scol) break

recroqueviller [R(ə)kRɔkəvije]: **se ~** vi (personne) to huddle up

recrudescence [R(ə)kRydesɑ̃s] nf fresh outbreak

recruter [R(ə)kRyte] vt to recruit

rectangle [Rɛktɑ̃gl] nm rectangle; **rectangulaire** adj rectangular

rectificatif [Rɛktifikatif] nm correction

rectifier [Rɛktifje] vt (calcul, adresse, paroles) to correct; (erreur) to rectify

rectiligne [Rɛktiliɲ] adj straight

recto [Rɛkto] nm front (of a page); **~ verso** on both sides (of the page)

reçu, e [R(ə)sy] pp de **recevoir** ▷ adj (candidat) successful; (admis, consacré) accepted ▷ nm (Comm) receipt; **je peux avoir un ~, s'il vous plaît?** can I have a receipt, please?

recueil [Rəkœj] nm collection; **recueillir** vt to collect; (voix, suffrages) to win; (accueillir: réfugiés, chat) to take in; **se recueillir** vi to gather one's thoughts, meditate

recul [R(ə)kyl] nm (éloignement) distance; (déclin) decline; **être en ~** to be on the decline; **avec du ~** with hindsight; **avoir un mouvement de ~** to recoil; **prendre du ~** to stand back; **reculé, e** adj remote; **reculer** vi to move back, back away; (Auto) to reverse, back (up); (fig) to (be

on the) decline ▷ vt to move back; (véhicule) to reverse, back (up); (date, décision) to postpone; **reculer devant** (danger, difficulté) to shrink from; **reculons: à reculons** adv backwards

récupérer [Rekypere] vt to recover, get back; (heures de travail) to make up; (déchets) to salvage ▷ vi to recover

récurer [RekyRe] vt to scour; **poudre à ~** scouring powder

reçut [Rəsy] vb voir **recevoir**

recycler [R(ə)sikle] vt (Tech) to recycle; **se ~** vi to retrain

rédacteur, -trice [Redaktœr, tRis] nm/f (journaliste) writer; subeditor; (d'ouvrage de référence) editor, compiler

rédaction [Redaksjɔ̃] nf writing; (rédacteurs) editorial staff; (Scol: devoir) essay, composition

redescendre [R(ə)desɑ̃dR] vi to go back down ▷ vt (pente etc) to go down

rédiger [Rediʒe] vt to write; (contrat) to draw up

redire [R(ə)diR] vt to repeat; **trouver à ~ à** to find fault with

redoubler [R(ə)duble] vi (tempête, violence) to intensify; (Scol) to repeat a year; **~ de patience/prudence** to be doubly patient/careful

redoutable [R(ə)dutabl] adj formidable, fearsome

redouter [R(ə)dute] vt to dread

redressement [R(ə)dRɛsmɑ̃] nm (économique) recovery

redresser [R(ə)dRese] vt (relever) to set upright; (pièce tordue) to straighten out; (situation, économie) to put right; **se ~** vi (personne) to sit ou stand up (straight); (économie) to recover

réduction [Redyksjɔ̃] nf reduction; **y a-t-il une ~ pour les étudiants?** is there a reduction for students?

réduire [RedɥiR] vt to reduce; (prix, dépenses) to cut, reduce; **réduit** nm (pièce) tiny room

rééducation [Reedykasjɔ̃] nf (d'un membre) re-education; (de délinquants, d'un blessé) rehabilitation

réel, le [Reɛl] adj real; **réellement** adv really

réexpédier [Reɛkspedje] vt (à l'envoyeur) to return, send back; (au destinataire) to send on, forward

refaire [R(ə)fɛR] vt to do again; (faire de nouveau: sport) to take up again; (réparer, restaurer) to do up

réfectoire [RefɛktwaR] nm refectory

référence [RefeRɑ̃s] nf reference; **références** nfpl (recommandations) reference sg

référer [RefeRe]: **se ~ à** vt to refer to

refermer [R(ə)fɛRme] vt to close ou shut again; **se ~** vi (porte) to close ou shut (again)

refiler [R(ə)file] vi (fam) to palm off

réfléchi, e [Refleʃi] adj (caractère) thoughtful; (action) well-thought-out; (Ling) reflexive; **c'est tout ~** my mind's made up

réfléchir [RefleʃiR] vt to reflect ▷ vi to think; **~ à** to think about

reflet [R(ə)flɛ] nm reflection; (sur l'eau etc) sheen no pl, glint; **refléter** vt to reflect; **se refléter** vi to be reflected

réflexe [Reflɛks] nm, adj reflex

réflexion [Reflɛksjɔ̃] nf (de la lumière etc) reflection; (fait de penser) thought; (remarque) remark; **~ faite, à la ~** on reflection

réflexologie [Reflɛksɔlɔʒi] nf reflexology

réforme [RefɔRm] nf reform; (Rel): **la R~** the Reformation; **réformer** vt to reform; (Mil) to declare unfit for service

refouler [R(ə)fule] vt (envahisseurs) to drive back; (larmes) to force back; (désir, colère) to repress

refrain [R(ə)fRɛ̃] nm refrain, chorus

refréner [Rəfʀene], **réfréner** [RefRene] vt to curb, check

réfrigérateur [RefRiʒeRatœR] nm refrigerator, fridge

refroidir [R(ə)fRwadiR] vt to cool; (fig: personne) to put off ▷ vi to cool (down); **se ~** vi (temps) to get cooler ou colder; (fig: ardeur) to cool (off); **refroidissement** nm (grippe etc) chill

refuge [R(ə)fyʒ] nm refuge; **réfugié, e** adj, nm/f refugee; **réfugier: se réfugier** vi to take refuge

refus [R(ə)fy] nm refusal; **ce n'est pas de ~** I won't say no, it's welcome; **refuser** vt to refuse; (Scol: candidat) to fail; **refuser qch à qn** to refuse sb sth; **refuser du monde** to have to turn people away; **se refuser à faire** to refuse to do

regagner [R(ə)gaɲe] vt (faveur) to win back; (lieu) to get back to

régal [Regal] nm treat; **régaler: se régaler** vi to have a delicious meal; (fig) to enjoy o.s.

regard [R(ə)gaR] nm (coup d'œil) look, glance; (expression) look (in one's eye); **au ~ de** (loi, morale) from the point of view of; **en ~ de** in comparison with

regardant, e [R(ə)gaRdɑ̃, ɑ̃t] adj (économe) tight-fisted; **peu ~ (sur)** very free (about)

regarder [R(ə)gaRde] vt to look at; (film, télévision, match) to watch; (concerner) to concern ▷ vi to look; **ne pas ~ à la dépense** to spare no expense; **~ qn/qch comme** to regard sb/sth as

régie [Reʒi] nf (Comm, Industrie) state-owned company; (Théâtre, Cinéma) production; (Radio, TV) control room

régime [Reʒim] nm (Pol) régime; (Méd) diet; (Admin: carcéral, fiscal etc) system; (de bananes, dattes) bunch; **se mettre au/suivre un ~** to go on/be on a diet

régiment [Reʒimɑ̃] nm regiment

région [Reʒjɔ̃] nf region; **régional, e, -aux** adj regional

régir [ReʒiR] vt to govern

régisseur [ReʒisœR] nm (d'un domaine) steward; (Cinéma, TV) assistant director; (Théâtre) stage manager

registre [RəʒistR] nm register

réglage [Reglaʒ] nm adjustment

règle [Regl] nf (instrument) ruler; (loi) rule; **règles** nfpl (menstruation) period sg; **en ~** in order; **en ~ générale** as a (general) rule

réglé, e [Regle] adj (vie) well-ordered; (arrangé) settled

règlement [Regləmɑ̃] nm (paiement) settlement; (arrêté) regulation; (règles, statuts) regulations pl, rules pl; **réglementaire** adj conforming to the regulations; (tenue) regulation cpd; **réglementation** nf (règles) regulations; **réglementer** vt to regulate

régler [Regle] vt (conflit, facture) to settle; (personne) to settle up with; (mécanisme, machine) to regulate, adjust; (thermostat etc) to set, adjust

réglisse [Reglis] nf liquorice

règne [Rɛɲ] nm (d'un roi etc, fig) reign; **le ~ végétal/animal** the vegetable/animal kingdom; **régner** vi (roi) to rule, reign; (fig) to reign

regorger [R(ə)gɔRʒe] vi: **~ de** to overflow with, be bursting with

regret [R(ə)gRɛ] nm regret; **à ~** with regret; **sans ~** with no regrets; **regrettable** adj regrettable; **regretter** vt to regret; (personne) to miss; **je regrette mais ...** I'm sorry but ...

regrouper [R(ə)gRupe] vt (grouper) to group together; (contenir) to include, comprise; **se ~** vi to gather (together)

régulier, -ière [Regylje, jɛR] adj (gén) regular; (vitesse, qualité) steady; (égal: couche, ligne) even; (Transports: ligne, service) scheduled, regular; (légal) lawful, in order; (honnête) straight, on the level; **régulièrement** adv regularly; (uniformément) evenly

rehausser [Rəose] vt (relever) to heighten, raise; (fig: souligner) to set off, enhance

rein [Rɛ̃] nm kidney; **reins** nmpl (dos) back sg

reine [Rɛn] nf queen

reine-claude [Rɛnklod] nf greengage

réinscriptible [Reɛ̃skRiptibl] adj (CD, DVD) rewritable

réinsertion [Reɛ̃sɛRsjɔ̃] nf (de délinquant) reintegration, rehabilitation

réintégrer [Reɛ̃tegRe] vt (lieu) to return to; (fonctionnaire) to reinstate

rejaillir [R(ə)ʒajiR] vi to splash up; **~ sur** (fig: scandale) to rebound on; (: gloire) to be reflected on

rejet [Rəʒɛ] nm rejection; **rejeter** vt (relancer) to throw back; (écarter) to reject; (déverser) to throw out, discharge; (vomir) to bring ou throw up; **rejeter la responsabilité de qch sur qn** to lay the responsibility for sth at sb's door

rejoindre [R(ə)ʒwɛ̃dR] vt (famille, régiment) to rejoin, return to; (lieu) to get (back) to; (suj: route etc) to meet, join; (rattraper) to catch up (with); **se ~** vi to meet; **je te rejoins à la gare** I'll see ou meet you at the station

réjouir [ReʒwiR] vt to delight; **se ~ (de qch/de faire)** to be delighted (about sth/to do); **réjouissances** nfpl (fête) festivities

relâche [Rəlɑʃ] nm ou nf: **sans ~** without respite ou a break; **relâché, e** adj loose, lax; **relâcher** vt (libérer) to release; (desserrer) to loosen; **se relâcher** vi (discipline) to become loose ou lax; (élève etc) to slacken off

relais [R(ə)lɛ] nm (Sport): **(course de) ~** relay (race); **prendre le ~ (de)** to take over (from); **relais routier** ≈ transport café (BRIT), ≈ truck stop (US)

relancer [R(ə)lɑ̃se] vt (balle) to throw back; (moteur) to restart; (fig) to boost, revive; (harceler): **~ qn** to pester sb

relatif, -ive [R(ə)latif, iv] adj relative

relation [R(ə)lasjɔ̃] nf (rapport) relation(ship); (connaissance) acquaintance; **relations** nfpl (rapports) relations; (connaissances) connections; **être/entrer en ~(s) avec** to be/get in contact with

relaxer [Rəlakse]: **se ~** vi to relax

relayer [R(ə)leje] vt (collaborateur, coureur etc) to relieve; **se ~** vi (dans une activité) to take it in turns

reléguer [R(ə)lege] vt to relegate

relevé, e [Rəl(ə)ve] adj (manches) rolled-up; (sauce) highly-seasoned ▷ nm (de compteur) reading; **relevé bancaire** ou **de compte** bank statement

relève [Rəlɛv] nf (personne) relief; **prendre la ~** to take over

relever [Rəl(ə)ve] vt (meuble) to stand up again; (personne tombée) to help up; (vitre, niveau de vie) to raise; (inf) to turn up; (style) to elevate; (plat, sauce) to season; (sentinelle, équipe) to relieve; (fautes) to pick out; (défi) to accept, take up; (noter: adresse etc) to take down, note; (: plan) to sketch; (compteur) to read; (ramasser: cahiers) to collect, take in; **se ~** vi (se remettre debout) to get up; **~ de** (maladie) to be recovering from; (être du ressort de) to be a matter for; (fig) to pertain to; **~ qn de** (fonctions) to relieve sb of; **~ la tête** to look up

relief [Rəljɛf] nm relief; **mettre en ~** (fig) to bring out, highlight

relier [ʀəlje] vt to link up; (livre) to bind; **~ qch à** to link sth to

religieux, -euse [ʀ(ə)liʒjø, jøz] adj religious ▷ nm monk

religion [ʀ(ə)liʒjɔ̃] nf religion

relire [ʀ(ə)liʀ] vt (à nouveau) to reread, read again; (vérifier) to read over

reluire [ʀ(ə)lɥiʀ] vi to gleam

remanier [ʀ(ə)manje] vt to reshape, recast; (Pol) to reshuffle

remarquable [ʀ(ə)maʀkabl] adj remarkable

remarque [ʀ(ə)maʀk] nf remark; (écrite) note

remarquer [ʀ(ə)maʀke] vt (voir) to notice; **se ~** vi to be noticeable; **faire ~ (à qn) que** to point out (to sb) that; **faire ~ qch (à qn)** to point sth out (to sb); **remarquez, ...** mind you ...; **se faire ~** to draw attention to o.s.

rembourrer [ʀɑ̃buʀe] vt to stuff

remboursement [ʀɑ̃buʀsəmɑ̃] nm (de dette, d'emprunt) repayment; (de frais) refund; **rembourser** vt to pay back, repay; (frais, billet etc) to refund; **se faire rembourser** to get a refund

remède [ʀ(ə)mɛd] nm (médicament) medicine; (traitement, fig) remedy, cure

remémorer [ʀ(ə)memɔʀe]: **se ~** vt to recall, recollect

remerciements [ʀəmɛʀsimɑ̃] nmpl thanks; **(avec) tous mes ~** (with) grateful ou many thanks

remercier [ʀ(ə)mɛʀsje] vt to thank; (congédier) to dismiss; **~ qn de/d'avoir fait** to thank sb for/for having done

remettre [ʀ(ə)mɛtʀ] vt (replacer) to put back; (vêtement) to put back on; (ajouter) to add; (ajourner) : **~ qch (à)** to postpone sth (until); **se ~** vi: **se ~ (de)** to recover (from); **~ qch à qn** (donner: lettre, clé etc) to hand over sth to sb; (: prix, décoration) to present sb with sth; **se ~ à faire qch** to start doing sth again; **s'en ~ à** to leave it (up) to

remise [ʀ(ə)miz] nf (rabais) discount; (local) shed; **remise de peine** reduction of sentence; **remise des prix** prize-giving; **remise en cause** ou **question** calling into question, challenging; **remise en jeu** (Football) throw-in

remontant [ʀ(ə)mɔ̃tɑ̃] nm tonic, pick-me-up

remonte-pente [ʀ(ə)mɔ̃tpɑ̃t] nm ski-lift

remonter [ʀ(ə)mɔ̃te] vi to go back up; (prix, température) to go up again ▷ vt (pente) to go up; (fleuve) to sail (ou swim etc) up; (manches, pantalon) to roll up; (col) to turn up; (niveau, limite) to raise; (fig: personne) to buck up; (qch de démonté) to put back together, reassemble; (montre) to wind up; **~ le moral à qn** to raise sb's spirits; **~ à** (dater de) to date ou go back to

remords [ʀ(ə)mɔʀ] nm remorse no pl; **avoir des ~** to feel remorse

remorque [ʀ(ə)mɔʀk] nf trailer; **remorquer** vt to tow; **remorqueur** nm tug(boat)

remous [ʀəmu] nm (d'un navire) (back)wash no pl; (de rivière) swirl, eddy ▷ nmpl (fig) stir sg

remparts [ʀɑ̃paʀ] nmpl walls, ramparts

remplaçant, e [ʀɑ̃plasɑ̃, ɑ̃t] nm/f replacement, stand-in; (Scol) supply teacher

remplacement [ʀɑ̃plasmɑ̃] nm replacement; **faire des ~s** (professeur) to do supply teaching; (secrétaire) to temp

remplacer [ʀɑ̃plase] vt to replace; **~ qch/qn par** to replace sth/sb with

rempli, e [ʀɑ̃pli] adj (emploi du temps) full, busy; **~ de** full of, filled with

remplir [ʀɑ̃pliʀ] vt to fill (up); (questionnaire) to fill out ou up; (obligations, fonction, condition) to fulfil; **se ~** vi to fill up

remporter [ʀɑ̃pɔʀte] vt (marchandise) to take away; (fig) to win, achieve

remuant, e [ʀəmɥɑ̃, ɑ̃t] adj restless

remue-ménage [ʀ(ə)mymenaʒ] nm inv commotion

remuer [ʀəmɥe] vt to move; (café, sauce) to stir ▷ vi to move; **se ~** vi to move; (fam: s'activer) to get a move on

rémunérer [ʀemyneʀe] vt to remunerate

renard [ʀ(ə)naʀ] nm fox

renchérir [ʀɑ̃ʃeʀiʀ] vi (fig): **~ (sur)** (en paroles) to add something (to)

rencontre [ʀɑ̃kɔ̃tʀ] nf meeting; (imprévue) encounter; **aller à la ~ de qn** to go and meet sb; **rencontrer** vt to meet; (mot, expression) to come across; (difficultés) to meet with; **se rencontrer** vi to meet

rendement [ʀɑ̃dmɑ̃] nm (d'un travailleur, d'une machine) output; (d'un champ) yield

rendez-vous [ʀɑ̃devu] nm appointment; (d'amoureux) date; (lieu) meeting place; **donner ~ à qn** to arrange to meet sb; **avoir/prendre ~ (avec)** to have/make an appointment (with); **j'ai ~ avec ...** I have an appointment with ...; **je voudrais prendre ~** I'd like to make an appointment

rendre [ʀɑ̃dʀ] vt (restituer) to give back, return; (invitation) to return, repay; (vomir) to bring up; (exprimer, traduire) to render; (faire devenir): **~ qn célèbre/qch possible** to make sb famous/sth possible; **se ~** vi (capituler) to surrender, give o.s. up; (aller): **se ~ quelque part** to go somewhere; **~ la monnaie à qn** to give sb his change; **se ~ compte de qch** to realize sth

rênes [ʀɛn] nfpl reins

renfermé, e [ʀɑ̃fɛʀme] adj (fig) withdrawn ▷ nm: **sentir le ~** to smell stuffy

renfermer [ʀɑ̃fɛʀme] vt to contain

renforcer [ʀɑ̃fɔʀse] vt to reinforce; **renfort: renforts** nmpl reinforcements; **à grand renfort de** with a great deal of

renfrogné, e [ʀɑ̃fʀɔɲe] adj sullen

renier [ʀənje] vt (personne) to disown, repudiate; (foi) to renounce

renifler [ʀ(ə)nifle] vi, vt to sniff

renne [ʀɛn] nm reindeer inv

renom [ʀənɔ̃] nm reputation; (célébrité) renown; **renommé, e** adj celebrated, renowned; **renommée** nf fame

renoncer [ʀ(ə)nɔ̃se]: **~ à** vt to give up; **~ à faire** to give up the idea of doing

renouer [ʀənwe] vt: **~ avec** (habitude) to take up again

renouveler [ʀ(ə)nuv(ə)le] vt to renew; (exploit, méfait) to repeat; **se ~** vi (incident) to recur, happen again; **renouvellement** nm (remplacement) renewal

rénover [ʀenɔve] vt (immeuble) to renovate, do up; (quartier) to redevelop

renseignement [ʀɑ̃sɛɲmɑ̃] nm information no pl, piece of information; **(guichet des) ~s** information office; **(service des) ~s** (Tél) directory enquiries (BRIT), information (US)

renseigner [ʀɑ̃seɲe] vt: **~ qn (sur)** to give information to sb (about); **se ~** vi to ask for information, make inquiries

rentabilité [ʀɑ̃tabilite] nf profitability

rentable [ʀɑ̃tabl] adj profitable

rente [ʀɑ̃t] nf private income; (pension) pension

rentrée [ʀɑ̃tʀe] nf: **~ (d'argent)** cash no pl coming in; **la ~ (des classes)** the start of the new school year

rentrer [ʀɑ̃tʀe] vi (revenir chez soi) to go to (ou come) (back) home; (entrer de nouveau) to go (ou come) back in; (entrer) to go (ou come) in; (air, clou: pénétrer) to go in; (revenu) to come in ▷ vt to bring in; (véhicule) to put away; (chemise dans pantalon etc) to tuck in; (griffes) to draw in; **le ventre** to pull in one's stomach; **~ dans** (heurter) to crash into; **~ dans l'ordre** to be back to normal; **~ dans ses frais** to recover one's expenses; **je rentre mardi** I'm going ou coming home on Tuesday

renverse [ʀɑ̃vɛʀs] **à la ~** adv backwards

renverser [ʀɑ̃vɛʀse] vt (faire tomber: chaise, verre) to knock over, overturn; (liquide, contenu) to spill, upset; (piéton) to knock down; (retourner) to turn upside down; (: ordre des mots etc) to reverse; (fig: gouvernement etc) to overthrow; (fam: stupéfier) to bowl over; **se ~** vi (verre, vase) to fall over; (contenu) to spill

renvoi [ʀɑ̃vwa] nm (d'employé) dismissal; (d'élève) expulsion; (référence) cross-reference; (éructation) belch; **renvoyer** vt to send back; (congédier) to dismiss; (élève: définitivement) to expel; (lumière) to reflect; (ajourner): **renvoyer qch (à)** to put sth off ou postpone sth (until)

repaire [ʀ(ə)pɛʀ] nm den

répandre [ʀepɑ̃dʀ] vt (renverser) to spill; (étaler, diffuser) to spread; (odeur) to give off; **se ~** vi to spill; (se propager) to spread; **répandu, e** adj (opinion, usage) widespread

réparation [ʀepaʀasjɔ̃] nf repair

réparer [ʀepaʀe] vt to repair; (fig: offense) to make up for, atone for; (: oubli, erreur) to put right; **où est-ce que je peux le faire ~?** where can I get it fixed?

repartie [ʀepaʀti] nf retort; **avoir de la ~** to be quick at repartee

repartir [ʀ(ə)paʀtiʀ] vi to leave again; (voyageur) to set off again; (fig) to get going again; **~ à zéro** to start from scratch (again)

répartir [ʀepaʀtiʀ] vt (pour attribuer) to share out; (pour disperser, disposer) to divide up; (poids) to distribute; **se ~** vt (travail, rôles) to share out between themselves; **répartition** nf (des richesses etc) distribution

repas [ʀ(ə)pɑ] nm meal

repassage [ʀ(ə)pasaʒ] nm ironing

repasser [ʀ(ə)pase] vi to come (ou go) back ▷ vt (vêtement, tissu) to iron; (examen) to retake, resit; (film) to show again; (leçon) revoir) to go over (again)

repentir [ʀəpɑ̃tiʀ] nm repentance; **se ~** vi to repent; **se ~ d'avoir fait qch** (regretter) to regret having done sth

répercussions [ʀepɛʀkysjɔ̃] nfpl (fig) repercussions

répercuter [ʀepɛʀkyte]: **se ~** vi (bruit) to reverberate; (fig): **se ~ sur** to have repercussions on

repère [ʀ(ə)pɛʀ] nm mark; (monument, événement) landmark

repérer [ʀ(ə)peʀe] vt (fam: erreur, personne) to spot; (: endroit) to locate; **se ~** vi to find one's way about

répertoire [ʀepɛʀtwaʀ] nm (liste) (alphabetical) list; (carnet) index notebook; (Inform) folder, directory; (d'un artiste) repertoire

répéter [ʀepete] vt to repeat; (préparer: leçon) to learn, go over; (Théâtre) to rehearse; **se ~** vi (redire) to repeat o.s.; (se reproduire) to be repeated, recur; **pouvez-vous ~, s'il vous plaît?** can you repeat that, please?

répétition [ʀepetisjɔ̃] nf repetition; (Théâtre) rehearsal; **~ générale** (final) dress rehearsal

répit [ʀepi] nm respite; **sans ~** without letting up

replier [ʀ(ə)plije] vt (rabattre) to fold down ou over; **se ~** vi (troupes, armée) to withdraw, fall back; (sur soi-même) to withdraw into o.s.

réplique [ʀeplik] nf (repartie, fig) reply; (Théâtre) line; (copie) replica; **répliquer** vi to reply; (riposter) to retaliate

répondeur [ʀepɔ̃dœʀ] nm: **~ (automatique)** (Tél) answering machine

répondre [ʀepɔ̃dʀ] vi to answer, reply; (freins) to respond; **~ à** to reply to, answer; (affection, salut) to return; (provocation) to respond to; (correspondre à: besoin) to answer; (: conditions) to meet; (: description) to match; (avec impertinence): **~ à qn** to answer sb back; **~ de** to answer for

réponse [ʀepɔ̃s] nf answer, reply; **en ~ à** in reply to

reportage [ʀ(ə)pɔʀtaʒ] nm report

reporter¹ [ʀəpɔʀtɛʀ] nm reporter

reporter² [ʀəpɔʀte] vt (ajourner): **~ qch (à)** to postpone sth (until); (transférer): **~ qch sur** to transfer sth to; **se ~ à** (époque) to think back to; (document) to refer to

repos [ʀ(ə)po] nm rest; (tranquillité) peace (and quiet); (Mil): **~!** stand at ease!; **ce n'est pas de tout ~!** it's no picnic!

reposant, e [ʀ(ə)pozɑ̃, ɑ̃t] adj restful

reposer [ʀ(ə)poze] vt (verre, livre) to put down; (délasser) to rest ▷ vi: **laisser ~** (pâte) to leave to stand; **se ~** vi to rest; **se ~ sur qn** to rely on sb; **~ sur** (fig) to rest on

repoussant, e [ʀ(ə)pusɑ̃, ɑ̃t] adj repulsive

repousser [ʀ(ə)puse] vi to grow again ▷ vt to repel, repulse; (offre) to turn down, reject; (personne) to push back; (différer) to put back

reprendre [ʀ(ə)pʀɑ̃dʀ] vt (objet prêté, donné) to take back; (prisonnier, ville) to recapture; (firme, entreprise) to take over; (le travail) to resume; (emprunter: argument, idée) to take up, use; (refaire: article etc) to go over again; (vêtement) to alter; (réprimander) to tell off; (corriger) to correct; (chercher): **je viendrai te ~ à 4 h** I'll come and fetch you at 4; (se resservir de): **~ du pain/un œuf** to take (ou eat) more bread/another egg ▷ vi (classes, pluie) to start (up) again; (activités, travaux, combats) to resume, start (up) again; (affaires) to pick up; (dire): **reprit-il** he went on; **~ des forces** to recover one's strength; **~ courage** to take new heart; **~ la route** to resume one's journey, set off again; **~ haleine** ou **son souffle** to get one's breath back

représentant, e [ʀ(ə)pʀezɑ̃tɑ̃, ɑ̃t] nm/f representative

représentation [ʀ(ə)pʀezɑ̃tasjɔ̃] nf (symbole, image) representation; (spectacle) performance

représenter [ʀ(ə)pʀezɑ̃te] vt to represent; (donner: pièce, opéra) to perform; **se ~** vt (se figurer) to imagine

répression [ʀepʀesjɔ̃] nf repression

réprimer [ʀepʀime] vt (émotions) to suppress; (peuple etc) to repress

repris [ʀ(ə)pʀi] nm: **~ de justice** ex-prisoner, ex-convict

reprise [ʀ(ə)pʀiz] nf (recommencement) resumption; (économique) recovery; (TV) repeat; (Comm) trade-in, part exchange; (raccommodage) mend; **à plusieurs ~s** on several occasions

repriser [ʀ(ə)pʀize] vt (chaussette, lainage) to darn; (tissu) to mend

reproche [ʀ(ə)pʀɔʃ] nm (remontrance) reproach; **faire des ~s à qn** to reproach sb; **sans ~(s)** beyond reproach;

reprocher vt: **reprocher qch à qn** to reproach ou blame sb for sth; **reprocher qch à** (critiquer) to have sth against

reproduction [ʀ(ə)pʀɔdyksjɔ̃] nf reproduction

reproduire [ʀ(ə)pʀɔdɥiʀ] vt to reproduce; **se ~** vi (Bio) to reproduce; (recommencer) to recur, re-occur

reptile [ʀɛptil] nm reptile

république [ʀepyblik] nf republic

répugnant, e [ʀepynɑ̃, ɑ̃t] adj disgusting

répugner [ʀepyne]: **~ à** vt : **~ à qn** to repel ou disgust sb; **~ à faire** to be loath ou reluctant to do

réputation [ʀepytasjɔ̃] nf reputation; **réputé, e** adj renowned

requérir [ʀəkeʀiʀ] vt (nécessiter) to require, call for

requête [ʀəkɛt] nf request

requin [ʀəkɛ̃] nm shark

requis, e [ʀəki, iz] adj required

RER sigle m (= réseau express régional) Greater Paris high-speed train service

rescapé, e [ʀɛskape] nm/f survivor

rescousse [ʀɛskus] nf: **aller à la ~ de qn** to go to sb's aid ou rescue

réseau, x [ʀezo] nm network

réservation [ʀezɛʀvasjɔ̃] nf booking, reservation; **j'ai confirmé ma ~ par fax/e-mail** I confirmed my booking by fax/e-mail

réserve [ʀezɛʀv] nf (retenue) reserve; (entrepôt) storeroom; (restriction, d'Indiens) reservation; (de pêche, chasse) preserve; **de ~** (provisions etc) in reserve

réservé, e [ʀezɛʀve] adj reserved; **chasse/pêche ~e** private hunting/fishing

réserver [ʀezɛʀve] vt to reserve; (chambre, billet etc) to book, reserve; (fig: destiner) to have in store; (garder): **~ qch pour/à** to keep ou save sth for; **je voudrais ~ une chambre pour deux personnes** I'd like to book a double room; **j'ai réservé une table au nom de ...** I booked a table in the name of ...

réservoir [ʀezɛʀvwaʀ] nm tank

résidence [ʀezidɑ̃s] nf residence; **résidence secondaire** second home; **résidence universitaire** hall of residence (BRIT), dormitory (US); **résidentiel, le** adj residential; **résider** vi: **résider à/dans/en** to reside in; **résider dans** (fig) to lie in

résidu [ʀezidy] nm residue no pl

résigner [ʀezine]: **se ~** vi: **se ~ (à qch/à faire)** to resign o.s. (to sth/to doing)

résilier [ʀezilje] vt to terminate

résistance [ʀezistɑ̃s] nf resistance; (de réchaud, bouilloire: fil) element

résistant, e [ʀezistɑ̃, ɑ̃t] adj (personne) robust, tough; (matériau) strong, hard-wearing

résister [ʀeziste] vi to resist; **~ à** (assaut, tentation) to resist; (supporter: gel etc) to withstand; (désobéir à) to stand up to, oppose

résolu, e [ʀezɔly] pp de **résoudre** ▷ adj: **être ~ à qch/faire** to be set upon sth/doing

résolution [ʀezɔlysjɔ̃] nf (fermeté, décision) resolution; (d'un problème) solution

résolve etc [ʀezɔlv] vb voir **résoudre**

résonner [ʀezɔne] vi (cloche, pas) to reverberate, resound; (salle) to be resonant

résorber [ʀezɔʀbe]: **se ~** vi (fig: chômage) to be reduced; (: déficit) to be absorbed

résoudre [ʀezudʀ] vt to solve; **se ~ à faire** to bring o.s. to do

respect [ʀɛspɛ] nm respect; **tenir en ~** to keep at bay; **présenter ses ~s à qn** to pay one's respects to sb; **respecter** vt to respect; **respectueux, -euse** adj respectful

respiration [ʀɛspiʀasjɔ̃] nf breathing no pl

respirer [ʀɛspiʀe] vi to breathe; (fig: se détendre) to get one's breath; (: se rassurer) to breathe again ▷ vt to breathe (in), inhale; (manifester: santé, calme etc) to exude

resplendir [ʀɛsplɑ̃diʀ] vi to shine; (fig): **~ (de)** to be radiant (with)

responsabilité [ʀɛspɔ̃sabilite] nf responsibility; (légale) liability

responsable [ʀɛspɔ̃sabl] adj responsible ▷ nm/f (coupable) person responsible; (personne compétente) person in charge; (de parti, syndicat) official; **~ de** responsible for

ressaisir [ʀ(ə)seziʀ]: **se ~** vi to regain one's self-control

ressasser [ʀ(ə)sase] vt to keep going over

ressemblance [ʀ(ə)sɑ̃blɑ̃s] nf resemblance, similarity, likeness

ressemblant, e [ʀ(ə)sɑ̃blɑ̃, ɑ̃t] adj (portrait) lifelike, true to life

ressembler [ʀ(ə)sɑ̃ble]: **~ à** vt to be like, resemble; (visuellement) to look like; **se ~** vi to be (ou look) alike

ressentiment [ʀ(ə)sɑ̃timɑ̃] nm resentment

ressentir [ʀ(ə)sɑ̃tiʀ] vt to feel; **se ~ de** to feel (ou show) the effects of

resserrer [ʀ(ə)seʀe] vt (nœud, boulon) to tighten (up); (fig: liens) to strengthen

resservir [ʀ(ə)seʀviʀ] vi to do ou serve again; **~ qn (d'un plat)** to give sb a second helping (of a dish); **se ~ de** (plat) to take a second helping of; (outil etc) to use again

ressort [ʀasɔʀ] nm (pièce) spring; (énergie) spirit; (recours): **en dernier ~** as a last resort; (compétence): **être du ~ de** to fall within the competence of

ressortir [ʀasɔʀtiʀ] vi (à nouveau) to come out (again); (contraster) to stand out; **~ de** to emerge from; **faire ~** (fig: souligner) to bring out

ressortissant, e [ʀ(ə)sɔʀtisɑ̃, ɑ̃t] nm/f national

ressources [ʀ(ə)suʀs] nfpl (moyens) resources

ressusciter [ʀesysite] vt (fig) to revive, bring back ▷ vi to rise (from the dead)

restant, e [ʀɛstɑ̃, ɑ̃t] adj remaining ▷ nm: **le ~ (de)** the remainder (of); **un ~ de** (de trop) some left-over

restaurant [ʀɛstɔʀɑ̃] nm restaurant; **pouvez-vous m'indiquer un bon ~?** can you recommend a good restaurant?

restauration [ʀɛstɔʀasjɔ̃] nf restoration; (hôtellerie) catering; **restauration rapide** fast food

restaurer [ʀɛstɔʀe] vt to restore; **se ~** vi to have something to eat

reste [ʀɛst] nm (restant): **le ~ (de)** the rest (of); (de trop): **un ~ (de)** some left-over; **restes** nmpl (nourriture) left-overs; (d'une cité etc, dépouille mortelle) remains; **du ~, au ~** besides, moreover

rester [ʀɛste] vi to stay, remain; (subsister) to remain, be left; (durer) to last ▷ vb impers: **il reste du pain/2 œufs** there's some bread/there are 2 eggs left (over); **restons-en là** let's leave it at that; **il me reste assez de temps** I have enough time left; **il ne me reste plus qu'à ...** I've just got to ...

restituer [ʀɛstitɥe] vt (objet, somme): **~ qch (à qn)** to return sth (to sb)

restreindre [ʀɛstʀɛ̃dʀ] vt to restrict, limit

restriction [ʀɛstʀiksjɔ̃] nf restriction

résultat [ʀezylta] nm result; **résultats** nmpl (d'examen, d'élection) results pl

résulter [ʀezylte]: **~ de** vt to result from, be the result of

résumé [ʀezyme] nm summary, résumé; **en ~** in brief; (pour conclure) to sum up

résumer [ʀezyme] vt (texte) to summarize; (récapituler) to sum up

résurrection [ʀezyʀɛksjɔ̃] nf resurrection

rétablir [ʀetabliʀ] vt to restore, re-establish; **se ~** (guérir) to recover; (silence, calme) to return, be restored; **rétablissement** nm restoring; (guérison) recovery

retaper [ʀ(ə)tape] (fam) vt (maison, voiture etc) to do up; (revigorer) to buck up

retard [ʀ(ə)taʀ] nm (d'une personne attendue) lateness no pl; (sur l'horaire, un programme) delay; (fig: scolaire, mental etc) backwardness; **en ~ (de 2 heures)** (2 hours) late; **avoir du ~** to be late; (sur un programme) to be behind (schedule); **prendre du ~** (train, avion) to be delayed; **sans ~** without delay; **désolé d'être en ~** sorry I'm late; **le vol a deux heures de ~** the flight is two hours late

retardataire [ʀ(ə)taʀdatɛʀ] nm/f latecomer

retardement [ʀ(ə)taʀdəmã]: **à ~** adj delayed action cpd; **bombe à ~** time bomb

retarder [ʀ(ə)taʀde] vt to delay; (montre) to put back ▷ vi (montre) to be slow; **~ qn (d'une heure)** (sur un horaire) to delay sb (an hour); **~ qch (de 2 jours)** (départ, date) to put sth back (2 days)

retenir [ʀət(ə)niʀ] vt (garder, retarder) to keep, detain; (maintenir: objet qui glisse, fig: colère, larmes) to hold back; (se rappeler) to retain; (réserver) to reserve; (accepter: proposition etc) to accept; (fig: empêcher d'agir): **~ qn (de faire)** to hold sb back (from doing); (prélever): **~ qch (sur)** to deduct sth (from); **se ~** vi (se raccrocher): **se ~ à** to hold onto; (se contenir): **se ~ de faire** to restrain o.s. from doing; **~ son souffle** to hold one's breath

retentir [ʀ(ə)tãtiʀ] vi to ring out; **retentissant, e** adj resounding

retenue [ʀət(ə)ny] nf (prélèvement) deduction; (Scol) detention; (modération) (self-)restraint

réticence [ʀetisãs] nf hesitation, reluctance no pl; **réticent, e** adj hesitant, reluctant

rétine [ʀetin] nf retina

retiré, e [ʀ(ə)tiʀe] adj (vie) secluded; (lieu) remote

retirer [ʀ(ə)tiʀe] vt (vêtement, lunettes) to take off, remove; (argent, plainte) to withdraw; (reprendre: bagages, billets) to collect, pick up; (extraire): **~ qch de** to take sth out of, remove sth from

retomber [ʀ(ə)tɔ̃be] vi (à nouveau) to fall again; (atterrir: après un saut etc) to land; (échoir): **~ sur qn** to fall on sb

rétorquer [ʀetɔʀke] vt: **~ (à qn) que** to retort (to sb) that

retouche [ʀ(ə)tuʃ] nf (sur vêtement) alteration; **retoucher** vt (photographie) to touch up; (texte, vêtement) to alter

retour [ʀ(ə)tuʀ] nm return; **au ~** (en route) on the way back; **à mon ~** when I get/got back; **être de ~ (de)** to be back (from); **par ~ du courrier** by return of post; **quand serons-nous de ~?** when do we get back?

retourner [ʀ(ə)tuʀne] vt (dans l'autre sens: matelas, crêpe etc) to turn (over); (: sac, vêtement) to turn inside out; (fam: bouleverser) to shake; (renvoyer, restituer): **~ qch à qn** to return sth to sb ▷ vi (aller, revenir): **~ quelque part/à** to go back ou return somewhere/to; **se ~** vi (tourner la

tête) to turn round; **~ à** (état, activité) to return to, go back to; **se ~ contre** (fig) to turn against

retrait [ʀ(ə)tʀɛ] nm (d'argent) withdrawal; **en ~** set back; **retrait du permis (de conduire)** disqualification from driving (BRIT), revocation of driver's license (US)

retraite [ʀ(ə)tʀɛt] nf (d'un employé) retirement; (revenu) pension; (d'une armée, Rel) retreat; **prendre sa ~** to retire; **retraite anticipée** early retirement; **retraité, e** adj retired ▷ nm/f pensioner

retrancher [ʀ(ə)tʀãʃe] vt (nombre, somme): **~ qch de** to take ou deduct sth from; **se ~ derrière/dans** to take refuge behind/in

rétrécir [ʀetʀesiʀ] vt (vêtement) to take in ▷ vi to shrink; **se ~** (route, vallée) to narrow

rétro [ʀetʀo] adj inv: **la mode ~** the nostalgia vogue

rétroprojecteur [ʀetʀopʀɔʒɛktœʀ] nm overhead projector

rétrospective [ʀetʀɔspɛktiv] nf (Art) retrospective; (Cinéma) season, retrospective; **rétrospectivement** adv in retrospect

retrousser [ʀ(ə)tʀuse] vt to roll up

retrouvailles [ʀ(ə)tʀuvaj] nfpl reunion sg

retrouver [ʀ(ə)tʀuve] vt (fugitif, objet perdu) to find; (calme, santé) to regain; (revoir) to see again; (rejoindre) to meet (again), join; **se ~** vi to meet; (s'orienter) to find one's way; **se ~ quelque part** to find o.s. somewhere; **s'y ~** (y voir clair) to make sense of it; (rentrer dans ses frais) to break even; **je ne retrouve plus mon portefeuille** I can't find my wallet (BRIT) ou billfold (US)

rétroviseur [ʀetʀovizœʀ] nm (rear-view) mirror

réunion [ʀeynjɔ̃] nf (séance) meeting

réunir [ʀeyniʀ] vt (rassembler) to gather together; (inviter: amis, famille) to have round, have in; (cumuler: qualités etc) to combine; (rapprocher: ennemis) to bring together (again), reunite; (rattacher: parties) to join (together); **se ~** vi (se rencontrer) to meet

réussi, e [ʀeysi] adj successful

réussir [ʀeysiʀ] vi to succeed, be successful; (à un examen) to pass ▷ vt to make a success of; **~ à faire** to succeed in doing; **~ à qn** (être bénéfique à) to agree with sb; **réussite** nf success; (Cartes) patience

revaloir [ʀ(ə)valwaʀ] vt: **je vous revaudrai cela** I'll repay you some day; (en mal) I'll pay you back for this

revanche [ʀ(ə)vãʃ] nf revenge; (sport) revenge match; **en ~** on the other hand

rêve [ʀɛv] nm dream; **de ~** dream cpd; **faire un ~** to have a dream

réveil [ʀevɛj] nm waking up no pl; (fig) awakening; (pendule) alarm (clock); **au ~** on waking (up); **réveiller** vt (personne) to wake up; (fig) to awaken, revive; **se réveiller** vi to wake up; **pouvez-vous me réveiller à 7 heures, s'il vous plaît?** could I have an alarm call at 7am, please?

réveillon [ʀevɛjɔ̃] nm Christmas Eve; (de la Saint-Sylvestre) New Year's Eve; **réveillonner** vi to celebrate Christmas Eve (ou New Year's Eve)

révélateur, -trice [ʀevelatœʀ, tʀis] adj: **~ (de qch)** revealing (sth)

révéler [ʀevele] vt to reveal; **se ~** vi to be revealed, reveal itself ▷ vb +attrib: **se ~ difficile/aisé** to prove difficult/easy

revenant, e [ʀ(ə)vənã, ãt] nm/f ghost

revendeur, -euse [ʀ(ə)vãdœʀ, øz] nm/f (détaillant) retailer; (de drogue) (drug-)dealer

revendication [R(ə)vɑ̃dikasjɔ̃] nf claim, demand
revendiquer [R(ə)vɑ̃dike] vt to claim, demand; (*responsabilité*) to claim
revendre [R(ə)vɑ̃dR] vt (*d'occasion*) to resell; (*détailler*) to sell; **à ~** (*en abondance*) to spare
revenir [Rəv(ə)niR] vi to come back; (*coûter*): **~ cher/à 100 euros (à qn)** to cost (sb) a lot/100 euros; **~ à** (*reprendre: études, projet*) to return to, go back to; (*équivaloir à*) to amount to; **~ à qn** (*part, honneur*) to go to sb, be sb's; (*souvenir, nom*) to come back to sb; **~ sur** (*question, sujet*) to go back over; (*engagement*) to go back on; **~ à soi** to come round; **n'en pas ~**: **je n'en reviens pas** I can't get over it; **~ sur ses pas** to retrace one's steps; **cela revient à dire que/au même** it amounts to saying that/the same thing; **faire ~** (*Culin*) to brown
revenu [Rəv(ə)ny] nm income; **revenus** nmpl income sg
rêver [Reve] vi, vt to dream; **~ de/à** to dream of
réverbère [RevɛRbɛR] nm street lamp ou light; **réverbérer** vt to reflect
revers [R(ə)vɛR] nm (*de feuille, main*) back; (*d'étoffe*) wrong side; (*de pièce, médaille*) back, reverse; (*Tennis, Ping-Pong*) backhand; (*de veste*) lapel; (*fig: échec*) setback
revêtement [R(ə)vɛtmɑ̃] nm (*des sols*) flooring; (*de chaussée*) surface
revêtir [R(ə)vetiR] vt (*habit*) to don, put on; (*prendre: importance, apparence*) to take on; **~ qch de** to cover sth with
rêveur, -euse [Revœʀ, øz] adj dreamy ▷ nm/f dreamer
revient [Rəvjɛ̃] vb voir **revenir**
revigorer [R(ə)vigɔRe] vt (*air frais*) to invigorate, brace up; (*repas, boisson*) to revive, buck up
revirement [R(ə)viRmɑ̃] nm change of mind; (*d'une situation*) reversal
réviser [Revize] vt to revise; (*machine*) to overhaul, service
révision [Revizjɔ̃] nf revision; (*de voiture*) servicing no pl
revivre [R(ə)vivR] vi (*reprendre des forces*) to come alive again ▷ vt (*épreuve, moment*) to relive
revoir [RəvwaR] vt to see again; (*réviser*) to revise ▷ nm: **au ~** goodbye
révoltant, e [Revɔltɑ̃, ɑ̃t] adj revolting, appalling
révolte [Revɔlt] nf rebellion, revolt
révolter [Revɔlte] vt to revolt; **se ~ (contre)** to rebel (against)
révolu, e [Revɔly] adj past; (*Admin*): **âgé de 18 ans ~s** over 18 years of age
révolution [Revɔlysjɔ̃] nf revolution; **révolutionnaire** adj, nm/f revolutionary
revolver [RevɔlvɛR] nm gun; (*à barillet*) revolver
révoquer [Revɔke] vt (*fonctionnaire*) to dismiss; (*arrêt, contrat*) to revoke
revue [R(ə)vy] nf review; (*périodique*) review, magazine; (*de music-hall*) variety show; **passer en ~** (*mentalement*) to go through
rez-de-chaussée [Red(ə)ʃose] nm inv ground floor
RF sigle f = **République française**
Rhin [Rɛ̃] nm Rhine
rhinocéros [RinɔseRɔs] nm rhinoceros
Rhône [Ron] nm Rhone
rhubarbe [Rybarb] nf rhubarb
rhum [Rɔm] nm rum
rhumatisme [Rymatism] nm rheumatism no pl
rhume [Rym] nm cold; **rhume de cerveau** head cold; **le rhume des foins** hay fever

ricaner [Rikane] vi (*avec méchanceté*) to snigger; (*bêtement*) to giggle
riche [Riʃ] adj rich; (*personne, pays*) rich, wealthy; **~ en** rich in; **richesse** nf wealth; (*fig: de sol, musée etc*) richness; **richesses** nfpl (*ressources, argent*) wealth sg; (*fig: trésors*) treasures
ricochet [Rikɔʃɛ] nm: **faire des ~s** to skip stones
ride [Rid] nf wrinkle
rideau, x [Rido] nm curtain; **rideau de fer** (*boutique*) metal shutter(s)
rider [Ride] vt to wrinkle; **se ~** vi to become wrinkled
ridicule [Ridikyl] adj ridiculous ▷ nm: **le ~** ridicule; **ridiculiser** vt to ridicule; **se ridiculiser** vi to make a fool of o.s.

MOT-CLÉ

rien [Rjɛ̃] pron 1: **(ne) ... rien** nothing, *tournure négative + anything*; **qu'est-ce que vous avez? - rien** what have you got? - nothing; **il n'a rien dit/fait** he said/did nothing; he hasn't said/done anything; **n'avoir peur de rien** to be afraid ou frightened of nothing, not to be afraid ou frightened of anything; **il n'a rien** (*n'est pas blessé*) he's all right; **ça ne fait rien** it doesn't matter; **de rien!** not at all!
2: **rien de**: **rien d'intéressant** nothing interesting; **rien d'autre** nothing else; **rien du tout** nothing at all
3: **rien que** just, only; nothing but; **rien que pour lui faire plaisir** only ou just to please him; **rien que la vérité** nothing but the truth; **rien que cela** that alone ▷ nm: **un petit rien** (*cadeau*) a little something; **des riens** trivia pl; **un rien de** a hint of; **en un rien de temps** in no time at all

rieur, -euse [R(i)jœʀ, R(i)jøz] adj cheerful
rigide [Riʒid] adj stiff; (*fig*) rigid; strict
rigoler [Rigɔle] vi (*rire: rire*) to laugh; (*s'amuser*) to have (some) fun; (*plaisanter*) to be joking ou kidding; **rigolo, -ote** (*fam*) adj funny ▷ nm/f comic; (*péj*) fraud, phoney
rigoureusement [RiguRøzmɑ̃] adv (*vrai*) absolutely; (*interdit*) strictly
rigoureux, -euse [RiguRø, øz] adj rigorous; (*hiver*) hard, harsh
rigueur [RigœR] nf rigour; **"tenue de soirée de ~"** "formal dress only"; **à la ~** at a pinch; **tenir ~ à qn de qch** to hold sth against sb
rillettes [Rijɛt] nfpl potted meat (*made from pork or goose*)
rime [Rim] nf rhyme
rinçage [Rɛ̃saʒ] nm rinsing (out); (*opération*) rinse
rincer [Rɛ̃se] vt to rinse; (*récipient*) to rinse out
ringard, e [Rɛ̃gaR, aRd] (*fam*) adj old-fashioned
riposter [Ripɔste] vi to retaliate ▷ vt: **~ que** to retort that
rire [RiR] vi to laugh; (*se divertir*) to have fun ▷ nm laugh; **le ~** laughter; **~ de** to laugh at; **pour ~** (*pas sérieusement*) for a joke ou a laugh
risible [Rizibl] adj laughable
risque [Risk] nm risk; **le ~** danger; **à ses ~s et périls** at his own risk; **risqué, e** adj risky; (*plaisanterie*) risqué, daring; **risquer** vt to risk; (*allusion, question*) to venture, hazard; **ça ne risque rien** it's quite safe; **risquer de**: **il risque de se tuer** he could get himself killed; **ce qui risque de se produire** what might ou could well happen; **il ne risque pas de recommencer** there's

no chance of him doing that again; **se risquer à faire** (*tenter*) to venture *ou* dare to do

issoler [ʀisɔle] vi, vt: **(faire) ~** to brown

istourne [ʀisturn] nf discount

ite [ʀit] nm rite; (*fig*) ritual

ivage [ʀivaʒ] nm shore

ival, e, -aux [ʀival, o] adj, nm/f rival; **rivaliser** vi: **rivaliser avec** (*personne*) to rival, vie with; **rivalité** nf rivalry

ive [ʀiv] nf shore; (*de fleuve*) bank; **riverain, e** nm/f riverside (*ou* lakeside) resident; (*d'une route*) local resident

ivière [ʀivjɛʀ] nf river

iz [ʀi] nm rice; **rizière** nf paddy-field, ricefield

RMI sigle m (= revenu minimum d'insertion) ≈ income support (BRIT), ≈ welfare (US)

RN sigle f = **route nationale**

obe [ʀɔb] nf dress; (*de juge*) robe; (*pelage*) coat; **robe de chambre** dressing gown; **robe de mariée** wedding dress; **robe de soirée** evening dress

obinet [ʀɔbinɛ] nm tap (BRIT), faucet (US)

obot [ʀɔbo] nm robot; **robot de cuisine** food processor

obuste [ʀɔbyst] adj robust, sturdy; **robustesse** nf robustness, sturdiness

oc [ʀɔk] nm rock

ocade [ʀɔkad] nf bypass

ocaille [ʀɔkaj] nf loose stones pl; (*jardin*) rockery, rock garden

oche [ʀɔʃ] nf rock

ocher [ʀɔʃe] nm rock

ocheux, -euse [ʀɔʃø, øz] adj rocky

odage [ʀɔdaʒ] nm: **en ~** running in

ôder [ʀode] vi to roam about; (*de façon suspecte*) to lurk (about *ou* around); **rôdeur, -euse** nm/f prowler

ogne [ʀɔɲ] (*fam*) nf: **être en ~** to be in a temper

ogner [ʀɔɲe] vt to clip; **~ sur** (*fig*) to cut down *ou* back on

ognons [ʀɔɲɔ̃] nmpl (Culin) kidneys

oi [ʀwa] nm king; **la fête des Rois, les Rois** Twelfth Night

ôle [ʀol] nm role, part

ollers [ʀɔlœʀ] nmpl Rollerblades®

omain, e [ʀɔmɛ̃, ɛn] adj Roman ▷ nm/f: **R~, e** Roman

oman, e [ʀɔmã, an] adj (Archit) Romanesque ▷ nm novel; **roman policier** detective story

omancer [ʀɔmãse] vt (*agrémenter*) to romanticize; **romancier, -ière** nm/f novelist; **romanesque** adj (*amours, aventures*) storybook cpd; (*sentimental: personne*) romantic

oman-feuilleton [ʀɔmãfœjtɔ̃] nm serialized novel

omanichel, le [ʀɔmaniʃɛl] (*péj*) nm/f gipsy

omantique [ʀɔmãtik] adj romantic

omarin [ʀɔmaʀɛ̃] nm rosemary

Rome [ʀɔm] n Rome

ompre [ʀɔ̃pʀ] vt to break; (*entretien, fiançailles*) to break off ▷ vi (*fiancés*) to break it off; **se ~** vi to break; **rompu, e** adj (*fourbu*) exhausted

onces [ʀɔ̃s] nfpl brambles

onchonner [ʀɔ̃ʃɔne] (*fam*) vi to grouse, grouch

ond, e [ʀɔ̃, ʀɔ̃d] adj round; (*joues, mollets*) well-rounded; (*fam: ivre*) tight ▷ nm (*cercle*) ring; (*fam: sou*): **je n'ai plus un ~** I haven't a penny left; **en ~** (*s'asseoir, danser*) in a ring; **ronde** nf (*gén: de surveillance*) rounds pl, patrol; (*danse*) round (dance); (*Mus*) semibreve (BRIT), whole note (US); **à la ronde** (*alentour*): **à 10 km à la ronde** for 10 km round;

rondelet, te adj plump

rondelle [ʀɔ̃dɛl] nf (*tranche*) slice, round; (*Tech*) washer

rond-point [ʀɔ̃pwɛ̃] nm roundabout

ronflement [ʀɔ̃fləmã] nm snore, snoring

ronfler [ʀɔ̃fle] vi to snore; (*moteur, poêle*) to hum

ronger [ʀɔ̃ʒe] vt to gnaw (at); (*suj: vers, rouille*) to eat into; **se ~ les ongles** to bite one's nails; **se ~ les sangs** to worry o.s. sick; **rongeur** nm rodent

ronronner [ʀɔ̃ʀɔne] vi to purr

rosbif [ʀɔsbif] nm: **du ~** roasting beef; (*cuit*) roast beef

rose [ʀoz] nf rose ▷ adj pink; **rose bonbon** adj inv candy pink

rosé, e [ʀoze] adj pinkish; **(vin) ~** rosé

roseau, x [ʀozo] nm reed

rosée [ʀoze] nf dew

rosier [ʀozje] nm rosebush, rose tree

rossignol [ʀɔsiɲɔl] nm (*Zool*) nightingale

rotation [ʀɔtasjɔ̃] nf rotation

roter [ʀɔte] (*fam*) vi to burp, belch

rôti [ʀoti] nm: **du ~** roasting meat; (*cuit*) roast meat; **un ~ de bœuf/porc** a joint of beef/pork

rotin [ʀɔtɛ̃] nm rattan (cane); **fauteuil en ~** cane (arm)chair

rôtir [ʀotiʀ] vi, vt (*aussi*: **faire ~**) to roast; **rôtisserie** nf (*restaurant*) steakhouse; (*traiteur*) roast meat shop; **rôtissoire** nf (roasting) spit

rotule [ʀɔtyl] nf kneecap

rouage [ʀwaʒ] nm cog(wheel), gearwheel; **les ~s de l'État** the wheels of State

roue [ʀu] nf wheel; **roue de secours** spare wheel

rouer [ʀwe] vt: **~ qn de coups** to give sb a thrashing

rouge [ʀuʒ] adj, nm/f red ▷ nm red; **(vin) ~** red wine; **sur la liste ~** ex-directory (BRIT), unlisted (US); **passer au ~** (*signal*) to go red; (*automobiliste*) to go through a red light; **rouge à joue** blusher; **rouge (à lèvres)** lipstick; **rouge-gorge** nm robin (redbreast)

rougeole [ʀuʒɔl] nf measles sg

rougeoyer [ʀuʒwaje] vi to glow red

rouget [ʀuʒɛ] nm mullet

rougeur [ʀuʒœʀ] nf redness; (*Méd: tache*) red blotch

rougir [ʀuʒiʀ] vi to turn red; (*de honte, timidité*) to blush, flush; (*de plaisir, colère*) to flush

rouille [ʀuj] nf rust; **rouillé, e** adj rusty; **rouiller** vt to rust ▷ vi to rust, go rusty

roulant, e [ʀulã, ãt] adj (*meuble*) on wheels; (*tapis etc*) moving; **escalier ~** escalator

rouleau, x [ʀulo] nm roll; (*à mise en plis, à peinture, vague*) roller; **rouleau à pâtisserie** rolling pin

roulement [ʀulmã] nm (*rotation*) rotation; (*bruit*) rumbling no pl, rumble; **travailler par ~** to work on a rota (BRIT) *ou* rotation (US) basis; **roulement (à billes)** ball bearings pl; **roulement de tambour** drum roll

rouler [ʀule] vt to roll; (*papier, tapis*) to roll up; (*Culin: pâte*) to roll out; (*fam: duper*) to do, con ▷ vi (*bille, boule*) to roll; (*voiture, train*) to go, run; (*automobiliste*) to drive; (*bateau*) to roll; **se ~ dans** (*boue*) to roll in; (*couverture*) to roll o.s. (up) in

roulette [ʀulɛt] nf (*de table, fauteuil*) castor; (*de dentiste*) drill; (*jeu*) roulette; **à ~s** on castors; **ça a marché comme sur des ~s** (*fam*) it went off very smoothly

roulis [ʀuli] nm roll(ing)

roulotte [ʀulɔt] nf caravan

roumain, e [ʀumɛ̃, ɛn] adj Rumanian ▷ nm/f: **R~, e** Rumanian

Roumanie [rumani] nf Rumania
rouquin, e [rukɛ̃, in] (péj) nm/f redhead
rouspéter [ruspete] (fam) vi to moan
rousse [Rus] adj voir **roux**
roussir [RusiR] vt to scorch ▷ vi (Culin): **faire ~** to brown
route [Rut] nf road; (fig: chemin) way; (itinéraire, parcours) route; (fig: voie) road, path; **il y a 3h de ~** it's a 3-hour ride ou journey; **en ~** on the way; **en ~!** let's go!; **mettre en ~** to start up; **se mettre en ~** to set off; **quelle ~ dois-je prendre pour aller à ...?** which road do I take for ...?; **route nationale** ≈ A road (BRIT), ≈ state highway (US); **routier, -ière** adj road cpd ▷ nm (camionneur) (long-distance) lorry (BRIT) ou truck (US) driver; (restaurant) ≈ transport café (BRIT), ≈ truck stop (US)
routine [Rutin] nf routine; **routinier, -ière** (péj) adj (activité) humdrum; (personne) addicted to routine
rouvrir [RuvRiR] vt, vi to reopen, open again; **se ~** vi to reopen, open again
roux, rousse [Ru, Rus] adj red; (personne) red-haired ▷ nm/f redhead
royal, e, -aux [Rwajal, o] adj royal; (cadeau etc) fit for a king
royaume [Rwajom] nm kingdom; (fig) realm; **le Royaume-Uni** the United Kingdom
royauté [Rwajote] nf (régime) monarchy
ruban [Rybã] nm ribbon; **ruban adhésif** adhesive tape
rubéole [Rybeɔl] nf German measles sg, rubella
rubis [Rybi] nm ruby
rubrique [RybRik] nf (titre, catégorie) heading; (Presse: article) column
ruche [Ryʃ] nf hive
rude [Ryd] adj (au toucher) rough; (métier, tâche) hard, tough; (climat) severe, harsh; (bourru) harsh, rough; (fruste: manières) rugged, tough; (fam: fameux) jolly good; **rudement** (fam) adv (très) terribly
rudimentaire [RydimãtɛR] adj rudimentary, basic
rudiments [Rydimã] nmpl: **avoir des ~ d'anglais** to have a smattering of English
rue [Ry] nf street
ruée [Rɥe] nf rush
ruelle [Rɥɛl] nf alley(-way)
ruer [Rɥe] vi (cheval) to kick out; **se ~** vi: **se ~ sur** to pounce on; **se ~ vers/dans/hors de** to rush ou dash towards/into/out of
rugby [Rygbi] nm rugby (football)
rugir [RyʒiR] vi to roar
rugueux, -euse [Rygø, øz] adj rough
ruine [Rɥin] nf ruin; **ruiner** vt to ruin; **ruineux, -euse** adj ruinous
ruisseau, x [Rɥiso] nm stream, brook
ruisseler [Rɥis(ə)le] vi to stream
rumeur [RymœR] nf (nouvelle) rumour; (bruit confus) rumbling
ruminer [Rymine] vt (herbe) to ruminate; (fig) to ruminate on ou over, chew over
rupture [RyptyR] nf (séparation, désunion) break-up, split; (de négociations etc) breakdown; (de contrat) breach; (dans continuité) break
rural, e, -aux [RyRal, o] adj rural, country cpd
ruse [Ryz] nf: **la ~** cunning, craftiness; (pour tromper) trickery; **une ~** a trick, a ruse; **rusé, e** adj cunning, crafty
russe [Rys] adj Russian ▷ nm/f: **R~** Russian ▷ nm (Ling) Russian
Russie [Rysi] nf: **la ~** Russia

rustine® [Rystin] nf rubber repair patch (for bicycle tyre)
rustique [Rystik] adj rustic
rythme [Ritm] nm rhythm; (vitesse) rate; (: de la vie) pace, tempo; **rythmé, e** adj rhythmic(al)

S

s' [s] pron voir **se**
sa [sa] adj voir **son'**
sable [sabl] nm sand
sablé [sable] nm shortbread biscuit
sabler [sable] vt (contre le verglas) to grit; **~ le champagne** to drink champagne
sabot [sabo] nm clog; (de cheval) hoof; **sabot de frein** brake shoe
saboter [sabote] vt to sabotage; (bâcler) to make a mess of, botch
sac [sak] nm bag; (à charbon etc) sack; **mettre à ~** to sack; **sac à dos** rucksack; **sac à main** handbag; **sac de couchage** sleeping bag; **sac de voyage** travelling bag
saccadé, e [sakade] adj jerky; (respiration) spasmodic
saccager [sakaʒe] vt (piller) to sack; (dévaster) to create havoc in
saccharine [sakaRin] nf saccharin
sachet [saʃɛ] nm (small) bag; (de sucre, café) sachet; **du potage en ~** packet soup; **sachet de thé** tea bag
sacoche [sakɔʃ] nf (gén) bag; (de bicyclette) saddlebag
sacré, e [sakRe] adj sacred; (fam: satané) blasted; (: fameux): **un ~ toupet** a heck of a cheek
sacrement [sakRəmã] nm sacrament
sacrifice [sakRifis] nm sacrifice; **sacrifier** vt to sacrifice
sacristie [sakRisti] nf (catholique) sacristy; (protestante) vestry
sadique [sadik] adj sadistic
safran [safRã] nm saffron
sage [saʒ] adj wise; (enfant) good

sage-femme [saʒfam] nf midwife
sagesse [saʒɛs] nf wisdom
Sagittaire [saʒitɛʀ] nm: **le ~** Sagittarius
Sahara [saaʀa] nm: **le ~** the Sahara (desert)
saignant, e [sɛɲɑ̃, ɑ̃t] adj (viande) rare
saigner [seɲe] vi to bleed ▷ vt to bleed; (animal) to kill (by bleeding); **~ du nez** to have a nosebleed
saillir [sajiʀ] vi to project, stick out; (veine, muscle) to bulge
sain, e [sɛ̃, sɛn] adj healthy; **~ et sauf** safe and sound, unharmed; **~ d'esprit** sound in mind, sane
saindoux [sɛ̃du] nm lard
saint, e [sɛ̃, sɛ̃t] adj holy ▷ nm/f saint; **le Saint Esprit** the Holy Spirit ou Ghost; **la Sainte Vierge** the Blessed Virgin; **la Saint-Sylvestre** New Year's Eve; **sainteté** nf holiness
sais etc [sɛ] vb voir **savoir**
saisie [sezi] nf seizure; **saisie (de données)** (data) capture
saisir [seziʀ] vt to take hold of, grab; (fig: occasion) to seize; (comprendre) to grasp; (entendre) to get, catch; (données) to capture; (Culin) to fry quickly; (Jur: biens, publication) to seize; **saisissant, e** adj startling, striking
saison [sɛzɔ̃] nf season; **haute/basse/morte ~** high/low/slack season; **saisonnier, -ière** adj seasonal
salade [salad] nf (Bot) lettuce etc; (Culin) (green) salad; (fam: confusion) tangle, muddle; **salade composée** mixed salad; **salade de fruits** fruit salad; **saladier** nm (salad) bowl
salaire [salɛʀ] nm (annuel, mensuel) salary; (hebdomadaire, journalier) pay, wages pl; **salaire minimum interprofessionnel de croissance** index-linked guaranteed minimum wage
salarié, e [salaʀje] adj nm/f salaried employee; wage-earner
salaud [salo] (fam!) nm sod (!), bastard (!)
sale [sal] adj dirty, filthy; (fam: mauvais) nasty
salé, e [sale] adj (mer, goût) salty; (Culin: amandes, beurre etc) salted; (: gâteaux) savoury; (fam: grivois) spicy; (: facture) steep
saler [sale] vt to salt
saleté [salte] nf (état) dirtiness; (crasse) dirt, filth; (tache etc) dirt no pl; (fam: méchanceté) dirty trick; (: camelote) rubbish no pl; (: obscénité) filthy thing (to say)
salière [saljɛʀ] nf saltcellar
salir [saliʀ] vt to (make) dirty; (fig: quelqu'un) to soil the reputation of; **se ~** vi to get dirty; **salissant, e** adj (tissu) which shows the dirt; (travail) dirty, messy
salle [sal] nf room; (d'hôpital) ward; (de restaurant) dining room; (d'un cinéma) auditorium; (: public) audience; **salle à manger** dining room; **salle d'attente** waiting room; **salle de bain(s)** bathroom; **salle de classe** classroom; **salle de concert** concert hall; **salle d'eau** shower-room; **salle d'embarquement** (à l'aéroport) departure lounge; **salle de jeux** (pour enfants) playroom; **salle de séjour** living room; **salle des ventes** saleroom
salon [salɔ̃] nm lounge, sitting room; (mobilier) lounge suite; (exposition) exhibition, show; **salon de coiffure** hairdressing salon; **salon de thé** tearoom
salope [salɔp] (fam!) nf bitch (!); **saloperie** (fam!) nf (action) dirty trick; (chose sans valeur) rubbish no pl
salopette [salɔpɛt] nf dungarees pl; (d'ouvrier) overall(s)
salsifis [salsifi] nm salsify
salubre [salybʀ] adj healthy, salubrious

saluer [salɥe] vt (pour dire bonjour, fig) to greet; (pour dire au revoir) to take one's leave; (Mil) to salute
salut [saly] nm (geste) wave; (parole) greeting; (Mil) salute; (sauvegarde) safety; (Rel) salvation ▷ excl (fam: bonjour) hi (there); (: au revoir) see you, bye
salutations [salytasjɔ̃] nfpl greetings; **Veuillez agréer, Monsieur, mes ~ distinguées** yours faithfully
samedi [samdi] nm Saturday
SAMU [samy] sigle m (= service d'assistance médicale d'urgence) ≈ ambulance (service) (BRIT), ≈ paramedics pl (US)
sanction [sɑ̃ksjɔ̃] nf sanction; **sanctionner** vt (loi, usage) to sanction; (punir) to punish
sandale [sɑ̃dal] nf sandal
sandwich [sɑ̃dwi(t)ʃ] nm sandwich; **je voudrais un ~ au jambon/fromage** I'd like a ham/cheese sandwich
sang [sɑ̃] nm blood; **en ~** covered in blood; **se faire du mauvais ~** to fret, get in a state; **sang-froid** nm calm, sangfroid; **de sang-froid** in cold blood; **sanglant, e** adj bloody
sangle [sɑ̃gl] nf strap
sanglier [sɑ̃glije] nm (wild) boar
sanglot [sɑ̃glo] nm sob; **sangloter** vi to sob
sangsue [sɑ̃sy] nf leech
sanguin, e [sɑ̃gɛ̃, in] adj blood cpd
sanitaire [sanitɛʀ] adj health cpd; **sanitaires** nmpl (lieu) bathroom sg
sans [sɑ̃] prép without; **un pull ~ manches** a sleeveless jumper; **~ faute** without fail; **~ arrêt** without a break; **~ ça** (fam) otherwise; **~ qu'il s'en aperçoive** without him ou his noticing; **sans-abri** nmpl homeless; **sans-emploi** nm/f inv unemployed person; **les sans-emploi** the unemployed; **sans-gêne** adj inv inconsiderate
santé [sɑ̃te] nf health; **en bonne ~** in good health; **boire à la ~ de qn** to drink (to) sb's health; **à ta/votre ~!** cheers!
saoudien, ne [saudjɛ̃, jɛn] adj Saudi Arabian ▷ nm/f: **S~, ne** Saudi Arabian
saoul, e [su, sul] adj = **soûl**
saper [sape] vt to undermine, sap
sapeur-pompier [sapœʀpɔ̃pje] nm fireman
saphir [safiʀ] nm sapphire
sapin [sapɛ̃] nm fir (tree); (bois) fir; **sapin de Noël** Christmas tree
sarcastique [saʀkastik] adj sarcastic
Sardaigne [saʀdɛɲ] nf: **la ~** Sardinia
sardine [saʀdin] nf sardine
SARL sigle f (= société à responsabilité limitée) ≈ plc (BRIT), ≈ Inc. (US)
sarrasin [saʀazɛ̃] nm buckwheat
satané, e [satane] (fam) adj confounded
satellite [satelit] nm satellite
satin [satɛ̃] nm satin
satire [satiʀ] nf satire; **satirique** adj satirical
satisfaction [satisfaksjɔ̃] nf satisfaction
satisfaire [satisfɛʀ] vt to satisfy; **~ à** (conditions) to meet; **satisfaisant, e** adj (acceptable) satisfactory; **satisfait, e** adj satisfied; **satisfait de** happy ou satisfied with
saturer [satyʀe] vt to saturate
sauce [sos] nf sauce; (avec un rôti) gravy; **sauce tomate** tomato sauce; **saucière** nf sauceboat
saucisse [sosis] nf sausage
saucisson [sosisɔ̃] nm (slicing) sausage

sauf, sauve [sof, sov] adj unharmed, unhurt; (fig: honneur) intact, saved ▷ prép except; **laisser la vie sauve à qn** to spare sb's life; **~ si** (à moins que) unless; **~ erreur** if I'm not mistaken; **~ avis contraire** unless you hear to the contrary

sauge [soʒ] nf sage

saugrenu, e [sogʀəny] adj preposterous

saule [sol] nm willow (tree)

saumon [somɔ̃] nm salmon inv

saupoudrer [sopudʀe] vt: **~ qch de** to sprinkle sth with

saur [sɔʀ] adj m: **hareng ~** smoked herring, kipper

saut [so] nm jump; (discipline sportive) jumping; **faire un ~ chez qn** to pop over to sb's (place); **saut à l'élastique** bungee jumping; **saut à la perche** pole vaulting; **saut en hauteur/longueur** high/long jump; **saut périlleux** somersault

sauter [sote] vi to jump, leap; (exploser) to blow up, explode; (: fusibles) to blow; (se détacher) to pop out (ou off) ▷ vt to jump (over), leap (over); (fig: omettre) to skip, miss (out); **faire ~** to blow up; (Culin) to sauté; **~ à la corde** to skip; **~ au cou de qn** to fly into sb's arms; **~ sur une occasion** to jump at an opportunity; **~ aux yeux** to be (quite) obvious

sauterelle [sotʀɛl] nf grasshopper

sautiller [sotije] vi (oiseau) to hop; (enfant) to skip

sauvage [sovaʒ] adj (gén) wild; (peuplade) savage; (farouche: personne) unsociable; (barbare) wild, savage; (non officiel) unauthorized, unofficial; **faire du camping ~** to camp in the wild ▷ nm/f savage; (timide) unsociable type

sauve [sov] adj f voir **sauf**

sauvegarde [sovgaʀd] nf safeguard; (Inform) backup; **sauvegarder** vt to safeguard; (Inform: enregistrer) to save; (: copier) to back up

sauve-qui-peut [sovkipø] excl run for your life!

sauver [sove] vt to save; (porter secours à) to rescue; (récupérer) to salvage, rescue; **se ~** vi (s'enfuir) to run away; (fam: partir) to be off; **sauvetage** nm rescue; **sauveteur** nm rescuer; **sauvette**: **à la sauvette** adv (se marier etc) hastily, hurriedly; **sauveur** nm saviour (BRIT), savior (US)

savant, e [savɑ̃, ɑ̃t] adj scholarly, learned ▷ nm scientist

saveur [savœʀ] nf flavour; (fig) savour

savoir [savwaʀ] vt to know; (être capable de): **il sait nager** he can swim ▷ nm knowledge; **se ~** vi (être connu) to be known; **je ne sais pas** I don't know; **je ne sais pas parler français** I don't speak French; **savez-vous où je peux …?** do you know where I can …?; **je n'en sais rien** I (really) don't know; **à ~** that is, namely; **faire ~ qch à qn** to let sb know sth; **pas que je sache** not as far as I know

savon [savɔ̃] nm (produit) soap; (morceau) bar of soap; (fam): **passer un ~ à qn** to give sb a good dressing-down; **savonner** vt to soap; **savonnette** nf bar of soap

savourer [savuʀe] vt to savour; **savoureux, -euse** adj tasty; (fig: anecdote) spicy, juicy

saxo(phone) [sakso(fɔn)] nm sax(ophone)

scabreux, -euse [skabʀø, øz] adj risky; (indécent) improper, shocking

scandale [skɑ̃dal] nm scandal; **faire un ~** (scène) to make a scene; (Jur) to create a disturbance; **faire ~** to scandalize people; **scandaleux, -euse** adj scandalous, outrageous

scandinave [skɑ̃dinav] adj Scandinavian ▷ nm/f: **S~** Scandinavian

Scandinavie [skɑ̃dinavi] nf Scandinavia

scarabée [skaʀabe] nm beetle

scarlatine [skaʀlatin] nf scarlet fever

scarole [skaʀɔl] nf endive

sceau, x [so] nm seal

sceller [sele] vt to seal

scénario [senaʀjo] nm scenario

scène [sɛn] nf (gén) scene; (estrade, fig: théâtre) stage; **entrer en ~** to come on stage; **mettre en ~** (Théâtre) to stage; (Cinéma) to direct; **faire une ~ (à qn)** to make a scene (with sb); **scène de ménage** domestic scene

sceptique [sɛptik] adj sceptical

schéma [ʃema] nm (diagramme) diagram, sketch; **schématique** adj diagrammatic(al), schematic; (fig) oversimplified

sciatique [sjatik] nf sciatica

scie [si] nf saw

sciemment [sjamɑ̃] adv knowingly

science [sjɑ̃s] nf science; (savoir) knowledge; **sciences humaines/sociales** social sciences; **sciences naturelles** (Scol) natural science sg, biology sg; **sciences po** political science ou studies pl; **science-fiction** nf science fiction; **scientifique** adj scientific ▷ nm/f scientist; (étudiant) science student

scier [sje] vt to saw; (retrancher) to saw off; **scierie** nf sawmill

scintiller [sɛ̃tije] vi to sparkle; (étoile) to twinkle

sciure [sjyʀ] nf: **~ (de bois)** sawdust

sclérose [skleʀoz] nf: **sclérose en plaques** multiple sclerosis

scolaire [skɔlɛʀ] adj school cpd; **scolariser** vt to provide with schooling/schools; **scolarité** nf schooling

scooter [skutœʀ] nm (motor) scooter

score [skɔʀ] nm score

scorpion [skɔʀpjɔ̃] nm (signe): **le S~** Scorpio

scotch [skɔtʃ] nm (whisky) scotch, whisky; **S~®** (adhésif) Sellotape® (BRIT), Scotch® tape (US)

scout, e [skut] adj, nm scout

script [skʀipt] nm (écriture) printing; (Cinéma) (shooting) script

scrupule [skʀypyl] nm scruple

scruter [skʀyte] vt to scrutinize; (l'obscurité) to peer into

scrutin [skʀytɛ̃] nm (vote) ballot; (ensemble des opérations) poll

sculpter [skylte] vt to sculpt; (bois) to carve; **sculpteur** nm sculptor; **sculpture** nf sculpture

SDF sigle m: **sans domicile fixe** homeless person; **les ~** the homeless

○ MOT-CLÉ

se [sə], **s'** pron **1** (emploi réfléchi) oneself; (: masc) himself; (: fém) herself; (: sujet non humain) itself; (: pl) themselves; **se savonner** to soap o.s.

2 (réciproque) one another, each other; **ils s'aiment** they love one another ou each other

3 (passif): **cela se répare facilement** it is easily repaired

4 (possessif): **se casser la jambe/se laver les mains** to break one's leg/wash one's hands

séance [seɑ̃s] nf (d'assemblée) meeting, session; (de tribunal) sitting, session; (musicale, Cinéma, Théâtre) performance

seau, x [so] nm bucket, pail

sec, sèche [sɛk, sɛʃ] adj dry; (raisins, figues) dried; (cœur: insensible) hard, cold ▷ nm: **tenir au ~** to keep in a dry place ▷ adv dry; **je le bois ~** I drink it straight ou neat; **à ~** (puits) dried up

sécateur [sekatœʀ] nm secateurs pl (BRIT), shears pl

sèche [sɛʃ] adj f voir **sec**; **sèche-cheveux** nm inv hair-drier; **sèche-linge** nm inv tumble dryer; **sèchement** adv (répondre) drily

sécher [seʃe] vt to dry; (dessécher: peau, blé) to dry (out); (: étang) to dry up; (fam: cours) to skip ▷ vi to dry; to dry out; to dry up; (fam: candidat) to be stumped; **se ~** (après le bain) to dry o.s.; **sécheresse** nf dryness; (absence de pluie) drought; **séchoir** nm drier

second, e [s(ə)ɡɔ̃, ɔd] adj second ▷ nm (assistant) second in command; (Navig) first mate ▷ nf (Scol) year 11 (BRIT), tenth grade (US); (Aviat, Rail etc) second class; **voyager en ~e** to travel second-class; **secondaire** adj secondary; **seconde²** nf second; **seconder** vt to assist

secouer [s(ə)kwe] vt to shake; (passagers) to rock; (traumatiser) to shake (up)

secourir [s(ə)kuʀiʀ] vt (venir en aide à) to assist, aid; **secourisme** nm first aid; **secouriste** nm/f first-aid worker

secours [s(ə)kuʀ] nm help, aid, assistance ▷ nmpl aid sg; **au ~!** help!; **appeler au ~** to shout ou call for help; **porter ~ à qn** to give sb assistance, help sb; **les premiers ~** first aid sg

secousse [s(ə)kus] nf jolt, bump; (électrique) shock; (fig: psychologique) jolt, shock

secret, -ète [sɛkʀɛ, ɛt] adj secret; (fig: renfermé) reticent, reserved ▷ nm secret; (discrétion absolue): **le ~** secrecy; **en ~** in secret, secretly; **secret professionel** professional secrecy

secrétaire [s(ə)kʀetɛʀ] nm/f secretary ▷ nm (meuble) writing desk; **secrétaire de direction** private ou personal secretary; **secrétaire d'État** junior minister; **secrétariat** nm (profession) secretarial work; (bureau) office; (: d'organisation internationale) secretariat

secteur [sɛktœʀ] nm sector; (zone) area; (Élec): **branché sur ~** plugged into the mains (supply)

section [sɛksjɔ̃] nf section; (de parcours d'autobus) fare stage; (Mil: unité) platoon; **sectionner** vt to sever

sécu [seky] abrf = **sécurité sociale**

sécurité [sekyʀite] nf (absence de danger) safety; (absence de troubles) security; **système de ~** security system; **être en ~** to be safe; **la sécurité routière** road safety; **la sécurité sociale** ≈ (the) Social Security (BRIT), ≈ Welfare (US)

sédentaire [sedɑ̃tɛʀ] adj sedentary

séduction [sedyksjɔ̃] nf seduction; (charme, attrait) appeal, charm

séduire [seduiʀ] vt to charm; (femme: abuser de) to seduce; **séduisant, e** adj (femme) seductive; (homme, offre) very attractive

ségrégation [seɡʀeɡasjɔ̃] nf segregation

seigle [sɛɡl] nm rye

seigneur [sɛɲœʀ] nm lord

sein [sɛ̃] nm breast; (entrailles) womb; **au ~ de** (équipe, institution) within

séisme [seism] nm earthquake

seize [sɛz] num sixteen; **seizième** num sixteenth

séjour [seʒuʀ] nm stay; (pièce) living room; **séjourner** vi to stay

sel [sɛl] nm salt; (fig: piquant) spice

sélection [selɛksjɔ̃] nf selection; **sélectionner** vt to select

self-service [sɛlfsɛʀvis] adj, nm self-service

selle [sɛl] nf saddle; **selles** nfpl (Méd) stools; **seller** vt to saddle

selon [s(ə)lɔ̃] prép according to; (en se conformant à) in accordance with; **~ que** according to whether; **~ moi** as I see it

semaine [s(ə)mɛn] nf week; **en ~** during the week, on weekdays

semblable [sɑ̃blabl] adj similar; (de ce genre): **de ~s mésaventures** such mishaps ▷ nm fellow creature ou man; **~ à** similar to, like

semblant [sɑ̃blɑ̃] nm: **un ~ de ...** a semblance of ...; **faire ~ (de faire)** to pretend (to do)

sembler [sɑ̃ble] vb + attrib to seem ▷ vb impers: **il semble (bien) que/inutile de** it (really) seems ou appears that/useless to; **il me semble que** it seems to me that; **comme bon lui semble** as he sees fit

semelle [s(ə)mɛl] nf sole; (intérieure) insole, inner sole

semer [s(ə)me] vt to sow; (fig: éparpiller) to scatter; (: confusion) to spread; (fam: poursuivants) to lose, shake off; **semé de** (difficultés) riddled with

semestre [s(ə)mɛstʀ] nm half-year; (Scol) semester

séminaire [seminɛʀ] nm seminar

semi-remorque [səmiʀəmɔʀk] nm articulated lorry (BRIT), semi(trailer) (US)

semoule [s(ə)mul] nf semolina

sénat [sena] nm senate; **sénateur** nm senator

Sénégal [seneɡal] nm: **le ~** Senegal

sens [sɑ̃s] nm (Physiol,) sense; (signification) meaning, sense; (direction) direction; **à mon ~** to my mind; **dans le ~ des aiguilles d'une montre** clockwise; **dans le ~ contraire des aiguilles d'une montre** anticlockwise; **dans le mauvais ~** (aller) the wrong way, in the wrong direction; **le bon ~** common sense; **sens dessus dessous** upside down; **sens interdit/unique** one-way street

sensation [sɑ̃sasjɔ̃] nf sensation; **à ~** (péj) sensational; **faire ~** to cause ou create a sensation; **sensationnel, le** adj (fam) fantastic, terrific

sensé, e [sɑ̃se] adj sensible

sensibiliser [sɑ̃sibilize] vt: **~ qn à** to make sb sensitive to

sensibilité [sɑ̃sibilite] nf sensitivity

sensible [sɑ̃sibl] adj sensitive; (aux sens) perceptible; (appréciable: différence, progrès) appreciable, noticeable; **~ à** sensitive to; **sensiblement** adv (à peu près): **ils sont sensiblement du même âge** they are approximately the same age; **sensiblerie** nf sentimentality

sensuel, le [sɑ̃sɥɛl] adj (personne) sensual; (musique) sensuous

sentence [sɑ̃tɑ̃s] nf (jugement) sentence

sentier [sɑ̃tje] nm path

sentiment [sɑ̃timɑ̃] nm feeling; **recevez mes ~s respectueux** (personne nommée) yours sincerely; (personne non nommée) yours faithfully; **sentimental, e, -aux** adj sentimental; (vie, aventure) love cpd

sentinelle [sɑ̃tinɛl] nf sentry

sentir [sɑ̃tiʀ] vt (par l'odorat) to smell; (par le goût) to taste; (au toucher, fig) to feel; (répandre une odeur de) to smell of; (: ressemblance) to smell like ▷ vi to smell; **~ mauvais** to smell bad; **se ~ bien** to feel good; **se ~ mal** (être indisposé) to feel unwell ou ill; **se ~ le courage/la**

force de faire to feel brave/strong enough to do; **il ne peut pas le ~** (fam) he can't stand him; **je ne me sens pas bien** I don't feel well

séparation [separasjɔ̃] nf separation; (cloison) division, partition

séparé, e [separe] adj (distinct) separate; (époux) separated; **séparément** adv separately

séparer [separe] vt to separate; (désunir) to drive apart; (détacher): **~ qch de** to pull sth (off) from; **se ~** vi (époux, amis) to separate, part; (se diviser: route etc) to divide; **se ~ de** (époux) to separate ou part from; (employé, objet personnel) to part with

sept [sɛt] num seven; **septante** (BELGIQUE, SUISSE) adj inv seventy

septembre [sɛptɑ̃bʀ] nm September

septicémie [sɛptisemi] nf blood poisoning, septicaemia

septième [sɛtjɛm] num seventh

séquelles [sekɛl] nfpl after-effects; (fig) aftermath sg

serbe [sɛʀb(ə)] adj Serbian

Serbie [sɛʀbi] nf: **la ~** Serbia

serein, e [səʀɛ̃, ɛn] adj serene

sergent [sɛʀʒɑ̃] nm sergeant

série [seʀi] nf series inv; (de clés, casseroles, outils) set; (catégorie: Sport) rank; **en ~** in quick succession; (Comm) mass cpd; **de ~** (voiture) standard; **hors ~** (Comm) custom-built; **série noire** (crime) thriller

sérieusement [seʀjøzmɑ̃] adv seriously

sérieux, -euse [seʀjø, jøz] adj serious; (élève, employé) reliable, responsible; (client, maison) reliable, dependable ▷ nm seriousness; (d'une entreprise etc) reliability; **garder son ~** to keep a straight face; **prendre qch/qn au ~** to take sth/sb seriously

serin [s(ə)ʀɛ̃] nm canary

seringue [s(ə)ʀɛ̃g] nf syringe

serment [sɛʀmɑ̃] nm (juré) oath; (promesse) pledge, vow

sermon [sɛʀmɔ̃] nm sermon

séropositif, -ive [seʀopozitif, iv] adj (Méd) HIV positive

serpent [sɛʀpɑ̃] nm snake; **serpenter** vi to wind

serpillière [sɛʀpijɛʀ] nf floorcloth

serre [sɛʀ] nf (Agr) greenhouse; **serres** nfpl (griffes) claws, talons

serré, e [seʀe] adj (habits) tight; (fig: lutte, match) tight, close-fought; (passagers etc) (tightly) packed; (réseau) dense; **avoir le cœur ~** to have a heavy heart

serrer [seʀe] vt (tenir) to grip ou hold tight; (comprimer, coincer) to squeeze; (poings, mâchoires) to clench; (suj: vêtement) to be too tight for; (ceinture, nœud, vis) to tighten ▷ vi: **~ à droite** to keep ou get over to the right

serrure [seʀyʀ] nf lock; **serrurier** nm locksmith

sert etc [sɛʀ] vb voir **servir**

servante [sɛʀvɑ̃t] nf (maid) servant

serveur, -euse [sɛʀvœʀ, øz] nm/f waiter (waitress)

serviable [sɛʀvjabl] adj obliging, willing to help

service [sɛʀvis] nm service; (assortiment de vaisselle) set, service; (bureau: de la vente etc) department, section; (travail) duty; **premier ~** (série de repas) first sitting; **être de ~** to be on duty; **faire le ~** to serve; **rendre un ~ à qn** to do sb a favour; (objet: s'avérer utile) to come in useful ou handy for sb; **mettre en ~** to put into service ou operation; **~ compris/non compris** service included/not included; **hors ~** out of order; **service après vente** after sales service; **service d'ordre** police (ou stewards) in charge of maintaining order; **service militaire**

military service; **services secrets** secret service sg

serviette [sɛʀvjɛt] nf (de table) (table) napkin, serviette; (de toilette) towel; (porte-documents) briefcase; **serviette hygiénique** sanitary towel

servir [sɛʀviʀ] vt to serve; (au restaurant) to wait on; (au magasin) to serve, attend to ▷ vi (Tennis) to serve; (Cartes) to deal; **se ~** vi (prendre d'un plat) to help o.s.; **vous êtes servi?** are you being served?; **~ à qn** (diplôme, livre) to be of use to sb; **~ à qch/faire** (outil etc) to be used for sth/doing; **ça ne sert à rien** it's no use; **~ (à qn) de** to serve as (for sb); **se ~ de** (plat) to help o.s. to; (voiture, outil, relations) to use; **sers-toi!** help yourself!

serviteur [sɛʀvitœʀ] nm servant

ses [se] adj voir **son¹**

seuil [sœj] nm doorstep; (fig) threshold

seul, e [sœl] adj (sans compagnie) alone; (unique): **un ~ livre** only one book, a single book ▷ adv (vivre) alone, on one's own ▷ nm, nf: **il en reste un(e) ~(e)** there's only one left; **le ~ livre** the only book; **parler tout ~** to talk to oneself; **faire qch (tout) ~** to do sth (all) on one's own ou (all) by oneself; **à lui (tout) ~** single-handed, on his own; **se sentir ~** to feel lonely; **seulement** adv only; **non seulement ... mais aussi** ou **encore** not only ... but also

sève [sɛv] nf sap

sévère [sevɛʀ] adj severe

sexe [sɛks] nm sex; (organes génitaux) genitals, sex organs; **sexuel, le** adj sexual

shampooing [ʃɑ̃pwɛ̃] nm shampoo

Shetland [ʃɛtlãd] n: **les îles ~** the Shetland Islands, Shetland

short [ʃɔʀt] nm (pair of) shorts pl

Ⓞ **MOT-CLÉ**

si [si] adv 1 (oui) yes; **"Paul n'est pas venu" — "si!"** "Paul hasn't come" — "yes, he has!"; **je vous assure que si** I assure you he did ou she is too
2 (tellement) so; **si gentil/rapidement** so kind/fast; **(tant et) si bien que** so much so that; **si rapide qu'il soit** however fast he may be
▷ conj if; **si tu veux** if you want; **je me demande si** I wonder if ou whether; **si seulement** if only
▷ nm (Mus) B; (en chantant la gamme) ti

Sicile [sisil] nf: **la ~** Sicily

SIDA [sida] sigle m (= syndrome immuno-déficitaire acquis) AIDS sg

sidéré, e [sidere] adj staggered

sidérurgie [sideʀyʀʒi] nf steel industry

siècle [sjɛkl] nm century

siège [sjɛʒ] nm seat; (d'entreprise) head office; (d'organisation) headquarters pl; (Mil) siege; **siège social** registered office; **siéger** vi to sit

sien, ne [sjɛ̃, sjɛn] pron: **le (la) ~(ne), les ~(ne)s** (homme) his; (femme) hers; (chose, animal) its

sieste [sjɛst] nf (afternoon) snooze ou nap; **faire la ~** to have a snooze ou nap

sifflement [sifləmɑ̃] nm: **un ~** a whistle

siffler [sifle] vi (gén) to whistle; (en respirant) to wheeze; (serpent, vapeur) to hiss ▷ vt (chanson) to whistle; (chien etc) to whistle for; (fille) to whistle at; (pièce, orateur) to hiss, boo; (fin du match, départ) to blow one's whistle for; (fam: verre) to guzzle

sifflet [siflɛ] nm whistle; **coup de ~** whistle

siffloter [siflɔte] *vi, vt* to whistle

sigle [sigl] *nm* acronym

signal, -aux [siɲal, o] *nm* signal; (*indice, écriteau*) sign; **donner le ~ de** to give the signal for; **signal d'alarme** alarm signal; **signalement** *nm* description, particulars *pl*

signaler [siɲale] *vt* to indicate; (*personne: faire un signe*) to signal; (*vol, perte*) to report; (*faire remarquer*): **~ qch à qn/(à qn) que** to point out sth to sb/(to sb) that; **je voudrais ~ un vol** I'd like to report a theft

signature [siɲatyʀ] *nf* signature; (*action*) signing

signe [siɲ] *nm* sign; (*Typo*) mark; **faire un ~ de la main** to give a sign with one's hand; **faire ~ à qn** (*fig: contacter*) to get in touch with sb; **faire ~ à qn d'entrer** to motion (to) sb to come in; **signer** *vt* to sign; **se signer** *vi* to cross o.s.; **où dois-je signer?** where do I sign?

significatif, -ive [siɲifikatif, iv] *adj* significant

signification [siɲifikasjɔ̃] *nf* meaning

signifier [siɲifje] *vt* (*vouloir dire*) to mean; (*faire connaître*): **~ qch (à qn)** to make sth known (to sb)

silence [silɑ̃s] *nm* silence; (*Mus*) rest; **garder le ~** to keep silent, say nothing; **silencieux, -euse** *adj* quiet, silent ▷ *nm* silencer

silhouette [silwɛt] *nf* outline, silhouette; (*allure*) figure

sillage [sijaʒ] *nm* wake

sillon [sijɔ̃] *nm* furrow; (*de disque*) groove; **sillonner** *vt* to criss-cross

simagrées [simagʀe] *nfpl* fuss *sg*

similaire [similɛʀ] *adj* similar; **similicuir** *nm* imitation leather; **similitude** *nf* similarity

simple [sɛ̃pl] *adj* simple; (*non multiple*) single ▷ *nm*: **~ messieurs/dames** men's/ladies' singles *sg* ▷ *nm/f*: **~ d'esprit** simpleton

simplicité [sɛ̃plisite] *nf* simplicity; **en toute ~** quite simply

simplifier [sɛ̃plifje] *vt* to simplify

simuler [simyle] *vt* to sham, simulate

simultané, e [simyltane] *adj* simultaneous

sincère [sɛ̃sɛʀ] *adj* sincere; **sincèrement** *adv* sincerely; (*pour parler franchement*) honestly, really; **sincérité** *nf* sincerity

Singapour [sɛ̃gapuʀ] *nm* Singapore

singe [sɛ̃ʒ] *nm* monkey; (*de grande taille*) ape; **singer** *vt* to ape, mimic; **singeries** *nfpl* antics

singulariser [sɛ̃gylaʀize] *vt*: **se ~** *vi* to call attention to o.s.

singularité [sɛ̃gylaʀite] *nf* peculiarity

singulier, -ière [sɛ̃gylje, jɛʀ] *adj* remarkable, singular ▷ *nm* singular

sinistre [sinistʀ] *adj* sinister ▷ *nm* (*incendie*) blaze; (*catastrophe*) disaster; (*Assurances*) damage (*giving rise to a claim*); **sinistré, e** *adj* disaster-stricken ▷ *nm/f* disaster victim

sinon [sinɔ̃] *conj* (*autrement, sans quoi*) otherwise, or else; (*sauf*) except, other than; (*si ce n'est*) if not

sinueux, -euse [sinɥø, øz] *adj* winding

sinus [sinys] *nm* (*Anat*) sinus; (*Géom*) sine; **sinusite** *nf* sinusitis

sirène [siʀɛn] *nf* siren; **sirène d'alarme** fire alarm; (*en temps de guerre*) air-raid siren

sirop [siʀo] *nm* (*à diluer: de fruit etc*) syrup; (*pharmaceutique*) syrup, mixture; **~ pour la toux** cough mixture

siroter [siʀɔte] *vt* to sip

sismique [sismik] *adj* seismic

site [sit] *nm* (*paysage, environnement*) setting; (*d'une ville etc: emplacement*) site; **site (pittoresque)** beauty spot; **sites touristiques** places of interest; **site Web** (*Inform*) website

sitôt [sito] *adv*: **~ parti** as soon as he *etc* had left; **~ que** as soon as; **pas de ~** not for a long time

situation [sitɥasjɔ̃] *nf* situation; (*d'un édifice, d'une ville*) position, location; **situation de famille** marital status

situé, e [sitɥe] *adj* situated

situer [sitɥe] *vt* to site, situate; (*en pensée*) to set, place; **se ~** *vi* to be situated

six [sis] *num* six; **sixième** *num* sixth ▷ *nf* (*Scol*) year 7 (BRIT), sixth grade (US)

skaï® [skaj] *nm* Leatherette®

ski [ski] *nm* (*objet*) ski; (*sport*) skiing; **faire du ~** to ski; **ski de fond** cross-country skiing; **ski nautique** water-skiing; **ski de piste** downhill skiing; **ski de randonnée** cross-country skiing; **skier** *vi* to ski; **skieur, -euse** *nm/f* skier

slip [slip] *nm* (*sous-vêtement*) pants *pl*, briefs *pl*; (*de bain: d'homme*) trunks *pl*; (*: du bikini*) (bikini) briefs *pl*

slogan [slɔgɑ̃] *nm* slogan

Slovaquie [slɔvaki] *nf*: **la ~** Slovakia

SMIC [smik] *sigle m* = **salaire minimum interprofessionnel de croissance**

smoking [smɔkiŋ] *nm* dinner *ou* evening suit

SMS *sigle m* = **short message service**; (*service*) SMS; (*message*) text message

SNCF *sigle f* (= *Société nationale des chemins de fer français*) French railways

snob [snɔb] *adj* snobbish ▷ *nm/f* snob; **snobisme** *nm* snobbery, snobbishness

sobre [sɔbʀ] *adj* (*personne*) temperate, abstemious; (*élégance, style*) sober

sobriquet [sɔbʀikɛ] *nm* nickname

social, e, -aux [sɔsjal, jo] *adj* social

socialisme [sɔsjalism] *nm* socialism; **socialiste** *nm/f* socialist

société [sɔsjete] *nf* society; (*sportive*) club; (*Comm*) company; **la ~ de consommation** the consumer society; **société anonyme** ≈ limited (BRIT) *ou* incorporated (US) company

sociologie [sɔsjɔlɔʒi] *nf* sociology

socle [sɔkl] *nm* (*de colonne, statue*) plinth, pedestal; (*de lampe*) base

socquette [sɔkɛt] *nf* ankle sock

sœur [sœʀ] *nf* sister; (*religieuse*) nun, sister

soi [swa] *pron* oneself; **en ~** (*intrinsèquement*) in itself; **cela va de ~** that *ou* it goes without saying; **soi-disant** *adj inv* so-called ▷ *adv* supposedly

soie [swa] *nf* silk; **soierie** *nf* (*tissu*) silk

soif [swaf] *nf* thirst; **avoir ~** to be thirsty; **donner ~ à qn** to make sb thirsty

soigné, e [swaɲe] *adj* (*tenue*) well-groomed, neat; (*travail*) careful, meticulous

soigner [swaɲe] *vt* (*malade, maladie: suj: docteur*) to treat; (*suj: infirmière, mère*) to nurse, look after; (*travail, détails*) to take care over; (*jardin, invités*) to look after; **soigneux, -euse** *adj* (*propre*) tidy, neat; (*appliqué*) painstaking, careful

soi-même [swamɛm] *pron* oneself

soin [swɛ̃] *nm* (*application*) care; (*propreté, ordre*) tidiness, neatness *ou* care; **soins** *nmpl* (*à un malade, blessé*) treatment *sg*, medical attention sg; (hygiène) care sg; **prendre ~ de** to take care of, look after; **prendre ~ de faire** to take care to do; **les premiers ~s** first aid sg

soir [swaʀ] nm evening; **ce ~** this evening, tonight; **à ce ~!** I see you this evening (ou tonight)!; **sept/dix heures du ~** seven in the evening/ten at night; **demain ~** tomorrow evening, tomorrow night; **soirée** nf evening; (réception) party

soit¹ [swa] vb voir **être** ▷ conj (à savoir) namely; (ou): **~ ... ~** either ... or; **~ que ... ~ que** ou **ou que** whether ... or whether

soit² [swat] adv so be it, very well

soixantaine [swasɑ̃tɛn] nf: **une ~ (de)** sixty or so, about sixty; **avoir la ~** (âge) to be around sixty

soixante [swasɑ̃t] num sixty; **soixante-dix** num seventy

soja [sɔʒa] nm soya; (graines) soya beans pl; **germes de ~** beansprouts

sol [sɔl] nm ground; (de logement) floor; (Agr) soil; (Mus) G; (: en chantant la gamme) so(h)

solaire [sɔlɛʀ] adj (énergie etc) solar; (crème etc) sun cpd

soldat [sɔlda] nm soldier

solde [sɔld] nf pay ▷ nm (Comm) balance; **soldes** nm ou f pl (articles) sale goods; (vente) sales; **en ~** at sale price; **solder** vt (marchandise) to sell at sale price, sell off

sole [sɔl] nf sole inv (fish)

soleil [sɔlɛj] nm sun; (lumière) sun(light); (temps ensoleillé) sun(shine); **il fait du ~** it's sunny; **au ~** in the sun

solennel, le [sɔlanɛl] adj solemn

solfège [sɔlfɛʒ] nm musical theory

solidaire [sɔlidɛʀ] adj: **être ~s** to show solidarity, stand ou stick together; **être ~ de** (collègues) to stand by; **solidarité** nf solidarity; **par solidarité (avec)** in sympathy (with)

solide [sɔlid] adj solid; (mur, maison, meuble) solid, sturdy; (connaissances, argument) sound; (personne, estomac) robust, sturdy ▷ nm solid

soliste [sɔlist] nm/f soloist

solitaire [sɔlitɛʀ] adj (sans compagnie) solitary, lonely; (lieu) lonely ▷ nm/f (ermite) recluse; (fig: ours) loner

solitude [sɔlityd] nf loneliness; (tranquillité) solitude

solliciter [sɔlisite] vt (personne) to appeal to; (emploi, faveur) to seek

sollicitude [sɔlisityd] nf concern

soluble [sɔlybl] adj soluble

solution [sɔlysjɔ̃] nf solution; **solution de facilité** easy way out

solvable [sɔlvabl] adj solvent

sombre [sɔ̃bʀ] adj dark; (fig) gloomy; **sombrer** vi (bateau) to sink; **sombrer dans** (misère, désespoir) to sink into

sommaire [sɔmɛʀ] adj (simple) basic; (expéditif) summary ▷ nm summary

somme [sɔm] nf (Math) sum; (quantité) amount; (argent) sum, amount ▷ nm: **faire un ~** to have a (short) nap; **en ~** all in all; **~ toute** all in all

sommeil [sɔmɛj] nm sleep; **avoir ~** to be sleepy; **sommeiller** vi to doze

sommet [sɔmɛ] nm top; (d'une montagne) summit, top; (fig: de la perfection, gloire) height

sommier [sɔmje] nm (bed) base

somnambule [sɔmnɑ̃byl] nm/f sleepwalker

somnifère [sɔmnifɛʀ] nm sleeping drug no pl (ou pill)

somnoler [sɔmnɔle] vi to doze

somptueux, -euse [sɔptɥø, øz] adj sumptuous

son¹, sa [sɔ̃, sa] (pl **ses**) adj (antécédent humain: mâle) his; (: femelle) her; (: valeur indéfinie) one's, his/her; (antécédent non humain) its

son² [sɔ̃] nm sound; (de blé) bran

sondage [sɔ̃daʒ] nm: **sondage (d'opinion)** (opinion) poll

sonde [sɔ̃d] nf (Navig) lead ou sounding line; (Méd) probe; (Tech: de forage) borer, driller

sonder [sɔ̃de] vt (Navig) to sound; (Tech) to bore, drill; (fig: personne) to sound out; **~ le terrain** (fig) to test the ground

songe [sɔ̃ʒ] nm dream; **songer** vi: **songer à** (penser à) to think over; (envisager) to consider, think of; **songer que** to think that; **songeur, -euse** adj pensive

sonnant, e [sɔnɑ̃, ɑ̃t] adj: **à 8 heures ~es** on the stroke of 8

sonné, e [sɔne] adj (fam) cracked; **il est midi ~** it's gone twelve

sonner [sɔne] vi to ring ▷ vt (cloche) to ring; (glas, tocsin) to sound; (portier, infirmière) to ring for; **~ faux** (instrument) to sound out of tune; (rire) to ring false

sonnerie [sɔnʀi] nf (son) ringing; (sonnette) bell; (de portable) ringtone; **sonnerie d'alarme** alarm bell

sonnette [sɔnɛt] nf bell; **sonnette d'alarme** alarm bell

sonore [sɔnɔʀ] adj (voix) sonorous, ringing; (salle) resonant; (film, signal) sound cpd; **sonorisation** nf (équipement: de salle de conférences) public address system, P.A. system; (: de discothèque) sound system; **sonorité** nf (de piano, violon) tone; (d'une salle) acoustics pl

sophistiqué, e [sɔfistike] adj sophisticated

sorbet [sɔʀbɛ] nm water ice, sorbet

sorcier [sɔʀsje] nm sorcerer

sordide [sɔʀdid] adj (lieu) squalid; (action) sordid

sort [sɔʀ] nm (destinée) fate; (condition) lot; (magique) curse, spell; **tirer au ~** to draw lots

sorte [sɔʀt] nf sort, kind; **de la ~** in that way; **de (telle) ~ que** so that; **en quelque ~** in a way; **faire en ~ que** to see to it that; **quelle ~ de ...?** what kind of ...?

sortie [sɔʀti] nf (issue) way out, exit; (remarque drôle) sally; (promenade) outing; (le soir: au restaurant etc) night out; (Comm: d'un disque) release; (: d'un livre) publication; (: d'un modèle) launching; **où est la ~?** where's the exit?; **sortie de bain** (vêtement) bathrobe

sortilège [sɔʀtilɛʒ] nm (magic) spell

sortir [sɔʀtiʀ] vi (gén) to come out; (partir, se promener, aller au spectacle) to go out; (numéro gagnant) to come up ▷ vt (gén) to take out; (produit, modèle) to bring out; (fam: dire) to come out with; **~ avec qn** to be going out with sb; **s'en ~** (malade) to pull through; (d'une difficulté etc) to get through; **~ de** (endroit) to go (ou come) out of, leave; (provenir de) to come from; (compétence) to be outside

sosie [sɔzi] nm double

sot, sotte [so, sɔt] adj silly, foolish ▷ nm/f fool; **sottise** nf (caractère) silliness, foolishness; (action) silly ou foolish thing

sou [su] nm: **près de ses ~s** tight-fisted; **sans le ~** penniless

soubresaut [subʀəso] nm start; (cahot) jolt

souche [suʃ] nf (d'arbre) stump; (de carnet) counterfoil (BRIT), stub

souci [susi] nm (inquiétude) worry; (préoccupation) concern; (Bot) marigold; **se faire du ~** to worry; **soucier**: **se soucier de** vt to care about; **soucieux, -euse** adj concerned, worried

soucoupe [sukup] nf saucer; **soucoupe volante** flying saucer

soudain, e [sudɛ̃, ɛn] adj (douleur, mort) sudden ▷ adv suddenly, all of a sudden

Soudan [sudã] nm: **le ~** Sudan

soude [sud] nf soda

souder [sude] vt (avec fil à souder) to solder; (par soudure autogène) to weld; (fig) to bind together

soudure [sudyʀ] nf soldering; welding; (joint) soldered joint; weld

souffle [sufl] nm (en expirant) breath; (en soufflant) puff, blow; (respiration) breathing; (d'explosion, de ventilateur) blast; (du vent) blowing; **être à bout de ~** to be out of breath; **un ~ d'air** a breath of air

soufflé, e [sufle] adj (fam: stupéfié) staggered ▷ nm (Culin) soufflé

souffler [sufle] vi (gén) to blow; (haleter) to puff (and blow) ▷ vt (feu, bougie) to blow out; (chasser: poussière etc) to blow away; (Tech: verre) to blow; (dire): **~ qch à qn** to whisper sth to sb

souffrance [sufʀãs] nf suffering; **en ~** (affaire) pending

souffrant, e [sufʀã, ãt] adj unwell

souffre-douleur [sufʀadulœʀ] nm inv butt, underdog

souffrir [sufʀiʀ] vi to suffer, be in pain ▷ vt to suffer, endure; (supporter) to bear, stand; **~ de** (maladie, froid) to suffer from; **elle ne peut pas le ~** she can't stand ou bear him

soufre [sufʀ] nm sulphur

souhait [swɛ] nm wish; **tous nos ~s pour la nouvelle année** (our) best wishes for the New Year; **à vos ~s!** bless you!; **souhaitable** adj desirable

souhaiter [swete] vt to wish for; **~ la bonne année à qn** to wish sb a happy New Year; **~ que** to hope that

soûl, e [su, sul] adj drunk ▷ nm: **tout son ~** to one's heart's content

soulagement [sulaʒmã] nm relief

soulager [sulaʒe] vt to relieve

soûler [sule] vt: **~ qn** to get sb drunk; (suj: boisson) to make sb drunk; (fig) to make sb's head spin ou reel; **se ~** vi to get drunk

soulever [sul(ə)ve] vt to lift; (poussière) to send up; (enthousiasme) to arouse; (question, débat) to raise; **se ~** vi (peuple) to rise up; (personne couchée) to lift o.s. up

soulier [sulje] nm shoe

souligner [suliɲe] vt to underline; (fig) to emphasize, stress

soumettre [sumɛtʀ] vt (pays) to subject, subjugate; (rebelle) to put down, subdue; **~ qch à qn** (projet etc) to submit sth to sb; **se ~ (à)** to submit (to)

soumis, e [sumi, iz] adj submissive; **soumission** nf submission

soupçon [supsɔ̃] nm suspicion; (petite quantité): **un ~ de** a hint ou touch of; **soupçonner** vt to suspect; **soupçonneux, -euse** adj suspicious

soupe [sup] nf soup

souper [supe] vi to have supper ▷ nm supper

soupeser [supəze] vt to weigh in one's hand(s); (fig) to weigh up

soupière [supjɛʀ] nf (soup) tureen

soupir [supiʀ] nm sigh; **pousser un ~ de soulagement** to heave a sigh of relief

soupirer [supiʀe] vi to sigh

souple [supl] adj supple; (fig: règlement, caractère)

flexible; (: démarche, taille) lithe, supple; **souplesse** nf suppleness; (de caractère) flexibility

source [suʀs] nf (point d'eau) spring; (d'un cours d'eau, fig) source; **de bonne ~** on good authority

sourcil [suʀsi] nm (eye)brow; **sourciller** vi: **sans sourciller** without turning a hair ou batting an eyelid

sourd, e [suʀ, suʀd] adj deaf; (bruit) muffled; (douleur) dull ▷ nm/f deaf person; **faire la ~e oreille** to turn a deaf ear; **sourdine** nf (Mus) mute; **en sourdine** softly, quietly; **sourd-muet, sourde-muette** adj deaf-and-dumb ▷ nm/f deaf-mute

souriant, e [suʀjã, jãt] adj cheerful

sourire [suʀiʀ] nm smile ▷ vi to smile; **~ à qn** to smile at sb; (fig: plaire à) to appeal to sb; (suj: chance) to smile on sb; **garder le ~** to keep smiling

souris [suʀi] nf mouse

sournois, e [suʀnwa, waz] adj deceitful, underhand

sous [su] prép under; **~ la pluie** in the rain; **~ terre** underground; **~ peu** shortly, before long; **sous-bois** inv undergrowth

souscrire [suskʀiʀ]: **~ à** vt to subscribe to

sous...: **sous-directeur, -trice** nm/f assistant manager(-manageress); **sous-entendre** vt to imply, infer; **sous-entendu, e** adj implied ▷ nm innuendo, insinuation; **sous-estimer** vt to underestimate; **sous-jacent, e** adj underlying; **sous-louer** vt to sublet; **sous-marin, e** adj (flore, faune) submarine; (pêche) underwater ▷ nm submarine; **sous-pull** nm thin poloneck jersey; **soussigné, e** adj: **je soussigné** I the undersigned; **sous-sol** nm basement; **sous-titre** nm subtitle

soustraction [sustʀaksjɔ̃] nf subtraction

soustraire [sustʀɛʀ] vt to subtract, take away; (dérober): **~ qch à qn** to remove sth from sb; **se ~ à** (autorité etc) to elude, escape from

sous...: **sous-traitant** nm sub-contractor; **sous-traiter** vt to sub-contract; **sous-vêtements** nmpl underwear sg

soutane [sutan] nf cassock, soutane

soute [sut] nf hold

soutenir [sut(ə)niʀ] vt to support; (assaut, choc) to stand up to, withstand; (intérêt, effort) to keep up; (assurer): **~ que** to maintain that; **soutenu, e** adj (efforts) sustained, unflagging; (style) elevated

souterrain, e [suteʀɛ̃, ɛn] adj underground ▷ nm underground passage

soutien [sutjɛ̃] nm support; **soutien-gorge** nm bra

soutirer [sutiʀe] vt: **~ qch à qn** to squeeze ou get sth out of sb

souvenir [suv(ə)niʀ] nm (réminiscence) memory; (objet) souvenir ▷ vb: **se ~ de** to remember; **se ~ que** to remember that; **en ~ de** in memory ou remembrance of; **avec mes affectueux/meilleurs ~s, ...** with love from, .../regards, ...

souvent [suvã] adv often; **peu ~** seldom, infrequently

souverain, e [suv(ə)ʀɛ̃, ɛn] nm/f sovereign, monarch

soyeux, -euse [swajø, øz] adj silky

spacieux, -euse [spasjø, jøz] adj spacious, roomy

spaghettis [spageti] nmpl spaghetti sg

sparadrap [spaʀadʀa] nm sticking plaster (BRIT), Bandaid® (US)

spatial, e, -aux [spasjal, jo] adj (Aviat) space cpd

speaker, ine [spikœʀ, kʀin] nm/f announcer

spécial, e, -aux [spesjal, jo] adj special; (bizarre) peculiar; **spécialement** adv especially, particularly;

(tout exprès) specially; **spécialiser**: **se spécialiser** vi to specialize; **spécialiste** nm/f specialist; **spécialité** nf speciality; (branche) special field

spécifier [spesifje] vt to specify, state

spécimen [spesimen] nm specimen

spectacle [spɛktakl] nm (scène) sight; (représentation) show; (industrie) show business; **spectaculaire** adj spectacular

spectateur, -trice [spɛktatœr, tris] nm/f (Cinéma etc) member of the audience; (Sport) spectator; (d'un événement) onlooker, witness

spéculer [spekyle] vi to speculate

spéléologie [speleɔlɔʒi] nf potholing

sperme [spɛrm] nm semen, sperm

sphère [sfɛr] nf sphere

spirale [spiral] nf spiral

spirituel, le [spiritɥɛl] adj spiritual; (fin, piquant) witty

splendide [splãdid] adj splendid

spontané, e [spɔ̃tane] adj spontaneous; **spontanéité** nf spontaneity

sport [spɔr] nm sport ▷ adj inv (vêtement) casual; **faire du ~** to do sport; **sports d'hiver** winter sports; **sportif, -ive** adj (journal, association, épreuve) sports cpd; (allure, démarche) athletic; (attitude, esprit) sporting

spot [spɔt] nm (lampe) spot(light); (annonce): **spot (publicitaire)** commercial (break)

square [skwar] nm public garden(s)

squelette [skəlɛt] nm skeleton; **squelettique** adj scrawny

SRAS [sras] sigle m (= syndrome respiratoire aigu sévère) SARS

Sri Lanka [srilãka] nm: **le ~** Sri Lanka

stabiliser [stabilize] vt to stabilize

stable [stabl] adj stable, steady

stade [stad] nm (Sport) stadium; (phase, niveau) stage

stage [staʒ] nm (cours) training course; **~ de formation (professionnelle)** vocational (training) course; **~ de perfectionnement** advanced training course; **stagiaire** nm/f, adj trainee

stagner [stagne] vi to stagnate

stand [stãd] nm (d'exposition) stand; (de foire) stall; **stand de tir** (à la foire, Sport) shooting range

standard [stãdar] adj inv standard ▷ nm switchboard; **standardiste** nm/f switchboard operator

standing [stãdiŋ] nm standing; **de grand ~** luxury

starter [starter] nm (Auto) choke

station [stasjɔ̃] nf station; (de bus) stop; (de villégiature) resort; **station de ski** ski resort; **station de taxis** taxi rank (BRIT) ou stand (US); **stationnement** nm parking; **stationner** vi to park; **station-service** nf service station

statistique [statistik] nf (science) statistics sg; (rapport, étude) statistic ▷ adj statistical

statue [staty] nf statue

statu quo [statykwo] nm status quo

statut [staty] nm status; **statuts** nmpl (Jur, Admin) statutes; **statutaire** adj statutory

Sté abr = **société**

steak [stɛk] nm steak; **~ haché** hamburger

sténo(graphie) [steno(grafi)] nf shorthand

stérile [steril] adj sterile

stérilet [sterilɛ] nm coil, loop

stériliser [sterilize] vt to sterilize

stimulant [stimylã] nm (fig) stimulus, incentive;

(physique) stimulant

stimuler [stimyle] vt to stimulate

stipuler [stipyle] vt to stipulate

stock [stɔk] nm stock; **stocker** vt to stock

stop [stɔp] nm (Auto: écriteau) stop sign; (: feu arrière) brake-light; **faire du ~** (fam) to hitch(hike); **stopper** vt, vi to stop, halt

store [stɔr] nm blind; (de magasin) shade, awning

strabisme [strabism] nm squinting

strapontin [strapɔ̃tɛ̃] nm jump ou foldaway seat

stratégie [strateʒi] nf strategy; **stratégique** adj strategic

stress [strɛs] nm stress; **stressant, e** adj stressful; **stresser** vt: **stresser qn** to make sb (feel) tense

strict, e [strikt] adj strict; (tenue, décor) severe, plain; **le ~ nécessaire/minimum** the bare essentials/minimum

strident, e [stridã, ãt] adj shrill, strident

strophe [strɔf] nf verse, stanza

structure [stryktyr] nf structure; **~s d'accueil** reception facilities

studieux, -euse [stydjø, jøz] adj studious

studio [stydjo] nm (logement) (one-roomed) flatlet (BRIT) ou apartment (US); (d'artiste, TV etc) studio

stupéfait, e [stypefɛ, ɛt] adj astonished

stupéfiant, e [stypefjã, jãt] adj (étonnant) stunning, astounding ▷ nm (Méd) drug, narcotic

stupéfier [stypefje] vt (étonner) to stun, astonish

stupeur [stypœr] nf astonishment

stupide [stypid] adj stupid; **stupidité** nf stupidity; (parole, acte) stupid thing (to do ou say)

style [stil] nm style

stylé, e [stile] adj well-trained

styliste [stilist] nm/f designer

stylo [stilo] nm: **~ (à encre)** (fountain) pen; **stylo (à) bille** ball-point pen

su, e [sy] pp de **savoir** ▷ nm: **au su de** with the knowledge of

suave [sɥav] adj sweet

subalterne [sybaltɛrn] adj (employé, officier) junior; (rôle) subordinate, subsidiary ▷ nm/f subordinate

subconscient [sypkɔ̃sjã] nm subconscious

subir [sybir] vt (affront, dégâts) to suffer; (opération, châtiment) to undergo

subit, e [sybi, it] adj sudden; **subitement** adv suddenly, all of a sudden

subjectif, -ive [sybʒɛktif, iv] adj subjective

subjonctif [sybʒɔ̃ktif] nm subjunctive

subjuguer [sybʒyge] vt to captivate

submerger [sybmɛrʒe] vt to submerge; (fig) to overwhelm

subordonné, e [sybɔrdɔne] adj, nm/f subordinate

subrepticement [sybrɛptismã] adv surreptitiously

subside [sybzid] nm grant

subsidiaire [sybzidjɛr] adj: **question ~** deciding question

subsister [sybziste] vi (rester) to remain, subsist; (survivre) to live on

substance [sypstãs] nf substance

substituer [sypstitɥe] vt: **~ qn/qch à** to substitute sb/sth for; **se ~ à qn** (évincer) to substitute o.s. for sb

substitut [sypstity] nm (succédané) substitute

subterfuge [sybtɛrfyʒ] nm subterfuge

subtil, e [syptil] adj subtle

subvenir [sybvənir]: **~ à** vt to meet

subvention [sybvɑ̃sjɔ̃] nf subsidy, grant; **subventionner** vt to subsidize

suc [syk] nm (Bot) sap; (de viande, fruit) juice

succéder [syksede]: **~ à** vt to succeed; **se ~** vi (accidents, années) to follow one another

succès [syksɛ] nm success; **avoir du ~** to be a success, be successful; **à ~** successful; **succès de librairie** bestseller

successeur [syksesœʀ] nm successor

successif, -ive [syksesif, iv] adj successive

succession [syksesjɔ̃] nf (série, Pol) succession; (Jur: patrimoine) estate, inheritance

succomber [sykɔ̃be] vi to die, succumb; (fig): **~ à** to succumb to

succulent, e [sykylɑ̃, ɑ̃t] adj (repas, mets) delicious

succursale [sykyʀsal] nf branch

sucer [syse] vt to suck; **sucette** (bonbon) lollipop; (de bébé) dummy (BRIT), pacifier (US)

sucre [sykʀ] nm (substance) sugar; (morceau) lump of sugar, sugar lump ou cube; **sucre d'orge** barley sugar; **sucre en morceaux/cristallisé/en poudre** lump/granulated/caster sugar; **sucre glace** icing sugar (BRIT), confectioner's sugar (US); **sucré, e** adj (produit alimentaire) sweetened; (au goût) sweet; **sucrer** vt (thé, café) to sweeten, put sugar in; **sucreries** nfpl (bonbons) sweets, sweet things; **sucrier** nm (récipient) sugar bowl

sud [syd] nm: **le ~** the south ▷ adj inv south; (côte) south, southern; **au ~** (situation) in the south; (direction) to the south; **au ~ de** (to the) south of; **sud-africain, e** adj South African ▷ nm/f: **Sud-Africain, e** South African; **sud-américain, e** adj South American ▷ nm/f: **Sud-Américain, e** South American; **sud-est** nm, adj inv south-east; **sud-ouest** nm, adj inv south-west

Suède [sɥɛd] nf: **la ~** Sweden; **suédois, e** adj Swedish ▷ nm/f: **Suédois, e** Swede ▷ nm (Ling) Swedish

suer [sɥe] vi to sweat; (suinter) to ooze; **sueur** nf sweat; **en sueur** sweating, in a sweat; **donner des sueurs froides à qn** to put sb in(to) a cold sweat

suffire [syfiʀ] vi (être assez): **~ (à qn/pour qch/pour faire)** to be enough ou sufficient (for sb/for sth/to do); **il suffit d'une négligence ...** it only takes one act of carelessness ...; **il suffit qu'on oublie pour que ...** one only needs to forget for ...; **ça suffit!** that's enough!

suffisamment [syfizamɑ̃] adv sufficiently, enough; **~ de** sufficient, enough

suffisant, e [syfizɑ̃, ɑ̃t] adj sufficient; (résultats) satisfactory; (vaniteux) self-important, bumptious

suffixe [syfiks] nm suffix

suffoquer [syfɔke] vt to choke, suffocate; (stupéfier) to stagger, astound ▷ vi to choke, suffocate

suffrage [syfʀaʒ] nm (Pol: voix) vote

suggérer [sygʒeʀe] vt to suggest; **suggestion** nf suggestion

suicide [sɥisid] nm suicide; **suicider: se suicider** vi to commit suicide

suie [sɥi] nf soot

suisse [sɥis] adj Swiss ▷ nm: **S~** Swiss pl inv ▷ nf: **la S~** Switzerland; **la S~ romande/allemande** French-speaking/German-speaking Switzerland

suite [sɥit] nf (continuation: d'énumération etc) rest, remainder; (: de feuilleton) continuation; (: film etc sur le même thème) sequel; (série) series, succession; (conséquence) result; (ordre, liaison logique) coherence; (appartement, Mus) suite; (escorte) retinue, suite; **suites** nfpl (d'une maladie etc) effects; **prendre la ~ de** (directeur

etc) to succeed, take over from; **donner ~ à** (requête, projet) to follow up; **faire ~ à** to follow; **(faisant) ~ à votre lettre du ...** further to your letter of the ...; **de ~** (d'affilée) in succession; (immédiatement) at once; **par la ~** afterwards, subsequently; **à la ~** one after the other; **à la ~ de** (derrière) behind; (en conséquence de) following

suivant, e [sɥivɑ̃, ɑ̃t] adj next, following ▷ prép (selon) according to; **au ~!** next!

suivi, e [sɥivi] adj (effort, qualité) consistent; (cohérent) coherent; **très/peu ~** (cours) well-/poorly-attended

suivre [sɥivʀ] vt (gén) to follow; (Scol: cours) to attend; (comprendre) to keep up with; (Comm: article) to continue to stock ▷ vi to follow; (élève: assimiler) to keep up; **se ~** vi (accidents etc) to follow one another; **faire ~** (lettre) to forward; **"à ~"** "to be continued"

sujet, te [syʒɛ, ɛt] adj: **être ~ à** (vertige etc) to be liable ou subject to ▷ nm/f (d'un souverain) subject ▷ nm subject; **au ~ de** about; **sujet de conversation** topic ou subject of conversation; **sujet d'examen** (Scol) examination question

super [sypɛʀ] (fam) adj inv terrific, great, fantastic, super

superbe [sypɛʀb] adj magnificent, superb

superficie [sypɛʀfisi] nf (surface) area

superficiel, le [sypɛʀfisjɛl] adj superficial

superflu, e [sypɛʀfly] adj superfluous

supérieur, e [sypeʀjœʀ] adj (lèvre, étages, classes) upper; (plus élevé: température, niveau, enseignement): **~ (à)** higher (than); (meilleur: qualité, produit): **~ (à)** superior (to); (excellent, hautain) superior ▷ nm, nf superior; **supériorité** nf superiority

supermarché [sypɛʀmaʀʃe] nm supermarket

superposer [sypɛʀpoze] vt (faire chevaucher) to superimpose; **lits superposés** bunk beds

superpuissance [sypɛʀpɥisɑ̃s] nf super-power

superstitieux, -euse [sypɛʀstisjø, jøz] adj superstitious

superviser [sypɛʀvize] vt to supervise

supplanter [syplɑ̃te] vt to supplant

suppléant, e [sypleɑ̃, ɑ̃t] adj (professeur) supply cpd; (juge, fonctionnaire) deputy cpd ▷ nm/f (professeur) supply teacher

suppléer [syplee] vt (ajouter: mot manquant etc) to supply, provide; (compenser: lacune) to fill in; **~ à** to make up for

supplément [syplemɑ̃] nm supplement; (de frites etc) extra portion; **un ~ de travail** extra ou additional work; **payer un ~** to pay an additional charge; **le vin est en ~** wine is extra; **supplémentaire** adj additional, further; (train, bus) relief cpd, extra

supplications [syplikasjɔ̃] nfpl pleas, entreaties

supplice [syplis] nm torture no pl

supplier [syplije] vt to implore, beseech

support [sypɔʀ] nm support; (publicitaire) medium; (audio-visuel) aid

supportable [sypɔʀtabl] adj (douleur) bearable

supporter[1] [sypɔʀtɛʀ] nm supporter, fan

supporter[2] [sypɔʀte] vt (conséquences, épreuve) to bear, endure; (défauts, personne) to put up with; (suj: chose: chaleur etc) to withstand; (: personne: chaleur, vin) to be able to take

supposer [sypoze] vt to suppose; (impliquer) to presuppose; **à ~ que** supposing (that)

suppositoire [sypozitwaʀ] nm suppository

suppression [sypʀesjɔ̃] nf (voir supprimer) cancellation;

removal; deletion

supprimer [syprime] vt (congés, service d'autobus etc) to cancel; (emplois, privilèges, témoin gênant) to do away with; (cloison, cause, anxiété) to remove; (clause, mot) to delete

suprême [syprɛm] adj supreme

 MOT-CLÉ

sur [syr] prép 1 (position) on; (par-dessus) over; (au-dessus) above; **pose-le sur la table** put it on the table; **je n'ai pas d'argent sur moi** I haven't any money on me
2 (direction) towards; **en allant sur Paris** going towards Paris; **sur votre droite** on ou to your right
3 (à propos de) on, about; **un livre/une conférence sur Balzac** a book/lecture on ou about Balzac
4 (proportion) out of; **un sur 10** one in 10; (Scol) one out of 10
5 (mesures) by; **4 m sur 2** 4 m by 2
6 (succession): **avoir accident sur accident** to have one accident after the other

sûr, e [syr] adj sure, certain; (digne de confiance) reliable; (sans danger) safe; (diagnostic, goût) reliable; **le plus - est de** the safest thing is to; **sûr de soi** self-assured, self-confident

surcharge [syrʃarʒ] nf (de passagers, marchandises) excess load; **surcharger** vt to overload

surcroît [syrkrwa] nm: **un - de** additional +nom; **par ou de -** moreover; **en -** in addition

surdité [syrdite] nf deafness

sûrement [syrmã] adv (certainement) certainly; (sans risques) safely

surenchère [syrɑ̃ʃɛr] nf (aux enchères) higher bid; **surenchérir** vi to bid higher; (fig) to try and outbid each other

surestimer [syrɛstime] vt to overestimate

sûreté [syrte] nf (sécurité) safety; (exactitude: de renseignements etc) reliability; (d'un geste) steadiness; **mettre en -** to put in a safe place; **pour plus de -** as an extra precaution, to be on the safe side

surf [sœrf] nm surfing

surface [syrfas] nf surface; (superficie) surface area; **une grande -** a supermarket; **faire -** to surface; **en -** near the surface; (fig) superficially

surfait, e [syrfɛ, ɛt] adj overrated

surfer [syrfe] vi: **- sur Internet** to surf ou browse the Internet

surgelé, e [syrʒəle] adj (deep-)frozen ▷ nm: **les -s** (deep-)frozen food

surgir [syrʒir] vi to appear suddenly; (fig: problème, conflit) to arise

sur...: surhumain, e adj superhuman; **sur-le-champ** adv immediately; **surlendemain** nm: **le surlendemain (soir)** two days later (in the evening); **le surlendemain de** two days after; **surmenage** nm overwork(ing); **surmener: se surmener** vi to overwork

surmonter [syrmɔ̃te] vt (vaincre) to overcome; (être au-dessus de) to top

surnaturel, le [syrnatyrɛl] adj, nm supernatural

surnom [syrnɔ̃] nm nickname

surnombre [syrnɔ̃br] nm: **être en -** to be too many (ou one too many)

surpeuplé, e [syrpœple] adj overpopulated

surplace [syrplas] nm: **faire du -** to mark time

surplomber [syrplɔ̃be] vt, vi to overhang

surplus [syrply] nm (Comm) surplus; (reste): **- de bois** wood left over

surprenant, e [syrprənã, ãt] adj amazing

surprendre [syrprãdr] vt (étonner) to surprise; (tomber sur: intrus etc) to catch; (entendre) to overhear

surpris, e [syrpri, iz] adj: **- (de/que)** surprised (at/ that); **surprise** nf surprise; **faire une surprise à qn** to give sb a surprise; **surprise-partie** nf party

sursaut [syrso] nm start, jump; **- de (énergie, indignation)** sudden fit ou burst of; **en -** with a start; **sursauter** vi to (give a) start, jump

sursis [syrsi] nm (Jur: gén) suspended sentence; (fig) reprieve

surtout [syrtu] adv (avant tout, d'abord) above all; (spécialement, particulièrement) especially; **-, ne dites rien!** whatever you do don't say anything!; **- pas!** certainly ou definitely not!; **- que ...** especially as ...

surveillance [syrvejãs] nf watch; (Police, Mil) surveillance; **sous - médicale** under medical supervision

surveillant, e [syrvejã, ãt] nm/f (de prison) warder; (Scol) monitor

surveiller [syrveje] vt (enfant, élèves, bagages) to watch, keep an eye on; (prisonnier, suspect) to keep (a) watch on; (territoire, bâtiment) to keep watch over; (travaux, cuisson) to supervise; (Scol: examen) to invigilate; **- son langage/sa ligne** to watch one's language/figure

survenir [syrvənir] vi (incident, retards) to occur, arise; (événement) to take place

survêtement [syrvɛtmã] nm tracksuit

survie [syrvi] nf survival; **survivant, e** nm/f survivor; **survivre** vi to survive; **survivre à (accident etc)** to survive

survoler [syrvɔle] vt to fly over; (fig: livre) to skim through

survolté, e [syrvɔlte] adj (fig) worked up

sus [sy(s)]: **en - de** prép in addition to, over and above; **en -** in addition

susceptible [syseptibl] adj touchy, sensitive; **- de faire** (hypothèse) liable to do

susciter [sysite] vt (admiration) to arouse; (ennuis): **- (à qn)** to create (for sb)

suspect, e [syspɛ(kt), ɛkt] adj suspicious; (témoignage, opinions) suspect ▷ nm/f suspect; **suspecter** vt to suspect; (honnêteté de qn) to question, have one's suspicions about

suspendre [syspãdr] vt (accrocher: vêtement): **- qch (à)** to hang sth up (on); (interrompre, démettre) to suspend

suspendu, e [syspãdy] adj (accroché): **- à** hanging on (ou from); (perché): **- au-dessus de** suspended over

suspens [syspã]: **en -** adv (affaire) in abeyance; **tenir en -** to keep in suspense

suspense [syspɛns, syspãs] nm suspense

suspension [syspãsjɔ̃] nf suspension; (lustre) light fitting ou fitment

suture [sytyr] nf (Méd): **point de -** stitch

svelte [svɛlt] adj slender, svelte

SVP abr (= s'il vous plaît) please

sweat [swit] nm (fam) sweatshirt

sweat-shirt [switʃœrt] (pl -s) nm sweatshirt

syllabe [si(l)lab] nf syllable

symbole [sɛ̃bɔl] nm symbol; **symbolique** adj

symbolic(al); (*geste, offrande*) token *cpd*; **symboliser** *vt*
to symbolize
symétrique [simetʀik] *adj* symmetrical
sympa [sɛ̃pa] (*fam*) *adj inv* nice; **sois ~, prête-le moi** be a
pal and lend it to me
sympathie [sɛ̃pati] *nf* (*inclination*) liking; (*affinité*)
friendship; (*condoléances*) sympathy; **j'ai beaucoup de ~
pour lui** I like him a lot; **sympathique** *adj* nice, friendly
sympathisant, e [sɛ̃patizɑ̃, ɑ̃t] *nm/f* sympathizer
sympathiser [sɛ̃patize] *vi* (*voisins etc: s'entendre*) to get
on (BRIT) *ou* along (US) (well)
symphonie [sɛ̃fɔni] *nf* symphony
symptôme [sɛ̃ptom] *nm* symptom
synagogue [sinagɔg] *nf* synagogue
syncope [sɛ̃kɔp] *nf* (*Méd*) blackout; **tomber en ~** to
faint, pass out
syndic [sɛ̃dik] *nm* (*d'immeuble*) managing agent
syndical, e, -aux [sɛ̃dikal, o] *adj* (*trade*) union *cpd*;
syndicaliste *nm/f* trade unionist
syndicat [sɛ̃dika] *nm* (*d'ouvriers, employés*) (*trade*) union;
syndicat d'initiative tourist office; **syndiqué, e** *adj*
belonging to a (*trade*) union; **syndiquer: se syndiquer**
vi to form a trade union; (*adhérer*) to join a trade union
synonyme [sinɔnim] *adj* synonymous ▷ *nm* synonym;
~ de synonymous with
syntaxe [sɛ̃taks] *nf* syntax
synthèse [sɛ̃tɛz] *nf* synthesis
synthétique [sɛ̃tetik] *adj* synthetic
Syrie [siʀi] *nf*: **la ~** Syria
systématique [sistematik] *adj* systematic
système [sistɛm] *nm* system; **le ~ D** resourcefulness

t' [t] *pron voir* **te**
ta [ta] *adj voir* **ton**[1]
tabac [taba] *nm* tobacco; (*magasin*) tobacconist's (shop)
tabagisme [tabaʒism] *nm*: **tabagisme passif** passive
smoking
table [tabl] *nf* table; **à ~!** dinner *etc* is ready!; **se mettre
à ~** to sit down to eat; **mettre la ~** to lay the table; **une
~ pour 4, s'il vous plaît** a table for 4, please; **table à
repasser** ironing board; **table de cuisson** hob; **table de
nuit** *ou* **de chevet** bedside table; **table des matières**
(table of) contents *pl*; **table d'orientation** viewpoint
indicator; **table roulante** trolley (BRIT), tea wagon (US)
tableau, x [tablo] *nm* (*peinture*) painting; (*reproduction,
fig*) picture; (*panneau*) board; (*schéma*) table, chart;
tableau d'affichage notice board; **tableau de bord**
dashboard; (*Aviat*) instrument panel; **tableau noir**
blackboard
tablette [tablɛt] *nf* (*planche*) shelf; **tablette de
chocolat** bar of chocolate
tablier [tablije] *nm* apron
tabou [tabu] *nm* taboo
tabouret [tabuʀɛ] *nm* stool
tac [tak] *nm*: **il m'a répondu du ~ au ~** he answered me
right back
tache [taʃ] *nf* (*saleté*) stain, mark; (*Art, de couleur, lumière*)
spot; **tache de rousseur** freckle
tâche [tɑʃ] *nf* task
tacher [taʃe] *vt* to stain, mark
tâcher [taʃe] *vi*: **~ de faire** to try *ou* endeavour to do
tacheté, e [taʃte] *adj* spotted
tact [takt] *nm* tact; **avoir du ~** to be tactful
tactique [taktik] *adj* tactical ▷ *nf* (*technique*) tactics *sg*;
(*plan*) tactic
taie [tɛ] *nf*: **~ (d'oreiller)** pillowslip, pillowcase
taille [tɑj] *nf* cutting; (*d'arbre etc*) pruning; (*milieu du
corps*) waist; (*hauteur*) height; (*grandeur*) size; **de ~ à faire**
capable of doing; **de ~** sizeable; **taille-crayon(s)** *nm*
pencil sharpener
tailler [taje] *vt* (*pierre, diamant*) to cut; (*arbre, plante*) to
prune; (*vêtement*) to cut out; (*crayon*) to sharpen

tailleur [tɑjœʀ] *nm* (*couturier*) tailor; (*vêtement*) suit; **en ~** (*assis*) cross-legged

taillis [tɑji] *nm* copse

taire [tɛʀ] *vi*: **faire ~ qn** to make sb be quiet; **se ~** *vi* to be silent *ou* quiet; **taisez-vous!** be quiet!

Taiwan [tajwan] *nf* Taiwan

talc [talk] *nm* talc, talcum powder

talent [talɑ̃] *nm* talent

talkie-walkie [tokiwoki] *nm* walkie-talkie

talon [talɔ̃] *nm* heel; (*de chèque, billet*) stub, counterfoil (BRIT); **talons plats/aiguilles** flat/stiletto heels

talus [taly] *nm* embankment

tambour [tɑ̃buʀ] *nm* (*Mus, aussi Tech*) drum; (*musicien*) drummer; (*porte*) revolving door(s *pl*); **tambourin** *nm* tambourine

Tamise [tamiz] *nf*: **la ~** the Thames

tamisé, e [tamize] *adj* (*fig*) subdued, soft

tampon [tɑ̃pɔ̃] *nm* (*coton, d'ouate*) wad, pad; (*amortisseur*) buffer; (*bouchon*) plug, stopper; (*cachet, timbre*) stamp; (*mémoire*) **~** (*Inform*) buffer; **tampon (hygiénique)** tampon; **tamponner** *vt* (*timbres*) to stamp; (*heurter*) to crash *ou* ram into; **tamponneuse** *adj f*: **autos tamponneuses** dodgems

tandem [tɑ̃dɛm] *nm* tandem

tandis [tɑ̃di]: **~ que** *conj* while

tanguer [tɑ̃ge] *vi* to pitch (and toss)

tant [tɑ̃] *adv* so much; **~ de** (*sable, eau*) so much; (*gens, livres*) so many; **~ que** as long as; (*autant que*) as much as; **~ mieux** that's great; (*avec une certaine réserve*) so much the better; **~ pis** too bad; (*conciliant*) never mind; **~ bien que mal** as well as can be expected

tante [tɑ̃t] *nf* aunt

tantôt [tɑ̃to] *adv* (*parfois*): **~ ... ~** now ... now; (*cet après-midi*) this afternoon

taon [tɑ̃] *nm* horsefly

tapage [tapaʒ] *nm* uproar, din

tapageur, -euse [tapaʒœʀ, øz] *adj* noisy; (*voyant*) loud, flashy

tape [tap] *nf* slap

tape-à-l'œil [tapalœj] *adj inv* flashy, showy

taper [tape] *vt* (*porte*) to bang, slam; (*enfant*) to slap; (*dactylographier*) to type (out); (*fam: emprunter*): **~ qn de 10 euros** to touch sb for 10 euros ▷ *vi* (*soleil*) to beat down; **se ~** *vt* (*repas*) to put away; (*fam: corvée*) to get landed with; **~ sur qn** to thump sb; (*fig*) to run sb down; **~ sur un clou** to hit a nail; **~ sur la table** to bang on the table; **~ à** (*porte etc*) to knock on; **~ dans** (*se servir*) to dig into; **~ des mains/pieds** to clap one's hands/stamp one's feet; **~ (à la machine)** to type

tapi, e [tapi] *adj* (*blotti*) crouching; (*caché*) hidden away

tapis [tapi] *nm* carpet; (*petit*) rug; **tapis de sol** (*de tente*) groundsheet; **tapis de souris** (*Inform*) mouse mat; **tapis roulant** (*pour piétons*) moving walkway; (*pour bagages*) carousel

tapisser [tapise] *vt* (*avec du papier peint*) to paper; (*recouvrir*): **~ qch (de)** to cover sth (with); **tapisserie** *nf* (*tenture, broderie*) tapestry; (*papier peint*) wallpaper; **tapissier-décorateur** *nm* interior decorator

tapoter [tapote] *vt* (*joue, main*) to pat; (*objet*) to tap

taquiner [takine] *vt* to tease

tard [taʀ] *adv* late; **plus ~** later (on); **au plus ~** at the latest; **sur le ~** late in life; **il est trop ~** it's too late

tarder [taʀde] *vi* (*chose*) to be a long time coming; (*personne*): **~ à faire** to delay doing; **il me tarde d'être** | am longing to be; **sans (plus) ~** without (further) delay

tardif, -ive [taʀdif, iv] *adj* late

tarif [taʀif] *nm*: **~ des consommations** price list; **~s postaux/douaniers** postal/customs rates; **~ des taxis** taxi fares; **~ plein/réduit** (*train*) full/reduced fare; (*téléphone*) peak/off-peak rate

tarir [taʀiʀ] *vi* to dry up, run dry

tarte [taʀt] *nf* tart; **~ aux fraises** strawberry tart; **~ Tatin** ≈ apple upside-down tart

tartine [taʀtin] *nf* slice of bread; **tartine de miel** slice of bread and honey; **tartiner** *vt* to spread; **fromage à tartiner** cheese spread

tartre [taʀtʀ] *nm* (*des dents*) tartar; (*de bouilloire*) fur, scale

tas [tɑ] *nm* heap, pile; (*fig*): **un ~ de** heaps of, lots of; **en ~** in a heap *ou* pile; **formé sur le ~** trained on the job

tasse [tɑs] *nf* cup; **tasse à café** coffee cup

tassé, e [tɑse] *adj*: **bien ~** (*café etc*) strong

tasser [tɑse] *vt* (*terre, neige*) to pack down; (*entasser*): **~ qch dans** to cram sth into; **se ~** *vi* (*se serrer*) to squeeze up; (*s'affaisser*) to settle; (*fig*) to settle down

tâter [tɑte] *vt* to feel; (*fig*) to try out; **se ~** (*hésiter*) to be in two minds; **~ de** (*prison etc*) to have a taste of

tatillon, ne [tatijɔ̃, ɔn] *adj* pernickety

tâtonnement [tɑtɔnmɑ̃] *nm*: **par ~s** (*fig*) by trial and error

tâtonner [tɑtɔne] *vi* to grope one's way along

tâtons [tɑtɔ̃]: **à ~** *adv*: **chercher/avancer à ~** to grope around for/grope one's way forward

tatouage [tatwaʒ] *nm* tattoo

tatouer [tatwe] *vt* to tattoo

taudis [todi] *nm* hovel, slum

taule [tol] (*fam*) *nf* nick (*fam*), prison

taupe [top] *nf* mole

taureau, x [tɔʀo] *nm* bull; (*signe*): **le T~** Taurus

taux [to] *nm* rate; (*d'alcool*) level; **taux d'intérêt** interest rate

taxe [taks] *nf* tax; (*douanière*) duty; **toutes ~s comprises** inclusive of tax; **la boutique hors ~s** the duty-free shop; **taxe à la valeur ajoutée** value-added tax; **taxe de séjour** tourist tax

taxer [takse] *vt* (*personne*) to tax; (*produit*) to put a tax on, tax

taxi [taksi] *nm* taxi; (*chauffeur: fam*) taxi driver; **pouvez-vous m'appeler un ~, s'il vous plaît?** can you call me a taxi, please?

Tchécoslovaquie [tʃekɔslɔvaki] *nf* Czechoslovakia; **tchèque** *adj* Czech ▷ *nm/f*: **Tchèque** Czech ▷ *nm* (*Ling*) Czech; **la République tchèque** the Czech Republic

Tchétchénie [tʃetʃeni] *nf*: **la ~** Chechnya

te, t' [tə] *pron you*; (*réfléchi*) yourself

technicien, ne [tɛknisjɛ̃, jɛn] *nm/f* technician

technico-commercial, e, -aux [tɛknikokɔmɛʀsjal, jo] *adj*: **agent ~** sales technician

technique [tɛknik] *adj* technical ▷ *nf* technique; **techniquement** *adv* technically

techno [tɛkno] *nf* (*Mus*) techno (music)

technologie [tɛknɔlɔʒi] *nf* technology; **technologique** *adj* technological

teck [tɛk] *nm* teak

tee-shirt [tiʃœʀt] *nm* T-shirt, tee-shirt

teindre [tɛ̃dʀ] *vt* to dye; **se ~ les cheveux** to dye one's hair; **teint, e** *adj* dyed ▷ *nm* (*du visage*) complexion; (*momentané*) colour ▷ *nf* shade; **grand teint** colourfast

teinté, e [tɛ̃te] adj: **~ de** (fig) tinged with
teinter [tɛ̃te] vt (verre, papier) to tint; (bois) to stain
teinture [tɛ̃tyʀ] nf dye; **teinture d'iode** tincture of iodine; **teinturerie** nf dry cleaner's; **teinturier** nm dry cleaner

tel, telle [tɛl] adj (pareil) such; (comme): **~ un/des ...** like a/like ...; (indéfini) such-and-such a; (intensif): **un ~/de ~s ...** such (a)/such ...; **rien de ~** nothing like it; **~ que** like, such as; **~ quel** as it is ou stands (ou was etc); **venez ~ jour** come on such and such a day

télé [tele] (fam) nf TV; **à la ~** on TV ou telly
télé...: **télécabine** nf (benne) cable car; **télécarte** nf phonecard; **téléchargeable** adj downloadable; **téléchargement** nm (action) downloading; (fichier) download; **télécharger** vt to download; **télécommande** nf remote control; **télécopieur** nm fax machine; **télédistribution** nf cable TV; **télégramme** nm telegram; **télégraphier** vt to telegraph, cable; **téléguider** vt to radio-control; **télématique** nf telematics sg; **téléobjectif** nm telephoto lens sg; **télépathie** nf telepathy; **téléphérique** nm cable car
téléphone [telefɔn] nm telephone; **avoir le ~** to be on the (tele)phone; **au ~** on the phone; **téléphoner** vi to make a phone call; **téléphoner à** to phone, call up; **est-ce que je peux téléphoner d'ici?** can I make a call from here?; **téléphonique** adj (tele)phone cpd
télé...: **téléréalité** nf reality TV
télescope [telɛskɔp] nm telescope
télescoper [telɛskɔpe] vt to smash up; **se ~** (véhicules) to concertina
télé...: **téléscripteur** nm teleprinter; **télésiège** nm chairlift; **téléski** nm ski-tow; **téléspectateur, -trice** nm/f (television) viewer; **télétravail** nm telecommuting; **télévente** nf telesales; **téléviseur** nm television set; **télévision** nf television; **à la télévision** on television; **télévision numérique** digital TV; **télévision par câble/satellite** cable/satellite television
télex [telɛks] nm telex
telle [tɛl] adj voir **tel**; **tellement** adv (tant) so much; (si) so; **tellement de** (sable, eau) so much; (gens, livres) so many; **il s'est endormi tellement il était fatigué** he was so tired (that) he fell asleep; **pas tellement** not (all) that much; not (all) that +adjectif
téméraire [temeʀɛʀ] adj reckless, rash
témoignage [temwaɲaʒ] nm (Jur: déclaration) testimony no pl, evidence no pl; (rapport, récit) account; (fig: d'affection etc: cadeau) token, mark; (: geste) expression
témoigner [temwaɲe] vt (intérêt, gratitude) to show ▷ vi (Jur) to testify, give evidence; **~ de** to bear witness to, testify to
témoin [temwɛ̃] nm witness ▷ adj: **appartement ~** show flat (BRIT); **être ~ de** to witness; **témoin oculaire** eyewitness
tempe [tɑ̃p] nf temple
tempérament [tɑ̃peʀamɑ̃] nm temperament, disposition; **à ~** (vente) on deferred (payment) terms; (achat) by instalments, hire purchase cpd
température [tɑ̃peʀatyʀ] nf temperature; **avoir ou faire de la ~** to be running ou have a temperature
tempête [tɑ̃pɛt] nf storm; **tempête de sable/neige** sand/snowstorm
temple [tɑ̃pl] nm temple; (protestant) church

temporaire [tɑ̃pɔʀɛʀ] adj temporary
temps [tɑ̃] nm (atmosphérique) weather; (durée) time; (époque) time, times pl; (Ling) tense; (Mus) beat; (Tech) stroke; **un ~ de chien** (fam) rotten weather; **quel ~ fait-il?** what's the weather like?; **il fait beau/mauvais ~** the weather is fine/bad; **avoir le ~/tout son ~** to have time/plenty of time; **en ~ de paix/guerre** in peacetime/wartime; **en ~ utile ou voulu** in due time ou course; **ces derniers ~** lately; **dans quelque ~** in a (little) while; **de ~ en ~, de ~ à autre** from time to time; **à ~** (partir, arriver) in time; **à ~ complet, à plein ~** full-time; **à ~ partiel, à mi-~** part-time; **dans le ~** at one time; **temps d'arrêt** pause, halt; **temps libre** free ou spare time; **temps mort** (Comm) slack period
tenable [t(ə)nabl] adj bearable
tenace [tənas] adj persistent
tenant, e [tənɑ̃, ɑ̃t] nm/f (Sport): **~ du titre** title-holder
tendance [tɑ̃dɑ̃s] nf tendency; (opinions) leanings pl, sympathies pl; (évolution) trend; **avoir ~ à** to have a tendency to, tend to
tendeur [tɑ̃dœʀ] nm (attache) elastic strap
tendre [tɑ̃dʀ] adj tender; (bois, roche, couleur) soft ▷ vt (élastique, peau) to stretch; (corde) to tighten; (muscle) to tense; (fig: piège) to set, lay; (donner): **~ qch à qn** to hold sth out to sb; (offrir) to offer sb sth; **se ~** vi (corde) to tighten; (relations) to become strained; **~ à qch/à faire** to tend towards sth/to do; **~ l'oreille** to prick up one's ears; **~ la main/le bras** to hold out one's hand/stretch out one's arm; **tendrement** adv tenderly; **tendresse** nf tenderness
tendu, e [tɑ̃dy] pp de **tendre** ▷ adj (corde) tight; (muscles) tensed; (relations) strained
ténèbres [tenɛbʀ] nfpl darkness sg
teneur [tənœʀ] nf content; (d'une lettre) terms pl, content
tenir [t(ə)niʀ] vt to hold; (magasin, hôtel) to run; (promesse) to keep ▷ vi to hold; (neige, gel) to last; **se ~** vi (avoir lieu) to be held, take place; (être: personne) to stand; **~ à** (personne, objet) to be attached to; (réputation) to care about; **~ à faire** to be determined to do; **~ de** (ressembler à) to take after; **ça ne tient qu'à lui** it is entirely up to him; **~ qn pour** to regard sb as; **~ qch de qn** (histoire) to have heard ou learnt sth from sb; (qualité, défaut) to have inherited ou got sth from sb; **~ dans** to fit into; **~ compte de qch** to take sth into account; **~ les comptes** to keep the books; **~ bon** to stand fast; **~ le coup** to hold out; **~ au chaud** (café, plat) to keep hot; **un manteau qui tient chaud** a warm coat; **tiens/tenez, voilà le stylo** there's the pen!; **tiens, voilà Alain!** look, here's Alain!; **tiens?** (surprise) really?; **se ~ droit** to stand (ou sit) up straight; **bien se ~** to behave well; **se ~ à qch** to hold on to sth; **s'en ~ à qch** to confine o.s. to sth
tennis [tenis] nm tennis; (court) tennis court ▷ nm ou f pl (aussi: **chaussures de ~**) tennis ou gym shoes; **tennis de table** table tennis; **tennisman** nm tennis player
tension [tɑ̃sjɔ̃] nf tension; (Méd) blood pressure; **avoir de la ~** to have high blood pressure
tentation [tɑ̃tasjɔ̃] nf temptation
tentative [tɑ̃tativ] nf attempt
tente [tɑ̃t] nf tent
tenter [tɑ̃te] vt (éprouver, attirer) to tempt; (essayer): **~ qch/de faire** to attempt ou try sth/to do; **~ sa chance** to try one's luck
tenture [tɑ̃tyʀ] nf hanging

tenu, e [t(ə)ny] *pp de* **tenir** ▷ *adj* (*maison, comptes*): **bien ~** well-kept; (*obligé*): **~ de faire** obliged to do ▷ *nf* (*vêtements*) clothes *pl*; (*comportement*) (good) manners *pl*, good behaviour; (*d'une maison*) upkeep; **en petite ~e** scantily dressed *ou* clad

ter [tɛʀ] *adj*: **16 ~ 16b** *ou* B

terme [tɛʀm] *nm* term; (*fin*) end; **à court/long ~** *adj* short-/long-term ▷ *adv* in the short/long term; **avant ~** (*Méd*) prematurely; **mettre un ~ à** to put an end *ou* a stop to; **en bons ~s** on good terms

terminaison [tɛʀminɛzɔ̃] *nf* (*Ling*) ending

terminal, -aux [tɛʀminal, o] *nm* terminal; **terminale** *nf* (*Scol*) ≈ year 13 (BRIT), ≈ twelfth grade (US)

terminer [tɛʀmine] *vt* to finish; **se ~** *vi* to end; **quand est-ce que le spectacle se termine?** when does the show finish?

terne [tɛʀn] *adj* dull

ternir [tɛʀniʀ] *vt* to dull; (*fig*) to sully, tarnish; **se ~** *vi* to become dull

terrain [tɛʀɛ̃] *nm* (*sol, fig*) ground; (*Comm: étendue de terre*) land *no pl*; (*parcelle*) plot (of land); (*à bâtir*) site; **sur le ~** (*fig*) on the field; **terrain d'aviation** airfield; **terrain de camping** campsite; **terrain de football/rugby** football/rugby pitch (BRIT) *ou* field (US); **terrain de golf** golf course; **terrain de jeu** games field; (*pour les petits*) playground; **terrain de sport** sports ground; **terrain vague** waste ground *no pl*

terrasse [tɛʀas] *nf* terrace; **à la ~** (*café*) outside; **terrasser** *vt* (*adversaire*) to floor; (*suj: maladie etc*) to strike down

terre [tɛʀ] *nf* (*gén, aussi Élec*) earth; (*substance*) soil, earth; (*opposé à mer*) land *no pl*; (*contrée*) land; **terres** *nfpl* (*terrains*) lands, land *sg*; **en ~** (*pipe, poterie*) clay *cpd*; **à ~** *ou* **par ~** (*mettre, être, s'asseoir*) on the ground (*ou* floor); (*jeter, tomber*) to the ground, down; **terre à terre** *adj inv* (*considération, personne*) down-to-earth; **terre cuite** terracotta; **la terre ferme** dry land; **terre glaise** clay

terreau [tɛʀo] *nm* compost

terre-plein [tɛʀplɛ̃] *nm* platform; (*sur chaussée*) central reservation

terrestre [tɛʀɛstʀ] *adj* (*surface*) earth's, of the earth; (*Bot, Zool, Mil*) land *cpd*; (*Rel*) earthly

terreur [tɛʀœʀ] *nf* terror *no pl*

terrible [tɛʀibl] *adj* terrible, dreadful; (*fam*) terrific; **pas ~** nothing special

terrien, ne [tɛʀjɛ̃, jɛn] *adj*: **propriétaire ~** landowner ▷ *nm/f* (*non martien etc*) earthling

terrier [tɛʀje] *nm* burrow, hole; (*chien*) terrier

terrifier [tɛʀifje] *vt* to terrify

terrine [tɛʀin] *nf* (*récipient*) terrine; (*Culin*) pâté

territoire [tɛʀitwaʀ] *nm* territory

terroriser [tɛʀɔʀize] *vt* to terrorize

terrorisme [tɛʀɔʀism] *nm* terrorism; **terroriste** *nm/f* terrorist

tertiaire [tɛʀsjɛʀ] *adj* tertiary ▷ *nm* (*Écon*) service industries *pl*

tes [te] *adj voir* **ton¹**

test [tɛst] *nm* test

testament [tɛstamɑ̃] *nm* (*Jur*) will; (*Rel*) Testament; (*fig*) legacy

tester [tɛste] *vt* to test

testicule [tɛstikyl] *nm* testicle

tétanos [tetanos] *nm* tetanus

têtard [tɛtaʀ] *nm* tadpole

tête [tɛt] *nf* head; (*cheveux*) hair *no pl*; (*visage*) face; **de ~** (*comme adj: wagon etc*) front *cpd*; (*comme adv: calculer*) in one's head, mentally; **perdre la ~** (*fig: s'affoler*) to lose one's head; (: *devenir fou*) to go off one's head; **tenir ~ à qn** to stand up to sb; **la ~ en bas** with one's head down; **la ~ la première** (*tomber*) headfirst; **faire une ~** (*Football*) to head the ball; **faire la ~** (*fig*) to sulk; **en ~** at the front; (*Sport*) in the lead; **à la ~ de** at the head of; **à ~ reposée** in a more leisurely moment; **n'en faire qu'à sa ~** to do as one pleases; **en avoir par-dessus la ~** to be fed up; **en ~ à ~** in private, alone together; **de la ~ aux pieds** from head to toe; **tête de lecture** (*playback*) head; **tête de liste** (*Pol*) chief candidate; **tête de mort** skull and crossbones; **tête de série** (*Tennis*) seeded player, seed; **tête de Turc** (*fig*) whipping boy; butt; **tête-à-queue** *nm inv*: **faire un tête-à-queue** to spin round

téter [tete] *vt*: **~ (sa mère)** to suck at one's mother's breast, feed

tétine [tetin] *nf* teat; (*sucette*) dummy (BRIT), pacifier (US)

têtu, e [tety] *adj* stubborn, pigheaded

texte [tɛkst] *nm* text; (*morceau choisi*) passage

textile [tɛkstil] *adj* textile *cpd* ▷ *nm* textile; **le ~** the textile industry

Texto® [tɛksto] *nm* text message

texture [tɛkstyʀ] *nf* texture

TGV *sigle m* (= *train à grande vitesse*) high-speed train

thaïlandais, e [tajlɑdɛ, ɛz] *adj* Thai ▷ *nm/f*: **T~, e** Thai

Thaïlande [tailɑd] *nf* Thailand

thé [te] *nm* tea; **~ au citron** lemon tea; **~ au lait** tea with milk; **prendre le ~** to have tea; **faire le ~** to make the tea

théâtral, e, -aux [teatʀal, o] *adj* theatrical

théâtre [teatʀ] *nm* theatre; (*péj: simulation*) playacting; (*fig: lieu*): **le ~ de** the scene of; **faire du ~** to act

théière [tejɛʀ] *nf* teapot

thème [tɛm] *nm* theme; (*Scol: traduction*) prose (composition)

théologie [teɔlɔʒi] *nf* theology

théorie [teɔʀi] *nf* theory; **théorique** *adj* theoretical

thérapie [teʀapi] *nf* therapy

thermal, e, -aux [tɛʀmal, o] *adj*: **station ~e** spa; **cure ~e** water cure

thermomètre [tɛʀmɔmɛtʀ] *nm* thermometer

thermos® [tɛʀmos] *nm ou nf*: **(bouteille) thermos** vacuum *ou* Thermos® flask

thermostat [tɛʀmɔsta] *nm* thermostat

thèse [tɛz] *nf* thesis

thon [tɔ̃] *nm* tuna (fish)

thym [tɛ̃] *nm* thyme

Tibet [tibɛ] *nm*: **le ~** Tibet

tibia [tibja] *nm* shinbone, tibia; (*partie antérieure de la jambe*) shin

TIC *sigle fpl* (= *technologies de l'information et de la communication*) ICT *sg*

tic [tik] *nm* tic, (*nervous*) twitch; (*de langage etc*) mannerism

ticket [tikɛ] *nm* ticket; **ticket de caisse** receipt; **je peux avoir un ticket de caisse, s'il vous plaît?** can I have a receipt, please?

tiède [tjɛd] *adj* lukewarm; (*vent, air*) mild, warm; **tiédir** *vi* to cool; (*se réchauffer*) to grow warmer

tien, ne [tjɛ̃, tjɛn] *pron*: **le(la) ~(ne), les ~(ne)s** yours; **à la ~e!** cheers!

tiens [tjɛ̃] *vb, excl voir* **tenir**

tiercé [tjɛʀse] nm *system of forecast betting giving first 3 horses*

tiers, tierce [tjɛʀ, tjɛʀs] adj third ▷ nm (Jur) third party; (fraction) third; **le tiers monde** the Third World

tige [tiʒ] nf stem; (baguette) rod

tignasse [tiɲas] (péj) nf mop of hair

tigre [tigʀ] nm tiger; **tigré, e** adj (rayé) striped; (tacheté) spotted; (chat) tabby; **tigresse** nf tigress

tilleul [tijœl] nm lime (tree), linden (tree); (boisson) lime-blossom) tea

timbre [tɛ̃bʀ] nm (tampon) stamp; (aussi: **~-poste**) (postage) stamp; (Mus: de voix, instrument) timbre, tone

timbré, e [tɛ̃bʀe] (fam) adj cracked

timide [timid] adj shy; (timoré) timid; **timidement** adv shyly; timidly; **timidité** nf shyness; timidity

tintamarre [tɛ̃tamaʀ] nm din, uproar

tinter [tɛ̃te] vi to ring, chime; (argent, clefs) to jingle

tique [tik] nf (parasite) tick

tir [tiʀ] nm (sport) shooting; (fait au manière de tirer) firing no pl; (rafale) fire; (stand) shooting gallery; **tir à l'arc** archery

tirage [tiʀaʒ] nm (action) printing; (Photo) print; (de journal) circulation; (de livre: nombre d'exemplaires) (print) run; (: édition) edition; (de loterie) draw; **par ~ au sort** by drawing lots

tire [tiʀ] nf: **vol à la ~** pickpocketing

tiré, e [tiʀe] adj (traits) drawn; **~ par les cheveux** far-fetched

tire-bouchon [tiʀbuʃɔ̃] nm corkscrew

tirelire [tiʀliʀ] nf moneybox

tirer [tiʀe] vt (gén) to pull; (trait, rideau, carte, conclusion, chèque) to draw; (langue) to stick out; (en faisant feu: balle, coup) to fire; (: animal) to shoot; (journal, livre, photo) to print; (Football: corner etc) to take ▷ vi (faire feu) to fire; (faire du tir, Football) to shoot; **se ~** vi (fam) to push off; **s'en ~** (éviter le pire) to get off; (survivre) to pull through; (se débrouiller) to manage; **~ qch de** (extraire) to take ou pull sth out of; **~ qn de** (embarras etc) to help ou get sb out of; **~ sur** (corde) to pull on ou at; (faire feu sur) to shoot ou fire at; (pipe) to draw on; (approcher de: couleur) to verge ou border on; **~ à l'arc/la carabine** to shoot with a bow and arrow/with a rifle; **~ à sa fin** to be drawing to a close; **~ qch au clair** to clear sth up; **~ au sort** to draw lots; **~ parti de** to take advantage of; **~ profit de** to profit from; **~ les cartes** to read ou tell the cards

tiret [tiʀe] nm dash

tireur [tiʀœʀ] nm gunman; **tireur d'élite** marksman

tiroir [tiʀwaʀ] nm drawer; **tiroir-caisse** nm till

tisane [tizan] nf herb tea

tisser [tise] vt to weave

tissu [tisy] nm fabric, material, cloth no pl; (Anat, Bio) tissue; **tissu-éponge** nm (terry) towelling no pl

titre [titʀ] nm (gén) title; (de journal) headline; (diplôme) qualification; (Comm) security; **en ~** (champion) official; **à juste ~** rightly; **à quel ~?** on what grounds?; **à aucun ~** on no account; **au même ~ (que)** in the same way (as); **à ~ d'information** for (your) information; **à ~ gracieux** free of charge; **à ~ d'essai** on a trial basis; **à ~ privé** in a private capacity; **titre de propriété** title deed; **titre de transport** ticket

tituber [titybe] vi to stagger (along)

titulaire [titylɛʀ] adj (Admin) with tenure ▷ nm/f (de permis) holder; **être ~ de** (diplôme, permis) to hold

toast [tost] nm slice ou piece of toast; (de bienvenue) (welcoming) toast; **porter un ~ à qn** to propose ou drink a toast to sb

toboggan [tɔbɔgã] nm slide; (Auto) flyover

toc [tɔk] excl: **~, ~** knock knock ▷ nm: **en ~** fake

tocsin [tɔksɛ̃] nm alarm (bell)

tohu-bohu [tɔybɔy] nm hubbub

toi [twa] pron you

toile [twal] nf (tableau) canvas; **de** ou **en ~** (pantalon) cotton; (sac) canvas; **la T~** (Internet) the Web; **toile cirée** oilcloth; **toile d'araignée** cobweb; **toile de fond** (fig) backdrop

toilette [twalɛt] nf (habits) outfit; **toilettes** nfpl (w.-c.) toilet sg; **faire sa ~** to have a wash, get washed; **articles de ~** toiletries; **où sont les ~s?** where's the toilet?

toi-même [twamɛm] pron yourself

toit [twa] nm roof; **toit ouvrant** sunroof

toiture [twatyʀ] nf roof

Tokyo [tɔkjo] n Tokyo

tôle [tol] nf (plaque) steel ou iron sheet; **tôle ondulée** corrugated iron

tolérable [tɔleʀabl] adj tolerable

tolérant, e [tɔleʀã, ãt] adj tolerant

tolérer [tɔleʀe] vt to tolerate; (Admin: hors taxe etc) to allow

tollé [tɔ(l)le] nm outcry

tomate [tɔmat] nf tomato; **~s farcies** stuffed tomatoes

tombe [tɔ̃b] nf (sépulture) grave; (avec monument) tomb

tombeau, x [tɔ̃bo] nm tomb

tombée [tɔ̃be] nf: **à la ~ de la nuit** at nightfall

tomber [tɔ̃be] vi to fall; (fièvre, vent) to drop; **laisser ~** (objet) to drop; (personne) to let down; (activité) to give up; **laisse ~!** forget it!; **faire ~** to knock over; **~ sur** (rencontrer) to bump into; **~ de fatigue/sommeil** to drop from exhaustion/be falling asleep on one's feet; **ça tombe bien** that's come at the right time; **il est bien tombé** he's been lucky; **à l'eau** (projet) to fall through; **~ en panne** to break down

tombola [tɔ̃bɔla] nf raffle

tome [tom] nm volume

ton¹, ta [tɔ̃, ta] (pl tes) adj your

ton² [tɔ̃] nm (gén) tone; (couleur) shade, tone; **de bon ~** in good taste

tonalité [tɔnalite] nf (au téléphone) dialling tone

tondeuse [tɔ̃døz] nf (à gazon) (lawn)mower; (du coiffeur) clippers pl; (pour les moutons) shears pl

tondre [tɔ̃dʀ] vt (pelouse, herbe) to mow; (haie) to cut, clip; (mouton, toison) to shear; (cheveux) to crop

tongs [tɔ̃g] nfpl flip-flops

tonifier [tɔnifje] vt (peau, organisme) to tone up

tonique [tɔnik] adj fortifying ▷ nm tonic

tonne [tɔn] nf metric ton, tonne

tonneau, x [tɔno] nm (à vin, cidre) barrel; **faire des ~x** (voiture, avion) to roll over

tonnelle [tɔnɛl] nf bower, arbour

tonner [tɔne] vi to thunder; **il tonne** it is thundering, there's some thunder

tonnerre [tɔnɛʀ] nm thunder

tonus [tɔnys] nm energy

top [tɔp] nm: **au 3ème ~** at the 3rd stroke ▷ adj: **~ secret** top secret

topinambour [tɔpinãbuʀ] nm Jerusalem artichoke

torche [tɔʀʃ] nf torch

torchon [tɔʀʃɔ̃] nm cloth; (à vaisselle) tea towel ou cloth

tordre [tɔʀdʀ] vt (chiffon) to wring; (barre, fig: visage) to twist; **se ~** vi: **se ~ le poignet/la cheville** to twist one's wrist/ankle; **se ~ de douleur/rire** to be doubled up with pain/laughter; **tordu, e** adj bent; (fig) crazy

tornade [tɔʀnad] nf tornado

torrent [tɔʀɑ̃] nm mountain stream

torsade [tɔʀsad] nf: **un pull à ~s** a cable sweater

torse [tɔʀs] nm chest; (Anat, Sculpture) torso; **~ nu** stripped to the waist

tort [tɔʀ] nm (défaut) fault; **torts** nmpl (Jur) fault sg; **avoir ~** to be wrong; **être dans son ~** to be in the wrong; **donner ~ à qn** to lay the blame on sb; **causer du ~ à qn** to harm sb; **à ~** wrongly; **à ~ et à travers** wildly

torticolis [tɔʀtikɔli] nm stiff neck

tortiller [tɔʀtije] vt to twist; (moustache) to twirl; **se ~** vi to wriggle; (en dansant) to wiggle

tortionnaire [tɔʀsjɔnɛʀ] nm torturer

tortue [tɔʀty] nf tortoise; (d'eau douce) terrapin; (d'eau de mer) turtle

tortueux, -euse [tɔʀtyø, øz] adj (rue) twisting; (fig) tortuous

torture [tɔʀtyʀ] nf torture; **torturer** vt to torture; (fig) to torment

tôt [to] adv early; **~ ou tard** sooner or later; **si ~** so early; (déjà) so soon; **plus ~** earlier; **au plus ~** at the earliest

total, e, -aux [tɔtal, o] adj, nm total; **au ~** in total; (fig) on the whole; **faire le ~** to work out the total; **totalement** adv totally; **totaliser** vt to total; **totalitaire** adj totalitarian; **totalité** nf: **la totalité de** all (of); the whole +sg; **en totalité** entirely

toubib [tubib] (fam) nm doctor

touchant, e [tuʃɑ̃, ɑ̃t] adj touching

touche [tuʃ] nf (de piano, de machine à écrire) key; (de téléphone) button; (Peinture et fig) stroke, touch; (fig: de nostalgie) touch; (Football: aussi: **remise en ~**) throw-in; (aussi: **ligne de ~**) touch-line; **touche dièse** (de téléphone, clavier) hash key

toucher [tuʃe] nm touch ▷ vt to touch; (palper) to feel; (atteindre: d'un coup de feu etc) to hit; (concerner) to concern, affect; (contacter) to reach, contact; (recevoir: récompense) to receive, get; (: salaire) to draw, get; (: chèque) to cash; **se ~** (être en contact) to touch; **au ~** to the touch; **à ~** to touch; (concerner) to have to do with, concern; **je vais lui en ~ un mot** I'll have a word with him about it; **~ au but** (fig) to near one's goal; **~ à sa fin** to be drawing to a close

touffe [tuf] nf tuft

touffu, e [tufy] adj thick, dense

toujours [tuʒuʀ] adv always; (encore) still; (constamment) forever; **~ plus** more and more; **pour ~** forever; **~ est-il que** the fact remains that; **essaie ~** (you can) try anyway

toupie [tupi] nf (spinning) top

tour¹ [tuʀ] nf tower; (immeuble) high-rise block (BRIT) ou building (US); (Échecs) castle, rook; **tour de contrôle** nf control tower; **la tour Eiffel** the Eiffel Tower

tour² [tuʀ] nm (excursion) trip, (à pied) stroll, walk; (en voiture) run, ride; (Sport: aussi: **~ de piste**) lap; (d'être servi ou de jouer etc) turn; (de roue etc) revolution; (Pol: aussi: **~ de scrutin**) ballot; (ruse, de prestidigitation) trick; (de potier) wheel; (à bois, métaux) lathe; (circonférence): **de 3 m de ~** 3 m round, with a circumference ou girth of 3 m; **faire le ~ de** to go round; (à pied) to walk round; **c'est au ~ de Renée** it's Renée's turn; **à ~ de rôle, à ~ de rôle** in turn; **tour de chant** nm song recital; **tour de force**

tour de force; **tour de garde** nm spell of duty; **tour d'horizon** nm (fig) general survey; **tour de taille/tête** nm waist/head measurement; **un 33 tours** an LP; **un 45 tours** a single

tourbe [tuʀb] nf peat

tourbillon [tuʀbijɔ̃] nm whirlwind; (d'eau) whirlpool; (fig) whirl, swirl; **tourbillonner** vi to whirl (round)

tourelle [tuʀɛl] nf turret

tourisme [tuʀism] nm tourism; **agence de ~** tourist agency; **faire du ~** to go touring; (en ville) to go sightseeing; **touriste** nm/f tourist; **touristique** adj tourist cpd; (région) touristy

tourment [tuʀmɑ̃] nm torment; **tourmenter** vt to torment; **se tourmenter** to fret, worry o.s.

tournage [tuʀnaʒ] nm (Cinéma) shooting

tournant [tuʀnɑ̃] nm (de route) bend; (fig) turning point

tournée [tuʀne] nf (du facteur etc) round; (d'artiste, politicien) tour; (au café) round (of drinks)

tourner [tuʀne] vt to turn; (sauce, mélange) to stir; (Cinéma: faire les prises de vues) to shoot; (: produire) to make ▷ vi to turn; (moteur) to run; (taximètre) to tick away; (lait etc) to turn (sour); **se ~** vi to turn round; **tournez à gauche/droite au prochain carrefour** turn left/right at the next junction; **mal ~** to go wrong; **~ autour de** to go round; (péj) to hang round; **~ à/en** to turn into; **~ qn en ridicule** to ridicule sb; **~ le dos à** (mouvement) to turn one's back on; (position) to have one's back to; **~ de l'œil** to pass out; **se ~ vers** to turn towards; (fig) to turn to; **se ~ les pouces** to twiddle one's thumbs

tournesol [tuʀnəsɔl] nm sunflower

tournevis [tuʀnəvis] nm screwdriver

tournoi [tuʀnwa] nm tournament

tournure [tuʀnyʀ] nf (Ling) turn of phrase; (évolution): **la ~ de qch** the way sth is developing; **tournure d'esprit** turn ou cast of mind

tourte [tuʀt] nf pie

tourterelle [tuʀtəʀɛl] nf turtledove

tous [tu] adj, pron voir **tout**

Toussaint [tusɛ̃] nf: **la ~** All Saints' Day

tousser [tuse] vi to cough

MOT-CLÉ

tout, e [tu, tut] (mpl **tous**, fpl **toutes**) adj **1** (avec article singulier) all; **tout le lait** all the milk; **toute la nuit** all night, the whole night; **tout le livre** the whole book; **tout un pain** a whole loaf; **tout le temps** all the time; the whole time; **tout le monde** everybody; **c'est tout le contraire** it's quite the opposite

2 (avec article pluriel) every, all; **tous les livres** all the books; **toutes les nuits** every night; **toutes les fois** every time; **toutes les trois/deux semaines** every third/other ou second week, every three/two weeks; **tous les deux** both ou each of us (ou them ou you); **toutes les trois** all three of us (ou them ou you)

3 (sans article): **à tout âge** at any age; **pour toute nourriture, il avait ...** his only food was ...

▷ pron everything, all; **il a tout fait** he's done everything; **je les vois tous** I can see them all ou all of them; **nous y sommes tous allés** all of us went, we all went; **c'est tout** that's all; **en tout** in all; **tout ce qu'il sait** all he knows

▷ nm whole; **le tout** all of it (ou them); **le tout est de ...**

the main thing is to ...; **pas du tout** not at all
▷ adv **1** (très, complètement) very; **tout près** very near; **le tout premier** the very first; **tout seul** all alone; **le livre tout entier** the whole book; **tout en haut** right at the top; **tout droit** straight ahead
2: **tout en** while; **tout en travaillant** while working, as he etc works ou worked
3: **tout d'abord** first of all; **tout à coup** suddenly; **tout à fait** absolutely; **tout à l'heure** a short while ago; (futur) in a short while, shortly; **à tout à l'heure!** see you later!; **tout de même** all the same; **tout de suite** immediately, straight away; **tout simplement** quite simply

:outefois [tutfwa] adv however

:outes [tut] adj, pron voir **tout**

:out-terrain [tuterɛ̃] adj: **vélo ~** mountain bike; **véhicule ~** four-wheel drive

:oux [tu] nf cough

:oxicomane [tɔksikɔman] nm/f drug addict

:oxique [tɔksik] adj toxic

:rac [trak] nm (au théâtre, en public) stage fright; (aux examens) nerves pl; **avoir le ~** (au théâtre, en public) to have stage fright; (aux examens) to be feeling nervous

:racasser [trakase] vt to worry, bother; **se ~** to worry

:race [tras] nf (empreintes) tracks pl; (marques, aussi fig) mark; (quantité infime, indice, vestige) trace; **traces de pas** footprints

:racer [trase] vt to draw; (piste) to open up

:ract [trakt] nm tract, pamphlet

:racteur [traktœr] nm tractor

:raction [traksjɔ̃] nf: **~ avant/arrière** front-wheel/rear-wheel drive

:radition [tradisjɔ̃] nf tradition; **traditionnel, le** adj traditional

:raducteur, -trice [tradyktœr, tris] nm/f translator

:raduction [tradyksjɔ̃] nf translation

:raduire [traduir] vt to translate; (exprimer) to convey; **~ qn en justice** to bring sb before the courts; **pouvez-vous me ~ ceci?** can you translate this for me?

:rafic [trafik] nm traffic; **trafic d'armes** arms dealing; **trafiquant, e** nm/f trafficker; (d'armes) dealer; **trafiquer** (péj) vt (vin) to doctor; (moteur, document) to tamper with

:ragédie [traʒedi] nf tragedy; **tragique** adj tragic

:rahir [trair] vt to betray; **trahison** nf betrayal; (Jur) treason

:rain [trɛ̃] nm (Rail) train; (allure) pace; **être en ~ de faire qch** to be doing sth; **c'est bien le ~ pour ...?** is this the train for ...?; **train d'atterrissage** undercarriage; **train de vie** lifestyle; **train électrique** (jouet) (electric) train set

:raîne [trɛn] nf (de robe) train; **être à la ~** to lag behind

:raîneau, x [trɛno] nm sleigh, sledge

:raîner [trene] vt (remorque) to pull; (enfant, chien) to drag ou trail along ▷ vi (robe, manteau) to trail; (être en désordre) to lie around; (aller lentement) to dawdle (along); (vagabonder, agir lentement) to hang about; (durer) to drag on; **se ~** vi: **se ~ par terre** to crawl (on the ground); **~ les pieds** to drag one's feet

:rain-train [trɛ̃trɛ̃] nm humdrum routine

:raire [trer] vt to milk

:rait [trɛ] nm (ligne) line; (de dessin) stroke; (caractéristique) feature, trait; **traits** nmpl (du visage) features; **d'un ~** (boire) in one gulp; **de ~** (animal) draught; **avoir ~ à** to concern; **trait d'union** hyphen

traitant, e [trɛtɑ̃, ɑ̃t] adj (shampooing) medicated; **votre médecin ~** your usual ou family doctor

traite [trɛt] nf (Comm) draft; (Agr) milking; **d'une ~** without stopping

traité [trete] nm treaty

traitement [trɛtmɑ̃] nm treatment; (salaire) salary; **traitement de données** data processing; **traitement de texte** word processing; (logiciel) word processing package

traiter [trete] vt to treat; (qualifier): **~ qn d'idiot** to call sb a fool ▷ vi to deal; **~ de** to deal with

traiteur [trɛtœr] nm caterer

traître, -esse [trɛtr, trɛtrɛs] adj (dangereux) treacherous ▷ nm traitor

trajectoire [traʒɛktwar] nf path

trajet [traʒɛ] nm (parcours, voyage) journey; (itinéraire) route; (distance à parcourir) distance; **il y a une heure de ~** the journey takes one hour

trampoline [trɑ̃pɔlin] nm trampoline

tramway [tramwɛ] nm tram(way); (voiture) tram(car) (BRIT), streetcar (US)

tranchant, e [trɑ̃ʃɑ̃, ɑ̃t] adj sharp; (fig) peremptory ▷ nm (d'un couteau) cutting edge; (de la main) edge; **à double ~** double-edged

tranche [trɑ̃ʃ] nf (morceau) slice; (arête) edge; **~ d'âge/de salaires** age/wage bracket

tranché, e [trɑ̃ʃe] adj (couleurs) distinct; (opinions) clear-cut

trancher [trɑ̃ʃe] vt to cut, sever ▷ vi to take a decision; **~ avec** to contrast sharply with

tranquille [trɑ̃kil] adj quiet; (rassuré) easy in one's mind, with one's mind at rest; **se tenir ~** (enfant) to be quiet; **laisse-moi/laisse-ça ~** leave me/it alone; **avoir la conscience ~** to have a clear conscience; **tranquillisant** nm tranquillizer; **tranquillité** nf peace (and quiet); (d'esprit) peace of mind

transférer [trɑ̃sfere] vt to transfer; **transfert** nm transfer

transformation [trɑ̃sfɔrmasjɔ̃] nf change, alteration; (radicale) transformation; (Rugby) conversion; **transformations** nfpl (travaux) alterations

transformer [trɑ̃sfɔrme] vt to change; (radicalement) to transform; (vêtement) to alter; (matière première, appartement, Rugby) to convert; **(se) ~ en** to turn into

transfusion [trɑ̃sfyzjɔ̃] nf: **~ sanguine** blood transfusion

transgénique [trɑ̃sʒenik] adj transgenic

transgresser [trɑ̃sgrese] vt to contravene

transi, e [trɑ̃zi] adj numb (with cold), chilled to the bone

transiger [trɑ̃ziʒe] vi to compromise

transit [trɑ̃zit] nm transit; **transiter** vi to pass in transit

transition [trɑ̃zisjɔ̃] nf transition; **transitoire** adj transitional

transmettre [trɑ̃smɛtr] vt (passer): **~ qch à qn** to pass sth on to sb; (Tech, Tél, Méd) to transmit; (TV, Radio: retransmettre) to broadcast; **transmission** nf transmission

transparent, e [trɑ̃sparɑ̃, ɑ̃t] adj transparent

transpercer [trɑ̃spɛrse] vt (froid, pluie) to go through, pierce; (balle) to go through

transpiration [trɑ̃spirasjɔ̃] nf perspiration

transpirer [trɑ̃spire] vi to perspire

transplanter [tʀɑ̃splɑ̃te] vt (Méd, Bot) to transplant
transport [tʀɑ̃spɔʀ] nm transport; **transports en commun** public transport sg; **transporter** vt to carry, move; (Comm) to transport, convey; **transporteur** nm haulage contractor (BRIT), trucker (US)
transvaser [tʀɑ̃svɑze] vt to decant
transversal, e, -aux [tʀɑ̃svɛʀsal, o] adj (rue) which runs across; **coupe ~e** cross section
trapèze [tʀapɛz] nm (au cirque) trapeze
trappe [tʀap] nf trap door
trapu, e [tʀapy] adj squat, stocky
traquenard [tʀaknaʀ] nm trap
traquer [tʀake] vt to track down; (harceler) to hound
traumatiser [tʀomatize] vt to traumatize
travail, -aux [tʀavaj] nm (gén) work; (tâche, métier) work no pl, job; (Écon, Méd) labour; **être sans ~** (employé) to be unemployed; voir aussi **travaux**; **travail (au) noir** moonlighting
travailler [tʀavaje] vi to work; (bois) to warp ▷ vt (bois, métal) to work; (objet d'art, discipline) to work on; **cela le travaille** it is on his mind; **travailleur, -euse** adj hard-working ▷ nm/f worker; **travailleur social** social worker; **travailliste** adj ≈ Labour cpd
travaux [tʀavo] nmpl (de réparation, agricoles etc) work sg; (sur route) roadworks pl; (de construction) building (work); **travaux des champs** farmwork sg; **travaux dirigés** (Scol) tutorial sg; **travaux forcés** hard labour no pl; **travaux manuels** (Scol) handicrafts; **travaux ménagers** housework no pl; **travaux pratiques** (Scol) practical work; (en laboratoire) lab work
travers [tʀavɛʀ] nm fault, failing; **en ~ (de)** across; **au ~ (de)/à ~** through; **de ~** (nez, bouche) crooked; (chapeau) askew; **comprendre de ~** to misunderstand; **regarder de ~** (fig) to look askance at
traverse [tʀavɛʀs] nf (de voie ferrée) sleeper; **chemin de ~** shortcut
traversée [tʀavɛʀse] nf crossing; **combien de temps dure la ~?** how long does the crossing take?
traverser [tʀavɛʀse] vt (gén) to cross; (ville, tunnel, aussi: percer, fig) to go through; (suj: ligne, trait) to run across
traversin [tʀavɛʀsɛ̃] nm bolster
travesti [tʀavɛsti] nm transvestite
trébucher [tʀebyʃe] vi: **~ (sur)** to stumble (over), trip (against)
trèfle [tʀefl] nm (Bot) clover; (Cartes: couleur) clubs pl; (: carte) club; **~ à quatre feuilles** four-leaf clover
treize [tʀɛz] num thirteen; **treizième** num thirteenth
tréma [tʀema] nm diaeresis
tremblement [tʀɑ̃bləmɑ̃] nm: **tremblement de terre** earthquake
trembler [tʀɑ̃ble] vi to tremble, shake; **~ de (froid, fièvre)** to shiver ou tremble with; (peur) to shake ou tremble with; **~ pour qn** to fear for sb
trémousser [tʀemuse]: **se ~** vi to jig about, wriggle about
trempé, e [tʀɑ̃pe] adj soaking (wet), drenched; (Tech) tempered
tremper [tʀɑ̃pe] vt to soak, drench; (aussi: **faire ~, mettre à ~**) to soak; (plonger): **~ qch dans** to dip sth in(to) ▷ vi to soak; (fig): **~ dans** to be involved ou have a hand in; **se ~** vi to have a quick dip
tremplin [tʀɑ̃plɛ̃] nm springboard; (Ski) ski-jump
trentaine [tʀɑ̃tɛn] nf: **une ~ (de)** thirty or so, about thirty; **avoir la ~** (âge) to be around thirty

trente [tʀɑ̃t] num thirty; **être sur son ~ et un** to be wearing one's Sunday best; **trentième** num thirtieth
trépidant, e [tʀepidɑ̃, ɑ̃t] adj (fig: rythme) pulsating; (: vie) hectic
trépigner [tʀepiɲe] vi to stamp (one's feet)
très [tʀɛ] adv very; much +pp, highly +pp
trésor [tʀezɔʀ] nm treasure; **Trésor (public)** public revenue; **trésorerie** nf (gestion) accounts pl; (bureaux) accounts department; **difficultés de trésorerie** cash problems, shortage of cash ou funds; **trésorier, -ière** nm/f treasurer
tressaillir [tʀesajiʀ] vi to shiver, shudder
tressauter [tʀesote] vi to start, jump
tresse [tʀɛs] nf braid, plait; **tresser** vt (cheveux) to braid, plait; (fil, jonc) to plait; (corbeille) to weave; (corde) to twis
tréteau, x [tʀeto] nm trestle
treuil [tʀœj] nm winch
trêve [tʀɛv] nf (Mil, Pol) truce; (fig) respite; **~ de ...** enough of this ...
tri [tʀi] nm: **faire le ~ (de)** to sort out; **le (bureau de) ~** (Postes) the sorting office
triangle [tʀijɑ̃gl] nm triangle; **triangulaire** adj triangular
tribord [tʀibɔʀ] nm: **à ~** to starboard, on the starboard side
tribu [tʀiby] nf tribe
tribunal, -aux [tʀibynal, o] nm (Jur) court; (Mil) tribunal
tribune [tʀibyn] nf (estrade) platform, rostrum; (débat) forum; (d'église, de tribunal) gallery; (de stade) stand
tribut [tʀiby] nm tribute
tributaire [tʀibytɛʀ] adj: **être ~ de** to be dependent on
tricher [tʀiʃe] vi to cheat; **tricheur, -euse** nm/f cheat(er)
tricolore [tʀikɔlɔʀ] adj three-coloured; (français) red, white and blue
tricot [tʀiko] nm (technique, ouvrage) knitting no pl; (vêtement) jersey, sweater; **~ de peau** vest; **tricoter** vt to knit
tricycle [tʀisikl] nm tricycle
trier [tʀije] vt to sort out; (Postes, fruits) to sort
trimestre [tʀimɛstʀ] nm (Scol) term; (Comm) quarter; **trimestriel, le** adj quarterly; (Scol) end-of-term
trinquer [tʀɛ̃ke] vi to clink glasses
triomphe [tʀijɔ̃f] nm triumph; **triompher** vi to triumph, win; **triompher de** to triumph over, overcom
tripes [tʀip] nfpl (Culin) tripe sg
triple [tʀipl] adj triple ▷ nm: **le ~ (de)** (comparaison) three times as much (as); **en ~ exemplaire** in triplicate; **tripler** vi, vt to triple, treble
triplés, -ées [tʀiple] nm/fpl triplets
tripoter [tʀipote] vt to fiddle with
triste [tʀist] adj sad; (couleur, temps, journée) dreary, (péj) **~ personnage/affaire** sorry individual/affair; **tristess** nf sadness
trivial, e, -aux [tʀivjal, jo] adj coarse, crude; (commun) mundane
troc [tʀɔk] nm barter
trognon [tʀɔɲɔ̃] nm (de fruit) core; (de légume) stalk
trois [tʀwa] num three; **troisième** num third ▷ nf (Scol) year 10 (BRIT), ninth grade (US); **le troisième âge** (périod de vie) one's retirement years; (personnes âgées) senior citizens pl
trombe [tʀɔ̃b] nf: **des ~s d'eau** a downpour; **en ~** like

a whirlwind

rombone [tʀɔ̃bɔn] nm (Mus) trombone; (de bureau) paper clip

rompe [tʀɔp] nf (d'éléphant) trunk; (Mus) trumpet, horn

romper [tʀɔ̃pe] vt to deceive; (vigilance, poursuivants) to elude; **se ~** vi to make a mistake, be mistaken; **se ~ de voiture/jour** to take the wrong car/get the day wrong; **se ~ de 3 cm/20 euros** to be out by 3 cm/20 euros; **je me suis trompé de route** I took the wrong road

rompette [tʀɔ̃pɛt] nf trumpet; **en ~** (nez) turned-up

rompeur, -euse [tʀɔ̃pœʀ, øz] adj deceptive

ronc [tʀɔ̃] nm (Bot, Anat) trunk; (d'église) collection box

rançon [tʀɔ̃sɔ̃] nm section; **tronçonner** vt to saw up; **tronçonneuse** nf chainsaw

rône [tʀon] nm throne

rop [tʀo] adv (+vb) too much; (+adjectif, adverbe) too; **~ (nombreux)** too many; **~ peu (nombreux)** too few; **~ (souvent)** too often; **~ (longtemps)** (for) too long; **~ de** (nombre) too many; (quantité) too much; **de ~, en ~: des livres en ~** a few books too many; **du lait en ~** too much milk; **3 livres/3 euros de ~** 3 books too many/3 euros too much; **ça coûte ~ cher** it's too expensive

ropical, e, -aux [tʀɔpikal, o] adj tropical

ropique [tʀɔpik] nm tropic

rop-plein [tʀoplɛ̃] nm (tuyau) overflow ou outlet (pipe); (liquide) overflow

roquer [tʀɔke] vt: **~ qch contre** to barter ou trade sth for; (fig) to swap sth for

rot [tʀo] nm trot; **trotter** vi to trot

rottinette [tʀɔtinɛt] nf (child's) scooter

rottoir [tʀɔtwaʀ] nm pavement (BRIT), sidewalk (US); **faire le ~** (péj) to walk the streets; **trottoir roulant** moving walkway, travellator

rou [tʀu] nm hole; (fig) gap; (Comm) deficit; **trou d'air** air pocket; **trou de mémoire** blank, lapse of memory

roublant, e [tʀublɑ̃, ɑ̃t] adj disturbing

rouble [tʀubl] adj (liquide) cloudy; (image, photo) blurred; (affaire) shady, murky ▷ adv: **voir ~** to have blurred vision ▷ nm agitation; **troubles** nmpl (Pol) disturbances, troubles, unrest sg; (Méd) trouble sg, disorders; **trouble-fête** nm spoilsport

roubler [tʀuble] vt to disturb; (liquide) to make cloudy; (intriguer) to bother; **se ~** vi (personne) to become flustered ou confused

rouer [tʀue] vt to make a hole (ou holes) in

rouille [tʀuj] (fam) nf: **avoir la ~** to be scared to death

roupe [tʀup] nf troop; **troupe (de théâtre)** (theatrical) company

roupeau, x [tʀupo] nm (de moutons) flock; (de vaches) herd

rousse [tʀus] nf case, kit; (d'écolier) pencil case; **aux ~s de** (fig) on the heels ou tail of; **trousse à outils** toolkit; **trousse de toilette** toilet bag

rousseau, x [tʀuso] nm (de mariée) trousseau; **trousseau de clefs** bunch of keys

rouvaille [tʀuvaj] nf find

rouver [tʀuve] vt to find; (rendre visite): **aller/venir ~ qn** to go/come and see sb; **se ~** vi (être) to be: **je trouve que** I find ou think that; **~ à boire/critiquer** to find something to drink/criticize; **se ~ mal** to pass out

ruand [tʀyɑ̃] nm gangster; **truander** vt: **se faire truander** to be swindled

ruc [tʀyk] nm (astuce) way, trick; (de cinéma, prestidigitateur) trick, effect; (chose) thing, thingumajig;

avoir le ~ to have the knack; **c'est pas mon ~** (fam) it's not really my thing

truffe [tʀyf] nf truffle; (nez) nose

truffé, e [tʀyfe] adj (Culin) garnished with truffles; **~ de** (fig: citations) peppered with; (: fautes) riddled with; (: pièges) bristling with

truie [tʀɥi] nf sow

truite [tʀɥit] nf trout inv

truquage [tʀykaʒ] nm special effects pl

truquer [tʀyke] vt (élections, serrure, dés) to fix

TSVP sigle (= tournez svp) PTO

TTC sigle (= toutes taxes comprises) inclusive of tax

tu' [ty] pron you; **dire tu à qn** to use the "tu" form to sb

tu², e [ty] pp de **taire**

tuba [tyba] nm (Mus) tuba; (Sport) snorkel

tube [tyb] nm tube; (chanson) hit

tuberculose [tybɛʀkyloz] nf tuberculosis

tuer [tɥe] vt to kill; **se ~** vi to be killed; (suicide) to kill o.s.; **se ~ au travail** (fig) to work o.s. to death; **tuerie** nf slaughter no pl

tue-tête [tytɛt]: **à ~** adv at the top of one's voice

tueur [tɥœʀ] nm killer; **tueur à gages** hired killer

tuile [tɥil] nf tile; (fam) spot of bad luck, blow

tulipe [tylip] nf tulip

tuméfié, e [tymefje] adj puffed-up, swollen

tumeur [tymœʀ] nf growth, tumour

tumulte [tymylt] nm commotion; **tumultueux, -euse** adj stormy, turbulent

tunique [tynik] nf tunic

Tunis [tynis] n Tunis

Tunisie [tynizi] nf: **la ~** Tunisia; **tunisien, ne** adj Tunisian ▷ nm/f: **Tunisien, ne** Tunisian

tunnel [tynɛl] nm tunnel; **le ~ sous la Manche** the Channel Tunnel

turbulent, e [tyʀbylɑ̃, ɑ̃t] adj boisterous, unruly

turc, turque [tyʀk] adj Turkish ▷ nm/f: **T~, Turque** Turk/Turkish woman ▷ nm (Ling) Turkish

turf [tyʀf] nm racing; **turfiste** nm/f racegoer

Turquie [tyʀki] nf: **la ~** Turkey

turquoise [tyʀkwaz] nf turquoise ▷ adj inv turquoise

tutelle [tytɛl] nf (Jur) guardianship; (Pol) trusteeship; **sous la ~ de** (fig) under the supervision of

tuteur [tytœʀ] nm (Jur) guardian; (de plante) stake, support

tutoyer [tytwaje] vt: **~ qn** to address sb as "tu"

tuyau, x [tɥijo] nm pipe; (flexible) tube; (fam) tip; **tuyau d'arrosage** hosepipe; **tuyau d'échappement** exhaust pipe; **tuyauterie** nf piping no pl

TVA sigle f (= taxe à la valeur ajoutée) VAT

tympan [tɛ̃pɑ̃] nm (Anat) eardrum

type [tip] nm type; (fam) chap, guy ▷ adj typical, classic

typé, e [tipe] adj ethnic

typique [tipik] adj typical

tyran [tiʀɑ̃] nm tyrant; **tyrannique** adj tyrannical

tzigane [dzigan] adj gipsy, tzigane

ulcère [ylsɛʀ] nm ulcer
ultérieur, e [ylteʀjœʀ] adj later, subsequent; **remis à une date ~e** postponed to a later date; **ultérieurement** adv later, subsequently
ultime [yltim] adj final

 MOT-CLÉ

un, une [œ̃, yn] art indéf a; (devant voyelle) an; **un garçon/vieillard** a boy/an old man; **une fille** a girl
▷ pron one; **l'un des meilleurs** one of the best; **l'un ..., l'autre** (the) one ..., the other; **les uns ..., les autres** some ..., others; **l'un et l'autre** both (of them); **l'un ou l'autre** either (of them); **l'un l'autre** each other; **les uns les autres** one another; **pas un seul** not a single one; **un par un** one by one
▷ num one; **une pomme seulement** one apple only, just one apple
▷ nf: **la une** (Presse) the front page

unanime [ynanim] adj unanimous; **unanimité** nf: **à l'unanimité** unanimously
uni, e [yni] adj (ton, tissu) plain; (surface) smooth, even; (famille) close(-knit); (pays) united
unifier [ynifje] vt to unite, unify
uniforme [ynifɔʀm] adj uniform; (surface, ton) even ▷ nm uniform; **uniformiser** vt (systèmes) to standardize
union [ynjɔ̃] nf union; **union de consommateurs** consumers' association; **union libre: vivre en union libre** (en concubinage) to cohabit; **Union européenne** European Union; **Union soviétique** Soviet Union
unique [ynik] adj (seul) only; (exceptionnel) unique; (le même): **un prix/système ~** a single price/system; **fils/fille ~** only son/daughter, only child; **sens ~** one-way street; **uniquement** adv only, solely; (juste) only, merely
unir [yniʀ] vt (nations) to unite; (en mariage) to unite, join together; **s'~** vi to unite; (en mariage) to be joined together
unitaire [yniteʀ] adj: **prix ~** unit price
unité [ynite] nf unit; (harmonie, cohésion) unity

univers [yniveʀ] nm universe; **universel, le** adj universal
universitaire [yniveʀsiteʀ] adj university cpd; (diplôme, études) academic, university cpd ▷ nm/f academic
université [yniveʀsite] nf university
urbain, e [yʀbɛ̃, ɛn] adj urban, city cpd, town cpd; **urbanisme** nm town planning
urgence [yʀʒɑ̃s] nf urgency; (Méd etc) emergency; **d'~** adj emergency cpd ▷ adv as a matter of urgency; **(service des) ~s** casualty
urgent, e [yʀʒɑ̃, ɑ̃t] adj urgent
urine [yʀin] nf urine; **urinoir** nm (public) urinal
urne [yʀn] nf (électorale) ballot box; (vase) urn
urticaire [yʀtikɛʀ] nf nettle rash
us [ys] nmpl: **us et coutumes** (habits and) customs
usage [yzaʒ] nm (emploi, utilisation) use; (coutume) custom; **à l'~** with use; **à l'~ de** (pour) for (use of); **en ~** in use; **hors d'~** out of service; **à ~ interne** (Méd) to be taken (internally); **à ~ externe** (Méd) for external use only; **usagé, e** adj (usé) worn; **usager, -ère** nm/f user
usé, e [yze] adj worn; (banal: argument etc) hackneyed
user [yze] vt (outil) to wear down; (vêtement) to wear out (matière) to wear away; (consommer: charbon etc) to use; **s'~** vi (tissu, vêtement) to wear out; **~ de** (moyen, procédé) to use, employ; (droit) to exercise
usine [yzin] nf factory
usité, e [yzite] adj common
ustensile [ystɑ̃sil] nm implement; **ustensile de cuisine** kitchen utensil
usuel, le [yzɥɛl] adj everyday, common
usure [yzyʀ] nf wear
utérus [yteʀys] nm uterus, womb
utile [ytil] adj useful
utilisation [ytilizasjɔ̃] nf use
utiliser [ytilize] vt to use
utilitaire [ytilitɛʀ] adj utilitarian
utilité [ytilite] nf usefulness no pl; **de peu d'~** of little use ou help
utopie [ytɔpi] nf utopia

worthwhile

valet [valε] nm manservant; (Cartes) jack

valeur [valœʀ] nf (gén) value; (mérite) worth, merit; (Comm: titre) security; **valeurs** nfpl (morales) values; **mettre en ~** (détail) to highlight; (objet décoratif) to show off to advantage; **avoir de la ~** to be valuable; **sans ~** worthless; **prendre de la ~** to go up ou gain in value

valide [valid] adj (en bonne santé) fit; (valable) valid; **valider** vt to validate

valise [valiz] nf (suit)case; **faire ses ~s** to pack one's bags

vallée [vale] nf valley

vallon [valɔ̃] nm small valley

valoir [valwaʀ] vi (être valable) to hold, apply ▷ vt (prix, valeur, effort) to be worth; (causer): **~ qch à qn** to earn sb sth; **se ~** vi to be of equal merit; (péj) to be two of a kind; **faire ~** (droits, prérogatives) to assert; **se faire ~** to make the most of o.s.; **à ~ sur** to be deducted from; **vaille que vaille** somehow or other; **cela ne me dit rien qui vaille** I don't like the look of it at all; **ce climat ne me vaut rien** this climate doesn't suit me; **le coup** ou **la peine** to be worth the trouble ou worth it; **~ mieux: il vaut mieux se taire** it's better to say nothing; **ça ne vaut rien** it's worthless; **que vaut ce candidat?** how good is this applicant?

valse [vals] nf waltz

vandalisme [vɑ̃dalism] nm vandalism

vanille [vanij] nf vanilla

vanité [vanite] nf vanity; **vaniteux, -euse** adj vain, conceited

vanne [van] nf gate; (fig) joke

vannerie [vanʀi] nf basketwork

vantard, e [vɑ̃taʀ, aʀd] adj boastful

vanter [vɑ̃te] vt to speak highly of, praise; **se ~** vi to boast, brag; **se ~ de** to pride o.s. on; (péj) to boast of

vapeur [vapœʀ] nf steam; (émanation) vapour, fumes pl; **vapeurs** nfpl (bouffées) vapours; **à ~** steam-powered, steam cpd; **cuit à la ~** steamed; **vaporeux, -euse** adj (flou) hazy, misty; (léger) filmy; **vaporisateur** nm spray; **vaporiser** vt (parfum etc) to spray

varappe [vaʀap] nf rock climbing

vareuse [vaʀøz] nf (blouson) pea jacket; (d'uniforme) tunic

variable [vaʀjabl] adj variable; (temps, humeur) changeable; (divers: résultats) varied, various

varice [vaʀis] nf varicose vein

varicelle [vaʀisεl] nf chickenpox

varié, e [vaʀje] adj varied; (divers) various; **hors d'œuvre ~s** selection of hors d'œuvres

varier [vaʀje] vi to vary; (temps, humeur) to change ▷ vt to vary; **variété** nf variety; **variétés** nfpl: **spectacle/ émission de variétés** variety show

variole [vaʀjɔl] nf smallpox

Varsovie [vaʀsɔvi] n Warsaw

vas [va] vb voir **aller**; **~-y!** [vazi] go on!

vase [vɑz] nm vase ▷ nf silt, mud; **vaseux, -euse** adj silty, muddy; (fig: confus) woolly, hazy; (: fatigué) woozy

vasistas [vazistas] nm fanlight

vaste [vast] adj vast, immense

vautour [votuʀ] nm vulture

vautrer [votʀe] vb: **se ~ dans/sur** to wallow in/sprawl on

va-vite [vavit]: **à la ~** adv in a rush ou hurry

VDQS sigle (= vin délimité de qualité supérieure) label

V

va [va] vb voir **aller**

vacance [vakɑ̃s] nf (Admin) vacancy; **vacances** nfpl holiday(s pl (BRIT)), vacation sg (US); **les grandes ~s** the summer holidays; **prendre des/ses ~s** to take a holiday/one's holiday(s); **aller en ~s** to go on holiday; **je suis ici en ~s** I'm here on holiday; **vacancier, -ière** nm/f holiday-maker

vacant, e [vakɑ̃, ɑ̃t] adj vacant

vacarme [vakaʀm] nm (bruit) racket

vaccin [vaksɛ̃] nm vaccine; (opération) vaccination; **vaccination** nf vaccination; **vacciner** vt to vaccinate; **être vacciné contre qch** (fam) to be cured of sth

vache [vaʃ] nf (Zool) cow; (cuir) cowhide ▷ adj (fam) rotten, mean; **vachement** (fam) adv (très) really; (pleuvoir, travailler) a hell of a lot; **vacherie** nf (action) dirty trick; (remarque) nasty remark

vaciller [vasije] vi to sway, wobble; (bougie, lumière) to flicker; (fig) to be failing, falter

va-et-vient [vaevjɛ̃] nm inv (de personnes, véhicules) comings and goings pl, to-ings and fro-ings pl

vagabond [vagabɔ̃] nm (rôdeur) tramp, vagrant; (voyageur) wanderer; **vagabonder** vi to roam, wander

vagin [vaʒɛ̃] nm vagina

vague [vag] nf wave ▷ adj vague; (regard) faraway; (manteau, robe) loose(-fitting); (quelconque): **un ~ bureau/cousin** some office/cousin or other; **vague de fond** ground swell; **vague de froid** cold spell

vaillant, e [vajɑ̃, ɑ̃t] adj (courageux) gallant; (robuste) hale and hearty

vain, e [vɛ̃, vεn] adj vain; **en ~** in vain

vaincre [vɛ̃kʀ] vt to defeat; (fig) to conquer, overcome; **vaincu, e** nm/f defeated party; **vainqueur** nm victor; (Sport) winner

vaisseau, x [veso] nm (Anat) vessel; (Navig) ship, vessel; **vaisseau spatial** spaceship

vaisselier [vesəlje] nm dresser

vaisselle [vesεl] nf (service) crockery; (plats etc à laver) (dirty) dishes pl; **faire la ~** to do the washing-up (BRIT) ou the dishes

valable [valabl] adj valid; (acceptable) decent,

guaranteeing the quality of wine

veau, x [vo] nm (Zool) calf; (Culin) veal; (peau) calfskin

vécu, e [veky] pp de **vivre**

vedette [vədɛt] nf (artiste etc) star; (canot) motor boat; (police) launch

végétal, e, -aux [veʒetal, o] adj vegetable ▷ nm vegetable, plant; **végétalien, ne** adj, nm/f vegan

végétarien, ne [veʒetarjɛ̃, jɛn] adj, nm/f vegetarian; **avez-vous des plats ~s?** do you have any vegetarian dishes?

végétation [veʒetasjɔ̃] nf vegetation; **végétations** nfpl (Méd) adenoids

véhicule [veikyl] nm vehicle; **véhicule utilitaire** commercial vehicle

veille [vɛj] nf (état) wakefulness; (jour): **la ~ (de)** the day before; **la ~ au soir** the previous evening; **à la ~ de** on the eve of; **la ~ de Noël** Christmas Eve; **la ~ du jour de l'An** New Year's Eve

veillée [veje] nf (soirée) evening; (réunion) evening gathering; **veillée (funèbre)** wake

veiller [veje] vi to stay up ▷ vt (malade, mort) to watch over, sit up with; **~ à** to attend to, see to; **~ à ce que** to make sure that; **~ sur** to watch over; **veilleur** nm: **veilleur de nuit** night watchman; **veilleuse** nf (lampe) night light; (Auto) sidelight; (flamme) pilot light

veinard, e [vɛnaʀ, aʀd] nm/f lucky devil

veine [vɛn] nf (Anat, du bois etc) vein; (filon) vein, seam; (fam: chance): **avoir de la ~** to be lucky

véliplanchiste [veliplɑ̃ʃist] nm/f windsurfer

vélo [velo] nm bike, cycle; **faire du ~** to go cycling; **vélomoteur** nm moped

velours [v(ə)luʀ] nm velvet; **velours côtelé** corduroy; **velouté, e** adj velvety ▷ nm: **velouté de tomates** cream of tomato soup

velu, e [vəly] adj hairy

vendange [vɑ̃dɑ̃ʒ] nf (aussi: **~s**) grape harvest; **vendanger** vi to harvest the grapes

vendeur, -euse [vɑ̃dœʀ, øz] nm/f shop assistant ▷ nm (Jur) vendor, seller

vendre [vɑ̃dʀ] vt to sell; **~ qch à qn** to sell sb sth; **"à ~"** "for sale"

vendredi [vɑ̃dʀədi] nm Friday; **vendredi saint** Good Friday

vénéneux, -euse [venenø, øz] adj poisonous

vénérien, ne [veneʀjɛ̃, jɛn] adj venereal

vengeance [vɑ̃ʒɑ̃s] nf vengeance no pl, revenge no pl

venger [vɑ̃ʒe] vt to avenge; **se ~** vi to avenge o.s.; **se ~ de qch** to avenge o.s. for sth, take one's revenge for sth; **se ~ de qn** to take revenge on sb; **se ~ sur** to take revenge on

venimeux, -euse [vənimø, øz] adj poisonous, venomous; (fig: haineux) venomous, vicious

venin [vənɛ̃] nm venom, poison

venir [v(ə)niʀ] vi to come; **~ de** to come from; **~ de faire: je viens d'y aller/de le voir** I've just been there/seen him; **s'il vient à pleuvoir** if it should rain; **j'en viens à croire que** I have come to believe that; **où veux-tu en ~?** what are you getting at?; **faire ~** (docteur, plombier) to call (out)

vent [vɑ̃] nm wind; **il y a du ~** it's windy; **c'est du ~** it's all hot air; **dans le ~** (fam) trendy

vente [vɑ̃t] nf sale; **la ~** (activité) selling; (secteur) sales pl; **mettre en ~** (produit) to put on sale; (maison, objet personnel) to put up for sale; **vente aux enchères**

auction sale; **vente de charité** jumble sale

venteux, -euse [vɑ̃tø, øz] adj windy

ventilateur [vɑ̃tilatœʀ] nm fan

ventiler [vɑ̃tile] vt to ventilate

ventouse [vɑ̃tuz] nf (de caoutchouc) suction pad

ventre [vɑ̃tʀ] nm (Anat) stomach; (légèrement péj) belly; (utérus) womb; **avoir mal au ~** to have stomach ache (BRIT) ou a stomach ache (US)

venu, e [v(ə)ny] pp de **venir** ▷ adj: **bien ~** timely; **mal ~** out of place; **être mal ~ à** ou **de faire** to have no grounds for doing, be in no position to do

ver [vɛʀ] nm worm; (des fruits etc) maggot; (du bois) woodworm no pl; voir aussi **vers**; **ver à soie** silkworm; **ver de terre** earthworm; **ver luisant** glow-worm; **ver solitaire** tapeworm

verbe [vɛʀb] nm verb

verdâtre [vɛʀdɑtʀ] adj greenish

verdict [vɛʀdik(t)] nm verdict

verdir [vɛʀdiʀ] vi, vt to turn green; **verdure** nf greenery

véreux, -euse [veʀø, øz] adj worm-eaten; (malhonnête) shady, corrupt

verge [vɛʀʒ] nf (Anat) penis

verger [vɛʀʒe] nm orchard

verglacé, e [vɛʀglase] adj icy, iced-over

verglas [vɛʀgla] nm (black) ice

véridique [veʀidik] adj truthful

vérification [veʀifikasjɔ̃] nf (action) checking no pl; (contrôle) check

vérifier [veʀifje] vt to check; (corroborer) to confirm, bear out

véritable [veʀitabl] adj real; (ami, amour) true; **un ~ désastre** an absolute disaster

vérité [veʀite] nf truth; **en ~** really, actually

verlan [vɛʀlɑ̃] nm (fam) (back) slang

vermeil, le [vɛʀmɛj] adj ruby red

vermine [vɛʀmin] nf vermin pl

vermoulu, e [vɛʀmuly] adj worm-eaten

verni, e [vɛʀni] adj (fam) lucky; **cuir ~** patent leather

vernir [vɛʀniʀ] vt (bois, tableau, ongles) to varnish; (poterie) to glaze; **vernis** nm (enduit) varnish; glaze; (fig) veneer; **vernis à ongles** nail polish ou varnish; **vernissage** nm (d'une exposition) preview

vérole [veʀɔl] nf (variole) smallpox

verre [vɛʀ] nm glass; (de lunettes) lens sg; **boire** ou **prendre un ~** to have a drink; **verres de contact** contact lenses; **verrière** nf (paroi vitrée) glass wall; (toit vitré) glass roof

verrou [veʀu] nm (targette) bolt; **mettre qn sous les ~s** to put sb behind bars; **verrouillage** nm locking; **verrouillage centralisé** central locking; **verrouiller** vt (porte) to bolt; (ordinateur) to lock

verrue [veʀy] nf wart

vers [vɛʀ] nm line ▷ nmpl (poésie) verse sg ▷ prép (en direction de) toward(s); (près de) around (about); (temporel) about, around

versant [vɛʀsɑ̃] nm slopes pl, side

versatile [vɛʀsatil] adj fickle, changeable

verse [vɛʀs]: **à ~** adv: **il pleut à ~** it's pouring (with rain)

Verseau [vɛʀso] nm: **le ~** Aquarius

versement [vɛʀsəmɑ̃] nm payment; **en 3 ~s** in 3 instalments

verser [vɛʀse] vt (liquide, grains) to pour; (larmes, sang) to shed; (argent) to pay; **~ qch sur un compte** to pay sth into an account

version [vɛʀsjɔ̃] nf version; (Scol) translation (into the mother tongue); **film en ~ originale** film in the original language

verso [vɛʀso] nm back; **voir au ~** see over(leaf)

vert, e [vɛʀ, vɛʀt] adj green; (vin) young; (vigoureux) sprightly ▷ nm green; **les V~s** (Pol) the Greens

vertèbre [vɛʀtɛbʀ] nf vertebra

vertement [vɛʀtəmɑ̃] adv (réprimander) sharply

vertical, e, -aux [vɛʀtikal, o] adj vertical; **verticale** nf vertical; **à la verticale** vertically; **verticalement** adv vertically

vertige [vɛʀtiʒ] nm (peur du vide) vertigo; (étourdissement) dizzy spell; (fig) fever; **vertigineux, -euse** adj breathtaking

vertu [vɛʀty] nf virtue; **en ~ de** in accordance with; **vertueux, -euse** adj virtuous

verve [vɛʀv] nf witty eloquence; **être en ~** to be in brilliant form

verveine [vɛʀvɛn] nf (Bot) verbena, vervain; (infusion) verbena tea

vésicule [vezikyl] nf vesicle; **vésicule biliaire** gall-bladder

vessie [vesi] nf bladder

veste [vɛst] nf jacket; **veste droite/croisée** single-/double-breasted jacket

vestiaire [vɛstjɛʀ] nm (au théâtre etc) cloakroom; (de stade etc) changing-room (BRIT), locker-room (US)

vestibule [vɛstibyl] nm hall

vestige [vɛstiʒ] nm relic; (fig) vestige; **vestiges** nmpl (de ville) remains

vestimentaire [vɛstimɑ̃tɛʀ] adj (détail) of dress; (élégance) sartorial; **dépenses ~s** clothing expenditure

veston [vɛstɔ̃] nm jacket

vêtement [vɛtmɑ̃] nm garment, item of clothing; **vêtements** nmpl clothes

vétérinaire [veteʀinɛʀ] nm/f vet, veterinary surgeon

vêtir [vetiʀ] vt to clothe, dress

vêtu, e [vety] pp de **vêtir** ▷ adj: **~ de** dressed in, wearing

vétuste [vetyst] adj ancient, timeworn

veuf, veuve [vœf, vœv] adj widowed ▷ nm widower

veuve [vœv] nf widow

vexant, e [vɛksɑ̃, ɑ̃t] adj (contrariant) annoying; (blessant) hurtful

vexation [vɛksasjɔ̃] nf humiliation

vexer [vɛkse] vt: **~ qn** to hurt sb's feelings; **se ~** vi to be offended

viable [vjabl] adj viable; (économie, industrie etc) sustainable

viande [vjɑ̃d] nf meat; **je ne mange pas de ~** I don't eat meat

vibrer [vibʀe] vi to vibrate; (son, voix) to be vibrant; (fig) to be stirred; **faire ~** to (cause to) vibrate; (fig) to stir, thrill

vice [vis] nm vice; (défaut) fault ▷ préfixe: **~...** vice-; **vice de forme** legal flaw ou irregularity

vicié, e [visje] adj (air) polluted, tainted; (Jur) invalidated

vicieux, -euse [visjø, jøz] adj (pervers) lecherous; (rétif) unruly ▷ nm/f lecher

vicinal, e, -aux [visinal, o] adj: **chemin ~** by-road, byway

victime [viktim] nf victim; (d'accident) casualty

victoire [viktwaʀ] nf victory

victuailles [viktɥaj] nfpl provisions

vidange [vidɑ̃ʒ] nf (d'un fossé, réservoir) emptying; (Auto) oil change; (de lavabo: bonde) waste outlet; **vidanges** nfpl (matières) sewage sg; **vidanger** vt to empty

vide [vid] adj empty ▷ nm (Physique) vacuum; (espace) (empty) space, gap; (futilité, néant) void; **avoir peur du ~** to be afraid of heights; **emballé sous ~** vacuum packed; **à ~** (sans occupants) empty; (sans charge) unladen

vidéo [video] nf video ▷ adj: **cassette ~** video cassette; **jeu ~** video game; **vidéoclip** nm music video; **vidéoconférence** nf videoconference

vide-ordures [vidɔʀdyʀ] nm inv (rubbish) chute

vider [vide] vt to empty; (Culin: volaille, poisson) to gut, clean out; **se ~** vi to empty; **~ les lieux** to quit ou vacate the premises; **videur** nm (de boîte de nuit) bouncer, doorman

vie [vi] nf life; **être en ~** to be alive; **sans ~** lifeless; **à ~** for life; **que faites-vous dans la ~?** what do you do?

vieil [vjɛj] adj m voir **vieux**; **vieillard** nm old man; **vieille** adj, nf voir **vieux**; **vieilleries** nfpl old things; **vieillesse** nf old age; **vieillir** vi (prendre de l'âge) to grow old; (population, vin) to age; (doctrine, auteur) to become dated ▷ vt to age; **vieillissement** nm growing old; ageing

Vienne [vjɛn] nf Vienna

viens [vjɛ̃] vb voir **venir**

vierge [vjɛʀʒ] adj virgin; (page) clean, blank ▷ nf virgin; (signe): **la V~** Virgo

Vietnam, Viet-Nam [vjɛtnam] nm Vietnam; **vietnamien, ne** adj Vietnamese ▷ nm/f: **Vietnamien, ne** Vietnamese

vieux, vieil, vieille [vjø, vjɛj] adj old ▷ nm/f old man (woman); **les vieux** nmpl old people; **un petit ~** a little old man; **mon ~/ma vieille** (fam) old man/girl; **prendre un coup de ~** to put years on; **vieux garçon** bachelor; **vieux jeu** adj inv old-fashioned

vif, vive [vif, viv] adj (animé) lively; (alerte, brusque, aigu) sharp; (lumière, couleur) bright; (air) crisp; (vent, émotion) keen; (fort: regret, déception) great, deep; (vivant): **brûlé ~** burnt alive; **de vive voix** personally; **avoir l'esprit ~** to be quick-witted; **piquer qn au ~** to cut sb to the quick; **à ~** (plaie) open; **avoir les nerfs à ~** to be on edge

vigne [viɲ] nf (plante) vine; (plantation) vineyard; **vigneron** nm wine grower

vignette [viɲɛt] nf (Admin) ≈ (road) tax disc (BRIT), ≈ license plate sticker (US); (de médicament) price label (used for reimbursement)

vignoble [viɲɔbl] nm (plantation) vineyard; (vignes d'une région) vineyards pl

vigoureux, -euse [viguʀø, øz] adj vigorous, robust

vigueur [vigœʀ] nf vigour; **entrer en ~** to come into force; **en ~** current

vilain, e [vilɛ̃, ɛn] adj (laid) ugly; (affaire, blessure) nasty; (pas sage: enfant) naughty; **vilain mot** naughty ou bad word

villa [villa] nf (detached) house; **~ en multipropriété** time-share villa

village [vilaʒ] nm village; **villageois, e** adj village cpd ▷ nm/f villager

ville [vil] nf town; (importante) city; (administration): **la ~** the (town) council, the local authority; **ville d'eaux** spa; **ville nouvelle** new town

vin [vɛ̃] nm wine; **avoir le ~ gai** to get happy after a few drinks; **vin d'honneur** reception (with wine and snacks); **vin de pays** local wine; **vin ordinaire** ou **de table** table wine

vinaigre [vinɛgʀ] nm vinegar; **vinaigrette** nf

vinaigrette, French dressing

vindicatif, -ive [vɛ̃dikatif, iv] *adj* vindictive

vingt [vɛ̃] *num* twenty; **~-quatre heures sur ~-quatre** twenty-four hours a day, round the clock; **vingtaine** *nf*: **une vingtaine (de)** about twenty, twenty or so; **vingtième** *num* twentieth

vinicole [vinikɔl] *adj* wine *cpd*, wine-growing

vinyle [vinil] *nm* vinyl

viol [vjɔl] *nm* (*d'une femme*) rape; (*d'un lieu sacré*) violation

violacé, e [vjɔlase] *adj* purplish, mauvish

violemment [vjɔlamã] *adv* violently

violence [vjɔlãs] *nf* violence

violent, e [vjɔlã, ãt] *adj* violent; (*remède*) drastic

violer [vjɔle] *vt* (*femme*) to rape; (*sépulture, loi, traité*) to violate

violet, te [vjɔlɛ, ɛt] *adj, nm* purple, mauve; **violette** *nf* (*fleur*) violet

violon [vjɔlõ] *nm* violin; (*fam: prison*) lock-up; **violon d'Ingres** hobby; **violoncelle** *nm* cello; **violoniste** *nm/f* violinist

vipère [vipɛʀ] *nf* viper, adder

virage [viʀaʒ] *nm* (*d'un véhicule*) turn; (*d'une route, piste*) bend

virée [viʀe] *nf* trip; (*à pied*) walk; (*longue*) walking tour; (*dans les cafés*) tour

virement [viʀmã] *nm* (*Comm*) transfer

virer [viʀe] *vt* (*Comm*): **~ qch (sur)** to transfer sth (into); (*fam: expulser*): **~ qn** to kick sb out ▷ *vi* to turn; (*Chimie*) to change colour; **~ au bleu/rouge** to turn blue/red; **~ de bord** to tack

virevolter [viʀvɔlte] *vi* to twirl around

virgule [viʀgyl] *nf* comma; (*Math*) point

viril, e [viʀil] *adj* (*propre à l'homme*) masculine; (*énergique, courageux*) manly, virile

virtuel, le [viʀtɥɛl] *adj* potential; (*théorique*) virtual

virtuose [viʀtɥoz] *nm/f* (*Mus*) virtuoso; (*gén*) master

virus [viʀys] *nm* virus

vis¹ [vi] *vb voir* **voir**; **vivre**

vis² [vis] *nf* screw

visa [viza] *nm* (*sceau*) stamp; (*validation de passeport*) visa

visage [vizaʒ] *nm* face

vis-à-vis [vizavi] *prép*: **~ de qn** to(wards) sb; **en ~** facing each other

visées [vize] *nfpl* (*intentions*) designs

viser [vize] *vi* to aim ▷ *vt* to aim at; (*concerner*) to be aimed or directed at; (*apposer un visa sur*) to stamp, visa; **~ à qch/faire** to aim at sth/at doing *ou* to do

visibilité [vizibilite] *nf* visibility

visible [vizibl] *adj* visible; (*disponible*): **est-il ~?** can he see me?, will he see visitors?

visière [vizjɛʀ] *nf* (*de casquette*) peak; (*qui s'attache*) eyeshade

vision [vizjõ] *nf* vision; (*sens*) (eye)sight, vision; (*fait de voir*): **la ~ de** the sight of; **visionneuse** *nf* viewer

visiophone [vizjɔfɔn] *nm* videophone

visite [vizit] *nf* visit; **~ médicale** medical examination; **~ accompagnée** *ou* **guidée** guided tour; **la ~ guidée commence à quelle heure?** what time does the guided tour start?; **faire une ~ à qn** to call on sb, pay sb a visit; **rendre ~ à qn** to visit sb, pay sb a visit; **être en ~ (chez qn)** to be visiting (sb); **avoir de la ~** to have visitors; **heures de ~** (*hôpital, prison*) visiting hours

visiter [vizite] *vt* to visit; **visiteur, -euse** *nm/f* visitor

vison [vizõ] *nm* mink

visser [vise] *vt*: **~ qch** (*fixer, serrer*) to screw sth on

visuel, le [vizɥɛl] *adj* visual

vital, e, -aux [vital, o] *adj* vital

vitamine [vitamin] *nf* vitamin

vite [vit] *adv* (*rapidement*) quickly, fast; (*sans délai*) quickly; (*sous peu*) soon; **~!** quick!; **faire ~** to be quick; **le temps passe ~** time flies

vitesse [vites] *nf* speed; (*Auto: dispositif*) gear; **prendre de la ~** to pick up *ou* gather speed; **à toute ~** at full *ou* top speed; **en ~** (*rapidement*) quickly; (*en hâte*) in a hurry

viticulteur [vitikyltœʀ] *nm* wine grower

vitrage [vitʀaʒ] *nm*: **double ~** double glazing

vitrail, -aux [vitʀaj, o] *nm* stained-glass window

vitre [vitʀ] *nf* (*window*) pane; (*de portière, voiture*) window; **vitré, e** *adj* glass *cpd*

vitrine [vitʀin] *nf* (*shop*) window; (*petite armoire*) display cabinet; **en ~** in the window

vivable [vivabl] *adj* (*personne*) livable-with; (*maison*) fit to live in

vivace [vivas] *adj* (*arbre, plante*) hardy; (*fig*) indestructible, inveterate

vivacité [vivasite] *nf* liveliness, vivacity

vivant, e [vivã, ãt] *adj* (*qui vit*) living, alive; (*animé*) lively; (*preuve, exemple*) living ▷ *nm*: **du ~ de qn** in sb's lifetime; **les ~s** the living

vive [viv] *adj voir* **vif** ▷ *vb voir* **vivre** ▷ *excl*: **~ le roi!** long live the king!; **vivement** *adv* deeply ▷ *excl*: **vivement les vacances!** roll on the holidays!

vivier [vivje] *nm* (*étang*) fish tank; (*réservoir*) fishpond

vivifiant, e [vivifjã, jãt] *adj* invigorating

vivoter [vivɔte] *vi* (*personne*) to scrape a living, get by; (*fig: affaire etc*) to struggle along

vivre [vivʀ] *vi, vt* to live; (*période*) to live through; **vivres** *nmpl* provisions, food supplies; **~ de** to live on; **il vit encore** he is still alive; **se laisser ~** to take life as it comes; **ne plus ~** (*être anxieux*) to live on one's nerves; **il a vécu** (*eu une vie aventureuse*) he has seen life; **être facile à ~** to be easy to get on with; **faire ~ qn** (*pourvoir à sa subsistance*) to provide (a living) for sb

vlan [vlã] *excl* wham!, bang!

VO [veo] *nf*: **film en VO** film in the original version; **en VO sous-titrée** in the original version with subtitles

vocabulaire [vɔkabylɛʀ] *nm* vocabulary

vocation [vɔkasjõ] *nf* vocation, calling

vœu, x [vø] *nm* wish; (*promesse*) vow; **faire ~ de** to take a vow of; **tous nos ~x de bonne année, meilleurs ~x** best wishes for the New Year

vogue [vɔg] *nf* fashion, vogue; **en ~** in fashion, in vogue

voici [vwasi] *prép* (*pour introduire, désigner*) here is +*sg*, here are +*pl*; **et ~ que ...** and now it (*ou* he) ...; *voir aussi* **voilà**

voie [vwa] *nf* way; (*Rail*) track, line; (*Auto*) lane; **être en bonne ~** to be going well; **mettre qn sur la ~** to put sb on the right track; **pays en ~ de développement** developing country; **être en ~ d'achèvement/de rénovation** to be nearing completion/in the process of renovation; **par ~ buccale** *ou* **orale** orally; **route à ~ unique** single-track road; **route à 2/3 ~s** 2-/3-lane road; **voie de garage** (*Rail*) siding; **voie express** expressway; **voie ferrée** track; railway line (BRIT), railroad (US); **la voie lactée** the Milky Way; **la voie publique** the public highway

voilà [vwala] *prép* (*en désignant*) there is +*sg*, there are +*pl*; **les ~** *ou* **voici** here *ou* there they are; **en ~** *ou* **voici**

un here's one, there's one; **voici mon frère et ~ ma sœur** this is my brother and that's my sister; **~ ou voici deux ans** two years ago; **~ ou voici deux ans que it's** two years since; **et ~!** there we are!; **~ tout** that's all; **~ ou voici** (en offrant etc) there ou here you are; **tiens! ~ Paul** look! there's Paul

voile [vwal] *nm* veil; (tissu léger) net ▷ *nf* sail; (sport) sailing; **voiler** *vt* to veil; (fausser: roue) to buckle; (: bois) to warp; **se voiler** *vi* (lune, regard) to mist over; (voix) to become husky; (roue, disque) to buckle; (planche) to warp; **voilier** *nm* sailing ship; (de plaisance) sailing boat; **voilure** *nf* (de voilier) sails *pl*

voir [vwar] *vi, vt* to see; **se ~** *vi* (être visible) to show; (se fréquenter) to see each other; (se produire) to happen; **cela se voit** (c'est visible) that's obvious, it shows; **faire ~ qch à qn** to show sb sth; **en faire ~ à qn** (fig) to give sb a hard time; **ne pas pouvoir ~ qn** not to be able to stand sb; **voyons!** let's see now; (indignation etc) come on!; **ça n'a rien à ~ avec lui** that has nothing to do with him

voire [vwar] *adv* even

voisin, e [vwazɛ̃, in] *adj* (proche) neighbouring; (contigu) next; (ressemblant) connected ▷ *nm/f* neighbour; **voisinage** *nm* (proximité) proximity; (environs) vicinity; (quartier, voisins) neighbourhood

voiture [vwatyr] *nf* car; (wagon) coach, carriage; **voiture de course** racing car; **voiture de sport** sports car

voix [vwa] *nf* voice; (Pol) vote; **à haute ~** aloud; **à ~ basse** in a low voice; **à 2/4 ~** (Mus) in 2/4 parts; **avoir ~ au chapitre** to have a say in the matter

vol [vɔl] *nm* (d'oiseau, d'avion) flight; (larcin) theft; **~ régulier** scheduled flight; **à ~ d'oiseau** as the crow flies; **au ~: attraper qch au ~** to catch sth as it flies past; **en ~** in flight; **je voudrais signaler un ~** I'd like to report a theft; **vol à main armée** armed robbery; **vol à voile** gliding; **vol libre** hang-gliding

volage [vɔlaʒ] *adj* fickle

volaille [vɔlaj] *nf* (oiseaux) poultry *pl*; (viande) poultry *no pl*; (oiseau) fowl

volant, e [vɔlɑ̃, ɑ̃t] *adj voir* **feuille** *etc* ▷ *nm* (d'automobile) (steering) wheel; (de commande) wheel; (objet lancé) shuttlecock; (bande de tissu) flounce

volcan [vɔlkɑ̃] *nm* volcano

volée [vɔle] *nf* (Tennis) volley; **à la ~: rattraper à la ~** to catch in mid-air; **à toute ~** (sonner les cloches) vigorously; (lancer un projectile) with full force

voler [vɔle] *vi* (avion, oiseau, fig) to fly; (voleur) to steal ▷ *vt* (objet) to steal; (personne) to rob; **~ qch à qn** to steal sth from sb; **on m'a volé mon portefeuille** my wallet (BRIT) ou billfold (US) has been stolen; **il ne l'a pas volé!** he asked for it!

volet [vɔle] *nm* (de fenêtre) shutter; (de feuillet, document) section

voleur, -euse [vɔlœr, øz] *nm/f* thief ▷ *adj* thieving; **"au ~!"** "stop thief!"

volontaire [vɔlɔ̃tɛr] *adj* (acte, enrôlement, prisonnier) voluntary; (oubli) intentional; (caractère, personne: décidé) self-willed ▷ *nm/f* volunteer

volonté [vɔlɔ̃te] *nf* (faculté de vouloir) will; (énergie, fermeté) will(power); (souhait, désir) wish; **à ~** as much as one likes; **bonne ~** goodwill, willingness; **mauvaise ~** lack of goodwill, unwillingness

volontiers [vɔlɔ̃tje] *adv* (avec plaisir) willingly, gladly; (habituellement, souvent) readily, willingly; **voulez-vous**

boire quelque chose? - ~! would you like something to drink? - yes, please!

volt [vɔlt] *nm* volt

volte-face [vɔltəfas] *nf inv* **faire ~** to turn round

voltige [vɔltiʒ] *nf* (Équitation) trick riding; (au cirque) acrobatics *sg*; **voltiger** *vi* to flutter (about)

volubile [vɔlybil] *adj* voluble

volume [vɔlym] *nm* volume; (Géom: solide) solid; **volumineux, -euse** *adj* voluminous, bulky

volupté [vɔlypte] *nf* sensual delight ou pleasure

vomi [vɔmi] *nm* vomit; **vomir** *vi* to vomit, be sick ▷ *vt* to vomit, bring up; (fig) to belch out, spew out; (exécrer) to loathe, abhor

vorace [vɔras] *adj* voracious

vos [vo] *adj voir* **votre**

vote [vɔt] *nm* vote; **vote par correspondance/ procuration** postal/proxy vote; **voter** *vi* to vote ▷ *vt* (projet de loi) to vote for; (loi, réforme) to pass

votre [vɔtr] (pl **vos**) *adj* your

vôtre [vɔtr] *pron*: **le ~, la ~, les ~s** yours; **les ~s** (fig) your family ou folks; **à la ~** (toast) your (good) health!

vouer [vwe] *vt*: **~ sa vie à** (étude, cause etc) to devote one's life to; **~ une amitié éternelle à qn** to vow undying friendship to sb

MOT-CLÉ

vouloir [vulwar] *nm*: **le bon vouloir de qn** sb's goodwill; sb's pleasure

▷ *vt* **1** (exiger, désirer) to want; **vouloir faire/que qn fasse** to want to do/sb to do; **voulez-vous du thé?** would you like ou do you want some tea?; **que me veut-il?** what does he want with me?; **sans le vouloir** (involontairement) without meaning to, unintentionally; **je voudrais ceci/faire** I would ou I'd like this/to do; **le hasard a voulu que ...** as fate would have it ...; **la tradition veut que ...** it is a tradition that ...

2 (consentir): **je veux bien** (bonne volonté) I'll be happy to; (concession) fair enough, that's fine; **je peux le faire, si vous voulez** I can do it if you like; **oui, si on veut** (en quelque sorte) yes, if you like; **veuillez attendre** please wait; **veuillez agréer ...** (formule épistolaire: personne nommée) yours sincerely; (personne non nommée) yours faithfully

3: **en vouloir à qn** to bear sb a grudge; **s'en vouloir (de)** to be annoyed with o.s. (for); **il en veut à mon argent** he's after my money

4: **vouloir de: l'entreprise ne veut plus de lui** the firm doesn't want him any more; **elle ne veut pas de son aide** she doesn't want his help

5: **vouloir dire** to mean

voulu, e [vuly] *adj* (requis) required, requisite; (délibéré) deliberate, intentional; *voir aussi* **vouloir**

vous [vu] *pron* you; (objet indirect) (to) you; (réfléchi: sg) yourself; (: pl) yourselves; (réciproque) each other ▷ *nm*: **employer le ~** (vouvoyer) to use the "vous" form; **~-même** yourself; **~-mêmes** yourselves

vouvoyer [vuvwaje] *vt*: **~ qn** to address sb as "vous"

voyage [vwajaʒ] *nm* journey, trip; (fait de voyager): **le ~** travel(ling); **partir/être en ~** to go off/be away on a journey ou trip; **faire bon ~** to have a good journey; **votre ~ s'est bien passé?** how was your journey?; **voyage d'affaires/d'agrément** business/pleasure trip; **voyage de noces** honeymoon; **nous sommes en voyage de noces** we're on honeymoon; **voyage organisé** package tour

voyager [vwajaʒe] vi to travel; **voyageur, -euse** nm/f traveller; (passager) passenger; **voyageur de commerce** sales representative, commercial traveller

voyant, e [vwajɑ̃, ɑ̃t] adj (couleur) loud, gaudy ▷ nm (signal) (warning) light

voyelle [vwajɛl] nf vowel

voyou [vwaju] nm hooligan

vrac [vʀak]: **en ~** adv (au détail) loose; (en gros) in bulk; (en désordre) in a jumble

vrai, e [vʀɛ] adj (véridique: récit, faits) true; (non factice, authentique) real; **à ~ dire** to tell the truth; **vraiment** adv really; **vraisemblable** adj likely; (excuse) convincing; **vraisemblablement** adj probably; **vraisemblance** nf likelihood; (romanesque) verisimilitude

vrombir [vʀɔ̃biʀ] vi to hum

VRP sigle m (= voyageur, représentant, placier) sales rep (fam)

VTT sigle m (= vélo tout-terrain) mountain bike

vu, e [vy] pp de **voir** ▷ adj: **bien/mal vu** (fig: personne) popular/unpopular; (: chose) approved/disapproved of ▷ prép (en raison de) in view of; **vu que** in view of the fact that

vue [vy] nf (fait de voir): **la ~ de** the sight of; (sens, faculté) (eye)sight; (panorama, image, photo) view; **vues** nfpl (idées) views; (dessein) designs; **hors de ~** out of sight; **avoir en ~** to have in mind; **tirer à ~** to shoot on sight; **à ~ d'œil** visibly; **à première ~** at first sight; **de ~** by sight; **perdre de ~** to lose sight of; **en ~** (visible) in sight; (célèbre) in the public eye; **en ~ de faire** with a view to doing; **perdre la ~** to lose one's (eye)sight; **avoir ~ sur** (suj: fenêtre) to have a view of; **vue d'ensemble** overall view

vulgaire [vylgɛʀ] adj (grossier) vulgar, coarse; (ordinaire) commonplace, mundane; (péj: quelconque): **de ~s touristes** common tourists; (Bot, Zool: non latin) common; **vulgariser** vt to popularize

vulnérable [vylneʀabl] adj vulnerable

wagon [vagɔ̃] nm (de voyageurs) carriage; (de marchandises) truck, wagon; **wagon-lit** nm sleeper, sleeping car; **wagon-restaurant** nm restaurant ou dining car

wallon, ne [walɔ̃, ɔn] adj Walloon ▷ nm (Ling) Walloon ▷ nm/f: **W~, ne** Walloon

watt [wat] nm watt

W-C sigle mpl (= water-closet(s)) toilet

Web [wɛb] nm inv: **le ~** the (World Wide) Web; **webmaster** [-mastœr], **webmestre** [-mɛstʀ] nm/f webmaster

week-end [wikɛnd] nm weekend

western [wɛstɛʀn] nm western

whisky [wiski] (pl **whiskies**) nm whisky

yaourt [jauʀt] *nm* yoghourt; **~ nature/aux fruits** plain/fruit yogurt
yeux [jø] *nmpl de* **œil**
yoga [jɔga] *nm* yoga
yoghourt [jɔguʀt] *nm* = **yaourt**
yougoslave [jugɔslav] (*Histoire*) *adj* Yugoslav(ian) ▷ *nm/f*: **Y~** Yugoslav
Yougoslavie [jugɔslavi] (*Histoire*) *nf* Yugoslavia; **l'ex-~** the former Yugoslavia

xénophobe [gzenɔfɔb] *adj* xenophobic ▷ *nm/f* xenophobe
xérès [gzeʀɛs] *nm* sherry
xylophone [gzilɔfɔn] *nm* xylophone

zapper [zape] *vi* to zap
zapping [zapiŋ] *nm*: **faire du ~** to flick through the channels
zèbre [zɛbʀ(ə)] *nm* (*Zool*) zebra; **zébré, e** *adj* striped, streaked
zèle [zɛl] *nm* zeal; **faire du ~** (*péj*) to be over-zealous; **zélé, e** *adj* zealous
zéro [zeʀo] *nm* zero, nought (*BRIT*); **au-dessous de ~** below zero (Centigrade) *ou* freezing; **partir de ~** to start from scratch; **trois (buts) à ~** 3 (goals to) nil
zeste [zɛst] *nm* peel, zest
zézayer [zezeje] *vi* to have a lisp
zigzag [zigzag] *nm* zigzag; **zigzaguer** *vi* to zigzag
Zimbabwe [zimbabwe] *nm*: **le ~** Zimbabwe
zipper [zipe] *vt* (*Inform*) to zip
zizi [zizi] *nm* (*langage enfantin*) willy
zodiaque [zɔdjak] *nm* zodiac
zona [zona] *nm* shingles *sg*
zone [zon] *nf* zone, area; (*fam: quartiers pauvres*): **la ~** the slums; **zone bleue** = restricted parking area; **zone industrielle** industrial estate
zoo [zo(o)] *nm* zoo
zoologie [zɔɔlɔʒi] *nf* zoology; **zoologique** *adj* zoological
zut [zyt] *excl* dash (it)! (*BRIT*), nuts! (*US*)

y [i] *adv* (*à cet endroit*) there; (*dessus*) on it (*ou* them); (*dedans*) in it (*ou* them) ▷ *pron* (*about ou* on *ou* of) it (*d'après le verbe employé*); **j'y pense** I'm thinking about it; **ça y est!** that's it!; *voir aussi* **aller; avoir**
yacht [jɔt] *nm* yacht

have an **abortion** se faire avorter

 KEYWORD

about [əˈbaʊt] adv **1** (approximately) environ, à peu près; **about a hundred/thousand** etc environ cent/mille etc, une centaine (de)/un millier (de) etc; **it takes about 10 hours** ça prend environ or à peu près 10 heures; **at about 2 o'clock** vers 2 heures; **I've just about finished** j'ai presque fini
2 (referring to place) çà et là, de-ci de-là; **to run about** courir çà et là; **to walk about** se promener, aller et venir; **they left all their things lying about** ils ont laissé traîner toutes leurs affaires
3: **to be about to do sth** être sur le point de faire qch
▷ prep **1** (relating to) au sujet de, à propos de; **a book about London** un livre sur Londres; **what is it about?** de quoi s'agit-il?; **we talked about it** nous en avons parlé; **what** or **how about doing this?** et si nous faisions ceci?
2 (referring to place) dans; **to walk about the town** se promener dans la ville

above [əˈbʌv] adv au-dessus ▷ prep au-dessus de; (more than) plus de; **mentioned ~** mentionné ci-dessus; **~ all** par-dessus tout, surtout

abroad [əˈbrɔːd] adv à l'étranger

abrupt [əˈbrʌpt] adj (steep, blunt) abrupt(e); (sudden, gruff) brusque

abscess [ˈæbsɪs] n abcès m

absence [ˈæbsəns] n absence f

absent [ˈæbsənt] adj absent(e); **absent-minded** adj distrait(e)

absolute [ˈæbsəluːt] adj absolu(e); **absolutely** [æbsəˈluːtlɪ] adv absolument

absorb [əbˈzɔːb] vt absorber; **to be ~ed in a book** être plongé(e) dans un livre; **absorbent cotton** n (US) coton m hydrophile; **absorbing** adj absorbant(e); (book, film etc) captivant(e)

abstain [əbˈsteɪn] vi: **to ~ (from)** s'abstenir (de)

abstract [ˈæbstrækt] adj abstrait(e)

absurd [əbˈsəːd] adj absurde

abundance [əˈbʌndəns] n abondance f

abundant [əˈbʌndənt] adj abondant(e)

abuse n [əˈbjuːs] (insults) insultes fpl, injures fpl; (ill-treatment) mauvais traitements mpl; (of power etc) abus m ▷ vt [əˈbjuːz] (insult) insulter; (ill-treat) malmener; (power etc) abuser de; **abusive** adj grossier(-ière), injurieux(-euse)

abysmal [əˈbɪzməl] adj exécrable; (ignorance etc) sans bornes

academic [ækəˈdɛmɪk] adj universitaire; (person: scholarly) intellectuel(-le); (pej: issue) oiseux(-euse), purement théorique ▷ n universitaire m/f; **academic year** n (University) année f universitaire; (Scol) année scolaire

academy [əˈkædəmɪ] n (learned body) académie f; (school) collège m; **~ of music** conservatoire m

accelerate [ækˈsɛləreɪt] vt, vi accélérer; **acceleration** [æksɛləˈreɪʃən] n accélération f; **accelerator** n (BRIT) accélérateur m

accent [ˈæksɛnt] n accent m

accept [əkˈsɛpt] vt accepter; **acceptable** adj acceptable; **acceptance** n acceptation f

---

A [eɪ] n (Mus) la m

 KEYWORD

a [eɪ, ə] (before vowel or silent h **an**) indef art **1** un(e); **a book** un livre; **an apple** une pomme; **she's a doctor** elle est médecin
2 (instead of the number "one") un(e); **a year ago** il y a un an; **a hundred/thousand** etc **pounds** cent/mille etc livres
3 (in expressing ratios, prices etc): **3 a day/week** 3 par jour/semaine; **10 km an hour** 10 km à l'heure; **£5 a person** 5£ par personne; **30p a kilo** 30p le kilo

A2 n (BRIT: Scol) deuxième partie de l'examen équivalent au baccalauréat

A.A. n abbr (BRIT: = Automobile Association) ≈ ACF m; (= Alcoholics Anonymous) AA

A.A.A. n abbr (= American Automobile Association) ≈ ACF m

aback [əˈbæk] adv: **to be taken ~** être décontenancé(e)

abandon [əˈbændən] vt abandonner

abattoir [ˈæbətwɑː] n (BRIT) abattoir m

abbey [ˈæbɪ] n abbaye f

abbreviation [əbriːvɪˈeɪʃən] n abréviation f

abdomen [ˈæbdəmən] n abdomen m

abduct [æbˈdʌkt] vt enlever

abide [əˈbaɪd] vt souffrir, supporter; **I can't ~ it/him** je ne le supporte pas; **abide by** vt fus observer, respecter

ability [əˈbɪlɪtɪ] n compétence f, capacité f; (skill) talent m

able [ˈeɪbl] adj compétent(e); **to be ~ to do sth** pouvoir faire qch, être capable de faire qch

abnormal [æbˈnɔːməl] adj anormal(e)

aboard [əˈbɔːd] adv à bord ▷ prep à bord de; (train) dans

abolish [əˈbɔlɪʃ] vt abolir

abolition [æbəˈlɪʃən] n abolition f

abort [əˈbɔːt] vt (Med) faire avorter; (Comput, fig) abandonner; **abortion** [əˈbɔːʃən] n avortement m; **to**

access ['ækses] n accès m; **to have ~ to** (information, library etc) avoir accès à, pouvoir utiliser or consulter; (person) avoir accès auprès de; **accessible** [æk'sesəbl] adj accessible

accessory [æk'sesərɪ] n accessoire m; **~ to** (Law) accessoire à

accident ['æksɪdənt] n accident m; (chance) hasard m; **I've had an ~** j'ai eu un accident; **by ~** (by chance) par hasard; (not deliberately) accidentellement; **accidental** [æksɪ'dɛntl] adj accidentel(le); **accidentally** [æksɪ'dɛntəlɪ] adv accidentellement; **Accident and Emergency Department** n (BRIT) service m des urgences; **accident insurance** n assurance f accident

acclaim [ə'kleɪm] vt acclamer ▷ n acclamations fpl

accommodate [ə'kɔmədeɪt] vt loger, recevoir; (oblige, help) obliger; (car etc) contenir

accommodation (US **accommodations**) [əkɔmə'deɪʃən(z)] n(pl) logement m

accompaniment [ə'kʌmpənɪmənt] n accompagnement m

accompany [ə'kʌmpənɪ] vt accompagner

accomplice [ə'kʌmplɪs] n complice m/f

accomplish [ə'kʌmplɪʃ] vt accomplir; **accomplishment** n (skill: gen pl) talent m; (completion) accomplissement m; (achievement) réussite f

accord [ə'kɔːd] n accord m ▷ vt accorder; **of his own ~** de son plein gré; **accordance** n: **in accordance with** conformément à; **according: according to** prep selon; **accordingly** adv (appropriately) en conséquence; (as a result) par conséquent

account [ə'kaunt] n (Comm) compte m; (report) compte rendu, récit m; **accounts** npl (Comm: records) comptabilité f, comptes; **of no ~** sans importance; **on ~** en acompte; **to buy sth on ~** acheter qch à crédit; **on no ~** en aucun cas; **on ~ of** à cause de; **to take into ~**, **take ~ of** tenir compte de; **account for** vt fus (explain) expliquer, rendre compte de; (represent) représenter; **accountable** adj: **accountable (to)** responsable (devant); **accountant** n comptable m/f; **account number** n numéro m de compte

accumulate [ə'kjuːmjuleɪt] vt accumuler, amasser ▷ vi s'accumuler, s'amasser

accuracy ['ækjurəsɪ] n exactitude f, précision f

accurate ['ækjurɪt] adj exact(e), précis(e); (device) précis; **accurately** adv avec précision

accusation [ækju'zeɪʃən] n accusation f

accuse [ə'kjuːz] vt: **to ~ sb (of sth)** accuser qn (de qch); **accused** n (Law) accusé(e)

accustomed [ə'kʌstəmd] adj: **~ to** habitué(e) or accoutumé(e) à

ace [eɪs] n as m

ache [eɪk] n mal m, douleur f ▷ vi (be sore) faire mal, être douloureux(-euse); **my head ~s** j'ai mal à la tête

achieve [ə'tʃiːv] vt (aim) atteindre; (victory, success) remporter, obtenir; **achievement** n exploit m, réussite f; (of aims) réalisation f

acid ['æsɪd] adj, n acide (m)

acknowledge [ək'nɔlɪdʒ] vt (also: **~ receipt of**) accuser réception de; (fact) reconnaître; **acknowledgement** n (of letter) accusé m de réception

acne ['æknɪ] n acné m

acorn ['eɪkɔːn] n gland m

acoustic [ə'kuːstɪk] adj acoustique

acquaintance [ə'kweɪntəns] n connaissance f

acquire [ə'kwaɪəʳ] vt acquérir; **acquisition** [ækwɪ'zɪʃən] n acquisition f

acquit [ə'kwɪt] vt acquitter; **to ~ o.s. well** s'en tirer très honorablement

acre ['eɪkəʳ] n acre f (= 4047 m²)

acronym ['ækrənɪm] n acronyme m

across [ə'krɔs] prep (on the other side) de l'autre côté de; (crosswise) en travers de ▷ adv de l'autre côté; en travers; **to run/swim ~** traverser en courant/à la nage; **~ from** en face de

acrylic [ə'krɪlɪk] adj, n acrylique (m)

act [ækt] n acte m, action f; (Theat: part of play) acte m; (: of performer) numéro m; (Law) loi f ▷ vi agir; (Theat) jouer; (pretend) jouer la comédie ▷ vt (role) jouer, tenir; **to catch sb in the ~** prendre qn sur le fait or en flagrant délit; **to ~ as** servir de; **act up** (inf) vi (person) se conduire mal; (knee, back, injury) jouer des tours; (machine) être capricieux(-ieuse); **acting** adj suppléant(e), par intérim ▷ n (activity): **to do some acting** faire du théâtre (or du cinéma)

action ['ækʃən] n action f; (Mil) combat(s) m(pl); (Law) procès m, action en justice; **out of ~** hors de combat; (machine etc) hors d'usage; **to take ~** agir, prendre des mesures; **action replay** n (BRIT TV) ralenti m

activate ['æktɪveɪt] vt (mechanism) actionner, faire fonctionner

active ['æktɪv] adj actif(-ive); (volcano) en activité; **actively** adv activement; (discourage) vivement

activist ['æktɪvɪst] n activiste m/f

activity [æk'tɪvɪtɪ] n activité f; **activity holiday** n vacances actives

actor ['æktəʳ] n acteur m

actress ['æktrɪs] n actrice f

actual ['æktjuəl] adj réel(le), véritable; (emphatic use) lui-même (elle-même)

actually ['æktjuəlɪ] adv réellement, véritablement; (in fact) en fait

acupuncture ['ækjupʌŋktʃəʳ] n acupuncture f

acute [ə'kjuːt] adj aigu(ë); (mind, observer) pénétrant(e)

A.D. adv abbr (= Anno Domini) ap. J.-C.

ad [æd] n abbr = **advertisement**

adamant ['ædəmənt] adj inflexible

adapt [ə'dæpt] vt adapter ▷ vi: **to ~ (to)** s'adapter (à); **adapter, adaptor** n (Elec) adaptateur m; (for several plugs) prise f multiple

add [æd] vt ajouter; (figures: also: **to ~ up**) additionner ▷ vi (fig): **it doesn't ~ up** cela ne rime à rien; **add up to** vt fus (Math) s'élever à; (fig: mean) signifier

addict ['ædɪkt] n toxicomane m/f; (fig) fanatique m/f; **addicted** [ə'dɪktɪd] adj: **to be addicted to** (drink, drugs) être adonné(e) à; (fig: football etc) être un(e) fanatique de; **addiction** [ə'dɪkʃən] n (Med) dépendance f; **addictive** [ə'dɪktɪv] adj qui crée une dépendance

addition [ə'dɪʃən] n (adding up) addition f; (thing added) ajout m; **in ~** de plus, de surcroît; **in ~ to** en plus de; **additional** adj supplémentaire

additive ['ædɪtɪv] n additif m

address [ə'drɛs] n adresse f; (talk) discours m, allocution f ▷ vt adresser; (speak to) s'adresser à; **my ~ is ...** mon adresse, c'est ...; **address book** n carnet m d'adresses

adequate ['ædɪkwɪt] adj (enough) suffisant(e); (satisfactory) satisfaisant(e)

adhere [əd'hɪəʳ] vi: **to ~ to** adhérer à; (fig: rule, decision) se tenir à

adhesive [əd'hiːzɪv] n adhésif m; **adhesive tape** n (BRIT) ruban m adhésif; (US Med) sparadrap m

adjacent [ə'dʒeɪsənt] adj adjacent(e), contigu(ë); **~ to** adjacent e

adjective ['ædʒɛktɪv] n adjectif m

adjoining [ə'dʒɔɪnɪŋ] adj voisin(e), adjacent(e), attenant(e)

adjourn [ə'dʒəːn] vt ajourner ▷ vi suspendre la séance; lever la séance; clore la session

adjust [ə'dʒʌst] vt (machine) ajuster, régler; (prices, wages) rajuster ▷ vi: **to ~ (to)** s'adapter (à); **adjustable** adj réglable; **adjustment** n (of machine) ajustage m, réglage m; (of prices, wages) rajustement m; (of person) adaptation f

administer [əd'mɪnɪstə'] vt administrer; **administration** [ədmɪnɪs'treɪʃən] n (management) administration f; (government) gouvernement m; **administrative** [əd'mɪnɪstrətɪv] adj administratif(-ive)

administrator [əd'mɪnɪstreɪtə'] n administrateur(-trice)

admiral ['ædmərəl] n amiral m

admiration [ædmə'reɪʃən] n admiration f

admire [əd'maɪə'] vt admirer; **admirer** n (fan) admirateur(-trice)

admission [əd'mɪʃən] n admission f; (to exhibition, night club etc) entrée f; (confession) aveu m

admit [əd'mɪt] vt laisser entrer; admettre; (agree) reconnaître, admettre; (crime) reconnaître avoir commis; **"children not ~ted"** "entrée interdite aux enfants"; **admit to** vt fus reconnaître, avouer; **admittance** n admission f, (droit m d')entrée f; **admittedly** adv il faut en convenir

adolescent [ædəu'lɛsnt] adj, n adolescent(e)

adopt [ə'dɔpt] vt adopter; **adopted** adj adoptif(-ive), adopté(e); **adoption** [ə'dɔpʃən] n adoption f

adore [ə'dɔː'] vt adorer

adorn [ə'dɔːn] vt orner

Adriatic (Sea) [eɪdrɪ'ætɪk-] n, adj: **the Adriatic (Sea)** la mer Adriatique, l'Adriatique f

adrift [ə'drɪft] adv à la dérive

adult ['ædʌlt] n adulte m/f ▷ adj (grown-up) adulte; (for adults) pour adultes; **adult education** n éducation f des adultes

adultery [ə'dʌltərɪ] n adultère m

advance [əd'vɑːns] n avance f ▷ vt avancer ▷ vi s'avancer; **in ~** en avance, d'avance; **to make ~s to sb** (gen) faire des propositions à qn; (amorously) faire des avances à qn; **~ booking** location f; **~ notice, ~ warning** préavis m; (verbal) avertissement m; **do I need to book in ~?** est-ce qu'il faut réserver à l'avance?; **advanced** adj avancé(e); (Scol: studies) supérieur(e)

advantage [əd'vɑːntɪdʒ] n (also Tennis) avantage m; **to take ~ of** (person) exploiter; (opportunity) profiter de

advent ['ædvənt] n avènement m, venue f; **A~** (Rel) avent m

adventure [əd'vɛntʃə'] n aventure f; **adventurous** [əd'vɛntʃərəs] adj aventureux(-euse)

adverb ['ædvəːb] n adverbe m

adversary ['ædvəsərɪ] n adversaire m/f

adverse ['ædvəːs] adj (effect) négatif(-ive); (weather, publicity) mauvais(e); (wind) contraire

advert ['ædvəːt] n abbr (BRIT) = **advertisement**

advertise ['ædvətaɪz] vi faire de la publicité or de la réclame; (in classified ads etc) mettre une annonce ▷ vt faire de la publicité or de la réclame pour; (in classified ads etc) mettre une annonce pour vendre; **to ~ for** (staff) recruter par (voie d')annonce; **advertisement** [əd'vəːtɪsmənt] n (Comm) publicité f, réclame f; (in classified ads etc) annonce f; **advertiser** n annonceur m; **advertising** n publicité f

advice [əd'vaɪs] n conseils mpl; (notification) avis m; **a piece of ~** un conseil; **to take legal ~** consulter un avocat

advisable [əd'vaɪzəbl] adj recommandable, indiqué(e)

advise [əd'vaɪz] vt conseiller; **to ~ sb of sth** aviser or informer qn de qch; **to ~ against sth/doing sth** déconseiller qch/conseiller de ne pas faire qch; **adviser, advisor** n conseiller(-ère); **advisory** adj consultatif(-ive)

advocate n ['ædvəkɪt] (lawyer) avocat (plaidant); (upholder) défenseur m, avocat(e) ▷ vt ['ædvəkeɪt] recommander, prôner; **to be an ~ of** être partisan(e) de

Aegean [iː'dʒiːən] n, adj: **the ~ (Sea)** la mer Égée, l'Égée f

aerial ['ɛərɪəl] n antenne f ▷ adj aérien(ne)

aerobics [ɛə'rəubɪks] n aérobic m

aeroplane ['ɛərəpleɪn] n (BRIT) avion m

aerosol ['ɛərəsɔl] n aérosol m

affair [ə'fɛə'] n affaire f; (also: **love ~**) liaison f; aventure f

affect [ə'fɛkt] vt affecter; (subj: disease) atteindre; **affected** adj affecté(e); **affection** n affection f; **affectionate** adj affectueux(-euse)

afflict [ə'flɪkt] vt affliger

affluent ['æfluənt] adj (person, family, surroundings) aisé(e), riche; **the ~ society** la société d'abondance

afford [ə'fɔːd] vt (behaviour) se permettre; (provide) fournir, procurer; **can we ~ a car?** avons-nous de quoi acheter or les moyens d'acheter une voiture?; **affordable** adj abordable

Afghanistan [æf'gænɪstæn] n Afghanistan m

afraid [ə'freɪd] adj effrayé(e); **to be ~ of or to** avoir peur de; **I am ~ that** je crains que + sub; **I'm ~ so/not** oui/non, malheureusement

Africa ['æfrɪkə] n Afrique f; **African** adj africain(e) ▷ n Africain(e); **African-American** adj afro-américain(e) ▷ n Afro-Américain(e)

after ['ɑːftə'] prep, adv après ▷ conj après que; **it's quarter ~ two** (US) il est deux heures et quart; **~ having done/~ he left** après avoir fait/ après son départ; **to name sb ~ sb** donner à qn le nom de qn; **to ask ~ sb** demander des nouvelles de qn; **what/who are you ~?** que/qui cherchez-vous?; **~ you!** après vous!; **~ all** après tout; **after-effects** npl (of disaster, radiation, drink etc) répercussions fpl; (of illness) séquelles fpl, suites fpl; **aftermath** n conséquences fpl; **afternoon** n après-midi m or f; **after-shave (lotion)** n lotion f après-rasage; **aftersun (lotion/cream)** n après-soleil m inv; **afterwards** (US **afterward**) adv après

again [ə'gɛn] adv de nouveau, encore (une fois); **to do sth ~** refaire qch; **~ and ~** à plusieurs reprises

against [ə'gɛnst] prep contre; (compared to) par rapport à

age [eɪdʒ] n âge m ▷ vt, vi vieillir; **he is 20 years of ~** il a 20 ans; **to come of ~** atteindre sa majorité; **it's been ~s since I saw you** ça fait une éternité que je ne t'ai pas vu; **~d 10** âgé(e) de 10 ans; **age group** n tranche f d'âge; **age limit** n limite f d'âge

agency ['eɪdʒənsɪ] n agence f

agenda [ə'dʒɛndə] n ordre m du jour

agent ['eɪdʒənt] n agent m; (firm) concessionnaire m

aggravate ['ægrəveɪt] vt (situation) aggraver; (annoy) exaspérer, agacer

aggression [ə'grɛʃən] n agression f

aggressive [ə'grɛsɪv] adj agressif(-ive)

agile ['ædʒaɪl] adj agile

agitated ['ædʒɪteɪtɪd] adj inquiet(-ète)

AGM n abbr (= annual general meeting) AG f

ago [ə'gəu] adv: **2 days ~** il y a 2 jours; **not long ~** il n'y a pas longtemps; **how long ~?** il y a combien de temps (de cela)?

agony ['ægənɪ] n (pain) douleur f atroce; (distress) angoisse f; **to be in ~** souffrir le martyre

agree [ə'gri:] vt (price) convenir de ▷ vi: **to ~ with** (person) être d'accord avec; (statements etc) concorder avec; (Ling) s'accorder avec; **to ~ to do** accepter de or consentir à faire; **to ~ to sth** consentir à qch; **to ~ that** (admit) convenir or reconnaître que; **garlic doesn't ~ with me** je ne supporte pas l'ail; **agreeable** adj (pleasant) agréable; (willing) consentant(e), d'accord; **agreed** adj (time, place) convenu(e); **agreement** n accord m; **in agreement** d'accord

agricultural [ægrɪ'kʌltʃərəl] adj agricole

agriculture ['ægrɪkʌltʃə'] n agriculture f

ahead [ə'hɛd] adv en avant; devant; **go right** or **straight ~** (direction) allez tout droit; **go ~!** (permission) allez-y!; **~ of** devant; (fig: schedule etc) en avance sur; **~ of time** en avance

aid [eɪd] n aide f; (device) appareil m ▷ vt aider; **in ~ of** en faveur de

aide [eɪd] n (person) assistant(e)

AIDS [eɪdz] n abbr (= acquired immune (or immuno-)deficiency syndrome) SIDA m

ailing ['eɪlɪŋ] adj (person) souffreteux(euse); (economy) malade

ailment ['eɪlmənt] n affection f

aim [eɪm] vt: **to ~ sth (at)** (gun, camera) braquer or pointer qch (sur); (missile) lancer qch (à or contre or en direction de); (remark, blow) destiner or adresser qch (à) ▷ vi (also: **to take ~**) viser ▷ n (objective) but m; (skill): **his ~ is bad** il vise mal; **to ~** viser; (fig) viser (à); **to ~ to do** avoir l'intention de faire

ain't [eɪnt] (inf) = **am not**; **aren't**; **isn't**

air [ɛə'] n air m ▷ vt aérer; (idea, grievance, views) mettre sur le tapis ▷ cpd (currents, attack etc) aérien(ne); **to throw sth into the ~** (ball etc) jeter qch en l'air; **by ~** par avion; **to be on the ~** (Radio, TV: programme) être diffusé(e); (: station) émettre; **airbag** n airbag m; **airbed** n (BRIT) matelas m pneumatique; **airborne** adj (plane) en vol; **as soon as the plane was airborne** dès que l'avion eut décollé; **air-conditioned** adj climatisé(e), à air conditionné; **air conditioning** n climatisation f; **aircraft** n inv avion m; **airfield** n terrain m d'aviation; **Air Force** n Armée f de l'air; **air hostess** n (BRIT) hôtesse f de l'air; **airing cupboard** n (BRIT) placard qui contient la chaudière et dans lequel on met le linge à sécher; **airlift** n pont aérien; **airline** n ligne aérienne, compagnie aérienne; **airliner** n avion m de ligne; **airmail** n: **by airmail** par avion; **airplane** n (US) avion m; **airport** n aéroport m; **air raid** n attaque aérienne; **airsick** adj: **to be airsick** avoir le mal de l'air; **airspace** n espace aérien; **airstrip** n terrain m d'atterrissage; **air terminal** n aérogare f; **airtight** adj hermétique; **air-traffic controller** n aiguilleur m du ciel; **airy** adj bien aéré(e);

(manners) dégagé(e)

aisle [aɪl] n (of church: central) allée f centrale; (: side) nef f latérale, bas-côté m; (in theatre, supermarket) allée; (on plane) couloir m; **aisle seat** n place f côté couloir

ajar [ə'dʒɑ:'] adj entrouvert(e)

à la carte [ælæ'kɑ:t] adv à la carte

alarm [ə'lɑ:m] n alarme f ▷ vt alarmer; **alarm call** n coup m de fil pour réveiller; **could I have an alarm call at 7 am, please?** pouvez-vous me réveiller à 7 heures, s'il vous plaît?; **alarm clock** n réveille-matin m inv, réveil m; **alarmed** adj (frightened) alarmé(e); (protected by an alarm) protégé(e) par un système d'alarme; **alarming** adj alarmant(e)

Albania [æl'beɪnɪə] n Albanie f

albeit [ɔ:l'bi:ɪt] conj bien que + sub, encore que + sub

album ['ælbəm] n album m

alcohol ['ælkəhɔl] n alcool m; **alcohol-free** adj sans alcool; **alcoholic** [ælkə'hɔlɪk] adj, n alcoolique (m/f)

alcove ['ælkəuv] n alcôve f

ale [eɪl] n bière f

alert [ə'lə:t] adj alerte, vif (vive); (watchful) vigilant(e) ▷ n alerte f ▷ vt alerter; **on the ~** sur le qui-vive; (Mil) en état d'alerte

algebra ['ældʒɪbrə] n algèbre m

Algeria [æl'dʒɪərɪə] n Algérie f

Algerian [æl'dʒɪərɪən] adj algérien(ne) ▷ n Algérien(ne)

Algiers [æl'dʒɪəz] n Alger

alias ['eɪlɪəs] adv alias ▷ n faux nom, nom d'emprunt

alibi ['ælɪbaɪ] n alibi m

alien ['eɪlɪən] n (from abroad) étranger(-ère); (from outer space) extraterrestre ▷ adj: **~ (to)** étranger(-ère) (à); **alienate** vt aliéner; (subj: person) s'aliéner

alight [ə'laɪt] adj en feu ▷ vi mettre pied à terre; (passenger) descendre; (bird) se poser

align [ə'laɪn] vt aligner

alike [ə'laɪk] adj semblable, pareil(le) ▷ adv de même; **to look ~** se ressembler

alive [ə'laɪv] adj vivant(e); (active) plein(e) de vie

KEYWORD

all [ɔ:l] adj (singular) tout(e); (plural) tous (toutes); **all day** toute la journée; **all night** toute la nuit; **all men** tous les hommes; **all five** tous les cinq; **all the books** tous les livres; **all his life** toute sa vie
▷ pron **1** tout; **I ate it all**, **I ate all of it** j'ai tout mangé; **all of us went** nous y sommes tous allés; **all of the boys went** tous les garçons y sont allés; **is that all?** c'est tout?; (in shop) ce sera tout?
2 (in phrases): **above all** surtout, par-dessus tout; **after all** après tout; **at all**: **not at all** (in answer to question) pas du tout; (in answer to thanks) je vous en prie!; **I'm not at all tired** je ne suis pas du tout fatigué(e); **anything at all will do** n'importe quoi fera l'affaire; **all in all** tout bien considéré, en fin de compte
▷ adv: **all alone** tout(e) seul(e); **it's not as hard as all that** ce n'est pas si difficile que ça; **all the more/the better** d'autant plus/mieux; **all but** presque, pratiquement; **the score is 2 all** le score est de 2 partout

Allah ['ælə] n Allah m

allegation [ælɪ'geɪʃən] n allégation f

alleged [ə'lɛdʒd] adj prétendu(e); **allegedly** adv à ce que l'on prétend, paraît-il

allegiance [ə'liːdʒəns] n fidélité f, obéissance f
allergic [ə'ləːdʒɪk] adj: **~ to** allergique à; **I'm ~ to penicillin** je suis allergique à la pénicilline
allergy [ˈælədʒɪ] n allergie f
alleviate [ə'liːvɪeɪt] vt soulager, adoucir
alley [ˈælɪ] n ruelle f
alliance [ə'laɪəns] n alliance f
allied [ˈælaɪd] adj allié(e)
alligator [ˈælɪgeɪtəʳ] n alligator m
all-in [ˈɔːlɪn] adj, adv (BRIT: charge) tout compris
allocate [ˈæləkeɪt] vt (share out) répartir, distribuer; **to ~ sth to** (duties) assigner or attribuer qch à; (sum, time) allouer qch à
allot [ə'lɔt] vt (share out) répartir, distribuer; **to ~ sth to** (time) allouer qch à; (duties) assigner qch à
all-out [ˈɔːlaut] adj (effort etc) total(e)
allow [ə'lau] vt (practice, behaviour) permettre, autoriser; (sum to spend etc) accorder, allouer; (sum, time estimated) compter, prévoir; (claim, goal) admettre; (concede): **to ~ that** convenir que; **to ~ sb to do** permettre à qn de faire, autoriser qn à faire; **he is ~ed to ...** on lui permet de ...; **allow for** vt fus tenir compte de; **allowance** n (money received) allocation f; (: from parent etc) subside m; (: for expenses) indemnité f; (us: pocket money) argent m de poche; (Tax) somme f déductible du revenu imposable, abattement m; **to make allowances for** (person) essayer de comprendre; (thing) tenir compte de
all right adv (feel, work) bien; (as answer) d'accord
ally n [ˈælaɪ] allié m ▷ vt [ə'laɪ]: **to ~ o.s. with** s'allier avec
almighty [ɔːl'maɪtɪ] adj tout(e)-puissant(e); (tremendous) énorme
almond [ˈɑːmənd] n amande f
almost [ˈɔːlməust] adv presque
alone [ə'ləun] adj, adv seul(e); **to leave sb ~** laisser qn tranquille; **to leave sth ~** ne pas toucher à qch; **let ~ ...** sans parler de ...; encore moins ...
along [ə'lɔŋ] prep le long de ▷ adv: **is he coming ~ with us?** vient-il avec nous?; **he was hopping/limping ~** il venait or avançait en sautillant/boitant; **~ with** avec, en plus de; (person) en compagnie de; **all ~** (all the time) depuis le début; **alongside** prep (along) le long de; (beside) à côté de ▷ adv bord à bord; côte à côte
aloof [ə'luːf] adj distant(e) ▷ adv: **to stand ~** se tenir à l'écart or à distance
aloud [ə'laud] adv à haute voix
alphabet [ˈælfəbɛt] n alphabet m
Alps [ælps] npl: **the ~** les Alpes fpl
already [ɔːl'rɛdɪ] adv déjà
alright [ˈɔːl'raɪt] adv (BRIT) = **all right**
also [ˈɔːlsəu] adv aussi
altar [ˈɔltəʳ] n autel m
alter [ˈɔltəʳ] vt, vi changer; **alteration** [ɔltə'reɪʃən] n changement m, modification f; **alterations** npl (Sewing) retouches fpl; (Archit) modifications fpl
alternate adj [ɔl'təːnɪt] alterné(e), alternant(e), alternatif(-ive); (us) = **alternative** ▷ vi [ˈɔltəːneɪt] alterner; **to ~ with** alterner avec; **on ~ days** un jour sur deux, tous les deux jours
alternative [ɔl'təːnətɪv] adj (solution, plan) autre, de remplacement; (lifestyle) parallèle ▷ n (choice) alternative f; (other possibility) autre possibilité f; **~ medicine** médecine alternative, médecine douce; **alternatively** adv: **alternatively one could ...** une autre or l'autre solution serait de ...

although [ɔːl'ðəu] conj bien que + sub
altitude [ˈæltɪtjuːd] n altitude f
altogether [ɔːltə'gɛðəʳ] adv entièrement, tout à fait; (on the whole) tout compte fait; (in all) en tout
aluminium [ælju'mɪnɪəm] (BRIT aluminum) [ə'luːmɪnəm] (us) n aluminium m
always [ˈɔːlweɪz] adv toujours
Alzheimer's (disease) [ˈæltshaɪməz-] n maladie f d'Alzheimer
am [æm] vb see **be**
a.m. adv abbr (= ante meridiem) du matin
amalgamate [ə'mælgəmeɪt] vt, vi fusionner
amass [ə'mæs] vt amasser
amateur [ˈæmətəʳ] n amateur m
amaze [ə'meɪz] vt stupéfier; **to be ~d (at)** être stupéfait(e) (de); **amazed** adj stupéfait(e); **amazement** n surprise f, étonnement m; **amazing** adj étonnant(e), incroyable; (bargain, offer) exceptionnel(le)
Amazon [ˈæməzən] n (Geo) Amazone f
ambassador [æm'bæsədəʳ] n ambassadeur m
amber [ˈæmbəʳ] n ambre m; **at ~** (BRIT Aut) à l'orange
ambiguous [æm'bɪgjuəs] adj ambigu(ë)
ambition [æm'bɪʃən] n ambition f; **ambitious** [æm'bɪʃəs] adj ambitieux(-euse)
ambulance [ˈæmbjuləns] n ambulance f; **call an ~!** appelez une ambulance!
ambush [ˈæmbuʃ] n embuscade f ▷ vt tendre une embuscade à
amen [ˈɑːmɛn] excl amen
amend [ə'mɛnd] vt (law) amender; (text) corriger; **to make ~s** réparer ses torts, faire amende honorable; **amendment** n (to law) amendement m; (to text) correction f
amenities [ə'miːnɪtɪz] npl aménagements mpl, équipements mpl
America [ə'mɛrɪkə] n Amérique f; **American** adj américain(e) ▷ n Américain(e); **American football** n (BRIT) football m américain
amicable [ˈæmɪkəbl] adj amical(e); (Law) à l'amiable
amid(st) [ə'mɪd(st)] prep parmi, au milieu de
ammunition [æmju'nɪʃən] n munitions fpl
amnesty [ˈæmnɪstɪ] n amnistie f
among(st) [ə'mʌŋ(st)] prep parmi, entre
amount [ə'maunt] n (sum of money) somme f; (total) montant m; (quantity) quantité f; nombre m ▷ vi: **to ~ to** (total) s'élever à; (be same as) équivaloir à, revenir à
amp(ère) [ˈæmp(ɛəʳ)] n ampère m
ample [ˈæmpl] adj ample, spacieux(-euse); (enough): **this is ~** c'est largement suffisant; **to have ~ time/room** avoir bien assez de temps/place
amplifier [ˈæmplɪfaɪəʳ] n amplificateur m
amputate [ˈæmpjuteɪt] vt amputer
Amtrak [ˈæmtræk] (us) n société mixte de transports ferroviaires interurbains pour voyageurs
amuse [ə'mjuːz] vt amuser; **amusement** n amusement m; (pastime) distraction f; **amusement arcade** n salle f de jeu; **amusement park** n parc m d'attractions
amusing [ə'mjuːzɪŋ] adj amusant(e), divertissant(e)
an [æn, ən, n] indef art see **a**
anaemia [ə'niːmɪə] (us **anemia**) n anémie f
anaemic [ə'niːmɪk] (us **anemic**) adj anémique
anaesthetic [ænɪs'θɛtɪk] (us **anesthetic**) n anesthésique m
analog(ue) [ˈænəlɔg] adj (watch, computer) analogique

analogy [əˈnælədʒɪ] n analogie f

analyse [ˈænəlaɪz] (US **analyze**) vt analyser; **analysis** (pl **analyses**) [əˈnæləsɪs, -siːz] n analyse f; **analyst** [ˈænəlɪst] n (political analyst etc) analyste m/f; (US) psychanalyste m/f

analyze [ˈænəlaɪz] vt (US) = **analyse**

anarchy [ˈænəkɪ] n anarchie f

anatomy [əˈnætəmɪ] n anatomie f

ancestor [ˈænsɪstəʳ] n ancêtre m, aïeul m

anchor [ˈæŋkəʳ] n ancre f ▷ vi (also: **to drop ~**) jeter l'ancre, mouiller ▷ vt mettre à l'ancre; (fig): **to ~ sth to** fixer qch à

anchovy [ˈæntʃəvɪ] n anchois m

ancient [ˈeɪnʃənt] adj ancien(ne), antique; (person) d'un âge vénérable; (car) antédiluvien(ne)

and [ænd] conj et; **~ so on** et ainsi de suite; **try ~ come** tâchez de venir; **come ~ sit here** venez vous asseoir ici; **he talked ~ talked** il a parlé pendant des heures; **better ~ better** de mieux en mieux; **more ~ more** de plus en plus

Andorra [ænˈdɔːrə] n (principauté f d')Andorre f

anemia etc [əˈniːmɪə] (US) = **anaemia** etc

anesthetic [ænɪsˈθetɪk] (US) = **anaesthetic**

angel [ˈeɪndʒəl] n ange m

anger [ˈæŋɡəʳ] n colère f

angina [ænˈdʒaɪnə] n angine f de poitrine

angle [ˈæŋɡl] n angle m; **from their ~** de leur point de vue

angler [ˈæŋɡləʳ] n pêcheur(-euse) à la ligne

Anglican [ˈæŋɡlɪkən] adj, n anglican(e)

angling [ˈæŋɡlɪŋ] n pêche f à la ligne

angrily [ˈæŋɡrɪlɪ] adv avec colère

angry [ˈæŋɡrɪ] adj en colère, furieux(-euse); (wound) enflammé(e); **to be ~ with sb/at sth** être furieux contre qn/de qch; **to get ~** se fâcher, se mettre en colère

anguish [ˈæŋɡwɪʃ] n angoisse f

animal [ˈænɪməl] n animal m ▷ adj animal(e)

animated [ˈænɪmeɪtɪd] adj animé(e)

animation [ænɪˈmeɪʃən] n (of person) entrain m; (of street, Cine) animation f

aniseed [ˈænɪsiːd] n anis m

ankle [ˈæŋkl] n cheville f

annex [ˈæneks] n (BRIT: also: **~e**) annexe f ▷ vt [əˈneks] annexer

anniversary [ænɪˈvəːsərɪ] n anniversaire m

announce [əˈnauns] vt annoncer; (birth, death) faire part de; **announcement** n annonce f; (for births etc: in newspaper) avis m de faire-part; (: letter, card) faire-part m; **announcer** n (Radio, TV: between programmes) speaker(ine) f; (: in a programme) présentateur(-trice)

annoy [əˈnɔɪ] vt agacer, ennuyer, contrarier; **don't get ~ed!** ne vous fâchez pas!; **annoying** adj agaçant(e), contrariant(e)

annual [ˈænjuəl] adj annuel(le) ▷ n (Bot) plante annuelle; (book) album m; **annually** adv annuellement

annum [ˈænəm] n see **per**

anonymous [əˈnɒnɪməs] adj anonyme

anorak [ˈænəræk] n anorak m

anorexia [ænəˈreksɪə] n (also: **~ nervosa**) anorexie f

anorexic [ænəˈreksɪk] adj, n anorexique (m/f)

another [əˈnʌðəʳ] adj: **~ book** (one more) un autre livre, encore un livre, un livre de plus; (a different one) un autre livre ▷ pron un(e) autre, encore un(e), un(e) de plus; see also **one**

answer [ˈɑːnsəʳ] n réponse f; (to problem) solution f ▷ vi répondre ▷ vt (reply to) répondre à; (problem) résoudre; (prayer) exaucer; **in ~ to your letter** suite à or en réponse à votre lettre; **to ~ the phone** répondre (au téléphone); **to ~ the bell** or **the door** aller or venir ouvrir (la porte); **answer back** vi répondre, répliquer; **answerphone** n (esp BRIT) répondeur m (téléphonique)

ant [ænt] n fourmi f

Antarctic [æntˈɑːktɪk] n: **the ~** l'Antarctique m

antelope [ˈæntɪləup] n antilope f

antenatal [ˈæntɪˈneɪtl] adj prénatal(e)

antenna (pl **~e**) [ænˈtenə, -niː] n antenne f

anthem [ˈænθəm] n: **national ~** hymne national

anthology [ænˈθɒlədʒɪ] n anthologie f

anthrax [ˈænθræks] n anthrax m

anthropology [ænθrəˈpɒlədʒɪ] n anthropologie f

anti [ˈæntɪ] prefix anti-; **antibiotic** [ˈæntɪbaɪˈɒtɪk] n antibiotique m; **antibody** [ˈæntɪbɒdɪ] n anticorps m

anticipate [ænˈtɪsɪpeɪt] vt s'attendre à, prévoir; (wishes, request) aller au devant de, devancer; **anticipation** [æntɪsɪˈpeɪʃən] n attente f

anticlimax [ˈæntɪˈklaɪmæks] n déception f

anticlockwise [ˈæntɪˈklɒkwaɪz] (BRIT) adv dans le sens inverse des aiguilles d'une montre

antics [ˈæntɪks] npl singeries fpl

anti: **antidote** [ˈæntɪdəut] n antidote m, contrepoison m; **antifreeze** [ˈæntɪfriːz] n antigel m; **anti-globalization** n antimondialisation f; **antihistamine** [æntɪˈhɪstəmɪn] n antihistaminique m; **antiperspirant** [æntɪˈpəːspɪrənt] n déodorant m

antique [ænˈtiːk] n (ornament) objet m d'art ancien; (furniture) meuble ancien ▷ adj ancien(ne); **antique shop** n magasin m d'antiquités

antiseptic [æntɪˈseptɪk] adj, n antiseptique (m)

antisocial [ˈæntɪˈsəuʃəl] adj (unfriendly) peu liant(e), insociable; (against society) antisocial(e)

antlers [ˈæntləz] npl bois mpl, ramure f

anxiety [æŋˈzaɪətɪ] n anxiété f; (keenness): **~ to do** grand désir or impatience f de faire

anxious [ˈæŋkʃəs] adj (très) inquiet(-ète); (always worried) anxieux(-euse); (worrying) angoissant(e); (keen): **~ to do/that** qui tient beaucoup à faire/à ce que + sub; impatient(e) de faire/que + sub

 KEYWORD

any [ˈenɪ] adj **1** (in questions etc: singular) du, de l', de la; (: plural) des; **do you have any butter/children/ink?** avez-vous du beurre/des enfants/de l'encre?

2 (with negative) de, d'; **I don't have any money/books** je n'ai pas d'argent/de livres

3 (no matter which) n'importe quel(le); (each and every) tout(e), chaque; **choose any book you like** vous pouvez choisir n'importe quel livre; **any teacher you ask will tell you** n'importe quel professeur vous le dira

4 (in phrases): **in any case** de toute façon; **any day now** d'un jour à l'autre; **at any moment** à tout moment, d'un instant à l'autre; **at any rate** en tout cas; **any time** n'importe quand; **he might come (at) any time** il pourrait venir n'importe quand; **come (at) any time** venez quand vous voulez

▷ pron **1** (in questions etc) en; **have you got any?** est-ce que vous en avez?; **can any of you sing?** est-ce que parmi vous il y en a qui savent chanter?

2 (with negative) en; **I don't have any (of them)** je n'en ai pas, je n'en ai aucun

3 (no matter which one(s)) n'importe lequel (or laquelle); (anybody) n'importe qui; **take any of those books (you like)** vous pouvez prendre n'importe lequel de ces livres ▷ adv **1** (in questions etc): **do you want any more soup/sandwiches?** voulez-vous encore de la soupe/des sandwichs?; **are you feeling any better?** est-ce que vous vous sentez mieux?

2 (with negative): **I can't hear him any more** je ne l'entends plus; **don't wait any longer** n'attendez pas plus longtemps; **anybody** pron n'importe qui; (in interrogative sentences) quelqu'un; (in negative sentences): **I don't see anybody** je ne vois personne; **if anybody should phone ...** si quelqu'un téléphone ...; **anyhow** adv quoi qu'il en soit; (haphazardly) n'importe comment; **do it anyhow you like** faites-le comme vous voulez; **she leaves things just anyhow** elle laisse tout traîner; **I shall go anyhow** j'irai de toute façon; **anyone** pron **= anybody**; **anything** pron (no matter what) n'importe quoi; (in questions) quelque chose; (with negative) ne ... rien; **can you see anything?** tu vois quelque chose?; **if anything happens to me ...** s'il m'arrive quoi que ce soit ...; **you can say anything you like** vous pouvez dire ce que vous voulez; **anything will do** n'importe quoi fera l'affaire; **he'll eat anything** il mange de tout; **anytime** adv (at any moment) d'un moment à l'autre; (whenever) n'importe quand; **anyway** adv de toute façon; **anyway, I couldn't come even if I wanted to** de toute façon, je ne pouvais pas venir même si je le voulais; **I shall go anyway** j'irai quand même; **why are you phoning, anyway?** au fait, pourquoi tu me téléphones?; **anywhere** adv n'importe où; (in interrogative sentences) quelque part; (in negative sentences): **I can't see him anywhere** je ne le vois nulle part; **can you see him anywhere?** tu le vois quelque part?; **put the books down anywhere** pose les livres n'importe où; **anywhere in the world** (no matter where) n'importe où dans le monde

apart [ə'pɑːt] adv (to one side) à part; de côté; à l'écart; (separately) séparément; **to take/pull ~ apart** démonter; **10 miles/a long way ~** à 10 miles/très éloignés l'un de l'autre; **~ from** prep à part, excepté

apartment [ə'pɑːtmənt] n (us) appartement m, logement m; (room) chambre f; **apartment building** n (us) immeuble m; maison divisée en appartements

apathy ['æpəθɪ] n apathie f, indifférence f

ape [eɪp] n (grand) singe ▷ vt singer

aperitif [ə'perɪtɪf] n apéritif m

aperture ['æpətʃjuə^r] n orifice m, ouverture f; (Phot) ouverture (du diaphragme)

APEX ['eɪpɛks] n abbr (Aviat: = advance purchase excursion) APEX m

apologize [ə'pɔlədʒaɪz] vi: **to ~ (for sth to sb)** s'excuser (de qch auprès de qn), présenter des excuses (à qn pour qch)

apology [ə'pɔlədʒɪ] n excuses fpl

apostrophe [ə'pɔstrəfɪ] n apostrophe f

appal [ə'pɔːl] (us **appall**) vt consterner, atterrer; horrifier; **appalling** adj épouvantable; (stupidity) consternant(e)

apparatus [æpə'reɪtəs] n appareil m, dispositif m; (in gymnasium) agrès mpl

apparent [ə'pærənt] adj apparent(e); **apparently** adv apparemment

appeal [ə'piːl] vi (Law) faire or interjeter appel ▷ n (Law) appel m; (request) appel; prière f; (charm) attrait m, charme m; **to ~ for** demander (instamment); implorer; **to ~ to** (beg) faire appel à; (be attractive) plaire à; **it doesn't ~ to me** cela ne m'attire pas; **appealing** adj (attractive) attrayant(e)

appear [ə'pɪə^r] vi apparaître, se montrer; (Law) comparaître; (publication) paraître, sortir, être publié(e); (seem) paraître, sembler; **it would ~ that** il semble que; **to ~ in Hamlet** jouer dans Hamlet; **to ~ on TV** passer à la télé; **appearance** n apparition f; parution f; (look, aspect) apparence f, aspect m

appendices [ə'pendɪsiːz] npl of **appendix**

appendicitis [əpendɪ'saɪtɪs] n appendicite f

appendix (pl **appendices**) [ə'pendɪks, -siːz] n appendice m

appetite ['æpɪtaɪt] n appétit m

appetizer ['æpɪtaɪzə^r] n (food) amuse-gueule m; (drink) apéritif m

applaud [ə'plɔːd] vt, vi applaudir

applause [ə'plɔːz] n applaudissements mpl

apple ['æpl] n pomme f; **apple pie** n tarte f aux pommes

appliance [ə'plaɪəns] n appareil m

applicable [ə'plɪkəbl] adj applicable; **to be ~ to** (relevant) valoir pour

applicant ['æplɪkənt] n: **~ (for)** candidat(e) (à)

application [æplɪ'keɪʃən] n application f; (for a job, a grant etc) demande f; candidature f; **application form** n formulaire m de demande

apply [ə'plaɪ] vt: **to ~ (to)** (paint, ointment) appliquer (sur); (law, etc) appliquer (à) ▷ vi: **to ~** (ask) s'adresser à; (be suitable for, relevant to) s'appliquer à; **to ~ (for)** (permit, grant) faire une demande (en vue d'obtenir); (job) poser sa candidature (pour), faire une demande d'emploi (concernant); **to ~ o.s. to** s'appliquer à

appoint [ə'pɔɪnt] vt (to post) nommer, engager; (date, place) fixer, désigner; **appointment** n (to post) nomination f; (job) poste m; (arrangement to meet) rendez-vous m; **to have an appointment** avoir un rendez-vous; **to make an appointment (with)** prendre rendez-vous (avec); **I'd like to make an appointment** je voudrais prendre rendez-vous

appraisal [ə'preɪzl] n évaluation f

appreciate [ə'priːʃɪeɪt] vt (like) apprécier, faire cas de; (be grateful for) être reconnaissant(e) de; (be aware of) comprendre, se rendre compte de ▷ vi (Finance) prendre de la valeur; **appreciation** [əpriːʃɪ'eɪʃən] n appréciation f; (gratitude) reconnaissance f; (Finance) hausse f, valorisation f

apprehension [æprɪ'henʃən] n appréhension f, inquiétude f

apprehensive [æprɪ'hensɪv] adj inquiet(-ète), appréhensif(-ive)

apprentice [ə'prentɪs] n apprenti m

approach [ə'prəutʃ] vi approcher ▷ vt (come near) approcher de; (ask, apply to) s'adresser à; (subject, passer-by) aborder ▷ n approche f; accès m, abord m; démarche f (intellectuelle)

appropriate adj [ə'prəuprɪɪt] (tool etc) qui convient, approprié(e); (moment, remark) opportun(e) ▷ vt [ə'prəuprɪeɪt] (take) s'approprier

approval [ə'pruːvəl] n approbation f; **on ~** (Comm) à

l'examen

approve [ə'pruːv] vt approuver; **approve of** vt fus (thing) approuver; (person): **they don't ~ of her** ils n'ont pas bonne opinion d'elle

approximate [ə'prɔksimit] adj approximatif(-ive); **approximately** adv approximativement

Apr. abbr = **April**

apricot ['eiprikɔt] n abricot m

April ['eiprəl] n avril m; **April Fools' Day** n le premier avril

apron ['eiprən] n tablier m

apt [æpt] adj (suitable) approprié(-e); (likely): **~ to do** susceptible de faire; ayant tendance à faire

aquarium [ə'kwɛəriəm] n aquarium m

Aquarius [ə'kwɛəriəs] n le Verseau

Arab ['ærəb] n Arabe m/f ▷ adj arabe

Arabia [ə'reibiə] n Arabie f; **Arabian** adj arabe; **Arabic** ['ærəbik] adj, n arabe (m)

arbitrary ['ɑːbitrəri] adj arbitraire

arbitration [ɑːbi'treiʃən] n arbitrage m

arc [ɑːk] n arc m

arcade [ɑː'keid] n arcade f; (passage with shops) passage m, galerie f; (with games) salle f de jeu

arch [ɑːtʃ] n arche f; (of foot) cambrure f, voûte f plantaire ▷ vt arquer, cambrer

archaeology [ɑːki'ɔlədʒi] (US **archeology**) n archéologie f

archbishop [ɑːtʃ'biʃəp] n archevêque m

archeology [ɑːki'ɔlədʒi] (US) = **archaeology**

architect ['ɑːkitekt] n architecte m; **architectural** [ɑːki'tektʃərəl] adj architectural(e); **architecture** n architecture f

archive ['ɑːkaiv] n (often pl) archives fpl

Arctic ['ɑːktik] adj arctique ▷ n: **the ~** l'Arctique m

are [ɑːʳ] vb see **be**

area ['ɛəriə] n (Geom) superficie f; (zone) région f; (: smaller) secteur m; (in room) coin m; (knowledge, research) domaine m; **area code** (US) n (Tel) indicatif m de zone

arena [ə'riːnə] n arène f

aren't [ɑːnt] = **are not**

Argentina [ɑːdʒən'tiːnə] n Argentine f; **Argentinian** [ɑːdʒən'tiniən] adj argentin(e) ▷ n Argentin(e)

arguably ['ɑːgjuəbli] adv: **it is ~ ...** on peut soutenir que c'est ...

argue ['ɑːgjuː] vi (quarrel) se disputer; (reason) argumenter; **to ~ that** objecter or alléguer que, donner comme argument que

argument ['ɑːgjumənt] n (quarrel) dispute f, discussion f; (reasons) argument m

Aries ['ɛəriz] n le Bélier

arise (pt **arose**, pp **~n**) [ə'raiz, ə'rəuz, ə'rizn] vi survenir, se présenter

arithmetic [ə'riθmətik] n arithmétique f

arm [ɑːm] n bras m ▷ vt armer; **arms** npl (weapons, Heraldry) armes fpl; **~ in ~** bras dessus bras dessous; **armchair** ['ɑːmtʃɛəʳ] n fauteuil m

armed [ɑːmd] adj armé(e); **armed forces** npl: **the armed forces** les forces armées; **armed robbery** n vol m à main armée

armour (US **armor**) ['ɑːməʳ] n armure f; (Mil: tanks) blindés mpl

armpit ['ɑːmpit] n aisselle f

armrest ['ɑːmrest] n accoudoir m

army ['ɑːmi] n armée f

A road n (BRIT) ≈ route nationale

aroma [ə'rəumə] n arôme m; **aromatherapy** n aromathérapie f

arose [ə'rəuz] pt of **arise**

around [ə'raund] adv (tout) autour; (nearby) dans les parages ▷ prep autour de; (near) près de; (fig: about) environ; (: date, time) vers; **is he ~?** est-il dans les parages or là?

arouse [ə'rauz] vt (sleeper) éveiller; (curiosity, passions) éveiller, susciter; (anger) exciter

arrange [ə'reindʒ] vt arranger; **to ~ to do sth** prévoir de faire qch; **arrangement** n arrangement m; **arrangements** npl (plans etc) arrangements mpl, dispositions fpl

array [ə'rei] n (of objects) déploiement m, étalage m

arrears [ə'riəz] npl arriéré m; **to be in ~ with one's rent** devoir un arriéré de loyer

arrest [ə'rest] vt arrêter; (sb's attention) retenir, attirer ▷ n arrestation f; **under ~** en état d'arrestation

arrival [ə'raivl] n arrivée f; **new ~** nouveau venu/ nouvelle venue; (baby) nouveau-né(e)

arrive [ə'raiv] vi arriver; **arrive at** vt fus (decision, solution) parvenir à

arrogance ['ærəgəns] n arrogance f

arrogant ['ærəgənt] adj arrogant(e)

arrow ['ærəu] n flèche f

arse [ɑːs] n (BRIT inf!) cul m (!)

arson ['ɑːsn] n incendie criminel

art [ɑːt] n art m; **Arts** npl (Scol) les lettres fpl; **art college** n école f des beaux-arts

artery ['ɑːtəri] n artère f

art gallery n musée m d'art; (saleroom) galerie f de peinture

arthritis [ɑː'θraitis] n arthrite f

artichoke ['ɑːtitʃəuk] n artichaut m; **Jerusalem ~** topinambour m

article ['ɑːtikl] n article m

articulate adj [ɑː'tikjulit] (person) qui s'exprime clairement et aisément; (speech) bien articulé(e), prononcé(e) clairement ▷ vb [ɑː'tikjuleit] ▷ vi articuler, parler distinctement ▷ vt articuler

artificial [ɑːti'fiʃəl] adj artificiel(le)

artist ['ɑːtist] n artiste m/f; **artistic** [ɑː'tistik] adj artistique

art school n ≈ école f des beaux-arts

 KEYWORD

as [æz] conj **1** (time: moment) comme, alors que; à mesure que; **he came in as I was leaving** il est arrivé comme je partais; **as the years went by** à mesure que les années passaient; **as from tomorrow** à partir de demain

2 (since, because) comme, puisque; **he left early as he had to be home by 10** comme il or puisqu'il devait être de retour avant 10h, il est parti de bonne heure

3 (referring to manner, way) comme; **do as you wish** faites comme vous voudrez; **as she said** comme elle disait

▷ adv **1** (in comparisons): **as big as** aussi grand que; **twice as big as** deux fois plus grand que; **as much** or **many as** autant que; **as much money/many books as** autant d'argent/de livres que; **as soon as** dès que

2 (concerning): **as for** or **to that** quant à cela, pour ce qui est de cela

3: **as if** or **though** comme si; **he looked as if he was ill** il avait l'air d'être malade; *see also* **long**; **such**; **well**
▷ *prep* (*in the capacity of*) en tant que, en qualité de; **he works as a driver** il travaille comme chauffeur; **as chairman of the company, he …** en tant que président de la société, il …; **he gave me it as a present** il me l'a offert, il m'en a fait cadeau

a.s.a.p. *abbr* = **as soon as possible**
asbestos [æz'bɛstəs] *n* asbeste *m*, amiante *m*
ascent [ə'sɛnt] *n* (*climb*) ascension *f*
ash [æʃ] *n* (*dust*) cendre *f*; (*also*: **~ tree**) frêne *m*
ashamed [ə'ʃeɪmd] *adj* honteux(-euse), confus(e); **to be ~ of** avoir honte de
ashore [ə'ʃɔːʳ] *adv* à terre
ashtray ['æʃtreɪ] *n* cendrier *m*
Ash Wednesday *n* mercredi *m* des Cendres
Asia ['eɪʃə] *n* Asie *f*; **Asian** *n* (*from Asia*) Asiatique *m/f*; (BRIT: *from Indian subcontinent*) Indo-Pakistanais(-e) ▷ *adj* asiatique; indo-pakistanais(-e)
aside [ə'saɪd] *adv* de côté; à l'écart ▷ *n* aparté *m*
ask [ɑːsk] *vt* demander; (*invite*) inviter; **to ~ sb sth/to do sth** demander à qn qch/de faire qch; **to ~ sb about sth** questionner qn au sujet de qch; se renseigner auprès de qn au sujet de qch; **to ~ (sb) a question** poser une question (à qn); **to ~ sb to dinner** inviter qn au restaurant; **ask for** *vt fus* demander; **it's just ~ing for trouble** or **for it** ce serait chercher des ennuis
asleep [ə'sliːp] *adj* endormi(e); **to fall ~** s'endormir
AS level *n abbr* (= *Advanced Subsidiary level*) première partie de l'examen équivalent au baccalauréat
asparagus [əs'pærəgəs] *n* asperges *fpl*
aspect ['æspɛkt] *n* aspect *m*; (*direction in which a building etc faces*) orientation *f*, exposition *f*
aspirations [æspə'reɪʃənz] *npl* (*hopes, ambition*) aspirations *fpl*
aspire [əs'paɪəʳ] *vi*: **to ~ to** aspirer à
aspirin ['æsprɪn] *n* aspirine *f*
ass [æs] *n* âne *m*; (*inf*) imbécile *m/f*; (*us inf!*) cul *m* (!)
assassin [ə'sæsɪn] *n* assassin *m*; **assassinate** *vt* assassiner
assault [ə'sɔːlt] *n* (*Mil*) assaut *m*; (*gen: attack*) agression *f* ▷ *vt* attaquer; (*sexually*) violenter
assemble [ə'sɛmbl] *vt* assembler ▷ *vi* s'assembler, se rassembler
assembly [ə'sɛmblɪ] *n* (*meeting*) rassemblement *m*; (*parliament*) assemblée *f*; (*construction*) assemblage *m*
assert [ə'səːt] *vt* affirmer, déclarer; (*authority*) faire valoir; (*innocence*) protester de; **assertion** [ə'səːʃən] *n* assertion *f*, affirmation *f*
assess [ə'sɛs] *vt* évaluer, estimer; (*tax, damages*) établir or fixer le montant de; (*person*) juger la valeur de; **assessment** *n* évaluation *f*, estimation *f*; (*of tax*) fixation *f*
asset ['æsɛt] *n* avantage *m*, atout *m*; (*person*) atout *m*; **assets** *npl* (Comm) capital *m*; avoir(s) *m(pl)*; actif *m*
assign [ə'saɪn] *vt* (*date*) fixer, arrêter; **to ~ sth to** (*task*) assigner qch à; (*resources*) affecter qch à; **assignment** *n* (*task*) mission *f*; (*homework*) devoir *m*
assist [ə'sɪst] *vt* aider, assister; **assistance** *n* aide *f*, assistance *f*; **assistant** *n* assistant(e), adjoint(e); (BRIT: *also*: **shop assistant**) vendeur(-euse)
associate *adj*, *n* [ə'səʊʃɪt] associé(e) ▷ *vb* [ə'səʊʃɪeɪt]

▷ *vt* associer ▷ *vi*: **to ~ with sb** fréquenter qn
association [əsəʊsɪ'eɪʃən] *n* association *f*
assorted [ə'sɔːtɪd] *adj* assorti(e)
assortment [ə'sɔːtmənt] *n* assortiment *m*; (*of people*) mélange *m*
assume [ə'sjuːm] *vt* supposer; (*responsibilities etc*) assumer; (*attitude, name*) prendre, adopter
assumption [ə'sʌmpʃən] *n* supposition *f*, hypothèse *f*; (*of power*) assomption *f*, prise *f*
assurance [ə'ʃʊərəns] *n* assurance *f*
assure [ə'ʃʊəʳ] *vt* assurer
asterisk ['æstərɪsk] *n* astérisque *m*
asthma ['æsmə] *n* asthme *m*
astonish [ə'stɒnɪʃ] *vt* étonner, stupéfier; **astonished** *adj* étonné(e); **to be astonished at** être étonné(e) de; **astonishing** *adj* étonnant(e), stupéfiant(e); **I find it astonishing that …** je trouve incroyable que … + *sub*; **astonishment** *n* (grand) étonnement *m*, stupéfaction *f*
astound [ə'staund] *vt* stupéfier, sidérer
astray [ə'streɪ] *adv*: **to go ~** s'égarer; (*fig*) quitter le droit chemin; **to lead ~** (*morally*) détourner du droit chemin
astrology [əs'trɒlədʒɪ] *n* astrologie *f*
astronaut ['æstrənɔːt] *n* astronaute *m/f*
astronomer [əs'trɒnəməʳ] *n* astronome *m*
astronomical [æstrə'nɒmɪkl] *adj* astronomique
astronomy [əs'trɒnəmɪ] *n* astronomie *f*
astute [əs'tjuːt] *adj* astucieux(-euse), malin(-igne)
asylum [ə'saɪləm] *n* asile *m*; **asylum seeker** [-siːkəʳ] *n* demandeur(-euse) d'asile

○ **KEYWORD**

at [æt] *prep* **1** (*referring to position, direction*) à; **at the top** au sommet; **at home/school** à la maison or chez soi/à l'école; **at the baker's** à la boulangerie, chez le boulanger; **to look at sth** regarder qch
2 (*referring to time*): **at 4 o'clock** à 4 heures; **at Christmas** à Noël; **at night** la nuit; **at times** par moments, parfois
3 (*referring to rates, speed etc*) à; **at £1 a kilo** une livre le kilo; **two at a time** deux à la fois; **at 50 km/h** à 50 km/h
4 (*referring to manner*): **at a stroke** d'un seul coup; **at peace** en paix
5 (*referring to activity*): **to be at work** (*in the office etc*) être au travail; (*working*) travailler; **to play at cowboys** jouer aux cowboys; **to be good at sth** être bon en qch
6 (*referring to cause*): **shocked/surprised/annoyed at sth** choqué par/étonné de/agacé par qch; **I went at his suggestion** j'y suis allé sur son conseil
7 (*symbol*) arobase *f*

ate [eɪt] *pt of* **eat**
atheist ['eɪθɪɪst] *n* athée *m/f*
Athens ['æθɪnz] *n* Athènes
athlete ['æθliːt] *n* athlète *m/f*
athletic [æθ'lɛtɪk] *adj* athlétique; **athletics** *n* athlétisme *m*
Atlantic [ət'læntɪk] *adj* atlantique ▷ *n*: **the ~ (Ocean)** l'(océan *m*) Atlantique *m*
atlas ['ætləs] *n* atlas *m*
A.T.M. *n abbr* (= *Automated Telling Machine*) guichet *m* automatique
atmosphere ['ætməsfɪəʳ] *n* (*air*) atmosphère *f*; (*fig: of place etc*) atmosphère, ambiance *f*

atom ['ætəm] n atome m; **atomic** [ə'tɔmɪk] adj atomique; **atom(ic) bomb** n bombe f atomique

A to Z® n (map) plan m des rues

atrocity [ə'trɔsɪtɪ] n atrocité f

attach [ə'tætʃ] vt (gen) attacher; (document, letter) joindre; **to be ~ed to sb/sth** (to like) être attaché à qn/qch; **attachment** n (tool) accessoire m; (Comput) fichier m joint; (love): **attachment (to)** affection f (pour), attachement m (à)

attack [ə'tæk] vt attaquer; (task etc) s'attaquer à ▷ n attaque f; **heart ~** crise f cardiaque; **attacker** n attaquant m; agresseur m

attain [ə'teɪn] vt (also: **to ~ to**) parvenir à, atteindre; (knowledge) acquérir

attempt [ə'tɛmpt] n tentative f ▷ vt essayer, tenter

attend [ə'tɛnd] vt (course) suivre; (meeting, talk) assister à; (school, church) aller à, fréquenter; (patient) soigner, s'occuper de; **attend to** vt fus (needs, affairs etc) s'occuper de; (customer) s'occuper de, servir; **attendance** n (being present) présence f; (people present) assistance f; **attendant** n employé(e); gardien(ne) ▷ adj concomitant(e), qui accompagne or s'ensuit

attention [ə'tɛnʃən] n attention f ▷ excl (Mil) garde-à-vous!; **for the ~ of** (Admin) à l'attention de

attic ['ætɪk] n grenier m, combles mpl

attitude ['ætɪtjuːd] n attitude f

attorney [ə'tɜːnɪ] n (us: lawyer) avocat m; **Attorney General** n (BRIT) ≈ procureur général; (us) ≈ garde m des Sceaux, ministre m de la Justice

attract [ə'trækt] vt attirer; **attraction** [ə'trækʃən] n (gen pl: pleasant things) attraction f, attrait m; (Physics) attraction; (fig: towards sb, sth) attirance f; **attractive** adj séduisant(e), attrayant(e)

attribute n ['ætrɪbjuːt] attribut m ▷ vt [ə'trɪbjuːt]: **to ~ sth to** attribuer qch à

aubergine ['əʊbəʒiːn] n aubergine f

auburn ['ɔːbən] adj auburn inv, châtain roux inv

auction ['ɔːkʃən] n (also: **sale by ~**) vente f aux enchères ▷ vt (also: **to sell by ~**) vendre aux enchères

audible ['ɔːdɪbl] adj audible

audience ['ɔːdɪəns] n (people) assistance f, public m; (on radio) auditeurs mpl; (at theatre) spectateurs mpl; (interview) audience f

audit ['ɔːdɪt] vt vérifier

audition [ɔː'dɪʃən] n audition f

auditor ['ɔːdɪtə*] n vérificateur m des comptes

auditorium [ɔːdɪ'tɔːrɪəm] n auditorium m, salle f de concert or de spectacle

Aug. abbr = **August**

August ['ɔːgəst] n août m

aunt [ɑːnt] n tante f; **auntie, aunty** n diminutive of **aunt**

au pair ['əʊ'pɛə*] n (also: **~ girl**) jeune fille f au pair

aura ['ɔːrə] n atmosphère f; (of person) aura f

austerity [ɔs'tɛrɪtɪ] n austérité f

Australia [ɔs'treɪlɪə] n Australie f; **Australian** adj australien(ne) ▷ n Australien(ne)

Austria ['ɔstrɪə] n Autriche f; **Austrian** adj autrichien(ne) ▷ n Autrichien(ne)

authentic [ɔː'θɛntɪk] adj authentique

author ['ɔːθə*] n auteur m

authority [ɔː'θɔrɪtɪ] n autorité f; (permission) autorisation (formelle); **the authorities** les autorités fpl, l'administration f

authorize ['ɔːθəraɪz] vt autoriser

auto ['ɔːtəu] n (us) auto f, voiture f; **autobiography** [ɔːtəbaɪ'ɔgrəfɪ] n autobiographie f; **autograph** ['ɔːtəgrɑːf] n autographe m ▷ vt signer, dédicacer; **automatic** [ɔːtə'mætɪk] adj automatique ▷ n (gun) automatique m; (car) voiture f à transmission automatique; **automatically** adv automatiquement; **automobile** ['ɔːtəməbiːl] n (us) automobile f; **autonomous** [ɔː'tɔnəməs] adj autonome; **autonomy** [ɔː'tɔnəmɪ] n autonomie f

autumn ['ɔːtəm] n automne m

auxiliary [ɔːg'zɪlɪərɪ] adj, n auxiliaire (m/f)

avail [ə'veɪl] vt: **to ~ o.s. of** user de; profiter de ▷ n: **to no ~** sans résultat, en vain, en pure perte

availability [əveɪlə'bɪlɪtɪ] n disponibilité f

available [ə'veɪləbl] adj disponible

avalanche ['ævəlɑːnʃ] n avalanche f

Ave. abbr = **avenue**

avenue ['ævənjuː] n avenue f; (fig) moyen m

average ['ævərɪdʒ] n moyenne f ▷ adj moyen(ne) ▷ vt (a certain figure) atteindre or faire etc en moyenne; **on ~** en moyenne

avert [ə'vɜːt] vt (danger) prévenir, écarter; (one's eyes) détourner

avid ['ævɪd] adj avide

avocado [ævə'kɑːdəu] n (BRIT: also: **~ pear**) avocat m

avoid [ə'vɔɪd] vt éviter

await [ə'weɪt] vt attendre

awake [ə'weɪk] adj éveillé(e) ▷ vb (pt awoke, pp awoken) ▷ vt éveiller ▷ vi s'éveiller; **to be ~** être réveillé(e)

award [ə'wɔːd] n (for bravery) récompense f; (prize) prix m; (Law: damages) dommages-intérêts mpl ▷ vt (prize) décerner; (Law: damages) accorder

aware [ə'wɛə*] adj: **~ of** (conscious) conscient(e) de; (informed) au courant de; **to become ~ of/that** prendre conscience de/que; se rendre compte de/que; **awareness** n conscience f, connaissance f

away [ə'weɪ] adv (au) loin; (movement): **she went ~** elle est partie ▷ adj (not here, not there) absent(e); (Sport): **to play ~** jouer à l'extérieur; **~ from** loin de; **two kilometres ~** à (une distance de) deux kilomètres, à deux kilomètres de distance; **two hours ~ by car** à deux heures de voiture or de route; **the holiday was two weeks ~** il restait deux semaines jusqu'aux vacances; **he's ~ for a week** il est parti (pour) une semaine; **to take sth ~ from sb** prendre qch à qn; **to take sth ~ from sth** (subtract) ôter qch de qch; **to work/pedal ~** travailler/pédaler à cœur joie; **to fade ~** (colour) s'estomper; (sound) s'affaiblir

awe [ɔː] n respect mêlé de crainte, effroi mêlé d'admiration; **awesome** ['ɔːsəm] (us) adj (inf: excellent) génial(e)

awful ['ɔːfəl] adj affreux(-euse); **an ~ lot of** énormément de; **awfully** adv (very) terriblement, vraiment

awkward ['ɔːkwəd] adj (clumsy) gauche, maladroit(e); (inconvenient) peu pratique; (embarrassing) gênant(e)

awoke [ə'wəuk] pt of **awake**

awoken [ə'wəukən] pp of **awake**

axe [æks] (us **ax**) n hache f ▷ vt (project etc) abandonner; (jobs) supprimer

axle ['æksl] n essieu m

ay(e) [aɪ] excl (yes) oui

azalea [ə'zeɪlɪə] n azalée f

B [biː] n (Mus): **B** si m
B.A. abbr (Scol) = **Bachelor of Arts**
baby ['beɪbɪ] n bébé m; **baby carriage** n (US) voiture f d'enfant; **baby-sit** vi garder les enfants; **baby-sitter** n baby-sitter m/f; **baby wipe** n lingette f (pour bébé)
bachelor ['bætʃələʳ] n célibataire m; **B~ of Arts/Science (BA/BSc)** ≈ licencié(e) ès or en lettres/sciences
back [bæk] n (of person, horse) dos m; (of hand) dos, revers m; (of house) derrière m; (of car, train) arrière m; (of chair) dossier m; (of page) verso m; (of crowd): **can the people at the ~ hear me properly?** est-ce que les gens du fond peuvent m'entendre?; (Football) arrière m; **~ to front** à l'envers ▷ vt (financially) soutenir (financièrement); (candidate: also: **~ up**) soutenir, appuyer; (horse: at races) parier or miser sur; (car) (faire) reculer ▷ vi reculer; (car etc) faire marche arrière ▷ adj (in compounds) de derrière, à l'arrière; **~ seat/wheel** (Aut) siège m/roue f arrière inv; **~ payments/rent** arriéré m de paiements/loyer; **~ garden/room** jardin/pièce sur l'arrière ▷ adv (not forward) en arrière; (returned): **he's ~** il est rentré, il est de retour; **he ran ~** il est revenu en courant; (restitution): **throw the ball ~** renvoie la balle; **can I have it ~?** puis-je le ravoir?, peux-tu me le rendre?; (again): **he called ~** il a rappelé; **back down** vi rabattre de ses prétentions; **back out** vi (of promise) se dédire; **back up** vt (person) soutenir; (Comput) faire une copie de sauvegarde de; **backache** n mal m au dos; **backbencher** (BRIT) n membre du parlement sans portefeuille; **backbone** n colonne vertébrale, épine dorsale; **back door** n porte f de derrière; **backfire** vi (Aut) pétarader; (plans) mal tourner; **backgammon** n trictrac m; **background** n arrière-plan m; (of events) situation f, conjoncture f; (basic knowledge) éléments mpl de base; (experience) formation f; **family background** milieu familial; **backing** n (fig) soutien m, appui m; **backlog** n: **backlog of work** travail m en retard; **backpack** n sac m à dos; **backpacker** n randonneur(-euse); **backslash** n barre oblique inversée; **backstage** adv dans les coulisses; **backstroke** n dos crawlé; **backup** adj (train, plane) supplémentaire, de réserve; (Comput) de sauvegarde ▷ n (support) appui

m, soutien m; (Comput: also: **backup file**) sauvegarde f; **backward** adj (movement) en arrière; (person, country) arriéré(e), attardé(e); **backwards** adv (move, go) en arrière; (read a list) à l'envers, à rebours; (fall) à la renverse; (walk) à reculons; **backyard** n arrière-cour f
bacon ['beɪkən] n bacon m, lard m
bacteria [bæk'tɪərɪə] npl bactéries fpl
bad [bæd] adj mauvais(e); (child) vilain(e); (mistake, accident) grave; (meat, food) gâté(e), avarié(e); **his ~ leg** sa jambe malade; **to go ~** (meat, food) se gâter; (milk) tourner
bade [bæd] pt of **bid**
badge [bædʒ] n insigne m; (of policeman) plaque f; (stickon, sew-on) badge m
badger ['bædʒəʳ] n blaireau m
badly ['bædlɪ] adv (work, dress etc) mal; **to reflect ~ on sb** donner une mauvaise image de qn; **~ wounded** grièvement blessé; **he needs it ~** il en a absolument besoin; **~ off** adj, adv dans la gêne
bad-mannered ['bæd'mænəd] adj mal élevé(e)
badminton ['bædmɪntən] n badminton m
bad-tempered ['bæd'tempəd] adj (by nature) ayant mauvais caractère; (on one occasion) de mauvaise humeur
bag [bæg] n sac m; **~s of** (inf: lots of) des tas de; **baggage** n bagages mpl; **baggage allowance** n franchise f de bagages; **baggage reclaim** n (at airport) livraison f des bagages; **baggy** adj avachi(e), qui fait des poches; **bagpipes** npl cornemuse f
bail [beɪl] n caution f ▷ vt (prisoner: also: **grant ~ to**) mettre en liberté sous caution; (boat: also: **~ out**) écoper; **to be released on ~** être libéré(e) sous caution; **bail out** vt (prisoner) payer la caution de
bait [beɪt] n appât m ▷ vt appâter; (fig: tease) tourmenter
bake [beɪk] vt (faire) cuire au four ▷ vi (bread etc) cuire (au four); (make cakes etc) faire de la pâtisserie; **baked beans** npl haricots blancs à la sauce tomate; **baked potato** n pomme f de terre en robe des champs; **baker** n boulanger m; **bakery** n boulangerie f; **baking** n (process) cuisson f; **baking powder** n levure f (chimique)
balance ['bæləns] n équilibre m; (Comm: sum) solde m; (remainder) reste m; (scales) balance f ▷ vt mettre or faire tenir en équilibre; (pros and cons) peser; (budget) équilibrer; (account) balancer; (compensate) compenser, contrebalancer; **~ of trade/payments** balance commerciale/des comptes or paiements; **balanced** adj (personality, diet) équilibré(e); (report) objectif(-ive); **balance sheet** n bilan m
balcony ['bælkənɪ] n balcon m; **do you have a room with a ~?** avez-vous une chambre avec balcon?
bald [bɔːld] adj (person) chauve; (tyre) lisse
ball [bɔːl] n boule f; (football) ballon m; (for tennis, golf) balle f; (dance) bal m; **to play ~** jouer au ballon (or à la balle); (fig) coopérer
ballerina [bælə'riːnə] n ballerine f
ballet ['bæleɪ] n ballet m; (art) danse f (classique); **ballet dancer** n danseur(-euse) de ballet
balloon [bə'luːn] n ballon m
ballot ['bælət] n scrutin m
ballpoint (pen) ['bɔːlpɔɪnt-] n stylo m à bille
ballroom ['bɔːlrum] n salle f de bal
Baltic ['bɔːltɪk] n: **the ~ (Sea)** la (mer) Baltique
bamboo [bæm'buː] n bambou m
ban [bæn] n interdiction f ▷ vt interdire

banana [bə'nɑːnə] n banane f
band [bænd] n bande f; (at a dance) orchestre m; (Mil) musique f, fanfare f
bandage ['bændɪdʒ] n bandage m, pansement m ▷ vt (wound, leg) mettre un pansement or un bandage sur
Band-Aid® ['bændeɪd] n (us) pansement adhésif
B. & B. n abbr = **bed and breakfast**
bandit ['bændɪt] n bandit m
bang [bæŋ] n détonation f; (of door) claquement m; (blow) coup (violent) ▷ vt frapper (violemment); (door) claquer ▷ vi détoner; claquer
Bangladesh [bæŋglə'deʃ] n Bangladesh m
Bangladeshi [bæŋglə'deʃɪ] adj du Bangladesh ▷ n habitant(e) du Bangladesh
bangle ['bæŋgl] n bracelet m
bangs [bæŋz] npl (us: fringe) frange f
banish ['bænɪʃ] vt bannir
banister(s) ['bænɪstə(z)] n(pl) rampe f (d'escalier)
banjo (pl -es or -s) ['bændʒəu] n banjo m
bank [bæŋk] n banque f; (of river, lake) bord m, rive f; (of earth) talus m, remblai m ▷ vi (Aviat) virer sur l'aile; **bank on** vt fus miser or tabler sur; **bank account** n compte m en banque; **bank balance** n solde m bancaire; **bank card** (BRIT) n carte f d'identité bancaire; **bank charges** npl (BRIT) frais mpl de banque; **banker** n banquier m; **bank holiday** n (BRIT) jour férié (où les banques sont fermées); **banking** n opérations fpl bancaires; profession f de banquier; **bank manager** n directeur m d'agence (bancaire); **banknote** n billet m de banque
bankrupt ['bæŋkrʌpt] adj en faillite; **to go ~** faire faillite; **bankruptcy** n faillite f
bank statement n relevé m de compte
banner ['bænə'] n bannière f
bannister(s) ['bænɪstə(z)] n(pl) = **banister(s)**
banquet ['bæŋkwɪt] n banquet m, festin m
baptism ['bæptɪzəm] n baptême m
baptize [bæp'taɪz] vt baptiser
bar [bɑː'] n (pub) bar m; (counter) comptoir m, bar; (rod: of metal etc) barre f; (of window etc) barreau m; (of chocolate) tablette f, plaque f; (fig: obstacle) obstacle m; (prohibition) mesure f d'exclusion; (Mus) mesure f ▷ vt (road) barrer; (person) exclure; (activity) interdire; **~ of soap** savonnette f; **behind ~s** (prisoner) derrière les barreaux; **the B~** (Law) le barreau; **~ none** sans exception
barbaric [bɑː'bærɪk] adj barbare
barbecue ['bɑːbɪkjuː] n barbecue m
barbed wire ['bɑːbd-] n fil m de fer barbelé
barber ['bɑːbə'] n coiffeur m (pour hommes); **barber's (shop)** (us **barber (shop)**) n salon m de coiffure (pour hommes)
bar code n code m à barres, code-barre m
bare [bɛə'] adj nu(e) ▷ vt mettre à nu, dénuder; (teeth) montrer; **barefoot** adj, adv nu-pieds, (les) pieds nus; **barely** adv à peine
bargain ['bɑːgɪn] n (transaction) marché m; (good buy) affaire f, occasion f ▷ vi (haggle) marchander; (negotiate) négocier, traiter; **into the ~** par-dessus le marché; **bargain for** vt fus (inf): **he got more than he ~ed for!** il en a eu pour son argent!
barge [bɑːdʒ] n péniche f; **barge in** vi (walk in) faire irruption; (interrupt talk) intervenir mal à propos
bark [bɑːk] n (of tree) écorce f; (of dog) aboiement m ▷ vi aboyer

barley ['bɑːlɪ] n orge f
barmaid ['bɑːmeɪd] n serveuse f (de bar), barmaid f
barman ['bɑːmən] n serveur m (de bar), barman m
barn [bɑːn] n grange f
barometer [bə'rɒmɪtə'] n baromètre m
baron ['bærən] n baron m; **baroness** n baronne f
barracks ['bærəks] npl caserne f
barrage ['bærɑːʒ] n (Mil) tir m de barrage; (dam) barrage m; (of criticism) feu m
barrel ['bærəl] n tonneau m; (of gun) canon m
barren ['bærən] adj stérile
barrette [bə'ret] (us) n barrette f
barricade [bærɪ'keɪd] n barricade f
barrier ['bærɪə'] n barrière f
barring ['bɑːrɪŋ] prep sauf
barrister ['bærɪstə'] n (BRIT) avocat (plaidant)
barrow ['bærəu] n (cart) charrette f à bras
bartender ['bɑːtendə'] n (us) serveur m (de bar), barman m
base [beɪs] n base f ▷ vt (opinion, belief): **to ~ sth on** baser or fonder qch sur ▷ adj vil(e), bas(se)
baseball ['beɪsbɔːl] n base-ball m; **baseball cap** n casquette f de base-ball
Basel [bɑːl] n = **Basle**
basement ['beɪsmənt] n sous-sol m
bases ['beɪsiːz] npl of **basis**
bash [bæʃ] vt (inf) frapper, cogner
basic ['beɪsɪk] adj (precautions, rules) élémentaire; (principles, research) fondamental(e); (vocabulary, salary) de base; (minimal) réduit(e) au minimum, rudimentaire; **basically** adv (in fact) en fait; (essentially) fondamentalement; **basics** npl: **the basics** l'essentiel m
basil ['bæzl] n basilic m
basin ['beɪsn] n (vessel, also Geo) cuvette f, bassin m; (BRIT: for food) bol m; (also: **wash~**) lavabo m
basis (pl **bases**) ['beɪsɪs, -siːz] n base f; **on a part-time/trial ~** à temps partiel/à l'essai
basket ['bɑːskɪt] n corbeille f; (with handle) panier m; **basketball** n basket-ball m
Basle [bɑːl] n Bâle
Basque [bæsk] adj basque ▷ n Basque m/f; **the ~ Country** le Pays basque
bass [beɪs] n (Mus) basse f
bastard ['bɑːstəd] n enfant naturel(le), bâtard(e); (inf!) salaud m (!)
bat [bæt] n chauve-souris f; (for baseball etc) batte f; (BRIT: for table tennis) raquette f ▷ vt: **he didn't ~ an eyelid** il n'a pas sourcillé or bronché
batch [bætʃ] n (of bread) fournée f; (of papers) liasse f; (of applicants, letters) paquet m
bath (pl -s) [bɑːθ, bɑːðz] n bain m; (bathtub) baignoire f ▷ vt baigner, donner un bain à; **to have a ~** prendre un bain; see also **baths**
bathe [beɪð] vi se baigner ▷ vt baigner; (wound etc) laver
bathing ['beɪðɪŋ] n baignade f; **bathing costume** (us **bathing suit**) n maillot m de bain
bath: **bathrobe** n peignoir m de bain; **bathroom** n salle f de bains; **baths** [bɑːðz] npl (BRIT: also: **swimming baths**) piscine f; **bath towel** n serviette f de bain; **bathtub** n baignoire f
baton ['bætən] n bâton m; (Mus) baguette f; (club) matraque f
batter ['bætə'] vt battre ▷ n pâte f à frire; **battered** adj

(hat, pan) cabossé(e); **battered wife/child** épouse/
enfant maltraité(e) or martyr(e)

battery ['bætərɪ] n (for torch, radio) pile f; (Aut, Mil)
batterie f; **battery farming** n élevage m en batterie

battle ['bætl] n bataille f, combat m ▷ vi se battre, lutter;
battlefield n champ m de bataille

bay [beɪ] n (of sea) baie f; (BRIT: for parking) place f de
stationnement; (: for loading) aire f de chargement; **B~ of
Biscay** golfe m de Gascogne; **to hold sb at ~** tenir qn à
distance or en échec

bay leaf n laurier m

bazaar [bə'zɑːʳ] n (shop, market) bazar m; (sale) vente f
de charité

BBC n abbr (= British Broadcasting Corporation) office de la
radiodiffusion et télévision britannique

B.C. adv abbr (= before Christ) av. J.-C.

O KEYWORD

be [biː] (pt **was, were**, pp **been**) aux vb **1** (with present
participle: forming continuous tenses): **what are you
doing?** que faites-vous?; **they're coming tomorrow**
ils viennent demain; **I've been waiting for you for 2
hours** je t'attends depuis 2 heures
2 (with pp: forming passives) être; **to be killed** être
tué(e); **the box had been opened** la boîte avait été
ouverte; **he was nowhere to be seen** on ne le voyait
nulle part
3 (in tag questions): **it was fun, wasn't it?** c'était drôle,
n'est-ce pas?; **he's good-looking, isn't he?** il est beau,
n'est-ce pas?; **she's back, is she?** elle est rentrée, n'est-
ce pas or alors?
4 (+to +infinitive): **the house is to be sold** (necessity)
la maison doit être vendue; (future) la maison va être
vendue; **he's not to open it** il ne doit pas l'ouvrir
▷ vb + complement **1** (gen) être; **I'm English** je suis
anglais(e); **I'm tired** je suis fatigué(e); **I'm hot/cold** j'ai
chaud/froid; **he's a doctor** il est médecin; **be careful/
good/quiet!** faites attention/soyez sages/taisez-
vous!; **2 and 2 are 4** 2 et 2 font 4
2 (of health) aller; **how are you?** comment allez-vous?;
I'm better now je vais mieux maintenant; **he's very ill**
il est très malade
3 (of age) avoir; **how old are you?** quel âge avez-vous?;
I'm sixteen (years old) j'ai seize ans
4 (cost) coûter; **how much was the meal?** combien a
coûté le repas?; **that'll be £5, please** ça fera 5 livres, s'il
vous plaît; **this shirt is £17** cette chemise coûte 17 livres
▷ vi **1** (exist, occur etc) être, exister; **the prettiest girl
that ever was** la fille la plus jolie qui ait jamais existé;
is there a God? y a-t-il un dieu?; **be that as it may** quoi
qu'il en soit; **so be it** soit
2 (referring to place) être, se trouver; **I won't be here
tomorrow** je ne serai pas là demain
3 (referring to movement) aller; **where have you been?**
où êtes-vous allé(s)?
▷ impers vb **1** (referring to time) être; **it's 5 o'clock** il est 5
heures; **it's the 28th of April** c'est le 28 avril
2 (referring to distance): **it's 10 km to the village** le
village est à 10 km
3 (referring to the weather) faire; **it's too hot/cold** il
fait trop chaud/froid; **it's windy today** il y a du vent
aujourd'hui
4 (emphatic): **it's me/the postman** c'est moi/le

facteur; **it was Maria who paid the bill** c'est Maria qui
a payé la note

beach [biːtʃ] n plage f ▷ vt échouer

beacon ['biːkən] n (lighthouse) fanal m; (marker) balise f

bead [biːd] n perle f; (of dew, sweat) goutte f; **beads** npl
(necklace) collier m

beak [biːk] n bec m

beam [biːm] n (Archit) poutre f; (of light) rayon m ▷ vi
rayonner

bean [biːn] n haricot m; (of coffee) grain m; **beansprouts**
npl pousses fpl or germes mpl de soja

bear [bɛəʳ] n ours m ▷ vb (pt **bore**, pp **borne**) ▷ vt
porter; (endure) supporter, rapporter ▷ vi: **to ~
right/left** obliquer à droite/gauche, se diriger vers la
droite/gauche

beard [bɪəd] n barbe f

bearer ['bɛərəʳ] n porteur m; (of passport etc) titulaire m/f

bearing ['bɛərɪŋ] n maintien m, allure f; (connection)
rapport m; (Tech): **(ball) bearings** npl roulement m (à
billes)

beast [biːst] n bête f; (inf: person) brute f

beat [biːt] n battement m; (Mus) temps m, mesure f; (of
policeman) ronde f ▷ vt, vi (pt ~, pp **~en**) battre; **off the
~en track** hors des chemins or sentiers battus; **to ~ it**
(inf) ficher le camp; **beat up** vt (inf: person) tabasser;
beating n raclée f

beautiful ['bjuːtɪful] adj beau (belle); **beautifully** adv
admirablement

beauty ['bjuːtɪ] n beauté f; **beauty parlour** (us **beauty
parlor**) [-'pɑːlə] n institut m de beauté; **beauty salon** n
institut m de beauté; **beauty spot** n (on skin) grain m de
beauté; (BRIT Tourism) site naturel (d'une grande beauté)

beaver ['biːvəʳ] n castor m

became [bɪ'keɪm] pt of **become**

because [bɪ'kɔz] conj parce que; **~ of** prep à cause de

beckon ['bɛkən] vt (also: **~ to**) faire signe (de venir) à

become [bɪ'kʌm] vi devenir; **to ~ fat/thin** grossir/
maigrir; **to ~ angry** se mettre en colère

bed [bɛd] n lit m; (of flowers) parterre m; (of coal, clay)
couche f; (of sea, lake) fond m; **to go to ~** aller se coucher;
bed and breakfast n (terms) chambre et petit déjeuner;
(place) ≈ chambre f d'hôte; **bedclothes** npl couvertures
fpl et draps mpl; **bedding** n literie f; **bed linen** n draps
mpl de lit (et taies fpl d'oreillers), literie f; **bedroom** n
chambre f (à coucher); **bedside** n: **at sb's bedside**
au chevet de qn; **bedside lamp** n lampe f de chevet;
bedside table n table f de chevet; **bedsit(ter)** n (BRIT)
chambre meublée, studio m; **bedspread** n couvre-lit m,
dessus-de-lit m; **bedtime** n: **it's bedtime** c'est l'heure
de se coucher

bee [biː] n abeille f

beech [biːtʃ] n hêtre m

beef [biːf] n bœuf m; **roast ~** rosbif m; **beefburger** n
hamburger m; **Beefeater** n hallebardier m (de la tour
de Londres)

been [biːn] pp of **be**

beer [bɪəʳ] n bière f; **beer garden** n (BRIT) jardin m d'un
pub (où l'on peut emmener ses consommations)

beet [biːt] n (vegetable) betterave f; (us: also: **red ~**)
betterave (potagère)

beetle ['biːtl] n scarabée m, coléoptère m

beetroot ['biːtruːt] n (BRIT) betterave f

before [bɪ'fɔːʳ] prep (of time) avant; (of space) devant

▷ *conj* avant que + *sub*; avant de ▷ *adv* avant; **~ going** avant de partir; **~ she goes** avant qu'elle (ne) parte; **the week ~** la semaine précédente or d'avant; **I've never seen it ~** c'est la première fois que je le vois; **beforehand** *adv* au préalable, à l'avance

beg [bɛg] *vi* mendier ▷ *vt* mendier; *(forgiveness, mercy etc)* demander; *(entreat)* supplier; **to ~ sb to do sth** supplier qn de faire qch; *see also* **pardon**

began [bɪ'gæn] *pt of* **begin**

beggar ['bɛgə'] *n* mendiant(e)

begin [bɪ'gɪn] *(pt* **began**, *pp* **begun)** *vt*, *vi* commencer; **to ~ doing** *or* **to do sth** commencer à faire qch; **beginner** *n* débutant(e); **beginning** *n* commencement *m*, début *m*

begun [bɪ'gʌn] *pp of* **begin**

behalf [bɪ'hɑːf] *n*: **on ~ of** *(us)*: **in ~ of** *(representing)* de la part de; *(for benefit of)* pour le compte de; **on my/his ~** de ma/sa part

behave [bɪ'heɪv] *vi* se conduire, se comporter; *(well: also:* **~ o.s.)** se conduire bien *or* comme il faut; **behaviour** *(us* **behavior)** *n* comportement *m*, conduite *f*

behind [bɪ'haɪnd] *prep* derrière; *(time)* en retard sur; *(supporting)*: **to be ~ sb** soutenir qn ▷ *adv* derrière; en retard ▷ *n* derrière *m*; **~ the scenes** dans les coulisses; **to be ~ (schedule) with sth** être en retard dans qch

beige [beɪʒ] *adj* beige

Beijing [beɪ'dʒɪŋ] *n* Pékin

being ['biːɪŋ] *n* être *m*; **to come into ~** prendre naissance

belated [bɪ'leɪtɪd] *adj* tardif(-ive)

belch [bɛltʃ] *vi* avoir un renvoi, roter ▷ *vt* *(also:* **~ out**: *smoke etc)* vomir, cracher

Belgian ['bɛldʒən] *adj* belge, de Belgique ▷ *n* Belge *m/f*

Belgium ['bɛldʒəm] *n* Belgique *f*

belief [bɪ'liːf] *n* *(opinion)* conviction *f*; *(trust, faith)* foi *f*

believe [bɪ'liːv] *vt*, *vi* croire, estimer; **to ~ in** *(God)* croire en; *(ghosts, method)* croire à; **believer** *n* *(in idea, activity)* partisan(e); *(Rel)* croyant(e)

bell [bɛl] *n* cloche *f*; *(small)* clochette *f*, grelot *m*; *(on door)* sonnette *f*; *(electric)* sonnerie *f*

bellboy ['bɛlbɔɪ] *(us* **bellhop)** ['bɛlhɔp] *n* groom *m*, chasseur *m*

bellow ['bɛləu] *vi* *(bull)* meugler; *(person)* brailler

bell pepper *n* *(esp us)* poivron *m*

belly ['bɛlɪ] *n* ventre *m*; **belly button** *(inf)* nombril *m*

belong [bɪ'lɔŋ] *vi*: **to ~ to** appartenir à; *(club etc)* faire partie de; **this book ~s here** ce livre va ici, la place de ce livre est ici; **belongings** *npl* affaires *fpl*, possessions *fpl*

beloved [bɪ'lʌvɪd] *adj* (bien-)aimé(e), chéri(e)

below [bɪ'ləu] *prep* sous, au-dessous de ▷ *adv* en dessous; en contre-bas; **see ~** voir plus bas *or* plus loin *or* ci-dessous

belt [bɛlt] *n* ceinture *f*; *(Tech)* courroie *f* ▷ *vt* *(thrash)* donner une raclée à; **beltway** *n* *(us Aut)* route *f* de ceinture; (: *motorway)* périphérique *m*

bemused [bɪ'mjuːzd] *adj* médusé(e)

bench [bɛntʃ] *n* banc *m*; *(in workshop)* établi *m*; **the B~** *(Law: judges)* la magistrature, la Cour

bend [bɛnd] *vb* *(pt*, *pp* **bent)** ▷ *vt* courber; *(leg, arm)* plier ▷ *vi* se courber ▷ *n* *(BRIT: in road)* virage *m*, tournant *m*; *(in pipe, river)* coude *m*; **bend down** *vi* se baisser; **bend over** *vi* se pencher

beneath [bɪ'niːθ] *prep* sous, au-dessous de; *(unworthy of)* indigne de ▷ *adv* dessous, au-dessous, en bas

beneficial [bɛnɪ'fɪʃəl] *adj*: **~ (to)** salutaire (pour), bénéfique (à)

benefit ['bɛnɪfɪt] *n* avantage *m*, profit *m*; *(allowance of money)* allocation *f* ▷ *vt* faire du bien à, profiter à ▷ *vi*: **he'll ~ from it** cela lui fera du bien, il y gagnera *or* s'en trouvera bien

Benelux ['bɛnɪlʌks] *n* Bénélux *m*

benign [bɪ'naɪn] *adj* *(person, smile)* bienveillant(e), affable; *(Med)* bénin(-igne)

bent [bɛnt] *pt*, *pp of* **bend** ▷ *n* inclination *f*, penchant *m* ▷ *adj*: **to be ~ on** être résolu(e) à

bereaved [bɪ'riːvd] *n*: **the ~** la famille du disparu

beret ['bɛreɪ] *n* béret *m*

Berlin [bəː'lɪn] *n* Berlin

Bermuda [bəː'mjuːdə] *n* Bermudes *fpl*

Bern [bəːn] *n* Berne

berry ['bɛrɪ] *n* baie *f*

berth [bəːθ] *n* *(bed)* couchette *f*; *(for ship)* poste *m* d'amarrage, mouillage *m* ▷ *vi* *(in harbour)* venir à quai; *(at anchor)* mouiller

beside [bɪ'saɪd] *prep* à côté de; *(compared with)* par rapport à; **that's ~ the point** ça n'a rien à voir; **to be ~ o.s. (with anger)** être hors de soi; **besides** *adv* en outre, de plus ▷ *prep* en plus de; *(except)* excepté

best [bɛst] *adj* meilleur(e) ▷ *adv* le mieux; **the ~ part of** *(quantity)* la plus grande partie de; **at ~** au mieux; **to make the ~ of sth** s'accommoder de qch (du mieux que l'on peut); **to do one's ~** faire de son mieux; **to the ~ of my knowledge** pour autant que je sache; **to the ~ of my ability** du mieux que je pourrai; **best-before date** *n* date *f* de limite d'utilisation or de consommation; **best man** *(irreg)* *n* garçon *m* d'honneur; **bestseller** *n* best-seller *m*, succès *m* de librairie

bet [bɛt] *n* pari *m* ▷ *vt*, *vi* *(pt*, *pp* **~** *or* **~ted)** parier; **to ~ sb sth** parier qch à qn

betray [bɪ'treɪ] *vt* trahir

better ['bɛtə'] *adj* meilleur(e) ▷ *adv* mieux ▷ *vt* améliorer ▷ *n*: **to get the ~ of** triompher de, l'emporter sur; **you had ~ do it** vous feriez mieux de le faire; **he thought ~ of it** il s'est ravisé; **to get ~** *(Med)* aller mieux; *(improve)* s'améliorer

betting ['bɛtɪŋ] *n* paris *mpl*; **betting shop** *n* *(BRIT)* bureau *m* de paris

between [bɪ'twiːn] *prep* entre ▷ *adv* au milieu, dans l'intervalle

beverage ['bɛvərɪdʒ] *n* boisson *f* (*gén* sans alcool)

beware [bɪ'wɛə'] *vt*: **to ~ (of)** prendre garde (à); **"~ of the dog"** "(attention) chien méchant"

bewildered [bɪ'wɪldəd] *adj* dérouté(e), ahuri(e)

beyond [bɪ'jɔnd] *prep* *(in place, time)* au-delà de; *(exceeding)* au-dessus de ▷ *adv* au-delà; **~ doubt** hors de doute; **~ repair** irréparable

bias ['baɪəs] *n* *(prejudice)* préjugé *m*, parti pris; *(preference)* prévention *f*; **bias(s)ed** *adj* partial(e), montrant un parti pris

bib [bɪb] *n* bavoir *m*

Bible ['baɪbl] *n* Bible *f*

bicarbonate of soda [baɪ'kɑːbənɪt-] *n* bicarbonate *m* de soude

biceps ['baɪsɛps] *n* biceps *m*

bicycle ['baɪsɪkl] *n* bicyclette *f*; **bicycle pump** *n* pompe *f* à vélo

bid [bɪd] *n* offre *f*; *(at auction)* enchère *f*; *(attempt)* tentative *f* ▷ *vb* *(pt* **~** *or* **bade**, *pp* **~** *or* **~den)** ▷ *vi* faire une enchère *or* offre ▷ *vt* faire une enchère *or* offre de; **to ~ sb good day** souhaiter le bonjour à qn; **bidder** *n*: **the**

highest bidder le plus offrant
bidet ['biːdeɪ] n bidet m
big [bɪg] adj (in height: person, building, tree) grand(e); (in bulk, amount: person, parcel, book) gros(se); **bigheaded** adj prétentieux(-euse); **big toe** n gros orteil
bike [baɪk] n vélo m; **bike lane** n piste f cyclable
bikini [bɪˈkiːnɪ] n bikini m
bilateral [baɪˈlætərl] adj bilatéral(e)
bilingual [baɪˈlɪŋgwəl] adj bilingue
bill [bɪl] n note f, facture f; (in restaurant) addition f, note f; (Pol) projet m de loi; (us: banknote) billet m (de banque); (notice) affiche f; (of bird) bec m; **put it on my ~** mettez-le sur mon compte; **"post no ~s"** "défense d'afficher"; **to fit** or **fill the ~** (fig) faire l'affaire; **billboard** (us) n panneau m d'affichage; **billfold** ['bɪlfəʊld] n (us) portefeuille m
billiards ['bɪljədz] n (jeu m de) billard m
billion ['bɪljən] n (BRIT) billion m (million de millions); (us) milliard m
bin [bɪn] n boîte f; (BRIT: also: **dust~, litter ~**) poubelle f; (for coal) coffre m
bind [baɪnd] (pt, pp **bound**) [baʊnd] vt attacher; (book) relier; (oblige) obliger, contraindre ▷ n (inf: nuisance) scie f
binge [bɪndʒ] n (inf): **to go on a ~** faire la bringue
bingo ['bɪŋgəʊ] n sorte de jeu de loto pratiqué dans des établissements publics
binoculars [bɪˈnɒkjuləz] npl jumelles fpl
bio... [baɪə] prefix: **biochemistry** n biochimie f; **biodegradable** ['baɪəʊdɪ'greɪdəbl] adj biodégradable; **biography** [baɪˈɒgrəfɪ] n biographie f; **biological** adj biologique; **biology** [baɪˈɒlədʒɪ] n biologie f; **biometric** [baɪəˈmɛtrɪk] adj biométrique
birch [bəːtʃ] n bouleau m
bird [bəːd] n oiseau m; (BRIT inf: girl) nana f; **bird flu** n grippe f aviaire; **bird of prey** n oiseau m de proie; **birdwatching** n ornithologie f (d'amateur)
Biro® ['baɪrəʊ] n stylo m à bille
birth [bəːθ] n naissance f; **to give ~ to** donner naissance à, mettre au monde; (subj: animal) mettre bas; **birth certificate** n acte m de naissance; **birth control** n (policy) limitation f des naissances; (methods) méthode(s) contraceptive(s); **birthday** n anniversaire m ▷ cpd (cake, card etc) d'anniversaire; **birthmark** n envie f, tache f de vin; **birthplace** n lieu m de naissance
biscuit ['bɪskɪt] n (BRIT) biscuit m; (us) petit pain au lait
bishop ['bɪʃəp] n évêque m; (Chess) fou m
bistro ['biːstrəʊ] n petit restaurant m, bistrot m
bit [bɪt] pt of **bite** ▷ n morceau m; (Comput) bit m, élément m binaire; (of tool) mèche f; (of horse) mors m; **a ~ of** un peu de; **a ~ mad/dangerous** un peu fou/risqué; **~ by ~** petit à petit
bitch [bɪtʃ] n (dog) chienne f; (inf!) salope f(!), garce f
bite [baɪt] vt, vi (pt **bit**, pp **bitten**) mordre; (insect) piquer ▷ n morsure f; (insect bite) piqûre f; (mouthful) bouchée f; **let's have a ~ (to eat)** mangeons un morceau; **to ~ one's nails** se ronger les ongles
bitten ['bɪtn] pp of **bite**
bitter ['bɪtəʳ] adj amer(-ère); (criticism) cinglant(e); (icy: weather, wind) glacial(e) ▷ n (BRIT: beer) bière f (à forte teneur en houblon)
bizarre [bɪˈzɑːʳ] adj bizarre
black [blæk] adj noir(e) ▷ n (colour) noir m; (person): **B-** noir(e) ▷ vt (BRIT Industry) boycotter; **to give sb a ~ eye** pocher l'œil à qn, faire un œil au beurre noir à qn; **to be in the ~** (in credit) avoir un compte créditeur; **~ and**

blue (bruised) couvert(e) de bleus; **black out** vi (faint) s'évanouir; **blackberry** n mûre f; **blackbird** n merle m; **blackboard** n tableau noir; **black coffee** n café noir; **blackcurrant** n cassis m; **black ice** n verglas m; **blackmail** n chantage m ▷ vt faire chanter, soumettre au chantage; **black market** n marché noir; **blackout** n panne f d'électricité; (in wartime) black-out m; (TV) interruption f d'émission; (fainting) syncope f; **black pepper** n poivre noir; **black pudding** n boudin (noir); **Black Sea** n: **the Black Sea** la mer Noire
bladder ['blædəʳ] n vessie f
blade [bleɪd] n lame f; (of propeller) pale f; **a ~ of grass** un brin d'herbe
blame [bleɪm] n faute f, blâme m ▷ vt: **to ~ sb/sth for sth** attribuer à qn/qch la responsabilité de qch; reprocher qch à qn/qch; **I'm not to ~** ce n'est pas ma faute
bland [blænd] adj (taste, food) doux (douce), fade
blank [blæŋk] adj blanc (blanche); (look) sans expression, dénué(e) d'expression ▷ n espace m vide, blanc m; (cartridge) cartouche f à blanc; **his mind was a ~** il avait la tête vide
blanket ['blæŋkɪt] n couverture f; (of snow, cloud) couche f
blast [blɑːst] n explosion f; (shock wave) souffle m; (of air, steam) bouffée f ▷ vt faire sauter or exploser
blatant ['bleɪtənt] adj flagrant(e), criant(e)
blaze [bleɪz] n (fire) incendie m; (fig) flamboiement m ▷ vi (fire) flamber; (fig) flamboyer, resplendir ▷ vt: **to ~ a trail** (fig) montrer la voie; **in a ~ of publicity** à grand renfort de publicité
blazer ['bleɪzəʳ] n blazer m
bleach [bliːtʃ] n (also: **household ~**) eau f de Javel ▷ vt (linen) blanchir; **bleachers** npl (us Sport) gradins mpl (en plein soleil)
bleak [bliːk] adj morne, désolé(e); (weather) triste, maussade; (smile) lugubre; (prospect, future) morose
bled [blɛd] pt, pp of **bleed**
bleed (pt, pp **bled**) [bliːd, blɛd] vt saigner; (brakes, radiator) purger ▷ vi saigner; **my nose is ~ing** je saigne du nez
blemish ['blɛmɪʃ] n défaut m; (on reputation) tache f
blend [blɛnd] n mélange m ▷ vt mélanger ▷ vi (colours etc: also: **~ in**) se mélanger, se fondre, s'allier; **blender** n (Culin) mixeur m
bless (pt, pp **~ed** or **blest**) [blɛs, blɛst] vt bénir; **~ you!** (after sneeze) à tes souhaits!; **blessing** n bénédiction f; (godsend) bienfait m
blew [bluː] pt of **blow**
blight [blaɪt] vt (hopes etc) anéantir, briser
blind [blaɪnd] adj aveugle ▷ n (for window) store m ▷ vt aveugler; **the blind** npl les aveugles mpl; **blind alley** n impasse f; **blindfold** n bandeau m ▷ adj, adv les yeux bandés ▷ vt bander les yeux à
blink [blɪŋk] vi cligner des yeux; (light) clignoter
bliss [blɪs] n félicité f, bonheur m sans mélange
blister ['blɪstəʳ] n (on skin) ampoule f, cloque f; (on paintwork) boursouflure f ▷ vi (paint) se boursoufler, se cloquer
blizzard ['blɪzəd] n blizzard m, tempête f de neige
bloated ['bləʊtɪd] adj (face) bouffi(e); (stomach, person) gonflé(e)
blob [blɒb] n (drop) goutte f; (stain, spot) tache f
block [blɒk] n bloc m; (in pipes) obstruction f; (toy) cube

m; *(of buildings)* pâté *m* (de maisons) ▷ *vt* bloquer; *(fig)* faire obstacle à; **the sink is ~ed** l'évier est bouché; **~ of flats** *(BRIT)* immeuble *(locatif)*; **mental ~** blocage *m*; **block up** *vt* boucher; **blockade** [blɔ'keɪd] *n* blocus *m* ▷ *vt* faire le blocus de; **blockage** *n* obstruction *f*; **blockbuster** *n* *(film, book)* grand succès; **block capitals** *npl* majuscules *fpl* d'imprimerie; **block letters** *npl* majuscules *fpl*

blog [blɔg] *n* blog *m*, blogue *m*

bloke [blɛuk] *n* *(BRIT inf)* type *m*

blond(e) [blɔnd] *adj*, *n* blond(e)

blood [blʌd] *n* sang *m*; **blood donor** *n* donneur(-euse) de sang; **blood group** *n* groupe sanguin; **blood poisoning** *n* empoisonnement *m* du sang; **blood pressure** *n* tension (artérielle); **bloodshed** *n* effusion *f* de sang, carnage *m*; **bloodshot** *adj*: **bloodshot eyes** yeux injectés de sang; **bloodstream** *n* sang *m*, système sanguin; **blood test** *n* analyse *f* de sang; **blood transfusion** *n* transfusion *f* de sang; **blood type** *n* groupe sanguin; **blood vessel** *n* vaisseau sanguin; **bloody** *adj* sanglant(e); *(BRIT infl)*: **this bloody ...** ce foutu ..., ce putain de ... (!) ▷ *adv*: **bloody strong/good** *(BRIT: infl)* vachement *or* sacrément fort/bon

bloom [bluːm] *n* fleur *f* ▷ *vi* être en fleur

blossom ['blɔsəm] *n* fleur(s) *f(pl)* ▷ *vi* être en fleurs; *(fig)* s'épanouir

blot [blɔt] *n* tache *f* ▷ *vt* tacher; *(ink)* sécher

blouse [blauz] *n* *(feminine garment)* chemisier *m*, corsage *m*

blow [blɛu] *n* coup *m* ▷ *vb* *(pt blew, pp ~n)* ▷ *vi* souffler ▷ *vt* *(instrument)* jouer de; *(fuse)* faire sauter; **to ~ one's nose** se moucher; **blow away** *vi* s'envoler ▷ *vt* chasser, faire s'envoler; **blow out** *vi* *(fire, flame)* s'éteindre; *(tyre)* éclater; *(fuse)* sauter; **blow up** *vi* exploser, sauter ▷ *vt* faire sauter; *(tyre)* gonfler; *(Phot)* agrandir; **blow-dry** *n* *(hairstyle)* brushing *m*

blown [blɛun] *pp* of **blow**

blue [bluː] *adj* bleu(e); *(depressed)* triste; **~ film/joke** film *m*/histoire *f* pornographique; **out of the ~** *(fig)* à l'improviste, sans qu'on s'y attende; **bluebell** *n* jacinthe *f* des bois; **blueberry** *n* myrtille *f*, airelle *f*; **blue cheese** *n* *(fromage)* bleu *m*; **blues** *npl*: **the blues** *(Mus)* le blues; **to have the blues** *(inf: feeling)* avoir le cafard; **bluetit** *n* mésange bleue

bluff [blʌf] *vi* bluffer ▷ *n* bluff *m*; **to call sb's ~** mettre qn au défi d'exécuter ses menaces

blunder ['blʌndər] *n* gaffe *f*, bévue *f* ▷ *vi* faire une gaffe *or* une bévue

blunt [blʌnt] *adj* *(knife)* émoussé(e), peu tranchant(e); *(pencil)* mal taillé(e); *(person)* brusque, ne mâchant pas ses mots

blur [bləːr] *n* *(shape)*: **to become a ~** devenir flou ▷ *vt* brouiller, rendre flou(e); **blurred** *adj* flou(e)

blush [blʌʃ] *vi* rougir ▷ *n* rougeur *f*; **blusher** *n* rouge *m* à joues

board [bɔːd] *n* *(wooden)* planche *f*; *(on wall)* panneau *m*; *(for chess etc)* plateau *m*; *(cardboard)* carton *m*; *(committee)* conseil *m*, comité *m*; *(in firm)* conseil d'administration; *(Naut, Aviat)*: **on ~** à bord ▷ *vt* *(ship)* monter à bord de; *(train)* monter dans; **full ~** *(BRIT)* pension complète; **half ~** *(BRIT)* demi-pension *f*; **~ and lodging** *n* chambre *f* avec pension; **to go by the ~** *(hopes, principles)* être abandonné(e); **board game** *n* jeu *m* de société; **boarding card** *n* *(Aviat, Naut)* carte *f* d'embarquement;

boarding pass *n* *(BRIT)* = **boarding card**; **boarding school** *n* internat *m*, pensionnat *m*; **board room** *n* salle *f* du conseil d'administration

boast [bɛust] *vi*: **to ~ (about or of)** se vanter (de)

boat [bɛut] *n* bateau *m*; *(small)* canot *m*; barque *f*

bob [bɔb] *vi* *(boat, cork on water: also: ~ up and down)* danser, se balancer

bobby pin ['bɔbɪ-] *n* *(US)* pince *f* à cheveux

body ['bɔdɪ] *n* corps *m*; *(of car)* carrosserie *f*; *(fig: society)* organe *m*, organisme *m*; **body-building** *n* body-building *m*, culturisme *m*; **bodyguard** *n* garde *m* du corps; **bodywork** *n* carrosserie *f*

bog [bɔg] *n* tourbière *f* ▷ *vt*: **to get ~ged down (in)** *(fig)* s'enliser (dans)

bogus ['bɛugəs] *adj* bidon *inv*; fantôme

boil [bɔɪl] *vt* (faire) bouillir ▷ *vi* bouillir ▷ *n* *(Med)* furoncle *m*; **to come to the** *or* *(US)* **a ~** bouillir; **boil down** *vi* *(fig)*: **to ~ down to** se réduire *or* ramener à; **boil over** *vi* déborder; **boiled egg** *n* œuf *m* à la coque; **boiled potatoes** *n* pommes *fpl* à l'anglaise *or* à l'eau; **boiler** *n* chaudière *f*; **boiling** ['bɔɪlɪŋ] *adj*: **I'm boiling (hot)** *(inf)* je crève de chaud; **boiling point** *n* point *m* d'ébullition

bold [bɛuld] *adj* hardi(e), audacieux(-euse); *(pej)* effronté(e); *(outline, colour)* franc (franche), tranché(e), marqué(e)

bollard ['bɔləd] *n* *(BRIT Aut)* borne lumineuse *or* de signalisation

bolt [bɛult] *n* verrou *m*; *(with nut)* boulon *m* ▷ *adv*: **~ upright** droit(e) comme un piquet ▷ *vt* *(door)* verrouiller; *(food)* engloutir ▷ *vi* se sauver, filer (comme une flèche); *(horse)* s'emballer

bomb [bɔm] *n* bombe *f* ▷ *vt* bombarder; **bombard** [bɔm'bɑːd] *vt* bombarder; **bomber** *n* *(Aviat)* bombardier *m*; *(terrorist)* poseur *m* de bombes; **bomb scare** *n* alerte *f* à la bombe

bond [bɔnd] *n* lien *m*; *(binding promise)* engagement *m*, obligation *f*; *(Finance)* obligation; **bonds** *npl* *(chains)* chaînes *fpl*; **in ~** *(of goods)* en entrepôt

bone [bɛun] *n* os *m*; *(of fish)* arête *f* ▷ *vt* désosser; ôter les arêtes de

bonfire ['bɔnfaɪər] *n* feu *m* (de joie); *(for rubbish)* feu *m*

bonnet ['bɔnɪt] *n* bonnet *m*; *(BRIT: of car)* capot *m*

bonus ['bɛunəs] *n* *(money)* prime *f*; *(advantage)* avantage *m*

boo [buː] *excl* hou!, peuh! ▷ *vt* huer

book [buk] *n* livre *m*; *(of stamps, tickets etc)* carnet *m*; *(Comm)*: **books** *npl* comptes *mpl*, comptabilité *f* ▷ *vt* *(ticket)* prendre; *(seat, room)* réserver; *(football player)* prendre le nom de, donner un carton à; **I ~ed a table in the name of ...** j'ai réservé une table au nom de ...; **book in** *vi* *(BRIT: at hotel)* prendre sa chambre; **book up** *vt* réserver; **the hotel is ~ed up** l'hôtel est complet; **bookcase** *n* bibliothèque *f* (meuble); **booking** *n* *(BRIT)* réservation *f*; **I confirmed my booking by fax/e-mail** j'ai confirmé ma réservation par fax/e-mail; **booking office** *n* *(BRIT)* bureau *m* de location; **book-keeping** *n* comptabilité *f*; **booklet** *n* brochure *f*; **bookmaker** *n* bookmaker *m*; **bookmark** *n* *(for book)* marque-page *m*; *(Comput)* signet *m*; **bookseller** *n* libraire *m/f*; **bookshelf** *n* *(single)* étagère *f* (à livres); *(bookcase)* bibliothèque *f*; **bookshop, bookstore** *n* librairie *f*

boom [buːm] *n* *(noise)* grondement *m*; *(in prices, population)* forte augmentation; *(busy period)* boom *m*, vague *f* de prospérité ▷ *vi* gronder; prospérer

boost [buːst] n stimulant m, remontant m ▷ vt stimuler

boot [buːt] n botte f; (for hiking) chaussure f (de marche); (ankle boot) bottine f; (BRIT: of car) coffre m ▷ n (Comput) lancer, mettre en route; **to ~** (in addition) par-dessus le marché, en plus

booth [buːð] n (at fair) baraque (foraine); (of telephone etc) cabine f; (also: **voting ~**) isoloir m

booze [buːz] (inf) n boissons fpl alcooliques, alcool m

border ['bɔːdər] n bordure f; bord m; (of a country) frontière f; **borderline** n (fig) ligne f de démarcation

bore [bɔːʳ] pt of **bear** ▷ vt (person) ennuyer, raser; (hole) percer; (well, tunnel) creuser ▷ n (person) raseur(-euse); (boring thing) barbe f; (of gun) calibre m; **bored** adj: **to be bored** s'ennuyer; **boredom** n ennui m

boring ['bɔːrɪŋ] adj ennuyeux(-euse)

born [bɔːn] adj: **to be ~** naître; **I was ~ in 1960** je suis né en 1960

borne [bɔːn] pp of **bear**

borough ['bʌrə] n municipalité f

borrow ['bɔrəʊ] vt: **to ~ sth (from sb)** emprunter qch (à qn)

Bosnia(-Herzegovina) ['bɔːsnɪə(hɜːtsə'gəʊvɪːnə)] n Bosnie-Herzégovine f; **Bosnian** ['bɔznɪən] adj bosniaque, bosnien(ne) ▷ n Bosniaque m/f, Bosnien(ne)

bosom ['buzəm] n poitrine f; (fig) sein m

boss [bɔs] n patron(ne) ▷ vt (also: **~ about, ~ around**) mener à la baguette; **bossy** adj autoritaire

both [bəʊθ] adj les deux, l'un(e) et l'autre ▷ pron: **~ (of them)** les deux, tous (toutes) (les) deux, l'un(e) et l'autre; **~ of us went, we ~ went** nous y sommes allés tous les deux ▷ adv: **~ A and B** A et B

bother ['bɔðər] vt (worry) tracasser; (needle, bait) importuner, ennuyer; (disturb) déranger ▷ vi (also: **~ o.s.**) se tracasser, se faire du souci ▷ n (trouble) ennuis mpl; **to ~ doing** prendre la peine de faire; **don't ~** ce n'est pas la peine; **it's no ~** aucun problème

bottle ['bɔtl] n bouteille f; (baby's) biberon m; (of perfume, medicine) flacon m ▷ vt mettre en bouteille(s); **bottle bank** n conteneur m (de bouteilles); **bottle-opener** n ouvre-bouteille m

bottom ['bɔtəm] n (of container, sea etc) fond m; (buttocks) derrière m; (of page, list) bas m; (of mountain, tree, hill) pied m ▷ adj (shelf, step) du bas

bought [bɔːt] pt, pp of **buy**

boulder ['bəʊldəʳ] n gros rocher (gén lisse, arrondi)

bounce [baʊns] vi (ball) rebondir; (cheque) être refusé (étant sans provision) ▷ vt faire rebondir ▷ n (rebound) rebond m; **bouncer** n (inf: at dance, club) videur m

bound [baʊnd] pt, pp of **bind** ▷ n (gen pl) limite f; (leap) bond m ▷ vi (leap) bondir ▷ vt (limit) borner ▷ adj: **to be ~ to do sth** (obliged) être obligé(e) or avoir obligation de faire qch; **he's ~ to fail** (likely) il est sûr d'échouer, son échec est inévitable or assuré; **~ by** (law, regulation) engagé(e) par; **~ for** à destination de; **out of ~s** dont l'accès est interdit

boundary ['baʊndrɪ] n frontière f

bouquet ['buːkeɪ] n bouquet m

bourbon ['buəbən] n (us: also: **~ whiskey**) bourbon m

bout [baʊt] n période f; (of malaria etc) accès m, crise f, attaque f; (Boxing etc) combat m, match m

boutique [buːˈtiːk] n boutique f

bow¹ [bəʊ] n nœud m; (weapon) arc m; (Mus) archet m

bow² [baʊ] n (with body) révérence f, inclination f (du buste or corps); (Naut: also: **~s**) proue f ▷ vi faire une révérence, s'incliner

bowels [baʊəlz] npl intestins mpl; (fig) entrailles fpl

bowl [bəʊl] n (for eating) bol m; (for washing) cuvette f; (ball) boule f ▷ vi (Cricket) lancer (la balle); **bowler** n (Cricket) lanceur m (de la balle); (BRIT: also: **bowler hat**) (chapeau m) melon m; **bowling** n (game) jeu m de boules, jeu de quilles; **bowling alley** n bowling m; **bowling green** n terrain m de boules (gazonné et carré); **bowls** n (jeu m de) boules fpl

bow tie [bəʊ-] n nœud m papillon

box [bɔks] n boîte f; (also: **cardboard ~**) carton m; (Theat) loge f ▷ vt mettre en boîte ▷ vi boxer, faire de la boxe; **boxer** ['bɔksər] n (person) boxeur m; **boxer shorts** npl caleçon m; **boxing** ['bɔksɪŋ] n (sport) boxe f; **Boxing Day** n (BRIT) le lendemain de Noël; **boxing gloves** npl gants mpl de boxe; **boxing ring** n ring m; **box junction** n (BRIT Aut) zone f (de carrefour) d'accès réglementé; **box office** n bureau m de location

boy [bɔɪ] n garçon m; **boy band** n boys band m

boycott ['bɔɪkɔt] n boycottage m ▷ vt boycotter

boyfriend ['bɔɪfrɛnd] n (petit) ami

bra [brɑː] n soutien-gorge m

brace [breɪs] n (support) attache f, agrafe f; (BRIT: also: **~s: on teeth**) appareil m (dentaire); (tool) vilebrequin m ▷ vt (support) consolider, soutenir; **braces** npl (BRIT: for trousers) bretelles fpl; **to ~ o.s.** (fig) se préparer mentalement

bracelet ['breɪslɪt] n bracelet m

bracket ['brækɪt] n (Tech) tasseau m, support m; (group) classe f, tranche f; (also: **brace ~**) accolade f; (also: **round ~**) parenthèse f; (also: **square ~**) crochet m ▷ vt mettre entre parenthèses; **in ~s** entre parenthèses or crochets

brag [bræg] vi se vanter

braid [breɪd] n (trimming) galon m; (of hair) tresse f, natte f

brain [breɪn] n cerveau m; **brains** npl (intellect, food) cervelle f

braise [breɪz] vt braiser

brake [breɪk] n frein m ▷ vt, vi freiner; **brake light** n feu m de stop

bran [bræn] n son m

branch [brɑːntʃ] n branche f; (Comm) succursale f; (: of bank) agence f; **branch off** vi (road) bifurquer; **branch out** vi diversifier ses activités

brand [brænd] n marque (commerciale) ▷ vt (cattle) marquer (au fer rouge); **brand name** n nom m de marque; **brand-new** adj tout(e) neuf (neuve), flambant neuf (neuve)

brandy ['brændɪ] n cognac m

brash [bræʃ] adj effronté(e)

brass [brɑːs] n cuivre m (jaune), laiton m; **the ~** (Mus) les cuivres; **brass band** n fanfare f

brat [bræt] n (pej) mioche m/f, môme m/f

brave [breɪv] adj courageux(-euse), brave ▷ vt braver, affronter; **bravery** n bravoure f, courage m

brawl [brɔːl] n rixe f, bagarre f

Brazil [brə'zɪl] n Brésil m; **Brazilian** adj brésilien(ne) ▷ n Brésilien(ne)

breach [briːtʃ] vt ouvrir une brèche dans ▷ n (gap) brèche f; (breaking): **~ of contract** rupture f de contrat; **~ of the peace** attentat m à l'ordre public

bread [brɛd] n pain m; **breadbin** n (BRIT) boîte f or huche f à pain; **breadbox** n (us) boîte f or huche f à pain; **breadcrumbs** npl miettes fpl de pain; (Culin) chapelure f, panure f

breadth [brɛtθ] n largeur f

break [breɪk] (pt broke, pp broken) vt casser, briser; (promise) rompre; (law) violer ▷ vi se casser, se briser; (weather) tourner; (storm) éclater; (day) se lever ▷ n (gap) brèche f; (fracture) cassure f; (rest) interruption f, arrêt m; (: short) pause f; (: at school) récréation f; (chance) chance f, occasion f favorable; **to ~ one's leg** etc se casser la jambe etc; **to ~ a record** battre un record; **to ~ the news to sb** annoncer la nouvelle à qn; **break down** vt (door etc) enfoncer; (figures, data) décomposer, analyser ▷ vi s'effondrer; (Med) faire une dépression (nerveuse); (Aut) tomber en panne; **my car has broken down** ma voiture est en panne; **break in** vt (horse etc) dresser ▷ vi (burglar) entrer par effraction; (interrupt) interrompre; **break into** vt fus (house) s'introduire o pénétrer par effraction dans; **break off** vi (speaker) s'interrompre; (branch) se rompre ▷ vt (talks, engagement) rompre; **break out** vi éclater, se déclarer; (prisoner) s'évader; **to ~ out in spots** se couvrir de boutons; **break up** vi (partnership) cesser, prendre fin; (marriage) se briser; (crowd, meeting) se séparer; (ship) se disloquer; (Scol: pupils) être en vacances; (line) couper; **the line's** or **you're ~ing up** ça coupe ▷ vt fracasser, casser; (fight etc) interrompre, faire cesser; (marriage) désunir; **breakdown** n (Aut) panne f; (in communications, marriage) rupture f; (Med: also: **nervous breakdown**) dépression f (nerveuse); (of figures) ventilation f, répartition f; **breakdown truck** (us **breakdown van**) n dépanneuse f

breakfast ['brɛkfəst] n petit déjeuner m; **what time is ~?** le petit déjeuner est à quelle heure?

break: **break-in** n cambriolage m; **breakthrough** n percée f

breast [brɛst] n (of woman) sein m; (chest) poitrine f; (of chicken, turkey) blanc m; **breast-feed** vt, vi (irreg: like **feed**) allaiter; **breast-stroke** n brasse f

breath [brɛθ] n haleine f, souffle m; **to take a deep ~** respirer à fond; **out of ~** à bout de souffle, essoufflé(e)

Breathalyser® ['brɛθəlaɪzə'] (BRIT) n alcootest m

breathe [briːð] vt, vi respirer; **breathe in** vi inspirer ▷ vt aspirer; **breathe out** vt, vi expirer; **breathing** n respiration f

breath: **breathless** adj essoufflé(e), haletant(e); **breathtaking** adj stupéfiant(e), à vous couper le souffle; **breath test** n alcootest m

bred [brɛd] pt, pp of **breed**

breed [briːd] (pt, pp **bred**) vt élever, faire l'élevage de ▷ vi se reproduire ▷ n race f, variété f

breeze [briːz] n brise f

breezy ['briːzɪ] adj (day, weather) venteux(-euse); (manner) désinvolte; (person) jovial(e)

brew [bruː] vt (tea) faire infuser; (beer) brasser ▷ vi (fig) se préparer, couver; **brewery** n brasserie f (fabrique)

bribe [braɪb] n pot-de-vin m ▷ vt acheter; soudoyer; **bribery** n corruption f

bric-a-brac ['brɪkəbræk] n bric-à-brac m

brick [brɪk] n brique f; **bricklayer** n maçon m

bride [braɪd] n mariée f, épouse f; **bridegroom** n marié m, époux m; **bridesmaid** n demoiselle f d'honneur

bridge [brɪdʒ] n pont m; (Naut) passerelle f (de commandement); (of nose) arête f; (Cards, Dentistry) bridge m ▷ vt (gap) combler

bridle ['braɪdl] n bride f

brief [briːf] adj bref (brève) ▷ n (Law) dossier m, cause

f; (gen) tâche f ▷ vt mettre au courant; **briefs** npl slip m; **briefcase** n serviette f; porte-documents m inv; **briefing** n instructions fpl; (Press) briefing m; **briefly** adv brièvement

brigadier [brɪgə'dɪə'] n brigadier général

bright [braɪt] adj brillant(e); (room, weather) clair(e); (person: clever) intelligent(e), doué(e); (: cheerful) gai(e); (idea) génial(e); (colour) vif (vive)

brilliant ['brɪljənt] adj brillant(e); (light, sunshine) éclatant(e); (inf: great) super

brim [brɪm] n bord m

brine [braɪn] n (Culin) saumure f

bring (pt, pp **brought**) [brɪŋ, brɔːt] vt (thing) apporter; (person) amener; **bring about** vt provoquer, entraîner; **bring back** vt rapporter; (person) ramener; **bring down** vt (lower) abaisser; (shoot down) abattre; (government) faire s'effondrer; **bring in** vt (person) faire entrer; (object) rentrer; (Pol: legislation) introduire; (produce: income) rapporter; **bring on** vt (illness, attack) provoquer; (player, substitute) amener; **bring out** vt sortir; (meaning) faire ressortir, mettre en relief; **bring up** vt élever; (carry up) monter; (question) soulever; (food: vomit) vomir, rendre

brink [brɪŋk] n bord m

brisk [brɪsk] adj vif (vive); (abrupt) brusque; (trade etc) actif(-ive)

bristle ['brɪsl] n poil m ▷ vi se hérisser

Brit [brɪt] n abbr (inf: = British person) Britannique m/f

Britain ['brɪtən] n (also: **Great ~**) la Grande-Bretagne

British ['brɪtɪʃ] adj britannique ▷ npl: **the ~** les Britanniques mpl; **British Isles** npl: **the British Isles** les îles fpl Britanniques

Briton ['brɪtən] n Britannique m/f

Brittany ['brɪtənɪ] n Bretagne f

brittle ['brɪtl] adj cassant(e), fragile

B road n (BRIT) ≈ route départementale

broad [brɔːd] adj large; (distinction) général(e); (accent) prononcé(e); **in ~ daylight** en plein jour; **broadband** n transmission f à haut débit; **broad bean** n fève f; **broadcast** n émission f ▷ vb (pt, pp **broadcast**) ▷ vt (Radio) radiodiffuser; (TV) téléviser ▷ vi émettre; **broaden** vt élargir; **to broaden one's mind** élargir ses horizons ▷ vi s'élargir; **broadly** adv en gros, généralement; **broad-minded** adj large d'esprit

broccoli ['brɔkəlɪ] n brocoli m

brochure ['brəʊʃjʊə'] n prospectus m, dépliant m

broil [brɔɪl] (us) vt rôtir

broiler ['brɔɪlə'] n (fowl) poulet m (à rôtir); (us: grill) gril m

broke [brəʊk] pt of **break** ▷ adj (inf) fauché(e)

broken ['brəʊkn] pp of **break** ▷ adj (stick, leg etc) cassé(e); (machine: also: **~ down**) fichu(e); **in ~ French/English** dans un français/anglais approximatif or hésitant

broker ['brəʊkə'] n courtier m

bronchitis [brɔŋ'kaɪtɪs] n bronchite f

bronze [brɔnz] n bronze m

brooch [brəʊtʃ] n broche f

brood [bruːd] n couvée f ▷ vi (person) méditer (sombrement), ruminer

broom [brum] n balai m; (Bot) genêt m

Bros. abbr (Comm: = brothers) Frères

broth [brɔθ] n bouillon m de viande et de légumes

brothel ['brɔθl] n maison close, bordel m

brother ['brʌðə'] n frère m; **brother-in-law** n beau-frère m

brought [brɔːt] *pt, pp of* **bring**

brow [brau] *n* front *m*; *(eyebrow)* sourcil *m*; *(of hill)* sommet *m*

brown [braun] *adj* brun(e), marron *inv*; *(hair)* châtain *inv*; *(tanned)* bronzé(e) ▷ *n (colour)* brun *m*, marron *m* ▷ *vt* brunir; *(Culin)* faire dorer, faire roussir; **brown bread** *n* pain *m* bis

Brownie ['brauni] *n* jeannette *f* éclaireuse (cadette)

brown rice *n* riz *m* complet

brown sugar *n* cassonade *f*

browse [brauz] *vi (in shop)* regarder *(sans acheter)*; **to ~ through a book** feuilleter un livre; **browser** *n (Comput)* navigateur *m*

bruise [bruːz] *n* bleu *m*, ecchymose *f*, contusion *f* ▷ *vt* contusionner, meurtrir

brunette [bruːˈnet] *n* (femme) brune

brush [brʌʃ] *n* brosse *f*; *(for painting)* pinceau *m*; *(for shaving)* blaireau *m*; *(quarrel)* accrochage *m*, prise *f* de bec ▷ *vt* brosser; *(also:* **~ past**, **~ against**) effleurer, frôler

Brussels ['brʌslz] *n* Bruxelles

Brussels sprout [-spraut] *n* chou *m* de Bruxelles

brutal ['bruːtl] *adj* brutal(e)

B.Sc. *n abbr* = **Bachelor of Science**

BSE *n abbr* = *(bovine spongiform encephalopathy)* ESB *f*, BSE *f*

bubble ['bʌbl] *n* bulle *f* ▷ *vi* bouillonner, faire des bulles; *(sparkle, fig)* pétiller; **bubble bath** *n* bain moussant; **bubble gum** *n* chewing-gum *m*; **bubblejet printer** ['bʌbldʒet-] *n* imprimante *f* à bulle d'encre

buck [bʌk] *n* mâle *m* (d'un lapin, lièvre, daim etc); *(us inf)* dollar *m* ▷ *vi* ruer, lancer une ruade; **to pass the ~** *(to sb)* se décharger de la responsabilité (sur qn)

bucket ['bʌkɪt] *n* seau *m*

buckle ['bʌkl] *n* boucle *f* ▷ *vt (belt etc)* boucler, attacher ▷ *vi (warp)* tordre, gauchir; *(: wheel)* se voiler

bud [bʌd] *n* bourgeon *m*; *(of flower)* bouton *m* ▷ *vi* bourgeonner; *(flower)* éclore

Buddhism ['budɪzəm] *n* bouddhisme *m*

Buddhist ['budɪst] *adj* bouddhiste ▷ *n* Bouddhiste *m/f*

buddy ['bʌdɪ] *n (us)* copain *m*

budge [bʌdʒ] *vt* faire bouger ▷ *vi* bouger

budgerigar ['bʌdʒərɪgɑːʳ] *n* perruche *f*

budget ['bʌdʒɪt] *n* budget *m* ▷ *vi*: **to ~ for sth** inscrire qch au budget

budgie ['bʌdʒɪ] *n* = **budgerigar**

buff [bʌf] *adj (couleur f)* chamois *m* ▷ *n (inf: enthusiast)* mordu(e)

buffalo (*pl* **~** *or* **-es**) ['bʌfələu] *n (BRIT)* buffle *m*; *(US)* bison *m*

buffer ['bʌfəʳ] *n* tampon *m*; *(Comput)* mémoire *f* tampon

buffet *n* ['bufeɪ] *(food BRIT: bar)* buffet *m* ▷ *vt* ['bʌfɪt] secouer, ébranler; **buffet car** *n (BRIT Rail)* voiture-bar *f*

bug [bʌg] *n (bedbug etc)* punaise *f*; *(esp us: any insect)* insecte *m*, bestiole *f*; *(fig: germ)* virus *m*, microbe *m*; *(spy device)* dispositif *m* d'écoute (électronique), micro clandestin; *(Comput: of program)* erreur *f* ▷ *vt (room)* poser des micros dans; *(inf: annoy)* embêter

buggy ['bʌgɪ] *n* poussette *f*

build [bɪld] *n (of person)* carrure *f*, charpente *f* ▷ *vt (pt, pp* **built**) construire, bâtir; **build up** *vt* accumuler, amasser; *(business)* développer; *(reputation)* bâtir; **builder** *n* entrepreneur *m*; **building** *n (trade)* construction *f*; *(structure)* bâtiment *m*, construction *f*; *(: residential, offices)* immeuble *m*; **building site** *n* chantier *m* (de construction); **building society** *n (BRIT)* société *f* de

crédit immobilier

built [bɪlt] *pt, pp of* **build**; **built-in** *adj (cupboard)* encastré(e); *(device)* incorporé(e); intégré(e); **built-up** *adj*: **built-up area** zone urbanisée

bulb [bʌlb] *n (Bot)* bulbe *m*, oignon *m*; *(Elec)* ampoule *f*

Bulgaria [bʌlˈgeərɪə] *n* Bulgarie *f*; **Bulgarian** *adj* bulgare ▷ *n* Bulgare *m/f*

bulge [bʌldʒ] *n* renflement *m*, gonflement *m* ▷ *vi* faire saillie; présenter un renflement; *(pocket, file)*: **to be bulging with** être plein(e) à craquer de

bulimia [bəˈlɪmɪə] *n* boulimie *f*

bulimic [bjuːˈlɪmɪk] *adj,n* boulimique *(m/f)*

bulk [bʌlk] *n* masse *f*, volume *m*; **in ~** *(Comm)* en gros, en vrac; **the ~ of** la plus grande *or* grosse partie de; **bulky** *adj* volumineux(-euse), encombrant(e)

bull [bul] *n* taureau *m*; *(male elephant, whale)* mâle *m*

bulldozer ['buldəuzəʳ] *n* bulldozer *m*

bullet ['bulɪt] *n* balle *f* (de fusil etc)

bulletin ['bulɪtɪn] *n* bulletin *m*, communiqué *m*; *(also:* **news ~**) *(bulletin d')informations fpl*; **bulletin board** *n (Comput)* messagerie *f* (électronique)

bullfight ['bulfaɪt] *n* corrida *f*, course *f* de taureaux; **bullfighter** *n* torero *m*; **bullfighting** *n* tauromachie *f*

bully ['bulɪ] *n* brute *f*, tyran *m* ▷ *vt* tyranniser, rudoyer

bum [bʌm] *n (inf: BRIT: backside)* derrière *m*; *(: esp us: tramp)* vagabond(e), traîne-savates *m/f inv*; *(: idler)* glandeur *m*

bumblebee ['bʌmblbiː] *n* bourdon *m*

bump [bʌmp] *n (blow)* coup *m*, choc *m*; *(jolt)* cahot *m*; *(on road etc, on head)* bosse *f* ▷ *vt* heurter, cogner; *(car)* emboutir; **bump into** *vt fus* rentrer dans, tamponner; *(inf: meet)* tomber sur; **bumper** *n* pare-chocs *m inv* ▷ *adj*: **bumper crop/harvest** récolte/moisson exceptionnelle; **bumpy** *adj (road)* cahoteux(-euse); **it was a bumpy flight/ride** on a été secoués dans l'avion/la voiture

bun [bʌn] *n (cake)* petit gâteau; *(bread)* petit pain au lait; *(of hair)* chignon *m*

bunch [bʌntʃ] *n (of flowers)* bouquet *m*; *(of keys)* trousseau *m*; *(of bananas)* régime *m*; *(of people)* groupe *m*; **bunches** *npl (in hair)* couettes *fpl*; **~ of grapes** grappe *f* de raisin

bundle ['bʌndl] *n* paquet *m* ▷ *vt (also:* **~ up**) faire un paquet de; *(put)*: **to ~ sth/sb into** fourrer *or* enfourner qch/qn dans

bungalow ['bʌngələu] *n* bungalow *m*

bungee jumping ['bʌndʒiːˈdʒʌmpɪŋ] *n* saut *m* à l'élastique

bunion ['bʌnjən] *n* oignon *m (au pied)*

bunk [bʌŋk] *n* couchette *f*; **bunk beds** *npl* lits superposés

bunker ['bʌŋkəʳ] *n (coal store)* soute *f* à charbon; *(Mil, Golf)* bunker *m*

bunny ['bʌnɪ] *n (also:* **~ rabbit**) lapin *m*

buoy [bɔɪ] *n* bouée *f*; **buoyant** *adj (ship)* flottable; *(carefree)* gai(e), plein(e) d'entrain; *(Comm: market, economy)* actif(-ive)

burden ['bəːdn] *n* fardeau *m*, charge *f* ▷ *vt* charger; *(oppress)* accabler, surcharger

bureau (*pl* **~x**) ['bjuərəu, -z] *n (BRIT: writing desk)* bureau *m*, secrétaire *m*; *(us: chest of drawers)* commode *f*; *(office)* bureau, office *m*

bureaucracy [bjuəˈrɔkrəsɪ] *n* bureaucratie *f*

bureaucrat ['bjuərəkræt] *n* bureaucrate *m/f*, rond-de-cuir *m*

bureau de change [-də'ʃɑ̃ʒ] (*pl* **bureaux de change**) *n* bureau *m* de change

bureaux ['bjuərəuz] *npl of* **bureau**

burger ['bə:gə'] *n* hamburger *m*

burglar ['bə:glə'] *n* cambrioleur *m*; **burglar alarm** *n* sonnerie *f* d'alarme; **burglary** *n* cambriolage *m*

Burgundy ['bə:gəndɪ] *n* Bourgogne *f*

burial ['berɪəl] *n* enterrement *m*

burn [bə:n] *vt, vi* (*pt, pp* **-ed** *or* **-t**) brûler ⊳ *n* brûlure *f*; **burn down** *vt* incendier, détruire par le feu; **burn out** *vt* (*writer etc*): **to ~ o.s. out** s'user (à force de travailler); **burning** *adj* (*building, forest*) en flammes; (*issue, question*) brûlant(e); (*ambition*) dévorant(e)

Burns' Night [bə:nz-] *n* fête écossaise à la mémoire du poète Robert Burns

burnt [bə:nt] *pt, pp of* **burn**

burp [bə:p] (*inf*) *n* rot *m* ⊳ *vi* roter

burrow ['bʌrəu] *n* terrier *m* ⊳ *vi* (*rabbit*) creuser un terrier; (*rummage*) fouiller

burst [bə:st] (*pt, pp* **~**) *vt* faire éclater; (*river: banks etc*) rompre ⊳ *vi* éclater; (*tyre*) crever ⊳ *n* explosion *f*; (*also:* **~ pipe**) fuite *f* (*due à une rupture*); **a ~ of enthusiasm/ energy** un accès d'enthousiasme/d'énergie; **to ~ into flames** s'enflammer soudainement; **to ~ out laughing** éclater de rire; **to ~ into tears** fondre en larmes; **to ~ open** *vi* s'ouvrir violemment *or* soudainement; **to be ~ing with** (*container*) être plein(e) (à craquer) de, regorger de; (*fig*) être débordant(e) de; **burst into** *vt fus* (*room etc*) faire irruption dans

bury ['berɪ] *vt* enterrer

bus (*pl* **~es**) [bʌs, 'bʌsɪz] *n* autobus *m*; **bus conductor** *n* receveur(-euse) *m/f* de bus

bush [buʃ] *n* buisson *m*; (*scrub land*) brousse *f*; **to beat about the ~** tourner autour du pot

business ['bɪznɪs] *n* (*matter, firm*) affaire *f*; (*trading*) affaires *fpl*; (*job, duty*) travail *m*; **to be away on ~** être en déplacement d'affaires; **it's none of my ~** cela ne me regarde pas, ce ne sont pas mes affaires; **he means ~** il ne plaisante pas, il est sérieux; **business class** *n* (*on plane*) classe *f* affaires; **businesslike** *adj* sérieux(-euse), efficace; **businessman** (*irreg*) *n* homme *m* d'affaires; **business trip** *n* voyage *m* d'affaires; **businesswoman** (*irreg*) *n* femme *f* d'affaires

busker ['bʌskə'] *n* (*BRIT*) artiste ambulant(e)

bus: **bus pass** *n* carte *f* de bus; **bus shelter** *n* abribus *m*; **bus station** *n* gare routière; **bus-stop** *n* arrêt *m* d'autobus

bust [bʌst] *n* buste *m*; (*measurement*) tour *m* de poitrine ⊳ *adj* (*inf: broken*) fichu(e), fini(e); **to go ~** faire faillite

bustling ['bʌslɪŋ] *adj* (*town*) très animé(e)

busy ['bɪzɪ] *adj* occupé(e); (*shop, street*) très fréquenté(e); (*US: telephone, line*) occupé ⊳ *vt*: **to ~ o.s.** s'occuper; **busy signal** *n* (*US*) tonalité *f* occupé *inv*

KEYWORD

but [bʌt] *conj* mais; **I'd love to come, but I'm busy** j'aimerais venir mais je suis occupé; **he's not English but French** il n'est pas anglais mais français; **but that's far too expensive!** mais c'est bien trop cher!
⊳ *prep* (*apart from, except*) sauf, excepté; **nothing but** rien d'autre que; **we've had nothing but trouble** nous n'avons eu que des ennuis; **no-one but him can do it** lui seul peut le faire; **who but a lunatic would do such a**

thing? qui sinon un fou ferait une chose pareille?; **but for you/your help** sans toi/ton aide; **anything but that** tout sauf *or* excepté ça, tout mais pas ça
⊳ *adv* (*just, only*) ne ... que; **she's but a child** elle n'est qu'une enfant; **had I but known** si seulement j'avais su; **I can but try** je peux toujours essayer; **all but finished** pratiquement terminé

butcher ['butʃə'] *n* boucher *m* ⊳ *vt* massacrer; (*cattle etc for meat*) tuer; **butcher's (shop)** *n* boucherie *f*

butler ['bʌtlə'] *n* maître *m* d'hôtel

butt [bʌt] *n* (*cask*) gros tonneau; (*of gun*) crosse *f*; (*of cigarette*) mégot *m*; (*BRIT fig: target*) cible *f* ⊳ *vt* donner un coup de tête à

butter ['bʌtə'] *n* beurre *m* ⊳ *vt* beurrer; **buttercup** *n* bouton *m* d'or

butterfly ['bʌtəflaɪ] *n* papillon *m*; (*Swimming: also:* **~ stroke**) brasse *f* papillon

buttocks ['bʌtəks] *npl* fesses *fpl*

button ['bʌtn] *n* bouton *m*; (*US: badge*) pin *m* ⊳ *vt* (*also:* **~ up**) boutonner ⊳ *vi* se boutonner

buy [baɪ] (*pt, pp* **bought**) *vt* acheter ⊳ *n* achat *m*; **to ~ sb sth/sth from sb** acheter qch à qn; **to ~ sb a drink** offrir un verre *or* à boire à qn; **can I ~ you a drink?** je vous offre un verre?; **where can I ~ some postcards?** où est-ce que je peux acheter des cartes postales?; **buy out** *vt* (*partner*) désintéresser; **buy up** *vt* acheter en bloc, rafler; **buyer** *n* acheteur(-euse) *m/f*

buzz [bʌz] *n* bourdonnement *m*; (*inf: phone call*): **to give sb a ~** passer un coup de fil à qn ⊳ *vi* bourdonner; **buzzer** *n* timbre *m* électrique

KEYWORD

by [baɪ] *prep* **1** (*referring to cause, agent*) par, de; **killed by lightning** tué par la foudre; **surrounded by a fence** entouré d'une barrière; **a painting by Picasso** un tableau de Picasso

2 (*referring to method, manner, means*): **by bus/car** en autobus/voiture; **by train** par le *or* en train; **to pay by cheque** payer par chèque; **by moonlight/candlelight** à la lueur de la lune/d'une bougie; **by saving hard, he ...** à force d'économiser, il ...

3 (*via, through*) par; **we came by Dover** nous sommes venus par Douvres

4 (*close to, past*) à côté de; **the house by the school** la maison à côté de l'école; **a holiday by the sea** des vacances au bord de la mer; **she went by me** elle est passée à côté de moi; **I go by the post office every day** je passe devant la poste tous les jours

5 (*with time: not later than; during*): **by daylight** à la lumière du jour; **by night** la nuit, de nuit; **by 4 o'clock** avant 4 heures; **by this time tomorrow** d'ici demain à la même heure; **by the time I got here it was too late** lorsque je suis arrivé il était déjà trop tard

6 (*amount*) à; **by the kilo/metre** au kilo/au mètre; **paid by the hour** payé à l'heure

7 (*Math: measure*): **to divide/multiply by 3** diviser/ multiplier par 3; **a room 3 metres by 4** une pièce de 3 mètres sur 4; **it's broader by a metre** c'est plus large d'un mètre

8 (*according to*) d'après, selon; **it's 3 o'clock by my watch** il est 3 heures à ma montre; **it's all right by me** je n'ai rien contre

9: (all) by oneself etc tout(e) seul(e)
▷ adv **1** see **go; pass** etc
2: by and by un peu plus tard, bientôt; **by and large** dans l'ensemble

bye(-bye) ['baɪ('baɪ)] excl au revoir!, salut!
by-election ['baɪɪlɛkʃən] n (BRIT) élection (législative) partielle
bypass ['baɪpɑːs] n rocade f; (Med) pontage m ▷ vt éviter
byte [baɪt] n (Comput) octet m

C

C [siː] n (Mus): **C** do m
cab [kæb] n taxi m; (of train, truck) cabine f
cabaret ['kæbəreɪ] n (show) spectacle m de cabaret
cabbage ['kæbɪdʒ] n chou m
cabin ['kæbɪn] n (house) cabane f, hutte f; (on ship) cabine f; (on plane) compartiment m; **cabin crew** n (Aviat) équipage m
cabinet ['kæbɪnɪt] n (Pol) cabinet m; (furniture) petit meuble à tiroirs et rayons; (also: **display ~**) vitrine f, petite armoire vitrée; **cabinet minister** n ministre m (membre du cabinet)
cable ['keɪbl] n câble m ▷ vt câbler, télégraphier; **cable car** n téléphérique m; **cable television** n télévision f par câble
cactus (pl **cacti**) ['kæktəs, -taɪ] n cactus m
café ['kæfeɪ] n ≈ café(-restaurant) m (sans alcool)
cafeteria [kæfɪ'tɪərɪə] n cafétéria f
caffein(e) ['kæfiːn] n caféine f
cage [keɪdʒ] n cage f
cagoule [kə'guːl] n K-way® m
Cairo ['kaɪərəʊ] n le Caire
cake [keɪk] n gâteau m; **~ of soap** savonnette f
calcium ['kælsɪəm] n calcium m

calculate ['kælkjuleɪt] vt calculer; (estimate: chances, effect) évaluer; **calculation** [kælkju'leɪʃən] n calcul m; **calculator** n calculatrice f
calendar ['kæləndəʳ] n calendrier m
calf (pl **calves**) [kɑːf, kɑːvz] n (of cow) veau m; (of other animals) petit m; (also: **~skin**) veau m, vachette f; (Anat) mollet m
calibre (US **caliber**) ['kælɪbəʳ] n calibre m
call [kɔːl] vt appeler; (meeting) convoquer ▷ vi appeler; (visit: also: **~ in, ~ round**) passer ▷ n (shout) appel m, cri m; (also: **telephone ~**) coup m de téléphone; **to be on ~** être de permanence; **to be ~ed** s'appeler; **can I make a ~ from here?** est-ce que je peux téléphoner d'ici?; **call back** vi (return) repasser; (Tel) rappeler ▷ vt (Tel) rappeler; **can you ~ back later?** pouvez-vous rappeler plus tard?; **call for** vt fus (demand) demander; (fetch) passer prendre; **call in** vt (doctor, expert, police) appeler, faire venir; **call off** vt annuler; **call on** vt fus (visit) rendre visite à, passer voir; (request): **to ~ on sb to do** inviter qn à faire; **call out** vi pousser un cri ou des cris; **call up** vt (Mil) appeler, mobiliser; (Tel) appeler; **callbox** n (BRIT) cabine f téléphonique; **call centre** (US **call center**) n centre m d'appels; **caller** n (Tel) personne f qui appelle; (visitor) visiteur m
callous ['kæləs] adj dur(e), insensible
calm [kɑːm] adj calme ▷ n calme m ▷ vt calmer, apaiser; **calm down** vi se calmer, s'apaiser ▷ vt calmer, apaiser; **calmly** ['kɑːmlɪ] adv calmement, avec calme
Calor gas® ['kæləʳ-] n (BRIT) butane m, butagaz® m
calorie ['kælərɪ] n calorie f
calves [kɑːvz] npl of **calf**
Cambodia [kæm'bəʊdɪə] n Cambodge m
camcorder ['kæmkɔːdəʳ] n caméscope m
came [keɪm] pt of **come**
camel ['kæməl] n chameau m
camera ['kæmərə] n appareil-photo m; (Cine, TV) caméra f; **in ~** à huis clos, en privé; **cameraman** n caméraman m; **camera phone** n téléphone m avec appareil photo numérique intégré
camouflage ['kæməflɑːʒ] n camouflage m ▷ vt camoufler
camp [kæmp] n camp m ▷ vi camper ▷ adj (man) efféminé(e)
campaign [kæm'peɪn] n (Mil, Pol etc) campagne f ▷ vi (also fig) faire campagne; **campaigner** n: **campaigner for** partisan(e) de; **campaigner against** opposant(e) à
camp: campbed n (BRIT) lit m de camp; **camper** n campeur(-euse); (vehicle) camping-car m; **campground** (US) n (terrain m de) camping m; **camping** n camping m; **to go camping** faire du camping; **campsite** n (terrain m de) camping m
campus ['kæmpəs] n campus m
can¹ [kæn] n (of milk, oil, water) bidon m; (tin) boîte f (de conserve) ▷ vt mettre en conserve

KEYWORD

can² [kæn] (negative **cannot, can't**, conditional and pt **could**) aux vb **1** (be able to) pouvoir; **you can do it if you try** vous pouvez le faire si vous essayez; **I can't hear you** je ne t'entends pas
2 (know how to) savoir; **I can swim/play tennis/drive** je sais nager/jouer au tennis/conduire; **can you speak French?** parlez-vous français?

3 (may) pouvoir; **can I use your phone?** puis-je me servir de votre téléphone?
4 (expressing disbelief, puzzlement etc): **it can't be true!** ce n'est pas possible!; **what CAN he want?** qu'est-ce qu'il peut bien vouloir?
5 (expressing possibility, suggestion etc): **he could be in the library** il est peut-être dans la bibliothèque; **she could have been delayed** il se peut qu'elle ait été retardée

Canada ['kænədə] n Canada m; **Canadian** [kə'neɪdɪən] adj canadien(ne) ▷ n Canadien(ne)
canal [kə'næl] n canal m
canary [kə'neərɪ] n canari m, serin m
cancel ['kænsəl] vt annuler; (train) supprimer; (party, appointment) décommander; (cross out) barrer, rayer; (cheque) faire opposition à; **I would like to ~ my booking** je voudrais annuler ma réservation; **cancellation** [kænsə'leɪʃən] n annulation f; suppression f
Cancer ['kænsə'] n (Astrology) le Cancer
cancer ['kænsə'] n cancer m
candidate ['kændɪdeɪt] n candidat(e)
candle ['kændl] n bougie f; (in church) cierge m; **candlestick** n (also: **candle holder**) bougeoir m; (bigger, ornate) chandelier m
candy ['kændɪ] n sucre candi; (us) bonbon m; **candy bar** (us) n barre f chocolatée; **candyfloss** n (BRIT) barbe f à papa
cane [keɪn] n canne f; (for baskets, chairs etc) rotin m ▷ vt (BRIT Scol) administrer des coups de bâton à
canister ['kænɪstə'] n boîte f (gén en métal); (of gas) bombe f
cannabis ['kænəbɪs] n (drug) cannabis m
canned ['kænd] adj (food) en boîte, en conserve; (inf: music) enregistré(e); (BRIT inf: drunk) bourré(e); (us inf: worker) mis(e) à la porte
cannon (pl ~ or ~s) ['kænən] n (gun) canon m
cannot ['kænɔt] = **can not**
canoe [kə'nu:] n pirogue f; (Sport) canoë m; **canoeing** n (sport) canoë m
canon ['kænən] n (clergyman) chanoine m; (standard) canon m
can-opener [-'əupnə'] n ouvre-boîte m
can't [kɑ:nt] = **can not**
canteen [kæn'ti:n] n (eating place) cantine f; (BRIT: of cutlery) ménagère f
canter ['kæntə'] vi aller au petit galop
canvas ['kænvəs] n toile f
canvass ['kænvəs] vi (Pol): **to ~ for** faire campagne pour ▷ vt (citizens, opinions) sonder
canyon ['kænjən] n cañon m, gorge (profonde)
cap [kæp] n casquette f; (for swimming) bonnet m de bain; (of pen) capuchon m; (of bottle) capsule f; (BRIT: contraceptive: also: **Dutch ~**) diaphragme m ▷ vt (outdo) surpasser; (put limit on) plafonner
capability [keɪpə'bɪlɪtɪ] n aptitude f, capacité f
capable ['keɪpəbl] adj capable
capacity [kə'pæsɪtɪ] n (of container) capacité f, contenance f; (ability) aptitude f
cape [keɪp] n (garment) cape f; (Geo) cap m
caper ['keɪpə'] n (Culin: gen pl) câpre f; (prank) farce f
capital ['kæpɪtl] n (also: **~ city**) capitale f; (money) capital m; (also: **~ letter**) majuscule f; **capitalism** n

capitalisme m; **capitalist** adj, n capitaliste m/f; **capital punishment** n peine capitale
Capitol ['kæpɪtl] n: **the ~** le Capitole
Capricorn ['kæprɪkɔ:n] n le Capricorne
capsize [kæp'saɪz] vt faire chavirer ▷ vi chavirer
capsule ['kæpsju:l] n capsule f
captain ['kæptɪn] n capitaine m
caption ['kæpʃən] n légende f
captivity [kæp'tɪvɪtɪ] n captivité f
capture ['kæptʃə'] vt (prisoner, animal) capturer; (town) prendre; (attention) capter; (Comput) saisir ▷ n capture f; (of data) saisie f de données
car [kɑ:'] n voiture f, auto f; (us Rail) wagon m, voiture f
carafe [kə'ræf] n carafe f
caramel ['kærəml] n caramel m
carat ['kærət] n carat m
caravan ['kærəvæn] n caravane f; **caravan site** n (BRIT) camping m pour caravanes
carbohydrate [kɑ:bəu'haɪdreɪt] n hydrate m de carbone; (food) féculent m
carbon ['kɑ:bən] n carbone m; **carbon dioxide** [-daɪ'ɔksaɪd] n gaz m carbonique, dioxyde m de carbone; **carbon monoxide** [-mɔ'nɔksaɪd] n oxyde m de carbone
car boot sale n: **carburettor** (us **carburetor**) [kɑ:bju'retə'] n carburateur m
card [kɑ:d] n carte f; (material) carton m; **cardboard** n carton m; **card game** n jeu m de cartes
cardigan ['kɑ:dɪgən] n cardigan m
cardinal ['kɑ:dɪnl] adj cardinal(e); (importance) capital(e) ▷ n cardinal m
cardphone ['kɑ:dfəun] n téléphone m à carte (magnétique)
care [kɛə'] n soin m, attention f; (worry) souci m ▷ vi: **to ~ about** (feel interest for) se soucier de, s'intéresser à; (person: love) être attaché(e) à; **in sb's ~** à la garde de qn, confié à qn; **~ of** (on letter) chez; **to take ~ (to do)** faire attention (à faire); **to take ~ of** vt s'occuper de; **I don't ~** ça m'est bien égal, peu m'importe; **I couldn't ~ less** cela m'est complètement égal, je m'en fiche complètement; **care for** vt fus s'occuper de; (like) aimer
career [kə'rɪə'] n carrière f ▷ vi (also: **~ along**) aller à toute allure
care: **carefree** adj sans souci, insouciant(e); **careful** adj soigneux(-euse); (cautious) prudent(e); **(be) careful!** (fais) attention!; **carefully** adv avec soin, soigneusement; prudemment; **caregiver** (us) n (professional) travailleur social; (unpaid) personne qui s'occupe d'un proche qui est malade; **careless** adj négligent(e); (heedless) insouciant(e); **carelessness** n manque m de soin, négligence f; insouciance f; **carer** ['kɛərə'] n (professional) travailleur social; (unpaid) personne qui s'occupe d'un proche qui est malade; **caretaker** n gardien(ne), concierge m/f
car-ferry ['kɑ:fɛrɪ] n (on sea) ferry(-boat) m; (on river) bac m
cargo (pl ~es) ['kɑ:gəu] n cargaison f, chargement m
car hire n (BRIT) location f de voitures
Caribbean [kærɪ'bi:ən] adj, n: **the ~ (Sea)** la mer des Antilles or des Caraïbes
caring ['kɛərɪŋ] adj (person) bienveillant(e); (society, organization) humanitaire
carnation [kɑ:'neɪʃən] n œillet m
carnival ['kɑ:nɪvl] n (public celebration) carnaval m; (us: funfair) fête foraine

carol ['kærəl] n: (**Christmas**) ~ chant m de Noël

carousel [kærə'sɛl] n (for luggage) carrousel m; (US) manège m

car park (BRIT) n parking m, parc m de stationnement

carpenter ['kɑːpɪntəʳ] n charpentier m; (joiner) menuisier m

carpet ['kɑːpɪt] n tapis m ▷ vt recouvrir (d'un tapis); **fitted ~** (BRIT) moquette f

car rental n (US) location f de voitures

carriage ['kærɪdʒ] n (BRIT Rail) wagon m; (horse-drawn) voiture f; (of goods) transport m; (: cost) port m; **carriageway** n (BRIT: part of road) chaussée f

carrier ['kærɪəʳ] n transporteur m, camionneur m; (company) entreprise f de transport; (Med) porteur(-euse); **carrier bag** n (BRIT) sac m en papier or en plastique

carrot ['kærət] n carotte f

carry ['kærɪ] vt (subj: person) porter; (: vehicle) transporter; (involve: responsibilities etc) comporter, impliquer; (Med: disease) être porteur de ▷ vi (sound) porter; **to get carried away** (fig) s'emballer, s'enthousiasmer; **carry on** vi (continue) continuer ▷ vt (conduct: business) diriger; (: conversation) entretenir; (continue: business, conversation) continuer; **to ~ on with sth/doing** continuer qch/à faire; **carry out** vt (orders) exécuter; (investigation) effectuer

cart [kɑːt] n charrette f ▷ vt (inf) transporter

carton ['kɑːtən] n (box) carton m; (of yogurt) pot m (en carton)

cartoon [kɑː'tuːn] n (Press) dessin m (humoristique); (satirical) caricature f; (comic strip) bande dessinée; (Cine) dessin animé

cartridge ['kɑːtrɪdʒ] n (for gun, pen) cartouche f

carve [kɑːv] vt (meat: also: ~ **up**) découper; (wood, stone) tailler, sculpter; **carving** n (in wood etc) sculpture f

car wash n station f de lavage (de voitures)

case [keɪs] n cas m; (Law) affaire f, procès m; (box) caisse f, boîte f; (for glasses) étui m; (BRIT: also: **suit~**) valise f; **in ~ of** en cas de; **in ~ he** au cas où il; **just in ~** à tout hasard; **in any ~** en tout cas, de toute façon

cash [kæʃ] n argent m; (Comm) (argent m) liquide m ▷ vt encaisser; **to pay (in) ~** payer (en argent) comptant or en espèces; **~ with order/on delivery** (Comm) payable or paiement à la commande/livraison; **I haven't got any ~** je n'ai pas de liquide; **cashback** n (discount) remise f; (at supermarket etc) retrait m (à la caisse); **cash card** n carte f de retrait; **cash desk** n (BRIT) caisse f; **cash dispenser** n distributeur m automatique de billets

cashew [kæ'fuː] n (also: ~ **nut**) noix f de cajou

cashier [kæ'ʃɪəʳ] n caissier(-ère)

cashmere ['kæʃmɪəʳ] ~ n cachemire m

cash point n distributeur m automatique de billets

cash register n caisse enregistreuse

casino [kə'siːnəu] n casino m

casket ['kɑːskɪt] n coffret m; (US: coffin) cercueil m

casserole ['kæsərəul] n (pot) cocotte f; (food) ragoût m (en cocotte)

cassette [kæ'sɛt] n cassette f; **cassette player** n lecteur m de cassettes

cast [kɑːst] (vb: pt, pp ~) vt (throw) jeter; (shadow: lit) projeter; (: fig) jeter; (glance) jeter ▷ n (Theat) distribution f; (also: **plaster ~**) plâtre m; **to ~ sb as Hamlet** attribuer à qn le rôle d'Hamlet; **to ~ one's vote** voter, exprimer son suffrage; **to ~ doubt on** jeter un doute sur; **cast off**

vi (Naut) larguer les amarres; (Knitting) arrêter les mailles

castanets [kæstə'nɛts] npl castagnettes fpl

caster sugar ['kɑːstə-] n (BRIT) sucre m semoule

cast-iron ['kɑːstaɪən] adj (lit) de or en fonte; (fig: will) de fer; (alibi) en béton

castle ['kɑːsl] n château m; (fortress) château-fort m; (Chess) tour f

casual ['kæʒjul] adj (by chance) de hasard, fait(e) au hasard, fortuit(e); (irregular: work etc) temporaire; (unconcerned) désinvolte; **~ wear** vêtements mpl sport inv

casualty ['kæʒjultɪ] n accidenté(e), blessé(e); (dead) victime f, mort(e); (BRIT: Med: department) urgences fpl

cat [kæt] n chat m

Catalan ['kætəlæn] adj catalan(e)

catalogue (US **catalog**) ['kætəlɔg] n catalogue m ▷ vt cataloguer

catalytic converter [kætə'lɪtɪkkən'vɜːtəʳ] n pot m catalytique

cataract ['kætərækt] n (also Med) cataracte f

catarrh [kə'tɑːʳ] n rhume m chronique, catarrhe f

catastrophe [kə'tæstrəfɪ] n catastrophe f

catch [kætʃ] (pt, pp **caught**) vt attraper; (person: by surprise) prendre, surprendre; (understand) saisir; (get entangled) accrocher ▷ vi (fire) prendre; (get entangled) s'accrocher ▷ n (fish etc) prise f; (hidden problem) attrape f, (Tech) loquet m; cliquet m; **to ~ sb's attention** or **eye** attirer l'attention de qn; **to ~ fire** prendre feu; **to ~ sight of** apercevoir; **catch up** vi (with work) se rattraper, combler son retard ▷ vt (also: ~ **up with**) rattraper

catching ['kætʃɪŋ] adj (Med) contagieux(-euse)

category ['kætɪgərɪ] n catégorie f

cater ['keɪtəʳ] vi: **to ~ for** (BRIT: needs) satisfaire, pourvoir à; (: readers, consumers) s'adresser à, pourvoir aux besoins de; (Comm: parties etc) préparer des repas pour

caterpillar ['kætəpɪləʳ] n chenille f

cathedral [kə'θiːdrəl] n cathédrale f

Catholic ['kæθəlɪk] (Rel) adj catholique ▷ n catholique m/f

Catseye® ['kæts'aɪ] n (BRIT Aut) (clou m à) catadioptre m

cattle ['kætl] npl bétail m, bestiaux mpl

catwalk ['kætwɔːk] n passerelle f; (for models) podium m (de défilé de mode)

caught [kɔːt] pt, pp of **catch**

cauliflower ['kɔlɪflauəʳ] n chou-fleur m

cause [kɔːz] n cause f ▷ vt causer

caution ['kɔːʃən] n prudence f; (warning) avertissement m ▷ vt avertir, donner un avertissement à; **cautious** adj prudent(e)

cave [keɪv] n caverne f, grotte f; **cave in** vi (roof etc) s'effondrer

caviar(e) ['kævɪɑːʳ] n caviar m

cavity ['kævɪtɪ] n cavité f; (Med) carie f

cc abbr (= cubic centimetre) cm³; (on letter etc) = **carbon copy**

CCTV n abbr = **closed-circuit television**

CD n abbr (= compact disc) CD m; **CD burner** n graveur m de CD; **CD player** n platine f laser; **CD-ROM** [siːdiːˈrɔm] n abbr (= compact disc read-only memory) CD-ROM m inv; **CD writer** n graveur m de CD

cease [siːs] vt, vi cesser; **ceasefire** n cessez-le-feu m

cedar ['siːdəʳ] n cèdre m

ceilidh ['keɪlɪ] n bal m folklorique écossais or irlandais

ceiling ['siːlɪŋ] n (also fig) plafond m

celebrate ['sɛlɪbreɪt] vt, vi célébrer; **celebration** [sɛlɪ'breɪʃən] n célébration f

celebrity [sɪ'lɛbrɪtɪ] n célébrité f

celery ['sɛlərɪ] n céleri m (en branches)

cell [sɛl] n (gen) cellule f; (Elec) élément m (de pile)

cellar ['sɛləʳ] n cave f

cello ['tʃɛləʊ] n violoncelle m

Cellophane® ['sɛləfeɪn] n cellophane® f

cellphone ['sɛlfəʊn] n téléphone m cellulaire

Celsius ['sɛlsɪəs] adj Celsius inv

Celtic ['kɛltɪk, 'sɛltɪk] adj celte, celtique

cement [sə'mɛnt] n ciment m

cemetery ['sɛmɪtrɪ] n cimetière m

censor ['sɛnsəʳ] n censeur m ▷ vt censurer; **censorship** n censure f

census ['sɛnsəs] n recensement m

cent [sɛnt] n (unit of dollar, euro) cent m (= un centième du dollar, de l'euro); see also **per**

centenary [sɛn'tiːnərɪ] (US **centennial**) [sɛn'tɛnɪəl] n centenaire m

center ['sɛntəʳ] (US) = **centre**

centi... [sɛntɪ] prefix: **centigrade** adj centigrade; **centimetre** (US **centimeter**) n centimètre m; **centipede** ['sɛntɪpiːd] n mille-pattes m inv

central ['sɛntrəl] adj central(e); **Central America** n Amérique centrale; **central heating** n chauffage central; **central reservation** n (BRIT Aut) terre-plein central

centre (US **center**) ['sɛntəʳ] n centre m ▷ vt centrer; **centre-forward** n (Sport) avant-centre m; **centre-half** n (Sport) demi-centre m

century ['sɛntjʊrɪ] n siècle m; **in the twentieth ~** au vingtième siècle

CEO n abbr (US) = **chief executive officer**

ceramic [sɪ'ræmɪk] adj céramique

cereal ['siːrɪəl] n céréale f

ceremony ['sɛrɪmənɪ] n cérémonie f; **to stand on ~** faire des façons

certain ['səːtən] adj certain(e); **to make ~ of** s'assurer de; **for ~** certainement, sûrement; **certainly** adv certainement; **certainty** n certitude f

certificate [sə'tɪfɪkɪt] n certificat m

certify ['səːtɪfaɪ] vt certifier; (award diploma to) conférer un diplôme etc à; (declare insane) déclarer malade mental(e)

cf. abbr (= compare) cf., voir

CFC n abbr (= chlorofluorocarbon) CFC m

chain [tʃeɪn] n (gen) chaîne f ▷ vt (also: **~ up**) enchaîner, attacher (avec une chaîne); **chain-smoke** vi fumer cigarette sur cigarette

chair [tʃɛəʳ] n chaise f; (armchair) fauteuil m; (of university) chaire f; (of meeting) présidence f ▷ vt (meeting) présider; **chairlift** n télésiège m; **chairman** n président m; **chairperson** n président(e); **chairwoman** n présidente f

chalet ['ʃæleɪ] n chalet m

chalk [tʃɔːk] n craie f; **chalkboard** (US) n tableau noir

challenge ['tʃælɪndʒ] n défi m ▷ vt défier; (statement, right) mettre en question, contester; **to ~ sb to do** mettre qn au défi de faire; **challenging** adj (task, career) qui représente un défi or une gageure; (tone, look) de défi, provocateur(-trice)

chamber ['tʃeɪmbəʳ] n chambre f; (BRIT Law: gen pl) cabinet m; **~ of commerce** chambre de commerce;

chambermaid n femme f de chambre

champagne [ʃæm'peɪn] n champagne m

champion ['tʃæmpɪən] n (also of cause) champion(ne); **championship** n championnat m

chance [tʃɑːns] n (luck) hasard m; (opportunity) occasion f, possibilité f; (hope, likelihood) chances fpl; (risk) risque m ▷ vt (risk) risquer ▷ adj fortuit(e), de hasard; **to take a ~** prendre un risque; **by ~** par hasard; **to ~ it** risquer le coup, essayer

chancellor ['tʃɑːnsələʳ] n chancelier m; **Chancellor of the Exchequer** [-ɪks'tʃɛkəʳ] (BRIT) n chancelier m de l'Échiquier

chandelier [ʃændə'lɪəʳ] n lustre m

change [tʃeɪndʒ] vt (alter, replace: Comm: money) changer; (switch, substitute: hands, trains, clothes, one's name etc) changer de ▷ vi (gen) changer; (change clothes) se changer; (be transformed): **to ~ into** se changer or transformer en ▷ n changement m; (money) monnaie f; **to ~ gear** (Aut) changer de vitesse; **to ~ one's mind** changer d'avis; **a ~ of clothes** des vêtements de rechange; **for a ~** pour changer; **do you have ~ for £10?** vous avez la monnaie de 10 livres?; **where can I ~ some money?** où est-ce que je peux changer de l'argent?; **keep the ~!** gardez la monnaie!; **change over** vi (swap) échanger; (change: drivers etc) changer; (change sides: players etc) changer de côté; **to ~ over from sth to sth** passer de qch à qch; **changeable** adj (weather) variable; **change machine** n distributeur m de monnaie; **changing room** n (BRIT: in shop) salon m d'essayage; (: Sport) vestiaire m

channel ['tʃænl] n (TV) chaîne f; (waveband, groove, fig: medium) canal m; (of river, sea) chenal m ▷ vt canaliser; **the (English) C~** la Manche; **Channel Islands** npl: **the Channel Islands** les îles fpl Anglo-Normandes; **Channel Tunnel** n: **the Channel Tunnel** le tunnel sous la Manche

chant [tʃɑːnt] n chant m; (Rel) psalmodie f ▷ vt chanter, scander

chaos ['keɪɔs] n chaos m

chaotic [keɪ'ɔtɪk] adj chaotique

chap [tʃæp] n (BRIT inf: man) type m

chapel ['tʃæpl] n chapelle f

chapped [tʃæpt] adj (skin, lips) gercé(e)

chapter ['tʃæptəʳ] n chapitre m

character ['kærɪktəʳ] n caractère m; (in novel, film) personnage m; (eccentric person) numéro m, phénomène m; **characteristic** ['kærɪktə'rɪstɪk] adj, n caractéristique (f); **characterize** ['kærɪktəraɪz] vt caractériser

charcoal ['tʃɑːkəʊl] n charbon m de bois; (Art) charbon

charge [tʃɑːdʒ] n (accusation) accusation f; (Law) inculpation f; (cost) prix (demandé) ▷ vt (gun, battery, Mil: enemy) charger; (customer, sum) faire payer ▷ vi foncer; **charges** npl (costs) frais mpl; (BRIT Tel): **to reverse the ~s** téléphoner en PCV; **to take ~ of** se charger de; **to be in ~ of** être responsable de, s'occuper de; **to ~ sb (with)** (Law) inculper qn (de); **charge card** n carte f de client (émise par un grand magasin); **charger** n (also: **battery charger**) chargeur m

charismatic [kærɪz'mætɪk] adj charismatique

charity ['tʃærɪtɪ] n charité f; (organization) institution f charitable or de bienfaisance, œuvre f (de charité); **charity shop** n (BRIT) boutique vendant des articles d'occasion au profit d'une organisation caritative

charm [tʃɑːm] n charme m; (on bracelet) breloque f ▷ vt

charmer, enchanter; **charming** adj charmant(e)

chart [tʃɑːt] n tableau m, diagramme m; graphique m; (map) carte marine ▷ vt dresser or établir la carte de; (sales, progress) établir la courbe de; **charts** npl (Mus) hit-parade m; **to be in the ~s** (record, pop group) figurer au hit-parade

charter ['tʃɑːtər] vt (plane) affréter ▷ n (document) charte f; **chartered accountant** n (BRIT) expert-comptable m; **charter flight** n charter m

chase [tʃeɪs] vt poursuivre, pourchasser; (also: ~ away) chasser ▷ n poursuite f, chasse f

chat [tʃæt] vi (also: **have a ~**) bavarder, causer; (on Internet) chatter ▷ n conversation f; **chat up** vt (BRIT inf: girl) baratiner; **chat room** n (Internet) forum m de discussion; **chat show** n (BRIT) talk-show m

chatter ['tʃætər] vi (person) bavarder, papoter ▷ n bavardage m, papotage m; **my teeth are ~ing** je claque des dents

chauffeur ['ʃəʊfər] n chauffeur m (de maître)

chauvinist ['ʃəʊvɪnɪst] n (also: **male ~**) phallocrate m, macho m; (nationalist) chauvin(e)

cheap [tʃiːp] adj bon marché inv, pas cher (chère); (reduced: ticket) à prix réduit; (: fare) réduit(e); (joke) facile, d'un goût douteux; (poor quality) à bon marché, de qualité médiocre ▷ adv à bon marché, pour pas cher; **can you recommend a ~ hotel/restaurant, please?** pourriez-vous m'indiquer un hôtel/restaurant bon marché?; **cheap day return** n billet m d'aller et retour réduit (valable pour la journée); **cheaply** adv à bon marché, à bon compte

cheat [tʃiːt] vi tricher; (in exam) copier ▷ vt tromper, duper; (rob): **to ~ sb out of sth** escroquer qch à qn ▷ n tricheur(-euse) m/f; escroc m; **cheat on** vt fus tromper

Chechnya [tʃtʃnjɑː] n Tchétchénie f

check [tʃek] vt vérifier; (passport, ticket) contrôler; (halt) enrayer; (restrain) maîtriser ▷ vi (official etc) se renseigner ▷ n vérification f; contrôle m; (curb) frein m; (BRIT: bill) addition f; (: us) = **cheque**; (pattern: gen pl) carreaux mpl; **to ~ with sb** demander à qn; **check in** vi (in hotel) remplir sa fiche (d'hôtel); (at airport) se présenter à l'enregistrement ▷ vt (luggage) (faire) enregistrer; **check off** vt (tick off) cocher; **check out** vi (in hotel) régler sa note ▷ vt (investigate: story) vérifier; **check up** vi: **to ~ up (on sth)** vérifier (qch); **to ~ up on sb** se renseigner sur le compte de qn; **checkbook** (us) = **chequebook**; **checked** adj (pattern, cloth) à carreaux; **checkers** n (us) jeu m de dames; **check-in** n (also: **check-in desk**: at airport) enregistrement m; **checking account** n (us) compte courant; **checklist** n liste f de contrôle; **checkmate** n échec et mat m; **checkout** n (in supermarket) caisse f; **checkpoint** n contrôle m; **checkroom** (us) n consigne f; **checkup** n (Med) examen médical, check-up m

cheddar ['tʃedər] n (also: **~ cheese**) cheddar m

cheek [tʃiːk] n joue f; (impudence) toupet m, culot m; **what a ~!** quel toupet!; **cheekbone** n pommette f; **cheeky** adj effronté(e), culotté(e)

cheer [tʃɪər] vt acclamer, applaudir; (gladden) réjouir, réconforter ▷ vi applaudir ▷ n (gen pl) acclamations fpl, applaudissements mpl; bravos mpl, hourras mpl; **~s!** à la vôtre!; **cheer up** vi se dérider, reprendre courage ▷ vt remonter le moral à or de, dérider, égayer; **cheerful** adj gai(e), joyeux(-euse)

cheerio [tʃɪərɪˈəʊ] excl (BRIT) salut!, au revoir!

cheerleader ['tʃɪəliːdər] n membre d'un groupe de majorettes qui chantent et dansent pour soutenir leur équipe pendant les matchs de football américain

cheese [tʃiːz] n fromage m; **cheeseburger** n cheeseburger m; **cheesecake** n tarte f au fromage

chef [ʃef] n chef (cuisinier)

chemical ['kemɪkl] adj chimique ▷ n produit m chimique

chemist ['kemɪst] n (BRIT: pharmacist) pharmacien(ne); (scientist) chimiste m/f; **chemistry** n chimie f; **chemist's (shop)** n (BRIT) pharmacie f

cheque (us **check**) [tʃek] n chèque m; **chequebook** (us **checkbook**) n chéquier m, carnet m de chèques; **cheque card** n (BRIT) carte f d'identité) bancaire

cherry ['tʃerɪ] n cerise f; (also: **~ tree**) cerisier m

chess [tʃes] n échecs mpl

chest [tʃest] n poitrine f; (box) coffre m, caisse f

chestnut ['tʃesnʌt] n châtaigne f; (also: **~ tree**) châtaignier m

chest of drawers n commode f

chew [tʃuː] vt mâcher; **chewing gum** n chewing-gum m

chic [ʃiːk] adj chic inv, élégant(e)

chick [tʃɪk] n poussin m; (inf) pépée f

chicken ['tʃɪkɪn] n poulet m; (inf: coward) poule mouillée; **chicken out** vi (inf) se dégonfler; **chickenpox** n varicelle f

chickpea ['tʃɪkpiː] n pois m chiche

chief [tʃiːf] n chef m ▷ adj principal(e); **chief executive** (us **chief executive officer**) n directeur(-trice) général(e); **chiefly** adv principalement, surtout

child (pl **~ren**) [tʃaɪld, 'tʃɪldrən] n enfant m/f; **child abuse** n maltraitance f d'enfants; (sexual) abus mpl sexuels sur des enfants; **child benefit** n (BRIT) = allocations familiales; **childbirth** n accouchement m; **child-care** n (for working parents) garde f des enfants (pour les parents qui travaillent); **childhood** n enfance f; **childish** adj puéril(e), enfantin(e); **child minder** n (BRIT) garde f d'enfants; **children** ['tʃɪldrən] npl of **child**

Chile ['tʃɪli] n Chili m

chill [tʃɪl] n (of water) froid m; (of air) fraîcheur f; (Med) refroidissement m, coup m de froid ▷ vt (person) faire frissonner; (Culin) mettre au frais, rafraîchir; **chill out** vi (inf: esp us) se relaxer

chil(l)i ['tʃɪli] n piment m (rouge)

chilly ['tʃɪli] adj froid(e), glacé(e); (sensitive to cold) frileux(-euse)

chimney ['tʃɪmni] n cheminée f

chimpanzee [tʃɪmpænˈziː] n chimpanzé m

chin [tʃɪn] n menton m

China ['tʃaɪnə] n Chine f

china ['tʃaɪnə] n (material) porcelaine f; (crockery) (vaisselle f en) porcelaine

Chinese [tʃaɪˈniːz] adj chinois(e) ▷ n (pl inv) Chinois(e); (Ling) chinois m

chip [tʃɪp] n (gen pl: Culin: BRIT) frite f; (: us: also: **potato ~**) chip m; (of wood) copeau m; (of glass, stone) éclat m; (also: **micro~**) puce f; (in gambling) fiche f ▷ vt (cup, plate) ébrécher; **chip shop** n (BRIT) friterie f

chiropodist [kɪˈrɒpədɪst] n (BRIT) pédicure m/f

chisel ['tʃɪzl] n ciseau m

chives ['tʃaɪvz] npl ciboulette f, civette f

chlorine ['klɔːriːn] n chlore m

choc-ice ['tʃɒkaɪs] n (BRIT) esquimau® m

chocolate ['tʃɒklɪt] n chocolat m

choice [tʃɔɪs] n choix m ▷ adj de choix

choir ['kwaɪər] n chœur m, chorale f

choke [tʃəʊk] vi étouffer ▷ vt étrangler; étouffer; (block) boucher, obstruer ▷ n (Aut) starter m

cholesterol [kəˈlestərɔl] n cholestérol m

choose (pt **chose**, pp **chosen**) [tʃuːz, tʃəʊz, ˈtʃəʊzn] vt choisir; **to ~ to do** décider de faire, juger bon de faire

chop [tʃɔp] vt (wood) couper (à la hache); (Culin: also: **~ up**) couper (fin), émincer, hacher (en morceaux) ▷ n (Culin) côtelette f; **chop down** vt (tree) abattre; **chop off** vt trancher; **chopsticks** ['tʃɔpstɪks] npl baguettes fpl

chord [kɔːd] n (Mus) accord m

chore [tʃɔːr] n travail m de routine; **household ~s** travaux mpl du ménage

chorus ['kɔːrəs] n chœur m; (repeated part of song, also fig) refrain m

chose [tʃəʊz] pt of **choose**

chosen ['tʃəʊzn] pp of **choose**

Christ [kraɪst] n Christ m

christen ['krɪsn] vt baptiser; **christening** n baptême m

Christian ['krɪstɪən] adj, n chrétien(ne); **Christianity** [krɪstɪˈænɪtɪ] n christianisme m; **Christian name** n prénom m

Christmas ['krɪsməs] n Noël m or f; **happy** or **merry ~!** joyeux Noël!; **Christmas card** n carte f de Noël; **Christmas carol** n chant m de Noël; **Christmas Day** n le jour de Noël; **Christmas Eve** n la veille de Noël; la nuit de Noël; **Christmas pudding** n (esp BRIT) Christmas pudding m; **Christmas tree** n arbre m de Noël

chrome [krəʊm] n chrome m

chronic ['krɔnɪk] adj chronique

chrysanthemum [krɪˈsænθəməm] n chrysanthème m

chubby ['tʃʌbɪ] adj potelé(e), rondelet(te)

chuck [tʃʌk] vt (inf) lancer, jeter; (BRIT: also: **~ up**: job) lâcher; **chuck out** vt (inf: person) flanquer dehors or à la porte; (rubbish etc) jeter

chuckle ['tʃʌkl] vi glousser

chum [tʃʌm] n copain (copine)

chunk [tʃʌŋk] n gros morceau

church [tʃəːtʃ] n église f; **churchyard** n cimetière m

churn [tʃəːn] n (for butter) baratte f; (also: **milk ~**) (grand) bidon à lait

chute [ʃuːt] n goulotte f; (also: **rubbish ~**) vide-ordures m inv; (BRIT: children's slide) toboggan m

chutney ['tʃʌtnɪ] n chutney m

CIA n abbr (= Central Intelligence Agency) CIA f

CID n abbr (= Criminal Investigation Department) ≈ P.J. f

cider ['saɪdər] n cidre m

cigar [sɪˈɡɑːr] n cigare m

cigarette [sɪɡəˈret] n cigarette f; **cigarette lighter** n briquet m

cinema ['sɪnəmə] n cinéma m

cinnamon ['sɪnəmən] n cannelle f

circle ['səːkl] n cercle m; (in cinema) balcon m ▷ vi faire or décrire des cercles ▷ vt (surround) entourer, encercler; (move round) faire le tour de, tourner autour de

circuit ['səːkɪt] n circuit m; (lap) tour m

circular ['səːkjʊlər] adj circulaire ▷ n circulaire f; (as advertisement) prospectus m

circulate ['səːkjʊleɪt] vi circuler ▷ vt faire circuler; **circulation** [səːkjʊˈleɪʃən] n circulation f; (of newspaper) tirage m

circumstances ['səːkəmstənsɪz] npl circonstances fpl; (financial condition) moyens mpl, situation financière

circus ['səːkəs] n cirque m

cite [saɪt] vt citer

citizen ['sɪtɪzn] n (Pol) citoyen(ne); (resident): **the ~s of this town** les habitants de cette ville; **citizenship** n citoyenneté f; (BRIT: Scol) ≈ éducation f civique

citrus fruits ['sɪtrəs-] npl agrumes mpl

city ['sɪtɪ] n (grande) ville f; **the C~** la Cité de Londres (centre des affaires); **city centre** n centre ville m; **city technology college** n (BRIT) établissement m d'enseignement technologique (situé dans un quartier défavorisé)

civic ['sɪvɪk] adj civique; (authorities) municipal(e)

civil ['sɪvɪl] adj civil(e); (polite) poli(e), civil(e); **civilian** [sɪˈvɪlɪən] adj, n civil(e)

civilization [sɪvɪlaɪˈzeɪʃən] n civilisation f

civilized ['sɪvɪlaɪzd] adj civilisé(e); (fig) où règnent les bonnes manières

civil: civil law n code civil; (study) droit civil; **civil rights** npl droits mpl civiques; **civil servant** n fonctionnaire m/f; **Civil Service** n fonction publique, administration f; **civil war** n guerre civile

CJD n abbr (= Creutzfeldt-Jakob disease) MCJ f

claim [kleɪm] vt (rights etc) revendiquer; (compensation) réclamer; (assert) déclarer, prétendre ▷ vi (for insurance) faire une déclaration de sinistre ▷ n revendication f; prétention f; (right) droit m; (insurance) **~** demande f d'indemnisation, déclaration f de sinistre; **claim form** n (gen) formulaire m de demande

clam [klæm] n palourde f

clamp [klæmp] n crampon m; (on workbench) valet m; (on car) sabot m de Denver ▷ vt attacher; (car) mettre un sabot à; **clamp down on** vt fus sévir contre, prendre des mesures draconiennes à l'égard de

clan [klæn] n clan m

clap [klæp] vi applaudir

claret ['klærət] n (vin m de) bordeaux m (rouge)

clarify ['klærɪfaɪ] vt clarifier

clarinet [klærɪˈnet] n clarinette f

clarity ['klærɪtɪ] n clarté f

clash [klæʃ] n (sound) choc m, fracas m; (with police) affrontement m; (fig) conflit m ▷ vi se heurter; être or entrer en conflit; (colours) jurer; (dates, events) tomber en même temps

clasp [klɑːsp] n (of necklace, bag) fermoir m ▷ vt serrer, étreindre

class [klɑːs] n (gen) classe f; (group, category) catégorie f ▷ vt classer, classifier

classic ['klæsɪk] adj classique ▷ n (author, work) classique m; **classical** adj classique

classification [klæsɪfɪˈkeɪʃən] n classification f

classify ['klæsɪfaɪ] vt classifier, classer

classmate ['klɑːsmeɪt] n camarade m/f de classe

classroom ['klɑːsrʊm] n (salle f de) classe f; **classroom assistant** n assistant(-e) d'éducation

classy ['klɑːsɪ] (inf) adj classe (inf)

clatter ['klætər] n cliquetis m ▷ vi cliqueter

clause [klɔːz] n clause f; (Ling) proposition f

claustrophobic [klɔːstrəˈfəʊbɪk] adj (person) claustrophobe; (place) où l'on se sent claustrophobe

claw [klɔː] n griffe f; (of bird of prey) serre f; (of lobster) pince f

clay [kleɪ] n argile f

clean [kliːn] adj propre; (clear, smooth) net(te); (record, reputation) sans tache; (joke, story) correct(e) ▷ vt nettoyer; **clean up** vt nettoyer; (fig) remettre de l'ordre dans; **cleaner** n (person) nettoyeur(-euse), femme f de ménage; (product) détachant m; **cleaner's** n (also: **dry cleaner's**) teinturier m; **cleaning** n nettoyage m

cleanser [klɛnzəʳ] n (for face) démaquillant m

clear [klɪəʳ] adj clair(e); (glass, plastic) transparent(e); (road, way) libre, dégagé(e); (profit, majority) net(te); (conscience) tranquille; (skin) frais (fraîche); (sky) dégagé(e) ▷ vt (road) dégager, déblayer; (table) débarrasser; (room etc: of people) faire évacuer; (cheque) compenser; (Law: suspect) innocenter; (obstacle) franchir or sauter sans heurter ▷ vi (weather) s'éclaircir; (fog) se dissiper ▷ adv: **~ of** à distance de, à l'écart de; **to ~ the table** débarrasser la table, desservir; **clear away** vt (things, clothes etc) enlever, retirer; **to ~ away the dishes** débarrasser la table; **clear up** vt ranger, mettre en ordre; (mystery) éclaircir, résoudre; **clearance** n (removal) déblayage m; (permission) autorisation f; **clear-cut** adj précis(e), nettement défini(e); **clearing** n (in forest) clairière f; **clearly** adv clairement; (obviously) de toute évidence; **clearway** n (BRIT) route f à stationnement interdit

clench [klɛntʃ] vt serrer

clergy [ˈkləːdʒɪ] n clergé m

clerk [klɑːk] (us) [kləːrk] n (BRIT) employé(e) de bureau; (us: salesman/woman) vendeur(-euse)

clever [ˈklɛvəʳ] adj (intelligent) intelligent(e); (skilful) habile, adroit(e); (device, arrangement) ingénieux(-euse), astucieux(-euse)

cliché [ˈkliːʃeɪ] n cliché m

click [klɪk] vi (Comput) cliquer ▷ vt: **to ~ one's tongue** faire claquer sa langue; **to ~ one's heels** claquer des talons; **to ~ on an icon** cliquer sur une icône

client [ˈklaɪənt] n client(e)

cliff [klɪf] n falaise f

climate [ˈklaɪmɪt] n climat m; **climate change** n changement m climatique

climax [ˈklaɪmæks] n apogée m, point culminant; (sexual) orgasme m

climb [klaɪm] vi grimper, monter; (plane) prendre de l'altitude ▷ vt (stairs) monter; (mountain) escalader; (tree) grimper à ▷ n montée f, escalade f; **to ~ over a wall** passer par dessus un mur; **climb down** vi (re)descendre; (BRIT fig) rabattre de ses prétentions; **climber** n (also: **rock climber**) grimpeur(-euse), varappeur(-euse); (plant) plante grimpante; **climbing** n (also: **rock climbing**) escalade f, varappe f

clinch [klɪntʃ] vt (deal) conclure, sceller

cling (pt, pp **clung**) [klɪŋ, klʌŋ] vi: **to ~ (to)** se cramponner (à), s'accrocher (à); (clothes) coller (à)

Clingfilm® [ˈklɪŋfɪlm] n film m alimentaire

clinic [ˈklɪnɪk] n clinique f; centre médical

clip [klɪp] n (for hair) barrette f; (also: **paper ~**) trombone m; (TV, Cinema) clip m ▷ vt (also: **~ together**: papers) attacher; (hair, nails) couper; (hedge) tailler; **clipping** n (from newspaper) coupure f de journal

cloak [kləuk] n grande cape f ▷ vt (fig) masquer, cacher; **cloakroom** n (for coats etc) vestiaire m; (BRIT: W.C.) toilettes fpl

clock [klɔk] n (large) horloge f; (small) pendule f; **clock in or on** (BRIT) vi (with card) pointer (en arrivant); (start work) commencer à travailler; **clock off or out** (BRIT) vi (with card) pointer (en partant); (leave work) quitter le travail; **clockwise** adv dans le sens des aiguilles d'une

montre; **clockwork** n rouages mpl, mécanisme m; (of clock) mouvement m (d'horlogerie) ▷ adj (toy, train) mécanique

clog [klɔg] n sabot m ▷ vt boucher, encrasser ▷ vi (also: **~ up**) se boucher, s'encrasser

clone [kləun] n clone m ▷ vt cloner

close¹ [kləus] adj (near): **~ (to)** près (de), proche (de); (contact, link, watch) étroit(e); (examination) attentif(-ive), minutieux(-euse); (contest) très serré(e); (weather) lourd(e), étouffant(e) ▷ adv près, à proximité; **~ to** prep près de; **~ by, ~ at hand** adj, adv tout(e) près; **a ~ friend** un ami intime; **to have a ~ shave** (fig) l'échapper belle

close² [kləuz] vt fermer ▷ vi (shop etc) fermer; (lid, door etc) se fermer; (end) se terminer, se conclure ▷ n (end) conclusion f; **what time do you ~?** à quelle heure fermez-vous?; **close down** vi fermer (définitivement); **closed** adj (shop etc) fermé(e)

closely [ˈkləuslɪ] adv (examine, watch) de près

closet [ˈklɔzɪt] n (cupboard) placard m, réduit m

close-up [ˈkləusʌp] n gros plan

closing time n heure f de fermeture

closure [ˈkləuʒəʳ] n fermeture f

clot [klɔt] n (of blood, milk) caillot m; (inf: person) ballot m ▷ vi (: external bleeding) se coaguler

cloth [klɔθ] n (material) tissu m, étoffe f; (BRIT: also: **tea ~**) torchon m; lavette f; (also: **table~**) nappe f

clothes [kləuðz] npl vêtements mpl, habits mpl; **clothes line** n corde f (à linge); **clothes peg** (us **clothes pin**) n pince f à linge

clothing [ˈkləuðɪŋ] n = **clothes**

cloud [klaud] n nuage m; **cloud over** vi se couvrir; (fig) s'assombrir; **cloudy** adj nuageux(-euse), couvert(e); (liquid) trouble

clove [kləuv] n clou m de girofle; **a ~ of garlic** une gousse d'ail

clown [klaun] n clown m ▷ vi (also: **~ about, ~ around**) faire le clown

club [klʌb] n (society) club m; (weapon) massue f, matraque f; (also: **golf ~**) club ▷ vt matraquer ▷ vi: **to ~ together** s'associer; **clubs** npl (Cards) trèfle m; **club class** n (Aviat) classe f club

clue [kluː] n indice m; (in crosswords) définition f; **I haven't a ~** je n'en ai pas la moindre idée

clump [klʌmp] n: **~ of trees** bouquet m d'arbres

clumsy [ˈklʌmzɪ] adj (person) gauche, maladroit(e); (object) malcommode, peu maniable

clung [klʌŋ] pt, pp of **cling**

cluster [ˈklʌstəʳ] n (petit) groupe; (of flowers) grappe f ▷ vi se rassembler

clutch [klʌtʃ] n (Aut) embrayage m; (grasp): **~es** étreinte f, prise f ▷ vt (grasp) agripper; (hold tightly) serrer fort; (hold on to) se cramponner à

cm abbr (= centimetre) cm

Co. abbr = **company, county**

c/o abbr (= care of) c/o, aux bons soins de

coach [kəutʃ] n (bus) autocar m; (horse-drawn) diligence f; (of train) voiture f, wagon m; (Sport: trainer) entraîneur(-euse); (school: tutor) répétiteur(-trice) ▷ vt (Sport) entraîner; (student) donner des leçons particulières à; **coach station** (BRIT) n gare routière; **coach trip** n excursion f en car

coal [kəul] n charbon m

coalition [kəuəˈlɪʃən] n coalition f

coarse [kɔːs] adj grossier(-ère), rude; (vulgar) vulgaire

coast [kəust] n côte f ▷ vi (car, cycle) descendre en roue libre; **coastal** adj côtier(-ère); **coastguard** n garde-côte m; **coastline** n côte f, littoral m

coat [kəut] n manteau m; (of animal) pelage m, poil m; (of paint) couche f ▷ vt couvrir, enduire; **coat hanger** n cintre m; **coating** n couche f, enduit m

coax [kəuks] vt persuader par des cajoleries

cob [kɔb] n see **corn**

cobbled [kɔbld] adj pavé(e)

cobweb [kɔbwɛb] n toile f d'araignée

cocaine [kə'keɪn] n cocaïne f

cock [kɔk] n (rooster) coq m; (male bird) mâle m ▷ vt (gun) armer; **cockerel** n jeune coq m

cockney [kɔknɪ] n cockney m/f (habitant des quartiers populaires de l'East End de Londres), ≈ faubourien(ne)

cockpit [kɔkpɪt] n (in aircraft) poste m de pilotage, cockpit m

cockroach [kɔkrəutʃ] n cafard m, cancrelat m

cocktail [kɔkteɪl] n cocktail m

cocoa [kəukəu] n cacao m

coconut [kəukənʌt] n noix f de coco

C.O.D. abbr = **cash on delivery**

cod [kɔd] n morue fraîche, cabillaud m

code [kəud] n code m; (Tel: area code) indicatif m

coeducational [kəuɛdju'keɪʃənl] adj mixte

coffee [kɔfɪ] n café m; **coffee bar** n (BRIT) café m; **coffee bean** n grain m de café; **coffee break** n pause-café f; **coffee maker** n cafetière f; **coffeepot** n cafetière f; **coffee shop** n café m; **coffee table** n (petite) table basse

coffin [kɔfɪn] n cercueil m

cog [kɔg] n (wheel) roue dentée; (tooth) dent f (d'engrenage)

cognac [kɔnjæk] n cognac m

coherent [kəu'hɪərənt] adj cohérent(e)

coil [kɔɪl] n rouleau m, bobine f; (contraceptive) stérilet m ▷ vt enrouler

coin [kɔɪn] n pièce f (de monnaie) ▷ vt (word) inventer

coincide [kəuɪn'saɪd] vi coïncider; **coincidence** [kəu'ɪnsɪdəns] n coïncidence f

Coke® [kəuk] n coca m

coke [kəuk] n (coal) coke m

colander [kɔləndə'] n passoire f (à légumes)

cold [kəuld] adj froid(e) ▷ n froid m; (Med) rhume m; **it's** ~ il fait froid; **to be** ~ (person) avoir froid; **to catch a** ~ s'enrhumer, attraper un rhume; **in** ~ **blood** de sang-froid; **cold cuts** (US) npl viandes froides; **cold sore** n bouton m de fièvre

coleslaw [kəulslɔ:] n sorte de salade de chou cru

colic [kɔlɪk] n colique(s) f(pl)

collaborate [kə'læbəreɪt] vi collaborer

collapse [kə'læps] vi s'effondrer, s'écrouler; (Med) avoir un malaise ▷ n effondrement m, écroulement m; (of government) chute f

collar [kɔlə'] n (of coat, shirt) col m; (for dog) collier m; **collarbone** n clavicule f

colleague [kɔli:g] n collègue m/f

collect [kə'lɛkt] vt rassembler; (pick up) ramasser; (as a hobby) collectionner; (BRIT: call for) (passer) prendre; (mail) faire la levée de, ramasser; (money owed) encaisser; (donations, subscriptions) recueillir ▷ vi (people) se rassembler; (dust, dirt) s'amasser; **to call** ~ (US Tel) téléphoner en PCV; **collection** [kə'lɛkʃən] n collection f; (of mail) levée f; (for money) collecte f, quête f;

collective [kə'lɛktɪv] adj collectif(-ive); **collector** n collectionneur m

college [kɔlɪdʒ] n collège m; (of technology, agriculture etc) institut m

collide [kə'laɪd] vi: **to** ~ (**with**) entrer en collision (avec)

collision [kə'lɪʒən] n collision f, heurt m

cologne [kə'ləun] n (also: **eau de** ~) eau f de cologne

colon [kəulən] n (sign) deux-points mpl; (Med) côlon m

colonel [kə:nl] n colonel m

colonial [kə'ləunɪəl] adj colonial(e)

colony [kɔlənɪ] n colonie f

colour etc (US **color** etc) [kʌlə'] n couleur f ▷ vt colorer; (dye) teindre; (paint) peindre; (with crayons) colorier; (news) fausser, exagérer ▷ vi (blush) rougir; **I'd like a different** ~ je le voudrais dans un autre coloris; **colour in** vt colorier; **colour-blind** adj daltonien(ne); **coloured** adj coloré(e); (photo) en couleur; **colour film** n (for camera) pellicule f (en) couleur; **colourful** adj coloré(e), vif (vive); (personality) pittoresque, haut(e) en couleurs; **colouring** n colorant m; (complexion) teint m; **colour television** n télévision f (en) couleur

column [kɔləm] n colonne f; (fashion column, sports column etc) rubrique f

coma [kəumə] n coma m

comb [kəum] n peigne m ▷ vt (hair) peigner; (area) ratisser, passer au peigne fin

combat [kɔmbæt] n combat m ▷ vt combattre, lutter contre

combination [kɔmbɪ'neɪʃən] n (gen) combinaison f

combine vb [kəm'baɪn] ▷ vt combiner ▷ vi s'associer; (Chem) se combiner ▷ n [kɔmbaɪn] (Econ) trust m; **to** ~ **sth with sth** (one quality with another) joindre ou allier qch à qch

come (pt **came**, pp ~) [kʌm, keɪm] vi **1** (movement towards) venir; **to** ~ **running** arriver en courant; **he's** ~ **here to work** il est venu ici pour travailler; ~ **with me** suivez-moi

2 (arrive) arriver; **to** ~ **home** rentrer (chez soi ou à la maison); **we've just** ~ **from Paris** nous arrivons de Paris
3 (reach): **to** ~ **to** (decision etc) parvenir à, arriver à; **the bill came to £40** la note s'est élevée à 40 livres
4 (occur): **an idea came to me** il m'est venu une idée
5 (be, become): **to** ~ **loose/undone** se défaire/desserrer; **I've** ~ **to like him** j'ai fini par bien l'aimer; **come across** vt fus rencontrer par hasard, tomber sur; **come along** vi (BRIT: pupil, work) faire des progrès, avancer; **come back** vi revenir; **come down** vi descendre; (prices) baisser; (buildings) s'écrouler; (: be demolished) être démoli(e); **come from** vt fus (source) venir de; (place) venir de, être originaire de; **come in** vi entrer; (train) arriver; (fashion) entrer en vogue; (on deal etc) participer; **come off** vi (button) se détacher; (attempt) réussir; **come on** vi (lights, electricity) s'allumer; (central heating) se mettre en marche; (pupil, work, project) faire des progrès, avancer; ~ **on!** viens! allons! allez!; **come out** vi sortir; (sun) se montrer; (book) paraître; (stain) s'enlever; (strike) cesser le travail, se mettre en grève; **come round** vi (after faint, operation) revenir à soi, reprendre connaissance; **come to** vi revenir à soi; **come up** vi monter; (sun) se lever; (problem) se poser; (event) survenir; (in conversation) être soulevé(e); **come up with** vt fus (money) fournir; **he came up with an idea** il a eu une idée, il a proposé quelque chose

comeback [kʌmbæk] n (Theat etc) rentrée f

comedian [kəˈmiːdɪən] n (comic) comique m; (Theat) comédien m

comedy [ˈkɒmɪdɪ] n comédie f; (humour) comique m

comet [ˈkɒmɪt] n comète f

comfort [ˈkʌmfət] n confort m, bien-être m; (solace) consolation f, réconfort m ▷ vt consoler, réconforter; **comfortable** adj confortable; (person) à l'aise; (financially) aisé(e); (patient) dont l'état est stationnaire; **comfort station** n (US) toilettes fpl

comic [ˈkɒmɪk] adj (also: **-al**) comique ▷ n (person) comique m; (BRIT: magazine: for children) magazine m de bandes dessinées or de BD; (: for adults) illustré m; **comic book** (US) n (for children) magazine m de bandes dessinées or de BD; (for adults) illustré m; **comic strip** n bande dessinée

comma [ˈkɒmə] n virgule f

command [kəˈmɑːnd] n ordre m, commandement m; (Mil: authority) commandement m; (mastery) maîtrise f ▷ vt (troops) commander; **to ~ sb to do** donner l'ordre or commander à qn de faire; **commander** n (Mil) commandant m

commemorate [kəˈmɛməreɪt] vt commémorer

commence [kəˈmɛns] vt, vi commencer; **commencement** (US) n (University) remise f des diplômes

commend [kəˈmɛnd] vt louer; (recommend) recommander

comment [ˈkɒmɛnt] n commentaire m ▷ vi: **to ~ on** faire des remarques sur; **"no ~"** "je n'ai rien à déclarer"; **commentary** [ˈkɒməntərɪ] n commentaire m; (Sport) reportage m (en direct); **commentator** [ˈkɒmənteɪtəʳ] n commentateur m; (Sport) reporter m

commerce [ˈkɒmə:s] n commerce m

commercial [kəˈmə:ʃəl] adj commercial(e) ▷ n (Radio, TV) annonce f publicitaire, spot m (publicitaire); **commercial break** n (Radio, TV) spot m (publicitaire)

commission [kəˈmɪʃən] n (committee, fee) commission f ▷ vt (work of art) commander, charger un artiste de l'exécution de; **out of ~** (machine) hors service; **commissioner** n (Police) préfet m (de police)

commit [kəˈmɪt] vt (act) commettre; (resources) consacrer; (to sb's care) confier (à); **to ~ o.s. (to do)** s'engager (à faire); **to ~ suicide** se suicider; **commitment** n engagement m; (obligation) responsabilité(s) (fpl)

committee [kəˈmɪtɪ] n comité m; commission f

commodity [kəˈmɒdɪtɪ] n produit m, marchandise f, article m

common [ˈkɒmən] adj (gen) commun(e); (usual) courant(e) ▷ n terrain communal; **commonly** adv communément, généralement; couramment; **commonplace** adj banal(e), ordinaire; **Commons** npl (BRIT Pol): **the (House of) Commons** la chambre des Communes; **common sense** n bon sens; **Commonwealth** n: **the Commonwealth** le Commonwealth

communal [ˈkɒmjuːnl] adj (life) communautaire; (for common use) commun(e)

commune n [ˈkɒmjuːn] (group) communauté f ▷ vi [kəˈmjuːn]: **to ~ with** (nature) communier avec

communicate [kəˈmjuːnɪkeɪt] vt communiquer, transmettre ▷ vi: **to ~ (with)** communiquer (avec)

communication [kəmjuːnɪˈkeɪʃən] n communication f

communion [kəˈmjuːnɪən] n (also: **Holy C~**) communion f

communism [ˈkɒmjunɪzəm] n communisme m; **communist** adj, n communiste m/f

community [kəˈmjuːnɪtɪ] n communauté f; **community centre** (US **community center**) n foyer socio-éducatif, centre m de loisirs; **community service** n ≈ travail m d'intérêt général, TIG m

commute [kəˈmjuːt] vi faire le trajet journalier (de son domicile à un lieu de travail assez éloigné) ▷ vt (Law) commuer; **commuter** n banlieusard(e) (qui fait un trajet journalier pour se rendre à son travail)

compact adj [kəmˈpækt] compact(e) ▷ n [ˈkɒmpækt] (also: **powder ~**) poudrier m; **compact disc** n disque compact; **compact disc player** n lecteur m de disques compacts

companion [kəmˈpænjən] n compagnon (compagne)

company [ˈkʌmpənɪ] n compagnie f; **to keep sb ~** tenir compagnie à qn; **company car** n voiture f de fonction; **company director** n administrateur(-trice)

comparable [ˈkɒmpərəbl] adj comparable

comparative [kəmˈpærətɪv] adj (study) comparatif(-ive); (relative) relatif(-ive); **comparatively** adv (relatively) relativement

compare [kəmˈpeəʳ] vt: **to ~ sth/sb with or to** comparer qch/qn avec or à ▷ vi: **to ~ (with)** se comparer (à); être comparable (à); **comparison** [kəmˈpærɪsn] n comparaison f

compartment [kəmˈpɑːtmənt] n (also Rail) compartiment m; **a non-smoking ~** un compartiment non-fumeurs

compass [ˈkʌmpəs] n boussole f; **compasses** npl (Math) compas m

compassion [kəmˈpæʃən] n compassion f, humanité f

compatible [kəmˈpætɪbl] adj compatible

compel [kəmˈpɛl] vt contraindre, obliger; **compelling** adj (fig: argument) irrésistible

compensate [ˈkɒmpənseɪt] vt indemniser, dédommager ▷ vi: **to ~ for** compenser; **compensation** [kɒmpənˈseɪʃən] n compensation f; (money) dédommagement m, indemnité f

compete [kəmˈpiːt] vi (take part) concourir; (vie): **to ~ (with)** rivaliser (avec), faire concurrence (à)

competent [ˈkɒmpɪtənt] adj compétent(e), capable

competition [kɒmpɪˈtɪʃən] n (contest) compétition f, concours m; (Econ) concurrence f

competitive [kəmˈpɛtɪtɪv] adj (Econ) concurrentiel(le); (sports) de compétition; (person) qui a l'esprit de compétition

competitor [kəmˈpɛtɪtəʳ] n concurrent(e)

complacent [kəmˈpleɪsnt] adj (trop) content(e) de soi

complain [kəmˈpleɪn] vi: **to ~ (about)** se plaindre (de); (in shop etc) réclamer (au sujet de); **complaint** n plainte f; (in shop etc) réclamation f; (Med) affection f

complement [ˈkɒmplɪmənt] n complément m; (esp of ship's crew etc) effectif complet ▷ vt (enhance) compléter; **complementary** [kɒmplɪˈmɛntərɪ] adj complémentaire

complete [kəmˈpliːt] adj complet(-ète); (finished) achevé(e) ▷ vt achever, parachever; (set, group) compléter; (a form) remplir; **completely** adv complètement; **completion** [kəmˈpliːʃən] n achèvement m; (of contract) exécution f

complex [ˈkɒmplɛks] adj complexe ▷ n (Psych, buildings

etc) complexe *m*

complexion [kəm'plekʃən] *n (of face)* teint *m*

compliance [kəm'plaɪəns] *n (submission)* docilité *f*; *(agreement):* ~ **with** le fait de se conformer à; **in ~ with** en conformité avec, conformément à

complicate ['kɒmplɪkeɪt] *vt* compliquer; **complicated** *adj* compliqué(e); **complication** [kɒmplɪ'keɪʃən] *n* complication *f*

compliment *n* ['kɒmplɪmənt] compliment *m* ▷ *vt* ['kɒmplɪment] complimenter; **complimentary** [kɒmplɪ'mentərɪ] *adj* flatteur(-euse); *(free)* à titre gracieux

comply [kəm'plaɪ] *vi:* **to ~ with** se soumettre à, se conformer à

component [kəm'pəunənt] *adj* composant(e), constituant(e) ▷ *n* composant *m*, élément *m*

compose [kəm'pəuz] *vt* composer; *(form):* **to be ~d of** se composer de; **to ~ o.s.** se calmer, se maîtriser; **composer** *n (Mus)* compositeur *m*; **composition** [kɒmpə'zɪʃən] *n* composition *f*

composure [kəm'pəuʒəʳ] *n* calme *m*, maîtrise *f* de soi

compound ['kɒmpaund] *n (Chem, Ling)* composé *m*; *(enclosure)* enclos *m*, enceinte *f* ▷ *adj* composé(e); *(fracture)* compliqué(e)

comprehension [kɒmprɪ'henʃən] *n* compréhension *f*

comprehensive [kɒmprɪ'hensɪv] *adj (very)* complet(-ète); ~ **policy** *(Insurance)* assurance *f* tous risques; **comprehensive (school)** *n (BRIT)* école secondaire non sélective avec libre circulation d'une section à l'autre, ≈ CES *m*

compress *vt* [kəm'pres] comprimer; *(text, information)* condenser ▷ *n* ['kɒmpres] *(Med)* compresse *f*

comprise [kəm'praɪz] *vt (also:* **be ~d of**) comprendre; *(constitute)* constituer, représenter

compromise ['kɒmprəmaɪz] *n* compromis *m* ▷ *vt* compromettre ▷ *vi* transiger, accepter un compromis

compulsive [kəm'pʌlsɪv] *adj (Psych)* compulsif(-ive); *(book, film etc)* captivant(e)

compulsory [kəm'pʌlsərɪ] *adj* obligatoire

computer [kəm'pju:təʳ] *n* ordinateur *m*; **computer game** *n* jeu *m* vidéo; **computer-generated** *adj* de synthèse; **computerize** *vt (data)* traiter par ordinateur; *(system, office)* informatiser; **computer programmer** *n* programmeur(-euse); **computer programming** *n* programmation *f*; **computer science** *n* informatique *f*; **computer studies** *npl* informatique *f*; **computing** [kəm'pju:tɪŋ] *n* informatique *f*

con [kɒn] *vt* duper; *(cheat)* escroquer ▷ *n* escroquerie *f*

conceal [kən'si:l] *vt* cacher, dissimuler

concede [kən'si:d] *vt* concéder ▷ *vi* céder

conceited [kən'si:tɪd] *adj* vaniteux(-euse), suffisant(e)

conceive [kən'si:v] *vt, vi* concevoir

concentrate ['kɒnsəntreɪt] *vi* se concentrer ▷ *vt* concentrer

concentration [kɒnsən'treɪʃən] *n* concentration *f*

concept ['kɒnsept] *n* concept *m*

concern [kən'sə:n] *n* affaire *f*; *(Comm)* entreprise *f*, firme *f*; *(anxiety)* inquiétude *f*, souci *m* ▷ *vt (worry)* inquiéter; *(involve)* concerner; *(relate to)* se rapporter à; **to be ~ed (about)** s'inquiéter (de), être inquiet(-ète) (au sujet de); **concerning** *prep* en ce qui concerne, à propos de

concert ['kɒnsət] *n* concert *m*; **concert hall** *n* salle *f* de concert

concerto [kən'tʃə:təu] *n* concerto *m*

concession [kən'seʃən] *n (compromise)* concession *f*; *(reduced price)* réduction *f*; **tax ~** dégrèvement fiscal; **"~s"** tarif réduit

concise [kən'saɪs] *adj* concis(e)

conclude [kən'klu:d] *vt* conclure; **conclusion** [kən'klu:ʒən] *n* conclusion *f*

concrete ['kɒnkri:t] *n* béton *m* ▷ *adj* concret(-ète); *(Constr)* en béton

concussion [kən'kʌʃən] *n (Med)* commotion (cérébrale)

condemn [kən'dem] *vt* condamner

condensation [kɒnden'seɪʃən] *n* condensation *f*

condense [kən'dens] *vi* se condenser ▷ *vt* condenser

condition [kən'dɪʃən] *n* condition *f*; *(disease)* maladie *f* ▷ *vt* déterminer, conditionner; **on ~ that** à condition que + *sub*, à condition de; **conditional** [kən'dɪʃənl] *adj* conditionnel(le); **conditioner** *n (for hair)* baume démêlant; *(for fabrics)* assouplissant *m*

condo ['kɒndəu] *n (us inf)* = **condominium**

condom ['kɒndəm] *n* préservatif *m*

condominium [kɒndə'mɪnɪəm] *n (us: building)* immeuble *m* (en copropriété); (: *rooms)* appartement *m* (dans un immeuble en copropriété)

condone [kən'dəun] *vt* fermer les yeux sur, approuver (tacitement)

conduct *n* ['kɒndʌkt] conduite *f* ▷ *vt* [kən'dʌkt] conduire; *(manage)* mener, diriger; *(Mus)* diriger; **to ~ o.s.** se conduire, se comporter; **conducted tour** *n (BRIT)* voyage organisé; *(of building)* visite guidée; **conductor** *n (of orchestra)* chef *m* d'orchestre; *(on bus)* receveur *m*; *(us: on train)* chef *m* de train; *(Elec)* conducteur *m*

cone [kəun] *n* cône *m*; *(for ice-cream)* cornet *m*; *(Bot)* pomme *f* de pin, cône

confectionery [kən'fekʃənrɪ] *n (sweets)* confiserie *f*

confer [kən'fəːʳ] *vt:* **to ~ sth on** conférer qch à ▷ *vi* conférer, s'entretenir

conference ['kɒnfərns] *n* conférence *f*

confess [kən'fes] *vt* confesser, avouer ▷ *vi (admit sth)* avouer; *(Rel)* se confesser; **confession** [kən'feʃən] *n* confession *f*

confide [kən'faɪd] *vi:* **to ~ in** s'ouvrir à, se confier à

confidence ['kɒnfɪdns] *n* confiance *f*; *(also:* **self-~**) assurance *f*, confiance en soi; *(secret)* confidence *f*; **in ~** *(speak, write)* en confidence, confidentiellement; **confident** *adj (self-assured)* sûr(e) de soi; *(sure)* sûr; **confidential** [kɒnfɪ'denʃəl] *adj* confidentiel(le)

confine [kən'faɪn] *vt* limiter, borner; *(shut up)* confiner, enfermer; **confined** *adj (space)* restreint(e), réduit(e)

confirm [kən'fəːm] *vt (report, Rel)* confirmer; *(appointment)* ratifier; **confirmation** [kɒnfə'meɪʃən] *n* confirmation *f*, ratification *f*

confiscate ['kɒnfɪskeɪt] *vt* confisquer

conflict *n* ['kɒnflɪkt] conflit *m*, lutte *f* ▷ *vi* [kən'flɪkt] *(opinions)* s'opposer, se heurter

conform [kən'fɔːm] *vi:* **to ~ (to)** se conformer (à)

confront [kən'frʌnt] *vt (two people)* confronter; *(enemy, danger)* affronter, faire face à; *(problem)* faire face à; **confrontation** [kɒnfrən'teɪʃən] *n* confrontation *f*

confuse [kən'fju:z] *vt (person)* troubler; *(situation)* embrouiller; *(one thing with another)* confondre; **confused** *adj (person)* dérouté(e), désorienté(e); *(situation)* embrouillé(e); **confusing** *adj* peu clair(e), déroutant(e); **confusion** [kən'fju:ʒən] *n* confusion *f*

congestion [kən'dʒestʃən] *n (Med)* congestion *f*; *(fig: traffic)* encombrement *m*

congratulate [kən'grætjuleɪt] vt: **to ~ sb (on)** féliciter qn (de); **congratulations** [kəngrætju'leɪʃənz] npl: **congratulations (on)** félicitations fpl (pour) ▷ excl: **congratulations!** (toutes mes) félicitations!

congregation [kɔŋɡrɪ'ɡeɪʃən] n assemblée f (des fidèles)

congress ['kɔŋɡrɛs] n congrès m; (Pol): **C~** Congrès m; **congressman** n membre m du Congrès; **congresswoman** n membre m du Congrès

conifer ['kɒnɪfə'] n conifère m

conjugate ['kɔndʒuɡeɪt] vt conjuguer

conjugation [kɔndʒə'ɡeɪʃən] n conjugaison f

conjunction [kən'dʒʌŋkʃən] n conjonction f; **in ~ with** (conjointement) avec

conjure ['kʌndʒə'] vi faire un tour de passe-passe

connect [kə'nɛkt] vt joindre, relier; (Elec) connecter; (Tel: caller) mettre en connexion; (: subscriber) brancher; (fig) établir un rapport entre, faire un rapprochement entre ▷ vi (train): **to ~ with** assurer la correspondance avec; **to be ~ed with** avoir un rapport avec; (have dealings with) avoir des rapports avec, être en relation avec; **connecting flight** n (vol m de) correspondance f; **connection** [kə'nɛkʃən] n relation f, lien m; (Elec) connexion f; (Tel) communication f; (train etc) correspondance f

conquer ['kɔŋkə'] vt conquérir; (feelings) vaincre, surmonter

conquest ['kɔŋkwɛst] n conquête f

cons [kɒnz] npl see **convenience**; **pro**

conscience ['kɔnʃəns] n conscience f

conscientious [kɔnʃɪ'ɛnʃəs] adj consciencieux(-euse)

conscious ['kɔnʃəs] adj conscient(e); (deliberate: insult, error) délibéré(e); **consciousness** n conscience f; (Med) connaissance f

consecutive [kən'sɛkjutɪv] adj consécutif(-ive); **on three ~ occasions** trois fois de suite

consensus [kən'sɛnsəs] n consensus m

consent [kən'sɛnt] n consentement m ▷ vi: **to ~ (to)** consentir (à)

consequence ['kɔnsɪkwəns] n suites fpl, conséquence f; (significance) importance f

consequently ['kɔnsɪkwəntlɪ] adv par conséquent, donc

conservation [kɔnsə'veɪʃən] n préservation f, protection f; (also: **nature ~**) défense f de l'environnement

conservative [kən'sə:vətɪv] adj conservateur(-trice); (cautious) prudent(e); **Conservative** adj, n (Brit Pol) conservateur(-trice)

conservatory [kən'sə:vətrɪ] n (room) jardin m d'hiver; (Mus) conservatoire m

consider [kən'sɪdə'] vt (study) considérer, réfléchir à; (take into account) penser à, prendre en considération; (regard, judge) considérer, estimer; **to ~ doing sth** envisager de faire qch; **considerable** adj considérable; **considerably** adv nettement; **considerate** adj prévenant(e), plein(e) d'égards; **consideration** [kənsɪdə'reɪʃən] n considération f; (reward) rétribution f, rémunération f; **considering** prep: **considering (that)** étant donné (que)

consignment [kən'saɪnmənt] n arrivage m, envoi m

consist [kən'sɪst] vi: **to ~ of** consister en, se composer de

consistency [kən'sɪstənsɪ] n (thickness) consistance f; (fig) cohérence f

consistent [kən'sɪstənt] adj logique, cohérent(e)

consolation [kɔnsə'leɪʃən] n consolation f

console¹ [kən'səul] vt consoler

console² ['kɔnsəul] n console f

consonant ['kɔnsənənt] n consonne f

conspicuous [kən'spɪkjuəs] adj voyant(e), qui attire l'attention

conspiracy [kən'spɪrəsɪ] n conspiration f, complot m

constable ['kʌnstəbl] n (Brit) ≈ agent m de police, gendarme m; **chief ~** ≈ préfet m de police

constant ['kɔnstənt] adj constant(e); incessant(e); **constantly** adv constamment, sans cesse

constipated ['kɔnstɪpeɪtɪd] adj constipé(e); **constipation** [kɔnstɪ'peɪʃən] n constipation f

constituency [kən'stɪtjuənsɪ] n (Pol: area) circonscription électorale; (: electors) électorat m

constitute ['kɔnstɪtjuːt] vt constituer

constitution [kɔnstɪ'tjuːʃən] n constitution f

constraint [kən'streɪnt] n contrainte f

construct [kən'strʌkt] vt construire; **construction** [kən'strʌkʃən] n construction f; **constructive** adj constructif(-ive)

consul ['kɔnsl] n consul m; **consulate** ['kɔnsjulɪt] n consulat m

consult [kən'sʌlt] vt consulter; **consultant** n (Med) médecin consultant; (other specialist) consultant m, (expert-)conseil m; **consultation** [kɔnsəl'teɪʃən] n consultation f; **consulting room** n (Brit) cabinet m de consultation

consume [kən'sjuːm] vt consommer; (subj: flames, hatred, desire) consumer; **consumer** n consommateur(-trice)

consumption [kən'sʌmpʃən] n consommation f

cont. abbr (= continued) suite

contact ['kɔntækt] n contact m; (person) connaissance f, relation f ▷ vt se mettre en contact or en rapport avec; **contact lenses** npl verres mpl de contact

contagious [kən'teɪdʒəs] adj contagieux(-euse)

contain [kən'teɪn] vt contenir; **to ~ o.s.** se contenir, se maîtriser; **container** n récipient m; (for shipping etc) conteneur m

contaminate [kən'tæmɪneɪt] vt contaminer

cont'd abbr (= continued) suite

contemplate ['kɔntəmpleɪt] vt contempler; (consider) envisager

contemporary [kən'tɛmpərərɪ] adj contemporain(e); (design, wallpaper) moderne ▷ n contemporain(e)

contempt [kən'tɛmpt] n mépris m, dédain m; **~ of court** (Law) outrage m à l'autorité de la justice

contend [kən'tɛnd] vt: **to ~ that** soutenir or prétendre que ▷ vi: **to ~ with** (compete) rivaliser avec; (struggle) lutter avec

content [kən'tɛnt] adj content(e), satisfait(e) ▷ vt contenter, satisfaire ▷ n ['kɔntɛnt] contenu m; (of fat, moisture) teneur f; **contents** npl (of container etc) contenu m; **(table of) ~s** table f des matières; **contented** adj content(e), satisfait(e)

contest n ['kɔntɛst] combat m, lutte f; (competition) concours m ▷ vt [kən'tɛst] contester, discuter; (compete for) disputer; (Law) attaquer; **contestant** [kən'tɛstənt] n concurrent(e); (in fight) adversaire m/f

context ['kɔntɛkst] n contexte m

continent ['kɔntɪnənt] n continent m; **the C~** (Brit) l'Europe continentale; **continental** [kɔntɪ'nɛntl] adj continental(e); **continental breakfast** n café (or thé) complet; **continental quilt** n (BRIT) couette f

continual [kən'tɪnjuəl] adj continuel(le); **continually** adv continuellement, sans cesse

continue [kən'tɪnjuː] vi continuer ▷ vt continuer; (start again) reprendre

continuity [kɔntɪ'njuːɪtɪ] n continuité f; (TV etc) enchaînement m

continuous [kən'tɪnjuəs] adj continu(e), permanent(e); (Ling) progressif(-ive); **continuous assessment** (BRIT) n contrôle continu; **continuously** adv (repeatedly) continuellement; (uninterruptedly) sans interruption

contour ['kɔntuəʳ] n contour m, profil m; (also: ~ **line**) courbe f de niveau

contraception [kɔntrə'sɛpʃən] n contraception f

contraceptive [kɔntrə'sɛptɪv] adj contraceptif(-ive), anticonceptionnel(le) ▷ n contraceptif m

contract n ['kɔntrækt] contrat m ▷ vb [kən'trækt] ▷ vi (become smaller) se contracter, se resserrer ▷ vt contracter; (Comm): **to ~ to do sth** s'engager (par contrat) à faire qch; **contractor** n entrepreneur m

contradict [kɔntrə'dɪkt] vt contredire; **contradiction** [kɔntrə'dɪkʃən] n contradiction f

contrary¹ ['kɔntrərɪ] adj contraire, opposé(e) ▷ n contraire m; **on the ~** au contraire; **unless you hear to the ~** sauf avis contraire

contrary² [kən'trɛərɪ] adj (perverse) contrariant(e), entêté(e)

contrast n ['kɔntrɑːst] contraste m ▷ vt [kən'trɑːst] mettre en contraste, contraster; **in ~ to** or **with** contrairement à, par opposition à

contribute [kən'trɪbjuːt] vi contribuer ▷ vt: **to ~ £10/an article to** donner 10 livres/un article à; **to ~ to** (gen) contribuer à; (newspaper) collaborer à; (discussion) prendre part à; **contribution** [kɔntrɪ'bjuːʃən] n contribution f; (BRIT: for social security) cotisation f; (to publication) article m; **contributor** n (to newspaper) collaborateur(-trice); (of money, goods) donateur(-trice)

control [kən'trəul] vt (process, machinery) commander; (temper) maîtriser; (disease) enrayer ▷ n maîtrise f; (power) autorité f; **controls** npl (of machine etc) commandes fpl; (on radio) boutons mpl de réglage; **to be in ~ of** être maître de, maîtriser; (in charge of) être responsable de; **everything is under ~** j'ai (or il a etc) la situation en main; **the car went out of ~** j'ai (or il a etc) perdu le contrôle du véhicule; **control tower** n (Aviat) tour f de contrôle

controversial [kɔntrə'vəːʃl] adj discutable, controversé(e)

controversy ['kɔntrəvəːsɪ] n controverse f, polémique f

convenience [kən'viːnɪəns] n commodité f; **at your ~** quand or comme cela vous convient; **all modern ~s**, **all mod cons** (BRIT) avec tout le confort moderne, tout confort

convenient [kən'viːnɪənt] adj commode

convent ['kɔnvənt] n couvent m

convention [kən'vɛnʃən] n convention f; (custom) usage m; **conventional** adj conventionnel(le)

conversation [kɔnvə'seɪʃən] n conversation f

conversely [kɔn'vəːslɪ] adv inversement, réciproquement

conversion [kən'vəːʃən] n conversion f; (BRIT: of house) transformation f, aménagement m; (Rugby)

transformation f

convert vt [kən'vəːt] (Rel, Comm) convertir; (alter) transformer; (house) aménager ▷ n ['kɔnvəːt] converti(e); **convertible** adj convertible ▷ n (voiture f) décapotable f

convey [kən'veɪ] vt transporter; (thanks) transmettre; (idea) communiquer; **conveyor belt** n convoyeur m, tapis roulant

convict vt [kən'vɪkt] déclarer (or reconnaître) coupable ▷ n ['kɔnvɪkt] forçat m, convict m; **conviction** [kən'vɪkʃən] n (Law) condamnation f; (belief) conviction f

convince [kən'vɪns] vt convaincre, persuader; **convinced** adj: **convinced of/that** convaincu(e) de/ que; **convincing** adj persuasif(-ive), convaincant(e)

convoy ['kɔnvɔɪ] n convoi m

cook [kuk] vt (faire) cuire ▷ vi cuire; (person) faire la cuisine ▷ n cuisinier(-ière); **cookbook** n livre m de cuisine; **cooker** n cuisinière f; **cookery** n cuisine f; **cookery book** n (BRIT) = **cookbook**; **cookie** n (US) biscuit m, petit gâteau sec; **cooking** n cuisine f

cool [kuːl] adj frais (fraîche), (not afraid) calme; (unfriendly) froid(e); (inf: trendy) cool inv (inf); (: great) super inv (inf) ▷ vt, vi rafraîchir, refroidir; **cool down** vi refroidir; (fig: person, situation) se calmer; **cool off** vi (become calmer) se calmer; (lose enthusiasm) perdre son enthousiasme

cop [kɔp] n (inf) flic m

cope [kəup] vi s'en sortir, tenir le coup; **to ~ with** (problem) faire face à

copper ['kɔpəʳ] n cuivre m; (BRIT: inf: policeman) flic m

copy ['kɔpɪ] n copie f; (book etc) exemplaire m ▷ vt copier; (imitate) imiter; **copyright** n droit m d'auteur, copyright m

coral ['kɔrəl] n corail m

cord [kɔːd] n corde f; (fabric) velours côtelé; (Elec) cordon m (d'alimentation), fil m (électrique); **cords** npl (trousers) pantalon m de velours côtelé; **cordless** adj sans fil

corduroy ['kɔːdərɔɪ] n velours côtelé

core [kɔːʳ] n (of fruit) trognon m, cœur m; (fig: of problem etc) cœur ▷ vt enlever le trognon or le cœur de

coriander [kɔrɪ'ændəʳ] n coriandre f

cork [kɔːk] n (material) liège m; (of bottle) bouchon m; **corkscrew** n tire-bouchon m

corn [kɔːn] n (BRIT: wheat) blé m; (US: maize) maïs m; (on foot) cor m; **~ on the cob** (Culin) épi m de maïs au naturel

corned beef ['kɔːnd-] n corned-beef m

corner ['kɔːnəʳ] n coin m; (in road) tournant m, virage m; (Football) corner m ▷ vt (trap: prey) acculer; (fig) coincer; (Comm: market) accaparer ▷ vi prendre un virage; **corner shop** (BRIT) n magasin m du coin

cornflakes ['kɔːnfleɪks] npl cornflakes mpl

cornflour ['kɔːnflauəʳ] n (BRIT) farine f de maïs, maïzena® f

cornstarch ['kɔːnstɑːtʃ] n (US) farine f de maïs, maïzena® f

Cornwall ['kɔːnwəl] n Cornouailles f

coronary ['kɔrənərɪ] n: **~ (thrombosis)** infarctus m (du myocarde), thrombose f coronaire

coronation [kɔrə'neɪʃən] n couronnement m

coroner ['kɔrənəʳ] n coroner m, officier de police judiciaire chargé de déterminer les causes d'un décès

corporal ['kɔːpərl] n caporal m, brigadier m ▷ adj: **~ punishment** châtiment corporel

corporate ['kɔːpərɪt] adj (action, ownership) en

commun; (Comm) de la société

corporation [kɔːpəˈreɪʃən] n (of town) municipalité f, conseil municipal; (Comm) société f

corps [kɔːʳ] (pl ~) [kɔːz] n corps m; **the diplomatic ~** le corps diplomatique; **the press ~** la presse

corpse [kɔːps] n cadavre m

correct [kəˈrɛkt] adj (accurate) correct(e), exact(e); (proper) correct, convenable ▷ vt corriger; **correction** [kəˈrɛkʃən] n correction f

correspond [kɔrɪsˈpɔnd] vi correspondre; **to ~ to sth** (be equivalent to) correspondre à qch; **correspondence** n correspondance f; **correspondent** n correspondant(e); **corresponding** adj correspondant(e)

corridor [ˈkɔrɪdɔːʳ] n couloir m, corridor m

corrode [kəˈrəud] vt corroder, ronger ▷ vi se corroder

corrupt [kəˈrʌpt] adj corrompu(e); (Comput) altéré(e) ▷ vt corrompre; (Comput) altérer; **corruption** n corruption f; (Comput) altération f (de données)

Corsica [ˈkɔːsɪkə] n Corse f

cosmetic [kɔzˈmɛtɪk] n produit m de beauté, cosmétique m ▷ adj (fig: reforms) symbolique, superficiel(le); **cosmetic surgery** n chirurgie f esthétique

cosmopolitan [kɔzməˈpɔlɪtn] adj cosmopolite

cost [kɔst] n coût m ▷ vb (pt, pp ~) ▷ vi coûter ▷ vt établir or calculer le prix de revient de; **costs** npl (Comm) frais mpl; (Law) dépens mpl; **how much does it ~?** combien ça coûte?; **to ~ sb time/effort** demander du temps/un effort à qn; **it ~ him his life/job** ça lui a coûté la vie/son emploi; **at all ~s** coûte que coûte, à tout prix

co-star [ˈkəustɑːʳ] n partenaire m/f

costly [ˈkɔstlɪ] adj coûteux(-euse)

cost of living n coût m de la vie

costume [ˈkɔstjuːm] n costume m; (BRIT: also: **swimming ~**) maillot m (de bain)

cosy (US **cozy**) [ˈkəuzɪ] adj (room, bed) douillet(te); **to be ~** (person) être bien (au chaud)

cot [kɔt] n (BRIT: child's) lit m d'enfant, petit lit; (US: campbed) lit de camp

cottage [ˈkɔtɪdʒ] n petite maison (à la campagne), cottage m; **cottage cheese** n fromage blanc (maigre)

cotton [ˈkɔtn] n coton m; (thread) fil m (de coton); **cotton on** vi (inf): **to ~ on (to sth)** piger (qch); **cotton bud** (BRIT) n coton-tige ® m; **cotton candy** (US) n barbe f à papa; **cotton wool** n (BRIT) ouate f, coton m hydrophile

couch [kautʃ] n canapé m; divan m

cough [kɔf] vi tousser ▷ n toux f; **I've got a ~** j'ai la toux; **cough mixture, cough syrup** n sirop m pour la toux

could [kud] pt of **can²**; **couldn't** = **could not**

council [ˈkaunsl] n conseil m; **city or town ~** conseil municipal; **council estate** n (BRIT) (quartier m or zone f de) logements loués à/par la municipalité; **council house** n (BRIT) maison f (à loyer modéré) louée par la municipalité; **councillor** (US **councilor**) n conseiller(-ère); **council tax** n (BRIT) impôts locaux

counsel [ˈkaunsl] n conseil m; (lawyer) avocat(e) ▷ vt: **to ~ (sb to do sth)** conseiller (à qn de faire qch); **counselling** (US **counseling**) n (Psych) aide psychosociale; **counsellor** (US **counselor**) n conseiller(-ère); (US Law) avocat m

count [kaunt] vt, vi compter ▷ n compte m; (nobleman) comte m; **count in** vt (inf): **to ~ sb in on sth** inclure qn dans qch; **count on** vt fus compter sur; **countdown** n

compte m à rebours

counter [ˈkauntəʳ] n comptoir m; (in post office, bank) guichet m; (in game) jeton m ▷ vt aller à l'encontre de, opposer ▷ adv: **~ to** à l'encontre de; contrairement à; **counterclockwise** (US) adv en sens inverse des aiguilles d'une montre

counterfeit [ˈkauntəfɪt] n faux m, contrefaçon f ▷ vt contrefaire ▷ adj faux(fausse)

counterpart [ˈkauntəpɑːt] n (of person) homologue m/f

countess [ˈkauntɪs] n comtesse f

countless [ˈkauntlɪs] adj innombrable

country [ˈkʌntrɪ] n pays m; (native land) patrie f; (as opposed to town) campagne f; (region) région f, pays; **country and western (music)** n musique f country; **country house** n manoir m, (petit) château; **countryside** n campagne f

county [ˈkauntɪ] n comté m

coup [kuː] (pl ~s) [kuːz] n (achievement) beau coup; (also: **~ d'état**) coup d'État

couple [ˈkʌpl] n couple m; **a ~ of** (two) deux; (a few) deux ou trois

coupon [ˈkuːpɔn] n (voucher) bon m de réduction; (detachable form) coupon m détachable, coupon-réponse m

courage [ˈkʌrɪdʒ] n courage m; **courageous** [kəˈreɪdʒəs] adj courageux(-euse)

courgette [kuəˈʒɛt] n (BRIT) courgette f

courier [ˈkurɪəʳ] n messager m, courrier m; (for tourists) accompagnateur(-trice)

course [kɔːs] n cours m; (of ship) route f; (for golf) terrain m; (part of meal) plat m; **of ~** adv bien sûr; **(no,) of ~ not!** bien sûr que non!, évidemment que non!; **~ of treatment** (Med) traitement m

court [kɔːt] n cour f; (Law) cour, tribunal m; (Tennis) court m ▷ vt (woman) courtiser, faire la cour à; **to take to ~** actionner ou poursuivre en justice

courtesy [ˈkəːtəsɪ] n courtoisie f, politesse f; **(by) ~ of** avec l'aimable autorisation de; **courtesy bus, courtesy coach** n navette gratuite

court: court-house [ˈkɔːthaus] n (US) palais m de justice; **courtroom** [ˈkɔːtrum] n salle f de tribunal; **courtyard** [ˈkɔːtjɑːd] n cour f

cousin [ˈkʌzn] n cousin(e); **first ~** cousin(e) germain(e)

cover [ˈkʌvəʳ] vt couvrir; (Press: report on) faire un reportage sur; (feelings, mistake) cacher; (include) englober; (discuss) traiter ▷ n (of book, Comm) couverture f; (of pan) couvercle m; (over furniture) housse f; (shelter) abri m; **covers** npl (on bed) couvertures; **to take ~** se mettre à l'abri; **under ~** à l'abri; **under ~ of darkness** à la faveur de la nuit; **under separate ~** (Comm) sous pli séparé; **cover up** vi: **to ~ up for sb** (fig) couvrir qn; **coverage** n (in media) reportage m; **cover charge** n couvert m (supplément à payer); **cover-up** n tentative f pour étouffer une affaire

cow [kau] n vache f ▷ vt effrayer, intimider

coward [ˈkauəd] n lâche m/f; **cowardly** adj lâche

cowboy [ˈkaubɔɪ] n cow-boy m

cozy [ˈkəuzɪ] adj (US) = **cosy**

crab [kræb] n crabe m

crack [kræk] n (split) fente f, fissure f; (in cup, bone) fêlure f; (in wall) lézarde f; (noise) craquement m, coup (sec); (Drugs) crack m ▷ vt fendre, fissurer; fêler; lézarder; (whip) faire claquer; (nut) casser; (problem) résoudre; (code) déchiffrer ▷ cpd (athlete) de première classe, d'élite; **crack down on** vt fus (crime) sévir contre, réprimer; **cracked** adj (cup, bone) fêlé(e); (broken) cassé(e); (wall) lézardé(e); (surface) craquelé(e); (inf) toqué(e), timbré(e); **cracker** n (also: **Christmas cracker**) pétard m; (biscuit) biscuit (salé), craquelin m

crackle ['krækl] vi crépiter, grésiller

cradle ['kreɪdl] n berceau m

craft [krɑːft] n métier (artisanal); (cunning) ruse f, astuce f; (boat: pl inv) embarcation f, barque f; (plane: pl inv) appareil m; **craftsman** (irreg) n artisan m ouvrier (qualifié); **craftsmanship** n métier m, habileté f

cram [kræm] vt (fill): **to ~ sth with** bourrer qch de; (put): **to ~ sth into** fourrer qch dans ▷ vi (for exams) bachoter

cramp [kræmp] n crampe f; **I've got ~ in my leg** j'ai une crampe à la jambe; **cramped** adj à l'étroit, très serré(e)

cranberry ['krænbərɪ] n canneberge f

crane [kreɪn] n grue f

crap [kræp] n (inf!: nonsense) conneries fpl (!); (: excrement) merde f (!)

crash [kræʃ] n (noise) fracas m; (of car, plane) collision f; (of business) faillite f ▷ vt (plane) écraser ▷ vi (plane) s'écraser; (two cars) se percuter, s'emboutir; (business) s'effondrer; **to ~ into** se jeter or se fracasser contre; **crash course** n cours intensif; **crash helmet** n casque (protecteur)

crate [kreɪt] n cageot m; (for bottles) caisse f

crave [kreɪv] vt, vi: **to ~ (for)** avoir une envie irrésistible de

crawl [krɔːl] vi ramper; (vehicle) avancer au pas ▷ n (Swimming) crawl m

crayfish ['kreɪfɪʃ] n (pl inv: freshwater) écrevisse f; (saltwater) langoustine f

crayon ['kreɪən] n crayon m (de couleur)

craze [kreɪz] n engouement m

crazy ['kreɪzɪ] adj fou (folle); **to be ~ about sb/sth** (inf) être fou de qn/qch

creak [kriːk] vi (hinge) grincer; (floor, shoes) craquer

cream [kriːm] n crème f ▷ adj (colour) crème inv; **cream cheese** n fromage m à la crème, fromage blanc; **creamy** adj crémeux(-euse)

crease [kriːs] n pli m ▷ vt froisser, chiffonner ▷ vi se froisser, se chiffonner

create [kriːˈeɪt] vt créer; **creation** [kriːˈeɪʃən] n création f; **creative** adj créatif(-ive); **creator** n créateur(-trice)

creature ['kriːtʃə'] n créature f

crèche [krɛʃ] n garderie f, crèche f

credentials [krɪˈdɛnʃlz] npl (references) références fpl; (identity papers) pièce f d'identité

credibility [krɛdɪˈbɪlɪtɪ] n crédibilité f

credible ['krɛdɪbl] adj digne de foi, crédible

credit ['krɛdɪt] n crédit m; (recognition) honneur m; (Scol) unité f de valeur ▷ vt (Comm) créditer; (believe: also: **give ~ to**) ajouter foi à, croire; **credits** npl (Cine) générique m; **to be in ~** (person, bank account) être créditeur(-trice); **to ~ sb with** (fig) prêter or attribuer à qn; **credit card** n carte f de crédit; **do you take credit cards?** acceptez-vous les cartes de crédit?

creek [kriːk] n (inlet) crique f, anse f; (us: stream) ruisseau m, petit cours d'eau

creep (pt, pp **crept**) [kriːp, krɛpt] vi ramper

cremate [krɪˈmeɪt] vt incinérer

crematorium (pl **crematoria**) [krɛməˈtɔːrɪəm, -ˈtɔːrɪə] n four m crématoire

crept [krɛpt] pt, pp of **creep**

crescent ['krɛsnt] n croissant m; (street) rue f (en arc de cercle)

cress [krɛs] n cresson m

crest [krɛst] n crête f; (of coat of arms) timbre m

crew [kruː] n équipage m; (Cine) équipe f (de tournage); **crew-neck** n col ras

crib [krɪb] n lit m d'enfant; (for baby) berceau m ▷ vt (inf) copier

cricket ['krɪkɪt] n (insect) grillon m, cri-cri m inv; (game) cricket m; **cricketer** n joueur m de cricket

crime [kraɪm] n crime m; **criminal** ['krɪmɪnl] adj, n criminel(le)

crimson ['krɪmzn] adj cramoisi(e)

cringe [krɪndʒ] vi avoir un mouvement de recul

cripple ['krɪpl] n boiteux(-euse), infirme m/f ▷ vt (person) estropier, paralyser; (ship, plane) immobiliser; (production, exports) paralyser

crisis (pl **crises**) ['kraɪsɪs, -siːz] n crise f

crisp [krɪsp] adj croquant(e); (weather) vif (vive); (manner etc) brusque; **crisps** (BRIT) npl (pommes fpl) chips fpl; **crispy** adj croustillant(e)

criterion (pl **criteria**) [kraɪˈtɪərɪən, -ˈtɪərɪə] n critère m

critic ['krɪtɪk] n critique m/f; **critical** adj critique; **criticism** ['krɪtɪsɪzəm] n critique f; **criticize** ['krɪtɪsaɪz] vt critiquer

Croat ['krəʊæt] adj, n = **Croatian**

Croatia [krəʊˈeɪʃə] n Croatie f; **Croatian** adj croate ▷ n Croate m/f; (Ling) croate m

crockery ['krɒkərɪ] n vaisselle f

crocodile ['krɒkədaɪl] n crocodile m

crocus ['krəʊkəs] n crocus m

croissant ['krwæsɔ̃] n croissant m

crook [kruk] n escroc m; (of shepherd) houlette f; **crooked** ['krukɪd] adj courbé(e), tordu(e); (action) malhonnête

crop [krɒp] n (produce) culture f; (amount produced) récolte f; (riding crop) cravache f ▷ vt (hair) tondre; **crop up** vi surgir, se présenter, survenir

cross [krɒs] n croix f; (Biol) croisement m ▷ vt (street etc) traverser; (arms, legs, Biol) croiser; (cheque) barrer ▷ adj en colère, fâché(e); **cross off** or **out** vt barrer, rayer; **cross over** vi traverser; **cross-Channel ferry** ['krɒsˈtʃænl-] n ferry m qui fait la traversée de la Manche; **crosscountry (race)** n cross(-country) m; **crossing** n (sea passage) traversée f; (also: **pedestrian crossing**) passage clouté; **how long does the crossing take?** combien de temps dure la traversée?; **crossing guard** (us) n contractuel qui fait traverser la rue aux enfants; **crossroads** n carrefour m; **crosswalk** n (us) passage clouté; **crossword** n mots mpl croisés

crotch [krɒtʃ] n (of garment) entrejambe m; (Anat) entrecuisse m

crouch [krautʃ] vi s'accroupir; (hide) se tapir; (before springing) se ramasser

crouton ['kruːtɒn] n croûton m

crow [krəʊ] n (bird) corneille f; (of cock) chant m du coq, cocorico m ▷ vi (cock) chanter

crowd [kraud] n foule f ▷ vt bourrer, remplir ▷ vi affluer, s'attrouper, s'entasser; **crowded** adj bondé(e), plein(e)

crown [kraun] n couronne f; (of head) sommet m de la tête; (of hill) sommet m ▷ vt (also tooth) couronner; **crown jewels** npl joyaux mpl de la Couronne

crucial ['kruːʃl] adj crucial(e), décisif(-ive)

crucifix ['kruːsɪfɪks] n crucifix m

crude [kruːd] adj (materials) brut(e); non raffiné(e); (basic) rudimentaire, sommaire; (vulgar) cru(e), grossier(-ière); **crude (oil)** n (pétrole) brut m

cruel [ˈkruəl] adj cruel(le); **cruelty** n cruauté f

cruise [kruːz] n croisière f ▷ vi (ship) croiser; (car) rouler; (aircraft) voler

crumb [krʌm] n miette f

crumble [ˈkrʌmbl] vt émietter ▷ vi (plaster etc) s'effriter; (land, earth) s'ébouler; (building) s'écrouler, crouler; (fig) s'effondrer

crumpet [ˈkrʌmpɪt] n petite crêpe (épaisse)

crumple [ˈkrʌmpl] vt froisser, friper

crunch [krʌntʃ] vt croquer; (underfoot) faire craquer, écraser; faire crisser ▷ n (fig) instant m or moment m critique, moment de vérité; **crunchy** adj croquant(e), croustillant(e)

crush [krʌʃ] n (crowd) foule f, cohue f; (love): **to have a ~ on sb** avoir le béguin pour qn; (drink): **lemon ~** citron pressé ▷ vt écraser; (crumple) froisser; (grind, break up: garlic, ice) piler; (: grapes) presser; (hopes) anéantir

crust [krʌst] n croûte f; **crusty** adj (bread) croustillant(e); (inf: person) revêche, bourru(e)

crutch [krʌtʃ] n béquille f; (also: **crotch**) entrejambe m

cry [kraɪ] vi pleurer; (shout: also: **~ out**) crier ▷ n cri m; **cry out** vi (call out, shout) pousser un cri ▷ vt crier

crystal [ˈkrɪstl] n cristal m

cub [kʌb] n petit m (d'un animal); (also: **~ scout**) louveteau m

Cuba [ˈkjuːbə] n Cuba m

cube [kjuːb] n cube m ▷ vt (Math) élever au cube

cubicle [ˈkjuːbɪkl] n (in hospital) box m; (at pool) cabine f

cuckoo [ˈkʊkuː] n coucou m

cucumber [ˈkjuːkʌmbəʳ] n concombre m

cuddle [ˈkʌdl] vt câliner, caresser ▷ vi se blottir l'un contre l'autre

cue [kjuː] n queue f de billard; (Theat etc) signal m

cuff [kʌf] n (BRIT: of shirt, coat etc) poignet m, manchette f; (US: on trousers) revers m; (blow) gifle f; **off the ~** adv à l'improviste; **cufflinks** n boutons m de manchette

cuisine [kwɪˈziːn] n cuisine f

cul-de-sac [ˈkʌldəsæk] n cul-de-sac m, impasse f

cull [kʌl] vt sélectionner ▷ n (of animals) abattage sélectif

culminate [ˈkʌlmɪneɪt] vi: **to ~ in** finir or se terminer par; (lead to) mener à

culprit [ˈkʌlprɪt] n coupable m/f

cult [kʌlt] n culte m

cultivate [ˈkʌltɪveɪt] vt cultiver

cultural [ˈkʌltʃərəl] adj culturel(le)

culture [ˈkʌltʃəʳ] n culture f

cumin [ˈkʌmɪn] n (spice) cumin m

cunning [ˈkʌnɪŋ] n ruse f, astuce f ▷ adj rusé(e), malin(-igne); (clever: device, idea) astucieux(-euse)

cup [kʌp] n tasse f; (prize, event) coupe f; (of bra) bonnet m

cupboard [ˈkʌbəd] n placard m

cup final n (BRIT Football) finale f de la coupe

curator [kjuəˈreɪtəʳ] n conservateur m (d'un musée etc)

curb [kəːb] vt refréner, mettre un frein à ▷ n (fig) frein m; (US) bord m du trottoir

curdle [ˈkəːdl] vi (se) cailler

cure [kjuəʳ] vt guérir; (Culin: salt) saler; (: smoke) fumer; (: dry) sécher ▷ n remède m

curfew [ˈkəːfjuː] n couvre-feu m

curiosity [kjuərɪˈɔsɪtɪ] n curiosité f

curious [ˈkjuərɪəs] adj curieux(-euse); **I'm ~ about him** il m'intrigue

curl [kəːl] n boucle f (de cheveux) ▷ vt, vi boucler; (tightly) friser; **curl up** vi s'enrouler; (person) se pelotonner; **curler** n bigoudi m, rouleau m; **curly** adj bouclé(e); (tightly curled) frisé(e)

currant [ˈkʌrnt] n raisin m de Corinthe, raisin sec; (fruit) groseille f

currency [ˈkʌrnsɪ] n monnaie f; **to gain ~** (fig) s'accréditer

current [ˈkʌrnt] n courant m ▷ adj (common) courant(e); (tendency, price, event) actuel(le); **current account** n (BRIT) compte courant; **current affairs** npl (questions fpl d') actualité f; **currently** adv actuellement

curriculum (pl **~s** or **curricula**) [kəˈrɪkjuləm, -lə] n programme m d'études; **curriculum vitae** [-ˈviːtaɪ] n curriculum vitae (CV) m

curry [ˈkʌrɪ] n curry m ▷ vt: **to ~ favour with** chercher à gagner la faveur or à s'attirer les bonnes grâces de; **curry powder** n poudre f de curry

curse [kəːs] vi jurer, blasphémer ▷ vt maudire ▷ n (spell) malédiction f; (problem, scourge) fléau m; (swearword) juron m

cursor [ˈkəːsəʳ] n (Comput) curseur m

curt [kəːt] adj brusque, sec(-sèche)

curtain [ˈkəːtn] n rideau m

curve [kəːv] n courbe f; (in the road) tournant m, virage m ▷ vi se courber; (road) faire une courbe; **curved** adj courbe

cushion [ˈkʊʃən] n coussin m ▷ vt (fall, shock) amortir

custard [ˈkʌstəd] n (for pouring) crème anglaise

custody [ˈkʌstədɪ] n (of child) garde f; (for offenders): **to take sb into ~** placer qn en détention préventive

custom [ˈkʌstəm] n coutume f, usage m; (Comm) clientèle f

customer [ˈkʌstəməʳ] n client(e)

customized [ˈkʌstəmaɪzd] adj personnalisé(e); (car etc) construit(e) sur commande

customs [ˈkʌstəmz] npl douane f; **customs officer** n douanier m

cut [kʌt] vb (pt, pp **~**) ▷ vt couper; (meat) découper; (reduce) réduire ▷ vi couper ▷ n coupure f; (of clothes) coupe f; (in salary etc) réduction f; (of meat) morceau m; **to ~ a tooth** percer une dent; **to ~ one's finger** se couper le doigt; **to get one's hair ~** se faire couper les cheveux; **I've ~ myself** je me suis coupé; **cut back** vt (plants) tailler; (production, expenditure) réduire; **cut down** vt (tree) abattre; (reduce) réduire; **cut off** vt couper; (fig) isoler; **cut out** vt (picture etc) découper; (remove) supprimer; **cut up** vt découper; **cutback** n réduction f

cute [kjuːt] adj mignon(ne), adorable

cutlery [ˈkʌtlərɪ] n couverts mpl

cutlet [ˈkʌtlɪt] n côtelette f

cut-price [ˈkʌtˈpraɪs] (US **cut-rate**) [ˈkʌtˈreɪt] adj au rabais, à prix réduit

cutting [ˈkʌtɪŋ] adj (fig) cinglant(e) ▷ n (BRIT: from newspaper) coupure f (de journal); (from plant) bouture f

CV n abbr = **curriculum vitae**

cwt abbr = **hundredweight(s)**

cyberspace [ˈsaɪbəspeɪs] n cyberespace m

cycle [ˈsaɪkl] n cycle m; (bicycle) bicyclette f, vélo m ▷ vi faire de la bicyclette; **cycle hire** n location f de vélos; **cycle lane, cycle path** n piste f cyclable; **cycling** n cyclisme m; **cyclist** n cycliste m/f

cyclone ['saɪkləʊn] n cyclone m
cylinder ['sɪlɪndər] n cylindre m
cymbals ['sɪmblz] npl cymbales fpl
cynical ['sɪnɪkl] adj cynique
Cypriot ['sɪprɪət] adj cypriote, chypriote ▷ n Cypriote m/f, Chypriote m/f
Cyprus ['saɪprəs] n Chypre f
cyst [sɪst] n kyste m; **cystitis** [sɪs'taɪtɪs] n cystite f
czar [zɑːr] n tsar m
Czech [tʃɛk] adj tchèque ▷ n Tchèque m/f; (Ling) tchèque m; **Czech Republic** n: **the Czech Republic** la République tchèque

d

D [diː] n (Mus): **D** ré m
dab [dæb] vt (eyes, wound) tamponner; (paint, cream) appliquer (par petites touches or rapidement)
dad, daddy [dæd, 'dædɪ] n papa m
daffodil ['dæfədɪl] n jonquille f
daft [dɑːft] adj (inf) idiot(e), stupide
dagger ['dægər] n poignard m
daily ['deɪlɪ] adj quotidien(ne), journalier(-ière) ▷ adv tous les jours
dairy ['dɛərɪ] n (shop) crèmerie f, laiterie f; (on farm) laiterie; **dairy produce** n produits laitiers
daisy ['deɪzɪ] n pâquerette f
dam [dæm] n (wall) barrage m; (water) réservoir m, lac m de retenue ▷ vt endiguer
damage ['dæmɪdʒ] n dégâts mpl, dommages mpl; (fig) tort m ▷ vt endommager, abîmer; (fig) faire du tort à; **damages** npl (Law) dommages-intérêts mpl
damn [dæm] vt condamner; (curse) maudire ▷ n (inf): **I don't give a ~** je m'en fous ▷ adj (inf: also: **~ed**): **this ~ ...** ce sacré or foutu ...; **~ (it)!** zut!
damp [dæmp] adj humide ▷ n humidité f ▷ vt (also: **~en**:

cloth, rag) humecter; (: enthusiasm etc) refroidir
dance [dɑːns] n danse f, (ball) bal m ▷ vi danser; **dance floor** n piste f de danse; **dancer** n danseur(-euse); **dancing** n danse f
dandelion ['dændɪlaɪən] n pissenlit m
dandruff ['dændrəf] n pellicules fpl
D & T n abbr (BRIT: Scol) = **design and technology**
Dane [deɪn] n Danois(e)
danger ['deɪndʒər] n danger m; **~!** (on sign) danger!; **in ~** en danger; **he was in ~ of falling** il risquait de tomber; **dangerous** adj dangereux(-euse)
dangle ['dæŋgl] vt balancer ▷ vi pendre, se balancer
Danish ['deɪnɪʃ] adj danois(e) ▷ n (Ling) danois m
dare [dɛər] vt: **to ~ sb to do** défier qn or mettre qn au défi de faire ▷ vi: **to ~ (to) do sth** oser faire qch; **I ~ say he'll turn up** il est probable qu'il viendra; **daring** adj hardi(e), audacieux(-euse) ▷ n audace f, hardiesse f
dark [dɑːk] adj (night, room) obscur(e), sombre; (colour, complexion) foncé(e), sombre ▷ n: **in the ~** dans le noir; **to be in the ~ about** (fig) ignorer tout de; **after ~** après la tombée de la nuit; **darken** vt obscurcir, assombrir ▷ vi s'obscurcir, s'assombrir; **darkness** n obscurité f; **darkroom** n chambre noire
darling ['dɑːlɪŋ] adj, n chéri(e)
dart [dɑːt] n fléchette f; (in sewing) pince f ▷ vi: **to ~ towards** se précipiter or s'élancer vers; **dartboard** n cible f (de jeu de fléchettes); **darts** n jeu m de fléchettes
dash [dæʃ] n (sign) tiret m; (small quantity) goutte f, larme f ▷ vt (throw) jeter or lancer violemment; (hopes) anéantir ▷ vi: **to ~ towards** se précipiter or se ruer vers
dashboard ['dæʃbɔːd] n (Aut) tableau m de bord
data ['deɪtə] npl données fpl; **database** n base f de données; **data processing** n traitement m (électronique) de l'information
date [deɪt] n date f; (with sb) rendez-vous m; (fruit) datte f ▷ vt dater; (person) sortir avec; **~ of birth** date de naissance; **to ~** adv à ce jour; **out of ~** périmé(e); **up to ~** à la page, mis(e) à jour, moderne; **dated** adj démodé(e)
daughter ['dɔːtər] n fille f; **daughter-in-law** n belle-fille f, bru f
daunting ['dɔːntɪŋ] adj décourageant(e), intimidant(e)
dawn [dɔːn] n aube f, aurore f ▷ vi (day) se lever; poindre; **it ~ed on him that ...** il lui vint à l'esprit que ...
day [deɪ] n jour m; (as duration) journée f; (period of time, age) époque f, temps m; **the ~ before** la veille, le jour précédent; **the ~ after, the following ~** le lendemain, le jour suivant; **the ~ before yesterday** avant-hier; **the ~ after tomorrow** après-demain; **by ~** de jour; **day-care centre** ['deɪkɛə-] n (for elderly etc) centre m d'accueil de jour; (for children) garderie f; **daydream** vi rêver (tout éveillé); **daylight** n (lumière f du) jour m; **day return** n (BRIT) billet m d'aller-retour (valable pour la journée); **daytime** n jour m, journée f; **day-to-day** adj (routine, expenses) journalier(-ière); **day trip** n excursion f (d'une journée)
dazed [deɪzd] adj abruti(e)
dazzle ['dæzl] vt éblouir, aveugler; **dazzling** adj (light) aveuglant(e), éblouissant(e); (fig) éblouissant(e)
DC abbr (Elec) = **direct current**
dead [dɛd] adj mort(e); (numb) engourdi(e), insensible; (battery) à plat ▷ adv (completely) absolument, complètement; (exactly) juste; **he was shot ~** il a été tué d'un coup de revolver; **~ tired** éreinté(e), complètement fourbu(e); **to stop ~** s'arrêter pile or net; **the line is ~** (Tel

la ligne est coupée; **dead end** n impasse f; **deadline** n date for heure f limite; **deadly** adj mortel(le); (weapon) meurtrier(-ière); **Dead Sea** n: **the Dead Sea** la mer Morte

deaf [dɛf] adj sourd(e); **deafen** vt rendre sourd(e); **deafening** adj assourdissant(e)

deal [di:l] n affaire f, marché m ▷ vt (pt, pp ~t) (blow) porter; (cards) donner, distribuer; **a great ~ of** beaucoup de; **deal with** vt fus (handle) s'occuper or se charger de; (be about: book etc) traiter de; **dealer** n (Comm) marchand m; (Cards) donneur m; **dealings** npl (in goods, shares) opérations fpl, transactions fpl; (relations) relations fpl, rapports mpl

dealt [dɛlt] pt, pp of **deal**

dean [di:n] n (Rel, BRIT Scol) doyen m; (US Scol) conseiller principal (conseillère principale) d'éducation

dear [dɪəʳ] adj cher (chère); (expensive) cher, coûteux(-euse) ▷ n: **my ~** mon cher (ma chère) ▷ excl: **~ me!** mon Dieu!; **D~ Sir/Madam** (in letter) Monsieur/ Madame; **D~ Mr/Mrs X** Cher Monsieur X (Chère Madame X); **dearly** adv (love) tendrement; (pay) cher

death [dɛθ] n mort f; (Admin) décès m; **death penalty** n peine f de mort; **death sentence** n condamnation f à mort

debate [dɪ'beɪt] n discussion f, débat m ▷ vt discuter, débattre

debit ['dɛbɪt] n débit m ▷ vt: **to ~ a sum to sb** or **to sb's account** porter une somme au débit de qn, débiter qn d'une somme; **debit card** n carte f de paiement

debris ['dɛbri:] n débris mpl, décombres mpl

debt [dɛt] n dette f; **to be in ~** avoir des dettes, être endetté(e)

debut ['deɪbju:] n début(s) m(pl)

Dec. abbr (= December) déc

decade ['dɛkeɪd] n décennie f, décade f

decaffeinated [dɪ'kæfɪneɪtɪd] adj décaféiné(e)

decay [dɪ'keɪ] n (of building) délabrement m; (also: **tooth ~**) carie f (dentaire) ▷ vi (rot) se décomposer, pourrir; (: teeth) se carier

deceased [dɪ'si:st] n: **the ~** le (la) défunt(e)

deceit [dɪ'si:t] n tromperie f, supercherie f; **deceive** [dɪ'si:v] vt tromper

December [dɪ'sɛmbəʳ] n décembre m

decency ['di:sənsɪ] n décence f

decent ['di:sənt] adj (proper) décent(e), convenable

deception [dɪ'sɛpʃən] n tromperie f

deceptive [dɪ'sɛptɪv] adj trompeur(-euse)

decide [dɪ'saɪd] vt (subj: person) décider; (question, argument) trancher, régler ▷ vi se décider, décider; **to ~ to do/that** décider de faire/que; **to ~ on** décider, se décider pour

decimal ['dɛsɪməl] adj décimal(e) ▷ n décimale f

decision [dɪ'sɪʒən] n décision f

decisive [dɪ'saɪsɪv] adj décisif(-ive); (manner, person) décidé(e), catégorique

deck [dɛk] n (Naut) pont m; (of cards) jeu m; (record deck) platine f; (of bus): **top ~** impériale f; **deckchair** n chaise longue

declaration [dɛklə'reɪʃən] n déclaration f

declare [dɪ'klɛəʳ] vt déclarer

decline [dɪ'klaɪn] n (decay) déclin m; (lessening) baisse f ▷ vt refuser, décliner ▷ vi décliner; (business) baisser

decorate ['dɛkəreɪt] vt (adorn, give a medal to) décorer; (paint and paper) peindre et tapisser; **decoration**
[dɛkə'reɪʃən] n (medal etc, adornment) décoration f; **decorator** n peintre m en bâtiment

decrease n ['di:kri:s] diminution f ▷ vt, vi [di:'kri:s] diminuer

decree [dɪ'kri:] n (Pol, Rel) décret m; (Law) arrêt m, jugement m

dedicate ['dɛdɪkeɪt] vt consacrer; (book etc) dédier; **dedicated** adj (person) dévoué(e), (Comput) spécialisé(e), dédié(e); **dedicated word processor** station f de traitement de texte; **dedication** [dɛdɪ'keɪʃən] n (devotion) dévouement m; (in book) dédicace f

deduce [dɪ'dju:s] vt déduire, conclure

deduct [dɪ'dʌkt] vt: **to ~ sth (from)** déduire qch (de), retrancher qch (de); **deduction** [dɪ'dʌkʃən] n (deducting, deducing) déduction f; (from wage etc) prélèvement m, retenue f

deed [di:d] n action f, acte m; (Law) acte notarié, contrat m

deem [di:m] vt (formal) juger, estimer

deep [di:p] adj profond(e); (voice) grave ▷ adv: **spectators stood 20 ~** il y avait 20 rangs de spectateurs; **4 metres ~** de 4 mètres de profondeur; **how ~ is the water?** l'eau a quelle profondeur?; **deep-fry** vt faire frire (dans une friteuse); **deeply** adv profondément; (regret, interested) vivement

deer [dɪəʳ] n (pl inv): (red) **~** cerf m; (fallow) **~** daim m; (roe) **~** chevreuil m

default [dɪ'fɔ:lt] n (Comput: also: **~ value**) valeur f par défaut; **by ~** (Law) par défaut, par contumace; (Sport) par forfait

defeat [dɪ'fi:t] n défaite f ▷ vt (team, opponents) battre

defect n ['di:fɛkt] défaut m ▷ vi [dɪ'fɛkt]: **to ~ to the enemy/the West** passer à l'ennemi/l'Ouest; **defective** [dɪ'fɛktɪv] adj défectueux(-euse)

defence (US **defense**) [dɪ'fɛns] n défense f

defend [dɪ'fɛnd] vt défendre; **defendant** n défendeur(-deresse); (in criminal case) accusé(e), prévenu(e); **defender** n défenseur m

defense [dɪ'fɛns] (US) = **defence**

defensive [dɪ'fɛnsɪv] adj défensif(-ive) ▷ n: **on the ~** sur la défensive

defer [dɪ'fə:ʳ] vt (postpone) différer, ajourner

defiance [dɪ'faɪəns] n défi m; **in ~ of** au mépris de; **defiant** [dɪ'faɪənt] adj provocant(e), de défi; (person) rebelle, intraitable

deficiency [dɪ'fɪʃənsɪ] n (lack) insuffisance f; (: Med) carence f; (flaw) faiblesse f; **deficient** [dɪ'fɪʃənt] adj (inadequate) insuffisant(e); **to be deficient in** manquer de

deficit ['dɛfɪsɪt] n déficit m

define [dɪ'faɪn] vt définir

definite ['dɛfɪnɪt] adj (fixed) défini(e), (bien) déterminé(e); (clear, obvious) net(te), manifeste; (certain) sûr(e); **he was ~ about it** il a été catégorique; **definitely** adv sans aucun doute

definition [dɛfɪ'nɪʃən] n définition f; (clearness) netteté f

deflate [di:'fleɪt] vt dégonfler

deflect [dɪ'flɛkt] vt détourner, faire dévier

defraud [dɪ'frɔ:d] vt: **to ~ sb of sth** escroquer qch à qn

defrost [di:'frɔst] vt (fridge) dégivrer; (frozen food) décongeler

defuse [di:'fju:z] vt désamorcer

defy [dɪ'faɪ] vt défier; (efforts etc) résister à; **it defies description** cela défie toute description

degree [dɪ'gri:] n degré m; (Scol) diplôme m (universitaire); **a (first) ~ in maths** (BRIT) une licence en maths; **by ~s** (gradually) par degrés; **to some ~** jusqu'à un certain point, dans une certaine mesure

dehydrated [di:haɪ'dreɪtɪd] adj déshydraté(e); (milk, eggs) en poudre

de-icer [di:'aɪsəʳ] n dégivreur m

delay [dɪ'leɪ] vt retarder; (payment) différer ▷ vi s'attarder ▷ n délai m, retard m; **to be ~ed** être en retard

delegate n ['dɛlɪgɪt] délégué(e) ▷ vt ['dɛlɪgeɪt] déléguer

delete [dɪ'li:t] vt rayer, supprimer; (Comput) effacer

deli ['dɛlɪ] n épicerie fine

deliberate adj [dɪ'lɪbərɪt] (intentional) délibéré(e); (slow) mesuré(e) ▷ vi [dɪ'lɪbəreɪt] délibérer, réfléchir; **deliberately** adv (on purpose) exprès, délibérément

delicacy ['dɛlɪkəsɪ] n délicatesse f; (choice food) mets fin or délicat, friandise f

delicate ['dɛlɪkɪt] adj délicat(e)

delicatessen [dɛlɪkə'tɛsn] n épicerie fine

delicious [dɪ'lɪʃəs] adj délicieux(-euse)

delight [dɪ'laɪt] n (grande) joie, grand plaisir ▷ vt enchanter; **she's a ~ to work with** c'est un plaisir de travailler avec elle; **to take ~ in** prendre grand plaisir à; **delighted** adj: **delighted (at** or **with sth)** ravi(e) (de qch); **to be delighted to do sth/that** être enchanté(e) or ravi(e) de faire qch/que; **delightful** adj (person) adorable; (meal, evening) merveilleux(-euse)

delinquent [dɪ'lɪŋkwənt] adj, n délinquant(e)

deliver [dɪ'lɪvəʳ] vt (mail) distribuer; (goods) livrer; (message) remettre; (speech) prononcer; (Med: baby) mettre au monde; **delivery** n (of mail) distribution f; (of goods) livraison f; (of speaker) élocution f; (Med) accouchement m; **to take delivery of** prendre livraison de

delusion [dɪ'lu:ʒən] n illusion f

de luxe [də'lʌks] adj de luxe

delve [dɛlv] vi: **to ~ into** fouiller dans

demand [dɪ'mɑ:nd] vt réclamer, exiger ▷ n exigence f; (claim) revendication f; (Econ) demande f; **in ~** demandé(e), recherché(e); **on ~** sur demande; **demanding** adj (person) exigeant(e); (work) astreignant(e)

demise [dɪ'maɪz] n décès m

demo ['dɛməu] n abbr (inf) = **demonstration**; (protest) manif f; (Comput) démonstration f

democracy [dɪ'mɔkrəsɪ] n démocratie f; **democrat** ['dɛməkræt] n démocrate m/f; **democratic** [dɛmə'krætɪk] adj démocratique

demolish [dɪ'mɔlɪʃ] vt démolir

demolition [dɛmə'lɪʃən] n démolition f

demon ['di:mən] n démon m

demonstrate ['dɛmənstreɪt] vt démontrer, prouver; (show) faire une démonstration de ▷ vi: **to ~ (for/against)** manifester (en faveur de/contre); **demonstration** [dɛmən'streɪʃən] n démonstration f; (Pol etc) manifestation f; **demonstrator** n (Pol etc) manifestant(e)

demote [dɪ'məut] vt rétrograder

den [dɛn] n (of lion) tanière f; (room) repaire m

denial [dɪ'naɪəl] n (of accusation) démenti m; (of rights, guilt, truth) dénégation f

denim ['dɛnɪm] n jean m; **denims** npl (blue-)jeans mpl

Denmark ['dɛnmɑːk] n Danemark m

denomination [dɪnɔmɪ'neɪʃən] n (money) valeur f; (Rel) confession f

denounce [dɪ'nauns] vt dénoncer

dense [dɛns] adj dense; (inf: stupid) obtus(e)

density ['dɛnsɪtɪ] n densité f; **single-/double-~ disk** (Comput) disquette f (à) simple/double densité

dent [dɛnt] n bosse f ▷ vt (also: **make a ~ in**) cabosser

dental ['dɛntl] adj dentaire; **dental floss** [-flɔs] n fil m dentaire; **dental surgery** n cabinet m de dentiste

dentist ['dɛntɪst] n dentiste m/f

dentures ['dɛntʃəz] npl dentier msg

deny [dɪ'naɪ] vt nier; (refuse) refuser

deodorant [di:'əudərənt] n déodorant m

depart [dɪ'pɑːt] vi partir; **to ~ from** (fig: differ from) s'écarter de

department [dɪ'pɑːtmənt] n (Comm) rayon m; (Scol) section f; (Pol) ministère m, département m; **department store** n grand magasin

departure [dɪ'pɑːtʃəʳ] n départ m; (fig): **a new ~** une nouvelle voie; **departure lounge** n salle f de départ

depend [dɪ'pɛnd] vi: **to ~ (up)on** dépendre de; (rely on) compter sur; **it ~s** cela dépend; **~ing on the result ...** selon le résultat ...; **dependant** n personne f à charge; **dependent** adj: **to be dependent (on)** dépendre (de) ▷ n = **dependant**

depict [dɪ'pɪkt] vt (in picture) représenter; (in words) (dé)peindre, décrire

deport [dɪ'pɔːt] vt déporter, expulser

deposit [dɪ'pɔzɪt] n (Chem, Comm, Geo) dépôt m; (of ore, oil) gisement m; (part payment) arrhes fpl, acompte m; (on bottle etc) consigne f; (for hired goods etc) cautionnement m, garantie f ▷ vt déposer; **deposit account** n compte m sur livret

depot ['dɛpəu] n dépôt m; (US: Rail) gare f

depreciate [dɪ'pri:ʃɪeɪt] vi se déprécier, se dévaloriser

depress [dɪ'prɛs] vt déprimer; (press down) appuyer sur, abaisser; (wages etc) faire baisser; **depressed** adj (person) déprimé(e); (area) en déclin, touché(e) par le sous-emploi; **depressing** adj déprimant(e); **depression** [dɪ'prɛʃən] n dépression f

deprive [dɪ'praɪv] vt: **to ~ sb of** priver qn de; **deprived** adj déshérité(e)

dept. abbr (= department) dép, dépt

depth [dɛpθ] n profondeur f; **to be in the ~s of despair** être au plus profond du désespoir; **to be out of one's ~** (BRIT: swimmer) ne plus avoir pied; (fig) être dépassé(e), nager

deputy ['dɛpjutɪ] n (second in command) adjoint(e); (Pol) député m; (US: also: **~ sheriff**) shérif adjoint ▷ adj: **~ hea** (Scol) directeur(-trice) adjoint(e), sous-directeur(-trice)

derail [dɪ'reɪl] vt: **to be ~ed** dérailler

derelict ['dɛrɪlɪkt] adj abandonné(e), à l'abandon

derive [dɪ'raɪv] vt: **to ~ sth from** tirer qch de; trouver q[...] dans ▷ vi: **to ~ from** provenir de, dériver de

descend [dɪ'sɛnd] vt, vi descendre; **to ~ from** descendr[...] de, être issu(e) de; **to ~ to** s'abaisser à; **descendant** n descendant(e); **descent** n descente f; (origin) origine f

describe [dɪs'kraɪb] vt décrire; **description** [dɪs'krɪpʃən] n description f; (sort) sorte f, espèce f

desert n ['dɛzət] désert m ▷ vb [dɪ'zəːt] ▷ vt déserter, abandonner ▷ vi (Mil) déserter; **deserted** [dɪ'zəːtɪd] adj désert(e)

deserve [dɪ'zəːv] vt mériter

design [dɪ'zaɪn] n (sketch) plan m, dessin m; (layout, shape) conception f, ligne f; (pattern) dessin, motif(s) m(pl); (of dress, car) modèle m; (art) design m, stylisme m; (intention) dessein m ▷ vt dessiner; (plan) concevoir; **design and technology** n (BRIT: Scol) technologie f

designate ['dezigneit] désigner ▷ adj ['dezignit] désigné(e)

designer [di'zainə'] n (Archit, Art) dessinateur(-trice); (Industry) concepteur m, designer m; (Fashion) styliste m/f

desirable [di'zaiərəbl] adj (property, location, purchase) attrayant(e)

desire [di'zaiə'] n désir m ▷ vt désirer, vouloir

desk [dɛsk] n (in office) bureau m; (for pupil) pupitre m; (BRIT: in shop, restaurant) caisse f; (in hotel, at airport) réception f; **desk-top publishing** ['dɛsktɔp-] n publication assistée par ordinateur, PAO f

despair [dis'pɛə'] n désespoir m ▷ vi: **to ~ of** désespérer de

despatch [dis'pætʃ] n, vt = **dispatch**

desperate ['dɛspərit] adj désespéré(e); (fugitive) prêt(e) à tout; **to be ~ for sth/to do sth** avoir désespérément besoin de qch/de faire qch; **desperately** adv désespérément; (very) terriblement, extrêmement; **desperation** [dɛspə'reiʃən] n désespoir m; **in (sheer) desperation** en désespoir de cause

despise [dis'paiz] vt mépriser

despite [dis'pait] prep malgré, en dépit de

dessert [di'zɔ:t] n dessert m; **dessertspoon** n cuiller f à dessert

destination [dɛsti'neiʃən] n destination f

destined ['dɛstind] adj: **~ for London** à destination de Londres

destiny ['dɛstini] n destinée f, destin m

destroy [dis'trɔi] vt détruire; (injured horse) abattre; (dog) faire piquer

destruction [dis'trʌkʃən] n destruction f

destructive [dis'trʌktiv] adj destructeur(-trice)

detach [di'tætʃ] vt détacher; **detached** adj (attitude) détaché(e); **detached house** n pavillon m, maison(nette) (individuelle)

detail ['di:teil] n détail m ▷ vt raconter en détail, énumérer; **in ~** en détail; **detailed** adj détaillé(e)

detain [di'tein] vt retenir; (in captivity) détenir

detect [di'tɛkt] vt déceler, percevoir; (Med, Police) dépister; (Mil, Radar, Tech) détecter; **detection** [di'tɛkʃən] n découverte f; **detective** n policier m; **private detective** détective privé; **detective story** n roman policier

detention [di'tɛnʃən] n détention f; (Scol) retenue f, consigne f

deter [di'tɔ:'] vt dissuader

detergent [di'tɔ:dʒənt] n détersif m, détergent m

deteriorate [di'tiəriəreit] vi se détériorer, se dégrader

determination [ditɜ:mi'neiʃən] n détermination f

determine [di'tɜ:min] vt déterminer; **to ~ to do** résoudre de faire, se déterminer à faire; **determined** adj (person) déterminé(e), décidé(e); **determined to do** décidé à faire

deterrent [di'tɛrənt] n effet m de dissuasion; force f de dissuasion

detest [di'tɛst] vt détester, avoir horreur de

detour ['di:tuə'] n détour m; (us Aut: diversion) déviation f

detract [di'trækt] vt: **to ~ from** (quality, pleasure) diminuer; (reputation) porter atteinte à

detrimental [dɛtri'mɛntl] adj: **~ to** préjudiciable ou nuisible à

devastating ['dɛvəsteitiŋ] adj dévastateur(-trice); (news) accablant(e)

develop [di'vɛləp] vt (gen) développer; (disease) commencer à souffrir de; (resources) mettre en valeur, exploiter; (land) aménager ▷ vi se développer; (situation, disease: evolve) évoluer; (facts, symptoms: appear) se manifester, se produire; **can you ~ this film?** pouvez-vous développer cette pellicule?; **developing country** n pays m en voie de développement; **development** n développement m; (of land) exploitation f; (new fact, event) rebondissement m, fait(s) nouveau(x)

device [di'vais] n (apparatus) appareil m, dispositif m

devil ['dɛvl] n diable m; démon m

devious ['di:viəs] adj (person) sournois(e), dissimulé(e)

devise [di'vaiz] vt imaginer, concevoir

devote [di'vəut] vt: **to ~ sth to** consacrer qch à; **devoted** adj dévoué(e); **to be devoted to** être dévoué(e) or très attaché(e) à; (book etc) être consacré(e) à; **devotion** n dévouement m, attachement m; (Rel) dévotion f, piété f

devour [di'vauə'] vt dévorer

devout [di'vaut] adj pieux(-euse), dévot(e)

dew [dju:] n rosée f

diabetes [daiə'bi:ti:z] n diabète m

diabetic [daiə'bɛtik] n diabétique m/f ▷ adj (person) diabétique

diagnose [daiəg'nəuz] vt diagnostiquer

diagnosis (pl **diagnoses**) [daiəg'nəusis, -si:z] n diagnostic m

diagonal [dai'ægənl] adj diagonal(e) ▷ n diagonale f

diagram ['daiəgræm] n diagramme m, schéma m

dial ['daiəl] n cadran m ▷ vt (number) faire, composer

dialect ['daiəlɛkt] n dialecte m

dialling code ['daiəliŋ-] (us **dial code**) n indicatif m (téléphonique); **what's the ~ for Paris?** quel est l'indicatif de Paris?

dialling tone ['daiəliŋ-] (us **dial tone**) n tonalité f

dialogue (us **dialog**) ['daiəlɔg] n dialogue m

diameter [dai'æmitə'] n diamètre m

diamond ['daiəmənd] n diamant m; (shape) losange m; **diamonds** npl (Cards) carreau m

diaper ['daiəpə'] n (us) couche f

diarrhoea (us **diarrhea**) [daiə'ri:ə] n diarrhée f

diary ['daiəri] n (daily account) journal m; (book) agenda m

dice [dais] n (pl inv) dé m ▷ vt (Culin) couper en dés or en cubes

dictate [dik'teit] vt dicter; **dictation** [dik'teiʃən] n dictée f

dictator [dik'teitə'] n dictateur m

dictionary ['dikʃənri] n dictionnaire m

did [did] pt of **do**

didn't [didnt] = **did not**

die [dai] vi mourir; **to be dying for sth** avoir une envie folle de qch; **to be dying to do sth** mourir d'envie de faire qch; **die down** vi se calmer, s'apaiser; **die out** vi disparaître, s'éteindre

diesel ['di:zl] n (vehicle) diesel m; (also: ~ oil) carburant m diesel, gas-oil m

diet ['daiət] n alimentation f; (restricted food) régime m ▷ vi (also: **be on a ~**) suivre un régime

differ ['difə'] vi: **to ~ from sth** (be different) être différent(e) de qch, différer de qch; **to ~ from sb over sth** ne pas être d'accord avec qn au sujet de qch; **difference** n différence f; (quarrel) différend m, désaccord m; **different** adj différent(e); **differentiate** [dɪfə'renʃɪeɪt] vi: **to differentiate between** faire une différence entre; **differently** adv différemment

difficult ['dɪfɪkəlt] adj difficile; **difficulty** n difficulté f

dig [dɪg] vt (pt, pp **dug**) (hole) creuser; (garden) bêcher ▷ n (prod) coup m de coude; (fig: remark) coup de griffe or de patte; (Archaeology) fouille f; **to ~ one's nails into** enfoncer ses ongles dans; **dig up** vt déterrer

digest vt [daɪ'dʒɛst] digérer ▷ n ['daɪdʒɛst] sommaire m, résumé m; **digestion** [dɪ'dʒɛstʃən] n digestion f

digit ['dɪdʒɪt] n (number) chiffre m (de 0 à 9); (finger) doigt m; **digital** adj (system, recording, radio) numérique, digital(e); (watch) à affichage numérique or digital; **digital camera** n appareil m photo numérique; **digital TV** n télévision f numérique

dignified ['dɪgnɪfaɪd] adj digne

dignity ['dɪgnɪtɪ] n dignité f

digs [dɪgz] npl (BRIT inf) piaule f, chambre meublée

dilemma [daɪ'lɛmə] n dilemme m

dill [dɪl] n aneth m

dilute [daɪ'luːt] vt diluer

dim [dɪm] adj (light, eyesight) faible; (memory, outline) vague, indécis(e); (room) sombre; (inf: stupid) borné(e), obtus(e) ▷ vt (light) réduire, baisser; (US Aut) mettre en code, baisser

dime [daɪm] n (US) pièce f de 10 cents

dimension [daɪ'mɛnʃən] n dimension f

diminish [dɪ'mɪnɪʃ] vt, vi diminuer

din [dɪn] n vacarme m

dine [daɪn] vi dîner; **diner** n (person) dîneur(-euse); (US: eating place) petit restaurant

dinghy ['dɪŋgɪ] n youyou m; (inflatable) canot m pneumatique; (also: **sailing ~**) voilier m, dériveur m

dingy ['dɪndʒɪ] adj miteux(-euse), minable

dining car ['daɪnɪŋ-] n (BRIT) voiture-restaurant f, wagon-restaurant m

dining room ['daɪnɪŋ-] n salle f à manger

dining table [daɪnɪŋ-] n table f de (la) salle à manger

dinner ['dɪnər] n (evening meal) dîner m; (lunch) déjeuner m; (public) banquet m; **dinner jacket** n smoking m; **dinner party** n dîner m; **dinner time** n (evening) heure f du dîner; (midday) heure du déjeuner

dinosaur ['daɪnəsɔːr] n dinosaure m

dip [dɪp] n (slope) déclivité f; (in sea) baignade f, bain m; (Culin) ≈ sauce f ▷ vt tremper, plonger; (BRIT Aut: lights) mettre en code, baisser ▷ vi plonger

diploma [dɪ'pləumə] n diplôme m

diplomacy [dɪ'pləuməsɪ] n diplomatie f

diplomat ['dɪpləmæt] n diplomate m; **diplomatic** [dɪplə'mætɪk] adj diplomatique

dipstick ['dɪpstɪk] n (BRIT Aut) jauge f de niveau d'huile

dire [daɪər] adj (poverty) extrême; (awful) affreux(-euse)

direct [daɪ'rɛkt] adj direct(e) ▷ vt (tell way) diriger, orienter; (letter, remark) adresser; (Cine, TV) réaliser; (Theat) mettre en scène; (order): **to ~ sb to do sth** ordonner à qn de faire qch ▷ adv directement; **can you ~ me to ...?** pouvez-vous m'indiquer le chemin de ...?; **direct debit** n (BRIT Banking) prélèvement m automatique

direction [dɪ'rɛkʃən] n direction f; **directions** npl (to a place) indications fpl; **~s for use** mode m d'emploi; **sense of ~** sens m de l'orientation

directly [dɪ'rɛktlɪ] adv (in straight line) directement, tout

droit; (at once) tout de suite, immédiatement

director [dɪ'rɛktər] n directeur m; (Theat) metteur m en scène; (Cine, TV) réalisateur(-trice)

directory [dɪ'rɛktərɪ] n annuaire m; (Comput) répertoire m; **directory enquiries** (US **directory assistance**) n (Tel: service) renseignements mpl

dirt [dəːt] n saleté f; (mud) boue f; **dirty** adj sale; (joke) cochon(ne) ▷ vt salir

disability [dɪsə'bɪlɪtɪ] n invalidité f, infirmité f

disabled [dɪs'eɪbld] adj handicapé(e); (maimed) mutilé(e)

disadvantage [dɪsəd'vɑːntɪdʒ] n désavantage m, inconvénient m

disagree [dɪsə'griː] vi (differ) ne pas concorder; (be against, think otherwise): **to ~ (with)** ne pas être d'accord (avec); **disagreeable** adj désagréable; **disagreement** n désaccord m, différend m

disappear [dɪsə'pɪər] vi disparaître; **disappearance** n disparition f

disappoint [dɪsə'pɔɪnt] vt décevoir; **disappointed** adj déçu(e); **disappointing** adj décevant(e); **disappointment** n déception f

disapproval [dɪsə'pruːvəl] n désapprobation f

disapprove [dɪsə'pruːv] vi: **to ~ of** désapprouver

disarm [dɪs'ɑːm] vt désarmer; **disarmament** [dɪs'ɑːməmənt] n désarmement m

disaster [dɪ'zɑːstər] n catastrophe f, désastre m; **disastrous** adj désastreux(-euse)

disbelief ['dɪsbə'liːf] n incrédulité f

disc [dɪsk] n disque m; (Comput) = **disk**

discard [dɪs'kɑːd] vt (old things) se débarrasser de; (fig) écarter, renoncer à

discharge vt [dɪs'tʃɑːdʒ] (duties) s'acquitter de; (waste etc) déverser; décharger; (patient) renvoyer (chez lui); (employee, soldier) congédier, licencier ▷ n ['dɪstʃɑːdʒ] (Elec, Med) émission f; (dismissal) renvoi m; licenciement m

discipline ['dɪsɪplɪn] n discipline f ▷ vt discipliner; (punish) punir

disc jockey n disque-jockey m (DJ)

disclose [dɪs'kləuz] vt révéler, divulguer

disco ['dɪskəu] n abbr discothèque f

discoloured [dɪs'kʌləd] (US **discolored**) adj décoloré(e), jauni(e)

discomfort [dɪs'kʌmfət] n malaise m, gêne f; (lack of comfort) manque m de confort

disconnect [dɪskə'nɛkt] vt (Elec, Radio) débrancher; (gas, water) couper

discontent [dɪskən'tɛnt] n mécontentement m

discontinue [dɪskən'tɪnjuː] vt cesser, interrompre; **"~d"** (Comm) "fin de série"

discount n ['dɪskaunt] remise f, rabais m ▷ vt [dɪs'kaunt] (report etc) ne pas tenir compte de

discourage [dɪs'kʌrɪdʒ] vt décourager

discover [dɪs'kʌvər] vt découvrir; **discovery** n découverte f

discredit [dɪs'krɛdɪt] vt (idea) mettre en doute; (person) discréditer

discreet [dɪ'skriːt] adj discret(-ète)

discrepancy [dɪ'skrɛpənsɪ] n divergence f, contradiction f

discretion [dɪ'skrɛʃən] n discrétion f; **at the ~ of** à la discrétion de

discriminate [dɪ'skrɪmɪneɪt] vi: **to ~ between**

tablir une distinction entre, faire la différence entre;
to ~ against pratiquer une discrimination contre;
discrimination [dɪskrɪmɪˈneɪʃən] n discrimination f;
(judgment) discernement m

discuss [dɪsˈkʌs] vt discuter de; (debate) discuter;
discussion [dɪsˈkʌʃən] n discussion f

disease [dɪˈziːz] n maladie f

disembark [dɪsɪmˈbɑːk] vt, vi débarquer

disgrace [dɪsˈɡreɪs] n honte f; (disfavour) disgrâce
▷ vt déshonorer, couvrir de honte; **disgraceful** adj
candaleux(-euse), honteux(-euse)

disgruntled [dɪsˈɡrʌntld] adj mécontent(e)

disguise [dɪsˈɡaɪz] n déguisement m ▷ vt déguiser; **in
~** déguisé(e)

disgust [dɪsˈɡʌst] n dégoût m, aversion f ▷ vt dégoûter,
écœurer

disgusted [dɪsˈɡʌstɪd] adj dégoûté(e), écœuré(e)

disgusting [dɪsˈɡʌstɪŋ] adj dégoûtant(e)

dish [dɪʃ] n plat m; **to do** or **wash the ~es** faire la
vaisselle; **dishcloth** n (for drying) torchon m; (for washing)
lavette f

dishonest [dɪsˈɒnɪst] adj malhonnête

dishtowel [ˈdɪʃtauəl] n (us) torchon m (à vaisselle)

dishwasher [ˈdɪʃwɔʃəʳ] n lave-vaisselle m

disillusion [dɪsɪˈluːʒən] vt désabuser, désenchanter

disinfectant [dɪsɪnˈfɛktənt] n désinfectant m

disintegrate [dɪsˈɪntɪɡreɪt] vi se désintégrer

disk [dɪsk] n (Comput) disquette f; **single-/double-sided
~** disquette une face/double face; **disk drive** n lecteur m
de disquette; **diskette** n (Comput) disquette f

dislike [dɪsˈlaɪk] n aversion f, antipathie f ▷ vt ne pas
aimer

dislocate [ˈdɪsləkeɪt] vt disloquer, déboîter

disloyal [dɪsˈlɔɪəl] adj déloyal(e)

dismal [ˈdɪzml] adj (gloomy) lugubre, maussade; (very
bad) lamentable

dismantle [dɪsˈmæntl] vt démonter

dismay [dɪsˈmeɪ] n consternation f ▷ vt consterner

dismiss [dɪsˈmɪs] vt congédier, renvoyer; (idea) écarter;
(Law) rejeter; **dismissal** n renvoi m

disobedient [dɪsəˈbiːdɪənt] adj désobéissant(e),
indiscipliné(e)

disobey [dɪsəˈbeɪ] vt désobéir à

disorder [dɪsˈɔːdəʳ] n désordre m; (rioting) désordres mpl;
(Med) troubles mpl

disorganized [dɪsˈɔːɡənaɪzd] adj désorganisé(e)

disown [dɪsˈəun] vt renier

dispatch [dɪsˈpætʃ] vt expédier, envoyer ▷ n envoi m,
expédition f; (Mil, Press) dépêche f

dispel [dɪsˈpɛl] vt dissiper, chasser

dispense [dɪsˈpɛns] vt (medicine) préparer (et vendre);
dispense with vt fus se passer de; **dispenser** n (device)
distributeur m

disperse [dɪsˈpəːs] vt disperser ▷ vi se disperser

display [dɪsˈpleɪ] n (of goods) étalage m; affichage m;
(Comput: information) visualisation f; (: device) visuel m;
(of feeling) manifestation f ▷ vt montrer; (goods) mettre à
l'étalage, exposer; (results, departure times) afficher; (pej)
faire étalage de

displease [dɪsˈpliːz] vt mécontenter, contrarier

disposable [dɪsˈpəuzəbl] adj (pack etc) jetable; (income)
disponible

disposal [dɪsˈpəuzl] n (of rubbish) évacuation f,
destruction f; (of property etc: by selling) vente f; (: by giving

away) cession f; **at one's ~** à sa disposition

dispose [dɪsˈpəuz] vi: **to ~ of** (unwanted goods) se
débarrasser de, se défaire de; (problem) expédier;
disposition [dɪspəˈzɪʃən] n disposition f; (temperament)
naturel m

disproportionate [dɪsprəˈpɔːʃənət] adj
disproportionné(e)

dispute [dɪsˈpjuːt] n discussion f; (also: **industrial ~**)
conflit m ▷ vt (question) contester; (matter) discuter

disqualify [dɪsˈkwɔlɪfaɪ] vt (Sport) disqualifier; **to ~ sb
for sth/from doing** rendre qn inapte à qch/à faire

disregard [dɪsrɪˈɡɑːd] vt ne pas tenir compte de

disrupt [dɪsˈrʌpt] vt (plans, meeting, lesson) perturber,
déranger; **disruption** [dɪsˈrʌpʃən] n perturbation f,
dérangement m

dissatisfaction [dɪssætɪsˈfækʃən] n mécontentement
m, insatisfaction f

dissatisfied [dɪsˈsætɪsfaɪd] adj: **~ (with)** insatisfait(e)
(de)

dissect [dɪˈsɛkt] vt disséquer

dissent [dɪˈsɛnt] n dissentiment m, différence f d'opinion

dissertation [dɪsəˈteɪʃən] n (Scol) mémoire m

dissolve [dɪˈzɔlv] vt dissoudre ▷ vi se dissoudre, fondre;
to ~ in(to) tears fondre en larmes

distance [ˈdɪstns] n distance f; **in the ~** au loin

distant [ˈdɪstnt] adj lointain(e), éloigné(e); (manner)
distant(e), froid(e)

distil (us **distill**) [dɪsˈtɪl] vt distiller; **distillery** n
distillerie f

distinct [dɪsˈtɪŋkt] adj distinct(e); (clear) marqué(e);
as ~ from par opposition à; **distinction** [dɪsˈtɪŋkʃən] n
distinction f; (in exam) mention f très bien; **distinctive**
adj distinctif(-ive)

distinguish [dɪsˈtɪŋɡwɪʃ] vt distinguer; **to ~ o.s.**
se distinguer; **distinguished** adj (eminent, refined)
distingué(e)

distort [dɪsˈtɔːt] vt déformer

distract [dɪsˈtrækt] vt distraire, déranger; **distracted**
adj (not concentrating) distrait(e); (worried) affolé(e);
distraction [dɪsˈtrækʃən] n distraction f

distraught [dɪsˈtrɔːt] adj éperdu(e)

distress [dɪsˈtrɛs] n détresse f ▷ vt affliger; **distressing**
adj douloureux(-euse), pénible

distribute [dɪsˈtrɪbjuːt] vt distribuer; **distribution**
[dɪstrɪˈbjuːʃən] n distribution f; **distributor** n (gen: Tech)
distributeur m; (Comm) concessionnaire m/f

district [ˈdɪstrɪkt] n (of country) région f; (of town)
quartier m; (Admin) district m; **district attorney** n (us)
≈ procureur m de la République

distrust [dɪsˈtrʌst] n méfiance f, doute m ▷ vt se
méfier de

disturb [dɪsˈtəːb] vt troubler; (inconvenience) déranger;
disturbance n dérangement m; (political etc)
troubles mpl; **disturbed** adj (worried, upset) agité(e),
troublé(e); **to be emotionally disturbed** avoir des
problèmes affectifs; **disturbing** adj troublant(e),
inquiétant(e)

ditch [dɪtʃ] n fossé m; (for irrigation) rigole f ▷ vt (inf)
abandonner; (person) plaquer

ditto [ˈdɪtəu] adv idem

dive [daɪv] n plongeon m; (of submarine) plongée f ▷ vi
plonger; **to ~ into** (bag etc) plonger la main dans; (place)
se précipiter dans; **diver** n plongeur m

diverse [daɪˈvəːs] adj divers(e)

diversion [daɪˈvəːʃən] n (BRIT Aut) déviation f; (distraction, Mil) diversion f

diversity [daɪˈvəːsɪtɪ] n diversité f, variété f

divert [daɪˈvəːt] vt (BRIT: traffic) dévier; (plane) dérouter; (train, river) détourner

divide [dɪˈvaɪd] vt diviser; (separate) séparer ▷ vi se diviser; **divided highway** (US) n route f à quatre voies

divine [dɪˈvaɪn] adj divin(e)

diving ['daɪvɪŋ] n plongée (sous-marine); **diving board** n plongeoir m

division [dɪˈvɪʒən] n division f; (separation) séparation f; (Comm) service m

divorce [dɪˈvɔːs] n divorce m ▷ vt divorcer d'avec; **divorced** adj divorcé(e); **divorcee** [dɪvɔːˈsiː] n divorcé(e)

D.I.Y. adj, n abbr (BRIT) = **do-it-yourself**

dizzy ['dɪzɪ] adj: **I feel ~** la tête me tourne, j'ai la tête qui tourne

DJ n abbr = **disc jockey**

DNA n abbr (= deoxyribonucleic acid) ADN m

KEYWORD

do [duː] (pt did, pp done) n (inf: party etc) soirée f, fête f ▷ vb **1** (in negative constructions) non traduit; **I don't understand** je ne comprends pas

2 (to form questions) non traduit; **didn't you know?** vous ne le saviez pas?; **what do you think?** qu'en pensez-vous?

3 (for emphasis, in polite expressions): **people do make mistakes sometimes** on peut toujours se tromper; **she does seem rather late** je trouve qu'elle est bien en retard; **do sit down/help yourself** asseyez-vous/servez-vous je vous en prie; **do take care!** faites bien attention à vous!

4 (used to avoid repeating vb): **she swims better than I do** elle nage mieux que moi; **do you agree? - yes, I do/no I don't** vous êtes d'accord? - oui/non; **she lives in Glasgow - so do I** elle habite Glasgow - moi aussi; **she didn't like it and neither did I** il n'a pas aimé ça, et nous non plus; **who broke it? - I did** qui l'a cassé? - c'est moi; **he asked me to help him and I did** il m'a demandé de l'aider, et c'est ce que j'ai fait

5 (in question tags): **you like him, don't you?** vous l'aimez bien, n'est-ce pas?; **I don't know him, do I?** je ne crois pas le connaître

▷ vt **1** (gen: carry out, perform etc) faire; (visit: city, museum) faire, visiter; **what are you doing tonight?** qu'est-ce que vous faites ce soir?; **what do you do?** (job) que faites-vous dans la vie?; **what can I do for you?** que puis-je faire pour vous?; **to do the cooking/washing-up** faire la cuisine/la vaisselle; **to do one's teeth/hair/nails** se brosser les dents/se coiffer/se faire les ongles

2 (Aut etc: distance) faire; (: speed) faire du; **we've done 200 km already** nous avons déjà fait 200 km; **the car was doing 100** la voiture faisait du 100 (à l'heure); **he can do 100 in that car** il peut faire du 100 (à l'heure) dans cette voiture-là

▷ vi **1** (act, behave) faire; **do as I do** faites comme moi

2 (get on, fare) marcher; **the firm is doing well** l'entreprise marche bien; **he's doing well/badly at school** ça marche bien/mal pour lui à l'école; **how do you do?** comment allez-vous?; (on being introduced) enchanté(e)!

3 (suit) aller; **will it do?** est-ce que ça ira?

4 (be sufficient) suffire, aller; **will £10 do?** est-ce que 10 livres suffiront?; **that'll do** ça suffit, ça ira; **that'll do!** (in annoyance) ça va or suffit comme ça!; **to make do (with)** se contenter (de)

do up vt (laces, dress) attacher; (buttons) boutonner; (zip) fermer; (renovate: room) refaire; (: house) remettre à neu

do with vt fus (need): **I could do with a drink/some help** quelque chose à boire/un peu d'aide ne serait pas de refus; **it could do with a wash** ça ne lui ferait pas de mal d'être lavé; (be connected with): **that has nothing to do with you** cela ne vous concerne pas; **I won't have anything to do with it** je ne veux pas m'en mêler

do without vi s'en passer; **if you're late for tea then you'll do without** si vous êtes en retard pour le dîner il faudra vous en passer

▷ vt fus se passer de; **I can do without a car** je peux me passer de voiture

dock [dɔk] n dock m; (wharf) quai m; (Law) banc m des accusés ▷ vi se mettre à quai; (Space) s'arrimer; **docks** npl (Naut) docks

doctor ['dɔktə'] n médecin m, docteur m; (PhD etc) docteur ▷ vt (drink) frelater; **call a ~!** appelez un docteu or un médecin!; **Doctor of Philosophy (PhD)** n (degree) doctorat m; (person) titulaire m/f d'un doctorat

document ['dɔkjumənt] n document m; **documentary** [dɔkjuˈmɛntərɪ] adj, n documentaire (m); **documentation** [dɔkjumənˈteɪʃən] n documentation f

dodge [dɔdʒ] n truc m; combine f ▷ vt esquiver, éviter

dodgy ['dɔdʒɪ] adj (inf: uncertain) douteux(-euse); (: shady) louche

does [dʌz] vb see **do**

doesn't ['dʌznt] = **does not**

dog [dɔg] n chien(ne) ▷ vt (follow closely) suivre de près; (fig: memory etc) poursuivre, harceler; **doggy bag** ['dɔgɪ n petit sac pour emporter les restes

do-it-yourself ['duːɪtjɔːˈsɛlf] n bricolage m

dole [dəul] n (BRIT: payment) allocation f de chômage; **on the ~** au chômage

doll [dɔl] n poupée f

dollar ['dɔlə'] n dollar m

dolphin ['dɔlfɪn] n dauphin m

dome [dəum] n dôme m

domestic [dəˈmɛstɪk] adj (duty, happiness) familial(e); (policy, affairs, flight) intérieur(e); (animal) domestique; **domestic appliance** n appareil ménager

dominant ['dɔmɪnənt] adj dominant(e)

dominate ['dɔmɪneɪt] vt dominer

domino ['dɔmɪnəu] (pl **-es**) n domino m; **dominoes** n (game) dominos mpl

donate [dəˈneɪt] vt faire don de, donner; **donation** [dəˈneɪʃən] n donation f, don m

done [dʌn] pp of **do**

donkey ['dɔŋkɪ] n âne m

donor ['dəunə'] n (of blood etc) donneur(-euse); (to charity) donateur(-trice); **donor card** n carte f de don d'organes

don't [dəunt] = **do not**

donut ['dəunʌt] (US) n = **doughnut**

doodle ['duːdl] vi griffonner, gribouiller

doom [duːm] n (fate) destin m ▷ vt: **to be ~ed to failure** être voué(e) à l'échec

door [dɔːʳ] n porte f; (Rail, car) portière f; **doorbell** n sonnette f; **door handle** n poignée f de porte; (of car) poignée de portière; **doorknob** n poignée f or bouton m de porte; **doorstep** n pas m de (la) porte, seuil m; **doorway** n (embrasure f de) porte f

dope [dəʊp] n (inf: drug) drogue f; (: person) andouille f ▷ vt (horse etc) doper

dormitory ['dɔːmɪtrɪ] n (BRIT) dortoir m; (US: hall of residence) résidence f universitaire

DOS [dɔs] n abbr (= disk operating system) DOS m

dosage ['dəʊsɪdʒ] n dose f; dosage m; (on label) posologie f

dose [dəʊs] n dose f

dot [dɔt] n point m; (on material) pois m ▷ vt: **~ted with** parsemé(e) de; **on the ~** à l'heure tapante; **dotcom** [dɔt'kɔm] n point com m, pointcom m; **dotted line** ['dɔtɪd-] n ligne pointillée; **to sign on the dotted line** signer à l'endroit indiqué or sur la ligne pointillée

double ['dʌbl] adj double ▷ adv (twice): **to cost ~ (sth)** coûter le double (de qch) or deux fois plus (que qch) ▷ n double m; (Cine) doublure f ▷ vt doubler; (fold) plier en deux ▷ vi doubler; **on the ~, at the ~** au pas de course; **double back** vi (person) revenir sur ses pas; **double bass** n contrebasse f; **double bed** n grand lit; **double-check** vt, vi revérifier; **double-click** vi (Comput) double-cliquer; **double-cross** vt doubler, trahir; **doubledecker** n autobus m à impériale; **double glazing** n (BRIT) double vitrage m; **double room** n chambre f pour deux; **doubles** n (Tennis) double m; **double yellow lines** npl (BRIT: Aut) double bande jaune marquant l'interdiction de stationner

doubt [daʊt] n doute m ▷ vt douter de; (suspect) douter; **no ~** sans doute; **to ~ that** douter que + sub; **doubtful** adj douteux(-euse); (person) incertain(e); **doubtless** adv sans doute, sûrement

dough [dəʊ] n pâte f; **doughnut** (US **donut**) n beignet m

dove [dʌv] n colombe f

Dover ['dəʊvəʳ] n Douvres

down [daʊn] n (fluff) duvet m ▷ adv en bas, vers le bas; (on the ground) par terre ▷ prep en bas de; (along) le long de ▷ vt (inf: drink) siffler; **to walk ~ a hill** descendre une colline; **to run ~ the street** descendre la rue en courant; **~ with X!** à bas X!; **down-and-out** n (tramp) clochard(e); **downfall** n chute f; ruine f; **downhill** adv: **to go downhill** descendre; (business) péricliter

Downing Street ['daʊnɪŋ-] n (BRIT): **10 ~** résidence du Premier ministre

down: **download** vt (Comput) télécharger; **downright** adj (lie etc) effronté(e); (refusal) catégorique

Down's syndrome [daʊnz-] n trisomie f

down: **downstairs** adv (on or to ground floor) au rez-de-chaussée; (on or to floor below) à l'étage inférieur; **down-to-earth** adj terre à terre inv; **downtown** adv en ville; **down under** adv en Australie or Nouvelle Zélande; **downward** ['daʊnwəd] adj, adv vers le bas; **downwards** ['daʊnwədz] adv vers le bas

doz. abbr = **dozen**

doze [dəʊz] vi sommeiller

dozen ['dʌzn] n douzaine f; **a ~ books** une douzaine de livres; **~s of** des centaines de

Dr. abbr (= doctor) Dr; (in street names) = **drive**

drab [dræb] adj terne, morne

draft [drɑːft] n (of letter, school work) brouillon m; (of literary work) ébauche f; (Comm) traite f; (US: call-up)

conscription f ▷ vt faire le brouillon de; (Mil: send) détacher; see also **draught**

drag [dræg] vt traîner; (river) draguer ▷ vi traîner ▷ n (inf) casse-pieds m/f; (women's clothing): **in ~** (en) travesti; **to ~ and drop** (Comput) glisser-poser

dragon ['drægn] n dragon m

dragonfly ['drægənflaɪ] n libellule f

drain [dreɪn] n égout m; (on resources) saignée f ▷ vt (land, marshes) drainer, assécher; (vegetables) égoutter; (reservoir etc) vider ▷ vi (water) s'écouler; **drainage** n (system) système m d'égouts; (act) drainage m; **drainpipe** n tuyau m d'écoulement

drama ['drɑːmə] n (art) théâtre m, art m dramatique; (play) pièce f; (event) drame m; **dramatic** [drə'mætɪk] adj (impressive) spectaculaire

drank [dræŋk] pt of **drink**

drape [dreɪp] vt draper; **drapes** npl (US) rideaux mpl

drastic ['dræstɪk] adj (measures) d'urgence, énergique; (change) radical(e)

draught (US **draft**) [drɑːft] n courant m d'air; **on ~** (beer) à la pression; **draught beer** n bière f (à la) pression; **draughts** n (BRIT: game) (jeu m de) dames fpl

draw [drɔː] (vb: pt **drew**, pp **~n**) vt tirer; (picture) dessiner; (attract) attirer; (line, circle) tracer; (money) retirer; (wages) toucher ▷ vi (Sport) faire match nul ▷ n match nul; **draw out** vi (lengthen) s'allonger ▷ vt (money) retirer; **draw up** vi (stop) s'arrêter ▷ vt (document) établir, dresser; (plan) formuler, dessiner; (chair) approcher; **drawback** n inconvénient m, désavantage m

drawer [drɔːʳ] n tiroir m

drawing ['drɔːɪŋ] n dessin m; **drawing pin** n (BRIT) punaise f; **drawing room** n salon m

drawn [drɔːn] pp of **draw**

dread [drɛd] n épouvante f, effroi m ▷ vt redouter, appréhender; **dreadful** adj épouvantable, affreux(-euse)

dream [driːm] n rêve m ▷ vt, vi (pt, pp **~ed** or **~t**) rêver; **dreamer** n rêveur(-euse)

dreamt [drɛmt] pt, pp of **dream**

dreary ['drɪərɪ] adj triste; monotone

drench [drɛntʃ] vt tremper

dress [drɛs] n robe f; (clothing) habillement m, tenue f ▷ vt habiller; (wound) panser ▷ vi: **to get ~ed** s'habiller; **dress up** vi s'habiller; (in fancy dress) se déguiser; **dress circle** n (BRIT) premier balcon; **dresser** n (furniture) vaisselier m; (: US) coiffeuse f, commode f; **dressing** n (Med) pansement m; (Culin) sauce f, assaisonnement m; **dressing gown** n (BRIT) robe f de chambre; **dressing room** n (Theat) loge f; (Sport) vestiaire m; **dressing table** n coiffeuse f; **dressmaker** n couturière f

drew [druː] pt of **draw**

dribble ['drɪbl] vi (baby) baver ▷ vt (ball) dribbler

dried [draɪd] adj (fruit, beans) sec (sèche); (eggs, milk) en poudre

drier ['draɪəʳ] n = **dryer**

drift [drɪft] n (of current etc) force f, direction f; (of snow) rafale f; coulée f; (: on ground) congère f; (general meaning) sens général ▷ vi (boat) aller à la dérive, dériver; (sand, snow) s'amonceler, s'entasser

drill [drɪl] n perceuse f; (bit) foret m; (of dentist) roulette f, fraise f; (Mil) exercice m ▷ vt percer; (troops) entraîner ▷ vi (for oil) faire un or des forage(s)

drink [drɪŋk] n boisson f; (alcoholic) verre m ▷ vt, vi (of

drank, *pp* **drunk**) boire; **to have a ~** boire quelque chose, boire un verre; **a ~ of water** un verre d'eau; **would you like a ~?** tu veux boire quelque chose?; **drink-driving** *n* conduite *f* en état d'ivresse; **drinker** *n* buveur(-euse); **drinking water** *n* eau *f* potable

drip [drɪp] *n* (*drop*) goutte *f*; (*Med: device*) goutte-à-goutte *m inv*; (*: liquid*) perfusion *f* ▷ *vi* tomber goutte à goutte; (*tap*) goutter

drive [draɪv] *n* promenade *f* or trajet *m* en voiture; (*also:* **~way**) allée *f*; (*energy*) dynamisme *m*, énergie *f*; (*push*) effort (concerté); campagne *f*; (*Comput: also:* **disk ~**) lecteur *m* de disquette ▷ *vb* (*pt* **drove**, *pp* **~n**) ▷ *vt* conduire; (*nail*) enfoncer; (*push*) chasser, pousser; (*Tech: motor*) actionner; entraîner ▷ *vi* (*be at the wheel*) conduire; (*travel by car*) aller en voiture; **left-/right-hand ~** (*Aut*) conduite *f* à gauche/droite; **to ~ sb mad** rendre qn fou (folle); **drive-in** *adj*, *n* (*esp us*) drive-in *m*

driven ['drɪvn] *pp of* **drive**

driver ['draɪvə'] *n* conducteur(-trice); (*of taxi, bus*) chauffeur *m*; **driver's license** *n* (*us*) permis *m* de conduire

driveway ['draɪvweɪ] *n* allée *f*

driving ['draɪvɪŋ] *n* conduite *f*; **driving instructor** *n* moniteur *m* d'auto-école; **driving lesson** *n* leçon *f* de conduite; **driving licence** *n* (*BRIT*) permis *m* de conduire; **driving test** *n* examen *m* du permis de conduire

drizzle ['drɪzl] *n* bruine *f*, crachin *m*

droop [druːp] *vi* (*flower*) commencer à se faner; (*shoulders, head*) tomber

drop [drɔp] *n* (*of liquid*) goutte *f*; (*fall*) baisse *f*; (*also:* **parachute ~**) saut *m* ▷ *vt* laisser tomber; (*voice, eyes, price*) baisser; (*passenger*) déposer ▷ *vi* tomber; **drop in** *vi* (*inf: visit*): **to ~ in (on)** faire un saut (chez), passer (chez); **drop off** *vi* (*sleep*) s'assoupir ▷ *vt* (*passenger*) déposer; **drop out** *vi* (*withdraw*) se retirer; (*student etc*) abandonner, décrocher

drought [draut] *n* sécheresse *f*

drove [drəuv] *pt of* **drive**

drown [draun] *vt* noyer ▷ *vi* se noyer

drowsy ['drauzɪ] *adj* somnolent(e)

drug [drʌg] *n* médicament *m*; (*narcotic*) drogue *f* ▷ *vt* droguer; **to be on ~s** se droguer; **drug addict** *n* toxicomane *m/f*; **drug dealer** *n* revendeur(-euse) de drogue; **druggist** *n* (*us*) pharmacien(ne)-droguiste; **drugstore** *n* (*us*) pharmacie-droguerie *f*, drugstore *m*

drum [drʌm] *n* tambour *m*; (*for oil, petrol*) bidon *m*; **drums** *npl* (*Mus*) batterie *f*; **drummer** *n* (joueur *m* de) tambour *m*

drunk [drʌŋk] *pp of* **drink** ▷ *adj* ivre, soûl(e) ▷ *n* (*also:* **~ard**) ivrogne *m/f*; **to get ~** se soûler; **drunken** *adj* ivre, soûl(e); (*rage, stupor*) ivrogne, d'ivrogne

dry [draɪ] *adj* sec (sèche); (*day*) sans pluie ▷ *vt* sécher; (*clothes*) faire sécher ▷ *vi* sécher; **dry off** *vi*, *vt* sécher; **dry up** *vi* (*river, supplies*) se tarir; **dry-cleaner's** *n* teinturerie *f*; **dry-cleaning** *n* (*process*) nettoyage *m* à sec; **dryer** *n* (*tumble-dryer*) sèche-linge *m inv*; (*for hair*) sèche-cheveux *m inv*

DSS *n abbr* (*BRIT*) = **Department of Social Security**

DTP *n abbr* (= *desktop publishing*) PAO *f*

dual ['djuəl] *adj* double; **dual carriageway** *n* (*BRIT*) route *f* à quatre voies

dubious ['djuːbɪəs] *adj* hésitant(e), incertain(e); (*reputation, company*) douteux(-euse)

duck [dʌk] *n* canard *m* ▷ *vi* se baisser vivement, baisser subitement la tête

due [djuː] *adj* (*money, payment*) dû (due); (*expected*) attendu(e); (*fitting*) qui convient ▷ *adv*: **~ north** droit vers le nord; **~ to** (*because of*) en raison de; (*caused by*) dû à; **the train is ~ at 8 a.m.** le train est attendu à 8 h; **she is ~ back tomorrow** elle doit rentrer demain; **he is ~ £10** on lui doit 10 livres; **to give sb his** *or* **her ~** être juste envers qn

duel ['djuəl] *n* duel *m*

duet [djuː'ɛt] *n* duo *m*

dug [dʌg] *pt*, *pp of* **dig**

duke [djuːk] *n* duc *m*

dull [dʌl] *adj* (*boring*) ennuyeux(-euse); (*not bright*) morne, terne; (*sound, pain*) sourd(e); (*weather, day*) gris(e), maussade ▷ *vt* (*pain, grief*) atténuer; (*mind, senses*) engourdir

dumb [dʌm] *adj* muet(te); (*stupid*) bête

dummy ['dʌmɪ] *n* (*tailor's model*) mannequin *m*; (*mock-up*) factice *m*, maquette *f*; (*BRIT: for baby*) tétine *f* ▷ *adj* faux (fausse), factice

dump [dʌmp] *n* (*also:* **rubbish ~**) décharge (publique); (*inf: place*) trou *m* ▷ *vt* (*put down*) déposer; déverser; (*get rid of*) se débarrasser de; (*Comput*) lister

dumpling ['dʌmplɪŋ] *n* boulette *f* (de pâte)

dune [djuːn] *n* dune *f*

dungarees [dʌŋgə'riːz] *npl* bleu(s) *m*(*pl*); (*for child, woman*) salopette *f*

dungeon ['dʌndʒən] *n* cachot *m*

duplex ['djuːplɛks] *n* (*us: also:* **~ apartment**) duplex *m*

duplicate *n* ['djuːplɪkət] double *m* ▷ *vt* ['djuːplɪkeɪt] faire un double de; (*on machine*) polycopier; **in ~** en deux exemplaires, en double

durable ['djuərəbl] *adj* durable; (*clothes, metal*) résistant(e), solide

duration [djuə'reɪʃən] *n* durée *f*

during ['djuərɪŋ] *prep* pendant, au cours de

dusk [dʌsk] *n* crépuscule *m*

dust [dʌst] *n* poussière *f* ▷ *vt* (*furniture*) essuyer, épousseter; (*cake etc*): **to ~ with** saupoudrer de; **dustbin** *n* (*BRIT*) poubelle *f*; **duster** *n* chiffon *m*; **dustman** *n* (*BRIT: irreg*) boueux *m*, éboueur *m*; **dustpan** *n* pelle *f* à poussière; **dusty** *adj* poussiéreux(-euse)

Dutch [dʌtʃ] *adj* hollandais(e), néerlandais(e) ▷ *n* (*Ling*) hollandais *m*, néerlandais *m* ▷ *adv*: **to go ~** *or* **dutch** (*inf*) partager les frais; **the Dutch** *npl* les Hollandais, les Néerlandais; **Dutchman** (*irreg*) *n* Hollandais *m*; **Dutchwoman** (*irreg*) *n* Hollandaise *f*

duty ['djuːtɪ] *n* devoir *m*; (*tax*) droit *m*, taxe *f*; **on ~** de service; (*at night etc*) de garde; **off ~** libre, pas de service or de garde; **duty-free** *adj* exempté(e) de douane, hors-taxe

duvet ['duːveɪ] *n* (*BRIT*) couette *f*

DVD *n abbr* (= *digital versatile or video disc*) DVD *m*; **DVD burner** *n* graveur *m* de DVD; **DVD player** *n* lecteur *m* de DVD; **DVD writer** *n* graveur *m* de DVD

dwarf (*pl* **dwarves**) [dwɔːf, dwɔːvz] *n* nain(e) ▷ *vt* écraser

dwell (*pt*, *pp* **dwelt**) [dwɛl, dwɛlt] *vi* demeurer; **dwell on** *vt fus* s'étendre sur

dwelt [dwɛlt] *pt*, *pp of* **dwell**

dwindle ['dwɪndl] *vi* diminuer, décroître

dye [daɪ] *n* teinture *f* ▷ *vt* teindre

dying ['daɪɪŋ] *adj* mourant(e), agonisant(e)

dynamic [daɪˈnæmɪk] *adj* dynamique
dynamite [ˈdaɪnəmaɪt] *n* dynamite *f*
dyslexia [dɪsˈlɛksɪə] *n* dyslexie *f*
dyslexic [dɪsˈlɛksɪk] *adj, n* dyslexique *m/f*

e

E [iː] *n* (*Mus*): **E** mi *m*
E111 *n abbr* (= *form E111*) formulaire *m* E111
each [iːtʃ] *adj* chaque ▷ *pron* chacun(e); **~ other**
l'un l'autre; **they hate ~ other** ils se détestent
(mutuellement); **they have 2 books ~** ils ont 2 livres
chacun; **they cost £5 ~** ils coûtent 5 livres (la) pièce
eager [ˈiːgər] *adj* (*person, buyer*) empressé(e); (*keen: pupil,
worker*) enthousiaste; **to be ~ to do sth** (*impatient*)
brûler de faire qch; (*keen*) désirer vivement faire qch; **to
be ~ for** (*event*) désirer vivement; (*vengeance, affection,
information*) être avide de
eagle [ˈiːgl] *n* aigle *m*
ear [ɪər] *n* oreille *f*; (*of corn*) épi *m*; **earache** *n* mal *m* aux
oreilles; **eardrum** *n* tympan *m*
earl [əːl] *n* comte *m*
earlier [ˈəːlɪər] *adj* (*date etc*) plus rapproché(e); (*edition
etc*) plus ancien(ne), antérieur(e) ▷ *adv* plus tôt
early [ˈəːlɪ] *adv* tôt, de bonne heure; (*ahead of time*) en
avance; (*near the beginning*) au début ▷ *adj* précoce,
qui se manifeste (*or se fait*) tôt *or* de bonne heure;
(*Christians, settlers*) premier(-ière); (*reply*) rapide;
(*death*) prématuré(e); (*work*) de jeunesse; **to have an ~
night/start** se coucher/partir tôt *or* de bonne heure;
in the ~ *or* **~ in the spring/19th century** au début *or*
commencement du printemps/19ème siècle; **early
retirement** *n* retraite anticipée
earmark [ˈɪəmɑːk] *vt*: **to ~ sth for** réserver *or* destiner
qch à
earn [əːn] *vt* gagner; (*Comm: yield*) rapporter; **to ~ one's
living** gagner sa vie
earnest [ˈəːnɪst] *adj* sérieux(-euse) ▷ *n*: **in ~** *adv*
sérieusement, pour de bon
earnings [ˈəːnɪŋz] *npl* salaire *m*; gains *mpl*; (*of company
etc*) profits *mpl*, bénéfices *mpl*
ear: **earphones** *npl* écouteurs *mpl*; **earplugs** *npl* boules
fpl Quiès®; (*to keep out water*) protège-tympans *mpl*;
earring *n* boucle *f* d'oreille
earth [əːθ] *n* (*gen, also BRIT Elec*) terre *f* ▷ *vt* (*BRIT Elec*)
relier à la terre; **earthquake** *n* tremblement *m* de terre,
séisme *m*
ease [iːz] *n* facilité *f*, aisance *f*; (*comfort*) bien-être *m*
▷ *vt* (*soothe: mind*) tranquilliser; (*reduce: pain, problem*)
atténuer; (: *tension*) réduire; (*loosen*) relâcher, détendre;
(*help pass*): **to ~ sth in/out** faire pénétrer/sortir qch
délicatement *or* avec douceur, faciliter la pénétration/la
sortie de qch; **at ~** à l'aise; (*Mil*) au repos
easily [ˈiːzɪlɪ] *adv* facilement; (*by far*) de loin
east [iːst] *n* est *m* ▷ *adj* (*wind*) d'est; (*side*) est *inv* ▷ *adv*
à l'est, vers l'est; **the E~** l'Orient *m*; (*Pol*) les pays *mpl* de
l'Est; **eastbound** *adj* en direction de l'est; (*carriageway*)
est *inv*
Easter [ˈiːstər] *n* Pâques *fpl*; **Easter egg** *n* œuf *m* de
Pâques
eastern [ˈiːstən] *adj* de l'est, oriental(e)
Easter Sunday *n* le dimanche de Pâques
easy [ˈiːzɪ] *adj* facile; (*manner*) aisé(e) ▷ *adv*: **to take it**
or **things ~** (*rest*) ne pas se fatiguer; (*not worry*) ne pas
(trop) s'en faire; **easy-going** *adj* accommodant(e),
facile à vivre
eat (*pt* **ate**, *pp* **~en**) [iːt, eɪt, ˈiːtn] *vt, vi* manger; **can
we have something to ~?** est-ce qu'on peut manger
quelque chose?; **eat out** *vi* manger au restaurant
eavesdrop [ˈiːvzdrɔp] *vi*: **to ~ (on)** écouter de façon
indiscrète
e-book [ˈiːbuk] *n* livre *m* électronique
e-business [ˈiːbɪznɪs] *n* (*company*) entreprise *f*
électronique; (*commerce*) commerce *m* électronique
EC *n abbr* (= *European Community*) CE *f*
eccentric [ɪkˈsɛntrɪk] *adj, n* excentrique *m/f*
echo, echoes [ˈɛkəu] *n* écho *m* ▷ *vt* répéter ▷ *vi*
résonner; faire écho
eclipse [ɪˈklɪps] *n* éclipse *f*
eco-friendly [iːkəuˈfrɛndlɪ] *adj* non nuisible à *or* qui ne
nuit pas à l'environnement
ecological [iːkəˈlɔdʒɪkəl] *adj* écologique
ecology [ɪˈkɔlədʒɪ] *n* écologie *f*
e-commerce [iːkɔməːs] *n* commerce *m* électronique
economic [iːkəˈnɔmɪk] *adj* économique; (*profitable*)
rentable; **economical** *adj* économique; (*person*)
économe; **economics** *n* (*Scol*) économie *f* politique ▷ *npl*
(*of project etc*) côté *m or* aspect *m* économique
economist [ɪˈkɔnəmɪst] *n* économiste *m/f*
economize [ɪˈkɔnəmaɪz] *vi* économiser, faire des
économies
economy [ɪˈkɔnəmɪ] *n* économie *f*; **economy class** *n*
(*Aviat*) classe *f* touriste; **economy class syndrome** *n*
syndrome *m* de la classe économique
ecstasy [ˈɛkstəsɪ] *n* extase *f*; (*Drugs*) ecstasy *m*; **ecstatic**
[ɛksˈtætɪk] *adj* extatique, en extase
eczema [ˈɛksɪmə] *n* eczéma *m*
edge [ɛdʒ] *n* bord *m*; (*of knife etc*) tranchant *m*, fil *m* ▷ *vt*
border; **on ~** (*fig*) crispé(e), tendu(e)
edgy [ˈɛdʒɪ] *adj* crispé(e), tendu(e)

edible ['ɛdɪbl] *adj* comestible; (*meal*) mangeable
Edinburgh ['ɛdɪnbərə] *n* Édimbourg
edit ['ɛdɪt] *vt* (*text, book*) éditer; (*report*) préparer;
(*film*) monter; (*magazine*) diriger; (*newspaper*) être le
rédacteur *or* la rédactrice en chef de; **edition** [ɪ'dɪʃən]
n édition *f*; **editor** *n* (*of newspaper*) rédacteur(-trice),
rédacteur(-trice) en chef; (*of sb's work*) éditeur(-trice);
(*also:* **film editor**) monteur(-euse); **political/foreign
editor** rédacteur politique/au service étranger;
editorial [ɛdɪ'tɔ:rɪəl] *adj* de la rédaction, éditorial(e)
▷ *n* éditorial *m*
educate ['ɛdjukeɪt] *vt* (*teach*) instruire; (*bring up*)
éduquer; **educated** ['ɛdjukeɪtɪd] *adj* (*person*) cultivé(e)
education [ɛdju'keɪʃən] *n* éducation *f*; (*studies*)
études *fpl*; (*teaching*) enseignement *m*, instruction *f*;
educational *adj* pédagogique; (*institution*) scolaire;
(*game, toy*) éducatif(-ive)
eel [i:l] *n* anguille *f*
eerie ['ɪərɪ] *adj* inquiétant(e), spectral(e), surnaturel(le)
effect [ɪ'fɛkt] *n* effet *m* ▷ *vt* effectuer; **effects** *npl*
(*property*) effets, affaires *fpl*; **to take ~** (*Law*) entrer en
vigueur, prendre effet; (*drug*) agir, faire son effet; **in ~** en
fait; **effective** *adj* efficace; (*actual*) véritable; **effectively**
adv efficacement; (*in reality*) effectivement, en fait
efficiency [ɪ'fɪʃənsɪ] *n* efficacité *f*, (*of machine, car*)
rendement *m*
efficient [ɪ'fɪʃənt] *adj* efficace; (*machine, car*) d'un bon
rendement; **efficiently** *adv* efficacement
effort ['ɛfət] *n* effort *m*; **effortless** *adj* sans effort,
aisé(e); (*achievement*) facile
e.g. *adv abbr* (= *exempli gratia*) par exemple, p. ex.
egg [ɛg] *n* œuf *m*; **hard-boiled/soft-boiled ~** œuf dur/à
la coque; **eggcup** *n* coquetier *m*; **egg plant** (*us*) *n*
aubergine *f*; **eggshell** *n* coquille *f* d'œuf; **egg white** *n*
blanc *m* d'œuf; **egg yolk** *n* jaune *m* d'œuf
ego ['i:gəu] *n* (*self-esteem*) amour-propre *m*; (*Psych*) moi *m*
Egypt ['i:dʒɪpt] *n* Égypte *f*; **Egyptian** [ɪ'dʒɪpʃən] *adj*
égyptien(ne) ▷ *n* Égyptien(ne)
Eiffel Tower ['aɪfəl-] *n* tour *f* Eiffel
eight [eɪt] *num* huit; **eighteen** *num* dix-huit;
eighteenth *num* dix-huitième; **eighth** *num* huitième;
eightieth ['eɪtɪɪθ] *num* quatre-vingtième
eighty ['eɪtɪ] *num* quatre-vingt(s)
Eire ['ɛərə] *n* République *f* d'Irlande
either ['aɪðə'] *adj* l'un ou l'autre; (*both, each*) chaque
▷ *pron*: **~ (of them)** l'un ou l'autre ▷ *adv* non plus ▷ *conj*: **~
good or bad** soit bon soit mauvais; **on ~ side** de chaque
côté; **I don't like ~** je n'aime ni l'un ni l'autre; **no, I don't
~** moi non plus; **which bike do you want? - ~ will do**
quel vélo voulez-vous? - n'importe lequel; **answer with ~
yes or no** répondez par oui ou par non
eject [ɪ'dʒɛkt] *vt* (*tenant etc*) expulser; (*object*) éjecter
elaborate *adj* [ɪ'læbərɪt] compliqué(e), recherché(e),
minutieux(-euse) ▷ *vb* [ɪ'læbəreɪt] ▷ *vt* élaborer ▷ *vi*
entrer dans les détails
elastic [ɪ'læstɪk] *adj, n* élastique (*m*); **elastic band** *n*
(*BRIT*) élastique *m*
elbow ['ɛlbəu] *n* coude *m*
elder ['ɛldə'] *adj* aîné(e) ▷ *n* (*tree*) sureau *m*; **one's ~s**
ses aînés; **elderly** *adj* âgé(e) ▷ *npl*: **the elderly** les
personnes âgées
eldest ['ɛldɪst] *adj, n*: **the ~ (child)** l'aîné(e) (des enfants)
elect [ɪ'lɛkt] *vt* élire; (*choose*): **to ~ to do** choisir de faire
▷ *adj*: **the president ~** le président désigné; **election**

n élection *f*; **electoral** *adj* électoral(e); **electorate** *n*
électorat *m*
electric [ɪ'lɛktrɪk] *adj* électrique; **electrical** *adj*
électrique; **electric blanket** *n* couverture chauffante;
electric fire *n* (*BRIT*) radiateur *m* électrique; **electrician**
[ɪlɛk'trɪʃən] *n* électricien *m*; **electricity** [ɪlɛk'trɪsɪtɪ]
n électricité *f*; **electric shock** *n* choc *m* or décharge *f*
électrique; **electrify** [ɪ'lɛktrɪfaɪ] *vt* (*Rail*) électrifier;
(*audience*) électriser
electronic [ɪlɛk'trɒnɪk] *adj* électronique; **electronic
mail** *n* courrier *m* électronique; **electronics** *n*
électronique *f*
elegance ['ɛlɪgəns] *n* élégance *f*
elegant ['ɛlɪgənt] *adj* élégant(e)
element ['ɛlɪmənt] *n* (*gen*) élément *m*; (*of heater, kettle
etc*) résistance *f*
elementary [ɛlɪ'mɛntərɪ] *adj* élémentaire; (*school,
education*) primaire; **elementary school** *n* (*us*) école
f primaire
elephant ['ɛlɪfənt] *n* éléphant *m*
elevate ['ɛlɪveɪt] *vt* élever
elevator ['ɛlɪveɪtə'] *n* (*in warehouse etc*) élévateur *m*,
monte-charge *m inv*; (*us: lift*) ascenseur *m*
eleven [ɪ'lɛvn] *num* onze; **eleventh** *num* onzième
eligible ['ɛlɪdʒəbl] *adj* éligible; (*for membership*)
admissible; **an ~ young man** un beau parti; **to be ~ for
sth** remplir les conditions requises pour qch
eliminate [ɪ'lɪmɪneɪt] *vt* éliminer
elm [ɛlm] *n* orme *m*
eloquent ['ɛləkwənt] *adj* éloquent(e)
else [ɛls] *adv*: **something ~** quelque chose d'autre, autre
chose; **somewhere ~** ailleurs, autre part; **everywhere ~**
partout ailleurs; **everyone ~** tous les autres; **nothing ~**
rien d'autre; **where ~?** à quel autre endroit?; **little ~** pas
grand-chose d'autre; **elsewhere** *adv* ailleurs, autre part
elusive [ɪ'lu:sɪv] *adj* insaisissable
e-mail ['i:meɪl] *n abbr* (= *electronic mail*) e-mail *m*, courriel
m ▷ *vt*: **to ~ sb** envoyer un e-mail *or* un courriel à qn;
e-mail address *n* adresse *f* e-mail
embankment [ɪm'bæŋkmənt] *n* (*of road, railway*)
remblai *m*, talus *m*; (*of river*) berge *f*, quai *m*; (*dyke*) digue *f*
embargo, embargoes [ɪm'bɑ:gəu] *n* (*Comm, Naut*)
embargo *m*; (*prohibition*) interdiction *f*
embark [ɪm'bɑ:k] *vi* embarquer ▷ *vt* embarquer; **to ~
on** (*journey etc*) commencer, entreprendre; (*fig*) se lancer
or s'embarquer dans
embarrass [ɪm'bærəs] *vt* embarrasser, gêner;
embarrassed *adj* gêné(e); **embarrassing** *adj*
gênant(e), embarrassant(e); **embarrassment** *n*
embarras *m*, gêne *f*, (*embarrassing thing, person*) source
f d'embarras
embassy ['ɛmbəsɪ] *n* ambassade *f*
embrace [ɪm'breɪs] *vt* embrasser, étreindre; (*include*)
embrasser ▷ *vi* s'embrasser, s'étreindre ▷ *n* étreinte *f*
embroider [ɪm'brɔɪdə'] *vt* broder; **embroidery** *n*
broderie *f*
embryo ['ɛmbrɪəu] *n* (*also fig*) embryon *m*
emerald ['ɛmərəld] *n* émeraude *f*
emerge [ɪ'mə:dʒ] *vi* apparaître; (*from room, car*) surgir;
(*from sleep, imprisonment*) sortir
emergency [ɪ'mə:dʒənsɪ] *n* (*crisis*) cas *m* d'urgence;
(*Med*) urgence *f*; **in an ~** en cas d'urgence; **state of ~**
m d'urgence; **emergency brake** (*us*) *n* frein *m* à main;
emergency exit *n* sortie *f* de secours; **emergency**

landing n atterrissage forcé; **emergency room** n (us: Med) urgences fpl; **emergency services** npl: **the emergency services** (fire, police, ambulance) les services mpl d'urgence

emigrate ['emigreit] vi émigrer; **emigration** [emi'greiʃən] n émigration f

eminent ['eminənt] adj éminent(e)

emissions [i'miʃənz] npl émissions fpl

emit [i'mit] vt émettre

emotion [i'məuʃən] n sentiment m; **emotional** adj (person) émotif(-ive), très sensible; (needs) affectif(-ive); (scene) émouvant(e); (tone, speech) qui fait appel aux sentiments

emperor ['empərər] n empereur m

emphasis (pl -ases) ['emfəsis, -si:z] n accent m; **to lay or place ~ on sth** (fig) mettre l'accent sur, insister sur

emphasize ['emfəsaiz] vt (syllable, word, point) appuyer or insister sur; (feature) souligner, accentuer

empire ['empaiər] n empire m

employ [im'plɔi] vt employer; **employee** [imploi'i:] n employé(e); **employer** n employeur(-euse); **employment** n emploi m; **employment agency** n agence for bureau m de placement

empower [im'pauər] vt: **to ~ sb to do** autoriser or habiliter qn à faire

empress ['empris] n impératrice f

emptiness ['emptinis] n vide m; (of area) aspect m désertique

empty ['empti] adj vide; (street, area) désert(e); (threat, promise) en l'air, vain(e) ▷ vt vider ▷ vi se vider; (liquid) s'écouler; **empty-handed** adj les mains vides

EMU n abbr (= European Monetary Union) UME f

emulsion [i'mʌlʃən] n émulsion f; (also: **~ paint**) peinture mate

enable [i'neibl] vt: **to ~ sb to do** permettre à qn de faire

enamel [i'næməl] n émail m; (also: **~ paint**) (peinture f) laque f

enchanting [in'tʃɑːntiŋ] adj ravissant(e), enchanteur(-eresse)

encl. abbr (on letters etc = enclosed) ci-joint(e); (= enclosure) PJ f

enclose [in'kləuz] vt (land) clôturer; (space, object) entourer; (letter etc) **to ~ (with)** joindre (à); **please find ~d** veuillez trouver ci-joint

enclosure [in'kləuʒər] n enceinte f

encore [ɔŋ'kɔːʳ] excl, n bis (m)

encounter [in'kauntər] n rencontre f ▷ vt rencontrer

encourage [in'kʌridʒ] vt encourager; **encouragement** n encouragement m

encouraging [in'kʌridʒiŋ] adj encourageant(e)

encyclop(a)edia [ensaiklau'pi:diə] n encyclopédie f

end [end] n fin f; (of table, street, rope etc) bout m, extrémité f ▷ vt terminer; (also: **bring to an ~, put an ~ to**) mettre fin à ▷ vi se terminer, finir; **in the ~** finalement; **on ~** (object) debout, dressé(e); **to stand on ~** (hair) se dresser sur la tête; **for hours on ~** pendant des heures (et des heures); **end up** vi: **to ~ up in** (condition) finir or se terminer par; (place) finir or aboutir à

endanger [in'deindʒər] vt mettre en danger; **an ~ed species** une espèce en voie de disparition

endearing [in'diəriŋ] adj attachant(e)

endeavour (us **endeavor**) [in'devər] n effort m; (attempt) tentative f ▷ vt: **to ~ to do** tenter or s'efforcer de faire

ending ['endiŋ] n dénouement m, conclusion f; (Ling) terminaison f

endless ['endlis] adj sans fin, interminable

endorse [in'dɔːs] vt (cheque) endosser; (approve) appuyer, approuver, sanctionner; **endorsement** n (approval) appui m, aval m; (BRIT: on driving licence) contravention f (portée au permis de conduire)

endurance [in'djuərəns] n endurance f

endure [in'djuər] vt (bear) supporter, endurer ▷ vi (last) durer

enemy ['enəmi] adj, n ennemi(e)

energetic [enə'dʒetik] adj énergique; (activity) très actif(-ive), qui fait se dépenser (physiquement)

energy ['enədʒi] n énergie f

enforce [in'fɔːs] vt (law) appliquer, faire respecter

engaged [in'geidʒd] adj (BRIT: busy, in use) occupé(e); (betrothed) fiancé(e); **to get ~** se fiancer; **the ~ the line's** la ligne est occupée; **engaged tone** n (BRIT Tel) tonalité f occupé inv

engagement [in'geidʒmənt] n (undertaking) obligation f, engagement m; (appointment) rendez-vous m inv; (to marry) fiançailles fpl; **engagement ring** n bague f de fiançailles

engaging [in'geidʒiŋ] adj engageant(e), attirant(e)

engine ['endʒin] n (Aut) moteur m; (Rail) locomotive f

engineer [endʒi'niər] n (BRIT: repairer) dépanneur m; (Navy, us Rail) mécanicien m; **engineering** n engineering m, ingénierie f; (of bridges, ships) génie m; (of machine) mécanique f

England ['ingland] n Angleterre f

English ['ingliʃ] adj anglais(e) ▷ n (Ling) anglais m; **the ~** npl les Anglais; **English Channel** n: **the English Channel** la Manche; **Englishman** (irreg) n Anglais m; **Englishwoman** (irreg) n Anglaise f

engrave [in'greiv] vt graver

engraving [in'greiviŋ] n gravure f

enhance [in'hɑːns] vt rehausser, mettre en valeur

enjoy [in'dʒɔi] vt aimer, prendre plaisir à; (have benefit of: health, fortune) jouir de; (: success) connaître; **to ~ o.s.** s'amuser; **enjoyable** adj agréable; **enjoyment** n plaisir m

enlarge [in'lɑːdʒ] vt accroître; (Phot) agrandir ▷ vi: **to ~ on** (subject) s'étendre sur; **enlargement** n (Phot) agrandissement m

enlist [in'list] vt recruter; (support) s'assurer ▷ vi s'engager

enormous [i'nɔːməs] adj énorme

enough [i'nʌf] adj: **~ time/books** assez or suffisamment de temps/livres ▷ adv: **big ~** assez or suffisamment grand ▷ pron: **have you got ~?** (en) avez-vous assez?; **~ to eat** assez à manger; **that's ~, thanks** cela suffit or c'est assez, merci; **I've had ~ of him** j'en ai assez de lui; **he has not worked ~** il n'a pas assez or suffisamment travaillé, il n'a pas travaillé assez or suffisamment; ... **which, funnily or oddly ~** ... qui, chose curieuse

enquire [in'kwaiər] vt, vi = **inquire**

enquiry [in'kwaiəri] n = **inquiry**

enrage [in'reidʒ] vt mettre en fureur or en rage, rendre furieux(-euse)

enrich [in'ritʃ] vt enrichir

enrol (us **enroll**) [in'rəul] vt inscrire ▷ vi s'inscrire; **enrolment** (us **enrollment**) n inscription f

en route [ɔn'ru:t] adv en route, en chemin

en suite ['ɔnswi:t] adj: **with ~ bathroom** avec salle de bains en attenante

ensure [ɪn'fʊəʳ] vt assurer, garantir

entail [ɪn'teɪl] vt entraîner, nécessiter

enter ['ɛntəʳ] vt (room) entrer dans, pénétrer dans; (club, army) entrer à; (competition) s'inscrire à or pour; (sb for a competition) (faire) inscrire; (write down) inscrire, noter; (Comput) entrer, introduire ▷ vi entrer

enterprise ['ɛntəpraɪz] n (company, undertaking) entreprise f; (initiative) (esprit m d')initiative f; **free ~** libre entreprise; **private ~** entreprise privée; **enterprising** adj entreprenant(e), dynamique; (scheme) audacieux(-euse)

entertain [ɛntə'teɪn] vt amuser, distraire; (invite) recevoir (à dîner); (idea, plan) envisager; **entertainer** n artiste m/f de variétés; **entertaining** adj amusant(e), distrayant(e); **entertainment** n (amusement) distraction f, divertissement m, amusement m; (show) spectacle m

enthusiasm [ɪn'θuːzɪæzəm] n enthousiasme m

enthusiast [ɪn'θuːzɪæst] n enthousiaste m/f; **enthusiastic** [ɪnθuːzɪ'æstɪk] adj enthousiaste; **to be enthusiastic about** être enthousiasmé(e) par

entire [ɪn'taɪəʳ] adj (tout) entier(-ère); **entirely** adv entièrement, complètement

entitle [ɪn'taɪtl] vt: **to ~ sb to sth** donner droit à qch à qn; **entitled** adj (book) intitulé(e); **to be entitled to do** avoir le droit de faire

entrance n ['ɛntrns] entrée f ▷ vt [ɪn'trɑːns] enchanter, ravir; **where's the ~?** où est l'entrée?; **to gain ~ to** (university etc) être admis à; **entrance examination** n examen m d'entrée or d'admission; **entrance fee** n (to museum etc) prix m d'entrée; (to join club etc) droit m d'inscription; **entrance ramp** n (us Aut) bretelle f d'accès; **entrant** n (in race etc) participant(e), concurrent(e); (BRIT: in exam) candidat(e)

entrepreneur ['ɔntrəprə'nəːʳ] n entrepreneur m

entrust [ɪn'trʌst] vt: **to ~ sth to** confier qch à

entry ['ɛntrɪ] n entrée f; (in register, diary) inscription f; **"no ~"** "défense d'entrer", "entrée interdite"; (Aut) "sens interdit"; **entry phone** n (BRIT) interphone m (à l'entrée d'un immeuble)

envelope ['ɛnvələup] n enveloppe f

envious ['ɛnvɪəs] adj envieux(-euse)

environment [ɪn'vaɪərnmənt] n (social, moral) milieu m; (natural world): **the ~** l'environnement m; **environmental** [ɪnvaɪərn'mɛntl] adj (of surroundings) du milieu; (issue, disaster) écologique; **environmentally** [ɪnvaɪərn'mɛntlɪ] adv: **environmentally sound/friendly** qui ne nuit pas à l'environnement

envisage [ɪn'vɪzɪdʒ] vt (foresee) prévoir

envoy ['ɛnvɔɪ] n envoyé(e); (diplomat) ministre m plénipotentiaire

envy ['ɛnvɪ] n envie f ▷ vt envier; **to ~ sb sth** envier qch à qn

epic ['ɛpɪk] n épopée f ▷ adj épique

epidemic [ɛpɪ'dɛmɪk] n épidémie f

epilepsy ['ɛpɪlɛpsɪ] n épilepsie f; **epileptic** adj, n épileptique m/f; **epileptic fit** n crise f d'épilepsie

episode ['ɛpɪsəud] n épisode m

equal ['iːkwl] adj égal(e) ▷ vt égaler; **~ to** (task) à la hauteur de; **equality** [iː'kwɔlɪtɪ] n égalité f; **equalize** vt, vi (Sport) égaliser; **equally** adv également, en parts égales; (treat) de la même façon; (pay) autant; (just as) tout aussi

equation [ɪ'kweɪʃən] n (Math) équation f

equator [ɪ'kweɪtəʳ] n équateur m

equip [ɪ'kwɪp] vt équiper; **to ~ sb/sth with** équiper or munir qn/qch de; **equipment** n équipement m; (electrical etc) appareillage m, installation f

equivalent [ɪ'kwɪvələnt] adj équivalent(e) ▷ n équivalent m; **to be ~ to** équivaloir à, être équivalent(e) à

ER abbr (BRIT: = Elizabeth Regina) la reine Elisabeth; (US: Med: = emergency room) urgences fpl

era ['ɪərə] n ère f, époque f

erase [ɪ'reɪz] vt effacer; **eraser** n gomme f

erect [ɪ'rɛkt] adj droit(e) ▷ vt construire; (monument) ériger, élever; (tent etc) dresser; **erection** [ɪ'rɛkʃən] n (Physiol) érection f; (of building) construction f

ERM n abbr (= Exchange Rate Mechanism) mécanisme m des taux de change

erode [ɪ'rəud] vt éroder; (metal) ronger

erosion [ɪ'rəuʒən] n érosion f

erotic [ɪ'rɔtɪk] adj érotique

errand ['ɛrnd] n course f, commission f

erratic [ɪ'rætɪk] adj irrégulier(-ière), inconstant(e)

error ['ɛrəʳ] n erreur f

erupt [ɪ'rʌpt] vi entrer en éruption; (fig) éclater; **eruption** [ɪ'rʌpʃən] n éruption f; (of anger, violence) explosion f

escalate ['ɛskəleɪt] vi s'intensifier; (costs) monter en flèche

escalator ['ɛskəleɪtəʳ] n escalier roulant

escape [ɪ'skeɪp] n évasion f, fuite f; (of gas etc) fuite ▷ vi s'échapper, fuir; (from jail) s'évader; (fig) s'en tirer; (leak) s'échapper ▷ vt échapper à; **to ~ from** (person) échapper à; (place) s'échapper de; (fig) fuir; **his name ~s me** son nom m'échappe

escort vt [ɪ'skɔːt] escorter ▷ n ['ɛskɔːt] (Mil) escorte f

especially [ɪ'spɛʃlɪ] adv (particularly) particulièrement; (above all) surtout

espionage ['ɛspɪənɑːʒ] n espionnage m

essay ['ɛseɪ] n (Scol) dissertation f; (Literature) essai m

essence ['ɛsns] n essence f; (Culin) extrait m

essential [ɪ'sɛnʃl] adj essentiel(le); (basic) fondamental(e); **essentials** npl éléments essentiels; **essentially** adv essentiellement

establish [ɪ'stæblɪʃ] vt établir; (business) fonder, créer; (one's power etc) asseoir, affirmer; **establishment** n établissement m; (founding) création f; (institution) établissement; **the Establishment** les pouvoirs établis, l'ordre établi

estate [ɪ'steɪt] n (land) domaine m, propriété f; (Law) biens mpl, succession f; (BRIT: also: **housing ~**) lotissement m; **estate agent** n (BRIT) agent immobilier; **estate car** n (BRIT) break m

estimate n ['ɛstɪmət] estimation f; (Comm) devis m ▷ vb ['ɛstɪmeɪt] vt estimer

etc abbr (= et cetera) etc

eternal [ɪ'təːnl] adj éternel(le)

eternity [ɪ'təːnɪtɪ] n éternité f

ethical ['ɛθɪkl] adj moral(e); **ethics** ['ɛθɪks] n éthique f ▷ npl moralité f

Ethiopia [iːθɪ'əupɪə] n Éthiopie f

ethnic ['ɛθnɪk] adj ethnique; (clothes, food) folklorique, exotique, propre aux minorités ethniques non-occidentales; **ethnic minority** n minorité f ethnique

e-ticket ['iːtɪkɪt] n billet m électronique

etiquette ['ɛtɪkɛt] n convenances fpl, étiquette f

EU n abbr (= European Union) UE f

euro ['juərəu] n (currency) euro m

Europe ['juərəp] n Europe f; **European** [juərə'piːən] adj européen(ne) ▷ n Européen(ne); **European Community** n Communauté européenne; **European Union** n Union européenne

Eurostar® ['juərəustɑː'] n Eurostar® m

evacuate [ɪ'vækjueɪt] vt évacuer

evade [ɪ'veɪd] vt échapper à; (question etc) éluder; (duties) se dérober à

evaluate [ɪ'væljueɪt] vt évaluer

evaporate [ɪ'væpəreɪt] vi s'évaporer; (fig: hopes, fear) s'envoler; (anger) se dissiper

eve [iːv] n: **on the ~ of** à la veille de

even ['iːvn] adj (level, smooth) régulier(-ière); (equal) égal(e); (number) pair(e) ▷ adv même; **~ if** même si + indic; **~ though** alors même que + cond; **~ more** encore plus; **~ faster** encore plus vite; **~ so** quand même; **not ~ pas même; ~ he was there** même lui était là; **~ on Sundays** même le dimanche; **to get ~ with sb** prendre sa revanche sur qn

evening ['iːvnɪŋ] n soir m; (as duration, event) soirée f; **in the ~** le soir; **evening class** n cours m du soir; **evening dress** n (man's) tenue f de soirée, smoking m; (woman's) robe f de soirée

event [ɪ'vent] n événement m; (Sport) épreuve f; **in the ~ of** en cas de; **eventful** adj mouvementé(e)

eventual [ɪ'ventʃuəl] adj final(e)

eventually [ɪ'ventʃuəlɪ] adv finalement

ever ['ɛvə'] adv jamais; (at all times) toujours; (in questions): **why ~ not?** mais enfin, pourquoi pas?; **the best ~** le meilleur qu'on ait jamais vu; **have you ~ seen it?** l'as-tu déjà vu?, as-tu eu l'occasion or t'est-il arrivé de le voir?; **~ since** (as adv) depuis; (as conj) depuis que; **~ so pretty** si joli; **evergreen** n arbre m à feuilles persistantes

○ **KEYWORD**

every ['ɛvrɪ] adj **1** (each) chaque; **every one of them** tous (sans exception); **every shop in town was closed** tous les magasins en ville étaient fermés
2 (all possible) tous (toutes) les; **I gave you every assistance** j'ai fait tout mon possible pour vous aider; **I have every confidence in him** j'ai entièrement or pleinement confiance en lui; **we wish you every success** nous vous souhaitons beaucoup de succès
3 (showing recurrence) tous les; **every day** tous les jours, chaque jour; **every other car** une voiture sur deux; **every other/third day** tous les deux/trois jours; **every now and then** de temps en temps; **everybody** = **everyone**; **everyday** adj (expression) courant(e), d'usage courant; (use) courant; (clothes, life) de tous les jours; (occurrence, problem) quotidien(ne); **everyone** pron tout le monde, tous pl; **everything** pron tout; **everywhere** adv partout; **everywhere you go you meet ...** où qu'on aille, on rencontre ...

evict [ɪ'vɪkt] vt expulser

evidence ['ɛvɪdns] n (proof) preuve(s) f(pl); (of witness) témoignage m; (sign): **to show ~ of** donner des signes de; **to give ~** témoigner, déposer

evident ['ɛvɪdnt] adj évident(e); **evidently** adv de toute évidence; (apparently) apparemment

evil ['iːvl] adj mauvais(e) ▷ n mal m

evoke [ɪ'vəuk] vt évoquer

evolution [iːvə'luːʃən] n évolution f

evolve [ɪ'vɔlv] vt élaborer ▷ vi évoluer, se transformer

ewe [juː] n brebis f

ex [eks] n (inf): **my ex** mon ex

ex- [eks] prefix ex-

exact [ɪg'zækt] adj exact(e) ▷ vt: **to ~ sth (from)** (signature, confession) extorquer qch (à); (apology) exiger qch (de); **exactly** adv exactement

exaggerate [ɪg'zædʒəreɪt] vt, vi exagérer; **exaggeration** [ɪgzædʒə'reɪʃən] n exagération f

exam [ɪg'zæm] n abbr (Scol) = **examination**

examination [ɪgzæmɪ'neɪʃən] n (Scol, Med) examen m; **to take** or **sit an ~** (BRIT) passer un examen

examine [ɪg'zæmɪn] vt (gen) examiner; (Scol, Law: person) interroger; **examiner** n examinateur(-trice)

example [ɪg'zɑːmpl] n exemple m; **for ~** par exemple

exasperated [ɪg'zɑːspəreɪtɪd] adj exaspéré(e)

excavate ['ekskəveɪt] vt (site) fouiller, excaver; (object) mettre au jour

exceed [ɪk'siːd] vt dépasser; (one's powers) outrepasser; **exceedingly** adv extrêmement

excel [ɪk'sel] vi exceller ▷ vt surpasser; **to ~ o.s.** se surpasser

excellence ['eksələns] n excellence f

excellent ['eksələnt] adj excellent(e)

except [ɪk'sept] prep (also: **~ for, ~ing**) sauf, excepté, à l'exception de ▷ vt excepter; **~ if/when** sauf si/quand; **~ that** excepté que, si ce n'est que; **exception** [ɪk'sepʃən] n exception f; **to take exception to** s'offusquer de; **exceptional** [ɪk'sepʃənl] adj exceptionnel(le); **exceptionally** [ɪk'sepʃənəlɪ] adv exceptionnellement

excerpt ['eksəːpt] n extrait m

excess [ɪk'ses] n excès m; **excess baggage** n excédent m de bagages; **excessive** adj excessif(-ive)

exchange [ɪks'tʃeɪndʒ] n échange m; (also: **telephone ~**) central m ▷ vt: **to ~ (for)** échanger (contre); **could I ~ this, please?** est-ce que je peux échanger ceci, s'il vous plaît?; **exchange rate** n taux m de change

excite [ɪk'saɪt] vt exciter; **excited** adj (tout (toute)) excité(e); **to get excited** s'exciter; **excitement** n excitation f; **exciting** adj passionnant(e)

exclaim [ɪk'skleɪm] vi s'exclamer; **exclamation** [ekskləˈmeɪʃən] n exclamation f; **exclamation mark** (us **exclamation point**) n point m d'exclamation

exclude [ɪk'skluːd] vt exclure

excluding [ɪk'skluːdɪŋ] prep: **~ VAT** la TVA non comprise

exclusion [ɪk'skluːʒən] n exclusion f

exclusive [ɪk'skluːsɪv] adj exclusif(-ive); (club, district) sélect(e); (item of news) en exclusivité; **~ of VAT** TVA non comprise; **exclusively** adv exclusivement

excruciating [ɪk'skruːʃɪeɪtɪŋ] adj (pain) atroce, déchirant(e); (embarrassing) pénible

excursion [ɪk'skəːʃən] n excursion f

excuse n [ɪk'skjuːs] excuse f ▷ vt [ɪk'skjuːz] (forgive) excuser; **to ~ sb from** (activity) dispenser qn de; **~ me!** excusez-moi!, pardon!; **now if you will ~ me, ...** maintenant, si vous (le) permettez ...

ex-directory ['eksdɪ'rektərɪ] adj (BRIT) sur la liste rouge

execute ['eksɪkjuːt] vt exécuter; **execution** [eksɪ'kjuːʃən] n exécution f

executive [ɪg'zekjutɪv] n (person) cadre m; (managing group) bureau m; (Pol) exécutif m ▷ adj exécutif(-ive); (position, job) de cadre

exempt [ɪg'zempt] adj: **~ from** exempté(e) or dispensé(e) de ▷ vt: **to ~ sb from** exempter or dispenser qn de

exercise [ˈeksəsaɪz] n exercice m ▷ vt exercer; (patience etc) faire preuve de; (dog) promener ▷ vi (also: **to take ~**) prendre de l'exercice; **exercise book** n cahier m

exert [ɪgˈzəːt] vt exercer, employer; **to ~ o.s.** se dépenser; **exertion** [ɪgˈzəːʃən] n effort m

exhale [eksˈheɪl] vt exhaler ▷ vi expirer

exhaust [ɪgˈzɔːst] n (also: **~ fumes**) gaz mpl d'échappement; (also: **~ pipe**) tuyau m d'échappement ▷ vt épuiser; **exhausted** adj épuisé(e); **exhaustion** [ɪgˈzɔːstʃən] n épuisement m; **nervous exhaustion** fatigue nerveuse

exhibit [ɪgˈzɪbɪt] n (Art) pièce f or objet m exposé(e); (Law) pièce à conviction ▷ vt (Art) exposer; (courage, skill) faire preuve de; **exhibition** [eksɪˈbɪʃən] n exposition f

exhilarating [ɪgˈzɪləreɪtɪŋ] adj grisant(e), stimulant(e)

exile [ˈeksaɪl] n exil m; (person) exilé(e) ▷ vt exiler

exist [ɪgˈzɪst] vi exister; **existence** n existence f; **existing** adj actuel(le)

exit [ˈeksɪt] n (also: **~**) où est la sortie?; **exit ramp** n (us Aut) bretelle f d'accès

exotic [ɪgˈzɔtɪk] adj exotique

expand [ɪkˈspænd] vt (area) agrandir; (quantity) accroître ▷ vi (trade, etc) se développer, s'accroître; (gas, metal) se dilater

expansion [ɪkˈspænʃən] n (territorial, economic) expansion f; (of trade, influence etc) développement m; (of production) accroissement m; (of population) croissance f; (of gas, metal) expansion, dilatation f

expect [ɪkˈspekt] vt (anticipate) s'attendre à, s'attendre à ce que + sub; (count on) compter sur, escompter; (require) demander, exiger; (suppose) supposer; (await: also baby) attendre ▷ vi: **to be ~ing** (pregnant woman) être enceinte; **expectation** [ekspekˈteɪʃən] n (hope) attente f, espérance(s) f(pl); (belief) attente

expedition [ekspəˈdɪʃən] n expédition f

expel [ɪkˈspel] vt chasser, expulser; (Scol) renvoyer, exclure

expenditure [ɪkˈspendɪtʃəˀ] n (act of spending) dépense f; (money spent) dépenses fpl

expense [ɪkˈspens] n (high cost) coût m; (spending) dépense f, frais mpl; **expenses** npl frais mpl; dépenses; **at the ~ of** (fig) aux dépens de; **expense account** n (note f de) frais m

expensive [ɪkˈspensɪv] adj cher (chère), coûteux(-euse); **it's too ~** ça coûte trop cher

experience [ɪkˈspɪərɪəns] n expérience f ▷ vt connaître; (feeling) éprouver; **experienced** adj expérimenté(e)

experiment [ɪkˈsperɪmənt] n expérience f ▷ vi faire une expérience; **experimental** [ɪksperɪˈmentl] adj expérimental(e)

expert [ˈekspəːt] adj expert(e) ▷ n expert m; **expertise** [ekspəːˈtiːz] n (grande) compétence

expire [ɪkˈspaɪəˀ] vi expirer; **expiry** n expiration f; **expiry date** n date f d'expiration; (on label) à utiliser avant ...

explain [ɪkˈspleɪn] vt expliquer; **explanation** [ekspləˈneɪʃən] n explication f

explicit [ɪkˈsplɪsɪt] adj explicite; (definite) formel(le)

explode [ɪkˈspləud] vi exploser

exploit n [ˈeksplɔɪt] exploit m ▷ vt [ɪkˈsplɔɪt] exploiter; **exploitation** [eksplɔɪˈteɪʃən] n exploitation f

explore [ɪkˈsplɔːˀ] vt explorer; (possibilities) étudier;

examiner; **explorer** n explorateur(-trice)

explosion [ɪkˈspləuʒən] n explosion f; **explosive** [ɪkˈspləusɪv] adj explosif(-ive) ▷ n explosif m

export vt [ekˈspɔːt] exporter ▷ n [ˈekspɔːt] exportation f ▷ cpd d'exportation; **exporter** n exportateur m

expose [ɪkˈspəuz] vt exposer; (unmask) démasquer, dévoiler; **exposed** adj (land, house) exposé(e); **exposure** [ɪkˈspəuʒəˀ] n exposition f; (publicity) couverture f; (Phot: speed) (temps m de) pose f; (: shot) pose; **to die of exposure** (Med) mourir de froid

express [ɪkˈspres] adj (definite) formel(le), exprès(-esse); (BRIT: letter etc) exprès inv ▷ n (train) rapide m ▷ vt exprimer; **expression** [ɪkˈspreʃən] n expression f; **expressway** n (us) voie f express (à plusieurs files)

exquisite [ekˈskwɪzɪt] adj exquis(e)

extend [ɪkˈstend] vt (visit, street) prolonger, remettre; (building) agrandir; (offer) présenter, offrir; (hand, arm) tendre ▷ vi (land) s'étendre; **extension** [ɪkˈstenʃən] n (of visit, street) prolongation f; (building) annexe f; (telephone: in offices) poste m; (: in private house) téléphone m supplémentaire; **extension cable, extension lead** n (Elec) rallonge f; **extensive** adj étendu(e), vaste; (damage, alterations) considérable; (inquiries) approfondi(e)

extent [ɪkˈstent] n étendue f; **to some ~** dans une certaine mesure; **to the ~ of ...** au point de ...; **to what ~?** dans quelle mesure?, jusqu'à quel point?; **to such an ~ that ...** à tel point que ...

exterior [ekˈstɪərɪəˀ] adj extérieur(e) ▷ n extérieur m

external [ekˈstəːnl] adj externe

extinct [ɪkˈstɪŋkt] adj (volcano) éteint(e); (species) disparu(e); **extinction** n extinction f

extinguish [ɪkˈstɪŋgwɪʃ] vt éteindre

extra [ˈekstrə] adj supplémentaire, de plus ▷ adv (in addition) en plus ▷ n supplément m; (perk) à-coté m; (Cine, Theat) figurant(e)

extract vt [ɪkˈstrækt] extraire; (tooth) arracher; (money, promise) soutirer ▷ n [ˈekstrækt] extrait m

extradite [ˈekstrədaɪt] vt extrader

extraordinary [ɪkˈstrɔːdnrɪ] adj extraordinaire

extravagance [ɪkˈstrævəgəns] n (excessive spending) prodigalités fpl; (thing bought) folie f, dépense excessive; **extravagant** adj extravagant(e); (in spending: person) prodigue, dépensier(-ière); (: tastes) dispendieux(-euse)

extreme [ɪkˈstriːm] adj, n extrême (m); **extremely** adv extrêmement

extremist [ɪkˈstriːmɪst] adj, n extrémiste m/f

extrovert [ˈekstrəvəːt] n extraverti(e)

eye [aɪ] n œil m ((yeux) pl); (of needle) trou m, chas m ▷ vt examiner; **to keep an ~ on** surveiller; **eyeball** n globe m oculaire; **eyebrow** n sourcil m; **eyedrops** npl gouttes fpl pour les yeux; **eyelash** n cil m; **eyelid** n paupière f; **eyeliner** n eye-liner m; **eyeshadow** n ombre f à paupières; **eyesight** n vue f; **eye witness** n témoin m oculaire

F [ɛf] n (Mus): **F** fa m

fabric ['fæbrɪk] n tissu m

fabulous ['fæbjuləs] adj fabuleux(-euse); (inf: super) formidable, sensationnel(le)

face [feɪs] n visage m, figure f; (expression) air m; (of clock) cadran m; (of cliff) paroi f; (of mountain) face f; (of building) façade f ▷ vt faire face à; (facts etc) accepter; **~ down** (person) à plat ventre; (card) face en dessous; **to lose/save ~** perdre/sauver la face; **to pull a ~** faire une grimace; **in the ~ of** (difficulties etc) face à, devant; **on the ~ of it** à première vue; **~ to ~** face à face; **face up to** vt fus faire face à, affronter; **face cloth** n (BRIT) gant m de toilette; **face pack** n (BRIT) masque m (de beauté)

facial ['feɪʃl] adj facial(e) ▷ n soin complet du visage

facilitate [fə'sɪlɪteɪt] vt faciliter

facilities [fə'sɪlɪtɪz] npl installations fpl, équipement m; **credit ~** facilités de paiement

fact [fækt] n fait m; **in ~** en fait

faction ['fækʃən] n faction f

factor ['fæktər] n facteur m; (of sun cream) indice m (de protection); **I'd like a ~ 15 suntan lotion** je voudrais une crème solaire d'indice 15

factory ['fæktərɪ] n usine f, fabrique f

factual ['fæktjuəl] adj basé(e) sur les faits

faculty ['fækəltɪ] n faculté f; (us: teaching staff) corps enseignant

fad [fæd] n (personal) manie f; (craze) engouement m

fade [feɪd] vi se décolorer, passer; (light, sound) s'affaiblir; (flower) se faner; **fade away** vi (sound) s'affaiblir

fag [fæg] n (BRIT inf: cigarette) clope f

Fahrenheit ['fɑ:rənhaɪt] n Fahrenheit m inv

fail [feɪl] vt (exam) échouer à; (candidate) recaler; (subj: courage, memory) faire défaut à ▷ vi échouer; (eyesight, health, light: also: **be ~ing**) baisser, s'affaiblir; (brakes) lâcher; **to ~ to do sth** (neglect) négliger de or ne pas faire qch; (be unable) ne pas arriver or parvenir à faire qch; **without ~** à coup sûr; sans faute; **failing** n défaut m ▷ prep faute de; **failing that** à défaut, sinon; **failure** ['feɪljər] n échec m; (person) raté(e); (mechanical etc) défaillance f

faint [feɪnt] adj faible; (recollection) vague; (mark) à peine visible ▷ n évanouissement m ▷ vi s'évanouir; **to feel ~** défaillir; **faintest** adj: **I haven't the faintest idea** je n'en ai pas la moindre idée; **faintly** adv faiblement; (vaguely) vaguement

fair [fɛər] adj équitable, juste; (hair) blond(e); (skin, complexion) pâle, blanc (blanche); (weather) beau (belle); (good enough) assez bon(ne); (sizeable) considérable ▷ adv: **to play ~** jouer franc jeu ▷ n foire f; (BRIT: funfair) fête (foraine); **fairground** n champ m de foire; **fair-haired** adj (person) aux cheveux clairs, blond(e); **fairly** adv (justly) équitablement; (quite) assez; **fair trade** n commerce m équitable; **fairway** n (Golf) fairway m

fairy ['fɛərɪ] n fée f; **fairy tale** n conte m de fées

faith [feɪθ] n foi f; (trust) confiance f; (sect) culte m, religion f; **faithful** adj fidèle; **faithfully** adv fidèlement; **yours faithfully** (BRIT: in letters) veuillez agréer l'expression de mes salutations les plus distinguées

fake [feɪk] n (painting etc) faux m; (person) imposteur m ▷ adj faux (fausse) ▷ vt (emotions) simuler; (painting) faire un faux de

falcon ['fɔ:lkən] n faucon m

fall [fɔ:l] n chute f; (decrease) baisse f; (us: autumn) automne m ▷ vi (pt **fell**, pp **~en**) tomber; (price, temperature, dollar) baisser; **falls** npl (waterfall) chute f d'eau, cascade f; **to ~ flat** vi (on one's face) tomber de tout son long, s'étaler; (joke) tomber à plat; (plan) échouer; **fall apart** vi (object) tomber en morceaux; **fall down** vi (person) tomber; (building) s'effondrer, s'écrouler; **fall for** vt fus (trick) se laisser prendre à; (person) tomber amoureux(-euse) de; **fall off** vi tomber; (diminish) baisser, diminuer; **fall out** vi (friends etc) se brouiller; (hair, teeth) tomber; **fall over** vi tomber (par terre); **fall through** vi (plan, project) tomber à l'eau

fallen ['fɔ:lən] pp of **fall**

fallout ['fɔ:laut] n retombées (radioactives)

false [fɔ:ls] adj faux (fausse); **under ~ pretences** sous un faux prétexte; **false alarm** n fausse alerte; **false teeth** npl (BRIT) fausses dents, dentier m

fame [feɪm] n renommée f, renom m

familiar [fə'mɪlɪər] adj familier(-ière); **to be ~ with sth** connaître qch; **familiarize** [fə'mɪlɪəraɪz] vt: **to familiarize o.s. with** se familiariser avec

family ['fæmɪlɪ] n famille f; **family doctor** n médecin m de famille; **family planning** n planning familial

famine ['fæmɪn] n famine f

famous ['feɪməs] adj célèbre

fan [fæn] n (folding) éventail m; (Elec) ventilateur m; (person) fan m, admirateur(-trice); (Sport) supporter m/f ▷ vt éventer; (fire, quarrel) attiser

fanatic [fə'nætɪk] n fanatique m/f

fan belt n courroie f de ventilateur

fan club n fan-club m

fancy ['fænsɪ] n (whim) fantaisie f, envie f; (imagination) imagination f ▷ adj (luxury) de luxe; (elaborate: jewellery, packaging) fantaisie inv ▷ vt (feel like, want) avoir envie de; (imagine) imaginer; **to take a ~ to** se prendre d'affection pour; s'enticher de; **he fancies her** elle lui plaît; **fancy dress** n déguisement m, travesti m

fan heater n (BRIT) radiateur soufflant

fantasize ['fæntəsaɪz] vi fantasmer

fantastic [fæn'tæstɪk] adj fantastique

fantasy ['fæntəsɪ] n imagination f, fantaisie f; (unreality) fantasme m

fanzine ['fænzi:n] n fanzine m
FAQ n abbr (= frequently asked question) FAQ f inv, faq f inv
far [fɑː^r] adj (distant) lointain(e), éloigné(e) ⊳ adv loin; **the ~ side/end** l'autre côté/bout; **it's not ~ (from here)** ce n'est pas loin (d'ici); **~ away, ~ off** au loin, dans le lointain; **~ better** beaucoup mieux; **~ from** loin de; **by ~** de loin, de beaucoup; **go as ~ as the bridge** allez jusqu'au pont; **as ~ as I know** pour autant que je sache; **how ~ is it to ...?** combien y a-t-il jusqu'à ...?; **how ~ have you got with your work?** où en êtes-vous dans votre travail?
farce [fɑːs] n farce f
fare [fɛə^r] n (on trains, buses) prix m du billet; (in taxi) prix de la course; (food) table f, chère f; **half ~** demi-tarif; **full ~** plein tarif
Far East n: **the ~** l'Extrême-Orient m
farewell [fɛə'wɛl] excl, n adieu m
farm [fɑːm] n ferme f ⊳ vt cultiver; **farmer** n fermier(-ière); **farmhouse** n (maison f de) ferme f, **farming** n agriculture f; (of animals) élevage m; **farmyard** n cour f de ferme
far-reaching ['fɑː'riːtʃɪŋ] adj d'une grande portée
fart [fɑːt] (inf!) vi péter
farther ['fɑːðə^r] adv plus loin ⊳ adj plus eloigné(e), plus lointain(e)
farthest ['fɑːðɪst] superlative of **far**
fascinate ['fæsɪneɪt] vt fasciner, captiver; **fascinated** adj fasciné(e)
fascinating ['fæsɪneɪtɪŋ] adj fascinant(e)
fascination [fæsɪ'neɪʃən] n fascination f
fascist ['fæʃɪst] adj, n fasciste m/f
fashion ['fæʃən] n mode f; (manner) façon f, manière f ⊳ vt façonner; **in ~** à la mode; **out of ~** démodé(e); **fashionable** adj à la mode; **fashion show** n défilé m de mannequins or de mode
fast [fɑːst] adj rapide; (clock): **to be ~** avancer; (dye, colour) grand or bon teint inv ⊳ adv vite, rapidement; (stuck, held) solidement ⊳ n jeûne m ⊳ vi jeûner; **~ asleep** profondément endormi
fasten ['fɑːsn] vt attacher, fixer; (coat) attacher, fermer ⊳ vi se fermer, s'attacher
fast food n fast food m, restauration f rapide
fat [fæt] adj gros(se) ⊳ n graisse f; (on meat) gras m; (for cooking) matière grasse
fatal ['feɪtl] adj (mistake) fatal(e); (injury) mortel(le); **fatality** [fə'tælɪtɪ] n (road death etc) victime f, décès m; **fatally** adv fatalement; (injured) mortellement
fate [feɪt] n destin m; (of person) sort m
father ['fɑːðə^r] n père m; **Father Christmas** n le Père Noël; **father-in-law** n beau-père m
fatigue [fə'tiːg] n fatigue f
fattening ['fætnɪŋ] adj (food) qui fait grossir
fatty ['fætɪ] adj (food) gras(se) ⊳ n (inf) gros (grosse)
faucet ['fɔːsɪt] n (us) robinet m
fault [fɔːlt] n faute f; (defect) défaut m; (Geo) faille f ⊳ vt trouver des défauts à, prendre en défaut; **it's my ~** c'est de ma faute; **to find ~ with** trouver à redire or à critiquer à; **at ~** fautif(-ive), coupable; **faulty** adj défectueux(-euse)
fauna ['fɔːnə] n faune f
favour etc (us **favor** etc) ['feɪvə^r] n faveur f; (help) service m ⊳ vt (proposition) être en faveur de; (pupil etc) favoriser; (team, horse) donner gagnant; **to do sb a ~** rendre un service à qn; **in ~ of** en faveur de; **to find ~ with sb**

trouver grâce aux yeux de qn; **favourable** adj favorable; **favourite** ['feɪvrɪt] adj, n favori(te)
fawn [fɔːn] n (deer) faon m ⊳ adj (also: **~-coloured**) fauve ⊳ vi: **to ~ (up)on** flatter servilement
fax [fæks] n (document) télécopie f, fax m; (machine) télécopieur m ⊳ vt envoyer par télécopie
FBI n abbr (us: = Federal Bureau of Investigation) FBI m
fear [fɪə^r] n crainte f, peur f ⊳ vt craindre; **for ~ of** de peur que + sub or de + infinitive; **fearful** adj craintif(-ive); (sight, noise) affreux(-euse), épouvantable; **fearless** adj intrépide
feasible ['fiːzəbl] adj faisable, réalisable
feast [fiːst] n festin m, banquet m; (Rel: also: **~ day**) fête f ⊳ vi festoyer
feat [fiːt] n exploit m, prouesse f
feather ['fɛðə^r] n plume f
feature ['fiːtʃə^r] n caractéristique f; (article) chronique f, rubrique f ⊳ vt (film) avoir pour vedette(s) ⊳ vi figurer (en bonne place); **features** npl (of face) traits mpl; **a (special) ~ on sth/sb** un reportage sur qch/qn; **feature film** n long métrage
Feb. abbr (= February) fév
February ['fɛbruərɪ] n février m
fed [fɛd] pt, pp of **feed**
federal ['fɛdərəl] adj fédéral(e)
federation [fɛdə'reɪʃən] n fédération f
fed up adj: **to be ~ (with)** en avoir marre or plein le dos (de)
fee [fiː] n rémunération f; (of doctor, lawyer) honoraires mpl; (of school, college etc) frais mpl de scolarité; (for examination) droits mpl
feeble ['fiːbl] adj faible; (attempt, excuse) pauvre; (joke) piteux(-euse)
feed [fiːd] n (of animal) nourriture f, pâture f; (on printer) mécanisme m d'alimentation f ⊳ vt (pt, pp **fed**) (person) nourrir; (BRIT: baby: breastfeed) allaiter; (: with bottle) donner le biberon à; (horse etc) donner à manger à; (machine) alimenter; (data etc) **to ~ sth into** enregistrer qch dans; **feedback** n (Elec) effet m Larsen; (from person) réactions fpl
feel [fiːl] n (sensation) sensation f; (impression) impression f ⊳ vt (pt, pp **felt**) (touch) toucher; (explore) tâter, palper; (cold, pain) sentir; (grief, anger) ressentir, éprouver; (think, believe): **to ~ (that)** trouver que; **to ~ hungry/cold** avoir faim/froid; **to ~ lonely/better** se sentir seul/mieux; **I don't ~ well** je ne me sens pas bien; **it ~s soft** c'est doux au toucher; **to ~ like** (want) avoir envie de; **feeling** n (physical) sensation f; (emotion, impression) sentiment m; **to hurt sb's feelings** froisser qn
feet [fiːt] npl of **foot**
fell [fɛl] pt of **fall** ⊳ vt (tree) abattre
fellow ['fɛləu] n type m; (comrade) compagnon m; (of learned society) membre m ⊳ cpd: **their ~ prisoners/ students** leurs camarades prisonniers/étudiants; **fellow citizen** n concitoyen(ne); **fellow countryman** n (irreg) compatriote m; **fellow men** npl semblables mpl; **fellowship** n (society) association f; (comradeship) amitié f, camaraderie f; (Scol) sorte de bourse universitaire
felony ['fɛlənɪ] n crime m, forfait m
felt [fɛlt] pt, pp of **feel** ⊳ n feutre m; **felt-tip** n (also: **felt-tip pen**) stylo-feutre m
female ['fiːmeɪl] n (Zool) femelle f; (pej: woman) bonne femme f ⊳ adj (Biol) femelle; (sex, character) féminin(e); (vote etc) des femmes

feminine ['fɛmɪnɪn] *adj* féminin(e)
feminist ['fɛmɪnɪst] *n* féministe *m/f*
fence [fɛns] *n* barrière *f* ▷ *vi* faire de l'escrime; **fencing** *n* (sport) escrime *m*
fend [fɛnd] *vi*: **to ~ for o.s.** se débrouiller (tout seul); **fend off** *vt* (attack etc) parer; (questions) éluder
fender ['fɛndə'] *n* garde-feu *m inv*; (on boat) défense *f*; (us: of car) aile *f*
fennel ['fɛnl] *n* fenouil *m*
ferment *vi* [fə'mɛnt] fermenter ▷ *n* ['fə:mɛnt] (fig) agitation *f*, effervescence *f*
fern [fə:n] *n* fougère *f*
ferocious [fə'rəuʃəs] *adj* féroce
ferret ['fɛrɪt] *n* furet *m*
ferry ['fɛrɪ] *n* (small) bac *m*; (large: also: **~boat**) ferry(-boat *m*) *m* ▷ *vt* transporter
fertile ['fə:taɪl] *adj* fertile; (Biol) fécond(e); **fertilize** ['fə:tɪlaɪz] *vt* fertiliser; (Biol) féconder; **fertilizer** *n* engrais *m*
festival ['fɛstɪvəl] *n* (Rel) fête *f*; (Art, Mus) festival *m*
festive ['fɛstɪv] *adj* de fête; **the ~ season** (BRIT: Christmas) la période des fêtes
fetch [fɛtʃ] *vt* aller chercher; (BRIT: sell for) rapporter
fête [feɪt] *n* fête *f*, kermesse *f*
fetus ['fi:təs] *n* (US) =**foetus**
feud [fju:d] *n* querelle *f*, dispute *f*
fever ['fi:və'] *n* fièvre *f*; **feverish** *adj* fiévreux(-euse), fébrile
few [fju:] *adj* (not many) peu de ▷ *pron* peu; **a ~** (as adj) quelques; (as pron) quelques-uns(-unes); **quite a ~ ...** *adj* un certain nombre de ..., pas mal de ...; **in the past ~ days** ces derniers jours; **fewer** *adj* moins de; **fewest** *adj* le moins nombreux
fiancé [fɪ'ɑ̃:ŋseɪ] *n* fiancé *m*; **fiancée** *n* fiancée *f*
fiasco [fɪ'æskəu] *n* fiasco *m*
fib [fɪb] *n* bobard *m*
fibre (US **fiber**) ['faɪbə'] *n* fibre *f*; **fibreglass** (US **Fiberglass®**) *n* fibre *f* de verre
fickle ['fɪkl] *adj* inconstant(e), volage, capricieux(-euse)
fiction ['fɪkʃən] *n* romans *mpl*, littérature *f* romanesque; (invention) fiction *f*; **fictional** *adj* fictif(-ive)
fiddle ['fɪdl] *n* (Mus) violon *m*; (cheating) combine *f*, escroquerie *f* ▷ *vt* (BRIT: accounts) falsifier, maquiller; **fiddle with** *vt fus* tripoter
fidelity [fɪ'dɛlɪtɪ] *n* fidélité *f*
fidget ['fɪdʒɪt] *vi* se trémousser, remuer
field [fi:ld] *n* champ *m*; (fig) domaine *m*, champ; (Sport: ground) terrain *m*; **field marshal** *n* maréchal *m*
fierce [fɪəs] *adj* (look, animal) féroce, sauvage; (wind, attack, person) (très) violent(e); (fighting, enemy) acharné(e)
fifteen [fɪf'ti:n] *num* quinze; **fifteenth** *num* quinzième
fifth [fɪfθ] *num* cinquième
fiftieth ['fɪftɪɪθ] *num* cinquantième
fifty ['fɪftɪ] *num* cinquante; **fifty-fifty** *adv* moitié-moitié ▷ *adj*: **to have a fifty-fifty chance (of success)** avoir une chance sur deux (de réussir)
fig [fɪg] *n* figue *f*
fight [faɪt] *n* (between persons) bagarre *f*; (argument) dispute *f*; (Mil) combat *m*; (against cancer etc) lutte *f* ▷ *vb* (pt, pp **fought**) *vt* se battre contre; (cancer, alcoholism, emotion) combattre, lutter contre; (election) se présenter à ▷ *vi* se battre; (argue) se disputer; (fig): **to ~ (for/against)** lutter (pour/contre); **fight back** *vi* rendre les coups; (after illness) reprendre le dessus ▷ *vt*

(tears) réprimer; **fight off** *vt* repousser; (disease, sleep, urge) lutter contre; **fighting** *n* combats *mpl*; (brawls) bagarres *fpl*
figure ['fɪgə'] *n* (Drawing, Geom) figure *f*; (number) chiffre *m*; (body, outline) silhouette *f*; (person's shape) ligne *f*, formes *fpl*; (person) personnage *m* ▷ *vt* (US: think) supposer ▷ *vi* (appear) figurer; (US: make sense) s'expliquer; **figure out** *vt* (understand) arriver à comprendre; (plan) calculer
file [faɪl] *n* (tool) lime *f*; (dossier) dossier *m*; (folder) dossier, chemise *f*; (: binder) classeur *m*; (Comput) fichier *m*; (row) file *f* ▷ *vt* (nails, wood) limer; (papers) classer; (Law: claim) faire enregistrer; déposer; **filing cabinet** *n* classeur *m* (meuble)
Filipino [fɪlɪ'pi:nəu] *adj* philippin(e) ▷ *n* (person) Philippin(e)
fill [fɪl] *vt* remplir; (vacancy) pourvoir à ▷ *n*: **to eat one's ~** manger à sa faim; **to ~ with** remplir de; **fill in** *vt* (hole) boucher; (form) remplir; **fill out** *vt* (form, receipt) remplir; **fill up** *vt* remplir ▷ *vi* (Aut) faire le plein
fillet ['fɪlɪt] *n* filet *m*; **fillet steak** *n* filet *m* de bœuf, tournedos *m*
filling ['fɪlɪŋ] *n* (Culin) garniture *f*, farce *f*; (for tooth) plombage *m*; **filling station** *n* station-service *f*, station *f* d'essence
film [fɪlm] *n* film *m*; (Phot) pellicule *f*, film; (of powder, liquid) couche *f*, pellicule ▷ *vt* (scene) filmer ▷ *vi* tourner; **I'd like a 36-exposure ~** je voudrais une pellicule de 36 poses; **film star** *n* vedette *f* de cinéma
filter ['fɪltə'] *n* filtre *m* ▷ *vt* filtrer; **filter lane** *n* (BRIT Aut: at traffic lights) voie *f* de dégagement; (: on motorway) voie *f* de sortie
filth [fɪlθ] *n* saleté *f*; **filthy** *adj* sale, dégoûtant(e); (language) ordurier(-ière), grossier(-ière)
fin [fɪn] *n* (of fish) nageoire *f*; (of shark) aileron *m*; (of diver) palme *f*
final ['faɪnl] *adj* final(e), dernier(-ière); (decision, answer) définitif(-ive) ▷ *n* (BRIT Sport) finale *f*; **finals** *npl* (Scol) examens *mpl* de dernière année; (US Sport) finale *f*; **finale** [fɪ'nɑ:lɪ] *n* finale *m*; **finalist** *n* (Sport) finaliste *m/f*; **finalize** *vt* mettre au point; **finally** *adv* (eventually) enfin, finalement; (lastly) en dernier lieu
finance [faɪ'næns] *n* finance *f* ▷ *vt* financer; **finances** *npl* finances *fpl*; **financial** [faɪ'nænʃəl] *adj* financier(-ière); **financial year** *n* année *f* budgétaire
find [faɪnd] *vt* (pt, pp **found**) trouver; (lost object) retrouver ▷ *n* trouvaille *f*, découverte *f*; **to ~ sb guilty** (Law) déclarer qn coupable; **find out** *vt* se renseigner sur; (truth, secret) découvrir; (person) démasquer ▷ *vi*: **to ~ out about** (make enquiries) se renseigner sur; (by chance) apprendre; **findings** *npl* (Law) conclusions *fpl*, verdict *m*; (of report) constatations *fpl*
fine [faɪn] *adj* (weather) beau (belle); (excellent) excellent(e); (thin, subtle, not coarse) fin(e); (acceptable) bien *inv* ▷ *adv* (well) très bien; (small) fin, finement ▷ *n* (Law) amende *f*; contravention *f* ▷ *vt* (Law) condamner à une amende; donner une contravention à; **he's ~** il va bien; **the weather is ~** il fait beau; **fine arts** *npl* beaux-arts *mpl*
finger ['fɪŋgə'] *n* doigt *m* ▷ *vt* palper, toucher; **index ~** index *m*; **fingernail** *n* ongle *m* (de la main); **fingerprint** *n* empreinte digitale; **fingertip** *n* bout *m* du doigt
finish ['fɪnɪʃ] *n* fin *f*; (Sport) arrivée *f*; (polish etc) finition *f* ▷ *vt* finir, terminer ▷ *vi* finir, se terminer; **to ~ doing sth**

finir de faire qch; **to ~ third** arriver or terminer troisième; **when does the show ~?** quand est-ce que le spectacle se termine?; **finish off** vt finir, terminer; (kill) achever; **finish up** vi, vt finir

Finland ['finlənd] n Finlande f; **Finn** n Finnois(e), Finlandais(e); **Finnish** adj finnois(e), finlandais(e) ▷ n (Ling) finnois m

fir [fəːᵊ] n sapin m

fire ['faɪəᵊ] n feu m; (accidental) incendie m; (heater) radiateur m ▷ vt (discharge): **to ~ a gun** tirer un coup de feu; (fig: interest) enflammer, animer; (inf: dismiss) mettre à la porte, renvoyer ▷ vi (shoot) tirer, faire feu; **~! au feu!**; **on ~** en feu; **to set ~ to sth, set sth on ~** mettre le feu à qch; **fire alarm** n avertisseur m d'incendie; **firearm** n arme f à feu; **fire brigade** n (us **fire department**) (régiment m de sapeurs-)pompiers mpl; **fire engine** n (BRIT) pompe f à incendie; **fire escape** n escalier m de secours; **fire exit** n issue for sortie f de secours; **fire extinguisher** n extincteur m; **fireman** (irreg) n pompier m; **fireplace** n cheminée f; **fire station** n caserne f de pompiers; **fire truck** (us) n = **fire engine**; **firewall** n (Internet) pare-feu m; **firewood** n bois m de chauffage; **fireworks** npl (display) feu(x) m(pl) d'artifice

firm [fəːm] adj ferme ▷ n compagnie f, firme f; **firmly** adv fermement

first [fəːst] adj premier(-ière) ▷ adv (before other people) le premier, la première; (before other things) en premier, d'abord; (when listing reasons etc) en premier lieu, premièrement; (in the beginning) au début ▷ n (person: in race) premier(-ière); (Aut) première f; **the ~ of January** le premier janvier; **at ~** au commencement, au début; **~ of all** tout d'abord, pour commencer; **first aid** n premiers secours or soins; **first-aid kit** n trousse f à pharmacie; **first-class** adj (ticket etc) de première classe; (excellent) excellent(e), exceptionnel(le); (post) en tarif prioritaire; **first-hand** adj de première main; **first lady** n (us) femme f du président; **firstly** adv premièrement, en premier lieu; **first name** n prénom m; **first-rate** adj excellent(e)

fiscal ['fɪskl] adj fiscal(e); **fiscal year** n exercice financier

fish [fɪʃ] n (pl inv) poisson m ▷ vt, vi pêcher; **~ and chips** poisson frit et frites; **fisherman** (irreg) n pêcheur m; **fishfinger** n pêcheur m; **fish fingers** npl (BRIT) bâtonnets de poisson (congelés); **fishing** n pêche f; **to go fishing** aller à la pêche; **fishing boat** n barque f de pêche; **fishing line** n ligne f (de pêche); **fishmonger** n (BRIT) marchand m de poisson; **fishmonger's (shop)** n (BRIT) poissonnerie f; **fish sticks** npl (us) = **fish fingers**; **fishy** adj (inf) suspect(e), louche

fist [fɪst] n poing m

fit [fɪt] adj (Med, Sport) en (bonne) forme; (proper) convenable, approprié(e) ▷ vt (subj: clothes) aller à; (put in, attach) installer, poser; (equip) garnir, munir; (suit) convenir à ▷ vi (clothes) aller; (parts) s'adapter; (in space, gap) entrer, s'adapter ▷ n (Med) accès m, crise f; (of anger) accès; (of hysterics, jealousy) crise; **~ to** (ready to) en état de; **~ for** (worthy) digne de; (capable) apte à; **to keep ~** se maintenir en forme; **this dress is a tight/good ~** cette robe est un peu juste/(me) va très bien; **a ~ of coughing** une quinte de toux; **by ~s and starts** par à-coups; **fit in** vi (add up) cadrer; (integrate) s'intégrer; (to new situation) s'adapter; **fitness** n (Med) forme f physique; **fitted** adj (jacket, shirt) ajusté(e); **fitted carpet** n moquette f; **fitted kitchen** n (BRIT) cuisine équipée; **fitted sheet** n drap-housse m; **fitting**

adj approprié(e) ▷ n (of dress) essayage m; (of piece of equipment) pose f, installation f; **fitting room** n (in shop) cabine f d'essayage; **fittings** npl installations fpl

five [faɪv] num cinq; **fiver** n (inf: BRIT) billet m de cinq livres; (: us) billet de cinq dollars

fix [fɪks] vt (date, amount etc) fixer; (sort out) arranger; (mend) réparer; (make ready: meal, drink) préparer ▷ n: **to be in a ~** être dans le pétrin; **fix up** vt (meeting) arranger; **to ~ sb up with sth** faire avoir qch à qn; **fixed** adj (prices etc) fixe; **fixture** n installation f (fixe); (Sport) rencontre f (au programme)

fizzy ['fɪzɪ] adj pétillant(e), gazeux(-euse)

flag [flæg] n drapeau m; (also: **~stone**) dalle f ▷ vi faiblir, fléchir; **flag down** vt héler, faire signe (de s'arrêter) à; **flagpole** n mât m

flair [flɛəᵊ] n flair m

flak [flæk] n (Mil) tir antiaérien; (inf: criticism) critiques fpl

flake [fleɪk] n (of rust, paint) écaille f; (of snow, soap powder) flocon m ▷ vi (also: **~ off**) s'écailler

flamboyant [flæm'bɔɪənt] adj flamboyant(e), éclatant(e); (person) haut(e) en couleur

flame [fleɪm] n flamme f

flamingo [flə'mɪŋgəu] n flamant m (rose)

flammable ['flæməbl] adj inflammable

flan [flæn] n (BRIT) tarte f

flank [flæŋk] n flanc m ▷ vt flanquer

flannel ['flænl] n (BRIT: also: **face ~**) gant m de toilette; (fabric) flanelle f

flap [flæp] n (of pocket, envelope) rabat m ▷ vt (wings) battre (de) ▷ vi (sail, flag) claquer

flare [flɛəᵊ] n (signal) signal lumineux; (Mil) fusée éclairante; (in skirt etc) évasement m; **flares** npl (trousers) pantalon m à pattes d'éléphant; **flare up** vi s'embraser; (fig: person) se mettre en colère, s'emporter; (: revolt) éclater

flash [flæʃ] n éclair m; (also: **news ~**) flash m (d'information); (Phot) flash ▷ vt (switch on) allumer (brièvement); (direct): **to ~ sth at** braquer qch sur; (send: message) câbler; (smile) lancer ▷ vi briller; jeter des éclairs; (light on ambulance etc) clignoter; **a ~ of lightning** un éclair; **in a ~** en un clin d'œil; **to ~ one's headlights** faire un appel de phares; **he ~ed by or past** il passa (devant nous) comme un éclair; **flashback** n flashback m, retour m en arrière; **flashbulb** n ampoule f de flash; **flashlight** n lampe f de poche

flask [flɑːsk] n flacon m, bouteille f; (also: **vacuum ~**) bouteille f thermos®

flat [flæt] adj plat(e); (tyre) dégonflé(e), à plat; (beer) éventé(e); (battery) à plat; (denial) catégorique; (Mus) bémol inv; (: voice) faux (fausse) ▷ n (BRIT: apartment) appartement m; (Aut) crevaison f, pneu crevé; (Mus) bémol m; **~ out** (work) sans relâche; (race) à fond; **flatten** vt (also: **flatten out**) aplatir; (crop) coucher; (house, city) raser

flatter ['flætəᵊ] vt flatter; **flattering** adj flatteur(-euse); (clothes etc) seyant(e)

flaunt [flɔːnt] vt faire étalage de

flavour etc (us **flavor** etc) ['fleɪvəᵊ] n goût m, saveur f; (of ice cream etc) parfum m ▷ vt parfumer, aromatiser; **vanilla-~ed** à l'arôme de vanille, vanillé(e); **what ~s do you have?** quels parfums avez-vous?; **flavouring** n arôme m (synthétique)

flaw [flɔː] n défaut m; **flawless** adj sans défaut

flea [fliː] n puce f; **flea market** n marché m aux puces

flee (pt, pp **fled**) [fliː, flɛd] vt fuir, s'enfuir de ▷ vi fuir, s'enfuir

fleece [fliːs] n (of sheep) toison f; (top) (laine f) polaire f ▷ vt (inf) voler, filouter

fleet [fliːt] n flotte f; (of lorries, cars etc) parc m; convoi m

fleeting ['fliːtɪŋ] adj fugace, fugitif(-ive); (visit) très bref (brève)

Flemish ['flɛmɪʃ] adj flamand(e) ▷ n (Ling) flamand m; **the ~** npl les Flamands

flesh [flɛʃ] n chair f

flew [fluː] pt of **fly**

flex [flɛks] n fil m or câble m électrique (souple) ▷ vt (knee) fléchir; (muscles) tendre; **flexibility** n flexibilité f; **flexible** adj flexible; (person, schedule) souple; **flexitime** (us **flextime**) n horaire m variable or à la carte

flick [flɪk] n petit coup m; (with finger) chiquenaude f ▷ vt donner un petit coup à; (switch) appuyer sur; **flick through** vt fus feuilleter

flicker ['flɪkə'] vi (light, flame) vaciller

flies [flaɪz] npl of **fly**

flight [flaɪt] n vol m; (escape) fuite f; (also: **~ of steps**) escalier m; **flight attendant** n steward m, hôtesse f de l'air

flimsy ['flɪmzɪ] adj peu solide; (clothes) trop léger(-ère); (excuse) pauvre, mince

flinch [flɪntʃ] vi tressaillir; **to ~ from** se dérober à, reculer devant

fling [flɪŋ] vt (pt, pp **flung**) jeter, lancer

flint [flɪnt] n silex m; (in lighter) pierre f (à briquet)

flip [flɪp] vt (throw) donner une chiquenaude à; (switch) appuyer sur; (us: pancake) faire sauter; **to ~ sth over** retourner qch

flip-flops ['flɪpflɒps] npl (esp BRIT) tongs fpl

flipper ['flɪpə'] n (of animal) nageoire f; (for swimmer) palme f

flirt [fləːt] vi flirter ▷ n flirteur(-euse)

float [fləut] n flotteur m; (in procession) char m; (sum of money) réserve f ▷ vi flotter

flock [flɒk] n (of sheep) troupeau m; (of birds) vol m; (of people) foule f

flood [flʌd] n inondation f; (of letters, refugees etc) flot m ▷ vt inonder ▷ vi (place) être inondé; (people): **to ~ into** envahir; **flooding** n inondation f; **floodlight** n projecteur m

floor [flɔː'] n sol m; (storey) étage m; (of sea, valley) fond m ▷ vt (knock down) terrasser; (baffle) désorienter; **ground ~** (us): **first ~** = rez-de-chaussée m; **first ~** (us): **second ~** premier étage; **what ~ is it on?** c'est à quel étage?; **floorboard** n planche f (du plancher); **flooring** n sol m; (wooden) plancher m; (covering) revêtement m de sol; **floor show** n spectacle m de variétés

flop [flɒp] n fiasco m ▷ vi (fail) faire fiasco; (fall) s'affaler, s'effondrer; **floppy** adj lâche, flottant(e) ▷ n (Comput: also: **floppy disk**) disquette f

flora ['flɔːrə] n flore f

floral ['flɔːrl] adj floral(e); (dress) à fleurs

florist ['flɒrɪst] n fleuriste m/f; **florist's (shop)** n magasin m or boutique f de fleuriste

flotation [fləu'teɪʃən] n (of shares) émission f; (of company) lancement m (en Bourse)

flour ['flauə'] n farine f

flourish ['flʌrɪʃ] vi prospérer ▷ n (gesture) moulinet m

flow [fləu] n (of water, traffic etc) écoulement m; (tide, influx) flux m; (of blood, Elec) circulation f; (of river) courant m ▷ vi couler; (traffic) s'écouler; (robes, hair) flotter

flower ['flauə'] n fleur f ▷ vi fleurir; **flower bed** n plate-bande f; **flowerpot** n pot m (à fleurs)

flown [fləun] pp of **fly**

fl. oz. abbr = **fluid ounce**

flu [fluː] n grippe f

fluctuate ['flʌktjueɪt] vi varier, fluctuer

fluent ['fluːənt] adj (speech, style) coulant(e), aisé(e); **he speaks ~ French, he's ~ in French** il parle le français couramment

fluff [flʌf] n duvet m; (on jacket, carpet) peluche f; **fluffy** adj duveteux(-euse); (toy) en peluche

fluid ['fluːɪd] n fluide m; (in diet) liquide m ▷ adj fluide; **fluid ounce** n (BRIT) = 0.028 l; 0.05 pints

fluke [fluːk] n coup m de veine

flung [flʌŋ] pt, pp of **fling**

fluorescent [fluə'rɛsnt] adj fluorescent(e)

fluoride ['fluəraɪd] n fluor m

flurry ['flʌrɪ] n (of snow) rafale f, bourrasque f; **a ~ of activity** un affairement soudain

flush [flʌʃ] n (on face) rougeur f; (fig: of youth etc) éclat m ▷ vt nettoyer à grande eau ▷ vi rougir ▷ adj (level): **~ with** au ras de, de niveau avec; **to ~ the toilet** tirer la chasse (d'eau)

flute [fluːt] n flûte f

flutter ['flʌtə'] n (of panic, excitement) agitation f; (of wings) battement m ▷ vi (bird) battre des ailes, voleter

fly [flaɪ] n (insect) mouche f; (on trousers: also: **flies**) braguette f ▷ vb (pt **flew**, pp **flown**) ▷ vt (plane) piloter; (passengers, cargo) transporter (par avion); (distance) parcourir ▷ vi voler; (passengers) aller en avion; (escape) s'enfuir, fuir; (flag) se déployer; **fly away, fly off** vi s'envoler; **fly-drive** n formule f avion plus voiture; **flying** n (activity) aviation f; (action) vol m ▷ adj: **flying visit** visite f éclair inv; **with flying colours** haut la main; **flying saucer** n soucoupe volante; **flyover** n (BRIT: overpass) pont routier

FM abbr (Radio: = frequency modulation) FM

foal [fəul] n poulain m

foam [fəum] n écume f; (on beer) mousse f; (also: **~ rubber**) caoutchouc m mousse ▷ vi (liquid) écumer; (soapy water) mousser

focus ['fəukəs] n (pl **~es**) foyer m; (of interest) centre m ▷ vt (field glasses etc) mettre au point ▷ vi: **to ~ (on)** (with camera) régler la mise au point (sur); (with eyes) fixer son regard (sur); (fig: concentrate) se concentrer; **out of/in ~** (picture) flou(e)/net(te); (camera) pas au point/au point

foetus (us **fetus**) ['fiːtəs] n fœtus m

fog [fɒg] n brouillard m; **foggy** adj: **it's foggy** il y a du brouillard; **fog lamp** (us **fog light**) n (Aut) phare m anti-brouillard

foil [fɔɪl] vt déjouer, contrecarrer ▷ n feuille f de métal; (kitchen foil) papier m d'alu(minium); **to act as a ~ to** (fig) servir de repoussoir or de faire-valoir à

fold [fəuld] n (bend, crease) pli m; (Agr) parc m à moutons; (fig) bercail m ▷ vt plier; **to ~ one's arms** croiser les bras; **fold up** vi (map etc) se plier, se replier; (business) fermer boutique ▷ vt (map etc) plier, replier; **folder** n (for papers) chemise f; (: binder) classeur m; (Comput) dossier m; **folding** adj (chair, bed) pliant(e)

foliage ['fəulɪdʒ] n feuillage m

folk [fəuk] npl gens mpl ▷ cpd folklorique; **folks** npl (inf: parents) famille f, parents mpl; **folklore** ['fəuklɔː'] n folklore m; **folk music** n musique f folklorique; (*contemporary*) musique folk, folk *m*; **folk song** *n* chanson *f* folklorique; (*contemporary*) chanson folk *inv*

follow ['fɔləu] *vt* suivre ▷ *vi* suivre; (*result*) s'ensuivre; **to ~ suit** (*fig*) faire de même; **follow up** *vt* (*letter, offer*) donner suite à; (*case*) suivre; **follower** *n* disciple *m/f*, partisan(e); **following** *adj* suivant(e) ▷ *n* partisans *mpl*, disciples *mpl*; **follow-up** *n* suite *f*, (*on file, case*) suivi *m*

fond [fɔnd] *adj* (*memory, look*) tendre, affectueux(-euse); (*hopes, dreams*) un peu fou (folle); **to be ~ of** aimer beaucoup

food [fu:d] *n* nourriture *f*; **food mixer** *n* mixeur *m*; **food poisoning** *n* intoxication *f* alimentaire; **food processor** *n* robot *m* de cuisine; **food stamp** *n* (*us*) bon *m* de nourriture (*pour indigents*)

fool [fu:l] *n* idiot(e); (*Culin*) mousse *f* de fruits ▷ *vt* berner, duper; **fool about, fool around** *vi* (*pej: waste time*) traînailler, glandouiller; (*: behave foolishly*) faire l'idiot or l'imbécile; **foolish** *adj* idiot(e), stupide; (*rash*) imprudent(e); **foolproof** *adj* (*plan etc*) infaillible

foot (*pl* **feet**) [fut, fi:t] *n* pied *m*; (*of animal*) patte *f*; (*measure*) pied *m* (= 30.48 cm; 12 inches) ▷ *vt* (*bill*) payer; **on ~** à pied; **footage** *n* (*Cine: length*) métrage *m*; (*: material*) séquences *fpl*; **foot-and-mouth (disease)** [futənd'mauθ-] *n* fièvre aphteuse; **football** *n* (*ball*) ballon *m* (de football); (*sport: BRIT*) football *m*; (*: us*) football américain; **footballer** *n* (*BRIT*) = **football player**; **football match** *n* (*BRIT*) match *m* de foot(ball); **football player** *n* footballeur(-euse), joueur(-euse) de football; (*us*) joueur(-euse) de football américain; **footbridge** *n* passerelle *f*; **foothills** *npl* contreforts *mpl*; **foothold** *n* prise *f* (de pied); **footing** *n* (*fig*) position *f*; **to lose one's footing** perdre pied; **footnote** *n* note *f* (en bas de page); **footpath** *n* sentier *m*; **footprint** *n* trace *f* (de pied); **footstep** *n* pas *m*; **footwear** *n* chaussures *fpl*

 KEYWORD

for [fɔː] *prep* **1** (*indicating destination, intention, purpose*) pour; **the train for London** le train pour (*or* à destination de) Londres; **he left for Rome** il est parti pour Rome; **he went for the paper** il est allé chercher le journal; **is this for me?** c'est pour moi?; **it's time for lunch** c'est l'heure du déjeuner; **what's it for?** ça sert à quoi?; **what for?** (*why*) pourquoi?; (*to what end*) pour quoi faire?, à quoi bon?; **for sale** à vendre; **to pray for peace** prier pour la paix

2 (*on behalf of, representing*) pour; **the MP for Hove** le député de Hove; **to work for sb/sth** travailler pour qn/qch; **I'll ask him for you** je vais lui demander pour toi; **G for George** G comme Georges

3 (*because of*) pour; **for this reason** pour cette raison; **for fear of being criticized** de peur d'être critiqué

4 (*with regard to*) pour; **it's cold for July** il fait froid pour juillet; **a gift for languages** un don pour les langues

5 (*in exchange for*): **I sold it for £5** je l'ai vendu 5 livres; **to pay 50 pence for a ticket** payer un billet 50 pence

6 (*in favour of*) pour; **are you for or against us?** êtes-vous pour ou contre nous?; **I'm all for it** je suis tout à fait pour; **vote for X** votez pour X

7 (*referring to distance*) pendant, sur; **there are roadworks for 5 km** il y a des travaux sur or pendant 5 km; **we walked for miles** nous avons marché pendant des kilomètres

8 (*referring to time*) pendant; depuis; pour; **he was away for 2 years** il a été absent pendant 2 ans; **she will be away for a month** elle sera absente (pendant) un mois; **it hasn't rained for 3 weeks** ça fait 3 semaines qu'il ne pleut pas, il ne pleut pas depuis 3 semaines; **I have known her for years** je la connais depuis des années; **can you do it for tomorrow?** est-ce que tu peux le faire pour demain?

9 (*with infinitive clauses*): **it is not for me to decide** ce n'est pas à moi de décider; **it would be best for you to leave** le mieux serait que vous partiez; **there is still time for you to do it** vous avez encore le temps de le faire; **for this to be possible ...** pour que cela soit possible ..

10 (*in spite of*): **for all that** malgré cela, néanmoins; **for all his work/efforts** malgré tout son travail/tous ses efforts; **for all his complaints, he's very fond of her** il a beau se plaindre, il l'aime beaucoup

▷ *conj* (*since, as: rather formal*) car

forbid (*pt* **forbad(e)**, *pp* **~den**) [fə'bɪd, -'bæd, -'bɪdn] *vt* défendre, interdire; **to ~ sb to do** défendre or interdire à qn de faire; **forbidden** *adj* défendu(e)

force [fɔːs] *n* force *f* ▷ *vt* forcer; (*push*) pousser (de force); **to ~ o.s. to do** se forcer à faire; **in ~** (*being used: rule, law, prices*) en vigueur; (*in large numbers*) en force; **forced** *adj* forcé(e); **forceful** *adj* énergique

ford [fɔːd] *n* gué *m*

fore [fɔː] *n*: **to the ~** en évidence; **forearm** *n* avant-bras *m inv*; **forecast** *n* prévision *f*; (*also: weather forecast*) prévisions *fpl* météorologiques, météo *f* ▷ *vt* (*irreg: like cast*) prévoir; **forecourt** *n* (*of garage*) devant *m*; **forefinger** *n* index *m*; **forefront** *n*: **in the forefront of** au premier rang or plan de; **foreground** *n* premier plan; **forehead** ['fɔrɪd] *n* front *m*

foreign ['fɔrɪn] *adj* étranger(-ère); (*trade*) extérieur(e); (*travel*) à l'étranger; **foreign currency** *n* devises étrangères; **foreigner** *n* étranger(-ère); **foreign exchange** *n* (*system*) change *m*; (*money*) devises *fpl*; **Foreign Office** *n* (*BRIT*) ministère *m* des Affaires étrangères; **Foreign Secretary** *n* (*BRIT*) ministre *m* des Affaires étrangères

fore: **foreman** (*irreg*) *n* (*in construction*) contremaître *m*; **foremost** *adj* le (la) plus en vue, premier(-ière) ▷ *adv*: **first and foremost** avant tout, tout d'abord; **forename** *n* prénom *m*

forensic [fə'rensɪk] *adj*: **~ medicine** médecine légale

foresee (*pt* **foresaw**, *pp* **~n**) [fɔː'siː, -'sɔː, -'siːn] *vt* prévoir; **foreseeable** *adj* prévisible

forest ['fɔrɪst] *n* forêt *f*; **forestry** *n* sylviculture *f*

forever [fə'rɛvə] *adv* pour toujours; (*fig: endlessly*) continuellement

foreword ['fɔːwəːd] *n* avant-propos *m inv*

forfeit ['fɔːfɪt] *vt* perdre

forgave [fə'geɪv] *pt of* **forgive**

forge [fɔːdʒ] *n* forge *f* ▷ *vt* (*signature*) contrefaire; (*wrought iron*) forger; **to ~ money** (*BRIT*) fabriquer de la fausse monnaie; **forger** *n* faussaire *m*; **forgery** *n* faux *m*, contrefaçon *f*

forget (*pt* **forgot**, *pp* **forgotten**) [fə'gɛt, -'gɔt, -'gɔtn] *vt, vi* oublier; **I've forgotten my key/passport** j'ai oublié ma clé/mon passeport; **forgetful** *adj* distrait(e), étourdi(e)

forgive (*pt* **forgave**, *pp* **~n**) [fə'gɪv, -'geɪv, -'gɪvn] *vt* pardonner; **to ~ sb for sth/for doing sth** pardonner qch à qn/à qn de faire qch

forgot [fəˈɡɒt] *pt of* **forget**

forgotten [fəˈɡɒtn] *pp of* **forget**

fork [fɔːk] *n* (*for eating*) fourchette *f*; (*for gardening*) fourche *f*; (*of roads*) bifurcation *f* ▷ *vi* (*road*) bifurquer

forlorn [fəˈlɔːn] *adj* (*deserted*) abandonné(e); (*hope, attempt*) désespéré(e)

form [fɔːm] *n* forme *f*; (*Scol*) classe *f*; (*questionnaire*) formulaire *m* ▷ *vt* former; (*habit*) contracter; **to ~ part of sth** faire partie de qch; **on top ~** en pleine forme

formal [ˈfɔːməl] *adj* (*offer, receipt*) en bonne et due forme; (*person*) cérémonieux(-euse); (*occasion, dinner*) officiel(le); (*garden*) à la française; (*clothes*) de soirée; **formality** [fɔːˈmælɪtɪ] *n* formalité *f*

format [ˈfɔːmæt] *n* format *m* ▷ *vt* (*Comput*) formater

formation [fɔːˈmeɪʃən] *n* formation *f*

former [ˈfɔːmə^r] *adj* ancien(ne); (*before n*) précédent(e); **the ~ ... the latter** le premier ... le second, celui-là ... celui-ci; **formerly** *adv* autrefois

formidable [ˈfɔːmɪdəbl] *adj* redoutable

formula [ˈfɔːmjulə] *n* formule *f*

fort [fɔːt] *n* fort *m*

forthcoming [fɔːθˈkʌmɪŋ] *adj* qui va paraître *or* avoir lieu prochainement; (*character*) ouvert(e), communicatif(-ive); (*available*) disponible

fortieth [ˈfɔːtɪɪθ] *num* quarantième

fortify [ˈfɔːtɪfaɪ] *vt* (*city*) fortifier; (*person*) remonter

fortnight [ˈfɔːtnaɪt] *n* (*BRIT*) quinzaine *f*, quinze jours *mpl*; **fortnightly** *adj* bimensuel(le) ▷ *adv* tous les quinze jours

fortress [ˈfɔːtrɪs] *n* forteresse *f*

fortunate [ˈfɔːtʃənɪt] *adj* heureux(-euse); (*person*) chanceux(-euse); **it is ~ that** c'est une chance que, il est heureux que; **fortunately** *adv* heureusement, par bonheur

fortune [ˈfɔːtʃən] *n* chance *f*; (*wealth*) fortune *f*; **fortune-teller** *n* diseuse *f* de bonne aventure

forty [ˈfɔːtɪ] *num* quarante

forum [ˈfɔːrəm] *n* forum *m*, tribune *f*

forward [ˈfɔːwəd] *adj* (*movement, position*) en avant, vers l'avant; (*not shy*) effronté(e); (*in time*) en avance ▷ *adv* (*also: ~s*) en avant ▷ *n* (*Sport*) avant *m* ▷ *vt* (*letter*) faire suivre; (*parcel, goods*) expédier; (*fig*) promouvoir, favoriser; **to move ~** avancer; **forwarding address** *n* adresse *f* de réexpédition

forward slash *n* barre *f* oblique

fossil [ˈfɒsl] *adj*, *n* fossile *m*

foster [ˈfɒstə^r] *vt* (*encourage*) encourager, favoriser; (*child*) élever (*sans adopter*); **foster child** *n* enfant élevé dans une famille d'accueil

foster parent *n* parent qui élève un enfant sans l'adopter

fought [fɔːt] *pt*, *pp of* **fight**

foul [faul] *adj* (*weather, smell, food*) infect(e); (*language*) ordurier(-ière); (*not shy*) (*Football*) faute *f* ▷ *vt* (*dirty*) salir, encrasser; **he's got a ~ temper** il a un caractère de chien; **foul play** *n* (*Law*) acte criminel

found [faund] *pt*, *pp of* **find** ▷ *vt* (*establish*) fonder; **foundation** [faunˈdeɪʃən] *n* (*act*) fondation *f*; (*base*) fondement *m*; (*also:* **foundation cream**) fond *m* de teint; **foundations** *npl* (*of building*) fondations *fpl*

founder [ˈfaundə^r] *n* fondateur *m* ▷ *vi* couler, sombrer

fountain [ˈfauntɪn] *n* fontaine *f*; **fountain pen** *n* stylo *m* (à encre)

four [fɔː^r] *num* quatre; **on all ~s** à quatre pattes; **four-letter word** *n* obscénité *f*, gros mot; **four-poster** *n* (*also:* **four-poster bed**) lit *m* à baldaquin; **fourteen** *num* quatorze; **fourteenth** *num* quatorzième; **fourth** *num* quatrième ▷ *n* (*Aut: also:* **fourth gear**) quatrième *f*; **four-wheel drive** *n* (*Aut: car*) voiture *f* à quatre roues motrices

fowl [faul] *n* volaille *f*

fox [fɒks] *n* renard *m* ▷ *vt* mystifier

foyer [ˈfɔɪeɪ] *n* (*in hotel*) vestibule *m*; (*Theat*) foyer *m*

fraction [ˈfrækʃən] *n* fraction *f*

fracture [ˈfræktʃə^r] *n* fracture *f* ▷ *vt* fracturer

fragile [ˈfrædʒaɪl] *adj* fragile

fragment [ˈfræɡmənt] *n* fragment *m*

fragrance [ˈfreɪɡrəns] *n* parfum *m*

frail [freɪl] *adj* fragile, délicat(e); (*person*) frêle

frame [freɪm] *n* (*of building*) charpente *f*; (*of human, animal*) charpente, ossature *f*; (*of picture*) cadre *m*; (*of door, window*) encadrement *m*, chambranle *m*; (*of spectacles: also:* **~s**) monture *f* ▷ *vt* (*picture*) encadrer; **~ of mind** disposition *f* d'esprit; **framework** *n* structure *f*

France [frɑːns] *n* la France

franchise [ˈfræntʃaɪz] *n* (*Pol*) droit *m* de vote; (*Comm*) franchise *f*

frank [fræŋk] *adj* franc (franche) ▷ *vt* (*letter*) affranchir; **frankly** *adv* franchement

frantic [ˈfræntɪk] *adj* (*hectic*) frénétique; (*distraught*) hors de soi

fraud [frɔːd] *n* supercherie *f*, fraude *f*, tromperie *f*; (*person*) imposteur *m*

fraught [frɔːt] *adj* (*tense: person*) très tendu(e); (: *situation*) pénible; **~ with** (*difficulties etc*) chargé(e) de, plein(e) de

fray [freɪ] *vt* effilocher ▷ *vi* s'effilocher

freak [friːk] *n* (*eccentric person*) phénomène *m*; (*unusual event*) hasard extraordinaire; (*pej: fanatic*): **health food ~** fana *m/f* or obsédé(e) de l'alimentation saine ▷ *adj* (*storm*) exceptionnel(le); (*accident*) bizarre

freckle [ˈfrɛkl] *n* tache *f* de rousseur

free [friː] *adj* libre; (*gratis*) gratuit(e) ▷ *vt* (*prisoner etc*) libérer; (*jammed object or person*) dégager; **is this seat ~?** la place est libre?; **~ (of charge)** gratuitement; **freedom** *n* liberté *f*; **Freefone®** *n* numéro vert; **free gift** *n* prime *f*; **free kick** *n* (*Sport*) coup franc; **freelance** *adj* (*journalist etc*) indépendant(e), free-lance *inv* ▷ *adv* en free-lance; **freely** *adv* librement; (*liberally*) libéralement; **Freepost®** *n* (*BRIT*) port payé; **free-range** *adj* (*egg*) de ferme; (*chicken*) fermier; **freeway** *n* (*US*) autoroute *f*; **free will** *n* libre arbitre *m*; **of one's own free will** de son plein gré

freeze [friːz] *vb* (*pt* **froze**, *pp* **frozen**) ▷ *vi* geler ▷ *vt* geler; (*food*) congeler; (*prices, salaries*) bloquer, geler ▷ *n* gel *m*; (*of prices, salaries*) blocage *m*; **freezer** *n* congélateur *m*; **freezing** *adj*: **freezing (cold)** (*room etc*) glacial(e); (*person, hands*) gelé(e), glacé(e) ▷ *n*: **3 degrees below freezing** 3 degrés au-dessous de zéro; **it's freezing** il fait un froid glacial; **freezing point** *n* point *m* de congélation

freight [freɪt] *n* (*goods*) fret *m*, cargaison *f*; (*money charged*) fret, prix *m* du transport; **freight train** *n* (*US*) train *m* de marchandises

French [frɛntʃ] *adj* français(e) ▷ *n* (*Ling*) français *m*; **the ~** *npl* les Français; **what's the ~ (word) for ...?** comment dit-on ... en français?; **French bean** *n* (*BRIT*)

haricot vert; **French bread** n pain m français; **French dressing** n (Culin) vinaigrette f; **French fried potatoes** (US **French fries**) npl (pommes de terre fpl) frites fpl; **Frenchman** (irreg) n Français m; **French stick** n ≈ baguette f; **French window** n porte-fenêtre f; **Frenchwoman** (irreg) n Française f

frenzy ['frɛnzɪ] n frénésie f

frequency ['friːkwənsɪ] n fréquence f

frequent adj ['friːkwənt] fréquent(e) ▷ vt [frɪˈkwɛnt] fréquenter; **frequently** ['friːkwəntlɪ] adv fréquemment

fresh [frɛʃ] adj frais (fraîche); (new) nouveau (nouvelle); (cheeky) familier(-ière), culotté(e); **freshen** vi (wind, air) fraîchir; **freshen up** vi faire un brin de toilette; **fresher** n (BRIT University: inf) bizuth m, étudiant(e) de première année; **freshly** adv nouvellement, récemment; **freshman** (US: irreg) n = **fresher**; **freshwater** adj (fish) d'eau douce

fret [frɛt] vi s'agiter, se tracasser

Fri abbr (= Friday) ve

friction ['frɪkʃən] n friction f, frottement m

Friday ['fraɪdɪ] n vendredi m

fridge [frɪdʒ] n (BRIT) frigo m, frigidaire® m

fried [fraɪd] adj frit(e); **~ egg** œuf m sur le plat

friend [frɛnd] n ami(e); **friendly** adj amical(e), (kind) sympathique, gentil(le); (place) accueillant(e); (Pol: country) ami(e) ▷ n (also: **friendly match**) match amical; **friendship** n amitié f

fries [fraɪz] (esp US) npl = **French fried potatoes**

frigate ['frɪgɪt] n frégate f

fright [fraɪt] n peur f, effroi m; **to give sb a ~** faire peur à qn; **to take ~** prendre peur, s'effrayer; **frighten** vt effrayer, faire peur à; **frightened** adj: **to be frightened (of)** avoir peur de(e); **frightening** adj effrayant(e); **frightful** adj affreux(-euse)

frill [frɪl] n (of dress) volant m; (of shirt) jabot m

fringe [frɪndʒ] n (BRIT: of hair) frange f; (edge: of forest etc) bordure f

Frisbee® ['frɪzbɪ] n Frisbee® m

fritter ['frɪtə*] n beignet m

frivolous ['frɪvələs] adj frivole

fro [frəu] see **to**

frock [frɔk] n robe f

frog [frɔg] n grenouille f; **frogman** (irreg) n homme-grenouille m

KEYWORD

from [frɔm] prep **1** (indicating starting place, origin etc) de; **where do you come from?**, **where are you from?** d'où venez-vous?; **where has he come from?** d'où arrive-t-il?; **from London to Paris** de Londres à Paris; **to escape from sb/sth** échapper à qn/qch; **a letter/telephone call from my sister** une lettre/un appel de ma sœur; **to drink from the bottle** boire à (même) la bouteille; **tell him from me that ...** dites-lui de ma part que ...

2 (indicating time) (à partir) de; **from one o'clock to** or **until** or **till two** d'une heure à deux heures; **from January (on)** à partir de janvier

3 (indicating distance) de; **the hotel is one kilometre from the beach** l'hôtel est à un kilomètre de la plage

4 (indicating price, number etc) de; **prices range from £10 to £50** les prix varient entre 10 livres et 50 livres; **the interest rate was increased from 9% to 10%** le taux d'intérêt est passé de 9% à 10%

5 (indicating difference) de; **he can't tell red from green** il ne peut pas distinguer le rouge du vert; **to be different from sb/sth** être différent de qn/qch

6 (because of, on the basis of): **from what he says** d'après ce qu'il dit; **weak from hunger** affaibli par la faim

front [frʌnt] n (of house, dress) devant m; (of coach, train) avant m; (promenade: also: **sea ~**) bord m de mer; (Mil, Pol, Meteorology) front m; (fig: appearances) contenance f, façade f ▷ adj de devant; (seat, wheel) avant inv ▷ vi: **in ~ (of)** devant; **front door** n porte f d'entrée; (of car) portière f avant; **frontier** ['frʌntɪə*] n frontière f; **front page** n première page; **front-wheel drive** n traction f avant

frost [frɔst] n gel m, gelée f; (also: **hoar~**) givre m; **frostbite** n gelures fpl; **frosting** n (esp US: on cake) glaçage m; **frosty** adj (window) couvert(e) de givre; (weather, welcome) glacial(e)

froth [frɔθ] n mousse f, écume f

frown [fraun] n froncement m de sourcils ▷ vi froncer les sourcils

froze [frəuz] pt of **freeze**

frozen ['frəuzn] pp of **freeze** ▷ adj (food) congelé(e); (very cold: person: Comm: assets) gelé(e)

fruit [fruːt] n (pl inv) fruit m; **fruit juice** n jus m de fruit; **fruit machine** n (BRIT) machine f à sous; **fruit salad** n salade f de fruits

frustrate [frʌsˈtreɪt] vt frustrer; **frustrated** adj frustré(e)

fry (pt, pp **fried**) [fraɪ, -d] vt (faire) frire; **small ~** le menu fretin; **frying pan** n poêle f (à frire)

ft. abbr = **foot**; **feet**

fudge [fʌdʒ] n (Culin) sorte de confiserie à base de sucre, de beurre et de lait

fuel [fjuəl] n (for heating) combustible m; (for engine) carburant m; **fuel tank** n (in vehicle) réservoir m de or à carburant

fulfil (US **fulfill**) [fulˈfɪl] vt (function, condition) remplir; (order) exécuter; (wish, desire) satisfaire, réaliser

full [ful] adj plein(e); (details, hotel, bus) complet(-ète); (busy: day) chargé(e); (skirt) ample, large ▷ adv: **to know ~ well that** savoir fort bien que; **I'm ~ (up)** j'ai bien mangé; **~ employment/fare** plein emploi/tarif; **a ~ two hours** deux bonnes heures; **at ~ speed** à toute vitesse; **in ~** (reproduce, quote, pay) intégralement; (write name etc) en toutes lettres; **full-length** adj (portrait) en pied; (coat) long(ue); **full-length film** long métrage; **full moon** n pleine lune; **full-scale** adj (model) grandeur nature inv; (search, retreat) complet(-ète), total(e); **full stop** n point m; **full-time** adj, adv (work) à plein temps; **fully** adv entièrement, complètement; (at least)

fumble ['fʌmbl] vi fouiller, tâtonner; **fumble with** vt fus tripoter

fume [fjuːm] vi (rage) rager; **fumes** npl vapeurs fpl, émanations fpl, gaz mpl

fun [fʌn] n amusement m, divertissement m; **to have ~** s'amuser; **for ~** pour rire; **to make ~ of** se moquer de

function ['fʌŋkʃən] n fonction f; (reception, dinner) cérémonie f, soirée officielle ▷ vi fonctionner

fund [fʌnd] n caisse f, fonds m; (source, store) source f, mine f; **funds** npl (money) fonds mpl

fundamental [fʌndəˈmɛntl] adj fondamental(e)

funeral ['fjuːnərəl] n enterrement m, obsèques fpl (more formal occasion); **funeral director** n entrepreneur m des

pompes funèbres; **funeral parlour** [-'pɑːləʳ] n (BRIT)
dépôt m mortuaire

funfair ['fʌnfɛəʳ] n (BRIT) fête (foraine)

fungus (pl **fungi**) ['fʌŋgəs, -gaɪ] n champignon m;
(mould) moisissure f

funnel ['fʌnl] n entonnoir m; (of ship) cheminée f

funny ['fʌnɪ] adj amusant(e), drôle; (strange)
curieux(-euse), bizarre

fur [fəːʳ] n fourrure f; (BRIT: in kettle etc) (dépôt m de) tartre
m; **fur coat** n manteau m de fourrure

furious ['fjuərɪəs] adj furieux(-euse); (effort) acharné(e)

furnish ['fəːnɪʃ] vt meubler; (supply) fournir; **furnishings**
npl mobilier m, articles mpl d'ameublement

furniture ['fəːnɪtʃəʳ] n meubles mpl, mobilier m; **piece
of ~** meuble m

furry ['fəːrɪ] adj (animal) à fourrure; (toy) en peluche

further ['fəːðəʳ] adj supplémentaire, autre; nouveau
(nouvelle) ▷ adv plus loin; (more) davantage; (moreover)
de plus ▷ vt faire avancer or progresser, promouvoir;
further education n enseignement m postscolaire
(recyclage, formation professionnelle); **furthermore** adv
de plus, en outre

furthest ['fəːðɪst] superlative of **far**

fury ['fjuərɪ] n fureur f

fuse (us **fuze**) [fjuːz] n fusible m; (for bomb etc) amorce f,
détonateur m ▷ vt, vi (metal) fondre; (BRIT: Elec): **to ~ the
lights** faire sauter les fusibles or les plombs; **fuse box** n
boîte f à fusibles

fusion ['fjuːʒən] n fusion f

fuss [fʌs] n (anxiety, excitement) chichis mpl, façons fpl;
(commotion) tapage m; (complaining, trouble) histoire(s)
f(pl); **to make a ~** faire des façons (or des histoires);
to make a ~ of sb dorloter qn; **fussy** adj (person)
tatillon(ne), difficile, chichiteux(-euse); (dress, style)
tarabiscoté(e)

future ['fjuːtʃəʳ] adj futur(e) ▷ n avenir m; (Ling) futur
m; **futures** npl (Comm) opérations fpl à terme; **in (the)
~ à l'avenir

fuze [fjuːz] n, vt, vi (us) = **fuse**

fuzzy ['fʌzɪ] adj (Phot) flou(e); (hair) crépu(e)

g

G [dʒiː] n (Mus): **G** sol m

g. abbr (= gram) g

gadget ['gædʒɪt] n gadget m

Gaelic ['geɪlɪk] adj, n (Ling) gaélique (m)

gag [gæg] n (on mouth) bâillon m; (joke) gag m ▷ vt
(prisoner etc) bâillonner

gain [geɪn] n (improvement) gain m; (profit) gain, profit m
▷ vt gagner ▷ vi (watch) avancer; **to ~ from/by** gagner
de/à; **to ~ on sb** (catch up) rattraper qn; **to ~ 3lbs (in
weight)** prendre 3 livres; **to ~ ground** gagner du terrain

gal. abbr = **gallon**

gala ['gɑːlə] n gala m

galaxy ['gæləksɪ] n galaxie f

gale [geɪl] n coup m de vent

gall bladder ['gɔːl-] n vésicule f biliaire

gallery ['gælərɪ] n (also: **art ~**) musée m ou (: private)
galerie; (: in theatre) dernier balcon

gallon ['gæln] n gallon m (BRIT = 4.543 l; US = 3.785 l)

gallop ['gæləp] n galop m ▷ vi galoper

gallstone ['gɔːlstəun] n calcul m (biliaire)

gamble ['gæmbl] n pari m, risque calculé ▷ vt, vi jouer;
to ~ on (fig) miser sur; **gambler** n joueur m; **gambling**
n jeu m

game [geɪm] n jeu m; (event) match m; (of tennis, chess,
cards) partie f; (Hunting) gibier m ▷ adj (willing): **to be ~
(for)** être prêt(e) (à or pour); **big ~** gros gibier; **games** npl
(Scol) sport m; (sport event) jeux; **games console** ['geɪmz-]
n console f de jeux vidéo; **game show** n jeu télévisé

gammon ['gæmən] n (bacon) quartier m de lard fumé;
(ham) jambon fumé or salé

gang [gæŋ] n bande f; (of workmen) équipe f

gangster ['gæŋstəʳ] n gangster m, bandit m

gap [gæp] n trou m; (in time) intervalle m; (difference): **~
(between)** écart m (entre)

gape [geɪp] vi (person) être or rester bouche bée; (hole,
shirt) être ouvert(e)

gap year n année que certains étudiants prennent pour
voyager ou pour travailler avant d'entrer à l'université

garage ['gærɑːʒ] n garage m; **garage sale** n vide-
grenier m

garbage ['gɑ:bɪdʒ] n (US: rubbish) ordures fpl, détritus mpl; (inf: nonsense) âneries fpl; **garbage can** n (US) poubelle f, boîte f à ordures; **garbage collector** n (US) éboueur m

garden ['gɑ:dn] n jardin m; **gardens** npl (public) jardin public; (private) parc m; **garden centre** (BRIT) n pépinière f, jardinerie f; **gardener** n jardinier m; **gardening** n jardinage m

garlic ['gɑ:lɪk] n ail m

garment ['gɑ:mənt] n vêtement m

garnish ['gɑ:nɪʃ] (Culin) vt garnir ▷ n décoration f

garrison ['gærɪsn] n garnison f

gas [gæs] n gaz m; (US: gasoline) essence f ▷ vt asphyxier; **I can smell ~** ça sent le gaz; **gas cooker** n (BRIT) cuisinière f à gaz; **gas cylinder** n bouteille f de gaz; **gas fire** n (BRIT) radiateur m à gaz

gasket ['gæskɪt] n (Aut) joint m de culasse

gasoline ['gæsəli:n] n (US) essence f

gasp [gɑ:sp] n halètement m; (of shock etc): **she gave a small ~ of pain** la douleur lui coupa le souffle ▷ vi haleter; (fig) avoir le souffle coupé

gas: **gas pedal** n (US) accélérateur m; **gas station** n (US) station-service f; **gas tank** n (US Aut) réservoir m d'essence

gate [geɪt] n (of garden) portail m; (of field, at level crossing) barrière f; (of building, town, at airport) porte f

gateau (pl **~x**) ['gætəu, -z] n gros gâteau m à la crème

gatecrash ['geɪtkræʃ] vt s'introduire sans invitation dans

gateway ['geɪtweɪ] n porte f

gather ['gæðər] vt (flowers, fruit) cueillir; (pick up) ramasser; (assemble: objects) rassembler; (: people) réunir; (: information) recueillir; (understand) comprendre; (Sewing) froncer ▷ vi (assemble) se rassembler; **to ~ speed** prendre de la vitesse; **gathering** n rassemblement m

gauge [geɪdʒ] n (instrument) jauge f ▷ vt jauger; (fig) juger de

gave [geɪv] pt of **give**

gay [geɪ] adj (homosexual) homosexuel(le); (colour) gai, vif (vive)

gaze [geɪz] n regard m fixe ▷ vi: **to ~ at** vt fixer du regard

GB abbr = **Great Britain**

GCSE n abbr (BRIT: = General Certificate of Secondary Education) examen passé à l'âge de 16 ans sanctionnant les connaissances de l'élève

gear [gɪər] n matériel m, équipement m; (Tech) engrenage m; (Aut) vitesse f ▷ vt (fig: adapt) adapter; **top** or (US) **high/low ~** quatrième (or cinquième)/première vitesse; **in ~** en prise; **gear up** vi: **to ~ up (to do)** se préparer (à faire); **gear box** n boîte f de vitesse; **gear lever** n levier m de vitesse; **gear shift** (US) n = **gear lever**; **gear stick** (BRIT) n = **gear lever**

geese [gi:s] npl of **goose**

gel [dʒel] n gelée f

gem [dʒem] n pierre précieuse

Gemini ['dʒemɪnaɪ] n les Gémeaux mpl

gender ['dʒendər] n genre m; (person's sex) sexe m

gene [dʒi:n] n (Biol) gène m

general ['dʒenərəl] n général m ▷ adj général(e); **in ~** en général; **general anaesthetic** (US **general anesthetic**) n anesthésie générale; **general election** n élection(s) législative(s); **generalize** vi généraliser; **generally** adv généralement; **general practitioner** n généraliste m/f;

general store n épicerie f

generate ['dʒenəreɪt] vt engendrer; (electricity) produire

generation [dʒenə'reɪʃən] n génération f; (of electricity etc) production f

generator ['dʒenəreɪtər] n générateur m

generosity [dʒenə'rɒsɪtɪ] n générosité f

generous ['dʒenərəs] adj généreux(-euse); (copious) copieux(-euse)

genetic [dʒɪ'netɪk] adj génétique; **~ engineering** ingénierie m génétique; **~ fingerprinting** système m d'empreinte génétique; **genetically modified** adj (food etc) génétiquement modifié(e); **genetics** n génétique f

Geneva [dʒɪ'ni:və] n Genève

genitals ['dʒenɪtlz] npl organes génitaux

genius ['dʒi:nɪəs] n génie m

gent [dʒent] n abbr (BRIT inf) = **gentleman**

gentle ['dʒentl] adj doux (douce); (breeze, touch) léger(-ère)

gentleman (irreg) ['dʒentlmən] n monsieur m; (well-bred man) gentleman m

gently ['dʒentlɪ] adv doucement

gents [dʒents] n W.-C. mpl (pour hommes)

genuine ['dʒenjuɪn] adj véritable, authentique; (person, emotion) sincère; **genuinely** adv sincèrement, vraiment

geographic(al) [dʒɪə'græfɪk(l)] adj géographique

geography [dʒɪ'ɒɡrəfɪ] n géographie f

geology [dʒɪ'ɒlədʒɪ] n géologie f

geometry [dʒɪ'ɒmɪtrɪ] n géométrie f

geranium [dʒɪ'reɪnɪəm] n géranium m

geriatric [dʒerɪ'ætrɪk] adj gériatrique ▷ n patient(e) gériatrique

germ [dʒɜ:m] n (Med) microbe m

German ['dʒɜ:mən] adj allemand(e) ▷ n Allemand(e); (Ling) allemand m; **German measles** n rubéole f

Germany ['dʒɜ:mənɪ] n Allemagne f

gesture ['dʒestjər] n geste m

KEYWORD

get [get] (pt, pp **got**, pp **gotten** (US)) vi **1** (become, be) devenir; **to get old/tired** devenir vieux/fatigué, vieillir/se fatiguer; **to get drunk** s'enivrer; **to get dirty** se salir; **to get married** se marier; **when do I get paid?** quand est-ce que je serai payé?; **it's getting late** il se fait tard

2 (go): **to get to/from** aller à/de; **to get home** rentrer chez soi; **how did you get here?** comment es-tu arrivé ici?

3 (begin) commencer or se mettre à; **to get to know sb** apprendre à connaître qn; **I'm getting to like him** je commence à l'apprécier; **let's get going** or **started** allons-y

4 (modal aux vb): **you've got to do it** il faut que vous le fassiez; **I've got to tell the police** je dois le dire à la police

▷ vt **1**: **to get sth done** (do) faire qch; (have done) faire faire qch; **to get sth/sb ready** préparer qch/qn; **to get one's hair cut** se faire couper les cheveux; **to get the car going** or **to go** (faire) démarrer la voiture; **to get sb to do sth** faire faire qch à qn

2 (obtain: money, permission, results) obtenir, avoir; (buy) acheter; (find: job, flat) trouver; (fetch: person, doctor, object) aller chercher; **to get sth for sb** procurer qch à qn; **get me Mr Jones, please** (on phone) passez-moi Mr Jones, s'il vous plaît; **can I get you a drink?** est-ce que je peux vous servir à boire?

3 (receive: present, letter) recevoir, avoir; (acquire: reputation) avoir; (prize) obtenir; **what did you get for your birthday?** qu'est-ce que tu as eu pour ton anniversaire?; **how much did you get for the painting?** combien avez-vous vendu le tableau?

4 (catch) prendre, saisir, attraper; (hit: target etc) atteindre; **to get sb by the arm/throat** prendre or saisir or attraper qn par le bras/à la gorge; **get him!** arrête-le!; **the bullet got him in the leg** il a pris la balle dans la jambe

5 (take, move): **to get sth to sb** faire parvenir qch à qn; **do you think we'll get it through the door?** on arrivera à le faire passer par la porte?

6 (catch, take: plane, bus etc) prendre; **where do I get the train for Birmingham?** où prend-on le train pour Birmingham?

7 (understand) comprendre, saisir; (hear) entendre; **I've got it!** j'ai compris!; **I don't get your meaning** je ne vois or comprends pas ce que vous voulez dire; **I didn't get your name** je n'ai pas entendu votre nom

8 (have, possess): **to have got** avoir; **how many have you got?** vous en avez combien?

9 (illness) avoir; **I've got a cold** j'ai le rhume; **she got pneumonia and died** elle a fait une pneumonie et elle en est morte

get away vi partir, s'en aller; (escape) s'échapper

get away with vt fus (punishment) en être quitte pour; (crime etc) se faire pardonner

get back vi (return) rentrer
▷ vt récupérer, recouvrer; **when do we get back?** quand serons-nous de retour?

get in vi entrer; (arrive home) rentrer; (train) arriver

get into vt fus entrer dans; (car, train etc) monter dans; (clothes) mettre, enfiler, endosser; **to get into bed/a rage** se mettre au lit/en colère

get off vi (from train etc) descendre; (depart: person, car) s'en aller
▷ vt (remove: clothes, stain) enlever
▷ vt fus (train, bus) descendre de; **where do I get off?** où est-ce que je dois descendre?

get on vi (at exam etc) se débrouiller; (agree): **to get on (with)** s'entendre (avec); **how are you getting on?** comment ça va?
▷ vt fus monter dans; (horse) monter sur

get out vi sortir; (of vehicle) descendre
▷ vt sortir

get out of vt fus sortir de; (duty etc) échapper à, se soustraire à

get over vt fus (illness) se remettre de

get through vi (Tel) avoir la communication; **to get through to sb** atteindre qn

get up vi (rise) se lever
▷ vt fus monter

getaway ['gɛtəweɪ] n fuite f

Ghana ['gɑːnə] n Ghana m

ghastly ['gɑːstlɪ] adj atroce, horrible

ghetto ['gɛtəu] n ghetto m

ghost [gəust] n fantôme m, revenant m

giant ['dʒaɪənt] n géant(e) ▷ adj géant(e), énorme

gift [gɪft] n cadeau m; (donation, talent) don m; **gifted** adj doué(e); **gift shop** (us **gift store**) n boutique f de cadeaux; **gift token, gift voucher** n chèque-cadeau m

gig [gɪg] n (inf: concert) concert m

gigabyte ['dʒɪgəbaɪt] n gigaoctet m

gigantic [dʒaɪˈgæntɪk] adj gigantesque

giggle ['gɪgl] vi pouffer, ricaner sottement

gills [gɪlz] npl (of fish) ouïes fpl, branchies fpl

gilt [gɪlt] n dorure f ▷ adj doré(e)

gimmick ['gɪmɪk] n truc m

gin [dʒɪn] n gin m

ginger ['dʒɪndʒə'] n gingembre m

gipsy ['dʒɪpsɪ] n = **gypsy**

giraffe [dʒɪˈrɑːf] n girafe f

girl [gəːl] n fille f, fillette f; (young unmarried woman) jeune fille; (daughter) fille; **an English ~** une jeune Anglaise; **girl band** n girls band m; **girlfriend** n (of girl) amie f; (of boy) petite amie; **Girl Guide** n (BRIT) éclaireuse f; (Roman Catholic) guide f; **Girl Scout** n (US) = **Girl Guide**

gist [dʒɪst] n essentiel m

give [gɪv] vb (pt **gave**, pp **~n**) ▷ vt donner ▷ vi (break) céder; (stretch: fabric) se prêter; **to ~ sb sth**, **~ sth to sb** donner qch à qn; (gift) offrir qch à qn; (message) transmettre qch à qn; **to ~ a cry/sigh** pousser un cri/un soupir; **give away** vt donner; (give free) faire cadeau de; (betray) donner, trahir; (disclose) révéler; **give back** vt rendre; **give in** vi céder ▷ vt donner; **give out** vt (food etc) distribuer; **give up** vi renoncer ▷ vt renoncer à; **to ~ up smoking** arrêter de fumer; **to ~ o.s. up** se rendre

given ['gɪvn] pp of **give** ▷ adj (fixed: time, amount) donné(e), déterminé(e) ▷ conj: **~ the circumstances ...** étant donné les circonstances ..., vu les circonstances ...; **~ that ...** étant donné que ...

glacier ['glæsɪə'] n glacier m

glad [glæd] adj content(e); **gladly** ['glædlɪ] adv volontiers

glamorous ['glæmərəs] adj (person) séduisant(e); (job) prestigieux(-euse)

glamour (US **glamor**) ['glæmə'] n éclat m, prestige m

glance [glɑːns] n coup m d'œil ▷ vi: **to ~ at** jeter un coup d'œil à

gland [glænd] n glande f

glare [glɛə'] n (of anger) regard furieux; (of light) lumière éblouissante; (of publicity) feux mpl ▷ vi briller d'un éclat aveuglant; **to ~ at** lancer un regard or des regards furieux à; **glaring** adj (mistake) criant(e), qui saute aux yeux

glass [glɑːs] n verre m; **glasses** npl (spectacles) lunettes fpl

glaze [gleɪz] vt (door) vitrer; (pottery) vernir ▷ n vernis m

gleam [gliːm] vi luire, briller

glen [glɛn] n vallée f

glide [glaɪd] vi glisser; (Aviat, bird) planer; **glider** n (Aviat) planeur m

glimmer ['glɪmə'] n lueur f

glimpse [glɪmps] n vision passagère, aperçu m ▷ vt entrevoir, apercevoir

glint [glɪnt] vi étinceler

glisten ['glɪsn] vi briller, luire

glitter ['glɪtə'] vi scintiller, briller

global ['gləubl] adj (world-wide) mondial(e); (overall) global(e); **globalization** n mondialisation f; **global warming** n réchauffement m de la planète

globe [gləub] n globe m

gloom [gluːm] n obscurité f; (sadness) tristesse f, mélancolie f; **gloomy** adj (person) morose; (place, outlook) sombre

glorious ['glɔːrɪəs] adj glorieux(-euse); (beautiful) splendide

glory ['glɔːrɪ] n gloire f; splendeur f

gloss [glɒs] n (shine) brillant m, vernis m; (also: **~ paint**) peinture brillante or laquée

glossary ['glɒsərɪ] n glossaire m, lexique m

glossy ['glɒsɪ] adj brillant(e), luisant(e) ▷ n (also: **~ magazine**) revue f de luxe

glove [glʌv] n gant m; **glove compartment** n (Aut) boîte f à gants, vide-poches m inv

glow [gləu] vi rougeoyer; (face) rayonner; (eyes) briller

glucose ['gluːkəus] n glucose m

glue [gluː] n colle f ▷ vt coller

GM abbr (= genetically modified) génétiquement modifié(e)

gm abbr (= gram) g

GMO n abbr (= genetically modified organism) OGM m

GMT abbr (= Greenwich Mean Time) GMT

gnaw [nɔː] vt ronger

go [gəu] vb (pt **went**, pp **gone**) ▷ vi aller; (depart) partir, s'en aller; (work) marcher; (break) céder; (time) passer; (be sold): **to go for £10** se vendre 10 livres; (become): **to go pale/mouldy** pâlir/moisir ▷ n (pl **goes**): **to have a go (at)** essayer (de faire); **to be on the go** être en mouvement; **whose go is it?** à qui est-ce de jouer?; **he's going to do it** il va le faire, il est sur le point de le faire; **to go for a walk** aller se promener; **to go dancing/shopping** aller danser/faire les courses; **to go and see sb, to go to see sb** aller voir qn; **how did it go?** comment est-ce que ça s'est passé?; **to go round the back/by the shop** passer par derrière/devant le magasin; **... to go** (us: food) ... à emporter; **go ahead** vi (take place) avoir lieu; (get going) y aller; **go away** vi partir, s'en aller; **go back** vi rentrer; revenir; (go again) retourner; **go by** vi (years, time) passer, s'écouler ▷ vt fus s'en tenir à; (believe) en croire; **go down** vi descendre; (number, price, amount) baisser; (ship) couler; (sun) se coucher ▷ vt fus descendre; **go for** vt fus (fetch) aller chercher; (like) aimer; (attack) s'en prendre à; attaquer; **go in** vi entrer; **go into** vt fus entrer dans; (investigate) étudier, examiner; (embark on) se lancer dans; **go off** vi partir, s'en aller; (food) se gâter; (milk) tourner; (bomb) sauter; (alarm clock) sonner; (alarm) se déclencher; (lights etc) s'éteindre; (event) se dérouler ▷ vt fus ne plus aimer; **the gun went off** le coup est parti; **go on** vi continuer; (happen) se passer ▷ vt fus (lights) s'allumer ▷ vt fus: **to go on doing** continuer à faire; **go out** vi sortir; (fire, light) s'éteindre; (tide) descendre; **to go out with sb** sortir avec qn; **go over** vi (ship) chavirer ▷ vt fus (check) revoir, vérifier; **go past** vt fus: **to go past sth** passer devant qch; **go round** vi (circulate: news, rumour) circuler; (revolve) tourner; (suffice) suffire (pour tout le monde); (visit): **to go round to sb's** passer chez qn; aller chez qn; (make a detour): **to go round (by)** faire un détour (par); **go through** vt fus (town etc) traverser; (search through) fouiller; (suffer) subir; **go up** vi monter; (price) augmenter ▷ vt fus gravir; **go with** vt fus aller avec; **go without** vt fus se passer de

go-ahead ['gəuəhed] adj dynamique, entreprenant(e) ▷ n feu vert

goal [gəul] n but m; **goalkeeper** n gardien m de but; **goal-post** n poteau m de but

goat [gəut] n chèvre f

gobble ['gɒbl] vt (also: **~ down, ~ up**) engloutir

god [gɒd] n dieu m; **G~** Dieu; **godchild** n filleul(e); **goddaughter** n filleule f; **goddess** n déesse f;

godfather n parrain m; **godmother** n marraine f; **godson** n filleul m

goggles ['gɒglz] npl (for skiing etc) lunettes (protectrices); (for swimming) lunettes de piscine

going ['gəuɪŋ] n (conditions) état m du terrain ▷ adj: **the ~ rate** le tarif (en vigueur)

gold [gəuld] n or m ▷ adj en or; (reserves) d'or; **golden** adj (made of gold) en or; (gold in colour) doré(e); **goldfish** n poisson m rouge; **goldmine** n mine f d'or; **gold-plated** adj plaqué(e) or inv

golf [gɒlf] n golf m; **golf ball** n balle f de golf; (on typewriter) boule f; **golf club** n club m de golf; (stick) club m, crosse f de golf; **golf course** n terrain m de golf; **golfer** n joueur(-euse) de golf

gone [gɒn] pp of **go**

gong [gɒŋ] n gong m

good [gud] adj bon(ne); (kind) gentil(le); (child) sage; (weather) beau (belle) ▷ n bien m; **goods** npl marchandise f, articles mpl; **~!** bon!, très bien!; **to be ~ at** être bon en; **to be ~ for** être bon pour; **it's no complaining** cela ne sert à rien de se plaindre; **to make ~** (deficit) combler; (losses) compenser; **for ~** (for ever) pour de bon, une fois pour toutes; **would you be ~ enough to ...?** auriez-vous la bonté or l'amabilité de ...?; **is this any ~?** (will it do?) est-ce que ceci fera l'affaire?, est-ce que cela peut vous rendre service?; (what's it like?) qu'est-ce que ça vaut?; **a ~ deal (of)** beaucoup (de); **a ~ many** beaucoup (de); **~ morning/afternoon!** bonjour!; **~ evening!** bonsoir!; **~ night!** bonsoir!; (on going to bed) bonne nuit!; **goodbye** excl au revoir!; **to say goodbye to sb** dire au revoir à qn; **Good Friday** n Vendredi saint; **good-looking** adj beau (belle), bien inv; **good-natured** adj (person) qui a un bon naturel; **goodness** n (of person) bonté f; **for goodness sake!** je vous en prie!; **goodness gracious!** mon Dieu!; **goods train** n (BRIT) train m de marchandises; **goodwill** n bonne volonté

goose (pl **geese**) [guːs, giːs] n oie f

gooseberry ['guzbərɪ] n groseille f à maquereau; **to play ~** (BRIT) tenir la chandelle

goose bumps, goose pimples npl chair f de poule

gorge [gɔːdʒ] n gorge f ▷ vt: **to ~ o.s. (on)** se gorger (de)

gorgeous ['gɔːdʒəs] adj splendide, superbe

gorilla [gə'rɪlə] n gorille m

gosh (inf) [gɒʃ] excl mince alors!

gospel ['gɒspl] n évangile m

gossip ['gɒsɪp] n (chat) bavardages mpl; (malicious) commérage m, cancans mpl; (person) commère f ▷ vi bavarder; cancaner, faire des commérages; **gossip column** n (Press) échos mpl

got [gɒt] pt, pp of **get**

gotten ['gɒtn] (us) pp of **get**

gourmet ['guəmeɪ] n gourmet m, gastronome m/f

govern ['gʌvən] vt gouverner; (influence) déterminer; **government** n gouvernement m; (BRIT: ministers) ministère m; **governor** n (of colony, state, bank) gouverneur m; (of school, hospital etc) administrateur(-trice); (BRIT: of prison) directeur(-trice)

gown [gaun] n robe f; (of teacher; BRIT: of judge) toge f

G.P. n abbr (Med) = **general practitioner**

grab [græb] vt saisir, empoigner ▷ vi: **to ~ at** essayer de saisir

grace [greɪs] n grâce f ▷ vt (honour) honorer; (adorn) orner; **5 days' ~** un répit de 5 jours; **graceful** adj gracieux(-euse), élégant(e); **gracious** ['greɪʃəs] adj bienveillant(e)

grade [greɪd] n (Comm: quality) qualité f; (size) calibre m; (type) catégorie f; (in hierarchy) grade m, échelon m; (Scol) note f; (us: school class) classe f; (: gradient) pente f ▷ vt classer; (by size) calibrer; **grade crossing** n (us) passage à niveau; **grade school** n (us) école f primaire

gradient ['greɪdɪənt] n inclinaison f, pente f

gradual ['grædjuəl] adj graduel(le), progressif(-ive); **gradually** adv peu à peu, graduellement

graduate n ['grædjuɪt] diplômé(e) d'université; (us: of high school) diplômé(e) de fin d'études ▷ vi ['grædjueɪt] obtenir un diplôme d'université (or de fin d'études); **graduation** [grædju'eɪʃən] n cérémonie f de remise des diplômes

graffiti [grə'fiːtɪ] npl graffiti mpl

graft [grɑːft] n (Agr, Med) greffe f; (bribery) corruption f ▷ vt greffer; **hard ~** (BRIT: inf) boulot acharné

grain [greɪn] n (single piece) grain m; (no pl: cereals) céréales fpl; (us: corn) blé m

gram [græm] n gramme m

grammar ['græmə'] n grammaire f; **grammar school** n (BRIT) ≈ lycée m

gramme [græm] n = **gram**

gran (inf) [græn] n (BRIT inf) mamie f (inf), mémé f (inf)

grand [grænd] adj magnifique, splendide; (gesture etc) noble; **grandad** (inf) n = **granddad**; **grandchild** (pl **~ren**) n petit-fils m, petite-fille f; **grandchildren** npl petits-enfants; **granddad** n (inf) papy m (inf), papi m (inf), pépé m (inf); **granddaughter** n petite-fille f; **grandfather** n grand-père m; **grandma** n (inf) = **gran**; **grandmother** n grand-mère f; **grandpa** n (inf) = **granddad**; **grandparents** npl grands-parents mpl; **grand piano** n piano m à queue; **Grand Prix** ['grɑ̃:'priː] n (Aut) grand prix automobile; **grandson** n petit-fils m

granite ['grænɪt] n granit m

granny ['grænɪ] n (inf) = **gran**

grant [grɑːnt] vt accorder; (a request) accéder à; (admit) concéder ▷ n (Scol) bourse f; (Admin) subside m, subvention f; **to take sth for ~ed** considérer qch comme acquis; **to take sb for ~ed** considérer qn comme faisant partie du décor

grape [greɪp] n raisin m

grapefruit ['greɪpfruːt] n pamplemousse m

graph [grɑːf] n graphique m, courbe f; **graphic** ['græfɪk] adj graphique; (vivid) vivant(e); **graphics** n (art) arts mpl graphiques; (process) graphisme m ▷ npl (drawings) illustrations fpl

grasp [grɑːsp] vt saisir ▷ n (grip) prise f; (fig) compréhension f, connaissance f

grass [grɑːs] n herbe f; (lawn) gazon m; **grasshopper** n sauterelle f

grate [greɪt] n grille f de cheminée ▷ vi grincer ▷ vt (Culin) râper

grateful ['greɪtful] adj reconnaissant(e)

grater ['greɪtə'] n râpe f

gratitude ['grætɪtjuːd] n gratitude f

grave [greɪv] n tombe f ▷ adj grave, sérieux(-euse)

gravel ['grævl] n gravier m

gravestone ['greɪvstəun] n pierre tombale

graveyard ['greɪvjɑːd] n cimetière m

gravity ['grævɪtɪ] n (Physics) gravité f, pesanteur f; (seriousness) gravité

gravy ['greɪvɪ] n jus m (de viande), sauce f (au jus de viande)

gray [greɪ] adj (us) = **grey**

graze [greɪz] vi paître, brouter ▷ vt (touch lightly) frôler, effleurer; (scrape) écorcher ▷ n écorchure f

grease [griːs] n (fat) graisse f; (lubricant) lubrifiant m ▷ vt graisser; lubrifier; **greasy** adj gras(se), graisseux(-euse); (hands, clothes) graisseux

great [greɪt] adj grand(e); (heat, pain etc) très fort(e), intense; (inf) formidable; **Great Britain** n Grande-Bretagne f; **great-grandfather** n arrière-grand-père m; **great-grandmother** n arrière-grand-mère f; **greatly** adv très, grandement; (with verbs) beaucoup

Greece [griːs] n Grèce f

greed [griːd] n (also: **~iness**) avidité f; (for food) gourmandise f; **greedy** adj avide; (for food) gourmand(e)

Greek [griːk] adj grec (grecque) ▷ n Grec (Grecque); (Ling) grec m

green [griːn] adj vert(e); (inexperienced) (bien) jeune, naïf(-ive); (ecological: product etc) écologique ▷ n (colour) vert m; (on golf course) green m; (stretch of grass) pelouse f; **greens** npl (vegetables) légumes verts; **green card** n (Aut) carte verte; (us: work permit) permis m de travail; **greengage** n reine-claude f; **greengrocer** n (BRIT) marchand m de fruits et légumes; **greengrocer's (shop)** n magasin m de fruits et légumes; **greenhouse** n serre f; **greenhouse effect** n: **the greenhouse effect** l'effet m de serre

Greenland ['griːnlənd] n Groenland m

green salad n salade verte

greet [griːt] vt accueillir; **greeting** n salutation f; **Christmas/birthday greetings** souhaits mpl de Noël/de bon anniversaire; **greeting(s) card** n carte f de vœux

grew [gruː] pt of **grow**

grey (us **gray**) [greɪ] adj gris(e); (dismal) sombre; **greyhaired** adj aux cheveux gris; **greyhound** n lévrier m

grid [grɪd] n grille f; (Elec) réseau m; **gridlock** n (traffic jam) embouteillage m

grief [griːf] n chagrin m, douleur f

grievance ['griːvəns] n doléance f, grief m; (cause for complaint) grief

grieve [griːv] vi avoir du chagrin; se désoler ▷ vt faire de la peine à, affliger; **to ~ for sb** pleurer qn

grill [grɪl] n (on cooker) gril m; (also: **mixed ~**) grillade(s) f(pl) ▷ vt (BRIT) griller; (inf: question) cuisiner

grille [grɪl] n grillage m; (Aut) calandre f

grim [grɪm] adj sinistre, lugubre; (serious, stern) sévère

grime [graɪm] n crasse f

grin [grɪn] n large sourire m ▷ vi sourire

grind [graɪnd] vb (pt, pp **ground**) ▷ vt écraser; (coffee, pepper etc) moudre; (us: meat) hacher ▷ n (work) corvée f

grip [grɪp] n (handclasp) poigne f; (control) prise f; (handle) poignée f; (holdall) sac m de voyage ▷ vt saisir, empoigner; (viewer, reader) captiver; **to come to ~s with** se colleter avec, en venir aux prises avec; **to ~ the road** (Aut) adhérer à la route; **gripping** adj prenant(e), palpitant(e)

grit [grɪt] n gravillon m; (courage) cran m ▷ vt (road) sabler; **to ~ one's teeth** serrer les dents

grits [grɪts] npl (us) gruau m de maïs

groan [grəun] n (of pain) gémissement m ▷ vi gémir

grocer ['grəusə'] n épicier m; **groceries** npl provisions fpl; **grocer's (shop), grocery** n épicerie f

groin [grɔɪn] n aine f

groom [gruːm] n (for horses) palefrenier m; (also: **bride~**) marié m ▷ vt (horse) panser; (fig): **to ~ sb for** former qn pour

groove [gruːv] n sillon m, rainure f

grope [grəup] vi tâtonner; **to ~ for** chercher à tâtons

gross [grəus] adj grossier(-ière); (Comm) brut(e); **grossly** adv (greatly) très, grandement

grotesque [grə'tɛsk] adj grotesque

ground [graund] pt, pp of **grind** ▷ n sol m, terre f; (land) terrain m, terres fpl; (Sport) terrain; (reason: gen pl) raison f; (US: also: ~ **wire**) terre f ▷ vt (plane) empêcher de décoller, retenir au sol; (US Elec) équiper d'une prise de terre; **grounds** npl (gardens etc) parc m, domaine m; (of coffee) marc m; **on the ~, to the ~** par terre; **to gain/lose ~** gagner/perdre du terrain; **ground floor** n (BRIT) rez-de-chaussée m; **groundsheet** n (BRIT) tapis m de sol; **groundwork** n préparation f

group [gruːp] n groupe m ▷ vt (also: ~ **together**) grouper ▷ vi (also: ~ **together**) se grouper

grouse [graus] n (pl inv: bird) grouse f (sorte de coq de bruyère) ▷ vi (complain) rouspéter, râler

grovel ['grɔvl] vi (fig) ramper (devant)

grow (pt **grew**, pp **~n**) [grəu, gruː, grəun] vi (plant) pousser, croître; (person) grandir; (increase) augmenter, se développer; (become) devenir; **to ~ rich/weak** s'enrichir/s'affaiblir ▷ vt cultiver, faire pousser; (hair, beard) laisser pousser; **grow on** vt fus: **that painting is ~ing on me** je finirai par aimer ce tableau; **grow up** vi grandir

growl [graul] vi grogner

grown [grəun] pp of **grow**; **grown-up** n adulte m/f, grande personne

growth [grəuθ] n croissance f, développement m; (what has grown) pousse f, poussée f; (Med) grosseur f, tumeur f

grub [grʌb] n larve f; (inf: food) bouffe f

grubby ['grʌbɪ] adj crasseux(-euse)

grudge [grʌdʒ] n rancune f ▷ vt: **to ~ sb sth** (in giving) donner qch à qn à contre-cœur; (resent) reprocher qch à qn; **to bear sb a ~ (for)** garder rancune or en vouloir à qn (de)

gruelling (US **grueling**) ['gruəlɪŋ] adj exténuant(e)

gruesome ['gruːsəm] adj horrible

grumble ['grʌmbl] vi rouspéter, ronchonner

grumpy ['grʌmpɪ] adj grincheux(-euse)

grunt [grʌnt] vi grogner

guarantee [gærən'tiː] n garantie f ▷ vt garantir

guard [gɑːd] n garde f; (one man) garde m; (BRIT Rail) chef m de train; (safety device: on machine) dispositif m de sûreté; (also: **fire~**) garde-feu m inv ▷ vt garder, surveiller; (protect): **to ~ sb/sth (against or from)** protéger qn/qch (contre); **to be on one's ~** (fig) être sur ses gardes; **guardian** n gardien(ne); (of minor) tuteur(-trice)

guerrilla [gə'rɪlə] n guérillero m

guess [gɛs] vi deviner ▷ vt deviner; (estimate) évaluer; (US) croire, penser ▷ n supposition f, hypothèse f; **to take** or **have a ~** essayer de deviner

guest [gɛst] n invité(e); (in hotel) client(e); **guest house** n pension f; **guest room** n chambre f d'amis

guidance ['gaɪdəns] n (advice) conseils mpl

guide [gaɪd] n (person) guide m/f; (book) guide m; (also: **Girl G~**) éclaireuse f; (Roman Catholic) guide f ▷ vt guider; **is there an English-speaking ~?** est-ce que l'un des guides parle anglais?; **guidebook** n guide m; **guide dog** n chien m d'aveugle; **guided tour** n visite guidée; **what time does the guided tour start?** la visite guidée

commence à quelle heure?; **guidelines** npl (advice) instructions générales, conseils mpl

guild [gɪld] n (History) corporation f; (sharing interests) cercle m, association f

guilt [gɪlt] n culpabilité f; **guilty** adj coupable

guinea pig ['gɪnɪ-] n cobaye m

guitar [gɪ'tɑːʳ] n guitare f; **guitarist** n guitariste m/f

gulf [gʌlf] n golfe m; (abyss) gouffre m

gull [gʌl] n mouette f

gulp [gʌlp] vi avaler sa salive; (from emotion) avoir la gorge serrée, s'étrangler ▷ vt (also: ~ **down**) avaler

gum [gʌm] n (Anat) gencive f; (glue) colle f; (also: **chewing-~**) chewing-gum m ▷ vt coller

gun [gʌn] n (small) revolver m, pistolet m; (rifle) fusil m, carabine f; (cannon) canon m; **gunfire** n fusillade f; **gunman** (irreg) n bandit armé; **gunpoint** n: **at gunpoint** sous la menace du pistolet (or fusil); **gunpowder** n poudre f à canon; **gunshot** n coup m de feu

gush [gʌʃ] vi jaillir; (fig) se répandre en effusions

gust [gʌst] n (of wind) rafale f

gut [gʌt] n intestin m, boyau m; **guts** npl (Anat) boyaux mpl; (inf: courage) cran m

gutter ['gʌtəʳ] n (of roof) gouttière f; (in street) caniveau m

guy [gaɪ] n (inf: man) type m; (also: **~rope**) corde f; (figure) effigie de Guy Fawkes

Guy Fawkes' Night [gaɪ'fɔːks-] n: **gym** [dʒɪm] n (also: **~nasium**) gymnase m; (also: **~nastics**) gym f; **gymnasium** n gymnase m; **gymnast** n gymnaste m/f; **gymnastics** n, npl gymnastique f; **gym shoes** npl chaussures fpl de gym(nastique)

gynaecologist (US **gynecologist**) [gaɪnɪ'kɔlədʒɪst] n gynécologue m/f

gypsy ['dʒɪpsɪ] n gitan(e), bohémien(ne)

haberdashery [hæbə'dæʃərɪ] n (BRIT) mercerie f
habit ['hæbɪt] n habitude f; (costume: Rel) habit m
habitat ['hæbɪtæt] n habitat m
hack [hæk] vt hacher, tailler ▷ n (pej: writer) nègre m;
hacker n (Comput) pirate m (informatique)
had [hæd] pt, pp of **have**
haddock (pl ~ or ~s) ['hædək] n églefin m; **smoked ~**
haddock m
hadn't ['hædnt] = **had not**
haemorrhage (US hemorrhage) ['hemərɪdʒ] n
hémorragie f
haemorrhoids (US hemorrhoids) ['hemərɔɪdz] npl
hémorroïdes fpl
haggle ['hægl] vi marchander
Hague [heɪg] n: **The ~ La** Haye
hail [heɪl] n grêle f ▷ vt (call) héler; (greet) acclamer ▷ vi
grêler; **hailstone** n grêlon m
hair [hɛəʳ] n cheveux mpl; (on body) poils mpl; (of animal)
pelage m; (single hair: on head) cheveu m; (: on body, of
animal) poil m; **to do one's ~** se coiffer; **hairband** n
(elasticated) bandeau m; (plastic) serre-tête m; **hairbrush**
n brosse f à cheveux; **haircut** n coupe f (de cheveux);
hairdo n coiffure f; **hairdresser** n coiffeur(-euse);
hairdresser's n salon m de coiffure, coiffeur m; **hair
dryer** n sèche-cheveux m, séchoir m; **hair gel** n gel m
pour cheveux; **hair spray** n laque f (pour les cheveux);
hairstyle n coiffure f; **hairy** adj poilu(e), chevelu(e); (inf:
frightening) effrayant(e)
hake (pl ~ or ~s) [heɪk] n colin m, merlu m
half [hɑːf] n (pl halves) moitié f; (of beer: also: ~ **pint**)
≈ demi m; (Rail, bus: also: ~ **fare**) demi-tarif m; (Sport:
of match) mi-temps f ▷ adj demi(e) ▷ adv (à) moitié,
à demi; **~ an hour** une demi-heure; **~ a dozen** une
demi-douzaine; **~ a pound** une demi-livre, ≈ 250 g; **two
and a ~** deux et demi; **to cut sth in ~** couper qch en
deux; **half board** n (BRIT: in hotel) demi-pension f; **half-
brother** n demi-frère m; **half day** n demi-journée f;
half fare n demi-tarif m; **half-hearted** adj tiède, sans
enthousiasme; **half-hour** n demi-heure f; **half-price**
adj à moitié prix ▷ adv (also: **at half-price**) à moitié prix;

half term n (BRIT Scol) vacances fpl (de demi-trimestre);
half-time n mi-temps f; **halfway** adv à mi-chemin;
halfway through sth au milieu de qch
hall [hɔːl] n salle f; (entrance way: big) hall m; (small) entrée
f; (US: corridor) couloir m; (mansion) château m, manoir m
hallmark ['hɔːlmɑːk] n poinçon m; (fig) marque f
hallo [hə'ləu] excl = **hello**
hall of residence n (BRIT) pavillon m or résidence f
universitaire
Halloween, Hallowe'en ['hæləu'iːn] n veille f de la
Toussaint
hallucination [həluːsɪ'neɪʃən] n hallucination f
hallway ['hɔːlweɪ] n (entrance) vestibule m; (corridor)
couloir m
halo ['heɪləu] n (of saint etc) auréole f
halt [hɔːlt] n halte f, arrêt m ▷ vt faire arrêter; (progress
etc) interrompre ▷ vi faire halte, s'arrêter
halve [hɑːv] vt (apple etc) partager ou diviser en deux;
(reduce by half) réduire de moitié
halves [hɑːvz] npl of **half**
ham [hæm] n jambon m
hamburger ['hæmbəːgəʳ] n hamburger m
hamlet ['hæmlɪt] n hameau m
hammer ['hæməʳ] n marteau m ▷ vt (nail) enfoncer;
(fig) éreinter, démolir ▷ vi (at door) frapper à coups
redoublés; **to ~ a point home to sb** faire rentrer qch
dans la tête de qn
hammock ['hæmək] n hamac m
hamper ['hæmpəʳ] vt gêner ▷ n panier m (d'osier)
hamster ['hæmstəʳ] n hamster m
hamstring ['hæmstrɪŋ] n (Anat) tendon m du jarret
hand [hænd] n main f; (of clock) aiguille f; (handwriting)
écriture f; (at cards) jeu m; (worker) ouvrier(-ière) m/f;
passer, donner; **to give sb a ~** donner un coup de main
à qn; **at ~** à portée de la main; **in ~** (situation) en main;
(work) en cours; **to be on ~** (person) être disponible;
(emergency services) se tenir prêt(e) (à intervenir); **to
~** (information etc) sous la main, à portée de la main;
on the one ~ ..., on the other ~ d'une part ..., d'autre
part; **hand down** vt passer; (tradition, heirloom)
transmettre; (US: sentence, verdict) prononcer; **hand
in** vt remettre; **hand out** vt distribuer; **hand over** vt
remettre; (powers etc) transmettre; **handbag** n sac m à
main; **hand baggage** n = **hand luggage**; **handbook** n
manuel m; **handbrake** n frein m à main; **handcuffs** npl
menottes fpl; **handful** n poignée f
handicap ['hændɪkæp] n handicap m ▷ vt
handicaper; **mentally/physically ~ped** handicapé(e)
mentalement/physiquement
handkerchief ['hæŋkətʃɪf] n mouchoir m
handle ['hændl] n (of door etc) poignée f; (of cup etc)
anse f; (of knife etc) manche m; (of saucepan) queue f; (for
winding) manivelle f ▷ vt toucher, manier; (deal with)
s'occuper de; (treat: people) prendre; **"~ with care"**
"fragile"; **to fly off the ~** s'énerver; **handlebar(s)** n(pl)
guidon m
hand: hand luggage n bagages mpl à main; **handmade**
adj fait(e) à la main; **handout** n (money) aide f, don m;
(leaflet) prospectus m; (at lecture) polycopié m; **hands-
free** adj (phone) mains libres inv ▷ n (also: **hands-free
kit**) kit m mains libres inv
handsome ['hænsəm] adj beau (belle); (profit)
considérable
handwriting ['hændraɪtɪŋ] n écriture f

handy ['hændɪ] *adj* (*person*) adroit(e); (*close at hand*) sous la main; (*convenient*) pratique

hang (*pt, pp* hung) [hæŋ, hʌŋ] *vt* accrocher; (*criminal*): (*pt, pp* ~ed) pendre ▷ *vi* pendre; (*hair, drapery*) tomber ▷ *n*: **to get the ~ of (doing) sth** (*inf*) attraper le coup pour faire qch; **hang about, hang around** *vi* traîner; **hang down** *vi* pendre; **hang on** *vi* (*wait*) attendre; **hang out** *vt* (*washing*) étendre (dehors) ▷ *vi* (*inf: live*) habiter, percher; (: *spend time*) traîner; **hang round** *vi* = **hang around**; **hang up** *vi* (*Tel*) raccrocher ▷ *vt* (*coat, painting etc*) accrocher, suspendre

hanger ['hæŋəʳ] *n* cintre *m*, portemanteau *m*

hang-gliding ['hæŋglaɪdɪn] *n* vol *m* libre or sur aile delta

hangover ['hæŋəʊvəʳ] *n* (*after drinking*) gueule *f* de bois

hankie, hanky ['hæŋkɪ] *n abbr* = **handkerchief**

happen ['hæpən] *vi* arriver, se passer, se produire; **what's ~ing?** que se passe-t-il?; **she ~ed to be free** il s'est trouvé (*or* se trouvait) qu'elle était libre; **as it ~s** justement

happily ['hæpɪlɪ] *adv* heureusement; (*cheerfully*) joyeusement

happiness ['hæpɪnɪs] *n* bonheur *m*

happy ['hæpɪ] *adj* heureux(-euse); **~ with** (*arrangements etc*) satisfait(e) de; **to be ~ to do** faire volontiers; **~ birthday!** bon anniversaire!

harass ['hærəs] *vt* accabler, tourmenter; **harassment** *n* tracasseries *fpl*

harbour, (*us* **harbor**) ['hɑ:bəʳ] *n* port *m* ▷ *vt* héberger, abriter; (*hopes, suspicions*) entretenir

hard [hɑ:d] *adj* dur(e); (*question, problem*) difficile; (*facts, evidence*) concret(-ète) ▷ *adv* (*work*) dur; (*think, try*) sérieusement; **to look ~ at** regarder fixement; (*thing*) regarder de près; **no ~ feelings!** sans rancune!; **to be ~ of hearing** être dur(e) d'oreille; **to be ~ done by** être traité(e) injustement; **hardback** *n* livre relié; **hardboard** *n* Isorel® *m*; **hard disk** *n* (*Comput*) disque dur; **harden** *vt* durcir; (*fig*) endurcir ▷ *vi* (*substance*) durcir

hardly ['hɑ:dlɪ] *adv* (*scarcely*) à peine; (*harshly*) durement; **~ anywhere/ever** presque nulle part/jamais

hard: **hardship** *n* (*difficulties*) épreuves *fpl*; (*deprivation*) privations *fpl*; **hard shoulder** *n* (*BRIT Aut*) accotement stabilisé; **hard-up** *adj* (*inf*) fauché(e); **hardware** *n* quincaillerie *f*; (*Comput, Mil*) matériel *m*; **hardware shop** (*us* **hardware store**) *n* quincaillerie *f*; **hard-working** *adj* travailleur(-euse), consciencieux(-euse)

hardy ['hɑ:dɪ] *adj* robuste; (*plant*) résistant(e) au gel

hare [hɛəʳ] *n* lièvre *m*

harm [hɑ:m] *n* mal *m*; (*wrong*) tort *m* ▷ *vt* (*person*) faire du mal *or* du tort à; (*thing*) endommager; **out of ~'s way** à l'abri du danger, en lieu sûr; **harmful** *adj* nuisible; **harmless** *adj* inoffensif(-ive)

harmony ['hɑ:mənɪ] *n* harmonie *f*

harness ['hɑ:nɪs] *n* harnais *m* ▷ *vt* (*horse*) harnacher; (*resources*) exploiter

harp [hɑ:p] *n* harpe *f* ▷ *vi*: **to ~ on about** revenir toujours sur

harsh [hɑ:ʃ] *adj* (*hard*) dur(e); (*severe*) sévère; (*unpleasant: sound*) discordant(e); (: *light*) cru(e)

harvest ['hɑ:vɪst] *n* (*of corn*) moisson *f*; (*of fruit*) récolte *f*; (*of grapes*) vendange *f* ▷ *vt* moissonner; récolter; vendanger

has [hæz] *vb see* **have**

hasn't ['hæznt] = **has not**

hassle ['hæsl] *n* (*inf: fuss*) histoire(s) *f(pl)*

haste [heɪst] *n* hâte *f*, précipitation *f*; **hasten** ['heɪsn] *vt* hâter, accélérer ▷ *vi* se hâter, s'empresser; **hastily** *adv* à la hâte; (*leave*) précipitamment; **hasty** *adj* (*decision, action*) hâtif(-ive); (*departure, escape*) précipité(e)

hat [hæt] *n* chapeau *m*

hatch [hætʃ] *n* (*Naut: also*: ~**way**) écoutille *f*; (*BRIT: also*: **service ~**) passe-plats *m inv* ▷ *vi* éclore

hatchback ['hætʃbæk] *n* (*Aut*) modèle *m* avec hayon arrière

hate [heɪt] *vt* haïr, détester ▷ *n* haine *f*; **hatred** ['heɪtrɪd] *n* haine *f*

haul [hɔ:l] *vt* traîner, tirer ▷ *n* (*of fish*) prise *f*; (*of stolen goods etc*) butin *m*

haunt [hɔ:nt] *vt* (*subj: ghost, fear*) hanter; (: *person*) fréquenter ▷ *n* repaire *m*; **haunted** *adj* (*castle etc*) hanté(e); (*look*) égaré(e), hagard(e)

○ **KEYWORD**

have [hæv] (*pt, pp* had) *aux vb* **1** (*gen*) avoir; être; **to have eaten/slept** avoir mangé/dormi; **to have arrived/gone** être arrivé(e)/allé(e); **having finished** *or* **when he had finished, he left** quand il a eu fini, il est parti; **we'd already eaten** nous avions déjà mangé

2 (*in tag questions*): **you've done it, haven't you?** vous l'avez fait, n'est-ce pas?

3 (*in short answers and questions*): **no I haven't!/yes we have!** mais non!/mais si!; **so I have!** ah oui!, oui c'est vrai!; **I've been there before, have you?** j'y suis déjà allé, et vous?

▷ *modal aux vb* (*be obliged*): **to have (got) to do sth** devoir faire qch, être obligé(e) de faire qch; **she has (got) to do it** elle doit le faire, il faut qu'elle le fasse; **you haven't to tell her** vous n'êtes pas obligé de le lui dire; (*must not*) ne le lui dites surtout pas; **do you have to book?** il faut réserver?

▷ *vt* **1** (*possess*) avoir; **he has (got) blue eyes/dark hair** il a les yeux bleus/les cheveux bruns

2 (*referring to meals etc*): **to have breakfast** prendre le petit déjeuner; **to have dinner/lunch** dîner/déjeuner; **to have a drink** prendre un verre; **to have a cigarette** fumer une cigarette

3 (*receive*) avoir, recevoir; (*obtain*) avoir; **may I have your address?** puis-je avoir votre adresse?; **you can have it for £5** vous pouvez l'avoir pour 5 livres; **I must have it for tomorrow** il me le faut pour demain; **to have a baby** avoir un bébé

4 (*maintain, allow*): **I won't have it!** ça ne se passera pas comme ça!; **we can't have that** nous ne tolérerons pas ça

5 (*by sb else*): **to have sth done** faire faire qch; **to have one's hair cut** se faire couper les cheveux; **to have sb do sth** faire faire qch à qn

6 (*experience, suffer*) avoir; **to have a cold/flu** avoir un rhume/la grippe; **to have an operation** se faire opérer; **she had her bag stolen** elle s'est fait voler son sac

7 (+*noun*): **to have a swim/walk** nager/se promener; **to have a bath/shower** prendre un bain/une douche; **let's have a look** regardons; **to have a meeting** se réunir; **to have a party** organiser une fête; **let me have a try** laissez-moi essayer

haven ['heɪvn] *n* port *m*; (*fig*) havre *m*

haven't ['hævnt] = **have not**

havoc ['hævək] n ravages mpl

Hawaii [hə'waɪ:] n (îles fpl) Hawaï m

hawk [hɔ:k] n faucon m

hawthorn ['hɔ:θɔ:n] n aubépine f

hay [heɪ] n foin m; **hay fever** n rhume m des foins; **haystack** n meule f de foin

hazard ['hæzəd] n (risk) danger m, risque m ▷ vt risquer, hasarder; **hazardous** adj hasardeux(-euse), risqué(e); **hazard warning lights** npl (Aut) feux mpl de détresse

haze [heɪz] n brume f

hazel ['heɪzl] n (tree) noisetier m ▷ adj (eyes) noisette inv; **hazelnut** n noisette f

hazy ['heɪzɪ] adj brumeux(-euse); (idea) vague

he [hi:] pron il; **it is he who ...** c'est lui qui ...; **here he is** le voici

head [hɛd] n tête f; (leader) chef m; (of school) directeur(-trice); (of secondary school) proviseur m ▷ vt (list) être en tête de; (group, company) être à la tête de; **~s or tails** pile ou face; **~ first** la tête la première; **~ over heels in love** follement or éperdument amoureux(-euse); **to ~ the ball** faire une tête; **head for** vt fus se diriger vers; (disaster) aller à; **head off** vt (threat, danger) détourner; **headache** n mal m de tête; **to have a headache** avoir mal à la tête; **heading** n titre m; (subject title) rubrique f; **headlamp** (BRIT) n = **headlight**; **headlight** n phare m; **headline** n titre m; **head office** n siège m, bureau m central; **headphones** npl casque m (à écouteurs); **headquarters** npl (of business) bureau or siège central; (Mil) quartier général m; **headroom** n (in car) hauteur f de plafond; (under bridge) hauteur limite; **headscarf** n foulard m; **headset** n = **headphones**; **headteacher** n directeur(-trice); (of secondary school) proviseur m; **head waiter** n maître m d'hôtel

heal [hi:l] vt, vi guérir

health [hɛlθ] n santé f; **health care** n services médicaux; **health centre** n (BRIT) centre m de santé; **health food** n aliment(s) naturel(s); **Health Service** n: **the Health Service** (BRIT) ≈ la Sécurité Sociale; **healthy** adj (person) en bonne santé; (climate, food, attitude etc) sain(e)

heap [hi:p] n tas m ▷ vt (also: **~ up**) entasser, amonceler; **she ~ed her plate with cakes** elle a chargé son assiette de gâteaux; **~s (of)** (inf: lots) des tas (de)

hear (pt, pp **~d**) [hɪə², hə:d] vt entendre; (news) apprendre ▷ vi entendre; **to ~ about** entendre parler de; (have news of) avoir des nouvelles de; **to ~ from sb** recevoir des nouvelles de qn

heard [hə:d] pt, pp of **hear**

hearing ['hɪərɪŋ] n (sense) ouïe f; (of witnesses) audition f; (of a case) audience f; **hearing aid** n appareil m acoustique

hearse [hə:s] n corbillard m

heart [hɑ:t] n cœur m; **hearts** npl (Cards) cœur; **at ~** au fond; **by ~** (learn, know) par cœur; **to lose/take ~** perdre/prendre courage; **heart attack** n crise f cardiaque; **heartbeat** n battement m de cœur; **heartbroken** adj: **to be heartbroken** avoir beaucoup de chagrin; **heartburn** n brûlures fpl d'estomac; **heart disease** n maladie f cardiaque

hearth [hɑ:θ] n foyer m, cheminée f

heartless ['hɑ:tlɪs] adj (person) sans cœur, insensible; (treatment) cruel(le)

hearty ['hɑ:tɪ] adj chaleureux(-euse); (appetite) solide;

(dislike) cordial(e); (meal) copieux(-euse)

heat [hi:t] n chaleur f; (Sport: also: **qualifying ~**) éliminatoire f ▷ vt chauffer; **heat up** vi (liquid) chauffer; (room) se réchauffer ▷ vt réchauffer; **heated** adj chauffé(e); (fig) passionné(e), échauffé(e), excité(e); **heater** n appareil m de chauffage; radiateur m; (in car) chauffage m; (water heater) chauffe-eau m

heather ['hɛðə²] n bruyère f

heating ['hi:tɪŋ] n chauffage m

heatwave ['hi:tweɪv] n vague f de chaleur

heaven ['hɛvn] n ciel m, paradis m; (fig) paradis; **heavenly** adj céleste, divin(e)

heavily ['hɛvɪlɪ] adv lourdement; (drink, smoke) beaucoup; (sleep, sigh) profondément

heavy ['hɛvɪ] adj lourd(e); (work, rain, user, eater) gros(se); (drinker, smoker) grand(e); (schedule, week) chargé(e)

Hebrew ['hi:bru:] adj hébraïque ▷ n (Ling) hébreu m

Hebrides ['hɛbrɪdi:z] npl: **the ~** les Hébrides fpl

hectare ['hɛktɑ:²] n (BRIT) hectare m

hectic ['hɛktɪk] adj (extremely busy) très chargé(e); (day) mouvementé(e); (lifestyle) trépidant(e)

he'd [hi:d] = **he would**; **he had**

hedge [hɛdʒ] n haie f ▷ vi se dérober ▷ vt: **to ~ one's bets** (fig) se couvrir

hedgehog ['hɛdʒhɔg] n hérisson m

heed [hi:d] vt (also: **take ~ of**) tenir compte de, prendre garde à

heel [hi:l] n talon m ▷ vt retalonner

hefty ['hɛftɪ] adj (person) costaud(e); (parcel) lourd(e); (piece, price) gros(se)

height [haɪt] n (of person) taille f, grandeur f; (of object) hauteur f; (of plane, mountain) altitude f; (high ground) hauteur, éminence f; (fig: of glory, fame, power) sommet m; (: of luxury, stupidity) comble m; **at the ~ of summer** au cœur de l'été; **heighten** vt hausser, surélever; (fig) augmenter

heir [ɛə²] n héritier m; **heiress** n héritière f

held [hɛld] pt, pp of **hold**

helicopter ['hɛlɪkɔptə²] n hélicoptère m

hell [hɛl] n enfer m; **oh ~!** (inf) merde!

he'll [hi:l] = **he will**; **he shall**

hello ['hɛləu] excl bonjour!; (to attract attention) hé!; (surprise) tiens!

helmet ['hɛlmɪt] n casque m

help [hɛlp] n aide f; (cleaner etc) femme f de ménage ▷ vt, vi aider; **~!** au secours!; **~ yourself** servez-vous; **can you ~ me?** pouvez-vous m'aider?; **can I ~ you?** (in shop) vous désirez?; **he can't ~ it** il n'y peut rien; **help out** vi aider ▷ vt: **to ~ sb out** aider qn; **helper** n aide m/f, assistant(e); **helpful** adj serviable, obligeant(e); (useful) utile; **helping** n portion f; **helpless** adj impuissant(e); (baby) sans défense; **helpline** n service m d'assistance téléphonique; (free) ≈ numéro vert

hem [hɛm] n ourlet m ▷ vt ourler

hemisphere ['hɛmɪsfɪə²] n hémisphère m

hemorrhage ['hɛmərɪdʒ] n (US) = **haemorrhage**

hemorrhoids ['hɛmərɔɪdz] npl (US) = **haemorrhoids**

hen [hɛn] n poule f; (female bird) femelle f

hence [hɛns] adv (therefore) d'où, de là; **2 years ~** d'ici 2 ans

hen night, hen party n soirée f entre filles (avant le mariage de l'une d'elles)

hepatitis [hɛpə'taɪtɪs] n hépatite f

her [hə:²] pron (direct) la, l' + vowel or h mute; (indirect) lui;

(stressed, after prep) elle ▷ adj son (sa), ses pl; see also **me; my**

herb [həːb] n herbe f; **herbal** adj à base de plantes; **herbal tea** n tisane f

herd [həːd] n troupeau m

here [hɪəʳ] adv ici; (time) alors ▷ excl tiens!, tenez!; **~!** (present) présent!; **~ is, ~ are** voici; **~ he/she is** le (la) voici

hereditary [hɪˈredɪtrɪ] adj héréditaire

heritage [ˈherɪtɪdʒ] n héritage m, patrimoine m

hernia [ˈhəːnɪə] n hernie f

hero (pl **~es**) [ˈhɪərəu] n héros m; **heroic** [hɪˈrəuɪk] adj héroïque

heroin [ˈherəuɪn] n héroïne f (drogue)

heroine [ˈherəuɪn] n héroïne f (femme)

heron [ˈherən] n héron m

herring [ˈherɪŋ] n hareng m

hers [həːz] pron le (la) sien(ne), les siens (siennes); see also **mine¹**

herself [həːˈself] pron (reflexive) se; (emphatic) elle-même; (after prep) elle; see also **oneself**

he's [hiːz] = **he is; he has**

hesitant [ˈhezɪtənt] adj hésitant(e), indécis(e)

hesitate [ˈhezɪteɪt] vi: **to ~ (about/to do)** hésiter (sur/à faire); **hesitation** [hezɪˈteɪʃən] n hésitation f

heterosexual [ˈhetərəuˈseksjuəl] adj, n hétérosexuel(le)

hexagon [ˈheksəgən] n hexagone m

hey [heɪ] excl hé!

heyday [ˈheɪdeɪ] n: **the ~ of** l'âge m d'or de, les beaux jours de

HGV n abbr = **heavy goods vehicle**

hi [haɪ] excl salut!; (to attract attention) hé!

hibernate [ˈhaɪbəneɪt] vi hiberner

hiccough, hiccup [ˈhɪkʌp] vi hoqueter ▷ n: **to have (the) ~s** avoir le hoquet

hid [hɪd] pt of **hide**

hidden [ˈhɪdn] pp of **hide** ▷ adj: **~ agenda** intentions non déclarées

hide [haɪd] n (skin) peau f ▷ vb (pt **hid**, pp **hidden**) ▷ vt cacher ▷ vi: **to ~ (from sb)** se cacher (de qn)

hideous [ˈhɪdɪəs] adj hideux(-euse), atroce

hiding [ˈhaɪdɪŋ] n (beating) correction f, volée f de coups; **to be in ~** (concealed) se tenir caché(e)

hi-fi [ˈhaɪfaɪ] adj, n abbr (= high fidelity) hi-fi f inv

high [haɪ] adj haut(e); (speed, respect, number) grand(e); (price) élevé(e); (wind) fort(e), violent(e); (voice) aigu(ë) ▷ adv haut, en haut; **20 m ~** haut(e) de 20 m; **~ in the air** haut dans le ciel; **highchair** n (child's) chaise haute; **high-class** adj (neighbourhood, hotel) chic inv, de grand standing; **higher education** n études supérieures; **high heels** npl talons hauts, hauts talons; **high jump** n (Sport) saut m en hauteur; **highlands** [ˈhaɪləndz] npl région montagneuse; **the Highlands** (in Scotland) les Highlands mpl; **highlight** n (fig: of event) point culminant ▷ vt (emphasize) faire ressortir, souligner; **highlights** npl (in hair) reflets mpl; **highlighter** n (pen) surligneur (lumineux); **highly** adv extrêmement, très; (unlikely) fort; (recommended, skilled, qualified) hautement; **to speak highly of** dire beaucoup de bien de; **highness** n: **His/Her Highness** son Altesse f; **high-rise** n (also: **high-rise block, high-rise building**) tour f (d'habitation); **high school** n lycée m; (us) établissement m d'enseignement supérieur; **high season** n (BRIT) haute saison; **high street** n (BRIT) grand-rue f; **high-tech**

(inf) adj de pointe; **highway** n (BRIT) route f; (US) route nationale; **Highway Code** n (BRIT) code m de la route

hijack [ˈhaɪdʒæk] vt détourner (par la force); **hijacker** n auteur m d'un détournement d'avion, pirate m de l'air

hike [haɪk] vi faire des excursions à pied ▷ n excursion f à pied, randonnée f; **hiker** n promeneur(-euse), excursionniste m/f; **hiking** n excursions fpl à pied, randonnée f

hilarious [hɪˈleərɪəs] adj (behaviour, event) désopilant(e)

hill [hɪl] n colline f; (fairly high) montagne f; (on road) côte f; **hillside** n (flanc m de) coteau m; **hill walking** n randonnée f de basse montagne; **hilly** adj vallonné(e), montagneux(-euse)

him [hɪm] pron (direct) le, l' + vowel or h mute; (stressed, indirect, after prep) lui; see also **me; himself** pron (reflexive) se; (emphatic) lui-même; (after prep) lui; see also **oneself**

hind [haɪnd] adj de derrière

hinder [ˈhɪndəʳ] vt gêner; (delay) retarder

hindsight [ˈhaɪndsaɪt] n: **with (the benefit of) ~** avec du recul, rétrospectivement

Hindu [ˈhɪnduː] n Hindou(e); **Hinduism** n (Rel) hindouisme m

hinge [hɪndʒ] n charnière f ▷ vi (fig): **to ~ on** dépendre de

hint [hɪnt] n allusion f; (advice) conseil m; (clue) indication f ▷ vt: **to ~ that** insinuer que ▷ vi: **to ~ at** faire une allusion à

hip [hɪp] n hanche f

hippie, hippy [ˈhɪpɪ] n hippie m/f

hippo [ˈhɪpəu] (pl **~s**) n hippopotame m

hippopotamus [hɪpəˈpotəməs] (pl **~es** or **hippopotami**) n hippopotame m

hippy [ˈhɪpɪ] n = **hippie**

hire [ˈhaɪəʳ] vt (BRIT: car, equipment) louer; (worker) embaucher, engager ▷ n location f; **for ~** à louer; (taxi) libre; **I'd like to ~ a car** je voudrais louer une voiture; **hire(d) car** n (BRIT) voiture f de location; **hire purchase** n (BRIT) achat m (or vente f) à tempérament or crédit

his [hɪz] pron le (la) sien(ne), les siens (siennes) ▷ adj son (sa), ses pl; see also **mine¹**; see also **my**

Hispanic [hɪsˈpænɪk] adj (in US) hispano-américain(e) ▷ n Hispano-Américain(e)

hiss [hɪs] vi siffler

historian [hɪˈstɔːrɪən] n historien(ne)

historic(al) [hɪˈstorɪk(l)] adj historique

history [ˈhɪstərɪ] n histoire f

hit [hɪt] vt (pt, pp **~**) frapper; (reach: target) atteindre, toucher; (collide with: car) entrer en collision avec, heurter; (fig: affect) toucher ▷ n coup m; (success) succès m; (song) tube m; (to website) visite f; (on search engine) résultat m de recherche; **to ~ it off with sb** bien s'entendre avec qn; **hit back** vi: **to ~ back at sb** prendre sa revanche sur qn

hitch [hɪtʃ] vt (fasten) accrocher, attacher; (also: **~ up**) remonter d'une saccade ▷ vi faire de l'autostop ▷ n (difficulty) anicroche f, contretemps m; **to ~ a lift** faire du stop; **hitch-hike** vi faire de l'auto-stop; **hitch-hiker** n auto-stoppeur(-euse); **hitch-hiking** n auto-stop m, stop m (inf)

hi-tech [ˈhaɪˈtek] adj de pointe

hitman [ˈhɪtmæn] (irreg) n (inf) tueur m à gages

HIV n abbr (= human immunodeficiency virus) HIV m, VIH m; **~-negative/positive** séronégatif(-ive)/positif(-ive)

hive [haɪv] n ruche f

hoard [hɔːd] n (of food) provisions fpl, réserves fpl; (of money) trésor m ▷ vt amasser

hoarse [hɔːs] adj enroué(e)

hoax [həʊks] n canular m

hob [hɔb] n plaque chauffante

hobble ['hɔbl] vi boitiller

hobby ['hɔbɪ] n passe-temps favori

hobo ['həʊbəʊ] n (us) vagabond m

hockey ['hɔkɪ] n hockey m; **hockey stick** n crosse f de hockey

hog [hɔg] n porc (châtré) ▷ vt (fig) accaparer; **to go the whole ~** aller jusqu'au bout

Hogmanay [hɔgmə'neɪ] n réveillon m du jour de l'An, Saint-Sylvestre f

hoist [hɔɪst] n palan m ▷ vt hisser

hold [həʊld] (pt, pp **held**) vt tenir; (contain) contenir; (meeting) tenir; (keep back) retenir; (believe) considérer; (possess) avoir ▷ vi (withstand pressure) tenir (bon); (be valid) valoir; (on telephone) attendre ▷ n prise f; (find) influence f; (Naut) cale f; **to catch** or **get (a) ~ of** saisir; **to get ~ of** (find) trouver; **~ the line!** (Tel) ne quittez pas!; **to ~ one's own** (fig) (bien) se défendre; **hold back** vt retenir; (secret) cacher; **hold on** vi tenir bon; (wait) attendre; **~ on!** (Tel) ne quittez pas!; **to ~ on to sth** (grasp) se cramponner à qch; (keep) conserver or garder qch; **hold out** vt offrir ▷ vi (resist): **to ~ out (against)** résister (devant), tenir bon (devant); **hold up** vt (raise) lever; (support) soutenir; (delay) retarder; (: traffic) ralentir; (rob) braquer; **holdall** n (BRIT) fourre-tout m inv; **holder** n (container) support m; (of ticket, record) détenteur(-trice); (of office, title, passport etc) titulaire m/f

hole [həʊl] n trou m

holiday ['hɔlədɪ] n (BRIT: vacation) vacances fpl; (day off) jour m de congé; (public) jour férié; **to be on ~** être en vacances; **I'm here on ~** je suis ici en vacances; **holiday camp** n (also: **holiday centre**) camp m de vacances; **holiday job** n (BRIT) boulot m (inf) de vacances; **holiday-maker** n (BRIT) vacancier(-ière); **holiday resort** n centre m de villégiature or de vacances

Holland ['hɔlənd] n Hollande f

hollow ['hɔləʊ] adj creux(-euse); (fig) faux (fausse) ▷ n creux m; (in land) dépression f (de terrain), cuvette f ▷ vt: **to ~ out** creuser, évider

holly ['hɔlɪ] n houx m

Hollywood ['hɔlɪwʊd] n Hollywood m

holocaust ['hɔləkɔːst] n holocauste m

holy ['həʊlɪ] adj saint(e); (bread, water) bénit(e); (ground) sacré(e)

home [həʊm] n foyer m, maison f; (country) pays natal, patrie f; (institution) maison ▷ adj de famille; (Econ, Pol) national(e), intérieur(e); (Sport: team) qui reçoit; (: match, win) sur leur or notre terrain ▷ adv chez soi, à la maison; au pays natal; (right in: nail etc) à fond; **at ~** chez soi, à la maison; **to go (or come) ~** rentrer (chez soi), rentrer à la maison (or au pays); **make yourself at ~** faites comme chez vous; **home address** n domicile permanent; **homeland** n patrie f; **homeless** adj sans foyer, sans abri; **homely** adj (plain) simple, sans prétention; (welcoming) accueillant(e); **home-made** adj fait(e) à la maison; **home match** n match m à domicile; **Home Office** n (BRIT) ministère m de l'Intérieur; **home owner** n propriétaire occupant; **home page** n (Comput) page f d'accueil; **Home Secretary** n (BRIT) ministre m de l'Intérieur; **homesick** adj: **to be homesick** avoir le

mal du pays; (missing one's family) s'ennuyer de sa famille; **home town** n ville natale; **homework** n devoirs mpl

homicide ['hɔmɪsaɪd] n (us) homicide m

homoeopathic (us **homeopathic**) [həʊmɪɔ'pæθɪk] adj (medicine) homéopathique; (doctor) homéopathe

homoeopathy (us **homeopathy**) [həʊmɪ'ɔpəθɪ] n homéopathie f

homosexual [hɔməʊ'sɛksjuəl] adj, n homosexuel(le)

honest ['ɔnɪst] adj honnête; (sincere) franc (franche); **honestly** adv honnêtement; franchement; **honesty** n honnêteté f

honey ['hʌnɪ] n miel m; **honeymoon** n lune f de miel, voyage m de noces; **we're on honeymoon** nous sommes en voyage de noces; **honeysuckle** n chèvrefeuille m

Hong Kong ['hɔŋ'kɔŋ] n Hong Kong

honorary ['ɔnərərɪ] adj honoraire; (duty, title) honorifique; **~ degree** diplôme m honoris causa

honour (us **honor**) ['ɔnə'] vt honorer ▷ n honneur m; **to graduate with ~s** obtenir sa licence avec mention; **honourable** (us **honorable**) adj honorable; **honours degree** n (Scol) ≈ licence f avec mention

hood [hʊd] n capuchon m; (of cooker) hotte f; (BRIT Aut) capote f; (us Aut) capot m; **hoodie** ['hʊdɪ] n (top) sweat m à capuche

hoof [huːf] (pl **~s** or **hooves**) [huːf, huːvz] n sabot m

hook [hʊk] n crochet m; (on dress) agrafe f; (for fishing) hameçon m ▷ vt accrocher; **off the ~** (Tel) décroché

hooligan ['huːlɪgən] n voyou m

hoop [huːp] n cerceau m

hooray [huː'reɪ] excl = **hurray**

hoot [huːt] vi (BRIT: Aut) klaxonner; (siren) mugir; (owl) hululer

Hoover® ['huːvə'] n (BRIT) aspirateur m ▷ vt: **to hoover** (room) passer l'aspirateur dans; (carpet) passer l'aspirateur sur

hooves [huːvz] npl of **hoof**

hop [hɔp] vi sauter; (on one foot) sauter à cloche-pied; (bird) sautiller

hope [həʊp] vt, vi espérer ▷ n espoir m; **I ~ so** je l'espère; **I ~ not** j'espère que non; **hopeful** adj (person) plein(e) d'espoir; (situation) prometteur(-euse), encourageant(e); **hopefully** adv (expectantly) avec espoir, avec optimisme; (one hopes) avec un peu de chance; **hopeless** adj désespéré(e); (useless) nul(le)

hops [hɔps] npl houblon m

horizon [hə'raɪzn] n horizon m; **horizontal** [hɔrɪ'zɔntl] adj horizontal(e)

hormone ['hɔːməʊn] n hormone f

horn [hɔːn] n corne f; (Mus) cor m; (Aut) klaxon m

horoscope ['hɔrəskəʊp] n horoscope m

horrendous [hə'rɛndəs] adj horrible, affreux(-euse)

horrible ['hɔrɪbl] adj horrible, affreux(-euse)

horrid ['hɔrɪd] adj (person) détestable; (weather, place, smell) épouvantable

horrific [hɔ'rɪfɪk] adj horrible

horrifying ['hɔrɪfaɪɪŋ] adj horrifiant(e)

horror ['hɔrə'] n horreur f; **horror film** n film m d'épouvante

hors d'œuvre [ɔː'dəːvrə] n hors d'œuvre m

horse [hɔːs] n cheval m; **horseback: on horseback** adj, adv à cheval; **horse chestnut** n (nut) marron m (d'Inde); (tree) marronnier m (d'Inde); **horsepower** n puissance f (en chevaux); (unit) cheval-vapeur m (CV); **horse-racing**

n courses *fpl* de chevaux; **horseradish** *n* raifort *m*; **horse riding** *n* (*BRIT*) équitation *f*

hose [həʊz] *n* (*also*: **~pipe**) tuyau *m*; (*also*: **garden ~**) tuyau d'arrosage; **hosepipe** *n* tuyau *m*; (*in garden*) tuyau d'arrosage

hospital ['hɔspɪtl] *n* hôpital *m*; **in ~** à l'hôpital; **where's the nearest ~?** où est l'hôpital le plus proche?

hospitality [hɔspɪ'tælɪtɪ] *n* hospitalité *f*

host [həʊst] *n* hôte *m*; (*TV, Radio*) présentateur(-trice), animateur(-trice); (*large number*): **a ~ of** une foule de; (*Rel*) hostie *f*

hostage ['hɔstɪdʒ] *n* otage *m*

hostel ['hɔstl] *n* foyer *m*; (*also*: **youth ~**) auberge *f* de jeunesse

hostess ['həʊstɪs] *n* hôtesse *f*; (*BRIT: also*: **air ~**) hôtesse de l'air; (*TV, Radio*) animatrice *f*

hostile ['hɔstaɪl] *adj* hostile

hostility [hɔ'stɪlɪtɪ] *n* hostilité *f*

hot [hɔt] *adj* chaud(e); (*as opposed to only warm*) très chaud; (*spicy*) fort(e); (*fig: contest*) acharné(e); (*topic*) brûlant(e); (*temper*) violent(e), passionné(e); **to be ~** (*person*) avoir chaud; (*thing*) être (très) chaud; (*weather*) faire chaud; **hot dog** *n* hot-dog *m*

hotel [həʊ'tɛl] *n* hôtel *m*

hot-water bottle [hɔt'wɔːtə-] *n* bouillotte *f*

hound [haʊnd] *vt* poursuivre avec acharnement ▷ *n* chien courant

hour ['aʊəʳ] *n* heure *f*; **hourly** *adj* toutes les heures; (*rate*) horaire

house *n* [haus] maison *f*; (*Pol*) chambre *f*; (*Theat*) salle *f*, auditoire *m* ▷ *vt* [hauz] (*person*) loger, héberger; **on the ~** (*fig*) aux frais de la maison; **household** *n* (*Admin etc*) ménage *m*; (*people*) famille *f*, maisonnée *f*; **householder** *n* propriétaire *m/f*; (*head of house*) chef *m* de famille; **housekeeper** *n* gouvernante *f*; **housekeeping** *n* (*work*) ménage *m*; (*money*) argent *m* du ménage; **housewife** (*irreg*) *n* ménagère *f*; femme *f* au foyer; **house wine** *n* cuvée *f* maison or du patron; **housework** *n* (travaux *mpl* du) ménage *m*

housing ['hauzɪŋ] *n* logement *m*; **housing development** (*BRIT* **housing estate**) *n* (*blocks of flats*) cité *f*; (*houses*) lotissement *m*

hover ['hɔvəʳ] *vi* planer; **hovercraft** *n* aéroglisseur *m*, hovercraft *m*

how [hau] *adv* comment; **~ are you?** comment allez-vous?; **~ do you do?** bonjour; (*on being introduced*) enchanté(e); **~ long have you been here?** depuis combien de temps êtes-vous là?; **~ lovely/awful!** que or comme c'est joli/affreux!; **~ much time/many people?** combien de temps/gens?; **~ much does it cost?** ça coûte combien?; **~ old are you?** quel âge avez-vous?; **~ tall is he?** combien mesure-t-il?; **~ is school?** ça va à l'école?; **~ was the film?** comment était le film?

however [hau'ɛvəʳ] *conj* pourtant, cependant ▷ *adv*: **~ I do it** de quelque manière que je m'y prenne; **~ cold it is** même s'il fait très froid; **~ did you do it?** comment y êtes-vous donc arrivé?

howl [haul] *n* hurlement *m* ▷ *vi* hurler; (*wind*) mugir

H.P. *n abbr* (*BRIT*) = **hire purchase**

h.p. *abbr* (*Aut*) = **horsepower**

HQ *n abbr* (= *headquarters*) QG *m*

hr(s) *abbr* (= *hour(s)*) h

HTML *n abbr* (= *hypertext markup language*) HTML *m*

hubcap ['hʌbkæp] *n* (*Aut*) enjoliveur *m*

huddle ['hʌdl] *vi*: **to ~ together** se blottir les uns contre les autres

huff [hʌf] *n*: **in a ~** fâché(e)

hug [hʌg] *vt* serrer dans ses bras; (*shore, kerb*) serrer ▷ *n*: **to give sb a ~** serrer qn dans ses bras

huge [hjuːdʒ] *adj* énorme, immense

hull [hʌl] *n* (*of ship*) coque *f*

hum [hʌm] *vt* (*tune*) fredonner ▷ *vi* fredonner; (*insect*) bourdonner; (*plane, tool*) vrombir

human ['hjuːmən] *adj* humain(e) ▷ *n* (*also*: **~ being**) être humain

humane [hjuː'meɪn] *adj* humain(e), humanitaire

humanitarian [hjuːmænɪ'tɛərɪən] *adj* humanitaire

humanity [hjuː'mænɪtɪ] *n* humanité *f*

human rights *npl* droits *mpl* de l'homme

humble [hʌmbl] *adj* humble, modeste

humid ['hjuːmɪd] *adj* humide; **humidity** [hjuː'mɪdɪtɪ] *n* humidité *f*

humiliate [hjuː'mɪlɪeɪt] *vt* humilier

humiliating [hjuː'mɪlɪeɪtɪŋ] *adj* humiliant(e)

humiliation [hjuːmɪlɪ'eɪʃən] *n* humiliation *f*

hummus ['huməs] *n* houm(m)ous *m*

humorous ['hjuːmərəs] *adj* humoristique

humour (*us* **humor**) ['hjuːməʳ] *n* humour *m*; (*mood*) humeur *f* ▷ *vt* (*person*) faire plaisir à; se prêter aux caprices de

hump [hʌmp] *n* bosse *f*

hunch [hʌntʃ] *n* (*premonition*) intuition *f*

hundred ['hʌndrəd] *num* cent; **~s of** des centaines de; **hundredth** [-ɪdθ] *num* centième

hung [hʌŋ] *pt, pp of* **hang**

Hungarian [hʌŋ'gɛərɪən] *adj* hongrois(e) ▷ *n* Hongrois(e); (*Ling*) hongrois *m*

Hungary ['hʌŋgərɪ] *n* Hongrie *f*

hunger ['hʌŋgəʳ] *n* faim *f* ▷ *vi*: **to ~ for** avoir faim de, désirer ardemment

hungry ['hʌŋgrɪ] *adj* affamé(e); **to be ~** avoir faim; **~ for** (*fig*) avide de

hunt [hʌnt] *vt* (*seek*) chercher; (*Sport*) chasser ▷ *vi* (*search*): **to ~ for** chercher (partout); (*Sport*) chasser ▷ *n* (*Sport*) chasse *f*; **hunter** *n* chasseur *m*; **hunting** *n* chasse *f*

hurdle ['həːdl] *n* (*Sport*) haie *f*; (*fig*) obstacle *m*

hurl [həːl] *vt* lancer (avec violence); (*abuse, insults*) lancer

hurrah, hurray [hu'rɑː, hu'reɪ] *excl* hourra!

hurricane ['hʌrɪkən] *n* ouragan *m*

hurry ['hʌrɪ] *n* hâte *f*, précipitation *f* ▷ *vi* se presser, se dépêcher ▷ *vt* (*person*) faire presser, faire se dépêcher; (*work*) presser; **to be in a ~** être pressé(e); **to do sth in a ~** faire qch en vitesse; **hurry up** *vi* se dépêcher

hurt [həːt] (*pt, pp* **~**) *vt* (*cause pain to*) faire mal à; (*injure, fig*) blesser ▷ *vi* faire mal ▷ *adj* blessé(e); **my arm ~s** j'ai mal au bras; **to ~ o.s.** se faire mal

husband ['hʌzbənd] *n* mari *m*

hush [hʌʃ] *n* calme *m*, silence *m* ▷ *vt* faire taire; **~!** chut!

husky ['hʌskɪ] *adj* (*voice*) rauque ▷ *n* chien *m* esquimau or de traîneau

hut [hʌt] *n* hutte *f*; (*shed*) cabane *f*

hyacinth ['haɪəsɪnθ] *n* jacinthe *f*

hydrangea [haɪ'dreɪndʒə] *n* hortensia *m*

hydrofoil ['haɪdrəfɔɪl] *n* hydrofoil *m*

hydrogen ['haɪdrədʒən] *n* hydrogène *m*

hygiene ['haɪdʒiːn] *n* hygiène *f*; **hygienic** [haɪ'dʒiːnɪk] *adj* hygiénique

hymn [hɪm] *n* hymne *m*; cantique *m*

hype [haɪp] n (inf) matraquage m publicitaire or médiatique
hypermarket ['haɪpəmɑːkɪt] (BRIT) n hypermarché m
hyphen ['haɪfn] n trait m d'union
hypnotize ['hɪpnətaɪz] vt hypnotiser
hypocrite ['hɪpəkrɪt] n hypocrite m/f
hypocritical [hɪpə'krɪtɪkl] adj hypocrite
hypothesis (pl **hypotheses**) [haɪ'pɔθɪsɪs, -siːz] n hypothèse f
hysterical [hɪ'stɛrɪkl] adj hystérique; (funny) hilarant(e)
hysterics [hɪ'stɛrɪks] npl: **to be in/have ~** (anger, panic) avoir une crise de nerfs; (laughter) attraper un fou rire

I [aɪ] pron je; (before vowel) j'; (stressed) moi
ice [aɪs] n glace f; (on road) verglas m ▷ vt (cake) glacer ▷ vi (also: **~ over**) geler; (also: **~ up**) se givrer; **iceberg** n iceberg m; **ice cream** n glace f; **ice cube** n glaçon m; **ice hockey** n hockey m sur glace
Iceland ['aɪslənd] n Islande f; **Icelander** n Islandais(e); **Icelandic** [aɪs'lændɪk] adj islandais(e) ▷ n (Ling) islandais m
ice: ice lolly n (BRIT) esquimau m; **ice rink** n patinoire f; **ice skating** n patinage m (sur glace)
icing ['aɪsɪŋ] n (Culin) glaçage m; **icing sugar** n (BRIT) sucre m glace
icon ['aɪkɔn] n icône f
ICT n abbr (BRIT: Scol: = information and communications technology) TIC fpl
icy ['aɪsɪ] adj glacé(e); (road) verglacé(e); (weather, temperature) glacial(e)
I'd [aɪd] = **I would; I had**
ID card n carte f d'identité
idea [aɪ'dɪə] n idée f
ideal [aɪ'dɪəl] n idéal m ▷ adj idéal(e); **ideally** [aɪ'dɪəlɪ]

adv (preferably) dans l'idéal; (perfectly): **he is ideally suited to the job** il est parfait pour ce poste
identical [aɪ'dɛntɪkl] adj identique
identification [aɪdɛntɪfɪ'keɪʃən] n identification f; **means of ~** pièce f d'identité
identify [aɪ'dɛntɪfaɪ] vt identifier
identity [aɪ'dɛntɪtɪ] n identité f; **identity card** n carte f d'identité; **identity theft** n usurpation f d'identité
ideology [aɪdɪ'ɔlədʒɪ] n idéologie f
idiom ['ɪdɪəm] n (phrase) expression f idiomatique; (style) style m
idiot ['ɪdɪət] n idiot(e), imbécile m/f
idle ['aɪdl] adj (doing nothing) sans occupation, désœuvré(e); (lazy) oisif(-ive), paresseux(-euse); (unemployed) au chômage; (machinery) au repos; (question, pleasures) vain(e), futile ▷ vi (engine) tourner au ralenti
idol ['aɪdl] n idole f
idyllic [ɪ'dɪlɪk] adj idyllique
i.e. abbr (= id est: that is) c. à d., c'est-à-dire
if [ɪf] conj si; **if necessary** si nécessaire, le cas échéant; **if so** si c'est le cas; **if not** sinon; **if only I could!** si seulement je pouvais!; see also **as; even**
ignite [ɪg'naɪt] vt mettre le feu à, enflammer ▷ vi s'enflammer
ignition [ɪg'nɪʃən] n (Aut) allumage m; **to switch on/off the ~** mettre/couper le contact
ignorance ['ɪgnərəns] n ignorance f
ignorant ['ɪgnərənt] adj ignorant(e); **to be ~ of** (subject) ne rien connaître en; (events) ne pas être au courant de
ignore [ɪg'nɔː] vt ne tenir aucun compte de; (mistake) ne pas relever; (person: pretend to not see) faire semblant de ne pas reconnaître; (: pay no attention to) ignorer
ill [ɪl] adj (sick) malade; (bad) mauvais(e) ▷ n mal m ▷ adv: **to speak/think ~ of sb** dire/penser du mal de qn; **to be taken ~** tomber malade
I'll [aɪl] = **I will; I shall**
illegal [ɪ'liːgl] adj illégal(e)
illegible [ɪ'lɛdʒɪbl] adj illisible
illegitimate [ɪlɪ'dʒɪtɪmət] adj illégitime
ill health n mauvaise santé
illiterate [ɪ'lɪtərət] adj illettré(e)
illness ['ɪlnɪs] n maladie f
illuminate [ɪ'luːmɪneɪt] vt (room, street) éclairer; (for special effect) illuminer
illusion [ɪ'luːʒən] n illusion f
illustrate ['ɪləstreɪt] vt illustrer
illustration [ɪlə'streɪʃən] n illustration f
I'm [aɪm] = **I am**
image ['ɪmɪdʒ] n image f; (public face) image de marque
imaginary [ɪ'mædʒɪnərɪ] adj imaginaire
imagination [ɪmædʒɪ'neɪʃən] n imagination f
imaginative [ɪ'mædʒɪnətɪv] adj imaginatif(-ive); (person) plein(e) d'imagination
imagine [ɪ'mædʒɪn] vt s'imaginer; (suppose) imaginer, supposer
imbalance [ɪm'bæləns] n déséquilibre m
imitate ['ɪmɪteɪt] vt imiter; **imitation** [ɪmɪ'teɪʃən] n imitation f
immaculate [ɪ'mækjulət] adj impeccable; (Rel) immaculé(e)
immature [ɪmə'tjuəʳ] adj (fruit) qui n'est pas mûr(e); (person) qui manque de maturité
immediate [ɪ'miːdɪət] adj immédiat(e); **immediately**

adv (*at once*) immédiatement; **immediately next to** juste à côté de

immense [ɪ'mɛns] *adj* immense, énorme; **immensely** *adv* (*+adj*) extrêmement; (*+vb*) énormément

immerse [ɪ'məːs] *vt* immerger, plonger; **to be ~d in** (*fig*) être plongé dans

immigrant ['ɪmɪgrənt] *n* immigrant(e); (*already established*) immigré(e); **immigration** [ɪmɪ'greɪʃən] *n* immigration *f*

imminent ['ɪmɪnənt] *adj* imminent(e)

immoral [ɪ'mɔrl] *adj* immoral(e)

immortal [ɪ'mɔːtl] *adj, n* immortel(le)

immune [ɪ'mjuːn] *adj*: **~ (to)** immunisé(e) (contre); **immune system** *n* système *m* immunitaire

immunize ['ɪmjunaɪz] *vt* immuniser

impact ['ɪmpækt] *n* choc *m*, impact *m*; (*fig*) impact

impair [ɪm'pɛəʳ] *vt* détériorer, diminuer

impartial [ɪm'pɑːʃl] *adj* impartial(e)

impatience [ɪm'peɪʃəns] *n* impatience *f*

impatient [ɪm'peɪʃənt] *adj* impatient(e); **to get** or **grow ~** s'impatienter

impeccable [ɪm'pɛkəbl] *adj* impeccable, parfait(e)

impending [ɪm'pɛndɪŋ] *adj* imminent(e)

imperative [ɪm'pɛrətɪv] *adj* (*need*) urgent(e), pressant(e); (*tone*) impérieux(-euse) ▷ *n* (*Ling*) impératif *m*

imperfect [ɪm'pəːfɪkt] *adj* imparfait(e); (*goods etc*) défectueux(-euse) ▷ *n* (*Ling: also:* **~ tense**) imparfait *m*

imperial [ɪm'pɪərɪəl] *adj* impérial(e); (BRIT: *measure*) légal(e)

impersonal [ɪm'pəːsənl] *adj* impersonnel(le)

impersonate [ɪm'pəːsəneɪt] *vt* se faire passer pour; (*Theat*) imiter

impetus ['ɪmpətəs] *n* impulsion *f*; (*of runner*) élan *m*

implant [ɪm'plɑːnt] *vt* (*Med*) implanter; (*fig: idea, principle*) inculquer

implement *n* ['ɪmplɪmənt] outil *m*, instrument *m*; (*for cooking*) ustensile *m* ▷ *vt* ['ɪmplɪmənt] exécuter

implicate ['ɪmplɪkeɪt] *vt* impliquer, compromettre

implication [ɪmplɪ'keɪʃən] *n* implication *f*; **by ~** indirectement

implicit [ɪm'plɪsɪt] *adj* implicite; (*complete*) absolu(e), sans réserve

imply [ɪm'plaɪ] *vt* (*hint*) suggérer, laisser entendre; (*mean*) indiquer, supposer

impolite [ɪmpə'laɪt] *adj* impoli(e)

import *vt* [ɪm'pɔːt] importer ▷ *n* ['ɪmpɔːt] (*Comm*) importation *f*; (*meaning*) portée *f*, signification *f*

importance [ɪm'pɔːtns] *n* importance *f*

important [ɪm'pɔːtnt] *adj* important(e); **it's not ~** c'est sans importance, ce n'est pas important

importer [ɪm'pɔːtəʳ] *n* importateur(-trice)

impose [ɪm'pəuz] *vt* imposer ▷ *vi*: **to ~ on sb** abuser de la gentillesse de qn; **imposing** *adj* imposant(e), impressionnant(e)

impossible [ɪm'pɔsɪbl] *adj* impossible

impotent ['ɪmpətnt] *adj* impuissant(e)

impoverished [ɪm'pɔvərɪʃt] *adj* pauvre, appauvri(e)

impractical [ɪm'præktɪkl] *adj* pas pratique; (*person*) qui manque d'esprit pratique

impress [ɪm'prɛs] *vt* impressionner, faire impression sur; (*mark*) imprimer, marquer; **to ~ sth on sb** faire bien comprendre qch à qn

impression [ɪm'prɛʃən] *n* impression *f*; (*of stamp, seal*)

empreinte *f*; (*imitation*) imitation *f*; **to be under the ~ that** avoir l'impression que

impressive [ɪm'prɛsɪv] *adj* impressionnant(e)

imprison [ɪm'prɪzn] *vt* emprisonner, mettre en prison; **imprisonment** *n* emprisonnement *m*; (*period*): **to sentence sb to 10 years' imprisonment** condamner qn à 10 ans de prison

improbable [ɪm'prɔbəbl] *adj* improbable; (*excuse*) peu plausible

improper [ɪm'prɔpəʳ] *adj* (*unsuitable*) déplacé(e), de mauvais goût; (*indecent*) indécent(e); (*dishonest*) malhonnête

improve [ɪm'pruːv] *vt* améliorer ▷ *vi* s'améliorer; (*pupil etc*) faire des progrès; **improvement** *n* amélioration *f*; (*of pupil etc*) progrès *m*

improvise ['ɪmprəvaɪz] *vt, vi* improviser

impulse ['ɪmpʌls] *n* impulsion *f*; **on ~** impulsivement, sur un coup de tête; **impulsive** [ɪm'pʌlsɪv] *adj* impulsif(-ive)

○ **KEYWORD**

in [ɪn] *prep* **1** (*indicating place, position*) dans; **in the house/the fridge** dans la maison/le frigo; **in the garden** dans le or au jardin; **in town** en ville; **in the country** à la campagne; **in school** à l'école; **in here/there** ici/là

2 (*with place names: of town, region, country*) **in London** à Londres; **in England** en Angleterre; **in Japan** au Japon; **in the United States** aux États-Unis

3 (*indicating time: during*): **in spring** au printemps; **in summer** en été; **in May/2005** en mai/2005; **in the afternoon** (dans) l'après-midi; **at 4 o'clock in the afternoon** à 4 heures de l'après-midi

4 (*indicating time: in the space of*) en; (: *future*) dans; **I did it in 3 hours/days** je l'ai fait en 3 heures/jours; **I'll see you in 2 weeks** *or* **in 2 weeks' time** je te verrai dans 2 semaines

5 (*indicating manner etc*) à; **in a loud/soft voice** à voix haute/basse; **in pencil** au crayon; **in writing** par écrit; **in French** en français; **the boy in the blue shirt** le garçon à *or* avec la chemise bleue

6 (*indicating circumstances*): **in the sun** au soleil; **in the shade** à l'ombre; **in the rain** sous la pluie; **a change in policy** un changement de politique

7 (*indicating mood, state*): **in tears** en larmes; **in anger** sous le coup de la colère; **in despair** au désespoir; **in good condition** en bon état; **to live in luxury** vivre dans le luxe

8 (*with ratios, numbers*): **1 in 10 households, 1 household in 10** 1 ménage sur 10; **20 pence in the pound** 20 pence par livre sterling; **they lined up in twos** ils se mirent en rangs (deux) par deux; **in hundreds** par centaines

9 (*referring to people, works*) chez; **the disease is common in children** c'est une maladie courante chez les enfants; **in (the works of) Dickens** chez Dickens, dans (l'œuvre de) Dickens

10 (*indicating profession etc*) dans; **to be in teaching** être dans l'enseignement

11 (*after superlative*) de; **the best pupil in the class** le meilleur élève de la classe

12 (*with present participle*): **in saying this** en disant ceci ▷ *adv*: **to be in** (*person: at home, work*) être là; (*train, ship,*

plane) être arrivé(e); (*in fashion*) être à la mode; **to ask sb in** inviter qn à entrer; **to run/limp** *etc* **in** entrer en courant/boitant *etc*
▷ *n*: **the ins and outs (of)** (*of proposal, situation etc*) les tenants et aboutissants (de)

inability [ɪnəˈbɪlɪtɪ] *n* incapacité *f*; **~ to pay** incapacité de payer

inaccurate [ɪnˈækjurət] *adj*. inexact(e); (*person*) qui manque de précision

inadequate [ɪnˈædɪkwət] *adj* insuffisant(e), inadéquat(e)

inadvertently [ɪnədˈvəːtntlɪ] *adv* par mégarde

inappropriate [ɪnəˈprəuprɪət] *adj* inopportun(e), mal à propos; (*word, expression*) impropre

inaugurate [ɪˈnɔːɡjureɪt] *vt* inaugurer; (*president, official*) investir de ses fonctions

Inc. *abbr* = **incorporated**

incapable [ɪnˈkeɪpəbl] *adj*: **~ (of)** incapable (de)

incense *n* [ˈɪnsɛns] encens *m* ▷ *vt* [ɪnˈsɛns] (*anger*) mettre en colère

incentive [ɪnˈsɛntɪv] *n* encouragement *m*, raison *f* de se donner de la peine

inch [ɪntʃ] *n* pouce *m* (=25 mm; 12 in a foot); **within an ~ of** à deux doigts de; **he wouldn't give an ~** (*fig*) il n'a pas voulu céder d'un pouce

incidence [ˈɪnsɪdns] *n* (*of crime, disease*) fréquence *f*

incident [ˈɪnsɪdnt] *n* incident *m*

incidentally [ɪnsɪˈdɛntəlɪ] *adv* (*by the way*) à propos

inclination [ɪnklɪˈneɪʃən] *n* inclination *f*; (*desire*) envie *f*

incline *n* [ˈɪnklaɪn] pente *f*, plan incliné ▷ *vb* [ɪnˈklaɪn] ▷ *vt* incliner ▷ *vi* (*surface*) s'incliner; **to be ~d to do** (*have a tendency to do*) avoir tendance à faire

include [ɪnˈkluːd] *vt* inclure, comprendre; **service is/is not ~d** le service est compris/n'est pas compris; **including** *prep* y compris; **inclusion** *n* inclusion *f*; **inclusive** *adj* inclus(e), compris(e); **inclusive of tax** taxes comprises

income [ˈɪnkʌm] *n* revenu *m*; (*from property etc*) rentes *fpl*; **income support** *n* (*BRIT*) ≈ revenu *m* minimum d'insertion, RMI *m*; **income tax** *n* impôt *m* sur le revenu

incoming [ˈɪnkʌmɪŋ] *adj* (*passengers, mail*) à l'arrivée; (*government, tenant*) nouveau (nouvelle)

incompatible [ɪnkəmˈpætɪbl] *adj* incompatible

incompetence [ɪnˈkɔmpɪtns] *n* incompétence *f*, incapacité *f*

incompetent [ɪnˈkɔmpɪtnt] *adj* incompétent(e), incapable

incomplete [ɪnkəmˈpliːt] *adj* incomplet(-ète)

inconsistent [ɪnkənˈsɪstnt] *adj* qui manque de constance; (*work*) irrégulier(-ière); (*statement*) peu cohérent(e); **~ with** en contradiction avec

inconvenience [ɪnkənˈviːnjəns] *n* inconvénient *m*; (*trouble*) dérangement *m* ▷ *vt* déranger

inconvenient [ɪnkənˈviːnjənt] *adj* malcommode; (*time, place*) mal choisi(e), qui ne convient pas; (*visitor*) importun(e)

incorporate [ɪnˈkɔːpəreɪt] *vt* incorporer; (*contain*) contenir

incorrect [ɪnkəˈrɛkt] *adj* incorrect(e); (*opinion, statement*) inexact(e)

increase *n* [ˈɪnkriːs] augmentation *f* ▷ *vi*, *vt* [ɪnˈkriːs] augmenter; **increasingly** *adv* de plus en plus

incredible [ɪnˈkrɛdɪbl] *adj* incroyable; **incredibly** *adv* incroyablement

incur [ɪnˈkəː] *vt* (*expenses*) encourir; (*anger, risk*) s'exposer à; (*debt*) contracter; (*loss*) subir

indecent [ɪnˈdiːsnt] *adj* indécent(e), inconvenant(e)

indeed [ɪnˈdiːd] *adv* (*confirming, agreeing*) en effet, effectivement; (*for emphasis*) vraiment; (*furthermore*) d'ailleurs; **yes ~!** certainement!

indefinitely [ɪnˈdɛfɪnɪtlɪ] *adv* (*wait*) indéfiniment

independence [ɪndɪˈpɛndns] *n* indépendance *f*; **Independence Day** *n* (*US*) fête de l'Indépendance américaine

independent [ɪndɪˈpɛndnt] *adj* indépendant(e); (*radio*) libre; **independent school** *n* (*BRIT*) école privée

index [ˈɪndɛks] *n* (*pl* **~es**) (*in book*) index *m*; (: *in library etc*) catalogue *m*; (*pl* **indices**) (*ratio, sign*) indice *m*

India [ˈɪndɪə] *n* Inde *f*; **Indian** *adj* indien(ne) ▷ *n* Indien(ne); **(American) Indian** Indien(ne) (d'Amérique)

indicate [ˈɪndɪkeɪt] *vt* indiquer ▷ *vi* (*BRIT Aut*): **to ~ left/right** mettre son clignotant à gauche/à droite; **indication** [ɪndɪˈkeɪʃən] *n* indication *f*, signe *m*; **indicative** [ɪnˈdɪkətɪv] *adj*: **to be indicative of sth** être symptomatique de qch ▷ *n* (*Ling*) indicatif *m*; **indicator** *n* (*sign*) indicateur *m*; (*Aut*) clignotant *m*

indices [ˈɪndɪsiːz] *npl of* **index**

indict [ɪnˈdaɪt] *vt* accuser; **indictment** *n* accusation *f*

indifference [ɪnˈdɪfrəns] *n* indifférence *f*

indifferent [ɪnˈdɪfrənt] *adj* indifférent(e); (*poor*) médiocre, quelconque

indigenous [ɪnˈdɪdʒɪnəs] *adj* indigène

indigestion [ɪndɪˈdʒɛstʃən] *n* indigestion *f*, mauvaise digestion

indignant [ɪnˈdɪgnənt] *adj*: **~ (at sth/with sb)** indigné(e) (de qch/contre qn)

indirect [ɪndɪˈrɛkt] *adj* indirect(e)

indispensable [ɪndɪˈspɛnsəbl] *adj* indispensable

individual [ɪndɪˈvɪdjuəl] *n* individu *m* ▷ *adj* individuel(le); (*characteristic*) particulier(-ière), original(e); **individually** *adv* individuellement

Indonesia [ɪndəˈniːzɪə] *n* Indonésie *f*

indoor [ˈɪndɔː] *adj* d'intérieur; (*plant*) d'appartement; (*swimming pool*) couvert(e); (*sport, games*) pratiqué(e) en salle; **indoors** [ɪnˈdɔːz] *adv* à l'intérieur

induce [ɪnˈdjuːs] *vt* (*persuade*) persuader; (*bring about*) provoquer; (*labour*) déclencher

indulge [ɪnˈdʌldʒ] *vt* (*whim*) céder à, satisfaire; (*child*) gâter ▷ *vi*: **to ~ in sth** (*luxury*) s'offrir qch, se permettre qch; (*fantasies etc*) se livrer à qch; **indulgent** *adj* indulgent(e)

industrial [ɪnˈdʌstrɪəl] *adj* industriel(le); (*injury*) du travail; (*dispute*) ouvrier(-ière); **industrial estate** *n* (*BRIT*) zone industrielle; **industrialist** *n* industriel *m*; **industrial park** *n* (*US*) zone industrielle

industry [ˈɪndəstrɪ] *n* industrie *f*; (*diligence*) zèle *m*, application *f*

inefficient [ɪnɪˈfɪʃənt] *adj* inefficace

inequality [ɪnɪˈkwɔlɪtɪ] *n* inégalité *f*

inevitable [ɪnˈɛvɪtəbl] *adj* inévitable; **inevitably** *adv* inévitablement, fatalement

inexpensive [ɪnɪkˈspɛnsɪv] *adj* bon marché *inv*

inexperienced [ɪnɪkˈspɪərɪənst] *adj* inexpérimenté(e)

inexplicable [ɪnɪkˈsplɪkəbl] *adj* inexplicable

infamous [ˈɪnfəməs] *adj* infâme, abominable

infant [ˈɪnfənt] *n* (*baby*) nourrisson *m*; (*young child*) petit(e) enfant

infantry ['ɪnfəntrɪ] n infanterie f

infant school n (BRIT) classes fpl préparatoires (entre 5 et 7 ans)

infect [ɪn'fekt] vt (wound) infecter; (person, blood) contaminer; **infection** [ɪn'fekʃən] n infection f; (contagion) contagion f; **infectious** [ɪn'fekʃəs] adj infectieux(-euse); (also fig) contagieux(-euse)

infer [ɪn'fə:ʳ] vt: **to ~ (from)** conclure (de), déduire (de)

inferior [ɪn'fɪərɪəʳ] adj inférieur(e); (goods) de qualité inférieure ▷ n inférieur(e); (in rank) subalterne m/f

infertile [ɪn'fə:taɪl] adj stérile

infertility [ɪnfə:'tɪlɪtɪ] n infertilité f, stérilité f

infested [ɪn'festɪd] adj: **~ (with)** infesté(e) (de)

infinite ['ɪnfɪnɪt] adj infini(e); (time, money) illimité(e); **infinitely** adv infiniment

infirmary [ɪn'fə:mərɪ] n hôpital m; (in school, factory) infirmerie f

inflamed [ɪn'fleɪmd] adj enflammé(e)

inflammation [ɪnflə'meɪʃən] n inflammation f

inflatable [ɪn'fleɪtəbl] adj gonflable

inflate [ɪn'fleɪt] vt (tyre, balloon) gonfler; (fig: exaggerate) grossir; (: increase) gonfler; **inflation** [ɪn'fleɪʃən] n (Econ) inflation f

inflexible [ɪn'fleksɪbl] adj inflexible, rigide

inflict [ɪn'flɪkt] vt: **to ~ on** infliger à

influence ['ɪnfluəns] n influence f ▷ vt influencer; **under the ~ of alcohol** en état d'ébriété; **influential** [ɪnflu'enʃl] adj influent(e)

influenza [ɪnflu'enzə] n grippe f

influx ['ɪnflʌks] n afflux m

info (inf) ['ɪnfəu] n (= information) renseignements mpl

inform [ɪn'fɔ:m] vt: **to ~ sb (of)** informer or avertir qn (de) ▷ vi: **to ~ on sb** dénoncer qn, informer contre qn

informal [ɪn'fɔ:ml] adj (person, manner, party) simple; (visit, discussion) dénué(e) de formalités; (announcement, invitation) non officiel(le); (colloquial) familier(-ère)

information [ɪnfə'meɪʃən] n information(s) f(pl); renseignements mpl; (knowledge) connaissances fpl; **a piece of ~** un renseignement; **information office** n bureau m de renseignements; **information technology** n informatique f

informative [ɪn'fɔ:mətɪv] adj instructif(-ive)

infra-red [ɪnfrə'red] adj infrarouge

infrastructure ['ɪnfrəstrʌktʃəʳ] n infrastructure f

infrequent [ɪn'fri:kwənt] adj peu fréquent(e), rare

infuriate [ɪn'fjuərɪeɪt] vt mettre en fureur

infuriating [ɪn'fjuərɪeɪtɪŋ] adj exaspérant(e)

ingenious [ɪn'dʒi:njəs] adj ingénieux(-euse)

ingredient [ɪn'gri:dɪənt] n ingrédient m; (fig) élément m

inhabit [ɪn'hæbɪt] vt habiter; **inhabitant** n habitant(e)

inhale [ɪn'heɪl] vt inhaler; (perfume) respirer; (smoke) avaler ▷ vi (breathe in) aspirer; (in smoking) avaler la fumée; **inhaler** n inhalateur m

inherent [ɪn'hɪərənt] adj: **~ (in or to)** inhérent(e) (à)

inherit [ɪn'herɪt] vt hériter (de); **inheritance** n héritage m

inhibit [ɪn'hɪbɪt] vt (Psych) inhiber; (growth) freiner; **inhibition** [ɪnhɪ'bɪʃən] n inhibition f

initial [ɪ'nɪʃl] adj initial(e) ▷ n initiale f ▷ vt parafer; **initials** npl initiales fpl; (as signature) parafe m; **initially** adv initialement, au début

initiate [ɪ'nɪʃɪeɪt] vt (start) entreprendre; amorcer; (enterprise) lancer; (person) initier; **to ~ proceedings against sb** (Law) intenter une action à qn, engager des poursuites contre qn

initiative [ɪ'nɪʃətɪv] n initiative f

inject [ɪn'dʒekt] vt injecter; (person): **to ~ sb with sth** faire une piqûre de qch à qn; **injection** [ɪn'dʒekʃən] n injection f, piqûre f

injure ['ɪndʒəʳ] vt blesser; (damage: reputation etc) compromettre; **to ~ o.s.** se blesser; **injured** adj (person, leg etc) blessé(e); **injury** n blessure f; (wrong) tort m

injustice [ɪn'dʒʌstɪs] n injustice f

ink [ɪŋk] n encre f; **ink-jet printer** ['ɪŋkdʒet-] n imprimante f à jet d'encre

inland adj ['ɪnlənd] intérieur(e) ▷ adv [ɪn'lænd] à l'intérieur, dans les terres; **Inland Revenue** n (BRIT) fisc m

in-laws ['ɪnlɔ:z] npl beaux-parents mpl; belle famille

inmate ['ɪnmeɪt] n (in prison) détenu(e); (in asylum) interné(e)

inn [ɪn] n auberge f

inner ['ɪnəʳ] adj intérieur(e); **inner-city** adj (schools, problems) de quartiers déshérités

inning ['ɪnɪŋ] n (us: Baseball) tour m de batte; **innings** npl (Cricket) tour de batte

innocence ['ɪnəsns] n innocence f

innocent ['ɪnəsnt] adj innocent(e)

innovation [ɪnəu'veɪʃən] n innovation f

innovative ['ɪnəu'veɪtɪv] adj novateur(-trice); (product) innovant(e)

in-patient ['ɪnpeɪʃənt] n malade hospitalisé(e)

input ['ɪnput] n (contribution) contribution f; (resources) ressources fpl; (Comput) entrée f (de données); (: data) données fpl ▷ vt (Comput) introduire, entrer

inquest ['ɪnkwest] n enquête (criminelle); (coroner's) enquête judiciaire

inquire [ɪn'kwaɪəʳ] vi demander ▷ vt demander; **to ~ about** s'informer de, se renseigner sur; **to ~ when/ where/whether** demander quand/où/si; **inquiry** n demande f de renseignements; (Law) enquête f, investigation f; **"inquiries"** "renseignements"

ins. abbr = **inches**

insane [ɪn'seɪn] adj fou (folle); (Med) aliéné(e)

insanity [ɪn'sænɪtɪ] n folie f; (Med) aliénation (mentale)

insect ['ɪnsekt] n insecte m; **insect repellent** n crème f anti-insectes

insecure [ɪnsɪ'kjuəʳ] adj (person) anxieux(-euse); (job) précaire; (building etc) peu sûr(e)

insecurity [ɪnsɪ'kjuərɪtɪ] n insécurité f

insensitive [ɪn'sensɪtɪv] adj insensible

insert vt [ɪn'sə:t] insérer ▷ n ['ɪnsə:t] insertion f

inside ['ɪn'saɪd] n intérieur m ▷ adj intérieur(e) ▷ adv à l'intérieur, dedans ▷ prep à l'intérieur de; (of time): **~ 10 minutes** en moins de 10 minutes; **to go ~** rentrer; **inside lane** n (Aut: in Britain) voie f de gauche; (: in US, Europe) voie f de droite; **inside out** adv à l'envers; (know) à fond; **to turn sth inside out** retourner qch

insight ['ɪnsaɪt] n perspicacité f; (glimpse, idea) aperçu m

insignificant [ɪnsɪg'nɪfɪknt] adj insignifiant(e)

insincere [ɪnsɪn'sɪəʳ] adj hypocrite

insist [ɪn'sɪst] vi insister; **to ~ on doing** insister pour faire; **to ~ on sth** exiger qch; **to ~ that** insister pour que + sub; (claim) maintenir or soutenir que; **insistent** adj insistant(e), pressant(e); (noise, action) ininterrompu(e)

insomnia [ɪn'sɔmnɪə] n insomnie f

inspect [ɪn'spɛkt] vt inspecter; (BRIT: ticket) contrôler; **inspection** [ɪn'spɛkʃən] n inspection f; (BRIT: of tickets) contrôle m; **inspector** n inspecteur(-trice); (BRIT: on buses, trains) contrôleur(-euse)

inspiration [ɪnspə'reɪʃən] n inspiration f; **inspire** [ɪn'spaɪəʳ] vt inspirer; **inspiring** adj inspirant(e)

instability [ɪnstə'bɪlɪtɪ] n instabilité f

install (US **instal**) [ɪn'stɔːl] vt installer; **installation** [ɪnstə'leɪʃən] n installation f

instalment (US **installment**) [ɪn'stɔːlmənt] n (payment) acompte m, versement partiel; (of TV serial etc) épisode m; **in ~s** (pay) à tempérament; (receive) en plusieurs fois

instance ['ɪnstəns] n exemple m; **for ~** par exemple; **in the first ~** tout d'abord, en premier lieu

instant ['ɪnstənt] n instant m ▷ adj immédiat(e), urgent(e); (coffee, food) instantané(e), en poudre; **instantly** adv immédiatement, tout de suite; **instant messaging** n messagerie f instantanée

instead [ɪn'stɛd] adv au lieu de cela; **~ of** au lieu de; **~ of sb** à la place de qn

instinct ['ɪnstɪŋkt] n instinct m; **instinctive** adj instinctif(-ive)

institute ['ɪnstɪtjuːt] n institut m ▷ vt instituer, établir; (inquiry) ouvrir; (proceedings) entamer

institution [ɪnstɪ'tjuːʃən] n institution f; (school) établissement m (scolaire); (for care) établissement (psychiatrique etc)

instruct [ɪn'strʌkt] vt: **to ~ sb in sth** enseigner qch à qn; **to ~ sb to do** charger qn or ordonner à qn de faire; **instruction** [ɪn'strʌkʃən] n instruction f; **instructions** npl (orders) directives fpl; **instructions for use** mode m d'emploi; **instructor** n professeur m; (for skiing, driving) moniteur m

instrument ['ɪnstrəmənt] n instrument m; **instrumental** [ɪnstru'mɛntl] adj (Mus) instrumental(e); **to be instrumental in sth/in doing sth** contribuer à qch/à faire qch

insufficient [ɪnsə'fɪʃənt] adj insuffisant(e)

insulate ['ɪnsjuleɪt] vt isoler; (against sound) insonoriser; **insulation** [ɪnsju'leɪʃən] n isolation f; (against sound) insonorisation f

insulin ['ɪnsjulɪn] n insuline f

insult n ['ɪnsʌlt] insulte f, affront m ▷ vt [ɪn'sʌlt] insulter, faire un affront à; **insulting** adj insultant(e), injurieux(-euse)

insurance [ɪn'ʃuərəns] n assurance f; **fire/life ~** assurance-incendie/-vie; **insurance company** n compagnie f or société f d'assurances; **insurance policy** n police f d'assurance

insure [ɪn'ʃuəʳ] vt assurer; **to ~ (o.s.) against** (fig) parer à

intact [ɪn'tækt] adj intact(e)

intake ['ɪnteɪk] n (Tech) admission f; (consumption) consommation f; (BRIT Scol): **an ~ of 200 a year** 200 admissions par an

integral ['ɪntɪgrəl] adj (whole) intégral(e); (part) intégrant(e)

integrate ['ɪntɪgreɪt] vt intégrer ▷ vi s'intégrer

integrity [ɪn'tɛgrɪtɪ] n intégrité f

intellect ['ɪntəlɛkt] n intelligence f; **intellectual** [ɪntə'lɛktjuəl] adj, n intellectuel(le)

intelligence [ɪn'tɛlɪdʒəns] n intelligence f; (Mil etc) informations fpl, renseignements mpl

intelligent [ɪn'tɛlɪdʒənt] adj intelligent(e)

intend [ɪn'tɛnd] vt (gift etc): **to ~ sth for** destiner qch à; **to ~ to do** avoir l'intention de faire

intense [ɪn'tɛns] adj intense; (person) véhément(e)

intensify [ɪn'tɛnsɪfaɪ] vt intensifier

intensity [ɪn'tɛnsɪtɪ] n intensité f

intensive [ɪn'tɛnsɪv] adj intensif(-ive); **intensive care** n: **to be in intensive care** être en réanimation; **intensive care unit** n service m de réanimation

intent [ɪn'tɛnt] n intention f ▷ adj attentif(-ive), absorbé(e); **to all ~s and purposes** en fait, pratiquement; **to be ~ on doing sth** être (bien) décidé à faire qch

intention [ɪn'tɛnʃən] n intention f; **intentional** adj intentionnel(le), délibéré(e)

interact [ɪntər'ækt] vi avoir une action réciproque; (people) communiquer; **interaction** [ɪntər'ækʃən] n interaction f; **interactive** adj (Comput) interactif, conversationnel(le)

intercept [ɪntə'sɛpt] vt intercepter; (person) arrêter au passage

interchange n ['ɪntətʃeɪndʒ] (exchange) échange m; (on motorway) échangeur m

intercourse ['ɪntəkɔːs] n: **sexual ~** rapports sexuels

interest ['ɪntrɪst] n intérêt m; (Comm: stake, share) participation f, intérêts mpl ▷ vt intéresser; **interested** adj intéressé(e); **to be interested in sth** s'intéresser à qch; **I'm interested in going** ça m'intéresse d'y aller; **interesting** adj intéressant(e); **interest rate** n taux m d'intérêt

interface ['ɪntəfeɪs] n (Comput) interface f

interfere [ɪntə'fɪəʳ] vi: **to ~ in** (quarrel) s'immiscer dans; (other people's business) se mêler de; **to ~ with** (object) tripoter, toucher à; (plans) contrecarrer; (duty) être en conflit avec; **interference** n (gen) ingérence f; (Radio, TV) parasites mpl

interim ['ɪntərɪm] adj provisoire; (post) intérimaire ▷ n: **in the ~** dans l'intérim

interior [ɪn'tɪərɪəʳ] n intérieur m ▷ adj intérieur(e); (minister, department) de l'intérieur; **interior design** n architecture f d'intérieur

intermediate [ɪntə'miːdɪət] adj intermédiaire; (Scol: course, level) moyen(ne)

intermission [ɪntə'mɪʃən] n pause f; (Theat, Cine) entracte m

intern vt [ɪn'tə:n] interner ▷ n [ɪntə:n] (US) interne m/f

internal [ɪn'tə:nl] adj interne; (dispute, reform etc) intérieur(e); **Internal Revenue Service** n (US) fisc m

international [ɪntə'næʃənl] adj international(e) ▷ n (BRIT Sport) international m

Internet [ɪntə'nɛt] n: **the ~** l'Internet m; **Internet café** n cybercafé m; **Internet Service Provider** n fournisseur m d'accès à Internet; **Internet user** n internaute m/f

interpret [ɪn'tə:prɪt] vt interpréter ▷ vi servir d'interprète; **interpretation** [ɪntə:prɪ'teɪʃən] n interprétation f; **interpreter** n interprète m/f; **could you act as an interpreter for us?** pourriez-vous nous servir d'interprète?

interrogate [ɪn'tɛrəugeɪt] vt interroger; (suspect etc) soumettre à un interrogatoire; **interrogation** [ɪntɛrəu'geɪʃən] n interrogation f; (by police) interrogatoire m

interrogative [ɪntə'rɔgətɪv] adj interrogateur(-trice)

▷ n (Ling) interrogatif m

interrupt [ɪntə'rʌpt] vt, vi interrompre; **interruption** [ɪntə'rʌpʃən] n interruption f

intersection [ɪntə'sɛkʃən] n (of roads) croisement m

interstate [ˈɪntərsteɪt] (US) n autoroute f (qui relie plusieurs États)

interval [ˈɪntəvl] n intervalle m; (BRIT: Theat) entracte m; (: Sport) mi-temps f; **at ~s** par intervalles

intervene [ɪntə'viːn] vi (time) s'écouler (entre-temps); (event) survenir; (person) intervenir

interview [ˈɪntəvjuː] n (Radio, TV etc) interview f; (for job) entrevue f ▷ vt interviewer; avoir une entrevue avec; **interviewer** n (Radio, TV etc) interviewer m

intimate adj [ˈɪntɪmət] intime; (friendship) profond(e); (knowledge) approfondi(e) ▷ vt [ˈɪntɪmeɪt] suggérer, laisser entendre; (announce) faire savoir

intimidate [ɪn'tɪmɪdeɪt] vt intimider

intimidating [ɪn'tɪmɪdeɪtɪŋ] adj intimidant(e)

into [ˈɪntu] prep dans; **~ pieces/French** en morceaux/français

intolerant [ɪn'tɔlərnt] adj: **~ (of)** intolérant(e) (de)

intranet [ˈɪntrənɛt] n intranet m

intransitive [ɪn'trænsɪtɪv] adj intransitif(-ive)

intricate [ˈɪntrɪkət] adj complexe, compliqué(e)

intrigue [ɪn'triːɡ] n intrigue f ▷ vt intriguer; **intriguing** adj fascinant(e)

introduce [ɪntrə'djuːs] vt introduire; (TV show etc) présenter; **to ~ sb (to sb)** présenter qn (à qn); **to ~ sb to** (pastime, technique) initier qn à; **introduction** [ɪntrə'dʌkʃən] n introduction f; (of person) présentation f; (to new experience) initiation f; **introductory** [ɪntrə'dʌktərɪ] adj préliminaire, introductif(-ive)

intrude [ɪn'truːd] vi (person) être importun(e); **to ~ on** or **into** (conversation etc) s'immiscer dans; **intruder** n intrus(e)

intuition [ɪntjuː'ɪʃən] n intuition f

inundate [ˈɪnʌndeɪt] vt: **to ~ with** inonder de

invade [ɪn'veɪd] vt envahir

invalid n [ˈɪnvəlɪd] malade m/f; (with disability) invalide m/f ▷ adj [ɪn'vælɪd] (not valid) invalide, non valide

invaluable [ɪn'væljuəbl] adj inestimable, inappréciable

invariably [ɪn'vɛərɪəblɪ] adv invariablement; **she is ~ late** elle est toujours en retard

invasion [ɪn'veɪʒən] n invasion f

invent [ɪn'vɛnt] vt inventer; **invention** [ɪn'vɛnʃən] n invention f; **inventor** n inventeur(-trice)

inventory [ˈɪnvəntrɪ] n inventaire m

inverted commas [ɪn'vəːtɪd-] npl (BRIT) guillemets mpl

invest [ɪn'vɛst] vt investir ▷ vi: **to ~ in** placer de l'argent or investir dans; (fig: acquire) s'offrir, faire l'acquisition de

investigate [ɪn'vɛstɪɡeɪt] vt étudier, examiner; (crime) faire une enquête sur; **investigation** [ɪnvɛstɪ'ɡeɪʃən] n (of crime) enquête f, investigation f

investigator [ɪn'vɛstɪɡeɪtər] n investigateur(-trice); **private ~** détective privé

investment [ɪn'vɛstmənt] n investissement m, placement m

investor [ɪn'vɛstər] n épargnant(e); (shareholder) actionnaire m/f

invisible [ɪn'vɪzɪbl] adj invisible

invitation [ɪnvɪ'teɪʃən] n invitation f

invite [ɪn'vaɪt] vt inviter; (opinions etc) demander; **inviting** adj engageant(e), attrayant(e)

invoice [ˈɪnvɔɪs] n facture f ▷ vt facturer

involve [ɪn'vɔlv] vt (entail) impliquer; (concern) concerner; (necessitate) nécessiter; **to ~ sb in** (theft etc) impliquer qn dans; (activity, meeting) faire participer qn à; **involved** adj (complicated) complexe; **to be involved in** (take part) participer à; **involvement** n (personal role) rôle m; (participation) participation f; (enthusiasm) enthousiasme m

inward [ˈɪnwəd] adj (movement) vers l'intérieur; (thought, feeling) profond(e), intime ▷ adv = **inwards**; **inwards** adv vers l'intérieur

IQ n abbr (= intelligence quotient) Q.I. m

IRA n abbr (= Irish Republican Army) IRA f

Iran [ɪ'rɑːn] n Iran m; **Iranian** [ɪ'reɪnɪən] adj iranien(ne) ▷ n Iranien(ne)

Iraq [ɪ'rɑːk] n Irak m; **Iraqi** adj irakien(ne) ▷ n Irakien(ne)

Ireland [ˈaɪələnd] n Irlande f

iris, irises [ˈaɪrɪs, -ɪz] n iris m

Irish [ˈaɪrɪʃ] adj irlandais(e) ▷ npl: **the ~** les Irlandais; **Irishman** (irreg) n Irlandais m; **Irishwoman** (irreg) n Irlandaise f

iron [ˈaɪən] n fer m; (for clothes) fer m à repasser ▷ adj de or en fer ▷ vt (clothes) repasser

ironic(al) [aɪ'rɔnɪk(l)] adj ironique; **ironically** adv ironiquement

ironing [ˈaɪənɪŋ] n (activity) repassage m; (clothes: ironed) linge repassé; (: to be ironed) linge à repasser; **ironing board** n planche f à repasser

irony [ˈaɪrənɪ] n ironie f

irrational [ɪ'ræʃənl] adj irrationnel(le); (person) qui n'est pas rationnel

irregular [ɪ'rɛɡjʊlər] adj irrégulier(-ière); (surface) inégal(e); (action, event) peu orthodoxe

irrelevant [ɪ'rɛləvənt] adj sans rapport, hors de propos

irresistible [ɪrɪ'zɪstɪbl] adj irrésistible

irresponsible [ɪrɪ'spɔnsɪbl] adj (act) irréfléchi(e); (person) qui n'a pas le sens des responsabilités

irrigation [ɪrɪ'ɡeɪʃən] n irrigation f

irritable [ˈɪrɪtəbl] adj irritable

irritate [ˈɪrɪteɪt] vt irriter; **irritating** adj irritant(e); **irritation** [ɪrɪ'teɪʃən] n irritation f

IRS n abbr (US) = **Internal Revenue Service**

is [ɪz] vb see **be**

ISDN n abbr (= Integrated Services Digital Network) RNIS m

Islam [ˈɪzlɑːm] n Islam m; **Islamic** [ɪz'lɑːmɪk] adj islamique

island [ˈaɪlənd] n île f; (also: **traffic ~**) refuge m (pour piétons); **islander** n habitant(e) d'une île, insulaire m/f

isle [aɪl] n île f

isn't [ˈɪznt] = **is not**

isolated [ˈaɪsəleɪtɪd] adj isolé(e)

isolation [aɪsə'leɪʃən] n isolement m

ISP n abbr = **Internet Service Provider**

Israel [ˈɪzreɪl] n Israël m; **Israeli** [ɪz'reɪlɪ] adj israélien(ne) ▷ n Israélien(ne)

issue [ˈɪʃuː] n question f, problème m; (of banknotes) émission f; (of newspaper) numéro m; (of book) publication f, parution f ▷ vt (rations, equipment) distribuer; (orders) donner; (statement) publier, faire; (certificate, passport) délivrer; (banknotes, cheques,

stamps) émettre, mettre en circulation; **at ~** en jeu, en cause; **to take ~ with sb (over sth)** exprimer son désaccord avec qn (sur qch)
IT *n abbr* = **information technology**

it [ɪt] *pron* **1** (*specific: subject*) il (elle); (*: direct object*) le (la, l'); (*: indirect object*) lui; **it's on the table** c'est or il (*or* elle) est sur la table; **I can't find it** je n'arrive pas à le trouver; **give it to me** donne-le-moi
2 (*after prep*): **about/from/of it** en; **I spoke to him about it** je lui en ai parlé; **what did you learn from it?** qu'est-ce que vous en avez retiré?; **I'm proud of it** j'en suis fier; **in/to it** y; **put the book in it** mettez-y le livre; **he agreed to it** il y a consenti; **did you go to it?** (*party, concert etc*) est-ce que vous y êtes allé(s)?
3 (*impersonal*) il; ce, cela, ça; **it's raining** il pleut; **it's Friday tomorrow** demain, c'est vendredi *or* nous sommes, vendredi; **it's 6 o'clock** il est 6 heures; **how far is it? — it's 10 miles** c'est loin? — c'est à 10 miles; **who is it? — it's me** qui est-ce? — c'est moi

Italian [ɪˈtæljən] *adj* italien(ne) ▷ *n* Italien(ne); (*Ling*) italien *m*
italics [ɪˈtælɪks] *npl* italique *m*
Italy [ˈɪtəlɪ] *n* Italie *f*
itch [ɪtʃ] *n* démangeaison *f* ▷ *vi* (*person*) éprouver des démangeaisons; (*part of body*) démanger; **I'm ~ing to do** l'envie me démange de faire; **itchy** *adj*: **my back is itchy** j'ai le dos qui me démange
it'd [ˈɪtd] = **it would**; **it had**
item [ˈaɪtəm] *n* (*gen*) article *m*; (*on agenda*) question *f*, point *m*; (*also*: **news ~**) nouvelle *f*
itinerary [aɪˈtɪnərərɪ] *n* itinéraire *m*
it'll [ˈɪtl] = **it will; it shall**
its [ɪts] *adj* son (sa), ses *pl*
it's [ɪts] = **it is; it has**
itself [ɪtˈsɛlf] *pron* (*reflexive*) se; (*emphatic*) lui-même (elle-même)
ITV *n abbr* (BRIT: = *Independent Television*) chaîne de télévision commerciale
I've [aɪv] = **I have**
ivory [ˈaɪvərɪ] *n* ivoire *m*
ivy [ˈaɪvɪ] *n* lierre *m*

jab [dʒæb] *vt*: **to ~ sth into** enfoncer *or* planter qch dans ▷ *n* (*Med: inf*) piqûre *f*
jack [dʒæk] *n* (*Aut*) cric *m*; (*Cards*) valet *m*
jacket [ˈdʒækɪt] *n* veste *f*, veston *m*; (*of book*) couverture *f*, jaquette *f*; **jacket potato** *n* pomme *f* de terre en robe des champs
jackpot [ˈdʒækpɔt] *n* gros lot
Jacuzzi® [dʒəˈkuːzɪ] *n* jacuzzi® *m*
jagged [ˈdʒægɪd] *adj* dentelé(e)
jail [dʒeɪl] *n* prison *f* ▷ *vt* emprisonner, mettre en prison; **jail sentence** *n* peine *f* de prison
jam [dʒæm] *n* confiture *f*; (*also*: **traffic ~**) embouteillage *m* ▷ *vt* (*passage etc*) encombrer, obstruer; (*mechanism, drawer etc*) bloquer, coincer; (*Radio*) brouiller ▷ *vi* (*mechanism, sliding part*) se coincer, se bloquer; (*gun*) s'enrayer; **to be in a ~** (*inf*) être dans le pétrin; **to ~ sth into** (*stuff*) entasser *or* comprimer qch dans; (*thrust*) enfoncer qch dans
Jamaica [dʒəˈmeɪkə] *n* Jamaïque *f*
jammed [dʒæmd] *adj* (*window etc*) coincé(e)
Jan *abbr* (= *January*) janv
janitor [ˈdʒænɪtəʳ] *n* (*caretaker*) concierge *m*
January [ˈdʒænjuərɪ] *n* janvier *m*
Japan [dʒəˈpæn] *n* Japon *m*; **Japanese** [dʒæpəˈniːz] *adj* japonais(e) ▷ *n* (*pl inv*) Japonais(e); (*Ling*) japonais *m*
jar [dʒɑːʳ] *n* (*stone, earthenware*) pot *m*; (*glass*) bocal *m* ▷ *vi* (*sound*) produire un son grinçant *or* discordant; (*colours etc*) détonner, jurer
jargon [ˈdʒɑːgən] *n* jargon *m*
javelin [ˈdʒævlɪn] *n* javelot *m*
jaw [dʒɔː] *n* mâchoire *f*
jazz [dʒæz] *n* jazz *m*
jealous [ˈdʒɛləs] *adj* jaloux(-ouse); **jealousy** *n* jalousie *f*
jeans [dʒiːnz] *npl* jean *m*
Jello® [ˈdʒɛləu] (*us*) *n* gelée *f*
jelly [ˈdʒɛlɪ] *n* (*dessert*) gelée *f*; (*us: jam*) confiture *f*; **jellyfish** *n* méduse *f*
jeopardize [ˈdʒɛpədaɪz] *vt* mettre en danger *or* péril
jerk [dʒɜːk] *n* secousse *f*, saccade *f*; (*of muscle*) spasme *m*; (*inf*) pauvre type *m* ▷ *vt* (*shake*) donner une secousse à;

(*pull*) tirer brusquement ▷ vi (*vehicles*) cahoter

jersey ['dʒɜːzɪ] n tricot m; (*fabric*) jersey m

Jesus ['dʒiːzəs] n Jésus

jet [dʒɛt] n (*of gas, liquid*) jet m; (*Aviat*) avion m à réaction, jet m; **jet lag** n décalage m horaire; **jet-ski** vi faire du jet-ski ou scooter des mers

jetty ['dʒɛtɪ] n jetée f, digue f

Jew [dʒuː] n Juif m

jewel ['dʒuːəl] n bijou m, joyau m; (*in watch*) rubis m; **jeweller** (*us* **jeweler**) n bijoutier(-ière), joaillier m; **jeweller's (shop)** (*us* **jewelry store**) n bijouterie f, joaillerie f; **jewellery** (*us* **jewelry**) n bijoux mpl

Jewish ['dʒuːɪʃ] adj juif (juive)

jigsaw ['dʒɪɡsɔː] n (*also:* **~ puzzle**) puzzle m

job [dʒɔb] n (*chore, task*) travail m, tâche f; (*employment*) emploi m, poste m, place f; **it's a good ~ that ...** c'est heureux or c'est une chance que ... + sub; **just the ~!** (c'est) juste or exactement ce qu'il faut!; **job centre** (*BRIT*) n ≈ ANPE f, ≈ Agence nationale pour l'emploi; **jobless** adj sans travail, au chômage

jockey ['dʒɔkɪ] n jockey m ▷ vi: **to ~ for position** manœuvrer pour être bien placé

jog [dʒɔɡ] vt secouer ▷ vi (*Sport*) faire du jogging; **to ~ sb's memory** rafraîchir la mémoire de qn; **jogging** n jogging m

join [dʒɔɪn] vt (*put together*) unir, assembler; (*become member of*) s'inscrire à; (*meet*) rejoindre, retrouver; (*queue*) se joindre à ▷ vi (*roads, rivers*) se rejoindre, se rencontrer ▷ n raccord m; **join in** vi se mettre de la partie ▷ vt fus se mêler à; **join up** vi (*meet*) se rejoindre; (*Mil*) s'engager

joiner ['dʒɔɪnə'] (*BRIT*) n menuisier m

joint [dʒɔɪnt] n (*Tech*) jointure f, joint m; (*Anat*) articulation f, jointure; (*BRIT Culin*) rôti m; (*inf: place*) boîte f; (*of cannabis*) joint ▷ adj commun(e); (*committee*) mixte, paritaire; (*winner*) ex aequo; **joint account** n compte joint; **jointly** adv ensemble, en commun

joke [dʒəuk] n plaisanterie f; (*also:* **practical ~**) farce f ▷ vi plaisanter; **to play a ~ on** jouer un tour à, faire une farce à; **joker** n (*Cards*) joker m

jolly ['dʒɔlɪ] adj gai(e), enjoué(e); (*enjoyable*) amusant(e), plaisant(e) ▷ adv (*BRIT inf*) rudement, drôlement

jolt [dʒəult] n cahot m, secousse f; (*shock*) choc m ▷ vt cahoter, secouer

Jordan ['dʒɔːdən] n (*country*) Jordanie f

journal ['dʒɜːnl] n journal m; **journalism** n journalisme m; **journalist** n journaliste m/f

journey ['dʒɜːnɪ] n voyage m; (*distance covered*) trajet m; **the ~ takes two hours** le trajet dure deux heures; **how was your ~?** votre voyage s'est bien passé?

joy [dʒɔɪ] n joie f; **joyrider** n voleur(-euse) de voiture (*qui fait une virée dans le véhicule volé*); **joy stick** n (*Aviat*) manche m à balai; (*Comput*) manche à balai, manette f (de jeu)

Jr abbr = **junior**

judge [dʒʌdʒ] n juge m ▷ vt juger; (*estimate: weight, size etc*) apprécier; (*consider*) estimer

judo ['dʒuːdəu] n judo m

jug [dʒʌɡ] n pot m, cruche f

juggle ['dʒʌɡl] vi jongler; **juggler** n jongleur m

juice [dʒuːs] n jus m; **juicy** adj juteux(-euse)

Jul abbr (= July) juil

July [dʒuːˈlaɪ] n juillet m

jumble ['dʒʌmbl] n fouillis m ▷ vt (*also:* **~ up**, **~ together**) mélanger, brouiller; **jumble sale** n (*BRIT*)

vente f de charité

jumbo ['dʒʌmbəu] adj (*also:* **~ jet**) (*avion*) gros porteur (à réaction)

jump [dʒʌmp] vi sauter, bondir; (*with fear etc*) sursauter; (*increase*) monter en flèche ▷ vt sauter, franchir ▷ n saut m, bond m; (*with fear etc*) sursaut m; (*fence*) obstacle m; **to ~ the queue** (*BRIT*) passer avant son tour

jumper ['dʒʌmpə'] n (*BRIT: pullover*) pull-over m; (*us: pinafore dress*) robe-chasuble f

jump leads (*us* **jumper cables**) npl câbles mpl de démarrage

Jun. abbr = **June**; **junior**

junction ['dʒʌŋkʃən] n (*BRIT: of roads*) carrefour m; (*of rails*) embranchement m

June [dʒuːn] n juin m

jungle ['dʒʌŋɡl] n jungle f

junior ['dʒuːnɪə'] adj, n: **he's ~ to me (by 2 years)**, he's **my ~ (by 2 years)** il est mon cadet (de 2 ans), il est plus jeune que moi (de 2 ans); **he's ~ to me** (*seniority*) il est en dessous de moi (dans la hiérarchie), j'ai plus d'ancienneté que lui; **junior high school** n (*us*) ≈ collège m d'enseignement secondaire; *see also* **high school**; **junior school** n (*BRIT*) école f primaire, cours moyen

junk [dʒʌŋk] n (*rubbish*) camelote f; (*cheap goods*) bric-à-brac m inv; **junk food** n snacks vite prêts (*sans valeur nutritive*)

junkie ['dʒʌŋkɪ] n (*inf*) junkie m, drogué(e)

junk mail n prospectus mpl; (*Comput*) messages mpl publicitaires

Jupiter ['dʒuːpɪtə'] n (*planet*) Jupiter f

jurisdiction [dʒuərɪs'dɪkʃən] n juridiction f; **it falls** or **comes within/outside our ~** cela rest ci/n'est pas de notre compétence or ressort

jury ['dʒuərɪ] n jury m

just [dʒʌst] adj juste ▷ adv: **he's ~ done it/left** il vient de le faire/partir; **~ right/two o'clock** exactement or juste ce qu'il faut/deux heures; **we were ~ going** nous partions; **I was ~ about to phone** j'allais téléphoner; **~ as he was leaving** au moment or à l'instant précis où il partait; **~ before/enough/here** juste avant/assez/là; **it's ~ me/a mistake** ce n'est que moi/(rien) qu'une erreur; **~ missed/caught** manqué/attrapé de justesse; **~ listen to this!** écoutez un peu ça!; **she's ~ as clever as you** elle est tout aussi intelligente que vous; **it's ~ as well that you ...** heureusement que vous ...; **~ a minute!**, **~ one moment!** un instant (s'il vous plaît)!

justice ['dʒʌstɪs] n justice f; (*us: judge*) juge m de la Cour suprême

justification [dʒʌstɪfɪ'keɪʃən] n justification f

justify ['dʒʌstɪfaɪ] vt justifier

jut [dʒʌt] vi (*also:* **~ out**) dépasser, faire saillie

juvenile ['dʒuːvənaɪl] adj juvénile; (*court, books*) pour enfants ▷ n adolescent(e)

K, k [keɪ] *abbr* (= *one thousand*) K; (= *kilobyte*) Ko
kangaroo [kæŋgə'ru:] *n* kangourou *m*
karaoke [kɑ:rə'əʊkɪ] *n* karaoké *m*
karate [kə'rɑ:tɪ] *n* karaté *m*
kebab [kə'bæb] *n* kébab *m*
keel [ki:l] *n* quille *f*; **on an even ~** (*fig*) à flot
keen [ki:n] *adj* (*eager*) plein(e) d'enthousiasme; (*interest, desire, competition*) vif (vive); (*eye, intelligence*) pénétrant(e); (*edge*) effilé(e); **to be ~ to do** *or* **on doing sth** désirer vivement faire qch, tenir beaucoup à faire qch; **to be ~ on sth/sb** aimer beaucoup qch/qn
keep [ki:p] (*pt, pp* **kept**) *vt* (*retain, preserve*) garder; (*hold back*) retenir; (*shop, accounts, promise, diary*) tenir; (*support*) entretenir; (*chickens, bees, pigs etc*) élever ▷ *vi* (*food*) se conserver; (*remain: in a certain state or place*) rester ▷ *n* (*of castle*) donjon *m*; (*food etc*): **enough for his ~** assez pour (*assurer*) sa subsistance; **to ~ doing sth** (*continue*) continuer à faire qch; (*repeatedly*) ne pas arrêter de faire qch; **to ~ sb from doing/sth from happening** empêcher qn de faire or que qn (*ne*) fasse/que qch (*n*)arrive; **to ~ sb happy/a place tidy** faire que qn soit content/qu'un endroit reste propre; **to ~ sth to o.s.** garder qch pour soi; **to ~ sth from sb** cacher qch à qn; **to ~ time** (*clock*) être à l'heure, ne pas retarder; **for ~s** (*inf*) pour de bon, pour toujours; **keep away** *vt*: **to ~ sth/sb away from sb** tenir qch/qn éloigné de qn ▷ *vi*: **to ~ away (from)** ne pas s'approcher (de); **keep back** *vt* (*crowds, tears, money*) retenir; (*conceal: information*) **to ~ sth back from sb** cacher qch à qn ▷ *vi* rester en arrière; **keep off** *vt* (*dog, person*) éloigner ▷ *vi*: **if the rain ~s off** s'il ne pleut pas; **~ your hands off!** pas touche! (*inf*); **"~ off the grass"** "pelouse interdite"; **keep on** *vi* continuer; **to ~ on doing** continuer à faire; **don't ~ on about it!** arrête (d'en parler)!; **keep out** *vt* empêcher d'entrer ▷ *vi* (*stay out*) rester en dehors; **"~ out"** "défense d'entrer"; **keep up** *vi* (*fig: in comprehension*) suivre ▷ *vt* continuer, maintenir; **to ~ up with sb** (*in work etc*) se maintenir au même niveau que qn; (*in race etc*) aller aussi vite que qn; **keeper** *n* gardien(ne); **keep-fit** *n* gymnastique *f* (d'entretien); **keeping** *n* (*care*) garde *f*; **in keeping with** en harmonie avec
kennel ['kɛnl] *n* niche *f*; **kennels** *npl* (*for boarding*) chenil *m*
Kenya ['kɛnjə] *n* Kenya *m*
kept [kɛpt] *pt, pp of* **keep**
kerb [kə:b] *n* (BRIT) bordure *f* du trottoir
kerosene ['kɛrəsi:n] *n* kérosène *m*
ketchup ['kɛtʃəp] *n* ketchup *m*
kettle ['kɛtl] *n* bouilloire *f*
key [ki:] *n* (*gen*;: *Mus*) clé *f*; (*of piano, typewriter*) touche *f*; (*on map*) légende *f* ▷ *adj* (*factor, role, area*) clé *inv* ▷ *vt* (*also*: **~ in**: *text*) saisir; **can I have my ~?** je peux avoir ma clé?; **a ~ issue** un problème fondamental; **keyboard** *n* clavier *m*; **keyhole** *n* trou *m* de la serrure; **keyring** *n* porte-clés *m*
kg *abbr* (= *kilogram*) K
khaki ['kɑ:kɪ] *adj, n* kaki *m*
kick [kɪk] *vt* donner un coup de pied à ▷ *vi* (*horse*) ruer ▷ *n* coup *m* de pied; (*inf: thrill*): **he does it for ~s** il le fait parce que ça l'excite, il le fait pour le plaisir; **to ~ the habit** (*inf*) arrêter; **kick off** *vi* (*Sport*) donner le coup d'envoi; **kick-off** *n* (*Sport*) coup *m* d'envoi
kid [kɪd] *n* (*inf: child*) gamin(e), gosse *m/f*; (*animal, leather*) chevreau *m* ▷ *vi* (*inf*) plaisanter, blaguer
kidnap ['kɪdnæp] *vt* enlever, kidnapper; **kidnapping** *n* enlèvement *m*
kidney ['kɪdnɪ] *n* (*Anat*) rein *m*; (*Culin*) rognon *m*; **kidney bean** *n* haricot *m* rouge
kill [kɪl] *vt* tuer ▷ *n* mise *f* à mort; **to ~ time** tuer le temps; **killer** *n* tueur(-euse); (*murderer*) meurtrier(-ière); **killing** *n* meurtre *m*; (*of group of people*) tuerie *f*, massacre *m*; (*inf*): **to make a killing** se remplir les poches, réussir un beau coup
kiln [kɪln] *n* four *m*
kilo ['ki:ləu] *n* kilo *m*; **kilobyte** *n* (*Comput*) kilo-octet *m*; **kilogram(me)** *n* kilogramme *m*; **kilometre** (*US* **kilometer**) ['kɪləmi:tə'] *n* kilomètre *m*; **kilowatt** *n* kilowatt *m*
kilt [kɪlt] *n* kilt *m*
kin [kɪn] *n see* **next-of-kin**
kind [kaɪnd] *adj* gentil(le), aimable ▷ *n* sorte *f*, espèce *f*; (*species*) genre *m*; **to be two of a ~** se ressembler; **in ~** (*Comm*) en nature; **~ of** (*inf: rather*) plutôt; **a ~ of** une sorte de; **what ~ of ...?** quelle sorte de ...?
kindergarten ['kɪndəgɑ:tn] *n* jardin *m* d'enfants
kindly ['kaɪndlɪ] *adj* bienveillant(e), plein(e) de gentillesse ▷ *adv* avec bonté; **will you ~ ...** auriez-vous la bonté or l'obligeance de ...
kindness ['kaɪndnɪs] *n* (*quality*) bonté *f*, gentillesse *f*
king [kɪŋ] *n* roi *m*; **kingdom** *n* royaume *m*; **kingfisher** *n* martin-pêcheur *m*; **king-size(d) bed** *n* grand lit (*de 1,95 m de large*)
kiosk ['ki:ɔsk] *n* kiosque *m*; (BRIT: *also*: **telephone ~**) cabine *f* (téléphonique)
kipper ['kɪpə'] *n* hareng fumé et salé
kiss [kɪs] *n* baiser *m* ▷ *vt* embrasser; **to ~ (each other)** s'embrasser; **kiss of life** *n* (BRIT) bouche à bouche *m*
kit [kɪt] *n* équipement *m*, matériel *m*; (*set of tools etc*) trousse *f*; (*for assembly*) kit *m*
kitchen ['kɪtʃɪn] *n* cuisine *f*
kite [kaɪt] *n* (*toy*) cerf-volant *m*
kitten ['kɪtn] *n* petit chat, chaton *m*
kitty ['kɪtɪ] *n* (*money*) cagnotte *f*
kiwi ['ki:wi:] *n* (*also*: **~ fruit**) kiwi *m*

km *abbr* (= *kilometre*) km
km/h *abbr* (= *kilometres per hour*) km/h
knack [næk] *n*: **to have the ~ (of doing)** avoir le coup (pour faire)
knee [ni:] *n* genou *m*; **kneecap** *n* rotule *f*
kneel [pt, pp **knelt**] [ni:l, nɛlt] *vi* (*also*: **~ down**) s'agenouiller
knelt [nɛlt] *pt, pp of* **kneel**
knew [nju:] *pt of* **know**
knickers ['nɪkəz] *npl* (BRIT) culotte *f* (de femme)
knife [naɪf] *n* (*pl* **knives**) couteau *m* ▷ *vt* poignarder, frapper d'un coup de couteau
knight [naɪt] *n* chevalier *m*; (*Chess*) cavalier *m*
knit [nɪt] *vt* tricoter ▷ *vi* tricoter; (*broken bones*) se ressouder; **to ~ one's brows** froncer les sourcils; **knitting** *n* tricot *m*; **knitting needle** *n* aiguille *f* à tricoter; **knitwear** *n* tricots *mpl*, lainages *mpl*
knives [naɪvz] *npl of* **knife**
knob [nɔb] *n* bouton *m*; (BRIT): **a ~ of butter** une noix de beurre
knock [nɔk] *vt* frapper; (*bump into*) heurter; (*fig: col*) dénigrer ▷ *vi* (*at door etc*): **to ~ at/on** frapper à/sur ▷ *n* coup *m*; **knock down** *vt* renverser; (*price*) réduire; **knock off** *vi* (*inf: finish*) s'arrêter (de travailler) ▷ *vt* (*vase, object*) faire tomber; (*inf: steal*) piquer; (*fig: from price etc*): **to ~ off £10** faire une remise de 10 livres; **knock out** *vt* assommer; (*Boxing*) mettre k.-o.; (*in competition*) éliminer; **knock over** *vt* (*object*) faire tomber; (*pedestrian*) renverser; **knockout** *n* (*Boxing*) knock-out *m*, K.-O. *m*; **knockout competition** (BRIT) compétition *f* avec épreuves éliminatoires
knot [nɔt] *n* (*gen*) nœud *m* ▷ *vt* nouer
know [nəu] *vt* (*pt* **knew**, *pp* **~n**) savoir; (*person, place*) connaître; **to ~ that** savoir que; **to ~ how to do** savoir faire; **to ~ how to swim** savoir nager; **to ~ about/of sth** (*event*) être au courant de qch; (*subject*) connaître qch; **I don't ~** je ne sais pas; **do you ~ where I can ...?** savez-vous où je peux ...?; **know-all** *n* (BRIT pej) je-sais-tout *m/f*; **know-how** *n* savoir-faire *m*, technique *f*, compétence *f*; **knowing** *adj* (*look etc*) entendu(e); **knowingly** *adv* (*on purpose*) sciemment; (*smile, look*) d'un air entendu; **know-it-all** *n* (US) = **know-all**
knowledge ['nɔlɪdʒ] *n* connaissance *f*; (*learning*) connaissances, savoir *m*; **without my ~** à mon insu; **knowledgeable** *adj* bien informé(e)
known [nəun] *pp of* **know** ▷ *adj* (*thief, facts*) notoire; (*expert*) expert(e)
knuckle ['nʌkl] *n* articulation *f* (des phalanges), jointure *f*
koala [kəu'ɑ:lə] *n* (*also*: **~ bear**) koala *m*
Koran [kɔ'rɑ:n] *n* Coran *m*
Korea [kə'rɪə] *n* Corée *f*; **Korean** *adj* coréen(ne) ▷ *n* Coréen(ne)
kosher ['kəuʃəʳ] *adj* kascher *inv*
Kosovar, Kosovan ['kɔsəvaʳ, 'kɔsəvən] *adj* kosovar(e)
Kosovo ['kɔsəvəu] *n* Kosovo *m*
Kuwait [ku'weɪt] *n* Koweït *m*

L *abbr* (BRIT Aut: = *learner*) signale un conducteur débutant
l. *abbr* (= *litre*) l
lab [læb] *n abbr* (= *laboratory*) labo *m*
label ['leɪbl] *n* étiquette *f*; (*brand: of record*) marque *f* ▷ *vt* étiqueter
labor *etc* ['leɪbəʳ] (US) = **labour** *etc*
laboratory [lə'bɔrətərɪ] *n* laboratoire *m*
Labor Day *n* (US, CANADA) fête *f* du travail (*le premier lundi de septembre*)
labor union *n* (US) syndicat *m*
Labour ['leɪbəʳ] *n* (BRIT Pol: also: **the ~ Party**) le parti travailliste, les travaillistes *mpl*
labour (US **labor**) ['leɪbəʳ] *n* (*work*) travail *m*; (*workforce*) main-d'œuvre *f* ▷ *vi*: **to ~ (at)** travailler dur (à), peiner (sur) ▷ *vt*: **to ~ a point** insister sur un point; **in ~** (*Med*) en travail; **labourer** *n* manœuvre *m*; **farm labourer** ouvrier *m* agricole
lace [leɪs] *n* dentelle *f*; (*of shoe etc*) lacet *m* ▷ *vt* (*shoe: also*: **~ up**) lacer
lack [læk] *n* manque *m* ▷ *vt* manquer de; **through** *or* **for ~ of** faute de, par manque de; **to be ~ing** manquer, faire défaut; **to be ~ing in** manquer de
lacquer ['lækəʳ] *n* laque *f*
lacy ['leɪsɪ] *adj* en dentelle; (*like lace*) comme de la dentelle
lad [læd] *n* garçon *m*, gars *m*
ladder ['lædəʳ] *n* échelle *f*; (BRIT: in tights) maille filée ▷ *vt, vi* (BRIT: tights) filer
ladle ['leɪdl] *n* louche *f*
lady ['leɪdɪ] *n* dame *f*; **"ladies and gentlemen ..."** "Mesdames (et) Messieurs ..."; **young ~** jeune fille *f*; (*married*) jeune femme *f*; **the ladies' (room)** les toilettes *fpl* des dames; **ladybird** (US **ladybug**) *n* coccinelle *f*
lag [læg] *n* retard *m* ▷ *vi* (*also*: **~ behind**) rester en arrière, traîner; (*fig*) rester à la traîne ▷ *vt* (*pipes*) calorifuger
lager ['lɑːgəʳ] *n* bière blonde
lagoon [lə'guːn] *n* lagune *f*
laid [leɪd] *pt, pp of* **lay**; **laid back** *adj* (*inf*) relaxe, décontracté(e)
lain [leɪn] *pp of* **lie**

lake [leɪk] n lac m

lamb [læm] n agneau m

lame [leɪm] adj (also fig) boiteux(-euse)

lament [lə'mɛnt] n lamentation f ▷ vt pleurer, se lamenter sur

lamp [læmp] n lampe f; **lamppost** n (BRIT) réverbère m; **lampshade** n abat-jour m inv

land [lænd] n (as opposed to sea) terre f(ferme); (country) pays m; (soil) terre; (piece of land) terrain m; (estate) terre(s), domaine(s) m(pl) ▷ vi (from ship) débarquer; (Aviat) atterrir; (fig: fall) (re)tomber ▷ vt (passengers, goods) débarquer; (obtain) décrocher; **to ~ sb with sth** (inf) coller qch à qn; **landing** n (from ship) débarquement m; (Aviat) atterrissage m; (of staircase) palier m; **landing card** n carte f de débarquement; **landlady** n propriétaire f, logeuse f; (of pub) patronne f; **landlord** n propriétaire m, logeur m; (of pub etc) patron m; **landmark** n (point m de) repère m; **to be a landmark** (fig) faire date or époque; **landowner** n propriétaire foncier or terrien; **landscape** n paysage m; **landslide** n (Geo) glissement m (de terrain); (fig: Pol) raz-de-marée (électoral)

lane [leɪn] n (in country) chemin m; (Aut: of road) voie f; (: line of traffic) file f; (in race) couloir m

language [ˈlæŋgwɪdʒ] n langage m; **what ~s do you speak?** quelles langues parlez-vous?; **bad ~** grossièretés fpl, langage grossier; **language laboratory** n laboratoire m de langues; **language school** n école f de langue

lantern [ˈlæntn] n lanterne f

lap [læp] n (of track) tour m (de piste); (of body): **in or on one's ~** sur les genoux ▷ vt (also: **~ up**) laper ▷ vi (waves) clapoter

lapel [lə'pɛl] n revers m

lapse [læps] n défaillance f, (in behaviour) écart m (de conduite) ▷ vi (Law) cesser d'être en vigueur; (contract) expirer; **to ~ into bad habits** prendre de mauvaises habitudes; **~ of time** laps m de temps, intervalle m

laptop (computer) [ˈlæptɒp-] n portable m

lard [lɑːd] n saindoux m

larder [ˈlɑːdə'] n garde-manger m inv

large [lɑːdʒ] adj grand(e); (person, animal) gros (grosse); **at ~** (free) en liberté; (generally) en général; pour la plupart; see also **by**; **largely** adv en grande partie; (principally) surtout; **large-scale** adj (map, drawing etc) à grande échelle; (fig) important(e)

lark [lɑːk] n (bird) alouette f; (joke) blague f, farce f

laryngitis [lærɪnˈdʒaɪtɪs] n laryngite f

lasagne [ləˈzænjə] n lasagne f

laser [ˈleɪzə'] n laser m; **laser printer** n imprimante f laser

lash [læʃ] n coup m de fouet; (also: **eye~**) cil m ▷ vt fouetter; (tie) attacher; **lash out** vi: **to ~ out (at or against sb/sth)** attaquer violemment (qn/qch)

lass [læs] (BRIT) n (jeune) fille f

last [lɑːst] adj dernier(-ière) ▷ adv en dernier; (most recently) la dernière fois; (finally) finalement ▷ vi durer; **~ week** la semaine dernière; **~ night** (evening) hier soir; (night) la nuit dernière; **at ~** enfin; **~ but one** avant-dernier(-ière); **lastly** adv en dernier lieu, pour finir; **last-minute** adj de dernière minute

latch [lætʃ] n loquet m; **latch onto** vt fus (cling to: person, group) s'accrocher à; (idea) se mettre en tête

late [leɪt] adj (not on time) en retard; (far on in day etc) tardif(-ive); (: edition, delivery) dernier(-ière); (dead)

défunt(e) ▷ adv tard; (behind time, schedule) en retard; **to be 10 minutes ~** avoir 10 minutes de retard; **sorry I'm ~** désolé d'être en retard; **it's too ~** il est trop tard; **of ~** dernièrement; **in ~ May** vers la fin (du mois) de mai, fin mai; **the ~ Mr X** feu M. X; **latecomer** n retardataire m/f; **lately** adv récemment; **later** (date etc) ultérieur(e); (version etc) plus récent(e) ▷ adv plus tard; **latest** [ˈleɪtɪst] adj tout(e) dernier(-ière); **at the latest** au plus tard

lather [ˈlɑːðə'] n mousse f (de savon) ▷ vt savonner

Latin [ˈlætɪn] n latin m ▷ adj latin(e); **Latin America** n Amérique latine; **Latin American** adj latino-américain(e), d'Amérique latine ▷ n Latino-Américain(e)

latitude [ˈlætɪtjuːd] n (also fig) latitude f

latter [ˈlætə'] adj deuxième, dernier(-ière) ▷ n: **the ~** ce dernier, celui-ci

laugh [lɑːf] n rire m ▷ vi rire; **(to do sth) for a ~** (faire qch) pour rire; **laugh at** vt fus se moquer de; (joke) rire de; **laughter** n rire m; (of several people) rires mpl

launch [lɔːntʃ] n lancement m; (also: **motor ~**) vedette f ▷ vt (ship, rocket, plan) lancer; **launch into** vt fus se lancer dans

launder [ˈlɔːndə'] vt laver; (fig: money) blanchir

Launderette® [lɔːnˈdrɛt] (BRIT: US **Laundromat®**) [ˈlɔːndrəmæt] n laverie f (automatique)

laundry [ˈlɔːndrɪ] n (clothes) linge m; (business) blanchisserie f; (room) buanderie f; **to do the ~** faire la lessive

lava [ˈlɑːvə] n lave f

lavatory [ˈlævətərɪ] n toilettes fpl

lavender [ˈlævəndə'] n lavande f

lavish [ˈlævɪʃ] adj (amount) copieux(-euse); (person: giving freely): **~ with** prodigue de ▷ vt: **to ~ sth on sb** prodiguer qch à qn; (money) dépenser qch sans compter pour qn

law [lɔː] n loi f; (science) droit m; **lawful** adj légal(e), permis(e); **lawless** adj (action) illégal(e); (place) sans loi

lawn [lɔːn] n pelouse f; **lawnmower** n tondeuse f à gazon

lawsuit [ˈlɔːsuːt] n procès m

lawyer [ˈlɔːjə'] n (consultant, with company) juriste m; (for sales, wills etc) ≈ notaire m; (partner, in court) ≈ avocat m

lax [læks] adj relâché(e)

laxative [ˈlæksətɪv] n laxatif m

lay [leɪ] pt of **lie** ▷ adj laïque; (not expert) profane ▷ vt (pt, pp **laid**) poser, mettre; (eggs) pondre; (trap) tendre; (plans) élaborer; **to ~ the table** mettre la table; **lay down** vt poser; (rules etc) établir; **to ~ down the law** (fig) faire la loi; **lay off** vt (workers) licencier; (provide: meal etc) fournir; **lay out** vt (design) dessiner, concevoir; (display) disposer; (spend) dépenser; **lay-by** n (BRIT) aire f de stationnement (sur le bas-côté)

layer [ˈleɪə'] n couche f

layman [ˈleɪmən] (irreg) n (Rel) laïque m; (non-expert) profane m

layout [ˈleɪaʊt] n disposition f, plan m, agencement m; (Press) mise f en page

lb. abbr (weight) = **pound**

lead¹ [liːd] n (front position) tête f; (distance, time ahead) avance f; (clue) piste f; (Elec) fil m; (for dog) laisse f; (Theat) rôle principal ▷ vb (pt, pp **led**) vt (guide) mener, conduire; (be leader of) être à la tête de ▷ vi (Sport) mener, être en tête; **to ~ to** (road, pipe) mener à, conduire à; (result in) conduire à; aboutir à; **to be in the ~** (Sport:

in race) mener, être en tête; (: *in match*) mener (à la marque); **to ~ sb to do sth** amener qn à faire qch; **to ~ the way** montrer le chemin; **lead up to** vt conduire à; (*in conversation*) en venir à

lead² [lɛd] n (*metal*) plomb m; (*in pencil*) mine f

leader ['liːdə'] n (*of team*) chef m; (*of party etc*) dirigeant(e), leader m; (*Sport: in league*) leader; (: *in race*) coureur m de tête; **leadership** n (*position*) direction f; **under the leadership of ...** sous la direction de ...; **qualities of leadership** qualités fpl de chef ou de meneur

lead-free ['lɛdfriː] adj sans plomb

leading ['liːdɪŋ] adj de premier plan; (*main*) principal(e); (*in race*) de tête

lead singer [liːd-] n (*in pop group*) (chanteur m) vedette f

leaf (pl **leaves**) [liːf, liːvz] n feuille f; (*of table*) rallonge f; **to turn over a new ~** (*fig*) changer de conduite or d'existence; **leaf through** vt (*book*) feuilleter

leaflet ['liːflɪt] n prospectus m, brochure f; (*Pol, Rel*) tract m

league [liːg] n ligue f; (*Football*) championnat m; **to be in ~ with** avoir partie liée avec, être de mèche avec

leak [liːk] n (*out: also fig*) fuite f ▷ vi (*pipe, liquid etc*) fuir; (*shoes*) prendre l'eau; (*ship*) faire eau ▷ vt (*liquid*) répandre; (*information*) divulguer

lean [liːn] adj maigre ▷ vb (pt, pp **~ed** or **~t**) ▷ vt: **to ~ sth on** appuyer qch sur ▷ vi (*slope*) pencher; (*rest*): **to ~ against** s'appuyer contre; être appuyé(e) contre; **to ~ on** s'appuyer sur; **lean forward** vi se pencher en avant; **lean over** vi se pencher ▷ pron; **leaning** n: **leaning (towards)** penchant m (pour)

leant [lɛnt] pt, pp of **lean**

leap [liːp] n bond m, saut m ▷ vi (pt, pp **~ed** or **~t**) bondir, sauter

leapt [lɛpt] pt, pp of **leap**

leap year n année f bissextile

learn (pt, pp **~ed** or **~t**) [ləːn, -t] vt, vi apprendre; **to ~ (how) to do sth** apprendre à faire qch; **to ~ about sth** (*Scol*) étudier qch; (*hear, read*) apprendre qch; **learner** n débutant(e); (*BRIT: also*: **learner driver**) (conducteur-trice) débutant(e); **learning** n savoir m

learnt [ləːnt] pp of **learn**

lease [liːs] n bail m ▷ vt louer à bail

leash [liːʃ] n laisse f

least [liːst] adj: **the ~** (+ *noun*) le (la) plus petit(e), le (la) moindre; (*smallest amount of*) le moins de ▷ pron: (**the**) **~ le moins** ▷ adv (+ *verb*) le moins; (+ *adj*): **the ~** le (la) moins; **the ~ money** le moins d'argent; **the ~ expensive** le (la) moins cher (chère); **the ~ possible effort** le moins d'effort possible; **at ~** au moins; (*or rather*) du moins; **you could at ~ have written** tu aurais au moins pu écrire; **not in the ~** le moins du monde

leather ['lɛðə'] n cuir m

leave [liːv] (vb: pt, pp **left**) vt laisser; (*go away from*) quitter; (*forget*) oublier ▷ vi partir, s'en aller ▷ n (*time off*) congé m; (*Mil, also: consent*) permission f; **what time does the train/bus ~?** le train/le bus part à quelle heure?; **to ~ sth to sb** (*money etc*) laisser qch à qn; **to be left** rester; **there's some milk left over** il reste du lait; **~ it to me!** laissez-moi faire!, je m'en occupe!; **on ~** en permission; **leave behind** vt (*also fig*) laisser; (*forget*) laisser, oublier; **leave out** vt oublier, omettre

leaves [liːvz] npl of **leaf**

Lebanon ['lɛbənən] n Liban m

lecture ['lɛktʃə'] n conférence f; (*Scol*) cours (magistral)

▷ vi donner des cours; enseigner ▷ vt (*scold*) sermonner, réprimander; **to give a ~ (on)** faire une conférence (sur), faire un cours (sur); **lecture hall** n amphithéâtre m; **lecturer** n (*speaker*) conférencier(-ière); (*BRIT: at university*) professeur m (d'université), prof m/f de fac (*inf*); **lecture theatre** n = **lecture hall**

led [lɛd] pt, pp of **lead¹**

ledge [lɛdʒ] n (*of window, on wall*) rebord m; (*of mountain*) saillie f, corniche f

leek [liːk] n poireau m

left [lɛft] pt, pp of **leave** ▷ adj gauche ▷ adv à gauche ▷ n gauche f; **there are two ~** il en reste deux; **on the ~, to the ~** à gauche; **the L~** (*Pol*) la gauche; **left-hand** adj: **the left-hand side** la gauche; **left-hand drive** n (*BRIT: vehicle*) véhicule m avec la conduite à gauche; **left-handed** adj gaucher(-ère); (*scissors etc*) pour gauchers; **left-luggage locker** n (*BRIT*) (casier m à) consigne f automatique; **left-luggage (office)** n (*BRIT*) consigne f; **left-overs** npl restes mpl; **left-wing** adj (*Pol*) de gauche

leg [lɛg] n jambe f; (*of animal*) patte f; (*of furniture*) pied m; (*Culin: of chicken*) cuisse f; (*of journey*) étape f; **1st/2nd ~** (*Sport*) match m aller/retour; **~ of lamb** (*Culin*) gigot m d'agneau

legacy ['lɛgəsɪ] n (*also fig*) héritage m, legs m

legal ['liːgl] adj (*permitted by law*) légal(e); (*relating to law*) juridique; **legal holiday** (*us*) n jour férié; **legalize** vt légaliser; **legally** adv légalement

legend ['lɛdʒənd] n légende f; **legendary** ['lɛdʒəndərɪ] adj légendaire

leggings ['lɛgɪŋz] npl caleçon m

legible ['lɛdʒəbl] adj lisible

legislation [lɛdʒɪs'leɪʃən] n législation f

legislative ['lɛdʒɪslətɪv] adj législatif(-ive)

legitimate [lɪ'dʒɪtɪmət] adj légitime

leisure ['lɛʒə'] n (*free time*) temps libre, loisirs mpl; **at ~** (*tout*) à loisir; **at your ~** (*later*) à tête reposée; **leisure centre** n (*BRIT*) centre m de loisirs; **leisurely** adj tranquille, fait(e) sans se presser

lemon ['lɛmən] n citron m; **lemonade** n (*fizzy*) limonade f; **lemon tea** n thé m au citron

lend (pt, pp **lent**) [lɛnd, lɛnt] vt: **to ~ sth (to sb)** prêter qch (à qn); **could you ~ me some money?** pourriez-vous me prêter de l'argent?

length [lɛŋθ] n longueur f; (*section: of road, pipe etc*) morceau m, bout m; **~ of time** durée f; **it is 2 metres in ~** cela fait 2 mètres de long; **at ~** (*at last*) enfin, à la fin; (*lengthily*) longuement; **lengthen** vt allonger, prolonger ▷ vi s'allonger; **lengthways** adv dans le sens de la longueur, en long; **lengthy** adj (très) long (longue)

lens [lɛnz] n lentille f; (*of spectacles*) verre m; (*of camera*) objectif m

Lent [lɛnt] n carême m

lent [lɛnt] pt, pp of **lend**

lentil ['lɛntl] n lentille f

Leo ['liːəu] n le Lion

leopard ['lɛpəd] n léopard m

leotard ['liːəʊtɑːd] n justaucorps m

leprosy ['lɛprəsɪ] n lèpre f

lesbian ['lɛzbɪən] n lesbienne f ▷ adj lesbien(ne)

less [lɛs] adj moins de ▷ pron, adv moins ▷ prep: **~ tax/10% discount** avant impôt/moins 10% de remise; **~ than that/you** moins que cela/vous; **~ than half** moins de la moitié; **~ than ever** moins que jamais; **~ and ~** de moins en moins; **the ~ he works ...** moins il travaille ...:

lessen vi diminuer, s'amoindrir, s'atténuer ▷ vt diminuer, réduire, atténuer; **lesser** ['lɛsəʳ] adj moindre; **to a lesser extent** or **degree** à un degré moindre

lesson ['lɛsn] n leçon f; **to teach sb a ~** (fig) donner une bonne leçon à qn

let (pt, pp ~) [lɛt] vt laisser; (BRIT: lease) louer; **to ~ sb do sth** laisser qn faire qch; **to ~ sb know sth** faire savoir qch à qn, prévenir qn de qch; **to ~ go** lâcher prise; **to ~ go of sth, to ~ sth go** lâcher qch; **~'s go** allons-y; **~ him come** qu'il vienne; **"to ~"** (BRIT) "à louer"; **let down** vt (lower) baisser; (BRIT: tyre) dégonfler; (disappoint) décevoir; **let in** vt laisser entrer; (visitor etc) faire entrer; **let off** vt (allow to leave) laisser partir; (not punish) ne pas punir; (firework etc) faire partir; (bomb) faire exploser; **let out** vt laisser sortir; (scream) laisser échapper; (BRIT: rent out) louer

lethal ['li:θl] adj mortel(le), fatal(e); (weapon) meurtrier(-ère)

letter ['lɛtəʳ] n lettre f; **letterbox** n (BRIT) boîte f aux or à lettres

lettuce ['lɛtɪs] n laitue f, salade f

leukaemia (US **leukemia**) [lu:'ki:mɪə] n leucémie f

level ['lɛvl] adj (flat) plat(e), plan(e), uni(e); (horizontal) horizontal(e) ▷ n niveau m ▷ vt niveler, aplanir; **"A" ~s** npl (BRIT) = baccalauréat m; **to be ~ with** au même niveau que; **to draw ~ with** (runner, car) arriver à la hauteur de, rattraper; **on the ~** (fig: honest) régulier(-ière); **level crossing** n (BRIT) passage m à niveau

lever ['li:vəʳ] n levier m; **leverage** n (influence): **leverage (on** or **with)** prise f (sur)

levy ['lɛvɪ] n taxe f, impôt m ▷ vt (tax) lever; (fine) infliger

liability [laɪə'bɪlətɪ] n responsabilité f; (handicap) handicap m

liable ['laɪəbl] adj (subject): **~ to** sujet(te) à, passible de; (responsible): **~ (for)** responsable (de); (likely): **~ to do** susceptible de faire

liaise [li:'eɪz] vi: **to ~ with** assurer la liaison avec

liar ['laɪəʳ] n menteur(-euse)

libel ['laɪbl] n diffamation f; (document) écrit m diffamatoire ▷ vt diffamer

liberal ['lɪbərl] adj libéral(e); (generous): **~ with** prodigue de, généreux(-euse) avec ▷ n: **L~** (Pol) libéral(e); **Liberal Democrat** n (BRIT) libéral(e)-démocrate m/f

liberate ['lɪbəreɪt] vt libérer

liberation [lɪbə'reɪʃən] n libération f

liberty ['lɪbətɪ] n liberté f; **to be at ~** (criminal) être en liberté; **at ~ to do** libre de faire; **to take the ~ of** prendre la liberté de, se permettre de

Libra ['li:brə] n la Balance

librarian [laɪ'brɛərɪən] n bibliothécaire m/f

library ['laɪbrərɪ] n bibliothèque f

Libya ['lɪbɪə] n Libye f

lice [laɪs] npl of **louse**

licence (US **license**) ['laɪsns] n autorisation f, permis m; (Comm) licence f; (Radio, TV) redevance f; (also: **driving ~**: US: also: **driver's license**) permis m de conduire

license ['laɪsns] n (US) = **licence**; **licensed** adj (for alcohol) patenté(e) pour la vente des spiritueux, qui a une patente de débit de boissons; (car) muni(e) de la vignette; **license plate** n (US Aut) plaque f minéralogique; **licensing hours** (BRIT) npl heures fpl d'ouvertures (des pubs)

lick [lɪk] vt lécher; (inf: defeat) écraser, flanquer une piquette or raclée à; **to ~ one's lips** (fig) se frotter les mains

lid [lɪd] n couvercle m; (eyelid) paupière f

lie [laɪ] n mensonge m ▷ vi (pt, pp ~d) (tell lies) mentir; (pt lay, pp lain) (rest) être étendu(e) or allongé(e) or couché(e); (in grave) être, se trouver, être; **to ~ low** (fig) se cacher, rester caché(e); **to tell ~s** mentir; **lie about, lie around** vi (things) traîner; (BRIT: person) traînasser, flemmarder; **lie down** vi se coucher, s'étendre

Liechtenstein ['lɪktənstaɪn] n Liechtenstein m

lie-in ['laɪɪn] n (BRIT): **to have a ~** faire la grasse matinée

lieutenant [lɛf'tɛnənt] (US) [lu:'tɛnənt] n lieutenant m

life (pl **lives**) [laɪf, laɪvz] n vie f; **to come to ~** (fig) s'animer; **life assurance** n (BRIT) = **life insurance**; **lifeboat** n canot m or chaloupe f de sauvetage; **lifeguard** n surveillant m de baignade; **life insurance** n assurance-vie f; **life jacket** n gilet m or ceinture f de sauvetage; **lifelike** adj qui semble vrai(e) or vivant(e), ressemblant(e); (painting) réaliste; **life preserver** n (US) gilet m or ceinture f de sauvetage; **life sentence** n condamnation f à vie or à perpétuité; **lifestyle** n style m de vie; **lifetime** n: **in his lifetime** de son vivant

lift [lɪft] vt soulever, lever; (end) supprimer, lever ▷ vi (fog) se lever ▷ n (BRIT: elevator) ascenseur m; **to give sb a ~** (BRIT) emmener or prendre qn en voiture; **can you give me a ~ to the station?** pouvez-vous m'emmener à la gare?; **lift up** vt soulever; **lift-off** n décollage m

light [laɪt] n lumière f; (lamp) lampe f; (Aut: rear light) feu m; (: headlamp) phare m; (for cigarette etc): **have you got a ~?** avez-vous du feu? ▷ vt (pt, pp ~ed or **lit**) (candle, cigarette, fire) allumer; (room) éclairer ▷ adj (room, colour) clair(e); (not heavy, also fig) léger(-ère); (not strenuous) peu fatigant(e); **lights** npl (traffic lights) feux mpl; **to come to ~** être dévoilé(e) or découvert(e); **in the ~ of** à la lumière de; étant donné; **light up** vi s'allumer; (face) s'éclairer; (smoke) allumer une cigarette or une pipe etc ▷ vt (illuminate) éclairer, illuminer; **light bulb** n ampoule f; **lighten** vt (light up) éclairer; (make lighter) éclaircir; (make less heavy) alléger; **lighter** n (also: **cigarette lighter**) briquet m; **light-hearted** adj gai(e), joyeux(-euse), enjoué(e); **lighthouse** n phare m; **lighting** n éclairage m; (in theatre) éclairages m; **lightly** adv légèrement; **to get off lightly** s'en tirer à bon compte

lightning ['laɪtnɪŋ] n foudre f; (flash) éclair m

lightweight ['laɪtweɪt] adj (suit) léger(-ère) ▷ n (Boxing) poids léger

like [laɪk] vt aimer (bien) ▷ prep comme ▷ adj semblable, pareil(le) ▷ n: **the ~** (pej) (d')autres du même genre or acabit; **his ~s and dislikes** ses goûts mpl or préférences fpl; **I would ~, I'd ~** je voudrais, j'aimerais; **would you ~ a coffee?** voulez-vous du café?; **to be/look ~ sb/sth** ressembler à qn/qch; **what's he ~?** comment est-il?; **what does it taste ~?** de quoi est-ce que ça a l'air?; **what does it taste ~?** quel goût est-ce que ça a?; **that's just ~ him** c'est bien de lui, ça lui ressemble; **do it ~ this** fais-le comme ceci; **it's nothing ~ ...** ce n'est pas du tout comme ...; **likeable** adj sympathique, agréable

likelihood ['laɪklɪhud] n probabilité f

likely ['laɪklɪ] adj (result, outcome) probable; (excuse) plausible; **he's ~ to leave** il va sûrement partir, il risque fort de partir; **not ~!** (inf) pas de danger!

likewise ['laɪkwaɪz] adv de même, pareillement

liking ['laɪkɪŋ] n (for person) affection f; (for thing) penchant m, goût m; **to be to sb's ~** être au goût de qn, plaire à qn

lilac ['laɪlək] n lilas m

Lilo® ['laɪləu] n matelas m pneumatique

lily ['lɪlɪ] n lis m; **~ of the valley** muguet m

limb [lɪm] n membre m

limbo ['lɪmbəu] n: **to be in ~** (fig) être tombé(e) dans l'oubli

lime [laɪm] n (tree) tilleul m; (fruit) citron vert, lime f; (Geo) chaux f

limelight ['laɪmlaɪt] n: **in the ~** (fig) en vedette, au premier plan

limestone ['laɪmstəun] n pierre f à chaux; (Geo) calcaire m

limit ['lɪmɪt] n limite f ▷ vt limiter; **limited** adj limité(e), restreint(e); **to be limited to** se limiter à, ne concerner que

limousine ['lɪməziːn] n limousine f

limp [lɪmp] n: **to have a ~** boiter ▷ vi boiter ▷ adj mou (molle)

line [laɪn] n (gen) ligne f; (stroke) trait m; (wrinkle) ride f; (rope) corde f; (wire) fil m; (of poem) vers m; (row, series) rangée f; (of people) file f, queue f; (railway track) voie f; (Comm: series of goods) article(s) m(pl), ligne de produits; (work) métier m ▷ vt: **to ~ (with)** (clothes) doubler (de); (box) garnir or tapisser (de); (subj: trees, crowd) border; **to stand in ~** (us) faire la queue; **in his ~ of business** dans sa partie, dans son rayon; **to be in ~ for sth** (fig) être en lice pour qch; **in ~ with** en accord avec, en conformité avec; **in a ~** aligné(e); **line up** vi s'aligner, se mettre en rang(s); (in queue) faire la queue ▷ vt aligner; (event) prévoir; (find) trouver; **to have sb/sth ~d up** avoir qn/qch en vue or de prévu(e)

linear ['lɪnɪər] adj linéaire

linen ['lɪnɪn] n linge m (de corps or de maison); (cloth) lin m

liner ['laɪnər] n (ship) paquebot m de ligne; (for bin) sac-poubelle m

line-up ['laɪnʌp] n (us: queue) file f; (also: **police ~**) parade f d'identification; (Sport) composition f de l'équipe f

linger ['lɪŋgər] vi s'attarder; traîner; (smell, tradition) persister

lingerie ['lænʒəriː] n lingerie f

linguist ['lɪŋgwɪst] n linguiste m/f; **to be a good ~** être doué(e) pour les langues; **linguistic** adj linguistique

lining ['laɪnɪŋ] n doublure f; (of brakes) garniture f

link [lɪŋk] n (connection) lien m, rapport m; (Internet) lien; (of a chain) maillon m ▷ vt relier, lier, unir; **links** npl (Golf) (terrain m de) golf m; **link up** vt relier ▷ vi (people) se rejoindre; (companies etc) s'associer

lion ['laɪən] n lion m; **lioness** n lionne f

lip [lɪp] n lèvre f; (of cup etc) rebord m; **lipread** vi lire sur les lèvres; **lip salve** [-sælv] n pommade f pour les lèvres, pommade rosat; **lipstick** n rouge m à lèvres

liqueur [lɪ'kjuər] n liqueur f

liquid ['lɪkwɪd] n liquide m ▷ adj liquide; **liquidizer** ['lɪkwɪdaɪzər] n (Brit Culin) mixer m

liquor ['lɪkər] n spiritueux m, alcool m; **liquor store** (us) n magasin m de vins et spiritueux

Lisbon ['lɪzbən] n Lisbonne f

lisp [lɪsp] n zézaiement m ▷ vi zézayer

list [lɪst] n liste f ▷ vt (write down) inscrire; (make list of) faire la liste de; (enumerate) énumérer

listen ['lɪsn] vi écouter; **to ~ to** écouter; **listener** n

auditeur(-trice)

lit [lɪt] pt, pp of **light**

liter ['liːtər] n (us) = **litre**

literacy ['lɪtərəsɪ] n degré m d'alphabétisation, fait m de savoir lire et écrire

literal ['lɪtərl] adj littéral(e); **literally** adv littéralement; (really) réellement

literary ['lɪtərərɪ] adj littéraire

literate ['lɪtərət] adj qui sait lire et écrire; (educated) instruit(e)

literature ['lɪtrɪtʃər] n littérature f; (brochures etc) copie f publicitaire, prospectus mpl

litre (us **liter**) ['liːtər] n litre m

litter ['lɪtər] n (rubbish) détritus mpl; (dirtier) ordures fpl; (young animals) portée f; **litter bin** n (Brit) poubelle f; **littered** adj: **littered with** (scattered) jonché(e) de

little ['lɪtl] adj (small) petit(e); (not much): **~ milk** peu de lait ▷ adv peu; **a ~** un peu (de); **a ~ milk** un peu de lait; **a ~ bit** un peu; **as ~ as possible** le moins possible; **~ by ~** petit à petit, peu à peu; **little finger** n auriculaire m, petit doigt

live¹ [laɪv] adj (animal) vivant(e), en vie; (wire) sous tension; (broadcast) (transmis(e)) en direct; (unexploded) non explosé(e)

live² [lɪv] vi vivre; (reside) vivre, habiter; **to ~ in London** habiter (à) Londres; **where do you ~?** où habitez-vous?; **live together** vi vivre ensemble, cohabiter; **live up to** vt fus se montrer à la hauteur de

livelihood ['laɪvlɪhud] n moyens mpl d'existence

lively ['laɪvlɪ] adj vif (vive), plein(e) d'entrain; (place, book) vivant(e)

liven up ['laɪvn-] vt (room etc) égayer; (discussion, evening) animer ▷ vi s'animer

liver ['lɪvər] n foie m

lives [laɪvz] npl of **life**

livestock ['laɪvstɔk] n cheptel m, bétail m

living ['lɪvɪŋ] adj vivant(e), en vie ▷ n: **to earn** or **make a ~** gagner sa vie; **living room** n salle f de séjour

lizard ['lɪzəd] n lézard m

load [ləud] n (weight) poids m; (thing carried) chargement m, charge f; (Elec, Tech) charge ▷ vt: **to ~ (with)** (also: **~ up**: lorry, ship) charger (de); (gun, camera) charger (avec); (Comput) charger; **a ~ of**, **~s of** (fig) un or des tas de, des masses de; **to talk a ~ of rubbish** (inf) dire des bêtises; **loaded** adj (dice) pipé(e); (question) insidieux(-euse); (inf: rich) bourré(e) de fric

loaf (pl **loaves**) [ləuf, ləuvz] n pain m, miche f ▷ vi (also: **~ about**, **~ around**) fainéanter, traîner

loan [ləun] n prêt m ▷ vt prêter; **on ~** prêté(e), en prêt

loathe [ləuð] vt détester, avoir en horreur

loaves [ləuvz] npl of **loaf**

lobby ['lɔbɪ] n hall m, entrée f; (Pol) groupe m de pression, lobby m ▷ vt faire pression sur

lobster ['lɔbstər] n homard m

local ['ləukl] adj local(e) ▷ n (Brit: pub) pub m or café m du coin; **the locals** npl les gens mpl du pays or du coin; **local anaesthetic** n anesthésie locale; **local authority** n collectivité locale, municipalité f; **local government** n administration locale or municipale; **locally** ['ləukəlɪ] adv localement; dans les environs or la région

locate [ləu'keɪt] vt (find) trouver, repérer; (situate) situer; **to be ~d in** être situé(e) or en

location [ləu'keɪʃən] n emplacement m; **on ~** (Cine) en extérieur

loch [lɔx] n lac m, loch m

lock [lɔk] n (of door, box) serrure f; (of canal) écluse f; (of hair) mèche f, boucle f ▷ vt (with key) fermer à clé ▷ vi (door etc) fermer à clé; (wheels) se bloquer; **lock in** vt enfermer; **lock out** vt enfermer dehors; (on purpose) mettre à la porte; **lock up** vt (person) enfermer; (house) fermer à clé ▷ vi tout fermer (à clé)

locker ['lɔkə^r] n casier m; (in station) consigne f automatique; **locker-room** (us) n (Sport) vestiaire m

locksmith ['lɔksmɪθ] n serrurier m

locomotive [ləukə'məutɪv] n locomotive f

locum ['ləukəm] n (Med) suppléant(e) de médecin etc

lodge [lɔdʒ] n pavillon m (de gardien); (also: **hunting ~**) pavillon de chasse ▷ vi (person): **to ~ with** être logé(e) chez, être en pension chez; (bullet) se loger ▷ vt (appeal etc) présenter; déposer; **to ~ a complaint** porter plainte; **lodger** n locataire m/f; (with room and meals) pensionnaire m/f

lodging ['lɔdʒɪŋ] n logement m

loft [lɔft] n grenier m; (apartment) grenier aménagé (en appartement) (gén dans ancien entrepôt ou fabrique)

log [lɔg] n (of wood) bûche f; (Naut) livre m ou journal m de bord; (of car) ≈ carte grise ▷ vt enregistrer; **log in, log on** vi (Comput) ouvrir une session, entrer dans le système; **log off, log out** vi (Comput) clore une session, sortir du système

logic ['lɔdʒɪk] n logique f; **logical** adj logique

logo ['ləugəu] n logo m

Loire [lwɑː] n: the (River) ~ la Loire

lollipop ['lɔlɪpɔp] n sucette f; **lollipop man/lady** (BRIT: irreg) n contractuel qui fait traverser la rue aux enfants

lolly ['lɔlɪ] n (inf: ice) esquimau m; (: lollipop) sucette f

London ['lʌndən] n Londres; **Londoner** n Londonien(ne)

lone [ləun] adj solitaire

loneliness ['ləunlɪnɪs] n solitude f, isolement m

lonely ['ləunlɪ] adj seul(e); (childhood etc) solitaire; (place) solitaire, isolé(e)

long [lɔŋ] adj long (longue) ▷ adv longtemps ▷ vi: **to ~ for sth/to do sth** avoir très envie de qch/de faire qch, attendre qch avec impatience/attendre de faire qch; **how ~ is this river/course?** quelle est la longueur de ce fleuve/la durée de ce cours?; **6 metres ~** (long) de 6 mètres; **6 months ~** qui dure 6 mois, de 6 mois; **all night ~** toute la nuit; **he no ~er comes** il ne vient plus; **I can't stand it any ~er** je ne peux plus le supporter; **~ before** longtemps avant; **before ~** (+ future) avant peu, dans peu de temps; (+ past) peu de temps après; **don't be ~!** fais vite!, dépêche-toi!; **I shan't be ~** je n'en ai pas pour longtemps; **at ~ last** enfin; **so** or **as ~ as** à condition que + sub; **long-distance** adj (race) de fond; (call) interurbain(e); **long-haul** adj (flight) long-courrier; **longing** n désir m, envie f; (nostalgia) nostalgie f ▷ adj plein(e) d'envie or de nostalgie

longitude ['lɔŋgɪtjuːd] n longitude f

long: **long jump** n saut m en longueur; **long-life** adj (batteries etc) longue durée inv; (milk) longue conservation; **long-sighted** adj (BRIT) presbyte; (fig) prévoyant(e); **long-standing** adj de longue date; **long-term** adj à long terme

loo [luː] n (BRIT inf) w.-c mpl, petit coin

look [luk] vi regarder; (seem) sembler, paraître, avoir l'air; (building etc): **to ~ south/on to the sea** donner au sud/sur la mer ▷ n regard m; (appearance) air m,

allure f, aspect m; **looks** npl (good looks) physique m, beauté f; **to ~ like** ressembler à; **to have a ~** regarder; **to have a ~ at sth** jeter un coup d'œil à qch; **~ (here)!** (annoyance) écoutez!; **look after** vt fus s'occuper de; (luggage etc: watch over) garder, surveiller; **look around** vi regarder autour de soi; **look at** vt fus regarder; (problem etc) examiner; **look back** vi: **to ~ back at sth/sb** se retourner pour regarder qch/qn; **to ~ back on** (event, period) évoquer, repenser à; **look down on** vt fus (fig) regarder de haut, dédaigner; **look for** vt fus chercher; **we're ~ing for a hotel/restaurant** nous cherchons un hôtel/restaurant; **look forward to** vt fus attendre avec impatience; **~ing forward to hearing from you** (in letter) dans l'attente de vous lire; **look into** vt fus (matter, possibility) examiner, étudier; **look out** vi (beware): **to ~ out (for)** prendre garde (à), faire attention (à); **~ out!** attention!; **look out for** vt fus (seek) être à la recherche de; (try to spot) guetter; **look round** vi (house, shop) faire le tour de ▷ vi (turn) regarder derrière soi, se retourner; **look through** vt fus (papers, book) examiner; (: briefly) parcourir; **look up** vi lever les yeux; (improve) s'améliorer ▷ vt (word) chercher; **look up to** vt fus avoir du respect pour; **lookout** n (tower etc) poste m de guet; (person) guetteur m; **to be on the lookout (for)** guetter

loom [luːm] vi (also: **~ up**) surgir; (event) paraître imminent(e); (threaten) menacer

loony ['luːnɪ] adj, n (inf) timbré(e), cinglé(e) m/f

loop [luːp] n boucle f ▷ vt: **to ~ sth round sth** passer qch autour de qch; **loophole** n (fig) porte f de sortie; échappatoire f

loose [luːs] adj (knot, screw) desserré(e); (clothes) vague, ample, lâche; (hair) dénoué(e), épars(e); (not firmly fixed) pas solide; (morals, discipline) relâché(e); (translation) approximatif(-ive) ▷ n: **to be on the ~** être en liberté; **~ connection** (Elec) mauvais contact; **to be at a ~ end** or (us) **at ~ ends** (fig) ne pas trop savoir quoi faire; **loosely** adv sans serrer; (imprecisely) approximativement; **loosen** vt desserrer, relâcher, défaire

loot [luːt] n butin m ▷ vt piller

lop-sided ['lɔp'saɪdɪd] adj de travers, asymétrique

lord [lɔːd] n seigneur m; **L~ Smith** lord Smith; **the L~** (Rel) le Seigneur; **my L~** (to noble) Monsieur le comte/le baron; (to judge) Monsieur le juge; (to bishop) Monseigneur; **good L~!** mon Dieu!; **Lords** npl (BRIT: Pol): **the (House of) Lords** (BRIT) la Chambre des Lords

lorry ['lɔrɪ] n (BRIT) camion m; **lorry driver** n (BRIT) camionneur m, routier m

lose (pt, pp **lost**) [luːz, lɔst] vt perdre ▷ vi perdre; **I've lost my wallet/passport** j'ai perdu mon portefeuille/passeport; **to ~ (time)** (clock) retarder; **lose out** vi être perdant(e); **loser** n perdant(e)

loss [lɔs] n perte f; **to make a ~** enregistrer une perte; **to be at a ~** être perplexe or embarrassé(e)

lost [lɔst] pt, pp of **lose** ▷ adj perdu(e); **to get ~** vi se perdre; **I'm ~** je me suis perdu; **~ and found property** n (us) objets trouvés; **~ and found** n (us) (bureau m des) objets trouvés; **lost property** n (BRIT) objets trouvés; **lost property office** or **department** (bureau m des) objets trouvés

lot [lɔt] n (at auctions, set) lot m; (destiny) sort m, destinée f; **the ~** (everything) le tout; (everyone) tous mpl, toutes fpl; **a ~** beaucoup; **a ~ of** beaucoup de; **~s of** des tas de; **to draw ~s (for sth)** tirer (qch) au sort

lotion ['ləuʃən] n lotion f

lottery ['lɔtəri] n loterie f

loud [laud] adj bruyant(e), sonore; (voice) fort(e); (condemnation etc) vigoureux(-euse); (gaudy) voyant(e), tapageur(-euse) ▷ adv (speak etc) fort; **out ~** tout haut; **loudly** adv fort, bruyamment; **loudspeaker** n haut-parleur m

lounge [laundʒ] n salon m; (of airport) salle f; (BRIT: also: **~ bar**) (salle de) café m or bar m ▷ vi (also: **~ about** or **around**) se prélasser, paresser

louse (pl **lice**) [laus, laɪs] n pou m

lousy ['lauzɪ] (inf) adj (bad quality) infect(e), moche; **I feel ~** je suis mal fichu(e)

love [lʌv] n amour m ▷ vt aimer; (caringly, kindly) aimer beaucoup; **I ~ chocolate** j'adore le chocolat; **to ~ to do** aimer beaucoup or adorer faire; **"15 ~"** (Tennis) "15 à rien or zéro"; **to be/fall in ~ with** être/tomber amoureux(-euse) de; **to make ~** faire l'amour; **~ from Anne, ~, Anne** affectueusement, Anne; **I ~ you** je t'aime; **love affair** n liaison (amoureuse); **love life** n vie sentimentale

lovely ['lʌvlɪ] adj (pretty) ravissant(e); (friend, wife) charmant(e); (holiday, surprise) très agréable, merveilleux(-euse)

lover ['lʌvəʳ] n amant m; (person in love) amoureux(-euse); (amateur): **a ~ of** un(e) ami(e) de, un(e) amoureux(-euse) de

loving ['lʌvɪŋ] adj affectueux(-euse), tendre, aimant(e)

low [ləu] adj bas (basse); (quality) mauvais(e), inférieur(e) ▷ adv bas ▷ n (Meteorology) dépression f; **to feel ~** se sentir déprimé(e); **he's very ~** (ill) il est bien bas or très affaibli; **to turn (down) ~** vt baisser; **to be ~ on** (supplies etc) être à court de; **to reach a new or an all-time ~** tomber au niveau le plus bas; **low-alcohol** adj à faible teneur en alcool, peu alcoolisé(e); **low-calorie** adj hypocalorique

lower ['ləuəʳ] adj inférieur(e) ▷ vt baisser; (resistance) diminuer; **to ~ o.s. to** s'abaisser à

low-fat ['ləu'fæt] adj maigre

loyal ['lɔɪəl] adj loyal(e), fidèle; **loyalty** n loyauté f, fidélité f; **loyalty card** n carte f de fidélité

L.P. n abbr = **long-playing record**

L-plates ['ɛlpleɪts] npl (BRIT) plaques fpl (obligatoires) d'apprenti conducteur

Lt n abbr (= lieutenant) Lt.

Ltd abbr (Comm: company: = limited) ≈ S.A.

luck [lʌk] n chance f; **bad ~** malchance f, malheur m; **good ~!** bonne chance!; **bad** or **hard** or **tough ~!** pas de chance!; **luckily** adv heureusement, par bonheur; **lucky** adj (person) qui a de la chance; (coincidence) heureux(-euse); (number etc) qui porte bonheur

lucrative ['lu:krətɪv] adj lucratif(-ive), rentable, qui rapporte

ludicrous ['lu:dɪkrəs] adj ridicule, absurde

luggage ['lʌgɪdʒ] n bagages mpl; **our ~ hasn't arrived** nos bagages ne sont pas arrivés; **could you send someone to collect our ~?** pourriez-vous envoyer quelqu'un chercher nos bagages?; **luggage rack** n (in train) porte-bagages m inv; (: on car) galerie f

lukewarm ['lu:kwɔ:m] adj tiède

lull [lʌl] n accalmie f; (in conversation) pause f ▷ vt: **to ~ sb to sleep** bercer qn pour qu'il s'endorme; **to be ~ed into a false sense of security** s'endormir dans une fausse sécurité

lullaby ['lʌləbaɪ] n berceuse f

lumber ['lʌmbəʳ] n (wood) bois m de charpente; (junk) bric-à-brac m inv ▷ vt (BRIT inf): **to ~ sb with sth/sb** coller or refiler qch/qn à qn

luminous ['lu:mɪnəs] adj lumineux(-euse)

lump [lʌmp] n morceau m; (in sauce) grumeau m; (swelling) grosseur f ▷ vt (also: **~ together**) réunir, mettre en tas; **lump sum** n somme globale or forfaitaire; **lumpy** adj (sauce) qui a des grumeaux; (bed) défoncé(e), peu confortable

lunatic ['lu:nətɪk] n fou (folle), dément(e) ▷ adj fou (folle), dément(e)

lunch [lʌntʃ] n déjeuner m ▷ vi déjeuner; **lunch break, lunch hour** n pause f de midi, heure f du déjeuner; **lunchtime** n: **it's lunchtime** c'est l'heure du déjeuner

lung [lʌŋ] n poumon m

lure [luəʳ] n (attraction) attrait m, charme m; (in hunting) appât m, leurre m ▷ vt attirer or persuader par la ruse

lurk [lə:k] vi se tapir, se cacher

lush [lʌʃ] adj luxuriant(e)

lust [lʌst] n (sexual) désir m (sexuel); (Rel) luxure f; (fig): **~ for** soif f de

Luxembourg ['lʌksəmbə:g] n Luxembourg m

luxurious [lʌg'zjuərɪəs] adj luxueux(-euse)

luxury ['lʌkʃərɪ] n luxe m ▷ cpd de luxe

Lycra® ['laɪkrə] n Lycra® m

lying ['laɪɪŋ] n mensonge(s) m(pl) ▷ adj (statement, story) mensonger(-ère), faux (fausse); (person) menteur(-euse)

Lyons ['ljɔ̃] n Lyon

lyrics ['lɪrɪks] npl (of song) paroles fpl

m. n abbr (= metre) m; (= million) M; (= mile) mi

M.A. n abbr (Scol) = **Master of Arts**

ma [mɑ:] (inf) n maman f

mac [mæk] n (BRIT) imper(méable m) m

macaroni [mækə'rəʊnɪ] n macaronis mpl

Macedonia [mæsɪ'dəʊnɪə] n Macédoine f;
Macedonian [mæsɪ'dəʊnɪən] adj macédonien(ne) ▷ n
Macédonien(ne); (Ling) macédonien m

machine [mə'ʃiːn] n machine f ▷ vt (dress etc) coudre à
la machine; (Tech) usiner; **machine gun** n mitrailleuse f;
machinery n machinerie f, machines fpl; (fig)
mécanisme(s) m(pl); **machine washable** adj (garment)
lavable en machine

macho ['mætʃəʊ] adj macho inv

mackerel ['mækrl] n (pl inv) maquereau m

mackintosh ['mækɪntɔʃ] n (BRIT) imperméable m

mad [mæd] adj fou (folle); (foolish) insensé(e); (angry)
furieux(-euse); **to be ~ (keen) about** or **on sth** (inf) être
follement passionné de qch, être fou de qch

Madagascar [mædə'gæskə'] n Madagascar m

madam ['mædəm] n madame f

mad cow disease n maladie f des vaches folles

made [meɪd] pt, pp of **make**; **made-to-measure** adj
(BRIT) fait(e) sur mesure; **made-up** ['meɪdʌp] adj (story)
inventé(e), fabriqué(e)

madly ['mædlɪ] adv follement; **~ in love** éperdument
amoureux(-euse)

madman ['mædmən] (irreg) n fou m, aliéné m

madness ['mædnɪs] n folie f

Madrid [mə'drɪd] n Madrid

Mafia ['mæfɪə] n maf(f)ia f

mag [mæg] n abbr (BRIT inf: = magazine) magazine m

magazine [mægə'ziːn] n (Press) magazine m, revue f;
(Radio, TV) magazine

maggot ['mægət] n ver m, asticot m

magic ['mædʒɪk] n magie f ▷ adj magique; **magical**
adj magique; (experience, evening) merveilleux(-euse);
magician [mə'dʒɪʃən] n magicien(ne)

magistrate ['mædʒɪstreɪt] n magistrat m; juge m

magnet ['mægnɪt] n aimant m; **magnetic** [mæg'nɛtɪk]
adj magnétique

magnificent [mæg'nɪfɪsnt] adj superbe, magnifique;
(splendid: robe, building) somptueux(-euse), magnifique

magnify ['mægnɪfaɪ] vt grossir; (sound) amplifier;
magnifying glass n loupe f

magpie ['mægpaɪ] n pie f

mahogany [mə'hɔgənɪ] n acajou m

maid [meɪd] n bonne f; (in hotel) femme f de chambre;
old ~ (pej) vieille fille

maiden name n nom m de jeune fille

mail [meɪl] n poste f; (letters) courrier m ▷ vt envoyer (par
la poste); **by ~** par la poste; **mailbox** n (us: also Comput)
boîte f aux lettres; **mailing list** n liste f d'adresses;
mailman (irreg) n (us) facteur m; **mail-order** n vente f or
achat m par correspondance

main [meɪn] adj principal(e) ▷ n (pipe) conduite
principale, canalisation f; **the ~s** (Elec) le secteur; **the
~ thing** l'essentiel m; **in the ~** dans l'ensemble; **main
course** n (Culin) plat m de résistance; **mainland** n
continent m; **mainly** adv principalement, surtout; **main
road** n grand axe, route nationale; **mainstream** n (fig)
courant principal; **main street** n rue f principale

maintain [meɪn'teɪn] vt entretenir; (continue)
maintenir, préserver; (affirm) soutenir; **maintenance**
['meɪntənəns] n entretien m; (Law: alimony) pension f
alimentaire

maisonette [meɪzə'nɛt] n (BRIT) appartement m en
duplex

maize [meɪz] n (BRIT) maïs m

majesty ['mædʒɪstɪ] n majesté f; (title): **Your M~** Votre
Majesté

major ['meɪdʒə'] n (Mil) commandant m ▷ adj
(important) important(e); (most important) principal(e);
(Mus) majeur(e) ▷ vi (us Scol): **to ~ (in)** se spécialiser (en)

Majorca [mə'jɔːkə] n Majorque f

majority [mə'dʒɔrɪtɪ] n majorité f

make [meɪk] vt (pt, pp made) faire; (manufacture) faire,
fabriquer; (earn) gagner; (decision) prendre; (friend) se
faire; (speech) faire, prononcer; (cause to be): **to ~ sb sad**
etc rendre qn triste etc; (force): **to ~ sb do sth** obliger
qn à faire qch, faire faire qch à qn; (equal): **2 and 2 ~
4** 2 et 2 font 4 ▷ n (manufacture) fabrication f; (brand)
marque f; **to ~ the bed** faire le lit; **to ~ a fool of sb**
(ridicule) ridiculiser qn; (trick) avoir or duper qn; **to ~ a
profit** faire un or des bénéfice(s); **to ~ a loss** essuyer
une perte; **to ~ it** (in time etc) y arriver; (succeed) réussir;
what time do you ~ it? quelle heure avez-vous?; **I ~ it
£249** d'après mes calculs ça fait 249 livres; **to be made
of** être en; **to ~ do with** se contenter de; se débrouiller
avec; **make off** vi filer; **make out** vt (write out: cheque)
faire; (decipher) déchiffrer; (understand) comprendre; (see)
distinguer; (claim, imply) prétendre, vouloir faire croire;
make up vt (invent) inventer, imaginer; (constitute)
constituer; (parcel, bed) faire ▷ vi se réconcilier; (with
cosmetics) se maquiller, se farder; **to be made up of** se
composer de; **make up for** vt fus compenser; (lost time)
rattraper; **makeover** ['meɪkəʊvə'] n (by beautician)
soins mpl de maquillage; (change of image) changement
m d'image; **maker** n fabricant m; (of film, programme)
réalisateur(-trice); **makeshift** adj provisoire,
improvisé(e); **make-up** n maquillage m

making ['meɪkɪŋ] n (fig): **in the ~** en formation or
gestation; **to have the ~s of** (actor, athlete) avoir l'étoffe
de

malaria [mə'lɛərɪə] n malaria f, paludisme m

Malaysia [mə'leɪzɪə] n Malaisie f

male [meɪl] n (Biol, Elec) mâle m ▷ adj (sex, attitude)
masculin(e); (animal) mâle; (child etc) du sexe masculin

malicious [mə'lɪʃəs] adj méchant(e), malveillant(e)

malignant [mə'lɪgnənt] adj (Med) malin(-igne)

mall [mɔːl] n (also: **shopping ~**) centre commercial

mallet ['mælɪt] n maillet m

malnutrition [mælnjuː'trɪʃən] n malnutrition f

malpractice [mæl'præktɪs] n faute professionnelle;
négligence f

malt [mɔːlt] n malt m ▷ cpd (whisky) pur malt

Malta ['mɔːltə] n Malte f; **Maltese** [mɔːl'tiːz] adj
maltais(e) ▷ n (pl inv) Maltais(e)

mammal ['mæml] n mammifère m

mammoth ['mæməθ] n mammouth m ▷ adj géant(e),
monstre

man (pl **men**) [mæn, mɛn] n homme m; (Sport) joueur
m; (Chess) pièce f ▷ vt (Naut: ship) garnir d'hommes;
(machine) assurer le fonctionnement de; (Mil: gun) servir;
(: post) être de service à; **an old ~** un vieillard; **~ and wife**
mari et femme

manage ['mænɪdʒ] vi se débrouiller; (succeed) y arriver,
réussir ▷ vt (business) gérer; (team, operation) diriger;
(control: ship) manier, manœuvrer; (: person) savoir
s'y prendre avec; **to ~ to do** se débrouiller pour faire;
(succeed) réussir à faire; **manageable** adj maniable; (task
etc) faisable; (number) raisonnable; **management** n

(running) administration f, direction f; *(people in charge: of business, firm)* dirigeants mpl, cadres mpl; *(: of hotel, shop, theatre)* direction; **manager** n *(of business)* directeur m; *(of institution etc)* administrateur m; *(of department, unit)* responsable m/f, chef m; *(of hotel etc)* gérant m; *(Sport)* manager m; *(of artist)* impresario m; **manageress** n directrice f, *(of hotel etc)* gérante f; **managerial** [mænɪˈdʒɪərɪəl] adj directorial(e); *(skills)* de cadre, de gestion; **managing director** n directeur général

mandarin [ˈmændərɪn] n *(also:* **~ orange**) mandarine f

mandate [ˈmændeɪt] n mandat m

mandatory [ˈmændətərɪ] adj obligatoire

mane [meɪn] n crinière f

maneuver [məˈnuːvəʳ] *(us)* = **manoeuvre**

mangetout [ˈmɒnʒˈtuː] n mange-tout m inv

mango *(pl* **-es**) [ˈmæŋɡəu] n mangue f

man: manhole n trou m d'homme; **manhood** n *(age)* âge m d'homme; *(manliness)* virilité f

mania [ˈmeɪnɪə] n manie f; **maniac** [ˈmeɪnɪæk] n maniaque m/f; *(fig)* fou (folle)

manic [ˈmænɪk] adj maniaque

manicure [ˈmænɪkjuəʳ] n manucure f

manifest [ˈmænɪfɛst] vt manifester ▷ adj manifeste, évident(e)

manifesto [mænɪˈfɛstəu] n *(Pol)* manifeste m

manipulate [məˈnɪpjuleɪt] vt manipuler; *(system, situation)* exploiter

man: mankind [mænˈkaɪnd] n humanité f, genre humain; **manly** adj viril(e); **man-made** adj artificiel(le); *(fibre)* synthétique

manner [ˈmænəʳ] n manière f, façon f; *(behaviour)* attitude f, comportement m; **manners** npl: **(good) ~s** (bonnes) manières f; **bad ~s** mauvaises manières; **all ~ of** toutes sortes de

manoeuvre *(us* **maneuver**) [məˈnuːvəʳ] vt *(move)* manœuvrer; *(manipulate: person)* manipuler; *(: situation)* exploiter ▷ n manœuvre f

manpower [ˈmænpauəʳ] n main-d'œuvre f

mansion [ˈmænʃən] n château m, manoir m

manslaughter [ˈmænslɔːtəʳ] n homicide m involontaire

mantelpiece [ˈmæntlpiːs] n cheminée f

manual [ˈmænjuəl] adj manuel(le) ▷ n manuel m

manufacture [mænjuˈfæktʃəʳ] vt fabriquer ▷ n fabrication f; **manufacturer** n fabricant m

manure [məˈnjuəʳ] n fumier m; *(artificial)* engrais m

manuscript [ˈmænjuskrɪpt] n manuscrit m

many [ˈmɛnɪ] adj beaucoup de, de nombreux(-euses) ▷ pron beaucoup, un grand nombre; **a great ~** un grand nombre (de); **~ a ...** bien des ..., plus d'un(e) ...

map [mæp] n carte f; *(of town)* plan m; **can you show it to me on the ~?** pouvez-vous me l'indiquer sur la carte?; **map out** vt tracer; *(fig: task)* planifier

maple [ˈmeɪpl] n érable m

Mar abbr = **March**

mar [mɑːʳ] vt gâcher, gâter

marathon [ˈmærəθən] n marathon m

marble [ˈmɑːbl] n marbre m; *(toy)* bille f

March [mɑːtʃ] n mars m

march [mɑːtʃ] vi marcher au pas; *(demonstrators)* défiler ▷ n marche f; *(demonstration)* manifestation f

mare [mɛəʳ] n jument f

margarine [mɑːdʒəˈriːn] n margarine f

margin [ˈmɑːdʒɪn] n marge f; **marginal** adj marginal(e);

marginal seat *(Pol)* siège disputé; **marginally** adv très légèrement, sensiblement

marigold [ˈmærɪɡəuld] n souci m

marijuana [mærɪˈwɑːnə] n marijuana f

marina [məˈriːnə] n marina f

marinade n [mærɪˈneɪd] marinade f

marinate [ˈmærɪneɪt] vt *(faire)* mariner

marine [məˈriːn] adj marin(e) ▷ n fusilier marin; *(us)* marine m

marital [ˈmærɪtl] adj matrimonial(e); **marital status** n situation f de famille

maritime [ˈmærɪtaɪm] adj maritime

marjoram [ˈmɑːdʒərəm] n marjolaine f

mark [mɑːk] n marque f; *(of skid etc)* trace f; *(BRIT Scol)* note f; *(oven temperature):* **(gas) ~ 4** thermostat m 4 ▷ vt *(also Sport: player)* marquer; *(stain)* tacher; *(BRIT Scol)* corriger, noter; **to ~ time** marquer le pas; **marked** adj *(obvious)* marqué(e), net(te); **marker** n *(sign)* jalon m; *(bookmark)* signet m

market [ˈmɑːkɪt] n marché m ▷ vt *(Comm)* commercialiser; **marketing** n marketing m; **marketplace** n place f du marché; *(Comm)* marché m; **market research** n étude f de marché

marmalade [ˈmɑːməleɪd] n confiture f d'oranges

maroon [məˈruːn] vt: **to be ~ed** être abandonné(e); *(fig)* être bloqué(e) ▷ adj *(colour)* bordeaux inv

marquee [mɑːˈkiː] n chapiteau m

marriage [ˈmærɪdʒ] n mariage m; **marriage certificate** n extrait m d'acte de mariage

married [ˈmærɪd] adj marié(e); *(life, love)* conjugal(e)

marrow [ˈmærəu] n *(of bone)* moelle f; *(vegetable)* courge f

marry [ˈmærɪ] vt épouser, se marier avec; *(subj: father, priest etc)* marier ▷ vi *(also:* **get married**) se marier

Mars [mɑːz] n *(planet)* Mars f

Marseilles [mɑːˈseɪ] n Marseille

marsh [mɑːʃ] n marais m, marécage m

marshal [ˈmɑːʃl] n maréchal m; *(us: fire, police)* ≈ capitaine m; *(for demonstration, meeting)* membre m du service d'ordre ▷ vt rassembler

martyr [ˈmɑːtəʳ] n martyr(e)

marvel [ˈmɑːvl] n merveille f ▷ vi: **to ~ (at)** s'émerveiller (de); **marvellous** *(us* **marvelous**) adj merveilleux(-euse)

Marxism [ˈmɑːksɪzəm] n marxisme m

Marxist [ˈmɑːksɪst] adj, n marxiste (m/f)

marzipan [ˈmɑːzɪpæn] n pâte f d'amandes

mascara [mæsˈkɑːrə] n mascara m

mascot [ˈmæskət] n mascotte f

masculine [ˈmæskjulɪn] adj masculin(e) ▷ n masculin m

mash [mæʃ] vt *(Culin)* faire une purée de; **mashed potato(es)** n(pl) purée f de pommes de terre

mask [mɑːsk] n masque m ▷ vt masquer

mason [ˈmeɪsn] n *(also:* **stone~**) maçon m; *(also:* **free~**) franc-maçon m; **masonry** n maçonnerie f

mass [mæs] n multitude f, masse f; *(Physics)* masse f; *(Rel)* messe f ▷ cpd *(communication)* de masse; *(unemployment)* massif(-ive) ▷ vi se masser; **masses** npl: **the ~es** les masses; **~es of** *(inf)* des tas de

massacre [ˈmæsəkəʳ] n massacre m

massage [ˈmæsɑːʒ] n massage m ▷ vt masser

massive [ˈmæsɪv] adj énorme, massif(-ive)

mass media npl mass-media mpl

mass-produce ['mæsprə'dju:s] vt fabriquer en série
mast [mɑ:st] n mât m; (Radio, TV) pylône m
master ['mɑ:stə'] n maître m; (in secondary school) professeur m; (in primary school) instituteur m; (title for boys): **M~ X** Monsieur X ▷ vt maîtriser; (learn) apprendre à fond; **M~ of Arts/Science (MA/MSc)** ≈ titulaire m/f d'une maîtrise (en lettres/science); **M~ of Arts/Science degree (MA/MSc)** n ≈ maîtrise f; **mastermind** n esprit supérieur ▷ vt diriger, être le cerveau de; **masterpiece** n chef-d'œuvre m
masturbate ['mæstəbeɪt] vi se masturber
mat [mæt] n petit tapis; (also: **door~**) paillasson m; (also: **table~**) set m de table ▷ adj = **matt**
match [mætʃ] n allumette f; (game) match m, partie f; (fig) égal(e) ▷ vt (also: **~ up**) assortir; (go well with) aller bien avec, s'assortir à; (equal) égaler, valoir ▷ vi être assorti(e); **to be a good ~** être bien assorti(e); **matchbox** n boîte f d'allumettes; **matching** adj assorti(e)
mate [meɪt] n (inf) copain (copine); (animal) partenaire m/f, mâle (femelle); (in merchant navy) second m ▷ vi s'accoupler
material [mə'tɪərɪəl] n (substance) matière f, matériau m; (cloth) tissu m, étoffe f; (information, data) données fpl ▷ adj matériel(le); (relevant: evidence) pertinent(e); **materials** npl (equipment) matériaux mpl
materialize [mə'tɪərɪəlaɪz] vi se matérialiser, se réaliser
maternal [mə'tə:nl] adj maternel(le)
maternity [mə'tə:nɪtɪ] n maternité f; **maternity hospital** n maternité f; **maternity leave** n congé m de maternité
math [mæθ] n (US: = **mathematics**) maths fpl
mathematical [mæθə'mætɪkl] adj mathématique
mathematician [mæθəmə'tɪʃən] n mathématicien(ne)
mathematics [mæθə'mætɪks] n mathématiques fpl
maths [mæθs] n abbr (BRIT: = **mathematics**) maths fpl
matinée ['mætɪneɪ] n matinée f
matron ['meɪtrən] n (in hospital) infirmière-chef f; (in school) infirmière f
matt [mæt] adj mat(e)
matter ['mætə'] n question f; (Physics) matière f, substance f; (Med: pus) pus m ▷ vi importer; **matters** npl (affairs, situation) la situation; **it doesn't ~** cela n'a pas d'importance; (I don't mind) cela ne fait rien; **what's the ~?** qu'est-ce qu'il y a?, qu'est-ce qui ne va pas?; **no ~ what** quoi qu'il arrive; **as a ~ of course** tout naturellement; **as a ~ of fact** en fait; **reading ~** (BRIT) de quoi lire, de la lecture
mattress ['mætrɪs] n matelas m
mature [mə'tjuə'] adj mûr(e); (cheese) fait(e); (wine) arrive(e) à maturité ▷ vi mûrir; (cheese, wine) se faire; **mature student** n étudiant(e) plus âgé(e) que la moyenne; **maturity** n maturité f
maul [mɔ:l] vt lacérer
mauve [məuv] adj mauve
max abbr = **maximum**
maximize ['mæksɪmaɪz] vt (profits etc, chances) maximiser
maximum ['mæksɪməm] (pl **maxima**) adj maximum ▷ n maximum m
May [meɪ] n mai m
may [meɪ] (conditional **might**) vi (indicating possibility): **he ~ come** il se peut qu'il vienne; (be allowed to): **~ I smoke?** puis-je fumer?; (wishes): **~ God bless you!** (que) Dieu vous bénisse!; **you ~ as well go** vous feriez aussi bien d'y aller
maybe ['meɪbi:] adv peut-être; **~ he'll ...** peut-être qu'il ...
May Day n le Premier mai
mayhem ['meɪhem] n grabuge m
mayonnaise [meɪə'neɪz] n mayonnaise f
mayor [mɛə'] n maire m; **mayoress** n (female mayor) maire m; (wife of mayor) épouse f du maire
maze [meɪz] n labyrinthe m, dédale m
MD n abbr (Comm) = **managing director**
me [mi:] pron me, m' + vowel or h mute; (stressed, after prep) moi; **it's me** c'est moi; **he heard me** il m'a entendu; **give me a book** donnez-moi un livre; **it's for me** c'est pour moi
meadow ['mɛdəu] n prairie f, pré m
meagre (us **meager**) ['mi:gə'] adj maigre
meal [mi:l] n repas m; (flour) farine f; **mealtime** n heure f du repas
mean [mi:n] adj (with money) avare, radin(e); (unkind) mesquin(e), méchant(e); (shabby) misérable; (average) moyen(ne) ▷ vt (pt, pp **~t**) (signify) signifier, vouloir dire; (refer to) faire allusion à, parler de; (intend): **to ~ to do** avoir l'intention de faire ▷ n moyenne f; **means** npl (way, money) moyens mpl; **by ~s of** (instrument) au moyen de; **by all ~s** je vous en prie; **to be ~t for** être destiné(e) à; **do you ~ it?** vous êtes sérieux?; **what do you ~?** que voulez-vous dire?
meaning ['mi:nɪŋ] n signification f, sens m; **meaningful** adj significatif(-ive); (relationship) valable; **meaningless** adj dénué(e) de sens
meant [mɛnt] pt, pp of **mean**
meantime ['mi:ntaɪm] adv (also: **in the ~**) pendant ce temps
meanwhile ['mi:nwaɪl] adv = **meantime**
measles ['mi:zlz] n rougeole f
measure ['mɛʒə'] vt, vi mesurer ▷ n mesure f; (ruler) règle (graduée)
measurements ['mɛʒəməntz] npl mesures fpl; **chest/ hip ~** tour m de poitrine/hanches
meat [mi:t] n viande f; **I don't eat ~** je ne mange pas de viande; **cold ~s** (BRIT) viandes froides; **meatball** n boulette f de viande
Mecca ['mɛkə] n la Mecque
mechanic [mɪ'kænɪk] n mécanicien m; **can you send a ~?** pouvez-vous nous envoyer un mécanicien?; **mechanical** adj mécanique
mechanism ['mɛkənɪzəm] n mécanisme m
medal ['mɛdl] n médaille f; **medallist** (us **medalist**) n (Sport) médaillé(e)
meddle ['mɛdl] vi: **to ~ in** se mêler de, s'occuper de; **to ~ with** toucher à
media ['mi:dɪə] npl media mpl ▷ npl of **medium**
mediaeval [mɛdɪ'i:vl] adj = **medieval**
mediate ['mi:dɪeɪt] vi servir d'intermédiaire
medical ['mɛdɪkl] adj médical(e) ▷ n (also: **~ examination**) visite médicale; (private) examen médical; **medical certificate** n certificat médical
medicated ['mɛdɪkeɪtɪd] adj traitant(e), médicamenteux(-euse)
medication [mɛdɪ'keɪʃən] n (drugs etc) médication f
medicine ['mɛdsɪn] n médecine f; (drug) médicament m

medieval [medr'i:vl] *adj* médiéval(e)
mediocre [mi:dr'əukə] *adj* médiocre
meditate ['mediteit] *vi*: **to ~ (on)** méditer (sur)
meditation [medr'teiʃən] *n* méditation *f*
Mediterranean [medrtə'reiniən] *adj* méditerranéen(ne); **the ~ (Sea)** la (mer) Méditerranée
medium ['mi:diəm] *adj* moyen(ne) ▷ *n* (*pl* media) (*means*) moyen *m*; (*pl ~s*) (*person*) médium *m*; **the happy ~** le juste milieu; **medium-sized** *adj* de taille moyenne; **medium wave** *n* (*Radio*) ondes moyennes, petites ondes
meek [mi:k] *adj* doux (douce), humble
meet (*pt, pp* met) [mi:t, met] *vt* rencontrer; (*by arrangement*) retrouver, rejoindre; (*for the first time*) faire la connaissance de; (*go and fetch*): **I'll ~ you at the station** j'irai te chercher à la gare; (*opponent, danger, problem*) faire face à; (*requirements*) satisfaire à, répondre à ▷ *vi* (*friends*) se rencontrer; se retrouver; (*in session*) se réunir; (*join: lines, roads*) se joindre; **nice ~ing you** ravi d'avoir fait votre connaissance; **meet up** *vi*: **to ~ up with sb** rencontrer qn; **meet with** *vt fus* (*difficulty*) rencontrer; **to ~ with success** être couronné(e) de succès; **meeting** *n* (*of group of people*) réunion *f*; (*between individuals*) rendez-vous *m*; **she's at** or **in a meeting** (*Comm*) elle est en réunion; **meeting place** *n* lieu *m* de (la) réunion; (*for appointment*) lieu de rendez-vous
megabyte ['megəbait] *n* (*Comput*) méga-octet *m*
megaphone ['megəfəun] *n* porte-voix *m inv*
megapixel ['megəpiksl] *n* mégapixel *m*
melancholy ['melənkəli] *n* mélancolie *f* ▷ *adj* mélancolique
melody ['melədi] *n* mélodie *f*
melon ['melən] *n* melon *m*
melt [melt] *vi* fondre ▷ *vt* faire fondre
member ['membə] *n* membre *m*; **Member of Congress** (*US*) *n* membre *m* du Congrès, ≈ député *m*; **Member of Parliament (MP)** *n* (*BRIT*) député *m*; **Member of the European Parliament (MEP)** *n* Eurodéputé *m*; **Member of the House of Representatives (MHR)** *n* (*US*) membre *m* de la Chambre des représentants; **Member of the Scottish Parliament (MSP)** *n* (*BRIT*) député *m* au Parlement écossais; **membership** *n* (*becoming a member*) adhésion *f*; admission *f*; (*the members*) membres *mpl*, adhérents *mpl*; **membership card** *n* carte *f* de membre
memento [mə'mentəu] *n* souvenir *m*
memo ['meməu] *n* note *f* (de service)
memorable ['memərəbl] *adj* mémorable
memorandum (*pl* memoranda) [memə'rændəm, -də] *n* note *f* (de service)
memorial [mi'mɔ:riəl] *n* mémorial *m* ▷ *adj* commémoratif(-ive)
memorize ['meməraiz] *vt* apprendre or retenir par cœur
memory ['meməri] *n* (*also Comput*) mémoire *f*; (*recollection*) souvenir *m*; **in ~ of** à la mémoire de; **memory card** *n* (*for digital camera*) carte *f* mémoire
men [men] *npl of* **man**
menace ['menis] *n* menace *f*; (*inf: nuisance*) peste *f*, plaie *f* ▷ *vt* menacer
mend [mend] *vt* réparer; (*darn*) raccommoder, repriser ▷ *n*: **on the ~** en voie de guérison; **to ~ one's ways** s'amender
meningitis [menin'dʒaitis] *n* méningite *f*

menopause ['menəupɔ:z] *n* ménopause *f*
men's room (*US*) *n*: **the men's room** les toilettes *fpl* pour hommes
menstruation [menstru'eiʃən] *n* menstruation *f*
menswear ['menzweə] *n* vêtements *mpl* d'hommes
mental ['mentl] *adj* mental(e); **mental hospital** *n* hôpital *m* psychiatrique; **mentality** [men'tæliti] *n* mentalité *f*; **mentally** *adv*: **to be mentally handicapped** être handicapé(e) mental(e); **the mentally ill** les malades mentaux
menthol ['menθɒl] *n* menthol *m*
mention ['menʃən] *n* mention *f* ▷ *vt* mentionner, faire mention de; **don't ~ it!** je vous en prie, il n'y a pas de quoi!
menu ['menju:] *n* (*set menu, Comput*) menu *m*; (*list of dishes*) carte *f*; **could we see the ~?** est-ce qu'on peut voir la carte?
MEP *n abbr* = **Member of the European Parliament**
mercenary ['mə:sinəri] *adj* (*person*) intéressé(e), mercenaire ▷ *n* mercenaire *m*
merchandise ['mə:tʃəndaiz] *n* marchandises *fpl*
merchant ['mə:tʃənt] *n* négociant *m*, marchand *m*; **merchant bank** *n* (*BRIT*) banque *f* d'affaires; **merchant navy** (*US* **merchant marine**) *n* marine marchande
merciless ['mə:silis] *adj* impitoyable, sans pitié
mercury ['mə:kjuri] *n* mercure *m*
mercy ['mə:si] *n* pitié *f*, merci *f*; (*Rel*) miséricorde *f*; **at the ~ of** à la merci de
mere [miə] *adj* simple; (*chance*) pur(e); **a ~ two hours** seulement deux heures; **merely** *adv* simplement, purement
merge [mə:dʒ] *vt* unir; (*Comput*) fusionner, interclasser ▷ *vi* (*colours, shapes, sounds*) se mêler; (*roads*) se joindre; (*Comm*) fusionner; **merger** *n* (*Comm*) fusion *f*
meringue [mə'ræŋ] *n* meringue *f*
merit ['merit] *n* mérite *m*, valeur *f* ▷ *vt* mériter
mermaid ['mə:meid] *n* sirène *f*
merry ['meri] *adj* gai(e); **M~ Christmas!** joyeux Noël!; **merry-go-round** *n* manège *m*
mesh [meʃ] *n* mailles *fpl*
mess [mes] *n* désordre *m*, fouillis *m*, pagaille *f*; (*muddle: of life*) gâchis *m*; (: *of economy*) pagaille *f*; (*dirt*) saleté *f*; (*Mil*) mess *m*, cantine *f*; **to be (in) a ~** être en désordre; **to be/get o.s. in a ~** (*fig*) être/se mettre dans le pétrin; **mess about** or **around** (*inf*) *vi* perdre son temps; **mess up** *vt* (*dirty*) salir; (*spoil*) gâcher; **mess with** (*inf*) *vt fus* (*challenge, confront*) se frotter à; (*interfere with*) toucher à
message ['mesidʒ] *n* message *m*; **can I leave a ~?** est-ce que je peux laisser un message?; **are there any ~s for me?** est-ce que j'ai des messages?
messenger ['mesindʒə] *n* messager *m*
Messrs, Messrs. ['mesəz] *abbr* (*on letters:* = messieurs) MM
messy ['mesi] *adj* (*dirty*) sale; (*untidy*) en désordre
met [met] *pt, pp of* **meet**
metabolism [me'tæbəlizəm] *n* métabolisme *m*
metal ['metl] *n* métal *m* ▷ *cpd* en métal; **metallic** [me'tælik] *adj* métallique
metaphor ['metəfə] *n* métaphore *f*
meteor ['mi:tiə] *n* météore *m*; **meteorite** ['mi:tiərait] *n* météorite *m* or *f*
meteorology [mi:tiə'rɔlədʒi] *n* météorologie *f*
meter ['mi:tə] *n* (*instrument*) compteur *m*; (*also*: **parking ~**) parc(o)mètre *m*; (*US: unit*) = **metre** ▷ *vt* (*Post*) affranchir à la machine

method ['mɛθəd] *n* méthode *f*; **methodical** [mɪ'θɔdɪkl] *adj* méthodique

methylated spirit ['mɛθɪleɪtɪd-] *n* (BRIT: also: **meths**) alcool *m* à brûler

meticulous [me'tɪkjuləs] *adj* méticuleux(-euse)

metre (US **meter**) ['miːtə*r*] *n* mètre *m*

metric ['mɛtrɪk] *adj* métrique

metro ['mɛtrəu] *n* métro *m*

metropolitan [mɛtrə'pɔlɪtən] *adj* métropolitain(e); **the M- Police** (BRIT) la police londonienne

Mexican ['mɛksɪkən] *adj* mexicain(e) ▷ *n* Mexicain(e)

Mexico ['mɛksɪkəu] *n* Mexique *m*

mg *abbr* (= milligram) mg

mice [maɪs] *npl of* **mouse**

micro... [maɪkrəu] *prefix*: **microchip** *n* (Elec) puce *f*; **microphone** *n* microphone *m*; **microscope** *n* microscope *m*; **microwave** *n* (also: **microwave oven**) four *m* à micro-ondes

mid [mɪd] *adj*: **~ May** la mi-mai; **~ afternoon** le milieu de l'après-midi; **in ~ air** en plein ciel; **he's in his ~ thirties** il a dans les trente-cinq ans; **midday** *n* midi *m*

middle ['mɪdl] *n* milieu *m*; (waist) ceinture *f*, taille *f* ▷ *adj* du milieu; (average) moyen(ne); **in the ~ of the night** au milieu de la nuit; **middle-aged** *adj* d'un certain âge, ni vieux ni jeune; **Middle Ages** *npl*: **the Middle Ages** le moyen âge; **middle-class** *adj* bourgeois(e); **middle class(es)** *n(pl)*: **the middle class(es)** ≈ les classes moyennes; **Middle East** *n*: **the Middle East** le Proche-Orient, le Moyen-Orient; **middle name** *n* second prénom; **middle school** *n* (US) école pour les enfants de 12 à 14 ans, ≈ collège *m*; (BRIT) école pour les enfants de 8 à 14 ans

midge [mɪdʒ] *n* moucheron *m*

midget ['mɪdʒɪt] *n* nain(e)

midnight ['mɪdnaɪt] *n* minuit *m*

midst [mɪdst] *n*: **in the ~ of** au milieu de

midsummer [mɪd'sʌmə*r*] *n* milieu *m* de l'été

midway [mɪd'weɪ] *adj, adv*: **~ (between)** à mi-chemin (entre); **~ through ...** au milieu de ..., en plein(e) ...

midweek [mɪd'wiːk] *adv* au milieu de la semaine, en pleine semaine

midwife (*pl* **midwives**) ['mɪdwaɪf, -vz] *n* sage-femme *f*

midwinter [mɪd'wɪntə*r*] *n* milieu *m* de l'hiver

might [maɪt] *vb see* **may** ▷ *n* puissance *f*, force *f*; **mighty** *adj* puissant(e)

migraine ['miːgreɪn] *n* migraine *f*

migrant ['maɪgrənt] *n* (bird, animal) migrateur *m*; (person) migrant(e) ▷ *adj* migrateur(-trice); migrant(e); (worker) saisonnier(-ière)

migrate [maɪ'greɪt] *vi* migrer

migration [maɪ'greɪʃən] *n* migration *f*

mike [maɪk] *n abbr* (= microphone) micro *m*

mild [maɪld] *adj* doux (douce); (reproach, infection) léger(-ère); (illness) bénin(-igne); (interest) modéré(e); (taste) peu relevé(e); **mildly** ['maɪldlɪ] *adv* doucement; légèrement; **to put it mildly** (inf) c'est le moins qu'on puisse dire

mile [maɪl] *n* mil(l)e *m* (= 1609 m); **mileage** *n* distance *f* en milles, ≈ kilométrage *m*; **mileometer** [maɪ'lɔmɪtə*r*] *n* compteur *m* kilométrique; **milestone** *n* borne *f*; (fig) jalon *m*

military ['mɪlɪtərɪ] *adj* militaire

militia [mɪ'lɪʃə] *n* milice *f*

milk [mɪlk] *n* lait *m* ▷ *vt* (cow) traire; (fig: person) dépouiller, plumer; (: situation) exploiter à fond; **milk**

chocolate *n* chocolat *m* au lait; **milkman** (irreg) *n* laitier *m*; **milky** *adj* (drink) au lait; (colour) laiteux(-euse)

mill [mɪl] *n* moulin *m*; (factory) usine *f*, fabrique *f*; (spinning mill) filature *f*; (flour mill) minoterie *f* ▷ *vt* moudre, broyer ▷ *vi* (also: **~ about**) grouiller

millennium (*pl* **~s** or **millennia**) [mɪ'lɛnɪəm, -'lɛnɪə] *n* millénaire *m*

milli... ['mɪlɪ] *prefix* milli...: **milligram(me)** *n* milligramme *m*; **millilitre** (US **milliliter**) ['mɪlɪliːtə*r*] *n* millilitre *m*; **millimetre** (US **millimeter**) *n* millimètre *m*

million ['mɪljən] *n* million *m*; **a ~ pounds** un million de livres sterling; **millionaire** [mɪljə'nɛə*r*] *n* millionnaire *m*; **millionth** [-θ] *num* millionième

milometer [maɪ'lɔmɪtə*r*] *n* = **mileometer**

mime [maɪm] *n* mime *m* ▷ *vt, vi* mimer

mimic ['mɪmɪk] *n* imitateur(-trice) ▷ *vt, vi* imiter, contrefaire

min. *abbr* (= minute(s)) mn.; (= minimum) min.

mince [mɪns] *vt* hacher ▷ *n* (BRIT Culin) viande hachée, hachis *m*; **mincemeat** *n* hachis de fruits secs utilisés en pâtisserie; (US) viande hachée, hachis *m*; **mince pie** *n* sorte de tarte aux fruits secs

mind [maɪnd] *n* esprit *m* ▷ *vt* (attend to, look after) s'occuper de; (be careful) faire attention à; (object to): **I don't ~ the noise** je ne crains pas le bruit, le bruit ne me dérange pas; **it is on my ~** cela me préoccupe; **to change one's ~** changer d'avis; **to my ~** à mon avis, selon moi; **to bear sth in ~** tenir compte de qch; **to have sb/sth in ~** avoir qn/qch en tête; **to make up one's ~** se décider; **do you ~ if ...?** est-ce que cela vous gêne si ...?; **I don't ~** cela ne me dérange pas; (don't care) ça m'est égal; **~ you, ...** remarquez, ...; **never ~** peu importe, ça ne fait rien; (don't worry) ne vous en faîtes pas; **"~ the step"** "attention à la marche"; **mindless** *adj* irréfléchi(e); (violence, crime) insensé(e); (boring: job) idiot(e)

mine¹ [maɪn] *pron* le (la) mien(ne), les miens (miennes); **a friend of ~** un de mes amis, un ami à moi; **this book is ~** ce livre est à moi

mine² [maɪn] *n* mine *f* ▷ *vt* (coal) extraire; (ship, beach) miner; **minefield** *n* champ *m* de mines; **miner** *n* mineur *m*

mineral ['mɪnərəl] *adj* minéral(e) ▷ *n* minéral *m*; **mineral water** *n* eau minérale

mingle ['mɪŋgl] *vi*: **to ~ with** se mêler à

miniature ['mɪnətʃə*r*] *adj* (en) miniature ▷ *n* miniature *f*

minibar ['mɪnɪbɑː*r*] *n* minibar *m*

minibus ['mɪnɪbʌs] *n* minibus *m*

minicab ['mɪnɪkæb] *n* (BRIT) taxi *m* indépendant

minimal ['mɪnɪml] *adj* minimal(e)

minimize ['mɪnɪmaɪz] *vt* (reduce) réduire au minimum; (play down) minimiser

minimum ['mɪnɪməm] *n* (*pl* **minima**) minimum *m* ▷ *adj* minimum

mining ['maɪnɪŋ] *n* exploitation minière

miniskirt ['mɪnɪskəːt] *n* mini-jupe *f*

minister ['mɪnɪstə*r*] *n* (BRIT Pol) ministre *m*; (Rel) pasteur *m*

ministry ['mɪnɪstrɪ] *n* (BRIT Pol) ministère *m*; (Rel): **to go into the ~** devenir pasteur

minor ['maɪnə*r*] *adj* petit(e), de peu d'importance; (Mus, poet, problem) mineur(e) ▷ *n* (Law) mineur(e)

minority [maɪ'nɔrɪtɪ] *n* minorité *f*

mint [mɪnt] *n* (plant) menthe *f*; (sweet) bonbon *m* à la menthe ▷ vt (coins) battre; **the (Royal) M~**, **the (US) M~** ≈ l'hôtel m de la Monnaie; **in ~ condition** à l'état de neuf

minus ['maɪnəs] n (also: **~ sign**) signe m moins ▷ prep moins; **12 ~ 6 equals 6** 12 moins 6 égal 6; **~ 24 °C** moins 24 °C

minute[1] n ['mɪnɪt] minute f; **minutes** npl (of meeting) procès-verbal m, compte rendu; **wait a ~!** (attendez) un instant!; **at the last ~** à la dernière minute

minute[2] adj [maɪ'njuːt] minuscule; (detailed) minutieux(-euse); **in ~ detail** par le menu

miracle ['mɪrəkl] n miracle m

miraculous [mɪ'rækjuləs] adj miraculeux(-euse)

mirage ['mɪrɑːʒ] n mirage m

mirror ['mɪrə[r]] n miroir m, glace f; (in car) rétroviseur m

misbehave [mɪsbɪ'heɪv] vi mal se conduire

misc. abbr = **miscellaneous**

miscarriage ['mɪskærɪdʒ] n (Med) fausse couche; **~ of justice** erreur f judiciaire

miscellaneous [mɪsɪ'leɪnɪəs] adj (items, expenses) divers(es); (selection) varié(e)

mischief ['mɪstʃɪf] n (naughtiness) sottises fpl; (playfulness) espièglerie f; (harm) mal m, dommage m; (maliciousness) méchanceté f; **mischievous** ['mɪstʃɪvəs] adj (playful, naughty) coquin(e), espiègle

misconception ['mɪskən'sepʃən] n idée fausse

misconduct [mɪs'kɒndʌkt] n inconduite f; **professional ~** faute professionnelle

miser ['maɪzə[r]] n avare m/f

miserable ['mɪzərəbl] adj (person, expression) malheureux(-euse); (conditions) misérable; (weather) maussade; (offer, donation) minable; (failure) pitoyable

misery ['mɪzərɪ] n (unhappiness) tristesse f; (pain) souffrances fpl; (wretchedness) misère f

misfortune [mɪs'fɔːtʃən] n malchance f, malheur m

misgiving [mɪs'gɪvɪŋ] n (apprehension) craintes fpl; **to have ~s about sth** avoir des doutes quant à qch

misguided [mɪs'gaɪdɪd] adj malavisé(e)

mishap ['mɪshæp] n mésaventure f

misinterpret [mɪsɪn'tɜːprɪt] vt mal interpréter

misjudge [mɪs'dʒʌdʒ] vt méjuger, se méprendre sur le compte de

mislay [mɪs'leɪ] vt (irreg: like **lay**) égarer

mislead [mɪs'liːd] vt (irreg: like **lead**) induire en erreur; **misleading** adj trompeur(-euse)

misplace [mɪs'pleɪs] vt égarer; **to be ~d** (trust etc) être mal placé(e)

misprint ['mɪsprɪnt] n faute f d'impression

misrepresent [mɪsreprɪ'zent] vt présenter sous un faux jour

Miss [mɪs] n Mademoiselle

miss [mɪs] vt (fail to get, attend, see) manquer, rater; (regret the absence of): **I ~ him/it** il/cela me manque ▷ n (shot) coup manqué; **we ~ed our train** nous avons raté notre train; **you can't ~ it** vous ne pouvez pas vous tromper; **miss out** vt (BRIT) oublier; **miss out on** vt fus (fun, party) rater, manquer; (chance, bargain) laisser passer

missile ['mɪsaɪl] n (Aviat) missile m; (object thrown) projectile m

missing ['mɪsɪŋ] adj manquant(e); (after escape, disaster: person) disparu(e); **to go ~** disparaître; **~ in action** (Mil) porté(e) disparu(e)

mission ['mɪʃən] n mission f; **on a ~ to sb** en mission

auprès de qn; **missionary** n missionnaire m/f

misspell ['mɪs'spel] vt (irreg: like **spell**) mal orthographier

mist [mɪst] n brume f ▷ vi (also: **~ over**, **~ up**) devenir brumeux(-euse); (BRIT: windows) s'embuer

mistake [mɪs'teɪk] n erreur f, faute f ▷ vt (irreg: like **take**) (meaning) mal comprendre; (intentions) se méprendre sur; **to ~ for** prendre pour; **by ~** par erreur, par inadvertance; **to make a ~** (in writing) faire une faute; (in calculating etc) faire une erreur; **there must be some ~** il doit y avoir une erreur, se tromper; **mistaken** pp of **mistake** ▷ adj (idea etc) erroné(e); **to be mistaken** faire erreur, se tromper

mister ['mɪstə[r]] n (inf) Monsieur m; see **Mr**

mistletoe ['mɪsltəu] n gui m

mistook [mɪs'tuk] pt of **mistake**

mistress ['mɪstrɪs] n maîtresse f; (BRIT: in primary school) institutrice f; (: in secondary school) professeur m

mistrust [mɪs'trʌst] vt se méfier de

misty ['mɪstɪ] adj brumeux(-euse); (glasses, window) embué(e)

misunderstand [mɪsʌndə'stænd] vt, vi (irreg: like **stand**) mal comprendre; **misunderstanding** n méprise f, malentendu m; **there's been a misunderstanding** il y a eu un malentendu

misunderstood [mɪsʌndə'stud] pt, pp of **misunderstand** ▷ adj (person) incompris(e)

misuse n [mɪs'juːs] mauvais emploi; (of power) abus m ▷ vt [mɪs'juːz] mal employer; abuser de

mitt(en) ['mɪt(n)] n moufle f; (fingerless) mitaine f

mix [mɪks] vt mélanger; (sauce, drink etc) préparer ▷ vi se mélanger; (socialize): **he doesn't ~ well** il est peu sociable ▷ n mélange m; **to ~ sth with sth** mélanger qch à qch; **cake ~** préparation f pour gâteau; **mix up** vt mélanger; (confuse) confondre; **to be ~ed up in sth** être mêlé(e) à qch ou impliqué(e) dans qch; **mixed** adj (feelings, reactions) contradictoire; (school, marriage) mixte; **mixed grill** n (BRIT) assortiment m de grillades; **mixed salad** n salade f de crudités; **mixed-up** adj (person) désorienté(e), embrouillé(e); **mixer** n (for food) batteur m, mixeur m; (drink) boisson gazeuse (servant à couper un alcool); (person): **he is a good mixer** il est très sociable; **mixture** n assortiment m, mélange m; (Med) préparation f; **mix-up** n: **there was a mix-up** il y a eu confusion

ml abbr (= millilitre(s)) ml

mm abbr (= millimetre) mm

moan [məun] n gémissement m ▷ vi gémir; (inf: complain): **to ~ (about)** se plaindre (de)

moat [məut] n fossé m, douves fpl

mob [mɒb] n foule f; (disorderly) cohue f ▷ vt assaillir

mobile ['məubaɪl] adj mobile ▷ n (Art) mobile m; **mobile home** n caravane f; **mobile phone** n téléphone portatif

mobility [məu'bɪlɪtɪ] n mobilité f

mobilize ['məubɪlaɪz] vt, vi mobiliser

mock [mɒk] vt ridiculiser; (laugh at) se moquer de ▷ adj faux (fausse); **mocks** npl (BRIT: Scol) examens blancs; **mockery** n moquerie f, raillerie f

mod cons ['mɒd'kɒnz] npl abbr (BRIT) = **modern conveniences**; see **convenience**

mode [məud] n mode m; (of transport) moyen m

model ['mɒdl] n modèle m; (person: for fashion) mannequin m; (: for artist) modèle m ▷ vt (with clay etc) modeler ▷ vi travailler comme mannequin ▷ adj *(railway: toy)* modèle réduit *inv*; *(child, factory)* modèle; **to ~ clothes** présenter des vêtements; **to ~ o.s. on** imiter

modem ['məʊdem] *n* modem *m*

moderate *adj* ['mɒdərət] modéré(e); *(amount, change)* peu important(e) ▷ *vb* ['mɒdəreɪt] ▷ *vi* se modérer, se calmer ▷ *vt* modérer

moderation [mɒdə'reɪʃən] *n* modération *f*, mesure *f*; **in ~** à dose raisonnable, pris(e) or pratiqué(e) modérément

modern ['mɒdən] *adj* moderne; **modernize** *vt* moderniser; **modern languages** *npl* langues vivantes

modest ['mɒdɪst] *adj* modeste; **modesty** *n* modestie *f*

modification [mɒdɪfɪ'keɪʃən] *n* modification *f*

modify ['mɒdɪfaɪ] *vt* modifier

module ['mɒdjuːl] *n* module *m*

mohair ['məʊhɛər] *n* mohair *m*

Mohammed [mə'hæmɛd] *n* Mahomet *m*

moist [mɔɪst] *adj* humide, moite; **moisture** ['mɔɪstʃər] *n* humidité *f*; *(on glass)* buée *f*; **moisturizer** ['mɔɪstʃəraɪzər] *n* crème hydratante

mold *etc* [məʊld] *(US)* = **mould** *etc*

mole [məʊl] *n* *(animal, spy)* taupe *f*; *(spot)* grain *m* de beauté

molecule ['mɒlɪkjuːl] *n* molécule *f*

molest [məʊ'lɛst] *vt* *(assault sexually)* attenter à la pudeur de

molten ['məʊltən] *adj* fondu(e); *(rock)* en fusion

mom [mɒm] *n* *(US)* = **mum**

moment ['məʊmənt] *n* moment *m*, instant *m*; **at the ~** en ce moment; **momentarily** ['məʊməntrɪlɪ] *adv* momentanément; *(US: soon)* bientôt; **momentary** *adj* momentané(e), passager(-ère); **momentous** [məʊ'mentəs] *adj* important(e), capital(e)

momentum [məʊ'mentəm] *n* élan *m*, vitesse acquise; *(fig)* dynamique *f*; **to gather ~** prendre de la vitesse; *(fig)* gagner du terrain

mommy ['mɒmɪ] *n* *(US: mother)* maman *f*

Mon *abbr* *(= Monday)* l.

Monaco ['mɒnəkəʊ] *n* Monaco *f*

monarch ['mɒnək] *n* monarque *m*; **monarchy** *n* monarchie *f*

monastery ['mɒnəstərɪ] *n* monastère *m*

Monday ['mʌndɪ] *n* lundi *m*

monetary ['mʌnɪtərɪ] *adj* monétaire

money ['mʌnɪ] *n* argent *m*; **to make ~** *(person)* gagner de l'argent; *(business)* rapporter; **money belt** *n* ceinture-portefeuille *f*; **money order** *n* mandat *m*

mongrel ['mʌŋɡrəl] *n* *(dog)* bâtard *m*

monitor ['mɒnɪtər] *n* *(TV, Comput)* écran *m*, moniteur *m* ▷ *vt* contrôler; *(foreign station)* être à l'écoute de; *(progress)* suivre de près

monk [mʌŋk] *n* moine *m*

monkey ['mʌŋkɪ] *n* singe *m*

monologue ['mɒnələɡ] *n* monologue *m*

monopoly [mə'nɒpəlɪ] *n* monopole *m*

monosodium glutamate [mɒnə'səʊdɪəm 'ɡluːtəmeɪt] *n* glutamate *m* de sodium

monotonous [mə'nɒtənəs] *adj* monotone

monsoon [mɒn'suːn] *n* mousson *f*

monster ['mɒnstər] *n* monstre *m*

month [mʌnθ] *n* mois *m*; **monthly** *adj* mensuel(le) ▷ *adv* mensuellement

Montreal [mɒntrɪ'ɔːl] *n* Montréal *m*

monument ['mɒnjumənt] *n* monument *m*

mood [muːd] *n* humeur *f*, disposition *f*; **to be in a**

good/bad ~ être de bonne/mauvaise humeur; **moody** *adj* *(variable)* d'humeur changeante, lunatique; *(sullen)* morose, maussade

moon [muːn] *n* lune *f*; **moonlight** *n* clair *m* de lune

moor [muər] *n* lande *f* ▷ *vt* *(ship)* amarrer ▷ *vi* mouiller

moose [muːs] *n* *(pl inv)* élan *m*

mop [mɒp] *n* balai *m* à laver; *(for dishes)* lavette *f* à vaisselle *f* ▷ *vt* éponger, essuyer; **~ of hair** tignasse *f*; **mop up** *vt* éponger

mope [məʊp] *vi* avoir le cafard, se morfondre

moped ['məʊpɛd] *n* cyclomoteur *m*

moral ['mɒrl] *adj* moral(e) ▷ *n* morale *f*; **morals** *npl* moralité *f*

morale [mɒ'rɑːl] *n* moral *m*

morality [mə'rælɪtɪ] *n* moralité *f*

morbid ['mɔːbɪd] *adj* morbide

O **KEYWORD**

more [mɔːr] *adj* **1** *(greater in number etc)* plus (de), davantage (de); **more people/work (than)** plus de gens/de travail (que)

2 *(additional)* encore (de); **do you want (some) more tea?** voulez-vous encore du thé?; **is there any more wine?** reste-t-il du vin?; **I have no** or **I don't have any more money** je n'ai plus d'argent; **it'll take a few more weeks** ça prendra encore quelques semaines

▷ *pron* plus, davantage; **more than 10** plus de 10; **it cost more than we expected** cela a coûté plus que prévu; **I want more** j'en veux plus or davantage; **is there any more?** est-ce qu'il en reste?; **there's no more** il n'y en a plus; **a little more** un peu plus; **many/much more** beaucoup plus, bien davantage

▷ *adv* plus; **more dangerous/easily (than)** plus dangereux/facilement (que); **more and more** de plus en plus; **more or less** plus ou moins; **more than ever** plus que jamais; **once more** encore une fois, une fois de plus

moreover [mɔː'rəʊvər] *adv* de plus

morgue [mɔːɡ] *n* morgue *f*

morning ['mɔːnɪŋ] *n* matin *m*; *(as duration)* matinée *f* ▷ *cpd* matinal(e); *(paper)* du matin; **in the ~** le matin; **7 o'clock in the ~** 7 heures du matin; **morning sickness** *n* nausées matinales

Moroccan [mə'rɒkən] *adj* marocain(e) ▷ *n* Marocain(e)

Morocco [mə'rɒkəʊ] *n* Maroc *m*

moron ['mɔːrɒn] *n* idiot(e), minus *m/f*

morphine ['mɔːfiːn] *n* morphine *f*

morris dancing ['mɒrɪs-] *n* *(BRIT)* danses folkloriques anglaises

Morse [mɔːs] *n* *(also: ~ code)* morse *m*

mortal ['mɔːtl] *adj, n* mortel(le)

mortar ['mɔːtər] *n* mortier *m*

mortgage ['mɔːɡɪdʒ] *n* hypothèque *f*; *(loan)* prêt *m* *(or* crédit *m)* hypothécaire ▷ *vt* hypothéquer

mortician [mɔː'tɪʃən] *n* *(US)* entrepreneur *m* de pompes funèbres

mortified ['mɔːtɪfaɪd] *adj* mort(e) de honte

mortuary ['mɔːtjuərɪ] *n* morgue *f*

mosaic [məʊ'zeɪɪk] *n* mosaïque *f*

Moscow ['mɒskəʊ] *n* Moscou *m*

Moslem ['mɒzləm] *adj, n* = **Muslim**

mosque [mɒsk] *n* mosquée *f*

mosquito (*pl* **-es**) [mɔsˈkiːtəu] *n* moustique *m*
moss [mɔs] *n* mousse *f*
most [məust] *adj* (*majority of*) la plupart de; (*greatest amount of*) le plus de ▷ *pron* la plupart ▷ *adv* le plus; (*very*) très, extrêmement; **the ~** le plus; **~ fish** la plupart des poissons; **the ~ beautiful woman in the world** la plus belle femme du monde; **~ of** (*with plural*) la plupart de; (*with singular*) la plus grande partie de; **~ of them** la plupart d'entre eux; **~ of the time** la plupart du temps; **I saw ~** (*a lot but not all*) j'en ai vu la plupart; (*more than anyone else*) c'est moi qui en ai vu le plus; **at the (very) ~** au plus; **to make the ~ of** profiter au maximum de; **mostly** *adv* (*chiefly*) surtout, principalement; (*usually*) généralement
MOT *n abbr* (BRIT) = **Ministry of Transport**; **the ~ (test)** visite technique (annuelle) obligatoire des véhicules à moteur
motel [məuˈtel] *n* motel *m*
moth [mɔθ] *n* papillon *m* de nuit; (*in clothes*) mite *f*
mother [ˈmʌðəʳ] *n* mère *f* ▷ *vt* (*pamper, protect*) dorloter; **motherhood** *n* maternité *f*; **mother-in-law** *n* belle-mère *f*; **mother-of-pearl** *n* nacre *f*; **Mother's Day** *n* fête *f* des Mères; **mother-to-be** *n* future maman; **mother tongue** *n* langue maternelle
motif [məuˈtiːf] *n* motif *m*
motion [ˈməuʃən] *n* mouvement *m*; (*gesture*) geste *m*; (*at meeting*) motion *f* ▷ *vt*, *vi*: **to ~ (to) sb to do sth** faire signe à qn de faire; **motionless** *adj* immobile, sans mouvement; **motion picture** *n* film *m*
motivate [ˈməutɪveɪt] *vt* motiver
motivation [məutɪˈveɪʃən] *n* motivation *f*
motive [ˈməutɪv] *n* motif *m*, mobile *m*
motor [ˈməutəʳ] *n* moteur *m*; (BRIT inf: vehicle) auto *f*; **motorbike** *n* moto *f*; **motorboat** *n* bateau *m* à moteur; **motorcar** *n* (BRIT) automobile *f*; **motorcycle** *n* moto *f*; **motorcyclist** *n* motocycliste *m/f*; **motoring** (BRIT) *n* tourisme *m* automobile; **motorist** *n* automobiliste *m/f*; **motor racing** (BRIT) *n* course *f* automobile; **motorway** *n* (BRIT) autoroute *f*
motto (*pl* **-es**) [ˈmɔtəu] *n* devise *f*
mould (US **mold**) [məuld] *n* moule *m*; (*mildew*) moisissure *f* ▷ *vt* mouler, modeler; (*fig*) façonner; **mouldy** *adj* moisi(e); (*smell*) de moisi
mound [maund] *n* monticule *m*, tertre *m*
mount [maunt] *n* (*hill*) mont *m*, montagne *f*; (*horse*) monture *f*; (*for picture*) carton *m* de montage ▷ *vt* monter; (*horse*) monter à; (*bike*) monter sur; (*picture*) monter sur carton ▷ *vi* (*inflation, tension*) augmenter; **mount up** *vi* s'élever, monter; (*bills, problems, savings*) s'accumuler
mountain [ˈmauntɪn] *n* montagne *f* ▷ *cpd* (de la) montagne; **mountain bike** *n* VTT *m*, vélo *m* tout terrain; **mountaineer** *n* alpiniste *m/f*; **mountaineering** *n* alpinisme *m*; **mountainous** *adj* montagneux(-euse); **mountain range** *n* chaîne *f* de montagnes
mourn [mɔːn] *vt* pleurer ▷ *vi*: **to ~ for sb** pleurer qn; **to ~ for sth** se lamenter sur qch; **mourner** *n* parent(e) or ami(e) du défunt; personne *f* en deuil or venue rendre hommage au défunt; **mourning** *n* deuil *m*; **in mourning** en deuil
mouse (*pl* **mice**) [maus, maɪs] *n* (*also Comput*) souris *f*; **mouse mat** *n* (*Comput*) tapis *m* de souris
moussaka [muˈsɑːkə] *n* moussaka *f*
mousse [muːs] *n* mousse *f*
moustache (US **mustache**) [məsˈtɑːʃ] *n*

moustache(s) *f(pl)*
mouth [mauθ, (*pl*) mauðz] *n* bouche *f*; (*of dog, cat*) gueule *f*; (*of river*) embouchure *f*; (*of hole, cave*) ouverture *f*; **mouthful** *n* bouchée *f*; **mouth organ** *n* harmonica *m*; **mouthpiece** *n* (*of musical instrument*) bec *m*, embouchure *f*; (*spokesperson*) porte-parole *m inv*; **mouthwash** *n* eau *f* dentifrice
move [muːv] *n* (*movement*) mouvement *m*; (*in game*) coup *m*; (: *turn to play*) tour *m*; (*change of house*) déménagement *m*; (*change of job*) changement *m* d'emploi ▷ *vt* déplacer, bouger; (*emotionally*) émouvoir; (*Pol: resolution etc*) proposer ▷ *vi* bouger, remuer; (*traffic*) circuler; (*also*: **~ house**) déménager; (*in game*) jouer; **can you ~ your car, please?** pouvez-vous déplacer votre voiture, s'il vous plaît?; **to ~ sb to do sth** pousser or inciter qn à faire qch; **to get a ~ on** se dépêcher, se remuer; **move back** *vi* revenir, retourner; **move off** *vi* s'éloigner, s'en aller; **move on** *vi* se remettre en route; **move out** *vi* (*of house*) déménager; **move over** *vi* se pousser, se déplacer; **move up** *vi* avancer; (*employee*) avoir de l'avancement; (*pupil*) passer dans la classe supérieure; **movement** *n* mouvement *m*
movie [ˈmuːvɪ] *n* film *m*; **movies** *npl*: **the ~s** le cinéma; **movie theater** (US) *n* cinéma *m*
moving [ˈmuːvɪŋ] *adj* en mouvement; (*touching*) émouvant(e)
mow (*pt* **-ed**, *pp* **-ed** or **-n**) [məu, -d, -n] *vt* faucher; (*lawn*) tondre; **mower** *n* (*also*: **lawnmower**) tondeuse *f* à gazon
Mozambique [məuzəmˈbiːk] *n* Mozambique *m*
MP *n abbr* (BRIT) = **Member of Parliament**
MP3 *n* mp3 *m*; **MP3 player** *n* lecteur *m* mp3
mpg *n abbr* (= *miles per gallon*) (30 mpg = 9,4 l. aux 100 km)
m.p.h. *abbr* (= *miles per hour*) (60 mph = 96 km/h)
Mr (US **Mr.**) [ˈmɪstəʳ] *n*: **Mr X** Monsieur X, M. X
Mrs (US **Mrs.**) [ˈmɪsɪz] *n*: **~ X** Madame X, Mme X
Ms (US **Ms.**) [mɪz] *n* (*Miss or Mrs*): **Ms X** Madame X, Mme X
MSP *n abbr* (= *Member of the Scottish Parliament*) député *m* au Parlement écossais
Mt *abbr* (*Geo*: = *mount*) Mt
much [mʌtʃ] *adj* beaucoup de ▷ *adv*, *n* or *pron* beaucoup; **we don't have ~ time** nous n'avons pas beaucoup de temps; **how ~ is it?** combien est-ce que ça coûte?; **it's not ~** ce n'est pas beaucoup; **too ~** trop (de); **so ~** tant (de); **I like it very/so ~** j'aime beaucoup/tellement ça; **as ~ as** autant de; **that's ~ better** c'est beaucoup mieux
muck [mʌk] *n* (*mud*) boue *f*; (*dirt*) ordures *fpl*; **muck up** *vt* (*inf: ruin*) gâcher, esquinter; (: *dirty*) salir; (: *exam, interview*) se planter à; **mucky** *adj* (*dirty*) boueux(-euse), sale
mucus [ˈmjuːkəs] *n* mucus *m*
mud [mʌd] *n* boue *f*
muddle [ˈmʌdl] *n* (*mess*) pagaille *f*, fouillis *m*; (*mix-up*) confusion *f* ▷ *vt* (*also*: **~ up**) brouiller, embrouiller; **to get in a ~** (*while explaining etc*) s'embrouiller
muddy [ˈmʌdɪ] *adj* boueux(-euse)
mudguard [ˈmʌdgɑːd] *n* garde-boue *m inv*
muesli [ˈmjuːzlɪ] *n* muesli *m*
muffin [ˈmʌfɪn] *n* (*roll*) petit pain rond et plat; (*cake*) petit gâteau au chocolat ou aux fruits
muffled [ˈmʌfld] *adj* étouffé(e), voilé(e)
muffler [ˈmʌfləʳ] *n* (*scarf*) cache-nez *m inv*; (US Aut) silencieux *m*

mug [mʌg] n (cup) tasse f (sans soucoupe); (: for beer) chope f; (inf: face) bouille f; (: fool) poire f ▷ vt (assault) agresser; **mugger** ['mʌgəʳ] n agresseur m; **mugging** n agression f

muggy ['mʌgɪ] adj lourd(e), moite

mule [mjuːl] n mule f

multicoloured (us **multicolored**) ['mʌltɪkʌləd] adj multicolore

multimedia ['mʌltɪ'miːdɪə] adj multimédia inv

multinational [mʌltɪ'næʃənl] n multinationale f ▷ adj multinational(e)

multiple ['mʌltɪpl] adj multiple ▷ n multiple m; **multiple choice (test)** n QCM m, questionnaire m à choix multiple; **multiple sclerosis** [-sklɪ'rəusɪs] n sclérose f en plaques

multiplex (cinema) ['mʌltɪpleks-] n (cinéma m) multisalles m

multiplication [mʌltɪplɪ'keɪʃən] n multiplication f

multiply ['mʌltɪplaɪ] vt multiplier ▷ vi se multiplier

multistorey ['mʌltɪ'stɔːrɪ] adj (BRIT: building) à étages; (: car park) à étages or niveaux multiples

mum [mʌm] n (BRIT) maman f ▷ adj: **to keep ~** ne pas souffler mot

mumble ['mʌmbl] vt, vi marmotter, marmonner

mummy ['mʌmɪ] n (BRIT: mother) maman f; (embalmed) momie f

mumps [mʌmps] n oreillons mpl

munch [mʌntʃ] vt, vi mâcher

municipal [mjuː'nɪsɪpl] adj municipal(e)

mural ['mjuərl] n peinture murale

murder ['məːdəʳ] n meurtre m, assassinat m ▷ vt assassiner; **murderer** n meurtrier m, assassin m

murky ['məːkɪ] adj sombre, ténébreux(-euse); (water) trouble

murmur ['məːməʳ] n murmure m ▷ vt, vi murmurer

muscle ['mʌsl] n muscle m; (fig) force f; **muscular** ['mʌskjʊləʳ] adj musculaire; (person, arm) musclé(e)

museum [mjuː'zɪəm] n musée m

mushroom ['mʌʃrum] n champignon m ▷ vi (fig) pousser comme un (or des) champignon(s)

music ['mjuːzɪk] n musique f; **musical** adj musical(e); (person) musicien(ne) ▷ n (show) comédie musicale; **musical instrument** n instrument m de musique; **musician** [mjuː'zɪʃən] n musicien(ne)

Muslim ['mʌzlɪm] adj, n musulman(e)

muslin ['mʌzlɪn] n mousseline f

mussel ['mʌsl] n moule f

must [mʌst] aux vb (obligation): **I ~ do it** je dois le faire, il faut que je le fasse; (probability): **he ~ be there by now** il doit y être maintenant, il y est probablement maintenant; (suggestion, invitation): **you ~ come and see me** il faut que vous veniez me voir ▷ n nécessité f, impératif m; **it's a ~** c'est indispensable; **I ~ have made a mistake** j'ai dû me tromper

mustache ['mʌstæʃ] n (us) = **moustache**

mustard ['mʌstəd] n moutarde f

mustn't ['mʌsnt] = **must not**

mute [mjuːt] adj, n muet(te)

mutilate ['mjuːtɪleɪt] vt mutiler

mutiny ['mjuːtɪnɪ] n mutinerie f ▷ vi se mutiner

mutter ['mʌtəʳ] vt, vi marmonner, marmotter

mutton ['mʌtn] n mouton m

mutual ['mjuːtʃuəl] adj mutuel(le), réciproque; (benefit, interest) commun(e)

muzzle ['mʌzl] n museau m; (protective device) muselière f; (of gun) gueule f ▷ vt museler

my [maɪ] adj mon (ma), mes pl; **my house/car/gloves** ma maison/ma voiture/mes gants; **I've washed my hair/cut my finger** je me suis lavé les cheveux/coupé le doigt; **is this my pen or yours?** c'est mon stylo ou c'est le vôtre?

myself [maɪ'self] pron (reflexive) me; (emphatic) moi-même; (after prep) moi; see also **oneself**

mysterious [mɪs'tɪərɪəs] adj mystérieux(-euse)

mystery ['mɪstərɪ] n mystère m

mystical ['mɪstɪkl] adj mystique

mystify ['mɪstɪfaɪ] vt (deliberately) mystifier; (puzzle) ébahir

myth [mɪθ] n mythe m; **mythology** [mɪ'θɔlədʒɪ] n mythologie f

n/a abbr (= not applicable) n.a.

nag [næg] vt (scold) être toujours après, reprendre sans arrêt

nail [neɪl] n (human) ongle m; (metal) clou m ▷ vt clouer; **to ~ sth to sth** clouer qch à qch; **to ~ sb down to a date/price** contraindre qn à accepter or donner une date/un prix; **nailbrush** n brosse f à ongles; **nailfile** n lime f à ongles; **nail polish** n vernis m à ongles; **nail polish remover** n dissolvant m; **nail scissors** npl ciseaux mpl à ongles; **nail varnish** n (BRIT) = **nail polish**

naïve [naɪ'iːv] adj naïf(-ïve)

naked ['neɪkɪd] adj nu(e)

name [neɪm] n nom m; (reputation) réputation f ▷ vt nommer; (identify: accomplice etc) citer; (price, date) fixer, donner; **by ~** par son nom; de nom; **in the ~ of** au nom de; **what's your ~?** comment vous appelez-vous?, quel est votre nom?; **namely** adv à savoir

nanny ['nænɪ] n bonne f d'enfants
nap [næp] n (sleep) (petit) somme
napkin ['næpkɪn] n serviette f (de table)
nappy ['næpɪ] n (BRIT) couche f
narcotics [nɑː'kɒtɪkz] npl (illegal drugs) stupéfiants mpl
narrative ['nærətɪv] n récit m ▷ adj narratif(-ive)
narrator [nə'reɪtər] n narrateur(-trice)
narrow ['nærəu] adj étroit(e); (fig) restreint(e), limité(e) ▷ vi (road) devenir plus étroit, se rétrécir; (gap, difference) se réduire; **to have a ~ escape** l'échapper belle; **narrow down** vt restreindre; **narrowly** adv: **he narrowly missed injury/the tree** il a failli se blesser/rentrer dans l'arbre; **he only narrowly missed the target** il a manqué la cible de peu or de justesse; **narrow-minded** adj à l'esprit étroit, borné(e); (attitude) borné(e)
nasal ['neɪzl] adj nasal(e)
nasty ['nɑːstɪ] adj (person: malicious) méchant(e); (: rude) très désagréable; (smell) dégoûtant(e); (wound, situation) mauvais(e), vilain(e)
nation ['neɪʃən] n nation f
national ['næʃənl] adj national(e) ▷ n (abroad) ressortissant(e); (when home) national(e); **national anthem** n hymne national; **national dress** n costume national; **National Health Service** n (BRIT) service national de santé, ≈ Sécurité Sociale; **National Insurance** n (BRIT) ≈ Sécurité Sociale; **nationalist** adj, n nationaliste m/f; **nationality** [næʃə'nælɪtɪ] n nationalité f; **nationalize** vt nationaliser; **national park** n parc national; **National Trust** n (BRIT) ≈ Caisse f nationale des monuments historiques et des sites
nationwide ['neɪʃənwaɪd] adj s'étendant à l'ensemble du pays; (problem) à l'échelle du pays entier
native ['neɪtɪv] n habitant(e) du pays, autochtone m/f ▷ adj du pays, indigène; (country) natal(e); (language) maternel(le); (ability) inné(e); **Native American** n Indien(ne) d'Amérique ▷ adj amérindien(ne); **native speaker** n locuteur natif
NATO ['neɪtəu] n abbr (= North Atlantic Treaty Organization) OTAN f
natural ['nætʃrəl] adj naturel(le); **natural gas** n gaz naturel; **natural history** n histoire naturelle; **naturally** adv naturellement; **natural resources** npl ressources naturelles
nature ['neɪtʃər] n nature f; **by ~** par tempérament, de nature; **nature reserve** n (BRIT) réserve naturelle
naughty ['nɔːtɪ] adj (child) vilain(e), pas sage
nausea ['nɔːsɪə] n nausée f
naval ['neɪvl] adj naval(e)
navel ['neɪvl] n nombril m
navigate ['nævɪgeɪt] vt (steer) diriger, piloter ▷ vi naviguer; (Aut) indiquer la route à suivre; **navigation** [nævɪ'geɪʃən] n navigation f
navy ['neɪvɪ] n marine f
navy-blue ['neɪvɪ'bluː] adj bleu marine inv
Nazi ['nɑːtsɪ] n Nazi(e)
NB abbr (= nota bene) NB
near [nɪər] adj proche ▷ adv près ▷ prep (also: **~ to**) près de ▷ vt approcher de; **in the ~ future** dans un proche avenir; **nearby** [nɪə'baɪ] adj proche ▷ adv tout près, à proximité; **nearly** adv presque; **I nearly fell** j'ai failli tomber; **it's not nearly big enough** ce n'est vraiment pas assez grand, c'est loin d'être assez grand; **near-sighted** adj myope
neat [niːt] adj (person, work) soigné(e); (room etc) bien

tenu(e) or rangé(e); (solution, plan) habile; (spirits) pur(e); **neatly** adv avec soin or ordre; (skilfully) habilement
necessarily ['nesɪsrɪlɪ] adv nécessairement; **not ~** pas nécessairement or forcément
necessary ['nesɪsrɪ] adj nécessaire; **if ~** si besoin est, le cas échéant
necessity [nɪ'sesɪtɪ] n nécessité f; chose nécessaire or essentielle
neck [nek] n cou m; (of horse, garment) encolure f; (of bottle) goulot m; **~ and ~** à égalité; **necklace** ['neklɪs] n collier m; **necktie** ['nektaɪ] n (esp US) cravate f
nectarine ['nektərɪn] n brugnon m, nectarine f
need [niːd] n besoin m ▷ vt avoir besoin de; **to ~ to do** devoir faire; avoir besoin de faire; **you don't ~ to go** vous n'avez pas besoin or vous n'êtes pas obligé de partir; **a signature is ~ed** il faut une signature; **there's no ~ to do ...** il n'y a pas lieu de faire ..., il n'est pas nécessaire de faire ...
needle ['niːdl] n aiguille f ▷ vt (inf) asticoter, tourmenter
needless ['niːdlɪs] adj inutile; **~ to say, ...** inutile de dire que ...
needlework ['niːdlwɜːk] n (activity) travaux mpl d'aiguille; (object) ouvrage m
needn't ['niːdnt] = **need not**
needy ['niːdɪ] adj nécessiteux(-euse)
negative ['negətɪv] n (Phot, Elec) négatif m; (Ling) terme m de négation ▷ adj négatif(-ive)
neglect [nɪ'glekt] vt négliger; (garden) ne pas entretenir; (duty) manquer à ▷ n (of person, duty, garden) le fait de négliger; (state of) **~** abandon m; **to ~ to do sth** négliger or omettre de faire qch; **to ~ one's appearance** se négliger
negotiate [nɪ'gəuʃɪeɪt] vi négocier ▷ vt négocier; (obstacle) franchir, négocier; **to ~ with sb for sth** négocier avec qn en vue d'obtenir qch
negotiation [nɪgəuʃɪ'eɪʃən] n négociation f, pourparlers mpl
negotiator [nɪ'gəuʃɪeɪtər] n négociateur(-trice)
neighbour (us **neighbor** etc) ['neɪbər] n voisin(e); **neighbourhood** n (place) quartier m; (people) voisinage m; **neighbouring** adj voisin(e), avoisinant(e)
neither ['naɪðər] adj, pron aucun(e) (des deux), ni l'un(e) ni l'autre ▷ conj: **~ do I** moi non plus ▷ adv: **~ good nor bad** ni bon ni mauvais; **~ of them** ni l'un ni l'autre
neon ['niːɒn] n néon m
Nepal [nɪ'pɔːl] n Népal m
nephew ['nevjuː] n neveu m
nerve [nɜːv] n nerf m; (bravery) sang-froid m, courage m; (cheek) aplomb m, toupet m; **nerves** npl (nervousness) nervosité f; **he gets on my ~s** il m'énerve
nervous ['nɜːvəs] adj nerveux(-euse); (anxious) inquiet(-ète), plein(e) d'appréhension; (timid) intimidé(e); **nervous breakdown** n dépression nerveuse
nest [nest] n nid m ▷ vi (se) nicher, faire son nid
Net [net] n (Comput): **the ~** (Internet) le Net
net [net] n filet m; (fabric) tulle f ▷ adj net(te) ▷ vt (fish etc) prendre au filet; **netball** n netball m
Netherlands ['neðələndz] npl: **the ~** les Pays-Bas mpl
nett [net] adj = **net**
nettle ['netl] n ortie f
network ['netwɜːk] n réseau m
neurotic [njuə'rɒtɪk] adj névrosé(e)
neuter ['njuːtər] adj neutre ▷ vt (cat etc) châtrer, couper

neutral ['nju:trəl] *adj* neutre ▷ *n* (*Aut*) point mort

never ['nɛvəʳ] *adv* (ne ...) jamais; **I ~ went** je n'y suis pas allé; **I've ~ been to Spain** je ne suis jamais allé en Espagne; **~ again** plus jamais; **~ in my life** jamais de ma vie; *see also* **mind**; **never-ending** *adj* interminable; **nevertheless** [nɛvəðə'lɛs] *adv* néanmoins, malgré tout

new [nju:] *adj* nouveau (nouvelle); (*brand new*) neuf (neuve); **New Age** New Age *m*; **newborn** *adj* nouveau-né(e); **newcomer** ['nju:kʌməʳ] *n* nouveau venu (nouvelle venue); **newly** *adv* nouvellement, récemment

news [nju:z] *n* nouvelle(s) *f(pl)*; (*Radio*, *TV*) informations *fpl*, actualités *fpl*; **a piece of ~** une nouvelle; **news agency** *n* agence *f* de presse; **newsagent** *n* (*BRIT*) marchand *m* de journaux; **newscaster** *n* (*Radio*, *TV*) présentateur(-trice); **news dealer** *n* (*US*) marchand *m* de journaux; **newsletter** *n* bulletin *m*; **newspaper** *n* journal *m*; **newsreader** *n* = **newscaster**

newt [nju:t] *n* triton *m*

New Year *n* Nouvel An; **Happy ~!** Bonne Année!; **New Year's Day** *n* le jour de l'An; **New Year's Eve** *n* la Saint-Sylvestre

New York [-'jɔ:k] *n* New York

New Zealand [-'zi:lənd] *n* Nouvelle-Zélande *f*; **New Zealander** *n* Néo-Zélandais(e)

next [nɛkst] *adj* (*in time*) prochain(e); (*seat*, *room*) voisin(e), d'à côté; (*meeting*, *bus stop*) suivant(e) ▷ *adv* la fois suivante; la prochaine fois; (*afterwards*) ensuite; **~ to** *prep* à côté de; **~ to nothing** presque rien; **~ time** *adv* la prochaine fois; **the ~ day** le lendemain, le jour suivant *or* d'après; **~ year** l'année prochaine; **~ please!** (*at doctor's etc*) au suivant!; **the week after ~** dans deux semaines; **next door** *adv* à côté ▷ *adj* (*neighbour*) d'à côté; **next-of-kin** *n* parent *m* le plus proche

NHS *n abbr* (*BRIT*) = **National Health Service**

nibble ['nɪbl] *vt* grignoter

nice [naɪs] *adj* (*holiday*, *trip*, *taste*) agréable; (*flat*, *picture*) joli(e); (*person*) gentil(le); (*distinction*, *point*) subtil(e); **nicely** *adv* agréablement; joliment; gentiment; subtilement

niche [ni:ʃ] *n* (*Archit*) niche *f*

nick [nɪk] *n* (*indentation*) encoche *f*; (*wound*) entaille *f*; (*BRIT inf*): **in good ~** en bon état ▷ *vt* (*cut*): **to ~ o.s.** se couper; (*inf*: *steal*) faucher, piquer; **in the ~ of time** juste à temps

nickel ['nɪkl] *n* nickel *m*; (*US*) pièce *f* de 5 cents

nickname ['nɪkneɪm] *n* surnom *m* ▷ *vt* surnommer

nicotine ['nɪkəti:n] *n* nicotine *f*

niece [ni:s] *n* nièce *f*

Nigeria [naɪ'dʒɪərɪə] *n* Nigéria *m or f*

night [naɪt] *n* nuit *f*; (*evening*) soir *m*; **at ~** la nuit; **by ~** de nuit; **last ~** (*evening*) hier soir; (*night-time*) la nuit dernière; **night club** *n* boîte *f* de nuit; **nightdress** *n* chemise *f* de nuit; **nightie** ['naɪtɪ] *n* chemise *f* de nuit; **nightlife** *n* vie *f* nocturne; **nightly** *adj* (*news*) du soir; (*by night*) nocturne ▷ *adv* (*every evening*) tous les soirs; (*every night*) toutes les nuits; **nightmare** *n* cauchemar *m*; **night school** *n* cours *mpl* du soir; **night shift** *n* équipe *f* de nuit; **night-time** *n* nuit *f*

nil [nɪl] *n* (*BRIT Sport*) zéro *m*

nine [naɪn] *num* neuf; **nineteen** *num* dix-neuf; **nineteenth** [naɪn'ti:nθ] *num* dix-neuvième; **ninetieth** ['naɪntɪɪθ] *num* quatre-vingt-dixième; **ninety** *num* quatre-vingt-dix

ninth [naɪnθ] *num* neuvième

nip [nɪp] *vt* pincer ▷ *vi* (*BRIT inf*): **to ~ out/down/up** sortir/descendre/monter en vitesse

nipple ['nɪpl] *n* (*Anat*) mamelon *m*, bout *m* du sein

nitrogen ['naɪtrədʒən] *n* azote *m*

 KEYWORD

no [nəu] (*pl* **noes**) *adv* (*opposite of "yes"*) non; **are you coming? — no (I'm not)** est-ce que vous venez? — non; **would you like some more? — no thank you** vous en voulez encore? — non merci
▷ *adj* (*not any*) (ne ...) pas de, (ne ...) aucun(e); **I have no money/books** je n'ai pas d'argent/de livres; **no student would have done it** aucun étudiant ne l'aurait fait; **"no smoking"** "défense de fumer"; **"no dogs"** "les chiens ne sont pas admis"
▷ *n* non *m*

nobility [nəu'bɪlɪtɪ] *n* noblesse *f*

noble ['nəubl] *adj* noble

nobody ['nəubədɪ] *pron* (ne ...) personne

nod [nɔd] *vi* faire un signe de (la) tête (*affirmatif ou amical*); (*sleep*) somnoler ▷ *vt*: **to ~ one's head** faire un signe de (la) tête; (*in agreement*) faire signe que oui ▷ *n* signe *m* de (la) tête; **nod off** *vi* s'assoupir

noise [nɔɪz] *n* bruit *m*; **I can't sleep for the ~** je n'arrive pas à dormir à cause du bruit; **noisy** *adj* bruyant(e)

nominal ['nɔmɪnl] *adj* (*rent*, *fee*) symbolique; (*value*) nominal(e)

nominate ['nɔmɪneɪt] *vt* (*propose*) proposer; (*appoint*) nommer; **nomination** [nɔmɪ'neɪʃən] *n* nomination *f*; **nominee** [nɔmɪ'ni:] *n* candidat agréé; personne nommée

none [nʌn] *pron* aucun(e); **~ of you** aucun d'entre vous, personne parmi vous; **I have ~ left** je n'en ai plus; **he's ~ the worse for it** il ne s'en porte pas plus mal

nonetheless ['nʌnðə'lɛs] *adv* néanmoins

non-fiction [nɔn'fɪkʃən] *n* littérature *f* non-romanesque

nonsense ['nɔnsəns] *n* absurdités *fpl*, idioties *fpl*; **~!** ne dites pas d'idioties!

non: **non-smoker** *n* non-fumeur *m*; **non-smoking** *adj* non-fumeur; **non-stick** *adj* qui n'attache pas

noodles ['nu:dlz] *npl* nouilles *fpl*

noon [nu:n] *n* midi *m*

no-one ['nəuwʌn] *pron* = **nobody**

nor [nɔ:ʳ] *conj* = **neither** ▷ *adv* *see* **neither**

norm [nɔ:m] *n* norme *f*

normal ['nɔ:ml] *adj* normal(e); **normally** *adv* normalement

Normandy ['nɔ:məndɪ] *n* Normandie *f*

north [nɔ:θ] *n* nord *m* ▷ *adj* nord *inv*; (*wind*) du nord ▷ *adv* au *or* vers le nord; **North Africa** *n* Afrique *f* du Nord; **North African** *adj* nord-africain(e), d'Afrique du Nord ▷ *n* Nord-Africain(e); **North America** *n* Amérique *f* du Nord; **North American** *n* Nord-Américain(e) ▷ *adj* nord-américain(e), d'Amérique du Nord; **northbound** ['nɔ:θbaund] *adj* (*traffic*) en direction du nord; (*carriageway*) nord *inv*; **north-east** *n* nord-est *m*; **northeastern** *adj* (du) nord-est *inv*; **northern** ['nɔ:ðən] *adj* du nord, septentrional(e); **Northern Ireland** *n* Irlande *f* du Nord; **North Korea** *n* Corée *f* du Nord; **North Pole** *n*: **the North Pole** le pôle Nord; **North**

Sea n: **the North Sea** la mer du Nord; **north-west** n nord-ouest m; **northwestern** ['nɔː'westən] adj (du) nord-ouest inv

Norway ['nɔːweɪ] n Norvège f; **Norwegian** [nɔː'wiːdʒən] adj norvégien(ne) ▷ n Norvégien(ne); (Ling) norvégien m

nose [nəuz] n nez m; (of dog, cat) museau m; (fig) flair m; **nose about, nose around** vi fouiner ou fureter (partout); **nosebleed** n saignement m de nez; **nosey** adj (inf) curieux(-euse)

nostalgia [nɔs'tældʒɪə] n nostalgie f

nostalgic [nɔs'tældʒɪk] adj nostalgique

nostril ['nɔstrɪl] n narine f; (of horse) naseau m

nosy ['nəuzɪ] (inf) adj = **nosey**

not [nɔt] adv (ne ...) pas; **he is** ~ or **isn't here** il n'est pas ici; **you must** ~ or **mustn't do that** tu ne dois pas faire ça; **I hope** ~ j'espère que non; ~ **at all** pas du tout; (after thanks) de rien; **it's too late, isn't it?** c'est trop tard, n'est-ce pas?; ~ **yet/now** pas encore/maintenant; see also **only**

notable ['nəutəbl] adj notable; **notably** adv (particularly) en particulier; (markedly) spécialement

notch [nɔtʃ] n encoche f

note [nəut] n note f; (letter) mot m; (banknote) billet m ▷ vt (also: ~ **down**) noter; (notice) constater; **notebook** n carnet m; (for shorthand etc) bloc-notes m; **noted** ['nəutɪd] adj réputé(e); **notepad** n bloc-notes m; **notepaper** n papier m à lettres

nothing ['nʌθɪŋ] n rien m; **he does** ~ il ne fait rien; ~ **new** rien de nouveau; **for** ~ (free) pour rien, gratuitement; (in vain) pour rien; ~ **at all** rien du tout; ~ **much** pas grand-chose

notice ['nəutɪs] n (announcement, warning) avis m ▷ vt remarquer, s'apercevoir de; **advance** ~ préavis m; **at short** ~ dans un délai très court; **until further** ~ jusqu'à nouvel ordre; **to give** ~, **hand in one's** ~ (employee) donner sa démission, démissionner; **to take** ~ **of** prêter attention à; **to bring sth to sb's** ~ porter qch à la connaissance de qn; **noticeable** adj visible

notice board n (BRIT) panneau m d'affichage

notify ['nəutɪfaɪ] vt: **to** ~ **sb of sth** avertir qn de qch

notion ['nəuʃən] n idée f; (concept) notion f; **notions** npl (US: haberdashery) mercerie f

notorious [nəu'tɔːrɪəs] adj notoire (souvent en mal)

notwithstanding [nɔtwɪθ'stændɪŋ] adv néanmoins ▷ prep en dépit de

nought [nɔːt] n zéro m

noun [naun] n nom m

nourish ['nʌrɪʃ] vt nourrir; **nourishment** n nourriture f

Nov. abbr (= November) nov

novel ['nɔvl] n roman m ▷ adj nouveau (nouvelle), original(e); **novelist** n romancier m; **novelty** n nouveauté f

November [nəu'vembə'] n novembre m

novice ['nɔvɪs] n novice m/f

now [nau] adv maintenant ▷ conj: ~ **(that)** maintenant (que); **right** ~ tout de suite; **by** ~ à l'heure qu'il est; **just** ~: **that's the fashion just** ~ c'est la mode en ce moment ou maintenant; ~ **and then**, ~ **and again** de temps en temps; **from** ~ **on** dorénavant; **nowadays** ['nauədeɪz] adv de nos jours

nowhere ['nəuwɛə'] adv (ne ...) nulle part

nozzle ['nɔzl] n (of hose) jet m, lance f; (of vacuum cleaner) suceur m

nr abbr (BRIT) = **near**

nuclear ['njuːklɪə'] adj nucléaire

nucleus (pl **nuclei**) ['njuːklɪəs, 'njuːklɪaɪ] n noyau m

nude [njuːd] adj nu(e) ▷ n (Art) nu m; **in the** ~ (tout(e)) nu(e)

nudge [nʌdʒ] vt donner un (petit) coup de coude à

nudist ['njuːdɪst] n nudiste m/f

nudity ['njuːdɪtɪ] n nudité f

nuisance ['njuːsns] n: **it's a** ~ c'est (très) ennuyeux or gênant; **he's a** ~ il est assommant or casse-pieds; **what a** ~! quelle barbe!

numb [nʌm] adj engourdi(e); (with fear) paralysé(e)

number ['nʌmbə'] n nombre m; (numeral) chiffre m; (of house, car, telephone, newspaper) numéro m ▷ vt numéroter; (amount to) compter; **a** ~ **of** un certain nombre de; **they were seven in** ~ ils étaient (au nombre de) sept; **to be** ~**ed among** compter parmi; **number plate** n (BRIT Aut) plaque f minéralogique or d'immatriculation; **Number Ten** n (BRIT: 10 Downing Street) résidence du Premier ministre

numerical [njuː'merɪkl] adj numérique

numerous ['njuːmərəs] adj nombreux(-euse)

nun [nʌn] n religieuse f, sœur f

nurse [nəːs] n infirmière f; (also: ~**maid**) bonne f d'enfants ▷ vt (patient, cold) soigner

nursery ['nəːsərɪ] n (room) nursery f; (institution) crèche f, garderie f; (for plants) pépinière f; **nursery rhyme** n comptine f, chansonnette f pour enfants; **nursery school** n école maternelle; **nursery slope** n (BRIT Ski) piste f pour débutants

nursing ['nəːsɪŋ] n (profession) profession f d'infirmière; (care) soins mpl; **nursing home** n clinique f; (for convalescence) maison f de convalescence or de repos; (for old people) maison de retraite

nurture ['nəːtʃə'] vt élever

nut [nʌt] n (of metal) écrou m; (fruit: walnut) noix f; (: hazelnut) noisette f; (: peanut) cacahuète f (terme générique en anglais)

nutmeg ['nʌtmeg] n (noix f) muscade f

nutrient ['njuːtrɪənt] n substance nutritive

nutrition [njuː'trɪʃən] n nutrition f, alimentation f

nutritious [njuː'trɪʃəs] adj nutritif(-ive), nourrissant(e)

nuts [nʌts] (inf) adj dingue

NVQ n abbr (BRIT) = **National Vocational Qualification**

nylon ['naɪlɔn] n nylon m ▷ adj de or en nylon

oak [əuk] n chêne m ▷ cpd de or en (bois de) chêne

O.A.P. n abbr (BRIT) = **old age pensioner**

oar [ɔːʳ] n aviron m, rame f

oasis (pl **oases**) [əu'eɪsɪs, əu'eɪsiːz] n oasis f

oath [əuθ] n serment m; (swear word) juron m; **on** (BRIT) or **under ~** sous serment; assermenté(e)

oatmeal ['əutmiːl] n flocons mpl d'avoine

oats [əuts] n avoine f

obedience [ə'biːdɪəns] n obéissance f

obedient [ə'biːdɪənt] adj obéissant(e)

obese [əu'biːs] adj obèse

obesity [əu'biːsɪtɪ] n obésité f

obey [ə'beɪ] vt obéir à; (instructions, regulations) se conformer à ▷ vi obéir

obituary [ə'bɪtjuərɪ] n nécrologie f

object n ['ɔbdʒɪkt] objet m; (purpose) but m, objet; (Ling) complément m d'objet ▷ vi [əb'dʒɛkt]: **to ~ to** (attitude) désapprouver; (proposal) protester contre, élever une objection contre; **I ~!** je proteste!; **he ~ed that ...** il a fait valoir or a objecté que ...; **money is no ~** l'argent n'est pas un problème; **objection** [əb'dʒɛkʃən] n objection f; **if you have no objection** si vous n'y voyez pas d'inconvénient; **objective** n objectif m ▷ adj objectif(-ive)

obligation [ɔblɪ'geɪʃən] n obligation f, devoir m; (debt) dette f (de reconnaissance)

obligatory [ə'blɪgətərɪ] adj obligatoire

oblige [ə'blaɪdʒ] vt (force): **to ~ sb to do** obliger or forcer qn à faire; (do a favour) rendre service à, obliger; **to be ~d to sb for sth** être obligé(e) à qn de qch

oblique [ə'bliːk] adj oblique; (allusion) indirect(e)

obliterate [ə'blɪtəreɪt] vt effacer

oblivious [ə'blɪvɪəs] adj: **~ of** oublieux(-euse) de

oblong ['ɔblɔŋ] adj oblong(ue) ▷ n rectangle m

obnoxious [əb'nɔkʃəs] adj odieux(-euse); (smell) nauséabond(e)

oboe ['əubəu] n hautbois m

obscene [əb'siːn] adj obscène

obscure [əb'skjuəʳ] adj obscur(e) ▷ vt obscurcir; (hide: sun) cacher

observant [əb'zəːvnt] adj observateur(-trice)

observation [ɔbzə'veɪʃən] n observation f; (by police etc) surveillance f

observatory [əb'zəːvətrɪ] n observatoire m

observe [əb'zəːv] vt observer; (remark) faire observer or remarquer; **observer** n observateur(-trice)

obsess [əb'sɛs] vt obséder; **obsession** [əb'sɛʃən] n obsession f; **obsessive** adj obsédant(e)

obsolete ['ɔbsəliːt] adj dépassé(e), périmé(e)

obstacle ['ɔbstəkl] n obstacle m

obstinate ['ɔbstɪnɪt] adj obstiné(e); (pain, cold) persistant(e)

obstruct [əb'strʌkt] vt (block) boucher, obstruer; (hinder) entraver; **obstruction** [əb'strʌkʃən] n obstruction f; (to plan, progress) obstacle m

obtain [əb'teɪn] vt obtenir

obvious ['ɔbvɪəs] adj évident(e), manifeste; **obviously** adv manifestement; (of course): **obviously!** bien sûr!; **obviously not!** évidemment pas!, bien sûr que non!

occasion [ə'keɪʒən] n occasion f; (event) événement m; **occasional** adj pris(e) (or fait(e) etc) de temps en temps; (worker, spending) occasionnel(le); **occasionally** adv de temps en temps, quelquefois

occult [ɔ'kʌlt] adj occulte ▷ n: **the ~** le surnaturel

occupant ['ɔkjupənt] n occupant m

occupation [ɔkju'peɪʃən] n occupation f; (job) métier m, profession f

occupy ['ɔkjupaɪ] vt occuper; **to ~ o.s. with** or **by doing** s'occuper à faire

occur [ə'kəːʳ] vi se produire; (difficulty, opportunity) se présenter; (phenomenon, error) se rencontrer; **to ~ to sb** venir à l'esprit de qn; **occurrence** [ə'kʌrəns] n (existence) présence f, existence f; (event) cas m, fait m

ocean ['əuʃən] n océan m

o'clock [ə'klɔk] adv: **it is 5 o'clock** il est 5 heures

Oct. abbr (= October) oct

October [ɔk'təubəʳ] n octobre m

octopus ['ɔktəpəs] n pieuvre f

odd [ɔd] adj (strange) bizarre, curieux(-euse); (number) impair(e); (not of a set) dépareillé(e); **60 ~** 60 et quelques; **at ~ times** de temps en temps; **the ~ one out** l'exception f; **oddly** adv bizarrement, curieusement; **odds** npl (in betting) cote f; **it makes no odds** cela n'a pas d'importance; **odds and ends** de petites choses; **at odds** en désaccord

odometer [ɔ'dɔmɪtəʳ] n (US) odomètre m

odour (US **odor**) ['əudəʳ] n odeur f

O   **KEYWORD**

of [ɔv, əv] prep **1** (gen) de; **a friend of ours** un de nos amis; **a boy of 10** un garçon de 10 ans; **that was kind of you** c'était gentil de votre part

2 (expressing quantity, amount, dates etc) de; **a kilo of flour** un kilo de farine; **how much of this do you need?** combien vous en faut-il?; **there were three of them** (people) ils étaient 3; (objects) il y en avait 3; **three of us went** 3 d'entre nous y sont allé(e)s; **the 5th of July** le 5 juillet; **a quarter of 4** (US) 4 heures moins le quart

3 (from, out of) en, de; **a statue of marble** une statue de or en marbre; **made of wood** (fait) en bois

---

off [ɔf] adj, adv (engine) coupé(e); (light, TV) éteint(e); (tap) fermé(e); (BRIT: food) mauvais(e), avancé(e);

(: *milk*) tourné(e); (*absent*) absent(e); (*cancelled*) annulé(e); (*removed*) retiré; **the lid was ~** le couvercle était retiré *or* n'était pas mis; (*away*): **to run/drive ~** partir en courant/en voiture ▷ *prep de*; **to be ~** (*to leave*) partir, s'en aller; **to be ~ sick** être absent pour cause de maladie; **a day ~** un jour de congé; **to have an ~ day** n'être pas en forme; **he had his coat ~** il avait enlevé son manteau; **10% ~** (*Comm*) 10% de rabais; **5 km ~ (the road)** à 5 km (de la route); **~ the coast** au large de la côte; **it's a long way ~** c'est loin (d'ici); **I'm ~ meat** je ne mange plus de viande; je n'aime plus la viande; **on the ~ chance** à tout hasard; **~ and on, on and ~** de temps à autre

offence (*us* **offense**) [əˈfɛns] *n* (*crime*) délit *m*, infraction *f*; **to take ~ at** se vexer de, s'offenser de

offend [əˈfɛnd] *vt* (*person*) offenser, blesser; **offender** *n* délinquant(e); (*against regulations*) contrevenant(e)

offense [əˈfɛns] *n* (*us*) = **offence**

offensive [əˈfɛnsɪv] *adj* offensant(e), choquant(e); (*smell etc*) très déplaisant(e); (*weapon*) offensif(-ive) ▷ *n* (*Mil*) offensive *f*

offer [ˈɔfəʳ] *n* offre *f*, proposition *f* ▷ *vt* offrir, proposer; **"on ~"** (*Comm*) "en promotion"

offhand [ɔfˈhænd] *adj* désinvolte ▷ *adv* spontanément

office [ˈɔfɪs] *n* (*place*) bureau *m*; (*position*) charge *f*, fonction *f*; **doctor's ~** (*us*) cabinet (médical); **to take ~** entrer en fonctions; **office block** (*us* **office building**) *n* immeuble *m* de bureaux; **office hours** *npl* heures *fpl* de bureau; (*us Med*) heures de consultation

officer [ˈɔfɪsəʳ] *n* (*Mil etc*) officier *m*; (*also*: **police ~**) agent *m* (de police); (*of organization*) membre *m* du bureau directeur

office worker *n* employé(e) de bureau

official [əˈfɪʃl] *adj* (*authorized*) officiel(le) ▷ *n* officiel *m*; (*civil servant*) fonctionnaire *m/f*; (*of railways, post office, town hall*) employé(e)

off: **off-licence** *n* (*BRIT*: *shop*) débit *m* de vins et de spiritueux; **off-line** *adj* (*Comput*) (en mode) autonome; (: *switched off*) non connecté(e); **off-peak** *adj* aux heures creuses; (*electricity, ticket*) au tarif heures creuses; **off-putting** *adj* (*BRIT*: *remark*) rébarbatif(-ive); (*person*) rebutant(e), peu engageant(e); **off-season** *adj*, *adv* hors-saison *inv*

offset [ˈɔfsɛt] *vt* (*irreg*: *like* **set**) (*counteract*) contrebalancer, compenser

offshore [ɔfˈʃɔːʳ] *adj* (*breeze*) de terre; (*island*) proche du littoral; (*fishing*) côtier(-ière)

offside [ˈɔfˈsaɪd] *adj* (*Sport*) hors jeu; (*Aut*: *in Britain*) de droite; (: *in US, Europe*) de gauche

offspring [ˈɔfsprɪŋ] *n* progéniture *f*.

often [ˈɔfn] *adv* souvent; **how ~ do you go?** vous y allez tous les combien?; **every so ~** de temps en temps, de temps à autre

oh [əu] *excl* ô!, oh!, ah!

oil [ɔɪl] *n* huile *f*; (*petroleum*) pétrole *m*; (*for central heating*) mazout *m* ▷ *vt* (*machine*) graisser; **oil filter** *n* (*Aut*) filtre *m* à huile; **oil painting** *n* peinture *f* à l'huile; **oil refinery** *n* raffinerie *f* de pétrole; **oil rig** *n* derrick *m*; (*at sea*) plate-forme pétrolière; **oil slick** *n* nappe *f* de mazout; **oil tanker** *n* (*ship*) pétrolier *m*; (*truck*) camion-citerne *m*; **oil well** *n* puits *m* de pétrole; **oily** *adj* huileux(-euse); (*food*) gras(se)

ointment [ˈɔɪntmənt] *n* onguent *m*

O.K., okay [ˈəuˈkeɪ] (*inf*) *excl* d'accord! ▷ *vt* approuver, donner son accord à ▷ *adj* (*not bad*) pas mal!; **is it O.K.?,**

are you O.K.? ça va?

old [əuld] *adj* vieux (vieille); (*person*) vieux, âgé(e); (*former*) ancien(ne), vieux, vieux; **how ~ are you?** quel âge avez-vous?; **he's 10 years ~** il a 10 ans, il est âgé de 10 ans; **~er brother/sister** frère/sœur aîné(e); **old age** *n* vieillesse *f*; **old-age pension** *n* (*BRIT*) (pension *f* de) retraite *f* (*de la sécurité sociale*); **old-age pensioner** *n* (*BRIT*) retraité(e); **old-fashioned** *adj* démodé(e); (*person*) vieux jeu *inv*; **old people's home** *n* (*esp BRIT*) maison *f* de retraite

olive [ˈɔlɪv] *n* (*fruit*) olive *f*; (*tree*) olivier *m* ▷ *adj* (*also*: **~-green**) (vert) olive *inv*; **olive oil** *n* huile *f* d'olive

Olympic [əuˈlɪmpɪk] *adj* olympique; **the ~ Games, the ~s** les Jeux *mpl* olympiques

omelet(te) [ˈɔmlɪt] *n* omelette *f*

omen [ˈəumən] *n* présage *m*

ominous [ˈɔmɪnəs] *adj* menaçant(e), inquiétant(e); (*event*) de mauvais augure

omit [əuˈmɪt] *vt* omettre

KEYWORD

on [ɔn] *prep* **1** (*indicating position*) sur; **on the table** sur la table; **on the wall** sur le *or* au mur; **on the left** à gauche
2 (*indicating means, method, condition etc*): **on foot** à pied; **on the train/plane** (*be*) dans le train/l'avion; (*go*) en train/avion; **on the telephone/radio/television** au téléphone/à la radio/à la télévision; **to be on drugs** se droguer; **on holiday** (*BRIT*): **on vacation** (*us*) en vacances
3 (*referring to time*): **on Friday** vendredi; **on Fridays** le vendredi; **on June 20th** le 20 juin; **a week on Friday** vendredi en huit; **on arrival** à l'arrivée; **on seeing this** en voyant cela
4 (*about, concerning*) sur, de; **a book on Balzac/physics** un livre sur Balzac/de physique
▷ *adv* **1** (*referring to dress*): **to have one's coat on** avoir (mis) son manteau; **to put one's coat on** mettre son manteau; **what's she got on?** qu'est-ce qu'elle porte?
2 (*referring to covering*): **screw the lid on tightly** vissez bien le couvercle
3 (*further, continuously*): **to walk** *etc* **on** continuer à marcher *etc*; **from that day on** depuis ce jour
▷ *adj* **1** (*in operation*: *machine*) en marche; (: *radio, TV, light*) allumé(e); (: *tap, gas*) ouvert(e); (: *brakes*) mis(e); **is the meeting still on?** (*not cancelled*) est-ce que la réunion a bien lieu?; (*in progress*) la réunion dure-t-elle encore?; **when is this film on?** quand passe ce film?
2 (*inf*): **that's not on!** (*not acceptable*) cela ne se fait pas!; (*not possible*) pas question!

once [wʌns] *adv* une fois; (*formerly*) autrefois ▷ *conj* une fois que + *sub*; **~ he had left/it was done** une fois qu'il fut parti/que ce fut terminé; **at ~** tout de suite, immédiatement; (*simultaneously*) à la fois; **all at ~** *adv* tout d'un coup; **~ a week** une fois par semaine; **~ more** encore une fois; **~ and for all** une fois pour toutes; **~ upon a time there was ...** il y avait une fois ..., il était une fois ...

oncoming [ˈɔnkʌmɪŋ] *adj* (*traffic*) venant en sens inverse

KEYWORD

one [wʌn] *num* un(e); **one hundred and fifty** cent cinquante; **one by one** un(e) à *or* par un(e); **one day**

un jour

▷ adj **1** (sole) seul(e), unique; **the one book which** l'unique or le seul livre qui; **the one man who** le seul (homme) qui

2 (same) même; **they came in the one car** ils sont venus dans la même voiture

▷ pron **1**: **this one** celui-ci (celle-ci); **that one** celui-là (celle-là); **I've already got one/a red one** j'en ai déjà un(e)/un(e) rouge; **which one do you want?** lequel voulez-vous?

2: **one another** l'un(e) l'autre; **to look at one another** se regarder

3 (impersonal) on; **one never knows** on ne sait jamais; **to cut one's finger** se couper le doigt; **one needs to eat** il faut manger

one-off [wʌnˈɒf] n (BRIT inf) exemplaire m unique

oneself [wʌnˈself] pron se; (after prep, also emphatic) soi-même; **to hurt ~** se faire mal; **to keep sth for ~** garder qch pour soi; **to talk to ~** se parler à soi-même; **by ~** tout seul

one: **one-shot** [wʌnˈʃɒt] (US) n = **one-off**; **one-sided** adj (argument, decision) unilatéral(e); **one-to-one** adj (relationship) univoque; **one-way** adj (street, traffic) à sens unique

ongoing [ˈɒngəʊɪŋ] adj en cours; (relationship) suivi(e)

onion [ˈʌnjən] n oignon m

on-line [ˈɒnlaɪn] adj (Comput) en ligne; (: switched on) connecté(e)

onlooker [ˈɒnlʊkəʳ] n spectateur(-trice)

only [ˈəʊnlɪ] adv seulement ▷ adj seul(e), unique ▷ conj seulement, mais; **an ~ child** un enfant unique; **not ~ ... but also** non seulement ... mais aussi; **I ~ took one** j'en ai seulement pris un, je n'en ai pris qu'un

on-screen [ɒnˈskriːn] adj à l'écran

onset [ˈɒnset] n début m; (of winter, old age) approche f

onto [ˈɒntu] prep = **on to**

onward(s) [ˈɒnwəd(z)] adv (move) en avant; **from that time ~** à partir de ce moment

oops [ʊps] excl houp!

ooze [uːz] vi suinter

opaque [əʊˈpeɪk] adj opaque

open [ˈəʊpn] adj ouvert(e); (car) découvert(e); (road, view) dégagé(e); (meeting) public(-ique); (admiration) manifeste ▷ vt ouvrir ▷ vi (flower, eyes, door, debate) s'ouvrir; (shop, bank, museum) ouvrir; (book etc: commence) commencer, débuter; **is it ~ to public?** est-ce ouvert au public?; **what time do you ~?** à quelle heure ouvrez-vous?; **in the ~ (air)** en plein air; **open up** vt ouvrir; (blocked road) dégager ▷ vi s'ouvrir; **open-air** adj en plein air; **opening** n ouverture f, (opportunity) occasion f, (work) débouché m; (job) poste vacant; **opening hours** npl heures fpl d'ouverture; **open learning** n enseignement universitaire à la carte, notamment par correspondance; (distance learning) télé-enseignement m; **openly** adv ouvertement; **open-minded** adj à l'esprit ouvert; **open-necked** adj à col ouvert; **open-plan** adj sans cloisons; **Open University** n (BRIT) cours universitaires par correspondance

opera [ˈɒpərə] n opéra m; **opera house** n opéra m; **opera singer** n chanteur(-euse) d'opéra

operate [ˈɒpəreɪt] vt (machine) faire marcher, faire fonctionner ▷ vi fonctionner; **to ~ on sb (for)** (Med) opérer qn (de)

operating room n (US: Med) salle f d'opération

operating theatre n (BRIT: Med) salle f d'opération

operation [ɒpəˈreɪʃən] n opération f; (of machine) fonctionnement m; **to have an ~ (for)** se faire opérer (de); **to be in ~** (machine) être en service; (system) être en vigueur; **operational** adj opérationnel(le); (ready for use) en état de marche

operative [ˈɒpərətɪv] adj (measure) en vigueur ▷ n (in factory) ouvrier(-ière)

operator [ˈɒpəreɪtəʳ] n (of machine) opérateur(-trice); (Tel) téléphoniste m/f

opinion [əˈpɪnjən] n opinion f, avis m; **in my ~** à mon avis; **opinion poll** n sondage m d'opinion

opponent [əˈpəʊnənt] n adversaire m/f

opportunity [ɒpəˈtjuːnɪtɪ] n occasion f; **to take the ~ to do** or **of doing** profiter de l'occasion pour faire

oppose [əˈpəʊz] vt s'opposer à; **to be ~d to sth** être opposé(e) à qch; **as ~d to** par opposition à

opposite [ˈɒpəzɪt] adj opposé(e); (house etc) d'en face ▷ adv en face ▷ prep en face de ▷ n opposé m, contraire m; (of word) contraire

opposition [ɒpəˈzɪʃən] n opposition f

oppress [əˈpres] vt opprimer

opt [ɒpt] vi: **to ~ for** opter pour; **to ~ to do** choisir de faire; **opt out** vi: **to ~ out of** choisir de ne pas participer à or ne pas adhérer

optician [ɒpˈtɪʃən] n opticien(ne)

optimism [ˈɒptɪmɪzəm] n optimisme m

optimist [ˈɒptɪmɪst] n optimiste m/f; **optimistic** [ɒptɪˈmɪstɪk] adj optimiste

optimum [ˈɒptɪməm] adj optimum

option [ˈɒpʃən] n choix m, option f; (Scol) matière f à option; **optional** adj facultatif(-ive)

or [ɔːʳ] conj ou; (with negative): **he hasn't seen or heard anything** il n'a rien vu ni entendu; **or else** sinon; ou bien

oral [ˈɔːrəl] adj oral(e) ▷ n oral m

orange [ˈɒrɪndʒ] n (fruit) orange f ▷ adj orange inv; **orange juice** n jus m d'orange; **orange squash** n orangeade f

orbit [ˈɔːbɪt] n orbite f ▷ vt graviter autour de

orchard [ˈɔːtʃəd] n verger m

orchestra [ˈɔːkɪstrə] n orchestre m; (US: seating) (fauteuils mpl d')orchestre

orchid [ˈɔːkɪd] n orchidée f

ordeal [ɔːˈdiːl] n épreuve f

order [ˈɔːdəʳ] n ordre m; (Comm) commande f ▷ vt ordonner; (Comm) commander; **in ~** en ordre; (of document) en règle; **out of ~** (not in correct order) en désordre; (machine) hors service; (telephone) en dérangement; **a machine in working ~** une machine en état de marche; **in ~ to do/that** pour faire/que + sub; **could I ~ now, please?** je peux commander, s'il vous plaît?; **to be on ~** être en commande; **to ~ sb to do** ordonner à qn de faire; **order form** n bon m de commande; **orderly** n (Mil) ordonnance f, (Med) garçon m de salle ▷ adj (room) en ordre; (mind) méthodique; (person) qui a de l'ordre

ordinary [ˈɔːdnrɪ] adj ordinaire, normal(e); (pej) ordinaire, quelconque; **out of the ~** exceptionnel(le)

ore [ɔːʳ] n minerai m

oregano [ɒrɪˈgɑːnəʊ] n origan m

organ [ˈɔːgən] n organe m; (Mus) orgue m, orgues fpl; **organic** [ɔːˈgænɪk] adj organique; (crops etc) biologique, naturel(le); **organism** n organisme m

organization [ɔːɡənaɪˈzeɪʃən] n organisation f

organize [ˈɔːɡənaɪz] vt organiser; **organized** [ˈɔːɡənaɪzd] adj (planned) organisé(e); (efficient) bien organisé; **organizer** n organisateur(-trice)

orgasm [ˈɔːɡæzəm] n orgasme m

orgy [ˈɔːdʒɪ] n orgie f

oriental [ɔːrɪˈɛntl] adj oriental(e)

orientation [ɔːrɪɛnˈteɪʃən] n (attitudes) tendance f; (in job) orientation f; (of building) orientation, exposition f

origin [ˈɒrɪdʒɪn] n origine f

original [əˈrɪdʒɪnl] adj original(e); (earliest) originel(le) ▷ n original m; **originally** adv (at first) à l'origine

originate [əˈrɪdʒɪneɪt] vi: to ~ from être originaire de; (suggestion) provenir de; to ~ in (custom) prendre naissance dans, avoir son origine dans

Orkney [ˈɔːknɪ] n (also: **the ~s, the ~ Islands**) les Orcades fpl

ornament [ˈɔːnəmənt] n ornement m; (trinket) bibelot m; **ornamental** [ɔːnəˈmɛntl] adj décoratif(-ive); (garden) d'agrément

ornate [ɔːˈneɪt] adj très orné(e)

orphan [ˈɔːfn] n orphelin(e)

orthodox [ˈɔːθədɒks] adj orthodoxe

orthopaedic (us **orthopedic**) [ɔːθəˈpiːdɪk] adj orthopédique

osteopath [ˈɒstɪəpæθ] n ostéopathe m/f

ostrich [ˈɒstrɪtʃ] n autruche f

other [ˈʌðəʳ] adj autre ▷ pron: **the ~ (one)** l'autre; **~s** (other people) d'autres b adv: **~ than** autrement que; à part; **the ~ day** l'autre jour; **otherwise** adv, conj autrement

Ottawa [ˈɒtəwə] n Ottawa

otter [ˈɒtəʳ] n loutre f

ouch [autʃ] excl aïe!

ought (pt ~) [ɔːt] aux vb: **I ~ to do it** je devrais le faire, il faudrait que je le fasse; **this ~ to have been corrected** cela aurait dû être corrigé; **he ~ to win** (probability) il devrait gagner

ounce [auns] n once f (28.35g; 16 in a pound)

our [ˈauəʳ] adj notre, nos pl; see also **my**; **ours** pron le (la) nôtre, les nôtres; see also **mine¹**; **ourselves** pron pl (reflexive, after preposition) nous; (emphatic) nous-mêmes; see also **oneself**

oust [aust] vt évincer

out [aut] adv dehors; (published, not at home etc) sorti(e); (light, fire) éteint(e); **~ there** là-bas; **he's ~** (absent) il est sorti; **to be ~ in one's calculations** s'être trompé dans ses calculs; **to run/back** etc ~ sortir en courant/en reculant etc; **~ loud** adv à haute voix; **~ of** prep (outside) en dehors de; (because of: anger etc) par; (from among): **10 ~ of 10** 10 sur 10; (without): **~ of petrol** sans essence, à court d'essence; **~ of order** (machine) en panne; (Tel: line) en dérangement; **outback** n (in Australia) intérieur m; **outbound** adj: **outbound (from/for)** en partance (de/pour); **outbreak** n (of violence) éruption f, explosion f; (of disease) de nombreux cas; **the outbreak of war south of the border** la guerre qui s'est déclarée au sud de la frontière; **outburst** n explosion f, accès m; **outcast** n exilé(e); (socially) paria m; **outcome** n issue f, résultat m; **outcry** n tollé (général); **outdated** adj démodé(e); **outdoor** adj de or en plein air; **outdoors** adv dehors; au grand air

outer [ˈautəʳ] adj extérieur(e); **outer space** n espace m cosmique

outfit [ˈautfɪt] n (clothes) tenue f

out: outgoing adj (president, tenant) sortant(e); (character) ouvert(e), extraverti(e); **outgoings** npl (BRIT: expenses) dépenses fpl; **outhouse** n appentis m, remise f

outing [ˈautɪŋ] n sortie f; excursion f

out: outlaw n hors-la-loi m inv ▷ vt (person) mettre hors la loi; (practice) proscrire; **outlay** n dépenses fpl; (investment) mise f de fonds; **outlet** n (for liquid etc) issue f, sortie f; (for emotion) exutoire m; (also: **retail outlet**) point m de vente; (us: Elec) prise f de courant; **outline** n (shape) contour m; (summary) esquisse f, grandes lignes ▷ vt (fig: theory, plan) exposer à grands traits; **outlook** n perspective f; (point of view) attitude f; **outnumber** vt surpasser en nombre; **out-of-date** adj (passport, ticket) périmé(e); (theory, idea) dépassé(e); (custom) désuet(-ète); (clothes) démodé(e); **out-of-doors** adv **=outdoors; out-of-the-way** adj loin de tout; **out-of-town** adj (shopping centre etc) en périphérie; **outpatient** n malade m/f en consultation externe; **outpost** n avant-poste m; **output** n rendement m, production f; (Comput) sortie f ▷ vt (Comput) sortir

outrage [ˈautreɪdʒ] n (anger) indignation f; (violent act) atrocité f, acte m de violence; (scandal) scandale m ▷ vt outrager; **outrageous** [autˈreɪdʒəs] adj atroce; (scandalous) scandaleux(-euse)

outright adv [autˈraɪt] complètement; (deny, refuse) catégoriquement; (ask) carrément; (kill) sur le coup ▷ adj [ˈautraɪt] complet(-ète); catégorique

outset [ˈautsɛt] n début m

outside [autˈsaɪd] n extérieur m ▷ adj extérieur(e) ▷ adv (au) dehors, à l'extérieur ▷ prep hors de, à l'extérieur de; (in front of) devant; **at the ~** (fig) au plus or maximum; **outside lane** n (Aut: in Britain) voie f de droite; (: in US, Europe) voie de gauche; **outside line** n (Tel) ligne extérieure; **outsider** n (stranger) étranger(-ère)

out: outsize adj énorme; (clothes) grande taille inv; **outskirts** npl faubourgs mpl; **outspoken** adj très franc (franche); **outstanding** adj remarquable, exceptionnel(le); (unfinished: work, business) en suspens, en souffrance; (debt) impayé(e); (problem) non réglé(e)

outward [ˈautwəd] adj (sign, appearances) extérieur(e); (journey) d'aller; **outwards** adv (esp BRIT) **=outward**

outweigh [autˈweɪ] vt l'emporter sur

oval [ˈəuvl] adj, n ovale m

ovary [ˈəuvərɪ] n ovaire m

oven [ˈʌvn] n four m; **oven glove** n gant m de cuisine; **ovenproof** adj allant au four; **oven-ready** adj prêt(e) à cuire

over [ˈəuvəʳ] adv (par-)dessus ▷ adj (or adv) (finished) fini(e), terminé(e); (too much) en plus ▷ prep sur; par-dessus; (above) au-dessus de; (on the other side of) de l'autre côté de; (more than) plus de; (during) pendant; (about, concerning): **they fell out ~ money/her** ils se sont brouillés pour des questions d'argent/à cause d'elle; **~ here** ici; **~ there** là-bas; **all ~** (everywhere) partout; **~ and ~ (again)** à plusieurs reprises; **~ and above** en plus de; **to ask sb ~** inviter qn (à passer); **to fall ~** tomber; **to turn sth ~** retourner qch

overall [ˈəuvərɔːl] adj (length) total(e); (study, impression) d'ensemble ▷ n (BRIT) blouse f ▷ adv [əuvərˈɔːl] dans l'ensemble, en général; **overalls** npl (boiler suit) bleus mpl (de travail)

overboard [ˈəuvəbɔːd] adv (Naut) par-dessus bord

overcame [əuvəˈkeɪm] pt of **overcome**

overcast ['əʊvəkɑːst] *adj* couvert(e)
overcharge [əʊvə'tʃɑːdʒ] *vt*: **to ~ sb for sth** faire payer qch trop cher à qn
overcoat ['əʊvəkəʊt] *n* pardessus *m*
overcome [əʊvə'kʌm] *vt* (*irreg: like* **come**) (*defeat*) triompher de; (*difficulty*) surmonter ▷ *adj* (*emotionally*) bouleversé(e); **~ with grief** accablé(e) de douleur
over: **overcrowded** *adj* (*city, country*) surpeuplé(e); **overdo** *vt* (*irreg: like* **do**) exagérer; (*overcook*) trop cuire; **to overdo it, to overdo things** (*work too hard*) en faire trop, se surmener; **overdone** [əʊvə'dʌn] *adj* (*vegetables, steak*) trop cuit(e); **overdose** *n* dose excessive; **overdraft** *n* découvert *m*; **overdrawn** *adj* (*account*) à découvert; **overdue** *adj* en retard; (*bill*) impayé(e); (*change*) qui tarde; **overestimate** *vt* surestimer
overflow *vi* [əʊvə'fləʊ] déborder ▷ *n* ['əʊvəfləʊ] (*also*: **~ pipe**) tuyau *m* d'écoulement, trop-plein *m*
overgrown [əʊvə'grəʊn] *adj* (*garden*) envahi(e) par la végétation
overhaul *vt* [əʊvə'hɔːl] réviser ▷ *n* ['əʊvəhɔːl] révision *f*
overhead *adv* [əʊvə'hɛd] au-dessus ▷ *adj, n* ['əʊvəhɛd] ▷ *adj* aérien(ne); (*lighting*) vertical(e) ▷ *n* (*us*) = **overheads**; **overhead projector** *n* rétroprojecteur *m*; **overheads** *npl* (*BRIT*) frais généraux
over: **overhear** *vt* (*irreg: like* **hear**) entendre (par hasard); **overheat** *vi* (*engine*) chauffer; **overland** *adj, adv* par voie de terre; **overlap** *vi* se chevaucher; **overleaf** *adv* au verso; **overload** *vt* surcharger; **overlook** *vt* (*have view of*) donner sur; (*miss*) oublier, négliger; (*forgive*) fermer les yeux sur
overnight *adv* [əʊvə'naɪt] (*happen*) durant la nuit; (*fig*) soudain ▷ *adj* ['əʊvənaɪt] d'une (*or* de) nuit; soudain(e); **to stay ~ (with sb)** passer la nuit (chez qn); **overnight bag** *n* nécessaire *m* de voyage
overpass ['əʊvəpɑːs] *n* (*us: for cars*) pont autoroutier; (: *for pedestrians*) passerelle *f*, pont *m*
overpower [əʊvə'paʊəʳ] *vt* vaincre; (*fig*) accabler; **overpowering** *adj* irrésistible; (*heat, stench*) suffocant(e)
over: **overreact** [əʊvəriː'ækt] *vi* réagir de façon excessive; **overrule** *vt* (*decision*) annuler; (*claim*) rejeter; (*person*) rejeter l'avis de; **overrun** *vt* (*irreg: like* **run**) (*Mil: country etc*) occuper; (*time limit etc*) dépasser ▷ *vi* dépasser le temps imparti
overseas [əʊvə'siːz] *adv* outre-mer; (*abroad*) à l'étranger ▷ *adj* (*trade*) extérieur(e); (*visitor*) étranger(-ère)
oversee [əʊvə'siː] *vt* (*irreg: like* **see**) surveiller
overshadow [əʊvə'ʃædəʊ] *vt* (*fig*) éclipser
oversight ['əʊvəsaɪt] *n* omission *f*, oubli *m*
oversleep [əʊvə'sliːp] *vi* (*irreg: like* **sleep**) se réveiller (trop) tard
overspend [əʊvə'spɛnd] *vi* (*irreg: like* **spend**) dépenser de trop
overt [əʊ'vəːt] *adj* non dissimulé(e)
overtake [əʊvə'teɪk] *vt* (*irreg: like* **take**) dépasser; (*BRIT: Aut*) dépasser, doubler
over: **overthrow** *vt* (*irreg: like* **throw**) (*government*) renverser; **overtime** *n* heures *fpl* supplémentaires
overtook [əʊvə'tʊk] *pt of* **overtake**
over: **overturn** *vt* renverser; (*decision, plan*) annuler ▷ *vi* se retourner; **overweight** *adj* (*person*) trop gros(se); **overwhelm** *vt* (*subj: emotion*) accabler, submerger; (*enemy, opponent*) écraser; **overwhelming** *adj* (*victory, defeat*) écrasant(e); (*desire*) irrésistible

ow [aʊ] *excl* aïe!
owe [əʊ] *vt* devoir; **to ~ sb sth, to ~ sth to sb** devoir qch à qn; **how much do I ~ you?** combien est-ce que je vous dois?; **owing to** *prep* à cause de, en raison de
owl [aʊl] *n* hibou *m*
own [əʊn] *vt* posséder ▷ *adj* propre; **a room of my ~** une chambre à moi, ma propre chambre; **to get one's ~ back** prendre sa revanche; **on one's ~** tout(e) seul(e); **own up** *vi* avouer; **owner** *n* propriétaire *m/f*; **ownership** *n* possession *f*
ox (*pl* **oxen**) [ɔks, 'ɔksn] *n* bœuf *m*
Oxbridge ['ɔksbrɪdʒ] *n* (*BRIT*) les universités d'Oxford et de Cambridge
oxen ['ɔksən] *npl of* **ox**
oxygen ['ɔksɪdʒən] *n* oxygène *m*
oyster ['ɔɪstəʳ] *n* huître *f*
oz. *abbr* = **ounce(s)**
ozone ['əʊzəʊn] *n* ozone *m*; **ozone friendly** *adj* qui n'attaque pas *or* qui préserve la couche d'ozone; **ozone layer** *n* couche *f* d'ozone

p *abbr* (*BRIT*) = **penny**; **pence**
P.A. *n abbr* = **personal assistant**; **public address system**
p.a. *abbr* = **per annum**
pace [peɪs] *n* pas *m*; (*speed*) allure *f*, vitesse *f* ▷ *vi*: **to ~ up and down** faire les cent pas; **to keep ~ with** aller à la même vitesse que; (*events*) se tenir au courant de; **pacemaker** *n* (*Med*) stimulateur *m* cardiaque; (*Sport: also*: **pacesetter**) meneur(-euse) de train
Pacific [pə'sɪfɪk] *n*: **the ~ (Ocean)** le Pacifique, l'océan *m* Pacifique
pacifier ['pæsɪfaɪəʳ] *n* (*us: dummy*) tétine *f*
pack [pæk] *n* paquet *m*; (*of hounds*) meute *f*; (*of thieves*,

wolves etc) bande f; (*of cards*) jeu m; (*us: of cigarettes*)
paquet m; (*back pack*) sac m à dos ▷ vt (*goods*) empaqueter,
emballer; (*in suitcase etc*) emballer; (*box*) remplir; (*cram*)
entasser ▷ vi: **to ~ (one's bags)** faire ses bagages; **pack
in** (BRIT inf) vi (*machine*) tomber en panne ▷ vt (*boyfriend*)
plaquer; **~ it in!** laisse tomber!; **pack off** vt: **to ~ sb off to**
expédier qn à; **pack up** (BRIT inf: *machine*) tomber en
panne; (: *person*) se tirer ▷ vt (*belongings*) ranger; (*goods,
presents*) empaqueter, emballer
package ['pækɪdʒ] n paquet m; (*also: ~ deal: agreement*)
marché global; (: *purchase*) forfait m; (Comput) progiciel
m ▷ vt (*goods*) conditionner; **package holiday** n (BRIT)
vacances organisées; **package tour** n voyage organisé
packaging ['pækɪdʒɪŋ] n (*wrapping materials*)
emballage m
packed [pækt] adj (*crowded*) bondé(e); **packed lunch**
(BRIT) n repas froid
packet ['pækɪt] n paquet m
packing ['pækɪŋ] n emballage m
pact [pækt] n pacte m, traité m
pad [pæd] n bloc(-notes m) m; (*to prevent friction*) tampon
m ▷ vt rembourrer; **padded** adj (*jacket*) matelassé(e);
(*bra*) rembourré(e)
paddle ['pædl] n (*oar*) pagaie f; (*us: for table tennis*)
raquette f de ping-pong ▷ vi (*with feet*) barboter, faire
trempette ▷ vt: **to ~ a canoe** etc pagayer; **paddling pool**
n petit bassin
paddock ['pædək] n enclos m; (Racing) paddock m
padlock ['pædlɔk] n cadenas m
paedophile (*us* **pedophile**) ['piːdəʊfaɪl] n pédophile m
page [peɪdʒ] n (*of book*) page f; (*also: ~ boy*) groom m,
chasseur m; (*at wedding*) garçon m d'honneur ▷ vt (*in
hotel etc*) (faire) appeler
pager ['peɪdʒə] n bip m (inf), Alphapage® m
paid [peɪd] pt, pp of **pay** ▷ adj (*work, official*) rémunéré(e);
(*holiday*) payé(e); **to put ~ to** (BRIT) mettre fin à, mettre
par terre
pain [peɪn] n douleur f; (*inf: nuisance*) plaie f; **to be
in ~** souffrir, avoir mal; **to take ~s to do** se donner
du mal pour faire; **painful** adj douloureux(-euse);
(*difficult*) difficile, pénible; **painkiller** n calmant m,
analgésique m; **painstaking** ['peɪnzteɪkɪŋ] adj (*person*)
soigneux(-euse); (*work*) soigné(e)
paint [peɪnt] n peinture f ▷ vt peindre; **to ~ the door
blue** peindre la porte en bleu; **paintbrush** n pinceau m;
painter n peintre m; **painting** n peinture f; (*picture*)
tableau m
pair [peə] n (*of shoes, gloves etc*) paire f; (*of people*) couple
m; **~ of scissors** (paire de) ciseaux mpl; **~ of trousers**
pantalon m
pajamas [pəˈdʒɑːməz] npl (*us*) pyjama(s) m(pl)
Pakistan [pɑːkɪˈstɑːn] n Pakistan m; **Pakistani** adj
pakistanais(e) ▷ n Pakistanais(e)
pal [pæl] n (inf) copain (copine)
palace ['pæləs] n palais m
pale [peɪl] adj pâle; **~ blue** adj bleu pâle inv
Palestine ['pælɪstaɪn] n Palestine f; **Palestinian**
[pælɪsˈtɪnɪən] adj palestinien(ne) ▷ n Palestinien(ne)
palm [pɑːm] n (Anat) paume f; (*also: ~ tree*) palmier m
▷ vt: **to ~ sth off on sb** (inf) refiler qch à qn
pamper ['pæmpə] vt gâter, dorloter
pamphlet ['pæmflət] n brochure f
pan [pæn] n (*also: sauce~*) casserole f; (*also: frying ~*)
poêle f

pancake ['pænkeɪk] n crêpe f
panda ['pændə] n panda m
pane [peɪn] n carreau m (de fenêtre), vitre f
panel ['pænl] n (*of wood, cloth etc*) panneau m; (Radio, TV)
panel m, invités mpl; (*for interview, exams*) jury m
panhandler ['pænhændlə] n (*us inf*) mendiant(e)
panic ['pænɪk] n panique f, affolement m ▷ vi s'affoler,
paniquer
panorama [pænəˈrɑːmə] n panorama m
pansy ['pænzɪ] n (Bot) pensée f
pant [pænt] vi haleter
panther ['pænθə] n panthère f
panties ['pæntɪz] npl slip m, culotte f
pantomime ['pæntəmaɪm] n (BRIT) spectacle m de
Noël
pants [pænts] n (BRIT: *woman's*) culotte f, slip m; (: *man's*)
slip, caleçon m; (*us: trousers*) pantalon m
pantyhose ['pæntɪhəʊz] (*us*) npl collant m
paper ['peɪpə] n papier m; (*also: wall~*) papier peint;
(*also: news~*) journal m; (*academic essay*) article m; (*exam*)
épreuve écrite ▷ adj en or de papier ▷ vt tapisser (de
papier peint); **papers** npl (*also: identity ~s*) papiers
mpl (d'identité); **paperback** n livre broché or non
relié; (*small*) livre m de poche; **paper bag** n sac m en
papier; **paper clip** n trombone m; **paper shop** n (BRIT)
marchand m de journaux; **paperwork** n papiers mpl;
(*pej*) paperasserie f
paprika ['pæprɪkə] n paprika m
par [pɑː] n (Golf) normale f du parcours; **on a ~
with** à égalité avec, au même niveau que
paracetamol [pærəˈsiːtəmɔl] (BRIT) n paracétamol m
parachute ['pærəʃuːt] n parachute m
parade [pəˈreɪd] n défilé m ▷ vt (*fig*) faire étalage de
▷ vi défiler
paradise ['pærədaɪs] n paradis m
paradox ['pærədɔks] n paradoxe m
paraffin ['pærəfɪn] n (BRIT): **~ (oil)** pétrole (lampant)
paragraph ['pærəgrɑːf] n paragraphe m
parallel ['pærəlel] adj: **~ (with or to)** parallèle (à); (*fig*)
analogue (à) ▷ n (*line*) parallèle f; (*fig, Geo*) parallèle m
paralysed ['pærəlaɪzd] adj paralysé(e)
paralysis (*pl* **paralyses**) [pəˈrælɪsɪs, -siːz] n paralysie f
paramedic [pærəˈmedɪk] n auxiliaire m/f médical(e)
paranoid ['pærənɔɪd] adj (Psych) paranoïaque;
(*neurotic*) paranoïde
parasite ['pærəsaɪt] n parasite m
parcel ['pɑːsl] n paquet m, colis m ▷ vt (*also: ~ up*)
empaqueter
pardon ['pɑːdn] n pardon m; (Law) grâce f ▷ vt
pardonner à; (Law) gracier; **~!** pardon!; **~ me!** (*after
burping etc*) excusez-moi!; **I beg your ~!** je suis désolé!;
(**I beg your**) **~?** (*us*): **~ me?** (*what
did you say?*) pardon?
parent ['peərənt] n (*father*) père m; (*mother*) mère
f; **parents** npl parents mpl; **parental** [pəˈrentl] adj
parental(e), des parents
Paris ['pærɪs] n Paris
parish ['pærɪʃ] n paroisse f; (BRIT: *civil*) ≈ commune f
Parisian [pəˈrɪzɪən] adj parisien(ne), de Paris ▷ n
Parisien(ne)
park [pɑːk] n parc m, jardin public ▷ vt garer ▷ vi se
garer; **can I ~ here?** est-ce que je peux me garer ici?
parking ['pɑːkɪŋ] n stationnement m; **"no ~"**
"stationnement interdit"; **parking lot** n (*us*) parking

m, parc *m* de stationnement; **parking meter** *n* parc(o)mètre *m*; **parking ticket** *n* P.-V. *m*

parkway ['pɑːkweɪ] *n* (*us*) route *f* express (*en site vert ou aménagé*)

parliament ['pɑːləmənt] *n* parlement *m*; **parliamentary** [pɑːlə'mɛntəri] *adj* parlementaire

Parmesan [pɑːmɪ'zæn] *n* (*also: ~ cheese*) Parmesan *m*

parole [pə'rəul] *n*: **on ~** en liberté conditionnelle

parrot ['pærət] *n* perroquet *m*

parsley ['pɑːslɪ] *n* persil *m*

parsnip ['pɑːsnɪp] *n* panais *m*

parson ['pɑːsn] *n* ecclésiastique *m*; (*Church of England*) pasteur *m*

part [pɑːt] *n* partie *f*; (*of machine*) pièce *f*; (*Theat etc*) rôle *m*; (*of serial*) épisode *m*; (*us: in hair*) raie *f* ▷ *adv* = **partly** ▷ *vt* séparer ▷ *vi* (*people*) se séparer; (*crowd*) s'ouvrir; **to take ~ in** participer à, prendre part à; **to take sb's ~** prendre le parti de qn, prendre parti pour qn; **for my ~** en ce qui me concerne; **for the most ~** en grande partie; dans la plupart des cas; **in ~** en partie; **to take sth in good/bad ~** prendre qch du bon/mauvais côté; **part with** *vt fus* (*person*) se séparer de; (*possessions*) se défaire de

partial ['pɑːʃl] *adj* (*incomplete*) partiel(le); **to be ~ to** aimer, avoir un faible pour

participant [pɑː'tɪsɪpənt] *n* (*in competition, campaign*) participant(e)

participate [pɑː'tɪsɪpeɪt] *vi*: **to ~ (in)** participer (à), prendre part (à)

particle ['pɑːtɪkl] *n* particule *f*; (*of dust*) grain *m*

particular [pə'tɪkjulə] *adj* (*specific*) particulier(-ière); (*special*) particulier, spécial(e); (*fussy*) difficile, exigeant(e); (*careful*) méticuleux(-euse); **in ~** en particulier, surtout; **particularly** *adv* particulièrement; (*in particular*) en particulier; **particulars** *npl* détails *mpl*; (*information*) renseignements *mpl*

parting ['pɑːtɪŋ] *n* séparation *f*; (*Brit: in hair*) raie *f*

partition [pɑː'tɪʃən] *n* (*Pol*) partition *f*, division *f*; (*wall*) cloison *f*

partly ['pɑːtlɪ] *adv* en partie, partiellement

partner ['pɑːtnə] *n* (*Comm*) associé(e); (*Sport*) partenaire *m/f*; (*spouse*) conjoint(e); (*lover*) ami(e); (*at dance*) cavalier(-ière); **partnership** *n* association *f*

part of speech *n* (*Ling*) partie *f* du discours

partridge ['pɑːtrɪdʒ] *n* perdrix *f*

part-time ['pɑːt'taɪm] *adj, adv* à mi-temps, à temps partiel

party ['pɑːtɪ] *n* (*Pol*) parti *m*; (*celebration*) fête *f*; (*: formal*) réception *f*; (*: in evening*) soirée *f*; (*group*) groupe *m*; (*Law*) partie *f*

pass [pɑːs] *vt* (*time, object*) passer; (*place*) passer devant; (*friend*) croiser; (*exam*) être reçu(e) à, réussir; (*overtake*) dépasser; (*approve*) approuver, accepter ▷ *vi* passer; (*Scol*) être reçu(e) or admis(e), réussir ▷ *n* (*permit*) laissez-passer *m inv*; (*membership card*) carte *f* d'accès or d'abonnement; (*in mountains*) col *m*; (*Sport*) passe *f*; (*Scol: also: ~ mark*): **to get a ~** être reçu(e) (sans mention); **to ~ sb sth** passer qch à qn; **could you ~ the salt/oil, please?** pouvez-vous me passer le sel/l'huile, s'il vous plaît?; **to make a ~ at sb** (*inf*) faire des avances à qn; **pass away** *vi* mourir; **pass by** *vi* passer ▷ *vt* (*ignore*) négliger; **pass on** *vt* (*hand on*): **to ~ on (to)** transmettre (à); **pass out** *vi* s'évanouir; **pass over** *vt* (*ignore*) passer sous silence; **pass up** *vt* (*opportunity*) laisser passer;

passable *adj* (*road*) praticable; (*work*) acceptable

passage ['pæsɪdʒ] *n* (*also: ~way*) couloir *m*; (*gen, in book*) passage *m*; (*by boat*) traversée *f*

passenger ['pæsɪndʒə] *n* passager(-ère)

passer-by [pɑːsə'baɪ] *n* passant(e)

passing place *n* (*Aut*) aire *f* de croisement

passion ['pæʃən] *n* passion *f*; **passionate** *adj* passionné(e); **passion fruit** *n* fruit *m* de la passion

passive ['pæsɪv] *adj* (*also Ling*) passif(-ive)

passport ['pɑːspɔːt] *n* passeport *m*; **passport control** *n* contrôle *m* des passeports; **passport office** *n* bureau *m* de délivrance des passeports

password ['pɑːswɜːd] *n* mot *m* de passe

past [pɑːst] *prep* (*in front of*) devant; (*further than*) au delà de, plus loin que; après; (*later than*) après ▷ *adv*: **to run ~** passer en courant ▷ *adj* passé(e); (*president etc*) ancien(ne) ▷ *n* passé *m*; **he's ~ forty** il a dépassé la quarantaine, il a plus de or passé quarante ans; **ten/ quarter ~ eight** huit heures dix/un or et quart; **for the ~ few/3 days** depuis quelques/3 jours; ces derniers/3 derniers jours

pasta ['pæstə] *n* pâtes *fpl*

paste [peɪst] *n* pâte *f*; (*Culin: meat*) pâté *m* (à tartiner); (*: tomato*) purée *f*, concentré *m*; (*glue*) colle *f* (de pâte) ▷ *vt* coller

pastel ['pæstl] *adj* pastel *inv* ▷ *n* (*Art: pencil*) (crayon *m*) pastel *m*; (*: drawing*) (dessin *m* au) pastel; (*colour*) ton *m* pastel *inv*

pasteurized ['pæstəraɪzd] *adj* pasteurisé(e)

pastime ['pɑːstaɪm] *n* passe-temps *m inv*, distraction *f*

pastor ['pɑːstə] *n* pasteur *m*

past participle [-'tɪsɪpl] *n* (*Ling*) participe passé

pastry ['peɪstrɪ] *n* pâte *f*; (*cake*) pâtisserie *f*

pasture ['pɑːstʃə] *n* pâturage *m*

pasty¹ *n* ['pæstɪ] petit pâté (en croûte)

pasty² ['peɪstɪ] *adj* (*complexion*) terreux(-euse)

pat [pæt] *vt* donner une petite tape à; (*dog*) caresser

patch [pætʃ] *n* (*of material*) pièce *f*; (*eye patch*) cache *m*; (*spot*) tache *f*; (*of land*) parcelle *f*; (*on tyre*) rustine *f* ▷ *vt* (*clothes*) rapiécer; **a bad ~** (*Brit*) une période difficile; **patchy** *adj* inégal(e); (*incomplete*) fragmentaire

pâté ['pæteɪ] *n* pâté *m*, terrine *f*

patent ['peɪtnt] (*us*) ['pætnt] *n* brevet *m* (d'invention) ▷ *vt* faire breveter ▷ *adj* patent(e), manifeste

paternal [pə'tɜːnl] *adj* paternel(le)

paternity leave [pə'tɜːnɪtɪ-] *n* congé *m* de paternité

path [pɑːθ] *n* chemin *m*, sentier *m*; (*in garden*) allée *f*; (*of missile*) trajectoire *f*

pathetic [pə'θɛtɪk] *adj* (*pitiful*) pitoyable; (*very bad*) lamentable, minable

pathway ['pɑːθweɪ] *n* chemin *m*, sentier *m*; (*in garden*) allée *f*

patience ['peɪʃns] *n* patience *f*; (*Brit: Cards*) réussite *f*

patient ['peɪʃnt] *n* malade *m/f*; (*of dentist etc*) patient(e) ▷ *adj* patient(e)

patio ['pætɪəu] *n* patio *m*

patriotic [pætrɪ'ɔtɪk] *adj* patriotique; (*person*) patriote

patrol [pə'trəul] *n* patrouille *f* ▷ *vt* patrouiller dans; **patrol car** *n* voiture *f* de police

patron ['peɪtrən] *n* (*in shop*) client(e); (*of charity*) patron(ne); **~ of the arts** mécène *m*

patronizing ['pætrənaɪzɪŋ] *adj* condescendant(e)

pattern ['pætən] *n* (*Sewing*) patron *m*; (*design*) motif *m*; **patterned** *adj* à motifs

pause [pɔːz] *n* pause *f*, arrêt *m* ▷ *vi* faire une pause, s'arrêter

pave [peɪv] *vt* paver, daller; **to ~ the way for** ouvrir la voie à

pavement ['peɪvmənt] *n* (BRIT) trottoir *m*; (US) chaussée *f*

pavilion [pə'vɪliən] *n* pavillon *m*; (Sport) stand *m*

paving ['peɪvɪŋ] *n* (material) pavé *m*, dalle *f*

paw [pɔː] *n* patte *f*

pawn [pɔːn] *n* (Chess, also fig) pion *m* ▷ *vt* mettre en gage; **pawnbroker** *n* prêteur *m* sur gages

pay [peɪ] *n* salaire *m*; (of manual worker) paie *f* ▷ *vb* (pt, pp **paid**) ▷ *vt* payer ▷ *vi* payer; (be profitable) être rentable; **can I ~ by credit card?** est-ce que je peux payer par carte de crédit?; **to ~ attention (to)** prêter attention (à); **to ~ sb a visit** rendre visite à qn; **to ~ one's respects to sb** présenter ses respects à qn; **pay back** *vt* rembourser; **pay for** *vt fus* payer; **pay in** *vt* verser; **pay off** *vt* (debts) régler, acquitter; (person) rembourser ▷ *vi* (scheme, decision) se révéler payant(e); **pay out** *vt* (money) payer, sortir de sa poche; **pay up** *vt* (amount) payer; **payable** *adj* payable; **to make a cheque payable to sb** établir un chèque à l'ordre de qn; **pay day** *n* jour *m* de paie; **pay envelope** *n* (US) paie *f*; **payment** *n* paiement *m*; (of bill) règlement *m*; (of deposit, cheque) versement *m*; **monthly payment** mensualité *f*; **payout** *n* (from insurance) dédommagement *m*; (in competition) prix *m*; **pay packet** *n* (BRIT) paie *f*; **pay phone** *n* cabine *f* téléphonique, téléphone public; **pay raise** *n* (US) = **pay rise**; **pay rise** *n* (BRIT) augmentation *f* (de salaire); **payroll** *n* registre *m* du personnel; **pay slip** *n* (BRIT) bulletin *m* de paie, feuille *f* de paie; **pay television** *n* chaînes *fpl* payantes

PC *n abbr* = **personal computer**; (BRIT) = **police constable** ▷ *adj abbr* = **politically correct**

p.c. *abbr* = **per cent**

PDA *n abbr* (= personal digital assistant) agenda *m* électronique

PE *n abbr* (= physical education) EPS *f*

pea [piː] *n* (petit) pois

peace [piːs] *n* paix *f*; (calm) calme *m*, tranquillité *f*; **peaceful** *adj* paisible, calme

peach [piːtʃ] *n* pêche *f*

peacock ['piːkɔk] *n* paon *m*

peak [piːk] *n* (mountain) pic *m*, cime *f*; (of cap) visière *f*; (fig: highest level) maximum *m*; (: of career, fame) apogée *m*; **peak hours** *npl* heures *fpl* d'affluence ou de pointe

peanut ['piːnʌt] *n* arachide *f*, cacahuète *f*; **peanut butter** *n* beurre *m* de cacahuète

pear [pɛəʳ] *n* poire *f*

pearl [pəːl] *n* perle *f*

peasant ['pɛznt] *n* paysan(ne)

peat [piːt] *n* tourbe *f*

pebble ['pɛbl] *n* galet *m*, caillou *m*

peck [pɛk] *vt* (also: **~ at**) donner un coup de bec à; (food) picorer ▷ *n* coup *m* de bec; (kiss) bécot *m*; **peckish** *adj* (BRIT inf): **I feel peckish** je mangerais bien quelque chose, j'ai la dent

peculiar [pɪ'kjuːliəʳ] *adj* (odd) étrange, bizarre, curieux(-euse); (particular) particulier(-ière); **~ to** particulier à

pedal ['pɛdl] *n* pédale *f* ▷ *vi* pédaler

pedalo ['pɛdələu] *n* pédalo *m*

pedestal ['pɛdəstl] *n* piédestal *m*

pedestrian [pɪ'dɛstrɪən] *n* piéton *m*; **pedestrian**

crossing *n* (BRIT) passage clouté; **pedestrianized** *adj*: **a pedestrianized street** une rue piétonne; **pedestrian precinct** (US **pedestrian zone**) *n* (BRIT) zone piétonne

pedigree ['pɛdɪgriː] *n* ascendance *f*; (of animal) pedigree *m* ▷ *cpd* (animal) de race

pedophile ['piːdəufaɪl] (US) *n* = **paedophile**

pee [piː] *vi* (inf) faire pipi, pisser

peek [piːk] *vi* jeter un coup d'œil (furtif)

peel [piːl] *n* pelure *f*, épluchure *f*; (of orange, lemon) écorce *f* ▷ *vt* peler, éplucher ▷ *vi* (paint etc) s'écailler; (wallpaper) se décoller; (skin) peler

peep [piːp] *n* (BRIT: look) coup d'œil furtif; (sound) pépiement *m* ▷ *vi* (BRIT) jeter un coup d'œil (furtif)

peer [pɪəʳ] *vi*: **to ~ at** regarder attentivement, scruter ▷ *n* (noble) pair *m*; (equal) pair, égal(e)

peg [pɛg] *n* (for coat etc) patère *f*; (BRIT: also: **clothes ~**) pince *f* à linge

pelican ['pɛlɪkən] *n* pélican *m*; **pelican crossing** *n* (BRIT Aut) feu *m* à commande manuelle

pelt [pɛlt] *vt*: **to ~ sb (with)** bombarder qn (de) ▷ *vi* (rain) tomber à seaux; (inf: run) courir à toutes jambes ▷ *n* peau *f*

pelvis ['pɛlvɪs] *n* bassin *m*

pen [pɛn] *n* (for writing) stylo *m*; (for sheep) parc *m*

penalty ['pɛnltɪ] *n* pénalité *f*; sanction *f*; (fine) amende *f*; (Sport) pénalisation *f*; (Football) penalty *m*; (Rugby) pénalité *f*

pence [pɛns] *npl of* **penny**

pencil ['pɛnsl] *n* crayon *m*; **pencil in** *vt* noter provisoirement; **pencil case** *n* trousse *f* (d'écolier); **pencil sharpener** *n* taille-crayon(s) *m inv*

pendant ['pɛndnt] *n* pendentif *m*

pending ['pɛndɪŋ] *prep* en attendant ▷ *adj* en suspens

penetrate ['pɛnɪtreɪt] *vt* pénétrer dans; (enemy territory) entrer en

penfriend ['pɛnfrɛnd] *n* (BRIT) correspondant(e)

penguin ['pɛŋgwɪn] *n* pingouin *m*

penicillin [pɛnɪ'sɪlɪn] *n* pénicilline *f*

peninsula [pə'nɪnsjulə] *n* péninsule *f*

penis ['piːnɪs] *n* pénis *m*, verge *f*

penitentiary [pɛnɪ'tɛnʃərɪ] *n* (US) prison *f*

penknife ['pɛnnaɪf] *n* canif *m*

penniless ['pɛnɪlɪs] *adj* sans le sou

penny (pl **pennies** or **pence**) ['pɛnɪ, 'pɛnɪz, pɛns] *n* (BRIT) penny *m*; (US) cent *m*

penpal ['pɛnpæl] *n* correspondant(e)

pension ['pɛnʃən] *n* (from company) retraite *f*; **pensioner** *n* (BRIT) retraité(e)

pentagon ['pɛntəgən] *n*: **the P~** (US Pol) le Pentagone

penthouse ['pɛnthaus] *n* appartement *m* (de luxe) en attique

penultimate [pɪ'nʌltɪmət] *adj* pénultième, avant-dernier(-ière)

people ['piːpl] *npl* gens *mpl*; personnes *fpl*; (inhabitants) population *f*; (Pol) peuple *m* ▷ *n* (nation, race) peuple *m*; **several ~ came** plusieurs personnes sont venues; **~ say that ...** on dit *ou* les gens disent que ...

pepper ['pɛpəʳ] *n* poivre *m*; (vegetable) poivron *m* ▷ *vt* (Culin) poivrer; **peppermint** *n* (sweet) pastille *f* de menthe

per [pəːʳ] *prep* par; **~ hour** (miles etc) à l'heure; (fee) (de) l'heure; **~ kilo** etc le kilo etc; **~ day/person** par jour/ personne; **~ annum** par an

perceive [pə'siːv] *vt* percevoir; (notice) remarquer,

s'apercevoir de

per cent adv pour cent

percentage [pə'sɛntɪdʒ] n pourcentage m

perception [pə'sɛpʃən] n perception f; (insight) sensibilité f

perch [pəːtʃ] n (fish) perche f; (for bird) perchoir m ▷ vi (se) percher

percussion [pə'kʌʃən] n percussion f

perennial [pə'rɛnɪəl] n (Bot) (plante f) vivace f, plante pluriannuelle

perfect ['pəːfɪkt] adj parfait(e) ▷ n (also: ~ **tense**) parfait m ▷ vt [pə'fɛkt] (technique, skill, work of art) parfaire; (method, plan) mettre au point; **perfection** [pə'fɛkʃən] n perfection f; **perfectly** ['pəːfɪktlɪ] adv parfaitement

perform [pə'fɔːm] vt (carry out) exécuter; (concert etc) jouer, donner ▷ vi (actor, musician) jouer; **performance** n représentation f, spectacle m; (of an artist) interprétation f; (Sport: of car, engine) performance f; (of company, economy) résultats mpl; **performer** n artiste m/f

perfume ['pəːfjuːm] n parfum m

perhaps [pə'hæps] adv peut-être

perimeter [pə'rɪmɪtəʳ] n périmètre m

period ['pɪərɪəd] n période f; (History) époque f; (Scol) cours m; (full stop) point m; (Med) règles fpl ▷ adj (costume, furniture) d'époque; **periodical** [pɪərɪ'ɔdɪkl] n périodique m; **periodically** adv périodiquement

perish ['pɛrɪʃ] vi périr, mourir; (decay) se détériorer

perjury ['pəːdʒərɪ] n (Law: in court) faux témoignage; (breach of oath) parjure m

perk [pəːk] n (inf) avantage m, à-côté m

perm [pəːm] n (for hair) permanente f

permanent ['pəːmənənt] adj permanent(e); **permanently** adv de façon permanente; (move abroad) définitivement; (open, closed) en permanence; (tired, unhappy) constamment

permission [pə'mɪʃən] n permission f, autorisation f

permit n ['pəːmɪt] permis m

perplex [pə'plɛks] vt (person) rendre perplexe

persecute ['pəːsɪkjuːt] vt persécuter

persecution [pəːsɪ'kjuːʃən] n persécution f

persevere [pəːsɪ'vɪəʳ] vi persévérer

Persian ['pəːʃən] adj persan(e); **the ~ Gulf** le golfe Persique

persist [pə'sɪst] vi: **to ~ (in doing)** persister (à faire), s'obstiner (à faire); **persistent** adj persistant(e), tenace

person ['pəːsn] n personne f; **in ~** en personne; **personal** adj personnel(le); **personal assistant** n secrétaire personnel(le); **personal computer** n ordinateur individuel, PC m; **personality** [pəːsə'nælɪtɪ] n personnalité f; **personally** adv personnellement; **to take sth personally** se sentir visé(e) par qch; **personal organizer** n agenda (personnel) (style Filofax®); (electronic) agenda électronique; **personal stereo** n Walkman® m, baladeur m

personnel [pəːsə'nɛl] n personnel m

perspective [pə'spɛktɪv] n perspective f

perspiration [pəːspɪ'reɪʃən] n transpiration f

persuade [pə'sweɪd] vt: **to ~ sb to do sth** persuader qn de faire qch, amener or décider qn à faire qch

persuasion [pə'sweɪʒən] n persuasion f; (creed) conviction f

persuasive [pə'sweɪsɪv] adj persuasif(-ive)

perverse [pə'vəːs] adj pervers(e); (contrary) entêté(e),

contrariant(e)

pervert n [pə'vəːt] perverti(e) ▷ vt [pə'vəːt] pervertir; (words) déformer

pessimism ['pɛsɪmɪzəm] n pessimisme m

pessimist ['pɛsɪmɪst] n pessimiste m/f; **pessimistic** [pɛsɪ'mɪstɪk] adj pessimiste

pest [pɛst] n animal m (or insecte m) nuisible; (fig) fléau m

pester ['pɛstəʳ] vt importuner, harceler

pesticide ['pɛstɪsaɪd] n pesticide m

pet [pɛt] n animal familier ▷ cpd (favourite) favori(e) ▷ vt (stroke) caresser, câliner; **teacher's ~** chouchou m du professeur; **~ hate** bête noire

petal ['pɛtl] n pétale m

petite [pə'tiːt] adj menu(e)

petition [pə'tɪʃən] n pétition f

petrified ['pɛtrɪfaɪd] adj (fig) mort(e) de peur

petrol ['pɛtrəl] n (BRIT) essence f; **I've run out of ~** je suis en panne d'essence

petroleum [pə'trəʊlɪəm] n pétrole m

petrol: petrol pump n (BRIT: in car, at garage) pompe f à essence; **petrol station** n (BRIT) station-service f; **petrol tank** n (BRIT) réservoir m d'essence

petticoat ['pɛtɪkəʊt] n jupon m

petty ['pɛtɪ] adj (mean) mesquin(e); (unimportant) insignifiant(e), sans importance

pew [pjuː] n banc m (d'église)

pewter ['pjuːtəʳ] n étain m

phantom ['fæntəm] n fantôme m

pharmacist ['fɑːməsɪst] n pharmacien(ne)

pharmacy ['fɑːməsɪ] n pharmacie f

phase [feɪz] n phase f, période f; **phase in** vt introduire progressivement; **phase out** vt supprimer progressivement

Ph.D. abbr = **Doctor of Philosophy**

pheasant ['fɛznt] n faisan m

phenomena [fə'nɔmɪnə] npl of **phenomenon**

phenomenal [fɪ'nɔmɪnl] adj phénoménal(e)

phenomenon (pl **phenomena**) [fə'nɔmɪnən, -nə] n phénomène m

Philippines ['fɪlɪpiːnz] npl (also: **Philippine Islands**): **the ~** les Philippines fpl

philosopher [fɪ'lɔsəfəʳ] n philosophe m

philosophical [fɪlə'sɔfɪkl] adj philosophique

philosophy [fɪ'lɔsəfɪ] n philosophie f

phlegm [flɛm] n flegme m

phobia ['fəʊbjə] n phobie f

phone [fəʊn] n téléphone m ▷ vt téléphoner à ▷ vi téléphoner; **to be on the ~** avoir le téléphone; (be calling) être au téléphone; **phone back** vt, vi rappeler; **phone up** vt téléphoner à ▷ vi téléphoner; **phone book** n annuaire m; **phone box** (US **phone booth**) n cabine f téléphonique; **phone call** n coup m de fil or de téléphone; **phonecard** n télécarte f; **phone number** n numéro m de téléphone

phonetics [fə'nɛtɪks] n phonétique f

phoney ['fəʊnɪ] adj faux (fausse), factice; (person) pas franc (franche)

photo ['fəʊtəʊ] n photo f; **photo album** n album m de photos; **photocopier** n copieur m; **photocopy** n photocopie f ▷ vt photocopier

photograph ['fəʊtəgræf] n photographie f ▷ vt photographier; **photographer** [fə'tɔgrəfəʳ] n photographe m/f; **photography** [fə'tɔgrəfɪ] n photographie f

phrase [freɪz] n expression f; (Ling) locution f ▷ vt exprimer; **phrase book** n recueil m d'expressions (pour touristes)

physical ['fɪzɪkl] adj physique; **physical education** n éducation f physique; **physically** adv physiquement

physician [fɪ'zɪʃən] n médecin m

physicist ['fɪzɪsɪst] n physicien(ne)

physics ['fɪzɪks] n physique f

physiotherapist [fɪzɪəu'θerəpɪst] n kinésithérapeute m/f

physiotherapy [fɪzɪəu'θerəpɪ] n kinésithérapie f

physique [fɪ'zi:k] n (appearance) physique m; (health etc) constitution f

pianist ['pi:ənɪst] n pianiste m/f

piano [pɪ'ænəu] n piano m

pick [pɪk] n (tool: also: **~-axe**) pic m, pioche f ▷ vt choisir; (gather) cueillir; (remove) prendre; (lock) forcer; **take your ~** faites votre choix; **the ~ of** le (la) meilleur(e) de; **to ~ one's nose** se mettre les doigts dans le nez; **to ~ one's teeth** se curer les dents; **to ~ a quarrel with sb** chercher noise à qn; **pick on** vt fus (person) harceler; **pick out** vt choisir; (distinguish) distinguer; **pick up** vi (improve) remonter, s'améliorer ▷ vt ramasser; (collect) passer prendre; (Aut: give lift to) prendre; (learn) apprendre; (Radio) capter; **to ~ up speed** prendre de la vitesse; **to ~ o.s. up** se relever

pickle ['pɪkl] n (also: **~s: as condiment**) pickles mpl ▷ vt conserver dans du vinaigre or dans de la saumure; **in a ~** (fig) dans le pétrin

pickpocket ['pɪkpɔkɪt] n pickpocket m

pick-up ['pɪkʌp] n (also: **~ truck**) pick-up m inv

picnic ['pɪknɪk] n pique-nique m ▷ vi pique-niquer; **picnic area** n aire f de pique-nique

picture ['pɪktʃəʳ] n (also TV) image f; (painting) peinture f, tableau m; (photograph) photo(graphie) f; (drawing) dessin m; (film) film m; (fig: description) description f ▷ vt (imagine) se représenter; **pictures** npl: **the ~s** (BRIT) le cinéma; **to take a ~ of sb/sth** prendre qn/qch en photo; **would you take a ~ of us, please?** pourriez-vous nous prendre en photo, s'il vous plaît?; **picture frame** n cadre m; **picture messaging** n picture messaging m, messagerie f d'images

picturesque [pɪktʃə'resk] adj pittoresque

pie [paɪ] n tourte f; (of fruit) tarte f; (of meat) pâté m en croûte

piece [pi:s] n morceau m; (item): **a ~ of furniture/advice** un meuble/conseil ▷ vt: **to ~ together** rassembler; **to take to ~s** démonter

pie chart n graphique m à secteurs, camembert m

pier [pɪəʳ] n jetée f

pierce [pɪəs] vt percer, transpercer; **pierced** adj (ears) percé(e)

pig [pɪg] n cochon m, porc m; (pej: unkind person) mufle m; (: greedy person) goinfre m

pigeon ['pɪdʒən] n pigeon m

piggy bank ['pɪgɪ-] n tirelire f

pigsty ['pɪgstaɪ] n porcherie f

pigtail ['pɪgteɪl] n natte f, tresse f

pike [paɪk] n (fish) brochet m

pilchard ['pɪltʃəd] n pilchard m (sorte de sardine)

pile [paɪl] n (pillar, of books) pile f; (heap) tas m; (of carpet) épaisseur f; **pile up** vi (accumulate) s'entasser, s'accumuler ▷ vt (put in heap) empiler, entasser; (accumulate) accumuler; **piles** npl hémorroïdes fpl; **pile-**

up n (Aut) télescopage m, collision f en série

pilgrim ['pɪlgrɪm] n pèlerin m

pilgrimage ['pɪlgrɪmɪdʒ] n pèlerinage m

pill [pɪl] n pilule f; **the ~** la pilule

pillar ['pɪləʳ] n pilier m

pillow ['pɪləu] n oreiller m; **pillowcase, pillowslip** n taie f d'oreiller

pilot ['paɪlət] n pilote m ▷ cpd (scheme etc) pilote, expérimental(e) ▷ vt piloter; **pilot light** n veilleuse f

pimple ['pɪmpl] n bouton m

PIN n abbr (= personal identification number) code m confidentiel

pin [pɪn] n épingle f; (Tech) cheville f ▷ vt épingler; **~s and needles** fourmis fpl; **to ~ sb down** (fig) coincer qn; **to ~ sth on sb** (fig) mettre qch sur le dos de qn

pinafore ['pɪnəfɔːʳ] n tablier m

pinch [pɪntʃ] n pincement m; (of salt etc) pincée f ▷ vt pincer; (inf: steal) piquer, chiper ▷ vi (shoe) serrer; **at a ~** à la rigueur

pine [paɪn] n (also: **~ tree**) pin m ▷ vi: **to ~ for** aspirer à, désirer ardemment

pineapple ['paɪnæpl] n ananas m

ping [pɪŋ] n (noise) tintement m; **ping-pong®** n ping-pong® m

pink [pɪŋk] adj rose ▷ n (colour) rose m

pinpoint ['pɪnpɔɪnt] vt indiquer (avec précision)

pint [paɪnt] n pinte f (BRIT = 0,57 l; US = 0,47 l); (BRIT inf) ≈ demi m, ≈ pot m

pioneer [paɪə'nɪəʳ] n pionnier m

pious ['paɪəs] adj pieux(-euse)

pip [pɪp] n (seed) pépin m; **pips** npl: **the ~s** (BRIT: time signal on radio) le top

pipe [paɪp] n tuyau m, conduite f; (for smoking) pipe f ▷ vt amener par tuyau; **pipeline** n (for gas) gazoduc m, pipeline m; (for oil) oléoduc m, pipeline; **piper** n (flautist) joueur(-euse) de pipeau; (of bagpipes) joueur(-euse) de cornemuse

pirate ['paɪərət] n pirate m ▷ vt (CD, video, book) pirater

Pisces ['paɪsiːz] n les Poissons mpl

piss [pɪs] vi (inf!) pisser (!); **pissed** (inf!) adj (BRIT: drunk) bourré(e); (US: angry) furieux(-euse)

pistol ['pɪstl] n pistolet m

piston ['pɪstən] n piston m

pit [pɪt] n trou m, fosse f; (also: **coal ~**) puits m de mine; (also: **orchestra ~**) fosse d'orchestre; (US: fruit stone) noyau m ▷ vt: **to ~ o.s. or one's wits against** se mesurer à

pitch [pɪtʃ] n (BRIT Sport) terrain m; (Mus) ton m; (fig: degree) degré m; (tar) poix f ▷ vt (throw) lancer; (tent) dresser ▷ vi (fall): **to ~ into/off** tomber dans/de; **pitch-black** adj noir(e) comme poix

pitfall ['pɪtfɔːl] n piège m

pith [pɪθ] n (of orange etc) intérieur m de l'écorce

pitiful ['pɪtɪful] adj (touching) pitoyable; (contemptible) lamentable

pity ['pɪtɪ] n pitié f ▷ vt plaindre; **what a ~!** quel dommage!

pizza ['pi:tsə] n pizza f

placard ['plækɑːd] n affiche f; (in march) pancarte f

place [pleɪs] n endroit m, lieu m; (proper position, job, rank, seat) place f; (home): **at/to his ~** chez lui ▷ vt (position) placer, mettre; (identify) situer; reconnaître; **to take ~** avoir lieu; **to change ~s with sb** changer de place avec qn; **out of ~** (not suitable) déplacé(e), inopportun(e); **in**

the first ~ d'abord, en premier; **place mat** n set m de table; (in linen etc) napperon m; **placement** n (during studies) stage m

placid ['plæsɪd] adj placide

plague [pleɪg] n (Med) peste f ▷ vt (fig) tourmenter

plaice [pleɪs] n (pl inv) carrelet m

plain [pleɪn] adj (in one colour) uni(e); (clear) clair(e), évident(e); (simple) simple; (not handsome) quelconque, ordinaire ▷ adv franchement, carrément ▷ n plaine f; **plain chocolate** n chocolat m à croquer; **plainly** adv clairement; (frankly) carrément, sans détours

plaintiff ['pleɪntɪf] n plaignant(e)

plait [plæt] n tresse f, natte f

plan [plæn] n plan m; (scheme) projet m ▷ vt (think in advance) projeter; (prepare) organiser ▷ vi faire des projets; **to ~ to do** projeter de faire

plane [pleɪn] n (Aviat) avion m; (also: **~ tree**) platane m; (tool) rabot m; (Art, Math etc) plan m; (fig) niveau m, plan m ▷ vt (with tool) raboter

planet ['plænɪt] n planète f

plank [plæŋk] n planche f

planning ['plænɪŋ] n planification f; **family ~** planning familial

plant [plɑːnt] n plante f; (machinery) matériel m; (factory) usine f ▷ vt planter; (bomb) déposer, poser; (microphone, evidence) cacher

plantation [plæn'teɪʃən] n plantation f

plaque [plæk] n plaque f

plaster ['plɑːstə^r] n plâtre m; (also: **~ of Paris**) plâtre à mouler; (BRIT: also: **sticking ~**) pansement adhésif ▷ vt plâtrer; (cover) **to ~ with** couvrir de; **plaster cast** n (Med) plâtre m; (model, statue) moule m

plastic ['plæstɪk] n plastique m ▷ adj (made of plastic) en plastique; **plastic bag** n sac m en plastique; **plastic surgery** n chirurgie f esthétique

plate [pleɪt] n (dish) assiette f; (sheet of metal, on door: Phot) plaque f; (in book) gravure f; (dental) dentier m

plateau (pl **~s** or **~x**) ['plætəu, -z] n plateau m

platform ['plætfɔːm] n (at meeting) tribune f; (stage) estrade f; (Rail) quai m; (Pol) plateforme f

platinum ['plætɪnəm] n platine m

platoon [plə'tuːn] n peloton m

platter ['plætə^r] n plat m

plausible ['plɔːzɪbl] adj plausible; (person) convaincant(e)

play [pleɪ] n jeu m; (Theat) pièce f (de théâtre) ▷ vt (game) jouer à; (team, opponent) jouer contre; (instrument) jouer de; (part, piece of music, note) jouer; (CD etc) passer ▷ vi jouer; **to ~ safe** ne prendre aucun risque; **play back** vt repasser, réécouter; **play up** vi (cause trouble) faire des siennes; **player** n joueur(-euse); (Mus) musicien(ne); **playful** adj enjoué(e); **playground** n cour f de récréation; (in park) aire f de jeux; **playgroup** n garderie f; **playing card** n carte f à jouer; **playing field** n terrain m de sport; **playschool** n = **playgroup**; **playtime** n (Scol) récréation f; **playwright** n dramaturge m

plc abbr (BRIT: = public limited company) ≈ SARL f

plea [pliː] n (request) appel m; (Law) défense f

plead [pliːd] vt plaider; (give as excuse) invoquer ▷ vi (Law) plaider; (beg): **to ~ with sb (for sth)** implorer qn (d'accorder qch); **to ~ guilty/not guilty** plaider coupable/non coupable

pleasant ['plɛznt] adj agréable

please [pliːz] excl s'il te (or vous) plaît ▷ vt plaire à ▷ vi (think fit): **do as you ~** faites comme il vous plaira; **~ yourself!** (inf) (faites) comme vous voulez!; **pleased** adj: **pleased (with)** content(e) (de); **pleased to meet you** enchanté (je suis heureux de faire votre connaissance)

pleasure ['plɛʒə^r] n plaisir m; **"it's a ~"** je vous en prie"

pleat [pliːt] n pli m

pledge [plɛdʒ] n (promise) promesse f ▷ vt promettre

plentiful ['plɛntɪful] adj abondant(e), copieux(-euse)

plenty ['plɛntɪ] n: **~ of** beaucoup de; (sufficient) (bien) assez de

pliers ['plaɪəz] npl pinces fpl

plight [plaɪt] n situation f critique

plod [plɔd] vi avancer péniblement; (fig) peiner

plonk [plɔŋk] (inf) n (BRIT: wine) pinard m, piquette f ▷ vt: **to ~ sth down** poser brusquement qch

plot [plɔt] n complot m, conspiration f; (of story, play) intrigue f; (of land) lot m de terrain, lopin m ▷ vt (mark out) tracer point par point; (Naut) pointer; (make graph of) faire le graphique de; (conspire) comploter ▷ vi comploter

plough (US **plow**) [plau] n charrue f ▷ vt (earth) labourer; **to ~ money into** investir dans; **ploughman's lunch** n (BRIT) assiette froide avec du pain, du fromage et des pickles

plow [plau] (US) = **plough**

ploy [plɔɪ] n stratagème m

pluck [plʌk] vt (fruit) cueillir; (musical instrument) pincer; (bird) plumer; **to ~ one's eyebrows** s'épiler les sourcils; **to ~ up courage** prendre son courage à deux mains

plug [plʌg] n (stopper) bouchon m, bonde f; (Elec) prise f de courant; (Aut: also: **spark(ing) ~**) bougie f ▷ vt (hole) boucher; (inf: advertise) faire du battage pour, matraquer; **plug in** vt (Elec) brancher; **plughole** n (BRIT) trou m (d'écoulement)

plum [plʌm] n (fruit) prune f

plumber ['plʌmə^r] n plombier m

plumbing ['plʌmɪŋ] n (trade) plomberie f; (piping) tuyauterie f

plummet ['plʌmɪt] vi (person, object) plonger; (sales, prices) dégringoler

plump [plʌmp] adj rondelet(te), dodu(e), bien en chair; **plump for** vt fus (inf: choose) se décider pour

plunge [plʌndʒ] n plongeon m; (fig) chute f ▷ vt plonger ▷ vi (fall) tomber, dégringoler; (dive) plonger; **to take the ~** se jeter à l'eau

pluperfect [pluː'pəːfɪkt] n (Ling) plus-que-parfait m

plural ['pluərl] adj pluriel(le) ▷ n pluriel m

plus [plʌs] n (also: **~ sign**) signe m plus; (advantage) atout m ▷ prep plus; **ten/twenty ~** plus de dix/vingt

ply [plaɪ] n (of wool) fil m ▷ vt (a trade) exercer ▷ vi (ship) faire la navette; **to ~ sb with drink** donner continuellement à boire à qn; **plywood** n contreplaqué m

P.M. n abbr (BRIT) = **prime minister**

p.m. adv abbr (= post meridiem) de l'après-midi

PMS n abbr (= premenstrual syndrome) syndrome prémenstruel

PMT n abbr (= premenstrual tension) syndrome prémenstruel

pneumatic drill [njuː'mætɪk-] n marteau-piqueur m

pneumonia [njuː'məunɪə] n pneumonie f

poach [pəutʃ] vt (cook) pocher; (steal) pêcher (or chasser) sans permis ▷ vi braconner; **poached** adj (egg) poché(e)

P.O. Box *n abbr* = **post office box**

pocket ['pɒkɪt] *n* poche *f* ▷ *vt* empecher; **to be (£5) out of ~** (BRIT) en être de sa poche (pour 5 livres); **pocketbook** *n* (US: *wallet*) portefeuille *m*; **pocket money** *n* argent *m* de poche

pod [pɒd] *n* cosse *f*

podcast *n* podcast *m*

podiatrist [pɔ'diːətrɪst] *n* (US) pédicure *m/f*

podium ['pəudɪəm] *n* podium *m*

poem ['pəuɪm] *n* poème *m*

poet ['pəuɪt] *n* poète *m*; **poetic** [pəu'ɛtɪk] *adj* poétique; **poetry** *n* poésie *f*

poignant ['pɔɪnjənt] *adj* poignant(e)

point [pɔɪnt] *n* point *m*; (*tip*) pointe *f*; (*in time*) moment *m*; (*in space*) endroit *m*; (*subject, idea*) point, sujet *m*; (*purpose*) but *m*; (*also*: **decimal ~**): **2 ~ 3 (2.3)** 2 virgule 3 (2,3); (BRIT Elec: *also*: **power ~**) prise *f* (de courant) ▷ *vt* (*show*) indiquer; (*gun etc*) braquer ▷ *vi*: **to ~ at** montrer du doigt; **points** *npl* (Rail) aiguillage *m*; **to make a ~ of doing sth** ne pas manquer de faire qch; **to get/miss the ~** comprendre/ne pas comprendre; **to come to the ~** en venir au fait; **there's no ~ (in doing)** cela ne sert à rien (de faire), à quoi ça sert?; **to be on the ~ of doing sth** être sur le point de faire qch; **point out** *vt* (*mention*) faire remarquer, souligner; **point-blank** *adv* (*fig*) catégoriquement; (*also*: **at point-blank range**) à bout portant; **pointed** *adj* (*shape*) pointu(e); (*remark*) plein(e) de sous-entendus; **pointer** *n* (*needle*) aiguille *f*; (*clue*) indication *f*; (*advice*) tuyau *m*; **pointless** *adj* inutile, vain(e); **point of view** *n* point *m* de vue

poison ['pɔɪzn] *n* poison *m* ▷ *vt* empoisonner; **poisonous** *adj* (*snake*) venimeux(-euse); (*substance, plant*) vénéneux(-euse); (*fumes*) toxique

poke [pəuk] *vt* (*jab with finger, stick etc*) piquer; pousser du doigt; (*put*): **to ~ sth in(to)** fourrer *or* enfoncer qch dans; **poke about** *vi* fureter; **poke out** *vi* (*stick out*) sortir

poker ['pəukər] *n* tisonnier *m*; (Cards) poker *m*

Poland ['pəulənd] *n* Pologne *f*

polar ['pəulər] *adj* polaire; **polar bear** *n* ours blanc

Pole [pəul] *n* Polonais(e)

pole [pəul] *n* (*of wood*) mât *m*, perche *f*; (Elec) poteau *m*; (Geo) pôle *m*; **pole bean** *n* (US) haricot *m* (à rames); **pole vault** *n* saut *m* à la perche

police [pə'liːs] *npl* police *f* ▷ *vt* maintenir l'ordre dans; **police car** *n* voiture *f* de police; **police constable** *n* (BRIT) agent *m* de police; **police force** *n* police *f*, forces *fpl* de l'ordre; **policeman** (*irreg*) *n* agent *m* de police, policier *m*; **police officer** *n* agent *m* de police; **police station** *n* commissariat *m* de police; **policewoman** (*irreg*) *n* femme-agent *f*

policy ['pɒlɪsɪ] *n* politique *f*; (*also*: **insurance ~**) police *f* (d'assurance)

polio ['pəulɪəu] *n* polio *f*

Polish ['pəulɪʃ] *adj* polonais(e) ▷ *n* (Ling) polonais *m*

polish ['pɒlɪʃ] *n* (*for shoes*) cirage *m*; (*for floor*) cire *f*, encaustique *f*; (*for nails*) vernis *m*; (*shine*) éclat *m*, poli *m*; (*fig: refinement*) raffinement *m* ▷ *vt* (*put polish on: shoes, wood*) cirer; (*make shiny*) astiquer, faire briller; **polish off** *vt* (*food*) liquider; **polished** *adj* (*fig*) raffiné(e)

polite [pə'laɪt] *adj* poli(e); **politeness** *n* politesse *f*

political [pə'lɪtɪkl] *adj* politique; **politically** *adv* politiquement; **politically correct** politiquement

correct(e)

politician [pɒlɪ'tɪʃən] *n* homme/femme politique, politicien(ne)

politics ['pɒlɪtɪks] *n* politique *f*

poll [pəul] *n* scrutin *m*, vote *m*; (*also*: **opinion ~**) sondage *m* (d'opinion) ▷ *vt* (*votes*) obtenir

pollen ['pɒlən] *n* pollen *m*

polling station *n* (BRIT) bureau *m* de vote

pollute [pə'luːt] *vt* polluer

pollution [pə'luːʃən] *n* pollution *f*

polo ['pəuləu] *n* polo *m*; **polo-neck** *adj* à col roulé ▷ *n* (*sweater*) pull *m* à col roulé; **polo shirt** *n* polo *m*

polyester [pɒlɪ'ɛstər] *n* polyester *m*

polystyrene [pɒlɪ'staɪriːn] *n* polystyrène *m*

polythene ['pɒlɪθiːn] *n* (BRIT) polyéthylène *m*; **polythene bag** *n* sac *m* en plastique

pomegranate ['pɒmɪgrænɪt] *n* grenade *f*

pompous ['pɒmpəs] *adj* pompeux(-euse)

pond [pɒnd] *n* étang *m*; (*stagnant*) mare *f*

ponder ['pɒndər] *vt* considérer, peser

pony ['pəunɪ] *n* poney *m*; **ponytail** *n* queue *f* de cheval; **pony trekking** *n* (BRIT) randonnée *f* équestre *or* à cheval

poodle ['puːdl] *n* caniche *m*

pool [puːl] *n* (*of rain*) flaque *f*; (*pond*) mare *f*; (*artificial*) bassin *m*; (*also*: **swimming ~**) piscine *f*; (*sth shared*) fonds commun; (*billiards*) poule *f* ▷ *vt* mettre en commun; **pools** *npl* (*football*) ≈ loto sportif

poor [puər] *adj* pauvre; (*mediocre*) médiocre, faible, mauvais(e) ▷ *npl*: **the ~** les pauvres *mpl*; **poorly** *adv* (*badly*) mal, médiocrement ▷ *adj* souffrant(e), malade

pop [pɒp] *n* (*noise*) bruit sec; (*Mus*) musique *f* pop; (*inf: drink*) soda *m*; (*us inf: father*) papa *m* ▷ *vt* (*put*) fourrer, mettre (rapidement) ▷ *vi* éclater; (*cork*) sauter; **pop in** *vi* entrer en passant; **pop out** *vi* sortir; **popcorn** *n* pop-corn *m*

pope [pəup] *n* pape *m*

poplar ['pɒplər] *n* peuplier *m*

popper ['pɒpər] *n* (BRIT) bouton-pression *m*

poppy ['pɒpɪ] *n* (*wild*) coquelicot *m*; (*cultivated*) pavot *m*

Popsicle® ['pɒpsɪkl] *n* (US) esquimau *m* (glace)

pop star *n* pop star *f*

popular ['pɒpjulər] *adj* populaire; (*fashionable*) à la mode; **popularity** [pɒpju'lærɪtɪ] *n* popularité *f*

population [pɒpju'leɪʃən] *n* population *f*

pop-up *adj* (Comput: *menu, window*) pop up *inv* ▷ *n* pop up *m inv*, fenêtre *f* pop up

porcelain ['pɔːslɪn] *n* porcelaine *f*

porch [pɔːtʃ] *n* porche *m*; (US) véranda *f*

pore [pɔːr] *n* pore *m* ▷ *vi*: **to ~ over** s'absorber dans, être plongé(e) dans

pork [pɔːk] *n* porc *m*; **pork chop** *n* côte *f* de porc; **pork pie** *n* pâté *m* de porc en croûte

porn [pɔːn] *adj* (*inf*) porno *n* (*inf*) porno *m*; **pornographic** [pɔːnə'græfɪk] *adj* pornographique; **pornography** [pɔː'nɔgrəfɪ] *n* pornographie *f*

porridge ['pɒrɪdʒ] *n* porridge *m*

port [pɔːt] *n* (*harbour*) port *m*; (Naut: *left side*) bâbord *m*; (*wine*) porto *m*; (Comput) port *m*, accès *m*; **~ of call** (port d')escale *f*

portable ['pɔːtəbl] *adj* portatif(-ive)

porter ['pɔːtər] *n* (*for luggage*) porteur *m*; (*doorkeeper*) gardien(ne); portier *m*

portfolio [pɔːt'fəulɪəu] *n* portefeuille *m*; (*of artist*) portfolio *m*

portion ['pɔːʃən] n portion f, part f

portrait ['pɔːtreɪt] n portrait m

portray [pɔː'treɪ] vt faire le portrait de; (in writing) dépeindre, représenter; (subj: actor) jouer

Portugal ['pɔːtjugl] n Portugal m

Portuguese [pɔːtju'giːz] adj portugais(e) ▷ n (pl inv) Portugais(e); (Ling) portugais m

pose [pəuz] n pose f ▷ vi poser; (pretend): **to ~ as** se faire passer pour ▷ vt poser; (problem) créer

posh [pɒʃ] adj (inf) chic inv

position [pə'zɪʃən] n position f; (job, situation) situation f ▷ vt mettre en place or en position

positive ['pɒzɪtɪv] adj positif(-ive); (certain) sûr(e), certain(e); (definite) formel(le), catégorique; **positively** adv (affirmatively, enthusiastically) de façon positive; (inf: really) carrément

possess [pə'zɛs] vt posséder; **possession** [pə'zɛʃən] n possession f; **possessions** npl (belongings) affaires fpl; **possessive** adj possessif(-ive)

possibility [pɒsɪ'bɪlɪtɪ] n possibilité f; (event) éventualité f

possible ['pɒsɪbl] adj possible; **as big as ~** aussi gros que possible; **possibly** adv (perhaps) peut-être; **I cannot possibly come** il m'est impossible de venir

post [pəust] n (BRIT: mail) poste f; (: letters, delivery) courrier m; (job, situation) poste m; (pole) poteau m ▷ vt (BRIT: send by post) poster; (: appoint): **to ~ to** affecter à; **where can I ~ these cards?** où est-ce que je peux poster ces cartes postales?; **postage** n tarifs mpl d'affranchissement; **postal** adj postal(e); **postal order** n mandat-(poste m) m; **postbox** n (BRIT) boîte f aux lettres (publique); **postcard** n carte postale; **postcode** n (BRIT) code postal

poster ['pəustə'] n affiche f

postgraduate ['pəust'grædjuət] n ≈ étudiant(e) de troisième cycle

postman ['pəustmən] (BRIT: irreg) n facteur m

postmark ['pəustmɑːk] n cachet m (de la poste)

post-mortem [pəust'mɔːtəm] n autopsie f

post office n (building) poste f; (organization): **the Post Office** les postes fpl

postpone [pəs'pəun] vt remettre (à plus tard), reculer

posture ['pɒstʃə'] n posture f; (fig) attitude f

postwoman ['pəust'wumən] (BRIT: irreg) n factrice f

pot [pɒt] n (for cooking) marmite f, casserole f; (teapot) théière f; (for coffee) cafetière f; (for plants, jam) pot m; (inf: marijuana) herbe f ▷ vt (plant) mettre en pot; **to go to ~** (inf) aller à vau-l'eau

potato (pl **~es**) [pə'teɪtəu] n pomme f de terre; **potato peeler** n épluche-légumes m

potent ['pəutnt] adj puissant(e); (drink) fort(e), très alcoolisé(e); (man) viril

potential [pə'tɛnʃl] adj potentiel(le) ▷ n potentiel m

pothole ['pɒthəul] n (in road) nid m de poule; (BRIT: underground) gouffre m, caverne f

pot plant n plante f d'appartement

potter ['pɒtə'] n potier m ▷ vi (BRIT): **to ~ around** or **about** bricoler; **pottery** n poterie f

potty ['pɒtɪ] n (child's) pot m

pouch [pautʃ] n (Zool) poche f; (for tobacco) blague f; (for money) bourse f

poultry ['pəultrɪ] n volaille f

pounce [pauns] vi: **to ~ (on)** bondir (sur), fondre (sur)

pound [paund] n livre f (weight = 453g, 16 ounces; money = 100 pence); (for dogs, cars) fourrière f ▷ vt (beat) bourrer de coups, marteler; (crush) piler, pulvériser ▷ vi (heart) battre violemment, taper; **pound sterling** n livre f sterling

pour [pɔː'] vt verser ▷ vi couler à flots; (rain) pleuvoir à verse; **to ~ sb a drink** verser or servir à boire à qn; **pour in** vi (people) affluer, se précipiter; (news, letters) arriver en masse; **pour out** vi (people) sortir en masse ▷ vt vider; (fig) déverser; (serve: a drink) verser; **pouring** adj: **pouring rain** pluie torrentielle

pout [paut] vi faire la moue

poverty ['pɒvətɪ] n pauvreté f, misère f

powder ['paudə'] n poudre f ▷ vt poudrer; **powdered milk** n lait m en poudre

power ['pauə'] n (strength, nation) puissance f, force f; (ability, Pol: of party, leader) pouvoir m; (of speech, thought) faculté f; (Elec) courant m; **to be in ~** être au pouvoir; **power cut** n (BRIT) coupure f de courant; **power failure** n panne f de courant; **powerful** adj puissant(e); (performance etc) très fort(e); **powerless** adj impuissant(e); **power point** n (BRIT) prise f de courant; **power station** n centrale f électrique

p.p. abbr (= per procurationem: by proxy) p.p.

PR n abbr = **public relations**

practical ['præktɪkl] adj pratique; **practical joke** n farce f; **practically** adv (almost) pratiquement

practice ['præktɪs] n pratique f; (of profession) exercice m; (at football etc) entraînement m; (business) cabinet m ▷ vt, vi (US) = **practise**; **in ~** (in reality) en pratique; **out of ~** rouillé(e)

practise (US **practice**) ['præktɪs] vt (work at: piano, backhand etc) s'exercer à, travailler; (train for: sport) s'entraîner à; (a sport, religion, method) pratiquer; (profession) exercer ▷ vi s'exercer, travailler; (train) s'entraîner; (lawyer, doctor) exercer; **practising** (US **practicing**) adj (Christian etc) pratiquant(e); (lawyer) en exercice

practitioner [præk'tɪʃənə'] n praticien(ne)

pragmatic [præg'mætɪk] adj pragmatique

prairie ['prɛərɪ] n savane f

praise [preɪz] n éloge(s) m(pl), louange(s) f(pl) ▷ vt louer, faire l'éloge de

pram [præm] n (BRIT) landau m, voiture f d'enfant

prank [præŋk] n farce f

prawn [prɔːn] n crevette f (rose); **prawn cocktail** n cocktail m de crevettes

pray [preɪ] vi prier; **prayer** [prɛə'] n prière f

preach [priːtʃ] vi prêcher; **preacher** n prédicateur n; (US: clergyman) pasteur m

precarious [prɪ'kɛərɪəs] adj précaire

precaution [prɪ'kɔːʃən] n précaution f

precede [prɪ'siːd] vt, vi précéder; **precedent** ['prɛsɪdənt] n précédent m; **preceding** [prɪ'siːdɪŋ] adj qui précède (or précédait)

precinct ['priːsɪŋkt] n (US: district) circonscription f, arrondissement m; **pedestrian ~** (BRIT) zone piétonnière; **shopping ~** (BRIT) centre commercial

precious ['prɛʃəs] adj précieux(-euse)

precise [prɪ'saɪs] adj précis(e); **precisely** adv précisément

precision [prɪ'sɪʒən] n précision f

predator ['prɛdətə'] n prédateur m, rapace m

predecessor ['priːdɪsɛsə'] n prédécesseur m

predicament [prɪ'dɪkəmənt] n situation f difficile

predict [prɪˈdɪkt] vt prédire; **predictable** adj prévisible; **prediction** [prɪˈdɪkʃən] n prédiction f
predominantly [prɪˈdɒmɪnəntlɪ] adv en majeure partie; (especially) surtout
preface [ˈprefəs] n préface f
prefect [ˈpriːfekt] n (BRIT: in school) élève chargé de certaines fonctions de discipline
prefer [prɪˈfəːr] vt préférer; **preferable** [ˈprefrəbl] adj préférable; **preferably** [ˈprefrəblɪ] adv de préférence; **preference** [ˈprefrəns] n préférence f
prefix [ˈpriːfɪks] n préfixe m
pregnancy [ˈpregnənsɪ] n grossesse f
pregnant [ˈpregnənt] adj enceinte adj f; (animal) pleine
prehistoric [ˈpriːhɪsˈtɔrɪk] adj préhistorique
prejudice [ˈpredʒudɪs] n préjugé m; **prejudiced** adj (person) plein(e) de préjugés; (in a matter) partial(e)
preliminary [prɪˈlɪmɪnərɪ] adj préliminaire
prelude [ˈpreljuːd] n prélude m
premature [ˈprematjuər] adj prématuré(e)
premier [ˈpremɪər] adj premier(-ière), principal(e) ▷ n (Pol: Prime Minister) premier ministre; (Pol: President) chef m de l'État
premiere [ˈpremɪəər] n première f
Premier League n première division
premises [ˈpremɪsɪz] npl locaux mpl; **on the ~** sur les lieux; sur place
premium [ˈpriːmɪəm] n prime f; **to be at a ~** (fig: housing etc) être très demandé(e), être rarissime
premonition [preməˈnɪʃən] n prémonition f
preoccupied [priːˈɔkjupaɪd] adj préoccupé(e)
prepaid [priːˈpeɪd] adj payé(e) d'avance
preparation [prepəˈreɪʃən] n préparation f; **preparations** npl (for trip, war) préparatifs mpl
preparatory school n école primaire privée; (US) lycée privé
prepare [prɪˈpɛər] vt préparer ▷ vi: **to ~ for** se préparer à
prepared [prɪˈpɛəd] adj: **~ for** préparé(e) à; **~ to** prêt(e) à
preposition [prepəˈzɪʃən] n préposition f
prep school n = **preparatory school**
prerequisite [priːˈrekwɪzɪt] n condition f préalable
preschool [ˈpriːˈskuːl] adj préscolaire; (child) d'âge préscolaire
prescribe [prɪˈskraɪb] vt prescrire
prescription [prɪˈskrɪpʃən] n (Med) ordonnance f; (: medicine) médicament m (obtenu sur ordonnance); **could you write me a ~?** pouvez-vous me faire une ordonnance?
presence [ˈprezns] n présence f; **in sb's ~** en présence de qn; **~ of mind** présence d'esprit
present [ˈpreznt] adj présent(e); (current) présent, actuel(le) ▷ n cadeau m; (actuality) présent m ▷ vt [prɪˈzent] présenter; (prize, medal) remettre; (give): **to ~ sb with sth** offrir qch à qn; **at ~** en ce moment; **to give sb a ~** offrir un cadeau à qn; **presentable** [prɪˈzentəbl] adj présentable; **presentation** [preznˈteɪʃən] n présentation f; (ceremony) remise f du cadeau (or de la médaille etc); (talk) exposé m; **present-day** adj contemporain(e), actuel(le); **presenter** [prɪˈzentər] n (BRIT Radio, TV) présentateur(-trice); **presently** adv (soon) tout à l'heure, bientôt; (with verb in past) peu après; (at present) en ce moment; **present participle** [-ˈpɑːtɪsɪpl] n participe m présent
preservation [prezəˈveɪʃən] n préservation f, conservation f

preservative [prɪˈzəːvətɪv] n agent m de conservation
preserve [prɪˈzəːv] vt (keep safe) préserver, protéger; (maintain) conserver, garder; (food) mettre en conserve ▷ n (for game, fish) réserve f; (often pl: jam) confiture f
preside [prɪˈzaɪd] vi présider
president [ˈprezɪdənt] n président(e); **presidential** [prezɪˈdenʃl] adj présidentiel(le)
press [pres] n (tool, machine, newspapers) presse f; (for wine) pressoir m ▷ vt (push) appuyer sur; (squeeze) presser, serrer; (clothes: iron) repasser; (insist): **to ~ sth on sb** presser qn d'accepter qch; (urge, entreat): **to ~ sb to do** or **into doing sth** pousser qn à faire qch ▷ vi appuyer; **we are ~ed for time** le temps nous manque; **to ~ for sth** faire pression pour obtenir qch; **press conference** n conférence f de presse; **pressing** adj urgent(e), pressant(e); **press stud** n (BRIT) bouton-pression m; **press-up** n (BRIT) traction f
pressure [ˈpreʃər] n pression f; (stress) tension f; **to put ~ on sb (to do sth)** faire pression sur qn (pour qu'il fasse qch); **pressure cooker** n cocotte-minute f; **pressure group** n groupe m de pression
prestige [presˈtiːʒ] n prestige m
prestigious [presˈtɪdʒəs] adj prestigieux(-euse)
presumably [prɪˈzjuːməblɪ] adv vraisemblablement
presume [prɪˈzjuːm] vt présumer, supposer
pretence (US **pretense**) [prɪˈtens] n (claim) prétention f; **under false ~s** sous des prétextes fallacieux
pretend [prɪˈtend] vt (feign) feindre, simuler ▷ vi (feign) faire semblant
pretense [prɪˈtens] n (US) = **pretence**
pretentious [prɪˈtenʃəs] adj prétentieux(-euse)
pretext [ˈpriːtekst] n prétexte m
pretty [ˈprɪtɪ] adj joli(e) ▷ adv assez
prevail [prɪˈveɪl] vi (win) l'emporter, prévaloir; (be usual) avoir cours; **prevailing** adj (widespread) courant(e), répandu(e); (wind) dominant(e)
prevalent [ˈprevələnt] adj répandu(e), courant(e)
prevent [prɪˈvent] vt: **to ~ (from doing)** empêcher (de faire); **prevention** [prɪˈvenʃən] n prévention f; **preventive** adj préventif(-ive)
preview [ˈpriːvjuː] n (of film) avant-première f
previous [ˈpriːvɪəs] adj (last) précédent(e); (earlier) antérieur(e); **previously** adv précédemment, auparavant
prey [preɪ] n proie f ▷ vi: **to ~ on** s'attaquer à; **it was ~ing on his mind** ça le rongeait or minait
price [praɪs] n prix m ▷ vt (goods) fixer le prix de; **priceless** adj sans prix, inestimable; **price list** n tarif m
prick [prɪk] n (sting) piqûre f ▷ vt piquer; **to ~ up one's ears** dresser or tendre l'oreille
prickly [ˈprɪklɪ] adj piquant(e), épineux(-euse); (fig: person) irritable
pride [praɪd] n fierté f; (pej) orgueil m ▷ vt: **to ~ o.s. on** se flatter de; s'enorgueillir de
priest [priːst] n prêtre m
primarily [ˈpraɪmərɪlɪ] adv principalement, essentiellement
primary [ˈpraɪmərɪ] adj primaire; (first in importance) premier(-ière), primordial(e) ▷ n (US: election) (élection f) primaire f; **primary school** n (BRIT) école f primaire
prime [praɪm] adj primordial(e), fondamental(e); (excellent) excellent(e) ▷ vt (fig) mettre au courant ▷ n: **in the ~ of life** dans la fleur de l'âge; **Prime Minister** n Premier ministre

primitive ['prɪmɪtɪv] adj primitif(-ive)
primrose ['prɪmrəuz] n primevère f
prince [prɪns] n prince m
princess [prɪn'ses] n princesse f
principal ['prɪnsɪpl] adj principal(e) ▷ n (head teacher) directeur m, principal m; (publish) publier; (write in capitals) écrire en majuscules; **out of** ~ épuisé(e);
principally adv principalement
principle ['prɪnsɪpl] n principe m; **in** ~ en principe; **on** ~ par principe
print [prɪnt] n (mark) empreinte f; (letters) caractères mpl; (fabric) imprimé m; (Art) gravure f, estampe f; (Phot) épreuve f ▷ vt imprimer; (publish) publier; (write in capitals) écrire en majuscules; **out of** ~ épuisé(e);
print out vt (Comput) imprimer; **printer** n (machine) imprimante f; (person) imprimeur m; **printout** n (Comput) sortie f imprimante
prior ['praɪəᵊ] adj antérieur(e), précédent(e); (more important) prioritaire ▷ adv: ~ **to doing** avant de faire
priority [praɪ'ɒrɪtɪ] n priorité f; **to have** or **take** ~ **over sth/sb** avoir la priorité sur qch/qn
prison ['prɪzn] n prison f ▷ cpd pénitentiaire; **prisoner** n prisonnier(-ière); **prisoner of war** n prisonnier(-ière) de guerre
pristine ['prɪstiːn] adj virginal(e)
privacy ['prɪvəsɪ] n intimité f, solitude f
private ['praɪvɪt] adj (not public) privé(e); (personal) personnel(le); (house, car, lesson) particulier(-ière); (quiet: place) tranquille ▷ n soldat m de deuxième classe; **"-"** (on envelope) "personnelle"; (on door) "privé"; **in** ~ en privé; **privately** adv en privé; (within oneself) intérieurement; **private property** n propriété privée; **private school** n école privée
privatize ['praɪvɪtaɪz] vt privatiser
privilege ['prɪvɪlɪdʒ] n privilège m
prize [praɪz] n prix m ▷ adj (example, idiot) parfait(e); (bull, novel) primé(e) ▷ vt priser, faire grand cas de; **prize-giving** n distribution f des prix; **prizewinner** n gagnant(e)
pro [prəu] n (inf: Sport) professionnel(le) ▷ prep pro ...; **pros** npl: **the** ~**s and cons** le pour et le contre
probability [prɒbə'bɪlɪtɪ] n probabilité f; **in all** ~ très probablement
probable ['prɒbəbl] adj probable
probably ['prɒbəblɪ] adv probablement
probation [prə'beɪʃən] n: **on** ~ (employee) à l'essai; (Law) en liberté surveillée
probe [prəub] n (Med, Space) sonde f; (enquiry) enquête f, investigation f ▷ vt sonder, explorer
problem ['prɒbləm] n problème m
procedure [prə'siːdʒəᵊ] n (Admin, Law) procédure f; (method) marche f à suivre, façon f de procéder
proceed [prə'siːd] vi (go forward) avancer; (act) procéder; (continue): **to** ~ **(with)** continuer, poursuivre; **to** ~ **to do** se mettre à faire; **proceedings** npl (measures) mesures fpl; (Law: against sb) poursuites fpl; (meeting) réunion f, séance f; (records) compte rendu; actes mpl; **proceeds** ['prəusiːdz] npl produit m, recette f
process ['prəuses] n processus m; (method) procédé m ▷ vt traiter
procession [prə'seʃən] n défilé m, cortège m; **funeral** ~ (on foot) cortège funèbre; (in cars) convoi m mortuaire
proclaim [prə'kleɪm] vt déclarer, proclamer
prod [prɒd] vt pousser
produce n ['prɒdjuːs] (Agr) produits mpl ▷ vt [prə'djuːs] produire; (show) présenter; (cause) provoquer,

causer; (Theat) monter, mettre en scène; (TV: programme) réaliser; (: play, film) mettre en scène; (Radio: programme) réaliser; (: play) mettre en ondes; **producer** n (Theat) metteur m en scène; (Agr, Comm, Cine) producteur m; (TV: of programme) réalisateur m; (: of play, film) metteur en scène; (Radio: of programme) réalisateur; (: of play) metteur en ondes
product ['prɒdʌkt] n produit m; **production** [prə'dʌkʃən] n production f; (Theat) mise f en scène; **productive** [prə'dʌktɪv] adj productif(-ive); **productivity** [prɒdʌk'tɪvɪtɪ] n productivité f
Prof. [prɒf] abbr (= professor) Prof
profession [prə'feʃən] n profession f; **professional** n professionnel(le) ▷ adj professionnel(le); (work) de professionnel
professor [prə'fesəᵊ] n professeur m (titulaire d'une chaire); (us: teacher) professeur m
profile ['prəufaɪl] n profil m
profit ['prɒfɪt] n (from trading) bénéfice m; (advantage) profit m ▷ vi: **to** ~ **(by** or **from)** profiter (de); **profitable** adj lucratif(-ive), rentable
profound [prə'faund] adj profond(e)
programme (us program) ['prəugræm] n (Comput: also BRIT) programme m; (Radio, TV) émission f ▷ vt programmer; **programmer** (us programer) n programmeur(-euse); **programming** (us programing) n programmation f
progress n ['prəugres] progrès m(pl) ▷ vi [prə'gres] progresser, avancer; **in** ~ en cours; **progressive** [prə'gresɪv] adj progressif(-ive); (person) progressiste
prohibit [prə'hɪbɪt] vt interdire, défendre
project n ['prɒdʒekt] (plan) projet m, plan m; (venture) opération f, entreprise f; (Scol: research) étude f, dossier m ▷ vb [prə'dʒekt] ▷ vt projeter ▷ vi (stick out) faire saillie, s'avancer; **projection** [prə'dʒekʃən] n projection f; (overhang) saillie f; **projector** [prə'dʒektəᵊ] n projecteur m
prolific [prə'lɪfɪk] adj prolifique
prolong [prə'lɒŋ] vt prolonger
prom [prɒm] n abbr = **promenade**; (us: ball) bal m d'étudiants; **the P-s** série de concerts de musique classique
promenade [prɒmə'nɑːd] n (by sea) esplanade f, promenade f
prominent ['prɒmɪnənt] adj (standing out) proéminent(e); (important) important(e)
promiscuous [prə'mɪskjuəs] adj (sexually) de mœurs légères
promise ['prɒmɪs] n promesse f ▷ vt, vi promettre; **promising** adj prometteur(-euse)
promote [prə'məut] vt promouvoir; (new product) lancer; **promotion** [prə'məuʃən] n promotion f
prompt [prɒmpt] adj rapide ▷ n (Comput) message m (de guidage) ▷ vt (cause) entraîner, provoquer; (Theat) souffler (son rôle or ses répliques) à; **at 8 o'clock** ~ à 8 heures précises; **to** ~ **sb to do** inciter or pousser qn à faire; **promptly** adv (quickly) rapidement, sans délai; (on time) ponctuellement
prone [prəun] adj (lying) couché(e) (face contre terre); (liable): ~ **to** enclin(e) à
prong [prɒŋ] n (of fork) dent f
pronoun ['prəunaun] n pronom m
pronounce [prə'nauns] vt prononcer; **how do you** ~ **it?** comment est-ce que ça se prononce?
pronunciation [prənʌnsɪ'eɪʃən] n prononciation f

proof [pru:f] n preuve f ▷ adj: **~ against** à l'épreuve de

prop [prɒp] n support m, étai m; (fig) soutien m ▷ vt (also: **~ up**) étayer, soutenir; **props** npl accessoires mpl

propaganda [prɒpə'gændə] n propagande f

propeller [prə'pɛlə'] n hélice f

proper ['prɒpə'] adj (suited, right) approprié(e), bon (bonne); (seemly) correct(e), convenable; (authentic) vrai(e), véritable; (referring to place): **the village ~ le** village proprement dit; **properly** adv correctement, convenablement; **proper noun** n nom m propre

property ['prɒpətɪ] n (possessions) biens mpl; (house etc) propriété f; (land) terres fpl, domaine m

prophecy ['prɒfɪsɪ] n prophétie f

prophet ['prɒfɪt] n prophète m

proportion [prə'pɔːʃən] n proportion f; (share) part f, partie f; **proportions** npl (size) dimensions fpl; **proportional, proportionate** adj proportionnel(le)

proposal [prə'pəuzl] n proposition f, offre f; (plan) projet m; (of marriage) demande f en mariage

propose [prə'pəuz] vt proposer, suggérer ▷ vi faire sa demande en mariage; **to ~ to do** avoir l'intention de faire

proposition [prɒpə'zɪʃən] n proposition f

proprietor [prə'praɪətə'] n propriétaire m/f

prose [prəuz] n prose f; (Scol: translation) thème m

prosecute ['prɒsɪkjuːt] vt poursuivre; **prosecution** [prɒsɪ'kjuːʃən] n poursuites fpl judiciaires; (accusing side: in criminal case) accusation f; (: in civil case) la partie plaignante; **prosecutor** n (lawyer) procureur m; (also: **public prosecutor**) ministère public; (us: plaintiff) plaignant(e)

prospect n ['prɒspɛkt] perspective f; (hope) espoir m, chances fpl ▷ vt, vi [prə'spɛkt] prospecter; **prospects** npl (for work etc) possibilités fpl d'avenir, débouchés mpl; **prospective** [prə'spɛktɪv] adj (possible) éventuel(le); (future) futur(e)

prospectus [prə'spɛktəs] n prospectus m

prosper ['prɒspə'] vi prospérer; **prosperity** [prɒ'spɛrɪtɪ] n prospérité f; **prosperous** adj prospère

prostitute ['prɒstɪtjuːt] n prostituée f; **male ~** prostitué m

protect [prə'tɛkt] vt protéger; **protection** [prə'tɛkʃən] n protection f; **protective** adj protecteur(-trice); (clothing) de protection

protein ['prəutiːn] n protéine f

protest n ['prəutɛst] protestation f ▷ vb [prə'tɛst] ▷ vi: **to ~ against/about** protester contre/à propos de; **to ~ (that)** protester que

Protestant ['prɒtɪstənt] adj, n protestant(e)

protester, protestor [prə'tɛstə'] n (in demonstration) manifestant(e)

protractor [prə'træktə'] n (Geom) rapporteur m

proud [praud] adj fier(-ère); (pej) orgueilleux(-euse)

prove [pruːv] vt prouver, démontrer ▷ vi: **to ~ correct** etc s'avérer juste etc; **to ~ o.s.** montrer ce dont on est capable

proverb ['prɒvəːb] n proverbe m

provide [prə'vaɪd] vt fournir; **to ~ sb with sth** fournir qch à qn; **provide for** vt fus (person) subvenir aux besoins de; (future event) prévoir; **provided** conj: **provided (that)** à condition que + sub; **providing** [prə'vaɪdɪŋ] conj à condition que + sub

province ['prɒvɪns] n province f; (fig) domaine m; **provincial** [prə'vɪnʃəl] adj provincial(e)

provision [prə'vɪʒən] n (supplying) fourniture f; approvisionnement m; (stipulation) disposition f; **provisions** npl (food) provisions fpl; **provisional** adj provisoire

provocative [prə'vɒkətɪv] adj provocateur(-trice), provocant(e)

provoke [prə'vəuk] vt provoquer

prowl [praul] vi (also: **~ about, ~ around**) rôder

proximity [prɒk'sɪmɪtɪ] n proximité f

proxy ['prɒksɪ] n: **by ~** par procuration

prudent ['pruːdnt] adj prudent(e)

prune [pruːn] n pruneau m ▷ vt élaguer

pry [praɪ] vi: **to ~ into** fourrer son nez dans

PS n abbr (= postscript) PS m

pseudonym ['sjuːdənɪm] n pseudonyme m

PSHE n abbr (BRIT: Scol: = personal, social and health education) cours d'éducation personnelle, sanitaire et sociale préparant à la vie adulte

psychiatric [saɪkɪ'ætrɪk] adj psychiatrique

psychiatrist [saɪ'kaɪətrɪst] n psychiatre m/f

psychic ['saɪkɪk] adj (also: **~al**) (méta)psychique; (person) doué(e) de télépathie or d'un sixième sens

psychoanalysis (pl **-ses**) [saɪkəuə'nælɪsɪs, -sɪːz] n psychanalyse f

psychological [saɪkə'lɒdʒɪkl] adj psychologique

psychologist [saɪ'kɒlədʒɪst] n psychologue m/f

psychology [saɪ'kɒlədʒɪ] n psychologie f

psychotherapy [saɪkəu'θɛrəpɪ] n psychothérapie f

pt abbr = **pint(s); point(s)**

PTO abbr (= please turn over) TSVP

pub [pʌb] n abbr (= public house) pub m

puberty ['pjuːbətɪ] n puberté f

public ['pʌblɪk] adj public(-ique) ▷ n public m; **in ~** en public; **to make ~** rendre public

publication [pʌblɪ'keɪʃən] n publication f

public: public company n société f anonyme; **public convenience** n (BRIT) toilettes fpl; **public holiday** n (BRIT) jour férié; **public house** n (BRIT) pub m

publicity [pʌb'lɪsɪtɪ] n publicité f

publicize ['pʌblɪsaɪz] vt (make known) faire connaître, rendre public; (advertise) faire de la publicité pour

public: public limited company n ≈ société f anonyme (SA) (cotée en Bourse); **publicly** adv publiquement, en public; **public opinion** n opinion publique; **public relations** n or npl relations publiques (RP); **public school** n (BRIT) école privée; (us) école publique; **public transport** (us **public transportation**) n transports mpl en commun

publish ['pʌblɪʃ] vt publier; **publisher** n éditeur m; **publishing** n (industry) édition f

pub lunch n repas m de bistrot

pudding ['pudɪŋ] n (BRIT: dessert) dessert m, entremets m; (sweet dish) pudding m, gâteau m

puddle ['pʌdl] n flaque f d'eau

puff [pʌf] n bouffée f ▷ vt (also: **~ out**: sails, cheeks) gonfler ▷ vi (pant) haleter; **puff pastry** (us **puff paste**) n pâte feuilletée

pull [pul] n (tug): **to give sth a ~** tirer sur qch ▷ vt tirer; (trigger) presser; (strain: muscle, tendon) se claquer ▷ vi tirer; **to ~ to pieces** mettre en morceaux; **to ~ one's punches** (also fig) ménager son adversaire; **to ~ one's weight** y mettre du sien; **to ~ o.s. together** se ressaisir; **to ~ sb's leg** (fig) faire marcher qn; **pull apart** vt (break) mettre en pièces, démantibuler; **pull away** vi (vehicle: move off) partir; (draw back) s'éloigner; **pull back** vt (lever *etc*) tirer sur; (*curtains*) ouvrir ▷ *vi* (*refrain*) s'abstenir; (*Mil: withdraw*) se retirer; **pull down** *vt* baisser, abaisser; (*house*) démolir; **pull in** *vi* (*Aut*) se ranger; (*Rail*) entrer en gare; **pull off** *vt* enlever, ôter; (*deal etc*) conclure; **pull out** *vi* démarrer, partir; (*Aut: come out of line*) déboîter ▷ *vt* (*from bag, pocket*) sortir; (*remove*) arracher; **pull over** *vi* (*Aut*) se ranger; **pull up** *vi* (*stop*) s'arrêter ▷ *vt* remonter; (*uproot*) déraciner, arracher

pulley ['pʊlɪ] *n* poulie *f*

pullover ['pʊləʊvəʳ] *n* pull-over *m*, tricot *m*

pulp [pʌlp] *n* (*of fruit*) pulpe *f*; (*for paper*) pâte *f* à papier

pulpit ['pʊlpɪt] *n* chaire *f*

pulse [pʌls] *n* (*of blood*) pouls *m*; (*of heart*) battement *m*; **pulses** *npl* (*Culin*) légumineuses *fpl*

puma ['pju:mə] *n* puma *m*

pump [pʌmp] *n* pompe *f*; (*shoe*) escarpin *m* ▷ *vt* pomper; **pump up** *vt* gonfler

pumpkin ['pʌmpkɪn] *n* potiron *m*, citrouille *f*

pun [pʌn] *n* jeu *m* de mots, calembour *m*

punch [pʌntʃ] *n* (*blow*) coup *m* de poing; (*tool*) poinçon *m*; (*drink*) punch *m* ▷ *vt* (*make a hole in*) poinçonner, perforer; (*hit*): **to ~ sb/sth** donner un coup de poing à qn/sur qch; **punch-up** *n* (*BRIT inf*) bagarre *f*

punctual ['pʌŋktjuəl] *adj* ponctuel(le)

punctuation [pʌŋktju'eɪʃən] *n* ponctuation *f*

puncture ['pʌŋktʃəʳ] *n* (*BRIT*) crevaison *f* ▷ *vt* crever

punish ['pʌnɪʃ] *vt* punir; **punishment** *n* punition *f*, châtiment *m*

punk [pʌŋk] *n* (*person: also*: **~ rocker**) punk *m/f*; (*music: also*: **~ rock**) le punk; (*us inf: hoodlum*) voyou *m*

pup [pʌp] *n* chiot *m*

pupil ['pju:pl] *n* élève *m/f*; (*of eye*) pupille *f*

puppet ['pʌpɪt] *n* marionnette *f*, pantin *m*

puppy ['pʌpɪ] *n* chiot *m*, petit chien

purchase ['pə:tʃɪs] *n* achat *m* ▷ *vt* acheter

pure [pjuəʳ] *adj* pur(e); **purely** *adv* purement

purify ['pjuərɪfaɪ] *vt* purifier, épurer

purity ['pjuərɪtɪ] *n* pureté *f*

purple ['pə:pl] *adj* violet(te); (*face*) cramoisi(e)

purpose ['pə:pəs] *n* intention *f*, but *m*; **on ~** exprès

purr [pə:ʳ] *vi* ronronner

purse [pə:s] *n* (*BRIT: for money*) porte-monnaie *m inv*; (*us: handbag*) sac *m* (à main) ▷ *vt* serrer, pincer

pursue [pə'sju:] *vt* poursuivre

pursuit [pə'sju:t] *n* poursuite *f*; (*occupation*) occupation *f*, activité *f*

pus [pʌs] *n* pus *m*

push [puʃ] *n* poussée *f* ▷ *vt* pousser; (*button*) appuyer sur; (*fig: product*) mettre en avant, faire de la publicité pour ▷ *vi* pousser; **to ~ for** (*better pay, conditions*) réclamer; **push in** *vi* s'introduire de force; **push off** *vi* (*inf*) filer, ficher le camp; **push on** *vi* (*continue*) continuer; **push over** *vt* renverser; **push through** *vi* (*in crowd*) se frayer un chemin; **pushchair** *n* (*BRIT*) poussette *f*; **pusher** *n* (*also*: **drug pusher**) revendeur(-euse) (de drogue), ravitailleur(-euse) (en drogue); **push-up** *n* (*us*) traction *f*

pussy(-cat) ['pʊsɪ-] *n* (*inf*) minet *m*

put (*pt, pp* **~**) [put] *vt* mettre; (*place*) poser, placer; (*say*) dire, exprimer; (*a question*) poser; (*case, view*) exposer, présenter; (*estimate*) estimer; **put aside** *vt* mettre de côté; **put away** *vt* (*store*) ranger; **put back** *vt* (*replace*) remettre, replacer; (*postpone*) remettre; **put by** *vt* (*money*) mettre de côté, économiser; **put down** *vt* (*parcel etc*) poser, déposer; (*in writing*) mettre par

écrit, inscrire; (*suppress: revolt etc*) réprimer, écraser; (*attribute*) attribuer; (*animal*) abattre; **put forward** *vt* (*ideas*) avancer, proposer; **put in** *vt* (*complaint*) soumettre; (*time, effort*) consacrer; **put off** *vt* (*postpone*) remettre à plus tard, ajourner; (*discourage*) dissuader; **put on** *vt* (*clothes, lipstick, CD*) mettre; (*light etc*) allumer; (*play etc*) monter; (*weight*) prendre; (*assume: accent, manner*) prendre; **put out** *vt* (*take outside*) mettre dehors; (*one's hand*) tendre; (*light etc*) éteindre; (*person: inconvenience*) déranger, gêner; **put through** *vt* (*Tel: caller*) mettre en communication; (*: call*) passer; (*plan*) faire accepter; **put together** *vt* mettre ensemble; (*assemble: furniture*) monter, assembler; (*meal*) préparer; **put up** *vt* (*raise*) lever, relever, remonter; (*hang*) accrocher; (*build*) construire, ériger; (*increase*) augmenter; (*accommodate*) loger; **put up with** *vt fus* supporter

putt [pʌt] *n* putt *m*; **putting green** *n* green *m*

puzzle ['pʌzl] *n* énigme *f*, mystère *m*; (*game*) jeu *m*, casse-tête *m*; (*jigsaw*) puzzle *m*; (*also*: **crossword ~**) mots croisés ▷ *vt* intriguer, rendre perplexe ▷ *vi*: **to ~ over** chercher à comprendre; **puzzled** *adj* perplexe; **puzzling** *adj* déconcertant(e), inexplicable

pyjamas [pɪ'dʒɑ:məz] *npl* (*BRIT*) pyjama *m*

pylon ['paɪlən] *n* pylône *m*

pyramid ['pɪrəmɪd] *n* pyramide *f*

Pyrenees [pɪrə'ni:z] *npl* Pyrénées *fpl*

q

quack [kwæk] *n* (*of duck*) coin-coin *m inv*; (*pej: doctor*) charlatan *m*

quadruple [kwɔ'dru:pl] *vt, vi* quadrupler

quail [kweɪl] *n* (*Zool*) caille *f* ▷ *vi*: **to ~ at** *or* **before** reculer devant

quaint [kweɪnt] *adj* bizarre; (*old-fashioned*) désuet(-ète);

(picturesque) au charme vieillot, pittoresque

quake [kweɪk] *vi* trembler ▷ *n abbr* = **earthquake**

qualification [kwɔlɪfɪˈkeɪʃən] *n (often pl: degree etc)* diplôme *m*; *(training)* qualification(s) *f(pl)*; *(ability)* compétence(s) *f(pl)*; *(limitation)* réserve *f*, restriction *f*

qualified [ˈkwɔlɪfaɪd] *adj (trained)* qualifié(e); *(professionally)* diplômé(e); *(fit, competent)* compétent(e), qualifié(e); *(limited)* conditionnel(le)

qualify [ˈkwɔlɪfaɪ] *vt* qualifier; *(modify)* atténuer, nuancer ▷ *vi*: **to ~ (as)** obtenir son diplôme (de); **to ~ (for)** remplir les conditions requises (pour); *(Sport)* se qualifier (pour)

quality [ˈkwɔlɪtɪ] *n* qualité *f*

qualm [kwɑːm] *n* doute *m*; scrupule *m*

quantify [ˈkwɔntɪfaɪ] *vt* quantifier

quantity [ˈkwɔntɪtɪ] *n* quantité *f*

quarantine [ˈkwɔrntiːn] *n* quarantaine *f*

quarrel [ˈkwɔrl] *n* querelle *f*, dispute *f* ▷ *vi* se disputer, se quereller

quarry [ˈkwɔrɪ] *n (for stone)* carrière *f*; *(animal)* proie *f*, gibier *m*

quart [kwɔːt] *n* ≈ litre *m*

quarter [ˈkwɔːtə] *n* quart *m*; *(of year)* trimestre *m*; *(district)* quartier *m*; *(US, CANADA: 25 cents)* (pièce *f* de) vingt-cinq cents *mpl* ▷ *vt* partager en quartiers *or* en quatre; *(Mil)* caserner, cantonner; **quarters** *npl* logement *m*; *(Mil)* quartiers *mpl*, cantonnement *m*; **a ~ of an hour** un quart d'heure; **quarter final** *n* quart *m* de finale; **quarterly** *adj* trimestriel(le) ▷ *adv* tous les trois mois

quartet(te) [kwɔːˈtɛt] *n* quatuor *m*; *(jazz players)* quartette *m*

quartz [kwɔːts] *n* quartz *m*

quay [kiː] *n (also:* **~side)** quai *m*

queasy [ˈkwiːzɪ] *adj*: **to feel ~** avoir mal au cœur

Quebec [kwɪˈbɛk] *n (city)* Québec; *(province)* Québec *m*

queen [kwiːn] *n (gen)* reine *f*; *(Cards etc)* dame *f*

queer [kwɪə] *adj* étrange, curieux(-euse); *(suspicious)* louche ▷ *n (inf: highly offensive)* homosexuel *m*

quench [kwɛntʃ] *vt*: **to ~ one's thirst** se désaltérer

query [ˈkwɪərɪ] *n* question *f* ▷ *vt (disagree with, dispute)* mettre en doute, questionner

quest [kwɛst] *n* recherche *f*, quête *f*

question [ˈkwɛstʃən] *n* question *f* ▷ *vt (person)* interroger; *(plan, idea)* mettre en question *or* en doute; **beyond ~** sans aucun doute; **out of the ~** hors de question; **questionable** *adj* discutable; **question mark** *n* point *m* d'interrogation; **questionnaire** [kwɛstʃəˈnɛə] *n* questionnaire *m*

queue [kjuː] *(BRIT)* *n* queue *f*, file *f* ▷ *vi (also:* **~ up)** faire la queue

quiche [kiːʃ] *n* quiche *f*

quick [kwɪk] *adj* rapide; *(mind)* vif (vive); *(agile)* agile, vif (vive) ▷ *n*: **cut to the ~** *(fig)* touché(e) au vif; **be ~!** dépêche-toi!; **quickly** *adv (fast)* vite, rapidement; *(immediately)* tout de suite

quid [kwɪd] *n (pl inv: BRIT inf)* livre *f*

quiet [ˈkwaɪət] *adj* tranquille, calme; *(voice)* bas(se); *(ceremony, colour)* discret(-ète) ▷ *n* tranquillité *f*, calme *m*; *(silence)* silence *m*; **quietly** *adv* tranquillement; *(silently)* silencieusement; *(discreetly)* discrètement

quilt [kwɪlt] *n* édredon *m*; *(continental quilt)* couette *f*

quirky [ˈkwɜːkɪ] *adj* singulier(-ère)

quit [kwɪt] *(pt, pp* **~** *or* **~ted)** *vt* quitter ▷ *vi (give up)*

abandonner, renoncer; *(resign)* démissionner

quite [kwaɪt] *adv (rather)* assez, plutôt; *(entirely)* complètement, tout à fait; **~ a few of them** un assez grand nombre d'entre eux; **that's not ~ right** ce n'est pas tout à fait juste; **~ (so)!** exactement!

quits [kwɪts] *adj*: **~ (with)** quitte (envers); **let's call it ~** restons-en là

quiver [ˈkwɪvə] *vi* trembler, frémir

quiz [kwɪz] *n (on TV)* jeu-concours *m* (télévisé); *(in magazine etc)* test *m* de connaissances ▷ *vt* interroger

quota [ˈkwəutə] *n* quota *m*

quotation [kwəuˈteɪʃən] *n* citation *f*; *(estimate)* devis *m*; **quotation marks** *npl* guillemets *mpl*

quote [kwəut] *n* citation *f*; *(estimate)* devis *m* ▷ *vt (sentence, author)* citer; *(price)* donner, soumettre ▷ *vi*: **to ~ from** citer; **quotes** *npl (inverted commas)* guillemets *mpl*

Rabat [rəˈbɑːt] *n* Rabat

rabbi [ˈræbaɪ] *n* rabbin *m*

rabbit [ˈræbɪt] *n* lapin *m*

rabies [ˈreɪbiːz] *n* rage *f*

RAC *n abbr (BRIT: = Royal Automobile Club)* ≈ ACF *m*

rac(c)oon [rəˈkuːn] *n* raton *m* laveur

race [reɪs] *n (species)* race *f*; *(competition, rush)* course *f* ▷ *vt (person)* faire la course avec ▷ *vi (compete)* faire la course, courir; *(pulse)* battre très vite; **race car** *n (US)* = **racing car**; **racecourse** *n* champ *m* de courses; **racehorse** *n* cheval *m* de course; **racetrack** *n* piste *f*

racial [ˈreɪʃl] *adj* racial(e)

racing [ˈreɪsɪŋ] *n* courses *fpl*; **racing car** *n (BRIT)* voiture *f* de course; **racing driver** *n (BRIT)* pilote *m* de course

racism [ˈreɪsɪzəm] *n* racisme *m*; **racist** [ˈreɪsɪst] *adj*, *n* raciste *m/f*

rack [ræk] n (for guns, tools) râtelier m; (for clothes) portant m; (for bottles) casier m; (also: **luggage ~**) filet m à bagages; (also: **roof ~**) galerie f; (also: **dish ~**) égouttoir m ▷ vt tourmenter; **to ~ one's brains** se creuser la cervelle

racket ['rækɪt] n (for tennis) raquette f; (noise) tapage m, vacarme m; (swindle) escroquerie f

racquet ['rækɪt] n raquette f

radar ['reɪdɑːʳ] n radar m

radiation [reɪdɪ'eɪʃən] n rayonnement m; (radioactive) radiation f

radiator ['reɪdɪeɪtəʳ] n radiateur m

radical ['rædɪkl] adj radical(e)

radio ['reɪdɪəʊ] n radio f ▷ vt (person) appeler par radio; **on the ~** à la radio; **radioactive** adj radioactif(-ive); **radio station** n station f de radio

radish ['rædɪʃ] n radis m

RAF n abbr (BRIT) = **Royal Air Force**

raffle ['ræfl] n tombola f

raft [rɑːft] n (craft: also: **life ~**) radeau m; (logs) train m de flottage

rag [ræg] n chiffon m; (pej: newspaper) feuille f, torchon m; (for charity) attractions organisées par les étudiants au profit d'œuvres de charité; **rags** npl haillons mpl

rage [reɪdʒ] n (fury) rage f, fureur f ▷ vi (person) être fou (folle) de rage; (storm) faire rage, être déchaîné(e); **it's all the ~** cela fait fureur

ragged ['rægɪd] adj (edge) inégal(e), qui accroche; (clothes) en loques; (appearance) déguenillé(e)

raid [reɪd] n (Mil) raid m; (criminal) hold-up m inv; (by police) descente f, rafle f ▷ vt faire un raid sur ou un hold-up dans ou une descente dans

rail [reɪl] n (on stair) rampe f; (on bridge, balcony) balustrade f; (of ship) bastingage m; (for train) rail m; **railcard** n (BRIT) carte f de chemin de fer; **railing(s)** n(pl) grille f; **railway** (US **railroad**) n chemin m de fer; (track) voie f ferrée; **railway line** n (BRIT) ligne f de chemin de fer; (track) voie ferrée; **railway station** n (BRIT) gare f

rain [reɪn] n pluie f ▷ vi pleuvoir; **in the ~** sous la pluie; **it's ~ing** il pleut; **rainbow** n arc-en-ciel m; **raincoat** n imperméable m; **raindrop** n goutte f de pluie; **rainfall** n chute f de pluie; (measurement) hauteur f des précipitations; **rainforest** n forêt tropicale; **rainy** adj pluvieux(-euse)

raise [reɪz] n augmentation f ▷ vt (lift) lever; hausser; (increase) augmenter; (morale) remonter; (standards) améliorer; (a protest, doubt) provoquer, causer; (a question) soulever; (cattle, family) élever; (crop) faire pousser; (army, funds) rassembler; (loan) obtenir; **to ~ one's voice** élever la voix

raisin ['reɪzn] n raisin sec

rake [reɪk] n (tool) râteau m; (person) débauché m ▷ vt (garden) ratisser

rally ['rælɪ] n (Pol etc) meeting m, rassemblement m; (Aut) rallye m; (Tennis) échange m ▷ vt rassembler, rallier; (support) gagner ▷ vi (sick person) aller mieux; (Stock Exchange) reprendre

RAM [ræm] n abbr (Comput: = random access memory) mémoire vive

ram [ræm] n bélier m ▷ vt (push) enfoncer; (crash into: vehicle) emboutir; (: lamppost etc) percuter

Ramadan [ræmə'dæn] n Ramadan m

ramble ['ræmbl] n randonnée f ▷ vi (walk) se promener, faire une randonnée; (pej: also: **~ on**) discourir, pérorer; **rambler** n promeneur(-euse), randonneur(-euse);

rambling adj (speech) décousu(e); (house) plein(e) de coins et de recoins; (Bot) grimpant(e)

ramp [ræmp] n (incline) rampe f; (Aut) dénivellation f; (in garage) pont m; **on/off** ~ (us Aut) bretelle f d'accès

rampage [ræm'peɪdʒ] n: **to be on the ~** se déchaîner

ran [ræn] pt of **run**

ranch [rɑːntʃ] n ranch m

random ['rændəm] adj fait(e) ou établi(e) au hasard; (Comput, Math) aléatoire ▷ n: **at ~** au hasard

rang [ræŋ] pt of **ring**

range [reɪndʒ] n (of mountains) chaîne f; (of missile, voice) portée f; (of products) choix m, gamme f; (also: **shooting ~**) champ m de tir; (also: **kitchen ~**) fourneau m (de cuisine) ▷ vt (place) mettre en rang, placer ▷ vi: **to ~ over** couvrir; **to ~ from ... to** aller de ... à

ranger ['reɪndʒəʳ] n garde m forestier

rank [ræŋk] n rang m; (Mil, status) grade m; (BRIT: also: **taxi ~**) station f de taxis ▷ vi: **to ~ among** compter ou se classer parmi ▷ adj (smell) nauséabond(e); **the ~ and file** (fig) la masse, la base

ransom ['rænsəm] n rançon f; **to hold sb to ~** (fig) exercer un chantage sur qn

rant [rænt] vi fulminer

rap [ræp] n (music) rap m ▷ vt (door) frapper sur ou à; (table etc) taper sur

rape [reɪp] n viol m; (Bot) colza m ▷ vt violer

rapid ['ræpɪd] adj rapide; **rapidly** adv rapidement; **rapids** npl (Geo) rapides mpl

rapist ['reɪpɪst] n auteur m d'un viol

rapport [ræ'pɔːʳ] n entente f

rare [reəʳ] adj rare; (Culin: steak) saignant(e); **rarely** adv rarement

rash [ræʃ] adj imprudent(e), irréfléchi(e) ▷ n (Med) rougeur f, éruption f; (of events) série f (noire)

rasher ['ræʃəʳ] n fine tranche (de lard)

raspberry ['rɑːzbərɪ] n framboise f

rat [ræt] n rat m

rate [reɪt] n (ratio) taux m, pourcentage m; (speed) vitesse f, rythme m; (price) tarif m ▷ vt (price) évaluer, estimer; (people) classer; **rates** npl (BRIT: property tax) impôts locaux; **to ~ sb/sth as** considérer qn/qch comme

rather ['rɑːðəʳ] adv (somewhat) assez, plutôt; (to some extent) un peu; **it's ~ expensive** c'est assez cher; (too much) c'est un peu cher; **there's ~ a lot** il y en a beaucoup; **I would** ou **I'd ~ go** j'aimerais mieux ou je préférerais partir; **or ~** (more accurately) ou plutôt

rating ['reɪtɪŋ] n (assessment) évaluation f; (score) classement m; (Finance) cote f; **ratings** npl (Radio) indice(s) m(pl) d'écoute; (TV) Audimat® m

ratio ['reɪʃɪəʊ] n proportion f; **in the ~ of 100 to 1** dans la proportion de 100 contre 1

ration ['ræʃən] n ration f ▷ vt rationner; **rations** npl (food) vivres mpl

rational ['ræʃənl] adj raisonnable, sensé(e); (solution, reasoning) logique; (Med: person) lucide

rat race n foire f d'empoigne

rattle ['rætl] n (of door, window) battement m; (of coins, chain) cliquetis m; (of train, engine) bruit m de ferraille; (for baby) hochet m ▷ vi cliqueter; (car, bus): **to ~ along** rouler en faisant un bruit de ferraille ▷ vt agiter (bruyamment); (inf: disconcert) décontenancer

rave [reɪv] vi (in anger) s'emporter; (with enthusiasm) s'extasier; (Med) délirer ▷ n (inf: party) rave f, soirée f techno

raven ['reɪvən] n grand corbeau

ravine [rə'viːn] n ravin m

raw [rɔː] adj (uncooked) cru(e); (not processed) brut(e); (sore) à vif, irrité(e); (inexperienced) inexpérimenté(e); **~ materials** matières premières

ray [reɪ] n rayon m; **~ of hope** lueur f d'espoir

razor ['reɪzəʳ] n rasoir m; **razor blade** n lame f de rasoir

Rd abbr = **road**

RE n abbr (BRIT) = **religious education**

re [riː] prep concernant

reach [riːtʃ] n portée f, atteinte f; (of river etc) étendue f ▷ vt atteindre, arriver à; (conclusion, decision) parvenir à ▷ vi s'étendre; **out of/within ~** (object) hors de/à portée; **reach out** vt tendre ▷ vi: **to ~ out (for)** allonger le bras (pour prendre)

react [riː'ækt] vi réagir; **reaction** [riː'ækʃən] n réaction f; **reactor** [riː'æktəʳ] n réacteur m

read (pt, pp **~**) [riːd, rɛd] vi lire ▷ vt lire; (understand) comprendre, interpréter; (study) étudier; (meter) relever; (subj: instrument etc) indiquer, marquer; **read out** vt lire à haute voix; **reader** n lecteur(-trice)

readily ['rɛdɪlɪ] adv volontiers, avec empressement; (easily) facilement

reading ['riːdɪŋ] n lecture f; (understanding) interprétation f; (on instrument) indications fpl

ready ['rɛdɪ] adj prêt(e); (willing) prêt, disposé(e); (available) disponible ▷ n: **at the ~** (Mil) prêt à faire feu; **when will my photos be ~?** quand est-ce que mes photos seront prêtes?; **to get ~** (as vi) se préparer; (as vt) préparer; **ready-cooked** adj précuit(e); **ready-made** adj tout(e) faite(e)

real [rɪəl] adj (world, life) réel(le); (genuine) véritable; (proper) vrai(e) ▷ adv (us inf: very) vraiment; **real ale** n bière traditionnelle; **real estate** n biens fonciers or immobiliers; **realistic** [rɪə'lɪstɪk] adj réaliste; **reality** [riː'ælɪtɪ] n réalité f

reality TV n téléréalité f

realization [rɪəlaɪ'zeɪʃən] n (awareness) prise f de conscience; (fulfilment: also: of asset) réalisation f

realize ['rɪəlaɪz] vt (understand) se rendre compte de, prendre conscience de; (a project, Comm: asset) réaliser

really ['rɪəlɪ] adv vraiment; **~?** vraiment?, c'est vrai?

realm [rɛlm] n royaume m; (fig) domaine m

realtor ['rɪəltɔːʳ] n (us) agent immobilier

reappear [riːə'pɪəʳ] vi réapparaître, reparaître

rear [rɪəʳ] adj de derrière, arrière inv; (Aut: wheel etc) arrière ▷ n arrière m ▷ vt (cattle, family) élever ▷ vi (also: **~ up**: animal) se cabrer

rearrange [riːə'reɪndʒ] vt réarranger

rear: **rear-view mirror** n (Aut) rétroviseur m; **rear-wheel drive** n (Aut) traction f arrière

reason ['riːzn] n raison f ▷ vi: **to ~ with sb** raisonner qn, faire entendre raison à qn; **it stands to ~ that** il va sans dire que; **reasonable** adj raisonnable; (not bad) acceptable; **reasonably** adv (behave) raisonnablement; (fairly) assez; **reasoning** n raisonnement m

reassurance [riːə'ʃuərəns] n (factual) assurance f, garantie f; (emotional) réconfort m

reassure [riːə'ʃuəʳ] vt rassurer

rebate ['riːbeɪt] n (on tax etc) dégrèvement m

rebel n ['rɛbl] rebelle m/f ▷ vi [rɪ'bɛl] se rebeller, se révolter; **rebellion** [rɪ'bɛljən] n rébellion f, révolte f; **rebellious** [rɪ'bɛljəs] adj rebelle

rebuild [riː'bɪld] vt (irreg: like **build**) reconstruire

recall vt [rɪ'kɔːl] rappeler; (remember) se rappeler, se souvenir de ▷ n ['riːkɔːl] rappel m; (ability to remember) mémoire f

rec'd abbr of **received**

receipt [rɪ'siːt] n (document) reçu m; (for parcel etc) accusé m de réception; (act of receiving) réception f; **receipts** npl (Comm) recettes fpl; **can I have a ~, please?** je peux avoir un reçu, s'il vous plaît?

receive [rɪ'siːv] vt recevoir; (guest) recevoir, accueillir; **receiver** n (Tel) récepteur m, combiné m; (Radio) récepteur; (of stolen goods) receleur(-euse); (for bankruptcies) administrateur m judiciaire

recent ['riːsnt] adj récent(e); **recently** adv récemment

reception [rɪ'sɛpʃən] n réception f; (welcome) accueil m, réception; **reception desk** n réception f; **receptionist** n réceptionniste m/f

recession [rɪ'sɛʃən] n (Econ) récession f

recharge [riː'tʃɑːdʒ] vt (battery) recharger

recipe ['rɛsɪpɪ] n recette f

recipient [rɪ'sɪpɪənt] n (of payment) bénéficiaire m/f; (of letter) destinataire m/f

recital [rɪ'saɪtl] n récital m

recite [rɪ'saɪt] vt (poem) réciter

reckless ['rɛkləs] adj (driver etc) imprudent(e); (spender etc) insouciant(e)

reckon ['rɛkən] vt (count) calculer, compter; (consider) considérer, estimer; (think): **I ~ (that) ...** je pense (que) ..., j'estime (que) ...

reclaim [rɪ'kleɪm] vt (land: from sea) assécher; (demand back) réclamer (le remboursement or la restitution de); (waste materials) récupérer

recline [rɪ'klaɪn] vi être allongé(e) or étendu(e)

recognition [rɛkəg'nɪʃən] n reconnaissance f; **transformed beyond ~** méconnaissable

recognize ['rɛkəgnaɪz] vt: **to ~ (by/as)** reconnaître (à/comme étant)

recollection [rɛkə'lɛkʃən] n souvenir m

recommend [rɛkə'mɛnd] vt recommander; **can you ~ a good restaurant?** pouvez-vous me conseiller un bon restaurant?; **recommendation** [rɛkəmən'deɪʃən] n recommandation f

reconcile ['rɛkənsaɪl] vt (two people) réconcilier; (two facts) concilier, accorder; **to ~ o.s. to** se résigner à

reconsider [riːkən'sɪdəʳ] vt reconsidérer

reconstruct [riːkən'strʌkt] vt (building) reconstruire; (crime, system) reconstituer

record n ['rɛkɔːd] rapport m, récit m; (of meeting etc) procès-verbal m; (register) registre m; (file) dossier m; (Comput) article m; (also: **police ~**) casier m judiciaire; (Mus: disc) disque m; (Sport) record m ▷ adj record inv ▷ vt [rɪ'kɔːd] (set down) noter; (Mus: song etc) enregistrer; **public ~s** archives fpl; **in ~ time** dans un temps record; **recorded delivery** n (BRIT Post): **to send sth recorded delivery** = envoyer qch en recommandé; **recorder** n (Mus) flûte f à bec; **recording** n (Mus) enregistrement m; **record player** n tourne-disque m

recount [rɪ'kaunt] vt raconter

recover [rɪ'kʌvəʳ] vt récupérer ▷ vi (from illness) se rétablir; (from shock) se remettre; **recovery** n récupération f; rétablissement m; (Econ) redressement m

recreate [riː'krɪ'eɪt] vt recréer

recreation [rɛkrɪ'eɪʃən] n (leisure) récréation f, détente f; **recreational drug** n drogue récréative; **recreational vehicle** n (us) camping-car m

recruit [rɪˈkruːt] n recrue f ▷ vt recruter; **recruitment** n recrutement m

rectangle [ˈrɛktæŋgl] n rectangle m; **rectangular** [rɛkˈtæŋgjuləʳ] adj rectangulaire

rectify [ˈrɛktɪfaɪ] vt (error) rectifier, corriger

rector [ˈrɛktəʳ] n (Rel) pasteur m

recur [rɪˈkəːʳ] vi se reproduire; (idea, opportunity) se retrouver; (symptoms) réapparaître; **recurring** adj (problem) périodique, fréquent(e); (Math) périodique

recyclable [riːˈsaɪkləbl] adj recyclable

recycle [riːˈsaɪkl] vt, vi recycler

recycling [riːˈsaɪklɪŋ] n recyclage m

red [rɛd] n rouge m; (Pol: pej) rouge m/f ▷ adj rouge; (hair) roux (rousse), ▷ adj rouge; (hair) roux (rousse); **in the ~** (account) à découvert; (business) en déficit; **Red Cross** n Croix-Rouge f; **redcurrant** n groseille f (rouge)

redeem [rɪˈdiːm] vt (debt) rembourser; (sth in pawn) dégager; (fig, also Rel) racheter

red: **red-haired** adj roux (rousse); **redhead** n roux (rousse); **red-hot** adj chauffé(e) au rouge, brûlant(e); **red light** n: **to go through a red light** (Aut) brûler un feu rouge; **red-light district** n quartier mal famé

red meat n viande f rouge

reduce [rɪˈdjuːs] vt réduire; (lower) abaisser; **"~ speed now"** (Aut) "ralentir"; **to ~ sb to tears** faire pleurer qn; **reduced** adj réduit(e); **"greatly reduced prices"** "gros rabais"; **at a reduced price** (goods) au rabais; (ticket etc) à prix réduit; **reduction** [rɪˈdʌkʃən] n réduction f, (of price) baisse f; (discount) rabais m; réduction; **is there a reduction for children/students?** y a-t-il une réduction pour les enfants/les étudiants?

redundancy [rɪˈdʌndənsɪ] n (BRIT) licenciement m, mise f au chômage

redundant [rɪˈdʌndnt] adj (BRIT: worker) licencié(e), mis(e) au chômage; (detail, object) superflu(e); **to be made ~** (worker) être licencié, être mis au chômage

reed [riːd] n (Bot) roseau m

reef [riːf] n (at sea) récif m, écueil m

reel [riːl] n bobine f, (Fishing) moulinet m; (Cine) bande f; (dance) quadrille écossais ▷ vi (sway) chanceler

ref [rɛf] n abbr (inf: = referee) arbitre m

refectory [rɪˈfɛktərɪ] n réfectoire m

refer [rɪˈfəːʳ] vt: **to ~ sb to** (inquirer, patient) adresser qn à; (reader: to text) renvoyer qn à ▷ vi: **to ~ to** (allude to) parler de, faire allusion à; (consult) se reporter à; (apply to) s'appliquer à

referee [rɛfəˈriː] n arbitre m; (BRIT: for job application) répondant(e) ▷ vt arbitrer

reference [ˈrɛfrəns] n référence f, renvoi m; (mention) allusion f, mention f; (for job application: letter) références; lettre f de recommandation; **with ~ to** en ce qui concerne; (Comm: in letter) me référant à; **reference number** n (Comm) numéro m de référence

refill vt [riːˈfɪl] remplir à nouveau; (pen, lighter etc) recharger ▷ n [ˈriːfɪl] (for pen etc) recharge f

refine [rɪˈfaɪn] vt (sugar, oil) raffiner; (taste) affiner; (idea, theory) peaufiner; **refined** adj (person, taste) raffiné(e); **refinery** n raffinerie f

reflect [rɪˈflɛkt] vt (light, image) réfléchir, refléter ▷ vi (think) réfléchir, méditer; **it ~s badly on him** cela le discrédite; **it ~s well on him** c'est tout à son honneur; **reflection** [rɪˈflɛkʃən] n réflexion f, (image) reflet m; **on reflection** réflexion faite

reflex [ˈriːflɛks] adj, n réflexe (m)

reform [rɪˈfɔːm] n réforme f ▷ vt réformer

refrain [rɪˈfreɪn] vi: **to ~ from doing** s'abstenir de faire ▷ n refrain m

refresh [rɪˈfrɛʃ] vt rafraîchir; (subj: food, sleep etc) redonner des forces à; **refreshing** adj (drink) rafraîchissant(e); (sleep) réparateur(-trice); **refreshments** npl rafraîchissements mpl

refrigerator [rɪˈfrɪdʒəreɪtəʳ] n réfrigérateur m, frigidaire m

refuel [riːˈfjuəl] vi se ravitailler en carburant

refuge [ˈrɛfjuːdʒ] n refuge m; **to take ~ in** se réfugier dans; **refugee** [rɛfjuˈdʒiː] n réfugié(e)

refund n [ˈriːfʌnd] remboursement m ▷ vt [rɪˈfʌnd] rembourser

refurbish [riːˈfəːbɪʃ] vt remettre à neuf

refusal [rɪˈfjuːzəl] n refus m; **to have first ~ on sth** avoir droit de préemption sur qch

refuse[1] [ˈrɛfjuːs] n ordures fpl, détritus mpl

refuse[2] [rɪˈfjuːz] vt, vi refuser; **to ~ to do sth** refuser de faire qch

regain [rɪˈgeɪn] vt (lost ground) regagner; (strength) retrouver

regard [rɪˈgɑːd] n respect m, estime f, considération f ▷ vt considérer; **to give one's ~s to** faire ses amitiés à; **"with kindest ~s"** "bien amicalement"; **as ~s, with ~ to** en ce qui concerne; **regarding** prep en ce qui concerne; **regardless** adv quand même; **regardless of** sans se soucier de

regenerate [rɪˈdʒɛnəreɪt] vt régénérer ▷ vi se régénérer

reggae [ˈrɛgeɪ] n reggae m

regiment [ˈrɛdʒɪmənt] n régiment m

region [ˈriːdʒən] n région f; **in the ~ of** (fig) aux alentours de; **regional** adj régional(e)

register [ˈrɛdʒɪstəʳ] n registre m; (also: **electoral ~**) liste électorale ▷ vt enregistrer, inscrire; (birth) déclarer; (vehicle) immatriculer; (letter) envoyer en recommandé; (subj: instrument) marquer ▷ vi s'inscrire; (at hotel) signer le registre; (make impression) être (bien) compris(e); **registered** adj (BRIT: letter) recommandé(e)

registered trademark n marque déposée

registrar [ˈrɛdʒɪstrɑːʳ] n officier m de l'état civil

registration [rɛdʒɪsˈtreɪʃən] n (act) enregistrement m; (of student) inscription f; (BRIT Aut: also: **~ number**) numéro m d'immatriculation

registry office [ˈrɛdʒɪstrɪ-] n (BRIT) bureau m de l'état civil; **to get married in a ~** se marier à la mairie

regret [rɪˈgrɛt] n regret m ▷ vt regretter; **regrettable** adj regrettable, fâcheux(-euse)

regular [ˈrɛgjuləʳ] adj régulier(-ière); (usual) habituel(le), normal(e); (soldier) de métier; (Comm: size) ordinaire ▷ n (client etc) habitué(e); **regularly** adv régulièrement

regulate [ˈrɛgjuleɪt] vt régler; **regulation** [rɛgjuˈleɪʃən] n (rule) règlement m; (adjustment) réglage m

rehabilitation [ˈriːəbɪlɪˈteɪʃən] n (of offender) réhabilitation f; (of addict) réadaptation f

rehearsal [rɪˈhəːsəl] n répétition f

rehearse [rɪˈhəːs] vt répéter

reign [reɪn] n règne m ▷ vi régner

reimburse [riːɪmˈbəːs] vt rembourser

rein [reɪn] n (for horse) rêne f

reincarnation [riːɪnkɑːˈneɪʃən] n réincarnation f

reindeer [ˈreɪndɪəʳ] n (pl inv) renne m

reinforce [riːɪnˈfɔːs] vt renforcer; **reinforcements** npl

(*Mil*) renfort(s) *m(pl)*
reinstate [riːɪnˈsteɪt] *vt* rétablir, réintégrer
reject *n* [ˈriːdʒɛkt] (*Comm*) article *m* de rebut ▷ *vt*
[rɪˈdʒɛkt] refuser; (*idea*) rejeter; **rejection** [rɪˈdʒɛkʃən] *n*
rejet *m*, refus *m*
rejoice [rɪˈdʒɔɪs] *vi*: to ~ (at or over) se réjouir (de)
relate [rɪˈleɪt] *vt* (*tell*) raconter; (*connect*) établir un
rapport entre ▷ *vi*: to ~ to (*connect*) se rapporter à; to ~
to sb (*interact*) entretenir des rapports avec qn; **related**
adj apparenté(e); **related to** (*subject*) lié(e) à; **relating
to** *prep* concernant
relation [rɪˈleɪʃən] *n* (*person*) parent(e); (*link*) rapport *m*,
lien *m*; **relations** *npl* (*relatives*) famille *f*; **relationship** *n*
rapport *m*, lien *m*; (*personal ties*) relations *fpl*, rapports;
(*also*: **family relationship**) lien de parenté; (*affair*)
liaison *f*
relative [ˈrɛlətɪv] *n* parent(e) ▷ *adj* relatif(-ive);
(*respective*) respectif(-ive); **relatively** *adv* relativement
relax [rɪˈlæks] *vi* (*muscle*) se relâcher; (*person: unwind*)
se détendre ▷ *vt* relâcher; (*mind, person*) détendre;
relaxation [riːlækˈseɪʃən] *n* relâchement *m*; (*of mind*)
détente *f*; (*recreation*) détente, délassement *m*; **relaxed**
adj relâché(e); détendu(e); **relaxing** *adj* délassant(e)
relay [ˈriːleɪ] *n* (*Sport*) course *f* de relais ▷ *vt* (*message*)
retransmettre, relayer
release [rɪˈliːs] *n* (*from prison, obligation*) libération *f*; (*of
gas etc*) émission *f*; (*of film etc*) sortie *f*; (*new recording*)
disque *m* ▷ *vt* (*prisoner*) libérer; (*book, film*) sortir; (*report,
news*) rendre public, publier; (*gas etc*) émettre, dégager;
(*free: from wreckage etc*) dégager; (*Tech: catch, spring etc*)
déclencher; (*let go: person, animal*) relâcher; (*: hand,
object*) lâcher; (*: grip, brake*) desserrer
relegate [ˈrɛləgeɪt] *vt* reléguer; (*Brit Sport*): **to be ~d**
descendre dans une division inférieure
relent [rɪˈlɛnt] *vi* se laisser fléchir; **relentless** *adj*
implacable; (*non-stop*) continuel(le)
relevant [ˈrɛləvənt] *adj* (*question*) pertinent(e);
(*corresponding*) approprié(e); (*fact*) significatif(-ive);
(*information*) utile
reliable [rɪˈlaɪəbl] *adj* (*person, firm*) sérieux(-euse), fiable;
(*method, machine*) fiable; (*news, information*) sûr(e)
relic [ˈrɛlɪk] *n* (*Rel*) relique *f*; (*of the past*) vestige *m*
relief [rɪˈliːf] *n* (*from pain, anxiety*) soulagement *m*; (*help,
supplies*) secours *m(pl)*; (*Art, Geo*) relief *m*
relieve [rɪˈliːv] *vt* (*pain, patient*) soulager; (*fear, worry*)
dissiper; (*bring help*) secourir; (*take over from: gen*) relayer;
(*: guard*) relever; **to ~ sb of sth** débarrasser qn de qch;
to ~ o.s. (*euphemism*) se soulager, faire ses besoins;
relieved *adj* soulagé(e)
religion [rɪˈlɪdʒən] *n* religion *f*
religious [rɪˈlɪdʒəs] *adj* religieux(-euse); (*book*) de piété;
religious education *n* instruction religieuse
relish [ˈrɛlɪʃ] *n* (*Culin*) condiment *m*; (*enjoyment*)
délectation *f* ▷ *vt* (*food etc*) savourer; **to ~ doing** se
délecter à faire
relocate [riːləuˈkeɪt] *vt* (*business*) transférer ▷ *vi* se
transférer, s'installer or s'établir ailleurs
reluctance [rɪˈlʌktəns] *n* répugnance *f*
reluctant [rɪˈlʌktənt] *adj* peu disposé(e), qui hésite;
reluctantly *adv* à contrecœur, sans enthousiasme
rely on [rɪˈlaɪ-] *vt fus* (*be dependent on*) dépendre de;
(*trust*) compter sur
remain [rɪˈmeɪn] *vi* rester; **remainder** *n* reste *m*;
(*Comm*) fin *f* de série; **remaining** *adj* qui reste; **remains**

npl restes *mpl*
remand [rɪˈmɑːnd] *n*: on ~ en détention préventive
▷ *vt*: **to be ~ed in custody** être placé(e) en détention
préventive
remark [rɪˈmɑːk] *n* remarque *f*, observation *f* ▷ *vt* (*faire*)
remarquer, dire; **remarkable** *adj* remarquable
remarry [riːˈmærɪ] *vi* se remarier
remedy [ˈrɛmədɪ] *n*: ~ (for) remède *m* (contre or à) ▷ *vt*
remédier à
remember [rɪˈmɛmbər] *vt* se rappeler, se souvenir
de; (*send greetings*): ~ me to him saluez-le de ma part;
Remembrance Day [rɪˈmɛmbrəns-] *n* (*Brit*) ≈ (le jour
de) l'Armistice *m*, ≈ le 11 novembre
remind [rɪˈmaɪnd] *vt*: **to ~ sb of sth** rappeler qch à qn;
to ~ sb to do faire penser à qn à faire, rappeler à qn qu'il
doit faire; **reminder** *n* (*Comm: letter*) rappel *m*; (*note etc*)
pense-bête *m*; (*souvenir*) souvenir *m*
reminiscent [rɛmɪˈnɪsnt] *adj*: ~ of qui rappelle, qui
fait penser à
remnant [ˈrɛmnənt] *n* reste *m*, restant *m*; (*of cloth*)
coupon *m*
remorse [rɪˈmɔːs] *n* remords *m*
remote [rɪˈməut] *adj* éloigné(e), lointain(e); (*person*)
distant(e); (*possibility*) vague; **remote control** *n*
télécommande *f*; **remotely** *adv* au loin; (*slightly*) très
vaguement
removal [rɪˈmuːvəl] *n* (*taking away*) enlèvement *m*;
suppression *f*; (*Brit: from house*) déménagement *m*; (*from
office: dismissal*) renvoi *m*; (*of stain*) nettoyage *m*; (*Med*)
ablation *f*; **removal man** (*irreg*) *n* (*Brit*) déménageur *m*;
removal van *n* (*Brit*) camion *m* de déménagement
remove [rɪˈmuːv] *vt* enlever, retirer; (*employee*) renvoyer;
(*stain*) faire partir; (*abuse*) supprimer; (*doubt*) chasser
Renaissance [rɪˈneɪsɑ̃s] *n*: the ~ la Renaissance
rename [riːˈneɪm] *vt* rebaptiser
render [ˈrɛndər] *vt* rendre
rendezvous [ˈrɔndɪvuː] *n* rendez-vous *m inv*
renew [rɪˈnjuː] *vt* renouveler; (*negotiations*) reprendre;
(*acquaintance*) renouer
renovate [ˈrɛnəveɪt] *vt* rénover; (*work of art*) restaurer
renowned [rɪˈnaund] *adj* renommé(e)
rent [rɛnt] *pt, pp* of **rend** ▷ *n* loyer *m* ▷ *vt* louer; **rental** *n*
(*for television, car*) (prix *m* de) location *f*
reorganize [riːˈɔːgənaɪz] *vt* réorganiser
rep [rɛp] *n abbr* (*Comm*) = **representative**
repair [rɪˈpɛər] *n* réparation *f* ▷ *vt* réparer; **in good/bad
~** en bon/mauvais état; **where can I get this ~ed?** où
est-ce que je peux faire réparer ceci?; **repair kit** *n* trousse
f de réparations
repay [riːˈpeɪ] *vt* (*irreg: like* **pay**) (*money, creditor*)
rembourser; (*sb's efforts*) récompenser; **repayment** *n*
remboursement *m*
repeat [rɪˈpiːt] *n* (*Radio, TV*) reprise *f* ▷ *vt* répéter;
(*promise, attack, also Comm: order*) renouveler; (*Scol: a
class*) redoubler ▷ *vi* répéter; **can you ~ that, please?**
pouvez-vous répéter, s'il vous plaît?; **repeatedly** *adv*
souvent, à plusieurs reprises; **repeat prescription**
n (*Brit*): **I'd like a repeat prescription** je voudrais
renouveler mon ordonnance
repellent [rɪˈpɛlənt] *adj* repoussant(e) ▷ *n*: **insect ~**
insectifuge *m*
repercussions [riːpəˈkʌʃənz] *npl* répercussions *fpl*
repetition [rɛpɪˈtɪʃən] *n* répétition *f*
repetitive [rɪˈpɛtɪtɪv] *adj* (*movement, work*)

répétitif(-ive); (speech) plein(e) de redites

replace [rɪ'pleɪs] vt (put back) remettre, replacer; (take the place of) remplacer; **replacement** n (substitution) remplacement m; (person) remplaçant(e)

replay ['riːpleɪ] n (of match) match rejoué; (of tape, film) répétition f

replica ['replɪkə] n réplique f, copie exacte

reply [rɪ'plaɪ] n réponse f ▷ vi répondre

report [rɪ'pɔːt] n rapport m; (Press etc) reportage m; (BRIT: also: **school ~**) bulletin m (scolaire); (of gun) détonation f ▷ vt rapporter, faire un compte rendu de; (Press etc) faire un reportage sur; (notify: accident) signaler; (: culprit) dénoncer ▷ vi (make a report) faire un rapport; (present o.s.): **to ~ (to sb)** se présenter (chez qn); **report card** n (US, SCOTTISH) bulletin m (scolaire); **reportedly** adv: **she is reportedly living in Spain** elle habiterait en Espagne; **he reportedly told them to ...** il leur aurait dit de ...; **reporter** n reporter m

represent [reprɪ'zent] vt représenter; (view, belief) présenter, expliquer; (describe): **to ~ sth as** présenter or décrire qch comme; **representation** [reprɪzen'teɪʃən] n représentation f; **representative** n représentant(e); (US Pol) député m ▷ adj représentatif(-ive), caractéristique

repress [rɪ'pres] vt réprimer; **repression** [rɪ'preʃən] n répression f

reprimand ['reprɪmɑːnd] n réprimande f ▷ vt réprimander

reproduce [riːprə'djuːs] vt reproduire ▷ vi se reproduire; **reproduction** [riːprə'dʌkʃən] n reproduction f

reptile ['reptaɪl] n reptile m

republic [rɪ'pʌblɪk] n république f; **republican** adj, n républicain(e)

reputable ['repjutəbl] adj de bonne réputation; (occupation) honorable

reputation [repju'teɪʃən] n réputation f

request [rɪ'kwest] n demande f; (formal) requête f ▷ vt: **to ~ (of or from sb)** demander (à qn); **request stop** n (BRIT: for bus) arrêt facultatif

require [rɪ'kwaɪə'] vt (need: subj: person) avoir besoin de; (: thing, situation) nécessiter, demander; (want) exiger; (order): **to ~ sb to do sth/sth of sb** exiger que qn fasse qch/qch de qn; **requirement** n (need) exigence f; besoin m; (condition) condition f (requise)

resat [riː'sæt] pt, pp of **resit**

rescue ['reskjuː] n (from accident) sauvetage m; (help) secours mpl ▷ vt sauver

research [rɪ'sɜːtʃ] n recherche(s) f(pl) ▷ vt faire des recherches sur

resemblance [rɪ'zembləns] n ressemblance f

resemble [rɪ'zembl] vt ressembler à

resent [rɪ'zent] vt être contrarié(e) par; **resentful** adj irrité(e), plein(e) de ressentiment; **resentment** n ressentiment m

reservation [rezə'veɪʃən] n (booking) réservation f; **to make a ~ (in an hotel/a restaurant/on a plane)** réserver or retenir une chambre/une table/une place; **reservation desk** n (US: in hotel) réception f

reserve [rɪ'zɜːv] n réserve f; (Sport) remplaçant(e) ▷ vt (seats etc) réserver, retenir; **reserved** adj réservé(e)

reservoir ['rezəvwɑː'] n réservoir m

reshuffle [riː'ʃʌfl] n: **Cabinet ~** (Pol) remaniement ministériel

residence ['rezɪdəns] n résidence f; **residence permit** n (BRIT) permis m de séjour

resident ['rezɪdənt] n (of country) résident(e); (of area, house) habitant(e); (in hotel) pensionnaire f ▷ adj résidant(e); **residential** [rezɪ'denʃəl] adj de résidence; (area) résidentiel(le); (course) avec hébergement sur place

residue ['rezɪdjuː] n reste m; (Chem, Physics) résidu m

resign [rɪ'zaɪn] vt (one's post) se démettre de ▷ vi démissionner; **to ~ o.s. to** (endure) se résigner à; **resignation** [rezɪg'neɪʃən] n (from post) démission f; (state of mind) résignation f

resin ['rezɪn] n résine f

resist [rɪ'zɪst] vt résister à; **resistance** n résistance f

resit vt [riː'sɪt] (BRIT): (pt, pp **resat**) (exam) repasser ▷ n ['riːsɪt] deuxième session f (d'un examen)

resolution [rezə'luːʃən] n résolution f

resolve [rɪ'zɔlv] n résolution f ▷ vt (decide): **to ~ to do** résoudre or décider de faire; (problem) résoudre

resort [rɪ'zɔːt] n (seaside town) station f balnéaire; (for skiing) station de ski; (recourse) recours m ▷ vi: **to ~ to** avoir recours à; **in the last ~** en dernier ressort

resource [rɪ'sɔːs] n ressource f; **resourceful** adj ingénieux(-euse), débrouillard(e)

respect [rɪs'pekt] n respect m ▷ vt respecter; **respectable** adj respectable; (quite good: result etc) honorable; **respectful** adj respectueux(-euse); **respective** adj respectif(-ive); **respectively** adv respectivement

respite ['respaɪt] n répit m

respond [rɪs'pɔnd] vi répondre; (react) réagir; **response** [rɪs'pɔns] n réponse f; (reaction) réaction f

responsibility [rɪspɔnsɪ'bɪlɪtɪ] n responsabilité f

responsible [rɪs'pɔnsɪbl] adj (liable): **~ (for)** responsable (de); (person) digne de confiance; (job) qui comporte des responsabilités; **responsibly** adv avec sérieux

responsive [rɪs'pɔnsɪv] adj (student, audience) réceptif(-ive); (brakes, steering) sensible

rest [rest] n repos m; (stop) arrêt m, pause f; (Mus) silence m; (support) support m, appui m; (remainder) reste m, restant m ▷ vi se reposer; (lean): **to ~ on/against** appuyer or reposer sur ▷ vt (lean): **to ~ sth on/against** appuyer qch sur/contre; **the ~ of them** les autres

restaurant ['restərɔŋ] n restaurant m; **restaurant car** n (BRIT Rail) wagon-restaurant m

restless ['restlɪs] adj agité(e)

restoration [restə'reɪʃən] n (of building) restauration f; (of stolen goods) restitution f

restore [rɪ'stɔː'] vt (building) restaurer; (sth stolen) restituer; (peace, health) rétablir; **to ~ to** (former state) ramener à

restrain [rɪs'treɪn] vt (feeling) contenir; (person): **to ~ (from doing)** retenir (de faire); **restraint** n (restriction) contrainte f; (moderation) retenue f; (of style) sobriété f

restrict [rɪs'trɪkt] vt restreindre, limiter; **restriction** [rɪs'trɪkʃən] n restriction f, limitation f

rest room n (US) toilettes fpl

restructure [riː'strʌktʃə'] vt restructurer

result [rɪ'zʌlt] n résultat m ▷ vi: **to ~ in** aboutir à, se terminer par; **as a ~ of** à la suite de

resume [rɪ'zjuːm] vt (work, journey) reprendre ▷ vi (work etc) reprendre

résumé ['reɪzjuːmeɪ] n (summary) résumé m; (US: curriculum vitae) curriculum vitae m inv

resuscitate [rɪˈsʌsɪteɪt] vt (Med) réanimer

retail [ˈriːteɪl] adj de or au détail ▷ adv au détail; **retailer** n détaillant(e)

retain [rɪˈteɪn] vt (keep) garder, conserver

retaliation [rɪtælɪˈeɪʃən] n représailles fpl, vengeance f

retarded [rɪˈtɑːdɪd] adj retardé(e)

retire [rɪˈtaɪəʳ] vi (give up work) prendre sa retraite; (withdraw) se retirer, partir; (go to bed) (aller) se coucher; **retired** adj (person) retraité(e); **retirement** n retraite f

retort [rɪˈtɔːt] vi riposter

retreat [rɪˈtriːt] n retraite f ▷ vi battre en retraite

retrieve [rɪˈtriːv] vt (sth lost) récupérer; (situation, honour) sauver; (error, loss) réparer; (Comput) rechercher

retrospect [ˈretrəspekt] n: **in ~** rétrospectivement, après coup; **retrospective** [retrəˈspektɪv] adj rétrospectif(-ive); (law) rétroactif(-ive) ▷ n (Art) rétrospective f

return [rɪˈtəːn] n (going or coming back) retour m; (of sth stolen etc) restitution f; (Finance: from land, shares) rapport m ▷ cpd (journey) de retour; (BRIT: ticket) aller et retour; (match) retour ▷ vi (person etc: come back) revenir; (: go back) retourner ▷ vt rendre; (bring back) rapporter; (send back) renvoyer; (put back) remettre; (Pol: candidate) élire; **returns** npl (Comm) recettes fpl; (Finance) bénéfices mpl; **many happy ~s (of the day)!** bon anniversaire!; **by ~ (of post)** par retour (du courrier); **in ~ (for)** en échange (de); **a ~ (ticket) for ...** un billet aller et retour pour ...; **return ticket** n (esp BRIT) billet m aller-retour

reunion [riːˈjuːnɪən] n réunion f

reunite [riːjuːˈnaɪt] vt réunir

revamp [riːˈvæmp] vt (house) retaper; (firm) réorganiser

reveal [rɪˈviːl] vt (make known) révéler; (display) laisser voir; **revealing** adj révélateur(-trice); (dress) au décolleté généreux or suggestif

revel [ˈrevl] vi: **to ~ in sth/in doing** se délecter de qch/à faire

revelation [revəˈleɪʃən] n révélation f

revenge [rɪˈvendʒ] n vengeance f; (in game etc) revanche f ▷ vt venger; **to take ~ (on)** se venger (sur)

revenue [ˈrevənjuː] n revenu m

Reverend [ˈrevərənd] adj (in titles): **the ~ John Smith** (Anglican) le révérend John Smith; (Catholic) l'abbé (John) Smith; (Protestant) le pasteur (John) Smith

reversal [rɪˈvəːsl] n (of opinion) revirement m; (of order) renversement m; (of direction) changement m

reverse [rɪˈvəːs] n contraire m, opposé m; (back) dos m, envers m; (of paper) verso m; (of coin) revers m; (Aut: also: ~ **gear**) marche arrière ▷ adj (order, direction) opposé(e), inverse ▷ vt (order, position) changer, inverser; (direction, policy) changer complètement de; (decision) annuler; (roles) renverser ▷ vi (BRIT Aut) faire marche arrière; **reverse-charge call** n (BRIT Tel) communication f en PCV; **reversing lights** npl (BRIT Aut) feux mpl de marche arrière or de recul

revert [rɪˈvəːt] vi: **to ~ to** revenir à, retourner à

review [rɪˈvjuː] n revue f; (of book, film) critique f; (of situation, policy) examen m, bilan m; (us: examination) examen ▷ vt passer en revue; faire la critique de; examiner

revise [rɪˈvaɪz] vt réviser, modifier; (manuscript) revoir, corriger ▷ vi (study) réviser; **revision** [rɪˈvɪʒn] n révision f

revival [rɪˈvaɪvəl] n reprise f; (recovery) rétablissement m; (of faith) renouveau m

revive [rɪˈvaɪv] vt (person) ranimer; (custom) rétablir; (economy) relancer; (hope, courage) raviver, faire renaître; (play, fashion) reprendre ▷ vi (person) reprendre connaissance; (: from ill health) se rétablir; (hope etc) renaître; (activity) reprendre

revolt [rɪˈvəult] n révolte f ▷ vi se révolter, se rebeller ▷ vt révolter, dégoûter; **revolting** adj dégoûtant(e)

revolution [revəˈluːʃən] n révolution f; (of wheel etc) tour m, révolution; **revolutionary** adj, n révolutionnaire (m/f)

revolve [rɪˈvɔlv] vi tourner

revolver [rɪˈvɔlvəʳ] n revolver m

reward [rɪˈwɔːd] n récompense f ▷ vt: **to ~ (for)** récompenser (de); **rewarding** adj (fig) qui (en) vaut la peine, gratifiant(e)

rewind [riːˈwaɪnd] vt (irreg: like wind) (tape) réembobiner

rewritable [riːˈraɪtəbl] adj (CD, DVD) réinscriptible

rewrite [riːˈraɪt] (pt rewrote, pp rewritten) vt récrire

rheumatism [ˈruːmətɪzəm] n rhumatisme m

Rhine [raɪn] n: **the (River) ~** le Rhin

rhinoceros [raɪˈnɔsərəs] n rhinocéros m

Rhône [rəun] n: **the (River) ~** le Rhône

rhubarb [ˈruːbɑːb] n rhubarbe f

rhyme [raɪm] n rime f; (verse) vers mpl

rhythm [ˈrɪðm] n rythme m

rib [rɪb] n (Anat) côte f

ribbon [ˈrɪbən] n ruban m; **in ~s** (torn) en lambeaux

rice [raɪs] n riz m; **rice pudding** n riz au lait

rich [rɪtʃ] adj riche; (gift, clothes) somptueux(-euse); **to be ~ in sth** être riche en qch

rid [rɪd] (pt, pp ~) vt: **to ~ sb of** débarrasser qn de; **to get ~ of** se débarrasser de

riddle [ˈrɪdl] n (puzzle) énigme f ▷ vt: **to be ~d with** être criblé(e) de; (fig) être en proie à

ride [raɪd] n promenade f, tour m; (distance covered) trajet m ▷ vb (pt rode, pp ridden) ▷ vi (as sport) monter (à cheval), faire du cheval; (go somewhere: on horse, bicycle) aller (à cheval or bicyclette etc); (travel: on bicycle, motor cycle, bus) rouler ▷ vt (a horse) monter; (distance) parcourir, faire; **to ~ a horse/bicycle** monter à cheval/à bicyclette; **to take sb for a ~** (fig) faire marcher qn; (cheat) rouler qn; **rider** n cavalier(-ière); (in race) jockey m; (on bicycle) cycliste m/f; (on motorcycle) motocycliste m/f

ridge [rɪdʒ] n (of hill) faîte m; (of roof, mountain) arête f; (on object) strie f

ridicule [ˈrɪdɪkjuːl] n ridicule m; dérision f ▷ vt ridiculiser, tourner en dérision; **ridiculous** [rɪˈdɪkjuləs] adj ridicule

riding [ˈraɪdɪŋ] n équitation f; **riding school** n manège m, école f d'équitation

rife [raɪf] adj répandu(e); **~ with** abondant(e) en

rifle [ˈraɪfl] n fusil m (à canon rayé) ▷ vt vider, dévaliser

rift [rɪft] n fente f, fissure f; (fig: disagreement) désaccord m

rig [rɪg] n (also: **oil ~**: on land) derrick m; (: at sea) plate-forme pétrolière f ▷ vt (election etc) truquer

right [raɪt] adj (true) juste, exact(e); (correct) bon (bonne); (suitable) approprié(e), convenable; (just) juste, équitable; (morally good) bien inv; (not left) droit(e) ▷ n (moral good) bien m; (title, claim) droit m; (not left) droite f ▷ adv (answer) correctement; (treat) bien, comme il faut; (not on the left) à droite ▷ vt redresser ▷ excl bon!; **do you have the ~ time?** avez-vous l'heure juste or exacte?; **to be ~** (person) avoir raison; (answer) être juste or correct(e); **by ~s** en toute justice; **on the ~** à droite; **to be in the ~** avoir raison; **~ in the middle** en plein milieu; **~ away** immédiatement; **right angle** n (Math) angle droit; **rightful** adj (heir) légitime; **right-hand** adj: **the right-hand side** la droite; **right-hand drive** n (BRIT) conduite f à droite; (vehicle) véhicule m avec la conduite à droite; **right-handed** adj droitier(-ière); **rightly** adv bien, correctement; (with reason) à juste titre; **right of way** n (on path etc) droit m de passage; (Aut) priorité f; **right-wing** adj (Pol) de droite

rigid ['rɪdʒɪd] adj rigide; (principle, control) strict(e)

rigorous ['rɪɡərəs] adj rigoureux(-euse)

rim [rɪm] n bord m; (of spectacles) monture f; (of wheel) jante f

rind [raɪnd] n (of bacon) couenne f; (of lemon etc) écorce f, zeste m; (of cheese) croûte f

ring [rɪŋ] n anneau m; (on finger) bague f; (also: **wedding ~**) alliance f; (of people, objects) cercle m; (of spies) réseau m; (of smoke etc) rond m; (arena) piste f, arène f; (for boxing) ring m; (sound of bell) sonnerie f ⊳ vb (pt **rang**, pp **rung**) ⊳ vi (telephone, bell) sonner; (person: by telephone) téléphoner; (ears) bourdonner; (also: **~ out**: voice, words) retentir ⊳ vt (BRIT Tel: also: **~ up**) téléphoner à, appeler; **to ~ the bell** sonner; **to give sb a ~** (Tel) passer un coup de téléphone or de fil à qn; **ring back** vt, vi (BRIT Tel) rappeler; **ring off** vi (BRIT Tel) raccrocher; **ring up** (BRIT) vt (Tel) téléphoner à, appeler; **ringing tone** n (BRIT Tel) tonalité f d'appel; **ringleader** n (of gang) chef m, meneur m; **ring road** n (BRIT) rocade f (motorway) périphérique m; **ringtone** n (on mobile) sonnerie f (de téléphone portable)

rink [rɪŋk] n (also: **ice ~**) patinoire f

rinse [rɪns] n rinçage m ⊳ vt rincer

riot ['raɪət] n émeute f, bagarres fpl ⊳ vi (demonstrators) manifester avec violence; (population) se soulever, se révolter; **to run ~** se déchaîner

rip [rɪp] n déchirure f ⊳ vt déchirer ⊳ vi se déchirer; **rip off** vt (inf: cheat) arnaquer; **rip up** vt déchirer

ripe [raɪp] adj (fruit) mûr(e); (cheese) fait(e)

rip-off ['rɪpɔf] n (inf): **it's a ~!** c'est du vol manifeste!, c'est de l'arnaque!

ripple ['rɪpl] n ride f, ondulation f; (of applause, laughter) cascade f ⊳ vi se rider, onduler

rise [raɪz] n (slope) côte f, pente f; (hill) élévation f; (increase: in wages: BRIT) augmentation f; (: in prices, temperature) hausse f, augmentation f; (fig: to power etc) ascension f ⊳ vi (pt **rose**, pp **~n**) s'élever, monter; (prices, numbers) augmenter, monter; (waters, river) monter; (sun, wind, person: from chair, bed) se lever; (also: **~ up**: tower, building) s'élever; (: rebel) se révolter; se rebeller; (in rank) s'élever; **to give ~ to** donner lieu à; **to ~ to the occasion** se montrer à la hauteur; **risen** ['rɪzn] pp of **rise**; **rising** adj (increasing: number, prices) en hausse; (tide) montant(e); (sun, moon) levant(e)

risk [rɪsk] n risque m ⊳ vt risquer; **to take** or **run the ~ of doing** courir le risque de faire; **at ~** en danger; **at one's own ~** à ses risques et périls; **risky** adj risqué(e)

rite [raɪt] n rite m; **the last ~s** les derniers sacrements

ritual ['rɪtjuəl] adj rituel(le) ⊳ n rituel m

rival ['raɪvl] n rival(e); (in business) concurrent(e) ⊳ adj rival(e); qui fait concurrence ⊳ vt (match) égaler; **rivalry** n rivalité f; (in business) concurrence f

river ['rɪvər] n rivière f; (major: also fig) fleuve m ⊳ cpd (port, traffic) fluvial(e); **up/down ~** en amont/aval; **riverbank** n rive f, berge f

rivet ['rɪvɪt] n rivet m ⊳ vt (fig) river, fixer

Riviera [rɪvɪ'eərə] n: **the (French) ~** la Côte d'Azur

road [rəud] n route f; (in town) rue f; (fig) chemin, voie f ⊳ cpd (accident) de la route; **major/minor ~** route principale or à priorité/voie secondaire; **which ~ do I take for ...?** quelle route dois-je prendre pour aller à...?; **roadblock** n barrage routier; **road map** n carte routière; **road rage** n comportement très agressif de certains usagers de la route; **road safety** n sécurité routière; **roadside** n bord m de la route, bas-côté m; **roadsign** n panneau m de signalisation; **road tax** n (BRIT Aut) taxe f sur les automobiles; **roadworks** npl travaux mpl (de réfection des routes)

roam [rəum] vi errer, vagabonder

roar [rɔːr] n rugissement m; (of crowd) hurlements mpl; (of vehicle, thunder, storm) grondement m ⊳ vi rugir; hurler; gronder; **to ~ with laughter** rire à gorge déployée; **to do a ~ing trade** faire des affaires en or

roast [rəust] n rôti m ⊳ vt (meat) (faire) rôtir; (coffee) griller, torréfier; **roast beef** n rôti m de bœuf, rosbif m

rob [rɔb] vt (person) voler; (bank) dévaliser; **to ~ sb of sth** voler or dérober qch à qn; (fig: deprive) priver qn de qch; **robber** n bandit m, voleur m; **robbery** n vol m

robe [rəub] n (for ceremony etc) robe f; (also: **bath~**) peignoir m; (us: rug) couverture f ⊳ vt revêtir (d'une robe)

robin ['rɔbɪn] n rouge-gorge m

robot ['rəubɔt] n robot m

robust [rəu'bʌst] adj robuste; (material, appetite) solide

rock [rɔk] n (substance) roche f, roc m; (boulder) rocher m, roche; (us: small stone) caillou m; (BRIT: sweet) = sucre m d'orge ⊳ vt (swing gently: cradle) balancer; (: child) bercer; (shake) ébranler, secouer ⊳ vi se balancer, être ébranlé(e) or secoué(e); **on the ~s** (drink) avec des glaçons; (marriage etc) en train de craquer; **rock and roll** n rock (and roll) m, rock'n'roll m; **rock climbing** n varappe f

rocket ['rɔkɪt] n fusée f; (Mil) fusée, roquette f; (Culin) roquette

rocking chair ['rɔkɪŋ-] n fauteuil m à bascule

rocky ['rɔkɪ] adj (hill) rocheux(-euse); (path) rocailleux(-euse)

rod [rɔd] n (metallic) tringle f; (Tech) tige f; (wooden) baguette f; (also: **fishing ~**) canne f à pêche

rode [rəud] pt of **ride**

rodent ['rəudnt] n rongeur m

rogue [rəug] n coquin(e)

role [rəul] n rôle m; **role-model** n modèle m à émuler

roll [rəul] n rouleau m; (of banknotes) liasse f; (also: **bread ~**) petit pain; (register) liste f; (sound of drums etc) roulement m ⊳ vt rouler; (also: **~ up**: string) enrouler; (also: **~ out**: pastry) étendre au rouleau, abaisser ⊳ vi rouler; **roll over** vi se retourner; **roll up** vi (inf: arrive) arriver, s'amener ⊳ vt (carpet, cloth, map) rouler; (sleeves) retrousser; **roller** n rouleau m; (wheel) roulette f; (for road) rouleau compresseur; (for hair) bigoudi m; **roller coaster** n montagnes fpl russes; **roller skates** npl patins mpl à roulettes; **roller-skating** n patin m à roulettes; **to go roller-skating** faire du patin à roulettes; **rolling pin** n rouleau m à pâtisserie

ROM [rɔm] n abbr (Comput: = read-only memory) mémoire morte, ROM f

Roman ['rəumən] adj romain(e) ⊳ n Romain(e); **Roman Catholic** adj, n catholique (m/f)

romance [rə'mæns] n (love affair) idylle f; (charm) poésie f; (novel) roman m à la rose

Romania etc [rəʊ'meɪnɪə] = **Rumania** etc

Roman numeral n chiffre romain

romantic [rə'mæntɪk] adj romantique; (novel, attachment) sentimental(e)

Rome [rəʊm] n Rome

roof [ru:f] n toit m; (of tunnel, cave) plafond m ▷ vt couvrir (d'un toit); **the ~ of the mouth** la voûte du palais; **roof rack** n (Aut) galerie f

rook [rʊk] n (bird) freux m; (Chess) tour f

room [ru:m] n (in house) pièce f; (also: **bed~**) chambre f (à coucher); (in school etc) salle f; (space) place f; **roommate** n camarade m/f de chambre; **room service** n service m des chambres (dans un hôtel); **roomy** adj spacieux(-euse); (garment) ample

rooster ['ru:stə'] n coq m

root [ru:t] n (Bot, Math) racine f; (fig: of problem) origine f, fond m ▷ vi (plant) s'enraciner

rope [rəʊp] n corde f; (Naut) cordage m ▷ vt (tie up or together) attacher; (climbers: also: **~ together**) encorder; (area: also: **~ off**) interdire l'accès à; (: divide off) séparer; **to know the ~s** (fig) être au courant, connaître les ficelles

rose [rəʊz] pt of **rise** ▷ n rose f; (also: **~bush**) rosier m

rosé ['rəʊzeɪ] n rosé m

rosemary ['rəʊzmərɪ] n romarin m

rosy ['rəʊzɪ] adj rose; **a ~ future** un bel avenir

rot [rɒt] n (decay) pourriture f; (fig: pej: nonsense) idioties fpl, balivernes fpl ▷ vt, vi pourrir

rota ['rəʊtə] n liste f, tableau m de service

rotate [rəʊ'teɪt] vt (revolve) faire tourner; (change round: crops) alterner; (: jobs) faire à tour de rôle ▷ vi (revolve) tourner

rotten ['rɒtn] adj (decayed) pourri(e); (dishonest) corrompu(e); (inf: bad) mauvais(e), moche; **to feel ~** (ill) être mal fichu(e)

rough [rʌf] adj (cloth, skin) rêche, rugueux(-euse); (terrain) accidenté(e); (path) rocailleux(-euse); (voice) rauque, rude; (person, manner: coarse) rude, fruste; (: violent) brutal(e); (district, weather) mauvais(e); (sea) houleux(-euse); (plan) ébauché(e); (guess) approximatif(-ive) ▷ n (Golf) rough m ▷ vt: **to ~ it** vivre à la dure; **to sleep ~** (BRIT) coucher à la dure; **roughly** adv (handle) rudement, brutalement; (speak) avec brusquerie; (make) grossièrement; (approximately) à peu près, en gros

roulette [ru:'let] n roulette f

round [raʊnd] adj rond(e) ▷ n rond m, cercle m; (BRIT: of toast) tranche f; (duty: of policeman, milkman etc) tournée f; (: of doctor) visites fpl; (game: of cards, in competition) partie f; (Boxing) round m; (of talks) série f ▷ vt (corner) tourner ▷ prep autour de ▷ adv: **right ~, all ~** tout autour; **~ of ammunition** cartouche f; **~ of applause** applaudissements mpl; **~ of drinks** tournée f; **~ of sandwiches** (BRIT) sandwich m; **the long way ~** (par) le chemin le plus long; **all (the) year ~** toute l'année; **it's just ~ the corner** (fig) c'est tout près; **to go ~ to sb's (house)** aller chez qn; **go ~ the back** passer par derrière; **enough to go ~** assez pour tout le monde; **she arrived ~ (about) noon** (BRIT) elle est arrivée vers midi; **~ the clock** 24 heures sur 24; **round off** vt (speech etc) terminer; **round up** vt rassembler; (criminals) effectuer une rafle de; (prices) arrondir (au chiffre supérieur); **roundabout**

n (BRIT Aut) rond-point m (à sens giratoire); (at fair) manège m (de chevaux de bois) ▷ adj (route, means) détourné(e); **round trip** n (voyage m) aller et retour m; **roundup** n rassemblement m; (of criminals) rafle f

rouse [raʊz] vt (wake up) réveiller; (stir up) susciter, provoquer; (interest) éveiller; (suspicions) susciter, éveiller

route [ru:t] n itinéraire m; (of bus) parcours m; (of trade, shipping) route f

routine [ru:'ti:n] adj (work) ordinaire, courant(e); (procedure) d'usage ▷ n (habits) habitudes fpl; (pej) train-train m; (Theat) numéro m

row¹ [rəʊ] n (line) rangée f; (of people, seats, Knitting) rang m; (behind one another: of cars, people) file f ▷ vi (in boat) ramer; (as sport) faire de l'aviron ▷ vt (boat) faire aller à la rame or à l'aviron; **in a ~** (fig) d'affilée

row² [raʊ] n (noise) vacarme m; (dispute) dispute f, querelle f; (scolding) réprimande f, savon m ▷ vi (also: **to have a ~**) se disputer, se quereller

rowboat ['rəʊbəʊt] n (US) canot m (à rames)

rowing ['rəʊɪŋ] n canotage m; (as sport) aviron m; **rowing boat** n (BRIT) canot m (à rames)

royal ['rɔɪəl] adj royal(e); **royalty** n (royal persons) (membres mpl de la) famille royale; (payment: to author) droits mpl d'auteur; (: to inventor) royalties fpl

rpm abbr (= revolutions per minute) t/mn (= tours/minute)

R.S.V.P. abbr (= répondez s'il vous plaît) RSVP

Rt. Hon. abbr (BRIT: = Right Honourable) titre donné aux députés de la Chambre des communes

rub [rʌb] n: **to give sth a ~** donner un coup de chiffon or de torchon à qch ▷ vt frotter; (person) frictionner; (hands) se frotter; **to ~ sb up** (BRIT) or **to ~ sb** (US) **the wrong way** prendre qn à rebrousse-poil; **rub in** vt (ointment) faire pénétrer; **rub off** vi partir; **rub out** vt effacer

rubber ['rʌbə'] n caoutchouc m; (BRIT: eraser) gomme f (à effacer); **rubber band** n élastique m; **rubber gloves** npl gants mpl en caoutchouc

rubbish ['rʌbɪʃ] n (from household) ordures fpl; (fig: pej) choses fpl sans valeur, camelote f; (nonsense) bêtises fpl, idioties fpl; **rubbish bin** n (BRIT) boîte f à ordures, poubelle f; **rubbish dump** n (BRIT: in town) décharge publique, dépotoir m

rubble ['rʌbl] n décombres mpl; (smaller) gravats mpl; (Constr) blocage m

ruby ['ru:bɪ] n rubis m

rucksack ['rʌksæk] n sac m à dos

rudder ['rʌdə'] n gouvernail m

rude [ru:d] adj (impolite: person) impoli(e); (: word, manners) grossier(-ière); (shocking) indécent(e), inconvenant(e)

ruffle ['rʌfl] vt (hair) ébouriffer; (clothes) chiffonner; (fig: person) **to get ~d** s'énerver

rug [rʌg] n petit tapis; (BRIT: blanket) couverture f

rugby ['rʌgbɪ] n (also: **~ football**) rugby m

rugged ['rʌgɪd] adj (landscape) accidenté(e); (features, character) rude

ruin ['ru:ɪn] n ruine f ▷ vt ruiner; (spoil: clothes) abîmer; (: event) gâcher; **ruins** npl (of building) ruine(s)

rule [ru:l] n règle f; (regulation) règlement m; (government) autorité f, gouvernement m ▷ vt (country) gouverner; (person) dominer; (decide) décider ▷ vi commander; (Law): **as a ~** normalement, en règle générale; **rule out** vt exclure; **ruler** n (sovereign) souverain(e); (leader) chef m (d'État); (for measuring) règle f; **ruling** adj (party) au pouvoir; (class) dirigeant(e) ▷ n (Law) décision f

rum [rʌm] n rhum m

Rumania [ruːˈmeɪnɪə] n Roumanie f; **Rumanian** adj roumain(e) ▷ n Roumain(e); (Ling) roumain m

rumble [ˈrʌmbl] n grondement m; (of stomach, pipe) gargouillement m ▷ vi gronder; (stomach, pipe) gargouiller

rumour (US **rumor**) [ˈruːməʳ] n rumeur f, bruit m (qui court) ▷ vt: **le bruit court que**

rump steak n romsteck m

run [rʌn] n (race) course f; (outing) tour m or promenade f (en voiture); (distance travelled) parcours m, trajet m; (series) suite f, série f; (Theat) série de représentations; (Ski) piste f; (Cricket, Baseball) point m; (in tights, stockings) maille filée, échelle f ▷ vb (pt **ran**, pp **~**) ▷ vt (business) diriger; (competition, course) organiser; (hotel, house) tenir; (race) participer à; (Comput: program) exécuter; (to pass: hand, finger): **to ~ sth over** promener or passer qch sur; (water, bath) faire couler; (Press: feature) publier ▷ vi courir; (pass: road etc) passer; (work: machine, factory) marcher; (bus, train) circuler; (continue: play) se jouer, être à l'affiche; (: contract) être valide or en vigueur; (flow: river, bath, nose) couler; (colours, washing) déteindre; (in election) être candidat, se présenter; **at a ~** au pas de course; **to go for a ~** aller courir or faire un peu de course à pied; (in car) faire un tour or une promenade (en voiture); **there was a ~ on** (meat, tickets) les gens se sont rués sur; **in the long ~** à la longue; **on the ~** en fuite; **I'll ~ you to the station** je vais vous emmener or conduire à la gare; **to ~ a risk** courir un risque; **run after** vt fus (to catch up) courir après; (chase) poursuivre; **run away** vi s'enfuir; **run down** vt (Aut: knock over) renverser; (BRIT: reduce: production) réduire progressivement; (: factory/shop) réduire progressivement la production/ l'activité de; (criticize) critiquer, dénigrer; **to be ~ down** (tired) être fatigué(e) or à plat; **run into** vt fus (meet: person) rencontrer par hasard; (: trouble) se heurter à; (collide with) heurter; **run off** vi s'enfuir ▷ vt (water) laisser s'écouler; (copies) tirer; **run out** vi (person) sortir en courant; (liquid) couler; (lease) expirer; (money) être épuisé(e); **run out of** vt fus se trouver à court de; **run over** vt (Aut) écraser ▷ vt fus (revise) revoir, reprendre; **run through** vt fus (recap) reprendre, revoir; (play) répéter; **run up** vi: **to ~ up against** (difficulties) se heurter à; **runaway** adj (horse) emballé(e); (truck) fou (folle); (person) fugitif(-ive); (child) fugueur(-euse)

rung [rʌŋ] pp of **ring** ▷ n (of ladder) barreau m

runner [ˈrʌnəʳ] n (in race: person) coureur(-euse); (: horse) partant m; (on sledge) patin m; (for drawer etc) coulisseau m; **runner bean** n (BRIT) haricot m (à rames); **runner-up** n second(e)

running [ˈrʌnɪŋ] n (in race etc) course f; (of business, organization) direction f, gestion f ▷ adj (water) courant(e); (commentary) suivi(e); **6 days ~** 6 jours de suite; **to be in/out of the ~ for sth** être/ne pas être sur les rangs pour qch

runny [ˈrʌnɪ] adj qui coule

run-up [ˈrʌnʌp] n (BRIT): **~ to sth** période f précédant qch

runway [ˈrʌnweɪ] n (Aviat) piste f (d'envol or d'atterrissage)

rupture [ˈrʌptʃəʳ] n (Med) hernie f

rural [ˈruərl] adj rural(e)

rush [rʌʃ] n (of crowd, Comm: sudden demand) ruée f; (hurry) hâte f; (of anger, joy) accès m; (current) flot m; (Bot) jonc

m ▷ vt (hurry) transporter or envoyer d'urgence ▷ vi se précipiter; **to ~ sth off** (do quickly) faire qch à la hâte; **rush hour** n heures fpl de pointe or d'affluence

Russia [ˈrʌʃə] n Russie f; **Russian** adj russe ▷ n Russe m/f; (Ling) russe m

rust [rʌst] n rouille f ▷ vi rouiller

rusty [ˈrʌstɪ] adj rouillé(e)

ruthless [ˈruːθlɪs] adj sans pitié, impitoyable

RV n abbr (US) = **recreational vehicle**

rye [raɪ] n seigle m

S

Sabbath [ˈsæbəθ] n (Jewish) sabbat m; (Christian) dimanche m

sabotage [ˈsæbətɑːʒ] n sabotage m ▷ vt saboter

saccharin(e) [ˈsækərɪn] n saccharine f

sachet [ˈsæʃeɪ] n sachet m

sack [sæk] n (bag) sac m ▷ vt (dismiss) renvoyer, mettre à la porte; (plunder) piller, mettre à sac; **to get the ~** être renvoyé(e) or mis(e) à la porte

sacred [ˈseɪkrɪd] adj sacré(e)

sacrifice [ˈsækrɪfaɪs] n sacrifice m ▷ vt sacrifier

sad [sæd] adj (unhappy) triste; (deplorable) triste, fâcheux(-euse); (inf: pathetic: thing) triste, lamentable; (: person) minable

saddle [ˈsædl] n selle f ▷ vt (horse) seller; **to be ~d with sth** (inf) avoir qch sur les bras

sadistic [səˈdɪstɪk] adj sadique

sadly [ˈsædlɪ] adv tristement; (unfortunately) malheureusement; (seriously) fort

sadness [ˈsædnɪs] n tristesse f

s.a.e. n abbr (BRIT: = stamped addressed envelope) enveloppe affranchie pour la réponse

safari [səˈfɑːrɪ] n safari m

safe [seɪf] adj (out of danger) hors de danger, en sécurité;

(*not dangerous*) sans danger; (*cautious*) prudent(e); (*sure: bet etc*) assuré(e) ▷ n coffre-fort m; **could you put this in the ~, please?** pourriez-vous mettre ceci dans le coffre-fort?; **~ and sound** sain(e) et sauf (sauve); **(just) to be on the ~ side** pour plus de sûreté, par précaution; **safely** *adv* (*assume, say*) sans risque d'erreur; (*drive, arrive*) sans accident; **safe sex** n rapports sexuels protégés
safety ['seɪftɪ] n sécurité f; **safety belt** n ceinture f de sécurité; **safety pin** n épingle f de sûreté or de nourrice
saffron ['sæfrən] n safran m
sag [sæg] vi s'affaisser, fléchir; (*hem, breasts*) pendre
sage [seɪdʒ] n (*herb*) sauge f; (*person*) sage m
Sagittarius [sædʒɪ'teərɪəs] n le Sagittaire
Sahara [sə'hɑːrə] n: **the ~ (Desert)** le (désert du) Sahara m
said [sɛd] pt, pp of **say**
sail [seɪl] n (*on boat*) voile f; (*trip*): **to go for a ~** faire un tour en bateau ▷ vt (*boat*) manœuvrer, piloter ▷ vi (*travel: ship*) avancer, naviguer; (*set off*) partir, prendre la mer; (*Sport*) faire de la voile; **they ~ed into Le Havre** ils sont entrés dans le port du Havre; **sailboat** n (*us*) bateau m à voiles, voilier m; **sailing** n (*Sport*) voile f; **to go sailing** faire de la voile; **sailing boat** n bateau m à voiles, voilier m; **sailor** n marin m, matelot m
saint [seɪnt] n saint(e)
sake [seɪk] n: **for the ~ of** (*out of concern for*) pour (l'amour de), dans l'intérêt de; (*out of consideration for*) par égard pour
salad ['sæləd] n salade f; **salad cream** n (*BRIT*) (sorte de) mayonnaise f; **salad dressing** n vinaigrette f
salami [sə'lɑːmɪ] n salami m
salary ['sælərɪ] n salaire m, traitement m
sale [seɪl] n vente f; (*at reduced prices*) soldes mpl; **sales** npl (*total amount sold*) chiffre m de ventes; **"for ~"** "à vendre"; **on ~** en vente; **sales assistant** (*us* **sales clerk**) n vendeur(-euse); **salesman** (*irreg*) n (*in shop*) vendeur m; **salesperson** (*irreg*) n (*in shop*) vendeur(-euse); **sales rep** n (*Comm*) représentant(e) m/f; **saleswoman** (*irreg*) n (*in shop*) vendeuse f
saline ['seɪlaɪn] adj salin(e)
saliva [sə'laɪvə] n salive f
salmon ['sæmən] n (*pl inv*) saumon m
salon ['sælɔn] n salon m
saloon [sə'luːn] n (*us*) bar m; (*BRIT Aut*) berline f; (*ship's lounge*) salon m
salt [sɔːlt] n sel m ▷ vt saler; **saltwater** adj (*fish etc*) (d'eau) de mer; **salty** adj salé(e)
salute [sə'luːt] n salut m; (*of guns*) salve f ▷ vt saluer
salvage ['sælvɪdʒ] n (*saving*) sauvetage m; (*things saved*) biens sauvés or récupérés ▷ vt sauver, récupérer
Salvation Army [sæl'veɪʃən-] n Armée f du Salut
same [seɪm] adj même ▷ pron: **the ~** le (la) même, les mêmes; **the ~ book as** le même livre que; **at the ~ time** en même temps; (*yet*) néanmoins; **all or just the ~** tout de même, quand même; **to do the ~** faire de même, en faire autant; **to do the ~ as sb** faire comme qn; **and the ~ to you!** et à vous de même!; (*after insult*) toi-même!
sample ['sɑːmpl] n échantillon m; (*Med*) prélèvement m ▷ vt (*food, wine*) goûter
sanction ['sæŋkʃən] n approbation f, sanction f ▷ vt cautionner, sanctionner; **sanctions** npl (*Pol*) sanctions
sanctuary ['sæŋktjuərɪ] n (*holy place*) sanctuaire m; (*refuge*) asile m; (*for wildlife*) réserve f
sand [sænd] n sable m ▷ vt (*also: ~* **down:** *wood etc*)

poncer
sandal ['sændl] n sandale f
sand: **sandbox** n (*us: for children*) tas m de sable; **sandcastle** n château m de sable; **sand dune** n dune f de sable; **sandpaper** n papier m de verre; **sandpit** n (*BRIT: for children*) tas m de sable; **sands** npl plage f (de sable); **sandstone** ['sændstəun] n grès m
sandwich ['sændwɪtʃ] n sandwich m ▷ vt (*also:* **~ in**) intercaler; **~ed between** pris en sandwich entre; **cheese/ham ~** sandwich au fromage/jambon
sandy ['sændɪ] adj sablonneux(-euse); (*colour*) sable inv, blond roux inv
sane [seɪn] adj (*person*) sain(e) d'esprit; (*outlook*) sensé(e), sain(e)
sang [sæŋ] pt of **sing**
sanitary towel (*us* **sanitary napkin**) ['sænɪtərɪ-] n serviette f hygiénique
sanity ['sænɪtɪ] n santé mentale; (*common sense*) bon sens
sank [sæŋk] pt of **sink**
Santa Claus [sæntə'klɔːz] n le Père Noël
sap [sæp] n (*of plants*) sève f ▷ vt (*strength*) saper, miner
sapphire ['sæfaɪə'] n saphir m
sarcasm ['sɑːkæzm] n sarcasme m, raillerie f
sarcastic [sɑː'kæstɪk] adj sarcastique
sardine [sɑː'diːn] n sardine f
SASE n abbr (*us* = self-addressed stamped envelope) enveloppe affranchie pour la réponse
sat [sæt] pt, pp of **sit**
Sat. abbr (= Saturday) sa
satchel ['sætʃl] n cartable m
satellite ['sætəlaɪt] n satellite m; **satellite dish** n antenne f parabolique; **satellite television** n télévision f par satellite
satin ['sætɪn] n satin m ▷ adj en or de satin, satiné(e)
satire ['sætaɪə'] n satire f
satisfaction [sætɪs'fækʃən] n satisfaction f
satisfactory [sætɪs'fæktərɪ] adj satisfaisant(e)
satisfied ['sætɪsfaɪd] adj satisfait(e); **to be ~ with sth** être satisfait de qch
satisfy ['sætɪsfaɪ] vt satisfaire, contenter; (*convince*) convaincre, persuader
Saturday ['sætədɪ] n samedi m
sauce [sɔːs] n sauce f; **saucepan** n casserole f
saucer ['sɔːsə'] n soucoupe f
Saudi Arabia ['saudɪ-] n Arabie f Saoudite
sauna ['sɔːnə] n sauna m
sausage ['sɔsɪdʒ] n saucisse f; (*salami etc*) saucisson m; **sausage roll** n friand m
sautéed ['səuteɪd] adj sauté(e)
savage ['sævɪdʒ] adj (*cruel, fierce*) brutal(e), féroce; (*primitive*) primitif(-ive), sauvage ▷ n sauvage m/f ▷ vt attaquer férocement
save [seɪv] vt (*person, belongings*) sauver; (*money*) mettre de côté, économiser; (*time*) (faire) gagner; (*keep*) garder; (*Comput*) sauvegarder; (*Sport: stop*) arrêter; (*avoid: trouble*) éviter ▷ vi (*also:* **~ up**) mettre de l'argent de côté ▷ n (*Sport*) arrêt m (du ballon) ▷ prep sauf, à l'exception de
savings ['seɪvɪŋz] npl économies fpl; **savings account** n compte m d'épargne; **savings and loan association** (*us*) n ≈ société f de crédit immobilier
savoury (*us* **savory**) ['seɪvərɪ] adj savoureux(-euse); (*dish: not sweet*) salé(e)
saw [sɔː] pt of **see** ▷ n (*tool*) scie f ▷ vt (*pt* **~ed**, *pp* **~ed** or

~n) scier; **sawdust** n sciure f

sawn [sɔːn] pp of **saw**

saxophone ['sæksəfəʊn] n saxophone m

say [seɪ] n: **to have one's ~** dire ce qu'on a à dire ▷ vt (pt, pp **said**) dire; **to have a ~** avoir voix au chapitre; **could you ~ that again?** pourriez-vous répéter ce que vous venez de dire?; **to ~ yes/no** dire oui/non; **my watch ~s 3 o'clock** ma montre indique 3 heures, il est 3 heures à ma montre; **that is to ~** c'est-à-dire, cela va sans dire, cela va de soi; **saying** n dicton m, proverbe m

scab [skæb] n croûte f, (pej) jaune m

scaffolding ['skæfəldɪŋ] n échafaudage m

scald [skɔːld] n brûlure f ▷ vt ébouillanter

scale [skeɪl] n (of fish) écaille f; (Mus) gamme f; (of ruler, thermometer etc) graduation f, échelle (graduée); (of salaries, fees etc) barème m; (of map, also size, extent) échelle f ▷ vt (mountain) escalader; **scales** npl balance f; (larger) bascule f; (also: **bathroom ~s**) pèse-personne m inv; **~ of charges** tableau m des tarifs; **on a large ~** sur une grande échelle, en grand

scallion ['skæljən] n (us: salad onion) ciboule f

scallop ['skɒləp] n coquille f Saint-Jacques; (Sewing) feston m

scalp [skælp] n cuir chevelu ▷ vt scalper

scalpel ['skælpl] n scalpel m

scam [skæm] n (inf) arnaque f

scampi ['skæmpɪ] npl langoustines (frites), scampi mpl

scan [skæn] vt (examine) scruter, examiner; (glance at quickly) parcourir; (TV, Radar) balayer ▷ n (Med) scanographie f

scandal ['skændl] n scandale m; (gossip) ragots mpl

Scandinavia [skændɪ'neɪvɪə] n Scandinavie f; **Scandinavian** adj scandinave ▷ n Scandinave m/f

scanner ['skænə'] n (Radar, Med) scanner m, scanographe m; (Comput) scanner, numériseur m

scapegoat ['skeɪpɡəʊt] n bouc m émissaire

scar [skɑː'] n cicatrice f ▷ vt laisser une cicatrice or une marque à

scarce [skeəs] adj rare, peu abondant(e); **to make o.s. ~** (inf) se sauver; **scarcely** adv à peine, presque pas

scare [skeə'] n peur f, panique f ▷ vt effrayer, faire peur à; **to ~ sb stiff** faire une peur bleue à qn; **bomb ~** alerte f à la bombe; **scarecrow** n épouvantail m; **scared** adj: **to be scared** avoir peur

scarf (pl **scarves**) [skɑːf, skɑːvz] n (long) écharpe f; (square) foulard m

scarlet ['skɑːlɪt] adj écarlate

scarves [skɑːvz] npl of **scarf**

scary ['skeərɪ] adj (inf) effrayant(e); (film) qui fait peur

scatter ['skætə'] vt éparpiller, répandre; (crowd) disperser ▷ vi se disperser

scenario [sɪ'nɑːrɪəʊ] n scénario m

scene [siːn] n (Theat, fig etc) scène f; (of crime, accident) lieu(x) m(pl), endroit m; (sight, view) spectacle m, vue f; **scenery** n (Theat) décor(s) m(pl); (landscape) paysage m; **scenic** adj offrant de beaux paysages or panoramas

scent [sɛnt] n parfum m, odeur f; (fig: track) piste f

sceptical (us **skeptical**) ['skeptɪkl] adj sceptique

schedule ['ʃedjuːl] (us) ['skedʒuːl] n programme m, plan m; (of trains) horaire m; (of prices etc) barème m, tarif m ▷ vt prévoir; **on ~** à l'heure (prévue); à la date prévue; **to be ahead of/behind ~** avoir de l'avance/du retard; **scheduled flight** n vol régulier

scheme [skiːm] n plan m, projet m; (plot) complot m,

combine f; (arrangement) arrangement m, classification f; (pension scheme etc) régime m ▷ vt, vi comploter, manigancer

schizophrenic [skɪtsə'frenɪk] adj schizophrène

scholar ['skɒlə'] n érudit(e); (pupil) boursier(-ère); **scholarship** n érudition f; (grant) bourse f (d'études)

school [skuːl] n (gen) école f; (secondary school) collège m, lycée m; (in university) faculté f; (us: university) université f ▷ cpd scolaire; **schoolbook** n livre m scolaire or de classe; **schoolboy** n écolier m; (at secondary school) collégien m, lycéen m; **schoolchildren** npl écoliers mpl; (at secondary school) collégiens mpl, lycéens mpl; **schoolgirl** n écolière f; (at secondary school) collégienne f, lycéenne f; **schooling** n instruction f, études fpl; **schoolteacher** n (primary) instituteur(-trice); (secondary) professeur m

science ['saɪəns] n science f; **science fiction** n science-fiction f; **scientific** [saɪən'tɪfɪk] adj scientifique; **scientist** n scientifique m/f; (eminent) savant m

sci-fi ['saɪfaɪ] n abbr (inf: = science fiction) SF f

scissors ['sɪzəz] npl ciseaux mpl; **a pair of ~** une paire de ciseaux

scold [skəʊld] vt gronder

scone [skɒn] n sorte de petit pain rond au lait

scoop [skuːp] n pelle f (à main); (for ice cream) boule f à glace; (Press) reportage exclusif or à sensation

scooter ['skuːtə'] n (motor cycle) scooter m; (toy) trottinette f

scope [skəʊp] n (capacity: of plan, undertaking) portée f, envergure f; (: of person) compétence f, capacités fpl; (opportunity) possibilités fpl

scorching ['skɔːtʃɪŋ] adj torride, brûlant(e)

score [skɔː'] n score m, décompte m des points; (Mus) partition f ▷ vt (goal, point) marquer; (success) remporter; (cut: leather, wood, card) entailler, inciser ▷ vi marquer des points; (Football) marquer un but; (keep score) compter les points; **on that ~** sur ce chapitre, à cet égard; **a ~ of** (twenty) vingt; **~s of** (fig) des tas de; **to ~ 6 out of 10** obtenir 6 sur 10; **score out** vt rayer, barrer, biffer; **scoreboard** n tableau m; **scorer** n (Football) auteur m du but; buteur m; (keeping score) marqueur m

scorn [skɔːn] n mépris m, dédain m

Scorpio ['skɔːpɪəʊ] n le Scorpion

scorpion ['skɔːpɪən] n scorpion m

Scot [skɒt] n Écossais(e)

Scotch [skɒtʃ] n whisky m, scotch m

Scotch tape® (us) n scotch® m, ruban adhésif

Scotland ['skɒtlənd] n Écosse f

Scots [skɒts] adj écossais(e); **Scotsman** (irreg) n Écossais m; **Scotswoman** (irreg) n Écossaise f; **Scottish** ['skɒtɪʃ] adj écossais(e); **Scottish Parliament** n Parlement écossais

scout [skaʊt] n (Mil) éclaireur m; (also: **boy ~**) scout m; **girl ~** (us) guide f

scowl [skaʊl] vi se renfrogner, avoir l'air maussade; **to ~ at** regarder de travers

scramble ['skræmbl] n (rush) bousculade f, ruée f ▷ vi grimper/descendre tant bien que mal; **to ~ for** se bousculer or se disputer pour (avoir); **to go scrambling** (Sport) faire du trial; **scrambled eggs** npl œufs brouillés

scrap [skræp] n bout m, morceau m; (fight) bagarre f; (also: **~ iron**) ferraille f ▷ vt jeter, mettre au rebut; (fig) abandonner, laisser tomber ▷ vi se bagarrer; **scraps** npl (waste) déchets mpl; **scrapbook** n album m

scrape [skreɪp] vt, vi gratter, racler ▷ n: **to get into a ~**

s'attirer des ennuis; **scrape through** vi (*exam etc*) réussir de justesse

scrap paper n papier m brouillon

scratch [skrætʃ] n égratignure f, rayure f; (*on paint*) éraflure f; (*from claw*) coup m de griffe ▷ vt (*rub*) (se) gratter; (*paint etc*) érafler; (*with claw, nail*) griffer ▷ vi (se) gratter; **to start from ~** partir de zéro; **to be up to ~** être à la hauteur; **scratch card** n carte f à gratter

scream [skri:m] n cri perçant, hurlement m ▷ vi crier, hurler

screen [skri:n] n écran m; (*in room*) paravent m; (*fig*) écran, rideau m ▷ vt masquer, cacher; (*from the wind etc*) abriter, protéger; (*film*) projeter; (*candidates etc*) filtrer; **screening** n (*of film*) projection f, (*Med*) test m (or tests) de dépistage; **screenplay** n scénario m; **screen saver** n (*Comput*) économiseur m d'écran

screw [skru:] n vis f ▷ vt (*also: ~ in*) visser; **screw up** vt (*paper etc*) froisser; **to ~ up one's eyes** se plisser les yeux; **screwdriver** n tournevis m

scribble ['skrɪbl] n gribouillage m ▷ vt, vi gribouiller, griffonner

script [skrɪpt] n (*Cine etc*) scénario m, texte m; (*writing*) (écriture f) script m

scroll [skrəʊl] n rouleau m ▷ vt (*Comput*) faire défiler (sur l'écran)

scrub [skrʌb] n (*land*) broussailles fpl ▷ vt (*floor*) nettoyer à la brosse; (*pan*) récurer; (*washing*) frotter

scruffy ['skrʌfɪ] adj débraillé(e)

scrum(mage) ['skrʌm(ɪdʒ)] n mêlée f

scrutiny ['skru:tɪnɪ] n examen minutieux

scuba diving ['sku:bə-] n plongée sous-marine (autonome)

sculptor ['skʌlptəʳ] n sculpteur m

sculpture ['skʌlptʃəʳ] n sculpture f

scum [skʌm] n écume f, mousse f; (*pej: people*) rebut m, lie f

scurry ['skʌrɪ] vi filer à toute allure; **to ~ off** détaler, se sauver

sea [si:] n mer f ▷ cpd marin(e), de (la) mer, maritime; **by** or **beside the ~** (*holiday, town*) au bord de la mer; **by ~ par mer**, en bateau; **out to ~** au large; (**out**) **at ~** en mer; **to be all at ~** (*fig*) nager complètement; **seafood** n fruits mpl de mer; **sea front** n bord m de mer; **seagull** n mouette f

seal [si:l] n (*animal*) phoque m; (*stamp*) sceau m, cachet m ▷ vt sceller; (*envelope*) coller; (: *with seal*) cacheter; **seal off** vt (*forbid entry to*) interdire l'accès à

sea level n niveau m de la mer

seam [si:m] n couture f; (*of coal*) veine f, filon m

search [sɜ:tʃ] n (*for person, thing, Comput*) recherche(s) f(pl); (*of drawer, pockets*) fouille f; (*Law: at sb's home*) perquisition f ▷ vt fouiller; (*examine*) examiner minutieusement; scruter ▷ vi: **to ~ for** chercher; **in ~ of** à la recherche de; **search engine** n (*Comput*) moteur m de recherche; **search party** n expédition f de secours

sea: **seashore** n rivage m, plage f, bord m de (la) mer; **seasick** adj: **to be seasick** avoir le mal de mer; **seaside** n bord m de mer; **seaside resort** n station f balnéaire

season ['si:zn] n saison f ▷ vt assaisonner, relever; **to be in/out of ~** être/ne pas être de saison; **seasonal** adj saisonnier(-ière); **seasoning** n assaisonnement m; **season ticket** n carte f d'abonnement

seat [si:t] n siège m; (*in bus, train: place*) place f; (*buttocks*) postérieur m; (*of trousers*) fond m ▷ vt faire asseoir,

placer; (*have room for*) avoir des places assises pour, pouvoir accueillir; **I'd like to book two ~s** je voudrais réserver deux places; **to be ~ed** être assis; **seat belt** n ceinture f de sécurité; **seating** n sièges fpl, places assises

sea: **sea water** n eau f de mer; **seaweed** n algues fpl

sec. abbr (= *second*) sec

secluded [sɪ'klu:dɪd] adj retiré(e), à l'écart

second ['sɛkənd] num deuxième, second(e) ▷ adv (*in race etc*) en seconde position ▷ n (*unit of time*) seconde f, (*Aut: also: ~ gear*) seconde; (*Comm: imperfect*) article m de second choix; (*BRIT Scol*) = licence f avec mention ▷ vt (*motion*) appuyer; **seconds** npl (*inf: food*) rab m (*inf*); **secondary** adj secondaire; **secondary school** n collège m; lycée m; **second-class** adj de deuxième classe; (*Rail*) de seconde (classe); (*Post*) au tarif réduit; (*pej*) de qualité inférieure ▷ adv (*Rail*) en seconde; (*Post*) au tarif réduit; **secondhand** adj d'occasion; (*information*) de seconde main; **secondly** adv deuxièmement; **second-rate** adj de deuxième ordre, de qualité inférieure; **second thoughts** npl: **to have second thoughts** changer d'avis; **on second thoughts** or **thought** (*US*) à la réflexion

secrecy ['si:krəsɪ] n secret m

secret ['si:krɪt] adj secret(-ète) ▷ n secret m; **in ~** adv en secret, secrètement, en cachette

secretary ['sɛkrətrɪ] n secrétaire m/f; **S~ of State (for)** (*Brit Pol*) ministre m (de)

secretive ['si:krətɪv] adj réservé(e); (*pej*) cachottier(-ière), dissimulé(e)

secret service n services secrets

sect [sɛkt] n secte f

section ['sɛkʃən] n section f; (*Comm*) rayon m; (*of document*) section, article m, paragraphe m; (*cut*) coupe f

sector ['sɛktəʳ] n secteur m

secular ['sɛkjʊləʳ] adj laïque

secure [sɪ'kjʊəʳ] adj (*free from anxiety*) sans inquiétude, sécurisé(e); (*firmly fixed*) solide, bien attaché(e) (or fermé(e) etc); (*in safe place*) en lieu sûr, en sûreté ▷ vt (*fix*) fixer, attacher; (*get*) obtenir, se procurer

security [sɪ'kjʊərɪtɪ] n sécurité f, mesures fpl de sécurité; (*for loan*) caution f, garantie f; **securities** npl (*Stock Exchange*) valeurs fpl, titres mpl; **security guard** n garde chargé de la sécurité; (*transporting money*) convoyeur m de fonds

sedan [sə'dæn] n (*US Aut*) berline f

sedate [sɪ'deɪt] adj calme; posé(e) ▷ vt donner des sédatifs à

sedative ['sɛdɪtɪv] n calmant m, sédatif m

seduce [sɪ'dju:s] vt séduire; **seductive** [sɪ'dʌktɪv] adj séduisant(e); (*smile*) séducteur(-trice); (*fig: offer*) alléchant(e)

see [si:] vb (*pt saw, pp ~n*) ▷ vt (*gen*) voir; (*accompany*): **to ~ sb to the door** reconduire or raccompagner qn jusqu'à la porte ▷ vi voir; **to ~ that** (*ensure*) veiller à ce que + sub, faire en sorte que + sub, s'assurer que; **~ you soon/ later/tomorrow!** à bientôt/plus tard/demain!; **see off** vt accompagner (à la gare or à l'aéroport etc); **see out** vt (*take to door*) raccompagner à la porte; **see through** vt mener à bonne fin ▷ vt fus voir clair dans; **see to** vt fus s'occuper de, se charger de

seed [si:d] n graine f; (*fig*) germe m; (*Tennis etc*) tête f de série; **to go to ~** (*plant*) monter en graine; (*fig*) se laisser aller

seeing ['si:ɪŋ] conj: **~ (that)** vu que, étant donné que

seek (pt, pp **sought** [si:k, sɔ:t] vt chercher, rechercher

seem [si:m] vi sembler, paraître; **there ~s to be ...** il semble qu'il y a ..., on dirait qu'il y a ...; **seemingly** adv apparemment

seen [si:n] pp of **see**

seesaw ['si:sɔ:] n (jeu m de) bascule f

segment ['sɛgmənt] n segment m; (of orange) quartier m

segregate ['sɛgrɪgeɪt] vt séparer, isoler

Seine [seɪn] n: **the (River) ~** la Seine

seize [si:z] vt (grasp) saisir, attraper; (take possession of) s'emparer de; (opportunity) saisir

seizure ['si:ʒəʳ] n (Med) crise f, attaque f; (of power) prise f

seldom ['sɛldəm] adv rarement

select [sɪ'lɛkt] adj choisi(e), d'élite; (hotel, restaurant, club) chic inv, sélect inv ▷ vt sélectionner, choisir; **selection** n sélection f, choix m; **selective** adj sélectif(-ive); (school) à recrutement sélectif

self [sɛlf] n (pl **selves**): **the ~** le moi inv ▷ prefix auto-; **self-assured** adj sûr(e) de soi, plein(e) d'assurance; **self-catering** adj (BRIT: flat) avec cuisine, où l'on peut faire sa cuisine; (: holiday) en appartement (or chalet etc) loué; **self-centred** (US **self-centered**) adj égocentrique; **self-confidence** n confiance f en soi; **self-confident** adj sûr(e) de soi, plein(e) d'assurance; **self-conscious** adj timide, qui manque d'assurance; **self-contained** adj (BRIT: flat) avec entrée particulière, indépendant(e); **self-control** n maîtrise f de soi; **self-defence** (US **self-defense**) n autodéfense f; (Law) légitime défense f; **self-drive** adj (BRIT): **self-drive car** voiture f de location; **self-employed** adj qui travaille à son compte; **self-esteem** n amour-propre m; **self-indulgent** adj qui ne se refuse rien; **self-interest** n intérêt personnel; **selfish** adj égoïste; **self-pity** n apitoiement m sur soi-même; **self-raising** [sɛlf'reɪzɪŋ] (US **self-rising**) [sɛlf'raɪzɪŋ] adj: **self-raising flour** farine f pour gâteaux (avec levure incorporée); **self-respect** n respect m de soi, amour-propre m; **self-service** adj, n libre-service (m), self-service (m)

sell (pt, pp **sold**) [sɛl, səuld] vt vendre ▷ vi se vendre; **to ~ at or for 10 euros** se vendre 10 euros; **sell off** vt liquider; **sell out** vi: **to ~ out (of sth)** (use up stock) vendre tout son stock (de qch); **sell-by-date** n date f limite de vente; **seller** n vendeur(-euse), marchand(e)

Sellotape® ['sɛləuteɪp] n (BRIT) scotch® m

selves [sɛlvz] npl of **self**

semester [sɪ'mɛstəʳ] n (esp US) semestre m

semi... ['sɛmɪ] prefix semi-, demi-; à demi, à moitié; **semicircle** n demi-cercle m; **semidetached (house)** n (BRIT) maison jumelée or jumelle; **semi-final** n demi-finale f

seminar ['sɛmɪnɑːʳ] n séminaire m

semi-skimmed ['sɛmɪ'skɪmd] adj demi-écrémé(e)

senate ['sɛnɪt] n sénat m; (US): **the S~** le Sénat; **senator** n sénateur m

send (pt, pp **sent**) [sɛnd, sɛnt] vt envoyer; **send back** vt renvoyer; **send for** vt fus (by post) se faire envoyer, commander par correspondance; **send in** vt (report, application, resignation) remettre; **send off** vt (goods) envoyer, expédier; (BRIT Sport: player) expulser or renvoyer du terrain; **send on** vt (BRIT: letter) faire suivre; (luggage etc: in advance) (faire) expédier à l'avance; **send out** vt (invitation) envoyer (par la poste); (emit: light, heat, signal) émettre; **send up** vt (person, price) faire monter; (BRIT: parody) mettre en boîte, parodier; **sender** n expéditeur(-trice); **send-off** n: **a good send-off** des adieux chaleureux

senile ['si:naɪl] adj sénile

senior ['si:nɪəʳ] adj (high-ranking) de haut niveau; (of higher rank): **to be ~ to sb** être le supérieur de qn; **senior citizen** n personne f du troisième âge; **senior high school** n (US) = lycée m

sensation [sɛn'seɪʃən] n sensation f; **sensational** adj qui fait sensation; (marvellous) sensationnel(le)

sense [sɛns] n sens m; (feeling) sentiment m; (meaning) sens, signification f; (wisdom) bon sens ▷ vt sentir, pressentir; **it makes ~** c'est logique; **senseless** adj insensé(e), stupide; (unconscious) sans connaissance; **sense of humour** (US **sense of humor**) n sens m de l'humour

sensible ['sɛnsɪbl] adj sensé(e), raisonnable; (shoes etc) pratique

sensitive ['sɛnsɪtɪv] adj: **~ (to)** sensible (à)

sensual ['sɛnsjuəl] adj sensuel(le)

sensuous ['sɛnsjuəs] adj voluptueux(-euse), sensuel(le)

sent [sɛnt] pt, pp of **send**

sentence ['sɛntns] n (Ling) phrase f; (Law: judgment) condamnation f, sentence f; (: punishment) peine f ▷ vt: **to ~ sb to death/to 5 years** condamner qn à mort/à 5 ans

sentiment ['sɛntɪmənt] n sentiment m; (opinion) opinion f, avis m; **sentimental** [sɛntɪ'mɛntl] adj sentimental(e)

Sep. abbr (= September) septembre

separate adj ['sɛprɪt] séparé(e); (organization) indépendant(e); (day, occasion, issue) différent(e) ▷ vb ['sɛpəreɪt] ▷ vt séparer; (distinguish) distinguer ▷ vi se séparer; **separately** adv séparément; **separates** npl (clothes) coordonnés mpl; **separation** [sɛpə'reɪʃən] n séparation f

September [sɛp'tɛmbəʳ] n septembre m

septic ['sɛptɪk] adj (wound) infecté(e); **septic tank** n fosse f septique

sequel ['si:kwl] n conséquence f; séquelles fpl; (of story) suite f

sequence ['si:kwəns] n ordre m, suite f; (in film) séquence f; (dance) numéro m

sequin ['si:kwɪn] n paillette f

Serb [sə:b] adj, n = **Serbian**

Serbia ['sə:bɪə] n Serbie f

Serbian ['sə:bɪən] adj serbe ▷ n Serbe m/f; (Ling) serbe m

sergeant ['sɑ:dʒənt] n sergent m; (Police) brigadier m

serial ['sɪərɪəl] n feuilleton m; **serial killer** n meurtrier m tuant en série; **serial number** n numéro m de série

series ['sɪərɪz] n série f; (Publishing) collection f

serious ['sɪərɪəs] adj sérieux(-euse); (accident etc) grave; **seriously** adv sérieusement; (hurt) gravement

sermon ['sə:mən] n sermon m

servant ['sə:vənt] n domestique m/f; (fig) serviteur n (servante)

serve [sə:v] vt (employer etc) servir, être au service de; (purpose) servir à; (customer, food, meal) servir; (subj: train) desservir; (apprenticeship) faire, accomplir; (prison term) faire; purger ▷ vi (Tennis) servir; (be useful): **to ~ as/for/to do** servir de/à/à faire ▷ n (Tennis) service m; **it ~s him right** c'est bien fait pour lui; **server** n (Comput) serveur m

service ['sə:vɪs] n (gen) service m; (Aut) révision f; (Rel) office m ▷ vt (car etc) réviser; **services** npl (Econ: tertiary sector) (secteur m) tertiaire m, secteur des services;

(BRIT: on motorway) station-service f; (Mil): **the S~s**
npl les forces armées; **to be of ~ to sb, to do sb a ~**
rendre service à qn; **~ included/not included** service
compris/non compris; **service area** n (on motorway)
aire f de services; **service charge** n (BRIT) service m;
serviceman (irreg) n militaire m; **service station** n
station-service f

serviette [sə:vɪ'et] n (BRIT) serviette f (de table)

session ['sɛʃən] n (sitting) séance f; **to be in ~** siéger, être
en session or en séance

set [set] n série f, assortiment m; (of tools etc) jeu m;
(Radio, TV) poste m; (Tennis) set m; (group of people) cercle
m, milieu m; (Cine) plateau m; (Theat: stage) scène f; (:
scenery) décor m; (Hairdressing) mise f en plis ▷ adj (fixed) fixe, déterminé(e); (ready) prêt(e)
▷ vb (pt, pp ~) ▷ vt (place) mettre, poser, placer; (fix,
establish) fixer; (: record) établir; (assign: task, homework)
donner; (exam) composer; (adjust) régler; (decide: rules
etc) fixer, choisir ▷ vi (sun) se coucher; (jam, jelly, concrete)
prendre; (bone) se ressouder; **to be ~ on doing** être
résolu(e) à faire; **to ~ to music** mettre en musique;
to ~ on fire mettre le feu à; **to ~ free** libérer; **to ~ sth
going** déclencher qch; **to ~ sail** partir, prendre la mer;
set aside vt mettre de côté; (time) garder; **set down** vt
(subj: bus, train) déposer; **set in** vi (infection, bad weather)
s'installer; (complications) survenir, surgir; **set off** vi se
mettre en route, partir ▷ vt (bomb) faire exploser; (cause
to start) déclencher; (show up well) mettre en valeur,
faire valoir; **set out** vi: **to ~ out (from)** partir (de) ▷ vt
(arrange) disposer; (state) présenter, exposer; **to ~ out to
do** entreprendre de faire; avoir pour but or intention de
faire; **set up** vt (organization) fonder, créer; **setback** n
(hitch) revers m, contretemps m; **set menu** n menu m

settee [se'ti:] n canapé m

setting ['setɪŋ] n cadre m; (of jewel) monture f; (position:
of controls) réglage m

settle ['setl] vt (argument, matter, account) régler;
(problem) résoudre; (Med: calm) calmer ▷ vi (bird, dust etc)
se poser; **to ~ for sth** accepter qch, se contenter de qch;
to ~ on sth opter or se décider pour qch; **settle down**
vi (get comfortable) s'installer; (become calmer) se calmer,
se ranger; (live quietly) se fixer; **settle in** vi s'installer;
settle up vi: **to ~ up with sb** régler (ce que l'on doit à)
qn; **settlement** n (payment) règlement m; (agreement)
accord m; (village etc) village m, hameau m

setup ['setʌp] n (arrangement) manière f dont les choses
sont organisées; (situation) situation f, allure f des choses

seven ['sevn] num sept; **seventeen** num dix-sept;
seventeenth [sevn'ti:nθ] num dix-septième; **seventh**
num septième; **seventieth** ['sevntɪɪθ] num soixante-
dixième; **seventy** num soixante-dix

sever ['sevə*] vt couper, trancher; (relations) rompre

several ['sevərl] adj, pron plusieurs pl; **~ of us** plusieurs
d'entre nous

severe [sɪ'vɪə*] adj (stern) sévère, strict(e); (serious) grave,
sérieux(-euse); (plain) sévère, austère

sew (pt ~ed, pp ~n) [səu, səud, səun] vt, vi coudre

sewage ['su:ɪdʒ] n vidange(s) f(pl)

sewer ['su:ə*] n égout m

sewing ['səuɪŋ] n couture f; (item(s)) ouvrage m; **sewing
machine** n machine f à coudre

sewn [səun] pp of **sew**

sex [sɛks] n sexe m; **to have ~ with** avoir des rapports
(sexuels) avec; **sexism** ['sɛksɪzəm] n sexisme m;

sexist adj sexiste; **sexual** ['sɛksjuəl] adj sexuel(le);
sexual intercourse n rapports sexuels; **sexuality**
[sɛksju'ælɪtɪ] n sexualité f; **sexy** adj sexy inv

shabby ['ʃæbɪ] adj miteux(-euse); (behaviour)
mesquin(e), méprisable

shack [ʃæk] n cabane f, hutte f

shade [ʃeɪd] n ombre f; (for lamp) abat-jour m inv; (of
colour) nuance f, ton m; (US: window shade) store m; (small
quantity): **a ~ of** un soupçon de ▷ vt abriter du soleil,
ombrager; **shades** npl (US: sunglasses) lunettes fpl de
soleil; **in the ~** à l'ombre; **a ~ smaller** un tout petit peu
plus petit

shadow ['ʃædəu] n ombre f ▷ vt (follow) filer; **shadow
cabinet** n (BRIT Pol) cabinet parallèle formé par le parti qui
n'est pas au pouvoir

shady ['ʃeɪdɪ] adj ombragé(e); (fig: dishonest) louche,
véreux(-euse)

shaft [ʃɑ:ft] n (of arrow, spear) hampe f; (Aut, Tech) arbre
m; (of mine) puits m; (of lift) cage f; (of light) rayon m,
trait m

shake [ʃeɪk] vb (pt shook, pp ~n) ▷ vt secouer; (bottle,
cocktail) agiter; (house, confidence) ébranler ▷ vi trembler;
to ~ one's head (in refusal etc) dire or faire non de la tête;
(in dismay) secouer la tête; **to ~ hands with sb** serrer la
main à qn; **shake off** vt secouer; (pursuer) se débarrasser
de; **shake up** vt secouer; **shaky** adj (hand, voice)
tremblant(e); (building) branlant(e), peu solide

shall [ʃæl] aux vb: **I ~ go** j'irai; **~ I open the door?** j'ouvre
la porte?; **I'll get the coffee, ~ I?** je vais chercher le café,
d'accord?

shallow ['ʃæləu] adj peu profond(e); (fig) superficiel(le),
qui manque de profondeur

sham [ʃæm] n frime f

shambles ['ʃæmblz] n confusion f, pagaïe f, fouillis m

shame [ʃeɪm] n honte f ▷ vt faire honte à; **it is a ~
(that/to do)** c'est dommage (que + sub/de faire); **what
a ~!** quel dommage!; **shameful** adj honteux(-euse),
scandaleux(-euse); **shameless** adj éhonté(e),
effronté(e)

shampoo [ʃæm'pu:] n shampooing m ▷ vt faire un
shampooing à

shandy ['ʃændɪ] n bière panachée

shan't [ʃɑ:nt] = **shall not**

shape [ʃeɪp] n forme f ▷ vt façonner, modeler; (sb's ideas,
character) former; (sb's life) déterminer ▷ vi (also: **~ up**:
events) prendre tournure; (: person) faire des progrès, s'en
sortir; **to take ~** prendre forme or tournure

share [ʃeə*] n part f; (Comm) action f ▷ vt partager;
(have in common) avoir en commun; **to ~ out (among
or between)** partager (entre); **shareholder** n (BRIT)
actionnaire m/f

shark [ʃɑːk] n requin m

sharp [ʃɑːp] adj (razor, knife) tranchant(e), bien
aiguisé(e); (point, voice) aigu(ë); (nose, chin) pointu(e);
(outline, increase) net(te); (cold, pain) vif (vive); (taste)
piquant(e), âcre; (Mus) dièse; (person: quick-witted) vif
(vive), éveillé(e); (: unscrupulous) malhonnête ▷ n (Mus)
dièse m ▷ adv: **at 2 o'clock ~** à 2 heures pile or tapantes;
sharpen vt aiguiser; (pencil) tailler; (fig) aviver;
sharpener n (also: **pencil sharpener**) taille-crayon(s) m
inv; **sharply** adv (turn, stop) brusquement; (stand out)
nettement; (criticize, retort) sèchement, vertement

shatter ['ʃætə*] vt briser; (fig: upset) bouleverser; (: ruin)
briser, ruiner ▷ vi voler en éclats, se briser; **shattered** adj

(*overwhelmed, grief-stricken*) bouleversé(e); (*inf: exhausted*) éreinté(e)

shave [ʃeɪv] vt raser ▷ vi se raser ▷ n: **to have a ~** se raser; **shaver** n (*also:* **electric shaver**) rasoir m électrique

shaving cream n crème f à raser

shaving foam n mousse f à raser

shavings [ʃeɪvɪŋz] npl (*of wood etc*) copeaux mpl

shawl [ʃɔːl] n châle m

she [ʃiː] pron elle

sheath [ʃiːθ] n gaine f, fourreau m, étui m; (*contraceptive*) préservatif m

shed [ʃed] n remise f, resserre f ▷ vt (*pt, pp ~*) (*leaves, fur etc*) perdre; (*tears*) verser, répandre; (*workers*) congédier

she'd [ʃiːd] = **she had**; **she would**

sheep [ʃiːp] n (*pl inv*) mouton m; **sheepdog** n chien m de berger; **sheepskin** n peau f de mouton

sheer [ʃɪə] adj (*utter*) pur(e), pur et simple; (*steep*) à pic, abrupt(e); (*almost transparent*) extrêmement fin(e) ▷ adv à pic, abruptement

sheet [ʃiːt] n (*on bed*) drap m; (*of paper*) feuille f; (*of glass, metal etc*) feuille, plaque f

sheik(h) [ʃeɪk] n cheik m

shelf (*pl* **shelves**) [ʃelf, ʃelvz] n étagère f, rayon m

shell [ʃel] n (*on beach*) coquillage m; (*of egg, nut etc*) coquille f; (*explosive*) obus m; (*of building*) carcasse f ▷ vt (*peas*) écosser; (*Mil*) bombarder (d'obus)

she'll [ʃiːl] = **she will**; **she shall**

shellfish [ʃelfɪʃ] n (*pl inv: crab etc*) crustacé m; (*: scallop etc*) coquillage m ▷ npl (*as food*) fruits mpl de mer

shelter [ʃeltə] n abri m, refuge m ▷ vt abriter, protéger; (*give lodging to*) donner asile à ▷ vi s'abriter, se mettre à l'abri; **sheltered** adj (*life*) retiré(e), à l'abri des soucis; (*spot*) abrité(e)

shelves [ʃelvz] npl of **shelf**

shelving [ʃelvɪŋ] n (*shelves*) rayonnage(s) m(pl)

shepherd [ʃepəd] n berger m ▷ vt (*guide*) guider, escorter; **shepherd's pie** n ≈ hachis m Parmentier

sheriff [ʃerɪf] (*us*) n shérif m

sherry [ʃerɪ] n xérès m, sherry m

she's [ʃiːz] = **she is**; **she has**

Shetland [ʃetlənd] n (*also:* **the ~s, the ~ Isles** *or* **Islands**) les îles fpl Shetland

shield [ʃiːld] n bouclier m; (*protection*) écran m de protection ▷ vt: **to ~ (from)** protéger (de or contre)

shift [ʃɪft] n (*change*) changement m; (*work period*) période f de travail; (*of workers*) équipe f, poste m ▷ vt déplacer, changer de place; (*remove*) enlever ▷ vi changer de place, bouger

shin [ʃɪn] n tibia m

shine [ʃaɪn] n éclat m, brillant m ▷ vb (*pt, pp* **shone**) ▷ vi briller ▷ vt (*torch*): **to ~ on** braquer sur; (*polish*): (*pt, pp* **~d**) faire briller or reluire

shingles [ʃɪŋɡlz] n (*Med*) zona m

shiny [ʃaɪnɪ] adj brillant(e)

ship [ʃɪp] n bateau m; (*large*) navire m ▷ vt transporter (par mer); (*send*) expédier (par mer); **shipment** n cargaison f; **shipping** n (*ships*) navires mpl; (*traffic*) navigation f; (*the industry*) industrie navale; (*transport*) transport m; **shipwreck** n épave f, (*event*) naufrage m ▷ vt: **to be shipwrecked** faire naufrage; **shipyard** n chantier naval

shirt [ʃəːt] n chemise f; (*woman's*) chemisier m; **in ~ sleeves** en bras de chemise

shit [ʃɪt] excl (*inf!*) merde (!)

shiver [ʃɪvə] n frisson m ▷ vi frissonner

shock [ʃɔk] n choc m; (*Elec*) secousse f, décharge f; (*Med*) commotion f, choc ▷ vt (*scandalize*) choquer, scandaliser; (*upset*) bouleverser; **shocking** adj (*outrageous*) choquant(e), scandaleux(-euse); (*awful*) épouvantable

shoe [ʃuː] n chaussure f, soulier m; (*also:* **horse~**) fer m à cheval ▷ vt (*pt, pp* **shod**) (*horse*) ferrer; **shoelace** n lacet m (de soulier); **shoe polish** n cirage m; **shoeshop** n magasin m de chaussures

shone [ʃɔn] pt, pp of **shine**

shook [ʃuk] pt of **shake**

shoot [ʃuːt] n (*on branch, seedling*) pousse f ▷ vb (*pt, pp* **shot**) ▷ vt (*game: hunt*) chasser; (*: aim at*) tirer; (*: kill*) abattre; (*person*) blesser/tuer d'un coup de fusil (*or de revolver*); (*execute*) fusiller; (*arrow*) tirer; (*gun*) tirer un coup de; (*Cine*) tourner ▷ vi (*with gun, bow*): **to ~ (at)** tirer (sur); (*Football*) shooter, tirer; **shoot down** vt (*plane*) abattre; **shoot up** vi (*fig: prices etc*) monter en flèche; **shooting** n (*shots*) coups mpl de feu; (*attack*) fusillade f; (*murder*) homicide m (*à l'aide d'une arme à feu*); (*Hunting*) chasse f

shop [ʃɔp] n magasin m; (*workshop*) atelier m ▷ vi (*also:* **go ~ping**) faire ses courses or ses achats; **shop assistant** n (*BRIT*) vendeur(-euse); **shopkeeper** n marchand(e), commerçant(e); **shoplifting** n vol m à l'étalage; **shopping** n (*goods*) achats mpl, provisions fpl; **shopping bag** n sac m (à provisions); **shopping centre** (*us* **shopping center**) n centre commercial; **shopping mall** n centre commercial; **shopping trolley** n (*BRIT*) Caddie® m; **shop window** n vitrine f

shore [ʃɔː] n (*of sea, lake*) rivage m, rive f ▷ vt: **to ~ (up)** étayer; **on ~** à terre

short [ʃɔːt] adj (*not long*) court(e); (*soon finished*) court, bref (brève); (*person, step*) petit(e); (*curt*) brusque, sec (sèche); (*insufficient*) insuffisant(e) ▷ n (*also:* **~ film**) court métrage; (*Elec*) court-circuit m; **to be ~ of sth** être à court de or manquer de qch; **in ~** bref; en bref; **~ of doing** à moins de faire; **everything ~ of** tout sauf; **it is ~ for** c'est l'abréviation or le diminutif de; **to cut ~** (*speech, visit*) abréger, écourter; **to fall ~ of** ne pas être à la hauteur de; **to run ~ of** arriver à court de, venir à manquer de; **to stop ~** s'arrêter net; **to stop ~ of** ne pas aller jusqu'à; **shortage** n manque m, pénurie f; **shortbread** n ≈ sablé m; **shortcoming** n défaut m; **short(crust) pastry** n (*BRIT*) pâte brisée; **shortcut** n raccourci m; **shorten** vt raccourcir; (*text, visit*) abréger; **shortfall** n déficit m; **shorthand** n (*BRIT*) sténo(graphie) f; **shortlist** n (*BRIT: for job*) liste f des candidats sélectionnés; **short-lived** adj de courte durée; **shortly** adv bientôt, sous peu; **shorts** npl: (**a pair of) shorts** un short; **short-sighted** adj (*BRIT*) myope; (*fig*) qui manque de clairvoyance; **short-sleeved** adj à manches courtes; **short story** n nouvelle f; **short-tempered** adj qui s'emporte facilement; **short-term** adj (*effect*) à court terme

shot [ʃɔt] pt, pp of **shoot** ▷ n coup m (de feu); (*try*) coup, essai m; (*injection*) piqûre f; (*Phot*) photo f; **to be a good/poor ~** (*person*) tirer bien/mal; **like a ~** comme une flèche; (*very readily*) sans hésiter; **shotgun** n fusil m de chasse

should [ʃud] aux vb: **I ~ go now** je devrais partir maintenant; **he ~ be there now** il devrait être arrivé maintenant; **I ~ go if I were you** si j'étais vous j'irais; **I ~ like to** j'aimerais bien, volontiers

shoulder ['ʃəʊldə'] n épaule f ▷ vt (fig) endosser, se charger de; **shoulder blade** n omoplate f

shouldn't ['ʃʊdnt] = **should not**

shout [ʃaʊt] n cri m ▷ vt crier ▷ vi crier, pousser des cris

shove [ʃʌv] vt pousser; (inf: put): **to ~ sth in** fourrer or ficher qch dans ▷ n poussée f

shovel ['ʃʌvl] n pelle f ▷ vt pelleter, enlever (or enfourner) à la pelle

show [ʃəʊ] n (of emotion) manifestation f, démonstration f; (semblance) semblant m, apparence f; (exhibition) exposition f, salon m; (Theat, TV) spectacle m; (Cine) séance f ▷ vb (pt **-ed**, pp **~n**) ▷ vt montrer; (film) passer; (courage etc) faire preuve de, manifester; (exhibit) exposer ▷ vi se voir, être visible; **can you ~ me where it is, please?** pouvez-vous me montrer où c'est?; **to be on ~** être exposé(e); **it's just for ~** c'est juste pour l'effet; **show in** vt faire entrer; **show off** vi (pej) crâner ▷ vt (display) faire valoir; (pej) faire étalage de; **show out** vt reconduire à la porte; **show up** vi (stand out) ressortir, (inf: turn up) se montrer ▷ vt (unmask) démasquer, dénoncer; (flaw) faire ressortir; **show business** n le monde du spectacle

shower ['ʃaʊə'] n (for washing) douche f; (rain) averse f; (of stones etc) pluie f, grêle f; (us: party) réunion organisée pour la remise de cadeaux ▷ vi prendre une douche, se doucher ▷ vt: **to ~ sb with** (gifts etc) combler qn de; **to have** or **take a ~** prendre une douche, se doucher; **shower cap** n bonnet m de douche; **shower gel** n gel m douche

showing ['ʃəʊɪŋ] n (of film) projection f

show jumping [-dʒʌmpɪŋ] n concours m hippique

shown [ʃəʊn] pp of **show**

show: **show-off** n (inf: person) crâneur(-euse), m'as-tu-vu(e); **showroom** n magasin m or salle f d'exposition

shrank [ʃræŋk] pt of **shrink**

shred [ʃrɛd] n (gen pl) lambeau m, petit morceau; (fig: of truth, evidence) parcelle f ▷ vt mettre en lambeaux, déchirer; (documents) détruire; (Culin: grate) râper; (: lettuce etc) couper en lanières

shrewd [ʃruːd] adj astucieux(-euse), perspicace; (business person) habile

shriek [ʃriːk] n cri perçant or aigu, hurlement m ▷ vt, vi hurler, crier

shrimp [ʃrɪmp] n crevette grise

shrine [ʃraɪn] n (place) lieu m de pèlerinage

shrink (pt **shrank**, pp **shrunk**) [ʃrɪŋk, ʃræŋk, ʃrʌŋk] vi rétrécir; (fig) diminuer; (also: **~ away**) reculer ▷ vt (wool) (faire) rétrécir ▷ n (inf: pej) psychanalyste m/f; **to ~ from (doing) sth** reculer devant (la pensée de faire) qch

shrivel ['ʃrɪvl] (also: **~ up**) vt ratatiner, flétrir ▷ vi se ratatiner, se flétrir

shroud [ʃraʊd] n linceul m ▷ vt: **~ed in mystery** enveloppé(e) de mystère

Shrove Tuesday ['ʃrəʊv-] n (le) Mardi gras

shrub [ʃrʌb] n arbuste m

shrug [ʃrʌg] n haussement m d'épaules ▷ vt, vi: **to ~ (one's shoulders)** hausser les épaules; **shrug off** vt faire fi de

shrunk [ʃrʌŋk] pp of **shrink**

shudder ['ʃʌdə'] n frisson m, frémissement m ▷ vi frissonner, frémir

shuffle ['ʃʌfl] vt (cards) battre; **to ~ (one's feet)** traîner les pieds

shun [ʃʌn] vt éviter, fuir

shut (pt, pp **~**) [ʃʌt] vt fermer ▷ vi (se) fermer; **shut down** vt fermer définitivement ▷ vi fermer définitivement; **shut up** vi (inf: keep quiet) se taire ▷ vt (close) fermer; (silence) faire taire; **shutter** n volet m; (Phot) obturateur m

shuttle ['ʃʌtl] n navette f; (also: **~ service**) (service m de) navette f; **shuttlecock** n volant m (de badminton)

shy [ʃaɪ] adj timide

siblings ['sɪblɪŋz] npl (formal) frères et sœurs mpl (de mêmes parents)

Sicily ['sɪsɪlɪ] n Sicile f

sick [sɪk] adj (ill) malade; (BRIT: vomiting): **to be ~** vomir; (humour) noir(e), macabre; **to feel ~** avoir envie de vomir, avoir mal au cœur; **to be ~ of** (fig) en avoir assez de; **sickening** adj (fig) écœurant(e), révoltant(e), répugnant(e); **sick leave** n congé m de maladie; **sickly** adj maladif(-ive), souffreteux(-euse); (causing nausea) écœurant(e); **sickness** n maladie f; (vomiting) vomissement(s) m(pl)

side [saɪd] n côté m; (of lake, road) bord m; (of mountain) versant m; (fig: aspect) côté, aspect m; (team: Sport) équipe f; (TV: channel) chaîne f ▷ adj (door, entrance) latéral(e) ▷ vi: **to ~ with sb** prendre le parti de qn, se ranger du côté de qn; **by the ~ of** au bord de; **~ by ~** côte à côte; **to rock from ~ to ~** se balancer; **to take ~s (with)** prendre parti (pour); **sideboard** n buffet m; **sideboards** (BRIT **sideburns**) npl (whiskers) pattes fpl; **side effect** n effet m secondaire; **sidelight** n (Aut) veilleuse f; **sideline** n (Sport) (ligne f de) touche f; (fig) activité f secondaire; **side order** n garniture f; **side road** n petite route, route transversale; **side street** n rue transversale; **sidetrack** vt (fig) faire dévier de son sujet; **sidewalk** n (US) trottoir m; **sideways** adv de côté

siege [siːdʒ] n siège m

sieve [sɪv] n tamis m, passoire f ▷ vt tamiser, passer (au tamis)

sift [sɪft] vt passer au tamis ou au crible; (fig) passer au crible

sigh [saɪ] n soupir m ▷ vi soupirer, pousser un soupir

sight [saɪt] n (faculty) vue f; (spectacle) spectacle m; (on gun) mire f ▷ vt apercevoir; **in ~** visible; (fig) en vue; **out of ~** hors de vue; **sightseeing** n tourisme m; **to go sightseeing** faire du tourisme

sign [saɪn] n (gen) signe m; (with hand etc) signe, geste m; (notice) panneau m, écriteau m; (also: **road ~**) panneau de signalisation ▷ vt signer; **where do I ~?** où dois-je signer?; **sign for** vt fus (item) signer le reçu pour; **sign in** vi signer le registre (en arrivant); **sign on** vi (BRIT: as unemployed) s'inscrire au chômage; (enrol) s'inscrire ▷ vt (employee) embaucher; **sign over** vt: **to ~ sth over to sb** céder qch par écrit à qn; **sign up** vi (Mil) s'engager; (for course) s'inscrire

signal ['sɪgnl] n signal m ▷ vi (Aut) mettre son clignotant ▷ vt (person) faire signe à; (message) communiquer par signaux

signature ['sɪgnətʃə'] n signature f

significance [sɪg'nɪfɪkəns] n signification f; importance f

significant [sɪg'nɪfɪkənt] adj significatif(-ive); (important) important(e), considérable

signify ['sɪgnɪfaɪ] vt signifier

sign language n langage m par signes

signpost ['saɪnpəʊst] n poteau indicateur

Sikh [si:k] *adj, n* Sikh *m/f*

silence ['saɪlns] *n* silence *m* ▷ *vt* faire taire, réduire au silence

silent ['saɪlnt] *adj* silencieux(-euse); (*film*) muet(te); **to keep** *or* **remain ~** garder le silence, ne rien dire

silhouette [sɪluː'ɛt] *n* silhouette *f*

silicon chip ['sɪlɪkən-] *n* puce *f* électronique

silk [sɪlk] *n* soie *f* ▷ *cpd* de *or* en soie

silly ['sɪlɪ] *adj* stupide, sot(te), bête

silver ['sɪlvə*ʳ*] *n* argent *m*; (*money*) monnaie *f* (en pièces d'argent); (*also*: **~ware**) argenterie *f* ▷ *adj* (*made of silver*) d'argent, en argent; (*in colour*) argenté(e); **silver-plated** *adj* plaqué/e argent

similar ['sɪmɪlə*ʳ*] *adj*: **~ (to)** semblable (à); **similarity** [sɪmɪ'lærɪtɪ] *n* ressemblance *f*, similarité *f*; **similarly** *adv* de la même façon, de même

simmer ['sɪmə*ʳ*] *vi* cuire à feu doux, mijoter

simple ['sɪmpl] *adj* simple; **simplicity** [sɪm'plɪsɪtɪ] *n* simplicité *f*; **simplify** ['sɪmplɪfaɪ] *vt* simplifier; **simply** *adv* simplement; (*without fuss*) avec simplicité; (*absolutely*) absolument

simulate ['sɪmjuleɪt] *vt* simuler, feindre

simultaneous [sɪməl'teɪnɪəs] *adj* simultané(e); **simultaneously** *adv* simultanément

sin [sɪn] *n* péché *m* ▷ *vi* pécher

since [sɪns] *adv, prep* depuis ▷ *conj* (*time*) depuis que; (*because*) puisque, étant donné que, comme; **~ then**, **ever ~** depuis ce moment-là

sincere [sɪn'sɪə*ʳ*] *adj* sincère; **sincerely** *adv* sincèrement; **Yours sincerely** (*at end of letter*) veuillez agréer, Monsieur (*or* Madame) l'expression de mes sentiments distingués *or* les meilleurs

sing (*pt* **sang**, *pp* **sung**) [sɪŋ, sæŋ, sʌŋ] *vt, vi* chanter

Singapore [sɪŋgə'pɔː] *n* Singapour *m*

singer ['sɪŋə*ʳ*] *n* chanteur(-euse)

singing ['sɪŋɪŋ] *n* (*of person, bird*) chant *m*

single ['sɪŋgl] *adj* seul(e), unique; (*unmarried*) célibataire; (*not double*) simple ▷ *n* (*BRIT*: *also*: **~ ticket**) aller *m* (simple); (*record*) 45 tours *m*; **singles** *npl* (*Tennis*) simple *m*; **every ~ day** chaque jour sans exception; **single out** *vt* choisir; (*distinguish*) distinguer; **single bed** *n* lit *m* d'une personne *or* à une place; **single file** *n*: **in single file** en file indienne; **single-handed** *adv* tout(e) seul(e), sans (aucune) aide; **single-minded** *adj* résolu(e), tenace; **single parent** *n* parent unique (*or* célibataire); **single-parent family** famille monoparentale; **single room** *n* chambre *f* à un lit *or* pour une personne

singular ['sɪŋgjulə*ʳ*] *adj* singulier(-ière); (*odd*) singulier, étrange; (*outstanding*) remarquable; (*Ling*) (au) singulier, du singulier ▷ *n* (Ling) singulier *m*

sinister ['sɪnɪstə*ʳ*] *adj* sinistre

sink [sɪŋk] *n* évier *m*; (*washbasin*) lavabo *m* ▷ *vb* (*pt* **sank**, *pp* **sunk**) ▷ *vt* (*ship*) (faire) couler, faire sombrer; (*foundations*) creuser ▷ *vi* couler, sombrer; (*ground etc*) s'affaisser; **to ~ into sth** (*chair*) s'enfoncer dans qch; **sink in** *vi* (*explanation*) rentrer (*inf*), être compris

sinus ['saɪnəs] *n* (*Anat*) sinus *m inv*

sip [sɪp] *n* petite gorgée *f* ▷ *vt* boire à petites gorgées

sir [sə*ʳ*] *n* monsieur *m*; **S~ John Smith** sir John Smith; **yes ~** oui Monsieur

siren ['saɪərn] *n* sirène *f*

sirloin ['səːlɔɪn] *n* (*also*: **~ steak**) aloyau *m*

sister ['sɪstə*ʳ*] *n* sœur *f*; (*nun*) religieuse *f*, (bonne) sœur; (*BRIT*: *nurse*) infirmière *f* en chef; **sister-in-law** *n* belle-sœur *f*

sit (*pt, pp* **sat**) [sɪt, sæt] *vi* s'asseoir; (*be sitting*) être assis(e); (*assembly*) être en séance, siéger; (*for painter*) poser ▷ *vt* (*exam*) passer, se présenter à; **sit back** *vi* (*in seat*) bien s'installer, se carrer; **sit down** *vi* s'asseoir; (*straight*) se redresser; (*not go to bed*) rester debout, ne pas se coucher

sitcom ['sɪtkɔm] *n abbr* (*TV*: = *situation comedy*) sitcom *f*, comédie *f* de situation

site [saɪt] *n* emplacement *m*, site *m*; (*also*: **building ~**) chantier *m* ▷ *vt* placer

sitting ['sɪtɪŋ] *n* (*of assembly etc*) séance *f*; (*in canteen*) service *m*; **sitting room** *n* salon *m*

situated ['sɪtjueɪtɪd] *adj* situé(e)

situation [sɪtju'eɪʃən] *n* situation *f*; **"~s vacant/ wanted"** (*BRIT*) offres/demandes d'emploi"

six [sɪks] *num* six; **sixteen** [sɪks'tiːn] *num* seize; **sixteenth** [sɪks'tiːnθ] *num* seizième; **sixth** ['sɪksθ] *num* sixième; **sixth form** *n* (*BRIT*) ≈ classes *fpl* de première et de terminale; **sixth-form college** *n* lycée *n'ayant que des classes de première et de terminale*; **sixtieth** ['sɪkstɪɪθ] *num* soixantième; **sixty** *num* soixante

size [saɪz] *n* dimensions *fpl*; (*of person*) taille *f*; (*of clothing*) taille; (*of shoes*) pointure *f*; (*of problem*) ampleur *f*; (*glue*) colle *f*; **sizeable** *adj* assez grand(e); (*amount, problem, majority*) assez important(e)

sizzle ['sɪzl] *vi* grésiller

skate [skeɪt] *n* patin *m*; (*fish*: *pl inv*) raie *f* ▷ *vi* patiner; **skateboard** *n* skateboard *m*, planche *f* à roulettes; **skateboarding** *n* skateboard *m*; **skater** *n* patineur(-euse); **skating** *n* patinage *m*; **skating rink** *n* patinoire *f*

skeleton ['skɛlɪtn] *n* squelette *m*; (*outline*) schéma *m*

skeptical ['skɛptɪkl] (*US*) = **sceptical**

sketch [skɛtʃ] *n* (*drawing*) croquis *m*, esquisse *f*; (*outline plan*) aperçu *m*; (*Theat*) sketch *m*, saynète *f* ▷ *vt* esquisser, faire un croquis *or* une esquisse de; (*plan etc*) esquisser

skewer ['skjuːə*ʳ*] *n* brochette *f*

ski [skiː] *n* ski *m* ▷ *vi* skier, faire du ski; **ski boot** *n* chaussure *f* de ski

skid [skɪd] *n* dérapage *m* ▷ *vi* déraper

ski: **skier** *n* skieur(-euse); **skiing** *n* ski *m*; **to go skiing** (aller) faire du ski

skilful (*US* **skillful**) ['skɪlful] *adj* habile, adroit(e)

ski lift *n* remonte-pente *m inv*

skill [skɪl] *n* (*ability*) habileté *f*, adresse *f*, talent *m*; (*requiring training*) compétences *fpl*; **skilled** *adj* habile, adroit(e); (*worker*) qualifié(e)

skim [skɪm] *vt* (*soup*) écumer; (*glide over*) raser, effleurer ▷ *vi*: **to ~ through** (*fig*) parcourir; **skimmed milk** (*US* **skim milk**) *n* lait écrémé

skin [skɪn] *n* peau *f* ▷ *vt* (*fruit etc*) éplucher; (*animal*) écorcher; **skinhead** *n* skinhead *m*; **skinny** *adj* maigre, maigrichon(ne)

skip [skɪp] *n* petit bond *or* saut *m*; (*BRIT*: *container*) benne *f* ▷ *vi* gambader, sautiller; (*with rope*) sauter à la corde ▷ *vt* (*pass over*) sauter

ski: **ski pass** *n* forfait-skieur(s) *m*; **ski pole** *n* bâton *m* de ski

skipper ['skɪpə*ʳ*] *n* (*Naut, Sport*) capitaine *m*; (*in race*) skipper *m*

skipping rope ['skɪpɪŋ-] (*US* **skip rope**) *n* (*BRIT*) corde *f* à sauter

skirt [skə:t] n jupe f ▷ vt longer, contourner
skirting board ['skə:tɪŋ-] n (BRIT) plinthe f
ski slope n piste f de ski
ski suit n combinaison f de ski
skull [skʌl] n crâne m
skunk [skʌŋk] n mouffette f
sky [skaɪ] n ciel m; **skyscraper** n gratte-ciel m inv
slab [slæb] n (of stone) dalle f; (of meat, cheese) tranche
épaisse
slack [slæk] adj (loose) lâche, desserré(e); (slow)
stagnant(e); (careless) négligent(e), peu sérieux(-euse) or
consciencieux(-euse); **slacks** npl pantalon m
slain [sleɪn] pp of **slay**
slam [slæm] vt (door) (faire) claquer; (throw) jeter
violemment, flanquer; (inf: criticize) éreinter, démolir
▷ vi claquer
slander ['slɑ:ndə'] n calomnie f; (Law) diffamation f
slang [slæŋ] n argot m
slant [slɑ:nt] n inclinaison f; (fig) angle m, point m de vue
slap [slæp] n claque f, gifle f; (on the back) tape f ▷ vt
donner une claque or une gifle (or une tape) à; **to ~ on**
(paint) appliquer rapidement ▷ adv (directly) tout droit,
en plein
slash [slæʃ] vt entailler, taillader; (fig: prices) casser
slate [sleɪt] n ardoise f ▷ vt (fig: criticize) éreinter, démolir
slaughter ['slɔ:tə'] n carnage m, massacre m; (of
animals) abattage m ▷ vt (animal) abattre; (people)
massacrer; **slaughterhouse** n abattoir m
Slav [slɑ:v] adj slave
slave [sleɪv] n esclave m/f ▷ vi (also: **~ away**) trimer,
travailler comme un forçat; **slavery** n esclavage m
slay (pt **slew**, pp **slain**) [sleɪ, slu:, sleɪn] vt (literary) tuer
sleazy ['sli:zɪ] adj miteux(-euse), minable
sled [slɛd] (US) = **sledge**
sledge [slɛdʒ] n luge f
sleek [sli:k] adj (hair, fur) brillant(e), luisant(e); (car, boat)
aux lignes pures or élégantes
sleep [sli:p] n sommeil m ▷ vi (pt, pp **slept**) dormir; **to
go to ~** s'endormir; **sleep in** vi (oversleep) se réveiller
trop tard; (on purpose) faire la grasse matinée; **sleep
together** vi (have sex) coucher ensemble; **sleeper** n
(person) dormeur(-euse); (BRIT Rail: on track) traverse
f; (: train) train-couchettes m; (: berth) couchette f;
sleeping bag n sac m de couchage; **sleeping
car** n wagon-lits m, voiture-lits f; **sleeping pill** n
somnifère m; **sleepover** n nuit f chez un copain or
une copine; **we're having a sleepover at Jo's** nous
allons passer la nuit chez Jo; **sleepwalk** vi marcher en
dormant; **sleepy** adj (fig) endormi(e)
sleet [sli:t] n neige fondue
sleeve [sli:v] n manche f; (of record) pochette f;
sleeveless adj (garment) sans manches
sleigh [sleɪ] n traîneau m
slender ['slɛndə'] adj svelte, mince; (fig) faible, ténu(e)
slept [slɛpt] pt, pp of **sleep**
slew [slu:] pt of **slay**
slice [slaɪs] n tranche f; (round) rondelle f; (utensil) spatule
f; (also: **fish ~**) pelle f à poisson ▷ vt couper en tranches
(or en rondelles)
slick [slɪk] adj (skilful) bien ficelé(e); (salesperson) qui a du
bagout ▷ n (also: **oil ~**) nappe f de pétrole, marée noire
slide [slaɪd] n (in playground) toboggan m; (Phot)
diapositive f; (BRIT: also: **hair ~**) barrette f; (in prices)
chute f, baisse f ▷ vb (pt, pp **slid**) ▷ vt (faire) glisser ▷ vi

glisser; **sliding** adj (door) coulissant(e)
slight [slaɪt] adj (slim) mince, menu(e); (frail) frêle;
(trivial) faible, insignifiant(e); (small) petit(e), léger(-ère)
before n ▷ n offense f, affront m ▷ vt (offend) blesser,
offenser; **not in the ~est** pas le moins du monde, pas du
tout; **slightly** adv légèrement, un peu
slim [slɪm] adj mince ▷ vi maigrir; (diet) suivre un régime
amaigrissant; **slimming** n amaigrissement m ▷ adj
(diet, pills) amaigrissant(e), pour maigrir; (food) qui ne
fait pas grossir
slimy ['slaɪmɪ] adj visqueux(-euse), gluant(e)
sling [slɪŋ] n (Med) écharpe f; (for baby) porte-bébé m;
(weapon) fronde f, lance-pierre f ▷ vt (pt, pp **slung**)
lancer, jeter
slip [slɪp] n faux pas; (mistake) erreur f, bévue f;
(underskirt) combinaison f; (of paper) petite feuille, fiche f
▷ vt (slide) glisser ▷ vi (slide) glisser; (move smoothly): **to ~
into/out of** se glisser or se faufiler dans/hors de; (decline)
baisser; **to ~ sth on/off** enfiler/enlever qch; **to give sb
the ~** fausser compagnie à qn; **a ~ of the tongue** un
lapsus; **slip up** vi faire une erreur, gaffer
slipped disc [slɪpt-] n déplacement m de vertèbre
slipper ['slɪpə'] n pantoufle f
slippery ['slɪpərɪ] adj glissant(e)
slip road n (BRIT: to motorway) bretelle f d'accès
slit [slɪt] n fente f; (cut) incision f ▷ vt (pt, pp **~**) fendre;
couper, inciser
slog [slɒg] n (BRIT: effort) gros effort; (: work) tâche
fastidieuse ▷ vi travailler très dur
slogan ['sləugən] n slogan m
slope [sləup] n pente f, côte f; (side of mountain) versant
m; (slant) inclinaison f ▷ vi: **to ~ down** être or descendre
en pente; **to ~ up** monter; **sloping** adj en pente,
incliné(e); (handwriting) penché(e)
sloppy ['slɒpɪ] adj (work) peu soigné(e), bâclé(e);
(appearance) négligé(e), débraillé(e)
slot [slɒt] n fente f ▷ vt: **to ~ sth into** encastrer or insérer
qch dans; **slot machine** n (BRIT: vending machine)
distributeur m (automatique), machine f à sous; (for
gambling) appareil m or machine à sous
Slovakia [sləu'vækɪə] n Slovaquie f
Slovene [sləu'vi:n] adj slovène ▷ n Slovène m/f; (Ling)
slovène m
Slovenia [sləu'vi:nɪə] n Slovénie f; **Slovenian** adj, n
= **Slovene**
slow [sləu] adj lent(e); (watch): **to be ~** retarder ▷ adv
lentement ▷ vt, vi ralentir; **"~"** (road sign) "ralenti"; **slow
down** vi ralentir; **slowly** adv lentement; **slow motion**
n: **in slow motion** au ralenti
slug [slʌg] n limace f; (bullet) balle f; **sluggish** adj (person)
mou (molle), lent(e); (stream, engine, trading) lent(e)
slum [slʌm] n (house) taudis m; **slums** npl (area)
quartiers mpl pauvres
slump [slʌmp] n baisse soudaine, effondrement m;
(Econ) crise f ▷ vi s'effondrer, s'affaisser
slung [slʌŋ] pt, pp of **sling**
slur [slə:'] n (smear): **~ (on)** atteinte f (à); insinuation f
(contre) ▷ vt mal articuler
slush [slʌʃ] n neige fondue
sly [slaɪ] adj (person) rusé(e); (smile, expression, remark)
sournois(e)
smack [smæk] n (slap) tape f; (on face) gifle f ▷ vt donner
une tape à; (on face) gifler; (on bottom) donner la fessée à
▷ vi: **to ~ of** avoir des relents de, sentir

small [smɔːl] adj petit(e); **small ads** npl (BRIT) petites annonces; **small change** n petite or menue monnaie

smart [smɑːt] adj élégant(e), chic inv; (clever) intelligent(e); (quick) vif (vive), prompt(e) ▷ vi faire mal, brûler; **smartcard** n carte à puce

smash [smæʃ] n (also: **--up**) collision f, accident m; (Mus) succès foudroyant ▷ vt casser, briser, fracasser; (opponent) écraser; (Sport: record) pulvériser ▷ vi se briser, se fracasser; s'écraser; **smashing** adj (inf) formidable

smear [smɪəʳ] n (stain) tache f; (mark) trace f; (Med) frottis m ▷ vt enduire; (make dirty) salir; **smear test** n (BRIT Med) frottis m

smell [smɛl] n odeur f; (sense) odorat m ▷ vb (pt, pp **smelt** or **~ed**) ▷ vt sentir ▷ vi (pej) sentir mauvais; **smelly** adj qui sent mauvais, malodorant(e)

smelt [smɛlt] pt, pp of **smell**

smile [smaɪl] n sourire m ▷ vi sourire

smirk [sməːk] n petit sourire suffisant or affecté

smog [smɔg] n brouillard mêlé de fumée

smoke [sməuk] n fumée f ▷ vt, vi fumer; **do you mind if I ~?** ça ne vous dérange pas que je fume?; **smoke alarm** n détecteur m de fumée; **smoked** adj (bacon, glass) fumé(e); **smoker** n (person) fumeur(-euse); (Rail) wagon m fumeurs; **smoking** n: **"no smoking"** (sign) "défense de fumer"; **smoky** adj enfumé(e); (taste) fumé(e)

smooth [smuːð] adj lisse; (sauce) onctueux(-euse); (flavour, whisky) moelleux(-euse); (movement) régulier(-ière), sans à-coups or heurts; (flight) sans secousses; (pej: person) doucereux(-euse), mielleux(-euse) ▷ vt (also: **~ out**) lisser, défroisser; (creases, difficulties) faire disparaître

smother ['smʌðəʳ] vt étouffer

SMS n abbr (= short message service) SMS m; **SMS message** n message m SMS

smudge [smʌdʒ] n tache f, bavure f ▷ vt salir, maculer

smug [smʌg] adj suffisant(e), content(e) de soi

smuggle ['smʌgl] vt passer en contrebande or en fraude; **smuggling** n contrebande f

snack [snæk] n casse-croûte m inv; **snack bar** n snack(-bar) m

snag [snæg] n inconvénient m, difficulté f

snail [sneɪl] n escargot m

snake [sneɪk] n serpent m

snap [snæp] n (sound) claquement m, bruit sec; (photograph) photo f, instantané m; adj subit(e), fait(e) sans réfléchir ▷ vt (fingers) faire claquer; (break) casser net ▷ vi se casser net or avec un bruit sec; (speak sharply) parler d'un ton brusque; **to ~ open/shut** s'ouvrir/se refermer brusquement; **snap at** vt fus (subj: dog) essayer de mordre; **snap up** vt sauter sur, saisir; **snapshot** n photo f, instantané m

snarl [snɑːl] vi gronder

snatch [snætʃ] n (small amount) ▷ vt saisir (d'un geste vif); (steal) voler; **to ~ some sleep** arriver à dormir un peu

sneak [sniːk] (US): (pt **snuck**) vi: **to ~ in/out** entrer/sortir furtivement or à la dérobée ▷ n (inf: pej: informer) faux jeton; **to ~ up on sb** s'approcher de qn sans faire de bruit; **sneakers** npl tennis mpl, baskets fpl

sneer [snɪəʳ] vi ricaner; **to ~ at sb/sth** se moquer de qn/qch avec mépris

sneeze [sniːz] vi éternuer

sniff [snɪf] vi renifler ▷ vt renifler, flairer; (glue, drug) sniffer, respirer

snigger ['snɪgəʳ] vi ricaner

snip [snɪp] n (cut) entaille f; (BRIT: inf: bargain) (bonne) occasion or affaire f ▷ vt couper

sniper ['snaɪpəʳ] n (marksman) tireur embusqué

snob [snɔb] n snob m/f

snooker ['snuːkəʳ] n sorte de jeu de billard

snoop [snuːp] vi: **to ~ about** fureter

snooze [snuːz] n petit somme ▷ vi faire un petit somme

snore [snɔːʳ] vi ronfler ▷ n ronflement m

snorkel ['snɔːkl] n (of swimmer) tuba m

snort [snɔːt] n grognement m ▷ vi grogner; (horse) renâcler

snow [snəu] n neige f ▷ vi neiger; **snowball** n boule f de neige; **snowdrift** n congère f; **snowman** (irreg) n bonhomme m de neige; **snowplough** (US **snowplow**) n chasse-neige m inv; **snowstorm** n tempête f de neige

snub [snʌb] vt repousser, snober ▷ n rebuffade f

snug [snʌg] adj douillet(te), confortable; (person) bien au chaud

KEYWORD

so [səu] adv 1 (thus, likewise) ainsi, de cette façon; **if so** si oui; **so do or have I** moi aussi; **it's 5 o'clock - so it is!** il est 5 heures - en effet! or c'est vrai!; **I hope/think so** je l'espère/le crois; **so far** jusqu'ici, jusqu'à maintenant; (in past) jusque-là
2 (in comparisons etc: to such a degree) si, tellement; **so big (that)** si or tellement grand (que); **she's not so clever as her brother** elle n'est pas aussi intelligente que son frère
3: **so much** adj, adv tant (de); **I've got so much work** j'ai tant de travail; **I love you so much** je vous aime tant; **so many** tant (de)
4 (phrases): **10 or so** à peu près or environ 10; **so long!** (inf: goodbye) au revoir!, à un de ces jours!; **so (what)?** (inf) (bon) et alors?, et après?
▷ conj 1 (expressing purpose): **so as to** pour faire, afin de faire; **so (that)** pour que or afin que + sub
2 (expressing result) donc, par conséquent; **so that** si bien que, de (telle) sorte que; **so that's the reason!** c'est donc (pour) ça!; **so you see, I could have gone** alors tu vois, j'aurais pu y aller

soak [səuk] vt faire or laisser tremper; (drench) tremper ▷ vi tremper; **soak up** vt absorber; **soaking** adj (also: **soaking wet**) trempé(e)

so-and-so ['səuənsəu] n (somebody) un(e) tel(le)

soap [səup] n savon m; **soap opera** n feuilleton télévisé (quotidienneté réaliste ou embellie); **soap powder** n lessive f, détergent m

soar [sɔːʳ] vi monter (en flèche), s'élancer; (building) s'élancer

sob [sɔb] n sanglot m ▷ vi sangloter

sober ['səubəʳ] adj qui n'est pas (or plus) ivre; (serious) sérieux(-euse), sensé(e); (colour, style) sobre, discret(-ète); **sober up** vi se dégriser

so-called ['səu'kɔːld] adj soi-disant inv

soccer ['sɔkəʳ] n football m

sociable ['səuʃəbl] adj sociable

social ['səuʃl] adj social(e); (sociable) sociable ▷ n (petite) fête; **socialism** n socialisme m; **socialist** adj, n socialiste (m/f); **socialize** vi: **to socialize with** (meet often) fréquenter; (get to know) lier connaissance or parler avec; **social life** n vie sociale; **socially** adv socialement, en société; **social security** n aide sociale; **social services** npl services sociaux; **social work** n assistance sociale; **social worker** n assistant(e) sociale(e)

society [sə'saɪətɪ] n société f; (club) société, association f; (also: **high ~**) (haute) société, grand monde

sociology [səʊsɪ'ɔlədʒɪ] n sociologie f

sock [sɔk] n chaussette f

socket ['sɔkɪt] n cavité f; (Elec: also: **wall ~**) prise f de courant

soda ['səʊdə] n (Chem) soude f; (also: **~ water**) eau f de Seltz; (us: also: **~ pop**) soda m

sodium ['səʊdɪəm] n sodium m

sofa ['səʊfə] n sofa m, canapé m; **sofa bed** n canapé-lit m

soft [sɔft] adj (not rough) doux (douce); (not hard) mou (molle); (not loud) doux, léger(-ère); (kind) doux, gentil(le); **soft drink** n boisson non alcoolisée; **soft drugs** npl drogues douces; **soften** ['sɔfn] vt (r)amollir; (fig) adoucir ▷ vi se ramollir; (fig) s'adoucir; **softly** adv doucement; (touch) légèrement; (kiss) tendrement; **software** n (Comput) logiciel m, software m

soggy ['sɔgɪ] adj (clothes) trempé(e); (ground) détrempé(e)

soil [sɔɪl] n (earth) sol m, terre f ▷ vt salir; (fig) souiller

solar ['səʊlər] adj solaire; **solar power** n énergie f solaire; **solar system** n système m solaire

sold [səʊld] pt, pp of **sell**

soldier ['səʊldʒər] n soldat m, militaire m

sold out adj (Comm) épuisé(e)

sole [səʊl] n (of foot) plante f; (of shoe) semelle f; (fish: pl inv) sole f ▷ adj seul(e), unique; **solely** adv seulement, uniquement

solemn ['sɔləm] adj solennel(le); (person) sérieux(-euse), grave

solicitor [sə'lɪsɪtər] n (BRIT: for wills etc) ≈ notaire m; (: in court) ≈ avocat m

solid ['sɔlɪd] adj (not liquid) solide; (not hollow: mass) compact(e); (: metal, rock, wood) massif(-ive) ▷ n solide m

solitary ['sɔlɪtərɪ] adj solitaire

solitude ['sɔlɪtjuːd] n solitude f

solo ['səʊləʊ] n solo m ▷ adv (fly) en solitaire; **soloist** n soliste m/f

soluble ['sɔljubl] adj soluble

solution [sə'luːʃən] n solution f

solve [sɔlv] vt résoudre

solvent ['sɔlvənt] adj (Comm) solvable ▷ n (Chem) (dis)solvant m

sombre (us **somber**) ['sɔmbər] adj sombre, morne

 KEYWORD

some [sʌm] adj **1** (a certain amount or number of): **some tea/water/ice cream** du thé/de l'eau/de la glace; **some children/apples** des enfants/pommes; **I've got some money but not much** j'ai de l'argent mais pas beaucoup
2 (certain: in contrasts): **some people say that ...** il y a des gens qui disent que ...; **some films were excellent, but most were mediocre** certains films étaient excellents, mais la plupart étaient médiocres
3 (unspecified): **some woman was asking for you** il y avait une dame qui vous demandait; **he was asking for some book (or other)** il demandait un livre quelconque; **some day** un de ces jours; **some day next week** un jour la semaine prochaine

▷ pron **1** (a certain number) quelques-un(e)s, certain(e)s: **I've got some** (books etc) j'en ai (quelques-uns); **some (of them) have been sold** certains ont été vendus
2 (a certain amount) un peu; **I've got some** (money, milk) j'en ai (un peu); **would you like some?** est-ce que vous en voulez?, en voulez-vous?; **could I have some of that cheese?** pourrais-je avoir un peu de ce fromage?; **I've read some of the book** j'ai lu une partie du livre
▷ adv: **some 10 people** quelque 10 personnes, 10 personnes environ; **somebody** ['sʌmbədɪ] pron = **someone**; **somehow** adv d'une façon ou d'une autre; (for some reason) pour une raison ou une autre; **someone** pron quelqu'un; **someplace** adv (us) = **somewhere**; **something** pron quelque chose m; **something interesting** quelque chose d'intéressant; **something to do** quelque chose à faire; **sometime** adv (in future) un de ces jours, un jour ou l'autre; (in past): **sometime last month** au cours du mois dernier; **sometimes** adv quelquefois, parfois; **somewhat** adv quelque peu, un peu; **somewhere** adv quelque part; **somewhere else** ailleurs, autre part

son [sʌn] n fils m

song [sɔŋ] n chanson f; (of bird) chant m

son-in-law ['sʌnɪnlɔː] n gendre m, beau-fils m

soon [suːn] adv bientôt; (early) tôt; **~ afterwards** peu après; see also **as**; **sooner** adv (time) plus tôt; (preference): **I would sooner do that** j'aimerais autant or je préférerais faire ça; **sooner or later** tôt ou tard

soothe [suːð] vt calmer, apaiser

sophisticated [sə'fɪstɪkeɪtɪd] adj raffiné(e), sophistiqué(e); (machinery) hautement perfectionné(e), très complexe

sophomore ['sɔfəmɔːr] n (us) étudiant(e) de seconde année

soprano [sə'prɑːnəu] n (singer) soprano m/f

sorbet ['sɔːbeɪ] n sorbet m

sordid ['sɔːdɪd] adj sordide

sore [sɔːr] adj (painful) douloureux(-euse), sensible ▷ n plaie f

sorrow ['sɔrəu] n peine f, chagrin m

sorry ['sɔrɪ] adj désolé(e); (condition, excuse, tale) triste, déplorable; **~!** pardon!, excusez-moi!; **~?** pardon?; **to feel ~ for** plaindre qn

sort [sɔːt] n genre m, espèce f, sorte f; (make: of coffee, car etc) marque f ▷ vt (also: **~ out**: select which to keep) trier; (classify) classer; (tidy) ranger; **sort out** vt (problem) résoudre, régler

SOS n SOS m

so-so ['səʊsəʊ] adv comme ci comme ça

sought [sɔːt] pt, pp of **seek**

soul [səʊl] n âme f

sound [saund] adj (healthy) en bonne santé, sain(e); (safe, not damaged) solide, en bon état; (reliable, not superficial) sérieux(-euse), solide; (sensible) sensé(e) ▷ adv: **~ asleep** profondément endormi(e) ▷ n (noise, volume) son m; (louder) bruit m; (Geo) détroit m, bras m de mer ▷ vt (alarm) sonner ▷ vi sonner, retentir; (fig: seem) sembler (être); **to ~ like** ressembler à; **sound bite** n phrase toute faite (pour être citée dans les médias); **soundtrack** n (of film) bande f sonore

soup [suːp] n soupe f, potage m

sour ['sauər] adj aigre; **it's ~ grapes** c'est du dépit

source [sɔːs] n source f

south [sauθ] n sud m ▷ adj sud inv; (wind) du sud ▷ adv au sud, vers le sud; **South Africa** n Afrique f du Sud; **South African** adj sud-africain(e) ▷ n Sud-Africain(e); **South America** n Amérique f du Sud; **South American** adj sud-américain(e) ▷ n Sud-Américain(e); **southbound** adj en direction du sud; (carriageway) sud inv; **south-east** n sud-est m; **southeastern** [sauθ'i:stən] adj du or au sud-est; **southern** ['sʌðən] adj (du) sud; méridional(e); **South Korea** n Corée f du Sud; **South of France** n: **the South of France** le Sud de la France, le Midi; **South Pole** n Pôle m Sud; **southward(s)** adv vers le sud; **south-west** n sud-ouest m; **southwestern** [sauθ'westən] adj du or au sud-ouest

souvenir [su:və'nɪəʳ] n souvenir m (objet)

sovereign ['sɔvrɪn] adj, n souverain(e)

sow¹ [səu] (pt ~**ed**, pp ~n) vt semer

sow² n [sau] truie f

soya ['sɔɪə] (us **soy**) [sɔɪ] n: ~ **bean** graine f de soja; ~ **sauce** sauce f au soja

spa [spɑ:] n (town) station thermale; (us: also: **health ~**) établissement m de cure de rajeunissement

space [speɪs] n (gen) espace m; (room) place f; espace; (length of time) laps m de temps ▷ cpd spatial(e) ▷ vt (also: ~ **out**) espacer; **spacecraft** n engin or vaisseau spatial; **spaceship** n = **spacecraft**

spacious ['speɪʃəs] adj spacieux(-euse), grand(e)

spade [speɪd] n (tool) bêche f, pelle f; (child's) pelle; **spades** npl (Cards) pique m

spaghetti [spə'gɛtɪ] n spaghetti mpl

Spain [speɪn] n Espagne f

spam [spæm] n (Comput) spam m

span [spæn] n (of bird, plane) envergure f; (of arch) portée f; (in time) espace m de temps, durée f ▷ vt enjamber, franchir; (fig) couvrir, embrasser

Spaniard ['spænjəd] n Espagnol(e)

Spanish ['spænɪʃ] adj espagnol(e), d'Espagne ▷ n (Ling) espagnol m; **the Spanish** npl les Espagnols

spank [spæŋk] vt donner une fessée à

spanner ['spænəʳ] n (BRIT) clé f (de mécanicien)

spare [spɛəʳ] adj de réserve, de rechange; (surplus) de or en trop, de reste ▷ n (part) pièce f de rechange, pièce détachée ▷ vt (do without) se passer de; (afford to give) donner, accorder, passer; (not hurt) épargner; **to ~** (surplus) en surplus, de trop; **spare part** n pièce f de rechange, pièce détachée; **spare room** n chambre f d'ami; **spare time** n moments mpl de loisir; **spare tyre** (us **spare tire**) n (Aut) pneu m de rechange; **spare wheel** n (Aut) roue f de secours

spark [spɑ:k] n étincelle f; **spark(ing) plug** n bougie f

sparkle ['spɑ:kl] n scintillement m, étincellement m, éclat m ▷ vi étinceler, scintiller

sparkling ['spɑ:klɪŋ] adj (wine) mousseux(-euse), pétillant(e); (water) pétillant(e), gazeux(-euse)

sparrow ['spærəu] n moineau m

sparse [spɑ:s] adj clairsemé(e)

spasm ['spæzəm] n (Med) spasme m

spat [spæt] pt, pp of **spit**

spate [speɪt] n (fig): ~ **of** avalanche f or torrent m de

spatula ['spætjulə] n spatule f

speak (pt **spoke**, pp **spoken**) [spi:k, spəuk, 'spəukn] vt (language) parler; (truth) dire ▷ vi parler; (make a speech) prendre la parole; **to ~ to sb/of** or **about sth** parler à qn/de qch; **I don't ~ French** je ne parle pas français; **do you ~ English?** parlez-vous anglais?; **can I ~ to ...?** est-ce

que je peux parler à ...?; **speaker** n (in public) orateur m; (also: **loudspeaker**) haut-parleur m; (for stereo etc) baffle m, enceinte f; (Pol): **the Speaker** (BRIT) le président de la Chambre des communes or des représentants; (US) le président de la Chambre

spear [spɪəʳ] n lance f ▷ vt transpercer

special ['spɛʃl] adj spécial(e); **special delivery** n (Post): **by special delivery** en express; **special effects** npl (Cine) effets spéciaux; **specialist** n spécialiste m/f; **speciality** [spɛʃɪ'ælɪtɪ] n (BRIT) spécialité f; **specialize** vi: **to specialize (in)** se spécialiser (dans); **specially** adv spécialement, particulièrement; **special needs** npl (BRIT) difficultés fpl d'apprentissage scolaire; **special offer** n (Comm) réclame f; **special school** n (BRIT) établissement m d'enseignement spécialisé; **specialty** n (US) = **speciality**

species ['spi:ʃi:z] n (pl inv) espèce f

specific [spə'sɪfɪk] adj (not vague) précis(e), explicite; (particular) particulier(-ière); **specifically** adv explicitement, précisément; (intend, ask, design) expressément, spécialement

specify ['spɛsɪfaɪ] vt spécifier, préciser

specimen ['spɛsɪmən] n spécimen m, échantillon m; (Med: of blood) prélèvement m; (: of urine) échantillon m

speck [spɛk] n petite tache, petit point; (particle) grain m

spectacle ['spɛktəkl] n spectacle m; **spectacles** npl (BRIT) lunettes fpl; **spectacular** [spɛk'tækjulɑʳ] adj spectaculaire

spectator [spɛk'teɪtəʳ] n spectateur(-trice)

spectrum (pl **spectra**) ['spɛktrəm, -rə] n spectre m; (fig) gamme f

speculate ['spɛkjuleɪt] vi spéculer; (try to guess): **to ~ about** s'interroger sur

sped [spɛd] pt, pp of **speed**

speech [spi:tʃ] n (faculty) parole f; (talk) discours m, allocution f; (manner of speaking) façon f de parler, langage m; (enunciation) élocution f; **speechless** adj muet(te)

speed [spi:d] n vitesse f; (promptness) rapidité f ▷ vi (pt, pp **sped**) (Aut: exceed speed limit) faire un excès de vitesse; **at full** or **top ~** à toute vitesse or allure; **speed up** (pt, pp ~**ed up**) vi aller plus vite, accélérer ▷ vt accélérer; **speedboat** n vedette f, hors-bord m inv; **speeding** n (Aut) excès m de vitesse; **speed limit** n limitation f de vitesse, vitesse maximale permise; **speedometer** [spɪ'dɔmɪtəʳ] n compteur m (de vitesse); **speedy** adj rapide, prompt(e)

spell [spɛl] n (also: **magic ~**) sortilège m, charme m; (period of time) (courte) période ▷ vt (pt, pp **spelt** or ~**ed**) (in writing) écrire, orthographier; (aloud) épeler; (fig) signifier; **to cast a ~ on sb** jeter un sort à qn; **he can't ~** il fait des fautes d'orthographe; **spell out** vt (explain): **to ~ sth out for sb** expliquer qch clairement à qn; **spellchecker** ['spɛltʃɛkəʳ] n (Comput) correcteur m or vérificateur m orthographique; **spelling** n orthographe f

spelt [spɛlt] pt, pp of **spell**

spend (pt, pp **spent**) [spɛnd, spɛnt] vt (money) dépenser; (time, life) passer; (devote) consacrer; **spending** n: **government spending** les dépenses publiques

spent [spɛnt] pt, pp of **spend** ▷ adj (cartridge, bullets) vide

sperm [spə:m] n spermatozoïde m; (semen) sperme m

sphere [sfɪəʳ] n sphère f; (fig) sphère, domaine m

spice [spaɪs] n épice f ▷ vt épicer

spicy ['spaɪsɪ] adj épicé(e), relevé(e); (fig) piquant(e)

spider ['spaɪdə^r] n araignée f
spike [spaɪk] n pointe f; (Bot) épi m
spill (pt, pp **spilt** or **~ed**) [spɪl, -t, -d] vt renverser; répandre ▷ vi se répandre; **spill over** vi déborder
spin [spɪn] n (revolution of wheel) tour m; (Aviat) (chute en) vrille f; (trip in car) petit tour, balade f; (on ball) effet m ▷ vb (pt, pp **spun**) ▷ vt (wool etc) filer; (wheel) faire tourner ▷ vi (turn) tourner, tournoyer
spinach ['spɪnɪtʃ] n épinards mpl
spinal ['spaɪnl] adj vertébral(e), spinal(e)
spinal cord n moelle épinière
spin doctor n (inf) personne employée pour présenter un parti politique sous un jour favorable
spin-dryer [spɪn'draɪə^r] n (BRIT) essoreuse f
spine [spaɪn] n colonne vertébrale; (thorn) épine f, piquant m
spiral ['spaɪərl] n spirale f ▷ vi (fig: prices etc) monter en flèche
spire ['spaɪə^r] n flèche f, aiguille f
spirit ['spɪrɪt] n (soul) esprit m, âme f; (ghost) esprit, revenant m; (mood) esprit, état m d'esprit; (courage) courage m, énergie f; **spirits** npl (drink) spiritueux mpl, alcool m; **in good ~s** de bonne humeur
spiritual ['spɪrɪtjuəl] adj spirituel(le); (religious) religieux(-euse)
spit [spɪt] n (for roasting) broche f; (spittle) crachat m; (saliva) salive f ▷ vi (pt, pp **spat**) cracher; (sound) crépiter; (rain) crachiner
spite [spaɪt] n rancune f, dépit m ▷ vt contrarier, vexer; **in ~ of** en dépit de, malgré; **spiteful** adj malveillant(e), rancunier(-ière)
splash [splæʃ] n (sound) plouf m; (of colour) tache f ▷ vt éclabousser ▷ vi (also: **~ about**) barboter, patauger; **splash out** vi (BRIT) faire une folie
splendid ['splendɪd] adj splendide, superbe, magnifique
splinter ['splɪntə^r] n (wood) écharde f; (metal) éclat m ▷ vi (wood) se fendre; (glass) se briser
split [splɪt] n fente f, déchirure f; (fig: Pol) scission f ▷ vb (pt, pp **~**) ▷ vt fendre, déchirer; (party) diviser; (work, profits) partager, répartir ▷ vi (break) se fendre, se briser; (divide) se diviser; **split up** vi (couple) se séparer, rompre; (meeting) se disperser
spoil (pt, pp **~ed** or **~t**) [spɔɪl, -d, -t] vt (damage) abîmer; (mar) gâcher; (child) gâter
spoilt [spɔɪlt] pt, pp of **spoil** ▷ adj (child) gâté(e); (ballot paper) nul(le)
spoke [spəuk] pt of **speak** ▷ n rayon m
spoken ['spəukn] pp of **speak**
spokesman ['spəuksmən] (irreg) n porte-parole m inv
spokesperson ['spəukspə:sn] (irreg) n porte-parole m inv
spokeswoman ['spəukswumən] (irreg) n porte-parole m inv
sponge [spʌndʒ] n éponge f; (Culin: also: **~ cake**) ≈ biscuit m de Savoie ▷ vt éponger ▷ vi: **to ~ off** or **on** vivre aux crochets de; **sponge bag** n (BRIT) trousse f de toilette
sponsor ['sponsə^r] n (Radio, TV, Sport) sponsor m; (for application) parrain m, marraine f; (BRIT: for fund-raising event) donateur(-trice) ▷ vt sponsoriser, parrainer, faire un don à; **sponsorship** n sponsoring m, parrainage m; dons mpl
spontaneous [spon'teɪnɪəs] adj spontané(e)
spooky ['spu:kɪ] adj (inf) qui donne la chair de poule
spoon [spu:n] n cuiller f; **spoonful** n cuillerée f

sport [spɔ:t] n sport m; (person) chic type m/chic fille f ▷ vt (wear) arborer; **sport jacket** n (US) = **sports jacket**; **sports car** n voiture f de sport; **sports centre** (BRIT) n centre sportif; **sports jacket** n (BRIT) veste f de sport; **sportsman** (irreg) n sportif m; **sports utility vehicle** n véhicule m de loisirs (de type SUV); **sportswear** n vêtements mpl de sport; **sportswoman** (irreg) n sportive f; **sporty** adj sportif(-ive)
spot [spot] n tache f; (dot: on pattern) pois m; (pimple) bouton m; (place) endroit m, coin m; (small amount): **a ~ of** un peu de ▷ vt (notice) apercevoir, repérer; **on the ~** sur place, sur les lieux; (immediately) sur le champ; **spotless** adj immaculé(e); **spotlight** n projecteur m; (Aut) phare m auxiliaire
spouse [spauz] n époux (épouse)
sprain [spreɪn] n entorse f, foulure f ▷ vt: **to ~ one's ankle** se fouler or se tordre la cheville
sprang [spræŋ] pt of **spring**
sprawl [sprɔ:l] vi s'étaler
spray [spreɪ] n jet m (en fines gouttelettes); (from sea) embruns mpl; (aerosol) vaporisateur m, bombe f; (for garden) pulvérisateur m; (of flowers) petit bouquet ▷ vt vaporiser, pulvériser; (crops) traiter
spread [spred] n (distribution) répartition f; (Culin) pâte f à tartiner; (inf: meal) festin m ▷ vb (pt, pp **~**) ▷ vt (paste, contents) étendre, étaler; (disease) répandre, propager; (wealth) répartir ▷ vi s'étendre; se répandre; se propager; (stain) s'étaler; **spread out** vi (people) se disperser; **spreadsheet** n (Comput) tableur m
spree [spri:] n: **to go on a ~** faire la fête
spring [sprɪŋ] n (season) printemps m; (leap) bond m, saut m; (coiled metal) ressort m; (of water) source f ▷ vi (pt **sprang**, pp **sprung**) ▷ vi bondir, sauter; **spring up** vi (problem) se présenter, surgir; (plant, buildings) surgir de terre; **spring onion** n (BRIT) ciboule f, cive f
sprinkle ['sprɪŋkl] vt: **to ~ water** etc **on, ~ with water** etc asperger d'eau etc; **to ~ sugar** etc **on, ~ with sugar** etc saupoudrer de sucre etc
sprint [sprɪnt] n sprint m ▷ vi courir à toute vitesse; (Sport) sprinter
sprung [sprʌŋ] pp of **spring**
spun [spʌn] pt, pp of **spin**
spur [spə:^r] n éperon m; (fig) aiguillon m ▷ vt (also: **~ on**) éperonner; aiguillonner; **on the ~ of the moment** sous l'impulsion du moment
spurt [spə:t] n jet m; (of blood) jaillissement m; (of energy) regain m, sursaut m ▷ vi jaillir, gicler
spy [spaɪ] n espion(ne) ▷ vi: **to ~ on** espionner, épier ▷ vt (see) apercevoir
sq. abbr = **square**
squabble ['skwɔbl] vi se chamailler
squad [skwɔd] n (Mil, Police) escouade f, groupe m; (Football) contingent m
squadron ['skwɔdrn] n (Mil) escadron m; (Aviat, Naut) escadrille f
squander ['skwɔndə^r] vt gaspiller, dilapider
square [skweə^r] n carré m; (in town) place f ▷ adj carré(e) ▷ vt (arrange) régler; arranger; (Math) élever au carré; (reconcile) concilier; **all ~** quitte; à égalité; **a ~ meal** un repas convenable; **2 metres ~** (de) 2 mètres sur 2; **1 ~ metre** 1 mètre carré; **square root** n racine carrée
squash [skwɔʃ] n (BRIT: drink): **lemon/orange ~** citronnade f/orangeade f; (Sport) squash m; (US: vegetable) courge f ▷ vt écraser

squat [skwɔt] *adj* petit(e) et épais(se), ramassé(e) ▷ *vi* (*also:* **~ down**) s'accroupir; **squatter** *n* squatter *m*

squeak [skwi:k] *vi* (*hinge, wheel*) grincer; (*mouse*) pousser un petit cri

squeal [skwi:l] *vi* pousser un or des cri(s) aigu(s) or perçant(s); (*brakes*) grincer

squeeze [skwi:z] *n* pression *f* ▷ *vt* presser; (*hand, arm*) serrer

squid [skwɪd] *n* calmar *m*

squint [skwɪnt] *vi* loucher

squirm [skwə:m] *vi* se tortiller

squirrel ['skwɪrəl] *n* écureuil *m*

squirt [skwə:t] *vi* jaillir, gicler ▷ *vt* faire gicler

Sr *abbr* = **senior**

Sri Lanka [srɪ'læŋkə] *n* Sri Lanka *m*

St *abbr* = **saint**; **street**

stab [stæb] *n* (*with knife etc*) coup *m* (de couteau *etc*); (*of pain*) lancée *f*; (*inf: try*): **to have a ~ at (doing) sth** s'essayer à (faire) qch ▷ *vt* poignarder

stability [stə'bɪlɪtɪ] *n* stabilité *f*

stable ['steɪbl] *n* écurie *f* ▷ *adj* stable

stack [stæk] *n* tas *m*, pile *f* ▷ *vt* empiler, entasser

stadium ['steɪdɪəm] *n* stade *m*

staff [stɑ:f] *n* (*work force*) personnel *m*; (*BRIT Scol: also:* **teaching ~**) professeurs *mpl*, enseignants *mpl*, personnel enseignant ▷ *vt* pourvoir en personnel

stag [stæg] *n* cerf *m*

stage [steɪdʒ] *n* scène *f*; (*platform*) estrade *f*; (*point*) étape *f*, stade *m*; (*profession*): **the ~** le théâtre ▷ *vt* (*play*) monter, mettre en scène; (*demonstration*) organiser; **in ~s** par étapes, par degrés

stagger ['stægə'] *vi* chanceler, tituber ▷ *vt* (*person: amaze*) stupéfier; (*hours, holidays*) étaler, échelonner; **staggering** *adj* (*amazing*) stupéfiant(e), renversant(e)

stagnant ['stægnənt] *adj* stagnant(e)

stag night, stag party *n* enterrement *m* de vie de garçon

stain [steɪn] *n* tache *f*; (*colouring*) colorant *m* ▷ *vt* tacher; (*wood*) teindre; **stained glass** (*decorative*) verre coloré; (*in church*) vitraux *mpl*; **stainless steel** *n* inox *m*, acier *m* inoxydable

staircase ['steəkeɪs] *n* = **stairway**

stairs [steəz] *npl* escalier *m*

stairway ['steəweɪ] *n* escalier *m*

stake [steɪk] *n* pieu *m*, poteau *m*; (*Comm: interest*) intérêts *mpl*; (*Betting*) enjeu *m* ▷ *vt* risquer, jouer; (*also:* **~ out:** *area*) marquer, délimiter; **to be at ~** être en jeu

stale [steɪl] *adj* (*bread*) rassis(e); (*food*) pas frais (fraîche); (*beer*) éventé(e); (*smell*) de renfermé; (*air*) confiné(e)

stalk [stɔ:k] *n* tige *f* ▷ *vt* traquer

stall [stɔ:l] *n* (*BRIT: in street, market etc*) éventaire *m*, étal *m*; (*in stable*) stalle *f* ▷ *vt* (*Aut*) caler; (*fig: delay*) retarder ▷ *vi* (*Aut*) caler; (*fig*) essayer de gagner du temps; **stalls** *npl* (*BRIT: in cinema, theatre*) orchestre *m*

stamina ['stæmɪnə] *n* vigueur *f*, endurance *f*

stammer ['stæmə'] *n* bégaiement *m* ▷ *vi* bégayer

stamp [stæmp] *n* timbre *m*; (*also:* **rubber ~**) tampon *m*; (*mark, also fig*) empreinte *f*; (*on document*) cachet *m* ▷ *vi* (*also:* **~ one's foot**) taper du pied ▷ *vt* (*letter*) timbrer; (*with rubber stamp*) tamponner; **stamp out** *vt* (*fire*) piétiner; (*crime*) éradiquer; (*opposition*) éliminer; **stamped addressed envelope** *n* (*BRIT*) enveloppe affranchie pour la réponse

stampede [stæm'pi:d] *n* ruée *f*; (*of cattle*) débandade *f*

stance [stæns] *n* position *f*

stand [stænd] *n* (*position*) position *f*; (*for taxis*) station *f* (de taxis); (*Comm*) étalage *m*, stand *m*; (*Sport: also:* **~s**) tribune *f*; (*also:* **music ~**) pupitre *m* ▷ *vb* (*pt, pp* **stood**) ▷ *vi* être or se tenir (debout); (*rise*) se lever, se mettre debout; (*be placed*) se trouver; (*remain: offer etc*) rester valable ▷ *vt* (*place*) mettre, poser; (*tolerate, withstand*) supporter; (*treat, invite*) offrir, payer; **to make a ~** prendre position; **to ~ for parliament** (*BRIT*) se présenter aux élections (*comme candidat à la députation*); **I can't ~ him** je ne peux pas le voir; **stand back** *vi* (*move back*) reculer, s'écarter; **stand by** *vi* (*be ready*) se tenir prêt(e) ▷ *vt fus* (*opinion*) s'en tenir à; (*person*) ne pas abandonner, soutenir; **stand down** *vi* (*withdraw*) se retirer; **stand for** *vt fus* (*signify*) représenter, signifier; (*tolerate*) supporter, tolérer; **stand in for** *vt fus* remplacer; **stand out** *vi* (*be prominent*) ressortir; **stand up** *vi* (*rise*) se lever, se mettre debout; **stand up for** *vt fus* défendre; **stand up to** *vt fus* tenir tête à, résister à

standard ['stændəd] *n* (*norm*) norme *f*, étalon *m*; (*level*) niveau *m* (voulu); (*criterion*) critère *m*; (*flag*) étendard *m* ▷ *adj* (*size etc*) ordinaire, normal(e); (*model, feature*) standard *inv*; (*practice*) courant(e); (*text*) de base; **standards** *npl* (*morals*) morale *f*, principes *mpl*; **standard of living** *n* niveau *m* de vie

stand-by ticket *n* (*Aviat*) billet *m* stand-by

standing ['stændɪŋ] *adj* debout *inv*; (*permanent*) permanent(e) ▷ *n* réputation *f*, rang *m*, standing *m*; **of many years'** ~ qui dure or existe depuis longtemps; **standing order** *n* (*BRIT: at bank*) virement *m* automatique, prélèvement *m* bancaire

stand: standpoint *n* point *m* de vue; **standstill** *n*: **at a standstill** à l'arrêt; (*fig*) au point mort; **to come to a standstill** s'immobiliser, s'arrêter

stank [stæŋk] *pt of* **stink**

staple ['steɪpl] *n* (*for papers*) agrafe *f* ▷ *adj* (*food, crop, industry etc*) de base principal(e) ▷ *vt* agrafer

star [stɑ:'] *n* étoile *f*; (*celebrity*) vedette *f* ▷ *vt* (*Cine*) avoir pour vedette; **stars** *npl* (*Astrology*) l'horoscope *m*

starboard ['stɑ:bəd] *n* tribord *m*

starch [stɑ:tʃ] *n* amidon *m*; (*in food*) fécule *f*

stardom ['stɑ:dəm] *n* célébrité *f*

stare [steə'] *n* regard *m* fixe ▷ *vi*: **to ~ at** regarder fixement

stark [stɑ:k] *adj* (*bleak*) désolé(e), morne ▷ *adv*: **~ naked** complètement nu(e)

start [stɑ:t] *n* commencement *m*, début *m*; (*of race*) départ *m*; (*sudden movement*) sursaut *m*; (*advantage*) avance *f*, avantage *m* ▷ *vt* commencer; (*cause: fight*) déclencher; (*rumour*) donner naissance à; (*fashion*) lancer; (*found: business, newspaper*) lancer, créer; (*engine*) mettre en marche ▷ *vi* (*begin*) commencer; (*begin journey*) partir, se mettre en route; (*jump*) sursauter; **when does the film ~?** à quelle heure est-ce que le film commence?; **to ~ doing** *or* **to do sth** se mettre à faire qch; **start off** *vi* commencer; (*leave*) partir; **start out** *vi* (*begin*) commencer; (*set out*) partir; **start up** *vi* commencer; (*car*) démarrer ▷ *vt* (*fight*) déclencher; (*business*) créer; (*car*) mettre en marche; **starter** *n* (*Aut*) démarreur *m*; (*Sport: official*) starter *m*; (*BRIT Culin*) entrée *f*; **starting point** *n* point *m* de départ

startle ['stɑ:tl] *vt* faire sursauter; donner un choc à; **startling** *adj* surprenant(e), saisissant(e)

starvation [stɑ:'veɪʃən] *n* faim *f*, famine *f*

starve [stɑ:v] vi mourir de faim ▷ vt laisser mourir de faim

state [steɪt] n état m; (Pol) État m ▷ vt (declare) déclarer, affirmer; (specify) indiquer, spécifier; **States** npl: **the S~s** les États-Unis; **to be in a ~** être dans tous ses états; **stately home** n manoir m or château m (ouvert au public); **statement** n déclaration f; (Law) déposition f; **state school** n école publique; **statesman** (irreg) n homme m d'État

static ['stætɪk] n (Radio) parasites mpl; (also: **~ electricity**) électricité f statique ▷ adj statique

station ['steɪʃən] n gare f; (also: **police ~**) poste m or commissariat m (de police) ▷ vt placer, poster

stationary ['steɪʃnərɪ] adj à l'arrêt, immobile

stationer's (shop) n (BRIT) papeterie f

stationery ['steɪʃnərɪ] n papier m à lettres, petit matériel de bureau

station wagon n (US) break m

statistic [stə'tɪstɪk] n statistique f; **statistics** n (science) statistique f

statue ['stætjuː] n statue f

stature ['stætʃər] n stature f; (fig) envergure f

status ['steɪtəs] n position f, situation f; (prestige) prestige m; (Admin, official position) statut m; **status quo** [-'kwəʊ] n: **the status quo** le statu quo

statutory ['stætjutrɪ] adj statutaire, prévu(e) par un article de loi

staunch [stɔːntʃ] adj sûr(e), loyal(e)

stay [steɪ] n (period of time) séjour m ▷ vi rester; (reside) loger; (spend some time) séjourner; **to ~ put** ne pas bouger; **to ~ the night** passer la nuit; **stay away** vi (from person, building) ne pas s'approcher; (from event) ne pas venir; **stay behind** vi rester en arrière; **stay in** vi (at home) rester à la maison; **stay on** vi rester; **stay out** vi (of house) ne pas rentrer; (strikers) rester en grève; **stay up** vi (at night) ne pas se coucher

steadily ['stedɪlɪ] adv (regularly) progressivement; (firmly) fermement; (walk) d'un pas ferme; (fixedly: look) sans détourner les yeux

steady ['stedɪ] adj stable, solide, ferme; (regular) constant(e), régulier(-ière); (person) calme, pondéré(e) ▷ vt assurer, stabiliser; (nerves) calmer; **a ~ boyfriend** un petit ami

steak [steɪk] n (meat) bifteck m, steak m; (fish, pork) tranche f

steal (pt **stole**, pp **stolen**) [stiːl, stəʊl, 'stəʊln] vt, vi voler; (move) se faufiler, se déplacer furtivement; **my wallet has been stolen** on m'a volé mon portefeuille

steam [stiːm] n vapeur f ▷ vt (Culin) cuire à la vapeur ▷ vi fumer; **steam up** vi (window) se couvrir de buée; **to get ~ed up about sth** (fig: inf) s'exciter à propos de qch; **steamy** adj humide; (window) embué(e); (sexy) torride

steel [stiːl] n acier m ▷ cpd d'acier

steep [stiːp] adj raide, escarpé(e); (price) très élevé(e), excessif(-ive) ▷ vt (faire) tremper

steeple ['stiːpl] n clocher m

steer [stɪər] vt diriger; (boat) gouverner; (lead: person) guider, conduire ▷ vi tenir le gouvernail; **steering** n (Aut) conduite f; **steering wheel** n volant m

stem [stem] n (of plant) tige f; (of glass) pied m ▷ vt contenir, endiguer; (attack, spread of disease) juguler

step [step] n pas m; (stair) marche f; (action) mesure f, disposition f ▷ vi: **to ~ forward/back** faire un pas en avant/arrière, avancer/reculer; **steps** npl (BRIT) = **stepladder**; **to be in/out of ~ (with)** (fig) aller dans le sens (de)/être déphasé(e) (par rapport à); **step down** vi (fig) se retirer, se désister; **step in** vi (fig) intervenir; **step up** vt (production, sales) augmenter; (campaign, efforts) intensifier; **stepbrother** n demi-frère m; **stepchild** (pl **~ren**) n beau-fils m, belle-fille f; **stepdaughter** n belle-fille f; **stepfather** n beau-père m; **stepladder** n (BRIT) escabeau m; **stepmother** n belle-mère f; **stepsister** n demi-sœur f; **stepson** n beau-fils m

stereo ['sterɪəʊ] n (sound) stéréo f; (hi-fi) chaîne f stéréo ▷ adj (also: **~phonic**) stéréo(phonique)

stereotype ['stɪərɪətaɪp] n stéréotype m ▷ vt stéréotyper

sterile ['sterаɪl] adj stérile; **sterilize** ['sterɪlaɪz] vt stériliser

sterling ['stɜːlɪŋ] adj (silver) de bon aloi, fin(e) ▷ n (currency) livre f sterling inv

stern [stɜːn] adj sévère ▷ n (Naut) arrière m, poupe f

steroid ['stɪərɔɪd] n stéroïde m

stew [stjuː] n ragoût m ▷ vt, vi cuire à la casserole

steward ['stjuːəd] n (Aviat, Naut, Rail) steward m; **stewardess** n hôtesse f

stick [stɪk] n bâton m; (for walking) canne f; (of chalk etc) morceau m ▷ vb (pt, pp **stuck**) ▷ vt (glue) coller; (thrust): **to ~ sth into** piquer or planter or enfoncer qch dans; (inf: put) mettre, fourrer; (: tolerate) supporter ▷ vi (adhere) tenir, coller; (remain) rester; (get jammed: door, lift) se bloquer; **stick out** vi dépasser, sortir; **stick up** vi dépasser, sortir; **stick up for** vt fus défendre; **sticker** n auto-collant m; **sticking plaster** n sparadrap m, pansement adhésif; **stick insect** n phasme m; **stick shift** n (US Aut) levier m de vitesses

sticky ['stɪkɪ] adj poisseux(-euse); (label) adhésif(-ive); (fig: situation) délicat(e)

stiff [stɪf] adj (gen) raide, rigide; (door, brush) dur(e); (difficult) difficile, ardu(e); (cold) froid(e), distant(e); (strong, high) fort(e), élevé(e) ▷ adv: **to be bored/ scared/frozen ~** s'ennuyer à mourir/être mort(e) de peur/froid

stifling ['staɪflɪŋ] adj (heat) suffocant(e)

stigma ['stɪgmə] n stigmate m

stiletto [stɪ'letəʊ] n (BRIT: also: **~ heel**) talon m aiguille

still [stɪl] adj immobile ▷ adv (up to this time) encore, toujours; (even) encore; (nonetheless) quand même, tout de même

stimulate ['stɪmjuleɪt] vt stimuler

stimulus (pl **stimuli**) ['stɪmjuləs, 'stɪmjulaɪ] n stimulant m; (Biol, Psych) stimulus m

sting [stɪŋ] n piqûre f; (organ) dard m ▷ vt, vi (pt, pp **stung**) piquer

stink [stɪŋk] n puanteur f ▷ vi (pt **stank**, pp **stunk**) puer, empester

stir [stɜːr] n agitation f, sensation f ▷ vt remuer ▷ vi remuer, bouger; **stir up** vt (trouble) fomenter, provoquer; **stir-fry** vt faire sauter ▷ n: **vegetable stir-fry** légumes sautés à la poêle

stitch [stɪtʃ] n (Sewing) point m; (Knitting) maille f; (Med) point de suture; (pain) point de côté ▷ vt coudre, piquer; (Med) suturer

stock [stɔk] n réserve f, provision f; (Comm) stock m; (Agr) cheptel m, bétail m; (Culin) bouillon m; (Finance) valeurs fpl, titres mpl; (descent, origin) souche f ▷ adj (fig: reply etc) classique ▷ vt (have in stock) avoir, vendre; **in ~** en stock, en magasin; **out of ~** épuisé(e); **to take ~ (of)**

faire le point; **~s and shares** valeurs (mobilières), titres; **stockbroker** ['stɒkbrəʊkə'] n agent m de change; **stock cube** n (BRIT Culin) bouillon-cube m; **stock exchange** n Bourse f (des valeurs); **stockholder** ['stɒkhəʊldə'] n (US) actionnaire m/f

stocking ['stɒkɪŋ] n bas m

stock market n Bourse f, marché financier

stole [stəʊl] pt of **steal** ▷ n étole f

stolen ['stəʊln] pp of **steal**

stomach ['stʌmək] n estomac m; (abdomen) ventre m ▷ vt supporter, digérer; **stomachache** n mal m à l'estomac ou au ventre

stone [stəʊn] n pierre f; (pebble) caillou m, galet m; (in fruit) noyau m; (Med) calcul m; (BRIT: weight) = 6.348 kg; 14 pounds ▷ cpd de or en pierre ▷ vt (person) lancer des pierres sur, lapider; (fruit) dénoyauter

stood [stʊd] pt, pp of **stand**

stool [stu:l] n tabouret m

stoop [stu:p] vi (also: **have a ~**) être voûté(e); (also: **~ down**: bend) se baisser, se courber

stop [stɒp] n arrêt m; (in punctuation) point m ▷ vt arrêter; (break off) interrompre; (also: **put a ~ to**) mettre fin à; (prevent) empêcher ▷ vi s'arrêter; (rain, noise etc) cesser, s'arrêter; **to ~ doing sth** cesser or arrêter de faire qch; **to ~ sb (from) doing sth** empêcher qn de faire qch; **~ it!** arrête!; **stop by** vi s'arrêter (au passage); **stop off** vi faire une courte halte; **stopover** n halte f; (Aviat) escale f; **stoppage** n (strike) arrêt m de travail; (obstruction) obstruction f

storage ['stɔːrɪdʒ] n emmagasinage m

store [stɔː'] n (stock) provision f, réserve f; (depot) entrepôt m; (BRIT: large shop) grand magasin; (US: shop) magasin m ▷ vt emmagasiner; (information) enregistrer; **stores** npl (food) provisions; **who knows what is in ~ for us?** qui sait ce que l'avenir nous réserve or ce qui nous attend?; **storekeeper** n (US) commerçant(e)

storey (US **story**) ['stɔːrɪ] n étage m

storm [stɔːm] n tempête f; (thunderstorm) orage m ▷ vi (fig) fulminer ▷ vt prendre d'assaut; **stormy** adj orageux(-euse)

story ['stɔːrɪ] n histoire f; (Press: article) article m; (US) = **storey**

stout [staʊt] adj (strong) solide; (fat) gros(se), corpulent(e) ▷ n bière f brune

stove [stəʊv] n (for cooking) fourneau m; (: small) réchaud m; (for heating) poêle m

straight [streɪt] adj droit(e); (hair) raide; (frank) honnête, franc (franche); (simple) simple ▷ adv (tout) droit; (drink) sec, sans eau; **to put or get ~** mettre en ordre, mettre de l'ordre dans; (fig) mettre au clair; **~ away, ~ off** (at once) tout de suite; **straighten** vt ajuster; (bed) arranger; **straighten out** vt (fig) débrouiller; **straighten up** vi (stand up) se redresser; **straightforward** adj simple; (frank) honnête, direct(e)

strain [streɪn] n (Tech) tension f, pression f; (physical) effort m; (mental) tension (nerveuse); (Med) entorse f; (breed: of plants) variété f; (: of animals) race f ▷ vt (fig: resources etc) mettre à rude épreuve, grever; (hurt: back etc) se faire mal à; (vegetables) égoutter; **strains** npl (Mus) accords mpl, accents mpl; **strained** adj (muscle) froissé(e); (laugh etc) forcé(e), contraint(e); (relations) tendu(e); **strainer** n passoire f

strait [streɪt] n (Geo) détroit m; **straits** npl: **to be in dire ~s** (fig) avoir de sérieux ennuis

strand [strænd] n (of thread) fil m, brin m; (of rope) toron m; (of hair) mèche f ▷ vt (boat) échouer; **stranded** adj en rade, en plan

strange [streɪndʒ] adj (not known) inconnu(e); (odd) étrange, bizarre; **strangely** adv étrangement, bizarrement; see also **enough**; **stranger** n (unknown) inconnu(e); (from somewhere else) étranger(-ère)

strangle ['stræŋgl] vt étrangler

strap [stræp] n lanière f, courroie f, sangle f; (of slip, dress) bretelle f

strategic [strə'tiːdʒɪk] adj stratégique

strategy ['strætɪdʒɪ] n stratégie f

straw [strɔː] n paille f; **that's the last ~!** ça c'est le comble!

strawberry ['strɔːbərɪ] n fraise f

stray [streɪ] adj (animal) perdu(e), errant(e); (scattered) isolé(e) ▷ vi s'égarer; **~ bullet** balle perdue

streak [striːk] n bande f, filet m; (in hair) raie f ▷ vt zébrer, strier

stream [striːm] n (brook) ruisseau m; (current) courant m, flot m; (of people) défilé m ininterrompu, flot ▷ vt (Scol) répartir par niveau ▷ vi ruisseler; **to ~ in/out** entrer/ sortir à flots

street [striːt] n rue f; **streetcar** n (US) tramway m; **street light** n réverbère m; **street map, street plan** n plan m des rues

strength [streŋθ] n force f; (of girder, knot etc) solidité f; **strengthen** vt renforcer; (muscle) fortifier; (building, Econ) consolider

strenuous ['strenjʊəs] adj vigoureux(-euse), énergique; (tiring) ardu(e), fatigant(e)

stress [stres] n (force, pressure) pression f; (mental strain) tension (nerveuse), stress m; (accent) accent m; (emphasis) insistance f ▷ vt insister sur, souligner; (syllable) accentuer; **stressed** adj (tense) stressé(e); (syllable) accentué(e); **stressful** adj (job) stressant(e)

stretch [stretʃ] n (of sand etc) étendue f ▷ vi s'étirer; (extend): **to ~ to** or **as far as** s'étendre jusqu'à ▷ vt tendre, étirer; (fig) pousser (au maximum); **at a ~** d'affilée; **stretch out** vi s'étendre ▷ vt (arm etc) allonger, tendre; (to spread) étendre

stretcher ['stretʃə'] n brancard m, civière f

strict [strɪkt] adj strict(e); **strictly** adv strictement

stride [straɪd] n grand pas, enjambée f ▷ vi (pt **strode**, pp **stridden**) marcher à grands pas

strike [straɪk] n grève f; (of oil etc) découverte f; (attack) raid m ▷ vb (pt, pp **struck**) ▷ vt frapper; (oil etc) trouver, découvrir; (make: agreement, deal) conclure ▷ vi faire grève; (attack) attaquer; (clock) sonner; **to go on** or **come out on ~** se mettre en grève, faire grève; **to ~ a match** frotter une allumette; **striker** n gréviste m/f; (Sport) buteur m; **striking** adj frappant(e), saisissant(e); (attractive) éblouissant(e)

string [strɪŋ] n ficelle f, fil m; (row: of beads) rang m; (Mus) corde f ▷ vt (pt, pp **strung**): **to ~ out** échelonner; **to ~ together** enchaîner; **the strings** npl (Mus) les instruments mpl à cordes; **to pull ~s** (fig) faire jouer le piston

strip [strɪp] n bande f; (Sport) tenue f ▷ vt (undress) déshabiller; (paint) décaper; (fig) dégarnir, dépouiller; (also: **~ down**: machine) démonter ▷ vi se déshabiller; **strip off** vt (paint etc) décaper ▷ vi (person) se déshabiller

stripe [straɪp] n raie f, rayure f; (Mil) galon m; **striped** adj rayé(e), à rayures

stripper ['strɪpə'] n strip-teaseuse f

strip-search ['strɪpsəːtʃ] vt: **to ~ sb** fouiller qn (en le faisant se déshabiller)

strive (pt **strove**, pp **~n**) [straɪv, strəʊv, 'strɪvn] vi: **to ~ to do/for sth** s'efforcer de faire/d'obtenir qch

strode [strəʊd] pt of **stride**

stroke [strəʊk] n coup m; (Med) attaque f; (Swimming: style) (sorte f de) nage f ▷ vt caresser; **at a ~** d'un (seul) coup

stroll [strəʊl] n petite promenade ▷ vi flâner, se promener nonchalamment; **stroller** n (US: for child) poussette f

strong [strɒŋ] adj (gen) fort(e); (healthy) vigoureux(-euse); (heart, nerves) solide; **they are 50 ~** ils sont au nombre de 50; **stronghold** n forteresse f, fort m; (fig) bastion m; **strongly** adv fortement, avec force; vigoureusement; solidement

strove [strəʊv] pt of **strive**

struck [strʌk] pt, pp of **strike**

structure ['strʌktʃə'] n structure f; (building) construction f

struggle ['strʌgl] n lutte f ▷ vi lutter, se battre

strung [strʌŋ] pt, pp of **string**

stub [stʌb] n (of cigarette) bout m, mégot m; (of ticket etc) talon m ▷ vt: **to ~ one's toe (on sth)** se heurter le doigt de pied (contre qch); **stub out** vt écraser

stubble ['stʌbl] n chaume m; (on chin) barbe f de plusieurs jours

stubborn ['stʌbən] adj têtu(e), obstiné(e), opiniâtre

stuck [stʌk] pt, pp of **stick** ▷ adj (jammed) bloqué(e), coincé(e)

stud [stʌd] n (on boots etc) clou m; (collar stud) bouton m de col; (earring) petite boucle d'oreille; (of horses: also: **~ farm**) écurie f, haras m; (also: **~ horse**) étalon m ▷ vt (fig): **~ded with** parsemé(e) or criblé(e) de

student ['stjuːdənt] n étudiant(e) ▷ adj (life) estudiantin(e), étudiant(e), d'étudiant; (residence, restaurant) universitaire; (loan, movement) étudiant; **student driver** n (US) (conducteur(-trice)) débutant(e); **students' union** n (BRIT: association) ≈ union f des étudiants; (: building) ≈ foyer m des étudiants

studio ['stjuːdɪəʊ] n studio m, atelier m; (TV etc) studio; **studio flat** (US **studio apartment**) n studio m

study ['stʌdɪ] n étude f; (room) bureau m ▷ vt étudier; (examine) examiner ▷ vi étudier, faire ses études

stuff [stʌf] n (gen) chose(s) f(pl), truc m; (belongings) affaires fpl, trucs; (substance) substance f ▷ vt rembourrer; (Culin) farcir; (inf: push) fourrer; **stuffing** n bourre f, rembourrage m; (Culin) farce f; **stuffy** adj (room) mal ventilé(e) or aéré(e); (ideas) vieux jeu inv

stumble ['stʌmbl] vi trébucher; **to ~ across** or **on** (fig) tomber sur

stump [stʌmp] n souche f; (of limb) moignon m ▷ vt: **to be ~ed** sécher, ne pas savoir que répondre

stun [stʌn] vt (blow) étourdir; (news) abasourdir, stupéfier

stung [stʌŋ] pt, pp of **sting**

stunk [stʌŋk] pp of **stink**

stunned [stʌnd] adj assommé(e); (fig) sidéré(e)

stunning ['stʌnɪŋ] adj (beautiful) étourdissant(e); (news etc) stupéfiant(e)

stunt [stʌnt] n (in film) cascade f, acrobatie f; (publicity) truc m publicitaire ▷ vt retarder, arrêter

stupid ['stjuːpɪd] adj stupide, bête; **stupidity**

[stjuː'pɪdɪtɪ] n stupidité f, bêtise f

sturdy ['stəːdɪ] adj (person, plant) robuste, vigoureux(-euse); (object) solide

stutter ['stʌtə'] n bégaiement m ▷ vi bégayer

style [staɪl] n style m; (distinction) allure f, cachet m, style; (design) modèle m; **stylish** adj élégant(e), chic inv; **stylist** n (hair stylist) coiffeur(-euse)

sub... [sʌb] prefix sub..., sous-; **subconscious** adj subconscient(e)

subdued [səb'djuːd] adj (light) tamisé(e); (person) qui a perdu de son entrain

subject n ['sʌbdʒɪkt] sujet m; (Scol) matière f ▷ adj [səb'dʒɛkt]: **to ~ to** soumettre à; **to be ~ to** (law) être soumis(e) à; **subjective** [səb'dʒɛktɪv] adj subjectif(-ive); **subject matter** n (content) contenu m

subjunctive [səb'dʒʌŋktɪv] n subjonctif m

submarine [sʌbmə'riːn] n sous-marin m

submission [səb'mɪʃən] n soumission f

submit [səb'mɪt] vt soumettre ▷ vi se soumettre

subordinate [sə'bɔːdɪnət] adj (junior) subalterne; (Grammar) subordonné(e) ▷ n subordonné(e)

subscribe [səb'skraɪb] vi cotiser; **to ~ to** (opinion, fund) souscrire à; (newspaper) s'abonner à; être abonné(e) à

subscription [səb'skrɪpʃən] n (to magazine etc) abonnement m

subsequent ['sʌbsɪkwənt] adj ultérieur(e), suivant(e); **subsequently** adv par la suite

subside [səb'saɪd] vi (land) s'affaisser; (flood) baisser; (wind, feelings) tomber

subsidiary [səb'sɪdɪərɪ] adj subsidiaire; accessoire; (BRIT Scol: subject) complémentaire ▷ n filiale f

subsidize ['sʌbsɪdaɪz] vt subventionner

subsidy ['sʌbsɪdɪ] n subvention f

substance ['sʌbstəns] n substance f

substantial [səb'stænʃl] adj substantiel(le); (fig) important(e)

substitute ['sʌbstɪtjuːt] n (person) remplaçant(e); (thing) succédané m ▷ vt: **to ~ sth/sb for** substituer qch/qn à, remplacer par qch/qn; **substitution** n substitution f

subtitles ['sʌbtaɪtlz] npl (Cine) sous-titres mpl

subtle ['sʌtl] adj subtil(e)

subtract [səb'trækt] vt soustraire, retrancher

suburb ['sʌbəːb] n faubourg m; **the ~s** la banlieue; **suburban** [sə'bəːbən] adj de banlieue, suburbain(e)

subway ['sʌbweɪ] n (BRIT: underpass) passage souterrain; (US: railway) métro m

succeed [sək'siːd] vi réussir ▷ vt succéder à; **to ~ in doing** réussir à faire

success [sək'sɛs] n succès m; réussite f; **successful** adj (business) prospère, qui réussit; (attempt) couronné(e) de succès; **to be successful (in doing)** réussir (à faire); **successfully** adv avec succès

succession [sək'sɛʃən] n succession f

successive [sək'sɛsɪv] adj successif(-ive)

successor [sək'sɛsə'] n successeur m

succumb [sə'kʌm] vi succomber

such [sʌtʃ] adj tel (telle); (of that kind): **~ a book** un livre de ce genre or pareil, un tel livre; (so much): **~ courage** un tel courage ▷ adv si; **~ a long trip** un si long voyage; **~ a lot of** tellement or tant de; **~ as** (like) tel (telle) que, comme; **as ~** adv en tant que tel (telle), à proprement parler; **such-and-such** adj tel ou tel (telle ou telle)

suck [sʌk] vt sucer; (breast, bottle) téter

Sudan [suˈdɑːn] n Soudan m
sudden [ˈsʌdn] adj soudain(e), subit(e); **all of a ~** soudain, tout à coup; **suddenly** adv brusquement, tout à coup, soudain
sue [suː] vt poursuivre en justice, intenter un procès à
suede [sweɪd] n daim m, cuir suédé
suffer [ˈsʌfəʳ] vt souffrir, subir; (bear) tolérer, supporter, subir ▷ vi souffrir; **to ~ from** (illness) souffrir de, avoir; **suffering** n souffrance(s) f(pl)
suffice [səˈfaɪs] vi suffire
sufficient [səˈfɪʃənt] adj suffisant(e)
suffocate [ˈsʌfəkeɪt] vi suffoquer; étouffer
sugar [ˈʃʊgəʳ] n sucre m ▷ vt sucrer
suggest [səˈdʒɛst] vt suggérer, proposer; (indicate) sembler indiquer; **suggestion** [səˈdʒɛstʃən] n suggestion f
suicide [ˈsuɪsaɪd] n suicide m; **~ bombing** attentat m suicide; see also **commit**; **suicide bomber** n kamikaze m/f
suit [suːt] n (man's) costume m, complet m; (woman's) tailleur m, ensemble m; (Cards) couleur f; (lawsuit) procès m ▷ vt (subj: clothes, hairstyle) aller à; (be convenient for) convenir à; (adapt): **to ~ sth to** adapter or approprier qch à; **well ~ed** (couple) faits l'un pour l'autre, très bien assortis; **suitable** adj qui convient; approprié(e), adéquat(e); **suitcase** n valise f
suite [swiːt] n (of rooms, also Mus) suite f; (furniture): **bedroom/dining room ~** (ensemble m de) chambre f à coucher/salle f à manger; **a three-piece ~** un salon (canapé et deux fauteuils)
sulfur [ˈsʌlfəʳ] (US) n = **sulphur**
sulk [sʌlk] vi bouder
sulphur (US **sulfur**) [ˈsʌlfəʳ] n soufre m
sultana [sʌlˈtɑːnə] n (fruit) raisin (sec) de Smyrne
sum [sʌm] n somme f; (Scol etc) calcul m; **sum up** vt résumer ▷ vi résumer
summarize [ˈsʌməraɪz] vt résumer
summary [ˈsʌmərɪ] n résumé m
summer [ˈsʌməʳ] n été m ▷ cpd d'été, estival(e); **(in the) ~** en été, pendant l'été; **summer holidays** npl grandes vacances; **summertime** n (season) été m
summit [ˈsʌmɪt] n sommet m; (also: **~ conference**) (conférence f au) sommet m
summon [ˈsʌmən] vt appeler, convoquer; **to ~ a witness** citer or assigner un témoin
Sun. abbr (= Sunday) dim
sun [sʌn] n soleil m; **sunbathe** vi prendre un bain de soleil; **sunbed** n lit pliant; (with sun lamp) lit à ultra-violets; **sunblock** n écran m total; **sunburn** n coup m de soleil; **sunburned, sunburnt** adj bronzé(e), hâlé(e); (painfully) brûlé(e) par le soleil
Sunday [ˈsʌndɪ] n dimanche m
sunflower [ˈsʌnflauəʳ] n tournesol m
sung [sʌŋ] pp of **sing**
sunglasses [ˈsʌnglɑːsɪz] npl lunettes fpl de soleil
sunk [sʌŋk] pp of **sink**
sun: sunlight n (lumière f du) soleil m; **sun lounger** n chaise longue; **sunny** adj ensoleillé(e); **it is sunny** il fait (du) soleil, il y a du soleil; **sunrise** n lever m du soleil; **sun roof** n (Aut) toit ouvrant; **sunscreen** n crème f solaire; **sunset** n coucher m du soleil; **sunshade** n (over table) parasol m; **sunshine** n (lumière f du) soleil m; **sunstroke** n insolation f, coup m de soleil; **suntan** n bronzage m; **suntan lotion** n lotion f or lait m solaire; **suntan oil** n huile f solaire

super [ˈsuːpəʳ] adj (inf) formidable
superb [suːˈpəːb] adj superbe, magnifique
superficial [suːpəˈfɪʃəl] adj superficiel(le)
superintendent [suːpərɪnˈtɛndənt] n directeur(-trice); (Police) ≈ commissaire m
superior [suˈpɪərɪəʳ] adj supérieur(e); (smug) condescendant(e), méprisant(e) ▷ n supérieur(e)
superlative [suˈpəːlətɪv] n (Ling) superlatif m
supermarket [ˈsuːpəmɑːkɪt] n supermarché m
supernatural [suːpəˈnætʃərəl] adj surnaturel(le) ▷ n: **the ~** le surnaturel
superpower [ˈsuːpəpauəʳ] n (Pol) superpuissance f
superstition [suːpəˈstɪʃən] n superstition f
superstitious [suːpəˈstɪʃəs] adj superstitieux(-euse)
superstore [ˈsuːpəstɔːʳ] n (BRIT) hypermarché m, grande surface
supervise [ˈsuːpəvaɪz] vt (children etc) surveiller; (organization, work) diriger; **supervision** [suːpəˈvɪʒən] n surveillance f; (monitoring) contrôle m; (management) direction f; **supervisor** n surveillant(e); (in shop) chef m de rayon
supper [ˈsʌpəʳ] n dîner m; (late) souper m
supple [ˈsʌpl] adj souple
supplement n [ˈsʌplɪmənt] supplément m ▷ vt [sʌplɪˈmɛnt] ajouter à, compléter
supplier [səˈplaɪəʳ] n fournisseur m
supply [səˈplaɪ] vt (provide) fournir; (equip) approvisionner or ravitailler (en); fournir (en) ▷ n provision f, réserve f; (supplying) approvisionnement m; **supplies** npl (food) vivres mpl; (Mil) subsistances fpl
support [səˈpɔːt] n (moral, financial etc) soutien m, appui m; (Tech) support m, soutien ▷ vt soutenir, supporter; (financially) subvenir aux besoins de; (uphold) être pour, être partisan de, appuyer; (Sport: team) être pour; **supporter** n (Pol etc) partisan(e); (Sport) supporter m
suppose [səˈpəuz] vt, vi supposer; imaginer; **to be ~d to do/be** être censé(e) faire/être; **supposedly** [səˈpəuzɪdlɪ] adv soi-disant; **supposing** conj si, à supposer que + sub
suppress [səˈprɛs] vt (revolt, feeling) réprimer; (information) faire disparaître; (scandal, yawn) étouffer
supreme [suˈpriːm] adj suprême
surcharge [ˈsəːtʃɑːdʒ] n surcharge f
sure [ʃuəʳ] adj (gen) sûr(e); (definite, convinced) sûr, certain(e); **~!** (of course) bien sûr!; **~ enough** effectivement; **to make ~ of sth/that** s'assurer de qch/que, vérifier qch/que; **surely** adv sûrement; certainement
surf [səːf] n (waves) ressac m ▷ vt: **to ~ the Net** surfer sur Internet, surfer sur le net
surface [ˈsəːfɪs] n surface f ▷ vt (road) poser un revêtement sur ▷ vi remonter à la surface; (fig) faire surface; **by ~ mail** par voie de terre; (by sea) par voie maritime
surfboard [ˈsəːfbɔːd] n planche f de surf
surfer [ˈsəːfəʳ] n (in sea) surfeur(-euse); **web** or **net ~** internaute m/f
surfing [ˈsəːfɪŋ] n surf m
surge [səːdʒ] n (of emotion) vague f ▷ vi déferler
surgeon [ˈsəːdʒən] n chirurgien m
surgery [ˈsəːdʒərɪ] n chirurgie f; (BRIT: room) cabinet m (de consultation); (also: **~ hours**) heures fpl de consultation

surname [ˈsɜːneɪm] n nom m de famille
surpass [səːˈpɑːs] vt surpasser, dépasser
surplus [ˈsɜːpləs] n surplus m, excédent m ▷ adj en surplus, de trop; (Comm) excédentaire
surprise [səˈpraɪz] n (gen) surprise f; (astonishment) étonnement m ▷ vt surprendre, étonner; **surprised** adj (look, smile) surpris(e), étonné(e); **to be surprised** être surpris; **surprising** adj surprenant(e), étonnant(e); **surprisingly** adv (easy, helpful) étonnamment, étrangement; **(somewhat) surprisingly, he agreed** curieusement, il a accepté
surrender [səˈrɛndəʳ] n reddition f, capitulation f ▷ vi se rendre, capituler
surround [səˈraund] vt entourer; (Mil etc) encercler; **surrounding** adj environnant(e); **surroundings** npl environs mpl, alentours mpl
surveillance [səːˈveɪləns] n surveillance f
survey n [ˈsɜːveɪ] enquête f, étude f; (in house buying etc) inspection f, (rapport m d')expertise f; (of land) levé m ▷ vt [səːˈveɪ] (situation) passer en revue; (examine carefully) inspecter; (building) expertiser; (land) faire le levé de; (look at) embrasser du regard; **surveyor** n (of building) expert m; (of land) (arpenteur m) géomètre m
survival [səˈvaɪvl] n survie f
survive [səˈvaɪv] vi survivre; (custom etc) subsister ▷ vt (accident etc) survivre à, réchapper de; (person) survivre à; **survivor** n survivant(e)
suspect adj, n [ˈsʌspɛkt] suspect(e) ▷ vt [səsˈpɛkt] soupçonner, suspecter
suspend [səsˈpɛnd] vt suspendre; **suspended sentence** n (Law) condamnation f avec sursis; **suspenders** npl (BRIT) jarretelles fpl; (US) bretelles fpl
suspense [səsˈpɛns] n attente f, incertitude f; (in film etc) suspense m; **to keep sb in ~** tenir qn en suspens, laisser qn dans l'incertitude
suspension [səsˈpɛnʃən] n (gen, Aut) suspension f; (of driving licence) retrait m provisoire; **suspension bridge** n pont suspendu
suspicion [səsˈpɪʃən] n soupçon(s) m(pl); **suspicious** adj (suspecting) soupçonneux(-euse), méfiant(e); (causing suspicion) suspect(e)
sustain [səsˈteɪn] vt soutenir; (subj: food) nourrir, donner des forces à; (damage) subir; (injury) recevoir
SUV n abbr (esp US: = sports utility vehicle) SUV m, véhicule m de loisirs
swallow [ˈswɔləu] n (bird) hirondelle f ▷ vt avaler; (fig: story) gober
swam [swæm] pt of **swim**
swamp [swɔmp] n marais m, marécage m ▷ vt submerger
swan [swɔn] n cygne m
swap [swɔp] n échange m, troc m ▷ vt: **to ~ (for)** échanger (contre), troquer (contre)
swarm [swɔːm] n essaim m ▷ vi (bees) essaimer; (people) grouiller; **to be ~ing with** grouiller de
sway [sweɪ] vi se balancer, osciller ▷ vt (influence) influencer
swear [swɛəʳ] (pt swore, pp sworn) vt, vi jurer; **swear in** vt assermenter; **swearword** n gros mot, juron m
sweat [swɛt] n sueur f, transpiration f ▷ vi suer
sweater [ˈswɛtəʳ] n tricot m, pull m
sweatshirt [ˈswɛtʃəːt] n sweat-shirt m
sweaty [ˈswɛtɪ] adj en sueur, moite or mouillé(e) de sueur

Swede [swiːd] n Suédois(e)
swede [swiːd] n (BRIT) rutabaga m
Sweden [ˈswiːdn] n Suède f; **Swedish** [ˈswiːdɪʃ] adj suédois(e) ▷ n (Ling) suédois m
sweep [swiːp] n (curve) grande courbe; (also: **chimney ~**) ramoneur m ▷ vb (pt, pp swept) ▷ vt balayer; (subj: current) emporter
sweet [swiːt] n (BRIT: pudding) dessert m; (candy) bonbon m ▷ adj doux (douce); (not savoury) sucré(e); (kind) gentil(le); (baby) mignon(ne); **sweetcorn** n maïs doux; **sweetener** [ˈswiːtnəʳ] n (Culin) édulcorant m; **sweetheart** n amoureux(-euse); **sweetshop** n (BRIT) confiserie f
swell [swɛl] n (of sea) houle f ▷ adj (US: inf: excellent) chouette ▷ vb (pt ~ed, pp swollen or ~ed) ▷ vt (increase) grossir, augmenter ▷ vi (increase) grossir, augmenter; (sound) s'enfler; (Med: also: ~ **up**) enfler; **swelling** n (Med) enflure f; (: lump) grosseur f
swept [swɛpt] pt, pp of **sweep**
swerve [swəːv] vi (to avoid obstacle) faire une embardée or un écart; (off the road) dévier
swift [swɪft] n (bird) martinet m ▷ adj rapide, prompt(e)
swim [swɪm] n: **to go for a ~** aller nager or se baigner ▷ vb (pt swam, pp swum) ▷ vi nager; (Sport) faire de la natation; (fig: head, room) tourner ▷ vt traverser (à la nage); **to ~ a length** nager une longueur; **swimmer** n nageur(-euse); **swimming** n nage f, natation f; **swimming costume** n (BRIT) maillot m (de bain); **swimming pool** n piscine f; **swimming trunks** npl maillot m de bain; **swimsuit** n maillot m (de bain)
swing [swɪŋ] n (in playground) balançoire f; (movement) balancement m, oscillations fpl; (change in opinion etc) revirement m ▷ vb (pt, pp swung) ▷ vt balancer, faire osciller; (also: ~ **round**) tourner, faire virer ▷ vi se balancer, osciller; (also: ~ **round**) virer, tourner; **to be in full ~** battre son plein
swipe card [swaɪp-] n carte f magnétique
swirl [swəːl] vi tourbillonner, tournoyer
Swiss [swɪs] adj suisse ▷ n (pl inv) Suisse(-esse)
switch [swɪtʃ] n (for light, radio etc) bouton m; (change) changement m, revirement m ▷ vt (change) changer; **switch off** vt éteindre; (engine, machine) arrêter; **could you ~ off the light?** pouvez-vous éteindre la lumière?; **switch on** vt allumer; (engine, machine) mettre en marche; **switchboard** n (Tel) standard m
Switzerland [ˈswɪtsələnd] n Suisse f
swivel [ˈswɪvl] vi (also: ~ **round**) pivoter, tourner
swollen [ˈswəulən] pp of **swell**
swoop [swuːp] n (by police etc) rafle f, descente f ▷ vi (bird: also: ~ **down**) descendre en piqué, piquer
swop [swɔp] n, vt = **swap**
sword [sɔːd] n épée f; **swordfish** n espadon m
swore [swɔːʳ] pt of **swear**
sworn [swɔːn] pp of **swear** ▷ adj (statement, evidence) donné(e) sous serment; (enemy) juré(e)
swum [swʌm] pp of **swim**
swung [swʌŋ] pt, pp of **swing**
syllable [ˈsɪləbl] n syllabe f
syllabus [ˈsɪləbəs] n programme m
symbol [ˈsɪmbl] n symbole m; **symbolic(al)** [sɪmˈbɔlɪk(l)] adj symbolique
symmetrical [sɪˈmɛtrɪkl] adj symétrique
symmetry [ˈsɪmɪtrɪ] n symétrie f
sympathetic [sɪmpəˈθɛtɪk] adj (showing pity)

compatissant(e); (*understanding*) bienveillant(e), compréhensif(-ive); **~ towards** bien disposé(e) envers

sympathize ['sɪmpəaɪz] *vi*: **to ~ with sb** plaindre qn; (*in grief*) s'associer à la douleur de qn; **to ~ with sth** comprendre qch

sympathy ['sɪmpəθɪ] *n* (*pity*) compassion *f*

symphony ['sɪmfənɪ] *n* symphonie *f*

symptom ['sɪmptəm] *n* symptôme *m*; indice *m*

synagogue ['sɪnəgɔg] *n* synagogue *f*

syndicate ['sɪndɪkɪt] *n* syndicat *m*, coopérative *f*; (*Press*) agence *f* de presse

syndrome ['sɪndrəʊm] *n* syndrome *m*

synonym ['sɪnənɪm] *n* synonyme *m*

synthetic [sɪn'θetɪk] *adj* synthétique

Syria ['sɪrɪə] *n* Syrie *f*

syringe [sɪ'rɪndʒ] *n* seringue *f*

syrup ['sɪrəp] *n* sirop *m*; (*BRIT: also*: **golden ~**) mélasse raffinée

system ['sɪstəm] *n* système *m*; (*Anat*) organisme *m*; **systematic** [sɪstə'mætɪk] *adj* systématique; méthodique; **systems analyst** *n* analyste-programmeur *m/f*

t

ta [tɑː] *excl* (*BRIT inf*) merci!

tab [tæb] *n* (*label*) étiquette *f*; (*on drinks can etc*) languette *f*; **to keep ~s on** (*fig*) surveiller

table ['teɪbl] *n* table *f* ▷ *vt* (*BRIT: motion etc*) présenter; **a ~ for 4, please** une table pour 4, s'il vous plaît; **to lay** *or* **set the ~** mettre le couvert *or* la table; **tablecloth** *n* nappe *f*; **table d'hôte** [tɑːbl'dəʊt] *adj* (*meal*) à prix fixe; **table lamp** *n* lampe décorative *or* de table; **tablemat** *n* (*for plate*) napperon *m*, set *m*; (*for hot dish*) dessous-de-plat *m inv*; **tablespoon** *n* cuiller *f* de service; (*also*: **tablespoonful**: *as measurement*) cuillerée *f* à soupe

tablet ['tæblɪt] *n* (*Med*) comprimé *m*; (*of stone*) plaque *f*

table tennis *n* ping-pong *m*, tennis *m* de table

tabloid ['tæblɔɪd] *n* (*newspaper*) quotidien *m* populaire

taboo [tə'buː] *adj*, *n* tabou (*m*)

tack [tæk] *n* (*nail*) petit clou; (*fig*) direction *f* ▷ *vt* (*nail*) clouer; (*sew*) bâtir ▷ *vi* (*Naut*) tirer un *or* des bord(s); **to ~ sth on to (the end of) sth** (*of letter, book*) rajouter qch à la fin de qch

tackle ['tækl] *n* matériel *m*, équipement *m*; (*for lifting*) appareil *m* de levage; (*Football, Rugby*) plaquage *m* ▷ *vt* (*difficulty, animal, burglar*) s'attaquer à; (*person: challenge*) s'expliquer avec; (*Football, Rugby*) plaquer

tacky ['tækɪ] *adj* collant(e); (*paint*) pas sec (sèche); (*pej: poor-quality*) minable; (: *showing bad taste*) ringard(e)

tact [tækt] *n* tact *m*; **tactful** *adj* plein(e) de tact

tactics ['tæktɪks] *npl* tactique *f*

tactless ['tæktlɪs] *adj* qui manque de tact

tadpole ['tædpəʊl] *n* têtard *m*

taffy ['tæfɪ] *n* (*US*) (bonbon *m* au) caramel *m*

tag [tæg] *n* étiquette *f*

tail [teɪl] *n* queue *f*; (*of shirt*) pan *m* ▷ *vt* (*follow*) suivre, filer; **tails** *npl* (*suit*) habit *m*; *see also* **head**

tailor ['teɪlər] *n* tailleur *m* (*artisan*)

Taiwan ['taɪ'wɑːn] *n* Taiwan (*no article*); **Taiwanese** [taɪwə'niːz] *adj* taïwanais(e) ▷ *n inv* Taïwanais(e)

take [teɪk] *vb* (*pt* **took**, *pp* **~n**) ▷ *vt* prendre; (*gain: prize*) remporter; (*require: effort, courage*) demander; (*tolerate*) accepter, supporter; (*hold: passengers etc*) contenir; (*accompany*) emmener, accompagner; (*bring, carry*) apporter, emporter; (*exam*) passer, se présenter à; **to ~ sth from** (*drawer etc*) prendre qch dans; (*person*) prendre qch à; **I ~ it that** je suppose que; **to be ~n ill** tomber malade; **it won't ~ long** ça ne prendra pas longtemps; **I was quite ~n with her/it** elle/cela m'a beaucoup plu; **take after** *vt fus* ressembler à; **take apart** *vt* démonter; **take away** *vt* (*carry off*) emporter; (*remove*) enlever; (*subtract*) soustraire; **take back** *vt* (*return*) rendre, rapporter; (*one's words*) retirer; **take down** *vt* (*building*) démolir; (*letter etc*) prendre, écrire; **take in** *vt* (*deceive*) tromper, rouler; (*understand*) comprendre, saisir; (*include*) couvrir, inclure; (*lodger*) prendre; (*dress, waistband*) reprendre; **take off** *vi* (*Aviat*) décoller ▷ *vt* (*remove*) enlever; **take on** *vt* (*work*) accepter, se charger de; (*employee*) prendre, embaucher; (*opponent*) accepter de se battre contre; **take out** *vt* sortir; (*remove*) enlever; (*invite*) sortir avec; **to ~ sth out of** (*out of drawer etc*) prendre qch dans; **to ~ sb out to a restaurant** emmener qn au restaurant; **take over** *vt* (*business*) reprendre ▷ *vi*: **to ~ over from sb** prendre la relève de qn; **take up** *vt* (*one's story*) reprendre; (*dress*) raccourcir; (*occupy: time, space*) prendre, occuper; (*engage in: hobby etc*) se mettre à; (*accept: offer, challenge*) accepter; **takeaway** (*BRIT*) *adj* (*food*) à emporter ▷ *n* (*shop, restaurant*) = magasin *m* qui vend des plats à emporter; **taken** *pp* of **take**; **is this seat taken?** la place est prise?; **takeoff** *n* (*Aviat*) décollage *m*; **takeout** *adj*, *n* (*US*) = **takeaway**; **takeover** *n* (*Comm*) rachat *m*; **takings** *npl* (*Comm*) recette *f*

talc [tælk] *n* (*also*: **~um powder**) talc *m*

tale [teɪl] *n* (*story*) conte *m*, histoire *f*; (*account*) récit *m*; **to tell ~s** (*fig*) rapporter

talent ['tælnt] *n* talent *m*, don *m*; **talented** *adj* doué(e), plein(e) de talent

talk [tɔːk] *n* (*a speech*) causerie *f*, exposé *m*; (*conversation*) discussion *f*; (*interview*) entretien *m*; (*gossip*) racontars *mpl* (*pej*) ▷ *vi* parler; (*chatter*) bavarder; **talks** *npl* (*Pol etc*) entretiens *mpl*; **to ~ about** parler de; **to ~ sb out of/into doing** persuader qn de ne pas faire/de faire; **to ~ shop** parler métier or affaires; **talk over** *vt* discuter (de); **talk show** *n* (*TV, Radio*) émission-débat *f*

tall [tɔːl] *adj* (*person*) grand(e); (*building, tree*) haut(e); **to be 6 feet ~** = mesurer 1 mètre 80

tambourine [tæmbə'riːn] *n* tambourin *m*

tame [teɪm] *adj* apprivoisé(e); (*fig: story, style*) insipide

tamper ['tæmpə^r] *vi*: **to ~ with** toucher à (*en cachette ou sans permission*)

tampon ['tæmpən] *n* tampon *m* hygiénique *or* périodique

tan [tæn] *n* (*also:* **sun~**) bronzage *m* ▷ *vt, vi* bronzer, brunir ▷ *adj* (*colour*) marron clair *inv*

tandem ['tændəm] *n* tandem *m*

tangerine [tændʒə'riːn] *n* mandarine *f*

tangle ['tæŋgl] *n* enchevêtrement *m*; **to get in(to) a ~** s'emmêler

tank [tæŋk] *n* réservoir *m*; (*for fish*) aquarium *m*; (*Mil*) char *m* d'assaut, tank *m*

tanker ['tæŋkə^r] *n* (*ship*) pétrolier *m*, tanker *m*; (*truck*) camion-citerne *m*

tanned [tænd] *adj* bronzé(e)

tantrum ['tæntrəm] *n* accès *m* de colère

Tanzania [tænzə'nɪə] *n* Tanzanie *f*

tap [tæp] *n* (*on sink etc*) robinet *m*; (*gentle blow*) petite tape *f* ▷ *vt* frapper *or* taper légèrement; (*resources*) exploiter, utiliser; (*telephone*) mettre sur écoute; **on ~** (*fig: resources*) disponible; **tap dancing** *n* claquettes *fpl*

tape [teɪp] *n* (*for tying*) ruban *m*; (*also:* **magnetic ~**) bande *f*(magnétique); (*cassette*) cassette *f*; (*sticky*) Scotch® *m* ▷ *vt* (*record*) enregistrer (au magnétoscope *or* sur cassette); (*stick*) coller avec du Scotch®; **tape measure** *n* mètre *m* à ruban; **tape recorder** *n* magnétophone *m*

tapestry ['tæpɪstrɪ] *n* tapisserie *f*

tar [tɑː] *n* goudron *m*

target ['tɑːgɪt] *n* cible *f*; (*fig: objective*) objectif *m*

tariff ['tærɪf] *n* (*Comm*) tarif *m*; (*taxes*) tarif douanier

tarmac ['tɑːmæk] *n* (*BRIT: on road*) macadam *m*; (*Aviat*) aire *f* d'envol

tarpaulin [tɑːˈpɔːlɪn] *n* bâche goudronnée

tarragon ['tærəgən] *n* estragon *m*

tart [tɑːt] *n* (*Culin*) tarte *f*; (*BRIT inf. pej: prostitute*) poule *f* ▷ *adj* (*flavour*) âpre, aigrelet(te)

tartan ['tɑːtn] *n* tartan *m* ▷ *adj* écossais(e)

tartar(e) sauce *n* sauce *f* tartare

task [tɑːsk] *n* tâche *f*; **to take to ~** prendre à partie

taste [teɪst] *n* goût *m*; (*fig: glimpse, idea*) idée *f*, aperçu *m* ▷ *vt* goûter ▷ *vi*: **to ~ of** (*fish etc*) avoir le *or* un goût de; **you can ~ the garlic (in it)** on sent bien l'ail; **to have a ~ of sth** goûter (à) qch; **can I have a ~?** je peux goûter?; **to be in good/bad** *or* **poor ~** être de bon/mauvais goût; **tasteful** *adj* de bon goût; **tasteless** *adj* (*food*) insipide; (*remark*) de mauvais goût; **tasty** *adj* savoureux(-euse), délicieux(-euse)

tatters ['tætəz] *npl*: **in ~** (*also:* **tattered**) en lambeaux

tattoo [təˈtuː] *n* tatouage *m*; (*spectacle*) parade *f* militaire ▷ *vt* tatouer

taught [tɔːt] *pt, pp* of **teach**

taunt [tɔːnt] *n* raillerie *f* ▷ *vt* railler

Taurus ['tɔːrəs] *n* le Taureau

taut [tɔːt] *adj* tendu(e)

tax [tæks] *n* (*on goods etc*) taxe *f*; (*on income*) impôts *mpl*, contributions *fpl* ▷ *vt* taxer; imposer; (*fig: patience etc*) mettre à l'épreuve; **tax disc** *n* (*BRIT Aut*) vignette *f* (automobile); **tax-free** *adj* exempt(e) d'impôts

taxi ['tæksɪ] *n* taxi *m* ▷ *vi* (*Aviat*) rouler (lentement) au sol; **can you call me a ~, please?** pouvez-vous m'appeler un taxi, s'il vous plaît?; **taxi driver** *n* chauffeur *m* de taxi; **taxi rank** (*BRIT* **taxi stand**) *n* station *f* de taxis

tax payer [-peɪə^r] *n* contribuable *m/f*

tax return *n* déclaration *f* d'impôts *or* de revenus

TB *n abbr* = **tuberculosis**

tea [tiː] *n* thé *m*; (*BRIT: snack: for children*) goûter *m*; **high ~** (*BRIT*) collation combinant goûter et dîner; **tea bag** *n* sachet *m* de thé; **tea break** *n* (*BRIT*) pause-thé *f*

teach (*pt, pp* **taught**) [tiːtʃ, tɔːt] *vt*: **to ~ sb sth, to ~ sth to sb** apprendre qch à qn; (*in school etc*) enseigner qch à qn ▷ *vi* enseigner; **teacher** *n* (*in secondary school*) professeur *m*; (*in primary school*) instituteur(-trice) *m/f*; **teaching** *n* enseignement *m*

tea: **tea cloth** *n* (*BRIT*) torchon *m*; **teacup** *n* tasse *f* à thé

tea leaves *npl* feuilles *fpl* de thé

team [tiːm] *n* équipe *f*; (*of animals*) attelage *m*; **team up** *vi*: **to ~ up (with)** faire équipe (avec)

teapot ['tiːpɔt] *n* théière *f*

tear¹ ['tɪə^r] *n* larme *f*; **in ~s** en larmes

tear² *n* [tɛə^r] déchirure *f* ▷ *vb* (*pt* **tore**, *pp* **torn**) ▷ *vt* déchirer ▷ *vi* se déchirer; **tear apart** *vt* (*also fig*) déchirer; **tear down** *vt* (*building, statue*) démolir; (*poster, flag*) arracher; **tear off** *vt* (*sheet of paper etc*) arracher; (*one's clothes*) enlever à toute vitesse; **tear up** *vt* (*sheet of paper etc*) déchirer, mettre en morceaux *or* pièces

tearful ['tɪəful] *adj* larmoyant(e)

tear gas [tɪə-] *n* gaz *m* lacrymogène

tearoom ['tiːruːm] *n* salon *m* de thé

tease [tiːz] *vt* taquiner; (*unkindly*) tourmenter

tea: **teaspoon** *n* petite cuiller; (*also:* **teaspoonful**: *as measurement*) ≈ cuillerée *f* à café; **teatime** *n* l'heure *f* du thé; **tea towel** *n* (*BRIT*) torchon *m* (à vaisselle)

technical ['tɛknɪkl] *adj* technique

technician [tɛk'nɪʃən] *n* technicien(ne)

technique [tɛk'niːk] *n* technique *f*

technology [tɛk'nɔlədʒɪ] *n* technologie *f*

teddy (bear) ['tɛdɪ-] *n* ours *m* (en peluche)

tedious ['tiːdɪəs] *adj* fastidieux(-euse)

tee [tiː] *n* (*Golf*) tee *m*

teen [tiːn] *adj* = **teenage** ▷ *n* (*US*) = **teenager**

teenage ['tiːneɪdʒ] *adj* (*fashions etc*) pour jeunes, pour adolescents; (*child*) qui est adolescent(e); **teenager** *n* adolescent(e)

teens [tiːnz] *npl*: **to be in one's ~** être adolescent(e)

teeth [tiːθ] *npl* of **tooth**

teetotal ['tiː'təutl] *adj* (*person*) qui ne boit jamais d'alcool

telecommunications ['tɛlɪkəmjuːnɪ'keɪʃənz] *n* télécommunications *fpl*

telegram ['tɛlɪgræm] *n* télégramme *m*

telegraph pole ['tɛlɪgrɑː-] *n* poteau *m* télégraphique

telephone ['tɛlɪfəun] *n* téléphone *m* ▷ *vt* (*person*) téléphoner à; (*message*) téléphoner; **to be on the ~** (*be speaking*) être au téléphone; **telephone book** *n* = **telephone directory**; **telephone booth** (*BRIT* **telephone box**) *n* cabine *f* téléphonique; **telephone**

call n appel m téléphonique; **telephone directory** n annuaire m (du téléphone); **telephone number** n numéro m de téléphone

telesales ['tɛlɪseɪlz] npl télévente f

telescope ['tɛlɪskəʊp] n télescope m

televise ['tɛlɪvaɪz] vt téléviser

television ['tɛlɪvɪʒən] n télévision f; **on ~** à la télévision; **television programme** n émission f de télévision

tell (pt, pp **told**) [tɛl, təʊld] vt dire; (relate: story) raconter; (distinguish): **to ~ sth from** distinguer qch de ▷ vi (talk): **to ~ of** parler de; (have effect) se faire sentir, se voir; **to ~ sb to do** dire à qn de faire; **to ~ the time** (know how to) savoir lire l'heure; **tell off** vt réprimander, gronder; **teller** n (in bank) caissier(-ière)

telly ['tɛlɪ] n abbr (BRIT inf: = television) télé f

temp [tɛmp] n (BRIT: = temporary worker) intérimaire m/f ▷ vi travailler comme intérimaire

temper ['tɛmpə'] n (nature) caractère m; (mood) humeur f; (fit of anger) colère f ▷ vt (moderate) tempérer, adoucir; **to be in a ~** être en colère; **to lose one's ~** se mettre en colère

temperament ['tɛmprəmənt] n (nature) tempérament m; **temperamental** [tɛmprə'mɛntl] adj capricieux(-euse)

temperature ['tɛmprətʃə'] n température f; **to have or run a ~** avoir de la fièvre

temple ['tɛmpl] n (building) temple m; (Anat) tempe f

temporary ['tɛmpərərɪ] adj temporaire, provisoire; (job, worker) temporaire

tempt [tɛmpt] vt tenter; **to ~ sb into doing** induire qn à faire; **temptation** n tentation f; **tempting** adj tentant(e); (food) appétissant(e)

ten [tɛn] num dix

tenant ['tɛnənt] n locataire m/f

tend [tɛnd] vt s'occuper de ▷ vi: **to ~ to do** avoir tendance à faire; **tendency** n ['tɛndənsɪ] n tendance f

tender ['tɛndə'] adj tendre; (delicate) délicat(e); (sore) sensible ▷ n (Comm: offer) soumission f; (money): **legal ~** cours légal ▷ vt offrir

tendon ['tɛndən] n tendon m

tenner ['tɛnə'] n (BRIT inf) billet m de dix livres

tennis ['tɛnɪs] n tennis m; **tennis ball** n balle f de tennis; **tennis court** n (court m de) tennis m; **tennis match** n match m de tennis; **tennis player** n joueur(-euse) de tennis; **tennis racket** n raquette f de tennis

tenor ['tɛnə'] n (Mus) ténor m

tenpin bowling ['tɛnpɪn-] n (BRIT) bowling m (à 10 quilles)

tense [tɛns] adj tendu(e) ▷ n (Ling) temps m

tension ['tɛnʃən] n tension f

tent [tɛnt] n tente f

tentative ['tɛntətɪv] adj timide, hésitant(e); (conclusion) provisoire

tenth [tɛnθ] num dixième

tent: tent peg n piquet m de tente; **tent pole** n montant m de tente

tepid ['tɛpɪd] adj tiède

term [tə:m] n terme m; (Scol) trimestre m ▷ vt appeler; **terms** npl (conditions) conditions fpl; (Comm) tarif m; **in the short/long ~** à court/long terme; **to come to ~s with** (problem) faire face à; **to be on good ~s with** bien s'entendre avec, être en bons termes avec

terminal ['tə:mɪnl] adj (disease) dans sa phase terminale; (patient) incurable ▷ n (Elec) borne f; (for oil, ore etc, also Comput) terminal m; (also: **air ~**) aérogare f; (BRIT: also: **coach ~**) gare routière

terminate ['tə:mɪneɪt] vt mettre fin à; (pregnancy) interrompre

termini ['tə:mɪnaɪ] npl of **terminus**

terminology [tə:mɪ'nɔlədʒɪ] n terminologie f

terminus (pl **termini**) ['tə:mɪnəs, 'tə:mɪnaɪ] n terminus m inv

terrace ['tɛrəs] n terrasse f; (BRIT: row of houses) rangée f de maisons (attenantes les unes aux autres); **the ~s** (BRIT Sport) les gradins mpl; **terraced** adj (garden) en terrasses; (in a row: house, cottage etc) attenant(e) aux maisons voisines

terrain [tɛ'reɪn] n terrain m (sol)

terrestrial [tɪ'rɛstrɪəl] adj terrestre

terrible ['tɛrɪbl] adj terrible, atroce; (weather, work) affreux(-euse), épouvantable; **terribly** adv terriblement; (very badly) affreusement mal

terrier ['tɛrɪə'] n terrier m (chien)

terrific [tə'rɪfɪk] adj (very great) fantastique, incroyable, terrible; (wonderful) formidable, sensationnel(le)

terrified ['tɛrɪfaɪd] adj terrifié(e); **to be ~ of sth** avoir très peur de qch

terrify ['tɛrɪfaɪ] vt terrifier; **terrifying** adj terrifiant(e)

territorial [tɛrɪ'tɔ:rɪəl] adj territorial(e)

territory ['tɛrɪtərɪ] n territoire m

terror ['tɛrə'] n terreur f; **terrorism** n terrorisme m; **terrorist** n terroriste m/f; **terrorist attack** n attentat m terroriste

test [tɛst] n (trial, check) essai m; (: of courage etc) épreuve f; (Med) examen m; (Chem) analyse f; (Scol) interrogation f de contrôle; (also: **driving ~**) (examen du) permis m de conduire ▷ vt essayer; mettre à l'épreuve; examiner; analyser; faire subir une interrogation (de contrôle) à

testicle ['tɛstɪkl] n testicule m

testify ['tɛstɪfaɪ] vi (Law) témoigner, déposer; **to ~ to sth** (Law) attester qch

testimony ['tɛstɪmənɪ] n (Law) témoignage m, déposition f

test: test match n (Cricket, Rugby) match international; **test tube** n éprouvette f

tetanus ['tɛtənəs] n tétanos m

text [tɛkst] n texte m; (on mobile phone) texto m, SMS m inv ▷ vt (inf) envoyer un texto ou SMS à; **textbook** n manuel m

textile ['tɛkstaɪl] n textile m

text message n texto m, SMS m inv

text messaging [-'mɛsɪdʒɪŋ] n messagerie textuelle

texture ['tɛkstʃə'] n texture f; (of skin, paper etc) grain m

Thai [taɪ] adj thaïlandais(e) ▷ n Thaïlandais(e)

Thailand ['taɪlænd] n Thaïlande f

Thames [tɛmz] n: **the (River) ~** la Tamise

than [ðæn, ðən] conj que; (with numerals): **more ~ 10/once** plus de 10/d'une fois; **I have more/less ~ you** j'en ai plus/moins que toi; **she has more apples ~ pears** elle a plus de pommes que de poires; **it is better to phone ~ to write** il vaut mieux téléphoner (plutôt) qu'écrire; **she is older ~ you think** elle est plus âgée que tu le crois

thank [θæŋk] vt remercier, dire merci à; **thanks** npl remerciements mpl ▷ excl merci!; **~ you (very much)** merci (beaucoup); **~ God** Dieu merci!; **~s to** prep grâce à; **thankfully** adv (fortunately) heureusement;

Thanksgiving (Day) n jour m d'action de grâce

 KEYWORD

that [ðæt] adj (demonstrative): (pl **those**) ce, cet + vowel or h mute, cette f; **that man/woman/book** cet homme/cette femme/ce livre; (not this) cet homme-là/cette femme-là/ce livre-là; **that one** celui-là (celle-là)
▷ pron **1** (demonstrative): (pl **those**) ce; (not this one) cela, ça; (that one) celui (celle); **who's that?** qui est-ce?; **what's that?** qu'est-ce que c'est?; **is that you?** c'est toi?; **I prefer this to that** je préfère ceci à cela or ça; **that's what he said** c'est or voilà ce qu'il a dit; **will you eat all that?** est-ce que tu vas manger tout ça?; **that is (to say)** c'est-à-dire, à savoir
2 (relative: subject) qui; (: object) que; (: after prep) lequel (laquelle), lesquels (lesquelles) pl; **the book that I read** le livre que j'ai lu; **the books that are in the library** les livres qui sont dans la bibliothèque; **all that I have** tout ce que j'ai; **the box that I put it in** la boîte dans laquelle je l'ai mis; **the people that I spoke to** les gens auxquels or à qui j'ai parlé
3 (relative: of time) où; **the day that he came** le jour où il est venu
▷ conj que; **he thought that I was ill** il pensait que j'étais malade
▷ adv (demonstrative): **I don't like it that much** ça ne me plaît pas tant que ça; **I didn't know it was that bad** je ne savais pas que c'était si or aussi mauvais; **it's about that high** c'est à peu près de cette hauteur

thatched [θætʃt] adj (roof) de chaume; **~ cottage** chaumière f

thaw [θɔː] n dégel m ▷ vi (ice) fondre; (food) dégeler ▷ vt (food) (faire) dégeler

 KEYWORD

the [ðiː, ðə] def art **1** (gen) le, la f, l' + vowel or h mute, les pl (NB: à + le(s) = **au(x)**; de + le = **du**; de + les = **des**); **the boy/girl/ink** le garçon/la fille/l'encre; **the children** les enfants; **the history of the world** l'histoire du monde; **give it to the postman** donne-le au facteur; **to play the piano/flute** jouer du piano/de la flûte
2 (+ adj to form n) le, la f, l' + vowel or h mute, les pl; **the rich and the poor** les riches et les pauvres; **to attempt the impossible** tenter l'impossible
3 (in titles): **Elizabeth the First** Elisabeth première; **Peter the Great** Pierre le Grand
4 (in comparisons): **the more he works, the more he earns** plus il travaille, plus il gagne de l'argent

theatre (US **theater**) [ˈθɪətəʳ] n théâtre m; (Med: also; **operating ~**) salle f d'opération

theft [θɛft] n vol m (larcin)

their [ðɛəʳ] adj leur, leurs pl; see also **my**; **theirs** pron le (la) leur, les leurs; see also **mine¹**

them [ðɛm, ðəm] pron (direct) les; (indirect) leur; (stressed, after prep) eux (elles); **give me a few of ~** donnez-m'en quelques uns (or quelques unes); see also **me**

theme [θiːm] n thème m; **theme park** n parc m à thème

themselves [ðəmˈsɛlvz] pl pron (reflexive) se; (emphatic, after prep) eux-mêmes (elles-mêmes); **between ~** entre eux (elles); see also **oneself**

then [ðɛn] adv (at that time) alors, à ce moment-là; (next) puis, ensuite; (and also) et puis ▷ conj (therefore) alors, dans ce cas ▷ adj: **the ~ president** le président d'alors or de l'époque; **by ~** (past) à ce moment-là; (future) d'ici là; **from ~ on** dès lors; **until ~** jusqu'à ce moment-là, jusque-là

theology [θɪˈɔlədʒɪ] n théologie f

theory [ˈθɪərɪ] n théorie f

therapist [ˈθɛrəpɪst] n thérapeute m/f

therapy [ˈθɛrəpɪ] n thérapie f

 KEYWORD

there [ðɛəʳ] adv **1**: **there is**, **there are** il y a; **there are 3 of them** (people, things) il y en a 3; **there is no-one here/no bread left** il n'y a personne/il n'y a plus de pain; **there has been an accident** il y a eu un accident
2 (referring to place) là, là-bas; **it's there** c'est là(-bas); **in/on/up/down there** là-dedans/là-dessus/là-haut/en bas; **he went there on Friday** il y est allé vendredi; **I want that book there** je veux ce livre-là; **there he is!** le voilà!
3: **there, there** (esp to child) allons, allons!

there: **thereabouts** adv (place) par là, près de là; (amount) environ, à peu près; **thereafter** adv par la suite; **thereby** adv ainsi; **therefore** adv donc, par conséquent

there's [ˈðɛəz] = **there is**; **there has**

thermal [ˈθəːml] adj thermique; **~ underwear** sous-vêtements mpl en Thermolactyl®

thermometer [θəˈmɔmɪtəʳ] n thermomètre m

thermostat [ˈθəːməustæt] n thermostat m

these [ðiːz] pl pron ceux-ci (celles-ci) ▷ pl adj ces; (not those): **~ books** ces livres-ci

thesis (pl **theses**) [ˈθiːsɪs, ˈθiːsiːz] n thèse f

they [ðeɪ] pl pron ils (elles); (stressed) eux (elles); **~ say that ...** (it is said that) on dit que ...; **they'd** = **they had**; **they would**; **they'll** = **they shall**; **they will**; **they're** = **they are**; **they've** = **they have**

thick [θɪk] adj épais(se); (stupid) bête, borné(e) ▷ n: **in the ~ of** au beau milieu de, en plein cœur de; **it's 20 cm ~** ça a 20 cm d'épaisseur; **thicken** vi s'épaissir ▷ vt (sauce etc) épaissir; **thickness** n épaisseur f

thief (pl **thieves**) [θiːf, θiːvz] n voleur(-euse)

thigh [θaɪ] n cuisse f

thin [θɪn] adj mince; (skinny) maigre; (soup) peu épais(se); (hair, crowd) clairsemé(e) ▷ vt (also: **~ down**: sauce, paint) délayer

thing [θɪŋ] n chose f; (object) objet m; (contraption) truc m; **things** npl (belongings) affaires fpl; **the ~ is ...** c'est que ...; **the best ~ would be to** le mieux serait de; **how are ~s?** comment ça va?; **to have a ~ about** (be obsessed by) être obsédé(e) par; (hate) détester; **poor ~!** le (or la) pauvre!

think (pt, pp **thought**) [θɪŋk, θɔːt] vi penser, réfléchir ▷ vt penser, croire; (imagine) s'imaginer; **what did you ~ of them?** qu'avez-vous pensé d'eux?; **to ~ about sth/sb** penser à qch/qn; **I'll ~ about it** je vais y réfléchir; **to ~ of doing** avoir l'idée de faire; **I ~ so/not** je crois or pense que oui/non; **to ~ well of** avoir une haute opinion de; **think over** vt bien réfléchir à; **think up** vt inventer, trouver

third [θəːd] num troisième ▷ n (fraction) tiers m; (Aut) troisième (vitesse) f; (BRIT Scol: degree) = licence f avec mention passable; **thirdly** adv troisièmement; **third**

party insurance n (BRIT) assurance f au tiers; **Third World** n: the Third World le Tiers-Monde

thirst [θəːst] n soif f; **thirsty** adj qui a soif, assoiffé(e); (work) qui donne soif; **to be thirsty** avoir soif

thirteen [θəːˈtiːn] num treize; **thirteenth** [-ˈtiːnθ] num treizième

thirtieth [ˈθəːtɪɪθ] num trentième

thirty [ˈθəːtɪ] num trente

○ KEYWORD

this [ðɪs] adj (demonstrative): (pl these) ce, cet + vowel or h mute, cette f; **this man/woman/book** cet homme/cette femme-ci/ce livre; (not that) cet homme-ci/cette femme-ci/ce livre-ci; **this one** celui-ci (celle-ci)
▷ pron (demonstrative): (pl these) ce; (not that one) celui-ci (celle-ci), ceci; **who's this?** qui est-ce?; **what's this?** qu'est-ce que c'est?; **I prefer this to that** je préfère ceci à cela; **this is where I live** c'est ici que j'habite; **this is what he said** voici ce qu'il a dit; **this is Mr Brown** (in introductions) je vous présente Mr Brown; (in photo) c'est Mr Brown; (on telephone) ici Mr Brown
▷ adv (demonstrative): **it was about this big** c'était à peu près de cette grandeur or grand comme ça; **I didn't know it was this bad** je ne savais pas que c'était si or aussi mauvais

thistle [ˈθɪsl] n chardon m

thorn [θɔːn] n épine f

thorough [ˈθʌrə] adj (search) minutieux(-euse); (knowledge, research) approfondi(e); (work, person) consciencieux(-euse); (cleaning) à fond; **thoroughly** adv (search) minutieusement; (study) en profondeur; (clean) à fond; (very) tout à fait

those [ðəʊz] pl pron ceux-là (celles-là) ▷ pl adj ces; (not these) ~ **books** ces livres-là

though [ðəʊ] conj bien que + sub, quoique + sub ▷ adv pourtant

thought [θɔːt] pt, pp of **think** ▷ n pensée f; (idea) idée f; (opinion) avis m; **thoughtful** adj (deep in thought) pensif(-ive); (serious) réfléchi(e); (considerate) prévenant(e); **thoughtless** adj qui manque de considération

thousand [ˈθaʊzənd] num mille; **one ~** mille; **two ~** deux mille; **~s of** des milliers de; **thousandth** num millième

thrash [θræʃ] vt rouer de coups; (as punishment) donner une correction à; (inf: defeat) battre à plate(s) couture(s)

thread [θrɛd] n fil m; (of screw) pas m, filetage m ▷ vt (needle) enfiler

threat [θrɛt] n menace f; **threaten** vi (storm) menacer ▷ vt: **to threaten sb with sth/to do** menacer qn de qch/de faire; **threatening** adj menaçant(e)

three [θriː] num trois; **three-dimensional** adj à trois dimensions; **three-piece suite** n salon m (canapé et deux fauteuils); **three-quarters** npl trois-quarts mpl; **three-quarters full** aux trois-quarts plein

threshold [ˈθrɛʃhəʊld] n seuil m

threw [θruː] pt of **throw**

thrill [θrɪl] n (excitement) émotion f, sensation forte; (shudder) frisson m ▷ vt (audience) électriser; **thrilled** adj: **thrilled (with)** ravi(e) de; **thriller** n film m (or roman m or pièce f) à suspense; **thrilling** adj (book, play etc) saisissant(e); (news, discovery) excitant(e)

thriving [ˈθraɪvɪŋ] adj (business, community) prospère

throat [θrəʊt] n gorge f; **to have a sore ~** avoir mal à la gorge

throb [θrɒb] vi (heart) palpiter; (engine) vibrer; **my head is ~bing** j'ai des élancements dans la tête

throne [θrəʊn] n trône m

through [θruː] prep à travers; (time) pendant, durant; (by means of) par, par l'intermédiaire de; (owing to) à cause de ▷ adj (ticket, train, passage) direct(e) ▷ adv à travers; **(from) Monday ~ Friday** (US) de lundi à vendredi; **to put sb ~ to sb** (Tel) passer qn à qn; **to be ~** (BRIT : Tel) avoir la communication; (esp US: have finished) avoir fini; **"no ~ traffic"** (US) "passage interdit"; **"no ~ road"** (BRIT) "impasse"; **throughout** prep (place) partout dans; (time) durant tout(e) le (la) ▷ adv partout

throw [θrəʊ] n jet m; (Sport) lancer m ▷ vt (pt **threw**, pp **~n**) lancer, jeter; (Sport) lancer; (rider) désarçonner; (fig) déconcerter; **to ~ a party** donner une réception; **throw away** vt jeter; (money) gaspiller; **throw in** vt (Sport: ball) remettre en jeu; (include) ajouter; **throw off** vt se débarrasser de; **throw out** vt jeter; (reject) rejeter; (person) mettre à la porte; **throw up** vi vomir

thru [θruː] (US) = **through**

thrush [θrʌʃ] n (Zool) grive f

thrust [θrʌst] vt (pt, pp ~) pousser brusquement; (push in) enfoncer

thud [θʌd] n bruit sourd

thug [θʌg] n voyou m

thumb [θʌm] n (Anat) pouce m ▷ vt: **to ~ a lift** faire de l'auto-stop, arrêter une voiture; **thumbtack** n (US) punaise f (clou)

thump [θʌmp] n grand coup; (sound) bruit sourd ▷ vt cogner sur ▷ vi cogner, frapper

thunder [ˈθʌndə] n tonnerre m ▷ vi tonner; (train etc): **to ~ past** passer dans un grondement or un bruit de tonnerre; **thunderstorm** n orage m

Thur(s) abbr (= Thursday) jeu

Thursday [ˈθəːzdɪ] n jeudi m

thus [ðʌs] adv ainsi

thwart [θwɔːt] vt contrecarrer

thyme [taɪm] n thym m

Tibet [tɪˈbɛt] n Tibet m

tick [tɪk] n (sound: of clock) tic-tac m; (mark) coche f; (Zool) tique f; (BRIT inf): **in a ~** dans un instant ▷ vi faire tic-tac ▷ vt (item on list) cocher; **tick off** vt (item on list) cocher; (person) réprimander, attraper

ticket [ˈtɪkɪt] n billet m; (for bus, tube) ticket m; (in shop: on goods) étiquette f; (for library) carte f; (also: **parking ~**) contravention f, p.-v. m; **ticket barrier** n (BRIT: Rail) portillon m automatique; **ticket collector** n contrôleur(-euse); **ticket inspector** n contrôleur(-euse); **ticket machine** n billetterie f automatique; **ticket office** n guichet m, bureau m de vente des billets

tickle [ˈtɪkl] vi chatouiller ▷ vt chatouiller; **ticklish** adj (person) chatouilleux(-euse); (problem) épineux(-euse)

tide [taɪd] n marée f; (fig: of events) cours m

tidy [ˈtaɪdɪ] adj (room) bien rangé(e); (dress, work) net (nette), soigné(e); (person) ordonné(e), qui a de l'ordre ▷ vt (also: **~ up**) ranger

tie [taɪ] n (string etc) cordon m; (BRIT: also: **neck~**) cravate f; (fig: link) lien m; (Sport: draw) égalité f de points; match nul ▷ vt (parcel) attacher; (ribbon) nouer ▷ vi (Sport) faire match nul; finir à égalité de points; **to ~ sth in a**

bow faire un nœud à or avec qch; **to ~ a knot in sth** faire un nœud à qch; **tie down** vt (fig): **to ~ sb down to** contraindre qn à accepter; **to feel ~d down** (by relationship) se sentir coincé(e); **tie up** vt (parcel) ficeler; (dog, boat) attacher; (prisoner) ligoter; (arrangements) conclure; **to be ~d up** (busy) être pris(e) or occupé(e)

tier [tɪəʳ] n gradin m; (of cake) étage m

tiger [ˈtaɪɡəʳ] n tigre m

tight [taɪt] adj (rope) tendu(e), raide; (clothes) étroit(e), très juste; (budget, programme, bend) serré(e); (control) strict(e), sévère; (inf: drunk) ivre, rond(e) ▷ adv (squeeze) très fort; (shut) à bloc, hermétiquement; **hold ~!** accrochez-vous bien!; **tighten** vt (rope) tendre; (screw) resserrer; (control) renforcer ▷ vi se tendre; se resserrer; **tightly** adv (grasp) bien, très fort; **tights** npl (BRIT) collant m

tile [taɪl] n (on roof) tuile f; (on wall or floor) carreau m

till [tɪl] n caisse (enregistreuse) ▷ prep, conj = **until**

tilt [tɪlt] vt pencher, incliner ▷ vi pencher, être incliné(e)

timber [ˈtɪmbəʳ] n (material) bois m de construction

time [taɪm] n temps m; (epoch: often pl) époque f, temps; (by clock) heure f; (moment) moment m; (occasion, also Math) fois f; (Mus) mesure f ▷ vt (race) chronométrer; (programme) minuter; (visit) fixer; (remark etc) choisir le moment de; **a long ~** un long moment, longtemps; **four at a ~** quatre à la fois; **for the ~ being** pour le moment; **from ~ to ~** de temps en temps; **at ~s** parfois; **in ~** (soon enough) à temps; (after some time) avec le temps, à la longue; (Mus) en mesure; **in a week's ~** dans une semaine; **in no ~** en un rien de temps; **any ~** n'importe quand; **on ~** à l'heure; **5 ~s 5** 5 fois 5; **what ~ is it?** quelle heure est-il?; **what ~ is the museum/shop open?** à quelle heure ouvre le musée/magasin?; **to have a good ~** bien s'amuser; **time limit** n limite f de temps, délai m; **timely** adj opportun(e); **timer** n (in kitchen) compte-minutes m inv; (Tech) minuteur m; **time-share** n maison f/appartement m en multipropriété; **timetable** n (Rail) (indicateur m) horaire m; (Scol) emploi m du temps; **time zone** n fuseau m horaire

timid [ˈtɪmɪd] adj timide; (easily scared) peureux(-euse)

timing [ˈtaɪmɪŋ] n (Sport) chronométrage m; **the ~ of his resignation** le moment choisi pour sa démission

tin [tɪn] n étain m; (also: ~ **plate**) fer-blanc m; (BRIT: can) boîte f (de conserve); (: for baking) moule m (à gâteau); (for storage) boîte f; **tinfoil** n papier m d'étain or d'aluminium

tingle [ˈtɪŋɡl] vi picoter; (person) avoir des picotements

tinker [ˈtɪŋkəʳ] n; **tinker with** vt fus bricoler, rafistoler

tinned [tɪnd] adj (BRIT: food) en boîte, en conserve

tin opener [-ˈaupnəʳ] n (BRIT) ouvre-boîte(s) m

tinsel [ˈtɪnsl] n guirlandes fpl de Noël (argentées)

tint [tɪnt] n teinte f; (for hair) shampooing colorant; **tinted** adj (hair) teint(e); (spectacles, glass) teinté(e)

tiny [ˈtaɪnɪ] adj minuscule

tip [tɪp] n (end) bout m; (gratuity) pourboire m; (BRIT: for rubbish) décharge f; (advice) tuyau m ▷ vt (waiter) donner un pourboire à; (tilt) incliner; (overturn: also: ~ **over**) renverser; (empty: also: ~ **out**) déverser; **how much should I ~?** combien de pourboire est-ce qu'il faut laisser?; **tip off** vt prévenir, avertir

tiptoe [ˈtɪptəu] n: **on ~** sur la pointe des pieds

tire [ˈtaɪəʳ] n (US) = **tyre** ▷ vt fatiguer ▷ vi se fatiguer; **tired** adj fatigué(e); **to be tired of** en avoir assez de, être las (lasse) de; **tire pressure** (US) = **tyre pressure**; **tiring**

adj fatigant(e)

tissue [ˈtɪʃuː] n tissu m; (paper handkerchief) mouchoir m en papier, kleenex® m; **tissue paper** n papier m de soie

tit [tɪt] n (bird) mésange f; **to give ~ for tat** rendre coup pour coup

title [ˈtaɪtl] n titre m

T-junction [ˈtiːˈdʒʌŋkʃən] n croisement m en T

TM n abbr = **trademark**

○ **KEYWORD**

to [tuː, tə] prep **1** (direction) à; (towards) vers; envers; **to go to France/Portugal/London/school** aller en France/ au Portugal/à Londres/à l'école; **to go to Claude's/the doctor's** aller chez Claude/le docteur; **the road to Edinburgh** la route d'Édimbourg

2 (as far as) (jusqu')à; **to count to 10** compter jusqu'à 10; **from 40 to 50 people** de 40 à 50 personnes

3 (with expressions of time): **a quarter to 5** 5 heures moins le quart; **it's twenty to 3** il est 3 heures moins vingt

4 (for, of) de; **the key to the front door** la clé de la porte d'entrée; **a letter to his wife** une lettre (adressée) à sa femme

5 (expressing indirect object) à; **to give sth to sb** donner qch à qn; **to talk to sb** parler à qn; **to be a danger to sb** être dangereux(-euse) pour qn

6 (in relation to) à; **3 goals to 2** 3 (buts) à 2; **30 miles to the gallon** ≈ 9,4 litres aux cent (km)

7 (purpose, result): **to come to sb's aid** venir au secours de qn, porter secours à qn; **to sentence sb to death** condamner qn à mort; **to my surprise** à ma grande surprise

▷ with vb **1** (simple infinitive): **to go/eat** aller/manger

2 (following another vb): **to want/try/start to do** vouloir/essayer de/commencer à faire

3 (with vb omitted): **I don't want to** je ne veux pas

4 (purpose, result) pour; **I did it to help you** je l'ai fait pour vous aider

5 (equivalent to relative clause): **I have things to do** j'ai des choses à faire; **the main thing is to try** l'important est d'essayer

6 (after adjective etc): **ready to go** prêt(e) à partir; **too old/young to ...** trop vieux/jeune pour ...

▷ adv: **push/pull the door to** tirez/poussez la porte

toad [təud] n crapaud m; **toadstool** n champignon (vénéneux)

toast [təust] n (Culin) pain grillé, toast m; (drink, speech) toast ▷ vt (Culin) faire griller; (drink to) porter un toast à; **toaster** n grille-pain m inv

tobacco [təˈbækəu] n tabac m

toboggan [təˈbɔɡən] n toboggan m; (child's) luge f

today [təˈdeɪ] adv, n (also fig) aujourd'hui (m)

toddler [ˈtɔdləʳ] n enfant m/f qui commence à marcher, bambin m

toe [təu] n doigt m de pied, orteil m; (of shoe) bout m ▷ vt: **to ~ the line** (fig) obéir, se conformer; **toenail** n ongle m de l'orteil

toffee [ˈtɔfɪ] n caramel m

together [təˈɡɛðəʳ] adv ensemble; (at same time) en même temps; **~ with** prep avec

toilet [ˈtɔɪlət] n (BRIT: lavatory) toilettes fpl, cabinets mpl; **to go to the ~** aller aux toilettes; **where's the ~?** où sont les toilettes?; **toilet bag** n (BRIT) nécessaire m de toilette; **toilet paper** n papier m hygiénique; **toiletries** npl articles mpl de toilette; **toilet roll** n rouleau m de papier hygiénique

token ['təukən] n (sign) marque f, témoignage m; (metal disc) jeton m ⊳ adj (fee, strike) symbolique; **book/record ~** (BRIT) chèque-livre/-disque m

Tokyo ['təukjəu] n Tokyo

told [təuld] pt, pp of **tell**

tolerant ['tɔlərnt] adj: **~ (of)** tolérant(e) (à l'égard de)

tolerate ['tɔləreɪt] vt supporter

toll [təul] n (tax, charge) péage m ⊳ vi (bell) sonner; **the accident ~ on the roads** le nombre des victimes de la route; **toll call** n (US Tel) appel m (à) longue distance; **toll-free** adj (US) gratuit(e) ⊳ adv gratuitement

tomato [təˈmɑːtəu] n (pl **~es**) n tomate f; **tomato sauce** n sauce f tomate

tomb [tuːm] n tombe f; **tombstone** n pierre tombale

tomorrow [təˈmɔrəu] adv, n (also fig) demain (m); **the day after ~** après-demain; **a week ~** demain en huit; **~ morning** demain matin

ton [tʌn] n tonne f (BRIT: = 1016 kg; US = 907 kg; metric = 1000 kg); **~s of** (inf) des tas de

tone [təun] n ton m; (of radio, also) tonalité f ⊳ vi (also: **~ in**) s'harmoniser; **tone down** vt (colour, criticism) adoucir

tongs [tɔŋz] npl pinces fpl; (for coal) pincettes fpl; (for hair) fer m à friser

tongue [tʌŋ] n langue f; **~ in cheek** adv ironiquement

tonic ['tɔnɪk] n (Med) tonique m; (also: **~ water**) Schweppes® m

tonight [təˈnaɪt] adv, n cette nuit; (this evening) ce soir

tonne [tʌn] n (BRIT: metric ton) tonne f

tonsil ['tɔnsl] n amygdale f; **tonsillitis** [tɔnsɪˈlaɪtɪs] n: **to have tonsillitis** avoir une angine or une amygdalite

too [tuː] adv (excessively) trop; (also) aussi; **~ much** (as adv) trop; (as adj) trop de; **~ many** adj trop de

took [tuk] pt of **take**

tool [tuːl] n outil m; **tool box** n boîte f à outils; **tool kit** n trousse f à outils

tooth (pl **teeth**) [tuːθ, tiːθ] n (Anat, Tech) dent f; **to brush one's teeth** se laver les dents; **toothache** n mal m de dents; **to have toothache** avoir mal aux dents; **toothbrush** n brosse f à dents; **toothpaste** n (pâte f) dentifrice m; **toothpick** n cure-dent m

top [tɔp] n (of mountain, head) sommet m; (of page, ladder) haut m; (of box, cupboard, table) dessus m; (lid: of box, jar) couvercle m; (: of bottle) bouchon m; (toy) toupie f; (Dress: blouse etc) haut; (: of pyjamas) veste f ⊳ adj du haut; (in rank) premier(-ière); (best) meilleur(e) ⊳ vt (exceed) dépasser; (be first in) être en tête de; **from ~ to bottom** de fond en comble; **on ~ of** sur; (in addition to) en plus de; **over the ~** (inf: behaviour etc) qui dépasse les limites; **top up** (US **top off**) vt (bottle) remplir; (salary) compléter; **to ~ up one's mobile (phone)** recharger son compte; **top floor** n dernier étage; **top hat** n haut-de-forme m

topic ['tɔpɪk] n sujet m, thème m; **topical** adj d'actualité

topless ['tɔplɪs] adj (bather etc) aux seins nus

topping ['tɔpɪŋ] n (Culin) couche de crème, fromage etc qui recouvre un plat

topple ['tɔpl] vt renverser, faire tomber ⊳ vi basculer; tomber

top-up ['tɔpʌp] n (for mobile phone) recharge f, minutes fpl; **top-up card** n (for mobile phone) recharge f

torch [tɔːtʃ] n torche f; (BRIT: electric) lampe f de poche

tore [tɔːʳ] pt of **tear²**

torment n ['tɔːmɛnt] tourment m ⊳ vt [tɔːˈmɛnt] tourmenter; (fig: annoy) agacer

torn [tɔːn] pp of **tear²**

tornado [tɔːˈneɪdəu] (pl **-es**) n tornade f

torpedo [tɔːˈpiːdəu] (pl **-es**) n torpille f

torrent ['tɔrnt] n torrent m; **torrential** [tɔˈrɛnʃl] adj torrentiel(le)

tortoise ['tɔːtəs] n tortue f

torture ['tɔːtʃəʳ] n torture f ⊳ vt torturer

Tory ['tɔːrɪ] adj, n (BRIT Pol) tory m/f, conservateur(-trice)

toss [tɔs] vt lancer, jeter; (BRIT: pancake) faire sauter; (head) rejeter en arrière ⊳ vi: **to ~ up for sth** (BRIT) jouer qch à pile ou face; **to ~ a coin** jouer à pile ou face; **to ~ and turn** (in bed) se tourner et se retourner

total ['təutl] adj total(e) ⊳ n total m ⊳ vt (add up) faire le total de, additionner; (amount to) s'élever à

totalitarian [təutælɪˈtɛərɪən] adj totalitaire

totally ['təutəlɪ] adv totalement

touch [tʌtʃ] n contact m, toucher m; (sense, skill: of pianist etc) toucher ⊳ vt (gen) toucher; (tamper with) toucher à; **a ~ of** (fig) un petit peu de; une touche de; **to get in ~ with** prendre contact avec; **to lose ~** (friends) se perdre de vue; **touch down** vi (Aviat) atterrir; (on sea) amerrir; **touchdown** n (Aviat) atterrissage m; (on sea) amerrissage m; (US Football) essai m; **touched** adj (moved) touché(e); **touching** adj touchant(e), attendrissant(e); **touchline** n (Sport) ligne f de touche f; **touch-sensitive** adj (keypad) à effleurement; (screen) tactile

tough [tʌf] adj dur(e); (resistant) résistant(é), solide; (meat) dur, coriace; (firm) inflexible; (task, problem, situation) difficile

tour ['tuəʳ] n voyage m; (also: **package ~**) voyage organisé; (of town, museum) tour m, visite f; (by band) tournée f ⊳ vt visiter; **tour guide** n (person) guide m/f

tourism ['tuərɪzm] n tourisme m

tourist ['tuərɪst] n touriste m/f ⊳ cpd touristique; **tourist office** n syndicat m d'initiative

tournament ['tuənəmənt] n tournoi m

tour operator n (BRIT) organisateur m de voyages, tour-opérateur m

tow [təu] vt remorquer; (caravan, trailer) tracter; **"on ~"** (US): **"in ~"** (Aut) "véhicule en remorque"; **tow away** vt (subj: police) emmener à la fourrière; (: breakdown service) remorquer

toward(s) [təˈwɔːd(z)] prep vers; (of attitude) envers, à l'égard de; (of purpose) pour

towel ['tauəl] n serviette f (de toilette); **towelling** n (fabric) tissu-éponge m

tower ['tauəʳ] n tour f; **tower block** n (BRIT) tour f (d'habitation)

town [taun] n ville f; **to go to ~** aller en ville; (fig) y mettre le paquet; **town centre** n (BRIT) centre m de la ville, centre-ville m; **town hall** n ≈ mairie f

tow truck n (US) dépanneuse f

toxic ['tɔksɪk] adj toxique

toy [tɔɪ] n jouet m; **toy with** vt fus jouer avec; (idea) caresser; **toyshop** n magasin m de jouets

trace [treɪs] n trace f ⊳ vt (draw) tracer, dessiner; (follow) suivre la trace de; (locate) retrouver

tracing paper ['treɪsɪŋ-] n papier-calque m

track [træk] n (mark) trace f; (path: gen) chemin m, piste f; (: of bullet etc) trajectoire f; (: of suspect, animal) piste; (Rail) voie ferrée, rails mpl; (on tape, Comput, Sport) piste; (on CD) piste f; (on record) plage f ▷ vt suivre la trace or la piste de; **to keep ~ of** suivre; **track down** vt (prey) trouver et capturer; (sth lost) finir par retrouver; **tracksuit** n survêtement m

tractor ['træktə] n tracteur m

trade [treɪd] n commerce m; (skill, job) métier m ▷ vi faire du commerce ▷ vt (exchange): **to ~ sth (for sth)** échanger qch (contre qch); **to ~ with/in** faire du commerce avec/le commerce de; **trade in** vt (old car etc) faire reprendre; **trademark** n marque f de fabrique; **trader** n commerçant(e), négociant(e); **tradesman** (irreg) n (shopkeeper) commerçant m; **trade union** n syndicat m

trading ['treɪdɪŋ] n affaires fpl, commerce m

tradition [trə'dɪʃən] n tradition f; **traditional** adj traditionnel(le)

traffic ['træfɪk] n trafic m; (cars) circulation f ▷ vi: **to ~ in** (pej: liquor, drugs) faire le trafic de; **traffic circle** n (us) rond-point m; **traffic island** n refuge m (pour piétons); **traffic jam** n embouteillage m; **traffic lights** npl feux mpl (de signalisation); **traffic warden** n contractuel(le)

tragedy ['trædʒədɪ] n tragédie f

tragic ['trædʒɪk] adj tragique

trail [treɪl] n (tracks) trace f, piste f; (path) chemin m, piste; (of smoke etc) traînée f ▷ vt (drag) traîner, tirer; (follow) suivre ▷ vi traîner; (in game, contest) être en retard; **trailer** n (Aut) remorque f; (us) caravane f; (Cine) bande-annonce f

train [treɪn] n train m; (in underground) rame f; (of dress) traîne f; (BRIT: series): **~ of events** série f d'événements ▷ vt (apprentice, doctor etc) former; (Sport) entraîner; (dog) dresser; (memory) exercer; (point: gun etc): **to ~ sth on** braquer qch sur ▷ vi recevoir sa formation; (Sport) s'entraîner; **one's ~ of thought** le fil de sa pensée; **what time does the ~ from Paris get in?** à quelle heure arrive le train de Paris?; **is this the ~ for …?** c'est bien le train pour…?; **trainee** [treɪ'ni:] n stagiaire m/f; (in trade) apprenti(e); **trainer** n (Sport) entraîneur(-euse); (of dogs etc) dresseur(-euse); **trainers** npl (shoes) chaussures fpl de sport; **training** n formation f; (Sport) entraînement m; (of dog etc) dressage m; **in training** (Sport) à l'entraînement; (fit) en forme; **training course** n cours m de formation professionnelle; **training shoes** npl chaussures fpl de sport

trait [treɪt] n trait m (de caractère)

traitor ['treɪtə] n traître m

tram [træm] n (BRIT: also: **~car**) tram(way) m

tramp [træmp] n (person) vagabond(e), clochard(e); (inf, pej: woman): **to be a ~** être coureuse

trample ['træmpl] vt: **to ~ (underfoot)** piétiner

trampoline ['træmpəli:n] n trampoline m

tranquil ['træŋkwɪl] adj tranquille; **tranquillizer** (us **tranquilizer**) n (Med) tranquillisant m

transaction [træn'zækʃən] n transaction f

transatlantic ['trænzət'læntɪk] adj transatlantique

transcript ['trænskrɪpt] n transcription f (texte)

transfer n ['trænsfə'] (gen, also Sport) transfert m; (Pol: of power) passation f; (of money) virement m; (picture, design) décalcomanie f; (: stick-on) autocollant m ▷ vt [træns'fə:'] transférer; passer; virer; **to ~ the charges** (BRIT Tel) téléphoner en P.C.V.

transform [træns'fɔ:m] vt transformer; **transformation** n transformation f

transfusion [træns'fju:ʒən] n transfusion f

transit ['trænzɪt] n: **in ~** en transit

transition [træn'zɪʃən] n transition f

transitive ['trænzɪtɪv] adj (Ling) transitif(-ive)

translate [trænz'leɪt] vt: **to ~ (from/into)** traduire (du/en); **can you ~ this for me?** pouvez-vous me traduire ceci?; **translation** [trænz'leɪʃən] n traduction f; (Scol: as opposed to prose) version f; **translator** n traducteur(-trice)

transmission [trænz'mɪʃən] n transmission f

transmit [trænz'mɪt] vt transmettre; (Radio, TV) émettre; **transmitter** n émetteur m

transparent [træns'pærnt] adj transparent(e)

transplant n ['trænsplɑ:nt] (Med) transplantation f

transport n ['trænspɔ:t] transport m ▷ vt [træns'pɔ:t] transporter; **transportation** [trænspɔ:'teɪʃən] n (moyen m de) transport m

transvestite [trænz'vestaɪt] n travesti(e)

trap [træp] n (snare, trick) piège m; (carriage) cabriolet m ▷ vt prendre au piège; (confine) coincer

trash [træʃ] n (pej: goods) camelote f; (: nonsense) sottises fpl; (us: rubbish) ordures fpl; **trash can** n (us) poubelle f

trauma ['trɔ:mə] n traumatisme m; **traumatic** [trɔ:'mætɪk] adj traumatisant(e)

travel ['trævl] n voyage(s) m(pl) ▷ vi voyager; (news, sound) se propager ▷ vt (distance) parcourir; **travel agency** n agence f de voyages; **travel agent** n agent m de voyages; **travel insurance** n assurance-voyage f; **traveller** (us **traveler**) n voyageur(-euse); **traveller's cheque** (us **traveler's check**) n chèque m de voyage; **travelling** (us **traveling**) n voyage(s) m(pl); **travel-sick** adj: **to get travel-sick** avoir le mal de la route (or de mer or de l'air); **travel sickness** n mal m de la route (or de mer or de l'air)

tray [treɪ] n (for carrying) plateau m; (on desk) corbeille f

treacherous ['tretʃərəs] adj traître(sse); (ground, tide) dont il faut se méfier

treacle ['tri:kl] n mélasse f

tread [tred] n (step) pas m; (sound) bruit m de pas; (of tyre) chape f, bande f de roulement ▷ vi (pt **trod**, pp **trodden**) marcher; **tread on** vt fus marcher sur

treasure ['treʒə'] n trésor m ▷ vt (value) tenir beaucoup à; **treasurer** n trésorier(-ière)

treasury ['treʒərɪ] n: **the T~** (us): **the T~ Department** ≈ le ministère des Finances

treat [tri:t] n petit cadeau, petite surprise ▷ vt traiter; **to ~ sb to sth** offrir qch à qn; **treatment** n traitement m

treaty ['tri:tɪ] n traité m

treble ['trebl] adj triple ▷ vt, vi tripler

tree [tri:] n arbre m

trek [trek] n (long walk) randonnée f; (tiring walk) longue marche, trotte f

tremble ['trembl] vi trembler

tremendous [trɪ'mendəs] adj (enormous) énorme; (excellent) formidable, fantastique

trench [trentʃ] n tranchée f

trend [trend] n (tendency) tendance f; (of events) cours m; (fashion) mode f; **trendy** adj (idea, person) dans le vent; (clothes) dernier cri inv

trespass ['trespəs] vi: **to ~ on** s'introduire sans permission dans; **"no ~ing"** "propriété privée", "défense d'entrer"

trial ['traɪəl] n (Law) procès m, jugement m; (test: of machine etc) essai m; **trials** npl (unpleasant experiences) épreuves fpl; **trial period** n période f d'essai

triangle ['traɪæŋgl] n (Math, Mus) triangle m

triangular [traɪ'æŋgjʊləʳ] adj triangulaire

tribe [traɪb] n tribu f

tribunal [traɪ'bjuːnl] n tribunal m

tribute ['trɪbjuːt] n tribut m, hommage m; **to pay ~** rendre hommage à

trick [trɪk] n (magic) tour m; (joke, prank) tour, farce f; (skill, knack) astuce f; (Cards) levée f ▷ vt attraper, rouler; **to play a ~ on sb** jouer un tour à qn; **that should do the ~** (fam) ça devrait faire l'affaire

trickle ['trɪkl] n (of water etc) filet m ▷ vi couler en un filet or goutte à goutte

tricky ['trɪkɪ] adj difficile, délicat(e)

tricycle ['traɪsɪkl] n tricycle m

trifle ['traɪfl] n bagatelle f; (Culin) ≈ diplomate m ▷ adv: **a ~ long** un peu long

trigger ['trɪgəʳ] n (of gun) gâchette f

trim [trɪm] adj (house, garden) bien tenu(e); (figure) svelte ▷ n (haircut etc) légère coupe; (on car) garnitures fpl ▷ vt (cut) couper légèrement; (decorate): **to ~ (with)** décorer (de); (Naut: a sail) gréer

trio ['triːəʊ] n trio m

trip [trɪp] n voyage m; (excursion) excursion f; (stumble) faux pas ▷ vi faire un faux pas, trébucher; **trip up** vi trébucher ▷ vt faire un croc-en-jambe à

triple ['trɪpl] adj triple

triplets ['trɪplɪts] npl triplés(-ées)

tripod ['traɪpɔd] n trépied m

triumph ['traɪʌmf] n triomphe m ▷ vi: **to ~ (over)** triompher (de); **triumphant** [traɪ'ʌmfənt] adj triomphant(e)

trivial ['trɪvɪəl] adj insignifiant(e); (commonplace) banal(e)

trod [trɔd] pt of **tread**

trodden ['trɔdn] pp of **tread**

trolley ['trɔlɪ] n chariot m

trombone [trɔm'bəʊn] n trombone m

troop [truːp] n bande f, groupe m; **troops** npl (Mil) troupes fpl; (: men) hommes mpl, soldats mpl

trophy ['trəʊfɪ] n trophée m

tropical ['trɔpɪkl] adj tropical(e)

trot [trɔt] n trot m ▷ vi trotter; **on the ~** (BRIT: fig) d'affilée

trouble ['trʌbl] n difficulté(s) f(pl), problème(s) m(pl); (worry) ennuis mpl, soucis mpl; (bother, effort) peine f; (Pol) conflit(s) m(pl), troubles mpl; (Med): **stomach etc ~** troubles gastriques etc ▷ vt (disturb) déranger, gêner; (worry) inquiéter ▷ vi: **to ~ to do** prendre la peine de faire; **troubles** npl (Pol etc) troubles; (personal) ennuis, soucis; **to be in ~** avoir des ennuis; (ship, climber etc) être en difficulté; **to have ~ doing sth** avoir du mal à faire qch; **it's no ~!** je vous en prie!; **the ~ is ...** le problème, c'est que ...; **what's the ~?** qu'est-ce qui ne va pas?; **troubled** adj (person) inquiet(-ète); (times, life) agité(e); **troublemaker** n élément perturbateur, fauteur m de troubles; **troublesome** adj (child) fatigant(e), difficile; (cough) gênant(e)

trough [trɔf] n (also: **drinking ~**) abreuvoir m; (also: **feeding ~**) auge f; (depression) creux m

trousers ['traʊzəz] npl pantalon m; **short ~** (BRIT) culottes courtes

trout [traʊt] n (pl inv) truite f

trowel ['traʊəl] n truelle f; (garden tool) déplantoir m

truant ['truənt] n: **to play ~** (BRIT) faire l'école buissonnière

truce [truːs] n trêve f

truck [trʌk] n camion m; (Rail) wagon m à plate-forme; **truck driver** n camionneur m

true [truː] adj vrai(e); (accurate) exact(e); (genuine) vrai, véritable; (faithful) fidèle; **to come ~** se réaliser

truly ['truːlɪ] adv vraiment, réellement; (truthfully) sans mentir; **yours ~** (in letter) je vous prie d'agréer, Monsieur (or Madame etc), l'expression de mes sentiments respectueux

trumpet ['trʌmpɪt] n trompette f

trunk [trʌŋk] n (of tree, person) tronc m; (of elephant) trompe f; (case) malle f; (us Aut) coffre m; **trunks** npl (also: **swimming ~s**) maillot m or slip m de bain

trust [trʌst] n confiance f; (responsibility): **to place sth in sb's ~** confier la responsabilité de qch à qn; (Law) fidéicommis m ▷ vt (rely on) avoir confiance en; (entrust): **to ~ sth to sb** confier qch à qn; (hope): **to ~ (that)** espérer (que); **to take sth on ~** accepter qch les yeux fermés; **trusted** adj en qui l'on a confiance; **trustworthy** adj digne de confiance

truth [truːθ, pl truːðz] n vérité f; **truthful** adj (person) qui dit la vérité; (answer) sincère

try [traɪ] n essai m, tentative f; (Rugby) essai ▷ vt (attempt) essayer, tenter; (test: sth new: also: **~ out**) essayer, tester; (Law: person) juger; (strain) éprouver ▷ vi essayer; **to ~ to do** essayer de faire; (seek) chercher à faire; **try on** vt (clothes) essayer; **trying** adj pénible

T-shirt ['tiːʃəːt] n tee-shirt m

tub [tʌb] n cuve f; (for washing clothes) baquet m; (bath) baignoire f

tube [tjuːb] n tube m; (BRIT: underground) métro m; (for tyre) chambre f à air

tuberculosis [tjubəːkjuˈləʊsɪs] n tuberculose f

tube station n (BRIT) station f de métro

tuck [tʌk] n vt (put) mettre; **tuck away** vt cacher, ranger; (money) mettre de côté; (building): **to be ~ed away** être caché(e); **tuck in** vt rentrer; (child) border ▷ vi (eat) manger de bon appétit; attaquer le repas; **tuck shop** n (BRIT Scol) boutique f à provisions

Tue(s) abbr (= Tuesday) ma

Tuesday ['tjuːzdɪ] n mardi m

tug [tʌg] n (ship) remorqueur m ▷ vt tirer (sur)

tuition [tjuːˈɪʃən] n (BRIT: lessons) leçons fpl; (: private) cours particuliers; (us: fees) frais mpl de scolarité

tulip ['tjuːlɪp] n tulipe f

tumble ['tʌmbl] n (fall) chute f, culbute f ▷ vi tomber, dégringoler; **to ~ to sth** (inf) réaliser qch; **tumble dryer** n (BRIT) séchoir m (à linge) à air chaud

tumbler ['tʌmbləʳ] n verre (droit), gobelet m

tummy ['tʌmɪ] n (inf) ventre m

tumour (us **tumor**) ['tjuːməʳ] n tumeur f

tuna ['tjuːnə] n (pl inv: also: **~ fish**) thon m

tune [tjuːn] n (melody) air m ▷ vt (Mus) accorder; (Radio, TV, Aut) régler, mettre au point; **to be in/out of ~** (instrument) être accordé/désaccordé; (singer) chanter juste/faux; **tune in** vi (Radio, TV): **to ~ in (to)** se mettre à l'écoute (de); **tune up** vi (musician) accorder son instrument

tunic ['tjuːnɪk] n tunique f

Tunis ['tjuːnɪs] n Tunis

Tunisia [tjuːˈnɪzɪə] n Tunisie f

Tunisian [tjuːˈnɪzɪən] adj tunisien(ne) ▷ n Tunisien(ne)

tunnel ['tʌnl] n tunnel m; (in mine) galerie f ▷ vi creuser un tunnel (or une galerie)

turbulence ['tə:bjuləns] n (Aviat) turbulence f

turf [tə:f] n gazon m; (clod) motte f (de gazon) ▷ vt gazonner

Turk [tə:k] n Turc (Turque)

Turkey ['tə:kɪ] n Turquie f

turkey ['tə:kɪ] n dindon m, dinde f

Turkish ['tə:kɪʃ] adj turc (turque) ▷ n (Ling) turc m

turmoil ['tə:mɔɪl] n trouble m, bouleversement m

turn [tə:n] n tour m; (in road) tournant m; (of mind, events) tournure f; (performance) numéro m; (Med) crise f, attaque f ▷ vt tourner; (collar, steak) retourner; (change): **to ~ sth into** changer qch en; (age) atteindre ▷ vi (object, wind, milk) tourner; (person: look back) se (re)tourner; (reverse direction) faire demi-tour; (become) devenir; **to ~ into** se changer en, se transformer en; **a good ~** un service; **it gave me quite a ~** ça m'a fait un coup; "**no left ~**" (Aut) "défense de tourner à gauche"; **~ left/right at the next junction** tournez à gauche/droite au prochain carrefour; **it's your ~** c'est (à) votre tour; **in ~** à son tour; à tour de rôle; **to take ~s** se relayer; **turn around** vi (person) se retourner ▷ vt (object) tourner; **turn away** vi se détourner, tourner la tête ▷ vt (reject: person) renvoyer; (: business) refuser; **turn back** vi revenir, faire demi-tour; **turn down** vt (refuse) rejeter, refuser; (reduce) baisser; (fold) rabattre; **turn in** vi (inf: go to bed) aller se coucher ▷ vt (fold) rentrer; **turn off** vi (from road) tourner ▷ vt (light, radio etc) éteindre; (tap) fermer; (engine) arrêter; **I can't ~ the heating off** je n'arrive pas à éteindre le chauffage; **turn on** vt (light, radio etc) allumer; (tap) ouvrir; (engine) mettre en marche; **I can't ~ the heating on** je n'arrive pas à allumer le chauffage; **turn out** vt (light, gas) éteindre; (produce) produire ▷ vi (voters, troops) se présenter; **to ~ out to be ...** s'avérer ..., se révéler ...; **turn over** vi (person) se retourner ▷ vt (object) retourner; (page) tourner; **turn round** vi faire demi-tour; (rotate) tourner; **turn to** vt fus: **to ~ to sb** s'adresser à qn; **turn up** vi (person) arriver, se pointer (inf); (lost object) être retrouvé(e) ▷ vt (collar) remonter; (radio, heater) mettre plus fort; **turning** n (in road) tournant m; **turning point** n (fig) tournant m, moment décisif

turnip ['tə:nɪp] n navet m

turn: **turnout** n (of voters) taux m de participation; **turnover** n (Comm: amount of money) chiffre m d'affaires; (: of goods) roulement m; (of staff) renouvellement m, changement m; **turnstile** n tourniquet m (d'entrée); **turn-up** n (BRIT: on trousers) revers m

turquoise ['tə:kwɔɪz] n (stone) turquoise f ▷ adj turquoise inv

turtle ['tə:tl] n tortue marine; **turtleneck (sweater)** n pullover m à col montant

tusk [tʌsk] n défense f (d'éléphant)

tutor ['tju:tə*] n (BRIT Scol: in college) directeur(-trice) d'études; (private teacher) précepteur(-trice); **tutorial** [tju:'tɔ:rɪəl] n (Scol) (séance f de) travaux mpl pratiques

tuxedo [tʌk'si:dəu] n (US) smoking m

TV [ti:'vi:] n abbr (= television) télé f, TV f

tweed [twi:d] n tweed m

tweezers ['twi:zəz] npl pince f à épiler

twelfth [twelfθ] num douzième

twelve [twelv] num douze; **at ~ (o'clock)** à midi; (midnight) à minuit

twentieth ['twentiiθ] num vingtième

twenty ['twenti] num vingt

twice [twais] adv deux fois; **~ as much** deux fois plus

twig [twig] n brindille f ▷ vt, vi (inf) piger

twilight ['twailait] n crépuscule m

twin [twin] adj, n jumeau(-elle) ▷ vt jumeler; **twin(-bedded) room** n chambre f à deux lits; **twin beds** npl lits mpl jumeaux

twinkle ['twiŋkl] vi scintiller; (eyes) pétiller

twist [twist] n torsion f, tour m; (in wire, flex) tortillon m; (bend: in road) tournant m; (in story) coup m de théâtre ▷ vt tordre; (weave) entortiller; (roll around) enrouler; (fig) déformer ▷ vi (road, river) serpenter; **to ~ one's ankle/wrist** (Med) se tordre la cheville/le poignet

twit [twit] n (inf) crétin(e)

twitch [twitʃ] n (pull) coup sec, saccade f; (nervous) tic m ▷ vi se convulser; avoir un tic

two [tu:] num deux; **to put ~ and ~ together** (fig) faire le rapprochement

type [taip] n (category) genre m, espèce f; (model) modèle m; (example) type m; (Typ) type, caractère m ▷ vt (letter etc) taper (à la machine); **typewriter** n machine f à écrire

typhoid ['taifɔid] n typhoïde f

typhoon [tai'fu:n] n typhon m

typical ['tipikl] adj typique, caractéristique; **typically** adv (as usual) comme d'habitude; (characteristically) typiquement

typing ['taipiŋ] n dactylo(graphie) f

typist ['taipist] n dactylo m/f

tyre (US **tire**) ['taiə*] n pneu m; **I've got a flat ~** j'ai un pneu crevé; **tyre pressure** n (BRIT) pression f (de gonflage)

uncanny [ʌnˈkænɪ] *adj* étrange, troublant(e)
uncertain [ʌnˈsəːtn] *adj* incertain(e); (*hesitant*)
hésitant(e); **uncertainty** *n* incertitude *f*, doutes *mpl*
unchanged [ʌnˈtʃeɪndʒd] *adj* inchangé(e)
uncle [ˈʌŋkl] *n* oncle *m*
unclear [ʌnˈklɪəʳ] *adj* (qui n'est) pas clair(e) or évident(e);
I'm still ~ about what I'm supposed to do je ne sais
pas encore exactement ce que je dois faire
uncomfortable [ʌnˈkʌmfətəbl] *adj* inconfortable,
peu confortable; (*uneasy*) mal à l'aise, gêné(e); (*situation*)
désagréable
uncommon [ʌnˈkɔmən] *adj* rare, singulier(-ière), peu
commun(e)
unconditional [ʌnkənˈdɪʃənl] *adj* sans conditions
unconscious [ʌnˈkɔnʃəs] *adj* sans connaissance,
évanoui(e); (*unaware*): ~ **(of)** inconscient(e) (de) ▷ *n*: **the
~** l'inconscient *m*
uncontrollable [ʌnkənˈtrəuləbl] *adj* (*child, dog*)
indiscipliné(e); (*temper, laughter*) irrépressible
unconventional [ʌnkənˈvɛnʃənl] *adj* peu
conventionnel(le)
uncover [ʌnˈkʌvəʳ] *vt* découvrir
undecided [ʌndɪˈsaɪdɪd] *adj* indécis(e), irrésolu(e)
undeniable [ʌndɪˈnaɪəbl] *adj* indéniable, incontestable
under [ˈʌndəʳ] *prep* sous; (*less than*) (de) moins de;
au-dessous de; (*according to*) selon, en vertu de ▷ *adv*
au-dessous; en dessous; ~ **there** là-dessous; ~ **the
circumstances** étant donné les circonstances; ~ **repair**
en (cours de) réparation; **undercover** *adj* secret(-ète),
clandestin(e); **underdone** *adj* (*Culin*) saignant(e); (:
pej) pas assez cuit(e); **underestimate** *vt* sous-
estimer, mésestimer; **undergo** *vt* (*irreg: like* **go**) subir;
(*treatment*) suivre; **undergraduate** *n* étudiant(e) (qui
prépare la licence); **underground** *adj* souterrain(e);
(*fig*) clandestin(e) ▷ *n* (*BRIT: railway*) métro *m*; (*Pol*)
clandestinité *f*; **undergrowth** *n* broussailles *fpl*, sous-
bois *m*; **underline** *vt* souligner; **undermine** *vt* saper,
miner; **underneath** [ʌndəˈniːθ] *adv* (en) dessous ▷ *prep*
sous, au-dessous de; **underpants** *npl* caleçon *m*, slip *m*;
underpass *n* (*BRIT: for pedestrians*) passage souterrain;
(: *for cars*) passage inférieur; **underprivileged** *adj*
défavorisé(e); **underscore** *vt* souligner; **undershirt** *n*
(*us*) tricot *m* de corps; **underskirt** *n* (*BRIT*) jupon *m*
understand [ʌndəˈstænd] *vt, vi* (*irreg: like* **stand**)
comprendre; **I don't ~** je ne comprends pas;
understandable *adj* compréhensible; **understanding**
adj compréhensif(-ive) ▷ *n* compréhension *f*; (*agreement*)
accord *m*
understatement [ˈʌndəsteɪtmənt] *n*: **that's an ~**
c'est (bien) peu dire, le terme est faible
understood [ʌndəˈstud] *pt, pp of* **understand** ▷ *adj*
entendu(e); (*implied*) sous-entendu(e)
undertake [ʌndəˈteɪk] *vt* (*irreg: like* **take**) (*job, task*)
entreprendre; (*duty*) se charger de; **to ~ to do sth**
s'engager à faire qch
undertaker [ˈʌndəteɪkəʳ] *n* (*BRIT*) entrepreneur *m* des
pompes funèbres, croque-mort *m*
undertaking [ˈʌndəteɪkɪŋ] *n* entreprise *f*; (*promise*)
promesse *f*
under: **underwater** *adv* sous l'eau ▷ *adj* sous-marin(e);
underway *adj*: **to be underway** (*meeting, investigation*)
être en cours; **underwear** *n* sous-vêtements *mpl*;
(*women's only*) dessous *mpl*; **underwent** *pt of* **undergo**;
underworld *n* (*of crime*) milieu *m*, pègre *f*

UFO [ˈjuːfəu] *n abbr* (= *unidentified flying object*) ovni *m*
Uganda [juːˈɡændə] *n* Ouganda *m*
ugly [ˈʌɡlɪ] *adj* laid(e), vilain(e); (*fig*) répugnant(e)
UHT *adj abbr* = **ultra-heat treated**; ~ **milk** lait *m* UHT *or*
longue conservation
UK *n abbr* = **United Kingdom**
ulcer [ˈʌlsəʳ] *n* ulcère *m*; **mouth** ~ aphte *f*
ultimate [ˈʌltɪmət] *adj* ultime, final(e); (*authority*)
suprême; **ultimately** *adv* (*at last*) en fin de compte;
(*fundamentally*) finalement; (*eventually*) par la suite
ultimatum (*pl* ~**s** *or* **ultimata**) [ˌʌltɪˈmeɪtəm, -tə] *n*
ultimatum *m*
ultrasound [ˈʌltrəsaund] *n* (*Med*) ultrason *m*
ultraviolet [ˈʌltrəˈvaɪəlɪt] *adj* ultraviolet(te)
umbrella [ʌmˈbrɛlə] *n* parapluie *m*; (*for sun*) parasol *m*
umpire [ˈʌmpaɪəʳ] *n* arbitre *m*; (*Tennis*) juge *m* de chaise
UN *n abbr* = **United Nations**
unable [ʌnˈeɪbl] *adj*: **to be ~ to** ne (pas) pouvoir, être
dans l'impossibilité de; (*not capable*) être incapable de
unacceptable [ʌnəkˈsɛptəbl] *adj* (*behaviour*)
inadmissible; (*price, proposal*) inacceptable
unanimous [juːˈnænɪməs] *adj* unanime
unarmed [ʌnˈɑːmd] *adj* (*person*) non armé(e); (*combat*)
sans armes
unattended [ʌnəˈtɛndɪd] *adj* (*car, child, luggage*) sans
surveillance
unattractive [ʌnəˈtræktɪv] *adj* peu attrayant(e);
(*character*) peu sympathique
unavailable [ʌnəˈveɪləbl] *adj* (*article, room, book*) (qui
n'est) pas disponible; (*person*) (qui n'est) pas libre
unavoidable [ʌnəˈvɔɪdəbl] *adj* inévitable
unaware [ʌnəˈwɛəʳ] *adj*: **to be ~ of** ignorer, ne pas
savoir, être inconscient(e) de; **unawares** *adv* à
l'improviste, au dépourvu
unbearable [ʌnˈbɛərəbl] *adj* insupportable
unbeatable [ʌnˈbiːtəbl] *adj* imbattable
unbelievable [ʌnbɪˈliːvəbl] *adj* incroyable
unborn [ʌnˈbɔːn] *adj* à naître
unbutton [ʌnˈbʌtn] *vt* déboutonner
uncalled-for [ʌnˈkɔːldfɔːʳ] *adj* déplacé(e), injustifié(e)

undesirable [ʌndɪˈzaɪərəbl] *adj* peu souhaitable; (*person, effect*) indésirable

undisputed [ˈʌndɪsˈpjuːtɪd] *adj* incontesté(e)

undo [ʌnˈduː] *vt* (*irreg: like* **do**) défaire

undone [ʌnˈdʌn] *pp of* **undo** ▷ *adj:* **to come ~** se défaire

undoubtedly [ʌnˈdautɪdlɪ] *adv* sans aucun doute

undress [ʌnˈdrɛs] *vi* se déshabiller

unearth [ʌnˈəːθ] *vt* déterrer; (*fig*) dénicher

uneasy [ʌnˈiːzɪ] *adj* mal à l'aise, gêné(e); (*worried*) inquiet(-ète); (*feeling*) désagréable; (*peace, truce*) fragile

unemployed [ʌnɪmˈplɔɪd] *adj* sans travail, au chômage ▷ *n:* **the ~** les chômeurs *mpl*

unemployment [ʌnɪmˈplɔɪmənt] *n* chômage *m*; **unemployment benefit** (*us* **unemployment compensation**) *n* allocation *f* de chômage

unequal [ʌnˈiːkwəl] *adj* inégal(e)

uneven [ʌnˈiːvn] *adj* inégal(e); (*quality, work*) irrégulier(-ière)

unexpected [ʌnɪkˈspɛktɪd] *adj* inattendu(e), imprévu(e); **unexpectedly** *adv* (*succeed*) contre toute attente; (*arrive*) à l'improviste

unfair [ʌnˈfɛəˈ] *adj:* **~ (to)** injuste (envers)

unfaithful [ʌnˈfeɪθful] *adj* infidèle

unfamiliar [ʌnfəˈmɪlɪəˈ] *adj* étrange, inconnu(e); **to be ~ with sth** mal connaître qch

unfashionable [ʌnˈfæʃnəbl] *adj* (*clothes*) démodé(e); (*place*) peu chic *inv*

unfasten [ʌnˈfɑːsn] *vt* défaire; (*belt, necklace*) détacher; (*open*) ouvrir

unfavourable (*us* **unfavorable**) [ʌnˈfeɪvrəbl] *adj* défavorable

unfinished [ʌnˈfɪnɪʃt] *adj* inachevé(e)

unfit [ʌnˈfɪt] *adj* (*physically: ill*) en mauvaise santé; (: *out of condition*) pas en forme; (*incompetent*): **~ (for)** impropre (à); (*work, service*) inapte (à)

unfold [ʌnˈfəuld] *vt* déplier ▷ *vi* se dérouler

unforgettable [ʌnfəˈgɛtəbl] *adj* inoubliable

unfortunate [ʌnˈfɔːtʃnət] *adj* malheureux(-euse); (*event, remark*) malencontreux(-euse); **unfortunately** *adv* malheureusement

unfriendly [ʌnˈfrɛndlɪ] *adj* peu aimable, froid(e)

unfurnished [ʌnˈfəːnɪʃt] *adj* non meublé(e)

unhappiness [ʌnˈhæpɪnɪs] *n* tristesse *f*, peine *f*

unhappy [ʌnˈhæpɪ] *adj* triste, malheureux(-euse); (*unfortunate: remark etc*) malheureux(-euse); (*not pleased*): **~ with** mécontent(e) de, peu satisfait(e) de

unhealthy [ʌnˈhɛlθɪ] *adj* (*gen*) malsain(e); (*person*) maladif(-ive)

unheard-of [ʌnˈhəːdɔv] *adj* inouï(e), sans précédent

unhelpful [ʌnˈhɛlpful] *adj* (*person*) peu serviable; (*advice*) peu utile

unhurt [ʌnˈhəːt] *adj* indemne, sain(e) et sauf (sauve)

unidentified [ʌnaɪˈdɛntɪfaɪd] *adj* non identifié(e); *see also* **UFO**

uniform [ˈjuːnɪfɔːm] *n* uniforme *m* ▷ *adj* uniforme

unify [ˈjuːnɪfaɪ] *vt* unifier

unimportant [ʌnɪmˈpɔːtənt] *adj* sans importance

uninhabited [ʌnɪnˈhæbɪtɪd] *adj* inhabité(e)

unintentional [ʌnɪnˈtɛnʃənəl] *adj* involontaire

union [ˈjuːnjən] *n* union *f*; (*also:* **trade ~**) syndicat *m* ▷ *cpd* du syndicat, syndical(e); **Union Jack** *n* drapeau du *Royaume-Uni*

unique [juːˈniːk] *adj* unique

unisex [ˈjuːnɪsɛks] *adj* unisexe

unit [ˈjuːnɪt] *n* unité *f*; (*section: of furniture etc*) élément *m*, bloc *m*; (*team, squad*) groupe *m*, service *m*; **kitchen ~** élément de cuisine

unite [juːˈnaɪt] *vt* unir ▷ *vi* s'unir; **united** *adj* uni(e); (*country, party*) unifié(e); (*efforts*) conjugué(e) *m*; **United Kingdom** *n* Royaume-Uni *m* (R.U.); **United Nations (Organization)** *n* (Organisation *f* des) Nations unies (ONU); **United States (of America)** *n* États-Unis *mpl*

unity [ˈjuːnɪtɪ] *n* unité *f*

universal [juːnɪˈvəːsl] *adj* universel(le)

universe [ˈjuːnɪvəːs] *n* univers *m*

university [juːnɪˈvəːsɪtɪ] *n* université *f* ▷ *cpd* (*student, professor*) d'université; (*education, year, degree*) universitaire

unjust [ʌnˈdʒʌst] *adj* injuste

unkind [ʌnˈkaɪnd] *adj* peu gentil(le), méchant(e)

unknown [ʌnˈnəun] *adj* inconnu(e)

unlawful [ʌnˈlɔːful] *adj* illégal(e)

unleaded [ʌnˈlɛdɪd] *n* (*also:* **~ petrol**) essence *f* sans plomb

unleash [ʌnˈliːʃ] *vt* (*fig*) déchaîner, déclencher

unless [ʌnˈlɛs] *conj:* **he leaves** à moins qu'il (ne) parte; **~ otherwise stated** sauf indication contraire

unlike [ʌnˈlaɪk] *adj* dissemblable, différent(e) ▷ *prep* à la différence de, contrairement à

unlikely [ʌnˈlaɪklɪ] *adj* (*result, event*) improbable; (*explanation*) invraisemblable

unlimited [ʌnˈlɪmɪtɪd] *adj* illimité(e)

unlisted [ˈʌnˈlɪstɪd] *adj* (*us Tel*) sur la liste rouge

unload [ʌnˈləud] *vt* décharger

unlock [ʌnˈlɔk] *vt* ouvrir

unlucky [ʌnˈlʌkɪ] *adj* (*person*) malchanceux(-euse); (*object, number*) qui porte malheur; **to be ~** (*person*) ne pas avoir de chance

unmarried [ʌnˈmærɪd] *adj* célibataire

unmistak(e)able [ʌnmɪsˈteɪkəbl] *adj* indubitable; qu'on ne peut pas ne pas reconnaître

unnatural [ʌnˈnætʃrəl] *adj* non naturel(le); (*perversion*) contre nature

unnecessary [ʌnˈnɛsəsərɪ] *adj* inutile, superflu(e)

UNO [ˈjuːnəu] *n abbr* = **United Nations Organization**

unofficial [ʌnəˈfɪʃl] *adj* (*news*) officieux(-euse), non officiel(le); (*strike*) ≈ sauvage

unpack [ʌnˈpæk] *vi* défaire sa valise ▷ *vt* (*suitcase*) défaire; (*belongings*) déballer

unpaid [ʌnˈpeɪd] *adj* (*bill*) impayé(e); (*holiday*) non-payé(e), sans salaire; (*work*) non rétribué(e)

unpleasant [ʌnˈplɛznt] *adj* déplaisant(e), désagréable

unplug [ʌnˈplʌg] *vt* débrancher

unpopular [ʌnˈpɔpjuləˈ] *adj* impopulaire

unprecedented [ʌnˈprɛsɪdɛntɪd] *adj* sans précédent

unpredictable [ʌnprɪˈdɪktəbl] *adj* imprévisible

unprotected [ˈʌnprəˈtɛktɪd] *adj* (*sex*) non protégé(e)

unqualified [ʌnˈkwɔlɪfaɪd] *adj* (*teacher*) non diplômé(e), sans titres; (*success*) sans réserve, total(e); (*disaster*) total(e)

unravel [ʌnˈrævl] *vt* démêler

unreal [ʌnˈrɪəl] *adj* irréel(le); (*extraordinary*) incroyable

unrealistic [ˈʌnrɪəˈlɪstɪk] *adj* (*idea*) irréaliste; (*estimate*) peu réaliste

unreasonable [ʌnˈriːznəbl] *adj* qui n'est pas raisonnable

unrelated [ʌnrɪˈleɪtɪd] *adj* sans rapport; (*people*) sans lien de parenté

unreliable [ʌnrɪˈlaɪəbl] *adj* sur qui (*or* quoi) on ne peut pas compter, peu fiable

unrest [ʌnˈrɛst] *n* agitation *f*, troubles *mpl*

unroll [ʌnˈrəʊl] *vt* dérouler

unruly [ʌnˈruːlɪ] *adj* indiscipliné(e)

unsafe [ʌnˈseɪf] *adj* (*in danger*) en danger; (*journey, car*) dangereux(-euse)

unsatisfactory [ˈʌnsætɪsˈfæktərɪ] *adj* peu satisfaisant(e)

unscrew [ʌnˈskruː] *vt* dévisser

unsettled [ʌnˈsɛtld] *adj* (*restless*) perturbé(e); (*unpredictable*) instable; uncertain(e); (*not finalized*) non résolu(e)

unsettling [ʌnˈsɛtlɪŋ] *adj* qui a un effet perturbateur

unsightly [ʌnˈsaɪtlɪ] *adj* disgracieux(-euse), laid(e)

unskilled [ʌnˈskɪld] *adj*: **~ worker** manœuvre *m*

unspoiled [ˈʌnˈspɔɪld], **unspoilt** [ˈʌnˈspɔɪlt] *adj* (*place*) non dégradé(e)

unstable [ʌnˈsteɪbl] *adj* instable

unsteady [ʌnˈstɛdɪ] *adj* mal assuré(e), chancelant(e), instable

unsuccessful [ʌnsəkˈsɛsful] *adj* (*attempt*) infructueux(-euse); (*writer, proposal*) qui n'a pas de succès; **to be ~** (*in attempting sth*) ne pas réussir; ne pas avoir de succès; (*application*) ne pas être retenu(e)

unsuitable [ʌnˈsuːtəbl] *adj* qui ne convient pas, peu approprié(e); (*time*) inopportun(e)

unsure [ʌnˈʃuər] *adj* pas sûr(e); **to be ~ of o.s.** ne pas être sûr de soi, manquer de confiance en soi

untidy [ʌnˈtaɪdɪ] *adj* (*room*) en désordre; (*appearance, person*) débraillé(e); (*person: in character*) sans ordre, désordonné; (*work*) peu soigné(e)

untie [ʌnˈtaɪ] *vt* (*knot, parcel*) défaire; (*prisoner, dog*) détacher

until [ənˈtɪl] *prep* jusqu'à; (*after negative*) avant ▷ *conj* jusqu'à ce que + *sub*; (*in past, after negative*) avant que + *sub*; **~ he comes** jusqu'à ce qu'il vienne, jusqu'à son arrivée; **~ now** jusqu'à présent, jusqu'ici; **~ then** jusque-là

untrue [ʌnˈtruː] *adj* (*statement*) faux (fausse)

unused[1] [ʌnˈjuːzd] *adj* (*new*) neuf (neuve)

unused[2] [ʌnˈjuːst] *adj*: **to be ~ to sth/to doing sth** ne pas avoir l'habitude de qch/de faire qch

unusual [ʌnˈjuːʒuəl] *adj* insolite, exceptionnel(le), rare; **unusually** *adv* exceptionnellement, particulièrement

unveil [ʌnˈveɪl] *vt* dévoiler

unwanted [ʌnˈwɔntɪd] *adj* (*child, pregnancy*) non désiré(e); (*clothes etc*) à donner

unwell [ʌnˈwɛl] *adj* souffrant(e); **to feel ~** ne pas se sentir bien

unwilling [ʌnˈwɪlɪŋ] *adj*: **to be ~ to do** ne pas vouloir faire

unwind [ʌnˈwaɪnd] *vb* (*irreg: like* **wind**) ▷ *vt* dérouler ▷ *vi* (*relax*) se détendre

unwise [ʌnˈwaɪz] *adj* imprudent(e), peu judicieux(-euse)

unwittingly [ʌnˈwɪtɪŋlɪ] *adv* involontairement

unwrap [ʌnˈræp] *vt* défaire; ouvrir

unzip [ʌnˈzɪp] *vt* ouvrir (la fermeture éclair de); (*Comput*) dézipper

KEYWORD

up [ʌp] *prep*: **he went up the stairs/the hill** il a monté l'escalier/la colline; **the cat was up a tree** le chat était dans un arbre; **they live further up the street** ils

habitent plus haut dans la rue; **go up that road and turn left** remontez la rue et tournez à gauche ▷ *adv* **1** en haut; en l'air; (*upwards, higher*): **up in the sky/ the mountains** (là-haut) dans le ciel/les montagnes; **put it a bit higher up** mettez-le un peu plus haut; **to stand up** (*get up*) se lever, se mettre debout; (*be standing*) être debout; **up there** là-haut; **up above** au-dessus

2: **to be up** (*out of bed*) être levé(e); (*prices*) avoir augmenté *or* monté; (*finished*): **when the year was up** à la fin de l'année

3: **up to** (*as far as*) jusqu'à; **up to now** jusqu'à présent

4: **to be up to** (*depending on*): **it's up to you** c'est à vous de décider; (*equal to*): **he's not up to it** (*job, task etc*) il n'en est pas capable; (*inf: be doing*): **what is he up to?** qu'est-ce qu'il peut bien faire?

▷ *n*: **ups and downs** hauts et bas *mpl*

up-and-coming [ʌpəndˈkʌmɪŋ] *adj* plein(e) d'avenir *or* de promesses

upbringing [ˈʌpbrɪŋɪŋ] *n* éducation *f*

update [ʌpˈdeɪt] *vt* mettre à jour

upfront [ʌpˈfrʌnt] *adj* (*open*) franc (franche) ▷ *adv* (*pay*) d'avance; **to be ~ about sth** ne rien cacher de qch

upgrade [ʌpˈgreɪd] *vt* (*person*) promouvoir; (*job*) revaloriser; (*property, equipment*) moderniser

upheaval [ʌpˈhiːvl] *n* bouleversement *m*; (*in room*) branle-bas *m*; (*event*) crise *f*

uphill [ʌpˈhɪl] *adj* qui monte; (*fig: task*) difficile, pénible ▷ *adv* (*face, look*) en amont, vers l'amont; **to go ~** monter

upholstery [ʌpˈhəʊlstərɪ] *n* rembourrage *m*; (*cover*) tissu d'ameublement; (*of car*) garniture *f*

upmarket [ʌpˈmɑːkɪt] *adj* (*product*) haut de gamme *inv*; (*area*) chic *inv*

upon [əˈpɔn] *prep* sur

upper [ˈʌpər] *adj* supérieur(e); du dessus ▷ *n* (*of shoe*) empeigne *f*; **upper-class** *adj* de la haute société, aristocratique; (*district*) élégant(e), huppé(e); (*accent, attitude*) caractéristique des classes supérieures

upright [ˈʌpraɪt] *adj* droit(e); (*fig*) droit, honnête

uprising [ˈʌpraɪzɪŋ] *n* soulèvement *m*, insurrection *f*

uproar [ˈʌprɔːr] *n* tumulte *m*, vacarme *m*; (*protests*) protestations *fpl*

upset *n* [ˈʌpsɛt] dérangement *m* ▷ *vt* [ʌpˈsɛt] (*irreg: like* **set**) (*glass etc*) renverser; (*plan*) déranger; (*person: offend*) contrarier; (*: grieve*) faire de la peine à; bouleverser ▷ *adj* [ʌpˈsɛt] contrarié(e); peiné(e); **to have a stomach ~** (BRIT) avoir une indigestion

upside down [ˈʌpsaɪd-] *adv* à l'envers; **to turn sth ~** (*fig: place*) mettre sens dessus dessous

upstairs [ʌpˈstɛəz] *adv* en haut ▷ *adj* (*room*) du dessus, d'en haut ▷ *n*: **the ~** l'étage *m*

up-to-date [ˈʌptəˈdeɪt] *adj* moderne; (*information*) très récent(e)

uptown [ˈʌptaʊn] (US) *adv* (*live*) dans les quartiers chics; (*go*) vers les quartiers chics ▷ *adj* des quartiers chics

upward [ˈʌpwəd] *adj* ascendant(e); vers le haut; **upward(s)** *adv* vers le haut; (*more than*): **upward(s) of** plus de

uranium [juəˈreɪnɪəm] *n* uranium *m*

Uranus [juəˈreɪnəs] *n* Uranus *f*

urban [ˈəːbən] *adj* urbain(e)

urge [əːdʒ] *n* besoin (impératif), envie (pressante) ▷ *vt* (*person*): **to ~ sb to do** exhorter qn à faire, pousser qn à faire, recommander vivement à qn de faire

urgency ['əːdʒənsɪ] n urgence f; (of tone) insistance f
urgent ['əːdʒənt] adj urgent(e); (plea, tone) pressant(e)
urinal ['juərɪnl] n (BRIT: place) urinoir m
urinate ['juərɪneɪt] vi uriner
urine ['juərɪn] n urine f
URL abbr (= uniform resource locator) URL f
US n abbr = **United States**
us [ʌs] pron nous; see also **me**
USA n abbr = **United States of America**
use n [juːs] emploi m, utilisation f; (usefulness) utilité
  f ▷ vt [juːz] se servir de, utiliser, employer; **in ~** en
  usage; **out of ~** hors d'usage; **to be of ~** servir, être
  utile; **it's no ~** ça ne sert à rien; **to have the ~ of** avoir
  l'usage de; **she ~d to do it** elle le faisait (autrefois), elle
  avait coutume de le faire; **to be ~d to** avoir l'habitude
  de, être habitué(e) à; **use up** vt finir, épuiser; (food)
  consommer; **used** [juːzd] adj (car) d'occasion; **useful**
  adj utile; **useless** adj inutile; (inf: person) nul(le); **user**
  n utilisateur(-trice), usager m; **user-friendly** adj
  convivial(e), facile d'emploi
usual ['juːʒuəl] adj habituel(le); **as ~** comme d'habitude;
  usually adv d'habitude, d'ordinaire
utensil [juːˈtɛnsl] n ustensile m; **kitchen ~s** batterie f
  de cuisine
utility [juːˈtɪlɪtɪ] n utilité f; (also: **public ~**) service
  public
utilize ['juːtɪlaɪz] vt utiliser; (make good use of) exploiter
utmost ['ʌtməust] adj extrême, le (la) plus grand(e) ▷ n:
  to do one's ~ faire tout son possible
utter ['ʌtəʳ] adj total(e), complet(-ète) ▷ vt prononcer,
  proférer; (sounds) émettre; **utterly** adv complètement,
  totalement
U-turn ['juːˈtəːn] n demi-tour m; (fig) volte-face f inv

v. abbr = **verse**; (= vide) v.; (= versus) c.; (= volt) V
vacancy ['veɪkənsɪ] n (BRIT: job) poste vacant; (room)
  chambre f disponible; **"no vacancies"** "complet"
vacant ['veɪkənt] adj (post) vacant(e); (seat etc) libre,
  disponible; (expression) distrait(e)
vacate [vəˈkeɪt] vt quitter
vacation [vəˈkeɪʃən] n (esp us) vacances fpl; **on
  ~** en vacances; **vacationer** (us **vacationist**) n
  vacancier(-ière)
vaccination [væksɪˈneɪʃən] n vaccination f
vaccine ['væksiːn] n vaccin m
vacuum ['vækjum] n vide m; **vacuum cleaner** n
  aspirateur m
vagina [vəˈdʒaɪnə] n vagin m
vague [veɪɡ] adj vague, imprécis(e); (blurred: photo,
  memory) flou(e)
vain [veɪn] adj (useless) vain(e); (conceited)
  vaniteux(-euse); **in ~** en vain
Valentine's Day ['væləntaɪnz-] n Saint-Valentin f
valid ['vælɪd] adj (document) valide, valable; (excuse)
  valable
valley ['vælɪ] n vallée f
valuable ['væljuəbl] adj (jewel) de grande valeur; (time,
  help) précieux(-euse); **valuables** npl objets mpl de valeur
value ['væljuː] n valeur f ▷ vt (fix price) évaluer,
  expertiser; (appreciate) apprécier; **values** npl (principles)
  valeurs fpl
valve [vælv] n (in machine) soupape f; (on tyre) valve f;
  (Med) valve, valvule f
vampire ['væmpaɪəʳ] n vampire m
van [væn] n (Aut) camionnette f
vandal ['vændl] n vandale m/f; **vandalism** n
  vandalisme m; **vandalize** vt saccager
vanilla [vəˈnɪlə] n vanille f
vanish ['vænɪʃ] vi disparaître
vanity ['vænɪtɪ] n vanité f
vapour (us **vapor**) ['veɪpəʳ] n vapeur f; (on window) buée f
variable ['vɛərɪəbl] adj variable; (mood) changeant(e)
variant ['vɛərɪənt] n variante f
variation [vɛərɪˈeɪʃən] n variation f; (in opinion)

changement m
varied ['vɛərɪd] *adj* varié(e), divers(e)
variety [və'raɪətɪ] *n* variété f; (*quantity*) nombre m, quantité f
various ['vɛərɪəs] *adj* divers(e), différent(e); (*several*) divers, plusieurs
varnish ['vɑ:nɪʃ] *n* vernis m ▷ *vt* vernir
vary ['vɛərɪ] *vt, vi* varier, changer
vase [vɑ:z] *n* vase m
Vaseline® ['væsɪli:n] *n* vaseline f
vast [vɑ:st] *adj* vaste, immense; (*amount, success*) énorme
VAT [væt] *n abbr* (BRIT: = *value added tax*) TVA f
vault [vɔ:lt] *n* (*of roof*) voûte f; (*tomb*) caveau m; (*in bank*) salle f des coffres; chambre forte ▷ *vt* (*also*: ~ **over**) sauter (d'un bond)
VCR *n abbr* = **video cassette recorder**
VDU *n abbr* = **visual display unit**
veal [vi:l] *n* veau m
veer [vɪəʳ] *vi* tourner; (*car, ship*) virer
vegan ['vi:gən] *n* végétalien(ne)
vegetable ['vedʒtəbl] *n* légume m ▷ *adj* végétal(e)
vegetarian [vedʒɪ'tɛərɪən] *adj, n* végétarien(ne); **do you have any ~ dishes?** avez-vous des plats végétariens?
vegetation [vedʒɪ'teɪʃən] *n* végétation f
vehicle ['vi:ɪkl] *n* véhicule m
veil [veɪl] *n* voile m
vein [veɪn] *n* veine f; (*on leaf*) nervure f
Velcro® ['vɛlkrəʊ] *n* velcro® m
velvet ['vɛlvɪt] *n* velours m
vending machine ['vɛndɪŋ-] *n* distributeur m automatique
vendor ['vɛndəʳ] *n* vendeur(-euse); **street ~** marchand ambulant
Venetian blind [vɪ'ni:ʃən-] *n* store vénitien
vengeance ['vɛndʒəns] *n* vengeance f; **with a ~** (*fig*) vraiment, pour de bon
venison ['vɛnɪsn] *n* venaison f
venom ['vɛnəm] *n* venin m
vent [vɛnt] *n* conduit m d'aération; (*in dress, jacket*) fente f ▷ *vt* (*fig: one's feelings*) donner libre cours à
ventilation [vɛntɪ'leɪʃən] *n* ventilation f, aération f
venture ['vɛntʃəʳ] *n* entreprise f ▷ *vt* risquer, hasarder ▷ *vi* s'aventurer, se risquer; **a business ~** une entreprise commerciale
venue ['vɛnju:] *n* lieu m
Venus ['vi:nəs] *n* (*planet*) Vénus f
verb [və:b] *n* verbe m; **verbal** *adj* verbal(e)
verdict ['və:dɪkt] *n* verdict m
verge [və:dʒ] *n* bord m; **"soft ~s"** (BRIT) "accotements non stabilisés"; **on the ~ of doing** sur le point de faire
verify ['vɛrɪfaɪ] *vt* vérifier
versatile ['və:sətaɪl] *adj* polyvalent(e)
verse [və:s] *n* vers mpl; (*stanza*) strophe f; (*in Bible*) verset m
version ['və:ʃən] *n* version f
versus ['və:səs] *prep* contre
vertical ['və:tɪkl] *adj* vertical(e)
very ['vɛrɪ] *adv* très ▷ *adj*: **the ~ book which** le livre même que; **the ~ last** le tout dernier; **at the ~ least** au moins; **~ much** beaucoup
vessel ['vɛsl] *n* (*Anat, Naut*) vaisseau m; (*container*) récipient m; *see also* **blood**

vest [vɛst] *n* (BRIT: *underwear*) tricot m de corps; (US: *waistcoat*) gilet m
vet [vɛt] *n abbr* (BRIT: = *veterinary surgeon*) vétérinaire m/f; (US: = *veteran*) ancien(ne) combattant(e) ▷ *vt* examiner minutieusement
veteran ['vɛtərn] *n* vétéran m; (*also*: **war ~**) ancien combattant
veterinary surgeon ['vɛtrɪnərɪ-] (BRIT), **veterinarian** [vɛtrɪ'nɛərɪən] (US) *n* vétérinaire m/f
veto ['vi:təʊ] *n* (*pl* **~es**) veto m ▷ *vt* opposer son veto à
via ['vaɪə] *prep* par, via
viable ['vaɪəbl] *adj* viable
vibrate [vaɪ'breɪt] *vi*: **to ~ (with)** vibrer (de)
vibration [vaɪ'breɪʃən] *n* vibration f
vicar ['vɪkəʳ] *n* pasteur m (*de l'Église anglicane*)
vice [vaɪs] *n* (*evil*) vice m; (*Tech*) étau m; **vice-chairman** *n* vice-président(e)
vice versa ['vaɪsɪ'və:sə] *adv* vice versa
vicinity [vɪ'sɪnɪtɪ] *n* environs mpl, alentours mpl
vicious ['vɪʃəs] *adj* (*remark*) cruel(le), méchant(e); (*blow*) brutal(e); (*dog*) méchant(e), dangereux(-euse); **a ~ circle** un cercle vicieux
victim ['vɪktɪm] *n* victime f
victor ['vɪktəʳ] *n* vainqueur m
Victorian [vɪk'tɔ:rɪən] *adj* victorien(ne)
victorious [vɪk'tɔ:rɪəs] *adj* victorieux(-euse)
victory ['vɪktərɪ] *n* victoire f
video ['vɪdɪəʊ] *n* (*video film*) vidéo f; (*also*: **~ cassette**) vidéocassette f; (*also*: **~ cassette recorder**) magnétoscope m ▷ *vt* (*with recorder*) enregistrer; (*with camera*) filmer; **video camera** *n* caméra f vidéo *inv*; **video (cassette) recorder** *n* magnétoscope m; **video game** *n* jeu m vidéo *inv*; **video shop** *n* vidéoclub m; **video tape** *n* bande f vidéo *inv*; (*cassette*) vidéocassette f
vie [vaɪ] *vi*: **to ~ with** lutter avec, rivaliser avec
Vienna [vɪ'ɛnə] *n* Vienne
Vietnam, Viet Nam ['vjɛt'næm] *n* Viêt-nam *or* Vietnam m; **Vietnamese** [vjɛtnə'mi:z] *adj* vietnamien(ne) ▷ *n* (*pl inv*) Vietnamien(ne)
view [vju:] *n* vue f; (*opinion*) avis m, vue f ▷ *vt* voir, regarder; (*situation*) considérer; (*house*) visiter; **on ~** (*in museum etc*) exposé(e); **in full ~ of sb** sous les yeux de qn; **in my ~** à mon avis; **in ~ of the fact that** étant donné que; **viewer** *n* (*TV*) téléspectateur(-trice); **viewpoint** *n* point m de vue
vigilant ['vɪdʒɪlənt] *adj* vigilant(e)
vigorous ['vɪgərəs] *adj* vigoureux(-euse)
vile [vaɪl] *adj* (*action*) vil(e); (*smell, food*) abominable; (*temper*) massacrant(e)
villa ['vɪlə] *n* villa f
village ['vɪlɪdʒ] *n* village m; **villager** *n* villageois(e)
villain ['vɪlən] *n* (*scoundrel*) scélérat m; (BRIT: *criminal*) bandit m; (*in novel etc*) traître m
vinaigrette [vɪneɪ'grɛt] *n* vinaigrette f
vine [vaɪn] *n* vigne f
vinegar ['vɪnɪgəʳ] *n* vinaigre m
vineyard ['vɪnjɑ:d] *n* vignoble m
vintage ['vɪntɪdʒ] *n* (*year*) année f, millésime m ▷ *cpd* (*car*) d'époque; (*wine*) de grand cru
vinyl ['vaɪnl] *n* vinyle m
viola [vɪ'əʊlə] *n* alto m
violate ['vaɪəleɪt] *vt* violer
violation [vaɪə'leɪʃən] *n* violation f; **in ~ of** (*rule, law*) en infraction à, en violation de

violence ['vaɪələns] n violence f
violent ['vaɪələnt] adj violent(e)
violet ['vaɪələt] adj (colour) violet(te) ▷ n (plant) violette f
violin [vaɪə'lɪn] n violon m
VIP n abbr (= very important person) VIP m
virgin ['vəːdʒɪn] n vierge f
Virgo ['vəːgəu] n la Vierge
virtual ['vəːtjuəl] adj (Comput, Physics) virtuel(le); (in effect): **it's a ~ impossibility** c'est quasiment impossible; **virtually** adv (almost) pratiquement; **virtual reality** n (Comput) réalité virtuelle
virtue ['vəːtju:] n vertu f; (advantage) mérite m, avantage m; **by ~ of** en vertu or raison de
virus ['vaɪərəs] n (Med, Comput) virus m
visa ['viːzə] n visa m
vise [vaɪs] n (us Tech) = **vice**
visibility [vɪzɪ'bɪlɪtɪ] n visibilité f
visible ['vɪzəbl] adj visible
vision ['vɪʒən] n (sight) vue f, vision f; (foresight, in dream) vision
visit ['vɪzɪt] n visite f; (stay) séjour m ▷ vt (person: us: also: **~ with**) rendre visite à; (place) visiter; **visiting hours** npl heures fpl de visite; **visitor** n visiteur(-euse); (to one's house) invité(e); **visitor centre** (us **visitor center**) n hall m or centre m d'accueil
visual ['vɪzjuəl] adj visuel(le); **visualize** vt se représenter
vital ['vaɪtl] adj vital(e); **of ~ importance (to sb/sth)** d'une importance capitale (pour qn/qch)
vitality [vaɪ'tælɪtɪ] n vitalité f
vitamin ['vɪtəmɪn] n vitamine f
vivid ['vɪvɪd] adj (account) frappant(e), vivant(e); (light, imagination) vif (vive)
V-neck ['viːnɛk] n décolleté m en V
vocabulary [vəu'kæbjuləri] n vocabulaire m
vocal ['vəukl] adj vocal(e); (articulate) qui n'hésite pas à s'exprimer, qui sait faire entendre ses opinions
vocational [vəu'keɪʃənl] adj professionnel(le)
vodka ['vɔdkə] n vodka f
vogue [vəug] n: **to be in ~** être en vogue or à la mode
voice [vɔɪs] n voix f ▷ vt (opinion) exprimer, formuler; **voice mail** n (system) messagerie f vocale; (device) boîte f vocale
void [vɔɪd] n vide m ▷ adj (invalid) nul(le); (empty): **~ of** vide de, dépourvu(e) de
volatile ['vɔlətaɪl] adj volatil(e); (fig: person) versatile; (: situation) explosif(-ive)
volcano (pl **-es**) [vɔl'keɪnəu] n volcan m
volleyball ['vɔlɪbɔːl] n volley(-ball) m
volt [vəult] n volt m; **voltage** n tension f, voltage m
volume ['vɔljuːm] n volume m; (of tank) capacité f
voluntarily ['vɔləntrɪlɪ] adv volontairement
voluntary ['vɔləntərɪ] adj volontaire; (unpaid) bénévole
volunteer [vɔlən'tɪə'] n volontaire m/f ▷ vt (information) donner spontanément ▷ vi (Mil) s'engager comme volontaire; **to ~ to do** se proposer pour faire
vomit ['vɔmɪt] n vomissure f ▷ vt, vi vomir
vote [vəut] n vote m, suffrage m; (votes cast) voix f, vote; (franchise) droit m de vote ▷ vt (chairman) élire; (propose): **to ~ that** proposer que + sub ▷ vi voter; **~ of thanks** discours m de remerciement; **voter** n électeur(-trice); **voting** n scrutin m, vote m
voucher ['vautʃə'] n (for meal, petrol, gift) bon m

vowel ['vauəl] n voyelle f
voyage ['vɔɪɪdʒ] n voyage m par mer, traversée f
vulgar ['vʌlgə'] adj vulgaire
vulnerable ['vʌlnərəbl] adj vulnérable
vulture ['vʌltʃə'] n vautour m

W

waddle ['wɔdl] vi se dandiner
wade [weɪd] vi: **to ~ through** marcher dans, patauger dans; (fig: book) venir à bout de
wafer ['weɪfə'] n (Culin) gaufrette f
waffle ['wɔfl] n (Culin) gaufre f ▷ vi parler pour ne rien dire; faire du remplissage
wag [wæg] vt agiter, remuer ▷ vi remuer
wage [weɪdʒ] n (also: **~s**) salaire m, paye f ▷ vt: **to ~ war** faire la guerre
wag(g)on ['wægən] n (horse-drawn) chariot m; (BRIT Rail) wagon m (de marchandises)
wail [weɪl] n gémissement m; (of siren) hurlement m ▷ vi gémir; (siren) hurler
waist [weɪst] n taille f, ceinture f; **waistcoat** n (BRIT) gilet m
wait [weɪt] n attente f ▷ vi attendre; **to ~ for sb/sth** attendre qn/qch; **to keep sb ~ing** faire attendre qn; **~ for me, please** attendez-moi, s'il vous plaît; **I can't ~ to ...** (fig) je meurs d'envie de ...; **to lie in ~ for** guetter; **wait on** vt fus servir; **waiter** n garçon m (de café), serveur m; **waiting list** n liste f d'attente; **waiting room** n salle f d'attente; **waitress** ['weɪtrɪs] n serveuse f
waive [weɪv] vt renoncer à, abandonner
wake [weɪk] vb (pt **woke** or **~d**, pp **woken** or **~d**) ▷ vt (also: **~ up**) réveiller ▷ vi (also: **~ up**) se réveiller ▷ n (for dead person) veillée f mortuaire; (Naut) sillage m
Wales [weɪlz] n pays m de Galles; **the Prince of ~** le

prince de Galles

walk [wɔːk] n promenade f; (short) petit tour; (gait) démarche f; (path) chemin m; (in park etc) allée f ▷ vi marcher; (for pleasure, exercise) se promener ▷ vt (distance) faire à pied; (dog) promener; **10 minutes' ~ from** à 10 minutes de marche de; **to go for a ~** se promener; faire un tour; **from all ~s of life** de toutes conditions sociales; **walk out** vi (go out) sortir; (as protest) partir (en signe de protestation); (strike) se mettre en grève; **to ~ out on sb** quitter qn; **walker** n (person) marcheur(-euse); **walkie-talkie** ['wɔːkɪ'tɔːkɪ] n talkie-walkie m; **walking** n marche f à pied; **walking shoes** npl chaussures fpl de marche; **walking stick** n canne f; **Walkman**® n Walkman® m; **walkway** n promenade f, cheminement piéton

wall [wɔːl] n mur m; (of tunnel, cave) paroi f

wallet ['wɔlɪt] n portefeuille m; **I can't find my ~** je ne retrouve plus mon portefeuille

wallpaper ['wɔːlpeɪpə^r] n papier peint ▷ vt tapisser

walnut ['wɔːlnʌt] n noix f; (tree, wood) noyer m

walrus (pl ~ or ~es) ['wɔːlrəs] n morse m

waltz [wɔːlts] n valse f ▷ vi valser

wand [wɔnd] n (also: **magic ~**) baguette f (magique)

wander ['wɔndə^r] vi (person) errer, aller sans but; (thoughts) vagabonder ▷ vt errer dans

want [wɔnt] vt vouloir; (need) avoir besoin de ▷ n: **for ~ of** par manque de, faute de; **to ~ to do** vouloir faire; **to ~ sb to do** vouloir que qn fasse; **wanted** adj (criminal) recherché(e) par la police; **"cook wanted"** "on recherche un cuisinier"

war [wɔː^r] n guerre f; **to make ~ (on)** faire la guerre (à)

ward [wɔːd] n (in hospital) salle f; (Pol) section électorale; (Law: child: also: **~ of court**) pupille m/f

warden ['wɔːdn] n (BRIT: of institution) directeur(-trice); (of park, game reserve) gardien(ne); (BRIT: also: **traffic ~**) contractuel(le)

wardrobe ['wɔːdrəub] n (cupboard) armoire f; (clothes) garde-robe f

warehouse ['wɛəhaus] n entrepôt m

warfare ['wɔːfɛə^r] n guerre f

warhead ['wɔːhɛd] n (Mil) ogive f

warm [wɔːm] adj chaud(e); (person, thanks, welcome, applause) chaleureux(-euse); **it's ~** il fait chaud; **I'm ~** j'ai chaud; **warm up** vi (person, room) se réchauffer; (athlete, discussion) s'échauffer ▷ vt (food) (faire) réchauffer; (water) (faire) chauffer; (engine) faire chauffer; **warmly** adv (dress) chaudement; (thank, welcome) chaleureusement; **warmth** n chaleur f

warn [wɔːn] vt avertir, prévenir; **to ~ sb (not) to do** conseiller à qn de (ne pas) faire; **warning** n avertissement m; (notice) avis m; **warning light** n avertisseur lumineux

warrant ['wɔrnt] n (guarantee) garantie f; (Law: to arrest) mandat m d'arrêt; (: to search) mandat de perquisition ▷ vt (justify, merit) justifier

warranty ['wɔrəntɪ] n garantie f

warrior ['wɔrɪə^r] n guerrier(-ière)

Warsaw ['wɔːsɔː] n Varsovie f

warship ['wɔːʃɪp] n navire m de guerre

wart [wɔːt] n verrue f

wartime ['wɔːtaɪm] n: **in ~** en temps de guerre

wary ['wɛərɪ] adj prudent(e)

was [wɔz] pt of **be**

wash [wɔʃ] vt laver ▷ vi se laver; (sea): **to ~ over/against** sth inonder/baigner qch ▷ n (clothes) lessive f; (washing programme) lavage m; (of ship) sillage m; **to have a ~** se laver, faire sa toilette; **wash up** vi (BRIT) faire la vaisselle; (US: have a wash) se débarbouiller; **washbasin** n lavabo m; **wash cloth** n (US) gant m de toilette; **washer** n (Tech) rondelle f, joint m; **washing** n (BRIT: linen etc: dirty) linge m; (: clean) lessive f; **washing line** n (BRIT) corde f à linge; **washing machine** n machine f à laver; **washing powder** n (BRIT) lessive f (en poudre)

Washington ['wɔʃɪŋtən] n Washington m

wash: washing-up n (BRIT) vaisselle f; **washing-up liquid** n (BRIT) produit m pour la vaisselle; **washroom** n (US) toilettes fpl

wasn't ['wɔznt] = **was not**

wasp [wɔsp] n guêpe f

waste [weɪst] n gaspillage m; (of time) perte f; (rubbish) déchets mpl; (also: **household ~**) ordures fpl ▷ adj (land, ground: in city) à l'abandon; (leftover): **~ material** déchets ▷ vt gaspiller; (time, opportunity) perdre; **waste ground** n (BRIT) terrain m vague; **wastepaper basket** n corbeille f à papier

watch [wɔtʃ] n montre f; (act of watching) surveillance f; (guard: Mil) sentinelle f; (: Naut) homme m de quart; (Naut: spell of duty) quart m ▷ vt (look at) observer; (: match, programme) regarder; (spy on, guard) surveiller; (be careful of) faire attention à ▷ vi regarder; (keep guard) monter la garde; **to keep ~** faire le guet; **watch out** vi faire attention; **watchdog** n chien m de garde; (fig) gardien(ne); **watch strap** n bracelet m de montre

water ['wɔːtə^r] n eau f ▷ vt (plant, garden) arroser ▷ vi (eyes) larmoyer; **in British ~s** dans les eaux territoriales Britanniques; **to make sb's mouth ~** mettre l'eau à la bouche de qn; **water down** vt (milk etc) couper avec de l'eau; (fig: story) édulcorer; **watercolour** (US **watercolor**) n aquarelle f; **watercress** n cresson m (de fontaine); **waterfall** n chute f d'eau; **watering can** n arrosoir m; **watermelon** n pastèque f; **waterproof** adj imperméable; **water-skiing** n ski m nautique

watt [wɔt] n watt m

wave [weɪv] n vague f; (of hand) geste m, signe m; (Radio) onde f; (in hair) ondulation f; (fig: of enthusiasm, strikes etc) vague ▷ vi faire signe de la main; (flag) flotter au vent; (grass) ondoyer ▷ vt (handkerchief) agiter; (stick) brandir; **wavelength** n longueur f d'ondes

waver ['weɪvə^r] vi vaciller; (voice) trembler; (person) hésiter

wavy ['weɪvɪ] adj (hair, surface) ondulé(e); (line) onduleux(-euse)

wax [wæks] n cire f; (for skis) fart m ▷ vt cirer; (car) lustrer; (skis) farter ▷ vi (moon) croître

way [weɪ] n chemin m, voie f; (distance) distance f; (direction) chemin, direction f; (manner) manière f; (habit) habitude f, façon; **which ~? — this ~/that ~** par où or de quel côté? — par ici/par là; **to lose one's ~** perdre son chemin; **on the ~ (to)** en route (pour); **to be on one's ~** être en route; **to be in the ~** bloquer le passage; (fig) gêner; **it's a long ~ away** c'est loin d'ici; **to go out of one's ~ to do** (fig) se donner beaucoup de mal pour faire; **to be under ~** (work, project) être en cours; **in a ~** dans un sens; **by the ~** à propos; **"~ in"** (BRIT) "entrée"; **"~ out"** (BRIT) "sortie"; **the ~ back** le chemin du retour; **"give ~"** (BRIT Aut) "cédez la priorité"; **no ~!** (inf) pas question!

W.C. n abbr (BRIT: = water closet) w.-c. mpl, waters mpl

we [wiː] pl pron nous

weak [wiːk] adj faible; (health) fragile; (beam etc) peu solide; (tea, coffee) léger(-ère); **weaken** vi faiblir ▷ vt affaiblir; **weakness** n faiblesse f; (fault) point m faible

wealth [welθ] n (money, resources) richesse(s) f(pl); (of details) profusion f; **wealthy** adj riche

weapon ['wepən] n arme f; **~s of mass destruction** armes fpl de destruction massive

wear [wɛəʳ] n (use) usage m; (deterioration through use) usure f ▷ vb (pt **wore**, pp **worn**) ▷ vt (clothes) porter; (put on) mettre; (damage: through use) user ▷ vi (last) faire de l'usage; (rub etc through) s'user; **sports/baby~** vêtements mpl de sport/pour bébés; **evening ~** tenue f de soirée; **wear off** vi disparaître; **wear out** vt user; (person, strength) épuiser

weary ['wɪərɪ] adj (tired) épuisé(e); (dispirited) las (lasse), abattu(e) ▷ vi: **to ~ of** se lasser de

weasel ['wiːzl] n (Zool) belette f

weather ['wɛðəʳ] n temps m ▷ vt (storm: lit, fig) essuyer; (crisis) survivre à; **under the ~** (fig: ill) mal fichu(e); **weather forecast** n prévisions fpl météorologiques, météo f

weave (pt **wove**, pp **woven**) [wiːv, wəuv, 'wəuvn] vt (cloth) tisser; (basket) tresser

web [web] n (of spider) toile f; (on duck's foot) palmure f; (fig) tissu m; (Comput): **the (World-Wide) W~** le Web; **web page** n (Comput) page f Web; **website** n (Comput) site m web

wed [wed] (pt, pp **-ded**) vt épouser ▷ vi se marier

Wed abbr (= Wednesday) me

we'd [wiːd] = **we had**; **we would**

wedding ['wedɪŋ] n mariage m; **wedding anniversary** n anniversaire m de mariage; **silver/golden wedding anniversary** noces fpl d'argent/d'or; **wedding day** n jour m du mariage; **wedding dress** n robe f de mariée; **wedding ring** n alliance f

wedge [wedʒ] n (of wood etc) coin m; (under door etc) cale f; (of cake) part f ▷ vt (fix) caler; (push) enfoncer, coincer

Wednesday ['wednzdɪ] n mercredi m

wee [wiː] adj (SCOTTISH) petit(e); tout(e) petit(e)

weed [wiːd] n mauvaise herbe ▷ vt désherber; **weedkiller** n désherbant m

week [wiːk] n semaine f; **a ~ today/on Tuesday** aujourd'hui/mardi en huit; **weekday** n jour m de semaine; (Comm) jour ouvrable; **weekend** n week-end m; **weekly** adv une fois par semaine, chaque semaine ▷ adj, n hebdomadaire (m)

weep [wiːp] (pt, pp **wept**) vi (person) pleurer

weigh [weɪ] vt, vi peser; **to ~ anchor** lever l'ancre; **weigh up** vt examiner

weight [weɪt] n poids m; **to put on/lose ~** grossir/maigrir; **weightlifting** n haltérophilie f

weir [wɪəʳ] n barrage m

weird [wɪəd] adj bizarre; (eerie) surnaturel(le)

welcome ['welkəm] adj bienvenu(e) ▷ n accueil m ▷ vt accueillir; (also: **bid ~**) souhaiter la bienvenue à; (be glad of) se réjouir de; **you're ~!** (after thanks) de rien, il n'y a pas de quoi

weld [weld] vt souder

welfare ['welfɛəʳ] n (wellbeing) bien-être m; (social aid) assistance sociale; **welfare state** n État-providence m

well [wel] n puits m ▷ adv bien ▷ adj: **to be ~** aller bien

▷ excl eh bien!; (relief also) bon!; (resignation) enfin!; **~ done!** bravo!; **get ~ soon!** remets-toi vite!; **to do ~** bien réussir; (business) prospérer; **as ~** (in addition) aussi, également; **as ~ as** aussi bien que or de; en plus de

we'll [wiːl] = **we will**; **we shall**

well: **well-behaved** adj sage, obéissant(e); **well-built** adj (person) bien bâti(e); **well-dressed** adj bien habillé(e), bien vêtu(e)

well-groomed ['-'gruːmd] adj très soigné(e)

wellies ['welɪz] (inf) npl (BRIT) = **wellingtons**

wellingtons ['welɪŋtənz] npl (also: **wellington boots**) bottes fpl en caoutchouc

well: **well-known** adj (person) bien connu(e); **well-off** adj aisé(e), assez riche; **well-paid** [wel'peɪd] adj bien payé(e)

Welsh [welʃ] adj gallois(e) ▷ n (Ling) gallois m; **the Welsh** npl (people) les Gallois; **Welshman** (irreg) n Gallois m; **Welshwoman** (irreg) n Galloise f

went [went] pt of **go**

wept [wept] pt, pp of **weep**

were [wəːʳ] pt of **be**

we're [wɪəʳ] = **we are**

weren't [wəːnt] = **were not**

west [west] n ouest m ▷ adj (wind) d'ouest; (side) ouest inv ▷ adv à or vers l'ouest; **the W~** l'Occident m, l'Ouest; **westbound** ['westbaund] adj en direction de l'ouest; (carriageway) ouest inv; **western** adj occidental(e), de or à l'ouest ▷ n (Cine) western m; **West Indian** adj antillais(e) ▷ n Antillais(e)

West Indies [-'ɪndɪz] npl Antilles fpl

wet [wet] adj mouillé(e); (damp) humide; (soaked: also: **~ through**) trempé(e); (rainy) pluvieux(-euse); **to get ~** se mouiller; **"~ paint"** "attention peinture fraîche"; **wetsuit** n combinaison f de plongée

we've [wiːv] = **we have**

whack [wæk] vt donner un grand coup à

whale [weɪl] n (Zool) baleine f

wharf (pl **wharves**) [wɔːf, wɔːvz] n quai m

○ KEYWORD

what [wɔt] adj **1** (in questions) quel(le); **what size is he?** quelle taille fait-il?; **what colour is it?** de quelle couleur est-ce?; **what books do you need?** quels livres vous faut-il?

2 (in exclamations): **what a mess!** quel désordre!; **what a fool I am!** que je suis bête!

▷ pron **1** (interrogative) que; de/à/en etc quoi; **what are you doing?** que faites-vous?, qu'est-ce que vous faites?; **what is happening?** qu'est-ce qui se passe?, que se passe-t-il?; **what are you talking about?** de quoi parlez-vous?; **what are you thinking about?** à quoi pensez-vous?; **what is it called?** comment est-ce que ça s'appelle?; **what about me?** et moi?; **what about doing ...?** et si on faisait ...?

2 (relative: subject) ce qui; (: direct object) ce que; (: indirect object) ce à quoi, ce dont; **I saw what you did/was on the table** j'ai vu ce que vous avez fait/ce qui était sur la table; **tell me what you remember** dites-moi ce dont vous vous souvenez; **what I want is a cup of tea** ce que je veux, c'est une tasse de thé

▷ excl (disbelieving) quoi!, comment!

whatever [wɔt'evəʳ] adj: **take ~ book you prefer**

prenez le livre que vous préférez, peu importe lequel; **~ book you take** quel que soit le livre que vous preniez ▷ *pron*: **do ~ is necessary** faites (tout) ce qui est nécessaire; **~ happens** quoi qu'il arrive; **no reason ~** *or* **whatsoever** pas la moindre raison; **nothing ~** *or* **whatsoever** rien du tout

whatsoever [wɒtsəu'ɛvər] *adj see* **whatever**

wheat [wi:t] *n* blé *m*, froment *m*

wheel [wi:l] *n* roue *f*; (*Aut*: **steering ~**) volant *m*; (*Naut*) gouvernail *m* ▷ *vt* (*pram etc*) pousser, rouler ▷ *vi* (*birds*) tournoyer; (*also*: **~ round**: *person*) se retourner, faire volte-face; **wheelbarrow** *n* brouette *f*; **wheelchair** *n* fauteuil roulant; **wheel clamp** *n* (*Aut*) sabot *m* (de Denver)

wheeze [wi:z] *vi* respirer bruyamment

KEYWORD

when [wɛn] *adv* quand; **when did he go?** quand est-ce qu'il est parti?
▷ *conj* **1** (*at, during, after the time that*) quand, lorsque; **she was reading when I came in** elle lisait quand *or* lorsque je suis entré
2 (*on, at which*): **on the day when I met him** le jour où je l'ai rencontré
3 (*whereas*) alors que; **I thought I was wrong when in fact I was right** j'ai cru que j'avais tort alors qu'en fait j'avais raison

whenever [wɛn'ɛvər] *adv* quand donc ▷ *conj* quand; (*every time that*) chaque fois que

where [wɛər] *adv, conj* où; **this is ~** c'est là que; **whereabouts** *adv* où donc ▷ *n*: **nobody knows his whereabouts** personne ne sait où il se trouve; **whereas** *conj* alors que; **whereby** *adv* (*formal*) par lequel (laquelle etc); **wherever** *adv* où donc ▷ *conj* où que + *sub*; **sit wherever you like** asseyez-vous (là) où vous voulez

whether [wɛðər] *conj* si; **I don't know ~ to accept or not** je ne sais pas si je dois accepter ou non; **it's doubtful ~ il** est peu probable que + *sub*; **~ you go or not** que vous y alliez ou non

KEYWORD

which [wɪtʃ] *adj* **1** (*interrogative: direct, indirect*) quel(le); **which picture do you want?** quel tableau voulez-vous?; **which one?** lequel (laquelle)?
2: **in which case** auquel cas; **we got there at 8pm, by which time the cinema was full** quand nous sommes arrivés à 20h, le cinéma était complet
▷ *pron* **1** (*interrogative*) lequel (laquelle), lesquels (lesquelles) *pl*; **I don't mind which** peu importe lequel; **which (of these) are yours?** lesquels sont à vous?; **tell me which you want** dites-moi lesquels *or* ceux que vous voulez
2 (*relative: subject*) qui; (: *object*) que; sur/vers etc lequel (laquelle) (*NB*: à + *lequel* = **auquel**; *de* + *lequel* = **duquel**); **the apple which you ate/which is on the table** la pomme que vous avez mangée/qui est sur la table; **the chair on which you are sitting** la chaise sur laquelle vous êtes assis; **the book of which you spoke** le livre dont vous avez parlé; **he said he knew, which is true/I was afraid of** il a dit qu'il le

savait, ce qui est vrai/ce que je craignais; **after which** après quoi

whichever [wɪtʃ'ɛvər] *adj*: **take ~ book you prefer** prenez le livre que vous préférez, peu importe lequel; **~ book you take** quel que soit le livre que vous preniez

while [waɪl] *n* moment *m* ▷ *conj* pendant que; (*as long as*) tant que; (*as, whereas*) alors que; (*though*) bien que + *sub*, quoique + *sub*; **for a ~** pendant quelque temps; **in a ~** dans un moment

whilst [waɪlst] *conj* = **while**

whim [wɪm] *n* caprice *m*

whine [waɪn] *n* gémissement *m*; (*of engine, siren*) plainte stridente ▷ *vi* gémir, geindre, pleurnicher; (*dog, engine, siren*) gémir

whip [wɪp] *n* fouet *m*; (*for riding*) cravache *f*; (*Pol: person*) chef *m* de file (*assurant la discipline dans son groupe parlementaire*) ▷ *vt* fouetter; (*snatch*) enlever (*or sortir*) brusquement; **whipped cream** *n* crème fouettée

whirl [wə:l] *vi* tourbillonner; (*dancers*) tournoyer ▷ *vt* faire tourbillonner; faire tournoyer

whisk [wɪsk] *n* (*Culin*) fouet *m* ▷ *vt* (*eggs*) fouetter, battre; **to ~ sb away** *or* **off** emmener qn rapidement

whiskers [ˈwɪskəz] *npl* (*of animal*) moustaches *fpl*; (*of man*) favoris *mpl*

whisky (*IRISH, US* **whiskey**) [ˈwɪskɪ] *n* whisky *m*

whisper [ˈwɪspər] *n* chuchotement *m* ▷ *vt, vi* chuchoter

whistle [ˈwɪsl] *n* (*sound*) sifflement *m*; (*object*) sifflet *m* ▷ *vi* siffler ▷ *vt* siffler, siffloter

white [waɪt] *adj* blanc (blanche); (*with fear*) blême ▷ *n* blanc *m*; (*person*) blanc (blanche); **White House** *n* (*US*): **the White House** la Maison-Blanche; **whitewash** *n* (*paint*) lait *m* de chaux ▷ *vt* blanchir à la chaux; (*fig*) blanchir

whiting [ˈwaɪtɪŋ] *n* (*pl inv: fish*) merlan *m*

Whitsun [ˈwɪtsn] *n* la Pentecôte

whittle [ˈwɪtl] *vt*: **to ~ away**, **to ~ down** (*costs*) réduire, rogner

whizz [wɪz] *vi* aller (*or passer*) à toute vitesse

who [hu:] *pron* qui

whoever [hu:'ɛvər] *pron*: **~ finds it** celui (celle) qui le trouve (, qui que ce soit), quiconque le trouve; **ask ~ you like** demandez à qui vous voulez; **~ he marries** qui que ce soit *or* quelle que soit la personne qu'il épouse; **~ told you that?** qui a bien pu vous dire ça?, qui donc vous a dit ça?

whole [həul] *adj* (*complete*) entier(-ière), tout(e); (*not broken*) intact(e), complet(-ète) ▷ *n* (*all*): **the ~ of** la totalité de, tout(e) le (la); (*entire unit*) tout *m*; **the ~ of the town** la ville tout entière; **on the ~**, **as a ~** dans l'ensemble; **wholefood(s)** *n(pl)* aliments complets; **wholeheartedly** [həul'hɑ:tɪdlɪ] *adv* sans réserve; **to agree wholeheartedly** être entièrement d'accord; **wholemeal** *adj* (*BRIT: flour, bread*) complet(-ète); **wholesale** *n* (*vente f en*) gros *m* ▷ *adj* (*price*) de gros; (*destruction*) systématique; **wholewheat** *adj* = **wholemeal**; **wholly** *adv* entièrement, tout à fait

KEYWORD

whom [hu:m] *pron* **1** (*interrogative*) qui; **whom did you see?** qui avez-vous vu?; **to whom did you give it?** à qui l'avez-vous donné?

2 (*relative*) que; à/de *etc* qui; **the man whom I saw/to whom I spoke** l'homme que j'ai vu/à qui j'ai parlé

whore [hɔːʳ] *n* (*inf: pej*) putain *f*

 KEYWORD

whose [huːz] *adj* **1** (*possessive: interrogative*): **whose book is this?, whose is this book?** à qui est ce livre?; **whose pencil have you taken?** à qui est le crayon que vous avez pris?, c'est le crayon de qui que vous avez pris?; **whose daughter are you?** de qui êtes-vous la fille? **2** (*possessive: relative*): **the man whose son you rescued** l'homme dont or de qui vous avez sauvé le fils; **the girl whose sister you were speaking to** la fille à qui or de laquelle vous parliez; **the woman whose car was stolen** la femme dont la voiture a été volée ▷ *pron* à qui; **whose is this?** à qui est ceci?; **I know whose it is** je sais à qui c'est

 KEYWORD

why [waɪ] *adv* pourquoi; **why not?** pourquoi pas? ▷ *conj*: **I wonder why he said that** je me demande pourquoi il a dit ça; **that's not why I'm here** ce n'est pas pour ça que je suis là; **the reason why** la raison pour laquelle ▷ *excl* eh bien!, tiens!; **why, it's you!** tiens, c'est vous!; **why, that's impossible!** voyons, c'est impossible!

wicked ['wɪkɪd] *adj* méchant(e); (*mischievous: grin, look*) espiègle, malicieux(-euse); (*crime*) pervers(e); (*inf: very good*) génial(e) (*inf*)
wicket ['wɪkɪt] *n* (*Cricket: stumps*) guichet *m*; (: *grass area*) espace compris entre les deux guichets
wide [waɪd] *adj* large; (*area, knowledge*) vaste, très étendu(e); (*choice*) grand(e) ▷ *adv*: **to open ~** ouvrir tout grand; **to shoot ~** tirer à côté; **it is 3 metres ~** cela fait 3 mètres de large; **widely** *adv* (*different*) radicalement; (*spaced*) sur une grande étendue; (*believed*) généralement; (*travel*) beaucoup; **widen** *vt* élargir ▷ *vi* s'élargir; **wide open** *adj* grand(e) ouvert(e); **widespread** *adj* (*belief etc*) très répandu(e)
widow ['wɪdəu] *n* veuve *f*; **widower** *n* veuf *m*
width [wɪdθ] *n* largeur *f*
wield [wiːld] *vt* (*sword*) manier; (*power*) exercer
wife (*pl* **wives**) [waɪf, waɪvz] *n* femme *f*, épouse *f*
wig [wɪg] *n* perruque *f*
wild [waɪld] *adj* sauvage; (*sea*) déchaîné(e); (*idea, life*) fou (folle); (*behaviour*) déchaîné(e), extravagant(e); (*inf: angry*) hors de soi, furieux(-euse) ▷ *n*: **the ~** la nature; **wilderness** ['wɪldənɪs] *n* désert *m*, région *f* sauvage; **wildlife** *n* faune *f* (et flore *f*); **wildly** *adv* (*behave*) de manière déchaînée; (*applaud*) frénétiquement; (*hit, guess*) au hasard; (*happy*) follement

 KEYWORD

will [wɪl] *aux vb* **1** (*forming future tense*): **I will finish it tomorrow** je le finirai demain; **I will have finished it by tomorrow** je l'aurai fini d'ici demain; **will you do it? - yes I will/no I won't** le ferez-vous? - oui/non **2** (*in conjectures, predictions*): **he will** or **he'll be there by**

now il doit être arrivé à l'heure qu'il est; **that will be the postman** ça doit être le facteur
3 (*in commands, requests, offers*): **will you be quiet!** voulez-vous bien vous taire!; **will you help me?** est-ce que vous pouvez m'aider?; **will you have a cup of tea?** voulez-vous une tasse de thé?; **I won't put up with it!** je ne le tolérerai pas!
▷ *vt* (*pt, pp* **willed**): **to will sb to do** souhaiter ardemment que qn fasse; **he willed himself to go on** par un suprême effort de volonté, il continua
▷ *n* volonté *f*; (*document*) testament *m*; **against one's will** à contre-cœur

willing ['wɪlɪŋ] *adj* de bonne volonté, serviable; **he's ~ to do it** il est disposé à le faire, il veut bien le faire; **willingly** *adv* volontiers
willow ['wɪləu] *n* saule *m*
willpower ['wɪl'pauəʳ] *n* volonté *f*
wilt [wɪlt] *vi* dépérir
win [wɪn] *n* (*in sports etc*) victoire *f* ▷ *vb* (*pt, pp* **won**) ▷ *vt* (*battle, money*) gagner; (*prize, contract*) remporter; (*popularity*) acquérir ▷ *vi* gagner; **win over** *vt* convaincre
wince [wɪns] *vi* tressaillir
wind¹ [wɪnd] *n* (*also* Med) vent *m*; (*breath*) souffle *m* ▷ *vt* (*take breath away*) couper le souffle à; **the ~(s)** (Mus) les instruments *mpl* à vent
wind² (*pt, pp* **wound**) [waɪnd, waund] *vt* enrouler; (*wrap*) envelopper; (*clock, toy*) remonter ▷ *vi* (*road, river*) serpenter; **wind down** *vt* (*car window*) baisser; (*fig: production, business*) réduire progressivement; **wind up** *vt* (*clock*) remonter; (*debate*) terminer, clôturer
windfall ['wɪndfɔːl] *n* coup *m* de chance
winding ['waɪndɪŋ] *adj* (*road*) sinueux(-euse); (*staircase*) tournant(e)
windmill ['wɪndmɪl] *n* moulin *m* à vent
window ['wɪndəu] *n* fenêtre *f*; (*in car, train: also:* **~pane**) vitre *f*; (*in shop etc*) vitrine *f*; **window box** *n* jardinière *f*; **window cleaner** *n* (*person*) laveur(-euse) de vitres; **window pane** *n* vitre *f*, carreau *m*; **window seat** *n* (*in vehicle*) place *f* côté fenêtre; **windowsill** *n* (*inside*) appui *m* de la fenêtre; (*outside*) rebord *m* de la fenêtre
windscreen ['wɪndskriːn] *n* pare-brise *m inv*; **windscreen wiper** *n* essuie-glace *m inv*
windshield ['wɪndʃiːld] (*us*) *n* = **windscreen**
windsurfing ['wɪndsəːfɪŋ] *n* planche *f* à voile
windy ['wɪndɪ] *adj* (*day*) de vent, venteux(-euse); (*place, weather*) venteux; **it's ~** il y a du vent
wine [waɪn] *n* vin *m*; **wine bar** *n* bar *m* à vin; **wine glass** *n* verre *m* à vin; **wine list** *n* carte *f* des vins; **wine tasting** *n* dégustation *f* (de vins)
wing [wɪŋ] *n* aile *f*; **wings** *npl* (Theat) coulisses *fpl*; **wing mirror** *n* (BRIT) rétroviseur latéral
wink [wɪŋk] *n* clin *m* d'œil ▷ *vi* faire un clin d'œil; (*blink*) cligner des yeux
winner ['wɪnəʳ] *n* gagnant(e)
winning ['wɪnɪŋ] *adj* (*team*) gagnant(e); (*goal*) décisif(-ive); (*charming*) charmeur(-euse)
winter ['wɪntəʳ] *n* hiver *m* ▷ *vi* hiverner; **in ~** en hiver; **winter sports** *npl* sports *mpl* d'hiver; **wintertime** *n* hiver *m*
wipe [waɪp] *n*: **to give sth a ~** donner un coup de torchon/de chiffon/d'éponge à qch ▷ *vt* essuyer; (*erase: tape*) effacer; **to ~ one's nose** se moucher; **wipe out** *vt* (*debt*) éteindre, amortir; (*memory*) effacer; (*destroy*)

anéantir; **wipe up** vt essuyer

wire [waɪəʳ] n fil m (de fer); (Elec) fil électrique; (Tel) télégramme m ▷ vt (house) faire l'installation électrique de; (also: **~ up**) brancher; (person: send telegram to) télégraphier à

wiring ['waɪərɪŋ] n (Elec) installation f électrique

wisdom ['wɪzdəm] n sagesse f; (of action) prudence f; **wisdom tooth** n dent f de sagesse

wise [waɪz] adj sage, prudent(e); (remark) judicieux(-euse)

wish [wɪʃ] n (desire) désir m; (specific desire) souhait m, vœu m ▷ vt souhaiter, désirer, vouloir; **best ~es** (on birthday etc) meilleurs vœux; **with best ~es** (in letter) bien amicalement; **to ~ sb goodbye** dire au revoir à qn; **he ~ed me well** il m'a souhaité bonne chance; **to ~ to do/sb to do** désirer or vouloir faire/que qn fasse; **to ~ for** souhaiter

wistful ['wɪstful] adj mélancolique

wit [wɪt] n (also: **~s**: intelligence) intelligence f, esprit m; (presence of mind) présence f d'esprit; (wittiness) esprit; (person) homme/femme d'esprit

witch [wɪtʃ] n sorcière f

O KEYWORD

with [wɪð, wɪθ] prep **1** (in the company of) avec; (at the home of) chez; **we stayed with friends** nous avons logé chez des amis; **I'll be with you in a minute** je suis à vous dans un instant

2 (descriptive): **a room with a view** une chambre avec vue; **the man with the grey hat/blue eyes** l'homme au chapeau gris/aux yeux bleus

3 (indicating manner, means, cause): **with tears in her eyes** les larmes aux yeux; **to walk with a stick** marcher avec une canne; **red with anger** rouge de colère; **to shake with fear** trembler de peur; **to fill sth with water** remplir qch d'eau

4 (in phrases): **I'm with you** (I understand) je vous suis; **to be with it** (inf: up-to-date) être dans le vent

withdraw [wɪθ'drɔ:] vt (irreg: like draw) retirer ▷ vi se retirer; **withdrawal** n retrait m; (Med) état m de manque; **withdrawn** pp of **withdraw** ▷ adj (person) renfermé(e)

withdrew [wɪθ'druː] pt of **withdraw**

wither ['wɪðəʳ] vi se faner

withhold [wɪθ'həuld] vt (irreg: like hold) (money) retenir; (decision) remettre; (permission): **to ~ (from)** (permission) refuser (à); (information): **to ~ (from)** cacher (à)

within [wɪð'ɪn] prep à l'intérieur de ▷ adv à l'intérieur; **~ his reach** à sa portée; **~ sight of** en vue de; **~ a mile of** à moins d'un mille de; **~ the week** avant la fin de la semaine

without [wɪð'aut] prep sans; **~ a coat** sans manteau; **~ speaking** sans parler; **to go** or **do ~ sth** se passer de qch

withstand [wɪθ'stænd] vt (irreg: like stand) résister à

witness ['wɪtnɪs] n (person) témoin m ▷ vt (event) être témoin de; (document) attester l'authenticité de; **to bear ~ to sth** témoigner de qch

witty ['wɪtɪ] adj spirituel(le), plein(e) d'esprit

wives [waɪvz] npl of **wife**

wizard ['wɪzəd] n magicien m

wk abbr = **week**

wobble ['wɔbl] vi trembler; (chair) branler

woe [wəu] n malheur m

woke [wəuk] pt of **wake**

woken ['wəukn] pp of **wake**

wolf (pl **wolves**) [wulf, wulvz] n loup m

woman (pl **women**) ['wumən, 'wɪmɪn] n femme f ▷ cpd: **~ doctor** femme f médecin; **~ teacher** professeur m femme

womb [wu:m] n (Anat) utérus m

women ['wɪmɪn] npl of **woman**

won [wʌn] pt, pp of **win**

wonder ['wʌndəʳ] n merveille f, miracle m; (feeling) émerveillement m ▷ vi: **to ~ whether/why** se demander si/pourquoi; **to ~ at** (surprise) s'étonner de; (admiration) s'émerveiller de; **to ~ about** songer à; **it's no ~ that** il n'est pas étonnant que + sub; **wonderful** adj merveilleux(-euse)

won't [wəunt] = **will not**

wood [wud] n (timber, forest) bois m; **wooden** adj en bois; (fig: actor) raide; (: performance) qui manque de naturel; **woodwind** n: **the woodwind** (Mus) les bois mpl; **woodwork** n menuiserie f

wool [wul] n laine f; **to pull the ~ over sb's eyes** (fig) en faire accroire à qn; **woollen** (us **woolen**) adj de or en laine; **woolly** (us **wooly**) adj laineux(-euse); (fig: ideas) confus(e)

word [wə:d] n mot m; (spoken) mot, parole f; (promise) parole; (news) nouvelles fpl ▷ vt rédiger, formuler; **in other ~s** en d'autres termes; **to have a ~ with sb** toucher un mot à qn; **to break/keep one's ~** manquer à sa parole/tenir (sa) parole; **wording** n termes mpl, langage m; (of document) libellé m; **word processing** n traitement m de texte; **word processor** n machine f de traitement de texte

wore [wɔːʳ] pt of **wear**

work [wə:k] n travail m; (Art, Literature) œuvre f ▷ vi travailler; (mechanism) marcher, fonctionner; (plan etc) marcher; (medicine) agir ▷ vt (clay, wood etc) travailler; (mine etc) exploiter; (machine) faire marcher or fonctionner; (miracles etc) faire; **works** n (BRIT: factory) usine f; **how does this ~?** comment est-ce que ça marche?; **the TV isn't ~ing** la télévision est en panne or ne marche pas; **to be out of ~** être au chômage or sans emploi; **to ~ loose** se défaire, se desserrer; **work out** vi (plans etc) marcher; (Sport) s'entraîner ▷ vt (problem) résoudre; (plan) élaborer; **it ~s out at £100** ça fait 100 livres; **worker** n travailleur(-euse), ouvrier(-ière); **work experience** n stage m; **workforce** n main-d'œuvre f; **working class** n classe ouvrière ▷ adj: **working-class** ouvrier(-ière), de la classe ouvrière; **working week** n semaine f de travail; **workman** (irreg) n ouvrier m; **work of art** n œuvre f d'art; **workout** n (Sport) séance f d'entraînement; **work permit** n permis m de travail; **workplace** n lieu m de travail; **worksheet** n (Scol) feuille f d'exercices; **workshop** n atelier m; **work station** n poste m de travail; **work surface** n plan m de travail; **worktop** n plan m de travail

world [wə:ld] n monde m ▷ cpd (champion) du monde; (power, war) mondial(e); **to think the ~ of sb** (fig) ne jurer que par qn; **World Cup** n: **the World Cup** (Football) la Coupe du monde; **world-wide** adj universel(le); **World-Wide Web** n: **the World-Wide Web** le Web

worm [wə:m] n (also: **earth~**) ver m

worn [wɔ:n] pp of **wear** ▷ adj usé(e); **worn-out** adj (object) complètement usé(e); (person) épuisé(e)

worried ['wʌrɪd] *adj* inquiet(-ète); **to be ~ about sth** être inquiet au sujet de qch

worry ['wʌrɪ] *n* souci *m* ▷ *vt* inquiéter ▷ *vi* s'inquiéter, se faire du souci; **worrying** *adj* inquiétant(e)

worse [wə:s] *adj* pire, plus mauvais(e) ▷ *adv* plus mal ▷ *n* pire *m*; **to get ~** (*condition, situation*) empirer, se dégrader; **a change for the ~** une détérioration; **worsen** *vt, vi* empirer; **worse off** *adj* moins à l'aise financièrement; (*fig*): **you'll be worse off this way** ça ira moins bien de cette façon

worship ['wə:ʃɪp] *n* culte *m* ▷ *vt* (*God*) rendre un culte à; (*person*) adorer

worst [wə:st] *adj* le (la) pire, le (la) plus mauvais(e) ▷ *adv* le plus mal ▷ *n* pire *m*; **at ~** au pis aller

worth [wə:θ] *n* valeur *f* ▷ *adj*: **to be ~** valoir; **it's ~ £5** cela en vaut la peine, ça vaut la peine; **it is ~ one's while (to do)** ça vaut le coup (*inf*) (de faire); **worthless** *adj* qui ne vaut rien; **worthwhile** *adj* (*activity*) qui en vaut la peine; (*cause*) louable;

worthy ['wə:ðɪ] *adj* (*person*) digne; (*motive*) louable; **~ of** digne de

KEYWORD

would [wud] *aux vb* **1** (*conditional tense*): **if you asked him he would do it** si vous le lui demandiez, il le ferait; **if you had asked him he would have done it** si vous le lui aviez demandé, il l'aurait fait

2 (*in offers, invitations, requests*): **would you like a biscuit?** voulez-vous un biscuit?; **would you close the door please?** voulez-vous fermer la porte, s'il vous plaît?

3 (*in indirect speech*): **I said I would do it** j'ai dit que je le ferais

4 (*emphatic*): **it WOULD have to snow today!** naturellement il neige aujourd'hui *or* il fallait qu'il neige aujourd'hui!

5 (*insistence*): **she wouldn't do it** elle n'a pas voulu *or* elle a refusé de le faire

6 (*conjecture*): **it would have been midnight** il devait être minuit; **it would seem so** on dirait bien

7 (*indicating habit*): **he would go there on Mondays** il y allait le lundi

wouldn't ['wudnt] = **would not**

wound¹ [wu:nd] *n* blessure *f* ▷ *vt* blesser

wound² [waund] *pt, pp of* **wind**

wove [wəuv] *pt of* **weave**

woven ['wəuvn] *pp of* **weave**

wrap [ræp] *vt* (*also*: **~ up**) envelopper; (*parcel*) emballer; (*wind*) enrouler; **wrapper** *n* (*on chocolate etc*) papier *m*; (BRIT: *of book*) couverture *f*; **wrapping** *n* (*of sweet, chocolate*) papier *m*; (*of parcel*) emballage *m*; **wrapping paper** *n* papier *m* d'emballage; (*for gift*) papier cadeau

wreath [ri:θ, (*pl*) ri:ðz] *n* couronne *f*

wreck [rɛk] *n* (*sea disaster*) naufrage *m*; (*ship*) épave *f*; (*vehicle*) véhicule accidenté; (*pej: person*) loque (humaine) ▷ *vt* démolir; (*fig*) briser, ruiner; **wreckage** *n* débris *mpl*; (*of building*) décombres *mpl*; (*of ship*) naufrage *m*

wren [rɛn] *n* (*Zool*) troglodyte *m*

wrench [rɛntʃ] *n* (*Tech*) clé *f* (à écrous); (*tug*) violent mouvement de torsion; (*fig*) déchirement *m* ▷ *vt* tirer violemment sur, tordre; **to ~ sth from** arracher qch (violemment) à *or* de

wrestle ['rɛsl] *vi*: **to ~ (with sb)** lutter (avec qn); **wrestler** *n* lutteur(-euse); **wrestling** *n* lutte *f*; (*also*: **all-in wrestling**: BRIT) catch *m*

wretched ['rɛtʃɪd] *adj* misérable

wriggle ['rɪgl] *vi* (*also*: **~ about**) se tortiller

wring (*pt, pp* **wrung**) [rɪŋ, rʌŋ] *vt* tordre; (*wet clothes*) essorer; (*fig*): **to ~ sth out of** arracher qch à

wrinkle ['rɪŋkl] *n* (*on skin*) ride *f*; (*on paper etc*) pli *m* ▷ *vt* rider, plisser ▷ *vi* se plisser

wrist [rɪst] *n* poignet *m*

write (*pt* **wrote**, *pp* **written**) [raɪt, rəut, 'rɪtn] *vt, vi* écrire; (*prescription*) rédiger; **write down** *vt* noter; (*put in writing*) mettre par écrit; **write off** *vt* (*debt*) passer aux profits et pertes; (*project*) mettre une croix sur; (*smash up: car etc*) démolir complètement; **write out** *vt* écrire, (*copy*) recopier; **write-off** *n* perte totale; **the car is a write-off** la voiture est bonne pour la casse; **writer** *n* auteur *m*, écrivain *m*

writing ['raɪtɪŋ] *n* écriture *f*; (*of author*) œuvres *fpl*; **in ~** par écrit; **writing paper** *n* papier *m* à lettres

written ['rɪtn] *pp of* **write**

wrong [rɒŋ] *adj* (*incorrect*) faux (fausse); (*incorrectly chosen: number, road etc*) mauvais(e); (*not suitable*) qui ne convient pas; (*wicked*) mal; (*unfair*) injuste ▷ *adv* mal ▷ *n* tort *m* ▷ *vt* faire du tort à, léser; **you are ~ to do it** tu as tort de le faire; **you are ~ about that, you've got it ~** tu te trompes; **what's ~?** qu'est-ce qui ne va pas?; **what's ~ with the car?** qu'est-ce qu'elle a, la voiture?; **to go ~** (*person*) se tromper; (*plan*) mal tourner; (*machine*) se détraquer; **I took a ~ turning** je me suis trompé de route; **wrongly** *adv* à tort; (*answer, do, count*) mal, incorrectement; **wrong number** *n* (*Tel*): **you have the wrong number** vous vous êtes trompé de numéro

wrote [rəut] *pt of* **write**

wrung [rʌŋ] *pt, pp of* **wring**

WWW *n abbr* = **World-Wide Web**; **the ~** le Web

XL abbr (= extra large) XL

Xmas ['ɛksməs] n abbr = **Christmas**

X-ray ['ɛksreɪ] n (ray) rayon m X; (photograph) radio(graphie) f ▷ vt radiographier

xylophone ['zaɪləfəʊn] n xylophone m

yacht [jɔt] n voilier m; (motor, luxury yacht) yacht m; **yachting** n yachting m, navigation f de plaisance

yard [jɑːd] n (of house etc) cour f; (us: garden) jardin m; (measure) yard m (= 914 mm; 3 feet); **yard sale** n (us)

brocante f (dans son propre jardin)

yarn [jɑːn] n fil m; (tale) longue histoire

yawn [jɔːn] n bâillement m ▷ vi bâiller

yd. abbr = **yard(s)**

yeah [jɛə] adv (inf) ouais

year [jɪəʳ] n an m, année f; (Scol etc) année; **to be 8 ~s old** avoir 8 ans; **an eight-~-old child** un enfant de huit ans; **yearly** adj annuel(le) ▷ adv annuellement; **twice yearly** deux fois par an

yearn [jəːn] vi: **to ~ for sth/to do** aspirer à qch/à faire

yeast [jiːst] n levure f

yell [jɛl] n hurlement m, cri m ▷ vi hurler

yellow ['jɛləʊ] adj, n jaune (m); **Yellow Pages®** npl (Tel) pages fpl jaunes

yes [jɛs] adv oui; (answering negative question) si ▷ n oui m; **to say ~ (to)** dire oui (à)

yesterday ['jɛstədɪ] adv, n hier (m); **~ morning/ evening** hier matin/soir; **all day ~** toute la journée d'hier

yet [jɛt] adv encore; (in questions) déjà ▷ conj pourtant, néanmoins; **it is not finished ~** ce n'est pas encore fini or toujours pas fini; **have you eaten ~?** vous avez déjà mangé?; **the best ~** le meilleur jusqu'ici or jusque-là; **as ~** jusqu'ici, encore

yew [juː] n if m

Yiddish ['jɪdɪʃ] n yiddish m

yield [jiːld] n production f, rendement m; (Finance) rapport m ▷ vt produire, rendre, rapporter; (surrender) céder ▷ vi céder; (us Aut) céder la priorité

yob(bo) ['jɔb(əʊ)] n (BRIT inf) loubar(d) m

yoga ['jəʊgə] n yoga m

yog(h)ourt n = **yog(h)urt**

yog(h)urt ['jɔgət] n yaourt m

yolk [jəʊk] n jaune m (d'œuf)

O **KEYWORD**

you [juː] pron **1** (subject) tu; (polite form) vous; (plural) vous; **you are very kind** vous êtes très gentil; **you French enjoy your food** vous autres Français, vous aimez bien manger; **you and I will go** toi et moi or vous et moi, nous irons; **there you are!** vous voilà!

2 (object: direct, indirect) te, t' + vowel; vous; **I know you** je te or vous connais; **I gave it to you** je te l'ai donné, je vous l'ai donné

3 (stressed) toi; vous; **I told YOU to do it** c'est à toi or vous que j'ai dit de le faire

4 (after prep, in comparisons) toi; vous; **it's for you** c'est pour toi or vous; **she's younger than you** elle est plus jeune que toi or vous

5 (impersonal: one) on; **fresh air does you good** l'air frais fait du bien; **you never know** on ne sait jamais; **you can't do that!** ça ne se fait pas!

you'd [juːd] = **you had**; **you would**

you'll [juːl] = **you will**; **you shall**

young [jʌŋ] adj jeune ▷ npl (of animal) petits mpl; (people): **the ~** les jeunes, la jeunesse; **my ~er brother** mon frère cadet; **youngster** n jeune m/f; (child) enfant m/f

your [jɔːʳ] adj ton (ta), tes pl; (polite form, pl) votre, vos pl; see also **my**

you're [juəʳ] = **you are**

yours [jɔːz] pron le (la) tien(ne), les tiens (tiennes); (polite form, pl) le (la) vôtre, les vôtres; **is it ~?** c'est à toi (or à vous)?; **a friend of ~** un(e) de tes (*or* de vos) amis; *see also* **faithfully**; **mine¹**; *see also* **sincerely**

yourself [jɔː'sɛlf] *pron (reflexive)* te; (: *polite form*) vous; (*after prep*) toi; vous; (*emphatic*) toi-même; vous-même; *see also* **oneself**; **yourselves** *pl pron* vous; (*emphatic*) vous-mêmes; *see also* **oneself**

youth [juːθ] *n* jeunesse *f*; (*young man*): (*pl* **~s**) jeune homme *m*; **youth club** *n* centre *m* de jeunes; **youthful** *adj* jeune; (*enthusiasm etc*) juvénile; **youth hostel** *n* auberge *f* de jeunesse

you've [juːv] = **you have**

Yugoslav ['juːgəʊslɑːv] *adj* yougoslave ▷ *n* Yougoslave *m/f*

Yugoslavia [juːgəʊ'slɑːvɪə] *n* (*Hist*) Yougoslavie *f*

zoom [zuːm] *vi*: **to ~ past** passer en trombe; **zoom lens** *n* zoom *m*

zucchini [zuː'kiːnɪ] *n(pl)* (*US*) courgette(s) *f(pl)*

Z

zeal [ziːl] *n* (*revolutionary etc*) ferveur *f*; (*keenness*) ardeur *f*, zèle *m*

zebra ['ziːbrə] *n* zèbre *m*; **zebra crossing** *n* (*BRIT*) passage clouté *or* pour piétons

zero ['zɪərəʊ] *n* zéro *m*

zest [zɛst] *n* entrain *m*, élan *m*; (*of lemon etc*) zeste *m*

zigzag ['zɪgzæg] *n* zigzag *m* ▷ *vi* zigzaguer, faire des zigzags

Zimbabwe [zɪm'bɑːbwɪ] *n* Zimbabwe *m*

zinc [zɪŋk] *n* zinc *m*

zip [zɪp] *n* (*also*: **~ fastener**) fermeture *f* éclair® *or* à glissière ▷ *vt* (*file*) zipper; (*also*: **~ up**) fermer (avec une fermeture éclair®); **zip code** *n* (*US*) code postal; **zip file** *n* (*Comput*) fichier *m* zip *inv*; **zipper** *n* (*US*) = **zip**

zit [zɪt] (*inf*) *n* bouton *m*

zodiac ['zəʊdɪæk] *n* zodiaque *m*

zone [zəʊn] *n* zone *f*

zoo [zuː] *n* zoo *m*

zoology [zuː'ɔlədʒɪ] *n* zoologie *f*